SHAKESPEARE
and his world

SHAKESPEARE

and his world

BY F. E. HALLIDAY

 THAMES AND HUDSON · LONDON

To BARBARA HEPWORTH in Friendship and Admiration

First published 1956
Reprinted 1970
All rights reserved
Printed in Great Britain
by Lowe & Brydone (Printers) Ltd London
Designed by George A. Adams
ISBN 0 500 13001 9

It is, unfortunately, a common delusion that little or nothing is known about the life of Shakespeare. In fact quite a lot is known. Thanks to the devoted labours of a succession of English and American scholars, from Malone and Halliwell-Phillipps in the eighteenth and nineteenth centuries to C. W. Wallace and Leslie Hotson in our own day, much has been discovered, and still is being discovered; far more, indeed, than we had any right to expect concerning a dramatist who lived the greater part of his life, and died, in an obscure provincial town. For it must be remembered that plays were not treated as serious literature when Shakespeare was alive, that after his death his work was temporarily eclipsed by the flashy drama of Beaumont and Fletcher, and that for the twenty years of the Civil War and Commonwealth the theatres were closed. It was, therefore, more than half a century after his death before the first fumbling attempts at research began, too late to glean much first-hand biographical information. But since then much has been unearthed from record and contemporary allusion, and the object of this book is quite simply to describe what we know about Shakespeare's life after three centuries of discovery, and to illuminate and animate the story by illustration.

It is doubly unfortunate that it should so generally be assumed that we know little about Shakespeare. For one thing, it has helped to foster the sentimental eighteenth century conception of Shakespeare as an inspired peasant, a conception that there is no longer any excuse for holding, yet one which in turn has encouraged the theory that such a man could not have written the plays attributed to him. A hundred years ago a Miss Delia Bacon proved to her own satisfaction that her namesake Francis Bacon was the author. Miss Bacon died insane, but her work was carried on by her disciples until they themselves were assailed by those who professed to have found 'the real Shakespeare' in one or other of a group of noble earls. Now we are told that the real author was Marlowe. Soon somebody in search of a hobby will discover the shadowy Elizabethan dramatist Wentworth Smith, and the Smithites will join in the cry.

Although this book has not been written to refute this nonsense, it should do something incidentally to dispel it. So far as I am aware nothing quite like it has been attempted before, and the illustration of so much biographical material, documents as well as portraits and places, should serve as a reassurance that the man who wrote the thirty-six plays of the Folio was William Shakespeare of Stratford-upon-Avon. It is a reasonable hypothesis.

F.E.H.

St. Ives
Cornwall
Summer 1956

CONTENTS

Warwick, from the low hills of Budbrooke

THERE HAVE BEEN SHAKESPEARES in Warwickshire since at least the middle of the thirteenth century, at which time a William Sakspere lived at Clopton on the outskirts of Stratford. This medieval William, however, was no great credit to the family, for, more than three hundred years before the birth of his famous namesake, he was hanged for robbery. 'Sakspere' is merely a simple variant of the name, which could be spelt in a bewildering number of ways, shading gradually into forms remoter and more remote from the generally accepted 'Shakespeare': Shakespert, Schakosper, Shexsper, Saxpere, Sash-pierre, Chacsper, Sadspere, Shaksbye, Shaxbee, and even Shakeschafte and Shakstaff. Seventeenth century antiquaries favoured a heroic derivation—'*Martial* in the *Warlike* sound of his Sur-name (whence some may conjecture him of a Military extraction), *Hasti-vibrans*, or Shake-speare'—but as only one Warwickshire family of Shakespeares is known to have held land by military tenure such a picturesque interpretation is open to doubt.

The poet's grandfather was probably the Richard Shakyspere who in 1525 was living at Budbrooke on the low hills that look eastward towards Warwick. A few years later he moved to the village of Snitterfield, three miles north of Stratford, where he farmed land on the manor of Robert Arden, the head of a

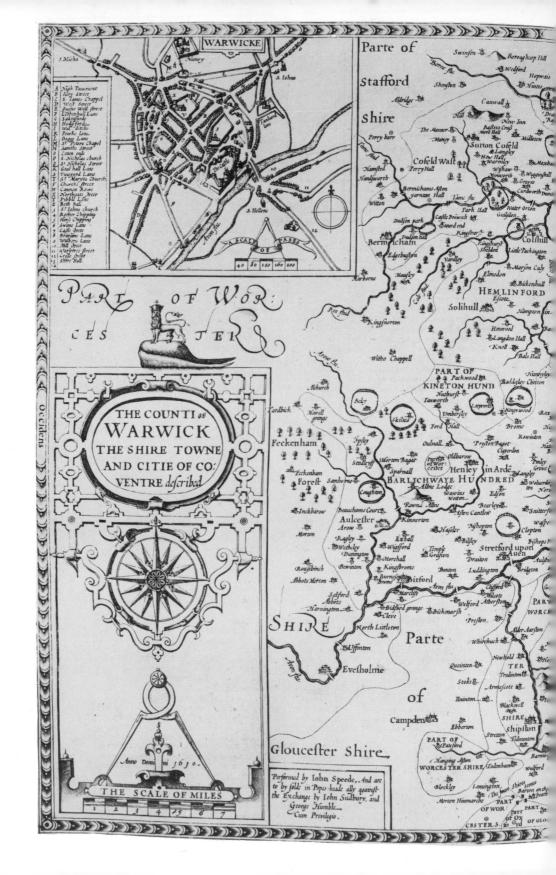

Warwickshire
in the time of
Shakespeare.
John Speed's
map, 1610

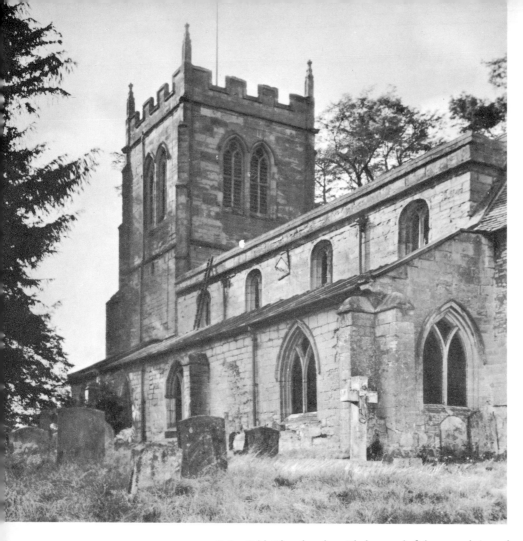

Snitterfield Church, where Shakespeare's father was christened

minor branch of an old and distinguished Warwickshire family. It was at Snitterfield that Richard's two sons, John and Henry, were born, probably in the fifteen-thirties, and christened in the parish church.

Robert Arden did not live at Snitterfield, but at Wilmcote, a village three or four miles to the west, where he had another estate. There, in his fine half-timbered farmhouse, backed by substantial barns and a great stone dovecote, he brought up a family of eight daughters, the youngest of whom was Mary. For almost thirty years Shakespeare's two grandfathers were neighbours, separated only by a few furlongs of road, and bound to one another by a common interest in the land, of which one was owner and the other tenant.

Robert Arden's house at Wilmcote, where Shakespeare's mother was born

Aston Cantlow Church, probably where Shakespeare's parents were married

John Shakespeare must have known Mary Arden ever since he was a small boy, and when, about 1550, he moved to Stratford, leaving his father and brother to carry on the farm at Snitterfield, he was still only a bare hour's walk from her home. No doubt the humble farmer's son felt it necessary to better his condition if ever he was to win the hand of the daughter of a country gentleman, however unpretentious, and in Stratford he set up as a glove-maker. His business prospered, and shortly after the death of Robert Arden in 1556 he married Mary, presumably in the church of Aston Cantlow, within the parish of which Wilmcote lies. It was a good match for the ambitious young man, for, apart from her name and social standing, Mary brought him two properties at Wilmcote, some hundred and fifty acres in all, and a share in the reversion of the Snitterfield estate.

But John too owned property. He was doing well, and just before his marriage invested money in two Stratford houses, one of which was in the row that ran along the north side of Henley Street at the top of the town. This was the one to the east of the 'Birthplace', in which he may already have been living as tenant. He had been in Henley Street for some time, for in 1552 he and his friend Adrian Quiney had been fined, not unreasonably, for making a dunghill in that thoroughfare. If, then, it was to the 'Birthplace' that he brought his bride, presumably he moved his business into the newly-bought house next door.

Their first child was born in September 1558. Nothing more is known of her, and it seems likely that she died in infancy, as did her sister, who was only five months old when she was buried in April, 1563. Perhaps both were victims of the plague, the fearful scourge that ravaged England with exceptional ferocity in 1563, and hope must have been seasoned with dread in the hearts of John and Mary Shakespeare as the time approached for the birth of their third child. But plague disappeared with the frosts of winter, and when pear and apple were breaking into blossom in the April of 1564 a son was born, perhaps on the 23rd. He was called William, and on the 26th 'Gulielmus filius Johannes Shakspere' was christened in the parish church of the Holy Trinity.

Queen Elizabeth was then a woman of thirty. Six years before she had succeeded to the throne of England, a backward and bankrupt island on the fringe merely of the new civilisation of the Renaissance. Thanks, however, to her remarkable courage and

Shakespeare's Birthplace

The first known view, 1769
Before restoration, 1847
During restoration, 1857
As it looks to-day

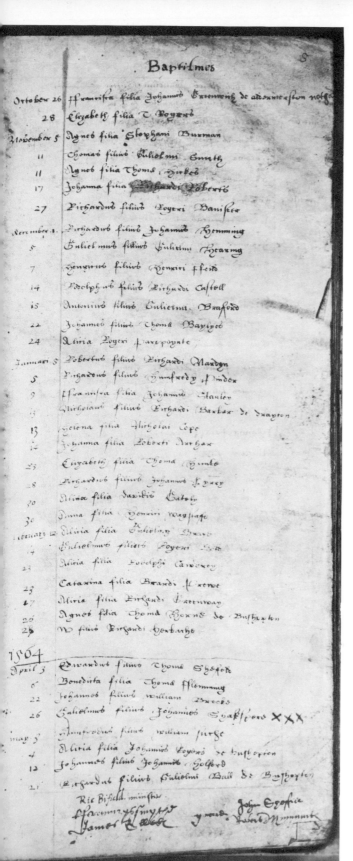

Queen Elizabeth I when she was thirty-five
and Shakespeare five

Baptism of 'William, son of John Shakspere', 26 April 1564
The entry in Stratford Parish Register

William Cecil, Lord Burghley,
Queen Elizabeth's chief minister

ability she had already set the country on the highroad to fortune. Above all, she had united the great majority of her people by establishing a moderate form of Protestantism as the official religion, though there still remained some disaffected Catholics, and on the other flank discontented Puritans who thought the Reformation had not gone far enough. In all her measures she had been advised and helped by her Secretary, William Cecil, Lord Burghley, who was to serve her with unwavering devotion almost to the end of her reign.

But one thing Elizabeth could not do, directly at least—summon up writers to enrich the literature of England which, since the death of Chaucer a hundred and fifty years before, had been lamentably barren. There were musicians equal to any in Europe, notably Thomas Tallis and his pupil William Byrd, but where were the poets? Indirectly, however, she might do much.

Then there was another thing that Elizabeth *would* not do—marry. She flirted and, for diplomatic ends, made a great show of marital intentions, but the most likely man seemed to be her favourite, Robert Dudley, Earl of Leicester, to whom she had just granted Kenilworth Castle. Leicester was unpopular and unacceptable—he was suspected of having murdered his first wife

Robert Dudley, Earl of Leicester,
Queen Elizabeth's first favourite

—but marry she must, for the heir to the throne was the flighty Catholic Mary,
Queen of Scots, who was on the point of marrying her vicious young cousin,
Lord Darnley. Cecil was in a frenzy of anxiety, yet Elizabeth remained
obstinately unmarried.

Every summer Elizabeth took a holiday in the form of a progress, or state
tour, when she and her Court, with immense quantities of baggage, descended
upon the houses of those chief subjects who were fortunate—or unfortunate—
enough to be within easy range of the capital. In August, 1566, she spent a
few days with Leicester at Kenilworth, calling on his brother, the Earl of
Warwick, at Warwick Castle, on her way to stay at Charlecote, the recently
rebuilt house of Sir Thomas Lucy near Stratford. It was probably as she left on
that August day that Shakespeare, then aged two and a half, caught his first

Charlecote, the home of Sir Thomas Lucy, where Elizabeth stayed

glimpse of the Queen as she passed under the great gateway and turned south towards Banbury and Oxford. Elizabeth would see no more of Stratford than the church on the far side of the river, gleaming in the morning sun.

The Church of the Holy Trinity stands at the south end of the town, its lofty chancel and tower (the spire was added after Shakespeare's day) mirrored in the waters of the Avon. For over two centuries it had been a collegiate church, served by priests who lived in the neighbouring College, but twenty years before Shakespeare's time the College had been dissolved, and the house occupied by the Combe family. From church and College the road bends left until it joins the broad street that intersects the little town from south to north. The houses are of brick and timber, for the nearest stone is that of the Cotswolds some miles away, and here at the very heart are the Gild buildings: the alms-houses, the Gildhall with the long schoolroom of the Grammar School above it, and the lovely spectral-grey Gild Chapel. The religious and social Gild of the Holy Cross had once been a power in the town, but like the College it had been suppressed, and the government was now in the hands of a bailiff, aldermen and capital burgesses. On the corner facing the Gild Chapel was New Place, a large half-timbered house built by Sir Hugh Clopton shortly

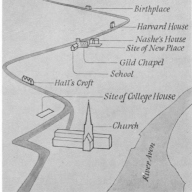

Stratford-upon-Avon. The road, imperishably associated
with Shakespeare, from his birthplace to the church

Holy Trinity Church, Stratford, where Shakespeare was baptised and buried ▶

The Gildhall with Schoolroom above

before he was buried in the church in 1492. Sir Hugh's also is the many-arched medieval bridge at the north end, the only link with London and the east, for the town was built entirely on the western bank of the river. When Shakespeare was a child it was a typical market town of some two thousand inhabitants, most of them engaged in agriculture or small-scale industry such as his father's trade of glove-making. No doubt the streets were filthy, but they were broad, and most of the houses had gardens. Then, from Henley Street the boy could roam through the remains of the Forest of Arden in the direction of Henley, Warwick, Alcester and Bidford, or he could cross the bridge and within an hour be at the foot of the Cotswolds, shapely uplands studded with beeches and grey limestone villages. And there was always the river for his delight.

The Gild Chapel, as Shakespeare saw it from New Place ▶

Clopton Bridge over the River Avon, Stratford's link with London

Education   In 1561 Richard Shakespeare had died at Snitterfield, where his younger son Henry now managed the farm. Henry was a shiftless character, always in difficulties, but his brother John pursued his prosperous career in Stratford. In 1565 he became an alderman, and by 1571, having held the coveted office of bailiff, was a sort of elder statesman, chief alderman of the borough and a justice of the peace. There were now three more children, Gilbert, Joan and Margaret. William, aged seven, was old enough to go to school.

It is high time that the mischievous conception of Shakespeare as an inspired peasant was finally dispelled. His mother was a member of a great family, his father an ambitious and exceptionally able man of business, and though there is no record (why should there be?) of his schooling, it is inconceivable that such parents would let slip the opportunity of sending him to the local grammar school. For the sons of burgesses the education was free up to the age of sixteen,

The Cotswolds near Stratford, much frequented by Shakespeare and the characters in his plays

The schoolroom where Shakespeare learned his Latin

and moreover it was one of the best schools in the country. We must, therefore, imagine Shakespeare during the decade of the seventies sitting at his desk in the schoolroom over the Council Chamber, where his father helped to shape the fortunes of the town, first at the feet of Simon Hunt, a devout Catholic at heart, and then of the Welshman, Thomas Jenkins, whom he was later lovingly to caricature as Sir Hugh Evans in *The Merry Wives*. The course would be a liberal one, chiefly in Latin, and with the aid of Lily's Latin Grammar he would work his way through the easy classics, fall in love with Ovid, read some Virgil, and perhaps some of the comedies of Plautus and tragedies of Seneca. His Bible was probably the popular Genevan version of 1560, rather than the official Bishops' Bible of 1568.

His schooldays were stirring times for England. Mary, Queen of Scots, having

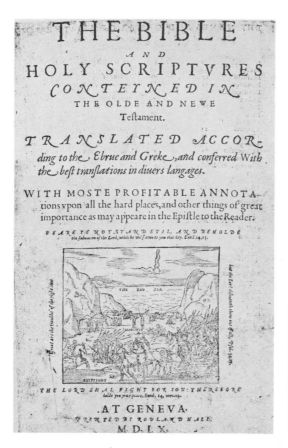

The Genevan, or 'Breeches', Bible

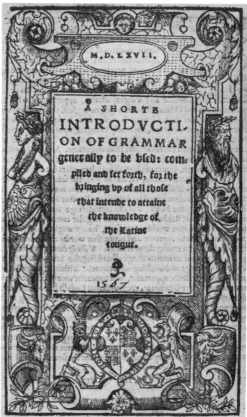

Lily's Latin Grammar, as used by Shakespeare

murdered her husband, had sought refuge in England where she was kept in close custody, and her son James VI, a sickly boy of Shakespeare's age, reigned in her stead. Then, the Counter-Reformation had been launched by the Pope. Philip II of Spain had driven his Protestant subjects in the Netherlands into revolt; France was in the throes of a religious war (it was while Elizabeth was staying at Charlecote on St. Bartholomew's day, 1572, that the Catholics had massacred the Huguenots in Paris); Elizabeth herself had been excommunicated, and there had been a Catholic rising and plots against her life. She still managed to keep England out of open war with Spain, but Drake was raiding the West Indies and Spanish Main, and in 1577 had set off on the voyage that was to take him round the world.

The seventies were also stirring times in the little world of the theatre. The

Sir Francis Drake after his voyage round the world, 1577-80

medieval miracle plays were still occasionally performed in the traditional
manner, as at Coventry, only twenty miles from Stratford, where a series of
biblical scenes was enacted by the gildsmen on movable stages, or 'pageants'.
Smaller places had to be content with more modest productions within the
arena formed by a circular bank of earth or by tiers of wooden steps erected to
accommodate the audience. Around the arena were ranged a number of canvas
'houses', rather like bathing-tents, representing the scenes in the play. The
mouth of hell was on the north side, and at the east was Heaven, a wooden hut
with the throne of God, approached by steps from a projecting stage. The actors
waited in their houses until called upon to perform, when they stepped into the
arena to play their parts, for it was here that almost all the action took place,
the stage being reserved for very exalted action in which God appeared.

But by the beginning of Elizabeth's reign the religious drama was already a curiosity, a relic of another age. In schools and at the university boys and young men were producing Latin plays in their dining-halls, and troupes of actors were wandering about the country performing 'interludes', knockabout farcical entertainments that were half acrobatic displays. The obvious place for their performance was in the medieval 'rounds', where they survived, or in the yard of an inn with its surrounding galleries. There were, however, more serious interludes, though scarcely plays in our sense of the word, written for private performance in the houses of the nobility and at Court. Small companies of players were retained to perform them, mainly in the Christmas season, after which they were free to pick up a living as best they could in London or the provinces. When Shakespeare was a boy, then, the drama was in a sorry state. The Reformation had almost killed the religious drama, and as yet the Renaissance had produced no comparable secular drama to take its place. Actors were treated as rogues and vagabonds, as many of them were, and there were no public theatres.

Miracle plays were still performed when Shakespeare was a boy

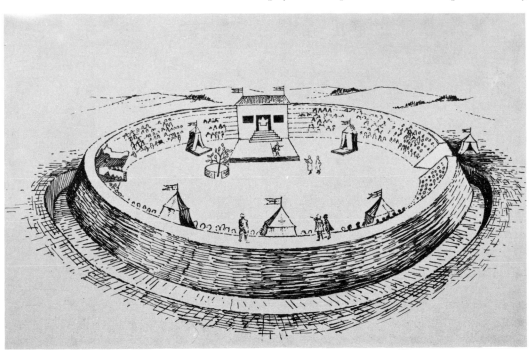

Shortly before Shakespeare's birth, however, there had been a development of great significance. Nicholas Udall, headmaster of Eton, had written a comedy modelled on Plautus for performance by boys, and Thomas Sackville and Thomas Norton a tragedy in the manner of Seneca, for presentation at Court by the students of the Inner Temple. The one, *Ralph Roister Doister,* is the first regular comedy in English, the other, *Gorboduc*, the first regular tragedy. Moreover *Gorboduc* was the first play to be written in blank verse. Here then were two plays whose classical dramatic structure might serve as a model to the shapeless episodic native interludes.

Then in the seventies came two more important developments. Acting was officially recognised as a legitimate profession, provided the player was under the patronage of a peer of the realm, and in 1576 the first public playhouse was built in London. The enterprise and vision were those of James Burbage, an obstinate ex-joiner and actor in the Earl of Leicester's company. Wisely he built The Theatre, as he proudly called it, in the rapidly expanding suburb of Shoreditch to the north of the City walls, beyond the control of the puritanical Corporation for whom the makeshift theatres in the City inns were 'meere brothel houses of Bauderie'. As we should expect, the Theatre was a combination of medieval round and inn-yard, a wooden amphitheatre of two or three galleries surrounding an open arena with projecting stage, in which the players could tumble about to their hearts' content.

Burbage soon had a competitor, for within a year the Curtain sprang up a few hundred yards nearer the City, cunningly placed to skim off a potential Theatre audience. There was also competition of another kind. The fastidious Elizabeth naturally preferred the more civilised and musical performances given by boys to the boisterous efforts of the uncouth adult actors, so that, encouraged by her favour, the Master of her choirboys rented a large room in the dissolved Blackfriars priory by the river, where they gave public performances of their

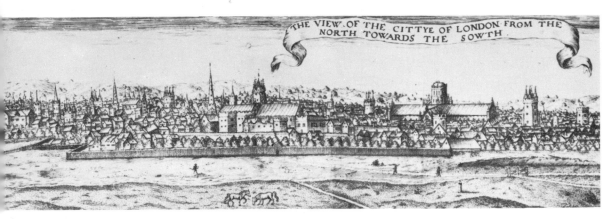

THE VIEW OF THE CITTYE OF LONDON FROM THE
NORTH TOWARDS THE SOWTH

London in 1600, showing the Curtain Theatre on the left

Title page of the first blank verse play

The Curtain Theatre,
where Shakespeare and his company
played from 1597 to 1599.
A detail from the view above

plays before production at Court. The choirboys of St. Paul's also had their little playhouse, so that by 1577 there were two open public theatres, and two roofed, or private, theatres. But again, where were the poets and dramatists to write for them?

Shakespeare, of course, knew nothing of these developments, though they had their effect even in Stratford. As early as 1569, when his father was bailiff, the Queen's Interluders, banished from Court for their incompetence, had visited the town, when they gave a first performance in the Council Chamber before being licensed to play elsewhere to the public. Then, in the seventies Stratford had become a regular centre for touring companies, notably the Earl of Leicester's, and naturally it was the Earl's company who helped to entertain the Queen when she stayed at Kenilworth in the summer of 1575. The 'Pleasures' were on a princely scale, and no doubt Shakespeare played truant on the day of the great water-pageant of the Lady of the Lake, and wondered at Arion riding on a dolphin's back.

In this year his father bought more Stratford property, but soon afterwards his fortunes began to decline. If he was a Catholic, as is possible, he may have

The site of the boys' theatre at Blackfriars

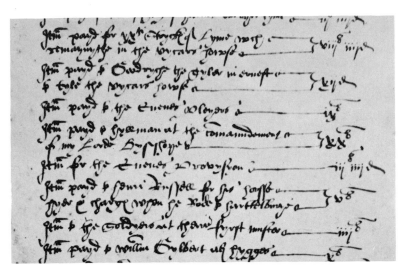

The entertainment of Queen Elizabeth referred to by Shakespeare in *A Midsummer Night's Dream*

been crippled by fines imposed under the increasingly severe recusancy measures, or he may have got involved in the affairs of his brother Henry, as he certainly did later, but whatever the cause, by 1579 he was reduced to mortgaging his wife's Wilmcote property and selling her share in the Snitterfield estate. The eight-year-old Anne died in the same year, but a third son, Richard, had been born in 1574, and to add to his troubles another child was expected soon. However, William would be sixteen in the following April, when he would leave school and be able to help in the business. This, then, was the position in the Henley Street house in the spring of 1580, as Drake approached Plymouth after his voyage round the world; John Shakespeare was in difficulties, and had five children to support: the baby Edmund, Richard aged six, Joan eleven, Gilbert fourteen, and William just sixteen. But William was now an asset rather than a liability, though one suspects that he was less interested in his father's business than in the three exciting books that had just been published: John Lyly's romance, *Euphues*, Thomas North's translation of Plutarch, and Edmund Spenser's *Shepherd's Calendar*, dedicated to Philip Sidney. The literary renaissance had begun.

In later life Shakespeare was to prove an admirable man of affairs, but as a boy he must have found the routine of business a deadly frustration, when he longed for leisure to read, and above all to write. Yet he would find some time for his adolescent scribbling, no doubt songs, sonnets and blank verse in the manner of Wyatt and Surrey, whose poems had been published shortly before his birth, and pastorals like those of the new man, Spenser. And in the course of the next two years, the hazel-eyed and auburn-haired boy—if we may trust

The *Golden Hind*, the ship in which Drake sailed round the world

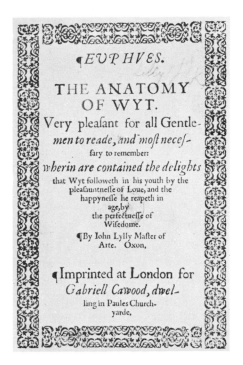

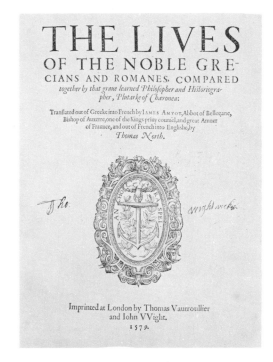

A book that influenced Shakespeare — The book used by Shakespeare for his Roman plays

the colouring on his monument—grew into a 'handsome, well-shaped' young man, just such a young man to entangle the heart of a woman.

Marriage

Across the meadows on the western fringe of Stratford lay the village of Shottery, and the thatched half-timbered farmhouse where Richard Hathaway lived with his second wife and numerous children. Richard died in 1581, and the next we hear of the family is of the proposed marriage of his eldest child, Anne, to 'William Shagspere'. Perhaps the ardent and frustrated boy of eighteen was infatuated by the woman eight years his senior, but Anne, whose chances of marriage were rapidly receding, did nothing to discourage him. By November 1582 it was impossible to conceal the fact that she was with child, and Shakespeare had to apply to the Bishop of Worcester for a special licence that would allow them to be married with only once asking of the banns. The clerk who recorded the issue of the licence muddled his entry and wrote that it was for 'Willelmum Shaxpere and Annam Whateley de Temple Grafton'. It was a very human error, for on the same day there had been a suit involving a certain William Whateley; and that it was an error is clear from the bond into which two Shottery farmers entered on the following day, November 28th, exempting

Temple Grafton Church, probably where Shakespeare and Anne Hathaway were married

Fulk Sandells and John Richardson guarantee the validity
of the proposed marriage of 'William Shagspere and Anne Hathwey'

The Hathaway farmhouse at Shottery

The clerk records the issue of a marriage licence
for 'William Shaxpere and Anne Whateley of Temple Grafton'

the bishop from liability if any irregularity should turn up after the hasty marriage. There was nothing unusual in the proceeding, and as Shakespeare was a minor he had to have such sureties. The couple would be married within a few days, probably at the village mentioned by the clerk, Temple Grafton, beyond Shottery, to escape over-curious eyes.

In accordance with the custom of the day Anne would join the family of John and Mary Shakespeare in Henley Street, where her first child, Susanna, was born in May, 1583. Her husband now seemed doomed to spend his days as a small trader in Stratford. It is true that his brother Gilbert was old enough to take his place in the family business, but William had trapped himself, or been trapped, by his marriage, and when in February, 1585 'Hamnet and Judeth sonne and daughter to William Shakspere' were christened there seemed to be no escape. Yet escape he did.

A late tradition has it that he was forced to 'fly his native country' by Sir Thomas Lucy of Charlecote, for poaching deer in his park, a picturesque though unlikely story based perhaps upon some petty trespass. According to another tradition he was for a time 'a schoolmaster in the country', some say at Dursley in the south Cotswolds, others at Rufford in Lancashire. Then there are those who think he went off to the Netherlands with the expeditionary force under Leicester, after the outbreak of open war with Spain in 1585, or,

The baptism of Shakespeare's children:
Susanna, 26 May 1583
The twins, Hamnet and Judith, 2 Feb. 1585

Hampton Lucy from Charlecote Park, scene of the poaching legend

most unlikely of all, to Italy. The chances are that he went to London when he could no longer bear the humdrum life to which he was condemned. Every year Stratford was visited by two or three companies of players, one of them Worcester's with their recent find, Edward Alleyn, two years younger than Shakespeare; and when five companies came in 1587 the attraction of London may well have proved irresistible. This was the year in which his Stratford contemporary, Richard Field, long apprenticed to a London printer, married his master's widow and took over the business. Perhaps Field had found an opening for him. In any event, Shakespeare probably went up to London in 1587, leaving his wife and three children in the care of his parents. His father seems to have been in a poor way at the time, for he had just been expelled from the borough Council, which he had not attended for many years, and

C

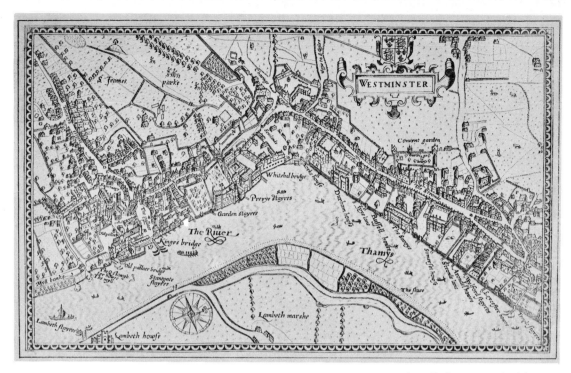

Westminster when Shakespeare arrived in 1587

sued for a debt of his brother Henry, which he had guaranteed. However, Gilbert was now twenty-one, and Joan, aged eighteen, would be a great help in the home. William was twenty-three.

London

There were two possible routes to London. After crossing Clopton bridge he could either fork right in the direction of Oxford, or he could go straight on through Banbury and Grendon, where he is said to have found the constable who was the original of Dogberry. The roads converged shortly before reaching Westminster, the seat of the central government where the great nobles had their town houses. As he walked wondering towards the City, he would pass between the old Palace of Westminster and the Abbey, and under the two gateways that connected Whitehall Palace, the Queen's principal residence, with its extension on the other side of the road. At Charing Cross he would turn east along the Strand, with Convent Garden and almost open country on the one hand, and on the other the great houses bordering the river, York House, Durham House, Somerset House, Leicester House, which must have set him thinking of Kenilworth. Then came the Inns of Court, like university colleges, where the lawyers learned their profession and the gentry how to manage their estates, and at Ludgate he entered the City.

Whitehall Palace and the great houses bordering the river

Westminster was splendid and spacious, though he had seen something like it before, at Oxford. But he had never seen anything like the City into which he now plunged, a city of 150,000 inhabitants, most of them huddled within the walls, though the suburbs to the north were rapidly growing. The brick and timber gabled houses of the merchants and shopkeepers were familiar enough, but it was the size of the place that was so unexpected and overwhelming, a town as big, or at least as populous, as a hundred Stratfords. The main thoroughfare led up Ludgate Hill, dominated by the decaying fabric of medieval St. Paul's, whose spire had fallen some years ago, and where Sir Philip Sidney had recently been buried. Then along Cheapside and Cornhill into Gracious Street, cutting through the City from south to north, the street of the great inns such as the Boar's Head, in whose yards plays were still performed. If he turned north he would soon find himself at Bishopsgate and on the road to the suburban Curtain and Theatre, if south he would come to the river and London Bridge. This was the only bridge across the Thames, many arched and lined with tall houses forming another street. Below was the Tower and the port of London, for only the smaller craft could sail beneath the arches. At the southern end, aloft on poles, were the heads of the traitors who had been

I V I T A S

The gally fuste

This description
Famous Citty LONDON
The yeare of Christe
yeare of the Moste W
Raigne of the Right
ELISABETH The
Sr Nicholas Moseley
Mator And Roger C
Wylde Sherifes of

Shakespeare's London

Mary, Queen of Scots,
executed shortly before
Shakespeare's arrival in London

executed after the discovery of the latest Catholic plot.

Shakespeare had arrived in London at one of the most exciting moments in its history. The plot had been to murder Elizabeth, rescue Mary, Queen of Scots, and with the help of Spain put her on the throne. Reluctantly Elizabeth had agreed that her cousin Mary was too dangerous to live longer, and in February she had been executed. The crisis of the war was at hand, for, in spite of Drake's dazzling raid on Cadiz, Philip II of Spain was building an Armada that would sail in the following year if not in this, and London was urgently preparing to meet invasion.

The year 1587 was also to prove one of the most exciting in the history of the theatre. If Shakespeare had crossed the river into Southwark, passed the church of St. Mary Overy, he would have come to Bankside, a region of prisons and brothels, where he would see—and smell—the Beargarden, and a similar cylindrical building just nearing completion, the Rose theatre. This was the work of Philip Henslowe, an enterprising and not over-scrupulous pawn-broker who foresaw a profitable future for the theatrical business. He had good reasons. There were now a number of reputable companies of players whose standard of acting was rapidly improving, and quite recently the Queen herself had taken a company of twelve of the leading players under her patronage. But more important, there had appeared a group of young university men who were writing plays that really were plays, and not mere knockabout entertainments.

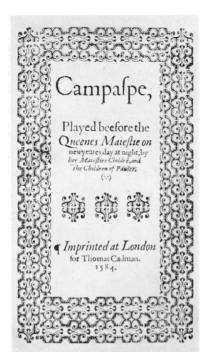

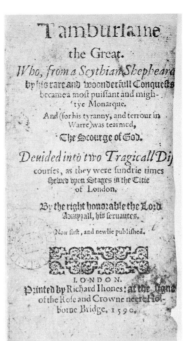

The first of Lyly's plays
to be performed at Court

Marlowe's *Tamburlaine*, one of
the first plays seen by
Shakespeare in London

There was John Lyly of Oxford, who had written a number of light sophis‚
ticated comedies for the children's company at Blackfriars. It is true that their
little private theatre had recently been closed—so much the better for the Rose—
but Lyly was popular with the Queen and still writing for the Children of
Paul's who played at their singing‚school near the cathedral, as well as at Court.
Then there was another, though less respectable Oxford man, George Peele, and
the brilliant and improvident Robert Greene of Cambridge. Perhaps Henslowe
had also met Peele's Oxford contemporary, Thomas Lodge, and Greene's young
friend Christopher Marlowe, just come down from Cambridge with the
manuscript of a play in his pocket. And it may have been at the newly opened
Rose a few months later that Shakespeare saw Edward Alleyn, now the leading
actor of the Admiral's company, play Tamburlaine. If so, it was a revelation,
and decisive in his choice of a career. It was also a revolution, for on that after‚
noon, as Alleyn declaimed the poetry of Marlowe, the modern English drama
was born.

Whatever the motives that brought Shakespeare to London, he now realised
that his true vocation was to write for the theatre, a course which meant that
the poetry he ached to write could become the very stuff of his profession. But
the plays had yet to be written, and in the meantime he had to earn a living.
The obvious course was to join a company of actors, for in that way he would
learn his craft from the inside and have a likely market for his wares.

The defeat of the Spanish Armada, July 1588 ▶

A company of actors consisted of about eight men, all of whom invested capital in a common stock of plays and apparel, sharing the profits in proportion to their investments, whence the name of 'sharers', or more picturesquely, 'full adventurers'. They had two or three boy apprentices whom they trained to play women's parts, for there were no actresses on the public stage for almost another century, and they hired a few novices, or old hands with no capital to invest, to play minor parts. It would be as a 'hireling' that Shakespeare found employ⁄ment, probably with the Queen's, the company for which Robert Greene was just beginning to write.

For some years, as we should expect, we hear nothing of the obscure actor and aspiring dramatist, and we must imagine him 'dressing' and rewriting old plays for his company, and trying his hand at original work, when he was not engaged in acting or rehearsing the numerous parts that he had to learn, for there was a different play each afternoon of the week, with a new one introduced into their repertory every fortnight or so. In the spring they performed in one of the public theatres, generally the Theatre, in the summer they went on tour, in 1589 getting as far afield as Carlisle, then back to their London theatre for an autumn season before retreating to one of the inns in Gracious Street for the winter, where they rehearsed the plays they were to present at Court.

The life of an actor with such a company, and at this time the Queen's was the most favoured of all, was a liberal education. Apart from the travel, the actors inevitably met the poets who wrote their plays, and mixed with the nobles and gallants of the Inns of Court who frequented their theatre, and sometimes invited them to perform in their dining⁄halls. Then at Christmas they per⁄formed before the Queen herself. Under Elizabeth the Court Revels began on December 26th and reached their climax on Twelfth Night, January 6th, with⁄in which Twelve Days of Christmas four or five plays were given, followed by two or three more before the beginning of Lent. Between 1587 and 1592 the Queen's Men gave fourteen of these Court performances, far more than any other company. However unpolished Shakespeare may have been when he arrived in London, it would not be long before he was at ease in the intellectual and courtly life of the capital, and he would have no difficulty in representing such a society in his plays.

Meanwhile, a new era had begun. The Armada had been destroyed, and the Spanish grip on the New World loosened. Leicester was dead, and his stepson, the handsome young Earl of Essex, had taken his place beside the aging Queen, quite eclipsing her other favourite, Sir Walter Raleigh. And, as if in celebration of these changes, the literature of England suddenly blossomed as never before. Sidney's *Arcadia* and his sonnets, and the first three books of Spenser's *Faerie Queene* were published, while in the theatre a dramatic revolution was carried

Queen Elizabeth after the destruction of the Armada

The Earl of Essex, the Queen's new favourite,
and Sir Walter Raleigh, Captain of the Guard

Sir Philip Sidney, killed in 1586,
whose sonnets inspired Shakespeare

The Redcross Knight, from *The Faerie Queene*,
published when Shakespeare was writing his first plays

through by Marlowe and the rest of the University Wits, now joined by Tom
Nashe. Then there was Thomas Kyd's *Spanish Tragedy*, a play of ghosts,
revenge and blood, that was to prove as perennially popular as Marlowe's
Tamburlaine, *Faustus* and *Jew of Malta*.

*Early Plays
and Poems*

Greene however had reached the end of his meteoric career. In September,
1592, consumed by his excesses, he lay dying in the house of a poor cobbler,
where he wrote his *Groatsworth of Wit*, an autobiographical fragment addressed
to his fellow dramatists, Marlowe, Nashe and Peele, imploring them to take
example from his fate and not to waste their wits in writing plays, from which
the only ones to profit were the players—puppets, antics, apes. But this was
not all. There was a young actor, no graduate and no gentleman, but a con-
ceited 'Shakescene', who had had the audacity to set up as dramatist and write
plays that the public preferred to his. The reference is unmistakably to Shakespeare, for 'Tygers hart wrapt in a Players hyde' is a parody of a line in *Henry VI,*

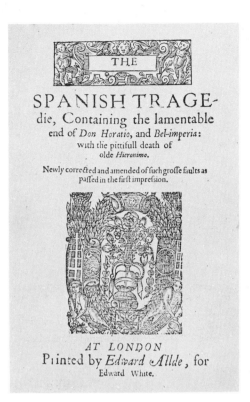

Greenes

Sweet boy, might I aduise thee, be aduisde, and get not many enemies by bitter wordes: inueigh against vaine men, for thou canst do it, no man better, no man so well: thou hast a libertie to reprooue all, and name none; for one being spoken to, all are offended; none being blamed no man is iniured. Stop shallow water still running, it will rage, or tread on a worme and it will turne: then blame not Schollers vexed with sharpe lines, if they reproue thy too much liberty of reproofe.

And thou no lesse deseruing than the other two, in some things rarer, in nothing inferiour; driuen (as my selfe) to extreme shifts, a litle haue I to say to thee: and were it not an idolatrous oth, I would sweare by sweet S. George, thou art vnworthy better hap, sith thou dependest on so meane a stay. Base minded men all three of you, if by my miserie you be not warnd: for vnto none of you (like mee) sought those burres to cleaue: those Puppets (I meane) that spake from our mouths, those Anticks garnisht in our colours. Is it not strange, that I, to whom they all haue beene beholding: is it not like that you, to whome they all haue beene beholding, shall (were yee in that case as I am now) bee both at once of them forsaken? Yes trust them not: for there is an vpstart Crow, beautified with our feathers, that with his Tygers hart wrapt in a Players hyde, supposes he is as well able to bombast out a blanke verse as the best of you: and beeing an absolute Iohannes fac totum, is in his owne conceit the onely Shake-scene in a countrey. O that I might intreat your rare wits to be imploied in more profitable courses: & let those Apes imitate your past excellence, and neuer more acquaint them with your admired inuentions. I knowe the best husband of you

Thomas Kyd's 'tragedy of revenge'   Robert Greene's attack on 'Shakescene'

Part Three. The Duke of York is addressing his captor, Queen Margaret:

> O tiger's heart wrapped in a woman's hide!
> How couldst thou drain the life-blood of the child,
> To bid the father wipe his eyes withal,
> And yet be seen to bear a woman's face?
> Women are soft, mild, pitiful and flexible;
> Thou stern, obdurate, flinty, rough, remorseless.
> Bid'st thou me rage? why, now thou hast thy wish:
> Wouldst have me weep? why, now thou hast thy will:
> For raging wind blows up incessant showers,
> And when the rage allays, the rain begins.

The verse, inflated, rhetorical and sententious, is a good example of Shakespeare's early style, modelled, as was only to be expected, on that of Marlowe.

49

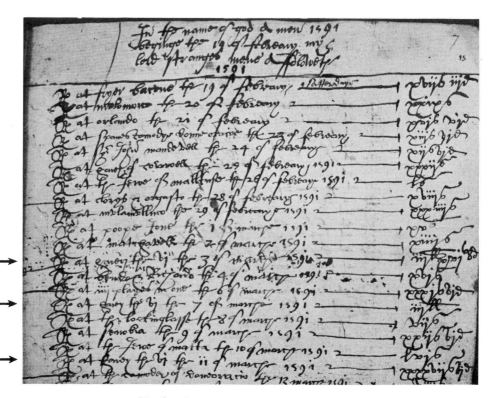

Henslowe's Diary, 1591(2): 'At harey the vj, £3.16.8'. The first record
of a performance of a Shakespeare play, *Henry VI*, Part 1

presence: than which, what can be a sharper reproofe to these degenerate effeminate dayes of ours.

    How would it haue ioyed braue Talbot (the terror of the
French) to thinke that after he had lyne two hundred yeares in
his Tombe, hee should triumphe againe on the Stage, and
haue his bones newe embalmed with the teares of ten thousand spectators at least, (at seuerall times) who in the Trage-
dian that represents his person, imagine they behold him fresh
bleeding.

    I will defend it against any Collian, or clubfisted Usurer of
them all, there is no immortalitie, can be giuen a man on earth
        F 3   like

Pierce Penilesse, 1592. Thomas Nashe's reference to the performance of *Henry VI*, Part 1

By the end of 1592, then, Shakespeare had written the three parts of *Henry VI* and made a considerable reputation as a dramatist. That he was a popular one is clear from the entry that Henslowe made in his accounts when Lord Strange's company played 'Harey the vj' (*Henry VI*, Part 1) at the Rose in the previous March. His takings were £3.16.8 (£100 of our money), the highest of the season, and its popularity is reflected in a passage of Nashe's *Pierce Penilesse*, describing the effect of the Talbot scenes in the play. Evidently Strange's had been buying up some of the stock of the Queen's, for they gave three of Greene's plays as well, all of them dismal failures financially.

Not unnaturally Shakespeare was offended by Greene's attack, and protested to the editor of the *Groatsworth of Wit*, Henry Chettle, who made a point of meeting him, and then in the Preface to his *Kind-Harts Dreame* handsomely apologised for leaving in the passage. It is the first description we have of Shakespeare, then aged twenty-eight, and it could scarcely be a more attractive one: civil in his demeanour, upright, well thought of by those in authority, an excellent actor and a graceful writer.

The worst enemies of the players were Puritans and plague. The Puritans, strongly entrenched in the City Corporation, would have liked to see the theatres plucked down and the prosperous and swaggering actors whipped and put to profitable employment, but since the Queen's open patronage of players they had been on the defensive. The most that Elizabeth and her Privy Council would allow was the closing of the theatres in time of plague, from which for

The first description of Shakespeare: Henry Chettle's apology in *Kind-Harts Dreame*, 1592

To the Gentlemen Readers.

sory, as if the originall fault had beene my fault, becaufe my felfe haue feene his demeanor no leffe ciuill than he exclent in the qualitie he profeffes: Befides, diuers of worfhip haue reported, his vp-rightnes of dealing, which argues his honefty, and his facetious grace in writting, that aprooues his Art. For the firft, whofe learning I reuerence, and at the perufing of Greenes Booke, ftroke out what then in confcience I thought he in fome dif-pleafure writ: or had it beene true, yet to publifh

the last ten years London had been virtually free; indeed there had been no serious outbreak since the year before Shakespeare's birth. But in the summer of 1592 the dreaded pestilence struck again, at the height of its fury claiming a thousand victims in a single week. The theatres were closed, and the companies driven unprofitably into the provinces to 'stalk upon boards and barrel-heads to an old cracked trumpet'. Winter brought no relief, 1593 was even worse, and it was the summer of 1594 before the theatres reopened.

What was Shakespeare doing during these two years? By this time we should expect him to be a sharer and no longer a hireling, but there is no record of his touring with any of the companies. A mere actor had no alternative to this unrewarding vagabondage, but Shakespeare was now primarily a writer and would be far more profitably employed in practising his craft. In Stratford he had a wife and three young children of whom he could have seen little for the last five years, and we may, I think, be pretty sure that it was with them that he spent the greater part of the period of plague. The Queen's made for Stratford soon after it began, and possibly he accompanied and left them there, arranging to rejoin them when the theatres reopened.

He would find his father still in trouble, having recently been included in a list of recusants for 'not comminge monethlie to the churche, it is sayd for feare of process for debtte'. This, however, is the last we hear of his misfortunes, probably because his successful son was able to help him put his affairs in order. They were busy years for the young dramatist. He had already written *Richard III*—creating incidentally his first great character—so rounding off the *Henry VI* trilogy, and now in his new-found happiness he turned naturally to comedy and lyric poetry. *The Comedy of Errors, The Taming of the Shrew* and *The Two Gentlemen of Verona* belong to this idyllic period, as do the early sonnets and the two long poems, *Venus and Adonis* and *The Rape of Lucrece*. Like Marlowe, he was still mainly interested in the poetry and the event, in telling a tragic, horrible, farcical or amorous story. His attitude to his characters, the serious ones at least, is detached, and there is something just a little callous in the way he moves his puppets and makes them speak and suffer. He was, in short, a healthy, happy and successful young poet of thirty. But the influence of Marlowe became progressively less, and the almost brutal martial music of his master's characteristic line was transformed into a more flexible and dancing measure, even in *Richard III*:

> *And now, instead of mounting barbed steeds*
> *To fright the souls of fearful adversaries,*
> *He capers nimbly in a lady's chamber*
> *To the lascivious pleasing of a lute.*

VENVS
AND ADONIS

Vilia miretur vulgus: mihi flauus Apollo
Pocula Caſtalia plena miniſtret aqua.

LONDON
Imprinted by Richard Field, and are to be ſold at
the ſigne of the white Greyhound in
Paules Church-yard.
1593.

The first work of Shakespeare
to be published

Venus and Adonis, the first of his works to be published, was beautifully printed by his friend Richard Field in 1593, and proved so popular that it went through nine editions in as many years. Every author tried to find a patron, and so he dedicated his poem hopefully to Henry Wriothesley, Earl of Southampton, a wealthy and influential young man of twenty, promising him a 'graver labour' if this amorous tale met with his approval. It did, and in the following year Field printed *The Rape of Lucrece* with another dedication to Southampton.

It was the publication of Sidney's sonnets that inspired Shakespeare to try his hand at the new form, and, as in Sidney's, a story runs obscurely through the sequence. They are addressed mainly to a beautiful young man who steals

D

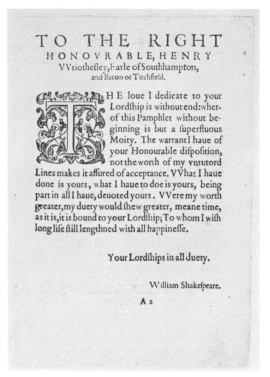

Dedication of *The Rape of Lucrece*

One of the two main claimants to be 'Mr. W.H.'
Henry Wriothesley, Earl of Southampton

away his mistress, a dark married woman, and then transfers his favour to another poet. Probably the story is almost as mythical as that of Venus and Adonis, and little more than a framework to support the poet's meditations on love and friendship. But when the sonnets were printed fifteen years later the publisher added an enigmatic dedication to 'Mr. W.H.', and who this W.H.— and the dark lady and rival poet—could have been has led to much throwing about of brains. There is no real clue to the lady and the poet—Chapman is the best guess—but it is of course tempting to believe that W.H. are the reversed initials of Henry Wriothesley, and that he, Shakespeare's patron, was the 'begetter' or inspirer of the sonnets. Some claim a more youthful peer, William Herbert, future Earl of Pembroke, who was only twelve in 1592. It is just possible, for Shakespeare probably knew Pembroke's mother, Sidney's sister,

Dedication of Shakespeare's
Sonnets to 'Mr.W.H.', by the
publisher, Thomas Thorpe

Another 'W.H.'
William Herbert,
Earl of Pembroke

In praise of Willobie *his* Auisa, *Hex-*ameton to the Author.

IN Lauine Land though Liuie boſt,
There hath beene ſeene a Conſtant *dame:*
Though Rome *lament that ſhe haue loſt*
The Gareland *of her rareſt fame,*
  Yet now we ſee, that here is found,
  As great a Faith *in* Engliſh *ground.*

Though Collatine *haue deerely bought,*
To high renowne, a laſting life,
And found, that moſt in vaine haue ſought,
To haue a Faire, *and* Conſtant *wife,*
  Yet Tarquyne *pluckt his gliſtering grape,*
  And Shake-ſpeare, *paints poore* Lucrece *rape.*

Willobie his Avisa, 1594. The first literary reference to Shakespeare by name

CANT. XLIIII.

Henrico Willobego. Italo-Hiſpalenſis.

H. W. being ſodenly infected with the contagion
of a fantaſticall fit, at the firſt ſight of *A,* pyneth a
while in ſecret griefe, at length not able any longer to
indure the burning heate of ſo feruent a humour, be-
wrayeth the ſecreſy of his diſeaſe vnto his familiar
frend W. S. who not long before had tryed the cur-
teſy

Was Henry Willoughby 'Mr. W.H.'?

and visited their house at Wilton, frequented by so many poets of the period. There is another possibility. In 1594 Henry Willoughby, an Oxford undergraduate, published *Willobie his Avisa,* a poem lamenting his unrequited love for the virtuous Avisa. In the prose introduction to one of the cantos H.W. tells how he confided his grief to his 'familiar friend W.S.', an 'old player' at the game of love, who had just recovered from a like passion. Perhaps H.W. is Mr. W.H., and that the reference is to Shakespeare and his affair with the dark lady is made slightly more probable by the mention of *The Rape of Lucrece* in the commendatory verses prefixed to the poem. At least the line has the merit of being the first literary reference to Shakespeare by name. But the hypothesis is not very convincing, and if W.H. really was Shakespeare's friend he may have been any one of a hundred young men of whom we have never heard. More prosaically, he may merely have been the man who secured a manuscript copy of the sonnets for Thomas Thorpe to publish without Shakespeare's permission.

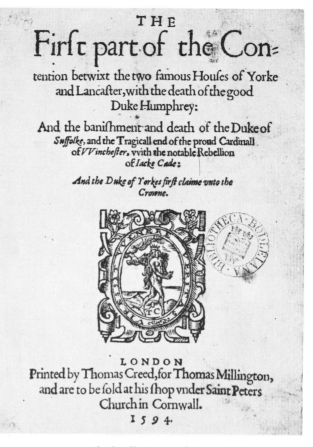

The 'Bad' Quarto of *Henry VI,* Part 2, 1594, one of the first of Shakespeare's plays to be published

Such literary piracy was only too common in Shakespeare's day, when there was no copyright in our sense of the word. All books, plays and pamphlets were supposed to be entered in the Register of the Stationers' Company, who protected the publisher, on payment of his sixpence, from any infringement of his rights, but there was nobody to protect the luckless author or the company of actors to whom he had sold a play—normally for £5 or £6—from an unscrupulous publisher who managed to get hold of a copy. The companies therefore took great care of their manuscript plays, rarely making more than one copy, but sometimes an actor memorised the text as best he could, wrote it out, and sold it to a publisher who issued the mangled version as the genuine article. This is what happened in 1594 to *Henry VI,* Part 2, published as *The First Part of the Contention.* Plays were normally issued as quartos, a term describing the

The first illustration to Shakespeare: a production of *Titus Andronicus*, c. 1594

size of the printed page, and these corrupt texts have been given the name of 'bad' quartos. There are at least six Shakespearean 'bad' quartos, of which the most famous is *Hamlet*.

When times were bad the companies were driven to sell some of their stock, and in this manner *Titus Andronicus* found its way into the market, probably appearing just before 2 *Henry VI*, thus becoming the first of Shakespeare's plays to be published. For times were very bad in 1594. The plague had played havoc with the companies. The Earl of Pembroke's had to pawn their clothes, the Queen's were broken and became a second-rate troupe of provincial players, and the only companies to weather the storm were the Admiral's (that is, the company of Lord Admiral Howard who had commanded the fleet against the Armada) and the Earl of Derby's, formerly Lord Strange's. Derby died in the spring, but the company had found another patron in Lord Hunsdon who, as Lord Chamberlain, was responsible for the conduct of the theatres and the presentation of plays at Court. As he was also Elizabeth's favourite cousin they could scarcely have found a more promising patron.

The Lord Chamberlain's Servant

When the theatres reopened, therefore, Shakespeare's choice of companies was really limited to two. Though both would be more than eager to have him and his new plays he threw in his lot with the Chamberlain's, with whom he was to stay for the rest of his career. Other members of that immortal fellowship were John Heminge, apparently a former colleague of Shakespeare's with the Queen's, Augustine Phillips the musician, Will Kempe the celebrated dancer and comedian, Henry Condell and Richard Burbage, younger son of James Burbage, owner of the Theatre. So it was to the Theatre that the Chamberlain's went in the wet summer of 1594, while their rivals, the Admiral's, under

Will Kempe dancing a morris

The patron of Shakespeare's company, and two of its leading members

Lord Chamberlain Hunsdon

Richard Burbage,
who played Shakespeare's heroes.
Possibly a self-portrait

Edward Alleyn of the Admiral's company,
who played Marlowe's tragic heroes

Henslowe and his new son-in-law Edward Alleyn, settled in again at the Rose on the other side of the river. Shakespeare took lodgings not far from the Theatre, in the neighbourhood of Bishopsgate.

He would find the theatrical scene strangely altered, for not only had the plague years quite transformed the actors' companies, they had also witnessed the virtual extinction of the men who had carried through the first stage of the dramatic revolution. Greene had died in 1592, a year later Marlowe had been killed in a brawl, and Kyd too was dead. Peele was dying, Lodge had turned adventurer and no longer wrote for the stage. Lyly had written nothing since the Paul's boys had ceased playing three years before, and Nashe was a pamphleteer rather than a playwright. At the age of thirty Shakespeare was left without rivals more formidable than Chettle and the 'peaking pageanter' Anthony Munday.

This was a serious position for Henslowe, now virtual owner of the Admiral's and their stock. Marlowe had been his man, and though he could go on producing his half-dozen plays he would have to find new men to supply new matter if he was to compete with Shakespeare and the Chamberlain's. His solution was a brilliant one from a commercial point of view. Less interested in quality than quantity and a rapid turnover of new plays, he set up a sort of dramatic workshop to which he enticed needy poets with the bait of steady

George Chapman, possibly the
rival poet of Shakespeare's *Sonnets*

The poet Michael Drayton,
Shakespeare's friend,
and a frequent visitor to Stratford

'Rare Ben Jonson', who 'loved Shakespeare, on this side idolatry, as much as any'

employment at a fixed, though admittedly not excessive, wage. In this way he attracted Munday and Chettle, and two of Shakespeare's contemporaries, Chapman and Drayton, true poets though with no particular aptitude for writing plays, and a number of younger men in their early twenties, a second generation as it were to replace the University Wits, including Thomas Heywood, Thomas Dekker, Ben Jonson and John Marston. Having collected his men he set them to work as a team in the mass-production of plays, each concentrating on what he could do best—tragedy, comedy, pathos, and so on. Munday, an ingenious spinner of plots, seems to have been in charge.

One of the plays manufactured by Munday and his men, or at least two of them, Chettle and Heywood, was *Sir Thomas More*, but when it went to the Master of the Revels to be licensed for production it was censored and returned for revision. Munday called in two more of his team to help, one being Dekker, and the other an unknown author who wrote three new pages describing More's pacification of a riot. These three pages are of profound importance, for the unknown author is thought by some scholars to be Shakespeare, and the writing to be his hand. If so, it is an invaluable aid to the correction of errors in the printed text of his plays, for we can understand the kind of mistake a printer might make when working from such a script, in which, for example, the letters *e, o* and *d* are easily confused. There is a strong case to be made for

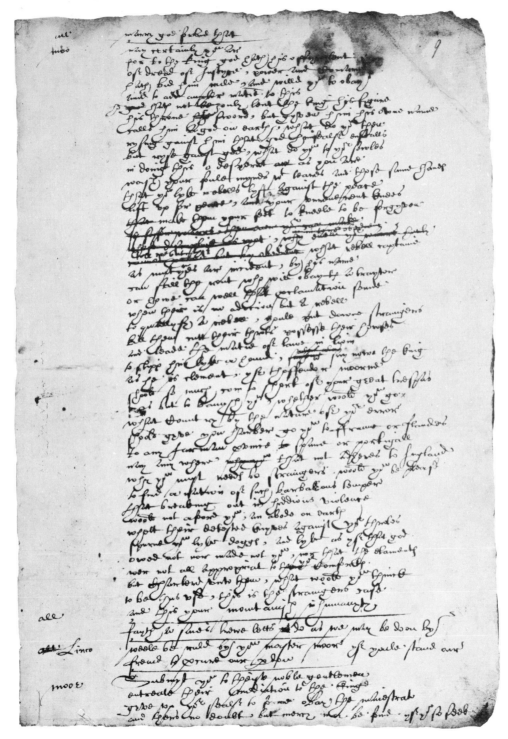

A page from *Sir Thomas More*, possibly in Shakespeare's handwriting

Shakespeare's hand, but inevitably it depends mainly on a comparison with authentic specimens of his writing, and of these there are only six, all of them signatures made some twenty years later. Then, it seems in the highest degree unlikely that Shakespeare would help to revise an Admiral's play produced as a counterblast to his own work for the Chamberlain's.

That he really was a member of the Chamberlain's is proved by the record of his being one of the payees for the company, along with Kempe and Burbage, for two Court performances at Greenwich Palace at Christmas 1594. They were paid £6.13.4 for each performance and £3.6.8 'by way of Her Majesty's reward', the customary handsome tip from the Queen when she herself was present; £20 in all, or about £600 to-day, an enviable sum for distribution among eight sharers, even after paying for their costumes, their hirelings and boys. There would be few other expenses, as the Revels Office supplied any properties they needed, including the lath and canvas 'houses' that served as scenes, as in the medieval plays. One of their 'comedies or Enterludes' would almost certainly be *The Comedy of Errors,* which they presented on the following night in the hall of Gray's Inn. This was the Inn's 'Grand Night', when they entertained their neighbours from the Inner Temple, the festivities proving so riotous that on the next day a mock trial was held in which a sorcerer was found guilty of foisting on them 'a company of base and common Fellows to make up our disorders with a Play of Errors and Confusion'.

Although the Admiral's gave as many Court performances as the Chamberlain's that Christmas, they lost ground in the following year, and by 1596 were completely eclipsed, the Chamberlain's giving all six performances. Shakespeare's lyrical vein seemed inexhaustible, and comedy, tragedy and history flowed from his pen, all crammed with the splendid poetry of the sonnets. What had the Admiral's to offer against *Love's Labour's Lost, A Midsummer Night's Dream, Romeo and Juliet,* and *Richard II*? And how could they compete with such poetry as this?—

> *For Orpheus' lute was strung with poets' sinews*
> *Whose golden touch could soften steel and stones,*
> *Make tigers tame and huge leviathans*
> *Forsake unsounded deeps to dance on sands.*

Or this?

> *Death, that hath suck'd the honey of thy breath,*
> *Hath had no power yet upon thy beauty:*
> *Thou art not conquer'd; beauty's ensign yet*
> *Is crimson in thy lips and in thy cheeks,*
> *And death's pale flag is not advanced there.*

Payment to Kempe, Shakespeare and Burbage
for a performance at Greenwich Palace, Christmas 1594

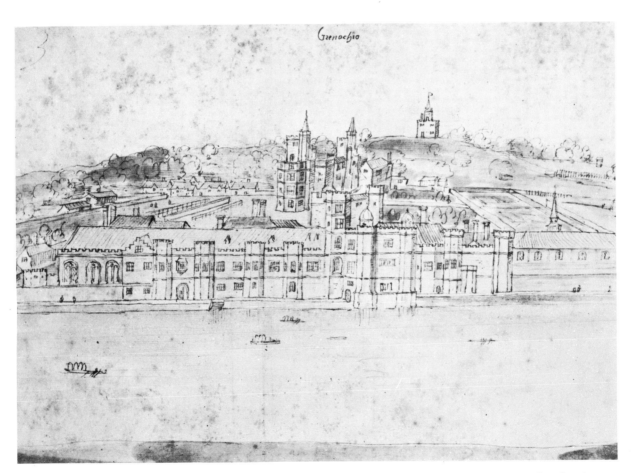

Greenwich Palace in 1594

65

The Hall of Gray's Inn, where *The Comedy of Errors* was performed in December 1594

But if Henslowe could not compete with the Chamberlain's at Court, he could at least provide his company and their audiences with a better theatre, and he spent more than £100 in painting and 'other repracyones' at the Rose. Such improvements and repairs were all the more necessary now that a rival had appeared on Bankside. This was Francis Langley, who in the course of 1595 built the 'finest and biggest' theatre in London, the Swan in Paris Garden, about a quarter of a mile further west.

Soon after its opening a Dutchman called de Witt saw a play there, and made a sketch. Unfortunately this has been lost, but a friend made a copy, and as this is our only contemporary illustration of the interior of an Elizabethan theatre it is of the first importance. Yet it must be treated with caution, for not only is it merely a copy, but the original drawing itself was no more than a sketch from memory, for if de Witt had been sitting in the theatre at the time he would not have drawn a bird's-eye view. However, it gives a good general

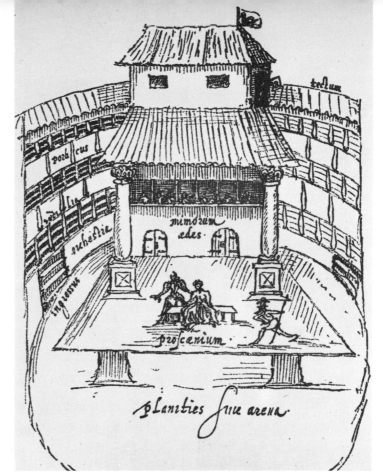

The Swan Theatre, built by Francis Langley,
~~ere Shakespeare and his company played in 1596-7

impression. Here are the galleries surrounding the arena with its apron stage,
partly sheltered by a canopy or 'shadow' supported on pillars. At the back is
the *mimorum aedes,* the actors' quarters or tiring-house, from which two doors
lead on to the stage. Above these is a gallery in which apparently are spectators,
and at the top is a hut, the medieval 'heavens', where thunder and other celestial
—and terrestrial—noises were manufactured. Presumably there is another
gallery, perhaps for musicians, hidden by the canopy. The most puzzling
feature is the absence of an upper stage, if the people in the gallery really are
spectators and not actors, and of a small curtained stage below. By this time,
when plays were no longer acrobatic entertainments, the 'groundlings' who
stood in the bottom gallery may have been turned into the yard, to the great
profit of the players, and it is now that we first hear of gallants hiring stools to
sit on the stage itself.

The Chamberlain's would be as interested as Henslowe in Langley's ven-

'Hamnet, son of William Shakspere', buried 11 August 1596

ture, though for another reason. The lease of the land on which the Theatre stood was running out, and if Burbage failed to get a renewal on reasonable terms, as seemed probable, the Swan would be a welcome alternative.

Stratford Affairs
So matters stood in the summer of 1596, when Shakespeare received news that his son, Hamnet, was desperately ill. Perhaps the boy died before he could reach Stratford, though it is impossible to read *King John*, which he was then writing, without finding a reflection of his anguish as he took the little body in his arms, in the line of Faulconbridge watching Hubert lift the body of the boy Arthur, 'How easy dost thou take all England up!' For Hamnet was his only son, all England to him in his grief. He was only eleven.

Yet so much remained. His wife Anne, it is true, was now forty, eight years his senior, and perhaps no very congenial companion for a poet accustomed to the life of London and the Court. But there was Hamnet's twin, Judith, and her sister Susanna, two years older. Then, his father and mother were still alive, and with them his sister and three brothers, for they were all as yet unmarried, Edmund, the youngest, being not much older than Hamnet. The Henley Street house was getting decidedly small for such a family, particularly since the great fires of the last two years, when one end had to be pulled down to prevent its catching alight. It had been a disastrous period, for more than two hundred buildings had been destroyed, most of them at the upper end of the town, and many of the Shakespeares' friends, including the Quineys and Sturleys, had been left homeless. But the new houses were going up, the finest being that of the bailiff, wealthy Thomas Rogers, in High Street.

When John Shakespeare had been bailiff, nearly thirty years before, eager in his prosperity to gentle his condition he had applied for a grant of arms, but during his years of adversity had had no heart to pursue the matter. Now that his fortunes had been restored, thanks to his successful son, he renewed the claim; for though Hamnet was dead, he had four sons, and the chances were that there would be other grandsons to inherit the rank of gentleman. A few months earlier William would have been as eager as his father, but now it must

The Stratford house built by Thomas Rogers, Shakespeare's neighbour and grandfather of John Harvard

68

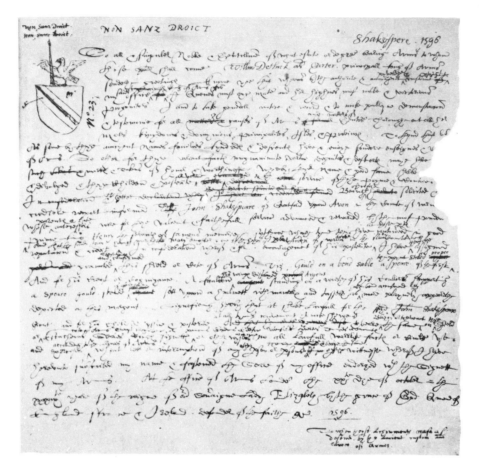

The Grant of Arms
to John Shakespeare

have seemed something of a vanity; yet there were Susanna and Judith to be considered, his brothers too, and he himself was not without ambition. So the application was made, and in October John Shakespeare, gentleman, was granted a coat of arms: 'Gould, on a bend sable, a speare of the first steeled argent. And for his creast or cognizaunce a faulcon, his wings displayed Argent standing on a wrethe of his coullers, supporting a speare gould steeled as aforesaid.'

Shakespeare was in no hurry to leave Stratford, for as the Chamberlain's were on tour there was no reason why he should return to London before they began rehearsals for the Revels, and perhaps it was during his protracted stay that he began the almost cynical and heartless *Merchant of Venice,* the last of the lyrical plays, in which his early poetry reaches perfection. When at length he did return he found the affairs of his company in some confusion. Lord Huns-don had died, and though his son had agreed to become their patron he was not the new Lord Chamberlain. This was Lord Cobham, no friend of the players, and the City Corporation made the most of their golden opportunity. They had failed to prevent the building of the Swan, according to them merely another place of meeting for 'theeves, horsestealers, whoremoongers, coozeners, connycatching persones, practizers of treason & such other lyke', but now they succeeded in persuading Cobham and the Privy Council to close the inn-theatres in the City. This was a severe blow, as the Chamberlain's used the Cross Keys in the winter, when the Theatre and Curtain proved too far afield, the way too miry, for London's citizens. So they came to terms with Langley, booked the Swan for the

Shakespeare's new patron, the second Lord Chamberlain Hunsdon

winter season, and Shakespeare moved his lodgings from Bishopsgate to Bankside. His association with Langley was soon to involve him in a quarrel.

Langley was on the worst of terms with one of the local Surrey magistrates, William Gardiner, whom he had publicly denounced, apparently with every justification, as 'a false perjured knave', scarcely a conciliatory phrase. The furious Gardiner thereupon enlisted the aid of his worthless stepson, William Wayte, and the two so threatened Langley that he sought legal protection from them, 'for fear of death, and so forth'. The danger was a real one in those turbulent days of swaggering gallants, when swords were light in their sheaths and constables as discreet as Dogberry. Marlowe had been had up for murder before he was himself killed with a dagger, and Jonson narrowly escaped hanging for running through a fellow actor with his sword. Gardiner would stick at nothing, and as a magistrate would certainly do his best to ruin Langley

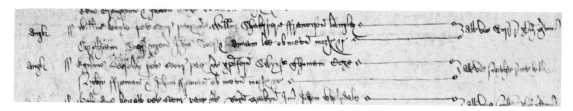

William Wayte craves sureties of the peace against William Shakspere and Francis Langley

Sir Thomas Lucy, buried in Charlecote church, 1600

by closing the Swan. No doubt this was why Shakespeare came to his aid, and why Wayte in his turn craved sureties of the peace against 'William Shakspere, Francis Langley' and two unknown women, Dorothy Soer and Anne Lee. Evidently Shakespeare was a dangerous opponent, though if Gardiner was the original of Justice Shallow he was a generous one, for the satire is nothing like as ferocious as that rascally magistrate deserved. But perhaps the fussy and ineffectual Shallow was a caricature of his Stratford neighbour and traditional persecutor, Sir Thomas Lucy.

He could not resist a hit at Lord Cobham, the man who had closed the Cross Keys to him and his company, and in his next play, *Henry IV,* gave the fat and uncourageous knight the name of his ancestor, Sir John Oldcastle. Cobham protested, and, to the great delight of his numerous enemies, Shakespeare changed the name to Falstaff, another historical character with a kind of alacrity in running away. The name stuck, and thenceforth Cobham was facetiously known as Falstaff. Shakespeare had his revenge. But in the spring of 1597 Lord Chamberlain Cobham died, unwept of the players, and to the great joy of Shakespeare and his fellows, their patron, the second Lord Hunsdon, was appointed to the vacant office. Once more they were the Lord Chamberlain's men.

Shortly after this Shakespeare was in Stratford again. He had money to invest, and like his father prudently put it into property. For some time he had had his eye on New Place, the 'praty howse of brike and tymber' opposite the Gild Chapel and his old school. The owner was William Underhill, 'a covetous and crafty man' who stood out for a stiff price, and in May Shakespeare paid him £60 for the house with its two barns, two gardens and two orchards. A few weeks later Underhill was poisoned by his crazy son.

There were repairs to be done, for the house was in poor condition, and the two parts of *Henry IV* are full of images that reveal Shakespeare's preoccupation with building—'The frame and huge foundation of the earth', 'like one that draws the model of a house', and so on. More prosaically, he sold a ton of stone to the Corporation for the repair of Clopton bridge, perhaps the remains of one of his tumble-down barns. This was his first house, and his delight in ordinary domestic occupations is reflected in the homely imagery that character-

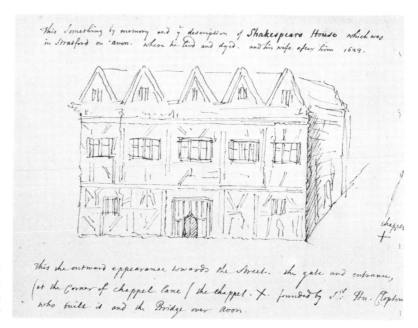

The house that Shakespeare bought in Stratford: New Place, 'a praty howse of brike and tymber'

ises the plays of this period, and indeed all his later work: 'Knit our powers to the arm of peace', 'like the bees, culling from every flower', for undoubtedly there were bees in the long-neglected garden that he was putting in order:

> *He cannot so precisely weed this land . . .*
> *His foes are so enrooted with his friends*
> *That, plucking to unfix an enemy,*
> *He doth unfasten so and shake a friend.*

And when he looked up from his gardening in the afternoon he saw the school-boys running 'east, west, north, south' along the crossroads at his corner, and naturally described the dispersal of an army as 'like a school broke up, Each hurries toward his home and sporting-place'—very different from their snail-like morning crawl, equally observed. His heart must have ached. Hamnet should have been among them.

The Middle Comedies

The death of Hamnet had a profound effect on Shakespeare, both as man and artist. He did not turn to tragic themes as a lesser man might have done; on the contrary, the plays of the next few years are the most seeming-happy of all. But there is a new mellowness and compassion, an extension of sympathy and understanding to characters of all classes and all ages. He was no longer a somewhat self-centred lover and poet identifying himself almost exclusively with the lovers and poets in his plays, but a dramatist with a passionate interest in all people, and the change was reflected in his style. The old lyrical elation was subdued and these historical and romantic comedies, from *Henry IV* to *Twelfth Night*, were written in a language much closer to that really spoken by men than anything that had gone before. We have only to compare the end of *The Merchant of Venice* with the opening of *Henry IV* to see the transition from the lovely but undramatic lyricism to a more natural and dramatic verse. Here is the Venetian Lorenzo:

> *The moon shines bright: in such a night as this,*
> *When the sweet wind did gently kiss the trees*
> *And they did make no noise, in such a night*
> *Troilus methinks mounted the Troyan walls,*
> *And sighed his soul toward the Grecian tents,*
> *Where Cressid lay that night.*

And here the English Harry:

> *So shaken as we are, so wan with care,*
> *Find we a time for frighted peace to pant,*
> *And breathe short-winded accents of new broils*
> *To be commenced in strands afar remote.*

The earlier plays had been mainly in verse, often in rhyme, and prose had been reserved for comic characters, significantly enough more memorable than most of the verse speakers, for lyric poetry is not the stuff of which men and women are made. But the plays of this group were for the most part written in prose, which now became the speech of kings as well as clowns, and out of it Shakespeare created many of his most lovable characters—Falstaff, Benedick, Beatrice and Rosalind. In short, lyric poetry gave way to dramatic prose, as dramatic prose was in turn to lead up to dramatic poetry.

It seems probable that after buying New Place Shakespeare no longer went on tour with his company, but whenever he could spent the summer in Stratford with his family. It would certainly pay the Chamberlain's handsomely to give their dramatist time to write the plays on which their prosperity so largely depended, and he is not likely to have demurred at such an arrangement. So we may imagine him settling into New Place in the summer of 1597 with his wife and two young daughters, writing *Henry IV*, and perhaps finding time to attend the wedding of his sister Joan, which probably took place somewhere in the neighbourhood of Stratford. Her husband was William Hart, a hatter, and the couple took over the rooms in the Henley Street house vacated by the family at New Place.

On his return to London Shakespeare found that there had been disturbing developments in his absence. Old James Burbage had died, and his sons Cuthbert and Richard had been unable to renew the lease of the land on which the Theatre stood. To make matters more difficult, Langley had got into trouble in July for allowing the Earl of Pembroke's players to produce a satirical comedy, *The Isle of Gulls*, at the Swan. On the grounds that it contained 'very seditious and sclanderous matter' the Privy Council ordered the closing of all the theatres, the imprisonment of some of the players and of the authors, one of whom was Nashe, who escaped, and the other Ben Jonson. Then when the general ban was lifted in October Langley was refused a renewal of his licence for the Swan as a theatre, and had to turn it into a sort of circus. Evidently Gardiner too had his revenge. This meant that the Theatre, Swan, and City inns were all closed to the Chamberlain's, while the Rose, of course, was occupied by the Admiral's. The only other theatre was the Curtain, not easily accessible in winter, and for the time being the Chamberlain's had to be content with this old and second-rate house.

Perhaps it was to help tide over this difficult period that they sold four of Shakespeare's plays to the publishers in 1597-98: *Richard II, Richard III, 1 Henry IV,* and *Love's Labour's Lost,* the first play to be published with his name. It should be noted that Shakespeare himself did not sell to the publishers, and had little control therefore over their production, the quality of which varied with the

The first play to be published
with Shakespeare's name

printer; William White, for example, made a poor job of the *Love's Labour's Lost* quarto, while Valentine Simmes produced a relatively good text of *Richard II*, though even he made 69 errors, and when he printed a second edition, after correcting 14, added 123 new ones. Plays simply were not treated as serious literature, and the best printers did not deal in them, and though Shakespeare might have insisted on seeing proofs, he was incurably easy-going and too deeply absorbed in what he was writing to trouble himself overmuch about what he had written.

Not everybody, however, took such a contemptuous view of plays as the stationers. In September, 1598, a schoolmaster called Francis Meres published his *Palladis Tamia: Wit's Treasury*, one section of which is a fantastic attempt to find classical parallels for contemporary English poets. As criticism it is quite valueless, but for the information that it gives about Shakespeare it is beyond price. It needed no 'Maister of Artes of both Universities' to tell us that he was considered the best dramatist of the day, both for comedy and tragedy, but only an intelligent contemporary in touch with writers and the theatre could have

mong al writers to be of an honeſt life and
vpright conuerſation:ſo *Michael Drayton*
(*què toties honoris & amoris cauſa nomino*)
among ſchollers, ſouldiours, Poets, and all
ſorts of people, is helde for a man of vertuous diſpoſition, honeſt conuerſation , and
wel gouerned cariage, which is almoſt miraculous among good wits in theſe declining and corrupt times, when there is nothing but rogery in villanous man, & whē
cheating and craſtines is counted the clea-
neſt wit, and ſoundeſt wiſedome.

As *Decius Auſonius Gallus in libris Fa-
ſtorum*, penned the occurrences of ȳ world
from the firſt creation of it to his time, that
is, to the raigne of the Emperor *Gratian*: ſo
Warner in his abſolute *Albions Englande*
hath moſt admirably penned the hiſtorie
of his own country from *Noah* to his time,
that is, to the raigne of Queene *Elizabeth*;
I haue heard him termd of the beſt wits of
both our Vniuerſities, our Engliſh *Homer*.

As *Euripedes* is the moſt ſententious a-
mong the Greek Poets:ſo is *Warner* amõg
our Engliſh Poets.

As the ſoule of *Euphorbus* was thought
to liue in *Pythagoras* : ſo the ſweete wittie
ſoule of *Ouid* liues in melliſluous & hony-
tongued *Shakeſpeare*, witnes his *Venus* and
Adonis, his *Lucrece* , his ſugred Sonnets
among

among his priuate friends, &c.

As *Plautus* and *Seneca* are accounted
the beſt for Comedy and Tragedy among
the Latines : ſo *Shakeſpeare* among ȳ Engliſh is the moſt excellent in both kinds for
the ſtage; for Comedy, witnes his *Gētlemē
of Verona*, his *Errors*, his *Loue labors loſt*, his
Loue labours wonne, his *Midſummers night
dreame*, & his *Merchant of Venice*: for Tragedy his *Richard the 2. Richard the 3. Henry the 4. King Iohn, Titus Andronicus* and
his *Romeo* and *Iuliet*.

As *Epius Stolo* ſaid, that the Muſes would
ſpeake with *Plautus* tongue, if they would
ſpeak Latin: ſo I ſay that the Muſes would
ſpeak with *Shakeſpeares* fine filed phraſe, if
they would ſpeake Engliſh.

As *Muſæus*, who wrote the loue of *Hero*
and *Leander*, had two excellent ſchollers,
Thamaras & *Hercules*: ſo hath he in England two excellent Poets, imitators of him
in the ſame argument and ſubiect, *Chriſto-
pher Marlow*, and *George Chapman*.

As *Ouid* ſaith of his worke;
*Iamȳ opus exegi, quod nec Iouis iva, nec ignis,
Nec poterit ferrum, nec edax abolere vetuſtas.*

And as *Horace* ſaith of his; *Exegi monu-
nentū ære perennius; Regaliȳ, ſitu pyramidū
uod non imber edax; Non Aquilo
poſſit diruere; aut innumerabilis*
O o 2, *annorum*

'Hony-tongued Shakespeare': a contemporary opinion

told us that his sonnets were then circulating among his friends, and recorded
twelve of the plays that he had written. Meres had a pedantic passion for balance
in his prose—six comedies set against six tragedies—which may account for his
omission of the three parts of *Henry VI*, and his not inappropriate title of
'Loue labours wonne' for, presumably, *The Taming of the Shrew*.

Palladis Tamia was fresh from the press when the Chamberlain's opened their
autumn season at the Curtain with Jonson's first important comedy, *Every Man
in his Humour*. There is a tradition that Shakespeare was responsible for his
company's acceptance of the play; certainly he acted in it, and Jonson's list of
the 'principall comœdians', appended later to the collected edition of his
Works, is the first definite record of his acting, and incidentally the first complete
cast of the company. Condell and Sly were now full adventurers, but Beeston
and Duke were hirelings, and never became sharers. The play was a portent,
a realistic comedy with a purpose, and a revolt against the romantic plays of
Shakespeare, of which Jonson made fun in his Prologue. Shakespeare replied
in *As You Like It* with a genial sketch of Jonson as the 'humorous' Jaques,

whose ambition was to 'cleanse the foul body of the infected world'. The two had little in common except genius, the one arrogant, pushing and intolerant, the other all sympathy for his fellow men, never making his work a vehicle for propaganda.

We have an example of Shakespeare's generosity at this very time. His friends, Adrian Quiney and his son Richard, had been badly hit by the fires at Stratford, and when Richard was in London shortly after the production of *Every Man in his Humour*, he wrote to Shakespeare urgently asking for a loan of £30 to help them out of their difficulties. Shakespeare lost no time in replying, or possibly went at once to see him at his lodging near St. Paul's, for on the same day Richard wrote home to say that his 'countryman' had promised them the money. It is the only fragment that remains of Shakespeare's correspondence.

There were other pressing claims upon his purse that winter. The Chamber- *The Globe* lain's had no intention of staying indefinitely at the Curtain, and after careful *Theatre* consideration had selected a site for a new theatre on Bankside, almost—to Henslowe's horror—opposite the Rose. On the 26th they played before the

This Comoedie was firſt
Acted, in the yeere
1 5 9 8.

By the then L. CHAMBERLAYNE
his Seruants.

The principall Comœdians were.

WILL SHAKESPEARE. RIC. BVRBADGE.
AVG. PHILIPS. IOH. HEMINGS.
HEN. CONDEL. THO. POPE.
WILL. SLYE. CHR. BEESTON.
WILL. KEMPE. IOH. DVKE.

With the allowance of the Maſter of REVELLS.

Cast of the first performance
of Ben Jonson's *Every Man in his Humour*

Richard Quiney asks Shakespeare for a loan, 25 Oct. 1598

Queen at Whitehall, and two days later carried out the audacious raid that they had been planning for some time. Although the Theatre was now on alien ground, it belonged, according to their interpretation of the lease, to the Burbage brothers, so arming themselves with axes they invaded the precinct and under the skilled direction of Peter Street, a carpenter, began its demolition. Then, as their opponents put it, 'they did in most forcible and ryotous manner take and carrye away from thence all the wood and timber'. There was a deal of wood and timber in the Theatre, and it must have been a strange sight to see Shakespeare and his companions trundling balks and beams along Bishopsgate, and over London Bridge to Bankside. There, on the marshy ground opposite the Rose, Street built another theatre for them. They called it the Globe, their sign being Hercules bearing the earth on his shoulders, symbol perhaps of their Herculean labour.

Street used what he could of the salvaged timber, but some of it was in poor condition, and the new Globe was by no means the old Theatre set up on a new site. The plays of 1599 were very different from those of 1576, for which James Burbage had prepared to cater before the dramatic revolution, and Shakespeare and his fellows knew from long experience exactly what they

The newly built Globe, opposite the Rose (misnamed 'The Stare')

wanted. Of course the audience must be made as comfortable as possible, but it was the stage that mattered. All the paraphernalia of trapdoors communicating with 'hell' beneath the apron stage were there, as well as corresponding quaint devices in the 'heavens', whence aerial visitations could be made. But the essential thing was the provision of a fully developed upper stage, projecting over the apron on the level of the middle gallery, and beneath this a curtained lower stage, which could be used to disclose more formal indoor scenes. Thus, with three stages and two levels, and the use of the yard if required, the most exacting of Shakespeare's plays could be produced, the action flowing unbroken over the whole of the playing-place. It was for this 'wooden O' that Shakespeare began to write *Henry V,* a history that would tax its resources to the utmost.

The Chamberlain's had now added a theatre to their common stock. Ten shares were created, half of them being allotted to the Burbage brothers, who had contributed the fabric of their Theatre, and the other five to those members of the company who paid for the building. Shakespeare was one of them— indeed, the Globe was described soon after its opening as 'a playhouse occupied by William Shakespeare and others'—so that to the income he earned as

S. PAULES CHURCH

Bow Church

THAMESIS

The Bear Gardne

The Globe

dramatist and actor he now added a tenth of the profits derived from the theatre itself. As dramatist he would receive about £10 for each play, as actor he was entitled to one eighth of the money paid for standing room and half that paid for seats in the galleries, as theatre-owner, or 'householder', to one tenth of the other half of the gallery takings. In addition there were the substantial rewards for Court performances. By the beginning of the new century his income was probably the equivalent of about £5,000 of our money, virtually free from tax. No wonder the actors at the Rose, all of them in debt to Henslowe, whose deliberate policy it was thus to keep them in his clutches, looked enviously at the free and prosperous association over the way, and Henslowe himself began to look about for another site for a theatre as far away from the Globe as possible.

While Shakespeare and his companions were dismantling the Theatre, Spenser had arrived in London, a refugee from Ireland, where his home had been sacked and burned by the rebels. He died a month later, apparently in poverty, and was buried in Westminster Abbey. Ireland was ablaze with rebellion, and the ambitious, unpredictable Essex persuaded the Queen to send him to extinguish it. In March he set out at the head of an army, taking with

A reconstruction of the Globe stage

him the Earl of Southampton as General of the Horse, and Shakespeare, nearing the end of *Henry V*, wrote:

> *Were now the general of our gracious empress,*
> *As in good time he may, from Ireland coming,*
> *Bringing rebellion broached on his sword,*
> *How many would the peaceful city quit*
> *To welcome him!*

But Essex did no such thing. After wasting the summer in futile marches he lost his nerve, made a truce with Tyrone, the rebel leader, deserted his army, and threw himself on Elizabeth's mercy. She placed him under arrest, and though soon released he was a discredited and ruined man, exiled from her favour and the Court. A dangerous man at this critical time, the old Queen's cousin and the people's darling, and the succession to the throne still unsettled.

Henry V was probably the play with which the Globe was opened in the

golden Legacie.

vp in his armes hee threw him against the grounde so violently,
that hee broake his necke, and so ended his dayes with his brother. At this vnlookt for massacre, the people murmured, and
were all in a deepe passion of pittie, but the Francklin, father
vnto these, neuer chaunged his countenance, but as a man of a
couragious resolution, tooke vp the bodies of his sonnes without shewe of outward discontent.

All this while stood Rosader and sawe this Tragedie : who
noting the vndoubted vertue of the Francklins minde, alighted of
from his Horse, and presently sat downe on the grasse, and commanded his boy to pul off his bootes, making him ready to try the
strength of this Champion, being furnished as he would, he clapt
the Francklin on the shoulder and said thus, Bold yeoman whose
sonnes haue ended the tearme of their yeares with honour, for
that I see thou scornest fortune with patience, and twhartest the
iniury of fate with content, in brooking the death of thy sonnes :
stand a while and either see me make a third in their Tragedie, or
else reuenge their fal with an honourable triumph, the Francklin
seeing so goodly a gentleman to giue him such curteous comfort,
gaue him hartie thankes, with promise to pray for his happy suc-
cesse. With that Rosader vailed bonnet to the King, and lightly
leapt within the lists, where noting more the companie then the
combataut, hee cast his eye vpon the troupe of Ladies that gliste-
red there lyke the starres of heauen, but at last Loue willing to
make him as amourous as hee was valiaunt, presented him
with the sight of Rosalynd, whose admirable beautie so in-
ueagled the eye of Rosader, that forgetting himselfe, hee stood
and feede his lookes on the fauour of Rosalyndes face, which
shee perceiuing, blusht : which was such a doubling of her beau-
teous excellence, that the bashful redde of Aurora, at the sight of
vnacquainted Phaeton, was not halfe so glorious :

The Normane seeing this young Gentleman fettered
in the lookes of the Ladyes, draue him out of his memen-
to with a shake by the shoulder : Rosader looking backe with
an angrie frowne, as if hee had been wakened from some plea-
saunt dreame, discouered to all by the furye of his countenance that hee was a man of some high thoughts ; but when they
C 2   all

The source of *As You Like It*

autumn of 1599, soon after Essex's disgrace. Shakespeare himself must have played the part of Chorus, and though in his Prologue he apologised for the new theatre's inadequacy for the presentation of 'so great an object', we can sense the pride he felt at introducing his audience to its girdling walls. He took no part in *Every Man out of his Humour*, which followed soon afterwards, a confused and tedious play, in which Jonson incidentally made game of Shakespeare's new gentility and motto, *Non sans droit*, by suggesting as an alternative *Not without mustard*.

The Chamberlain's had to raise money for the building of the Globe by selling some of their stock, and in 1600 offered four of Shakespeare's plays to the publishers: *The Merchant of Venice, A Midsummer Night's Dream, Much Ado about Nothing*, and 2 *Henry IV*. All were duly entered in the Stationers' Register, the last two together, a particularly interesting entry, for it is the first in which Shakespeare's name is recorded. A few days earlier the company had discovered that one of their hirelings had vamped up a version of *Henry V* with the intention of turning a dishonest penny by selling it to a stationer. They did their best to prevent publication, but it was no good, and the mutilated version joined the 'bad' quartos of 2, 3 *Henry VI* and *Romeo and Juliet* in the booksellers' shops near St. Paul's. *The Merry Wives of Windsor*, written at about this time, was soon to make a fifth.

Although Shakespeare was gradually being relieved of his duties as an actor, it was a particularly busy period for him. He was writing hard to supply the Globe with new plays that would make the venture a success, and help to pay off the loans they had been compelled to take up at a high rate of interest. Somehow in the course of 1599-1600 he managed to produce *Julius Caesar,* and *As You Like It,* based on Thomas Lodge's romance, *Rosalynde,* with music by Thomas Morley, and by the Christmas of 1600 he had a third play ready for the Revels. This was *Twelfth Night,* presented in the great hall of Whitehall Palace on Twelfth Night, 1601, as a compliment to Elizabeth's distinguished guest, the young Italian nobleman, Virginio Orsino, Duke of Bracciano. As a compliment to Elizabeth as well, who was expected to identify herself with Olivia, for according to the fiction of the Court she was still the Faery Queen against whose youth and beauty time was powerless. She was, in fact, sixty-eight, black-toothed, red-wigged and wrinkled. Nor was Shakespeare under any illusion about the destructive power of time. It is indeed a constant theme in his early poetry: 'wasteful time', 'devouring time', 'cormorant time'. Up till now he had seen age from the side of youth, but *Twelfth Night* is a transition, a reconciliation with time, an acceptance of the fact that he himself was no longer young, and henceforth he saw youth with compassionate eyes from the side of age. It is the last, as it is the most perfect, of his middle comedies.

Thomas Morley's setting of a Shakespeare song, from his *First Booke of Ayres,* 1600

Exactly a month later, on Friday, February 6th, half a dozen gentlemen called at the Globe and asked the Chamberlain's to put on a special performance of Shakespeare's *Richard II* the next day. They demurred, protesting that it was an old play that would attract but a poor audience. When they were offered forty shillings, however, they agreed, and on the Saturday afternoon played the tragedy of the deposing and killing of King Richard to a disappointed audience. The next morning three hundred armed men poured out of Essex House in the Strand, and headed by the Earl stormed up Ludgate and along Cheapside,

F

Ben Jonson gives Marston a pill

calling on the citizens to 'liberate' the Queen from her evil counsellors. Not a man joined them. The desperate Essex surrendered, and the rest of the leaders, including Southampton, were arrested. Ten days later they were brought to trial, found guilty of treason, and condemned to death, though Southampton's sentence was commuted to life imprisonment. On the 25th the old Queen's young favourite was executed at the Tower. The Chamberlain's had been unwittingly implicated in the rising, for the performance of *Richard II* was part of the plot—to remind the citizens that sovereigns might be deposed. They were questioned but found innocent, and on the eve of Essex's execution performed again at Whitehall.

The Admiral's gave three Court performances that Christmas, but they were no longer at the Rose. They had left Bankside to the Chamberlain's and moved over the river to Finsbury, north of Cripplegate, where Henslowe and Alleyn had built a fine new theatre, the Fortune, modelled on the Globe, though square in plan. More significant was the appearance, or reappearance, of two more companies at Court—the Children of Paul's and the Children of the Chapel. Shakespeare had never had to face the competition of the boys, for it was ten years since last they had been players. The Chamberlain's however, were themselves largely responsible for the venture. Before he died James Burbage had converted part of the Blackfriars buildings into a second private theatre, forming a hall some seventy feet long and fifty wide, equipped with a stage, galleries and seats. Protests from the residents had prevented his opening it, but in 1600 his sons leased it to the Master of the Chapel Children, and performances began again. Here was something new to tickle the jaded palates of the citizens, and they flocked to Blackfriars and the singing-school of Paul's. Though their choirmasters could not command the pen of Shakespeare, who wrote exclusively for his own company, they commissioned the best of the other dramatists, and so began the profitable War of the Theatres—profitable that is, for the boys, though not so for the adult companies.

Ben Jonson and John Marston were quarrelsome young

men with different ideas about the drama. In *Every Man out of his Humour* Jonson had parodied Marston's bombastic style, and Marston had replied by pillorying Jonson in one of the first plays given by the Paul's boys. Jonson countered with *Cynthia's Revels*, written for the Chapel, in which both Marston and his friend Dekker were ridiculed. Again Marston hit back in a Paul's play. London was delighted, and all agog to see what would happen next. They were not disappointed. In the autumn of 1601 the Chapel Children played Jonson's *Poetaster,* satirising Dekker as the playdresser Demetrius and Marston as the poetaster Crispinus. The two are arraigned before Caesar, and Jonson, as the virtuous Horace, gives Crispinus a pill to make him vomit up his windy words. A few weeks later came the reply of Dekker and Marston in *Satiromastix,* produced at Paul's. The arrogant Horace is hauled up before—of all people—William Rufus, and Demetrius and Crispinus are appointed his judges. They prefer not to give him pills, fearing the stench of the black insolence they would fetch up, but crown him with nettles and make him swear to abandon his exhibitionism and conceit. Jonson would have replied, but he had offended the government by satirising more than rival playwrights, and was silenced. It was the last round in the War of the Theatres.

At Cambridge that Christmas the undergraduates played an anonymous comedy called *The Return from Parnassus,* in which Kempe and Burbage are introduced praising their colleague Shakespeare who had taken the bumptious Jonson down a peg or two. But what Shakespeare had to do with the War of the Theatres, and what was the purge he gave Jonson is a mystery, though he did add a footnote to the squabble and the competition of the 'aery of children' in *Hamlet,* which he was then writing.

What was the purge that Shakespeare gave Jonson?

Shakespeare's comment on 'The War of the Theatres', from the first, the 'bad', quarto of *Hamlet,* 1603

The Old Stratford estate bought by Shakespeare in 1602

'This Indenture . . . Betweene . . . John Combe of Old Stretford . . .
And William Shakespere of Stretford vppon Avon . . . gentleman . . .'

He may have missed the climax of the wordy warfare, for his father had died in September, and presumably he was in Stratford for the funeral, or soon afterwards. Perhaps the 'merry cheeked old man' had been attended in his last illness by the young Bedfordshire doctor, John Hall, who had just begun to practise in the town. There were other changes in the Henley Street house. His sister Joan had recently given birth to a son, his first nephew, and his youngest brother, Edmund, had left Stratford to become, like him, a player. But his other brothers were still there, and it was to Gilbert that he assigned the business of negotiating the purchase of an estate from William Combe and his nephew John, 127 acres of agricultural land in Old Stratford, just to the north of the town. By the spring of 1602, therefore, Shakespeare was a landed gentleman with the finest house in Stratford. Moreover he was at the height of his powers, and on the threshold of his greatest achievements.

Elizabeth, however, was failing. After the Christmas Revels the Court moved up the river to Richmond where, on February 2nd, 1603, the Chamberlain's presented a play, possibly the recently completed *Hamlet*. If so, nothing could have been more appropriate, for Shakespeare never saw the Queen again, and he had made his farewell:

> *Good night, sweet prince,*
> *And flights of angels sing thee to thy rest!*

She died in the early morning of March 24th.

Richmond Palace, where Queen Elizabeth died, 24 March 1603

James I and VI

The Chamberlain's become the King's Men, 19 May 1603

Another and less heroic age had dawned. The new sovereign was James, King of Scotland, a well-meaning but obstinate, pedantic man of about Shakespeare's age, his Queen an extravagant Danish princess, the mother of his three young children, Henry, Elizabeth and Charles. James lost no time in re-arranging his Court after his own liking, advancing his supporters and discarding his opponents. Lord Burghley's son, Robert Cecil, was confirmed as chief minister and soon created Earl of Salisbury, Francis Bacon was knighted, Shakespeare's patron, Southampton, released from prison, and Raleigh committed to the Tower. The reorganisation of Court life soon involved theatrical affairs, and within two months of his accession James had taken Shakespeare and his fellows under his own patronage. This change of patrons did not in itself involve any change of fortune, for though they were Grooms of the Chamber equipped with the royal scarlet livery, they were unpaid, as their office was merely an honorary one. The change of sovereigns, however, did involve a change of fortune. Under Elizabeth an average of six or seven Court performances had been given each year, under James there were rarely less than twenty, and as the King's Men gave the majority of these it meant a considerable increase in their incomes. All the other London companies were taken under royal patronage. The Admiral's became Prince Henry's, a new company playing at the Curtain became Queen Anne's, and the Chapel Children at Blackfriars were now known as the Children of the Queen's Revels.

At the beginning of this new era Shakespeare was just thirty-nine. It was exactly ten years since his first work had been published, ten years since Marlowe had died, and in the course of that astonishing decade the 'upstart crow' had written some twenty plays, from *Love's Labour's Lost* and *Romeo and Juliet* to *Twelfth Night, Troilus and Cressida* and *Hamlet,* carrying the revolution begun

The King's Servant

91

Middle Temple Hall, where *Twelfth Night* was performed, 2 Feb. 1602

The first Shakespeare anecdote, as told by John Manningham of the Middle Temple, 1602

by the University Wits to heights undreamed of by the envious Greene. More-over, his achievement and example had produced a school of dramatists the like of which had never been seen before, and has never been seen since, in England or in any other country. Yet success had not spoiled him; he was still as modest and civil as Chettle had found him ten years before, and still as popular with 'divers of worship' at the Inns of Court, where his plays were performed and he was affectionately known as William the Conqueror.

Despite its promise the Jacobean age began inauspiciously. Plague came in with James, the theatres were closed, and 30,000 people died in London before they were reopened in the following spring. It was the worst visitation of Shakespeare's lifetime. The King's Men went on tour, performing *Hamlet* both at Oxford and Cambridge, with the result that one of their hirelings, probably he who played Marcellus, memorised and wrote a version for a publisher. So a sixth 'bad' quarto, the most famous of all, appeared in London at the height of the plague. Shakespeare himself probably retired to New Place to revise the recalcitrant *All's Well,* which had as yet not ended well, and to write *Measure for Measure,* a sombre and experimental comedy whose title reveals a more serious intent than its light-hearted predecessors, *Much Ado about Nothing, As You Like It, What You Will.* By November he had rejoined his company and was rehearsing for the Revels at Mortlake, up the river from London, when they received an order to to go to Wilton, the Earl of Pembroke's house near Salisbury. The Court was there, and on December 2nd Shakespeare and his fellows gave their first performance before the King, the play being, apparently, *As You Like It.* Soon afterwards James left Wilton for Hampton Court, where his first Christmas Revels were held. The King's gave seven plays, one of which was *A Midsummer Night's Dream,* and another Jonson's unsuccessful tragedy *Sejanus,* in which Shakespeare took part. It is the last record of his acting, and it may be that from now on he was free to devote all his time to writing and the

Wilton House. 'We have the man Shakespeare with us'— to present *As You Like It* before King James, 2 Dec. 1603

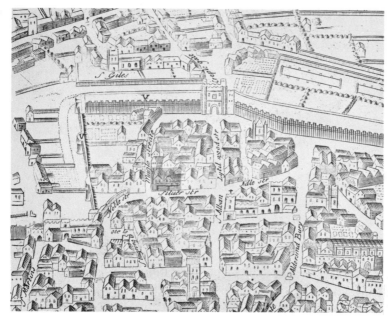

Christopher Mountjoy's house,
at the corner of Mugle Street and Silver Str
near Cripplegate,
where Shakespeare was lodging in 1604

producing of plays. In *Hamlet* we catch a glimpse of him coaching his fellows: 'Speak the speech, I pray you, as I pronounced it to you, trippingly on the tongue . . . Suit the action to the word, the word to the action, with this special observance, that you o'erstep not the modesty of nature.' The medieval tradition of ranting, of tearing a passion to tatters, died hard, but Shakespeare would have none of it in his company. His withdrawal from acting made room for new men, and the fellowship was increased from nine to twelve sharers.

By the end of February the plague was almost over, and Shakespeare found new London lodgings near Cripplegate, at the corner of Monkwell (Mugle) Street and Silver Street, in the house of Christopher Mountjoy, a maker of tires, the costly and elaborate headdresses worn by ladies. Here he got involved in a family affair. Mountjoy had a daughter Mary, whom he wished to see married to his apprentice Stephen Belott, and Shakespeare good-naturedly agreed to further the romance. He brought to bear on Belott what must have been his very considerable powers of persuasion, pointing out that there would be an enviable marriage portion with Mary, with hints perhaps of more to follow on her father's death. Stephen's diffidence was overcome. Shakespeare betrothed them by making them take each other's hand, and they were married in November. It was not the last that he was to hear of the matter.

The Great
Tragedies
It was probably at the Mountjoys' that he began to write *Othello*. The dramatic prose of his histories and comedies had taught him to write dramatic

The Somerset House Conference, 1604, when Shakespeare was on duty as a Groom of the Chamber

poetry, verse creative of character, perfected in *Hamlet* and *Measure for Measure*. Now, at the height of his powers, he applied this noble medium to the noblest of dramatic forms, tragedy. There is no need to assume that he was now, and for the next few years, himself in tragic mood; a man does not necessarily take to tragic themes because he is unhappy—Falstaff had been Shakespeare's reply to the disaster of Hamnet's death—but a great poet and dramatist will turn to tragedy if he wishes to create the highest form of art, and *Othello* is only the first of the series of tremendous tragedies that culminated in *Antony and Cleopatra* four years later. Even for Burbage, playing the tragic heroes at the Globe, the strain must have been considerable, but for Shakespeare it must have been almost unbearable, as month after month he lived the parts and suffered with the characters he was creating—for this complete self-identification is one of the main secrets of his art—suffered the jealousy of Othello, the madness of Timon and Lear, the remorse of Macbeth, the insane pride of Coriolanus and the despair of Antony.

In March the King was able to make his long delayed state progress through the City, and Shakespeare as a Groom of the Chamber was given his scarlet livery for the occasion. He was soon called upon to wear it again in an official capacity. In August Cecil negotiated peace with Spain, and the King's Men were appointed to attend the Spanish Ambassador Extraordinary at Somerset House. It was peace with honour, the most successful political event of the

95

'Shaxberd' at Whitehall. The Revels Account for 1604⁄5

reign. The twenty years' war with Spain was over. And yet those twenty anxious years had seen, had stimulated, the great Elizabethan literary renaissance.

No wonder the Revels that Christmas were joyful and prolonged, from the beginning of November to the end of February. Fortunately the accounts of the Master of the Revels for this season of 1604⁄5 have been preserved. Of the eleven plays presented by the King's Men at least seven were Shakespeare's: *Othello, The Merry Wives of Windsor, Measure for Measure, The Comedy of Errors, Love's Labour's Lost, Henry V* and *The Merchant of Venice,* which was given twice. They also gave two performances of Jonson's comedies.

Jonson claimed Scottish descent and was not slow to exploit this fortunate ancestry, in conjunction with the Queen's passion for extravagant display. In Elizabeth's reign the masque had been little more than a modest form of charade involving dressing up and dancing, but under Jonson it developed into an elaborate pageantry set off by the most spectacular scenic effects. The actors were the Queen herself and the great ones of the Court, the ladies wearing jewellery worth more than a monarch's revenue. To design the costumes and the scenery

Jonson secured the help of the rising young architect, Inigo Jones, and the long collaboration of these two great men began on Twelfth Night, 1605, with the *Masque of Blackness,* in which the Queen and her ladies appeared as blackamoors. During the next few years Jonson was establishing his position at Court by writing and rehearsing these ephemeral and lovely trifles, while Shakespeare was engaged with his great tragedies. *Timon of Athens* and the greater part of *King Lear* were probably written in 1605.

If Shakespeare was in Stratford as early as April he would certainly attend the wedding of Robert Harvard of Southwark and Katherine Rogers, the daughter of his neighbour Thomas Rogers, and even if he were not there would soon meet them at their home on Bankside, where their famous son, John Harvard, was born two years later. In the following month he lost an old friend, Augustine Phillips, one of the original members of the Chamberlain's company. The most loyal of men, he left legacies to most of his fellows, including 'a thirty shillings peece in gould' to Shakespeare. He seems to have been in Stratford by July, when he invested £440, a very large sum, in the tithes of the fields adjoining his estate to the north of the town. There he would meet his new neighbour at Clopton House, the wealthy young Catholic, Ambrose Rookwood. It is just possible that he was still at New Place at the beginning of November, for plague had returned to London and the theatres were closed. If so, he would see something of the excitement on the 6th. The

A design by Inigo Jones for the *Masque of Blackness*

Clopton House, Stratford,
a base for the Gunpowder Plot

Gunpowder Plot had miscarried, Guy Fawkes had been arrested, and the other conspirators had fled to their strongholds in the Midlands, one of which was Clopton House. It was raided by the borough constables, but Rookwood had flown. Two days later he was captured, and was executed with Fawkes in front of the Parliament House which they had attempted to blow up.

The King's Men gave ten plays that Christmas, and we can imagine James, after the performance of one of Shakespeare's histories, buttonholing the author and suggesting that as he had written so many plays about English history he might like to try his hand at a Scottish theme. Perhaps one of his ancestors. . . . He may not have added that he was expecting a visit from his brother-in-law, Christian IV of Denmark, in the summer. Plays by his own company would be an essential part of the entertainment, and Christian would certainly expect to see a performance of *The Prince of Denmark*. Apart from being the most appropriate of plays, *Hamlet* was also the most famous; quoted everywhere in London, it had been exported to Germany, and was even acted on the high seas. Shakespeare took the hint and, having finished *King Lear* (it was acted at Court in December), turned up the Scottish history in Holinshed's *Chronicles*,

What are these So wither'd, and so wild in their attire? The history of Macbeth, from Holinshed's *Chronicle*

was right displeasant to him and his people, as shoulde appeare in that it was a custome many yeares after, that no Knightes were made in Norway, excepte they were firste sworne to revenge the slaughter of theyr countreymen and frendes thus slayne in Scotland.

The othe that knights tooke in Norway, to revenge the death of theyr frendes.

The Scottes hauing wonne so notable a victory, after they had gathered and diuided the spoyle of the fielde, caused solemne processions to be made in all places of the realme, and thankes to be giuen to almightie God, that had sent them so fayre a day ouer their enimies.

Solemne processions for victory gotte.

But whylest the people were thus at theyr processions, worde was brought that a newe fleete of Danes was arriued at Kingcorne, sent thyther by Canute king of England in reuenge of his brothers Suenoes ouerthrow.

A power of Danes arriue at Kyncorne cut of England.

To resist these enimies, whiche were already landed, and busie in spoiling the countrey, Makbeth and Banquho were sente with the kings authoritie, who hauing with them a conuenient power, encountred the enimies, slewe parte of them, and chased the other to theyr shippes. They that escaped and got once to theyr shippes, obtayned of Makbeth for a great summe of golde, that suche of theyr freendes as were slaine at this last bickering might be buried in Saint Colmes Inche. In memorie whereof, many olde Sepultures are yet in the sayde Inche, there to be seene grauen with the armes of the Danes, as

The Danes vanquished by Makbeth and Banquho.

Danes buried in S. Colmes Inche.

the maner of burying noble men still is, and heretofore hath bene vsed.

A peace was also concluded at the same time betwixte the Danes and Scottishmen, ratified as some haue wryten in this wise. That from thence foorth the Danes shoulde neuer come into Scotlande to make any warres against the Scottes by any maner of meanes.

A peace concluded betwixt Scottes and Danes.

And these were the warres that Duncane had with forrayne enimics in the seuenth yeare of his reygne.

Shortly after happened a straunge and vncouth wonder, whiche afterwarde was the cause of muche trouble in the realme of Scotlande as ye shall after heare. It fortuned as Makbeth & Banquho iourneyed towarde Fores, where the king as then lay, they went sporting by the way togither without other companie, saue only themselues, passing through the woodes and fieldes, when sodenly in the middes of a launde, there met them iij. women in straunge & ferly apparell, resembling creatures of an elder worlde, whom when they attentiuely behelde, wondering much at the sight, The first of them spake & sayde: All hayle Makbeth Thane of Glammis (for he had lately entred into that dignitie and office by the death of his father Synel.) The ij. of them said: Hayle Makbeth Thane of Cawder: but the third sayde: All hayle Makbeth that hereafter shall be king of Scotland.

The prophesie of three women supposing to be the weird sisters or feiries.

Then Banquho, what maner of women (saith he) are you, that seeme so litle fauourable vnto me, where as to my fellow here, besides highe offices, yee assigne also the kingdome, appointyng foorth nothing for me at all? Yes sayth the firste of them, wee promise greater benefites vnto thee, than vnto him, for he shall reygne in in deede, but with an vnluckie ende: neyther shall he leaue any issue behinde him to succeede in his place, where contrarily thou in deede shalt not reygne at all, but of thee those shall be borne whiche shall gouerne the Scottishe kingdome by long order of continuall discent. Herewith the foresayde women vanished immediatly out of theyr sight. This was reputed at the first but some vayne fantasticall illusion by Makbeth and Banquho, in so muche that Banquho woulde call Makbeth in ieste kyng of Scot-

A thing to wonder at.

Q.ii.   Scot-

found the story of Macbeth, and began to write. Unfortunately Christian was preceded by plague, and the festivities had to be held outside the capital, so that it was at Greenwich that the King's Men presented before the royal rivals two plays, one of which must have been *Hamlet*. A few days later at Hampton Court, to the great satisfaction of James, *Hamlet* was capped by *Macbeth*.

Holinshed's *Chronicles*, uninspired though they were, had served Shakespeare well, but for his last two tragedies he turned to the noble prose of Sir Thomas North's translation of Plutarch, *The Lives of the Noble Grecians and Romans*. He may have finished *Coriolanus* and been already engaged on *Antony and Cleopatra* when, in June, 1607, his elder daughter Susanna, now a woman of twenty-four, married Dr. John Hall. The young physician was making a great reputation for himself, not only in Stratford, but throughout the county and even beyond. Some years later he began to compile a case-book, 'Observations' so well esteemed that they were translated from the original Latin and published twenty years after his death. By 1607 he could afford to live spaciously, so he bought a half-timbered house near the church, enlarged it to include an impressive consulting-room and dispensary, and there installed himself with his bride.

New Place would now have only two occupants for the greater part of the year, Anne and Judith, and Shakespeare looked round for companions for his wife and younger daughter. The new town clerk, Thomas Greene, was his distant cousin, married, with two small children, just the sort of family to enliven the big house, and before returning to London Shakespeare arranged that they should move into New Place, on the understanding that they would have to leave when he retired.

He was in no hurry to return, for plague had again closed the theatres, and his company was on tour. But he was back by November, and at Whitehall on December 28th for the presentation of a play. This may have been the day on which his young brother Edmund died, for he was buried in the church of St. Saviour's, only a few yards from the Globe, on the morning of the 31st. We do not know what company of players he had joined; perhaps he was a hireling with the King's, waiting for a vacancy as sharer in the fellowship, but we may be sure that it was his brother who paid for the expensive funeral, with the solemn tolling of the great bell.

A few months later Shakespeare lost his mother. She may have gone to live at New Place after the death of her husband, but more probably stayed in Henley Street with Joan and her two little grandsons. The house now belonged to Shakespeare, who let it to his sister and brother-in-law at a nominal rent, and perhaps his bachelor brothers moved into the eastern half where they still carried on their father's business. But more important to Shakespeare than the loss of his mother was the coming of a grandchild. In the previous February

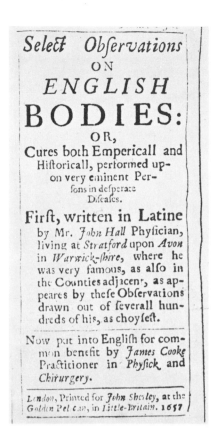

The case-book of Shakespeare's son-in-law   Hall's Croft, the home of Shakespeare's daughter, Susanna

Susanna had given birth to a daughter.

The birth of Elizabeth Hall in 1608 coincided with important developments in the affairs of the King's Men. The Children of the Revels had got into difficulties, and in August their manager surrendered the Blackfriars theatre to its owners, the Burbage brothers, who formed a syndicate of seven house-keepers, including Shakespeare, Heminge and Condell. The company now had another playhouse on the other side of the river as their winter quarters, an acquisition of immense significance. They were the first company of adult actors to perform regularly in a small roofed theatre, and obviously this involved a modification not only in their style of acting but in their type of play as well. The Globe was an open theatre, cold and draughty in winter, with room for an audience of two or three thousand, half of whom stood in the yard. The Black-friars was snug and intimate, and held only two or three hundred, all of whom were seated. Moreover, the audience at the Globe was a cross-section of society,

G

Two new dramatists engaged by the King's Men to write for their Blackfriars theatre: John Fletcher, Francis Beaumont

from courtier to carter, but only the wealthier and more educated classes could afford seats at Blackfriars. Something on a smaller scale than Shakespeare's titanic tragedies was called for, and the King's Men engaged two young dramatists who had already written for the boys at Blackfriars. So began the famous collaboration of Beaumont and Fletcher and their series of sweet, courtly, sentimental romances bearing little or no resemblance to real life. It was the beginning of the degeneration of the virile Elizabethan drama nurtured in the open theatres.

Shakespeare, too, began to write for the Blackfriars stage. Having brought his tragic art to perfection in *Antony and Cleopatra*, he turned again to romance, though more grave and lyrical in treatment than his middle comedies, and by November had written *Pericles,* the story of the sea-born Marina. There can be little doubt that the inspiration was his granddaughter, an inspiration carried over into his last three plays, in which the essential theme is the fortunes of his young heroines, Imogen, Perdita and Miranda. After the strain of four years of tragedy the relief must have been sweet indeed.

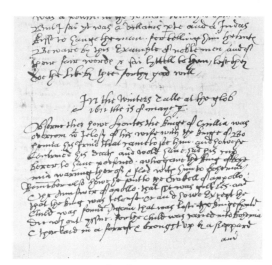

'In the Winters Talle at the glob
1611 the 15 of Maye.'
Simon Forman describes a performance

'His sugred Sonnets among his priuate friends'

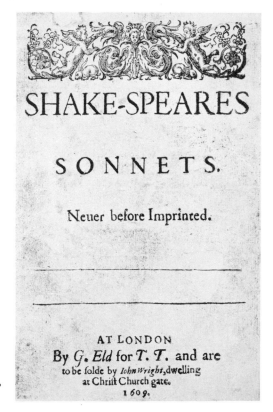

SHAKE-SPEARES

SONNETS.

Neuer before Imprinted.

AT LONDON
By *G. Eld* for *T. T.* and are
to be solde by *Iohn Wright,* dwelling
at Chriſt Church gate.
1609.

Perhaps the publication of *King Lear* in 1608, followed by *Pericles* and *Troilus and Cressida* in 1609, had something to do with raising money for the Black-friars venture, though the first two are sufficiently poor texts to warrant suspicion of piracy. The *Sonnets*, too, which at last appeared in 1609, may have been issued without Shakespeare's permission. These were the last of his works to be published in his lifetime, though the quartos that had already been printed con-tinued to go through new editions, and his popularity is further attested by the plays issued with his name by stationers more enterprising than honest. For example, *A Yorkshire Tragedy,* a King's play it is true, was published in 1608 as 'written by W. Shakspeare'.

Probably Shakespeare spent much of 1609 at New Place, as plague closed the theatres for most of the year. This annual recurrence of plague in London inevitably made him think of retirement to Stratford, but he decided to wait another year, and in September Thomas Greene made a note that he could 'stay another yere at newe place'. But 1610 was little better; by the end of June plague deaths were mounting, the theatres were closed again, the players once

The Last Years

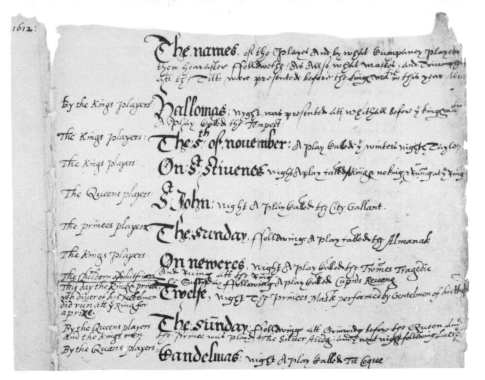

'A play Called the Tempest.' The Revels Account for 1611-12

more took to the road, and Shakespeare, now aged forty-six, gave up his London lodgings and retired to Stratford, where he finished *The Winter's Tale*.

Ironically enough, plague lifted soon after his move and did not affect London again while he lived, so that for the next year or two he probably spent as much time as ever with his company. He may have been with them when they crossed the river from Blackfriars to the Globe in April, and presented *Macbeth, The Winter's Tale* and *Cymbeline*. These were all seen by the physician and astrologer Simon Forman, who made notes on them in his *Booke of Plaies*. The pity is that they are merely summaries of the plots, the doctor in *Macbeth* being, apparently, his favourite character. If only he had written a description of the productions and of how Burbage played Macbeth and Leontes he could so easily have won the fame for which he thirsted, without the desperate recourse to suicide a few weeks later, on the day that he had predicted for his death.

In the previous autumn Shakespeare had read the accounts of the wreck of Sir George Somers on the Bermudas, and probably spoken to some of the survivors. The story moved him strangely, for storms and wrecks were much in his mind at this time, and in the course of 1611 he wrote his last and loveliest

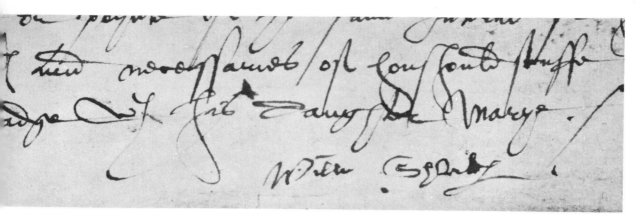

And more he cannot depose.' Shakespeare signs his deposition in the case of *Belott v. Mountjoy*, 11 May 1612

play, *The Tempest*. There can be little doubt that he was at Whitehall for its production on November 1st, when the Revels began. It was followed by *The Winter's Tale*, and altogether the King's Men gave twenty‑two plays that season, which was prolonged to the end of April.

He stayed in London a little longer. There was no alternative, for he had been called as witness in a case brought by Stephen Belott against his father‑in‑law, who had failed to make over the dowry promised with his daughter. On May 11th, 1612, 'William Shakespeare of Stratford vpon Aven, gentleman, of the age of xlviij yeres or thereaboutes' was questioned by a lawyer. It is strange to hear the echo of his voice. Yes, he had known the Mountjoys for some ten years, and had helped to persuade Stephen, 'a very good and industrious servant', to marry Mary. It was true that Mountjoy had promised a marriage portion, but how much it was he had quite forgotten, and he remembered nothing at all about a promised legacy. He was not very helpful, but there was no reason why he should remember such details after eight years, and having signed his deposition he made for Stratford. He had work to do.

His retirement, or semi‑retirement, would have been disastrous to the King's Men if Beaumont and Fletcher had not been there to supply them with new plays, rapidly becoming almost as popular as his own. When, therefore, Beau‑mont married an heiress and withdrew from the theatre they were in great distress. Fletcher needed the stimulus of a collaborator, and until he found another among the younger men they implored Shakespeare to write with him. It would not be very arduous work; if he would set the play going by intro‑ducing the main themes and characters Fletcher would see to the rest. Shake‑speare readily agreed and began to sketch out *Cardenio*, a play that has been lost, though it was produced at the Revels of 1612‑13. These were the most brilliant of the reign, in celebration of the marriage of James's daughter Elizabeth to

Princess Elizabeth and the Elector Palatine,
whose betrothal was celebrated by a performance of *The Tempest*

Queen Anne and Henry, Prince of Wales,
who died during his sister's
wedding festivities

the Elector Palatine, and Shakespeare must have been there to supervise the production of *The Tempest, Julius Caesar, Much Ado, Othello, The Winter's Tale,* and the two parts of *Henry IV. The Tempest* was almost certainly given on the eve of the betrothal, and we may, perhaps, imagine Shakespeare playing his last part that night as Prospero, blessing the young couple—for they were only children—and wishing them the happiness that was, alas, so soon to elude them.

The festivities were marred by the sudden death of Henry, Prince of Wales, a young man of great promise, but after a pause they were resumed. In March, before their conclusion, Shakespeare bought the gatehouse of the Blackfriars priory, near the theatre, raising part of the money by a mortgage, a transaction in which he was helped by his friends John Heminge and William Johnson, landlord of the Mermaid Tavern. It was at the Mermaid, near St. Paul's, that Shakespeare, Jonson, Fletcher, Donne and other leading wits used to forgather and dine on the first Friday of the month, when words were nimble and full of subtle flame. A few days later he was associated with another old friend, Dick

Shakespeare buys a London house. He and his trustee, the landlord of the Mermaid, sign the conveyance, 10 March 1613

The mortgage, 11 March 1613, with Shakespeare's signature

Burbage, in a very different matter. This was the designing and making for the Duke of Rutland of an 'impresa', a device painted on a pasteboard shield carried by his squire before a tilt. Burbage, we know, was an amateur painter, and it looks as though Shakespeare may have been one too.

In the middle of April the Elector and Elizabeth set out for Germany, and the Court left London. But Shakespeare probably lingered. Fletcher had recently finished the history of *Henry VIII* which he had half written for him, and it was soon to be produced at the Globe. Perhaps, however, he was already back in Stratford when, on that fatal Tuesday, June 29th, the Globe was burned to the ground during a performance of the play. The wadding from a gun fired on the entry of King Henry set fire to the thatch, and within an hour the galleries had crashed into the yard, and the heavens and hell were consumed together among the flaming timbers. The audience escaped by a miracle, 'only one man had his breeches set on fire, that would perhaps have broiled him, if he had not by the benefit of a provident wit put it out with bottle ale'. 'Nothing',

John Shakespeare's workshop converted into an inn

we are told, 'did perish but wood and straw and a few forsaken cloaks'. If the King's Men kept their stock of plays in the Globe, somehow they were saved, and with them the priceless manuscript plays of Shakespeare. The house-keepers had to shoulder the cost of rebuilding, and it may be that Shakespeare relinquished his share to a more active member of the company.

From now on he spent most of his time in Stratford. Gilbert and Richard had both died in the last year. Their father's old workshop was let and con-verted into an inn, known as the Swan and Maidenhead, and Joan and her family—there were now three boys—were left in sole possession of the Henley Street house. The pity was that there were no small boys in the Hall house, no grandsons. Elizabeth was the only child of Susanna, whom, incidentally, Shakespeare had to help to clear of an irresponsible and slanderous charge soon after his return from London. Some of his old friends, Richard Quiney among them, had gone, but others remained. There were, for example, Henry Walker, of whose young son he was godfather, his neighbours Hamnet and Judith Sadler, godparents of his own children, and next door but one to New Place was Julyne Shaw. The brothers John and Anthony Nash lived in Old Strat-ford, and at Clifford Chambers over the river was Sir Henry Rainsford with whom Michael Drayton sometimes stayed. Thomas Russell lived a little further afield in the manor house at Aldminster. Then there was the wealthy

John Combe, 'vpon whose name Shakespeere did merrily fann vp some witty and facetious verses'

bachelor and money-lender, John Combe. He died in July, 1614, on the day after the third great fire to ravage the town, and was buried by the altar in the parish church. He left £5 to Shakespeare, who probably found the sculptor to make his tomb and effigy, Gerard Johnson, the Bankside mason.

At this time Shakespeare was involved in a scheme to enclose the open fields bordering his estate. Although he was not one of the promoters, as a tithe-owner he would be affected, probably favourably. His attitude, however, is uncertain, and the main interest of the controversy lies in the notes made by Thomas Greene, who, as town clerk, was employed by the Corporation to prevent the enclosure. Shakespeare may have gone up to London in the spring for the opening of the new Globe theatre, rebuilt 'in far finer manner than before', with a tiled roof to the galleries instead of thatch, for he would want to see what Fletcher had made of his contribution to *The Two Noble Kinsmen*—not very much as it happened. He was certainly there in November with John Hall, when Greene, who was already up on enclosure business, called 'to see him howe he did' and to ask how things were going in Stratford. His 'Cosen

The painted room in the Crown Tavern, Oxford, where Shakespeare is said
to have lodged on his journeys between London and Stratford.
It was kept by John Davenant, and tradition has it that Shakespeare
was godfather of his son, William

Thomas Greene makes his last note on 'my Cosen Shakspeare'

The second Globe theatre and Beargarden. (The names are interchanged.) The Blackfriars theatre is probably the long building above and to the right of the flag

Shakspeare' assured him that although 'they meane in Aprill to servey the Land . . . there will be nothyng done at all'. He was right, though the controversy dragged on, and nearly a year later, in September, 1615, Greene inserted a note in his memoranda: 'W Shakspeares tellyng J Greene [Thomas's brother] that I was not able to beare the encloseinge of Welcombe'. It is the last record we have of Shakespeare before he made his will a few months later.

When he was in London at the end of 1614 he would meet Ben Jonson and learn of his project to publish a collected edition of his 'Works'. No doubt this set him thinking along the same lines, for, now that Fletcher had found new collaborators and the King's Men were no longer in urgent need of his help, how could he better employ his longed-for leisure than in preparing his own works for a similar collected edition? After all, he had been abominably careless about the publication of his plays. Half of them, indeed, had never been published, and some of these were scarcely in a state for the press; then, the printed texts of many of the remainder were most inaccurate, and four of the corrupt pirated quartos had never been replaced by a genuine version. There was plenty of work for the next year or two, and we may imagine him in 1615 revising and rewriting some of his manuscript plays, the still recalcitrant *All's Well that Ends Well,* for example, in his study at New Place.

By the beginning of 1616 preparations were afoot for the marriage of Judith and Thomas Quiney, son of his old friend Richard, and in January, being then 'in perfect health', he got Francis Collins, a Warwick solicitor, to draw up a will providing for both his daughters. A few weeks after the wedding, which was on February 10th, he was taken seriously ill. According to an old tradition, 'Shakespear, Drayton and Ben Jhonson had a merry meeting, and it seems drank too hard, for Shakespear died of a feavour there contracted'. It is possible. Drayton might have been at Clifford Chambers early in the year, though Jonson was probably much too busy with masques and revels at Whitehall. Perhaps the merry meeting, if there really was one, took place in London to celebrate the publication of Jonson's folio edition of his *Works*. If Shakespeare was taken ill there, he might have been a very sick man by the time he reached Stratford after riding ninety miles in cold March weather. But whatever happened, he sent for Collins again, and, after revising his will, signed it on March 25th. Anne was provided for by her widow's dower, and his only mention of her is the famous 'vnto my wief my second best bed'. It was the bed on which he was dying. To Judith he left a substantial marriage portion; to Joan £20, all his 'wearing Apparrell'—it would come in useful for her sons— and the Henley Street house for life. With a few exceptions all the rest of his estate was to go to Susanna and her heirs male, if any. The death of Hamnet had ruined his plan of founding a family, but Susanna's sons would at least be lineal descendants. It was a vain hope. Elizabeth was Susanna's only child, and Elizabeth, though twice married, had no children at all. Judith's three sons all died young, and only the collateral line of Joan and the Harts survived. Among the minor legatees were his 'ffellowes John Hemynge Richard Burbage & Henry Cundell', to whom he left 26s. 8d. 'a peece to buy them Ringes'. They were the sole survivors of the original Chamberlain's fellowship formed more than twenty years ago.

His brother-in-law was dying in Henley Street, and on April 17th 'Will. Hartt, hatter' was buried. Presumably Dr. Hall attended them both. He was to cure Michael Drayton, 'an excellent poet', of a fever, but an even more excellent poet he was unable to save. Shakespeare died a week after the funeral of Joan's husband, possibly on his fifty-second birthday. On April 25th he was taken from New Place, past the Gild Chapel and Grammar School, down the road to the church along which he had been carried to his christening exactly fifty-two years before, and buried in front of the altar. Gerard Johnson was commissioned to make the monument that was set up on the wall overlooking his grave.

'By me William Shakspeare.' The last of the three pages of his will

Males of the bodie of the said fourth sonne laufully ysseuinge in such maner as yt ys before Lymitted to be & remaine to the ffirst second & third sonnes of her bodie & to their heires males ... & for defalt of such yssue the said p[re]misse to be & remaine to my ... neece Susanna Hall & the heires males of her bodie lawfully yssuinge ... & for default of such yssue to the right heires of me the said William Shakspeare for ever Item I gyve & bequeath to my said Daughter Judith my broad silver gilt bole All the rest of my goode Chattell Leases plate Jewels & Householde stuffe whatsoever after my dettes and Legasies paied & my funerall expences dischargd I gyve devise & bequeath to my Sonne in Lawe John Hall gent & my Daughter Susanna his wife whom I ordeine & make executors of this my Last will & testam[en]t And I doe intreat & Appoint Thomas Russell Esquier & ffraunces Collins gent to be overseers hereof And doe revoke All former wills & publish this to be my Last will & testam[en]t In witnes whereof I have herevnto put my Seale ... the Daie & Yeare first above written.

witnes to the publishing
hereof   ffra: Collyns
Julyus Shawe
John Robinson
Hamnet Sadler
Robert Whatcott

By me William Shakspeare

Probatum ...

'Will Shakspere gent'.
The entry of his burial
in Stratford Parish Register

Shakespeare's monument and grave within the sanctuary of Holy Trinity Church, Stratfor

What then? What remained? Why all this pother about a provincial boy
who made a fortune out of the theatre? The question was answered seven years
later when Heminge and Condell completed the work that Shakespeare had
entrusted to them, the editing of his plays and their publication in a single
volume. Had it not been for their devotion half of them, including *Twelfth
Night* and *Macbeth, Antony and Cleopatra* and *The Tempest,* might have perished
unpublished, and of *Henry V* and three others we should have only the
mutilated versions of the 'bad' quartos. But Shakespeare's friends brought out
the precious manuscripts from the King's Men's store, some his originals, others
fair copies, and from these the yet unpublished plays were printed, as well as
those 'maimed and deformed by the frauds and stealthes of iniurious impostors'.
The remainder were set up from their quartos, corrected by reference to the
manuscripts. This, then, remained: the thirty-six plays of the Folio, perhaps the
greatest single creative achievement of man. It is a large claim.

Yet among the poets of the world there are only one or two with any claim
to be of Shakespeare's stature. Will you have pure lyric? There are the songs,
from 'Who is Silvia' in *The Two Gentlemen of Verona* to 'Full fathom five' in
The Tempest. Or sonnets? There are a hundred and fifty, from which one may
choose at random:

> *Shall I compare thee to a summer's day?*
> *Thou art more lovely and more temperate:*
> *Rough winds do shake the darling buds of May,*
> *And summer's lease hath all too short a date.*

or,

> *When lofty trees I see barren of leaves,*
> *Which erst from heat did canopy the herd,*
> *And summer's green all girded up in sheaves,*
> *Born on the bier with white and bristly beard,*
> *Then of thy beauty do I question make,*
> *That thou among the wastes of time must go.*

The same princely poetry is the stuff of the early lyrical plays:

> *It was the lark, the herald of the morn,*
> *No nightingale: look, love, what envious streaks*
> *Do lace the severing clouds in yonder east:*
> *Night's candles are burned out, and jocund day*
> *Stands tiptoe on the misty mountain top.*

The monument overlooking the grav

And to a similar, though more intricate and golden lyricism Shakespeare returned in his last romances:

> *Daffodils,*
> *That come before the swallow dares, and take*
> *The winds of March with beauty; violets dim,*
> *But sweeter than the lids of Juno's eyes*
> *Or Cytherea's breath.*

Then, Shakespeare was doubly a maker, a creator not only of poetry but of people, and here no other poet approaches him. No other writer has ever created a comparable company of men and women, humble and exalted, grave and gay, comic and tragic, noble and ignoble: Launce, Bottom, Dogberry, Pistol, Autolycus, Juliet's nurse, Mistress Quickly; Falstaff, Touchstone, Jaques, Feste, Malvolio, Parolles, Benedick; Julia, Beatrice, Rosalind, Viola, Helena, Marina, Imogen, Perdita, Miranda; Richard II, Richard III, King John, Henry V, Hotspur, Brutus, Hamlet, Othello, Iago, Lear, Macbeth; Juliet, Desdemona, Cordelia, Volumnia, Lady Macbeth, Cleopatra—the list might be almost indefinitely extended. The wonder is that they are nothing but words, and the final wonder is the words themselves, the poetry in which they talk themselves alive. For they *are* the poetry. This *is* Juliet:

> *Come, gentle night, come, loving, black-brow'd night,*
> *Give me my Romeo; and, when he shall die,*
> *Take him and cut him out in little stars,*
> *And he will make the face of heaven so fine,*
> *That all the world will be in love with night.*

This Hamlet:

> *O good Horatio, what a wounded name,*
> *Things standing thus unknown, shall live behind me!*
> *If thou didst ever hold me in thy heart,*
> *Absent thee from felicity a while,*
> *And in this harsh world draw thy breath in pain,*
> *To tell my story.*

This Cleopatra:

> *O, see, my women,*
> *The crown o' the earth doth melt. My lord!*
> *O, wither'd is the garland of the war,*
> *The soldier's pole is fall'n: young boys and girls*
> *Are level now with men; the odds is gone,*
> *And there is nothing left remarkable*
> *Beneath the visiting moon.*

Title page of the First Foli

Mr. WILLIAM
SHAKESPEARES

COMEDIES,
HISTORIES, &
TRAGEDIES.

Published according to the True Originall Copies.

Martin Droeshout sculpsit London.

LONDON
Printed by Isaac Iaggard, and Ed. Blount. 1623

But this, we feel, is Shakespeare, one of the rare glimpses we catch of him in his plays:

> Our revels now are ended. These our actors,
> As I foretold you, were all spirits, and
> Are melted into air, into thin air:
> And, like the baseless fabric of this vision,
> The cloud-capp'd towers, the gorgeous palaces,
> The solemn temples, the great globe itself,
> Yea, all which it inherit shall dissolve,
> And, like this insubstantial pageant faded,
> Leave not a rack behind. We are such stuff
> As dreams are made on; and our little life
> Is rounded with a sleep.

Although Shakespeare is so elusive, because so protean, ever changing from one character to another, his spirit permeates the plays, and we read them not only for the poetry and the people we meet there, but also for the man he was. That is what, above all, makes them so consolatory. We read them for his genial wisdom, his flooding noonday illumination of life, his gaiety and wit, his essential sanity: because he was the ideally normal man, whose far-ranging faculties were all perfectly attuned and harmonised. We read Shakespeare because he is the man whom we should all like to have for friend.

Here follow five pages from the First Foli

To the great Variety of Readers.

Rom the moſt able, to him that can but ſpell: There you are number'd. We had rather you were weighd. Eſpecially, when the fate of all Bookes depends vpon your capacities : and not of your heads alone, but of your purſes. Well! It is now publique, & you wil ſtand for your priuiledges wee know : to read, and cenſure. Do ſo, but buy it firſt. That doth beſt commend a Booke, the Stationer ſaies. Then, how odde ſoeuer your braines be, or your wiſedomes, make your licence the ſame, and ſpare not. Iudge your ſixe-pen'orth, your ſhillings worth, your fiue ſhillings worth at a time, or higher, ſo you riſe to the iuſt rates, and welcome. But, what euer you do, Buy. Cenſure will not driue a Trade, or make the Iacke go. And though you be a Magiſtrate of wit, and ſit on the Stage at *Black-Friers*, or the *Cock-pit*, to arraigne Playes dailie, know, theſe Playes haue had their triall alreadie, and ſtood out all Appeales ; and do now come forth quitted rather by a Decree of Court, then any purchas'd Letters of commendation.

It had bene a thing, we confeſſe, worthie to haue bene wiſhed, that the Author himſelfe had liu'd to haue ſet forth, and ouerſeen his owne writings ; But ſince it hath bin ordain'd otherwiſe, and he by death departed from that right, we pray you do not envie his Friends, the office of their care, and paine, to haue collected & publiſh'd them ; and ſo to haue publiſh'd them, as where (before) you were abuſ'd with diuerſe ſtolne, and ſurreptitious copies, maimed, and deformed by the frauds and ſtealthes of iniurious impoſtors, that expos'd them : euen thoſe, are now offer'd to your view cur'd, and perfect of their limbes ; and all the reſt, abſolute in their numbers, as he conceiued thē. Who, as he was a happie imitator of Nature, was a moſt gentle expreſſer of it. His mind and hand went together : And what he thought, he vttered with that eaſineſſe, that wee haue ſcarſe recciued ſrom him a blot in his papers. But it is not our prouince, who onely gather his works, and giue them you, to praiſe him. It is yours that reade him. And there we hope, to your diuers capacities, you will finde enough, both to draw, and hold you : for his wit can no more lie hid, then it could be loſt. Reade him, therefore ; and againe, and againe : And if then you doe not like him, ſurely you are in ſome manifeſt danger, not to vnderſtand him. And ſo we leaue you to other of his Friends, whom if you need, can bee your guides : if you neede them not, you can leade your ſelues, and others. And ſuch Readers we wiſh him.

A 3   *Iohn Heminge.*
Henrie Condell.

William Sly,
one of the original members of Shakespeare's company
John Lowin,
who played Falstaff, and in the part of Henry VIII
'had his instructions from Mr. Shakespear himself'
Nathan Field,
playwright as well as player,
who replaced Shakespeare in the King's Company

The Workes of William Shakespeare,

containing all his Comedies, Histories, and
Tragedies: Truely set forth, according to their first ORJGJNALL.

The Names of the Principall Actors
in all these Playes.

Illiam Shakespeare.

Richard Burbadge.

John Hemmings.

Augustine Phillips.

William Kempt.

Thomas Poope.

George Bryan.

Henry Condell.

William Slye.

Richard Cowly.

John Lowine.

Samuell Crosse.

Alexander Cooke.

Samuel Gilburne.

Robert Armin.

William Ostler.

Nathan Field.

John Underwood.

Nicholas Tooley.

William Ecclestone.

Joseph Taylor.

Robert Benfield.

Robert Goughe.

Richard Robinson.

John Shancke.

John Rice.

A CATALOGVE

of the seuerall Comedies, Histories, and Tragedies contained in this Volume.

124

THE
TEMPEST.

Actus primus, Scena prima.

A tempestuous noise of Thunder and Lightning heard: Enter a Ship-master, and a Boteswaine.

Master.

BOte-swaine.

Botes. Heere Master : What cheere ?

Mast. Good : Speake to th'Mariners : fall too't, yarely, or we run our selues a ground, bestirre, bestirre.   *Exit.*

Enter Mariners.

Botes. Heigh my hearts, cheerely, cheerely my harts : yare, yare : Take in the toppe-sale : Tend to th'Masters whistle : Blow till thou burst thy winde, if roome enough.

Enter Alonso, Sebastian, Anthonio, Ferdinando,
Gonzalo, and others.

Alon. Good Boteswaine haue care : where's the Master ? Play the men.

Botes. I pray now keepe below.

Anth. Where is the Master, Boson ?

Botes. Do you not heare him ? you marre our labour, Keepe your Cabines : you do assist the storme.

Gonz. Nay, good be patient.

Botes. When the Sea is : hence, what cares these roarers for the name of King ? to Cabine; silence : trouble vs not.

Gon. Good, yet remember whom thou hast aboord.

Botes. None that I more loue then my selfe. You are a Counsellor, if you can command these Elements to silence, and worke the peace of the present, wee will not hand a rope more, vse your authoritie : If you cannot, giue thankes you haue liu'd so long, and make your selfe readie in your Cabine for the mischance of the houre, if it so hap. Cheerely good hearts : out of our way I say.   *Exit.*

Gon. I haue great comfort from this fellow: methinks he hath no drowning marke vpon him, his complexion is perfect Gallowes : stand fast good Fate to his hanging, make the rope of his destiny our cable, for our owne doth little aduantage : If he be not borne to bee hang'd, our case is miserable.   *Exit.*

Enter Boteswaine.

Botes. Downe with the top-Mast : yare, lower, lower, bring her to Try with Maine-course. A plague——
A cry within.   Enter Sebastian, Anthonio & Gonzalo.

vpon this howling: they are lowder then the weather, or our office : yet againe ? What do you heere? Shal we giue ore and drowne, haue you a minde to sinke ?

Sebas. A poxe o'your throat, you bawling, blasphemous incharitable Dog.

Botes. Worke you then.

Anth. Hang cur, hang, you whoreson insolent Noysemaker, we are lesse afraid to be drownde, then thou art.

Gonz. I'le warrant him for drowning, though the Ship were no stronger then a Nutt-shell, and as leaky as an vnstanched wench.

Botes. Lay her a hold, a hold, set her two courses off to Sea againe, lay her off.

Enter Mariners wet.

Mari. All lost, to prayers, to prayers, all lost.

Botes. What must our mouths be cold ?

Gonz. The King, and Prince, at prayers, let's assist them, for our case is as theirs.

Sebas. I'am out of patience.

An. We are meerly cheated of our liues by drunkards, This wide-chopt-rascall, would thou mightst lye drowning the washing of ten Tides.

Gonz. Hee'l be hang'd yet, Though euery drop of water sweare against it, And gape at widst to glut him.   *A confused noyse within.*

Mercy on vs. We split, we split, Farewell my wife, and children, Farewell brother : we split, we split, we split.

Anth. Let's all sinke with' King

Seb. Let's take leaue of him.   *Exit.*

Gonz. Now would I giue a thousand furlongs of Sea, for an Acre of barren ground : Long heath, Browne firrs, any thing; the wills aboue be done, but I would faine dye a dry death.   *Exit.*

Scena Secunda.

Enter Prospero and Miranda.

Mira. If by your Art (my deerest father) you haue Put the wild waters in this Rore, alay them:
The skye it seemes would powre down stinking pitch, But that the Sea, mounting to th' welkins cheeke, Dashes the fire out. Oh! I haue suffered With those that I saw suffer: A braue vessell

A   (Who

Make no Collection of it. Let him shew
His skill in the construction.

Luc. Philarmonus.

Sooth. Heere, my good Lord.

Luc. Read, and declare the meaning.

Reades.

WHen as a Lyons whelpe, shall to himselfe vnknown, without seeking finde, and bee embrac'd by a peece of tender
Ayre: And when from a stately Cedar shall be lopt branches,
which being dead many yeares, shall after renue, bee ioyned to
the old Stocke, and freshly grow, then shall Posthumus end his
miseries, Britaine be fortunate, and flourish in Peace and Plen-
tie.

Thou *Leonatus* art the Lyons Whelpe,
The fit and apt Construction of thy name
Being *Leonatus*, doth import so much:
The peece of tender Ayre, thy vertuous Daughter,
Which we call *Mollis Aer*, and *Mollis Aer*
We terme it *Mulier*; which *Mulier* I diuine
Is this most constant Wife, who euen now
Answering the Letter of the Oracle,
Vnknowne to you vnsought, were clipt about
With this most tender Aire.

Cym. This hath some seeming.

Sooth. The lofty Cedar, Royall *Cymbeline*
Personates thee: And thy lopt Branches, point
Thy two Sonnes forth: who by *Belarius* stolne
For many yeares thought dead, are now reuiu'd
To the Maiesticke Cedar ioyn'd; whose Issue

Promises Britaine, Peace and Plenty.

Cym. Well,
My Peace we will begin: And *Caius Lucius*,
Al:hough the Victor, we submit to *Cesar*,
And to the Romane Empire; promising
To pay our wonted Tribute, from the which
We were dissuaded by our wicked Queene,
Whom heauens in Iustice both on her, and hers,
Haue laid most heauy hand.

Sooth. The fingers of the Powres aboue, do tune
The harmony of this Peace: the Vision
Which I made knowne to *Lucius* ere the stroke
Of yet this scarse-cold-Battaile, at this instant
Is full accomplish'd. For the Romaine Eagle
From South to West, on wing soaring aloft
Lessen'd her selfe, and in the Beames o'th'Sun
So vanish'd; which fore-shew'd our Princely Eagle
Th'Imperiall *Cesar*, should againe vnite
His Fauour, with the Radiant *Cymbeline*,
Which shines heere in the West.

Cym. Laud we the Gods,
And let our crooked Smoakes climbe to their Nostrils
From our blest Altars. Publish we this Peace
To all our Subiects. Set we forward: Let
A Roman, and a Brittish Ensigne waue
Friendly together: so through *Luds-Towne* march,
And in the Temple of great Iupiter
Our Peace wee'l ratifie: Seale it with Feasts.
Set on there: Neuer was a Warre did cease
(Ere bloodie hands were wash'd) with such a Peace.

Exeunt.

FINIS.

*Printed at the Charges of W. Jaggard, Ed. Blount, I. Smithweeke,
and W. Aspley, 1623.*

GOOD FREND FOR IESVS SAKE FORBEARE,
TO DIGG THE DVST ENCLOASED HEARE.
BLESE BE Y MAN Y SPARES THES STONES,
AND CVRST BE HE Y MOVES MY BONES.

Sweet Swan of Auon! *what a fight it were*
 To fee thee in our waters yet appeare,
And make thofe flights vpon the bankes of Thames,
 That fo did take Eliza, *and our* Iames !
But ftay, I fee thee in the Hemifphere
 Aduanc'd, and made a Conftellation there !
Shine forth, thou Starre of Poets, *and with rage,*
 Or influence, chide, or cheere the drooping Stage;
Which, fince thy flight frō hence, hath mourn'd like night,
 And defpaires day, but for thy Volumes light.

BEN: IONSON.

The Family of Shakespeare

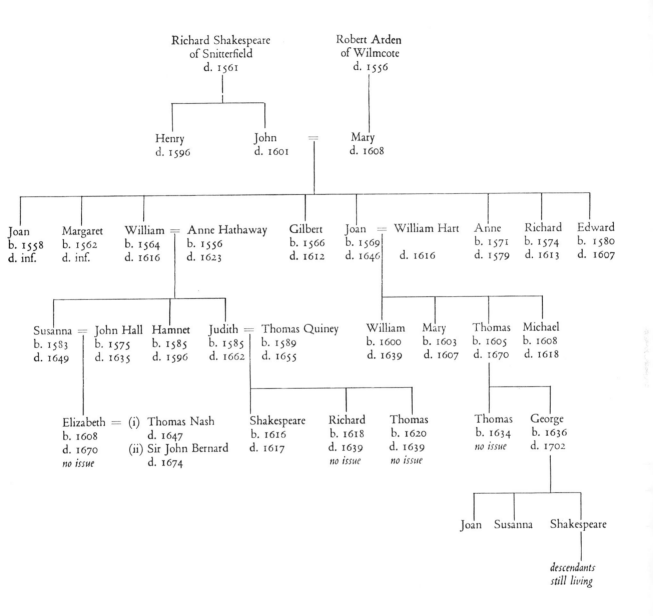

Richard Shakespeare
of Snitterfield
d. 1561

Robert **Arden**
of Wilmcote
d. 1556

Henry
d. 1596

John
d. 1601

=

Mary
d. 1608

Joan
b. 1558
d. inf.

Margaret
b. 1562
d. inf.

William
b. 1564
d. 1616

=

Anne Hathaway
b. 1556
d. 1623

Gilbert
b. 1566
d. 1612

Joan
b. 1569
d. 1646

=

William Hart
d. 1616

Anne
b. 1571
d. 1579

Richard
b. 1574
d. 1613

Edward
b. 1580
d. 1607

Susanna
b. 1583
d. 1649

=

John Hall
b. 1575
d. 1635

Hamnet
b. 1585
d. 1596

Judith
b. 1585
d. 1662

=

Thomas Quiney
b. 1589
d. 1655

William
b. 1600
d. 1639

Mary
b. 1603
d. 1607

Thomas
b. 1605
d. 1670

Michael
b. 1608
d. 1618

Elizabeth
b. 1608
d. 1670
no issue

=

(i) Thomas Nash
d. 1647

(ii) Sir John Bernard
d. 1674

Shakespeare
b. 1616
d. 1617

Richard
b. 1618
d. 1639
no issue

Thomas
b. 1620
d. 1639
no issue

Thomas
b. 1634
no issue

George
b. 1636
d. 1702

Joan   Susanna   Shakespeare

*descendants
still living*

ACKNOWLEDGEMENTS

I acknowledge with gratitude the courtesy of those who have given permission for the reproduction of material in their possession, and I take this opportunity of thanking Mr Levi Fox, Director of Shakespeare's Birthplace, Mr John Summerson, Curator of the Sir John Soane Museum, and Mr Arthur Boyars for their help in obtaining some of the illustrations.

F.E.H.

Frontispiece. This leaden statue of Shakespeare on the wall of the Town Hall at Stratford was presented to the Corporation in 1769 by David Garrick, who organised the Jubilee of that year. It is the work of John Cheere, brother of Sir Henry Cheere, a pupil of Scheemakers. *Photograph by Edwin Smith.*

Page

7 WARWICK FROM BUDBROOKE. *Photograph by Edwin Smith.*

8-9 WARWICKSHIRE IN 1610. Drawn by John Speed for his *Theatre of the Empire of Great Britain,* and engraved by Jodocus Hondius. *British Museum.*

10 SNITTERFIELD CHURCH. Presumably John Shakespeare was christened here, though the register begins only in 1561. *Photograph by Edwin Smith.*

11 ROBERT ARDEN'S HOUSE, WILMCOTE. A typical early 16th century building, with timber frame on a stone foundation. Bought by the Trustees of Shakespeare's Birthplace in 1930. *Photograph by Edwin Smith.*

12 ASTON CANTLOW CHURCH. There is no record of the marriage of John Shakespeare and Mary Arden, as the register begins after that date. *Photograph by Edwin Smith.*

13 SHAKESPEARE'S BIRTHPLACE in 1769, the year of the Garrick Jubilee. The houses are built about a central chimney stack on a stone foundation, the oak frame tied by rafters, the panels filled with wattle and daub. The first known illustration: a drawing by Richard Greene in *The Gentleman's Magazine.*

THE BIRTHPLACE IN 1847. A modern print from a negative taken at the time of its sale to the Birthplace Committee for £3,000. The living-room had been converted into a butcher's shop (see p. 108). *Trustees of Shakespeare's Birthplace.*

THE BIRTHPLACE IN 1857. Restoration in progress. *Trustees of Shakespeare's Birthplace.*

THE BIRTHPLACE TO-DAY. In 1891 an Act of Parliament incorporated the Trustees and Guardians of Shakespeare's Birthplace, responsible for maintaining property associated with Shakespeare. *Photograph by Edwin Smith.*

14 ENTRY OF SHAKESPEARE'S BAPTISM in the register of Holy Trinity Church, Stratford. In 1600 entries from 1558 onwards were transcribed into this register, each page being signed by the vicar, Richard Byfield, and the churchwardens. *Trustees of Shakespeare's Birthplace.*

ELIZABETH I in 1569, apparently her first portrait as Queen. The painting, by Hans Eworth, forms part of an allegorical group, a kind of Judgment of Paris, in which Elizabeth awards the apple to herself instead of to one of the three goddesses. *From the painting at Hampton Court, by gracious permission of H.M. the Queen.*

15 WILLIAM CECIL, by an unknown artist. Cecil was born in 1520, created Lord Burghley in 1571, Lord Treasurer in 1572, and died in 1598. *National Portrait Gallery*

16 ROBERT DUDLEY, by an unknown artist. Born in 1532, created Earl of Leicester in 1564, he died in 1588. He was the uncle of Philip Sidney and stepfather of the Earl of Essex. *By permission of the Trustees of the Wallace Collection.*

17 CHARLECOTE HOUSE, rebuilt *c.* 1558. Elizabeth knighted Thomas Lucy when she

stayed here in 1566. *Photograph by Edwin Smith.*

18 STRATFORD-UPON-AVON. This aerial view shows all the principal places associated with Shakespeare. *Aerofilms Ltd.*

19 CHURCH OF THE HOLY TRINITY, STRATFORD. The original building is early 13th century, the aisles were added in 1330, the chancel *c.* 1480, and the spire in the 18th century. *Photograph by Edwin Smith.*

20 THE GILDHALL AND SCHOOLROOM. The upper chamber of the Gildhall was converted into the schoolroom of the grammar school in 1564, in place of the old schoolhouse in the quad. Beyond the Gild Chapel is the site of New Place, and beyond that again the house of Thomas Nash, first husband of Shakespeare's granddaughter, Elizabeth Hall. *Photograph by Edwin Smith.*

21 THE GILD CHAPEL, rebuilt by Sir Hugh Clopton, *c.* 1490. There are medieval wall paintings inside. *Photograph by Edwin Smith.*

22 CLOPTON BRIDGE OVER THE AVON. Dr Caroline Spurgeon made the ingenious suggestion that the eddy under the last arch on the far side of the river inspired the description of Collatine's grief in *The Rape of Lucrece:*

As through an arch the violent roaring tide
Outruns the eye that doth behold his haste,
Yet in the eddy boundeth in his pride
Back to the strait that forced him on so fast,
In rage sent out, recall'd in rage, being past:
Even so his sighs, his sorrows, make a saw,
To push grief on and back the same grief draw.

Photograph by Edwin Smith.

23 THE COTSWOLD ESCARPMENT. Meon Hill, near Wincot, four miles south of Stratford. 'Marian Hacket, the fat ale-wife' of *The Taming of the Shrew,* lived at Wincot: In 1591

'Sara Hacket, the daughter of Robert Hacket' was baptised at Quinton, within the parish of which Wincot lies. *Photograph by Edwin Smith.*

24 STRATFORD GRAMMAR SCHOOL. The schoolroom was originally the over-hall of the Gild of the Holy Cross. *Photograph by Edwin Smith.*

25 THE GENEVAN BIBLE, 1560. Prepared in Geneva by refugee reformers during the Marian persecution, it is sometimes known as the 'Breeches Bible', from its rendering of *Genesis* iii. 7: 'They sewed fig tree leaves together and made themselves breeches'. *British Museum.*

LILY'S LATIN GRAMMAR, 1567, the First (English) Part. William Lily was the first High Master of St Paul's School, and grandfather of the dramatist John Lyly. *Folger Shakespeare Library, Washington.*

26 SIR FRANCIS DRAKE (*c.* 1540-96), aged 43. *British Museum.*

27 PERRAN ROUND. Only two medieval theatres remain, both in Cornwall. The interior of Perran Round is 130 feet across, the banks about 12 feet high. A tunnel, or 'conveyor', ran under the stage, ending in a pit near the middle of the arena. This reconstruction, by the author, is based mainly on stage directions in the Cornish miracle plays.

28-29 LONDON FROM THE NORTH, *c.* 1600. An engraving, apparently unique, inserted in the manuscript journal of Abram Booth, an agent of the Dutch East India Company. *Library of the University of Utrecht.*

29 THE CURTAIN THEATRE, built by Henry Laneman, 1576-7. Detail from the left of the *View of London.* The neighbouring Theatre had been removed, and this is the only known view of one of the two first London playhouses.

29 *Gorboduc*, 1565: the first edition, surreptitiously printed. It is the first English tragedy to be written in the classical Senecan manner. *Huntington Library, San Marino, California.*

30 BLACKFRIARS FROM BANKSIDE. The boys' theatre was in one of the buildings behind Blackfriars Stairs (see p. 111). From J. C. Visscher's View of London, dated 1616. Visscher, who may never have been in London, based his panorama on Norden's *View* in *Civitas Londini* (p. 40-41). *British Museum.*

31 THE QUEEN'S INTERLUDERS AT STRATFORD. The payment is the third entry. From the Stratford Council Book, 1568-9. *Trustees of Shakespeare's Birthplace.*

'THE HONORABLE ENTERTAINEMENT gieuen to the Queenes Maiestie in Progresse, at Elvetham,' 1591. Shakespeare probably had this woodcut from this pamphlet in mind when in *A Midsummer Night's Dream*, II. i he makes Oberon describe a water pageant with fireworks, and Elizabeth as 'a fair vestal throned by the west'. The Elvetham Entertainment must have resembled the one at Kenilworth. *British Museum.*

32 THE GOLDEN HIND. In April, 1581, Elizabeth knighted Drake on board when it anchored at Deptford. There it was preserved for a century before being broken up. From the map of Drake's voyage, by Jodocus Hondius. *British Museum.*

33 *Euphues*, 1579: the first edition. Shakespeare parodied rather than imitated euphuism, the artificial speech of the period; for example, Falstaff in 1 *Henry IV:* 'Though the camomile, the more it is trodden on the faster it grows, yet youth, the more it is wasted the sooner it wears.' *British Museum.*

PLUTARCH'S *Lives*, translated by Sir Thomas North: the first edition, 1579. Richard Field,

the Stratford boy, was apprenticed to Vautrollier, the finest printer of his age (see p. 53). *British Museum.*

34 TEMPLE GRAFTON CHURCH, a drawing by James Saunders *c.* 1800. It was rebuilt in the 19th century, and unfortunately the register does not begin until 1695. *Trustees of Shakespeare's Birthplace.*

SHAKESPEARE'S MARRIAGE BOND. The first four lines, in Latin, are the bond proper, in which Sandells and Richardson bind themselves in a surety of £40 on behalf of Shakespeare. The remainder is in English: 'The condicion of this obligacion ys suche that if herafter there shall not appere any Lawfull Lett or impediment . . . but that William Shagspere . . . and Anne Hathwey of Stratford . . . maiden may lawfully solennize matrimony together . . . then the said obligacion to be voyd . . .' *Diocesan Registry, Worcester.*

35 THE HATHAWAY FARMHOUSE at Shottery, originally called Hewland. In the 18th century it was converted into three cottages, acquired by the Birthplace Trustees in 1892. *Photograph by Edwin Smith.*

SHAKESPEARE'S MARRIAGE LICENCE. The clerk's erroneous entry in the Bishop of Worcester's Register: 'Item eodem die similis emanavit licencia inter Wm Shaxpere et Annam Whateley de Temple Grafton.' 'Item, on the same day [27 Nov. 1582] a similar licence was issued between W.S. and A.W. of T.G.' *Diocesan Registry, Worcester.*

36 THE BAPTISM OF SHAKESPEARE'S CHILDREN. The entries in the register of Holy Trinity Church. *Trustees of Shakespeare's Birthplace.*

37 HAMPTON LUCY FROM CHARLECOTE PARK. 'Lettyce the Daughter', and 'Jeames the sonne of Henrye Shakespere' were christened

I

in Hampton Lucy church in 1582 and 1585 respectively. James was buried there in Sept. 1589. This Henry Shakespeare was probably the poet's uncle. *Photograph by Edwin Smith.*

38 WESTMINSTER, from John Norden's *Speculum Britanniae,* 1593. *British Museum.*

39 WHITEHALL, from J. C. Visscher's *View of London* (see p. 30 note). *British Museum.*

40-41 VIEW OF LONDON, 1600, from *Civitas Londini,* drawn by John Norden. This is the source of Visscher's *View* (see p. 30). The Swan and Beargarden are clearly visible. Almost hidden in the trees to the south-east of the Beargarden are the Rose and Globe. All are shown as polygonal, possibly an error or an 'artistic' touch by the unknown engraver. *Royal Library, Stockholm.*

42 MARY, QUEEN OF SCOTS in 1578, aged 36. A portrait attributed to P. Oudry. *National Portrait Gallery.*

43 *Campaspe,* 1584: the first edition. John Lyly (*c.* 1554-1606) was the author of *Euphues* (p. 33). *British Museum.*

Tamburlaine, 1590: the first edition. Though there is little direct evidence that Marlowe wrote the play there is no doubt that it is his. *Bodleian Library, Oxford.*

44-45 THE SPANISH ARMADA. The medallions show the commanders of the English ships. By Hendrick Cornelius Vroom (1566-1619), from *The Tapestry Hangings in the House of Lords,* by John Pine, 1739. *British Museum.*

47 ROBERT DEVEREUX, 2nd EARL OF ESSEX (1567-1601). Painted in 1597 by an unknown artist. *National Portrait Gallery.*

SIR WALTER RALEIGH (*c.* 1552-1618). Painted in Armada year by an unknown

artist. For thirteen years before his execution he was imprisoned by James I. *National Portrait Gallery.*

QUEEN ELIZABETH, aged 59. Painted by an unknown artist to commemorate her visit in 1592 to Ditchley, Oxfordshire, on which county she is standing. *National Portrait Gallery.*

48 SIR PHILIP SIDNEY. He was only thirty-two when mortally wounded in the Netherlands at the beginning of the war with Spain, 1586. The quotation is from the elegy of his friend, Fulke Greville. *National Portrait Gallery: artist unknown.*

The Faerie Queene. St George and the Dragon, from the first edition of Books I-III, 1590. *British Museum.*

49 *The Spanish Tragedy,* the first extant edition, 1592(?). Kyd was probably the author of the original lost play of *Hamlet,* Shakespeare's version of which is the most famous of all tragedies of revenge. *British Museum.*

Greenes Groatsworth of Wit, 1592. 'Sweete boy' is Nashe; 'thou no less deserving' probably Peele. Marlowe is addressed as 'the famous gracer of Tragedians . . . who hath said . . . There is no God'. *British Museum.*

50 HENSLOWE'S *Diary* is really an account book in which he entered his receipts. The entries are headed, 'In the name of god Amen 1591 begininge the 19 of Febreary my lord Stranges mene as ffoloweth 1591'. The new year then began on March 25th, so that February 1591 is 1592 according to our reckoning. The first entry is Greene's *Friar Bacon,* 17s. 3d.; the third Greene's *Orlando Furioso,* 16s. 6d.; the seventh Marlowe's *Jew of Malta,* 50s. Shakespeare's 1 *Henry VI* is the twelfth, its receipts £3 16s. 8d., the highest of the season, its popularity so great that it was given fifteen times. Henslowe died a few

weeks before Shakespeare. *Dulwich College, by permission of the Governors.*

50 *Pierce Penilesse,* 1592: the first edition. Nashe is defending plays, and the Talbot reference is almost certainly to Shakespeare's I *Henry VI. British Museum.*

51 *Kind-Harts Dreame: Conteining fiue Apparitions, with their Inuectiues against abuses raigning,* 1592: the first edition. One of the apparitions is Greene, 'of face amible, of body well proportioned'. *British Museum.*

53 *Venus and Adonis,* the first quarto. Field had now taken over the Vautrollier press and used the same device (see p. 33). The quotation is from Ovid's *Amores* I. xv., rendered by Marlowe:

Let base-conceited wits admire vile things:
Fair Phoebus lead me to the Muses' springs.

British Museum.

54 *The Rape of Lucrece.* The only quarto, all other editions being in octavo. *Bodleian Library, Oxford.*

HENRY WRIOTHESLEY, 3rd EARL OF SOUTHAMPTON (1573-1630). A painting in the possession of the Duke of Portland at Welbeck Abbey.

55 WILLIAM HERBERT, 3rd EARL OF PEMBROKE (1580-1630). The Folio of 1623 was dedicated to him and his brother, the Earl of Montgomery. A painting by Van Dyck in the possession of Lord Herbert at Wilton House.

Shakespeare's Sonnets, 1609, the only early edition. Thorpe became a member of the Stationers' Company in 1594 and was active for thirty years. *British Museum.*

56 *Willobie His Avisa,* 1594. Henry Willoughby was related by marriage to Thomas Russell,

one of the overseers of Shakespeare's will. *British Museum.*

57 *The First Part of the Contention,* the 'bad' quarto of 2 *Henry VI,* so bad that until recently it was thought to be the source-play used by Shakespeare. *Bodleian Library, Oxford.*

58 *Titus Andronicus,* a drawing probably made by Henry Peacham in 1594. It illustrates, not quite accurately, the first scene: 'Tamora pleadinge for her sonnes going to execution'. Aaron the Moor, and presumably therefore, Othello, is conceived as a negro, and there is some attempt at historical costume for the chief characters. From the *Harley Papers* in the possession of the Marquis of Bath at Longleat.

59 WILLIAM KEMPE, from the title page of his *Nine Days' Wonder,* 1600, an account of his dance from London to Norwich in 1599. He died a few years later. *Bodleian Library, Oxford.*

HENRY CAREY, 1st LORD HUNSDON (c. 1524-96). Lord Chamberlain, and the nephew of Anne Boleyn. *British Museum.*

RICHARD BURBAGE (c. 1568-1619), played 'young Hamlett, ould Heironymoe, Kind Leer, the greued Moore, and more beside'. He and Alleyn were the greatest actors of the age. *Dulwich College, by permission of the Governors.*

60 EDWARD ALLEYN (1566-1626). He retired in 1604, having made a fortune. His first wife was Henslowe's stepdaughter, his second the daughter of John Donne. He founded Dulwich College, where this portrait is preserved. *By permission of the Governors.*

61 GEORGE CHAPMAN (c. 1559-1634). Shakespeare's sonnet 86, 'Was it the proud full sail of his great verse', may refer to Chapman. He is chiefly remembered for his translation of Homer, which inspired Keats. *British Museum.*

61 MICHAEL DRAYTON (1563-1631). The girl he loved married Sir Henry Rainsford of Clifford Chambers, near Stratford, where he used to stay. *National Portrait Gallery: artist unknown.*

62 BENJAMIN JONSON (1572-1637). He complained that 'Shakespeare wanted art', meaning that he did not follow the classical 'rules', yet he wrote the splendid elegy in the Folio, 'To the memory of my beloved, Mr William Shakespeare'. Apparently the portrait is a copy of one at Knole by Gerard Honthorst. *National Portrait Gallery.*

63 *Sir Thomas More.* The last of the three pages, lines 96-147, thought by some to be in Shakespeare's handwriting. The passage begins,

all marry god forbid that
moo nay certainly yo^u ar
for to the king god hath his offyc lent
of dread of Iustyce, power and
Comaund
hath bid him rule, and willd yo^u to
obay

The manuscript, *Harley* 7368, is in the British Museum.

65 SHAKESPEARE AS PAYEE. 'To Willm Kempe Willm Shakespeare & Richarde Burbage seruantes to the Lord Chambleyne vpon the councelles warr^t dated at Whitehall xv^{to} Martii 1594 for twoe seuerall comedies or Enterludes shewed by them before her Matie in xrmas tyme laste paste viz^d vpon St Stephens daye & Innocentes daye xiii^l vj^s viij^d and by waye of her ma^{tes} Rewarde vj^l xiij^s iiij^d.' From the accounts of the Treasurer of the Chamber. *Public Record Office.*

GREENWICH PALACE, originally called Pleasaunce or Placentia. Here Henry VII died, and Henry VIII, Mary and Elizabeth were born. Demolished by Charles II, Greenwich Hospital was built on its site by Wren. A drawing by Anthony van Wyndgaerde. *Ashmolean Museum, Oxford.*

66 THE HALL OF GRAY'S INN, built 1556-60, and gutted during an air raid in 1941. *Copyright Raphael Tuck & Sons Ltd.*

67 THE SWAN THEATRE. The sketch was discovered by the German scholar, K. T. Gaedertz in 1888, from which date modern research may be said to begin. De Witt added a note that the Swan was built of a concrete of flints, with wooden columns painted to resemble marble, and that it would seat 3,000.

68 ENTRY OF HAMNET'S DEATH, in the register of Holy Trinity Church, Stratford. *Trustees of Shakespeare's Birthplace.*

69 HARVARD HOUSE. The date, 1596, can be seen on the centre boss beneath the middle window. John Harvard (1607-38) went to America and bequeathed money and books to the College that became Harvard University. *Photograph by Edwin Smith.*

70 THE GRANT OF ARMS. Line 13 reads that 'John Shakespeare of Stratford vppon Avon in the counte of Warwick whose parentes and late antecessors were for their valiant and faithful services advanced and rewarded by the most prudent prince King Henry the seventh . . .' It may be so, though there is no record of such services, and the citation may have been a fiction to justify the grant, which was in fact challenged in 1602 by Ralph Broke, York Herald. *A photograph supplied by the Shakespeare Birthplace Trust of the draft in the College of Arms.*

71 GEORGE CAREY, 2nd LORD HUNSDON (1547-1603). A miniature, in the possession of the Duke of Buccleuch, by the great Elizabethan 'limner' Nicholas Hilliard. It has recently been questioned whether this really

is a portrait of Lord Hunsdon. *From a print in the Victoria and Albert Museum.*

71 WILLIAM WAYTE'S PETITION, Nov. 1596, from the rolls of the Court of Queen's Bench, discovered by Dr Leslie Hotson in 1930. The abbreviated Latin, expanded, reads:

Anglia. *scire scilicet* Willelmus Wayte petit securitates pacis versus Willelmum Shakspere, Franciscum Langley, Dorotheam Soer uxorem Johannis Soer & Annam Lee, ob metum mortis &c.

England. Be it known that W.W. craves sureties of the peace against W.S., F.L., D.S., wife of John Soer, & A.L. for fear of death &c. *Public Record Office.*

72 SIR THOMAS LUCY (1532-1600), the effigy in Charlecote church. His wife, Joyce, 'in love to her husband most faithful and true', died in 1596. *Photograph by Edwin Smith.*

73 NEW PLACE. The original 'grete house', built by Sir Hugh Clopton and bought by Shakespeare, was pulled down about 1702. This drawing, the only known authentic illustration, was made by George Vertue 'by memory' in 1737, and represents the Church Street front, 'a long gallery &c and for servants', the 'real dwelling house' being behind. *British Museum.*

75 THE SITE OF NEW PLACE. The second New Place, 'a handsome brick house', was pulled down in 1759 by its irate owner, Rev. Francis Gastrell, because he thought the rates too high. To-day only the foundations remain. *Photograph by Edwin Smith.*

77 *Love's Labour's Lost,* the first quarto. *British Museum.*

78 *Palladis Tamia: Wits Treasury,* 1598, is the second of a short series of books called *Wit's Commonwealth,* by various authors. Francis Meres (1565-1647) was a graduate of both Cambridge and Oxford. In 1602 he became rector and schoolmaster at Wing, Rutland. *British Museum.*

79 *Every Man in his Humour,* cast of the first performance, from the Folio edition of Jonson's *Works,* 1616. *British Museum.*

80 RICHARD QUINEY'S LETTER. It begins, 'Loveinge Contreyman, I am bolde of yowe as of a ffrende, craveinge yowre helpe with xxx^{ll} vppon Mr Bushells & my securytee or Mr Myttons with me. Mr Rosswell is nott come to London as yeate & I have especiall cawse. Yowe shall ffrende me muche in helpeinge me out of all the debettes I owe in London, I thancke god, & muche quiet my mynde which wolde nott be indebted. I am nowe towardes the Cowrte . . .'

Richard was on his way to see the Privy Council in a successful attempt to get taxation relief for Stratford, badly hit by the fires. He died in 1602, during his second term as bailiff. *Trustees of Shakespeare's Birthplace.*

81 BANKSIDE, 1600, from *Civitas Londini,* by John Norden. The Rose is miscalled 'The Star', a name otherwise unknown. All the theatres are shown as cylindrical, the most authoritative indication of their shape. *Royal Library, Stockholm.*

82 BANKSIDE, from Visscher's *View* (see note to p. 30). Visscher, copying Norden's *View* (p. 40) failed to see the Globe and gave its name to the Rose. The theatres are shown as polygonal. *British Museum.*

83 THE GLOBE THEATRE. There may have been rails round the apron stage when it was built, though the first real evidence is in Middleton's *Black Book,* 1604: 'the stage-rails of this earthen globe'. *A reconstruction by the author.*

84 THE STATIONERS' REGISTER, 1600. '23 Augusti. Andrew Wyse William Aspley. Entred for their copies vnder the handes of

the wardens Two bookes, the one called Muche a Doo about nothinge. Thother the second parte of the history of Kinge Henry the iiijth with the humours of Sir John Falstaff: Wrytten by master Shakespere. xijd.' *Stationers' Hall, by permission of the Worshipful Company of Stationers.*

84 *Rosalynde: Euphues Golden Legacie,* 1590, written by Thomas Lodge on his voyage to the Azores. *British Museum.*

85 'IT WAS A LOVER AND HIS LASS.' Morley was one of the greatest of Elizabethan composers, particularly of lute songs and madrigals. He died, aged 46, in 1603. He was probably a friend of Shakespeare's. His setting of the song comes from a unique copy of his *First Booke of Ayres,* 1600, in the Folger Shakespeare Library, Washington.

86 *Poetaster or The Arraignment:* the first quarto, 1602. *British Museum.*

87 *The Returne from Pernassus: or the Scourge of Simony.* 'Publiquely acted by the Students in Saint Iohns Colledge in Cambridge.' The first quarto, 1606. *British Museum.*

The Tragicall Historie of Hamlet Prince of Denmarke. 'By William Shake-speare. As it hath beene diuerse times acted by his Highnesse seruants in the Cittie of London: as also in the two Vniuersities of Cambridge and Oxford, and else-where.' The 'bad' quarto, 1603; how bad may be seen by comparing this passage with the full text in II.ii. *Bodleian Library, Oxford.*

88 SHAKESPEARE'S ESTATE of 127 acres at Old Stratford. *Photograph by Edwin Smith.*

THE CONVEYANCE of the Old Stratford estate, 1 May 1602. 'This indenture . . . Betweene William Combe of Warrwicke . . . Esquier, and John Combe of Olde Stretford . . . gentleman, on the one partie,

And William Shakespere of Stretford vppon Avon . . . gentleman, on thother partye, Witnesseth that . . . in consideracion of the somme of three hundred and twentie poundes . . .' It was 'Sealed and deliuered to Gilbert Shakespere, to the vse of the within named William Shakespere'. *Trustees of Shakespeare's Birthplace.*

89 RICHMOND PALACE, the medieval Sheen. Rebuilt by Henry VII, James I gave it to Prince Henry, after whose death it fell into decay. There are morris dancers in the foreground. A painting of about 1620 by an unknown artist. *By permission of the Syndics of the Fitzwilliam Museum, Cambridge.*

90 JAMES I and VI, 1610. Probably by John de Critz. *By permission of the Trustees of the National Maritime Museum, Greenwich.*

91 THE SPECIAL COMMISSION appointing 'William Shackespeare and others' the King's Servants, 19 May 1603. 'James by the grace of god . . . Knowe yee that Wee . . . haue licenced . . . theise our Servauntes Lawrence Fletcher, William Shakespeare, Richard Burbage, Augustyne Phillippes, Iohn Heninges, Henrie Condell, William Sly, Robert Armyn, Richard Cowly, and the rest of theire Assosiates to vse and exercise the Arte and faculty of playinge Comedies, Tragedies, histories, Enterludes . . . aswell for the recreation of our lovinge Subjectes, as for our Solace and pleasure.' Fletcher came from Scotland with James, and was merely an honorary member of the company. *Public Record Office.*

92 MIDDLE TEMPLE HALL. 'At our feast wee had a play called Twelue Night or What You Will, much like the Commedy of Errores.' From the *Diary* of John Manningham. *Picture Post Library.*

THE FIRST SHAKESPEARE ANECDOTE, 13 March 1602. 'Vpon a tyme when Burbidge played Rich. 3. there was a citizen greue soe farr in liking with him that before shee went from the play shee appointed him to come that night vnto hir by the name of Ri: the 3. Shakespeare overhearing their conclusion went before, was intertained, and at his game ere Burbidge came. Then message being brought that Rich. the 3.ᵈ was at the dore, Shakespeare caused returne to be made that William the Conquerour was before Rich. the 3. Shakespeare's name William. *(Mr Curle)?* From the *Diary* of John Manningham. His informant, Edward Curle, was a fellow student at the Middle Temple. *British Museum.*

93 WILTON HOUSE. The central part is all that remains of the original Tudor house, rebuilt by Inigo Jones after the fire of about 1647. Lady Pembroke is said to have written to her son, 'We have the man Shakespeare with us'. *National Building Record.*

94 MOUNTJOY'S HOUSE. From the map of London attributed to Ralph Agas, printed in 1633. *British Museum.*

95 THE SOMERSET HOUSE CONFERENCE, August 1604. The English delegation, on the right, consists of Sir Robert Cecil; the Earl of Northampton; Charles Blount, Earl of Devon, who defeated Tyrone after Essex's failure; the Earl of Nottingham, Lord Admiral at the time of the Armada, and patron of the company of players; Thomas Sackville, Earl of Dorset, part author of *Gorboduc.* The leader of the Spanish delegation is the Constable of Castile, on whom Shakespeare and the King's men attended. The painting is attributed to M. Gheeraerts II. *National Portrait Gallery.*

96 THE REVELS ACCOUNTS for 1604-5, made out by the Master of the Revels, Edmund Tilney, showing expenses incurred for the Court performance of plays. Only two

Accounts of the period of Shakespeare's career have survived. *Public Record Office.*

97 *The Masque of Blackness.* One of the twelve masquers. 'The colours azure and silver, but returned on the top with a scroll and antique dressing of feathers, and jewels interlaced with ropes of pearl. And for the front, ear, neck and wrists, the ornament was of the most choice and orient pearl.' *Devonshire Collection, Chatsworth. By permission of the Trustees of the Chatsworth Settlement.*

98 CLOPTON HOUSE: the old doorway. The rest of the house was rebuilt about 1700. *Photograph by Edwin Smith.*

99 *The Chronicles of England, Scotland and Ireland, 1577*: the first edition. When Raphael Holinshed died, about 1580, he was steward of the manor of Packwood, near Stratford. *British Museum.*

101 *Select Observations,* by John Hall (1575-1635). Unfortunately his notes begin after Shakespeare's death, but he records how he cured his wife and daughter of various ailments. *Trustees of Shakespeare's Birthplace.*

HALL'S CROFT. The house was bought by the Shakespeare Birthplace Trust in 1949. *Photograph by Edwin Smith.*

102 JOHN FLETCHER (1579-1625). Born at Rye, Sussex, he probably went to Cambridge. His father was Bishop of London. *National Portrait Gallery: artist unknown.*

FRANCIS BEAUMONT (1584-1616). The son of Sir Francis Beaumont, he was an Oxford and Inner Temple man. According to John Aubrey, Beaumont and Fletcher 'lived together on the Banke Side, not far from the Playhouse, both batchelors; lay together; had one wench in the house between them, which they did so admire; the same cloathes and cloake, &c., between them'. In the possession of Lord Sackville at Knole. *Artist unknown.*

103 SIMON FORMAN's *Booke of Plaies*. Forman (1552-1611), an Oxford man, practised in London, where he was imprisoned for having no diploma, though eventually he was granted one by Cambridge. He died 12 Sept. 1611 while crossing the Thames in a boat, probably by suicide. His note begins, 'Obserue ther howe Lyontes the kinge of Cicillia was overcom with Jelosy of his wife with the kinge of Bohemia his frind . . .' On the next page he describes Autolycus, 'the Rog that cam in all tottered like coll pixci', and concludes, 'Beware of trustinge feined beggars or fawninge fellouss'. *Bodleian Library, Oxford.*

SHAKESPEARE's *Sonnets*, 1609. See note to p. 55.

104 THE REVELS ACCOUNT for 1611-12 (see p. 96 and note). Tilney died in 1610 and the Master of the Revels was now Sir George Buck. *A King and No King* and *Cupid's Revenge* are by Beaumont and Fletcher. *Tu Quoque* was the popular name for *The City Gallant*, a comedy by Jo. Cooke. *The Silver Age* and *Lucrece* are Heywood's. The authors of the other plays are unknown. *Public Record Office.*

105 SHAKESPEARE's DEPOSITION AND SIGNATURE in the case of *Belott v. Mountjoy*. Shakespeare's evidence, of which this is the conclusion, was written by a clerk. The last two lines, not quite complete in the illustration, read, '[he knoweth not what] implementes and necessaries of houshould stuffe [the defendant gaue the plaintiff] in marriadge with his daughter Marye.' The Belott-Mountjoy Suit was discovered by Prof. C. W. Wallace of the University of Nebraska in 1910. *Public Record Office.*

106 THE MARRIAGE OF PRINCESS ELIZABETH AND FREDERICK V, ELECTOR PALATINE, 14 February 1613. Frederick lost the crown of Bohemia and his Electorate, and died in 1632. Elizabeth, 'Queen of Hearts', died in England in 1662. She was the mother of Rupert of the Rhine, and grandmother of George I. From a German broadsheet, 1613. *British Museum.*

106 QUEEN ANNE (1574-1619). The daughter of Frederick II of Denmark, she married James in 1589 when he was king of Scotland only. A miniature by Isaac Oliver at Windsor Castle. *By gracious permission of H.M. the Queen.*

HENRY, PRINCE OF WALES (1594-1612). Instead of an enlightened Henry IX, England had Charles I and a Civil War. A miniature by Isaac Oliver. *By permission of the Syndics of the Fitzwilliam Museum, Cambridge.*

107 THE BLACKFRIARS GATEHOUSE: THE CONVEYANCE, 10 March 1613. 'William Shakespeare of Stratford Vpon Avon' pays Henry Walker £140 for a tenement 'part of which is erected over a great gate'. The famous Mermaid meetings took place on the first Friday of the month, and it was just at this time that Johnson was charged with serving meat instead of fish on Fridays in Lent. *Guildhall Library, London.*

THE BLACKFRIARS GATEHOUSE: THE MORTGAGE to Walker for £60, apparently as security against payment of the balance, 11 March 1613. Shakespeare leased the house to one John Robinson. It was destroyed by the Great Fire of 1666. *British Museum.*

108 THE SWAN AND MAIDENHEAD. About 1808 the eastern part of the Birthplace property was fronted with red brick (see p. 13). A lithograph by C. Graf, 1851. *Trustees of Shakespeare's Birthplace.*

109 JOHN COMBE. The verses that Shakespeare is said to have 'fanned up' are,
Ten in the hundred must lie in his graue,
But a hundred to ten whether God will him haue.

Who then must be interr'd in this Tombe?
Oh (quoth the Diuell) my John a Combe.

It is only a legend, and the verses are merely a variation on an old theme. *Photograph by Edwin Smith.*

110 THE CROWN TAVERN, OXFORD. Towards the end of his career in London Shakespeare probably made the journey to Stratford two or three times a year; Oxford was a convenient place to break the journey, and he may well have stayed with the Davenants and been godfather of William, born in 1606. On the other hand, he left 20s. to his godson William Walker, and there is no mention of William Davenant in his will. When Davenant was a knight, Poet Laureate and in his cups he used to like to think that Shakespeare was his father.

The Crown Tavern is now 3 Cornmarket Street, where the painted bedroom-walls were discovered in 1927. *Photograph by W. R. Rose, by permission of Mr E. W. Attwood.*

THOMAS GREENE'S NOTE. 'Sept. W Shakspeare's tellyng J Greene that J [I] was not able to beare the encloseinge of Welcombe.' This was inserted between the entry of 14 Aug.—'Mr Barber dyed'—and that of 5 Sept. —'his sending James for the executours of Mr Barber to agree as ys sayd with them for Mr Barbers interest.' Thomas Barber was a landowner, and the 'his' of the last entry is probably William Combe, the leader of the enclosure movement. The note on Shakespeare is not very clear, for Greene was a titheholder and would probably gain by enclosure. A fortnight before Shakespeare's death he was replaced as town clerk by Francis Collins. *Trustees of Shakespeare's Birthplace.*

111 THE SECOND GLOBE. After 1614 the 'Beere bayting house' was also a theatre, the Hope. From the *Long View* of London, 1647, by Wenceslas Hollar. *Guildhall Library, London.*

113 SHAKESPEARE'S WILL: the last page. Probably written by Collins's clerk, it begins, 'Males of the bodies of the said . . .' The 'Item, I gyve vnto my wief my second best bed with the furniture' is the insertion above the ninth line. John and Susanna Hall are residuary legatees and appointed executors, Thomas Russell and Francis Collins overseers. On the left are the witnesses' signatures, on the right the probate endorsement, 22 June 1616. Shakespeare signed each of the three sheets and probably wrote the 'By me'. These three signatures, the two of the Gatehouse transaction and that of the deposition are the only writing that can definitely be claimed as his (see p. 63 and note). *Somerset House, London.*

114 ENTRY OF SHAKESPEARE'S BURIAL in the register of Holy Trinity Church, Stratford. *Trustees of Shakespeare's Birthplace.*

115 THE CHANCEL OF HOLY TRINITY CHURCH. Shakespeare's monument is the first on the left wall, beyond the door, his grave in the sanctuary floor below. John Combe's tomb is to the left of the altar. *Photograph by Edwin Smith.*

117 SHAKESPEARE'S MONUMENT. The monument itself is marble, the bust of painted Cotswold stone. The Latin inscription reads:
In judgment a Nestor, in genius a Socrates, in art a Virgil:
The earth covers him, the people mourn him, Olympus has him.
Photograph by Edwin Smith.

119 THE FIRST FOLIO: TITLE PAGE. The engraving is by Martin Droeshout, son of a Flemish immigrant. He was only fifteen when Shakespeare died, and probably worked from a line drawing by some unknown artist. The engraving exists in two states, the second of which, more heavily worked, is reproduced here. This portrait and the bust, the proportions of which agree,

are the only two authentic likenesses of Shakespeare, though not necessarily very accurate ones. *British Museum.*

121 THE FIRST FOLIO: THE PREFACE. Note that Heminge and Condell claim to have replaced the 'bad' quarto texts by those of the original manuscripts, and that there was scarcely a 'blot' (erasure) in Shakespeare's papers.

122 WILLIAM SLY, died 1608. *Dulwich College, by permission of the Governors.*

JOHN LOWIN (1576-1669?). He became a sharer in 1604, and stayed with the company until the closing of the theatres in 1642, when he turned innkeeper. He played Morose, Volpone, Epicure Mammon and Bosola. *Ashmolean Museum, Oxford.*

NATHAN FIELD (1587-1620). As one of the Chapel Children he was a great favourite of Jonson's. *Dulwich College, by permission of the Governors.*

123 THE FIRST FOLIO: THE ACTOR LIST. These are the sharers in the Chamberlain's-King's company from 1594 to 1623. The list is approximately chronological.

124 THE FIRST FOLIO: THE CATALOGUE OF PLAYS. Only half of them had previously been published, and only fourteen with good texts. By an oversight *Troilus and Cressida,* the first play in the Tragedy section, was omitted from the Catalogue.

125 THE FIRST FOLIO: *The Tempest.* The last of Shakespeare's plays is the first in the Folio, and its stage directions the most detailed. Some plays merely give entries, others are divided only into acts, and six have no division at all.

126 THE FIRST FOLIO: *Cymbeline.* The last page.

127 THE GRAVE OF SHAKESPEARE. On his right lies Thomas Nash, first husband of his granddaughter, Elizabeth Hall, on his left his wife, Anne. *Photograph by Edwin Smith.*

128 JONSON'S ELEGY 'To the memory of my beloued, the Author, Mr. William Shakespeare, and what he hath left vs.' The last ten lines. From the First Folio.

INDEX OF ARTISTS

Page numbers in italics refer to the pictures

Acclaim for
FLIGHT OF THE EAGLE

An Indigo Best Book of the Year, 2013
Globe and Mail *national bestseller*
Vancouver Sun *Best of the Shelf*

"[Black] has written the most amazing book."

—Rush Limbaugh

"Conrad Black has put together a study that is as bold and thought-provoking as it is trenchant and entertaining."

—*The Weekly Standard*

"Unlike so many academic histories, every page of this book has the authentic touch of a historian who knows countless facts and figures by heart. When he mentions a warship, for example, you can be sure that he would be able to reel off all her vital statistics on demand."

—*National Review*

"Black writes with boundless energy, graceful lucidity, considerable learning."
—*Winnipeg Free Press*

"Fascinating, richly detailed."
—*Vancouver Sun*

"[A] sweeping dissertation on the rise of the United States as a dominant global superpower . . . . [Black is] a first-rate historian."
—*Toronto Star*

"[Black's] admiration for this country is on full display in this elegant survey of American history from the beginnings to the Obama administration, rendered in his distinctive rolling cadences. . . . Black's section on the Civil War is a model of concision . . . he manages to illuminate aspects of the conduct of the war that are frequently overlooked."
—*The American Spectator*

"A fascinating portrayal of greatness that follows America's rise from a British colony to the leader of the free world in just 200 years."
—*Welland Tribune*

"Conrad Black's *Flight of the Eagle* . . . begs to be read by anyone who wants a candid—dare I say warts and all—look at U.S. history."
—*The Huffington Post*

"[Black's] enthusiasm is contagious, his erudition bracing, and his breadth of knowledge impressive."
—*PJ Media*

"Arguably [Black's] most ambitious work to date."
—*Q*, CBC Radio One

FLIGHT OF THE EAGLE

ALSO BY CONRAD BLACK

Render Unto Caesar: The Life and Legacy of Maurice Duplessis

A Life in Progress

Franklin Delano Roosevelt: Champion of Freedom

Richard M. Nixon: A Life in Full

A Matter of Principle

CONRAD BLACK

FLIGHT

of the

EAGLE

The Grand Strategies That Brought America
from Colonial Dependence to World Leadership

ENCOUNTER BOOKS

NEW YORK • LONDON

First American edition published in 2013 by Encounter Books,
an activity of Encounter for Culture and Education, Inc.,
a nonprofit, tax exempt corporation.
Encounter Books website address: www.encounterbooks.com

Manufactured in the United States and printed on
acid-free paper. The paper used in this publication meets
the minimum requirements of ANSI/NISO Z39.48 1992
(R 1997) (*Permanence of Paper*).

First paperback edition published in 2014.
Paperback edition ISBN: 978-1-59403-758-0

THE LIBRARY OF CONGRESS HAS CATALOGUED
THE HARDCOVER EDITION AS FOLLOWS:
Black, Conrad.
Flight of the eagle: the grand strategies that brought America from colonial
dependence to world leadership/Conrad Black.
pages cm
Includes bibliographical references and index.
ISBN 978-1-59403-673-6 (hardcover: alk. paper)—ISBN 978-1-59403-674-3 (ebook)
1. United States—Foreign relations. 2. Strategic culture—United States—History.
3. United States—Foreign relations administration. 4. Presidents—United States—History. I. Title.
E183.7.B57 2013
327.73—dc23
2012038962

Chapter 1: Wikimedia Commons, Source: http://www.npg.si.edu/exh/brush/ben.htm.   *Chapter 2:* Library of Congress, Prints and Photographs Division, LC-USZ62-117116 DLC.   *Chapter 3:* Library of Congress, Prints and Photographs Division, LC-USZ62-117117 DLC.   *Chapter 4:* Library of Congress, Prints and Photographs Division, LC-USZ62-117120 DLC.   *Chapter 5:* Library of Congress, Prints and Photographs Division, LC-USZ62-13011 DLC.   *Chapter 6:* Library of Congress, Prints and Photographs Division, LC-USZ62-13016 DLC.   *Chapter 7:* Library of Congress, Prints and Photographs Division, LC-USZ62-13018 DLC.   *Chapter 8:* Library of Congress, Prints and Photographs Division, LC-USZ62-13026 DLC.   *Chapter 9:* Library of Congress, Prints and Photographs Division, LC-USZ62-13028 DLC.   *Chapter 10:* Library of Congress, Prints and Photographs Division, LC-USZ62-26759 DLC.   *Chapter 11:* Wikimedia Commons, Source: U.S. Naval Historical Center Photograph #: NH 67209: http://www.history.navy.mil/photos/sh-fornv/uk/uksh-p/pow12.htm. Donation of Vice Admiral Harry Sanders, USN (Retired), 1969.   *Chapter 12:* Library of Congress, Prints and Photographs Division, LC-USZ62-88849 DLC.   *Chapter 13:* Library of Congress, Prints and Photographs Division, LC-USZ62-117123 DLC.   *Chapter 14:* Library of Congress, Prints and Photographs Division, LC-USZ62-117124 DLC.   *Chapter 15:* Wikimedia Commons, Courtesy of the National Archives & Records Administration.   *Chapter 16:* Wikimedia Commons, Courtesy of Ronald Reagan Library, Source: http://www.reagan.utexas.edu/archives/photographs/photo.html

FOR LOYAL AMERICAN FRIENDS, IN PARTICULAR

Tina Brown and Harold Evans, Shelby Bryan and Anna Wintour, Domenico Buccigrossi, Ann Coulter, Thierry Despont, Julie Nixon Eisenhower, Mica Ertegun, Miguel Estrada, Pepe and Amelia Fanjul, Jack Fowler, Ron Genini, Carolyn Gurland, Roger and Susan Hertog, Laura Ingraham, Robert Jennings, Henry and Nancy Kissinger, Roger Kimball, Parker Ladd, Leonard Lauder, Rush Limbaugh, Seth Lipsky and Amity Shlaes, Norman and Sarah Murphy, Peggy Noonan, John and Melissa O'Sullivan, Larry Perotto, Robert Pirie, Norman Podhoretz and Midge Decter, David Pringle, Chris Ruddy, Donald and Melania Trump, Robert Emmett Tyrrell, George Will, Paul Wolfowitz, Paul Wright, Jayne Wrightsman, Ezra Zilkha, and Mort Zuckerman; and the late Bill Buckley and Bill Safire.

CONTENTS

Contents

THREE
The Indispensable Country, 1933–1957

FOUR
The Supreme Nation, 1957–2013

PREFACE TO THE PAPERBACK EDITION

Since the original publication of this book in May 2013, the inattention to the American strategic interest that has afflicted the country quite consistently for most of the more than 20 years after the end of the Cold War has become more evident. Concern for that strategic interest was vital to the unprecedentedly swift rise of America from colonial status to clear preeminence in a bipolar world in just 170 years, and to the status of the world's only superpower at the end of the Cold War 45 years after that. Thus the degeneration into civil war in Syria led to President Obama declining to take any role at all other than advising that the incumbent president of Syria had to go but doing nothing to achieve that end, then declaring the use of sarin gas by the regime on Syria's civilian population to be the crossing of a red line that required military retaliation and positioning the naval forces to do that (with cruise missiles), then abdicating the role of commander-in-chief to the Congress, sending his secretary of state to tell congressional leaders that such punitive action would be "unbelievably small," and, as congressional defeat loomed, dumping the issue into the eager and untrustworthy hands of the Russian gangster-president Vladimir Putin.

Having reversed the George W. Bush policy of promoting democracy even where this led to the elevation of very undemocratic movements, as in Lebanon and Gaza and the Palestinian West Bank, the Obama administration then abandoned America's long-time Egyptian ally, the authoritarian president Hosni Mubarak, when he came under general pressure. When the anti-democratic Muslim Brotherhood was elected to lead the government and set out to rewrite the new constitution unilaterally, somewhat in the manner of Salvador Allende in Chile in the early seventies, and then a military regime seized power in reaction, the administration remonstrated ineffectually and implausibly with the new regime in favor of the Brotherhood and its ousted and no longer overly popular leaders. The administration continued to provide Pakistan with aid that it knew was being sent on to a

Taliban faction in Afghanistan that was diligently murdering American and allied soldiers. As this is written, it is not clear that anything will have been accomplished by the sanctions placed on Iran, consistently less severe than those voted by the Congress, to frustrate that country's quest for a nuclear military capacity. The danger of that country becoming a nuclear power—followed by Turkey, Saudi Arabia, and Egypt—is a very disturbing one, and America's failure of leadership is largely responsible for the concern.

Truckling to the Palestinians over settlements, a red herring considering that Israel proved in Sinai and Gaza that it would uproot its settlers in compliance with a real peace and not just another land-for-peace scam, produced no progress in Israel-Palestine relations. The British effectively sold the same real estate to two opposed parties and there has never been any solution except to divide the old Palestine Mandate in two; fixating on settlements is just a delaying action. There will be no resolution until the Arabs accept Israel's legitimacy and right to exist as a Jewish state. Pretending to ignore Turkish posturing in the Arab world and saber-rattling at Israel, and the imposition of repressive measures within Turkey, has just encouraged more of it all. A retrenchment to the United States was disguised as a "pivot to Asia," though not very successfully. There is general skepticism in the world that the United States has any staying power. And in Iraq and Afghanistan, the expenditure of nearly 58,000 American casualties and two trillion dollars has not produced any discernible strategic benefit for the United States and its allies, and has strained those alliances. The elimination of the Saddam Hussein government in Baghdad and the killing or immobilization of significant numbers of terrorists have been useful, but not cost-effective.

There is no evidence that any serious strategic analysis has gone into any of this, but President Obama continues to claim that all developments are the product of his administration's skillful diplomacy, "backed by force." There is surprisingly wide acceptance within the United States of this now very familiar revisionist delusion. The disintegration of Ukraine was long seen as an occasion for patching relations with Russia and not as the central issue between the nativists and Western emulators in Central Europe, nor as the opportunity it is to extend the borders of the West and strengthen the hand of the party of international conciliation and domestic reform in Russia.

Generally, the withdrawal of the United States from its former over-exposed Cold War involvement in every corner of the earth is a good thing, and regional balances are developing in Europe and East Asia. All regions should be able to manage their own affairs, and the rationale for Franklin D. Roosevelt's launch of the United States into durable positions of normative and deterrent influence in

Western Europe and the Far East has been made less urgent by the disintegration of the Soviet Union, and by the comparative embrace of rational national behavior by the Chinese. Such withdrawals are more a demonstration of the success of the containment policy pursued between the Roosevelt/Truman administrations and those of Ronald Reagan and George H. W. Bush, than a manifestation of durable American irresolution. But such comprehensive initiatives should be carefully planned and executed and explained, and not just left to devolve in a series of inelegant improvisations as they have.

It remains a fortunate time for a country to lose its capacity for correct strategic analysis and policy formulation and execution. Western Europe is not under threat, and Germany is now tentatively exercising its potential, for the third time, as Europe's greatest power, but this time, unlike the imperial and Nazi experiences, in close alliance with its neighbors and trans-Atlantic allies, and entirely as a champion of democratic government and human liberty. This transformation of a unified Germany must rank as one of the very greatest achievements of American statesmanship, and one which will bear the fruit of stability and prosperity in Europe for a very long time. As this is written, Germany is instrumental in the apparent victory of the Western emulators over the Russian nativists and annexationists in Ukraine, despite the Russian seizure of Crimea, and possibly some other ethnic Russian sections of Ukraine as a consolation prize for its definitive loss of that central country that it had occupied for two centuries. China is flexing its muscles in the manner of inexperienced new powers (like Bismarck and Theodore Roosevelt), but is not really threatening anyone. And it should be possible to help coordinate a containment strategy, to the extent one is required, with Japan, India, Vietnam, Thailand, South Korea, the Philippines, Malaysia, Singapore, Australia, Indonesia, New Zealand, and Burma (where the Chinese overplayed their hand and have effectively been evicted as the chief influence). In Latin America, the economically sensible and reasonably democratic countries are steadily outpacing the detritus of the Castroite left in Argentina, Venezuela, and a few other countries.

As usual, except when countries have their backs to the wall and the United States is their principal hope for salvation, America's allies are happy enough to have a rather feckless regime floundering through these recent years in Washington, apart from the continuing accrual of very large government deficits in the United States. These deficits are made more unsettling by the fact that they are largely financed not by arm's-length auctions of government securities, but by the U.S. Federal Reserve, a subsidiary of the Treasury, purporting to "buy" the unsold securities with the issuance of notes for the purpose. The contribution of the United States to monetary instability has been very serious and uninterrupted throughout the Obama presidency. This defies one of the original justifications provided by George Washington for forming an "indissoluble Union": to create and maintain a valuable and reliable currency.

The threat to American strategic interests and national security, despite the terrorist nuisance which ultimately all governments will oppose, is not principally from outside the United States. American federal politics seem to have become almost dysfunctional, as very little can be got through the Congress, where the Republicans control the House of Representatives, and both parties shriek epithets at each other rather than compromise in the traditional and more productive way of American legislators. And the role of money in American government is becoming steadily more prevalent and disturbing.

There is plenty of evidence, including poor voter turnouts and low-quality candidates for national office, that the country is dismayed and is fearful of bad political management. But these are the times when countries can afford a comparatively great exposure to misgovernment. The United States remains fundamentally the world's most powerful country, and though China could mount a threat eventually, there is no historical evidence that China seeks more than a position of respect in the world and deference from its neighbors. Increasingly, as the United States rolls its forces back from the world, concerns about ineptitude in American strategic leadership are moderated by the absence of serious threats from other countries, and by the complete absence of any professed American vocation to occupy or otherwise intrude upon other countries.

As for the quality of American leadership, it is this author's contention that the Watergate fiasco effectively deterred the best possible candidates from seeking the highest offices for a whole generation, with the halcyon exception of the Reagan presidency. But the headship of the United States remains the greatest office within the gift of any people or political system. The office has not sought the man since Washington, but the men and women seeking the office will become worthy of it again. In a phrase of Charles de Gaulle about his own country in the fifties, the United States is "crossing the desert," but there is no reason to doubt that it will arrive in tolerably good health on the other side. All great nationalities possess the genius of renewal, as China and Germany, in very different ways, are demonstrating. The United States will surely find and elevate leaders who understand and are capable of continuing the successes of the principal statesmen whose strategic insights and execution are recounted in the following pages.

—Conrad Black
Toronto, March 2014

INTRODUCTORY NOTE

Henry A. Kissinger

A society's national strategy defines the goals it seeks to achieve and the contingencies it attempts to prevent. It unites a people's core interests, values, and apprehensions. This effort is not an academic undertaking, nor an element in a particular political platform. If it is to be effective, it must be embedded in the convictions and actions of a society over a period of time.

For the United States, the development of such a strategy has been a complex journey. No country has played such a decisive role in shaping international order, nor professed such deep ambivalence about its participation in it.

The United States was founded in large part as a conscious turning away from European concepts of international order. The founders declared independence during the heyday of the Westphalian international system, brought about at the end of the Thirty Years' War. The premises of this system were the sovereign control of states over their territories, domestic structure as the prerogative of the government—hence a doctrine of non-interference in other states' affairs—and an equilibrium between the great powers (expressing itself in the concept of a "balance of power").

The Founding Fathers skillfully used this system to establish American independence and security. Yet they stood intentionally aloof from it, declining to send fully empowered embassies to European courts. The European balance of power was useful to the new country, but not to the point of participating in its practical conduct. Rather, the United States relied on Britain to play the role of balancer and used the resultant equilibrium to ban a European role in the Western Hemisphere via the Monroe Doctrine.

When the United States reentered European affairs during World War I, President Woodrow Wilson announced America's war aims as a rejection of Westphalian principles. He denounced the balance of power and the practice of traditional diplomatic methods (decried as "secret diplomacy") as a major contributing cause of war. In their place he proclaimed the objective of self-determination as the organizing principle of the coming peace. As a result, the Treaty of Versailles, which ended the war, abandoned many of the established principles of the balance of power and of non-interference in domestic affairs. With the map of Europe redrawn, the United States thereupon withdrew from day-to-day global diplomacy.

When the United States assumed a global role in World War II, it did so in pursuit of historic objectives—preventing Europe or Asia from falling under the domination of a single power, particularly a hostile one. When this heroic undertaking succeeded, many Americans, including some in government, expected to be able to withdraw from the conduct of global policy.

Yet America was now the dominant country in the world. Concern with the balance of power shifted from internal European arrangements to the containment of Soviet expansionism globally, turning the international order operationally into a two-power world. The United States had emerged as the essential guarantor of allied security and international stability. Particularly in the North Atlantic region, America concentrated on mobilizing resources for an agreed mission. Washington saw its role as the director of the common enterprise of countering a specific challenge to peace, rather than as a participant in an equilibrium.

After the collapse of the Soviet Union, the international system gradually grew more multipolar. China emerged as a global economic power with an increasing military capacity. Traditional power centers ended periods of isolation, colonial rule, or underdevelopment and began to play influential international roles. Something like a global version of Westphalian diplomacy began to emerge—an equilibrium balancing the sometimes-compatible, sometimes-competitive aims of multiple sovereign units.

Through all these transformations, the United States has been torn between its faith in its exceptional nature and global mission, and the pressures of a public opinion skeptical of open-ended commitments in distant regions. The ideal of universal democracy-promotion, if adopted as an operational strategy, implies a doctrine of permanent domestic engineering across the world. Yet the prevailing American view has regarded foreign policy as a series of episodes with definitive conclusions; it recoiled from the ambiguities of a historical process in which goals are achieved incrementally, through imperfect stages.

As America evolved from a peripheral exception to international order to an essential component of it, it has been obliged to meld its noble ideals with a concept of the national interest sustainable across decades, administrations, and historical vicissitudes. America's moral convictions are essential to its national purpose and to popular support for its policies. An understanding of equilibrium, and a distinction between essential tasks and long-term aspirations, is necessary to sustain American efforts in a world of disparate cultures and multiple centers of power. America's ability to balance and synthesize these elements will define its future, and importantly shape twenty-first-century prospects for world order.

Conrad Black has brilliantly traced this evolution and framed thought-provoking questions about America's world role in the coming decades. He has related domestic to international pressures, and evoked the key events, strategies, and dilemmas inherent in America's rise. Through thoughtful sketches of the key actors—especially the presidents—and their policies, he has provided a book that will be indispensable reading for those who want to understand the past as well as sketch a roadmap for the future.

ONE

THE ASPIRANT STATE, 1754–1836

Benjamin Franklin

CHAPTER ONE

The Path to Independence

*The British and Americans Defeat
the French in America, 1754–1774*

1. THE GREAT POWERS AND THE AMERICAS

The long, swift rise of America to absolute preeminence in the world began in the obscure skirmishing of settlers, traders, natives, adventurers, and French and British (and some Spanish) soldiers and militiamen, more or less uniformed, in what is today the western parts of eastern seaboard states of the United States. Surges of idealism and desperation had propelled Quakers, Puritans, organized groups of Roman Catholics, more exotic non-conformists, and the routinely disaffected and abnormally adventurous to strike out for the New World. There was, with most, some notion of ultimately building a better society than those from which they had decamped. There was little thought, until well into the eighteenth century, of constructing there a political society that would influence the world. And there was almost no thought, until near the end of that century, that there would arise in America a country that would in physical and demographic strength, as well as moral example, lead the whole world.

Political conditions at the approach of what became the Seven Years' War (in America, the French and Indian Wars, in Russia and Sweden the Pomeranian War, in Austria and Prussia the Third Silesian War, and in India the Third Carnatic War) consisted of endless scrapping among the great continental powers along their borders. These were France; Austria, the polyglot Central European heir of the Holy Roman Empire; Russia; and, thrusting up to challenge Austria for leadership of the German center of Europe, Prussia. The other Great Power, Great Britain, when its Stuart Dynasty, half Protestant and half Roman Catholic, came to an end in 1714, recruited the Stuarts' distant but reliably Protestant cousins, starting with George I to IV, 1714–1830, to succeed them. George I and George II scarcely spoke English and spent much time in their native Hanover, a placid little principality of 750,000 which they continued to rule and where they didn't have to be bothered with an unruly parliament like that in London.

The lengthy British rule of the great Whigs, Sir Robert Walpole, Henry Pelham, and Pelham's brother, the Duke of Newcastle, 1721–1762, appeased the kings by using British money and power to secure Hanover. Apart from that, Britain cohered, before the king set up his own Church, to the policy of Thomas Cardinal Wolsey (1511–1529), Henry VIII's chancellor, who devised the practice, followed to recent times, of putting England's weight against whichever was the strongest of the continental powers (successively, roughly, Spain until the rise of Louis XIII's great minister, Cardinal Richelieu in 1624; France until the defeat of Napoleon in 1815; Germany until the defeat of Hitler in 1945; and Russia until the disintegration of the Soviet Union in 1991). An unprecedentedly benign Germany then resumed that position to no great consternation in Britain or elsewhere (Chapter 16).

Russia, under Peter the Great, Czar from 1689 to 1725, joined the ranks of the Great Powers at the start of the eighteenth century. For the purposes of this book, the first important Russian leader was the Empress Catherine the Great,[1] who reigned from 1762 to 1796, and we are also concerned with the Prussian king Frederick II, the Great (1740–1786), and the Austrian empress Maria Theresa (reigned from 1740 to 1780). These three rulers provided strong military and diplomatic government in Central and Eastern Europe in the last decades of the eighteenth century.

2. THE BRITISH EMPIRE AND EARLY SKIRMISHING IN AMERICA

William Pitt was the first leading British public figure to limn out a vision of a growing and flourishing British civilization on both sides of the Atlantic and in the East and West Indies, arising to give the British the status and strength of an incomparable giant straddling the great ocean. Even he pitched his vision, naturally, mainly in terms of ending, in Britain's favor, the great contest with France because of the scale and size and wealth the British nationality would grow into, vast and rich, and relatively secure as not having to fend off the invasions of adjoining landward neighbors. In Britain, his philippics against the French went down better than his visions of the New World. But as Pitt gained force and support in Britain, the leading Americans considered that the Thirteen Colonies were coming close to self-sufficiency, if the French threat in Canada could be disposed of, and could indeed then have a splendid autonomous political future, if they could coordinate better between themselves, and agree on their collective purpose. As the formal beginning of the new Anglo-French war approached, the most astute leaders of both Britain and America were groping for a raison d'être of the American project. In London and Westminster, going it alone was unthinkable for the colonies, and so was not given any thought. In America, if France could be driven from Canada, it was an idea whose attractions were bound to grow, and, if it were not headed off by a competing imperial vision, its time would come.

From the sixteenth to the end of the eighteenth century, European diplomacy was a minuet, with the partners constantly changing, but disputing the same

---

1.   During the Pugachev Revolt of 1774, which inflamed much of southern Russia, Catherine wrote to her friend the French philosopher and agitator Voltaire that that region had become infected because it was "inhabited by all the good-for-nothings of whom Russia has thought fit to rid herself over the past 40 years, rather in the same spirit that the American colonies were populated." The British made Homeric efforts to persuade Catherine to assist them against France, Spain, and the American colonists in coming years, but Catherine, though an Anglophile and well-disposed, sagely declined, even when offered Minorca as an inducement. (RKM402)

adjoining areas, a horribly expensive struggle between hired and often mercenary armies. The only country that had a vision that transcended this pattern of self-inflicted destruction, through the attrition of endless conflict on the frontiers, was Britain, with its concept of manipulating the balance of power while steadily expanding its empire overseas and asserting mastery of the world's oceans. This was the long-standing British strategy. France oscillated between trying to dominate Germany and trying to contest overseas theaters with Britain, and couldn't do both simultaneously. Prussia and Russia were trying to expand at the expense of their neighbors, which in Russia's case meant much of Eurasia. Austria, Turkey, and Spain were trying to hold on to what they had. Sweden and the Netherlands were second-tier opportunists and Portugal was outward-facing from Europe to an empire that was large for the size of the home country (in South America, Africa, India, and the Far East). By opposing larger Spain, Portugal gained the protection of the Royal Navy to maintain its empire, which it would not otherwise have been able to defend from larger predators.

The French, when they finally developed a plan, wanted to distract the British to the nether regions of empire and strike a mortal blow at the home island of Britain. Of these long-standing British and French strategic designs, the British generally succeeded in imposing theirs, and the French, perpetually unsure whether they wanted to make a crossing in force of the Rhine or the English Channel, never really came close to a serious invasion of the British Isles. (The Pyrenees and the Alps were less promising and tempting places of trespass, though they were occasionally traversed.)

By the 1750s there were just the first glimmerings of an American strategy, spontaneously derived but starting to receive direction to work with the British to remove the French from Canada and then favorably alter the relationship with Britain.

There was a loyalty in the colonies to the abstract entity of the Crown, and the impersonal wearer of the crown, but affections between the English and the Americans became frayed (as did relations between the Canadians and the French), and if the Crown (in the one case and the other) was seen as exclusively favoring the mother country, colonial fealty to the overseas king-protector would prove very fungible.

Combat was so routine in North America that even full-scale battles and reductions of opposing forts, involving the deaths of hundreds of men on both sides, did not provoke declarations of war. Until 1756, wars could be generated only by European matters. By the early 1750s, the race was on between the French, pushing down from the Great Lakes to the Ohio River and then to and down the

Mississippi, and the English (Americans in practice but constantly seeking British military reinforcement when challenged), settling and exploring ever westward, for control of the Ohio country and the vast hinterland of North America. Alert American landowners, including young George Washington, 21 in 1753, were large land acquirers west of the Alleghenies. The French, who had an entirely developed rival claim, constructed a series of forts connecting Quebec to their traders in Illinois. These forts were at Presque Isle on the south shore of Lake Erie, another on a tributary of the Allegheny River, a third on the Allegheny itself, and the fourth at the meeting of the Allegheny and Monongahela Rivers to form the Ohio, the site of the modern city of Pittsburgh (whose name gives a hint of the outcome of the Anglo-French rivalry).

The French fort at the forks of the Ohio was called Fort Duquesne, after the builder, a French naval officer who was entrusted with the Canadian military command, and mobilized 11,000 Canadians, trained them thoroughly by colonial standards, and pressed south with them organized into 165 companies, supported by thousands of Indians whom the French had enticed with generous offers of trading rights. The Indians tended to take the promises of the French more seriously than those of the English, because the French seemed much less inclined to people the New World themselves with immigration, rather than just taking what the fur trade and other commerce would yield. The British had planned a fort on the same site and the rivalry, in the names of Duquesne and Pitt, and over the same geography, presaged future conflicts over many colonial places claimed as a matter of right by different nationalities. Duquesne expended the lives of over 400 of his men and spent over four million *livres*, erecting his forts and developing trails between them, but the effort did wonders to galvanize American colonial opinion, especially in the unison of the chorus it raised up to London to repel the French interloper.

In the autumn of 1753 an enterprising 21-year-old Adjutant George Washington volunteered to carry a letter to the French at the forks of the Ohio, asking them to "desist" and withdraw. The governor of Virginia, Robert Dinwiddie, sent 200 men with Washington for this mission. Before Washington got clear of the Allegheny Mountains, one of Duquesne's officers had repulsed the British contingent that tried to occupy the coveted site, majestic to this day, where the Ohio River begins. Undaunted and showing a boldness, indeed impetuosity, a trait for which he would not be well-known at the height of his career, Washington chose to advance against the French, who greatly outnumbered him. Washington fell upon a 35-man French and Indian scouting party and killed the commander of the French unit, a M. Jumonville, and nine others. Accounts differ and Washington's own is a truncated and rather self-serving description of a provoked and measured response, rather than, as is claimed by the French and some of the colonial militiamen, a massacre begun by an Indian ally of the Americans who sank his hatchet into Jumonville's skull, preparatory to relieving him of his scalp. The young Adjutant Washington, after the astonishing precocity of carrying out an act of war of one Great Power on another, on the instructions of Dinwiddie, who had no authority to order anything of the kind, then sagely retreated to a hastily constructed stockade, christened—in a divine service where Washington, not a demonstrably religious man, presided—Fort Necessity.

It was a modest affair and was soon invested by 700 French and Canadians and 100 of their Indian allies. The French rained down musket-fire on the garrison, which Dinwiddie had bulked up to 400, and at sunset of the first day of the siege, Washington's force panicked and broke into the rum issue. The French mercifully offered the Americans, retirement from Fort Necessity provided they returned French prisoners, promised not to return to the Ohio Valley within a year, left two hostages behind as an earnest, and admitted the "assassination" of Jumonville. Washington accepted all this, having taken 30 dead and 70 wounded, compared with three French dead and a handful of wounded. He retired, with most of his men carrying the wounded and the corpses of their fallen comrades. Most of his force deserted and scattered at the first opportunity. He rightly counted himself lucky, but had effectively accepted responsibility for starting one of the most important wars of modern times, and with an uncivilized act at that. Washington has presented posterity a rather bowdlerized version of this fiasco and his subsequent renown has somewhat obscured the facts, though it must be said that he was personally brave and collected, and swiftly seized the prospect of honorable deliverance when it appeared.

Even the placatory British prime minister, Newcastle, was outraged and worried when he learned of this debacle. He relied on what he portentously described as his continental "system" of alliances with the Spanish, Austrian Empire, Danes, Hanover, and some other German states to contain France, while he launched a counter-blow in America. With George II's favored son, the Duke of Cumberland, Newcastle concerted a plan for sending two Irish regiments out to America under the command of Major General Edward Braddock, a spit-and-polish professional with no experience or knowledge at all of American warfare, to uproot the French fort system that Duquesne had built. Cumberland blew any security with public announcements about the new armed mission, which came to the attention of the French ambassador in London as to any informed person in the British capital. The French rushed to send reinforcements to Canada, though they suffered from the ice-shortened season for dispatching forces up the St. Lawrence.

3. THE OUTBREAK OF THE SEVEN YEARS' WAR

The English position in those colonies was not much strengthened by the arrival of Braddock and his Irishmen in February 1755. The colonists resented Braddock's high-handed manner and the British army's rules, which were that any British officer, even a lieutenant, could order about like pirates any colonial officer, even Washington and his few peers, and that the colonial militias were subject to British military discipline. This was heavy going for these rough and ready frontiersmen, who were unaccustomed to taking orders, other than at the approach of and during outright exchanges of live fire. Nor were they much enamored of submitting themselves to a regimen that was unsparing in meting out floggings and even drum-head executions.

From May to July 1754 in Albany, New York, there was what was called the Albany Congress, to pursue unity of the colonies. The leading figure at the Congress was the ambitious Philadelphia inventor, scientist, printer, postmaster, and diplomat Benjamin Franklin. Behind his jaunty humor there lurked a sophisticated political operator who would prove himself more than able to master the sternest and most tortuous challenges that could be posed in the chancelleries of Europe. He was already the principal public figure among the colonists, and Washington was a rising young officer and landowner, the one an amiable intellectual and sly maneuverer, the other a physically imposing and capable officer, though personally stiff and somewhat limited by being a plantation inheritor and, beyond elemental education, an autodidact. But both were investors in and advocates of trans-Allegheny development, and both had a vision of a rapidly expanding America that would brook no interference from the French, and whose attachment to the British was essentially much less a reflexive submission to the Crown than a tactical association with the presumed facilitator of their local ambitions.

Franklin had already done a stint as Pennsylvania's representative in London. However flickering might be their imperial enthusiasm, the colonists had no ability at this point to replace the British with any locally generated or spontaneous cohesion. The Albany Congress broke up in disharmony, and the Quaker majority in the Pennsylvania Assembly, dominated by and servile to the Penn family, roundly deserted Franklin and repudiated any notion of colonial union for the unholy purpose of armed combat, especially for the purpose of enriching the less pious of their number in extra-territorial speculation.

Braddock started off with a fantastically ambitious plan for blotting the French out of the continent, which Cumberland and his entourage had devised in complete ignorance of North American conditions or of the likely correlation of forces, and in defiance of Newcastle's chimerical hopes of avoiding war with France. Admiral Edward Boscawen was to blockade the Gulf of St. Lawrence, strangling New France of reinforcements. Braddock and his Irish regiments were to take Fort Duquesne, which was now a formidable fortress. Braddock named the governor of Massachusetts, William Shirley, a major general and told him to reactivate disbanded regiments and march to Niagara at the western end of Lake Ontario and seize the large French fort there, following which Braddock, who would clear the French out of the several hundred miles of French forts and garrisons between what are today Pittsburgh and Buffalo, would join forces for the final mopping-up of New France. It was an insane plan, made even more absurd by Braddock's impossible personality and incandescent contempt for the colonials.

Braddock rejected suggestions from a couple of the colonial governors that instead of attacking the southern French forts, including Duquesne, he attack with all his forces at Niagara, the northern terminus of the French supply route into the Ohio, Illinois, and Mississippi country. This would have been the correct strategy for concentrating all available force on the point of maximum vulnerability. Cumberland and the other London creators of the Braddock attack plan had no idea that the supposedly navigable rivers often had rapids and that the trails that were supposed to be avenues for British supply wagons were narrow and often soft underfoot and could only be used at a snail's pace, and a not very motivated snail at that. Nor were they aware that almost no Indians could now be induced to assist the British as guides or scouts and that only they knew their way to the designated targets. Washington prudently declined the command of a Virginia regiment and instead accepted to be an unpaid aide to Braddock, presumably, after his harrowing combat command debut at Fort Necessity, to avoid blame for another shambles, and to increase his chances for a British commission that would give him some status in the parent-country forces, which would clearly be needed in ever larger numbers if the French were to be successfully resisted.

Braddock also made the acquaintance of Benjamin Franklin. His severe demands for horses and supplies frightened the Pennsylvania legislature out of its Quaker aversion to the somewhat louche and worldly Franklin, who was sent as a placatory envoy to Braddock. Franklin, now America's most accomplished diplomat, as Washington was its foremost soldier, though nothing in the past of either indicated the heights they would achieve in the balance of their careers, exploited Braddock's unsuccessful foraging in Maryland and Virginia. Franklin sent boxes of fine food and good wine to the junior officers of Braddock's units, and Pennsylvania was thereafter excused from the general's rages against the colonials.

Braddock, with Washington at his side suffering from dysentery and acute hemorrhoids, plunged through the wilderness toward Fort Duquesne, his force's movements faithfully reported by Indians to the French commander, Contrecoeur, the victor of the Fort Necessity encounter and brother-in-law of the "assassinated" Jumonville. On July 10, Braddock's so-called "flying column" of about 1,500 men, including several hundred civilian workers and a number of the officers' whores, which had managed about five miles a day, was attacked by about 800 French, Canadians, and (in the majority) Indians. The attackers infiltrated the dense forests on each side of the road and without warning, disconcerting the English with the nerve-rattling screaming of the Indians, poured down precise, rapid sniper-fire. The well-trained British formed into rectangles in the road, consolidating themselves as better targets for the enemies they could not see, and were steadily mowed down. Braddock remained mounted, and acted with great bravery, as did Washington, who had two horses shot from under him. After several hours, Braddock was mortally wounded, and died on the retreat two days later. A rout began, with Washington trying manfully to prevent a complete shambles, organizing the transport of the wounded, and trying to keep the retreat in some sequence. The French took 23 dead Indians, and about 16 wounded, compared with about 1,000 British dead and wounded, scores of whom were scalped by the Indians. Fortunately for the British, and as was their custom, the Indians had no interest in following up on their victory beyond taking the heads and picking the pockets of the enemy and whatever could be had from their wagons. The wreckage of Braddock's flying column and the balance of his force arrived like a grim tornado in Philadelphia and, although they were in the searing heat of late July, demanded winter quarters.

The British did better in Acadia, and seized the French fort at the narrow isthmus connecting Cape Breton to Nova Scotia. There followed the expulsion ultimately of about 14,000 French and Franco-Indian civilians from Acadia (mainly Nova Scotia, and what are now New Brunswick and Prince Edward Island), an eerie foretaste of some greater deportations of helpless civilian populations in the centuries to come, an ethnic cleansing. The Acadians had generally refused an oath of allegiance to the British Crown, because of conflicting loyalties, a refusal to draw a hostile line with French and Indian relatives, and fear of being deprived of their right to practice as Roman Catholics and to retain their language. In about equal numbers, they were assimilated into New England, went to Louisiana and laid the base of the "Cajuns," returned to France, or returned to the area of their expulsion when conditions had improved. It was a shabby affair, and there was no excuse for it, though it was conducted less brutally than more modern deportations, including by the United States of its southeastern Indians.[2]

The British also had a modest success on Lake George, south of Montreal, where both sides took several hundred casualties and continued into the winter more or less as they had entered the spring, though with the French toiling to build a larger fort. Admiral Boscawen had seized two ships and several hundred soldiers, but the main French reinforcements for Canada, under General Montcalm, had arrived successfully in Quebec. The attack on Niagara, which was the only one of the projected operations that made much sense, was not launched in 1755, as planned. Despite repeated acts of war and probably 2,000 casualties or prisoners taken, while Britain stood clearly in the eyes of the world and such international law as there was as an aggressor, France and Britain were still officially at peace. The rout and death of Braddock and the failure of the rest of the British plan had heavy repercussions in London, where Newcastle's legendary talents at political survivorship would be put to a serious challenge. William Pitt's hour had almost arrived.

Implausibly, Newcastle still thought he might be able to avoid war with France in Europe. He was trying to maintain his continental "system" of alliances with Austria, the Netherlands, and Georgian Hanover and some neighboring German states, against France and Prussia, steadily emerging as the chief acquirer of German states and a potential rival in central Europe to Austria, whose empire was largely in the polyglot and irredentist Slavic and Italian wards of eastern and southern Europe. Newcastle proposed to try to add Russia to this alliance, to put a rod on Prussia's back, concerned always, Pitt and his faction claimed, more with the welfare of Hanover than of Britain.

The rise of Prussia under George II's brother-in-law, Frederick the Great, caused George II to fear Prussian designs on Hanover, as Frederick had already seized Silesia from Maria Theresa. Acting on this concern, Britain proposed and negotiated renewal of its defensive treaty with Russia in 1755. Frederick feared Russia even more than George feared Prussia, and after first rejecting an overture from Britain on news of the renewal of the Anglo-Russian treaty, Frederick proposed, and in January 1756, concluded with Britain, a non-aggression pact, which became one of mutual assistance should any aggressor disturb "the tranquility of Germany"—i.e., attack either Hanover or Prussia.

This appeared to be a brilliant consolidation of Hanoverian security, but Newcastle had outsmarted himself. Maria Theresa was so outraged at Britain's treaty

---

2. In contravention of binding treaties and the judgment of the U.S. Supreme Court.

with Prussia, from which she proposed to recover Silesia, that she terminated her alliance with Britain. Russia declined to ratify its treaty renewal with Britain; France renounced her treaty with Prussia and formed a new alliance with its rival of 250 years, Austria. This was the real beginning of the 200-year Franco-German conflict. Far from being secure, Hanover was now threatened by France and Austria.

In an attack that replicated his sudden seizure of Silesia, Frederick invaded the Austrian protectorate of Saxony in August 1756. Austria, France, and Russia declared war on Prussia. While it was reminiscent of the seizure of Silesia, the attack on Saxony, coming on the heels of the arrangements with Britain, also presaged the German attack on Poland immediately after the Nazi-Soviet Pact of 1939. And the cascade of treaty-triggered declarations of war would be somewhat replicated 158 years later at the outbreak of World War I (Chapters 8 and 10).

France would protect Austria, but Austria was not bound to assist France—it was sufficient incentive for the French to detach Austria from the British. These tergiversations became known as the Diplomatic Revolution of 1756.

In 1755, the Thirteen Colonies had about 1.5 million people, compared with a little more than four times that in Great Britain (excluding Ireland), around 15 million in France, 3.5 million in Prussia, and just under two million in the Netherlands. The American colonies had a faster rate of growth and higher standard of living than any of the major powers. They were politically primitive but, as events were to prove, had political leadership more talented than the governors the British haphazardly sent to rule over them, and even than the mature European powers themselves. The instances of statehood were already close to hand, though few thought in these terms, especially as the French menace loomed larger and more imminently than ever. The myth of the paltry obscurity of a handful of disparate and insignificant settlements, however, is much exaggerated, both by British snobbery and by the requirements of the mythos of America's birth.

As Newcastle scattered subsidies across Europe from the Rhine to Russia, to try to raise an alliance that would deter France from going to war in reprisal against Britain's acts of war in America, Pitt denounced the system of paying subsidies as cowardly and ineffectual with greater force and causticity than ever. His parliamentary remarks were especially vituperative given that he was a member of the government as paymaster of the armed forces, from which post he was finally dismissed in 1755. In 1756, Pitt claimed that Newcastle was deliberately leaving the British base in Minorca, in the Balearic Islands, under-defended, in order to represent the fall of it as evidence of the inadvisability of going to war with France. France had assembled a large naval force in Toulon, its main Mediterranean naval base, and attacked Minorca, which fell in the summer of 1756, despite an effort to protect the island by Admiral John Byng. Newcastle finally declared war on May 18, 1756, after hostilities had been in full swing in the Americas for two years. Partly in order to relieve himself of Pitt's charges, Newcastle had Byng court-martialed and persecuted him relentlessly, until he was, very unjustly, executed by firing squad in March 1757.

It was of no interest to the other powers what happened between the British and French in North America, and the British and French had no interest in Central and Eastern Europe, except the nostalgic British defense of Hanover. This took the form, in practice, of the British arming and paying extensive Hanoverian and Hessian armies, which they could deploy to North America when conditions in Germany allowed their release. The Netherlands, traditionally one of Newcastle's allies, was exhausted and had no interest in any of the contested areas and refused to be subsidized back into line as an ally. Sweden, however, was induced to join against Prussia. In its preliminaries this was the most American of all wars to date between the European powers.

Though their fleet was at Toulon, the French were preparing an army of up to 100,000 men in the Channel ports, for an invasion of Britain. Pitt, when he gained control of policy, wanted to mire France in Europe and deploy superior forces to America, India, and the Caribbean.

4. THE SEVEN YEARS' WAR, AMERICA

The French commander in Quebec as of May 1756, Montcalm, was an accomplished soldier, though he, too, despised the Indians, and had little use for the Canadians either, but he was a military genius in comparison with Cumberland's successor to Braddock, the Earl of Loudoun, a pompous military administrator who not only detested colonials and natives but had no idea of how to conduct a war or even a battle. He abruptly fired Massachusetts governor William Shirley in June 1756, and sent him off in disgrace, carrying the responsibility for some of Braddock's blunders. (It was the season of the scapegoat, as the official murder of the only slightly cautious Admiral Byng after the fall of Minorca had demonstrated.) Loudoun's lack of rapport with the colonial authorities surpassed even Braddock's.

Montcalm invested Fort Oswego, at the southeastern edge of Lake Ontario, with 3,000 men, in August 1756, and it quickly fell, with about 1,600 British taken prisoner. Montcalm was not sufficiently impressed with the duration or vigor of their resistance to allow the British to retreat under their own colors. This was the inauspicious start of the Loudoun incumbency, and even after this setback, the colonial governments were little disposed to assist the British military, despite all Loudoun's huffing and puffing. Once again, the worldly Franklin came to the rescue in Pennsylvania, and in exchange for a modest gift by the owners of most of the colony, the Penn family, the Assembly voted 55,000 pounds for "the King's use," a Franklinian euphemism that allowed the pacifist Quaker majority to pretend that it was not for military uses, a balm of conscience presumably made more emollient by the fact that the payment was destined to help prevent their occupation and capture by Montcalm's swashbuckling Catholic, French legionnaires. The Quaker caucus of legislators soon splintered on the issue of whether to offer bounties for Indian prisoners and scalps, and the Quaker domination of the Pennsylvania Assembly ended abruptly, at the hands of fellow colonials less troubled by the exigencies of war. Loudoun had had explicitly to threaten the use of force to gain quarters for his troops in Philadelphia, where an epidemic of dysentery and related ailments was feared. This was not a gesture best designed to build Anglo-American solidarity at the approach of the enemy. Again, Franklin produced the desired compromise, by assigning the soldiers a principal hospital, addressing under the same roof both the wrath of the commander and the threat to public health.

Loudoun had been promised the formidable total, for the American theater, of 17,000 troops, to seize Louisbourg in Nova Scotia, and ultimately Quebec; he left New York in a 100-ship force carrying 6,000 troops, the largest amphibious force ever launched in North America up to that time, bound for Louisbourg, on June 20, 1757. His force arrived at Halifax on June 30 and had to wait 10 days for the accompanying Royal Navy squadron that was to blast its way into Louisbourg harbor. There was a further wait for the abatement of fog. By that time, the French had concentrated a fleet of 18 warships at Louisbourg, and the Royal Navy commander, Admiral Francis Holborne, declared the mission impossible beginning so late in the season, and the whole force returned dismally to New York. While this was happening in late July 1757, Montcalm, at the head of 3,000 French, 3,000 Canadians, and a blood-curdling 2,000 Indians, who volunteered in large numbers, encouraged by French successes, had invested Fort William Henry at the south end of Lake George, the entrance to the Hudson Valley from Quebec. Montcalm's force included representatives from 33 different Indian tribes, or nations. Nearly half were Catholics who could be influenced, if not commanded, by the missionary priests that Montcalm brought for that purpose. The rest could be motivated to some degree by French officers and traders they had served with, but 2,000 Indians coming from up to 1,500 miles to enlist for an attack on the British were going to be a terribly unruly group once the issue was joined.

Colonel George Monro was defending the fort with 1,500 men. In late July Monro sent a reconnaissance in force up the lake. Most of it was seized by Indians and frightful barbarities ensued, including three Englishmen boiled in a pot for dinner, washed down with large quantities of rum the British had brought with them. Returning survivors warned Monro of the imminent dangers, though they did not know the extent of Montcalm's force. The French arrived in strength on August 3, including artillery, spearheaded by 1,500 naked Indians gliding swiftly up the lake in their canoes. Monro was advised to consider capitulation in a letter expressing the view of the governor of New York, which was taken by an Indian from the body of the courier, whom he had intercepted, and sent into Fort William Henry under a white flag, with an accompanying note from Montcalm that it was good advice. When Monro declined, Montcalm maintained continuous artillery fire for five days, and by August 9 the British garrison was very haggard and the walls of the fort had been smashed in several places.

Monro belatedly took the governor's advice and Montcalm chivalrously replicated the surrender terms of Minorca earlier in the summer: the British would promise to refrain from combat for 18 months and would leave an officer behind as hostage and return French prisoners, and would be allowed to leave with their belongings, under their colors, with a French escort to the next fort to the east. Montcalm would take all the stores and artillery left in the fort, and would care for the seriously wounded British and return them as their convalescent condition permitted. It was European war by officers and gentlemen to the highest standard.

Unfortunately, these terms did not conform in the slightest to Indian notions of the fruits of victory. The Indians were not consulted by Montcalm, and when they learned of these generous conditions, and of the resulting paucity of rewards for them, they first seized and scalped some of the wounded, and the following day, on the march to the nearest British fort, Fort Edward, they attacked the column from all sides and in the most terrifying manner, killing nearly 200 and capturing perhaps 500. Montcalm himself led his officers and men, accompanied by the placatory missionaries, to restore order and take back the prisoners seized by the Indians. Eventually Montcalm, the French governor, Vaudreuil, and others managed, sometimes by paying up to 30 bottles of brandy per ransomed prisoner, to liberate and return to Fort Edward all but about 200 prisoners, who, except for about 40 who joined Indian communities and remained there, were deemed to have been massacred. The incident was apparently concluded by a public, ritualistic, and instantly infamous boiling and eating of a British prisoner by his Indian captors outside Montreal on August 15, 1757.

It was a great victory for Montcalm and left all New York almost open to Montcalm's forces, which with further reinforcements now stood at about 11,000 seasoned fighters under a skilled commander. But as Montcalm and Vaudreuil immediately foresaw, the strategic implications of the terrible aftermath of the fall of Fort William Henry were potentially very bad for France. The Indians would henceforth be very difficult to persuade to join the French, as they didn't really care what side they were on and were only interested in the slave labor of prisoners and, along with scalps, the prestige they brought to returning individual warriors, and booty—especially liquor, firearms, ammunition, and gaudy trinkets. Montcalm could attempt to provide them with all of this except the prisoners and scalps, but the French had become heavy-handed in retrieving the captured British, from civilized and Christian disgust at the barbarities of their allies. It was difficult to imagine that of the three parties in the engagement, the British and French, with their colonial fellow-soldiers, were the enemies. The Indians would not assist if they had to fight the designated enemy and then the ostensible ally to get anything useful, and the French would not recruit allies who would sully the flag and faith of France with disgusting acts and have to be subdued, at great risk and cost of lives. Thus would vanish much of the French superior expertise at guerrilla war, and reconnaissance and path-finding in the trackless wilderness of much of the contested territory.

Even more worrisome, the French commanders knew, and were even in some sympathy with, what they correctly anticipated would be the British reaction. It would be represented to Britain and the colonies that what had occurred was completely normal behavior for the Catholic French and the Indians whom they had coached and encouraged, and that the aftermath of the capitulation agreement was indicative of the French regard for a pact between officers, and of French treachery generally.

The notorious failure of the colonial assemblies to assign the funds necessary to build and equip proper militias, and to coordinate with each other, was now over. Instead of the British having to send forces from across the Atlantic to enter into cat-and-mouse games with inhospitable locals, there was finally a sense that it was time for a showdown with the French and Indians in North America, and that it was a struggle of life and death and for the honor of British America, to avenge the massacred and punish the savages and their satanic French puppeteers. As always in mortal combat, these caricatures were travesties, and there was a general recognition that Montcalm personally had behaved with the exemplary courtesy and the moderation of a noble officer of the Old World (which was true, but he could have prearranged a buy-off of most of the Indians, if necessary, where appropriate, with the moral reinforcement of the missionaries). But the intensity of the war, and the fervor and determination with which it would be conducted by the British of both the New and Old Worlds, had changed radically.

Between August 7 and August 12, Connecticut and Massachusetts alone mobilized 12,000 militiamen and sent them to Fort Edward to deal a counterblow to Montcalm and, as it was fancied, his blood-stained Indian allies. In fact, Montcalm was exhausted of provisions and his Indian intelligence and logistical and reconnaissance expertise had defected, and he felt he had no alternative but to withdraw toward Montreal. Loudoun, returned from the fiasco in Nova Scotia, at least was heartened by the stiffening of colonial resolve to self-defense and cooperation with the British. There was not, however, such a spirit of solidarity that Loudoun was prepared to accede to Washington's request to take the Virginia regiment Washington had led and trained to a high standard directly into the British army, nor to give Washington the commission he had certainly earned.

Instead, he placed Washington directly under a British regimental colonel who immediately ordered him to supply immense requisitions for what was clearly outright embezzlement.[3] Greater coordination between the colonial assemblies was a great step forward, but Loudoun's continued oppressive condescensions, faithfully replicated by his subalterns, could only contribute to increased American contemplation of the long-term need for this chronically subordinate relationship. This was especially true when inflicted on a man of Washington's high character, loyalty, and impending influence on colonial opinion.

5. THE FIRST PHASE OF THE WAR IN EUROPE

The Russians, Austrians, Swedish, and French were all determined to slam the door on Frederick's effort to force his way onto the European scene as a Great Power, whereas the British were for as many land powers as possible in Europe, to facilitate their manipulation of the balance of power. A war in Europe having been unlikely a few months before, it was now a roaring conflict involving all the major powers. France, Austria, Sweden, and Russia should have been able to subdue Prussia, but the shared Pitt-Newcastle objective of so distracting France in Europe that it would be unable to commit equivalent forces to resist Britain's overseas ambitions might be attainable.

No American had any experience with European diplomatic affairs, and few were interested. Franklin, as the former and returning representative to London of Pennsylvania and a couple of other of the colonies, must have had some curiosity about these events, but his only recorded interest was in the distraction of France in Europe to facilitate its expulsion from North America. Pitt finally forced

---

3.   Fred Anderson, *Crucible of War: The Seven Years' War and the Fate of the Empire in British North America, 1754–1766*, London, Faber and Faber, 2000, p. 203.

Newcastle from office in November 1756, and returned to government the following month as secretary of state for all external matters except the main powers of Europe, under the Duke of Devonshire as prime minister, who had no real support and was just a compromise caretaker acceptable to Newcastle, Pitt, and George II. Newcastle remained the principal influence on the government. Pitt was again dismissed in April 1757, because of his opposition to the continental policy, as he wanted a fight to the finish with France and not the temporizing he imputed to Newcastle, and he continued to accuse Newcastle of murdering Byng to cover his own pusillanimity (with some reason).

By this time, Frederick had prorupted into Bohemia (the Czechs), aiming to knock the Austrians out of the war. In May 1757, he laid siege to Prague, next to Vienna and Budapest and Venice the greatest city in Maria Theresa's empire, but was defeated in June. Frederick was soon flung out of Bohemia and Silesia was largely recaptured by the Austrians.

With bad news pouring in, Pitt and Newcastle somewhat composed their differences, and formed a new ministry in June 1757. Newcastle was in charge of finances and Pitt of war policy. Cumberland was defeated in Hanover and forced to acquiesce in the withdrawal of Hanover from the war in October. Pitt managed to have this decision revisited at the end of the year (with a huge bribe to the native land of his monarchy, a practice he had always criticized), and Frederick scored two of the greatest victories of his career, at Rossbach against the French on November 5, 1757, and at Leuthen against the Austrians one month later. (This pushed the Austrians out of Silesia permanently, a bitter pill for Maria Theresa.)

In a long and almost unwaveringly unsuccessful military tradition, Pitt organized a series of amphibious "descents" on the French coast. The first of these was at Rochefort in September, and it failed, as did almost all such initiatives up to and including the Canadian landing at Dieppe in 1942 (Chapter 11). The brightest note, early in the war, was in India. Colonel Robert Clive, the deputy commander at Madras, had seized Calcutta, the principal city of Bengal, in early 1757, and made substantial advances from there. And Pitt created a militia, forerunner of the Home Guard, of 32,000, as a back-up force in case England were herself to see for the first time in 700 years the campfires of a real invader. One of the celebrated (but none too bellicose) recruits to this force would be the illustrious historian Edward Gibbon.[4] By the end of 1757, Pitt had already energized the war effort.

As 1758 dawned, William Pitt was firmly in control of the British war strategy and was canvassing the ranks of British officers to get aggressive, intelligent com-

---

4.   Anderson, *op. cit.*, p. 173.

manders for the overseas operations, like the brilliant Clive in India. Frederick's victories over the French and Austrians, and the return to war of Hanover, had pushed those powers back onto the defensive. In America, the colonies were stepping forward to their own defense more determined than ever to remove the threat to their existence posed by the French. If that goal could be attained, the future of the English-speaking world would depend on whether the war in America forged an unshakable solidarity of national victory between its two great components, or an American recognition that in the new circumstances, colonial subordinacy to Britain was a retardant, and not a spur, to the stirring and increasingly plausible ambitions of the New World. Without the French threat, America's need for the overlordship of the British would be much less obvious.

William Pitt's strategy was to tie down as many French as possible in Germany or as they waited for a chance to cross the Channel, which he was confident would not come, while pouring British resources into the Empire he was building. He grasped the importance of sea power and the huge advantage that accrued to Britain with a blue-water policy that put the British flag all around the world while the European powers squabbled and skirmished on their frontiers, as long as none of them became too over-powerful opposite the others. Partly to divert the French and partly, belatedly, to appease King George II, he dispatched the first British troops to the continent in many years, 9,000 regulars under the scion of Britain's greatest general up to that time (with the possible exception of Cromwell), the Duke of Marlborough, to Hanover.

The Hanoverian commander, Prince Ferdinand of Brunswick, pushed the French out of Hanover, recaptured the port of Emden in March, and stirred considerable anxiety in France by crossing the Rhine, a bold move for a small state. The French eventually drove him out, but he fulfilled Pitt's plan of distracting the French on their German frontier while he attacked them around the world. At the behest of an American slave-trader, Thomas Cumming, Pitt sent a force to clear the French out of Goree and Fort St. Louis, near the modern Dakar, and from the nearby mouth of the Gambia, in West Africa, and quickly took over a lucrative slave trade, shipping unfortunate natives to the mercies of the American plantation owners. Following a very modestly successful "descent" at Cherbourg, and the disastrous failure of his third "descent," at St. Cast, a worse fiasco than Rochefort in 1757, Pitt concluded that the Caribbean would be a more rewarding disposition of these amphibious forces.

Pitt solidified relations with Frederick of Prussia with the Anglo-Prussian Convention of April 1758, and a 670,000-pound annual subsidy to Prussia, at least several thousand times as much as in today's dollars. Frederick demonstrated an astonishing bellicosity as he rushed around the borders of his kingdom battling the Austrians, French, Swedes, and Russians. He showed the advantages of interior lines and demonstrated the weakness of these primitive alliances, as for years there was no coordination at all between the enemies of Prussia. Had they determined to attack from four directions at the same time, Frederick, talented commander though he was, would have been overwhelmed.

Frederick began 1758 with an invasion of Moravia (now the eastern Czech Republic), but the Austrians repulsed him after several months, ending his last attempt to seize territory directly from Maria Theresa. While France fenced with the Hanoverians, Frederick turned against Russia, which had occupied East Prussia, around Königsberg. Frederick drew a bloody battle with the Russians at Zorndorf in August 1758, but the Russians withdrew. In September the Prussians failed to expel the Swedes from Prussia, though Frederick did deflect them from Berlin, which was their target. In October, Frederick was again bested by Maria Theresa's army, though narrowly, in Saxony, but compelled her withdrawal from Saxony at the end of the year. Pitt's European strategy worked well in 1758, as Prussia and Hanover were magnets to the powers of the French-led coalition, and absorbed the blows of all, leaving Pitt almost free to bulk up his overseas strategy.

6. THE WAR IN AMERICA, 1758

In America, Loudoun had a dismal start to the year, and was horrified at the uncooperativeness of the colonial assemblies, who, while resisting his heavy-handed tyranny, recognized the French threat sufficiently to group ever more closely together, naming commissioners to meet and agree on force levels. Loudoun wrote Pitt on February 14, 1758, announcing what he represented as virtually a usurpation in America of the powers of the Crown by the collaboration of the New England governors. He summoned the governors to meet with him at Hartford a few days after writing Pitt, and revealed his campaign plans for the year: the now customary menu for new attacks on Louisbourg and Fort Duquesne, on Fort Carillon on Lake Champlain (Ticonderoga), and on Fort Frontenac at the mouth of Lake Ontario, near the modern Kingston. These plans were then lengthily debated in the Massachusetts Assembly, to the assured knowledge of the French.

This was the state of disorder Loudoun's bungling had created when the genius of Pitt revealed itself in letters delivered March 10 and obviously written before Loudoun's complaints to him of near-insurrection in his letter of February 14. Pitt sacked Loudoun and replaced him with Major General James Abercromby, "to repair the Losses and Disappointments of the last inactive and unhappy Campaign," and ordered that colonial officers would henceforth enjoy the same rank in the British forces, and the British government would undertake the cost of equipping the colonial forces to a serious standard, in furtherance of an "Irruption into Canada."[5] This was a series of giant leaps forward. The Massachusetts legislature, which had been balkily debating Loudoun's request for 2,128 men for weeks (and had, in effect refused him), agreed by voice vote on March 11, 1758, to raise 7,000 men. Within a month, the colonies had voted to raise 23,000 men for Abercromby. Only Maryland, divided by other issues, temporarily failed to increase its militia. As the colonies had over 1.5 million people (counting about 150,000 slaves), these levies of forces could be considerably extended, and given the preeminence of the Royal Navy in the North Atlantic, France was not going to be able to maintain a military balance in America. The combination of Pitt's enlightened policies and the French-Indian outrage at Fort William Henry the previous summer had stirred what amounted to national sentiment in the Thirteen Colonies. This would not subside, and was to endure and grow into a world-shaking historic force.

So also had American affection for Britain been stimulated. The problem with the colonists, which Braddock and Loudoun had not understood, was not that they were such slackers but that there was little unemployment or surplus labor in the colonies, because of the prosperity of agriculture and the requirements for growing trades in the towns to service a growing population settled ever more extensively. As a result, military service for minimal pay, as was the European norm, was not only an uncompetitive living financially but had been a long-term commitment to thankless servitude to overbearing and often corrupt British officers. At a stroke, Pitt had promised pay-levels equivalent to civilian work and the promotion of American officers, for a limited enlistment, in a holy crusade to crush the French and the Indians once and for all. It was an irresistible package to take advantage of the colonies' demographic advantage over French Canada of more than 15 to one. It was inspired policy, but it also reflected Pitt's complete lack of interest in administration. It was going to be expensive and was going to whet the autonomist appetites of the locals, but these were delayed reactions that would be dealt with after the immediate French threat had been excised.

The new British commander, Abercromby, was just an undistinguished conduit. Pitt brought in with him as army and navy chiefs of staff Field Marshal Lord Ligonier, and Admiral Lord Anson. Ligonier was 77 in 1757, and had served with distinction in heavy combat in every British war of the eighteenth century, starting with his close proximity to Marlborough in the last great battles against the armies of Louis XIV. He is generally reckoned the greatest British field commander between

---

5. Anderson, *op. cit.*, p. 226.

Marlborough and Wellington. Anson was one of the Royal Navy's great reformers, after a distinguished career as a combat serving officer, and he and Ligonier worked very smoothly together. Pitt told Ligonier he wanted young, aggressive officers without political influence. He wanted men who would fight to make their careers and achieve position and renown, and who would be dependent on him, Pitt, and not constantly scheming and trading with prominent members of Parliament or the entourage of the royal family.

Ligonier selected accordingly for the four missions that had been the ambitions of succeeding British commanders since before the war officially began. Jeffery Amherst, a 40-year-old colonel and regimental commander, was promoted to "Major General in America" to command the expedition against Louisbourg, assisted by the 31-year-old Lieutenant Colonel James Wolfe. The attack on Fort Duquesne was to be conducted by a 50-year-old Scottish doctor, Brigadier John Forbes; Ticonderoga (Fort Carillon) and Fort Frontenac were to be taken by the 33-year-old acting brigadier, Viscount Howe (though Abercromby himself was the nominal commander). Pitt had strengthened the forces in accord with his plan: 14,000 men under Amherst in the attack on Louisbourg; 25,000 men for the attacks on Ticonderoga and Frontenac and the "Irruption into Canada"; and Forbes had 7,000 men for the attack on Fort Duquesne.

Counting the militia of every able-bodied male between the ages of 16 and 60 (except for the numerous priesthood), Montcalm had 25,000 men in total, though the real total at any time was less than that, or all secular civilian occupations would have been denuded. The Indians, traditionally a powerful French ally, had vanished, either from smallpox, detection of the shifting balance of power, or anger at the debacle following the fall of Fort William Henry. Montcalm thus reaped the worst of two harvests: the spirit of vengeance of both the outraged English and the, as they considered themselves, betrayed Indians. He was also suffering from acute shortages of food, due to a poor harvest, and a shortage of some munitions. Montcalm's problems were further aggravated by the divisions of the civil administration, led by the governor, Pierre de Rigaud de Vaudreuil, and the financial director, or *Intendant*, François Bigot, and particularly the corrupt practices of Bigot, who held that office from 1744 on and had embezzled an immense fortune.

Gravely compounding French disadvantages, Louis XV had lost interest in colonial matters and was particularly tired of the military costs of Canada, which did not return him much. The fur trade was no possible justification for such a vast effort, and the French had much less natural disposition for overseas adventure than Britain, a relatively poor island nation with seafaring conducted along its entire perimeter. Pitt was able to blockade the French Mediterranean fleet at

Gibraltar, and many of the Atlantic ports, and Boscawen had raised appreciably his interdiction of arriving French ships in the Gulf of St. Lawrence. There were only two avenues for breaking into Canada and strangling the French presence up the St. Lawrence to Quebec, which required disposing of Louisbourg first, or from New York past Ticonderoga-Carillon and Lake Champlain toward Montreal. Pitt and Ligonier had prepared a heavy blow at each door.

The first test was Abercromby and Howe's move on Fort Carillon (Ticonderoga). They set up their headquarters on the recently smoldering ruins of Fort William Henry and amassed 16,000 men for the assault. They arrived by water, in a thousand small craft, and landed four miles from the French fort on July 5. Unfortunately, Howe was killed by a retreating French reconnaissance sniper, and Abercromby lacked the energy for what followed. Montcalm had arrived at Carillon and found it desperately under-prepared, in men and supplies and the state of the fortifications, to cope with an attack. He built concealed trenches and elevated gun emplacements, and moved some of his 3,600 men forward. Abercromby did not trouble to train his artillery on the fort, and ordered a charge uphill at the French on July 8, a thousand light troops followed by 7,000 Redcoats in parade precision, to the roll of drums and the skirl of bagpipes. The French held their fire until the British became disorganized in the forward trenches and impediments Montcalm had just had crafted from felled trees, and then cut the British down in droves. About 2,000 were killed or seriously wounded, as Abercromby, from behind the lines, ordered renewed attacks over the corpses and wounded of the previous failed charges all day. Then, as night fell, he ordered a retreat that became a panic and a rout, and many wounded and much supplies were abandoned. Montcalm thought at first it was a stratagem to lure him out, as Abercromby still had a great superiority of manpower and artillery and supplies. Abercromby stabilized his forces at the old Fort William Henry; Montcalm remained at Carillon until late August, and then had to release most of his men to return and bring in the harvest. He had, by his skill and decisive leadership, and Abercromby's incompetence, saved New France for another winter. But the British, under so determined a leader as Pitt, were not to be put off so easily.

The other access to Canada, via the St. Lawrence, was not approached with such hesitancy. Amherst had arrived in strength near Louisbourg on June 8 and began investing the town and fort. Louisbourg was a formidable installation, but the techniques for reducing a fortress in a siege were well-known and could not be countered if the attacking forces were adequately numerous and supplied and the besieged object could not be resupplied. Trenches were dug to bring siege guns forward and holes were blasted in the walls and other trenches were dug to enable columns of attackers to come forward and surge through the ruptured walls. Other artillery would fire over the walls and create as much havoc as possible for as long as was necessary. The British boxed in and gradually outgunned the French men o' war in the harbor, and invested the fort on all landward sides and were eventually able to pour fire from the naval squadron straight into the town. The French defended valiantly but had no chance of being relieved, and by July 26, the French commander, Drucour, asked for terms, as the British had at Fort William Henry.

The legacy of that frightful episode intruded. Instead of recognizing that the French had fought honorably and tenaciously, as they had (and had taken 400 dead and 1,300 wounded in a garrison of 5,000), and allowing them to retire under their colors and with their possessions, Amherst required that the entire garrison be taken as prisoners of war and the entire civilian population of 8,000 from the surrounding area be deported to France. This was the larger, second half of the removal of the Acadians from 1755, and was another outrage. But the British felt that the earlier, prewar precedent and the antics of the French and Indians at Fort William Henry would have justified even sterner measures. The fall of Louisbourg left the St. Lawrence wide open to the Royal Navy, though there was not time to organize an attack up-river in 1758.

The third British target, Fort Frontenac, at the eastern end of Lake Ontario where it empties into the St. Lawrence, fell easily on August 26, to a deft and stealthy approach by Colonel John Bradstreet at the head of 3,100 men against a garrison of only 110 soldiers, the rest having been taken forward by the troops-starved Montcalm. Bradstreet captured stores and bread for more than 4,000, plus all the lake-craft the French had on Lake Ontario. The supply route between Montreal and the Ohio and western Pennsylvania forts was now heavily interdicted.

Abercromby, who despite his lethargy and lack of imagination as a commander had moments of strategic boldness, ordered Forbes to take Fort Duquesne, which involved some sort of rapprochement with some of the Indian tribes (or nations, as they preferred to be called). Abercromby was then sacked by Pitt, in favor of Amherst. The Indians remembered Fort William Henry, and despite Montcalm's repulse of Abercromby at Carillon, they knew of the fall of Fort Frontenac and the approach of Forbes at the head of a large force. They spurned the request for alliance of the French commander at Duquesne, François-Marie Le Marchand de Lignery, and the Frenchman evacuated Fort Duquesne, blew it up on November 23, and withdrew his diminished garrison up the Allegheny for the winter. Pittsburgh would arise on the ashes of Fort Duquesne, Ligonier would be its most prosperous suburb, Duquesne a distinguished university, and for many years Forbes Field would be Duquesne's baseball stadium. The route was clear from Philadelphia into the Ohio country, and the French presence in North America had been eradicated except for Montreal, Quebec, a few lesser towns along the St. Lawrence and St. Maurice Rivers, and partially, New Orleans.

7. THE WAR IN THE WEST INDIES AND AFRICA, 1759

On the heels of his successful seizure of the Senegalese slave trade, Pitt followed the advice of a Jamaican sugar plantation owner, William Beckford (who was also a London alderman), and seized the French island of Guadeloupe, which had a sugar production equivalent to Jamaica's (20,000 tons a year), and was a staging port for attacks by French privateers against British sea commerce in the Caribbean. Possession of it would give Britain control of the sugar market and pricing procedure opposite most of Europe, and a bargaining chip to trade for Minorca, a valued base for the British fleet in the Mediterranean. (The British would take Martinique, too, in 1761.) A financial bonanza followed, as Martinique and Guadeloupe provided Britain with great quantities not only of sugar but of coffee, rum, molasses, and tropical fruit, and the wealth generated by these activities transformed the City doubters about Britain's rising debt to purring tabbies, financing these exotic industries. The cautious and envious Newcastle periodically advised Pitt that the London City financial community, which bought British bonds, had to believe in the war for it to be paid for; in fact, Pitt, as long as his military operations were successful, could have forced the country's bonds on the City, though it would have been a huge inconvenience. Pitt had sold his ability to deliver much of the world to British rule and profit, and to push France back into her own country, and he was delivering on his promise. There were 71,000 men in the Royal Navy and 91,000 in the army and it was proposed to add 10,000 to the army. Britain's capacity to build ships was at its outer limits. With the activities of Britain in America, the Caribbean, West Africa, and India, as well as Hanover, there were only about 10,000 troops, strengthened by the flabby and almost untrained home guard of 32,000, to protect the home islands in case of need.

For once, Montcalm would not be looking forward to the end of the Quebec winter. In Paris, it had been a dismal military year, and all Louis XV had to show for his exertions was to have thrown the paltry Hanoverians back across the Rhine. The Duke de Choiseul was named chief minister to go head-to-head with Pitt. His strategy would be the familiar one to mass the French navy to facilitate an invasion of England by the main French army, and leave it to Austria and Russia and the Swedes to give Frederick of Prussia a well-deserved thrashing, and give up the overseas campaigns as an improvident beau geste where France had little interest and less chance of success against the maritime-focused British. Of course, the problems with this were that Choiseul had no short-term ability to devote the forces necessary to build a fleet that could seriously threaten the British Isles; Pitt could always bribe Europeans into tearing scraps out of the frontiers of France; and the long-term strategic future was in vast continents and subcontinents, such as North America and India, and not in the *cordons sanglants*, slivers of territory between the Great Powers of Europe such as Flanders, Alsace-Lorraine, Silesia, and the trackless political wasteland of the Balkans, which changed hands back and forth at intervals for centuries.

Choiseul's impatience with the overseas operations was understandable, and coincided with the king's irritation at their cost and difficulty. But in building up an army of 100,000 in the Channel ports and waiting for an opportunity to attack across the Channel with naval superiority, he was seeking an instant gratification of a long-held wish that the British had never permitted to be filled. The only way to defeat Britain was successfully to occupy the home islands. This would require a substantially stronger navy than Britain's, as well as an army large enough to defeat and occupy England, while maintaining sufficient strength to repel an invasion by a land neighbor, while busy trying to subdue the British Isles. Thus the secret of crushing Britain, as was never realized by its greatest continental adversaries, was to be at peace with all continental powers, which would require a greater army than all continental rivals, and then to have a greater navy than Britain's. This would effectively require the combined naval and military force of the three other greatest powers in Europe. The geography and history of Europe never yielded any country such an advantage, and the British talent for dividing Europe with well-purchased and supported coalitions prevented that, even against leaders who dominated most of Europe for a time. This is why Britain has not been seriously invaded since the arrival of William the Conqueror in 1066. Choiseul's plan appealed to Gallic logic and King Louis XV's acute military frustration, but it had no basis in reality. Though there is no evidence that anyone was thinking in these terms in the eighteenth century, this is precisely the advantage, much magnified from Britain's modest means, that would eventually accrue to the Great Power of the Americas: no one could threaten it at home, and it would be able to intervene and promote coalitions in Europe and East Asia and the Middle East.

Pitt had successfully placated the king, and was loved by the masses, and the cautious Newcastle was little disposed to oppose him. As the normally waspy and envious Horace Walpole (the long-serving prime minister's belletrist son) remarked,

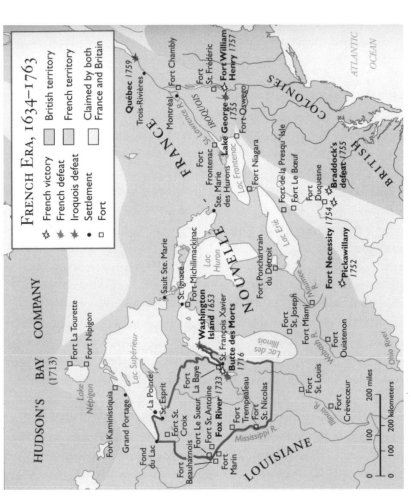

Seven Years War in America. Wisconsin Cartographers' Guild. WISCONSIN'S PAST AND PRESENT. © 1998 by the Regents of the University of Wisconsin System. Reprinted by permission of The University of Wisconsin Press.

"Our bells are worn threadbare with ringing for victories."[6] Pitt presented a budget for 1759 that, at 13 million pounds, was the greatest by far in British history and was more than half debt, with more than half the anticipated revenues committed to paying interest. To anyone who cared to notice, it was obvious that the quantum of this debt, especially if the war dragged on at all (and Pitt might take France's castaway colonies but neither Britain nor any other country had any power to threaten France herself), would grow and would have to be shared by all the British, including the more than 20 percent of Britons in the flourishing colonies of America. This was a time bomb.

8. THE FALL OF QUEBEC

Pitt sent out his military orders for 1759 on December 9, 1758. These were to include Amherst overwhelming French opposition along Lake Champlain and seizing Montreal, while James Wolfe, who had returned to London and settled in his club to recover his health and reported to Pitt that he was ready to go up the St. Lawrence, was so charged, and he left England for Canada on February 24. On July 25, 1759, Amherst's forces captured Fort Niagara, about 60 miles from what is now Toronto, and at the opposite end of Lake Ontario from Fort Frontenac, which Bradstreet had taken 11 months before. By this time, Wolfe's assault on Quebec was well underway. He landed 8,500 troops on Ile d'Orleans, a few miles down-river from Quebec, on June 28. Despite the immense importance of the battle for Quebec to the whole Western world, and the huge mythology that has been built about it, from both sides, it was an almost accidental and very close-run engagement. Heavily outnumbered and isolated, Montcalm defended Quebec with great skill and agility, inflicting heavy losses on Wolfe, whose problems were compounded by acute fevers, indigestion, and depressive attacks. He was reduced to asking the opinion of his brigade commanders (Robert Monckton, George Townshend, and James Murray), whom he despised, a sentiment that was fully requited. They recommended that he desist from further attacks on Quebec from down-river and that Wolfe move the British forces up, to the west of Quebec, and attack there, to separate Montcalm from landward reinforcements, and try to enfilade Quebec from what was presumed to be its more vulnerable aspect.

Precise advice on how to take Quebec came from Captain Robert Stobo, one of the prisoners handed over by Washington as an earnest when he evacuated Fort Necessity in 1755. Stobo had lived as a prisoner since, in Fort Duquesne and then Quebec, though he circulated easily in Quebec society, until apprehended as a spy

---

6. Anderson, *op. cit.*, p. 298.

for having smuggled out of Fort Duquesne, via an Indian, plans he had drawn of Duquesne that were found in the belongings of the deceased Braddock after the disaster on the Monongahela. Stobo escaped Quebec, spoke only to Wolfe, and advised him of a footpath up the cliffs at what has become known as Wolfe's Cove. Thus arose the plan for one of history's decisive military battles.[7]

Wolfe moved about 4,500 men on the tides up-river from Quebec, then down on the current in the early hours of September 12, mounted Stobo's path to a site above known as the Plains of Abraham, and overwhelmed a small French tent encampment. Wolfe was apparently beset by morose thoughts, as well as indecision, finding himself alone on the Plains. He ordered that disembarkations stop, but the landing officer assumed the order was mistaken and ignored it. Montcalm had been distracted by a carefully played ruse to the east of Quebec, and only arrived on the Plains after Wolfe's men had been drawn up across the Plains. By 9:30 in the morning Montcalm was concerned that the British were bringing up artillery from the ships and entrenching themselves in a manner that would become irreversible if didn't act, and ordered his men forward. In fact, Wolfe had had one of his attacks of inertia and the British were bringing up artillery but not entrenching; Montcalm had summoned a detachment of 2,000 of his best troops from the west, who he hoped would land in Wolfe's rear once battle was engaged.

There were about 4,500 men on each side, though the British had the advantage of better trained and disciplined forces. There is a good deal of anecdotal evidence that neither commander expected to survive the engagement about to begin. In this at least, their provisions were exact. The French attacked in rather ragged order, supported by Indians and irregular skirmishers who sniped from the sides. The British coolly held their fire, and the professionalism of the Redcoats paid handsome rewards—they drenched the French with artillery and pushed them into what became a rather uncoordinated but not panicky retreat to Quebec. Wolfe had been wounded early on the wrist, but was mortally hit by snipers in the chest and stomach as he joined the advance. Just before he died, he received the information that the French were vacating the field and that it was certainly a victory. Only a few minutes later, the column Montcalm had been hoping for arrived in the British rear, but the British, now commanded by Brigadier George Townshend, were able to deflect them. Montcalm had been severely wounded on

---

7. This version of events, long conventionally accepted, is not undisputed, and it is impossible to be certain of it because of Wolfe's premature death and the lack of corroboration of his alleged comments, but it still seems likely.

his retreat from the Plains, in his stomach and leg. He fell into a delirium and died at 4 a.m. the following morning.

The governor general of New France, the Marquis de Vaudreuil, took over. He ordered the forces Montcalm had been whipping into shape to the east of Quebec when Wolfe attacked from the west to retreat inland and westward; the remains of the army at the Plains to join them; both groups to join with the column that had arrived from the west just after they could have been decisive; Quebec to hang on as best it could; and the forces that managed to execute the maneuver to retreat toward Montreal, the final significant outpost of French rule in North America. (New Orleans was an unfortified, international crossroads of adventurers.) The French irregulars had no enthusiasm for prolonging the suspense at Quebec and accepted Townshend's generous surrender terms on September 18. Montcalm's deputy commander, François de Lévis, had taken over the fragmented units from Vaudreuil, had shaped them up, and was leading them crisply back to Quebec and was only a day's march away when Quebec surrendered.

The historic importance of the Battle of the Plains of Abraham, as determining the fate of Canada, and the expulsion of the French from North America, amplified by the drama of the two brave and capable commanders dying on the field, mythologically immortalized by the paintings of the death scenes by Benjamin West of Wolfe and by Louis Watteau of Montcalm, have obscured what a close and often farcical encounter it was. If Wolfe had approached Quebec more closely and quickly and put in hand the measures to start a siege, preventing westward sorties from the city, Montcalm would have been bottled up. If Montcalm had waited an hour before attacking, his relief force would have arrived in the British rear almost simultaneously. If Quebec had held out another two days, Lévis would have mauled Townshend very badly.

Because the British would now have to spend the winter in Quebec, 7,000 troops with 7,000 civilians, in a heavily damaged town with accommodation and food for the winter for just 7,000 and winter closing off the possibility of resupply, Brigadier Murray, to whom Townshend bequeathed command when he took the last ship out on October 18, formalized what would be a genuinely historic policy that would ramify constructively through centuries to come, of close and equal cooperation between the British and the French in Canada.

There would not be such rejoicing at the military capture of a town in North America until the fall of Atlanta to General Sherman 105 years later (Chapter 6), and in Britain, a thousand bonfires of celebration blazed. It was a particular relief to Pitt, as Wolfe's last dispatches had been quite gloomy. Pitt's eulogy of the fallen commander remains one of the classics of British parliamentary oratory: "The horror of the night, the precipice scaled by Wolfe, the empire he with a handful of men added to England, and the glorious catastrophe of contentedly terminating life where his fame began—ancient story may be ransacked and ostentatious philosophy thrown into the account before an episode can be found to rank with Wolfe's." A monument was raised to Wolfe in the slightly out-of-the-way place of Greenwich, only a few hundred yards from where the Meridian would be set (Chapter 7). The French were not so preoccupied with Quebec, though they found the succession of British victories very tiresome, but Choiseul's policy of an invasion of England had gained no traction. The French fleet at Toulon, which had taken Minorca, tried to skip the Mediterranean and gather in the Channel. The ever-vigilant Boscawen saw it sneak past Gibraltar, gave chase, destroyed five of the French ships at the Battle of Lagos (Portugal, not Nigeria), and blockaded the rest into Cádiz.

9. THE WAR IN EUROPE, 1759

But the main French naval forces, at Brest in Britanny, joined with returning forces from the Caribbean and sought to take advantage of traditionally stormy weather in the autumn to slip the blockade of Admiral Sir Edward Hawke, who had developed the technique of rotating several of his ships at a time home for refit, provisioning and home leave, and maintaining the watch constantly. Hawke and the French naval commander, the Count de Conflans, came to grips on November 20 in tempestuous weather in Quiberon Bay. A wild action ensued, in which there was no effort to coordinate between different ships in each command, and in the melee and the succeeding grounding of French ships in the Vilaine River, the British lost two ships and 300 men and the French ultimately 17 ships and 2,500 men. The French navy was in no position to conduct invasion barges across the Channel, even had the weather allowed, and Quiberon Bay was a victory on the scale of Drake's, and of Howe's and Nelson's to come. Pitt's strategy was triumphant, and Choiseul's, as designs based on the invasion of Britain inevitably are, was a complete failure.

The continental campaign had not gone well for the Anglo-Prussian alliance, however. Hanover was safe enough, but Frederick's bellicosity had caught up with him. The Russians won some victories on the Eastern Front, the Austrians forced the surrender of a Prussian corps at Maxen (13,000 men), and at Kunersdorf on August 12, in the greatest defeat of his career, Frederick lost half his army (21,000 men) to the Russians, who, not for the last time in the history of these countries, had been completely underestimated. The Austrians occupied Dresden, and Saxony, Frederick's initial prize in the war, was largely lost. Frederick contemplated abdication and even suicide and began frenzied importuning of

Pitt to convene a peace conference. Prince Louis of Brunswick, the Dutch regent and a presentable neutral, but the brother of the British ally Prince Ferdinand, duly invited the combatants to parlay, but the Austrians and Russians were not interested. Nor, really, were the French. No one, including the British banker of Frederick's military impetuosities (and his brother-in-law George II), much cared what happened to the Prussians.

The odd Anglo-Prussian alliance, with Pitt everywhere victorious and Frederick on the ropes, surged and staggered into 1760. Pitt was running out of French colonies to attack, but France had the largest army in Europe, and in the same measure that the British were determined to keep continental and especially French armies out of England, they had no land war capacity to do more in France than amphibious pin-pricks along the coast, which were almost always costly failures anyway. It was a stand-off, a shark and a lion. But a general peace could not be had until the Austrians and Russians wearied of the war with Prussia, which had Frederick, in a frenetic war of maneuver, endlessly showing the prowess of his well-trained troops, marching all about his frontiers repelling intruders at every hand. His opponents finally had a coordinated plan: The Austrians would again try to take Silesia and advance from Saxony, the Russians would attack from East Prussia, and whichever column encountered Frederick was to try to tie him up while the others made for Berlin.

The endless scrambling around the edges of a gradually imploding Prussia continued all year. Frederick, though outnumbered, ejected the Austrians from Silesia yet again. The Russians, with an Austrian contingent, briefly occupied Berlin in October, but withdrew as Frederick hastily returned. The Russian empress, Elizabeth, would be the only Russian leader to occupy Berlin until Joseph Stalin arrived at the Potsdam Conference in Frederick's palace in 1945, at the head of the 360 divisions of the Red Army (Chapter 11). The year of relentless warfare in Germany ended with the Battle of Torgau on November 2, west of Dresden, which was effectively a draw between the Austrians and Frederick's smaller army. Frederick's resourcefulness was starting to wear down his enemies, but even now, no serious peace discussions took place. The war in India also continued well for the British, and France had no capacity at all to resupply its forces there.

10. THE END OF THE WAR IN AMERICA, 1760

In America, Montreal was effectively the last prize. Lévis made a spirited effort to retake Quebec in April but was repulsed, and Amherst encroached on Montreal over the summer and it was surrendered, at least honorably and with generous terms for the civil population, by Governor Vaudreuil, on September 8, 1760. With the fall of Quebec and Montreal to the English, the war for North America was effectively over. In London, America's greatest intellectual, Benjamin Franklin, was back as the envoy of Pennsylvania, as of 1757, and he shared in the widespread concern in some American circles that Britain might bargain Canada back to France for Martinique and trade Guadeloupe for Minorca. All his conscient life up to this time, Franklin had cherished a view of the endless growth of America, and noted early regarding the growth of the American population, doubling every 20 years or so, that "it will in another century be more than the people of England, and the greatest number of Englishmen will be on this side of the water."[8] He strongly objected to the British custom of prescribing the death penalty for far too many offenses, and of substituting for the gallows the transportation of such convicts to America. He approved the imposition of tariffs on the convicts' admission (invalidated by the British Parliament), and even sponsored the return to Britain of a shipload of rattlesnakes as a gesture of thanks for the receipt in America of so many hardened criminals.[9]

Franklin chafed at unreasonable laws imposed from overseas, but continued to regard himself as an Englishman living in America. Franklin disapproved the emigration of Germans in such numbers that they might not assimilate to the English language,[10] but reasoned that the prosperity, relative absence of war, more abundant agriculture, standard of living, and general levels of nutrition and energy in America were so superior to those in Britain that America would surpass the British population without one more person embarking in Britain for America. Franklin was correct, and would have been even without the huge waves of assimilated immigration from central and southern Europe, or the famine-driven half of the entire Irish population that made ship for America and Canada in the middle of the next century. Franklin included such thoughts in his *Observations Concerning the Increase of Mankind.* He wrote nothing of his long-term notions of political organization of relations with the home country, but when the North American victory became clear, he agitated and lobbied strenuously for the British retention of Canada. As agent for Pennsylvania, Franklin rarely met Pitt (until later, less intense times for Pitt, when they became quite friendly), but he had a close relationship with Pitt's secretaries, Potter and Wood, and was continually pipelining in his urgings for the conquest and retention of Canada.

---

8. Edmund S. Morgan, *Benjamin Franklin*, New Haven, Yale University Press, 2002, p. 76.
9. Ibid. p. 74.
10. Ibid. p. 72.

When this appeared to be in hand, in 1760, it was assumed in Britain that peace was near, as the British sea superiority and French land superiority made it hard to discern where the war would continue. The Earl of Bath wrote a pamphlet promoting retention of Canada, and it was widely thought, but never confirmed and now seems unlikely, that Franklin effectively ghost-wrote much of it. Edmund Burke wrote a trenchant championship of retention of Guadeloupe and the return of Canada, as Louisbourg had been returned by the Peace of Aix-la-Chappelle in 1748. Franklin openly entered this controversy, writing "I have long been of opinion that the foundations of the future grandeur and stability of the British Empire lie in America; and though, like other foundations, they are low and little now, they are nevertheless broad and strong enough to support the greatest political structure that human wisdom ever erected. . . . If we keep it, all the country from the St. Lawrence to the Mississippi will in another century be filled with British people . . . the Atlantic sea will be covered with your trading ships; and your naval power, thence continually increasing, will extend your influence round the whole world, and awe the world. If the French remain in Canada, they will continually harass our colonies by the Indians, and impede, if not prevent their growth; your progress will at best be slow."[11] This was from a letter to Lord Kames but was reprinted in what became known as Franklin's *The Canada Pamphlet*.

Franklin was certainly prescient, but he was essentially sketching out the future of America, not Britain. There is no doubt that he thought America would surpass Britain, and given his frequent bouts of irritation with the British regime in America, it is hard to doubt that he at least had a two-track option: Britain and America together become unquestionably the greatest power in the world and sort out governance between them; or America, the mortal threat of France to strangle English-speaking America in its cradle having been graciously removed, would achieve the same prodigies without the British. What he did not know, and was not generally known, was that Pitt would have fought to the last musket ball himself to keep Canada, and Louis XV and Choiseul felt themselves well shot of the unprofitable, inaccessible, unremitting New France that Jacques Cartier had allegedly called, on discovering it, "The land God gave to Cain," and that Frederick the Great's (and Catherine the Great's) friend Voltaire dismissed as "a few acres of snow" (a description that rankles yet in Quebec, 250 years later). Even more improbably, the bountiful fisheries of Newfoundland caused Pitt to say that he would rather give up his right arm than a share of the fishing off the Grand Banks to France, and that he would surrender the Tower of London before

---

11. *The Works of Benjamin Franklin*, Philadelphia, Childs and Peterson, 1840, vol. 1, p. 255–256.

he would give up Newfoundland. Pitt was not just concerned with fish, because access to fisheries was what bred sailors and created the personnel for a navy, and cutting France off from such fisheries would have severely crimped its ability to rebuild its shattered navy.[12]

11. THE END OF THE SEVEN YEARS' WAR

Military fatigue and diplomatic confusion settled and thickened until the war finally ended. King George II died on October 25, 1760, and was succeeded by his young grandson, the preternaturally headstrong George III, who had no interest at all in Hanover and was opposed, partly from sharing his father's dislike of his grandfather, to any British assistance there. It was to appease George II that Walpole and Pelham had propped up Hanover. George III achieved the appointment of his former tutor, the Earl of Bute, as northern secretary in charge of European continental relations (for which post he was completely unqualified), assuring friction with Pitt, who retained the Southern Department (all foreign affairs except Europe). Bute wanted to wind the war down and shared his master's opposition to any involvement in continental wars.

In Europe in 1761, essentially the same familiar armies continued to mill about on the edges of Prussia in an increasing state of depletion and exhaustion. Choiseul managed in 1762 to bring Spain into the war against Britain, convincing the Spanish that now that Britain held the scepter of the seas, she would be poaching on the Spanish interests in Latin America next. (If true, that was all the more reason for Spain to have entered the war earlier, when she could have joined forces with a still navally viable France.) Faithful to a centuries-old alliance, Portugal rallied to England and declared war on Spain, which invaded its smaller neighbor. Again, the British sent an expeditionary force to help their protégé. Pitt had learned of the French-Spanish arrangement, and advocated a preemptive strike against the Spanish. The advice was rejected as improper under international law (which scarcely existed and when invoked was almost always pretextual), and from warweariness. Pitt resigned from the government, leaving Bute preeminent under the mighty survivor, Prime Minister the Duke of Newcastle, now 36 years in cabinet. He was now having severe problems paying for the war, as the government was charged, in effect, 25 percent interest and was still two million pounds short on the last year, facing the possible requirement simply to print banknotes and endure

---

12. Shortly after, Newfoundland settled into a long notoriety as a poor province. It went bankrupt as an autonomous dominion in the 1930s and more or less fell into the arms of Canada in 1949, but finally became wealthy with the development of off-shore oil in the early twenty-first century.

inflation, a horrible political and social nightmare. Newcastle, too, was abruptly turned out by George III and Bute on May 26, 1762, ending the very long (41 years) dominance of the Walpole-Pelham Whigs, years of vast success for Britain, in war and peace, and all over the world.

The French army, in one of the longest droughts of victory in its history, was unable to get by or through the Hanoverians; Czarina Elizabeth died, and was replaced by her dull-witted German nephew, Peter III, who worshipped Frederick the Great and abruptly withdrew from the war, mediated peace between Prussia and Sweden, and threatened Austria, before being overthrown, imprisoned, and murdered, in 1762, with the presumed complicity of his formidable wife, Catherine the Great, in one of history's most lop-sided marriages. She quickly restored the anti-Prussian slant of Russian policy.[13] Frederick, who was a man of considerable culture, wrote a couplet about Catherine: "The Russian Messalina, the Cossacks' whore, Gone to service lovers on the Stygian shore."[14]

As negotiations dragged desultorily on, the well-traveled Monckton seized Havana on August 14, 1762. Once again, there were celebrations in the streets in England. Peace was finally secured by the craftiness of Choiseul, a clever negotiator and diplomat, if an unsuccessful war strategist. Spain would fight to the death rather than acquiesce in the permanent loss of Havana. Britain would have to be bought off with something comparable. An insufficiently generous peace could produce a parliamentary revolt, and bring back Pitt, who would trim France back to the Ile-de-France, if he could bribe enough European armies to do it. The national debt of Great Britain had increased from 74.5 million pounds in 1755 to 133.25 million in 1763; 10 times the year's budget which was half deficit. This was almost more debt than Britain could bear without provoking taxpayers' revolts in both the home islands and America, and a default and rampant inflation were both completely out of the question.

It had been a brilliant but almost Pyrrhic victory for Pitt. France was a larger and richer country than Britain, but it too had a financial problem, so the pressure was on Choiseul to produce a peace that would be accepted by Spain, which he had induced late into the war and was not gasping for money and was prepared to delay peace to get Havana back. Choiseul gave Louisiana to Spain, in exchange for Spain ceding to Britain the territory from Mississippi to Georgia in return for Havana. Since Louis and Choiseul had no interest in North America, that worked

---

13. The death of the Czarina Elizabeth is celebrated as the miracle of the House of Brandenburg, and it was invoked by Goebbels and Hitler, inaccurately, in the desperation of their bunker, following the death of President Franklin D. Roosevelt in 1945 (Chapter 11).

14. Anderson, *op. cit.*, p. 493.

for everyone, and France took back her sugar islands, as well as the little Gulf of St. Lawrence islands of St. Pierre and Miquelon, from which to service her fishing fleet, which was guaranteed access to Newfoundland fishing. France gave back Minorca but kept Pondicherry in India and the West African slave trading stations. Britain ruled North America and India. Everyone had what he wanted most and the Peace of Paris was signed on February 10, 1763. Britain had the winning strategy, but in a perverse pattern that would be followed with other leaders who rescued it from wars that were going badly with Great Powers, it dispensed with the father of victory Pitt, as it would with his son for a brief peace with Napoleon, Lloyd George in 1922, and Churchill in 1945 (though not Palmerston after Crimea).

Five days later came the Treaty of Hubertusburg. Frederick the Great kept Silesia and Maria Theresa took back Saxony. Not for the last time, Germany had unleashed aggressive war, and not for the last time gained nothing tangible from it. Frederick promised to support Maria Theresa's son as next head of the Holy Roman Empire. But he had established Prussia as a Great Power, and had given the world an astonishing and minatory demonstration of Germany's military aptitudes and national tenacity. Furor Teutonicus was foreseeable (if not much foreseen). In Eastern Europe, Prussia was a doughty contender, but hundreds of thousands of lives had been lost in a war that, though it made Prussia a Great Power and enabled America to start thinking of independence, effected no significant changes to anything else in Europe. The 22-year-old George Washington had ignited a fateful conflict.

The Seven Years' War had been an utterly stupid war for everyone except the British and the Americans. They had gained a world, with a debt time bomb attached to it, and had perfected the technique, soon to be absolutely vital for compensating for France's much larger population and greater national wealth. France had surrendered much of the prestige she had enjoyed from Richelieu to Louis XIV. The zigzag of French decline had begun, with the most dismal war in its history, prior to the severe beatings it would suffer (110 and 180 years later) in two out of three contests with a united Germany. William Pitt had been the great war statesman, Frederick the Great the great commander, and the whimsical Philadelphian printer and scientist, Benjamin Franklin, the great strategic prophet.

12. ANGLO-AMERICAN RELATIONS AFTER 1763

The removal of France from North America made Britain dispensable to the American colonists, and the heavy costs of the British victory in the Seven Years' War and the increased cohesion the colonies achieved in the war altered the correlation of forces between Britain and America. The British did not notice this, but the more astute Americans did.

At first, all was well in Anglo-American relations, as the dispatch of the French was celebrated by both. As early as 1754, Franklin, renowned throughout the world as a scientist, and a prodigious talent in other areas as well, had exposed to his learned British friend Peter Collinson, a successful merchant but also a distinguished naturalist, his opinion that "Britain and her Colonies should be considered as one Whole, and not different states with separate Interests." He had abandoned his previous hope, broached but frustrated at the Albany Congress earlier in 1754 (which had been convened at the request of the British Board of Trade, a government ministry), for colonial unity of purpose and action. He still favored a Grand Council of all the colonies, chosen by the individual colonial assemblies and presided over by a President General, who would represent the monarch of Britain and America. This was the heart of his plan at Albany. The Grand Council would operate independently of the British Parliament. This largely prefigured constitutional dispositions in America and the British Commonwealth, but Franklin made little progress with it at this stage. The prime minister, Newcastle, completely ignored the proposal when it was presented to him by the Board of Trade in 1754.[15]

When Franklin had persuaded the Pennsylvania Assembly to set up a colonial militia after the catastrophe on the Monongahela, and accepted a colonelcy in it, so great was the concern about Pennsylvania's open western border that the British government vetoed the creation of the militia. British reaction to autonomous gestures in the colonies was reflexive and hostile. Franklin, an optimist, chose not to set too much store by that, and the ensuing war buried the hatchet between the British and their colonies (in the heads and torsos of their shared enemies). Even Franklin's astounding and relentless powers of persuasion made few converts to his idea of trans-Atlantic organization or any devolution like it when he returned as representative (lobbyist, in fact) for Pennsylvania in London in 1764 after a brief absence. He had already been elected a member of the Royal Society and soon was awarded honorary doctorates from St. Andrews and Oxford (and had as much right to be called Doctor as Samuel Johnson). The British greatly respected Franklin and much liked him, but they did not connect their regard for him with any notion that the American colonies possessed any aptitude or representative desire for self-government. Franklin gleaned a notion of what he was facing in 1760, when Collinson arranged a meeting with the president of the King's Privy Council, Lord Granville, one of the most influential members of the government. Granville wished to discuss the military scene in America, but added, in an unpromising

---

15. Morgan, *op. cit.*, pp. 86, 90.

aside, that "The king is the Legislator of the Colonies," and his will was "the law of the land." Franklin's polite remonstrations made no headway.[16]

When Franklin returned to London in 1764, his chief preoccupation, bizarrely, was to bring Pennsylvania more directly under British rule, in order to emancipate it from what he rightly considered the bigoted autocracy of the Penn family. He had fought against this in various capacities in Philadelphia and construed it as his duty to seek the most likely possible easement of the arbitrariness of the Penns, and so called for the prerogatives of the existing legislature to be gutted, prior to the establishment of a federal colonial authority. His wishes would come to pass, but not as he had initially foreseen. One of Franklin's closest British friends and one of the country's leading solicitors, Richard Jackson, told Franklin shortly after the Treaty of Paris was signed that Britain intended to keep 10,000 troops in America, at the expense of the colonies. Franklin replied that the more costs Britain inflicted on the colonies, the less revenue it could expect to have remitted to Britain, recognizing at once the problem the victorious Empire faced. "It is not worth your while. The more you oblige us to pay here, the less you can receive there." Six months later, Jackson, by then a member of Parliament, wrote to him that "200,000 pounds will infallibly be raised by Parliament on the plantations." Franklin replied that he was "not much alarm'd. . . . You will take care for your own sakes not to lay greater Burthens upon us than we can bear; for you cannot hurt us without hurting yourselves."[17] He wrote to Collinson in the same line: "I think there is scarce anything you can do that may be hurtful to us, but what will be as much or more so to you. This must be our chief security."[18]

13. THE STAMP ACT

Shortly after Franklin's return to London in 1764, debate began on the Stamp Act, which imposed a tax on printed and paper goods in the colonies, including even newspapers and decks of cards, and was so called because payment of the tax was certified by a stamp on the article taxed. Britain already had such a tax domestically. Pitt's brother-in-law, George Grenville (not to be confused with Lord Granville), was leader of the government in the House of Commons. In presenting the measure, Grenville claimed the right of Parliament to levy taxes anywhere in the Empire, which was not contested by his fellow legislators, but he gave the colonies a year to propose alternatives. None did so, although Franklin

---

16. Morgan, *op. cit.*, p. 114.
17. Ibid. p. 141.
18. Ibid. p. 142.

himself did. Franklin achieved prodigies of diplomatic access and advocacy, but he had no legitimate status at all, and was merely an information service from Pennsylvania and other colonies that engaged him, to the British government, establishment, and public. Franklin's proposal was to have Parliament establish a colonial credit office that would issue bills of credit in the colonies, and collect 6 percent for renewal of the bills each year, and these could be used as currency. Gold and silver currency were scarce in the colonies, as all transactions with Britain had to be paid in cash, and Parliament had forbidden the issuance of paper money in America. Franklin's theory was that this would be an adequately disguised tax, and would not be unpopular in America because of the desire there for paper money to replace an inordinate mass of informal IOUs. It isn't clear how the interest would have been collected, or how inflation would have been avoided, but at least it was creative thinking, and a start.

Franklin subscribed to the theory of his friendly acquaintance Edmund Burke that popular discussion of rights was a sure sign of misgovernment, and he watched with concern as the revenue-raising tax became a noisy trans-Atlantic debate about the right to tax. Franklin was shocked at the proportions of the outrage in the colonies when the stamp tax was imposed, in November 1765. There was in the stamp tax a move to tax harmonization in the Empire, but also to strike a preemptive blow for the untrammeled rights of the Imperial Parliament. The English suspected some of the colonial leaders of aspiring to independence, and that must have been correct.[19] But they acted in a way that could have been reasonably assumed to fan and inflame that sentiment, not defuse or douse it. The British political class assumed that while there were agitators for independence in America, they were opportunists, rabble-rousers, and scoundrels, and that the great majority were committed Englishmen, loyal to the Crown, come what may. That sentiment was strong, but what the British, from the king down, failed to grasp was that loyalty to the Crown in America depended on the wearer of the Crown appearing to be the impartial arbiter, when necessary, of the interests of all his subjects. If the king were to seem solely interested in upholding the British side of an argument with the Americans, that loyalty, in the face of the higher and more imminent patriotic interest of the colonists, supplemented by their material interests, would quickly evaporate. The British had not sent talented governors to America, with rare exceptions, and as has been mentioned, the conduct of the military expedition leaders had been heavy-handed with the colonists, and

19. Morgan, *op. cit.*, p. 152.

completely ineffectual with the French and Indians, prior to Pitt's taking control of the Seven Years' War in 1758.

The theory of parliamentary representation of all interests was strained, in part because Parliament was riddled with constituencies that had very few people in them, were controlled by influential individuals, and in any case did not represent the colonies at all, other than in the sense that the national interest of the home islands required some consideration of the Americans. (There were about 9.5 million people in the British Isles, including over two million Irish Roman Catholics who were a good deal more dissentient in spirit as subjects of the British Parliament than the Americans at their most unenthusiastic; there was an electorate of about 300,000, scattered extremely unevenly through about 540 constituencies, and the appointive and hereditary House of Lords had greater powers than the House of Commons.) Even had it been a broad suffrage with equal representation for all districts, it would still have been scandalous non-representation of the Americans, the wealthiest part of the British-governed world with, by the mid-1770s, about 30 percent of the population of Britain, about 70 percent of the population of Prussia, which had just held the great Austrian and Russian Empires at bay for almost seven years, and a greater population than the Netherlands or Sweden, noteworthy powers that had swayed the destinies of Europe at times in the previous 150 years. (Admittedly, about 8 percent of the Americans were unenfranchised slaves, who had only the rights their owners allowed from one moment to the next.)

On the other side, the Americans knew that Britain had saved them from a most unappetizing fate at the hands of the French, a prospect made more gruesome and horrifying by any contemplation of what the Indians might have done to make the lives of the colonists shorter and more uncongenial. All informed Americans knew that Britain had gone a long way into debt doing so, and as America was the most prosperous part of the Empire, it had some obligation to shoulder a proportionate share of the cost. It is impossible, at this remove, and buried as these matters now are in the folkloric mythology of the creation of the United States, to guess what degree of unvarnished cynicism might have hastened and made louder the American caterwauling about rights, and the corresponding failure to make any suggestion, apart from Franklin's worthy improvisation, of an alternative to the stamp tax to retire the debt incurred in the military salvation of America.

The Pennsylvania Assembly adopted a resolution strenuously condemning the Stamp Act, as did the Virginia Assembly, under the influence of the fiery orator Patrick Henry, who advised George III to contemplate the fate of Julius Caesar and Charles I (as if either the men or their fates were in the slightest similar, and seeming to condone their ends, an assassination and a pseudo-judicial murder, shortly leading in each case to the elevation of their heirs). The Virginians asserted that the tax was "illegal, unconstitutional, and unjust. . . . The inhabitants of this Colony are not bound to yield Obedience to any law or Ordinance whatever, designed to impose any Taxation whatever upon them," apart from those legislated in Virginia. This response was known as the Virginia Resolves and was emulated by most of the colonies. The British had designated collectors of the tax, who were pressured into refusing to collect it. With the tax in effect but not being collected, and demonstrations verging on violence around the colonies, nine of the colonies met in New York and declared that taxes could be imposed on the colonists only with their personal consent or that of their elected representatives. This was represented as part of the birthright of Englishmen. It was a stirring stand for individual liberty and rugged individualism, but was nonsense in fact. No sane person will volunteer to be taxed, other than in a severe community or national emergency, and Englishmen were taxed all the time with only a vote of an undemocratically elected House of Commons and a House of Lords that would recoil in horror at the thought that it was answerable to the taxpayers. (It should not be imagined that the colonial houses of assembly had a greatly larger percentage of representation on their voters' lists, although the procedure of what became known as gerrymandering [after the redistricting artistry of the fifth vice president, Elbridge Gerry] had not had the time to plumb the depths of electoral vote-rigging that existed in England.) The rights Englishmen possessed, which distinguished them from most nationalities, except for some Swiss, Dutch, and Scandinavians, were freedom of speech and assembly, and access to generally fairly independent courts, as well as some participatory legislative processes, and the Americans received them from and shared them with the British.

14. FRANKLIN'S DIPLOMACY IN LONDON, 1764–1767

The Americans, Franklin was convinced, didn't want independence, but they wanted an end to inferiority. They recognized the British right to regulate trade between parts of the Empire, but not to do anything that really touched the lives of the colonists. The problem with this outlook was that it amounted to Britain's having the high privilege of assuring the security of the colonists, at British expense, and no authority to require anything of the colonists in return. Even if such a thing could be negotiated for the future, it left Britain with the heavy cost of having thrown the French out of North America, to protect the colonists, with the beneficiaries loudly claiming that it was their birthright as Englishmen, and the most well-to-do group of Englishmen at that, to refuse to pay anything toward their own salvation. That would not work as the modus operandi of a functioning empire.

On the other side, the British imagined that they could do what they wished legislating over and for the colonists, that there was any truth to the fiction that the British Parliament represented the Americans, that the colonists, like those in Gibraltar or the Falkland Islands, had no capacity whatever for self-government, and that no American could possibly wish it except a few political demagogues and self-seekers. The Empire was not going to last long on such a flimsy foundation as that, either. It was in this deepening vortex that Franklin worked in London.

Franklin had thought of American representation in the British Parliament, but it was soon clear that matters had deteriorated too far for that. The Americans would not seek it, in the same measure that the British would not offer it. There was already an obvious danger of armed conflict, as there was much talk in London of sending the British army to collect the stamp tax. Fortunately the ministry changed, and Pitt's friend the Marquis of Rockingham became prime minister. Franklin met the new president of the Board of Trade, Lord Dartmouth, and proposed the suspension of the Stamp Act, until the colonies' debt levels, which he attributed to the fiscal rigors of the late war, had subsided. (They were modest compared with Britain's.) And then the Stamp Act could quietly expire. He also warned that the use of armed force to collect taxes in America would fail, as the soldiers would be induced to desert in large numbers by the higher pay scales of the American private sector, and by the impossibility of rounding up deserters in a country so vast and absorbent of dissenters.

On February 13, 1766, Franklin appeared before Parliament in effect to answer for America. He did so brilliantly. He protested American loyalty, which had been affected by the British imposition of "an internal tax." There had never been any objection to taxes on exports. Partly because of Franklin's efforts, the British repealed the Stamp Act in 1766, but accompanied that move with the Declaratory Act, which averred that Parliament had the right to legislate for the colonies "in all cases whatsoever." Franklin wasn't much bothered by that declaration, as long as nothing was done about it. He cherished a reform of the Empire that would cause Britain to shed even its right to excise taxes on exports. He was more convinced than ever that eventually America would surpass Britain and foresaw a gradual inversion of the relationship, that the American country would be the senior partner. A man of immense subtlety, congeniality, and diplomacy, Franklin exaggerated the ability of others to reason as thoughtfully as he did.

He wrote home very happily of "the august body" of the British Parliament having done the right and sensible thing in repealing the Stamp Act, and predicted imperial reform. By this Franklin meant a single monarch of the Empire, but the main constituent parts entirely self-governing, or coordinating through a grand assembly of representatives meeting in equality and dealing with matters of common interest, as he had proposed for the colonies themselves. The first option was close to what the British Commonwealth became 150 years later, between Britain and what were called the "white Dominions"—Canada, Australia, New Zealand, and, more or less, South Africa. Of course, all of those countries combined, and adding the United Kingdom, even today, have a population, as Franklin foresaw, that is not much more than half that of the U.S. The second option, with the grand assembly, was emulated to a substantial degree by the advocates of federalism at the Constitutional Convention in Philadelphia, where Franklin presided, in 1787 and 1788.

Franklin's optimism, as frequently happened in his long life, was unjustified. "Every man in England," he wrote, ". . . seems to jostle himself into the Throne with the King, and talks of 'our subjects in the colonies.'"[20] As usually happens in long-running disagreements, tempers escalated and a natural desire to settle the dispute violently steadily gained ground as a prospect. A similar process would be replicated between the slave-holding and free American states 90 years later (Chapters 6 and 7). The British could speak only of repression by force, tipsy with their Seven Years' War victories, especially as the Rockingham-Pitt regimes gave way to the king's friends, the reactionary governments of the Duke of Grafton and Frederick, Lord North. Franklin did not think the British possessed the least idea of how difficult it would be to suppress the colonists, and did not think they would succeed if they tried. It was painful for Benjamin Franklin, as for many. He wrote Lord Kames (Pitt's friend) that "I love Britain" and many British, and "I wish it prosperity." His sought-for union could disadvantage America briefly, but "America, an immense Territory favour'd by Nature with all advantages of Climate, Soil, great navigable Rivers and Lakes etc., must become a great Country, populous and mighty; and will in a less time than is generally conceived, be able to shake off any Shackles that may be imposed on her and perhaps place them on the Imposers."[21] This was Franklin's wistful hope, and prophetic view; while the British grumbled belligerently and garrulously about putting America in its place, the sun was already rising on the mighty and uncontainable power of the New World. Nothing could stifle, or, ultimately, equal it. America was the predestined nation.

---

20. Morgan, *op. cit.*, p. 161.
21. Ibid. p. 163.

15. THE TOWNSHEND TAXES

Franklin was already being overtaken by events. In 1767 the chancellor of the Exchequer, Charles Townshend, imposed a series of excise taxes on a range of English manufactures, including paper, glass, paint, and, eventually, tea, and provided for a board of customs commissioners to sit in America and collect the tax as the goods arrived. This must have been a gratuitous gesture to annoy the Americans, as the duty could have been levied in British ports as the goods left the country of origin. Franklin did not foresee that this would arouse his countrymen, but a new uproar occurred. The most important American of all, if a confrontation came, would be George Washington, the senior military officer in the colonies. He had not been overly successful as a senior officer, but was a capable and brave leader, a tall, impressive presence, and an astute businessman, though only a mid-level plantation owner. He had continued assiduously to invest in the western part of Virginia and in the Ohio country, and had steadily built his plantation at Mount Vernon, where he was sometimes a harsh slavemaster. Though largely self-educated, he was knowledgeable and worldly, despite the fact that he never left America. Unlike Franklin, he was not gregarious but rather slightly shy. But he was formidable and respected. He was a member of the Virginia House of Burgesses, and steered clear of the debate on the Stamp Act, ignoring the pyrotechnics of Patrick Henry and others, as did also the young plantation owner from Monticello, Thomas Jefferson, who entered the House at the age of 21 in 1764. Jefferson disliked public speaking, and was never good at it, but he was an elegant writer, a talented lawyer, a fine architect, and a learned polymath.

Washington reasoned that the Stamp Act raised the ire especially of "the speculators," by which he meant lawyers, publishers, and ship owners, whom he tended to disparage (not land and crop speculators like himself). Washington proposed that the Stamp Act be responded to with a general campaign to buy less from Britain, arguing that British merchants could be relied upon to agitate in ways that the Mother of Parliaments could not resist, whereas it could resist disaffected colonials. He believed such a partial boycott would provide "a necessary stimulus to industry" in America. He was as cool-headed as Franklin, but less intellectual, and tended to think as a businessman or military commander. He soon discontinued tobacco production at Mount Vernon, and went over to arts and crafts manufacturing to fill the void that he anticipated from strained relations with the British.[22]

---

22. James MacGregor Burns and Susan Dunn, *The Three Roosevelts: Patrician Leaders Who Transformed America*, New York, Grove Press, 2001, p. 16.

By 1769 Townshend's laws had caused Washington to toughen his stance and call for an outright general American boycott of British goods. More ominously, and getting well ahead of Franklin, who toiled to the end to avoid a complete rupture, Washington wrote that if "selfish, designing men . . . and clashing interests" made a boycott impractical, no one should "hesitate a moment" to take up arms, though this "should be the last resource."[23]

In May 1769, the Virginia burgesses adopted "An humble, dutiful, and loyal address" to George III to protect "the violated rights of America." The angry governor, a typical British Colonel Blimp (an inflexible and traditionalist stuffed shirt) figure, Lord Dunmore, dissolved the House of Burgesses, and its members repaired to the Raleigh Tavern for a venting of fierce oratory. After a fair bit of steam had been blown off, Washington spoke, and unveiled a plan he had worked out with his closest collaborator, George Mason, for total non-importation from Britain. Washington sold it, apart from other factors, as a way for Virginia merchants to simply renege on their often heavy debts to British suppliers. This plan was adopted, and gave Washington a rounded parliamentary status to add to his high standing as an officer and astute plantation owner and land buyer. Washington faithfully adhered to it at first, but it quickly became clear that, though the general boycott did hold in many other areas, Virginians and other Americans did not wish to give up their addiction to British luxury goods, and Washington abandoned his own boycott on British clothes and furniture after a few months. (Yet when he had his portrait painted by Charles Wilson Peale in 1772, he wore an old Virginia Regiment uniform he had not been in for 13 years. The colonel, as he now was, had a natural political flair.)

Franklin, in the front lines in London, equable though he was, was also hardening in his attitude. By the end of 1769, Parliament was considering the repeal of all the Townshend taxes except that on tea. Franklin told his British friends that no such repeal would be adequate to lift the non-importation campaign in America, unless it also applied to everything exported to America.[24] Parliament and the party leaders had determined that tea was the point where the line had to be drawn. There must be no more concessions to the colonists. By the early 1770s Franklin still loved England and watched the descent toward armed conflict with foreboding, relieved only by the esteem in which the English held him, even King George III.[25] In 1770, when a letter of his to a Massachusetts friend was

---

23. Burns and Dunn, *op. cit.*, p. 17.
24. Morgan, *op. cit.*, p. 171.
25. Ibid. p. 175.

read in the legislative assembly of that colony, Franklin was chosen to become representative for Massachusetts also, as he already had been for Georgia and for New Jersey, where Franklin's son William was the governor, as well as Pennsylvania.

A running battle went on with partial boycotts, a good deal of smuggling, and outbursts of civil disobedience. In the spring of 1773, the still young Jefferson (30, compared with Washington's 40 and Franklin's 67) had earned himself a reputation as a diligent and capable legislator and agreeable and thoughtful and intelligent companion, and he led a "committee of correspondence" to strengthen ties with other colonial legislators and coordinate responses to continuing British impositions. Townshend's tax on tea was continuously in place through the early 1770s. Once again, the British had no idea that the Americans would find this particularly objectionable. On December 16, 1773, members of the Sons of Liberty, a Boston autonomist organization led by vehement opponents of any subordination to Britain, such as John Adams's cousin Samuel Adams, disguised themselves as American Indians, stormed the tea ships, and threw 342 chests of tea into the harbor. This passed into history as the Boston Tea Party. The Sons of Liberty went to great lengths to show they were not an unruly mob, repairing locks on the ships' holds and punishing one of their members who had pocketed some tea leaves for his own use.

The Tea Party, as all the world knows, set the tinder and kindling alight. Parliament revoked the Charter of Massachusetts in early 1774, substituted a military government, and purported to shut down Boston Harbor until the value of the tea destroyed had been paid. The reaction among the colonies was uniform and very supportive of the Boston tea partiers. Thomas Jefferson drafted a resolution denouncing the "Intolerable Acts," as the parliamentary response was known. The resolution passed and Dunmore vetoed the measure. Jefferson then drafted a pious resolution calling for "a day of fasting and prayer" for the Boston protesters, which passed easily, and Dunmore again dissolved the House of Burgesses. (Jefferson too, like Washington and Franklin, was not a formally religious man—he was pitching this to others.) This time the legislators dispersed to the Apollo Room of the Raleigh Tavern in Williamsburg, and adopted a resolution calling for a "continental congress" from all the colonies to meet in Philadelphia to organize resistance to British rule. The strategy of a nation or people may be crafted deliberately by leaders, or may, in more primitive circumstances, evolve spontaneously from collective responses to events. The Americans were just moving from the second to the first. (Mainly) British people seeking a better life had come to America to find it. British grand strategy, devised by one of its greatest statesmen, William Pitt the Elder, had provided for the successful prosecution of a worldwide war against France, conspicuously in North America, empowering the Americans to reconfigure the nature of their relations with Britain. Pitt's successors did not grasp the complexities of the post-French era in North America, though Pitt and his most talented contemporaries did. And so had an emerging cadre of unusually capable Americans.

16. THE CONTINENTAL CONGRESS

Jefferson wrote some guidelines for the Virginia delegates to the Continental Congress that were judged too radical to be adopted, but one was published in London, *A Summary View of the Rights of British America*, with the author identified as "A Virginian." It is a learned but rabidly partisan constitutional-law treatise. Jefferson claimed that the colonists carried to the New World all the rights of free-born Englishmen, and that the unwritten constitution of England assured these rights as, according to the Virginian in question, the colonists had built the colonies "unaided" by the mother country, which was nonsense, of course, and ignored the chief subject of the dispute: the demand of the British to be assisted in recovering their huge investment to protect the colonies from the French. Jefferson claimed that the British were taking the view that the only rights the colonists had were those of conquered people, because the colonies were conquered. This was doubly nonsense, both substantively and because that was not the British position, which was that the Parliament of Great Britain represented all British subjects whether they participated in elections to it or not (another tenuous argument, but they abounded on both sides). Jefferson also improvised the sheer fiction that the pre–Norman Conquest Anglo-Saxons had a fundamental attachment to individual liberties, to which the colonists were legitimate heirs. They had no claim to be continuators of the Anglo-Saxons in Britain before 1066, and those Anglo-Saxons had no such system. The whole argument was moonshine, but it indicated the polemical and casuistic legal skill of Jefferson.

The Continental Congress met in the autumn of 1774 and called for a complete boycott of British goods, and adjourned to May 1775. Before that meeting occurred, the American Revolutionary War had begun. These three men, George Washington, Benjamin Franklin, and Thomas Jefferson, would be the most important of the prominent figures that conducted the American side, a surprisingly talented leadership group, given the colonies' population of now just under three million, though their distinction has been somewhat exaggerated by the American genius for hyperbole, for the recreated spectacle, and by the star system, which Jefferson largely originated with his fantastic polemical assertions at the new nation's birth.

The rebels would look to Washington to put together a fighting force from the previously rather unreliable militia (which Washington himself had despised), and successfully resist the battle-hardened British regulars, the Redcoats. Benjamin Franklin, the great diplomat and world-renowned intellectual, would be relied upon to recruit allies by exploiting the fissiparous European interplay of ever-changing balances of power, which always included a deep reservoir of resentment of whichever power had won the last European war, never mind that the suitor was the beneficiary of Britain's great victory. And Thomas Jefferson would be the chief expositor, not to say propagandist, to make the case that this was not a grubby contest about taxes, colonial ingratitude, and the rights of the martial victor and mother country (all of which it largely was), and to repackage it as an epochal struggle for the rights of man, vital to the hopes and dreams of everyone in the world. Instead of, as Austria would do in the following century, "astound the world with our ingratitude," America would raise a light unto the nations and uplift the masses of the world with a creative interpretation of its motives.

All three men were suffused with the vision of the rising America, predestined to mighty nationhood. They had the starting strategy for the vertiginous rise of America: Washington the military and commercial might, Franklin the intellectual leadership and diplomatic felicity, Jefferson the clarion of a new order of freedom (unencumbered by a number of incongruities, not least among them the institution of slavery, which all three enjoyed, although Franklin became an abolitionist). The combination of people and events was combustible and would produce both heat and light. Inconveniently prematurely perhaps, but inevitably, the American project would show the world what free men in a new world could do. From the start, the world was watching, and its astonishment at what has followed has not ceased, these 238 years.

George Washington

CHAPTER TWO

CHAPTER TWO

Independence

*The Americans and French Defeat
the British in America, 1774–1789*

1. THE END OF EMPIRE IN LONDON

Benjamin Franklin, such a constant figure in the rise and decline of Anglo-American relations through and after the Seven Years' War, remained in London as trans-Atlantic civil war in the English-speaking world doomfully approached. Franklin published letters with the governor of Massachusetts, Thomas Hutchinson, which inflamed opinion on both sides of the Atlantic. (In them, Franklin again, as he often had before, wrote that "The inhabitants of this country, in all probability, in a few years, will be more numerous than those of Great Britain and Ireland together." This was the core of Franklin's belief that America was sure to win.[1]

On January 29, 1774, the Privy Council summoned Franklin to be present to hear discussion of the Massachusetts Assembly's petition, and Franklin stood poker-faced, expressionless, while he was subjected to a vitriolic attack from the solicitor general of Great Britain, Alexander Wedderburn. The petition was rejected as "groundless, vexatious, and scandalous and calculated only for the seditious Purpose of keeping up a Spirit of Clamour and Discontent."[2] Two days later, Franklin was sacked as deputy postmaster general of America. Franklin retired as agent for Massachusetts, but continued for Pennsylvania. He demonstrated admirable repose of manner and was calm and courteous throughout this difficult time. His serenity was doubtless fortified by his long-held prediction of what would come and his unshakeable conviction that America was predestined to surpass Great Britain and all other nations of the world.

Parliament's response to the Boston Tea Party—the Intolerable Acts (or the Coercive Acts, as they were known in Britain)—substantially not only closed the Port of Boston and reduced the powers of the Massachusetts Assembly, it purportedly banned town meetings, curtailed trial by jury in the colony, and declared that British troops must be stationed in Boston and billeted and paid for by the locals at the whim of the commander of the troops. Franklin denounced the acts for provoking war with the colonies, "for a war it will be, as a national Cause when it is in fact only a ministerial one."[3]

Despite his many British friends, and the esteem in which he was held there, Franklin was also seen by the arch-imperialists as the evil visionary who transmitted messages back and forth with America, always twisting them toward increased

---

1.   Edmund S. Morgan, *Benjamin Franklin*, New Haven, Yale University Press, 2002, p. 191. It somewhat presaged Abraham Lincoln's addresses in the late 1850s when he warned the South that if it came to war, the North had too many people not to prevail (Chapter 6). With one as with the other, a knowledge of the demographic trend was a consoling trump card in the struggle both sought to avoid but considered likely.
2.   Ibid. p. 203.
3.   Ibid. p. 206.

disharmony. This was not a fair allegation and was essentially a famous case of blaming the messenger. Abrasive spirits were skyrocketing on both sides. Franklin proposed compensation of the East India Company for its loss of tea, and of Boston for the closing of the port, without success in either case.

In the autumn of 1774, the ban on town meetings was generally ignored, and what were known as "Resolves" were adopted in Massachusetts and delivered by the talented horseman Paul Revere to the Continental Congress meeting in Philadelphia, on September 18. They called for civil disobedience, dissolution of the courts, seizure of the money of the colonial government in Massachusetts, and intensive preparation for war. The Congress balked at this as too provocative, but prepared a bill of rights virtually seceding from the British jurisdiction and demanded an airtight boycott of all British goods. A petition to the king to uphold the colonies' side in the dispute was also included. A reintroduction of Franklin's Albany plan for inter-colonial parliamentary union was voted down as too much resembling the over-powerful Parliament against which they were virtually in revolt.

In August 1774, William Pitt, Earl of Chatham, who had not been accessible to Franklin during the Seven Years' War, though his chief secretaries were and they knew each other indirectly, called upon Franklin. They met again on December 26, right after Franklin had received and sent on to Chatham the Continental Congress resolutions. Chatham declared that the Congress had acted with such "Temper, Moderation, and Wisdom," that it was "the most honourable Assembly of Statesmen since those of the ancient Greeks and Romans in the most virtuous times." Chatham spoke in the House of Lords on January 20, 1775, ostentatiously greeting and speaking with Franklin in the lobby of the House and advocated withdrawal of British troops from Massachusetts, appointment of a commission to negotiate a settlement, and a general de-escalation. He feared for destruction of the Empire he had largely built and saw as clearly as Franklin did where the present course would shortly lead.

Chatham presented his bill to the House of Lords on January 29, 1775. It restricted Parliament's right to legislate in America to matters of trade, made any taxation in America conditional on consent of the taxed, and recognized the Continental Congress. All British statutes that the Congress had objected to from 1764 to 1774 were to be suspended or repealed. The ministry attacked it as the insidious work of Franklin, as if Britain's greatest living statesman were a mere mouthpiece. Chatham replied that the bill was his own, but that were he charged to resolve the mess the government and its predecessors had created, he would not hesitate to consult the man "whom all Europe held in high Estimation for his

Knowledge and Wisdom, and ranked with our Boyles and Newtons, who was an Honour not to the English Nation only, but to Human Nature."[4]

Such high praise from so great a man in so eminent a place indicated Franklin's unique standing as the premier American in the world, but Chatham's bill was vituperatively rejected. Franklin assimilated the praise as expressionlessly as he had endured being reviled the year before by the same objectors. This was the end, and he left a few weeks later and arrived in Philadelphia on May 5, 1775. The die was cast.

2. THE OUTBREAK OF WAR

On April 19, 1775, American militiamen and British Redcoats exchanged fire at Lexington and Concord, outside Boston, and the British conducted a ragged retreat back into Boston, harried by American irregulars sniping and skirmishing. The war had begun, though sequels were a time in coming. The Second Continental Congress met in Philadelphia just after Franklin's return to that city; formed, at least theoretically, a Continental Army (of the Massachusetts militia and six additional companies the Congress thought it could dispatch); and drafted Colonel George Washington, as the ranking British officer among Americans (who attended the Congress in the old blue uniform he had worn for his official portrait), and by now a committed imperial secessionist, as its commander.

John Adams (of Massachusetts) had proposed him, which gave something of a national character to his commission. Washington, in his previous career, had not been a particularly successful commanding officer, though he understood logistics and the basic requirements of leadership and had been conspicuously courageous. He had earned the respect of all by his sober demeanor and imposing appearance. He said he was unworthy of the honor, and declined to be paid, apart from his expenses. He was one of the wealthiest men in the colonies because of his astute management of his plantation, adding little factories to provide what the escalation of the boycott against Britain had required to be manufactured domestically. And British victories over the French now assured a steady inflow of settlers and appreciating land values in the Ohio country where he had been a very astute acquirer of land.

George Washington the semi-autodidact, the unsuccessful striver for a British army commission and combat glory, had made himself, by default as well as by his own distinguished bearing, the custodian of the hopes of a new country. To

---

4. Morgan, *op. cit.*, p. 217.

his wife and others, Washington wrote that he could not decline the draft of the Continental Congress to command the Continental Army; that to have done so would have caused censure to rain down upon him, for cowardice, fecklessness, and betrayal. Thus was born the mighty myth of the disinterested Cincinnatus, the unseeking officer and country squire summoned from his bucolic and familial pleasures to take in hand the cause of human liberty. Fortunately for the whole project, the propagation of its motives was to be chiefly in the hands of one of the most adept spin-doctors of world history in Thomas Jefferson.

Washington proceeded to Cambridge, Massachusetts, to take command of the minimalist, but grandiosely titled, Continental Army, ostensibly a force of 17,000. If he succeeded, he would be the father of a new and predestined nation. If he failed, he was running some risk of being hanged as a traitor. He had seen the ineptitude of British forces in America, except when they had overwhelming numbers, and he had certainly seen the insufferable incompetence and arrogance of British colonial administration, and shared Franklin's view of the golden future of America. Britain's greatest statesmen, Chatham (Pitt), Burke, and Fox, were in sympathy with the American project. In one of his greatest Demosthenean oratorical triumphs, Burke urged an almost spellbound but dissentient Parliament to "keep the poor, giddy, thoughtless people of our country from plunging headlong into this impious war."[5]

John Adams forged what would prove the axis of the first administration of the new state and the basis of what became the Federalist Party by being the chief propagator of the Washington legend. None of the general's (as he shortly became) successors in the great office he would hold and establish were better served by their touts and publicists than Washington was by Adams, who must have known there was some hyperbole in his comments, asserting in the summer of 1775 that the general was "a gentleman of one of the first fortunes upon the continent," who was "leaving his delicious retirement [aged 43], his family and friends, sacrificing his ease and hazarding all in the cause of his country." Washington's gamble should not be understated. But Britain was at least as divided as America, as Franklin told him. It had been one thing to land forces on the Atlantic littoral of America and proceed westward and north to deal with outnumbered and under-supplied French, while receiving the cooperation, however grudging, of 2.5 million colonists (not counting several hundred thousand slaves). It would be something else, altogether

---

5.   James MacGregor Burns and Susan Dunn, *The Three Roosevelts: Patrician Leaders Who Transformed America*, New York, Grove Press, 2001, p. 26.

more complicated, to land and sustain forces, or supply them by the tenuous routes from Canada, in sufficient numbers to subdue a rebellious population over an area four to five times as extensive as the British Isles.

The foolishness of the king and his advisers, who would be heckled mercilessly by Britain's greatest parliamentarians (illustrating that whatever the grievances of the Americans, Britain was not quite the tyranny they claimed), could probably be relied upon to produce a great many mistakes. And the principal European powers, especially France, after the drubbing it had so recently received at the hands of the British, would be only too happy to assist in any obstruction of British enjoyment of the spoils of their recent victory. The British were hugely overconfident, because they assumed that almost all the colonists were a good deal more attached to the mother country and the Crown than they were (and they took no account of the substantial segments of the American population that were of Dutch, French, and German origin). No conventional colony had successfully revolted in post-Hellenic times, but there had never been a colony like this millions of headstrong people in as sophisticated a society as the mother country, thousands of miles distant.

For Washington, principle and opportunity conjoined, and it seemed a risk worth taking. For Franklin, it was unfolding as he expected, once he had had a good look at delusional British intransigence, toward an outcome of which he was confident. For Jefferson, much younger and less prominent than the other two, it seemed the tide of events and an idea that could be glamorized and sold. As often happens when people initiate wars, it would be much longer and more difficult than either side imagined, but, the principal American founders must have reasoned, especially Franklin with his intimate knowledge of both sides, it should be easier to exhaust the patience of the British by attrition than to crush the spirit of the distant Americans. Though no one could have known this at the time, suppressing such a revolt, as would be shown in the colonial struggles of the twentith century, from South Africa to Algeria, would generally require at least as many soldiers as there were able-bodied rebels, something vastly beyond the capacities of the British in this case.

Yet the purpose of the conflict was still not unanimously clear in America. In a pattern that would be replicated, there was an incomplete consensus in America about a war already underway. The leading Virginians, especially Washington, Jefferson, and Patrick Henry, and the leading Massachusetts public men, such as John Adams and his cousin, Samuel Adams, claimed the British recourse to force had begun a war for independence. There was a good deal of opinion in New York, Pennsylvania, the Carolinas, and other colonies (or states) that was less militant, still royalist in principle, and was wary of being dragged into a futile war by Virginia plantation owners and Boston merchants.

On July 5, 1775, the Second Continental Congress sent King George III a final and unanimous petition (including Washington and Jefferson and Franklin), asking that he exercise the impartial, overarching legal and moral authority he enjoyed as sovereign of all the British, at home and across the seas, to resolve the dispute between America and the British Parliament. In one of the most catastrophic blunders of British history, he issued a proclamation on August 23, condemning "the traitorous correspondence, counsels, and comfort, of diverse wicked and desperate persons within this realm" and ordered all loyal subjects, whether civilian or military, to use their "utmost endeavors to withstand and suppress such rebellion and to disclose and make known all treasons and traitorous conspiracies." This drew the line, and many of the approximately one-third of Americans who were primarily loyal to the Crown prepared to depart for Britain or Canada; ultimately about 60,000 did depart (though estimates range up to 100,000),[6] three-quarters of them to Canada, where they raised the English-speaking share of the population from less than 20 to over 40 percent, a total of 165,000 people (100,000 French), compared with about 2.5 million free Americans and 300,000 slaves. (As Canada was too northerly for the cultivation of cotton, there was never any economic rationale for slavery in that country.)

The rest of colonial opinion firmed up admirably in support of rebellion, and Franklin, still in intense correspondence with his British friends, ignored the king, whom he took to be a suggestible hothead (with some reason), and lamented "the mangling hands of a few blundering ministers. . . . God will protect and prosper [America]; you will only exclude yourselves from any share in it," he wrote to an English friend.[7] It would be a civil war, and therefore the bitterest of conflicts. Franklin was durably estranged from his son Billy, the royal governor of New Jersey, and after a long and unsuccessful conversation lasting through much of the night in May, they parted, on unfriendly terms. Young Franklin was interned in Connecticut in the ensuing conflict and spent the balance of his life in Britain. They were reconciled after the war. Franklin, now well clear of the harassments of the Penns, was president of the Committee of Safety of Pennsylvania (a precursor to the title of the dreaded authors of the Terror of Prairial in France, in the world's next great revolution, less than 15 years off).

---

6.   Robert Harvey, *A Few Bloody Noses: The American War of Independence,* London, John Murray, 2001, p. 428.

7.   Morgan, *op. cit.,* p. 223.

He called for the construction of ships to harass British men o' war should they approach Philadelphia, and gave an outline of his proposed constitution for the new country in the Congress in the autumn of 1775. He claimed, then and later, to have been opposed to seeking alliances, but on December 9, 1775, he wrote to Charles Dumas, a learned and well-connected salonnier in The Hague, and asked for his informed opinion on the possibility of seeking aid in Europe against the British in a coming insurrection. While he was awaiting a response, the French government sent the Chevalier de Bonvouloir to America to investigate the military and diplomatic prospects. Franklin and his committee eagerly concerted hypotheses with the visitor. The Committee of Correspondence that Jefferson had helped establish, at Franklin's urging, sent Silas Deane to Paris with a mandate to determine whether alliance, or at least recognition, would be attainable from the French.

Thomas Paine's inflammatory pamphlet *Common Sense* called for independence and denounced monarchy generally, and had a huge sale and influence. Washington had sent a force to gain control of the British province of Quebec and persuade the French-speaking Canadians to join the incipient revolt. They captured Montreal but were sent packing before the walls of Quebec. Washington asked Franklin, as the Americans' preeminent diplomat, to try his hand at persuading the Canadians. Unfortunately for the cause, the government of Canada was in the hands of a governor so skillful that had he been given charge of America instead, he might have settled down the whole problem. Sir Guy Carleton, subsequently Lord Dorchester, had caused the British adoption of the Quebec Act in 1774, by which the French Canadians pledged allegiance to the British Crown and the British government pledged preservation of the French language, the Roman Catholic religion, and the civil law. Both sides adhered rigorously to their pledges.

For the French Canadians, there was a credibility problem in the American profession of friendship, as hostility to the French and to Roman Catholicism had been prominent in the attitudes of their late opponents in the French and Indian (Seven Years') Wars. Franklin was empowered to make no such pledge of continuity and cultural security, though he could probably have managed the religious and legal guarantees. But as citizens of a united amalgamation of emancipated colonies, the French population of 100,000 was sure to be subsumed in the English-speaking majority of three million. The Americans had been foraging off the land and were hugely unpopular with the locals, and they were effectively chased out of Canada. (Benedict Arnold, an able general, commanded, and underestimated at the outset, by almost 50 percent, the length of the long trek ahead of him. He led his force well, as he would continue to do as the most controversial figure in the war, but it was an impossible mission.)

From Lexington and Concord, possibly the most mythologized aspects of this entire conflict (no one knows which side fired the first shot "heard round the world"; Paul Revere did not ride alone, never got to Concord, and was arrested by the British in mid-ride; and Longfellow was perhaps the greatest myth-maker of all the fabulists who have had a hand in this, starting with Jefferson), the British repaired to Boston and the armies met at Bunker Hill on June 17, 1775. It was a bloody engagement, and the British retained control of Boston, but it was some-thing of a moral victory for the Americans to have held their own so tenaciously against a larger and better-trained force. The British lost about half of the 2,200 men engaged, and three times as many casualties as the Americans. Washington skillfully besieged Boston, and the British commander, General William Howe, withdrew by sea to Halifax on March 17, 1776.

The war largely adjourned, apart from the redoubled preparations of both sides, until the British reappeared at New York on June 25. Hundreds of transports commanded by the naval commander, Admiral Richard Lord Howe, brother of lands forces commander, General William Lord Howe, transported 30,000 men, a remarkable feat of amphibious warfare for the time. General Howe's second-in-command, Henry Clinton, had proposed going up the Hudson to what is now Morningside Heights, disembarking and cutting off Washington's retreat from his positions on Manhattan and Long Island, which might have been a decisive stroke, but General Howe disembarked on Staten Island on July 2, 1776.

3. THE DECLARATION OF INDEPENDENCE

John and Samuel Adams had pushed through the Congress by a narrow margin a bill ordering each colony to suppress what remained of British government within its borders. A committee was set up to declare the independence of the colonies, consisting of Jefferson (whose "felicity of expression," in Adams's words, was widely recognized), Franklin, Adams, Robert Livingston of New York, and Roger Sherman of Connecticut, representing five different colonies, though only Jefferson represented the South. Jefferson was tasked with writing the draft, which he did over nearly three weeks in the Philadelphia boarding house where he was living. He adapted his draft constitution of Virginia. Adams and Franklin had some substantive suggestions, which Jefferson incorporated, and the draft of the declaration was given to the Congress on June 28, 1776.

Jefferson addressed two objectives: the demonization of George III as a tyrant of Caligulan proportions, whose iniquities justified in themselves the revolt that was starting, and a universal declaration of human rights designed to put the new insurgent regime at the forefront of the Enlightenment's exaltation of human rights, from John Locke to Jean-Jacques Rousseau. The second purpose thunders out of the preamble (and also winds up the document): "We hold these truths to be self-evident: that all men are created equal; that they are endowed by their Creator with certain inalienable rights; that among these are life, liberty, and the pursuit of happiness; that to secure these rights, governments are instituted among men, deriving their just powers from the consent of the governed; that whenever any form of government becomes destructive of these ends, it is the right of the people to alter and abolish it, and to institute new government, laying its foundations on such principles, and organizing its powers in such form, as to them shall seem most likely to effect their safety and happiness."

These words, and the conclusion, pledging everything including "our sacred Honour" to fight for the achievement of independence, have enjoyed an immense historical resonance. Their stirring appeal to natural law and the concept of universal rights and the dignity of all men are justly celebrated, both for their eloquence and their historical importance. But they are a rather grandiose magnification of what was really a straight jurisdictional dispute, over the right of the British Parliament, whose authority had not previously been challenged in America, to levy taxes in America, largely to retire debts incurred in defending the colonists from the French and the Indians. The ill-considered actions of the British government had been as vigorously, and at least as stirringly, debated in the British Parliament as the intrepid accretions of the ambitions of the revolutionaries had been debated in their Congress.

Only the lead weight of the king's friends in Parliament (and this for the last time in British history), backed by the infelicitous combination of jingoism and the pomposity that generally afflicts the attitudes of imperial powers to their colonists, torqued up the press and official and public opinion to take such a strong line against the colonists. It must be said that the Americans had shown an athletic dexterity in shifting from importunity for assistance against France to extreme protectiveness about their right not to be taxed by a previously authoritative Parliament that had, on urgent request, rendered redemptionist services to the rebels. There is no clear absence of right for Britain to tax the colonists, especially at this time and for the reduction of debt subscribed for this purpose. And despite Jefferson's commendable improvisation of self-evident truths and inalienable rights adhering, by act of the Creator, to human life itself, Jefferson and many of the other delegates were slaveholders, and were deists or more distant believers in any notion of a Creator. And the British not only possessed and exercised as many of these rights and truths as the Americans, but they, and not Jefferson's bowdlerized rendering of Enlightenment philosophers, were the source of any American enjoyment of them. It was, in the abstract, a bit rich for these delegates to throw all this back in the face of the Mother of Parliaments, which, whatever its electoral chicaneries and shortcomings, was the world's, and America's, chief source of the rights claimed.

Of course, the British have their own myths, and the Glorious Revolution of 1687 and the Settlement Act of 1701 are pretty weak reeds on which to claim a great coruscation of self-government. The concepts of human rights, the rule of law, and responsible government had, with the utmost difficulty, taken some hold in a few places—Britain, Switzerland, the Netherlands, parts of Scandinavia, and, sketchily and tentatively, a few Italian and German principalities (where, as the future history of those countries would show, they were very fragile and easily revocable). America was not adding much to what already existed, except the genius of presentation and of the spectacle, which Jefferson may be said to have originated in America, as opposed to outright propaganda, a laurel that falls to Paine. These talents that Jefferson bestowed on the questing new regime have never departed the character and society of America, and have been much amplified by media technology, and with Washington's military leadership and Franklin's diplomatic brilliance, must be considered one of the original ingredients of the American story that would command and rivet the attention of the whole world for centuries after.

The other main element of the Declaration of Independence, the representation of George III as an epochal tyrant of satanic odiousness, like the blood libel on the American Indians as barbarous savages of no merit, as if they had not been the rightful inhabitants of the new nation before being rather brusquely displaced, were much more emphasized at the time of publication. And they have, naturally, not weathered the ages as successfully. George III was not a tyrant at all, and his greatest minister up to this time, Chatham (rivaled in all of his 60-year reign only by his son the younger William Pitt), was as strenuous a critic of his policy as the leading American revolutionaries. At the height of these events, the young Charles James Fox, just 26, told the House of Commons on October 26, 1775, nine months before the Declaration of Independence: "The Earl of Chatham, the king of Prussia [Frederick the Great], nay Alexander the Great never gained more in one campaign than the noble Lord North [then the prime minister] has lost—he has lost a whole continent." (Fox betrayed unjustified pessimism about Canada and in the interests of forensic hyperbole ignored Mexico, but he expressed accurately the contempt of the opposition for the king's policy.)

The attack on the Indians was understandable and they were primitive and often barbarous, but few people today would dispute that they had some rights of prior possession that were simply dismissed with a brutality that was cavalier and often aggravated by violations of treaties and agreements on the most spurious pretexts. The British were, if anything, more respectful of native rights than the colonists, and certainly British policy toward Indians in Canada was a good deal more civilized than American, and almost wholly untainted by the corruption that afflicted American policy to Indians from colonial to modern times.

The principal congressional edit of the Declaration was the removal of Jefferson's effort to blame the importation of slavery into the colonies on George III. This from Jefferson, who recognized the moral difficulty of slavery and its potential to disrupt the new country's future but could not bring himself to emancipate his slaves, and carried on a sexual relationship for 38 years with one (Sally Hemings), who bore him seven children and from whom most of his descendants came, is a brazen act of hypocrisy. Fortunately for Jefferson and the acoustical clarity of the call to the ages he was writing, his colleagues saw that the great pamphleteer was intoxicated with his own virtuosity, as man and craftsman, and excised that one allegation.

The British regarded the Americans as ingrates, and they were. The Americans regarded the British as overbearing and presumptuous meddlers, and they were. In the contest of public relations, Washington, Franklin, and Jefferson easily routed George III, a limited, ill-tempered, and intermittently mad young monarch of no particular ability. If Chatham, Burke, and Fox had been able to act in the king's name, there would have been a much narrower issue and a fiercely contested battle for public relations and intellectual rigor. The United States did indeed become a "shining city on a hill" and a "new order of the ages," but in the sense that it was a vast, almost virgin continent being set up politically at the cutting edge of democratic advances that in the Old World had only been reached in a few places, and after centuries of internecine struggles punctuated by violent revolutions and sanguinary changes of regime.

As a practical matter, the American Revolutionary War was a struggle between two almost equally advanced and very conditionalized democracies, and what governed was the correlation of forces as it evolved under the varying levels of military and diplomatic competence and political agility of the two sides. The American leaders doubtless persuaded themselves of a somewhat more exalted moral distinction between the parties. They were men of conviction, certainly, but they were also self-interested opportunists who saw the main chance, painted it with a thick coat of conjured virtue, and deserve the homage due to the bold, the brilliant, the steadfast, and, by a narrow margin, the just. On the legal and political facts, they do not deserve the hallelujah chorus ululated to them incessantly for 235 years by the clangorous American myth-making machine and its international converts.

The British made the classic historic error of trying to impose taxes on people from whom they could not ultimately collect them, not that they were such unjust taxes. And the British explanation of their actions was so inept that the Americans not only withheld the tax but largely grasped the moral-political leadership of the whole planet with a nascent regime already clad in star-spangled swaddling clothes. This was the strategic genius of American national nativity: it discarded the great oceanic powers in order, the French and the British, each with the assistance of the other, and covered this accomplishment in the indefectible virtue of the rights of man. This would be the American formula in centuries to come, under Lincoln, Wilson, the Roosevelts, and in the Cold War, generally with a stronger legal and moral case: the advantage of force and possession of virtue, both applied in carefully selected circumstances.

The Congress had received three resolutions from Richard Henry Lee of Virginia on June 7, 1776, proclaiming "that these united colonies are, and of right ought to be, free and independent states" and should dissolve all political association with Great Britain; proposing "articles of confederation and perpetual union"; and recommending that envoys be sent to France and other powers to seek alliance against Britain. These resolutions were adopted on July 2, and the Declaration of Independence, as all the world knows, was signed on July 4, 1776, though at first only by the president (John Hancock) and the secretary (Charles Thomson) of the Congress. Over the next year or so, most of the other delegates signed.

4. WAR, THE FIRST PHASE

It is not the purpose of this book to give a detailed military history of the Revolutionary War. It took Washington a few months to settle on the correct strategy, and it was to some degree forced upon him as the only remaining option, but it became in many respects the first modern guerrilla war. (Then and subsequently, guerrilla wars have only been conducted by powers that have not had the means to wage real wars.) The British could not occupy the entire insurrectionist territory, as Lord Amherst, who had enjoyed such success in the previous war, calculated that it would require 45,000 troops to occupy New York, Philadelphia, and Newport, and a standing army of at least 30,000 additional soldiers to be prepared to meet the main enemy army at any time. (Philadelphia was the second largest British city, though it only had 34,000 people, compared with London's 750,000, which was the second highest city population in the world after Beijing's, at about one million.) Amherst's optimum force levels were completely out of the question, because the worldwide strength of the British army was 50,000, only about 10,000 of them in North America. A substantial army was always necessary to assure continued control of the immense empire in India.

After eight years of war in America, the British army in all areas would only total 145,000, including 5,000 American loyalists and 30,000 hired Germans (as part of the old exchange with Hanover, which had so often availed itself of British forces). Even at the end of the war, there were just 57,000 of these in America. Washington started with 10,000 regulars and 7,000 militiamen at Boston, which attrition wore down to only 3,000 regulars within a year. Throughout the conflict, Washington rarely deployed more than about 8,000 regulars that moved with him. The Continental Army had about 150,000 members, plus around 100,000 militiamen, and wherever Washington and his later southern colonies commander, Nathanael Greene, went, there were ample forces to set aside what they were doing and rally to the revolutionary colors. John Adams and others had advocated an army of militiamen, but Washington, though his militia were relatively trained as events progressed, never lost his respect for trained professionals and his skepticism about part-time soldiers, who enlisted when the enemy was close by, grumbled at conditions and lack of pay, and melted as soon as they weren't under direct threat to their homes and families.

On August 29, 1776, after a very professional assault by the British, Washington withdrew in good order from Brooklyn to Manhattan. Washington declined to defend Manhattan more than perfunctorily, after tactically blundering badly in advancing his forces across the East River into Brooklyn, where they were roughly handled on land and could have been cut off by water. Both General Howe and Admiral Howe missed their chance out of, it was suggested, relative kinship and hopes for American surrender.[8] Washington did demonstrate great organizational ability and opportunism by evacuating back to Manhattan an army of 9,500 and all their guns in the night of August 30, ignominiously ending what was called the Battle of Long Island. Stronger and swifter action here too, by the Howes, could have done grievous early damage to the Revolution.

---

8. It was a little like the comparative gentleness that some have claimed limited the German approach at Dunkirk 164 years later (Chapter 9). Both interpretations are improbable.

Washington then developed a plan that became general for the war, and retreated to Westchester, drawing the British inland and away from their sea-borne communications and supplies, and into territory where they would have to expend troops protecting their lines against constant irregular harassment. Washington retreated first to White Plains and then to New Jersey, and the British did take 2,700 Americans prisoner at Fort Washington, at the far northern end of Manhattan on November 16. There were again great celebrations in Britain, as in Pitt's time, but it was an illusion; Washington was conducting a Fabian campaign, drawing and pulling British forces fruitlessly about the interior. In New Jersey, he was chiefly concerned to protect Philadelphia. Washington conducted an almost scorched-earth retreat to Trenton, New Jersey, on the Delaware River, and on into Pennsylvania on December 8, 1776, blowing up bridges and leaving the path of the warily advancing British strewn with obstacles and enfiladed by snipers.

At this point, one of Washington's greatest problems was the short and precise enlistments of most of his men. They could pack up and leave after six months, no matter how intensely at grips with the enemy they might be. Washington had pulled together a force of 6,000 on the Pennsylvania side of the Delaware, and just as he seemed in inexorable retreat and the Continental Congress quit Philadelphia for Baltimore, Washington, in the boldest and most original move of his military career to date, recrossed the Delaware, and on Christmas Day and December 26 attacked the British and their German allies at three points, exploiting a considerable post-Christmas hangover of the Germans. As the eminent British historian George Otto Trevelyan wrote: "It may be doubted whether so small a number of men ever employed so short a space of time with greater or more lasting results upon the history of the world."[9]

Washington had sent his skeptical and scheming second-in-command, General Horatio Gates, to Philadelphia, where he agitated to replace Washington, who gambled all the meager forces he had on this daring counter-attack, which moved on to the capture of Princeton and the advance to Morristown, about 10 miles west of the Hudson and Manhattan. It was a masterstroke and is the basis of much of Washington's claim to being a first-rate commander, albeit with small forces. This was where the armies sat, Washington in Morristown and Howe in New York, until the spring of 1777. With expiring enlistments and the months of hard slogging and fighting, Washington's forces had dwindled down to about

9.   William J. Casey, *Where and How the War Was Fought: An Armchair Tour of the American Revolution*, New York, Morrow, 1976, p. 91. This may have been the inspiration for Winston Churchill's comment on the Battle of Britain in 1940: "Never in the field of human conflict was so much owed by so many to so few."

3,000, against nearly 10 times as many under Howe. But Howe did not know how feeble his opponent's numbers were, only that if he attacked, the Americans would draw the British farther into America. Washington was able, as he put it, to "keep up an appearance"[10] and expressed "great surprise that we are still in a calm . . . much beyond my expectation" at the end of March. Howe made a feint with 18,000 men in late June, but Washington outmaneuvered him and the British withdrew to Staten Island. Howe embarked 15,000 men by sea from New York in July and generated great mystery about his destination, as Washington marched his forces to and fro trying to anticipate a landing. This finally occurred in late August near Philadelphia. The Battle of Brandywine ensued, in which the British forced an American withdrawal and inflicted more casualties than they sustained, but the Americans fought well and tenaciously and remained between Howe and Philadelphia, the capital through which Washington had marched his crisply turned-out forces in a morale-boosting parade on the way to the battlefield.

Washington did not have the forces to prevent a direct British march on Philadelphia from two directions by all Howe's forces, and the British captured the city with 18,000 men, more than one for every two inhabitants, on September 26, 1777, without opposition. The Congress had fled again and there remained many loyalists to welcome the British, but maintaining the sea-land supply lines to the occupying forces consumed a large number of troops to no practical military end. It should be remembered that while these operations were under way, almost all the rest of the Thirteen Colonies apart from New York were functionally independent and accustoming themselves to self-government. The British could muscle their way into the large towns but that did not return to them the forced, much less the voluntary, fealty of over two million insurrectionist Americans. On October 4, Washington provided a plan too intricate for his under-trained troops at Germantown just outside Philadelphia. He almost prevailed but had to retire, in good order, having taken about 1,000 casualties out of 11,000 mainly militiamen, to 500 British casualties in a force of 9,000 regulars.

British general John Burgoyne, who had been unwisely given the command in place of the able Carleton, had been approaching New York from Canada, along Lake Champlain, by Fort Ticonderoga (formerly Montcalm's Carillon), and in actions reminiscent of those in the same terrain less than 20 years before. The British plan was to cut New England and the western country off completely from the colonies south of New York, and take Philadelphia as a first step in pushing Washington into Virginia and gradually driving organized rebel military forces

---

10. Casey, *op. cit.*, p. 100.

south and bottling them up and destroying them in the Carolinas. When Burgoyne, who had been repulsed at Ticonderoga in 1776, descended the well-trodden route to New York in 1777, it was evacuated, but at the end of August 1777, some of his units suffered a severe defeat and nearly a thousand casualties in a confused action around Bennington, New York. The American commander was General Philip Schuyler, who was sacked for his trouble and replaced by the politically ambitious General Horatio Gates.

Gates had 7,000 men to block Burgoyne from taking Albany, and his force was increased by nearly 10,000 militiamen. If Burgoyne could reach Albany, it was expected that Howe could advance toward him both by land and on the Hudson and cut the colonies in two. There was an indecisive skirmish at Saratoga on September 19, 1777, and a clear American victory there on October 7, followed by the capture of Burgoyne and the surrender and deportation of his army of over 4,000 after a well-executed pursuit by Gates. This led to what was known as the Conway Cabal, in which there was an attempt to infiltrate the Congress and recruit Lafayette, a French nobleman leading some volunteers from among his Anglophobic countrymen, to assist in displacing Washington in Gates's favor. Washington, who was sensitive to the political currents, rallied Lafayette and squashed the plot. Gates was chastened and the other conspirators were punished. As the historian Robert Harvey remarked, Washington "had not yet proved himself to be a great general, but he was a masterly political operator."[11]

5. FRANCE JOINS THE WAR

Benjamin Franklin had arrived in Paris on December 4, 1776, to seek an alliance. For a time, he was saddled with the less devious and less diplomatic John Adams, who tended to engage his hosts on what he presented as their moral duty to assist the Americans. Franklin, one of the world's most technically sophisticated printers, established a small printing press in his house and began churning out effective, though outrageously inaccurate, pamphlets, alleging British atrocities and making wild claims of the success of American arms. Franklin's puckish sense of humor, as well as his subtle techniques of insinuation and polemical advocacy, were all well-served. Louis XVI was smarting from the cataract of defeats of the Seven Years' War. Franklin dressed very plainly in black and wore a fur hat, and played to perfection the role of the frontier philosopher and the Enlightenment scientist. Louis's foreign minister, the Count of Vergennes, had already persuaded the king to give a million *livres* secretly to the Americans, and despite the warnings of the

---

11. Harvey, *op. cit.*, p. 298.

king's finance minister, the astute A.R.J. Turgot, that the country could not afford to invest much in this effort, the king was lured both by vengeance and by the spirited performance of the Americans. The king and his advisers were even more impressed by Washington fighting it out so effectively at Germantown than they were by the American victories at Saratoga.[12]

Washington marched his now ragged army of 10,000 to Valley Forge, to monitor and, if possible, retake Philadelphia, and went into uncomfortable winter quarters there. He lost a quarter of his men to frostbite and other problems of exposure and malnutrition, but maintained morale; training was improved under the German adventurer Baron Friedrich von Steuben, Washington famously shared the rations of his men, and in the spring of 1778 new volunteers replenished his famished ranks.[13] The war had now been going on for over three years and the British were not close to subduing the rebellion, though they had occupied Philadelphia and New York. And on March 13, 1778, the French government announced a Treaty of Amity with America, a declaration of war on Britain in fact. Franklin's achievement in bringing France, despite its precarious finances, into the war and in support of republicanism and secessionism was an astonishing one. No parliament had sat in France since the young Richelieu had dismissed the Estates General in 1614 with such finality that it did not dare to reconvene until the start of the French Revolution 175 years later, to which revolution the exertions of the American Revolutionary War doubtless contributed. Yet France, instead of seeking a payoff from Britain to remain neutral, was wheedled by Franklin into assisting a movement that in its liberalism would infect much thinking in France, to the peril of the French monarchy. The entire history of diplomacy yields few triumphs so great and important to the world as this coup wrought by Franklin at the age of 72.

On the news from Paris and Saratoga, British policy was reappraised. As would frequently occur in subsequent distant wars against rebellious populations, the commander requested more forces and was removed. Howe, so successful in the Seven Years' War, asked for 10,000 more men.[14] Howe was replaced by General Henry Clinton, and Clinton was ordered to abandon Philadelphia and Rhode

---

12. Casey, *op. cit.*, p. 129. As would be the case in reverse between the British and Americans with the Battle of Britain 163 years later (Chapter 10), the argument for assistance was much strengthened by the performance of the petitioner.
13. The arrival of Von Steuben and other swashbucklers such as the Marquis de Lafayette and the Poles, Tadeusz Kosciusko and Casimir Pulaski, presaged the international attraction of future wars of pure popular motive, such as the Spanish Civil War of 1936–1939.
14. As General William Westmoreland would ask for 206,000 more men after the Tet offensive in Vietnam in 1968 and would be kicked upstairs to army chief of staff just before the commander-in-chief, President Lyndon Johnson, also withdrew (Chapter 14).

Island and to defend the West Indies, where French aggression was feared and which was still more highly prized not only than Canada, as was shown 15 years before, but even than what was left of the British interest in the Thirteen Colonies. Clinton redeployed some of his forces to Florida accordingly (a strategically insane disposition, since there were no enemy forces there and the territory was worthless militarily). Washington gave an army command to Lafayette, largely to encourage tangible French solidarity, and he shared in a skillful harassment of the Howe-Clinton army as it moved from Philadelphia toward New York.

At Monmouth Courthouse in late June, Washington was visible in the action all day on his white horse, showing conspicuous gallantry, and narrowly missed destroying Clinton's army, which crept away in the night and was embarked by the Royal Navy. (Washington destroyed the career of General Charles Lee, whom he used as a whipping boy with very excessive severity, for the escape of the British. He was a very political general.) At this point, and hereafter, it became clear that Washington's strategy was working and that success was likely if the French were of any real assistance. Admiral Count d'Estaing arrived at the mouth of the Delaware River in July 1778 with a substantial fleet, and then engaged in an unsuccessful attempt to displace the British at Newport, Rhode Island. There were British spoiling raids along the New England shore, and the other main actions in the balance of 1778 were in Georgia. The British had no strategy at all to win the war except attrition, which was operating more effectively against them than against the Americans. The war dragged on and the Americans became stronger and the British more exasperated.

In 1778 there was again the danger of invasion of England from France. With much of the British fleet tied up in the Americas, the French army was always large enough to threaten the home islands if it could be got across the Channel. The British and French fleets skirmished indecisively in the Channel in mid-July, but the damage to French rigging and supplies made an invasion effort unlikely in that year. The lack of success of d'Estaing's hovering around the American coast aroused sentiments that were to prove durable: "Americans who recalled the French and Indian Wars and looked upon the French as foreigners and papists, now also regarded them as foppish and cowardly. The aristocratic French looked upon the Americans as vulgar rabble." Lafayette almost fought a duel with an American after hearing "the name of France . . . the leading nation of the world, spoken . . . with disdain, by a herd of Yankees."[15] D'Estaing, as the French too were preoccupied

---

15. Harvey, *op. cit.*, pp. 307–308. Little of this has changed in the intervening centuries, though there were some celebratory moments with the Third Republic, including the one that produced the Statue of Liberty.

with the West Indies, took St. Vincent and Grenada after the British had seized St. Lucia. In India, the capable governor Warren Hastings (about to be unjustly persecuted by Edmund Burke) seized almost all the remaining French enclaves in the subcontinent.

This was to some degree the return of world war, because of the French element, but there was no plan to suppress the revolt that started it and the British planners henceforth really aimed only at breaking off and keeping some of the southern states and Florida, to make the core of a tropical and Caribbean empire. In a classic case of strategists believing what they wanted to believe rather than what was indicated by the objective facts, the British, to borrow a phrase from the Vietnam War, Americanized the war by trying to arm and encourage loyalists along the sea coast. It was nonsense, of course. The loyalists were never more than a third of the country at their most numerous and were less now, and the gap in the mismatch between the leadership talents and quality of command decisions between George III and Lord North on the one hand, and Washington and Franklin on the other, widened steadily. The British blundered into war with the Netherlands after seizing diplomatic correspondence bound for that country, on the high seas, and the blandishments of the French and two centuries of stunted envy brought the Spanish into the war against Britain in the summer of 1779, as it had in the Seven Years' War. The British remained convinced, on no evidence, that most Americans were opposed to the Revolution, and they now intended to assist loyalist groups within the colonies and not try to insert overwhelming force to suppress and occupy the country.

The whole concept was a fantasy, and Washington established himself at West Point, a fort north of New York, where he could move the Continental Army to New England or New Jersey and Philadelphia, as need arose. The British continued to occupy New York City, but apart from that, very few Americans saw much of them from then on, apart from the to-ing and fro-ing with small forces in the South. In the debate on America in Parliament in May 1779, General James Robertson gave the new rationale: "The object of the war was to enable the loyal subjects of America to get free from the tyranny of the rebels, and to let the colony follow its inclination, by returning to the king's government." This was building a revisionist airplane in the air.

On the American side, much has been made of Washington's failure to destroy the British though he had many chances, but he had pursued successfully his political/military strategy, of harassing and containing the British wherever they tried to advance, strengthening the quality of his fighting units, and facilitating the rise of rebel confidence and determination.

As had been the case in the years before the Revolution, the colonies tended to think of themselves and of military deliverance as an entitlement of miraculous origin. Just as they balked at paying their share of the cost of ejecting the French from North America, the colonies, as long as the Redcoats weren't coming across their own fields and through the kitchen door, tended to ignore the Continental Congress's calls for funds. The Congress, which had no authority over the individual states/colonies, droned self-interestedly and loquaciously on, taking pot shots at Washington and others who were risking all for the birth and life of a new nation. The British convinced themselves that the South was a loyalist heartland, and Clinton dispatched 3,500 by sea to Georgia and seized Savannah with a brilliant amphibious operation. Heady with this success, the normally rather diffident Clinton laid claim to Georgia and then marched for Charleston, the largest city in the South, but was stopped and sent swiftly back to Savannah, being as hotly pursued by the American general Benjamin Lincoln as Lincoln's lameness, obesity, and narcolepsy would allow. D'Estaing was persuaded to assist in a recapture of Savannah, but became impatient lest he be taken by surprise by the Royal Navy during the siege and ordered a disastrous attack across a swamp in which more than a quarter of the investing forces were killed. D'Estaing, unashamed at being the author of this fiasco, then withdrew to the West Indies, and Lincoln withdrew to Charleston.

6. THE SOUTHERN CAMPAIGN, 1779–1781

The Spanish posed something of a distraction for the British in western Georgia and Florida, and Clinton was enticed by the southern climes to try his hand at winter war with an amphibious expedition from New York to Charleston at the end of 1779. Like so much of most wars, and certainly this one, macabre farce ensued, as the fleet of over a hundred vessels was severely buffeted by storms, and broken up, and Clinton and the naval commander, Admiral Arbuthnot, hated each other. There was no such concentration of loyal support as the British imagined, and the coastal area of South Carolina had only 19,000 whites and 69,000 slaves, not a rich reservoir of political support even if most of the citizens had been monarchists. The British did finally reach Charleston and Clinton commanded the attack well, took the city, and treated the inhabitants generously. It was the greatest British victory of the war. Unfortunately, one of his cavalry commanders, Banastre Tarleton, soon overran some retreating Virginians near the North Carolina border at Waxhaw in June 1780, ignored a white flag, and massacred the American force, 350 men. This was a shocking breach of discipline and civilized standards of war-making, and resonated ominously. (His excuse was that his horse had been shot out from under him after he had ordered the charge and before he saw the flag of surrender, but this is not believable, as the killing continued for 25 minutes among the idle and prostrate Americans.)

The condition of the Revolution lapsed back to the implacable gloom of Valley Forge, as Washington wintered in Morristown under another heavy winter, with the Congress providing neither funds nor recruits. Washington's army of 15,000, with desertions and some deaths from exposure and malnutrition, dwindled to 5,000 in early 1780. This, coupled with the debacle at Charleston, seemed to bring American fortunes back to their lowest point in a war that had now sputtered on for five years. But it would be clear in time that the greatest impact of this trying time was on Washington's views of post-independence government. He railed at the venality and cowardice of the Congress and assemblies. He lamented that war profiteers had not been "hunted . . . down as the pests of society. I would to God that one of the most atrocious in each state was hung in gibbets upon a gallows five times as high as the one prepared by Hamen."[16] This galvanized Washington into a belief that only a strong, but non-monarchical, executive of a federal state in which the central government had authority in all non-local matters would govern successfully. Washington was as much a politician and administrator, and almost as much a financier, as a specialist in military strategy and tactics, and his conclusions in these trying times, which he navigated with great strength of character and astuteness, would ramify profoundly in the establishment of the state that would eventually emerge from these convulsions.

General Benedict Arnold, who had conducted the arduous march to Quebec, to be sent packing by the French Canadians in 1775, a very capable general who had been unfairly under-recognized because of his relative sympathies for the British (Washington had complained that he had not been promoted), deserted a command position, and missed arrest by a few minutes when he fled West Point in September 1780 and went over to the British, abandoning even his wife. He asked for 20,000 pounds, and received most of it, to lead American forces into a trap, squandering the lives of his men and forfeiting the respect of everyone, permanently, one of the most catastrophic career and public relations misjudgments in history. He wrote Washington, from the aptly named evacuation vessel, HMS *Vulture*: "The heart which is conscious of its own rectitude, cannot attempt to palliate a step which the world may censure as wrong." He asked for gentle treatment

---

16. Harvey, *op. cit.*, p. 334.

of his wife and child, which was accorded. He became a commander of loyalist forces in the war and continued to be a capable combat general.[17]

The British conciliated the Indians and most of them rallied to the British, who had, to the extent they could be distinguished from the American colonists, been more civil and reliable than the Americans. This was to prove more than adequate justification for the Americans, after the war, to redouble their repressions, exploitations, and betrayals of the Indians. A read of Jefferson's harangue on the evils of the Indians in the Declaration of Independence is instructive in that regard. Similarly, large numbers of slaves defected to the British, and as many as 60,000 of the slave population, now approximately 400,000, escaped to Canada and to Britain, or were shipped to free communities in West Africa, but in general, they were recaptured and ground down with even more severity than usual by the authors and adherents of the self-evident truths and inalienable rights with which the Creator had endowed all men.

Gates was appointed to the Southern Command by the Congress, over Washington's support of Nathanael Greene, and the victor of Saratoga quickly suffered the worst American defeat of the war, at Camden, North Carolina, compounded by his headlong flight on galloping horseback to nearly 200 miles from the field of his complete humiliation. He was relieved, and Greene, perhaps the ablest military commander of the war, on either side, replaced him. The French, who were none too impressed with the performance of their ally, sacked the feckless d'Estaing and replaced him with Count de Guichen, and dispatched 5,000 more troops under the capable Count de Rochambeau, and the British gave the Caribbean command to one of the greatest admirals of their prodigious naval history, Sir George Rodney. The Spanish also escalated their efforts, sending 12,000 troops to the Caribbean, of whom a disconcerting 5,000 died like galley slaves en route on the overcrowded, under-provisioned Spanish ships. The shift in naval emphasis to the West Indies assisted the American revolutionaries, and Washington welcomed Rochambeau and his 5,000 soldiers at Hartford on September 21, 1780. Guichen and Rodney engaged and skirmished and the French did well to draw the issue with so distinguished an opponent. The state of the conflict was briefly stable, as the final act began.

Greene found the wreckage of Gates's army, 1,400 "naked and dispirited" troops, at Hillsboro, on November 27, 1780, where the hero of Saratoga had fled after the Camden rout. He faced the British commander, the competent nephew of Prime Minister Robert Walpole, Lord Cornwallis, who had performed well throughout the Revolutionary War in various commands, and had shattered Gates at Camden. What

---

17. Harvey, *op. cit.*, p. 346.

was later reckoned, in Jefferson's pious words, "That joyful annunciation of that turn in the tide of success which ended the Revolutionary War" occurred on November 27, 1980, at King's Mountain, on the border between the Carolinas. A little over a thousand British and loyalists commanded by a fierce Scot, Patrick Ferguson, met 1,400 "overmountain" men, virtual hillbillies, commanded by their militia-leading landlords, John Sevier and Isaac Shelby, and almost the entire British force was killed or captured. The overmountain men were tall and lean and agile, had matted hair, and seemed like savages to their enemies, and behaved accordingly. The rulebook having been dispensed with by Tarleton at Waxhaw, the Americans massacred many of the British and left many more to be eaten by wolves. They marched 700 prisoners off, but many of those perished also. The small and almost inadvertent engagement demonstrated, as would many sequels in other distant partly colonial, partly guerrilla wars, that the side that is in revolt only has to win occasionally to keep the fires burning, and the overseas power becomes easily demoralized by any defeat.

The British were now facing not only the war's most able field commander in Greene and his deputy, Daniel Morgan, but also guerrilla warriors of genius, in Thomas Sumter and especially General Francis "Swamp Fox" Marion. Cornwallis moved cautiously from Camden toward Charlotte, and in January 1781, after the setback at King's Mountain, he sent Tarleton to deal with the very able Morgan, while he went into North Carolina after Greene. Tarleton charged impetuously uphill after Morgan, at Cowpens on January 13. Morgan had 200 militiamen fire twice and then retreat as if in rout, and as the British reached the crest of the hill, in probably the most finely executed action of the war, Morgan's main force poured fire onto the British, who broke and retreated, with the Americans on their heels. Tarleton bravely fought to the end, and was finally chased off with only 40 survivors, having lost over a thousand men to the Americans, who sustained only 70 casualties. Both armies regrouped and their combined forces met at Guilford Court House, North Carolina, on March 15, 1781, and Cornwallis did well to repel Greene, though outnumbered. It was not a decisive victory and the British lost 500 men to 300 American casualties. (Loyalists fighting with the British, when captured, often received a very rough and not infrequently mortal treatment; it had become a very nasty war.)

7. YORKTOWN

The Americans, with the advantage of interior lines, could reinforce Greene by land, but Cornwallis depended on supply from New York, and neither the timorous Clinton in New York nor the vacillating home government would send reinforcements. Finally, the masses of waiting loyalists upon whose existence the southern strategy was based didn't exist and the whole British Americanization plan was a fiasco. Cornwallis, faced with the necessity to fall back to Charleston and pursue a southern redoubt strategy with no prospects of long-term survival, or make a huge gamble to try to win the war, marched for Virginia. Cornwallis arrived at the head of 1,000 regulars at Petersburg, a city that would recur in American military history (Chapter 6), on May 20, 1781, and was joined by Benedict Arnold at the head of 4,000 loyalists. Virginia's governor, now Thomas Jefferson, had almost no forces, as almost all Virginians inclined to war-making were with Washington outside New York. Jefferson's many talents did not run to military preparations. Richmond was being defended by Lafayette with 500 militiamen. Washington's cousins offered supplies to a British contingent to prevent the sacking of Mount Vernon, eliciting a severe rebuke from the American commander, who would have preferred that "they had burnt my house and laid my plantation in ruins. . . . You should have reflected on the bad example of . . . making a voluntary offer of refreshments to them with a view to prevent a conflagration."[18]

Cornwallis vainly chased Lafayette around Virginia, enduring the attrition of minor skirmishes as well as the harassments of Clinton, who kept ordering him to detach and divert packets of troops for footling purposes. The British held New York, Wilmington, Charleston, and Savannah, but Washington, though enfeebled by desertions and mutinies, still held the rest of the North and Greene and Marion and Morgan roamed around the interior of the South at will. The British, after nearly seven years of fighting, could not suppress the revolt, and the Americans were still not able to win the decisive battle. But the inability of the British to win was permanent, as they were not winning over the population and could spare no more troops for the campaign. At some point, there was a danger that the Americans would win a main-force engagement, and reduce the British to mere perches on shore while domestic British support for this endless and costly attrition withered. And Britain could not keep large units of its navy endlessly overseas shuttling forces around the eastern shore of America. It was all right to chase the French and Spanish and Dutch fleets around, but not to leave them alone to transport a French army across the English Channel for months on end attending to distractions in America. Something finally had to give. The French had no confidence in the Americans and proposed a peace allowing both sides to keep what they held. Fortunately for the Americans, while Franklin led the opposition to such a settlement, George III would not concede an inch to the rebels.

Finally, Washington persuaded Rochambeau, who had been idling in Newport for a year, to bring his 4,000 men to join him in Westchester. The new French

---

18. Harvey, *op. cit.*, p. 391.

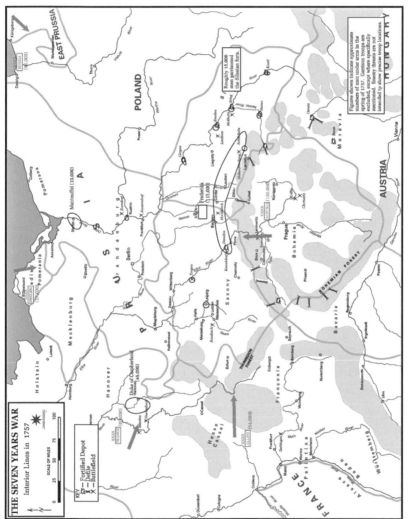

EAST PRUSSIA

POLAND

HUNGARY

AUSTRIA

Moravia

Bohemia

BOHEMIAN FOREST

Bavaria

Saxony

Brandenburg

Mecklenburg

Holstein

Hanover

Hesse Cassel

THÜRINGIAN FOREST

Franconia

FRANCE

Württemberg

Baden

Alsace

Lorraine

Pomerania

Berlin

Prague

Vienna

Seven Years War in Europe. Courtesy of the Department of History, United States Military Academy

admiral Count de Grasse, as much more capable and aggressive than Guichen as Guichen had been compared with the hapless d'Estaing, sailed from the Dominican Republic on August 14, 1781, with 3,300 soldiers on board. Washington, in one of his several acts of both tactical and strategic genius in the long war, pretended merely to be shifting forces around New York as he rushed south in forced marches, but he left only 3,500 men facing the indolent Clinton with 11,000 Redcoats in New York City. Washington and Rochambeau had a triumphant progress through the streets and banqueting halls of Philadelphia as de Grasse disembarked his forces in Chesapeake Bay in the first days of September. Unfortunately for the British, Admiral Rodney, after many successes in the West Indies, returned to Britain to restore his health and fortunes and defend himself in Parliament, and the bumbling Admiral Sir Thomas Graves was left to deal with de Grasse. Graves was afraid to enter Chesapeake Bay and was thus unable to evacuate Cornwallis, who was now encircled on land by over 15,000 French and Americans around Yorktown.

Clinton promised to relieve Cornwallis by land and send Graves back with adequate forces to disembark him, but neither occurred. Cornwallis had 8,300 men bottled up in Yorktown, at the southern end of Chesapeake Bay. Fearing British reinforcements by sea, as Clinton was not moving on the ground, Washington pressed the siege forward as quickly as he prudently could. The British surrendered on October 17, 1781. Cornwallis feigned illness and his second-in-command, Brigadier Charles O'Hara, handed his sword to Rochambeau, trying to maintain the pretense that the British had been defeated by the French alone. Washington had 8,500 men to Rochambeau's 7,000, and had first seen the possibilities for Yorktown, but the French had the artillery and de Grasse drove off Graves, so it was a largely French battle in a mainly American war. Rochambeau treated Cornwallis very graciously, even lending him 10,000 pounds when he did appear, and the British band played "The World Turned Upside Down" as they marched out. As when he had crossed the Delaware with inferior forces and defeated the British at Princeton and Trenton, Washington had acted boldly and brilliantly, seeing at once the opportunity to concentrate forces around Yorktown and marching his and Rochambeau's long-inactive forces at astounding speed through summer heat to the task. He was as brilliant in the swingeing stroke as he was implacable in the long periods of demoralizing inactivity, pecked at and aggravated by venal and spineless politicians.

Yorktown did not end the war but it was like Stalingrad, or Dien Bien Phu in Vietnam in 1954, or the Tet Offensive in 1968 (Chapters 11, 14, 15)—a dramatic (in the case of Tet, public relations, not military) victory that knocked the stuffings out of the morale of one side while lifting the other. As would happen to

America in the Vietnam War, Parliament finally rebelled against the king's policy and in November 1781 voted to refuse to approve any further offensive actions in America. Lord North was dismissed as prime minister after 12 disastrous years and the closest colleague of the late Earl of Chatham (who had died in 1778), the Marquis of Rockingham, was invested. (But power really resided in the conciliatory Earl of Shelburne, a friend of Franklin's, who was theoretically charged with the nonsensical mission of talking the Americans back into the British realm. The British were still not, and probably are not yet, sure of what the Americans were so upset about.) Charles James Fox was put in charge of negotiating an exit from the war, and sent Thomas Grenville to Paris to deal with Franklin.

As war gave way to diplomacy, Franklin, now 76, reemerged as the key figure in the American leadership. The French wished to take back some of what had been lost in the Seven Years' War; the Americans wanted unconditional independence for their territory and Canada; the British would give no more than they had to, but would prefer concessions to their belligerent American cousins (whom Rockingham and Fox had generally sympathized with) than to their ancient French foes. The Americans would not be a threat to them in the Americas, but French revival would. The French had effectively won the war for the Americans, with de Grasse, Rochambeau, and Lafayette, and had a strong moral argument opposite Franklin. The dithering Congress, fearing the inexhaustibly wily Franklin's affinity for the French, had sent the incorruptible John Adams to help shore him up. This was not necessary, and the French found Adams stiff, unilingual, and self-righteous. He shortly moved on to the Netherlands to try to negotiate a loan with the Dutch. (It was nonsense anyway, as the same Congress had purported to instruct the commissioners to be guided by the French, which Franklin, who in practice acted on his own account for America until late on, ignored, as he carried on complex, secret discussions with all sides, inscrutable behind his mask as the affable and frank American frontier patriot and absent-minded scientist.) Franklin had had great success contracting loans with France during the active phases of the war. He was not prepared to offer more than moral appreciation for moral claims, and the issue was resolved when Admiral Rodney returned to the West Indies, discovered a French-Spanish plan to seize Jamaica, and smashed the enemy fleet, taking the doughty de Grasse prisoner. This timely whipping awakened the French from their reverie about regaining an empire in the Americas.

With all sides acting with extreme duplicity, and the Spanish not even recognizing American independence and seeking a comeback in North America themselves, Franklin, suffering from kidney stones, handed over negotiations to the recently arrived minister to Spain, the very able John Jay, but with continuing guidance and retaining general oversight. The British hand was strengthened by the repulse in 1783 of one of the longest sieges in history, by the French and Spanish at Gibraltar after four years. Britain raised the ante, demanding payment of American prewar debts that had provoked the taxes and the insurrection in the first place, and compensation for the expropriated and displaced American loyalists. Jay and Franklin accepted to compensate the loyalists, but did so on behalf of the 13 individual states, as they were about, officially, to become, knowing that it was unlikely they would produce a brass farthing. The British agreed to this flimflam, dropped their debt claims in the broader context of secret side deals dividing between them navigation rights on the Mississippi, and conceding, as between them, everything east of that river to the Americans; i.e., the British were inviting the Americans to evict the Spanish, including from Florida. In the final Treaty of Paris, signed on September 3, 1783, Britain recognized American independence while retaining all of Canada and Newfoundland and its gains in the West Indies, returned Minorca again to Spain, but retained Gibraltar. Sir Guy Carleton, who was the last British commander in America, ignored Washington in the handover ceremonies in New York, and evacuated all 3,000 fugitive slaves from under plantationer Washington's nose.

The Spanish gained nothing, and the French had been swindled by Franklin into providing and by Washington into deploying the margin of victory, as well as vital financial support, and had nothing to show for it but more war debts and the flashing sparks of republicanism and democracy in the dry straw and tinder that now underlay the French monarchy and aristocracy. They might have judged from the British experience as the colonists' creditors how quickly the Americans would be repaying them.

Franklin had played the diplomatic cards brilliantly, and his construction, maintenance, and disassembly of the French alliance was one of the masterpieces of world diplomatic history, made more piquant by his masquerade as a guileless though witty yokel, pitched perfectly to the susceptibilities to narcissism and grandiosity of the French court, as he had previously so well gauged the temper of the ruling circles in London. Washington had made his mistakes but had been brilliant when necessary, and cautious when in error, and had maintained a largely unpaid, ragtag army in existence despite nearly eight demoralizing years of attrition and the endless prattling and meddling of contemptible politicians, masquerading as sovereign legislators in their forcibly itinerant Congress. Jefferson had not had a good war as a rather unresourceful war governor, but he had launched the great American claim to universal values and exceptionalism—a mystique that would grow and flourish for generations after the indispensable services of Washington and Franklin had receded into the mists of folklore and he would continue to propagate them in the new nation's highest offices and then in a long and esteemed retirement.

8. ARTICLES OF CONFEDERATION

Of the three resolutions of the Congress on Richard Henry Lee's motions in June 1776, independence had been achieved and Jefferson's independence declaration-drafting committee, like Washington's specific military command, had been overwhelmingly successful. So had Franklin's diplomatic mission. But the committee to produce "articles of confederation" had not produced a viable framework for a united country. The fulfillment of the founders' dreams would require that this subject be addressed before this brave new world would be fairly launched. The Congress had purported to spend about $200 million but had no power to tax and was dependent on the colonies, or states, to back its obligations. These jurisdictions were not much friendlier to central authority than they had been with the British, and efforts to pass a federal constitution, including Franklin's original effort and John Dickinson's sequel, were rejected. In November 1777, Articles of Confederation were approved which made the states sovereign and ignored federalism. In fact, the only authority in the shattered jurisdiction was General George Washington and his army. The strength, wisdom, and character of the example he set can be best understood by the results when the Latin American republics, 40 years later, revolted and yielded to the temptation of military rule. Washington rejected such overtures, and condemned petitions to Congress urging Greene and others to seize power after vehemently declining to do so himself.

Washington urged his countrymen "to express your utmost horror and detestation of the man who wishes, under specious pretenses, to overturn the liberties of our country, and who wickedly attempts to open the flood gates of civil discord, and deluge our rising empire in blood."[19] He consented reluctantly to the demobilization of the Continental Army, but warned that it remained to be seen whether the Revolution he had led to victory was "a blessing or a curse, not to the present age alone, for with our fate will the destiny of unborn millions be involved." He called for "an indissoluble Union of the States under one Federal Head"; the honoring of public debt; the establishment of armed forces; and a spirit of cooperation and sacrifice among all the states. Washington took leave of his comrades at New York on December 4, 1783, in probably the most emotional public occasion of American history, and on December 23 handed over his sword to the president of the Continental Congress (Thomas Mifflin, whom he

---

19. Harvey, *op. cit.*, p. 434.

despised and had fired as quartermaster general of the army), taking "leave of all my employments of public life." Mifflin replied with a majestic statement written by Jefferson, concluding somewhat ambiguously with "earnest prayers that a life so beloved may be fostered with all His care; that your days may be happy as they have been illustrious, and that He will finally give you that reward which this world will not give." Washington was not quite prepared to sign off on the possibilities of the present world, though he returned to Mount Vernon on Christmas Eve, and wrote to friends and even casual correspondents of his relief at being able now to live quietly on his estates.

In fact, he put himself at the disposition of the public and in the reserve of the new nation, the chief facilitator of the American project, with a greater right than anyone to require that the supreme sacrifices of the 15,000 or so Americans who had died and the devastation that had laid waste much of the country and reduced the economic product by about 45 percent[20] not have been in vain. He was charging the Congress with the task of justifying and completing the Revolution, knowing that the chances of it doing so were zero.

In Paris and Versailles, despite the abrasions of the peace process, Franklin was a national hero, even appointed by King Louis XVI to a scientific commission. He and Washington were almost universally admired, and Franklin was the lion of the salons of both London and Paris, in a manner probably never approached by anyone else. He became acquainted and often friendly with the leading *philosophes*, and counseled liberal reforms but warned against anything violent. As always, his advice was good, and as was often also true, it was not followed. He retired his commission in 1785, aged 79, and then stopped with friends in England, his immensely alluring personality and intelligence overcoming all the vexations of epochal disputes. He was reconciled with his son, the former governor of New Jersey, and returned to a hero's welcome in Philadelphia.

The Congress and all the states were printing money and the Congress eventually devalued all currency by 97.5 percent. Washington's brilliant but impulsive aide, Alexander Hamilton; Jefferson's understudy, James Madison; and Robert Morris, the Philadelphia financier who financed much of the war, proposed a 5 percent import duty, but a number of the states refused to cooperate. To some extent the states reneged on their financial obligations generated by the Revolutionary War, just as they had refused to contribute to the British to help pay for the eviction of the French from Canada. It was the same stingy impulse, but they were now largely, themselves, the creditors of their own almost worthless war debts.

---

20. Harvey, *op. cit.*, p. 438.

Poverty stalked the country except for parts of Pennsylvania and New York and New Jersey; debtors' courts were busy, and reformers such as Jefferson, whose talents were much more evident in peacetime as he abolished primogeniture and proposed universal education, broadened the franchise to assure a voice to the less prosperous. It was clear by 1785 that the system was not working, as the British, in particular, had predicted.

A land dispute between Maryland and Virginia had been settled amicably under Washington's auspices at Mount Vernon, and Washington asked the 34-year-old James Madison, a brilliant Virginian lawyer and legislator, to convene a meeting between representatives of the states to discuss interstate commerce. Five states were represented at Annapolis, Maryland, at the meeting in September 1786. Shays' Rebellion in late 1786 and January 1787, an uprising of destitute Massachusetts farmers, was put down by swiftly recruited militia, but led to suspension of some taxes, and emphasized the absurdity and impotence of the political system. Congress was reduced to asking the states to grant it the power to impose certain taxes, and New York vetoed this.

Twelve states, all but Rhode Island, then called for a constitutional convention to meet at Philadelphia in May 1787. Enthusiasm for the idea of a federal constitution was sketchy in many state elites. In Virginia, Washington and most of the rest of the 40 families that owned the great plantations favored a strong federal government. Jefferson was absent as minister in Paris (where he succeeded Franklin in 1785), and Jefferson's cousin, Edmund Randolph, was skeptical. Patrick Henry, the radical Virginian independence leader, disapproved the project and did not attend, though he was elected a delegate. John Adams was absent as minister in England (where he was graciously received by George III). Also absent were his anti-federalist cousin, Samuel Adams, and states' rights advocate John Hancock. The autonomist governor of New York, General George Clinton, boycotted, and the New York delegation was effectively led by the young and brilliant, but none too democratic or representative, Alexander Hamilton. Benjamin Franklin and Robert Morris led the Pennsylvanians. Some delegations were chosen by state assemblies, but some were supplemented by invitations from the conveners.

Washington was in the background, but he and Franklin, who had been proposing federal arrangements since the Albany Congress of 1754, were the real champions of a strong federal state. Washington's challenge to the state assemblies to justify the ideals of the Declaration of Independence and the long and bloody war that followed it had, as he expected, not been met. He would not seize power as many had urged when his army was demobilized, but he was conspicuously available now, to be the legitimately chosen father of the nation in peace as he had been in war. At the instigation of the 81-year old Franklin, Washington was elected president of the Constitutional Convention, and as host, in his splendid role of president of Pennsylvania, Franklin was elected chairman, the two indispensable founders of the nation ensconced at the head of the unfolding process. Franklin, suffering from gout and gallstones, was conveyed by sedan chair to and from the proceedings, by inmates of the municipal prison (with whom he was courteous and jaunty). The two grand strategists and chief elders of America were ready for the supreme effort to complete their work: the replacement of the French threat to British America, and of the British overlordship of a post-French America, with a government that could lead independent America to greatness and fulfill the promise of Jefferson's luxuriant Declaration of Independence.

9. THE CONSTITUTIONAL CONVENTION

Most of the delegates to the Constitutional Convention were effectively self-chosen. It was assumed that state governors and some senior figures of the legislatures could come ex officio. The Virginians arrived first, led by their governor, Edmund Randolph (Washington being present in his national capacity by common wish, ratified by his election as president of the Convention). At first, the advocates of states' rights and autonomy hung back, not wishing to be involved in a project whose aims they disapproved. As more states sent delegates and the sponsorship of Washington and Franklin lent it momentum and gravity, most decided that it could be contrary to their interests not to be present. By June, all the states except Rhode Island, which had been reduced almost to anarchy, and New Hampshire were present. There were 8 planters and farmers, 21 practicing lawyers and also some that were not active members of the profession, and 15 merchants. As in other parliaments and special conventions of the time, the working class and small farmers, not to mention the tenant farmers and indigent, were represented only in the altruistic afterthoughts of the more prosperous.

Washington stayed in Philadelphia with Robert Morris, the wealthy financier who had been the treasurer of the revolutionary government in fact, apart from what Franklin and Adams could raise overseas. Morris and the unrelated Gouverneur Morris were delegates, and among others who would be prominent were Rufus King of Massachusetts, Roger Sherman of Connecticut, William Livingston and William Paterson of New Jersey, Jared Ingersoll, and Thomas Mifflin and James Wilson of Pennsylvania, John Dickinson of Delaware, Daniel Carroll of Maryland, John Blair of Virginia, William Blount of North Carolina, and Pierce Butler and cousins Charles and Charles C. Pinckney of South Carolina, as well as Madison and Hamilton. The radical and populist elements were largely under-represented, though they certainly had their say when the time came to ratify the arrangements that emerged, in the legislatures of the several states. The discussions and side-arrangements of the Constitutional Convention are intricate and interesting, but are also not the subject of this book, which is rather concerned with the strategic direction and management of the United States, from its emergence as a concept to the time of writing. The governing arrangements of the country are immensely important to this narrative, but the precise interaction of men and events that produced them, beyond the designs of the country's chief political architects, are not.

On May 29, Randolph introduced the Virginia Plan, drafted by Madison, approved by Washington, and based on Jefferson's constitution of Virginia. Some of the states had lower houses broadly enfranchised, and upper houses elected by people who were larger taxpayers or property owners, who sometimes had life tenure. Some, like Pennsylvania, had a single house chosen by everyone who paid any tax, and there were various gradations in between. Jefferson was controversial, though a wealthy plantation and slave-owner, as he was a liberal who famously said: "My observations do not enable me to say I think integrity the characteristic of wealth."[21] The Virginia Plan had a two-house federal Congress—a popularly elected House of Representatives and a Senate chosen by the state legislatures. The Congress would choose the executive and judiciary and would have powers over all matters of interstate scale, reducing states to the level of local government. The smaller states objected that they would be swamped by the influence of the larger ones, and the populist elements saw this as a matrix for aristocratic and oligarchic rule, if not a centralized despotism scarcely less odious than the one from which they had all just successfully revolted. (There was some justice in both criticisms, which again highlights the fact that Britain was a relatively democratic country, and had become more so since the failure of the king's American policy imposed on an unconvinced and ultimately rebellious Parliament.)

The under-represented masses, insofar as they existed in these colonies where the largest city had just breasted the 40,000 mark, were in the larger states, and so both their spokesmen and the conservatives were unimpressed with the argument for equality of small states, as states were imaginary or arbitrary creations in America, not distinct cultural and linguistic entities as in Europe. Some of the smaller states' representatives, such as Gunning Bedford of Delaware, hinted that the aid of foreign allies of the small states might be solicited, to which Gouverneur Morris replied: "The country must be united. If persuasion does not unite it, the sword will. The gallows and halter will finish the work of the sword." Threats

---

21. Harvey, *op. cit.*, p. 444.

of bayonet attacks and the attentions of the hangman are pretty robust debating gambits, especially between recent victorious comrades-in-arms, who had crusaded for universal human rights.

A triangular arrangement was agreed, in an impressive model of constructive compromise, where both Washington and Franklin, who were largely silent in the formal proceedings but convened delegates singly and in small groups privately, played a capital part. All of the states would have equal representation in the Senate, whose members would be chosen not by the lower house, as in the Virginia Plan, but by the legislatures of the country's constituent states. The lower House of Representatives would be represented in proportion to its population, except the southern states took the position, en bloc, that they would not touch the notion of a federal state unless the slave population was factored into the weight given to the size of state delegations to the House of Representatives.

The compromise reached was that for purposes of calculating the representation of states in the House of Representatives, three-fifths of slaves would be counted. For these purposes, this effectively gave the slave states' free citizens 1.5 to 1.6 times the voting power of each eligible voter in free states. Though covered over in verbose piffle about different economic criteria for voting in different states, this was an ugly arrangement certain to breed and amplify resentment. Many thoughtful southerners, including Jefferson, had moral reservations about slavery, "a fire bell in the night," he later called it. Much more numerous were northerners, especially in the puritanical Northeast, who thought slavery an outright evil, shaming, blasphemous, and unchristian. Thus to adapt slavery to the comparative political advantage of the slaveholder was a bitter pill to swallow. The southerners even tried to exempt slavery from taxation in the Constitution but were unsuccessful, but did get a guarantee that slavery would be unchallenged for at least 30 years. Again, Franklin, who had become a quiet opponent of slavery and would become head of the Pennsylvania anti-slavery society, was instrumental in getting the compromise approved. He lobbied quietly with his usual argument that the triumph of American democracy was inevitable and that it would dwarf slave-holding cotton states as it would dwarf little Britain, and that what was needed was a long view.

There was passionate disagreement over the nature of the executive. Alexander Hamilton, who was a native of the West Indies, never had bought all the way into republicanism and favored an elected monarchy for set terms. This was generally seen as the sighting shot in Washington's claim to the headship of a new state, as long as it had a coherent federal framework. There were calls for an elected chief of state who would not be styled a king. Some thought Congress should elect the chief executive, some the people, and the populists and the large-state conservatives were on the same side of the argument again. Another, rather intricate compromise emerged: the president and the vice president (a nebulous position whose occupant had the right of succession between quadrennial elections and would preside over the Senate "like an unwanted poor relation in a wealthy family"),[22] would be chosen by an Electoral College of state representatives, in which each state would have as many electors as it had members of the two houses of Congress combined. This again pleased the populists by getting the vote closer to the people, and the large state delegates for recognizing their influence. In the event of an absence of a majority in the Electoral College, the election would be decided by the House of Representatives, with each state delegation casting a single vote reflecting the wishes of the majority of its congressmen.

There was an effort by the conservatives to restrict the vote in the lower house to propertied elements, on the theory that large employers would buy or otherwise control the votes of their employees. Madison and Franklin debunked this as likely to lead to another revolution. It was agreed that Congress could impeach and remove the chief executive, though the process would be a great deal more complicated than a mere vote of no-confidence as in the British Parliament. Members of the House would be elected to two-year terms and of the Senate to six-year terms, a third to be up for reelection every two years. It was an admirable compromise, but far from the exercise in pure democracy that was necessary to be consistent with the superlatives of the Declaration of Independence, and with other incitements to war against a nation that essentially had as popularly based and accountable a government, albeit on the basis of a shifting mass of practices and precedents rather than a constitution. The compromise went to a drafting committee, called the Committee of Style, consisting of William Samuel Johnson of Connecticut, Rufus King, Gouverneur Morris, Madison, and Hamilton, on September 8, 1787. The committee reported in four days later, and the Constitution was adopted by the weary delegates, after a general refusal to continue the convention to discuss a bill of rights.

The ratification process precipitated another prolonged crisis of horse-trading, threats, sulks, and blandishments. In Massachusetts, the two recalcitrants, John Hancock and Samuel Adams, relented in their hostility to the Constitution. Hancock presided over the state constitutional convention and it was suggested that he might be a fine candidate for vice president of the new republic. Samuel Adams, an almost deranged Anglophobe and relentless critic of any authority, even a presumptive one like Washington, agreed to support ratification in exchange for

22. Jeffrey St. John, *Constitutional Journal: A Correspondent's Report from the Convention of 1787*, Ottawa, Illinois, Jameson Books, 1987.

a bill of rights of individuals. This would take the form of a list of amendments to be recommended to the first Congress. On this basis, the new Constitution was adopted by a narrow margin, by 187 to 168 in Massachusetts, and by only 10 votes in New Hampshire and Virginia, despite the support of Washington, the absent Jefferson, the chief framer Madison, the rising James Monroe, and even Patrick Henry. And in New York, prodigies of persuasion by Alexander Hamilton notwithstanding, the Constitution was adopted by three votes in the legislature, over the objections of the four-term governor, General George Clinton (who served five more terms). North Carolina only ratified in 1789 and balky little Rhode Island in 1790, though there was by then no doubt that failure to ratify would have resulted in that little state's being subsumed into Connecticut and Massachusetts. The Bill of Rights was eventually agreed in 1791, and was adopted in the first 10 amendments to the Constitution.

By a hair's breadth, the new nation had endowed itself with a Constitution that would serve it well and become one of the most renowned and respected texts in human history. No famous law-giver since Moses (who was, after all, a messenger), from Hammurabi to Justinian to Napoleon, remotely approached the triumph of, principally, James Madison, who devised the system of checks and balances between three co-equal branches of government. So great was Madison's prestige, he wrote important messages for Washington, and on occasion, when the message was addressed to the House of Representatives, wrote the reply as well. Hamilton opposed a Bill of Rights, on the spurious grounds that it was unnecessary because the Constitution did not authorize the government to violate anyone's rights, betraying a faith in the benignity of official executive authority that makes it clear that Hamilton had no interest at all in individual rights. Madison himself was lukewarm initially, until Jefferson remonstrated with him and he saw that nothing less would get the Constitution ratified and adopted. Madison's achievement in producing a Constitution that secured federal authority, balanced the branches of a stable government, and assured individual rights, established him in the front rank of the nation's founders, and was another immense and fortuitous strategic milestone for the emerging country.

That it was adopted was a felicitous stroke for America, a happy launch that enabled the new nation to assure itself and offer to immigrants a regime of ordered liberty and a society of laws that was slightly less girt about by impediments of tradition and antique formalism than Britain's. Jefferson's genius at the propagation of the new American era electrified the world. The words of Gouverneur Morris's splendid preamble became and remained familiar to virtually every informed person in the world: "We the People of the United States, in order to form a more perfect Union, establish Justice, insure domestic Tranquility, provide for the common defense, promote the general Welfare, and secure the Blessings of Liberty to ourselves and our Posterity, do ordain and establish this Constitution for the United States of America." Those chiefly responsible for creating the circumstances that permitted, and generated the necessary support for, the promulgation of this document—Washington, Franklin, Jefferson, Hamilton, Madison, John Jay, and John Adams—did not doubt that it would guide the new country to glory and preeminence among nations, and that their work would long be discernible among men.

There was never much suspense about who would get the call as the first president; for the last time in the history of the country, someone would truly accept a draft to that office. Washington received the blandishments of Hamilton rather neutrally and expressed no interest in the presidency to anyone, saying only that he would accept it if to decline it would hurt the country. It is believable that he did not especially wish to be president, but not that he did not expect to be president. He was encouraged that supporters of the Constitution, called Federalists, won the congressional elections, and when the Electoral College gave all 69 votes to Washington voluntarily, without his ever having expressed even a private word of desire for the office, he had no choice but to accept, as he had accepted the command of the Continental Army. In what has proved an enduring tradition of using the vice presidency to provide regional balance, it was contested between John Adams and John Hancock. Washington made it known that he would be happy with Adams, a more staunch Federalist than Hancock and a personal loyalist, and Adams was narrowly chosen. George Washington, who in 1785 had described the notion of American unity as "a farce," was inaugurated the first president of the United States, eight weeks late, on April 30, 1789.[23] In the 35 years since the Seven Years' War effectively began in the backwoods of America (partly because of Washington's actions)—a war that established Prussia as a Great Power, delivered all of India to Britain, and expelled France from North America—the American colonists had developed a burning, independent patriotism and brilliant national leadership, had outmaneuvered the greatest nations in Europe, had electrified the world, had restored serious republican government to the world after an absence of 17 centuries, had politically formalized the Enlightenment by endowing themselves with novel but instantly respected political institutions, and had set forth in the world, as their greatest subsequent leader famously said, "dedicated to the proposition that all men are created equal." An epochal political and national experiment had been prepared by a brilliant sequence of strategic triumphs.

---

23. Burns and Dunn, *op. cit.*, p. 45.

Thomas Jefferson

CHAPTER THREE

Creating a New Republic
and Launching It in the
World, 1789–1809

1. THE WASHINGTON PRESIDENCY

There was no precedent for Washington. It had been centuries since there had been even a marginally serious republic and there had never been a constitutional one. The whole notion of constitutional government was fragmentary. In Britain, some of the Swiss cantons, parts of the Netherlands and Scandinavia, and a few of the German and Italian jurisdictions there were some institutional restraints on executive authority and some rights vested in individual citizens. But the Bill of Rights guarantees of due process, insurance against capricious prosecution, just compensation for seized property, the presumption of innocence for accused, access to counsel, prompt justice, reasonable bail (almost all of which have become pretty moth-eaten in practice at time of writing)[1] and the attribution of unallocated powers to the states or the people themselves showed at least a conceptual respect for individual liberties that was unique in the world and was widely acclaimed as such.

There was no assumption in the late eighteenth century that government had any purpose except defending the country, maintaining internal order, overseeing a currency of integrity, and generally administering laws and facilitating lawful and useful activities as defined from time to time. Washington had challenged the Continental Congress, when he took leave of his demobilized army in 1783, to maintain adequate armed forces, honor the Revolution's debts with a reliable currency, maintain an indissoluble union, and promote a spirit of sacrifice and cooperation among all the states. The Congress and the states had completely failed to do any of that, and he intended to provide them himself. He saw himself, with perfect justice, as the emblem and symbol of the nation, not only for having led the armies of the Revolution to victory and presided over the assembly that wrote the Constitution, but as the man summoned by popular and general demand, and without opposition, to take the headship of the new nation and, by his conduct, define its presidency. In his inaugural address, he spoke of an "indissoluble union between virtue and happiness, between duty and advantage, between the genuine maxims of an honest and magnanimous policy, and the solid rewards of public prosperity and felicity." This was a rather unspecific message of exhortations and velleities, more remarkable in its serenity by the fact that Washington had lost a lot of money during the Revolution and had to borrow $100 at 6 percent interest just to attend his own inauguration.[2]

---

1.   Disclosure requires reference to the author's legal travails as the actual basis of this reflection; they are fully described in my previous book, *A Matter of Principle*, and summarized in the last footnote of Chapter 16.

2.   Ron Chernow, *Washington: A Life*, New York, Penguin, 2010, p. 554.

Washington toured most of the country in stages, reassuring people with his majestic presence, and promised in famous letters to the Newport synagogue and to the Roman Catholics of America (through the bishop of Baltimore) that their congregants and co-religionists would not be discriminated against in the new nation as they probably had been in the countries they or their forebears had departed. To the Jews, he wrote: "The Government of the United States . . . gives to bigotry no sanction, to persecution no assistance. . . . May the children of the Stock of Abraham who dwell in this land, continue to merit and enjoy the good will of the other inhabitants; while every one shall sit under his own vine and fig tree, and there shall be none to make him afraid." To the Roman Catholics he wrote: "May the members of your society in America, animated alone by the pure spirit of Christianity and still conducting themselves as the faithful subjects of our free government, enjoy every spiritual and temporal felicity." He had not been as loquacious as Franklin in expressing confidence that the United States would relatively quickly become the premier nation of the world. But the whole ambiance of the new nation, the tenor of the wording of its earliest and most basic state papers, exuded confidence in the exalted and exceptional destiny of America, and of its unique and evangelical status as a light unto the whole world, showing the way forward for the rights of man and the organization of government. Implicit in this was America's predestined and natural right to expand across America and become a country on a grander scale than any European nation.

This notion of destiny and exceptionalism was in part simply true and evident in the world's only and revolutionary constitutional republic, in part reasonable supposition of growing immigration and the settling of the generally rich and largely vacant land westward to and beyond the Mississippi, and in part an act of levitation and denial, to rise above inconvenient facts, such as that there were other democracies in the world, that slavery was objectively evil, and that to patch the country together, indecent electoral Danegeld had had to be paid to the minority of the states where it was established. Washington, as president in Philadelphia, where the law was that after six months' residence slaves were automatically free, cycled his slaves in from Mount Vernon for a little over 20 weeks and then platooned them with others, to avoid emancipation of them. To be arbitrary, the American claim to moral leadership was one-third pure virtue, one-third ambitious but plausible striving, and one-third humbug and hypocrisy. The virtue would be strained at times but not discarded or altogether sullied; the ambitions of the most ardent patriots to world leadership would be attained in prodigies of courage, imagination, and diligence; but the fraud and corruption would constantly nag and periodically haunt the nation through all the astounding times ahead.

Foreign affairs were to be entrusted to a department of state, which was directed ad interim by John Jay, and then by the first secretary of state, Thomas Jefferson. At first, there was little to do in foreign affairs, though loose ends remained with the British, and France began her revolutionary perturbations with the storming of the Bastille prison in Paris less than three months after Washington's inauguration. The American fiscal shambles was to be addressed by the brilliant, bold, and vehement Alexander Hamilton as secretary of the Treasury. Armed forces were in the hands of the secretary of war, Henry Knox, a journeyman colleague from the Revolutionary War, who presided over a permanent army of 5,000, the navy, shipyards, the armory, and Indian affairs. He was not at all of the quality of Jefferson and Hamilton, and nor was the attorney general, Virginia's Governor Edmund Randolph, who did not have an office but took a retainer as the government's lawyer. In these brave and halcyon days, what became the United States Department of Justice was not even an embryo. Samuel Osgood was the first postmaster general. Washington's confidence in John Adams had been shaken by his advocacy of an all-militia army, and during his incumbency his office was, and would long remain, anomalous, although relations between the two men were satisfactorily revived later in the administration. It was a cabinet of only seven. But one of the very most important figures continued to be Congressman James Madison, who was Washington's most trusted adviser, the champion of the Bill of Rights, and generally recognized and deferred to as the principal author of the Constitution. This group of five (Washington, Jefferson, Hamilton, Adams, Madison), who with Franklin are generally considered the principal founders of the United States, continued through all of the decade, and Jefferson and Madison through the first quarter of the next century, as leaders of the new republic's public life, assuring and symbolizing continuity.

Washington's only rival as the very greatest American and co-founder of the nation, Benjamin Franklin, finally passed away on April 17, 1790, aged 84. He had seen the new government in and fairly launched. Benjamin Franklin was universally saluted as a great man, statesman, scientist, inventor, writer, and publisher, and especially as a unique, wholly admirable personality. When he was buried, approximately half the whole population of Philadelphia, about 20,000 people, crowded the few blocks to the Christ Church cemetery, and the casket was preceded by all the clergy of the city, of every denomination.[3]

The main focus of the administration was in the complex series of measures very skillfully formulated and advanced by Hamilton to create fiscal and monetary

---

3.   Walter Isaacson, *Benjamin Franklin: An American Life*, New York, Simon and Schuster, 2003, p. 470.

stability. Hamilton's plan came in three main proposals from January 1790 to March 1791: foreign debt, mainly in the hands of the former French and Dutch allies, was reckoned at $11.7 million, and was to be honored entirely with payment in guaranteed interest-bearing notes. The domestically held debt of the defunct Confederation and the states was estimated at about $67 million, and all of this was to be "assumed," which meant placed in a sinking fund where it would yield interest and be retired eventually. Hamilton had softened the onerousness of these assumptions of debt by quietly buying some of it at heavily discounted prices, but it was a very controversial plan. There was general agreement on the foreign debt but the uneven distribution of state debt led to fierce debate and it was initially narrowly rejected by the House of Representatives at the urging of Madison, but Hamilton arranged with Madison, in a deal brokered by Jefferson, that the debt-assumption proposals would be accepted in exchange for moving the capital of the country from Philadelphia to a new site on the Potomac adjacent to Virginia.

This instantly gave the U.S. government a respected fiscal status, competitive with the stronger European nations, put a lot of money in the hands of the administration's grateful friends, presaged a number of Keynesian and monetarist policies of 130 to 150 years later, created a lively American capital market, subordinated the states to the central government, and deprived the states of much of their argument for access to tax revenues, as their debt vanished.

Hamilton's second measure was the establishment of the Bank of the United States as the handler of large money transfers, the manager of the national debt, principal institutional lender, and issuer of supplementary currency as debt certificates. This generated heated constitutional argument with Jefferson, who considered it ultra vires to the government, but Hamilton's view of the "implicit powers" of the government prevailed with Washington and Congress. Only 35 at this time, Hamilton, who had caught Washington's attention as a young volunteer from the West Indies early in the Revolutionary War, was undoubtedly a man of genius, as all his contemporaries, including worldly figures such as the timeless French foreign minister, Talleyrand, agreed. Almost at a stroke he massively reinforced the basis of American government and union and planted the fast-growing seeds of American finance and the transition from an agricultural to an industrial economy, events that would change and astonish the whole world. A mint was established in January of 1791 to give America its own coinage and end the miscellaneous circulation of British, French, Spanish, and even German currency in America.

To ensure adequate revenue to deal with the debt assumption and the operations of the federal government, Hamilton proposed tariffs (with the additional benefit of stimulating manufacturing) and excise taxes, including a tax on distilled spirits. The tax fell heavily on the hinterland agricultural communities, as this was the chief destination of unsold grain for the distillation of spirits, and was strenuously challenged and often defied, in the Carolinas and Pennsylvania especially, and eventually led (in July 1794) to the Whiskey Rebellion in western Pennsylvania. Washington mobilized 15,000 militiamen, and under General Henry Lee, accompanied by former colonel Hamilton, the disobedience was suppressed. Two men were convicted of treason, but pardoned by Washington. The effect of these measures, including the unambiguous enforcement of the excise taxes, was to establish the unquestioned authority of the United States government as a fiscally responsible national administration that soon had a better international credit rating than the main European powers, and as an unchallengeably authoritative occupant of its constitutional jurisdictions, whose writ would run in all matters and throughout the land.

Hamilton's proposed measures for encouraging manufacturing were not immediately adopted, but were very prescient and even visionary. In a report of nearly 100,000 words, Hamilton outlined proposals that went beyond the House of Representatives' request for a plan to make the United States independent of foreign sources for military supplies. Hamilton "elaborated his grand vision of a powerful, integrated, and wealthy war-making nation that would be the equal of any in Europe, including Great Britain."[4] The political economy of the Federalists, hinted at in broad strokes by Washington and hammered into detailed proposals fit for legislation by Hamilton, was a fast track to an economic and military powerhouse. Despite the Jefferson-Madison advocacy of a rather bucolic and adjudicatory state, their political astuteness would bring them to the highest offices within a few years, where they were no less nationalistic than their Federalist predecessors. From right to left, country to city, South to North, patricians to the lower bourgeoisie, the small but talented American political class was straining like whippets to attract immigrants, settle the West, build industry, and make America a mighty nation in the world. And there was never the slightest hesitation to include military power and its application as a chief criterion of the new nation's potential influence.

Washington and his Treasury secretary not only had got control of the debt problem that had been building and festering for nearly 10 years and established a strong currency, but had done so in a manner that was in accord with the adopted Constitution and was susceptible only to technical legal arguments by Jefferson

---

4. Gordon S. Wood, *Empire of Liberty: A History of the Early Republic, 1789–1815*, Oxford and New York, Oxford University Press, 2009, p. 100.

and his followers, but not to comparisons with the unrepresented taxation and high-handed collection measures of the British. Almost at once, the new nation had a solid fiscal regime.

Where Washington desired a rather mystic national commitment to thrift, unity of purpose and sacrifice, with a balance between urban industry and agriculture, and Jefferson professed the greater virtue and desirability of rural life, Hamilton saw clearly the economic future and eschewed laissez-faire capitalism in favor of government participation to encourage centralized government, promotion of manufacturing and heavy industry, and a headlong pursuit of pure capitalism (pure apart from the fact that the government was channeling the direction of its progress). Hamilton saw the huge advantage the British and Dutch had over the other powers because of their private capital markets and sophisticated methods of funding public debt, compared with Colbert's authoritarian methods of official financial regimentation in France.

Jefferson, though an elitist, favored a broad suffrage. Washington trusted the people less than Jefferson, but wanted them ultimately responsible for their own government, with an edge for more accomplished people, which in practice meant wealthier ones. Hamilton was fairly liberal in matters of civil rights, but was both a monarchist at heart and a meritocratic authoritarian in matters of devising and implementing public policy. Adams the Bostonian, despite his personal and intra-party disputes with Hamilton, partly shared the political and economic designs of the New Yorker, while Madison sided with Jefferson, his fellow Virginia planta-tion owner. Jefferson's Enlightenment utopianism based on man's inert decency and capacity for self-improvement vied with a Hamiltonian blend of Hobbesian cynicism, Adam Smith capitalism, and far-sighted industrialism. As in all things, Washington hovered majestically above it all, seeking excellence in men and poli-cies and making it up as he went along. He thought Hamilton more practical in economic terms, but relied heavily on Madison for adaptation of the Constitution. It must be said that, on balance, the Constitution was so intelligently designed and the principal founders of the country so capable and highly motivated that the United States started its life with four to five decades of what would, in later periods, if not always at the time, be regarded as good government.

Washington had unsuccessfully demanded, and then promised, indissolubility of nationhood, adequate armed forces, fiscal integrity, and an example of incorrupt-ible sacrifice. Having led in the establishment of the new nation, he wished now to do all he could to maximize the likelihood of its swift growth and undisturbed progress among nations, which at that time numbered only the five Great Powers in Europe that came through the Seven Years' War (Britain, France, Austria, Russia and Prussia), the secondary powers (the Spanish, Portuguese, Ottoman, and Dutch Empires as well as Sweden, Denmark, Switzerland, and a few of the German and Italian kingdoms and principalities), and on rumor and belief, mysterious entities in the East, most conspicuously China. With its house increasingly in order, the United States was already reaching the upper levels of the second tier of powers, as its population passed the level of half of Britain's at about the end of Washington's presidency, when it reached 5 million to Britain's 10 million. And where the old empires were in decline, the United States, glamorized by its revolution and mythologized by the stirring tenor of its originating state papers, was, from its earliest days, a dazzling and steeply ascending comet among nations.

Washington was not trying to lead the Congress in a legislative program, beyond the instances and criteria of serious sovereign statehood that he had promised to pursue after the failure of the Congress and states to do so in the interregnum between Yorktown and Philadelphia, but he was determined to establish the presidency as a very republican but majestic office that was above faction, region, and partisanship. He alone was responsible for patronage and was very circumspect in resisting the importunity of office-seekers and filling the senior positions and federal bench with highly qualified people. (John Jay was a superlative choice as first chief justice.) Washington had an elegant (but not ostentatious) carriage, with six matched cream-colored horses, held rather ceremonious levees, and entertained somewhat opulently, with profusions of wigged footmen in full livery. Washington in public addresses referred to himself in the third person, and the iconography of his presidency, especially official portraits and medals, was an imitation of European monarchy. He never dined in a citizen's private home and traveled somewhat elaborately but not with absurd trappings, as in his trips about New England in 1789 and through the South in 1791. There were criticisms that he had monarchical flourishes but he had made it widely known that he would resist at any cost any suggestion of such a transition for the presidency, and he encouraged Madison to oppose Adams's effort to have the president referred to as "His Most Benign Majesty," which would have reduced the office to an absurdity. (Adams was a terrible fidget with styles of address, and ruminated nervously aloud in the Congress about what he would be called when President Washington visited the Congress, since that title would preempt his as president of the Senate. The answer effortlessly emerged: Mr. Vice President.)

The United States quickly achieved, though the retention of this felicitous balance would vary with Washington's successors, a fine combination of the solidity and dignity of monarchy with the spirit and effervescence of popular democracy. Not until the Fifth Republic of France, 165 years after the tumultuous founding of the First, would the fiercely contesting French national traditions of monarchy and republicanism be reconciled in a president with immense powers and a renewable seven-year term, an elected sovereign, the fusion (in Charles de Gaulle) of monarchy and republicanism. In other major European republics, such as Germany and Italy, the post–World War II presidents would be just stand-ins for deposed monarchs. In the United States, and in the latest of the French Republics, the president is chief of state and head of government. Madison devised and Washington inaugurated, this brilliant novelty of government.

Another indication of the grandiose ambitions of the new nation was the engagement of the French engineer Pierre-Charles l'Enfant to design a splendid capital of grand straight boulevards in what was an unpromising swamp but grew in one long lifetime to be an elegant and monumental capital of a great nation. None of the founders of the republic, and as far as can be discerned, none of its founding citizens either, dissented from the cult of predestined greatness that Washington, especially, but all of the founders according to their means and talents, lavished upon the national experiment as if from giant and constantly swinging incense-pots.

2. THE RIVALRY BETWEEN HAMILTON AND JEFFERSON

Under Jefferson's influence, Madison moved away from his friendship with Hamilton, which had flowered while Jefferson was in Paris, and Madison and Hamilton, with John Jay and a few others, were writing the Federalist Papers. Jefferson found Hamilton's cynicism, materialism, and brusqueness, his lack of the idealism of the contemplative Enlightenment and disrespect for the gracious civilities of France, jarring. He and Madison took to referring to Hamilton and his entourage as "speculators, stock-jobbers, and Tories," the last an especially odious word in the aftermath of the Revolution. With the death of Franklin, Jefferson was able to hold himself out as the worldly traveler and connoisseur of civilization at its rich sources, protesting all the while to be the true democrat, patrician and elitist though his notions of democracy were. Washington, who remained above attack, even after his whole-hearted support of Hamilton's suppression of the Whiskey Rebellion in 1794, was trying to run a government whose principal cabinet members were starting to splinter badly apart. The spirit of party and notion of opposition was not immediately respectable, but Jefferson and Madison began press attacks on Hamilton and Adams.

A battle developed between rival newspapers, John Fenno's strongly Federalist *Gazette of the United States*, founded in 1789, and Philip Freneau's opposition *National Gazette*, founded in 1790. Freneau was incentivized by being named an official interpreter by the State Department and his newspaper was a fire-breathing spigot of billingsgate and sensationalism directed at Hamilton, Adams, the Federalists, and, by implication, the president himself. The government was accused of promoting monarchism and an aristocracy, as well as a sleazy commercialism, and subverting republicanism and Jefferson's notions of democracy (which were, to say the least, idiosyncratic). Fenno took the gloves off at once and directly attacked Jefferson as a scheming and treacherous enemy of the Constitution. It was an improbable and swift descent into an ear-splitting slanging match between Fenno and Freneau.

British precedents were somewhat replicated, as Hamilton and Adams were portrayed by their enemies as "the court," the Tories around Washington's crowned majesty, while Jefferson and Madison fancied themselves the country gentry loyal opposition, with Jefferson having the aspect of the sly Whig grandee with popular, if far from egalitarian, affectations, a new Walpole. The Whigs became the Republican Party, and the Federalists evolved from the supporters of the Constitution, which soon had general adherence, so almost everyone was in that sense a federalist, to a more urban and commercial bloc that Freneau and his sponsors labeled, as tendentiously as possible, Tories. It was a preposterous state of affairs, as the two senior cabinet members hurled muck at each other, and Jefferson employed in the government an anti-government propagandist flinging vitriol at the administration of which Jefferson was a senior member. Washington urged Hamilton to reply to Jefferson, to reassure general opinion, and tried to assure Jefferson that there was no such plot against the Constitution and to promote monarchic leanings, as he feared and alleged.

Both Hamilton and Jefferson were urging Washington to take a second term, but the cabinet meetings by mid-1792 had the two senior cabinet secretaries quarrelling, as Jefferson said, like roosters. Washington wrote to both in July 1792, asking for "more charity for the opinions and acts of one another." Both men replied the same day to Washington, Hamilton in terms of forthright grievances against Jefferson's attacks on his policies and on Hamilton personally. Jefferson sent a rather labored attack on Hamilton and spent much of his letter defending the hiring of Freneau at the State Department. Given the brilliance and historic importance of the men, it was a disappointingly immature performance, a schoolyard shouting match, in which Hamilton seemed several grades more advanced than his rival. Jefferson wrote Washington that he would retire soon but that "I will not suffer my retirement to be clouded by the slanders of a man whose history, from the moment when history can stoop to notice him, is a tissue of machinations against the liberty of the country which has not only received and given him bread, but heaped its honors on his head"—pretty juvenile carping from the author of the

Declaration of Independence, and vulgar snobbery as well, toward the illegitimate son of a Scottish West Indian merchant who had rendered invaluable service to the new nation.[5]

3. WASHINGTON'S SECOND TERM

By simply not responding to endless requests from all sides that he allow himself to be selected for another presidential term, Washington backed into his reelection, again unanimously. Adams ran more strongly for vice president than he had four years before, clinging tightly to the president's coat-tails, and was irritated to have come only 77 votes to 50 ahead of the long-serving governor of New York, George Clinton, who just four years before had been one of the leading opponents of ratification of the Constitution. Hamilton had feared that Jefferson might manage to slip into the vice presidency over the less agile Adams. The Treasury secretary was less preoccupied with personal disparagements of Jefferson, but regarded him as "a man of sublimated and paradoxical imagination entertaining and propagating notions inconsistent with dignified and orderly government."[6] In January 1793, Jefferson's followers moved five motions of censure against Hamilton in the House of Representatives, all of which Hamilton had rejected handily, probably with the known support of the unanimously reacclaimed president.

Lost in the controversy was the testimony Washington's unanimous reelection gave to the unquestionable success, great dignity of office, and successful economic policies of the first presidential term. The American system was just starting to show its distinctive characteristics. It was at this time not acceptable for a man to campaign for an office, as the clever but mistrusted young New York lawyer Aaron Burr was said to have done, very unsuccessfully, for the vice presidency. Neither Hamilton nor Jefferson had stood for election to anything in the new constitutional regime, and when elections were contested, there was no campaign and the voter turnout was often as low as 5 percent.[7]

The emerging Democratic-Republican opposition was a two-headed beast from the beginning—disgruntled southern slaveholders, distressed by the urban, industrial, and commercial nature of Hamiltonism, and along with them the northerners, who were in rebellion against the financial establishment of Hamilton's friends. The first group wanted to put the brakes on the Hamilton economic system; the second wanted to accelerate it and make it more open and meritocratic. It would take no less talented

---

5.   Wood, *op. cit.*, p. 157.
6.   Ibid. p. 158.
7.   Ibid. p. 162.

a political chameleon than Jefferson to keep this broad church under the same roof and lead it anywhere useful. These were the origins of the modern Democratic Party. The anti-Federalists were called Republicans, and later, Democratic-Republicans, and were in fact what are now known as "Democrats." Jefferson sold the idea that the Federalists were essentially British Tories, monarchists, cronies, corrupt speculators, warring alike on the hard-working bourgeoisie and the virtuous and tranquil South, a society that was paternalistic, rather than exploitively slave-holding. (The Federalists eventually, in the 1820s, became National Republicans, then a decade later Whigs, and finally, in the 1850s, Republicans.)

The French Revolution had a huge impact on Europe, which lingers yet, but it proceeded in a haphazard, often absurd sequence. France was Europe's greatest nation by any measurement—27 million people in 1789, almost three times as populous as Britain, with the richest agriculture and most admired literature and intellectual community in Europe.

But Louis XIV's wars and monumental grandiosity, especially the Palace of Versailles, strained the treasury, which relied on taxation of the lower classes, and his wars, in the end, accomplished only a minor extension outwards of the northeast frontier. The wars of the eighteenth century were horribly expensive and achieved nothing for France, as in the American Revolutionary War, and the Seven Years' War had been a disaster.

Finally, in May 1789, to raise revenues, Louis summoned the Estates General, which had not met since Richelieu had dismissed it in 1614. The first estate, the clergy, had 300 of the 1,200 delegates, owned 10 percent of the country's land, and paid no tax. The second estate, the nobility, had 300 delegates and owned about 30 percent of the country's land, and about half of their delegates were somewhat reform-minded. The remaining 97 percent of the people were represented by the 600 delegates of the third estate, though most of them were lawyers, business people, and the bourgeoisie; the rural peasantry and urban poor, at least 60 percent of the population of France, were not represented other than in whatever altruistic thoughts their socioeconomic betters had for them.

After a few weeks, the first two estates tried to exclude the third, who repaired to a covered tennis court and, joined by 47 nobles, swore to pursue reform, which was not why they had been summoned. They declared themselves to be the National Assembly, and the king attempted to dissolve them on June 27. Riots ensued, culminating in the seizure of the Bastille, a prison and arsenal in Paris, on July 14. It contained only five counterfeiters and two deranged prisoners, and 250 barrels of gunpowder. (The half-mad dissolute, the Marquis de Sade, had been released a week before.) The governor of the Bastille was decapitated and his head bobbed on a pike at the head of tens of thousands of angry marching demonstrators, after they had blown up and burned down the Bastille.

On August 4, the National Assembly voted to abolish almost all aristocratic and clerical privileges, and on August 26 adopted a Declaration of the Rights of Man largely based on the American Declaration of Independence. On October 5, a mob of 5,000 women, and men dressed as women, marched to Versailles and compelled the return with them of the royal family to the Tuileries Palace (the Louvre) in central Paris, where they were more or less detained.

The Count Mirabeau was the principal figure of the National Assembly, and he was a constitutional monarchist who was adept at preventing the extremes from making inroads. Unfortunately, he suddenly died in March 1791, following a particularly frolicsome evening with two dancers he brought home with him after an evening at the opera. A new constitution establishing a monarchy of limited powers which Mirabeau had been working on was proclaimed on May 3, 1791. Maria Theresa's daughter, Queen Marie Antoinette, persuaded the king to flee Paris, which they did on June 20, 1791, disguised as servants. They crowded everybody into a slow carriage and foolishly stopped for the night at Varennes, not far from the frontier of the Austrian Netherlands, where the king was recognized, captured, and ignominiously returned to Paris.

The moderates felt betrayed by the king's flight and the extremists vindicated. Marie Antoinette's brother, Emperor Leopold II, asked for all Europe to help restore the French monarchy. On August 27, he and the Prussian king, Frederick William, joined by Louis's brother the Count d'Artois, met at Pillnitz and urged pan-European action to restore Louis to power. Nothing came of this except the rage of the National Assembly, which achieved its apotheosis with France's declaration of war on Austria in April 1792.

Except for one year, war would continue until 1815, taking about 750,000 French lives and a larger number of other nationalities as war engulfed Europe from Cádiz to Moscow and from Copenhagen to Naples and, briefly, spread into Egypt and Palestine. The Revolution moved steadily to the left and ever further from its declared goals, and violently devoured ever greater numbers of innocents, until the Committee of Public Safety, which had implemented the Reign of Terror, was itself executed on the guillotine, to the delight of the fickle, blood-thirsty mob. Reaction and corruption ensued, followed by the Bonapartist dictatorship and empire.

If the king had had any notion of how to govern, he would not have had to call the Estates General. If he had had any political acumen, he could easily have set himself at the head of the reformers and been the indispensable man. If he had even managed the flight to Varennes and beyond properly, he could have returned to Paris eventually, as his brothers did, in the baggage train of the Duke of Wellington's army.

One of the great watersheds of Western history was a sanguinary and tragicomic farce that presaged the ambiguity of the legacy of the Enlightenment itself. The moderate civilizing evolution advocated by Voltaire, Franklin, and their friends degenerated into terror, licentiousness, dictatorship, endless war, and futile reaction. The first claimants to emulation of the American Revolution soon became a horrifying cautionary tale.

France joined America as a republic in 1792—the first of five republics in France (to date), interspersed with a directory, consulate, two empires, two restorations, a "popular monarchy," two provisional governments, a government in exile, and an undefined "French State," governing in the name of a foreign occupier. The First Republic would last only three years.

American cartwheels of delight, solidarity, and legitimization of events in France would not be durable. Jefferson went impetuously cock-a-hoop for the French revolutionaries, delighted that the monarch to whom he had presented his letters of credence was executed as "a criminal," and soon subsumed into the breezy assurance that "The tree of liberty must be watered with the blood of tyrants." Jefferson was not only a bigoted and delusional Francophile and Anglophobe; he was a poseur. He sincerely believed that revolution was a discrete movement that must sweep Europe and ensconce America as its legitimizing trailblazer, or perish and imperil the American Revolution with it. Both Hamilton and Jefferson urged on Washington a proclamation of neutrality, which he did issue on April 22, 1793, and Jefferson's true colors as a romantic revolutionary sobered by a political opportunist and a champion of inherited and slave-holding property became more visible.

Unlike Thomas Paine and some other American true believers, Jefferson knew that what had occurred in America wasn't a revolution at all. It was a forced national disembarkation of the colonial power, a national self-empowerment, in which the land-owning and professional and leading commercial classes reinforced their control over the disaffected country, covering the whole drama in the stirring vocabulary of liberty and obscuring a tax dispute that flared into a continental war of liberation. What was unfolding in France was a much more profound and very violent upheaval temporarily destroying an entire civilization built in rich distinction over 15 centuries. What Jefferson professed to regard as a revolutionary movement productive of human liberty was just anarchism, soon seized by an authoritarian militarist and translated into an orgy of aggressive conquest and spoliation killing several million people across Europe, although France was certainly not solely responsible for the carnage. Jefferson ran with the revolutionaries and rode in a carriage with the established and inherited interests, and reconciled it all artfully, one of history's first and greatest limousine liberals. In 1793, he urged Madison to reply to Hamilton's successful denunciations of the French Revolution in newspapers and pamphlets. Madison dutifully tried, but his heart wasn't in it, and nor were the unfolding forces of history, as the French Revolution became steadily more impossible to defend.

Washington, Hamilton, and Jefferson all agreed that the United States must maintain its neutrality between France and Britain. In the sage beginning of what would be a vastly successful policy for nearly 150 years, the United States would generally abstain from Europe's quarrels, and grow steadily stronger as Europe's penchant for internecine bloodbaths became ever more sanguinary. Washington said that with 20 years of peace and economic growth, the United States would be fully capable to see off any European intruder. This was only slightly optimistic, and did not, of course, address America's own Achilles' heel, the ineluctable tumor of slavery.

4. RELATIONS WITH FRANCE AND BRITAIN

Problems between neutralist America and the compulsively belligerent revolutionary government of France were not long in coming. The French minister, the bumptious and completely unqualified "Citizen (Edmond Charles) Genêt," aged just 29, arrived at Charleston on April 8, 1793, and commissioned four privateers to prey upon British shipping in American waters and also commissioned overland attacks on British and Spanish targets on the borders of the United States. He proceeded, amid considerable celebrations and extravagant greetings, to Philadelphia, where he arrived on May 16. Washington received him coolly on May 18, and on June 5 Jefferson handed him a letter from the president telling him that his privateers could not infringe U.S. territorial waters and no prizes taken would be permitted in U.S. ports. The letter noted in the sparest terms a serious trespass on U.S. national sovereignty. Genêt promised to do as Washington demanded but soon rechristened a British vessel that had been taken as it was being refitted in a U.S. port, and when warned not to allow the ship to sail, he did so anyway and threatened to appeal over Washington's head to the American people. Both Hamilton and Madison, in the midst of their newspaper debate, supported the president. On August 2, the cabinet, including Jefferson, agreed with Washington's demand for Genêt's recall. Washington sent his full correspondence on the issue to the Congress with a message saying that Genêt was trying to plunge the U.S. into "war abroad and discord and anarchy at home."

The Democratic societies had been supporting Genêt, but the great majority of Americans backed Washington's firm and sensible response, and the whole affair then rapidly descended into farce. Genêt lingered in America but had no status, as the Revolution in France moved toward its most extreme phase. Genêt's successor, Joseph Fauchet, arrived in 1794 and demanded Genêt's arrest and extradition to France in chains. Washington, in a typical gentlemanly flourish, refused and gave him asylum, and Genêt became an American and married a daughter of Governor and future vice president George Clinton. Support for France was also diluted by Thomas Paine's pamphlet *The Age of Reason*, which sold scores of thousands of copies in America but was an attack on all religion, raised the strenuous opposition of all denominations, and brought the entire clergy of America into the Federalist camp, instantly cured of any sympathy for the French Revolution, which Paine had served as a member of the National Convention. It also destroyed much of his historical standing and caused otherwise kindred spirits to defect from his admirers, such as Theodore Roosevelt, who generally referred to him as "a filthy little atheist."[8]

The Treaty of 1783 had recognized American independence and ended the the American Revolutionary War but did not resolve all issues between the United States and Great Britain. Britain continued to occupy a series of forts and trading posts in the Northwest that were recognized as American but that the British still operated. The British justified their retention by the failure of the Americans to pay pre-revolutionary debts to British merchants and promised compensation to loyalists whose property had been confiscated. The British had promoted the creation of an Indian buffer state in the Ohio country, and the Americans believed that the British had incited attacks on American settlers and had generally retarded the western progress of the United States. Orders in council of June and November 1793 authorized the impressments into British service of American crews seized on the high seas, an act of war the Americans could not ignore (and Madison did not when his time came to deal with such matters).

Canadian and West Indian ports were closed to American ships, and the British, once war broke out with France in 1792, arrogated unto themselves the right to seize American cargoes intended for France, and to detain indefinitely American ships and sailors. The Federalists responded by making war-like noises and building up the country's armed forces, an army of 20,000 and a vigorous program of naval construction, following Washington's long-held maxim that to preserve peace one must prepare for war. The Jefferson-Madison Republicans wanted to avoid war but

---

8.   Daniel Ruddy, *Theodore Roosevelt's History of the United States in His Own Words*, New York, Harper Collins, 2010, p. 1.

engage in a complete boycott of any imports from Britain, which was impossible to enforce, punitive to certain regions, especially New England, and would have had no leverage opposite the British, since the United States provided only about 15 percent of their trade, which could be replaced. This was a mad suggestion, because tariffs on British imports were what chiefly financed Hamilton's sinking fund for Revolutionary War and Confederation debt, the country's standing army, and any incentivization to manufacturing such as the secretary of the Treasury proposed. In trade matters, the Americans had started out with a naïve idea of free trade with everyone, and the Confederation had empowered a commission of Franklin, Adams, and Jefferson to pursue such agreements with all countries. Only Prussia, Sweden, and Morocco agreed, countries with which America's trade was negligible.

The Federalist plan seemed to have helped motivate the British to end their policy of wholesale seizures of American shipping, which gave Washington the latitude he felt he needed to send John Jay to negotiate an agreement with the British. Madison and Jefferson were raving that any war preparations were part of a Hamiltonian plot to foist a military and monarchical dictatorship on the country in the guise of avenging wrongs from England, but that any effort to negotiate a settlement was the first step to dishonoring the nation with a sell-out of the republic's interests to the former abusive colonial master. As was his practice, Jefferson left it to Madison to make these implausible arguments, reserving the necessary room to maneuver and dissemble, as he did in the Genêt affair. Jefferson retired as secretary of state in July 1793, with effect at the end of that year. The crushing of the Whiskey Rebellion confirmed the Republicans' fear that Hamilton, behind the cloak of Washington's prestige, was cranking up to use the militia to curtail popular liberties.

Jay signed with the British a draft treaty on November 19, 1794, which assured the British withdrawal from the Northwest posts and forts by June 1, 1796; admitted U.S. vessels to British East Indian ports, and to West Indian ports if they did not carry over 70 tons of cargo; and renounced the right to ship from the West Indies cotton, molasses, sugar, and other staples. Joint commissions would take up pre-revolutionary debts, a dispute over the northeast border with Canada, and compensation for illegal seizures of American vessels. Trade between the two countries was upgraded to a most-favored-nation status. Impressment of sailors had been officially abandoned and compensation for impressed sailors and for deported slaves taken by the British were dropped as a complaint, as was, on the British side, compensation for loyalist property that had been seized. Various concerns about the Indians, including responsibility for their alleged aggressions, were not dealt with, leaving the Americans a free hand to resolve matters by force, as they were more than pleased to do.

There was fierce opposition from the Republicans (again, Jefferson and Madison), because of treatment of debts, West Indian shipping rights, and, for the southerners, fugitive slaves. Washington acknowledged that the agreement, known at the time and since as Jay's Treaty, was imperfect, but he recognized that given the correlation of forces, it was a commendable effort. Furthermore, it was brilliant general policy, because it levered on a military build-up to magnify the trade relationship with Britain, which sharply increased tariff and excise revenue and strengthened the American central government and directly increased and spread American prosperity. The sources of revenue safeguarded by Jay's Treaty, the tariffs, financed the military build-up that gave America the leverage to extract the revenue from its arrangements with Britain. The treaty, and Jefferson and Madison's response to it, showed the superiority of the Washington, Hamilton, Jay, and later Adams policy, which had been pioneered by Franklin, of playing on the British vulnerability in Canada and manipulating Britain and France against each other. It was profoundly sensible strategic thinking, rigorously implemented by Washington, Hamilton, and Jay.

The Jefferson-Madison policy of a trade embargo would have severely enfeebled America without much harming the British. Hamilton led the fight for ratification, against Madison, and the treaty was voted through by the Senate, except for the West Indian trade provisions. Madison led a battle in the House to block appropriations for enforcement. The House asked Washington for the papers of the treaty negotiations. Washington refused, establishing an important precedent. In April 1796, in a stunning defeat for Madison, even the appropriations were passed, as sensible opinion warmed to the virtues of Jay's Treaty, while the Reign of Terror unfolded in France in 1794 and during its seedy aftermath.

Randolph (again, Jefferson's cousin), who had succeeded Jefferson in the State Department, was accused of conspiring with Fauchet, the French minister, to sandbag the treaty, on the basis of captured letters, and resigned, in order to avoid being fired by Washington, and was replaced by Timothy Pickering, in August 1795. Hamilton retired as secretary of the Treasury and was replaced by Oliver Wolcott. Pickering had replaced the rather plodding Knox at the War Department, and was succeeded by James McHenry, though Washington was his own secretary of war, as many future presidents would be their own secretaries of state. (McHenry was only Washington's fourth choice for the War Department, and Pickering was his seventh choice for State—the atmosphere was becoming inflamed and many of the best-qualified people declined to enter public life.)[9] Hamilton continued

---

9. Wood, *op. cit.*, p. 234.

to be a strong influence and counselor to the president, and it was an entirely Federalist cabinet.

The British claims for pre-revolutionary debts were finally settled by mutual agreement in 1802 at $2.66 million. In October 1795, Thomas Pinckney, minister to Britain and special envoy to Spain, signed the Treaty of San Lorenzo with Spain, which conceded points Spain had sought to withhold from America when Jay had negotiated with the Spanish in 1786, especially the unfettered navigation of the Mississippi. In 1796, Washington and Pickering recalled James Monroe as minister to France, when it came to light that he had implied to the French that he could negotiate an American loan to France of $5 million, and showered his hosts with other obsequious deferences that completely exceeded his diplomatic remit.

Washington, Hamilton, and Jay's sensible and profitable and honorable foreign policy, to navigate around a general European war, was a complement to their very successful financial and economic policies. Hamilton's assumption of state debts had, as had been intended, led to a drastic reduction in state taxes and had encouraged a huge increase in American prosperity by all indices. American imports from Britain increased from $23.5 million in 1790 to $63 million in 1795, and American exports enjoyed a parallel increase in the same time. The European war and Jay's suddenly popular treaty had raised the demand and price for all agricultural commodities. Thus began, with as great a success as it ever enjoyed in subsequent centuries, including under Ronald Reagan 190 years later (Chapter 16), the application of tax cuts and supply side economics to American spending, saving, investment, and job creation. Although the administration was decisively successful, Washington, ever mindful of his reputation and a tireless enemy of the spirit of party and faction, had found the partisan back-biting tiresome, and declined publicly and in good time to seek a third term as president.

This was another immense contribution to the stability of American politics and to the public's trust in the presidency. It was notoriously clear that he could have retained his office as long as he wished, and his handing over of it, especially in the light of the blood-stained chaos and pelagic corruption in France, reflected great honor on him and on the young republic he had secured, had helped design, and had launched. His farewell address is generally considered another of the great state papers in the nation's history. A first version was written four years earlier by Madison and, without being delivered, was heavily modified by Hamilton, and then substantially refined by Washington himself. The message was delivered by hand and never publicly read by the president. It extolled the virtues of religion, morality, knowledge, and financial soundness, and then dealt at length with foreign policy and warned against "permanent, inveterate antipathies" and "passionate attachments" to other countries. Washington called for commercial relations but "as little political connection as possible" to foreign countries. "Temporary alliances" might be appropriate in "extraordinary emergencies." But the United States should "steer clear of permanent alliances," as it was "folly in one nation to look for disinterested favors from another."[10]

Washington and Franklin had been the principal American collaborators in the British removal of the French threat from America's borders, the first strategic initiative of the Americans, even if in a very secondary role to the British. He and Franklin were the principal architects of the first and most important autonomous American strategic undertaking: the revision of and American emancipation from the British relationship. They would have accepted a less abrupt and complete version of this than actually occurred, but not one more ambiguous in terms of emergent American sovereignty. Jefferson was the principal expositor and propagandist of the Revolution, and Washington, Franklin, Madison, and Hamilton were, in different ways, the chief authors of America's third move of strategic genius, the Constitution. Washington was the creator of the fourth great strategic achievement, a distinguished and respected presidency, and, importantly assisted by Hamilton, was the creator of an effective executive branch and, with Hamilton, of extremely imaginative and successful economic and foreign policies for the new nation. It had been a masterly progression.

George Washington had led the new nation successfully in war and in peace for a total of 23 years with no pay except out-of-pocket expenses, and had voluntarily surrendered his supreme offices when many wished him to continue in them. He would carry into retirement the profound admiration and gratitude of his countrymen and the well-earned esteem of the whole known world. The immense regard Americans had for him while he lived has withstood the closest historical analysis and has not wavered or declined in the more than two centuries since his death. He is universally recognized as having been a capable general, a fine statesman, an outstanding president, and one of history's great men.

5. JOHN ADAMS AS PRESIDENT AND THE CRISIS WITH FRANCE

John Adams and Thomas Jefferson were the two most prominent candidates to replace Washington, and General Thomas Pinckney ran to be Adams's vice president, and Aaron Burr, without encouragement from Jefferson, sought the same office. Ballots were not separated; Electoral College members each wrote two different

---

10. Wood, *op. cit.*, p. 208.

names on ballots, office unspecified. The person with the highest number of ballots became president, and the person in second place became vice president, provided there was a majority. Washington was concerned that, though Madison had done the dirty work, Jefferson had sponsored much criticism of him and that Jefferson's victory would be interpreted as a rejection of the outgoing president. He was also concerned that Virginia not seem to be entitled to permanent occupancy of the presidency, so he publicly endorsed Adams, who was elected by 71 electoral votes to 68 for Jefferson, 59 for Pinckney, and 30 for Burr. Jefferson, as recipient of the second-largest vote total, would take office as vice president. Wolcott, Pickering, and McHenry retained the Treasury, State, and War departments, and Hamilton's influence on them also continued. It had been a fine launch for the country, exalting the presidency, navigating the international currents, and building the foundations of prosperity and union. It was about to become more complicated, and more difficult, without Washington's fine judgment and immense prestige.

Both Jefferson and Hamilton were sensitive to criticism and reckless in their conduct and correspondence. Jefferson sent a letter to an Italian friend, Philip Mazzei, in 1796, which was republished in the United States the following year. Jefferson had written that "An Anglican, monarchical and aristocratical party" was subverting the Revolution, and America was being led astray by "apostates who have gone over to these heresies, men who were Samsons in the field and Solomons in the council, but who have had their heads shorn by the harlot England." (GSW235) This was widely interpreted as a slur on Washington, a step Jefferson had often skirted. He declined to comment and Washington would not deign to refer to it, and the controversy passed eventually. It did confirm that Jefferson's was the party of the Enlightenment, religious and industrial skepticism, the landed gentry, and the common people; but not of faith, capitalism, or a modern economic future.

Hamilton, who, though brilliant and courageous, was young and impetuous, had in 1792 had an adulterous affair with a Mrs. Maria Reynolds, and to avoid publicity, as he was the 37-year-old Treasury secretary, had paid blackmail to her husband. When interrogated by some opposition members of the Congress, including then senator James Monroe, about his private use of Treasury funds, Hamilton foolishly confessed the affair, and five years later it came to light. A duel between Hamilton and Monroe was narrowly avoided, ironically, as it would turn out, by the suave and ambitious Aaron Burr. Monroe too was a hothead, and almost challenged President Adams to a duel in 1797, after Adams described him as "a disgraced minister, recalled in displeasure for misconduct," only a slight exaggeration.

Despite the provision in the 1778 France-America Treaty of Friendship for free trade and navigation, France responded to Jay's Treaty like an angry uncle, and began seizing American ships without any pretext of legality, much as the British had been doing. It refused to receive General Charles Cotesworth Pinckney, brother of Adams's vice presidential running mate, whom Washington had sent to replace Monroe as minister in Paris after Monroe's recall. Adams called a special session of Congress for May 1797, accused the French of trying to drive a wedge between the government and the people of the U.S., and vowed that the United States would not cower in "a colonial spirit of fear and sense of inferiority," nor "be the miserable instruments of foreign influence."[11] Congress approved the calling up of 80,000 militiamen, the fortification of ports and harbors, and the completion of three frigates. Adams followed the successful precedent of his predecessor and tried to replicate the Jay mission to Britain in 1795. He considered sending Madison, a political foe but reliable patriot, but eventually sent the Federalists Charles C. Pinckney and John Marshall, a distinguished Virginia lawyer and assemblyman (who had declined Washington's offers of the War office and the ministry to Paris), and the Republican Elbridge Gerry, as a commission to iron out relations with France.

At this point, France had a string of astounding military successes, having harnessed the Revolution's exaltation of soul to a meritocratic basis of military promotion, which had thrown up some brilliant field commanders. The most conspicuous of these was the 28-year-old (in 1797) Napoleon Bonaparte, who, in one of history's great campaigns, had just flung the Austrian Empire out of Italy with a ragtag army that had not been properly clothed when he took it over. There were mutinies in the Royal Navy and food shortages in Britain, but the Admiralty assured Parliament that the British Isles would, yet again, be successfully defended as necessary. The French foreign minister, the preternaturally cunning former bishop Charles Maurice Talleyrand, who would have a scandalous but rich and brilliant career serving a kaleidoscope of successive conflicting French regimes in high offices for another 40 years, had lived in the United States during the Terror, and felt he knew American opinion. (Washington had refused to receive him because he was cohabiting with an African-American woman.) Talleyrand was unimpressed with American threats and was being secretly advised by his Jeffersonian friends not to give Adams another Jay's Treaty.

Subordinates of Talleyrand (later known as X, Y, and Z) told the American commissioners that the foreign minister would receive them only if they apologized for Adams's anti-French remarks to Congress in May, assumed France's debts to individual Americans, made France a sizeable loan on excellent terms, and paid Talleyrand a

11. Wood, *op. cit.*, p. 240.

direct bribe of 50,000 pounds (over $1 million today). They also said that France, which was now governing the Netherlands, Switzerland, and chunks of Germany and Italy, was taking the position that neutrality was tantamount to animosity and that American neutrality was unacceptable. Intoxicated with military success, the French were back to the mad official egotism, tinged with rampant corruption, of the Genêt school of diplomacy. Pinckney and Marshall indignantly departed, leaving the Republican Gerry behind because Talleyrand had implied that if all the commissioners departed, it could result in war. Gerry subscribed to the Jeffersonian admiration of France and belief in the imminent French crushing of Britain. (Gerry was no political angel himself, and though his name was pronounced with a hard G, his redistricting practices gave rise to the expression "gerrymandering" for refreshing congressional districts in the contorted shape of salamanders.)

Adams informed Congress of the failure of the mission to France in March 1798, and requested congressional approval of the arming of American merchant vessels. Jefferson denounced his former (and future) friend Adams's conduct as "almost insane" and, in a bitter debate that followed, called for release of the diplomatic correspondence, having no idea how incendiary it was. Adams obliged and the effect was devastating to Jefferson and the Republicans, whom Federalist orators had taken to referring to as Jacobins, to assimilate them to Robespierre and St. Just and the Terror that had sent thousands of innocents to the guillotine, before the leaders were toppled and taken on carts past jeering crowds to the guillotine in a principal public square and decapitated as a much-appreciated public entertainment, their severed heads held up to the delight of the blood-crazed masses. Adams regained control of Congress in 1798, and Congress embargoed all trade with France and canceled all treaties with that country, ordered 15 more warships, and approved a naval budget for 1799 greater than the entire history of American naval expenses prior to that. Washington was appointed commander-in-chief of the new army and Hamilton his second-in-command and inspector general. (Washington expressed concern that accepting the nomination might be seen as a "restless act, evincive of my discontent in retirement.")[12] An independent Navy Department was established with Benjamin Stoddart of Maryland as the first secretary.

Along with this military preparedness came a domestic political hysteria that would be replicated in America from time to time over the next 175 (or more) years. There suddenly arose a widespread paranoia about recent Irish, Dutch, German, and French immigrants, who were suspected of being French agents. (One of the targets was Albert Gallatin, the very capable Swiss immigrant who succeeded

---

12. Wood, *op. cit.*, p. 267.

Madison as Republican leader in the House of Representatives.) The Federalists rammed through a series of reactionary measures, as Adams ponderously replied to testimonials of loyalty and fealty from all over the country. Again and again in American history, such patriotic fervor would flair up and then subside quickly (like the brief spikes in reactive popularity in the Bush administrations roughly 200 years later), and leave the incumbent president looking like he oversold the crisis, mismanaged it, or tried to exploit it for partisan gain.

6. THE NATURALIZATION, ALIEN, AND SEDITION ACTS

In June and July 1798, Adams rushed through the Naturalization Act, which raised the period of residency needed for citizenship from five to 14 years (repealed in 1802); the Alien Act, which expired in 1802 and authorized the president to expel any alien judged dangerous or suspected of "treasonable or secret" ambitions; the Alien Enemies Act, which empowered the president to arrest, imprison, or expel in wartime any alien judged to be acting in the interest of an alien power; and the Sedition Act, which provided for fines and imprisonment for citizens or aliens who collaborate to frustrate the execution of national laws or prevent a federal officer from carrying out his duties, to aid or promote "any insurrection, riot, unlawful assembly, or combination," or to publish "any false, scandalous and malicious writing" disparaging the U.S. government, the Congress, or the president. The Sedition Act would expire in March 1801, but it was clearly aimed at partisan opponents, and the anti-publication section was used against 10 Republican editors, including James Thomson Callender, who had revealed Hamilton's affair with Mrs. Reynolds.

The Republicans were outraged by the Sedition Act, and not overly delighted with the rest of the program. Jefferson, an astute political tactician, however woolly he might be about international affairs and the economic future of the country, was a sincere supporter of civil liberties and wrote a series of resistant resolutions adopted by the new state of Kentucky (admitted with Vermont in 1792), while Madison composed resolutions for Virginia. Kentucky claimed a right to nullify federal legislation that violated the constitutional delegation of unallocated powers to the states and citizenry, while Virginia, under Madison's guidance, only charged states with having to "interpose for arresting the progress of evil."

Both states repeated their firm adherence to the Union, and softened their resolutions in response to the objections of other states, but for Jefferson to raise the flag of state nullification, on its own authority, of federal laws it judged ultra vires, was opening the door to severe internecine strife. This sequence created an extremely nasty atmosphere, and Adams, who had the advantage with the

XYZ affair and backlash against foreign meddlers, must be held responsible for allowing, and in some respects encouraging, the poisoning of the atmosphere, and especially the straight partisan prosecution of Republican editors. Washington would never have sponsored such extreme measures or allowed the atmosphere to become so overheated, though he did publicly support the Alien and Sedition Acts as necessary in the circumstances. (To give the measures some perspective, the British five years before had prescribed transportation to Australia for up to 14 years for any dissent from the war with France. The French Revolution brought down a frenzied atmosphere, particularly in France itself, where any offense, real or imagined, resulted, for a time, in immediate public execution.) The Sedition Act passed the House by only 44 to 41, and was actually milder than the existing seditious libel laws.

Hamilton was still very influential with the Federalists and with Wolcott, Pickering, and McHenry, and he aspired now to be the commander of the new army that was being created. When there was an uprising of German Americans in northeastern Pennsylvania in 1799, Hamilton urged drastic action. Adams sent 500 militiamen, who put the small disobedience down promptly and without casualties. The ringleader, John Fries, was condemned to death, but pardoned by Adams. Hamilton was advocating a new program he had cooked up, including war with France in alliance with Britain, to take over all of what are now the southern and central states of the U.S.; promotion of revolt in Latin America under American leadership by a large army he would command; higher taxes to pay for the large European-sized military establishment and an extensive system of roads and canals to accelerate population growth and economic development; a more extensive court system to regiment the population more closely; and the fragmentation of Virginia and some of the other large states to reduce their importance relative to the federal government (though fragmenting Virginia into three states would have tripled the number of Virginia senators).[13]

Hamilton, practicing law in New York and well away from Washington's guidance, had become an authoritarian militarist. Jefferson was backsliding toward an almost confederationist view. Adams held the political center, but without the grasp of the political arts necessary to make it a position of strength. He did move to excise Hamilton's influence in May and June 1800 by firing McHenry and Pickering, and named the formidable John Marshall secretary of state.

Adams also had moved to cut Hamilton off at the end of the limb by sending a new commission to France, after Talleyrand publicly stated that an American

---

13. Wood, *op. cit.*, p. 265.

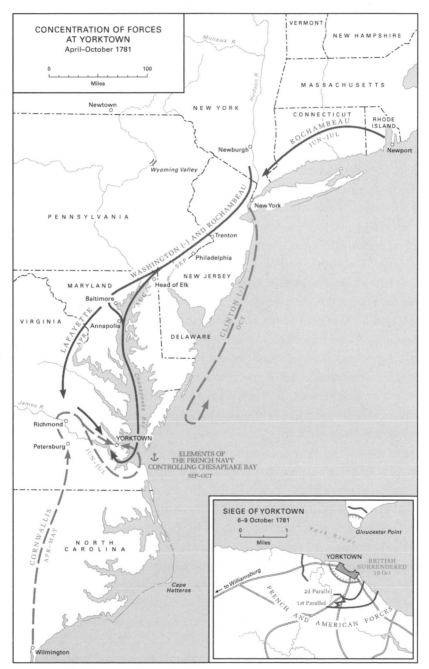

CONCENTRATION OF FORCES AT YORKTOWN
April–October 1781

0   100
Miles

VERMONT

NEW HAMPSHIRE

Mohawk R.

NEW YORK

MASSACHUSETTS

Newtown

CONNECTICUT

RHODE ISLAND

Hudson R.

Newburgh

ROCHAMBEAU
JUN–JUL

Newport

Wyoming Valley

New York

PENNSYLVANIA

WASHINGTON (–) AND ROCHAMBEAU

Trenton

CLINTON (–)
OCT

SEP
Philadelphia

AUG

MARYLAND

Head of Elk

NEW JERSEY

Baltimore

VIRGINIA

Annapolis

LAFAYETTE
APR.

DELAWARE

Chesapeake Bay

James R.

Richmond

Petersburg

JUN–JUL

YORKTOWN

ELEMENTS OF
THE FRENCH NAVY
CONTROLLING CHESAPEAKE BAY
SEP–OCT

CORNWALLIS
APR–MAY

NORTH
CAROLINA

Cape Hatteras

Wilmington

SIEGE OF YORKTOWN
6–9 October 1781

0   1
Miles

York River

Gloucester Point

YORKTOWN

BRITISH
SURRENDERED
19 Oct

to Williamsburg

2d Parallel

1st Parallel

FRENCH AND AMERICAN FORCES

American Revolutionary War. Courtesy of the U.S. Army Center of Military History

minister would be respectfully received. The new minister, William Vans Murray; the chief justice of the U.S., Oliver Ellsworth (John Jay had retired to become governor of New York, replacing Clinton); and the governor of North Carolina, William Davie (replacing Patrick Henry as a delegation member, who declined because of age and health and died shortly after the others departed in the spring of 1799) were the commissioners and were courteously received in Paris. All the saber-rattling had got the attention of the French, who did not need war with a fierce and rising America at this point, as they contemplated the ancient puzzle of how to suppress their trans-Channel foes, after Admiral Horatio Nelson had defeated the French Navy in the Battle of the Nile in October 1798, deferring indefinitely any possibility of a French invasion of England and stranding Bonaparte in Egypt. Adams was in danger of losing public opinion to Jefferson, but his policy was successful, as a new treaty with France, the Convention of 1800, was signed on September 30, 1800, superseding that of 1778 and ending any defensive alliance while normalizing relations with France.

George Washington had died just 17 days before the end of the century of which he had been one of the greatest historic figures, an event observed with universal respect. His last view of Mount Vernon, where he peacefully passed away, aged 67, was of his estate covered in snow. In his will he emancipated his slaves and provided financially for their welfare. General "Light Horse" Harry Lee, congressman (and father of General Robert E. Lee), in his moving official eulogy on December 26, 1799, spoke nothing but the truth in describing the late president as "first in war, first in peace, first in the hearts of his countrymen." The event caused only the briefest pause in the wild political blood-letting that had so appalled the deceased leader.

After a decade of its new constitutional arrangements, the United States had enjoyed a 70 percent gain in population and a tripling of the national economy, and had gone to the brink of war with first Britain and then France and extracted favorable arrangements with both. Washington had briefly lost public opinion with Jay's Treaty, and Adams lost many of his partisans with the Convention of 1800 without gaining much from Jefferson, who favored the French treaty but was still agitating the country over the kangaroo courts that convicted 10 of his editors. Adams, ex-diplomat as he was, proved strategically competent but politically vulnerable. Hamilton, who was becoming increasingly irrational, lashed out at Adams with a 54-page letter for the Federalist establishment acidulously assessing Adams's presidency, published with rejoicing by the Republicans as soon as they got hold of it in the summer of 1800. Hamilton was trying to promote Charles C. Pinckney's candidacy over Adams but must have known that the inevitable beneficiary would be Jefferson, whom Hamilton now perversely claimed to respect more than Adams.

7. JEFFERSON AS PRESIDENT

The divisions among the Federalists seemed to assure Republican victory in 1800. The main issues were the Alien and Sedition Acts, the increased taxes to pay for the larger military budget, and the revival of anti-British sentiment—while French-American relations started to improve, the British went back to seizing American ships and sailors. These were all negative issues for the Federalists, and the disaffection of Hamilton and his powerful faction redounded to Charles C. Pinckney's benefit opposite Adams but also helped the Republican candidates, Jefferson and Aaron Burr. The electoral votes came in 73 votes each for Jefferson and Burr, 65 for Adams, 64 for Pinckney, and one vote for John Jay. It could be assumed at first that this would assure Jefferson's election, but as no distinction was made on the ballots of the division of office between two candidates, it was a tie for the presidential vote, which Burr now professed to have been seeking. There being no majority, the election moved from the Electoral College to the House of Representatives, where the delegation of each state caucused to decide on a candidate and then cast a single vote for that candidate. The Federalists had the majority in the House and preferred the suave and charming but devious and, in policy terms ambiguous, Burr over their ancient foe, Jefferson.

But against this trend, Hamilton was convinced that Burr was a scoundrel and an opportunist, a cunning man of no integrity, and that Jefferson was preferable to Burr, as he was also to Adams, because of what Hamilton professed to consider a betrayal by Adams in seeking reconciliation with France. Hamilton applied his almost demonic energy to supporting Jefferson over Burr, as Adams and Pinckney had distinctly, though narrowly, lost. There were 35 ballots between February

and February 17, 1801, without a winner. There was discussion of a statutory declaration of a winner, and the Federalist House could have professed to elect Pinckney or even Hamilton president, though this would have badly snarled the process and opened it to challenge before the Supreme Court. Jefferson warned the governor of Virginia, his protégé James Monroe, that Virginia should be ready for armed resistance should any such effort be mounted.[14]

The Federalist senator from Delaware, James Bayard, received from a Maryland Republican, General Samuel Smith, what he professed to consider assurances from Jefferson that he would preserve the Hamilton financial program and Adams's new

---

14. Wood, *op. cit.*, p. 285.

navy and would only dismiss Federalist officeholders for cause. It was later denied that any such promises had come from Jefferson, but believing they had that comfort level, the Federalists arranged votes and abstentions within state congressional delegations that tilted the vote on the 36th ballot: 10 states for Jefferson to 4 for Burr, and 2 states unable to declare a choice. (Tennessee had become the 16th state in 1796.) The Jefferson Revolution had begun, and this opened the great, six-term reign of the Jefferson-Virginian Republicans. But it began narrowly and uncertainly. Jefferson and Madison had hinted at nullification of federal legislation, in Jefferson's case on behalf of Kentucky, on the determination of the state alone; and in the electoral controversy, Jefferson and Monroe had corresponded on the possibility of an armed Virginian resistance to a Federalist, legislated election victor, not necessarily an unconstitutional solution. These were profound fissures in the constitutional beliefs of the main political groups, and that is without considering the implications of the smoldering issue of slavery.

In one of his last and most important presidential acts, Adams appointed the very able lawyer and secretary of state, anti-Jeffersonian Virginian John Marshall, as chief justice of the United States, a post he would distinguishedly occupy for 34 years. John Adams, a competent statesman and man of inflexible integrity and patriotism, retired to his home in Quincy, Massachusetts, angry and disappointed, but having rendered conspicuous service, and generally respected if not afloat on waves of public affection. He would prove to be the first of four generations of his family of eminent, public-spirited Americans, and the longest-lived of any president of the U.S. until the twenty-first century.

Jefferson's inaugural address foresaw the steady growth in the power, extent, and prosperity of the nation. He had been an advocate of a small federal government, and thought the Articles of Confederation could have been amended to make an adequate framework, and that the presidency, as created, was an elected monarchy, "a bad edition of a Polish king."[15] Jefferson immediately set an informal tone to proceedings, dressed casually, delivered messages in writing, and received anyone who wanted to see him, simply, often in slippers, and in the order they appeared, very congenially. He sold Adams's elaborate coach and horses and traveled in a one-horse market-cart.

Whether the Federalists thought they had an understanding with Jefferson or not, he did shrink the army drastically, and with the very capable expatriate Swiss banker Albert Gallatin (who had been discommoded by the xenophobia of

---

15. By the time Jefferson was inaugurated, Poland had been carved up entirely by the Russian, Prussian, and Austrian Empires and had no king.

1798) as Treasury secretary, vacated tax fields, reduced spending, and reduced debt steadily through his presidency, even as the country continued to grow rapidly. He considered his administration to be Whig against the Federalist Tories, and he mastered the appearances of popular government. He considered the Bonapartist coup seizing power for the new consulate to be confirmation of his aversion to large standing armies, and had never seen any need for such a force anyway. He established the U.S. Military Academy at West Point to train Republican officers to replace the Washington-Adams military establishment, but ultimately to assure a non-political officer corps, a valuable and needed reform. Jefferson did allow himself to be persuaded by Gallatin of the merits of the Bank of the United States, and their various frugalities, especially reductions in the army and navy, helped cut the federal debt from $83 million to $57 million in eight years, despite a nearly 40 percent increase in the country's population, to about seven million.

Jefferson continued a nationalist tradition in the defense of the nation's interests in the world and its continued western expansion. Following the example of the British, the United States under its first two presidents had fallen into the habit of paying tribute to the Barbary pirates along the North African coast from Morocco east to what is now Libya. The Pasha of Tripoli (forerunner to Colonel Qaddaffi) increased his extortions for each ship and purported to declare war on the United States on May 14, 1801. Jefferson was less hostile to the navy than to the army, as it was less adaptable for use in domestic repression, and he dispatched a "Mediterranean squadron" that, led in the principal action by Lieutenant Stephen Decatur, destroyed the Pasha's principal vessel, the former USS *Philadelphia*. A blockade was imposed on the main pirate harbors, and the Pasha eventually thought better of it and signed a peace in June 1805. (Tribute, in reduced amounts, continued to be paid until 1816.)[16]

8. THE LOUISIANA PURCHASE

Louisiana was the name for a vast territory bounded by the Gulf of Mexico and to the east by the Mississippi, and extending to the Canadian border in what would become Montana while broadening east to Lake Huron and west almost to Oregon. It was 828,000 square miles, including most of what has ever since Jeffersonian times been considered the heartland of America. The territory, as part of the settlement of the Seven Years' War, was ceded by France to Spain in 1762, and as part

---

16.   Pope Pius VII said, as the Barbary pirates regularly seized hostages and held them for ransom, that "the United States had done more for the cause of Christianity than the most powerful nations of Christendom have done for ages." (Christopher Hitchens, "Jefferson Versus the Muslim Pirates," *City Journal*, Spring 2007.)

of Napoleon's imperial ambitions was taken back from Spain in the secret Treaty of San Ildefonso in October 1800, which was confirmed with the signing of the Treaty of Madrid in March 1801. Jefferson, despite his incandescent Francophilia, was alarmed by this and feared such a powerful and contiguous French presence. He was also worried that the westward growth of the country could be stunted by restrictive French administration of the port of New Orleans and meddling with Mississippi traffic. The Spanish government in New Orleans, continuing in the name of France, revoked the right of Americans to unload cargo in New Orleans in 1802. Even Jefferson had been appalled at the conduct of the French in the Genêt and XYZ affairs, which were the two chief diplomatic encounters to date between the United States and France. Jefferson wrote the American minister in Paris, Robert Livingston, in April 1802, that "The day that France takes New Orleans . . . we must marry ourselves to the British fleet and nation." This was an astonishing turn for the president, but demonstrated his clear-headed pursuit of the national and his own political interests when not permitted the luxury of his dilettantish biases. He told Livingston to negotiate an acquisition of a Gulf port and as much as he could of the lower Mississippi, or at least permanent and adequate rights in New Orleans.

On January 12, 1803, Jefferson named James Monroe—the former minister to France whom Washington had recalled, as Adams said, "in disgrace" for his fraternization with the Robespierrists and the Directory—as minister plenipotentiary to France to join Livingston in the negotiations and buy New Orleans and West Florida. The Congress had authorized $2 million, but Jefferson told Monroe to go to $10 million if he had to. By the time Monroe arrived in France in April, Napoleon had abandoned his ideas of a revived American empire, shocked at the unsuccessful decade-long effort to suppress a slave revolt in Haiti and wary of revived war with Britain, which continued to be invincible at sea. He did not wish to be starved out of North America as Louis XVI had been. Just before Monroe's arrival, Talleyrand asked Livingston what the U.S. would pay for the whole Louisiana Territory. Monroe took this up on his arrival a couple of days later and boldly seized the opportunity. Agreement was reached and signed on May 2, antedated to April 30, buying the whole territory for $15 million, including U.S. government assumption of $3.75 million of French debts to private American interests. Monroe and Livingston exceeded their authority but Jefferson was delighted, and the acquisition was easily approved by the Senate in October. It slightly tested the president's strict constructionist ideas, but, as always, he was able to adjust legal dogmas to suit a rational discharge of his office.

This was a brilliant, if entirely fortuitous, transaction that doubled the size of the country. Neither liberal historian Sean Willentz's commendation of Jefferson for increasing the nation's territory while shrinking its defense budget nor Theodore Roosevelt's outrageous lampoon of Jefferson and Madison (the secretary of state) was justified. Roosevelt called them "timid, well-meaning statesmen . . . pitted against the greatest warrior and law-giver, and one of the greatest diplomats of modern times, . . . who were unable to so much as appreciate that there was shame in the practice of venality, dishonesty, mendacity, cruelty and treachery." Napoleon and Talleyrand were as described,[17] but Napoleon knew he couldn't hold the territory against the British and Americans and correctly saw that the United States would rise up to rival and surpass the British. What he could not foresee was that the British would have the sagacity to tuck themselves in under the wing of the Americans as an indispensable ally when they could no longer lead the English-speaking world themselves. Jefferson's and Madison's and Monroe's conduct in the matter was astute, opportunistic, and entirely successful. In less than 50 years since the start of the Seven Years' War, the Americans had helped remove the French from their borders, achieved their independence, launched and established a stable republic with solid institutions and a strong currency, and more than doubled their original territory, peacefully. It had been a steadily more remarkable series of strategic successes, accomplished by a continuously remarkable group of men.

9. HAMILTON AND BURR

Jefferson's next foray into westward expansionism was the dispatch of the expedition of Merriweather Lewis and William Clark to the Pacific and back. Lewis was a military officer and had been assigned as an aide to Jefferson when he became president. Jefferson had never been west of the Appalachians, but his father had been a surveyor who had glimpsed the Ohio country and Jefferson had long cherished a powerful and romantic notion of the potential for the westward expansion of the country. Jefferson proposed to Lewis a full scientific and exploratory expedition to the Pacific coast, which had never been reached overland from America, only by the Scot Alexander Mackenzie in Canada. Lewis agreed and selected William Clark, a fellow army officer, as co-leader. The expedition was expanded to 26 people, including scientists, experts in Indian languages, and a contingent of soldiers trained in frontier life. They set off from St. Louis in the spring of 1804, and after 1,600 miles went into winter quarters in November near what became Bismarck, North Dakota. They resumed their westward progress in April 1805, and reached the Pacific Ocean on November 15. The return journey to St. Louis, Missouri, from March to September 1806, was more direct. The maps, wildlife and botanical drawings,

---

17. Ruddy, *op. cit.*, p. 89.

and diaries were of scientific value and captured the imagination of the country by focusing on the immense and abundant territory that beckoned to settlers (however disgruntled the indigenous population might be about it).

Jefferson's war with the Federalists, and settling of scores generally, ramified quite widely. His supporters successfully impeached and removed from office federal district judge John Pickering, and impeached but failed to remove Associate Supreme Court Justice Samuel Chase, who had condemned the malcontent John Fries and the scurrilous blackmailer James T. Callender.

After Aaron Burr had abruptly metamorphosed from a vice presidential into a presidential candidate in early 1801, there was a widespread feeling not only that he was a scoundrel but that the system was a disaster of intrigue and chaos waiting to happen. The response was the Twelfth Amendment to the Constitution, providing for separate balloting for president and vice president, which was ratified in September 1804, in time for the presidential election.

As the 1804 election approached, both Alexander Hamilton and Aaron Burr vanished from the political front lines, where they had long been prominent. Hamilton was one of the leaders of the Federalists in denying Burr the governorship of New York, which he sought when long-serving Governor George Clinton was tapped by Jefferson to take Burr's place as vice president. (John Jay only held the office for one term.) Hamilton joined the Republicans in crusading for Burr's opponent, Morgan Lewis. In one of his frequent effusions, Hamilton, twiddling his thumbs impatiently in New York while Jefferson lolled in the newly completed White House, denounced Burr—who was infuriated at the imputations to him of unscrupulousness and even treachery, and at being frozen entirely out of government by Jefferson—as "a dangerous man, and one who ought not to be trusted with the reins of government." In the manner of the times, this led to a duel, in which, at Weehawken, New Jersey, on July 11, 1804, Burr killed Hamilton. Thus, aged only 49, there perished the third of the six principal founders of the country. Hamilton was almost a demiurge, a financial and administrative genius and a very capable military officer in both staff and combat roles. He was a relentless political schemer and operator, and when not grounded by Washington, tended to fly off unguided, combustible, and with unpredictable results. He was a monarchist and an authoritarian at heart, but he had rendered immense services to the country and glimpsed more clearly than anyone else the true and necessary development of the American economy.

Of the other principal figures at the birth of the republic apart from Washington, Franklin, and Hamilton, Adams had retired, but Jefferson and Madison remained in great offices with work to do. Aaron Burr, who had been a brilliant politician and was a gifted lawyer and inveterate schemer, was finished politically. Having been judged guilty of trying to snitch away from Jefferson his election victory in 1800, and now having killed Hamilton, he was not presentable for high office, and wandered off to the West with great but, some thought, sinister ambitions. A helplessly controversial person, Burr would be back before the country soon again, in an exotic and unflattering light.

The disillusioned editor Callender, imprisoned under the Sedition Act, became annoyed that the administration would not repay him his fine and attacked Jefferson for fathering three children with his comely slave, Sally Hemings. Jefferson ignored the allegation, which was not reprinted in respectable publications and was dismissed as the malicious scandal-mongering of a convicted felon, who in any case died in July 1803 when he blundered into a river in Richmond, Virginia, in a drunken stupor. (Callender's allegations were correct, but not strictly relevant to Jefferson's competence to hold his office, legally or otherwise.)

General Charles Cotesworth Pinckney was nominated by the Federalists for president, and the Hamiltonian disciple and anti-slavery advocate Rufus King, minister to Great Britain and former senator from New York, was nominated for vice president. There was not really too much to run against, as Jefferson offered peace, prosperity, and a distinguished, unpretentious government, and he and Clinton won easily, 162 electoral votes to 14, and with about 72 percent of the votes.

After the death of Hamilton, Burr was indicted for murder but continued for eight months to be the vice president, in which capacity he presided in very statesmanlike and learned fashion over the impeachment trial of Justice Chase, which, to Jefferson's acute irritation, ended in acquittal. Burr devised his next and perhaps most grandiose plan. He spoke with the British and Spanish ministers to Washington about subsidizing the creation of a new jurisdiction that Burr would set up in the Southwest. Neither the subsequent judicial proceedings nor the efforts of historians have clarified whether Burr had any treasonable intent. The American military commander in the southern Mississippi region, General James Wilkinson (who commissioned Lieutenant Zebulon Montgomery Pike's expedition to the sources of the Mississippi and to Colorado, where Pike's Peak is named after him, and New Mexico, in 1806–1807), was illicitly taking competing emoluments from the French, British, and Spanish, to keep an eye out for their interests in the Southwest. Burr, a great national celebrity, much admired in some circles for clearing his honor by killing an illustrious opponent in a duel, padded around the area and supplied arms from his own resources to the Louisiana militia, and added his own tangible favors to those Wilkinson was receiving from foreign powers. Burr and Wilkinson had been friendly when both had been in the Continental Army.

As rumors became more intense and far-fetched that Burr was planning to set up his own country, carved out of American and Mexican territory, Jefferson had him charged with treason on November 26, 1806. Jefferson reported to the Congress in February 1807 that the former vice president's "guilt is placed beyond question," oblivious of the fact that Burr had already been released by a grand jury in Mississippi for lack of evidence, but rearrested in Alabama. He was taken to Richmond for trial, while Jefferson personally worked with the U.S. attorney in Richmond, George Hay, on the prosecution's case. Burr was a brilliant barrister and participated in the preparation of his own case, which, to Jefferson's dismay, was judged by Chief Justice John Marshall, self-assigned for the purpose to the Fourth Circuit. In April 1807, Marshall pitched out the treason charge and reduced it to conspiracy. Burr had many supporters, including Jefferson's cousin and successor as secretary of state and former U.S. attorney general, Edmund Randolph. Burr subpoenaed Jefferson, and the documentation between his officials and himself in respect of the case, and Marshall ruled that the president enjoyed no exemption, and that he would determine confidentially the relevance and degree of privilege and national security concerns of the material.

Burr excused Jefferson as a witness, and Jefferson helped establish an important precedent, which would be used in the Watergate affair in 1974, and handed over the material to Marshall. The trial, in August 1807, consisted of the evidence and cross-examination of the sole government witness, General Wilkinson, who was torn limb from limb by Burr and his counsel and appeared a good deal more guilty of reprehensible acts than the defendant. The jury found Burr not guilty, but in wording that implied it was not convinced that he was wholly innocent of wrongdoing. Burr departed for Europe until the murder charges against him over the Hamilton duel had been dropped, then returned to New York, where he lived quietly and successfully as a lawyer and figure of society until he died in 1836, aged 80. He was a great but unfocused talent, and was in superficial respects a forerunner to Richard Nixon, as an able politician who could not shake the suspicion of lack of probity. But Burr never got close to the presidency or great deeds.

10. RESPONDING TO WAR IN EUROPE

As war had resumed in Europe in 1803, it was not long before the high-handed conduct of the European powers, especially Britain, made America's maritime rights again become a scorching issue. Both Britain and France claimed the right to prevent neutral countries from trading with the other, which in practice, since Britain held the scepter of the sea, meant that America was soon back to the exasperating practice of having the British seize and search her ships, confiscate cargo, and remove alleged deserters and impress American seamen into British service. It was a straight oppression by the stronger naval power of the weaker, and international law walked the plank as soon as hostilities commenced. The British invoked the Rule of 1756, successfully imposed in the Seven Years' War, whereby European powers that had forbidden trade with its West Indian colonies in time of peace should not open trade up to neutrals in wartime. Thus phrased, it seemed to put the onus for simply squashing trade by imposition of naval force on the exporting country, though the victim would be the neutral carrier, trying to pick up from one combatant and use his neutrality to assure delivery that the combatant power with inferior naval strength (France) could not assure himself. The legalities were a little more complicated than they at first seemed. But it was all made excessively difficult by the British practice of not just inspecting American ships and seizing cargos but also dragooning American sailors, along with alleged defectors from the Royal Navy, into that navy.

The turning point came when a British court determined that the practice of the French delivering to American ports cargo that American ships then conveyed to French ports would be considered as direct commerce from the French West Indies unless the Americans could satisfy the intercepting British that they had intended originally for the voyage to terminate in an American port. This was not going to be easy to establish, but it was at least a variation on outright seizure, and the product of a British court decision and not just an executive naval command order. Madison reported the decision in a trenchantly worded report in January 1806, and the Senate condemned "unprovoked aggression" and the "violation of neutral rights." When Britain ignored American threats and protests, the Congress voted an embargo on an extensive list of items that the U.S. imported from Britain that it could produce itself or buy from other countries. The statute was only in effect from October to November 1806, when Jefferson asked for its suspension until after the election of his successor, in December 1808. European affairs vastly surpassed the efforts of America to make itself felt. In May 1806, Charles James Fox, again British foreign secretary, had declared an absolute naval blockade of the European Atlantic coast from Brest in northwest France to the mouth of the Elbe in Prussia.

At the end of 1806, Jefferson sent William Pinckney (a member of a temporarily ubiquitous family) to London to join the minister there, the already ubiquitous James Monroe, in trying to sort out an agreement with Britain, with the imposition of the trade embargo against British goods as a bargaining chip. The British weren't interested: a treaty was negotiated that produced only slight concessions on West Indian trade and none at all on British impressment of American sailors or the American ambition for payment of indemnities for British ship seizures. It was a painful lesson in the comparative importance of and correlation of forces between states, and Jefferson declined to send such a feeble arrangement to the Senate for ratification.

Napoleon replied to Fox with his Berlin Decree of November 21, 1806 (following his conquest of Prussia, a blitzkrieg as astounding as that of the German army in conquering France 134 years later). Napoleon purported to bar all commerce and communication between Britain and the entire continent of Europe. Jefferson then ordered new negotiations with Britain on the hopeful assumption that the British would prove more amenable after this initiative from the French emperor (who had promoted himself from first consul three years before). The British and French scarcely noticed the Americans as the greatest war in the history of the world until a hundred years later steadily grew in scope and intensity.

A very galling incident illustrated the dilemma of America and the limitations of its president's pacifistic impulses in June 1807, when the British frigate *Leopard* stopped the American frigate *Chesapeake* beyond the three-mile territorial limit off Norfolk, Virginia, and the American ship declined to have her crew inspected for British deserters. The British ship subdued the American vessel with four broadsides killing three and wounding 18 Americans. Four sailors were seized, of whom only one was a British deserter. The incident inflamed and unified American opinion, Jefferson estimated, beyond anything since Lexington and Concord 32 years before. The U.S. demand for an apology and indemnity was simply ignored by the British, in what was now the customary manner, and Jefferson was finally forced to gamble on his economic response policy, which had been passed over in favor of the Adams-Hamilton military threat of 1798. Jefferson secured congressional approval of an almost complete embargo against trade with all foreign governments (since virtually all accessible countries were now at war with each other) and closed American ports entirely to all British shipping.

This policy was an inexcusable misreading of what should have been obvious to Jefferson and his collaborators: that the United States would be the principal victim; that the embargo would have no impact on France, which controlled almost all of Europe west of Russia, south of Sweden, and north of the Ottoman Empire; and that the British would benefit from the loss of American competition, and would import foodstuffs from South America instead. American ships at sea when the embargo was imposed simply did not return to American ports and continued as international traders, enjoying the full cooperation of the Royal Navy with any American ship that ignored the American law. An immense smuggling business was carried on through Canada, with the cooperation not only of the British but of most New England and Upstate New York commercial interests.

The embargo did not prevent British ships from delivering cargos to the United States, but it forbade them to remove American exports, so many dropped off in northern U.S. ports and picked up return cargoes in Canada. And Napoleon, astounded at the absurdity of the American measure and partially justifying Theodore Roosevelt's disparagement of the comparative naïveté of Jefferson and Madison in dealing with such a man as he, seized all American shipping in French and French-controlled ports and waters, more than $10 million of shipping assets, claiming that any such ships were obviously British vessels with false papers, as no American would ignore Jefferson's embargo act.

Jefferson amplified his mistake with draconian enforcement orders, dispensing with the Fourth Amendment requirement for search warrants, ordering seizure by customs officials on suspicion of infractions of the embargo, deploying the armed forces along the Canadian border, and even determining that the Lake Champlain area was in a state of insurrection. None of these measures stopped smuggling on a massive scale, but they invited nullification actions by state legislatures (including by former secretary of state Pickering in New England), the withholding of state militias for enforcement purposes in New England, and unsuccessful constitutional challenges, and they involved clear impositions of force more objectionable than those for which Jefferson had urged revolt from George III in the most empurpled terms in the Declaration of Independence and elsewhere. The policy was an unmitigated economic, political, and moral disaster. The export industry declined by 75 percent and standards of living, especially in New England and the main Atlantic ports, plummeted. Finally, the Congress repealed the embargo and Jefferson signed this abandonment of his policy just three days before the inauguration of his successor, on March 1, 1809.

11. ASSESSING THOMAS JEFFERSON

Jefferson had been a good president up to the economic reprisals against the warring European powers. His simple and frugal manner of government, devolving much back on the states and promoting democratic values generally, was popular, and with Gallatin at the Treasury, prosperity continued to increase. The Louisiana Purchase and the Lewis and Clark and Pike expeditions were valuable in themselves in laying out settler routes and goals, and fired the nation's imagination with the organic growth of western settlement. Because the forceful handling of the Genêt and XYZ affairs by Washington, and the strong resistance, with clear military overtones, of Adams to the original maritime impressments and seizure crisis of 1798 had been successful, Jefferson had been spared the exposure of his ill-considered economic reprisals against larger economies of much less vulnerability than America's to misconceived and largely unenforceable laws. He was finally free to present and force through the docile Congress a policy that laid the U.S. economy low and exposed Jefferson as an innumerate blowhard and a hypocrite. He spent much of the last year of his presidency in an immobilized state, racked by migraines and digestive problems.

Only the happenstance of the Louisiana Purchase made Jefferson a more successful president than Adams, and in that as in previous offices, Jefferson did not have the steady judgment and self-control of Washington, any more than had the quirky and irascible Adams.

Yet, though Jefferson botched his mad essay at economic warfare, he was a great expander of the country, popularizer of the presidency, and decentralizer of government, and one of the most politically gifted and effective leaders in the country's history, clearly surpassed in this regard only by Franklin D. Roosevelt and possibly by Lincoln and Reagan also. His principal rival as the greatest intellectual in the presidency, Woodrow Wilson (though John Quincy Adams, John Adams's son, could also be a rival), wrestled 110 years later with similar maritime provocations in a European war, and had the same pacifistic tendencies as Jefferson, but, at the head of a much more powerful America, would make war rather than tolerate the humiliation of America. Jefferson had done little as the country's first secretary of state, and less, other than in partisan organization and political rough and tumble, as its second vice president. He was a talented president, but it is not accidental that he directed that his gravestone should refer to his status as author of the Declaration of Independence and the Virginia statute on the rights of man, and to his status as founder of the University of Virginia, and not to his great offices of state.

Only the reputation of the Democratic-Republicans as sincere adherents to popular government (which was not an imposture), and the continued erosion of the Federalists and the absence of a galvanizing figure to rally the opposition, prevented a political upheaval in the 1808 elections. Hamilton was sorely missed. Three of the candidates for national office from the previous election ran again. Jefferson followed the Washington precedent and retired after two terms, though he could presumably have been reelected, because of the disarray of his opponents and despite the fiasco of his trade policies. He was replaced by Madison as the presidential candidate of the Democratic-Republicans (Democrats, as they became, and Jefferson and Madison are celebrated as the founders of the modern Democratic Party), and George Clinton was again nominated for vice president. The Federalists again chose Charles Cotesworth Pinckney for president and Rufus King for vice president.

Some of the Jeffersonians splintered off under the half-mad but brilliant John Randolph of Roanoke, who was a states' rights and nullification advocate (he proposed that states could decide the federal government had exceeded its powers and simply nullify the application of the offending law within their own borders). The eastern Jeffersonians nominated George Clinton, on what amounted almost to a free-trade platform. Clinton thus became the first and to date only person in American history to be nominated and stand for election as president and as vice president in the same year. Technically, he was running against himself, as the same person could not simultaneously hold both positions. The Randolphites were known as the "Quids" (because Randolph said they were neither Democratic-Republicans nor Federalists, and were a "third something," or Tertium Quids—it was a mark of an erudite electorate that a splinter party acquired a Latin name). They nominated James Monroe for president, but he, unlike his administration colleague Clinton, declined to allow his name to stand against his old friend Madison. The vote was closer than in the previous election, but Madison and Clinton won, by 122 electoral votes to 47 for Pinckney and six for Clinton, who had the consolation of being reelected vice president by 113 to 47 for King. The Federalists made substantial gains in the Congress, but did not secure the majority of either house. Pinckney only received about 32 percent of the votes for president against about 55 percent for Madison.

The Americans suffered their first serious strategic setback, going back 50 years to the Seven Years' War, when Jefferson had said that taking Canada was "a mere matter of marching." It proved to be more complicated than that, but he didn't even endow his country with the men to make the march. If Jefferson had taken a leaf from the book of his predecessors, and built up a large army and equipped it, he could have threatened Britain with the permanent seizure of Canada, and could have forced some variance in the maritime provocations of the British. The application of simple grade-three arithmetic would have told him, as it told his opponents and the countries he was aiming to influence, that the policies he did adopt could not succeed, and their failure squandered a good deal of the political capital and credibility that had been built up by his comrades in the establishment of the United States—Washington, Franklin, Hamilton, and Adams.

This setback would be compounded by Madison, but was a lost opportunity, not a lasting defeat, and was more than overshadowed by the Louisiana Purchase. In strategic terms, the Jefferson presidency, though more ambiguous than its predecessors, continued America's advance, in a world where almost all other nations were wracked by war.

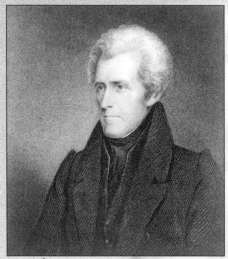

Andrew Jackson

CHAPTER FOUR

Reconciling with Britain Abroad, and with Slavery at Home, 1809–1836

1. JAMES MADISON AS PRESIDENT

Madison was the last principal founder of the nation still in harness. His presidency was heavily preoccupied with the perpetual crisis caused by the refusal of the British and French to take the United States and its sovereignty seriously. The novelty had worn off America, and Napoleon was a far more epochal and immense historic figure—other than in the most conventionally idealistic terms—than the American founders, and the struggle with him was entirely engrossing to Europe and terminally enervating to much of it, ultimately including France. Madison drifted through his first year, after the cancellation of Jefferson's embargo, which act included authorizing the president to resume trade with any country that signaled the end of violations of America's neutrality.

While in this mode, Madison was embarrassingly fleeced, first by the British and then by the French, as if in a stately early nineteenth century court quadrille. The British minister in Washington, David Erskine, told Madison's secretary of state, Robert Smith, that the British orders in council that had so offended America would be withdrawn on June 10, 1809. Madison responded with a proclamation on April 19 lifting the ban on trade with Great Britain. The British foreign secretary, George Canning, disavowed Erskine and pulled him as minister on May 30, and Madison reimposed the trade embargo on Britain on August 9, 1809. The next legislative tackling of the trade question was by the chairman of the House Foreign Affairs Committee, Nathaniel Macon, in early 1810. His bill stated that if either Britain or France relaxed its offensive measures, the president could prohibit trade with the other. (Only Britain and France were now players in this American game, which the subjects of their attempted reprisals barely seemed to notice.) Napoleon's foreign minister, the Duke de Cadore,[1] informed the American minister in Paris, John Armstrong, that France was ending its trade blockade. Madison, undismayed by the fiasco with Britain, announced on November 2, 1810, that the embargo against France had ended, and that commerce with Britain would end completely if it did not follow the French lead. In retaliation, Britain completely shut down New York as a port and redoubled the impressments of American sailors, before it came to light that Napoleon had not ended the anti-American trade exclusion at all. By then, such matters had been overtaken by more important and drastic events, as France had invaded Russia and America had gone back to war against Britain.

---

1. Talleyrand had concluded that Napoleon was mad and he had retired and made his peace with the Bourbons.

Madison did seize west Florida, which was the territory along the Gulf coast from the Mississippi to Mobile, Alabama, on October 27, 1810, as it had been Jefferson's and his contention that American sovereignty over this territory could be legally inferred from the Louisiana Purchase. But Madison continued, almost four years after the imposition of the self-defeating embargo, to shuffle and reshuffle ineffectual remedies to the systematic British and French violations of American sovereignty. If he had followed Washington's old dictum that peace should be pursued by preparing for war, and assembled an army capable of occupying Canada, Britain would have made concessions. Britain could not transfer the forces that would have been necessary to prevent an American occupation of Canada after it had committed its main army to the war in Spain in 1808. But Madison compounded Jefferson's error and never armed himself with a plausible stick with which to threaten the British, who continued to treat the United States like a banana republic, a practice in which Napoleon emulated or surpassed them with simple chicanery, as he had no navy (having been relieved of it by Viscount Nelson and other British admirals) with which fully to replicate Britain's outrages against America.

As the foreign policy problems worsened and the American foreign trade economy stagnated, apart from the formidable efforts of smugglers, the charter of the Bank of the United States came up for renewal. The tenacious Swiss banker and ethnologist Albert Gallatin, settling determinedly into his third full term as Treasury secretary, fought hard to renew the charter, with Madison's support. The administration lost in the House, and a tie in the Senate was broken by the vote of Vice President Clinton, against the government, an almost unheard-of rebuff to the president. It was another unfortunate blunder, because the Bank was, as Hamilton had designed it, and as Gallatin had seen, a fine financing vehicle—something that, despite Jefferson and Madison's aversion to debt and large government, would prove very necessary when, the following year, the United States found itself trying to fund a war against a Great Power. (Gallatin was a great authority on American Indian tribes, and here too his expertise could have been invaluable, as relations with the indigenous peoples were chronically and dishonestly mismanaged for generations.)

Finally, by 1811, American opinion was moving toward war with Britain despite all the Jefferson-Madison pusillanimity about porous and self-punitive economic embargoes. The formidable Shawnee chief, Tecumseh, and his brother, The Prophet, were being encouraged by the British to build up an Indian buffer zone on the northwest frontier, and there was frequent skirmishing with settlers in the summer of 1811. The governor of the Indiana Territory, General William Henry Harrison, was induced to move against Tecumseh, who had attempted to organize all the main tribes, bands, and nations, as they variously called themselves, including in the Southwest, into a great defensive confederation. The Indians attacked the approaching Harrison at dawn on November 7 at Tippecanoe, and a fierce struggle see-sawed all day until the Americans forced retreat on the Indians, and burned their village down. This entered into American legend, in the absence of real war against sophisticated enemies, as a great victory, and after 30 years for the legend to be magnified by the American promotional machine, Harrison would join a succession of 11 men from Washington to Eisenhower who would ride military renown into the presidency.

By 1811, the British promotion of the Indians would inflame opinion in the West and North as efficiently as the maritime abrasions had aroused the seaboard states, especially New England and New York. Coming forward in the Congress now were young and aggressive men from the West and the South, who were widely known, following the description of John Randolph of Roanoke, as "war hawks." Among the most prominent were Henry Clay of Kentucky, Speaker of the House in 1811; John C. Calhoun of South Carolina, who followed Macon as chairman of the House Foreign Affairs Committee; and Richard M. Johnson (who in 1813 would claim to have killed Tecumseh). They advocated an armed and aggressive response to the British.

2. THE WAR OF 1812

On November 5, 1811, Madison, clearly preparing to take the plunge that would have been easier and timelier years before after suitable preparations, blasted the antics of the British on the high seas ("hostile inflexibility in trampling on rights which no independent nation can relinquish"). He was no kinder to the French, who had hoodwinked him for a year into believing the continental blockade in the Berlin Decree of 1806 had been lifted, and finally called for additional commitments to national defense. On April 1, 1812, he asked the Congress for an immediate and general embargo for 60 days, and was empowered three days later to call up 100,000 militiamen from around the country for six months.

The war that was to follow was farcical in its beginning and in its end, and often in between. The Napoleonic blockade, enforced by the mighty French Grand Army, did cause serious hardship in Britain, and the prime minister, Spencer Percival, was contemplating easing the heavy-handed treatment of America when he became the only British prime minister to be assassinated, by a deranged man of incoherent political views, on May 11, 1812. He was replaced by Lord Liverpool, but the delay held up until June 23 the British suspension of the orders in council that blockaded America. On June 18, at Madison's request, Congress declared war on Great Britain.

Madison delivered his request for a declaration of war on June 1; seventeen days to extract the declaration, with New England, New York, New Jersey, and Delaware voting against, illustrated how not to go to war. The country was sharply divided from the start, far more than it had been on the issue of independence from Britain, or than the South would be about seceding or the North over subduing secession nearly 50 years later. Not until the latter stages of the Vietnam War would America be so divided while exchanging fire with an enemy. Madison identified impressments of American sailors, violation of U.S. neutrality and territorial waters, the blockade of U.S. ports, and the related refusal to retract the enabling orders in council (as if the provocations would have been less galling if they weren't declared official policy, but only judicial decisions) as the reasons for war. Indians were not mentioned.

Because of three full terms of mismanagement of America's war-making powers and strategic position opposite Great Britain, the United States did not enter the war with such advantages as it should have enjoyed. Britain had its main army in Spain and was in no position to send heavy units to America. Its navy was fully engaged enforcing the blockade on France and its allied and conquered territories. The United States had 30 times as many people as Canada, and the U.S. Navy, though only 16 ships, had advantages of proximity and resupply, and was manned entirely by carefully selected and trained men. Against that, its army was not trained at all, public opinion was fragmented badly from the start, and there was no capacity to raise money efficiently since the lapse of the Bank of the United States. Madison was responsible, building on Jefferson's woeful traditions in these matters, for all of these problems.

The British only cuffed the Americans about because they ruled the oceans and knew that the United States had no military capability to inconvenience them in Canada or the West Indies. Countries, like people, do what they think they can get away with, with impunity. Madison was ultimately correct to go to war, but it would not have been necessary if he had not been swindled so artistically by Napoleon. The war—late, poorly prepared both in war-making terms and in preparation of public opinion—was still the right thing to do if it were successful. If the United States had emerged from it in possession of Canada, none of the impotent saber-rattling and vapid posturing of the various embargoes would have counted for anything.

Madison, a profoundly pacifistic man, despite his eminent position as a revolutionary, did finally conclude that there was no option but war, and started with every opportunity to make the war a great success and another immense accretion to the territory of the United States. And he started it in high fettle, visiting each government department, rendering pep talks wearing a "little round hat and huge cockade."[2]

The original American military plan was a harking back to the unfulfilled dreams of the previous wars about the ease of taking Canada (which had only been done by Britain in 1759, by penetrating the vast St. Lawrence like an endoscopy and seizing Quebec). There were to be the now traditional three parallel approaches: General Henry Dearborn would scoot up Lake Champlain and take Montreal; General Stephen Van Rensselaer would cross into Canada at the Niagara River and take what was to become Toronto; and a westerly force under General William Hull would attack across the St. Clair River at what is now Detroit and clean up whatever was left. The Americans were poorly trained militia, and the previous Washington and Adams Administrations' commitment to a permanent general staff and the development of detailed provisional war plans had been abandoned. Thus, all that was imagined were predictable approaches toward Montreal and at the western ends of Lake Ontario and Lake Erie.

Hull's drive across the Detroit River into Canada was the first off, but it proceeded only a few miles and then he withdrew after a month, as he was rightly fearful of being cut off by Tecumseh, who had thrown his lot in with the British and Canadians following their capture of the American post on Michilimackinac Island. Hull abruptly surrendered Detroit to General Isaac Brock without any exchange of fire, and the Indians seized Fort Dearborn (Chicago) on August 15 and massacred the garrison. His entire force of 2,000 were instant POWs. Hull was court-martialed for cowardice and sentenced to death, but the sentence was commuted because of his Revolutionary War service, and he was dishonorably discharged.

As if for the convenience of the defenders, the Americans deferred the attack at Niagara until the complete rout and capture of the Detroit forces, and Brock awaited Rensselaer on the Niagara River starting in late August. (Rensselaer had no military experience, but he was a Federalist and was appointed by New York governor Daniel Tompkins in a move to placate political opposition.) After two months, the Americans attacked at Queenston Heights and won the engagement, killing Brock. As the struggle reached its climax, the New York reservists declined to assist the rest of the American force, because their obligation to do so did not extend beyond the borders of the state. The British repulsed the invaders, and Van Rensselaer retired and was replaced by General Alexander Smyth. Smyth

2.   Gordon S. Wood, *Empire of Liberty: A History of the Early Republic 1789–1815*, Oxford and New York, Oxford University Press, 2009, p. 660.

dithered for over a month before attempting another invasion of Canada, which was easily repulsed on November 28, and he was sacked. Dearborn set out from Plattsburg for Montreal on November 19, hoping to coordinate with Smyth. His New York reservists also refused to cross the border into Quebec, and Dearborn returned diffidently to Plattsburg. After this sequence of fiascoes, Madison fired the war secretary, William Eustis, and replaced him with John Armstrong, who proved abrasive and unsuitable.

In the first year of the conflict, the United States did do better on the ocean and on the Great Lakes, and in single-vessel combat more than held its own with the Royal Navy, which had swept the waters around Europe of adversaries. Monroe had been asked by Madison at the end of the year to test the waters with peace overtures to the British. Once again, Madison had completely misjudged the prospects. The United States had had such a ludicrous start to the war that the British had no incentive at all to negotiate. As part of the same ambivalence about the war, the United States had maintained a chargé in London even after the outbreak of war, and the chargé advised the British foreign secretary, Lord Castlereagh (Marquis of Londonderry), that peace could be had if the British would abandon impressment of American sailors, and blockades of American ports, and pay for damage to American ships and forts. Castlereagh declined to negotiate on that basis, and a British overture from Admiral Warren, who commanded their forces in Halifax, directly to Monroe was rejected by Monroe unless the British promised to abandon impressment. This was not acceptable and the desultory war continued into 1813.

3. THE 1812 ELECTION

The presidential election of 1812 saw the origin of what became a wartime tradition of the nomination of a peace candidate by the party out of office. George Clinton's capable nephew, De Witt Clinton, mayor of New York City and champion of the Erie Canal, which he later built, as governor, was nominated by the New York state antiwar Republicans, with former Empire loyalist Jared Ingersoll for vice president, and the Federalists, fading and fragmented, endorsed both candidates. With the antiwar Democratic-Republicans having defected, President Madison was unanimously renominated by the Democratic-Republican congressional caucus. George Clinton had died, and Elbridge Gerry was nominated for vice president with Madison.

Of the principal founders of the country, Franklin had been too old to participate in the government, and Washington, Hamilton, and Adams were men of affairs, practical officers, and people of commercial and administrative talent. None of them was particularly talented politically, other than, in the broadest sense,

Washington. Jefferson the great polemicist and political theorist and Madison the great constitutional expert did not possess great practical skills of administration or the instinct of the national interest other than in an idealized sense of natural expansion into unpopulated areas. They thought it was sufficient to raise the lamp to the world and have a balanced Constitution and economical government and all else would follow, and they suspected Adams and Hamilton of being commercially dominated warmongers, with fragile attachment to any notion of individual or popular rights (quite unfairly in the case of Adams).

There were limitations to the Adams-Hamilton view of a dominating state and powerful standing armed forces, counting nothing on the goodwill of nations or the halcyon powers of America's founding principles and institutions. But the first group, prominently including Franklin, had an unerring instinct for the national interest, for the self-interestedness of other countries, for the limitations of sonorous assertions of inalienable rights as substitutes for armed force and the will to use it. Their strategic grasp never faltered, where Jefferson and Madison allowed the United States to lapse back into neo-colonial irrelevance, having neither the strength to threaten British possession of Canada, nor the strategic weight and diplomatic finesse to hold any sort of balance between France and Britain in wars that involved all the European powers for decades.

But Jefferson and Madison were immensely skillful politically. Their unpretentious method of government, tendency to devolve government to the states, and emphasis on broadening the suffrage and generalizing availability and quality of education while reducing taxes all hugely endeared them to the country. Hamilton and Adams, who between them won only one serious election, Adams as president, and that only because of Washington's endorsement and by a narrow margin, had no such appeal or success. This was the problem of the Federalists, who began as supporters of the Constitution but once the Constitution was adopted and implemented never developed as a party and merely became a group of interests, and not such widespread interests at that—essentially the commercial and financial elites of New York, Philadelphia, and Boston. The Democratic-Republicans essentially controlled the whole political spectrum, and most of the political competition in the country was between its factions. In these circumstances, inept though Madison's delayed, hesitant, backing into war had been, unwise though it was to go to war as head of a divided country, if he ran the war intelligently, he had yet a great chance to pick the fine plum of Canada, not a huge population but a huge rich area.

The interesting precedent in the 1812 election was the emergence of an antiwar party. In future wars, whenever they were waged or at least discussed for long enough, support and opposition to the war tended to be the demarcation in the presidential election: Clay leading antiwar opposition to Polk over Mexico in 1844; McClelland against Lincoln in the Civil War in 1864; Eisenhower promising to end the Korean War, though on favorable terms, in 1952; McGovern opposing the Vietnam War against Nixon in 1972; and both John Kerry and Barack Obama somewhat, though perhaps ambiguously, against the Iraq War in 2004 and 2008. America's participation in World War I would be between elections, and Woodrow Wilson ran as the man who "kept us out of war" and then asked for a declaration of war six weeks after he was reinaugurated. Franklin D. Roosevelt promised peace through strength and all aid short of war for the democracies in 1940, and his opponent, Wendell Willkie, though he supported his program, accused FDR of leading the nation into war. The only direct attack on the United States in history, by the Japanese at Pearl Harbor, was so brazen, premeditated, and unannounced that there was practically unanimous support for participation in World War II when it came.

De Witt Clinton gave it a good try, but Madison prevailed, 128 electoral votes to 89, with Gerry winning 131 to 86 over Ingersoll. The Federalists, in what would be their last vigorous performance, made substantial congressional gains, as all the New England and Middle Atlantic states down to Virginia, except Vermont and Pennsylvania, went for the opposition.

4. THE WAR: THE CAMPAIGNS OF 1813

Despite the success of individual American sea captains in single-ship duels with the British, and despite the fact that the Royal Navy was blockading practically all of Europe from Bahia in Spain to the Baltic, and from Gibraltar to Naples, it was still able to dispatch the forces necessary to blockade the entire American Atlantic and Gulf coasts, and to keep the blockade almost airtight throughout the war, though it left New England and New York untroubled for a time, in order to encourage the domestic political opposition. But the blockade was extended to the northern tip of the American coast in 1814. Throughout this time, the British caused havoc along the whole coast, with shore raiding parties and amphibious hit-and-run missions. American privateers and commerce raiders did a great deal of damage around the British Isles and in southern sea lanes as time went on, forcing the British to convoy ships to and from the Americas, but the British blockade of the United States, while it spurred the development of domestic manufacturing, did raise prices and depress farm incomes.

The Americans made significant progress in 1813, though they paid dearly for the absence of a military commander of the quality of Washington, Greene, Marion, and Morgan, until late in the war. A group of Kentuckians, including Speaker Henry Clay, engaged William Henry Harrison, victor of Tippecanoe, to take charge of their militia and try to recapture Detroit. Madison then named Harrison a major general of the U.S. Army (he had been a major general of militia), and confirmed his orders. He had 10,000 men. The Americans were defeated at Frenchtown in January and suffered about 1,000 casualties, but they defeated the British and Tecumseh at Fort Meigs in May and at Fort Stephenson in August. Harrison was enabled to carry out his orders to retake Detroit only after the decisive victory of Captain Oliver Hazard Perry in the Battle of Lake Erie on September 10, 1813. (Perry had the advantage of experienced, salt-water navy veterans, against relatively inexperienced lake sailors.) Perry sent Harrison the famous message "We have met the enemy and they are ours." In June, the dying Captain James Lawrence, on board the *Chesapeake*, in a duel with the British *Shannon*, had given the more famous order "Don't give up the ship," which became the motto of the United States Navy. (Perry's flagship on Lake Erie was named *Lawrence* after him.) Harrison pushed into Canada at the western end of Lake Erie. It was in this campaign in September of 1813 that Tecumseh was killed by Colonel Richard Johnson at Moravian Town, with the result that the Indians wholly deserted the British and Canadians, removing great anxiety from the American northwest frontier communities. (Johnson would run successfully for vice president of the U.S. in 1836 on the memorable slogan "Rumpsey, Dumpsey, Who Killed Tecumseh?")

The American attack on Ontario at the Niagara point of entry, under General Henry Dearborn and Colonel Winfield Scott, was a good deal more professionally executed than the slapstick farce of the previous year. The Americans took York (Toronto), and against Dearborn's orders key buildings in the city were burned down, including the house of assembly and the governor's house. (The explorer General Zebulon Montgomery Pike was killed in the actions around Toronto, aged 52.) Dearborn was replaced by the egregious General James Wilkinson, Aaron Burr's former collaborator and allegedly a member of the Conway conspiracy against George Washington, who had fluffed up his own role in the victory of Saratoga while serving as General Gates's messenger to the Continental Congress conveying news of the victory and the surrender of Burgoyne. Typically, Madison had just finished trying to court-martial Wilkinson (who had also been fired as clothier general of the army for taking kickbacks on the material for uniforms), and Wilkinson had only been released on Christmas Day, 1811. He was one of American history's ultimate (more or less likeable) scoundrels.

Wilkinson was to attack along the St. Lawrence to Montreal, while General Wade Hampton followed the well-trodden path north along Lake Champlain, and the two armies were to converge and take Montreal, which was defended by 15,000 British soldiers, well dug in around the city. Hampton approached to the Chateauguay River, suffered a minor defeat in a skirmish, and withdrew his 4,000 men back into New York state. Wilkinson suffered a defeat of one section of his 10,000-man force and then ducked into winter quarters too, very prudently, in mid-October. It wasn't quite as absurd an attack toward Montreal as the previous year's, but was only a marginal improvement, and the Americans never threatened or came within 50 miles of Canada's largest city. The nature of the war escalated when the Americans burned a village near Niagara Falls. The British and Canadians seized Fort Niagara in December, wounding or capturing about 500 of the American defenders, and then the Indians laid waste some of the upper New York countryside around Niagara, and occupied and burned down Buffalo in the last couple of days of 1813. It was a little war but a nasty one.

The lack of enthusiasm for the war in the U.S. administration was never a secret, in 1813 as in 1812. America's able minister to Russia, President Adams's son John Quincy Adams, had encouraged the offer of mediation from the czar, Alexander I, who had ignored the Napoleonic blockade to facilitate American commerce with Denmark and with Russia itself. Once Napoleon had attacked Russia, in June 1812, Russia and Britain were firm allies, and the Russian emperor had some influence with Britain, especially after the Russian armies and the Russian winter had ground down Napoleon's Grand Army, which had intimidated all Europe for over eight years. Napoleon's defeat in Russia, and then, in October 1813, the first real battlefield defeat he sustained in his career, at Leipzig, at the hands of the combined Russian, Prussian, Austrian, and Swedish armies, as the British were finally driving the French out of Spain after more than six years of combat, signaled a decisive shift in the war in Europe.

The Americans could reasonably expect that the British would soon be in a position to send large numbers of battle-hardened troops and commanders to fight in America. The defeats on Lake Erie and at Detroit were in sharp contrast to the Duke of Wellington's victories in Spain. Castlereagh declined the intervention of the czar, but in November 1813 he sent a diplomatic message to Monroe offering direct negotiations. Madison and Monroe agreed and, contrary to normal practice, in which such negotiations are conducted secretly, Madison sought and achieved confirmation of a high-powered peace delegation to go to Ghent, in what is now Belgium, to negotiate. The American negotiating team would be the minister to Russia, Adams; the emissary who had been nominated to negotiate under the czar's aegis, James A. Bayard; Speaker of the House and war-hawk leader Henry Clay; the chargé in London, Jonathan Russell, and the Treasury secretary, Albert Gallatin.

Madison could scarcely have emphasized his desire for peace more clearly. The American group considerably outranked their British analogues, Lord Gambier, Henry Goulburn, and William Adams. At the conference, the Americans were a motley group, as Clay would sometimes return from a night of gambling and carousing to encounter the purposeful Adams having just concluded his morning prayers, but Gallatin shepherded them along and they were quite congenial.[3]

5. MILITARY AND DIPLOMATIC DEVELOPMENTS IN 1814

To Madison's considerable credit, he finally recognized the complete failure of his and Jefferson's hare-brained, counter-arithmetical commercial restriction policy—that it was riddled with smuggling and corruption, that is had done much more damage to the United States than to those against whom it had supposedly been applied, and that it had not motivated Britain to be less unreasonable. On March 31, 1814, he recommended to the Congress the abandonment and repeal of the entire program. Whatever may be said of the errors that led to these policies and their lengthy unsuccessful implementation, the president renounced them with a lack of official vanity and humbug that set an admirable precedent rarely followed in the subsequent history of his great office. Provision was made to protect new manufacturing industries with special tariffs for two years after peace should occur, but the repeal of the Embargo and Non-Importation Acts was approved easily by both houses of the Congress.

The late Tecumseh had managed to stir up the Creek Indians in Alabama, who seized Fort Mims, about 35 miles north of Mobile, and massacred more than half of the nearly 600 people in the fort, including a good many women and children. The major general of the Tennessee militia, Andrew Jackson, organized 2,000 volunteers (hence the identifying slogan of the state), and went on the warpath against the Creeks. There were a number of skirmishes won by both sides, but in March 1814, Jackson, now at the head of 3,000 men, overwhelmed the Creek stronghold at Horseshoe Bend, Alabama, killed approximately a thousand Indian braves, and carried off more than 500 Indian women and children as prisoners. In a treaty in August, the Creeks signed over two-thirds of their land to the United States. This came two weeks after the Generals Harrison and Lewis Cass signed the Treaty of Greenville with the Delaware, Miami, Seneca, Shawnee, and Wyandot Indians, in the coalition assembled by Tecumseh, in consequence of which those tribes again flipped sides and declared peace with the Americans and war on the British. These were not large forces involved (there had been more than 500,000

---

3. Wood, *op. cit.*, p. 695.

soldiers engaged on the two sides in the Battle of Leipzig), but the antics of the Indians were extremely disturbing to the settlers, and they tended to ignore Euro-American niceties about women and children. These generals wrote a new chapter in the American political lionization of generals, even when their fame arose in small engagements. Jackson, Harrison, and Cass would, between them, be major party nominees to the presidency six times between 1824 and 1848, and win three times, and the only one of them who did not become president, Lewis Cass, became secretary of state instead. Senior military officers would receive electoral votes for president or vice president in 27 of America's first 30 quadrennial elections, 1788–1904. Eleven of America's first 25 presidents would be distinguished military officers, and the first 30 elections would produce 15 terms with soldier-presidents and three with military vice presidents.

Castlereagh was about to become the co-star, along with Austria's Metternich and the imperishable Talleyrand and the Holy See's cunning delegate, Ercole Cardinal Consalvi, of the immense Congress of Vienna, which would reorder much of the world, Napoleon having gone into exile at Elba, off the Italian coast, in April. (Talleyrand sold the argument that Napoleon, whom he had served as foreign minister for eight years, was an impostor who had inflicted himself on France in Cromwellian manner, and that France, with Britain, Austria, Russia, and Prussia, was a fully fledged member of the Holy Alliance that had defeated Napoleon, a considerable feat of diplomatic advocacy.) Capable statesman as he was, Castlereagh pursued a negotiated peace and escalation of the War of 1812 at the same time. As his delegation sat down with the Americans at Ghent, the British sent 14,000 veterans of the Duke of Wellington's Peninsular Army to Canada in the summer of 1814, and the Royal Navy ignored Madison's olive branch in repealing the embargo and reinforced its blockading fleets against America. The British high command produced a much more imaginative plan to win the war than the humdrum American efforts to charge into Canada yet again by the Lake Champlain, Niagara, and Detroit approaches. They were also vastly more competent than those responsible for the British conduct of the American Revolutionary War. Twenty years of fighting Napoleon had sharpened their staff work and greatly fortified their officer talent.

A three-pronged attack was envisioned, in the footsteps of Montcalm and Burgoyne on the inevitable Lake Champlain and another go at the Niagara crossing; and amphibious attacks on Chesapeake Bay, just southeast of Washington, and at New Orleans. The U.S. regular army was only 34,000 men at the start of October 1814. There were as many as 100,000 militiamen and reservists, but they were scattered through all the states in various conditions of preparedness, command competence, experience, and equipment. The better reservist leaders, such as Jackson and Harrison, were very capable, and Jackson, who had survived hand-to-hand combat with Indians (including a hatchet-wound to the cranium), had been a drummer in the Revolutionary War, and had personally killed a number of men in military and civilian capacities, was a fierce personality who was about to stride to the forefront of national affairs and remain there for 30 years. The charlatan Wilkinson survived another court-martial but finally left the army for even greener financial pastures, trying in Burrite fashion to buy part of Mexico. Winfield Scott and Jackson were the rising figures in the army now.

The Americans launched a preemptive strike at Niagara, which yielded a fine American victory at Chippewa in July, led by General Winfield Scott, who took only about half the 500 casualties of the British. Scott would prove to be probably the greatest American general between Washington and Greene and the Civil War, and was now embarked on a career of 50 years as a military hero. (He, too, would be an unsuccessful presidential candidate, in 1852.) Three weeks later, there was a further action involving about 6,000 men evenly divided, at Lundy's Lane, near Niagara Falls. It was a stalemate, though the Americans withdrew, and both sides took about 850 casualties. The British failed to take Fort Erie, but the Americans vacated it anyway a few months later—another indecisive engagement almost within earshot of the thundering falls. The British attack down Lake Champlain was repulsed in a naval battle in September, although the Americans were out-numbered. The British commander, Sir George Prevost, who mishandled 11,000 well-trained soldiers, was sacked, but that would prove the last time in history these singularly unsuccessful routes of invasion in both directions, Niagara and Lake Champlain, would be exploited (other than by armies of amiable tourists moving in both directions at once).

The Chesapeake Bay landings would be more successful, and were really an elaboration on previous coastal raids all along the American littoral, and on Pitt's "descents" on France in the Seven Years' War. This British movement of their land forces in pin-pricks on the perimeter of their enemies, facilitated by their usual naval superiority, would continue through the World Wars, including Gallipoli and Zeebrugge in World War I (unsuccessful), and the Greek and Crete operations and Dieppe (Canadian forces) in World War II (also unsuccessful). The 4,000 men of the British attacking force departed directly from France for their American targets in June 1814, with a brief stop at Bermuda, and were landed on August 19, an ambitious undertaking in amphibious warfare for the time. The objective was to burn Washington to avenge the burning of Toronto (York) the previous year. The American commander, the inept General William Winder, failed with a ragtag of 7,000 reservists and sailors to stop 3,000 of Wellington's veterans at Bladensburg, nine miles from Washington, with Madison and the cabinet looking on and the Americans scattered as the British marched, unopposed, into Washington on August 24. The president and his cabinet colleagues fled (on foot in Madison's case, because of problems with his horse) in different directions and the government temporarily disintegrated.

The British burned the Capitol, and all the other government buildings except the patent office, including the White House, which Mrs. Madison had fled with a portrait of George Washington under her arm, after coolly organizing the removal of as much as possible; she was refused shelter by the irate wife of a farmer who had just been conscripted, an astounding, even endearing display of official disorder. The white paint slapped onto the executive mansion's seared outer walls gave the building its subsequent name. Apart from a couple of residences, a newspaper office, and the naval dock (which the Americans blew up themselves), the British forces showed correct discipline and avoided indiscriminate destruction or looting. The British left by sea on the 25th, unharried, and Madison and his colleagues returned on August 27, to a less-exuberant welcome from the citizenry. Madison again fired the secretary of war, John Armstrong, and now took the extreme step of replacing him with Monroe, who took over the War Department while retaining the State Department, a unique event in American history to this day. Monroe was now a virtual co-president, supervising the defense of the country and the negotiation of peace. The British had scored a great propaganda victory of little straight military significance, but their attempt to take Baltimore three weeks later failed. The Americans prepared thoroughly and repulsed the British from what was then one of America's largest cities. The unsuccessful British bombardment of Fort McHenry inspired Francis Scott Key to write the American national anthem, "The Star-Spangled Banner."

6. THE END OF THE WAR

The peace conference at Ghent continued through the autumn. The British opened by demanding a rewriting in their favor of the Canadian border through the northern New England states and Michigan and Minnesota, and the establishment of an Indian buffer state in the Northwest. The Americans demanded reparations and an end of impressments and the blockade. They rejected any changes of territorial boundaries from the start of the war, and claimed none. They had been faithful throughout to their demands, and it must be said that despite Madison's bumbling, and the frightful indignity of having their capital razed to the ground, they had shown considerable pluck, and fought their corner quite well after the initial debacle of their 1812 invasion of Canada. Madison, though he provoked acute nostalgia for the steady and formidable Washington as a war leader, showed remarkable honesty, partly naïve and partly the result of creeping resignation and the disillusioning cynicism of experience. When news of the burning of Washington reached the Congress of Vienna, the British stiffened their demands. When news of the American victory on Lake Champlain arrived, it was sobering.

The Duke of Wellington, the world's most illustrious military commander with Napoleon in involuntary retirement, was offered the command in Canada. He was not eager for it, as the United States now had over eight million people, and there was no possibility of subduing the whole country, or permanently gouging large parts out of it. The British had been at war for 21 of the previous 22 years, and had supported an immense navy constantly in action throughout that time, and armies of 75,000 to 90,000, most of the units steadily in action for the last six years in a very costly and severe war in Spain. (The duke had been Sir Arthur Wellesley when he departed for Spain in 1808, and when he returned he had the unprecedented pleasure of having his patents read in the House of Lords as baron, viscount, earl, marquis, and duke, recognizing his successive victories in that very long war in Spain and Portugal.)

Wellington was more interested in jointly leading the British in the Vienna discussions that rewrote the map of much of Europe than in embarking for a nebulous mission in Canada. He had commanded armies in India as well as Spain, and preferred not to do it again. This was all for the best, as Napoleon famously returned from Elba in March 1815 and conducted one more campaign, narrowly lost at Waterloo, where Wellington won one of the most important and closely contested battles in the history of the world. His absence could have been decisive, as the Prussian Blucher and whomever the British would have named in Wellington's stead could not have defeated Napoleon, generally reckoned the greatest military commander in history. (Waterloo was, after Leipzig, his only defeat in scores of battles, many of them won against heavy odds and by tactical tours de force of genius.)

The duke advised his government that after the American victory on Lake Champlain, the British were not entitled by the results on the ground to demand territorial concessions. On November 26, 1814, the British abandoned their demand for territorial concessions and an Indian buffer zone in the Northwest. As the world would now be at peace, impressments and blockades seemed, and were, a stale-dated issue. The British were not going to pay reparations and indemnities and the Americans didn't seriously expect them to, as the chief victor in Europe and now the most powerful nation in the world. The Americans made some uncontroversial fishing concessions, but that was all.

The long British struggle with France going back 500 years to Joan of Arc, and accentuated after the Reformation and the rise of national governments, and especially by Louis XIV and then the almost departed emperor, had finally been resolved in favor of Britain. The island nation was tired and strained by costs and casualties and the first stresses of the industrial age, and it didn't want an endless war in America, but it was not going to do more than end the war and leave things as they had been. And if the Americans tried to chase the British out of Canada now, they would find Wellington and his army tramping down the shores of Lake Champlain and across the Niagara River, and they would not remind anyone of General Burgoyne or Governor Prevost. The Treaty of Ghent was signed on December 24 and peace soon broke out.

True to its frequently absurd nature, and symmetrically with the fact that America declared war as the casus belli of the British blockade was being removed, the greatest battle of the war occurred two weeks after the peace was concluded, and so did not influence the results at all, but was important for other reasons. General Andrew Jackson had been named commander of the military district from New Orleans to Mobile, by Monroe, and characteristically ignored Monroe's orders not to disturb Spanish Florida, and seized Pensacola. When he learned of British forces approaching, he retired to Baton Rouge to be ready to repulse British landings wherever they appeared on the Gulf coast. The British landed 7,500 men under General Sir Edward Pakenham (the Duke of Wellington's brother-in-law) 40 miles east of New Orleans, starting on December 13.

Jackson bustled down to New Orleans starting on December 15 and was able to attack the British on December 23. He furiously constructed defensive positions around New Orleans, and Pakenham attacked Jackson's 4,500 men with 5,300 of his regulars on January 8, 1815. Jackson placed Tennessee and Kentucky marksmen with long rifles in forward trenches, and advantageously placed his artillery to smash the British line as well. The advance of the British, walking upright in tight formation, presented a splendid target. There was a second British advance after the first was driven back. It was a madly unimaginative attack plan by Pakenham, who was killed as his army was badly defeated and took over 2,000 casualties, compared with only eight American dead and 13 wounded. Jackson became America's greatest hero, its greatest warrior since Washington, and its most successful political leader since Jefferson, and eventually, with Washington, Jefferson, and Lincoln, one of the four most important American presidents in the first 140 years of its history.

News of the Battle of New Orleans reached the still fire-ravaged capital of the United States before the news of the Treaty of Ghent, and greatly salved

American sensibilities after the scorching there and the inelegant flight of the government. The treaty arrived on February 11, was ratified unanimously by the Senate (meeting in temporary quarters) on February 15, and proclaimed by Madison on February 17. It had been a silly little war in many ways; it should have been fought earlier and more wisely by the Americans, yet they suffered only 1,877 dead and 4,000 wounded. The economic cost had been heavy and the strain on national unity had been considerable. It was an opportunity lost and Madison went far too long with the foolishness of Jefferson's notions of economic war. Yet the United States had accomplished something in fighting successfully to keep its head up against the greatest powers in the world, and particularly the overwhelming master of the world's seas. The Royal Navy was deployed across all the world's oceans, "wherever wood could float" as Napoleon grudgingly said (with as large, in numbers of ships, and as far-flung a fleet as the United States would deploy at the end of World War I, when Admiral Nimitz's mighty Pacific Fleet took 400,000 men to sea when it sailed). The war's farcical aspect had been diluted by Madison's lack of pomposity and endearing preparedness to acknowledge error.

The Americans, though without so skillful a propagandist as Jefferson to tart up a rather squalid little war, apart from the successes of Perry and Jackson, still managed to present it as a milestone on the road to full national maturity. Gallatin, no Jefferson or Paine or Hamilton, but a formidable talent in a less-crowded field, declared: "The war has renewed and reinstated the national feelings and characters which the Revolution had given. The people . . . are more American; they feel and act more as a nation."[4] In the end, the last of the nation's founders to retire had finally, and reluctantly, done the honorable thing to defend the nation's honor and sovereignty, and, in his way, had done so successfully. Washington and Adams and Hamilton would have taken over Canada and ended up buying peace with a cash settlement. But it was just that, an opportunity lost, not a defeat, and considering the power of the opponent, it lightly enhanced America's status in the world. Ancient and mighty France had to endure the British army in Paris for a prolonged period. They didn't burn anything but they stayed as long as they pleased, and the Duke of Wellington "bought" the British embassy on the Faubourg St. Honore. Today it remains there, next to the United States embassy, and both are only a cricket ball or baseball's throw from the residence of the president of the (Fifth) Republic.

---

4. Daniel Walker Howe, *What Hath God Wrought: The Transformation of America, 1815–1848*, Oxford and New York, Oxford University Press, 2007, p. 71.

Madison, true to his nature and having learned his lesson, recommended retention of an army of 20,000, and most of the navy that had been built up, but the Congress reverted to its former condition, cut the army to 10,000, sold gunboats, and returned the Great Lakes to an unarmed state. Madison did have the pleasure of sending Captain Stephen Decatur to give the Dey of Algiers, and his analogues in Tunis and Tripoli, another good thrashing at sea with a 10-ship squadron, extracting concessions and return of hostages and tribute and reparations from the Barbary leaders and ending this problem (and legitimizing after all the wording of the Marine Corps anthem). A complete restoration of normal and favorable trade terms with Britain was agreed in a commercial convention in July 1816.

In one of the last major initiatives of his administration, Madison again sounded a little like his Federalist predecessors in supporting the rechartering of a Bank of the United States. This was recommended by the Treasury secretary, Alexander J. Dallas, as necessary to patch back together the chaotic state of the country's finances after the war with Britain. A very weak measure setting up a bank that would be severely circumscribed was passed by the Congress but vetoed by Madison. Then the men who would lead the Congress for the next 35 years, despite intermittent dalliances in the administration (all three would be secretaries of state)—John C. Calhoun, Henry Clay, and Daniel Webster—joined forces and put through a serious bill. Calhoun would speak for the South, Clay for the West and Midwest, and Webster for New England. Calhoun was a Democrat, as the Democratic-Republicans were about to be called officially, and the other two would emerge as Whigs, when the Federalists metamorphosed into that party, and their relations with each other were never especially warm. But they played an immense role, greater than any of the presidents between Jackson and Lincoln, except Polk, in the long denouement of the related problems of slavery and states' rights. The new bank would have $35 million of authorized capital, one-fifth posted by the federal government, which would name five of the 25 directors. The bank would receive federal government deposits and not pay interest on them, and in other respects resembled Hamilton's original bank. It would be a normative and stabilizing influence, controlling the money supply and maintaining reasonable consistency of credit in the country, through, eventually, 25 branches. The bank was one of Madison's principal presidential achievements.

In his very last material act as president, Madison vetoed a bill for federal construction of roads and canals that Calhoun, congressional leader of the South, had put forward, to be financed from the dividends of the Bank of the U.S. This was a remarkable acceptance by Calhoun of Hamilton's constitutional justification of implied powers, and showed also how far Calhoun would move, from advocating a generous interpretation of the federal government's powers to enact a measure for national unity and closer union, to where he would end his career, 35 years ahead. Madison remained true to his own concepts of the Constitution, imposing his veto with the unique authority of the principal draftsman.

The president honored the Washington and Jefferson tradition and declined to seek a third term. He would leave office a respected president, moderately popular for his unpretentious nature, thought slightly unserious after the British descent upon Washington, and remembered by the knowledgeable for his irreplaceable contributions to the Constitution.

7. JAMES MONROE AS PRESIDENT

Having held almost every other post, including senator, governor, minister to France and to Britain, and secretary of state and of war, James Monroe was almost a case of the office seeking the man. There was a challenge from the former minister to France, war secretary and current Treasury secretary William H. Crawford of Georgia, as a younger man (44, compared with Monroe's 58) and not a Virginian, unlike Monroe and three of the four presidents to date. The House caucus of the Democratic-Republicans chose the nominee and Monroe won this test 65 to 54. Vice President Gerry had died in office, and Monroe and his colleagues appeased New York with the selection for that position of that state's governor, Daniel D. (an improvised initial that did not stand for anything) Tompkins. Rufus King, respected political veteran and former vice presidential candidate, was nominated by the Federalists, who were no longer a coherent party, and did not offer a vice presidential candidate.

The result was a foregone conclusion; Monroe won 183 electoral votes to 34 for King, who took only Massachusetts, Connecticut, and Delaware. The Federalists vanished from the scene, in, as a Boston newspaper would describe it as Monroe toured New England, "an era of good feeling." Monroe, too, had come a long way having opposed the Constitution as too centralist, he now seemed more a follower of the first Virginian president than of the next two. In his inaugural address, he called for armed forces adequate to protect the nation's interests and a policy that would favor manufacturing. He had a strong administration, with Tompkins, John Quincy Adams as secretary of state, Crawford at the Treasury, John C. Calhoun at the War Department, and Richard Rush as attorney general. More talented than any cabinet since Washington's first administration, it more resembled such British coalitions as Pelham and Newcastle's "broad-bottom" government of 1744–1754, or Grenville and Fox's "government of all the talents" of 1806.

The long process of building a close Anglo-American relationship took its first step with what was called the Rush-Bagot Agreement of 1817, though it had been entirely agreed between Monroe and Castlereagh. It substantially disarmed the Great Lakes (which the Congress had unilaterally done anyway). It was also implicit that the same principle would govern the land frontier between the United States and Canada. This agreement would be supplemented by the Convention of 1818, signed for the United States again by Richard Rush, then minister in London, and by Albert Gallatin, now the minister in Paris. This convention extended the border along the 49th parallel from Lake of the Woods (northern Minnesota) to the Rocky Mountains, and agreed to negotiate the border through the Rockies to the Pacific in 10 years, in which time citizens of both signatory countries could move freely in the Far Pacific territory. The United States also obtained modest fishing concessions in Newfoundland waters.

The fierce and Anglophobic Andrew Jackson was placed in charge of American forces on the Georgia-Florida border, across which many runaway slaves and hostile Indians had fled. There were some incidents and Jackson's standing orders were to clear the area between the U.S. border and the Spanish forts. Jackson wrote to President Monroe that if he were advised, through "channels . . . that possession of the Floridas would be desirable to the United States . . . in sixty days it will be accomplished." He received no reply, which for as bellicose an American expansionist as Jackson was all the encouragement he needed to invade East Florida in April 1818.

He captured Pensacola in May and captured two English traders whom he accused of fomenting slave and Indian and even Spanish action against the United States (Alexander Arbuthnot and Robert Ambrister). Jackson hanged the first and shot the second. British and official American opinion condemned Jackson; Clay proposed censure in the House, and the war and Treasury secretaries, Calhoun and Crawford, agreed. The secretary of state, the very able John Quincy Adams, was negotiating with the Spanish for control of Florida. Jackson's antics considerably strengthened his bargaining position and he entirely approved Jackson's action. Public opinion rose up in support of the general, and neither Monroe nor the Congress took any action against him. Thus reinforced, Adams negotiated the cession to the U.S. of all Florida, and the western boundary of the Louisiana Purchase. Adams, son of the former president, had studied in France and the Netherlands, was a former senator, had served in diplomatic capacities as a teenager, and had served all the previous presidents, as minister in the Netherlands, Prussia, Russia, and Great Britain. He had been the senior diplomat in the Ghent peace delegation and would prove one of the most capable secretaries of state in American history.

8. THE MISSOURI COMPROMISE

At the end of 1819, there were 22 states in the Union, 11 free and 11 slave, with Maine and Missouri having applied for admission. The slave states, apart from Delaware, Maryland, Virginia, Georgia, and the Carolinas, were Kentucky, Tennessee, Alabama, Mississippi, and Louisiana. The free states, apart from those in the original 13, were Vermont, Ohio, Indiana, and Illinois. The northern states were growing more quickly than the southern states, as that was where most immigrants arrived, and Europeans, the source of most immigration, did not want to move to a semi-tropical climate, and were unfamiliar with dealing with people of African origin. Most Americans were in free states, and despite the three-fifths rule, the congressional delegations of the free states were substantially larger than those of the South. When amendments were proposed prohibiting slavery in the Missouri Territory, which was a large part of the Louisiana Purchase, there was very spirited reaction from southerners, and a series of heated debates and close votes, as the strains on a country half free and half slave, with a constitutional arrangement for favoring slave states in congressional delegations and presidential and vice presidential electoral votes, began, as was widely foreseen, to tear at national unity. After acrimonious and confused debate for nearly four months, a compromise proposed by Senator Jesse Thomas of Illinois was adopted. Maine and Missouri were admitted as states, Maine as a free state and Missouri without restriction on slavery, and the balance of the Louisiana Territory west of Missouri and north of the line 36°30 (the continuation of the Arkansas-Missouri border) would not be a slave-holding area.

This settled the issue down for a time, but it was perennial, and would become more intractable. The North now realized that slavery would not die on its own, though most considered it unchristian and an affront to the founding values of the country. The South realized that it would always be questioned and that it would always be on the moral defensive. "From [the Missouri Compromise] on few Americans had any illusions left about the awful reality of slavery in America."[5] Jefferson famously now called it "A fire bell in the night . . . the knell of the Union." He feared that all that he and "the generation of 1776" had accomplished to secure "self-government and happiness to their country" could be squandered "by the unwise and unworthy passions of their sons."[6] Yet he dismissed the Missouri question as "not a moral question, but one merely of power."

---

5.   Wood, *op. cit.*, p. 737.
6.   Ibid.

Monroe had so defused partisanship, the caucus of his party in the House of Representatives that was to choose the Democratic-Republican nominees for president and vice president could not assemble a quorum on the preannounced date. The Federalist Party was inactive, so no one was officially put forward by any party. President Monroe and Vice President Tompkins allowed their names to stand and there was no formal opposition. Monroe won 231 electoral votes to three abstentions and one vote cast for Adams (the secretary of state) by an elector who thought no one but Washington should have the honor of being elected unanimously. Tompkins collected 218 votes, with the others scattered, although he simultaneously ran as governor of New York, making it clear that if elected, he would serve in that office, leaving the secretary of state to succeed to the presidency should Monroe not complete his term. In the event, Tompkins lost the governor's race narrowly to De Witt Clinton, who went on to build the Erie Canal, connecting New York City to the Great Lakes, one of the world's most noteworthy feats of engineering at the time. It was 363 miles long, 40 feet wide and 4 feet deep, and had 83 locks to take vessels up 675 feet. It would have been only half as long if it had utilized Lake Ontario, but war with Britain was still thought quite possible, and Lake Ontario was more peopled on the northern side (Toronto) and was directly accessible from the St. Lawrence, so the Erie Canal runs parallel to the lake, about 10 miles south of it, from Lake Oneida to Lake Erie at Buffalo.

9. THE MONROE DOCTRINE

Starting in 1810, all of the Latin American countries began to agitate for independence from Spain and Portugal. Open revolts flickered and raged all over the Americas south of the United States. The colonial powers were evicted more effortlessly in some places than others, but they had nothing like the resources to try to maintain themselves that the British had had at their disposal 40 years before. The so-called Holy Alliance (France, Russia, Austria, Prussia; Britain withdrew from this ultra-conservative arrangement), a strange and almost mystical reactionary league to freeze Europe and much of the world as they were when the Congress of Vienna concluded, determined at Verona in November 1822 that members would all assist a restoration of absolute monarchy in Spain. France invaded Spain to this end, less than a decade after Wellington and the Spanish guerrillas had forced Napoleon's army out of Spain. Canning, who had replaced the (suicidally) deceased Castlereagh as foreign minister, suspected the French of aspiring to a Latin American empire, and when he did not receive adequate French assurances to disabuse himself of this concern, he proposed to Rush, the American minister in London, that Great Britain and the United States make a joint pact to keep other European powers out of Latin America. Monroe had already recognized the nascent Latin American republics and exchanged embassies with them (in May 1822). Rush told Canning that he did not have the authority to commit the U.S., but that he suspected the concept could have traction if Britain would join the United States in recognizing the new Latin American republics.

Monroe and, when he consulted them, Jefferson and Madison were enthusiastic about close cooperation with Great Britain, quite a turn for the old revolutionaries. Once America became active in the world, its leaders quickly found that the only foreign power it had much in common with was Britain—the language, the comparative liberality, and the stable political institutions. Adams demurred from his elders and predecessors (all four had been secretary of state and Adams, too, would be president.) Secretary of State Adams was not so convinced that the British were really renouncing colonial ambitions in Latin America; he had been jousting with the British over Cuba, and feared a nefarious attempt to establish a quid pro quo. He considered that the British alone would prevent other Europeans from asserting themselves in Latin America, as no one now disputed the absolute supremacy of the Royal Navy, virtually everywhere in the world. Adams was also concerned about the czar's assertion of rights in the Northwest, where the British had a minimal naval presence and little concern what the Russians did. In the light of these factors, Adams proposed distinctive American warnings to Russia and France, and the United States did not respond to Canning. Adams persuaded Monroe and the rest of the cabinet to issue a policy statement purporting to govern foreign activities in the Americas.

In his annual message to the Congress on December 2, 1823, the president enunciated what became known as the Monroe Doctrine, which was composed by Adams and himself. They made four points: The Americas would not be subject to further colonization by Europeans; there was a distinct political society in the Americas very different to that of Europe; the United States would consider any attempt to extend European influence in the Americas to be dangerous to the national security of the U.S., but existing European colonies and dependencies in the Americas were grandfathered as legitimate; and the United States renounced any interest in influencing events in Europe. There were some doubtful aspects of this formulation. The United States had much more in common with Britain than with the emerging, unstable dictatorships of Latin America, and the Royal Navy assured the integrity of the Americas at least for the first 40 years after Monroe promulgated his doctrine. The United States had no ability whatever to prevent British encroachments in South America, had they wished to make any. And the renunciation of an American role in Europe was not much of an act of restraint, as it had no capacity whatever to play any such role. On April 17, 1824, the U.S. signed with Russia a treaty in which Russia confined itself to activities in the Pacific Northwest of North America above longitude 54°40, and desisted from attempts to rule the Bering Sea exclusively for Russian fishing and whaling.

In general, international reaction to Monroe's speech was complete indifference, even in Latin America, but it would become an extremely important dispensation for the Americas after 1865, when the power of the United States was very great and unchallengeable in its own hemisphere. In the meantime, this was a brilliant diplomatic stroke by Monroe and Adams, as they managed to align their country's interest exactly with Britain's and appear to have more power than they did, while building a solid relationship with their former nemesis. Britain was now entering the greatest century of its influence in the world in its history, and the association of America with it was entirely on the basis of America's own national interest.

Monroe would follow his fellow Virginians and retire after two terms, having blended Jeffersonism with Hamiltonism, and having recovered some of Franklin's talent for diplomatic finesse, which seemed to give America a greater weight in the world than it really possessed. And the ill-conceived embargoes had been successful shields for the launch of manufacturing. That was not what was expected to happen by the squires of Monticello and Montpelier (Jefferson's and Madison's homes), but it was the beginning of an industrial capacity Hamilton had foreseen and that in the centuries to come would stupefy the world. After five presidencies and 50 years after the American Revolution began, the new republic was fairly launched.

Taken as a whole, in just one lifetime, from the start of the Seven Years' War to 1824, the Americans had had an astounding rise, from a colony with two million people to one of the world's six or seven most important countries, with over 11 million people. The problem of being half slave-holding and half free was the only shadow over America's prospects, but it was a dark and lengthening shadow. Jefferson, the unimpoverishable optimist, in his final years, yet had "twinges of fear of an impending disaster whose sources he never fully understood. He and his colleagues had created" (and nurtured) "a Union devoted to liberty that contained an inner flaw that nearly proved to be its undoing." Madison, who died 10 years after Jefferson and Adams, in 1836, left the posthumous word that "There was a serpent creeping with his deadly wiles" in the American "paradise."[7] So there was, and the great strategic challenge now was to keep the Union together until the forces of federalism in the North and West would be adequately motivated

---

7.   Wood, *op. cit.*, p. 738.

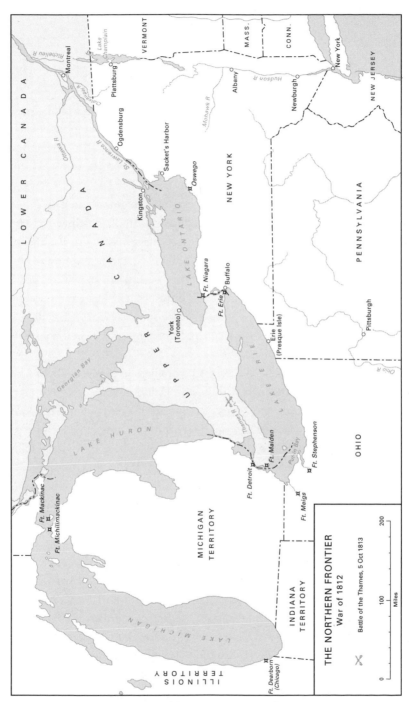

War of 1812. Courtesy of the U.S. Army Center of Military History

and powerful to suppress the slave states, if either moral revulsion at slavery or a preemptive insurrection made that necessary to preserve the Union.

10. THE 1824 ELECTION AND PRESIDENT JOHN QUINCY ADAMS

As the Virginia Dynasty ended, there was jockeying for the succession in Monroe's talented cabinet. John Quincy Adams, William Crawford, and John C. Calhoun were all presumed to be running for president, as was the populist general Andrew Jackson. The country was practically a one-party state, and the states objected to the practice of the Democratic-Republican caucus of the House of Representatives choosing the party's nominee and, effectively, the president. The Tennessee legislature selected General Jackson as a candidate in 1822, which was a year after Calhoun had thrown his hat in the ring, and so fierce was the rivalry that Crawford, who had great influence in the Senate, blocked the promotion of officers favored by Calhoun as war secretary, sometimes even when they were supported by the president himself. The Massachusetts and Kentucky legislatures nominated their favorite sons, Adams and the Speaker of the House, Henry Clay, all in 1822. Monroe launched the concept of the "lame duck" president, well before it was called that.

A stroke effectively eliminated Crawford, who had been selected by the House caucus in the traditional manner, in 1823, and Calhoun withdrew to run for vice president with both Jackson and Adams. Jackson ran in favor of popular election of the president, but against federally paid internal improvements, which were held to be intrusive by the federal government, and if permitted, likely to be followed by federal meddling in the status of slavery. Most of the candidates favored tariff protection for American manufacturing. The ballot yielded 99 electoral votes for Jackson, 84 for Adams, 41 for Crawford, and 37 for Clay. As there was no majority, the election went to the House of Representatives, which would consider only the top three candidates. Clay urged support for Adams and, as Speaker, exercised considerable influence, starting with causing the Kentucky congressmen to ignore the instruction of the state legislature to vote for Jackson, and vote for Adams instead. Adams won 13 states to seven for Jackson and four for Crawford. Clay accepted Adams's offer of secretary of state, leading to the allegation of a "corrupt bargain" by the two to throw the House election to Adams. There was never any evidence of this, but it was much bandied about, including by the erratic and volcanic John Randolph, who also described Adams and Clay as "the Puritan and the blackleg." This led to a duel, in which neither aggrieved party (Clay and Randolph) was injured. Calhoun was easily elected vice president.

After this election, the Adams and Clay groups became National Republicans, while the Jacksonians became the successors to Jefferson and Madison as Democratic-Republicans. Adams declined to politicize the civil service and dismissed only 12 federal government employees in his term, and those for objective cause. It was an admirable stance, but nothing was going to stop the charge of Jackson, swearing vengeance for the corrupt bargain and claiming to be the spear of the people as they seized control of government from the elites. In his address to the Congress in December 1825, Adams proposed an extensive program of roads and canals, a national university and observatory, and further exploration of the interior. It was an ambitious program, but one bound to offend the states' rights advocates, which included all the South and much of the Southwest, essentially because of fear of attacks on slavery. This was the key to discussion of federal aid to public works, and was indicative of self-defeating government minimalism. It was held that if the federal government had the power to build public works all over the country, there would then be nothing to stop it from tampering with slavery. The South was already retreating into a slave mentality. Calhoun, as president of the Senate, elevated many opponents of the administration, as he was now the South's leading political figure and used his position to advance his own status and not to support the administration (having probably received more votes for his office from followers of Jackson than of Adams).

The whole first half of 1826 was taken up with debate over U.S. attendance at the Panama Conference. This was a pan–Latin American meeting organized by the liberator of much of South America, Simón Bolívar, who was seeking a tight alliance between all the states against Spain or any outside interloper. He sought a continental assembly and the right to require military support and solidarity from all constituent states. Colombia and Mexico insisted that the United States be invited, and Adams agreed to be represented. This created awkwardnesses; where Adams and Clay believed that American preeminence in the hemisphere required American representation, Calhoun and Senator Martin Van Buren, a devious New York wheelhorse who would hold almost every elective office and champion different sides of many issues, opposed U.S. attendance, ostensibly because the Senate had not been consulted before Adams accepted the invitation, and because attendance would violate American opposition to intrusion in the affairs of other countries. The real reason for the concern of the South was that there would be black national leaders present and they did not wish to exalt the dignity of "negroes" ethnically indistinguishable from slaves.

The Congress supported the administration, after vigorous debate, but the representatives Adams sent did not arrive, one because of death en route. That there should have been a heated six-month debate on such a trivial issue illustrated the extreme sensitivity of the slavery issue. Southern leaders overreacted, reacted preemptively, and generally betrayed a nearly paranoid fear of criticism of slavery. Calhoun was the leader of this strain of opinion, and Van Buren went along with it only to cement his relations with Jackson, whom he saw more clearly than some as the coming man.

Thomas Jefferson, aged 83, and John Adams, aged 91, died on July 4, 1826, the fiftieth anniversary of the Declaration of Independence. Adams's last words were alleged to have been that "Jefferson survives." They had mended their quarrels of decades before and enjoyed an extensive and often eloquent correspondence. Adams had the pleasure, as the only president to this point to have been denied reelection, of seeing his son installed as president, at time of writing a feat replicated only by the Bushes. The senior Adams and Jefferson had seen a tremendous advance of the country they had done so much to establish, including a steady advance of popular government, a discarding of property and tax-paying qualifications for voting, and the movement in all states except Delaware and South Carolina of the selection of presidential electors from the state legislators directly to the voters.

The North-South divisions were aggravated by the tariff debates of the late twenties. Northern and central manufacturing states wanted higher tariffs for textiles and steel and iron goods, to protect their ever-growing domestic market, while the South wanted those goods to be cheaper, and did not want to provoke tariff retaliation by the wide range of foreign countries to which the South exported agricultural products and cotton. The South was fiercely attached to the principle of absolute equality with the North, which it was losing demographically, though it was maintained in the Senate. As the North grew more quickly, and tariffs prospered its own industries while handicapping those of the South, and the North aspersed slavery and the ownership by people of other human beings, southerners came to question in increasing numbers the value and utility of the Union to them.

As early as 1813, an in camera Federalist convention had met and proposed a series of constitutional amendments that included elimination of the three-fifths rule regarding the counting of slaves in calculating congressional representation and the composition of the Electoral College; the admission of new states and declaration of embargoes or of war only with two-thirds majorities of both houses of Congress; and the prohibition of a second presidential term and of successive presidents from the same state. The report of this convention arrived in Washington as the Treaty of Ghent arrived, and the issues died, especially after the vibrant 1824 presidential contest between a Deep South candidate, a New Englander, and two frontiersmen. But it indicated the stresses the Virginia Dynasty and the War of

1812 had caused. The grievances and sensibilities of the South would not be so easily appeased. Three of the four 1824 presidential candidates were slaveholders, three-quarters of the people were not, 15 percent of the people were black, and 15 percent of those were free. It was bound to become very complicated, very quickly.

Severe strains between the regions arose again over tariffs. The Jacksonians in control of the Congress determined to embarrass the president by proposing outrageously high tariffs ("The Tariff of Abominations") on a wide range of products, to ensure that all sections voted against it, and Jackson's supporters would take credit for its defeat in the South and West, which saw tariffs as a sop to the eastern and northern states, which would blame Adams for the defeat. This was the cynical design of the unholy alliance between Calhoun and Van Buren, and it backfired, because New England voted for the tariffs as supportive of the principle of protection, and the measure passed. Calhoun then baptized himself in political chicanery by total immersion, by leading South Carolina (six weeks after his reelection as vice president in 1828) to adopt a series of legislative resolutions protesting the constitutionality of the tariff Calhoun had himself co-sponsored on the assumption that it would be defeated. He also wrote, though he did not sign, a treatise that embraced the separatist concept of nullification—the ability of a state simply to declare that a federal law did not apply within that state. This was not compatible with any serious notion of the United States (though Jefferson had flirted with it after the Alien and Sedition Acts under the senior Adams). This constitutional heresy would prove almost inextinguishable, and was still being bandied about by southern segregationists in the 1960s. It was a public rumination on separatism: the acceptance of the benefits of the Union while eschewing anything thought to be burdensome. It was an outrage from the just-reelected vice president of the United States of America, Monroe's war secretary, and the co-author of a tariff whose adoption he now purported to find unconstitutional. The rot at the core of the American Union was already a life-threatening tumor.

11. THE RISE OF JACKSON

Jackson had retired as a senator in 1825, following the Tennessee legislature's nomination of him for president (presidential aspirants threw their hats into the ring much earlier in these times), and he accepted Calhoun as his running mate. Now, and henceforth, this party was called the Democrats, leaving "Republican" for adoption by a new force 30 years hence. President Adams was renominated by what was called the National Republican convention, meeting in Harrisburg. He took as his running mate, Richard Rush, former minister to Great Britain and attorney general and current secretary of war.

Jackson was now, in 1828, an unstoppable political force: as the demographic center of the country moved across the Appalachians, he was the hero of the frontiersmen and of the Old South, and of all who admired the spirit of expansion, the Revolutionary drummer boy turned national military hero. (He had won probably the greatest land battle in the country's history, the Battle of New Orleans, albeit after the end of the war in which it was supposedly fought. As Yorktown was largely won by the French, and as they were never at war again, it was certainly the greatest victory ever won by the Americans over the British.) Jackson was the selfless combat hero, the rugged man of the West, the guardian of the slave-holding South, and he was a slick political operator. He won the 1828 presidential election with 647,000 votes and 178 electoral votes to Adams's 509,000 votes and 83 electoral votes. New York state went for Jackson by 5,000 out of 276,000 because of the exertions of Martin Van Buren and William L. Marcy, who between them would be amply rewarded in the coming decades with a cornucopia of great offices. They were the leaders of the Albany Regency, the ruling political machinery in New York from the retirement of Tompkins and DeWitt Clinton to the rise of William Henry Seward and Thurlow Weed in the late 1930s.

John Quincy Adams is rivaled only by Thomas Jefferson and Thomas Woodrow Wilson as the greatest intellect ever to hold the presidency of the United States. He was one of the nation's very greatest secretaries of state and had an imaginative program as president, but was the representative of a region of declining importance and was saddled with the appearance and tone of a New England Brahmin and an overt opponent of slavery, as the fireball of Jacksonian democracy swept most of the country. Completely unaffected by the prestige of the presidency and of his family, he was elected to the House of Representatives, the only ex-president in the country's history except for Andrew Johnson to serve again in elective office after leaving the White House, and became one of the leaders of the abolitionist movement. He was a man of the utmost intelligence and integrity, but not an overly effective president and not a particularly astute national politician. He was profoundly esteemed in his last 17 years in Congress, right to his death in 1848 at the age of 79.

General Jackson was a startling change from the six Virginia and Massachusetts gentlemen who had preceded him to the nation's highest office. In his inaugural address, Jackson was quite restrained, promising economy in government and respect for the jurisdictions of states, a "just and liberal policy" toward the Indians, and what appeared to be a reform of the civil service. He was silent or enigmatic about tariffs, internal improvements, and the status of the Bank of the United States. He threw the White House open to the populace, which included a tremendous rout of rumbustious and reveling frontiersmen, and a rather bacchanalian occasion ensued, with windows being used as doors and considerable alcoholic consumption, though no vandalism or violence. It was a symbolic notice of a distinct change in tone from the former occupants.

Jackson did not hold regular cabinet meetings, and did not have a very distinguished cabinet, apart from Van Buren at State, but relied on a "kitchen cabinet" of less senior officials and friends. This would change in 1831. It shortly emerged that Jackson's idea of reform of the civil service was to sack a large number of people not identified with his own political rise and movement and replace them with loyalists. This affected about 20 percent of all federal employees in the Jackson years, and was dubbed "the Spoils System" by New York Senator William Marcy ("To the winner go the spoils"), Van Buren's side-kick in the Albany Regency.

Jackson allowed the Calhoun sponsorship of nullificationist ideas in South Carolina to go publicly uncontradicted through the first year of his administration, but it was known by the whole political community to be a ticking time bomb. A debate that began at the end of 1829 over the advisability of the federal government restricting and monitoring more closely the sale of public lands was soon represented by the formidable Senator Thomas Hart Benton of Missouri as an attempt by northeastern interests to control and retard the growth of the West. This quickly escalated as Senator Robert Hayne of South Carolina claimed that "the life of our system is the independence of our states" and imputed overbearing centralizing ambitions to the federal government. This smoked out the Senate's most formidable orator of all, Daniel Webster, who attacked those southerners who "Habitually speak of the Union in terms of indifference, or even of disparagement." The debate continued all through January 1830, as Hayne threw down the mask and espoused the sovereignty of the states and their right to unilateral nullification of federal laws. Webster replied that the states were sovereign only as far as the Constitution allowed that sovereignty is determined by the Constitution, that it resides with the government of the whole nation, and that state-federal disputes would be resolved by federal institutions and processes: federal courts, constitutional amendments, and free elections. Webster accused his opponents of sophistical arguments designed to weaken and undermine the national government in a dishonorable way. He concluded one of the most famous addresses ever rendered in the United States Senate: "Liberty and Union, now and forever, one and inseparable!" (January 27, 1830).

Hayne, who was understood to be speaking for his fellow South Carolinian and president of the Senate, Vice President Calhoun, replied to this with the familiar "compact" theory, that the states formed the federal government and had the legal capacity to judge when their rights were being infringed, and that the right of the states to reject federal laws was undiminished from before the Constitution was adopted. Webster had the better of the constitutional argument, as the adoption of and more than 40 years of adherence to the Constitution clearly conferred legitimacy on it, subject to interpretation, as the governmental law established by "We the people . . . for the United States of America." Calhoun and his fellow alarmed slaveholders were not going to render inoperative a document so thoroughly debated and ratified and enforced with specious arguments about a compact and with the miraculous revenance, after decades of invisibility and silence, of a selective right of nullification. These arguments were a goad, and a warning to the North, and the first stab at developing a plausible argument to justify secession, by force of arms if necessary.

Subtle differences became the subject of intense scrutiny in the divination of the nuances of federal or state attachments. This became quite commonplace in matters of toasts at official occasions. One early example was the Jefferson Day dinner in Washington on April 13, 1830, where Jackson proposed a toast to "Our Union; it must be preserved." And Calhoun responded: "The Union, next to our liberty most dear. May we always remember that it can only be preserved by distributing equally the benefits and burdens of the Union."

12. THE UNION AND SLAVERY

Battle lines were being drawn, but Jackson was playing a subtle and discreet game. He was a large slaveholder, and for his defense of New Orleans and seizure of Florida, his heavy-handed policy toward the Indians, and his respect for states' rights in public works matters, he had great popularity in the South. He was the incarnation of the frontiersman and had followed the settler's path and extended the country westward. And yet, as a nationalist who had finessed the tariff issue and emerged as a fierce defender of the Union, he was not necessarily unpopular in the North. He devised a policy that would serve the Union well and vitally. Jackson would guarantee slavery in the South and Southwest and resist any impeachment of it, and promote its westward expansion; and he would enforce the primacy and inviolability of the Union.

In the South, he would be the man who would make the Union work for the South and would be that region's unconquerable champion of the institution of slavery. In other regions, he was the guarantor of the Union; he would maintain the integrity of the United States at any cost. The North would tolerate slavery where it existed and in adjacent places to be settled, but not in the North, and the Union would survive. The South would accept the assurance of slavery where it existed and to the west of that, and would accept the Union. Jackson laid down this policy and enforced and bequeathed it. It was not a permanent arrangement, but it bought a vital 30 years, in which the Unionists became very much stronger than the slaveholders. This was a strategy of national self-preservation, geared to the inexorable economic and demographic rise and preeminence of the free states. It is not clear that Jackson thought beyond the co-preservation of the Union and of slavery, but tempered by the talents at compromise of Henry Clay and Daniel Webster, his rejection of nullification and of abolitionism was used by a generation of American public life as a shield behind which the numerical, economic, and moral strength of the free states came vastly to exceed those of the slave states.

The subject of internal improvements (public works) was a vexatious aspect of the same debate. Jackson's position that such interstate projects, or internationally significant versions such as the improvement of ports and harbors, were legitimate. But with the veto of the Maysville project, a highway entirely within the state of Kentucky, on May 27, 1830, Jackson sent a message to all sides: he was in favor of such projects where they really were matters involving more than one state, but not otherwise, and was for the division of available funds for redistribution to the states for selection of their own preferred objectives. This too, was a clever policy, as the North was concerned about federal aid to large projects, which Jackson supported; and the South was concerned with incursions from the federal government in local matters, which Jackson opposed.

The break between the president and the vice president would ramify into many fields. One of the sparks that set the long-accumulating tinder alight was the revelation to Jackson that Calhoun, as secretary of war in 1818, had favored censuring and punishing Jackson for his conduct in Florida. There was an acerbic exchange of correspondence between the two men, and all communication ended, with Jackson determined to be rid of Calhoun. The sly Van Buren (known as "The Red Fox of Kinderhook," referring to his hair-color, cunning, and place of residence), who had ingratiated himself quite profoundly with Jackson by oiling his New York political machine for the president, though formerly an ally of Calhoun's in presenting the Tariff of Abominations in an unsuccessful effort to embarrass President Adams, was now President Jackson's chief henchman in the purge of Calhoun. The ancient Florida quarrel just exacerbated the crisis caused by Calhoun's effort to reduce the Union to a periodic consultation with half of the states to see if they would accept the application of laws passed by what had been for 40 years the legislature of America.

A third ingredient in the boiling atmosphere was the attempted boycott of Secretary of War John Eaton's wife, Peggy O'Neal, a former barmaid. Mrs. Calhoun and other cabinet secretaries' wives refused contact with Mrs. Eaton, and when this absurd matter was raised at a cabinet meeting by Jackson, the only person who supported him was Van Buren, an egalitarian and a bachelor. To facilitate the house-cleaning, Van Buren and Eaton tendered their resignations, and Jackson sent Van Buren to London, eliminated the social problem with Eaton's wife by naming Eaton governor of Florida, sacked the rest to purge any influence of Calhoun, partly merged the kitchen and real cabinets, and added some stronger members. Calhoun blocked the confirmation of Van Buren to the London post, casting the deciding vote himself, in a brazenly provoking desertion of the administration, and Van Buren soon returned. The distinguished jurist and barrister and mayor of New York and codifier of the laws of Louisiana, Edward Livingston, went to State; the former minister to London, Louis McLane, took the Treasury; General Lewis Cass took over the War Department; Senator Levi Woodbury became secretary of the navy Amos Kendall soon became postmaster general; and the most durable and powerful of all except Jackson himself, Roger B. Taney, became attorney general. This swept the Calhoun elements out, and Calhoun's days as vice president were also numbered. Jackson strengthened his government and gave notice that he was not only fierce and belligerent, as had been well-known for 25 years, but also a skillful political infighter, such as had not been seen in the White House since the reign of the last general-in-residence. There was none of the philosophical stoicism of Jefferson or John Quincy Adams, the ambivalence of Madison or Monroe, or the rather self-defeating querulousness of John Adams. Jackson was a crafty, fanatical, and deadly opponent.

The firmness of Jackson's policy was its own reward; exalted though Britain was in the world, even its most powerful statesmen did not wish to cross swords with Old Hickory, as Jackson's followers called him. Lord Palmerston, who virtually invented gunboat diplomacy, and was not above threatening war on any state, and conducted several in a very long career that included 19 years in the junior but influential post of secretary at war, three years as home secretary, 16 years as foreign secretary, and nine years as prime minister, actively wished to avoid a tangle with Jackson, whom he knew would be like a porcupine and would make any test of strength not worth the trouble. Palmerston "always respected a powerful opponent and the references in his correspondence to General Jackson . . . show that here was a man not to be trifled with."[8]

The administration negotiated a very satisfactory reopening of complete trading access through the West Indian ports, a long-running grievance resolved. Jackson

---

8.   Jasper Riley, *Lord Palmerston*, London, Constable, 1970, p. 263.

also resolved claims for damage to American shipping against France, going back to 1815. In 1834, the French being in arrears, Jackson asked the Congress for reprisals against France, which then approved an installment under the reparation agreement, conditional on Jackson's apology for slights against France. This was an inexplicable French reversion to the insolence of the Genêt and XYZ affairs. Jackson replied that "The honor of my country shall never be stained by an apology from me for the statement of truth and the performance of duty." Jackson fired off ukases all day and sat on the terrace on temperate evenings, as he had for decades with his beloved but now deceased wife Rachel, both smoking large-bowled pipes and speaking softly of their happy but terribly eventful and tumultuous life together.

Jackson's policy toward Indians was also rather repressive, and was based on removing all Indians to west of the Mississippi, chiefly to free up land for more slaves baling cotton in the South. To this end, over 250,000 Indians were transported west, and many thousands died of illnesses contracted on the voyage. Treaties with Indians were routinely violated, especially when gold was discovered on Cherokee land in Georgia, and the Supreme Court overruled the state's expropriation of the gold-yielding property. Jackson allegedly said: "The chief justice [Marshall] has made his decision; now let him enforce it." Armed resistance to forced movement by the Sac and Fox Indians led to the Black Hawk War in 1832, but the resistance was futile. Jackson's enthusiasm for slavery and shabby treatment of the Indians are two great failings of his character and administration, though, again, they helped get the Union through a vital and vulnerable period.

The Nat Turner slave revolt in Southampton County, Virginia, August 13 to 23, 1831, killed 57 whites and over 100 blacks, and led to the execution of 20 slaves and the deterioration of slave-holding conditions throughout the South, restricting the movements of slaves, reducing their education levels, and making emancipation of individual slaves more difficult. There was great agitation in the South to prevent the dissemination of abolitionist propaganda through the mails. Jackson, ever faithful to his formula of safety for slavery in the South but no secession, proposed a bill banning such literature from the mails. Robert Hayne's successor as governor of South Carolina, George McDuffie, in a splendid local flourish, demanded the death penalty for such offenders, "without benefit of clergy."[9] The following year, the New England Anti-Slavery League was founded by William Lloyd Garrison, and there were similar organizations elsewhere in

---

9.   Richard B. Morris, *Encyclopedia of American History*, Sixth Edition, New York, Harper and Row, 1932, p. 209.

the North, as the entrenchment of positions on the issue on each side deepened slowly and ominously.

13. JACKSON'S SECOND TERM: NULLIFICATION AND THE NATIONAL BANK

Jackson had been renominated to the presidency without opposition by what was now officially called the Democratic Party, and having purged Calhoun, he secured the nomination for vice president of his friend and protégé Martin Van Buren. The National Republicans held a convention in Baltimore and nominated Henry Clay for president and John Sergeant of Pennsylvania for vice president. There was also an Anti-Masonic Party. The main campaign issue was Jackson's declared opposition to the renewal of the charter of the Bank of the United States. Jackson and Van Buren won easily, as they were the party of effective Unionism, and Jackson represented the Bank of the U.S. as an elitist and exploitive enterprise operated by corrupt plutocrats friendly with Clay. Jackson had about 55 percent of the vote and 219 electoral votes to 49 for Clay.

Although Calhoun had helped generate the nullification controversy with his co-sponsorship of the Tariff of Abominations, this fed the nullification argument, and Jackson advocated a reduction of some tariffs sensitive to South Carolina in 1832, to reduce frictions. But the nullification party won the South Carolina elections in October 1832. Calhoun had stopped acting through surrogates and overtly championed nullification in a number of speeches and letters, dressing it up in relatively plausible constitutional argument. A South Carolina state convention was called for November 19. The convention was largely boycotted by South Carolina's Unionists, and adopted a nullification ordinance, which declared the 1828 and 1832 tariffs nullified and forbade their collection in the state; required a state loyalty oath for all state employees except members of the legislature; forbade appeal to the U.S. Supreme Court of any matter arising from the ordinance; and stated that any use of force by the federal government against a state would be grounds for secession. The convention then voted to authorize and pay for a force of military resistance; this was taking matters to the verge of insurrection, and with the wrong president. Jackson ordered the war secretary to put the federal forts in Charleston Harbor on alert and put General Winfield Scott in command of all federal forces in South Carolina. About 8,000 South Carolina Unionists volunteered for the federal militia to suppress the nullifiers if necessary. For good measure, Jackson told a congressman that "If one drop of blood be shed there in defiance of the laws of the United States, I will hang the first man of them I can get my hands on to the first tree I can find." When South Carolina senator Robert

Hayne expressed skepticism to Senator Thomas Hart Benton that Jackson would follow through, Benton replied: "When Jackson begins to talk about hanging, they can begin to look for rope."[10] (Benton had been Jackson's aide at New Orleans, with the rank of colonel, and then represented his interests in Washington. They quarreled and Benton shot and wounded Jackson in a frontier brawl, though they were later reconciled. Among Benton's several famous sayings was: "I don't quarrel, but I fight, sir; and when I fight, a funeral follows." He and Jackson were birds of a feather, but he renounced slavery in later years, and thus was denied a sixth term as U.S. senator from Missouri.)

In his message to the Congress on December 4, 1832, Jackson recommended further downward revision of the tariff, and in his Proclamation to the People of South Carolina six days later (drafted by Livingston and a very substantial state paper), Jackson described nullification as a "practical absurdity" and reaffirmed the supremacy of a sovereign and indivisible federal government. No state could disobey federal law and none could leave the Union, and any attempt to do so "by armed force is treason." Calhoun resigned as vice president a couple of months before the end of his term, on December 28, having already been reelected to the U.S. Senate replacing Hayne, who had just been elected governor of South Carolina. South Carolina called for a general convention of other states in solidarity, but was rebuffed. On January 16, 1833, Jackson sent Congress his Force Bill, authorizing the collection of tariff duties in South Carolina by the U.S. Army if necessary, though what was actually foreseen was offshore collection, which would have made armed clashes less likely.

Daniel Webster again led the Unionist forces in debate, against Calhoun, and it was a memorable single-warrior combat, though Webster had the better of the argument and was the ne plus ultra of American political orators of the time. Henry Clay, exercising again his great talent for conciliating the apparently irreconcilable, introduced a compromise tariff. Both Jackson's Force Bill and Clay's tariff passed and both were signed into law by Jackson on March 2, 1833, two days before he was reinaugurated. Six weeks before, South Carolina, supposedly in response to Clay's approaching tariff bill, but certainly not without awareness of Jackson's aroused threats, suspended its nullification ordinance, and rescinded it when the tariff was enacted, but also purported to nullify the Force Bill.

By this powerful show of force and purpose, coupled with conciliatory gestures to slave-holding, Jackson had shut down any thought of insurrection for perhaps a generation. Henceforth the cause of Union would rest chiefly on the ability of

---

10. Howe, *op. cit.*, p. 406.

the free states to attract more immigration and spread westward more quickly than the more sluggish and agrarian slave states, so that insurrection would become unfeasible because of the greater strength of the Union states. This demonstrated Jackson's strategic grasp, even if intuitively, of how to keep the Union together. The young republic had made its point in the world, but the world could also see that it was threatened by internal contradictions. Jackson loved the Union more than he approved slavery, and the United States owes him much for deferring the supreme test between the two unequal halves of the country until the Unionists, by the narrowest of margins and with the benefit of the most distinguished leadership in the country's history, were strong enough to throttle the secessionists. Jackson may not have reacted for exactly this reason, but he saved the Union for a significant time at a decisive moment, and applied the only strategy that was going to preserve the country's full potential for national greatness and benign world influence.

The 81-year-old (in 1832) James Madison, like Jefferson, had been disconcerted when their party was taken over by the comparative ruffian and warmonger Jackson, but they also had come to recognize the danger posed by the slavery issue. Jackson had politely referred to Madison as "a great civilian" but added that "the mind of a philosopher could not dwell on blood and carnage with any composure."[11] Jackson had no such difficulties. He never lacked the steely resolve to deal severely with people and events. Once again, the American system seemed miraculously to have demonstrated that the office does seek the man, as it had turned up a leader who had terrible lapses of humanity, moderation, and scruple, but was providentially able to produce a policy of finely calibrated appeasement and intimidation of the slave-holding interest that would keep North and South together under the same constitutional roof for an indispensable further period of national maturation. By whatever combination of intuition, good fortune, and design, it was masterly strategy for the ultimate elimination of the Union's great internal weakness (slavery).

Jackson's next major step, the veto of the renewal of the charter of the Bank of the United States, stirred another immense controversy. Clay urged the head of the Bank, Nicholas Biddle, to submit his application for recharter four years early, in 1832, to force Jackson's hand and make an election issue of it. Biddle did so, and it was useful to Jackson, as the Bank was unpopular in the South and West, and seen as an elitist eastern organization that overly contracted credit in the faster-growing areas of the country. This also helped Jackson counter the nullifiers

---

11. Howe, *op. cit.*, p. 79.

and appear generally as the champion of the little people. Biddle was judged too restrictive of credit through his ability to enforce ratios on smaller banks, and he was not accorded the credit the Bank generally deserved for avoiding inflation and keeping an orderly money supply. Shutting the Bank down was a mistake other than politically. Both houses of the Congress voted to renew, but they could not override Jackson's veto. Jackson's actions proved to be unsuccessful, but not as catastrophically mistimed as Madison's inability to renew the charter in 1811.

Following the reelection of Jackson, Clay and Calhoun joined forces to get a House vote approving retention of government deposits in the Bank of the United States. Jackson felt he had won a clear mandate to get rid of the Bank, and Biddle thought his position justified his replying to Jackson's war on him and his Bank by tightening credit, which he did. By the end of 1833, Biddle's tactics had induced significant financial distress in the country, and Jackson had overcome a divided cabinet to remove federal government deposits from the Bank and place them in 23 state banks.

Jackson named Roger Taney, the attorney general, secretary of the Treasury to carry out the changes he sought, and as always with Jackson, there were insults and ruffled feathers all round. Clay got a censure vote against both Jackson and the Treasury through the Senate. Jackson's transgression was that he refused to hand over to the Senate a paper he had read to his cabinet about the Bank recharter question. Jackson lodged a protest that he had been accused of an impeachable offense without being given an opportunity to defend himself. The Senate declined to confirm Taney at Treasury, but Jackson had him serve ad interim, and named him successfully, over strenuous opposition, as chief justice of the United States in 1835 when John Marshall died after 34 years in his office.[12] Taney was the first senior American official who was a Roman Catholic; he would serve 29 years as chief justice, with very mixed results. Benton eventually had the censure of Jackson expunged.

Inflation was abetted by the use of land-sale speculators' notes as a form of transactional debt, and the huge increase in western land sales generated great increases in activity, and consequently in the de facto money supply, since these notes served as currency. Jackson ordered that only gold, silver, and in a few cases certain state-backed scrip would be accepted as payment in sales of federal lands. This turned inflation instantly into deflation, sharply reducing sales of federal lands and placing great strain on the state banks. Jackson's unnuanced decrees

---

12. It was the constant mournful tolling over Marshall's death that caused Philadelphia's Liberty Bell famously to crack irreparably.

in banking and monetary policy caused syncopated economic lurches that were often destructive to many, and reduced general levels of confidence in the rational administration of the country's affairs.

Presidents (J.Q.) Adams and Jackson had both offered to buy Texas from Mexico, without success. American settlement in Texas began in earnest with Moses Austin and his son Stephen F. Austin, and was agreed by successive Mexican governments until 1830, when Mexico outlawed slavery in Texas and forbade further American settlement there. Stephen Austin went to Mexico to negotiate with the president, the charming and imperishable scoundrel General Antonio López de Santa Anna, who was nine times president of his country (though serving only seven years), and called himself "the Napoleon of the West" among other encomia. Santa Anna arrested Austin and imprisoned him for eight months. A group of Texans asserted their independence in 1835. Santa Anna set out to crush Texas militarily, and invested the San Antonio fortress, the Alamo, on February 23, 1836, with 3,000 men. The fortress was defended by only 188 men, including folkloric figures William Travis and Davy Crockett. After 10 days, Santa Anna overwhelmed the defenders and all the Americans were massacred, as were several hundred other Americans at different locations in Texas.

On April 21, Sam Houston led several hundred men stealthily across the San Jacinto River, near what is today the city of Houston, and defeated about 1,200 Mexicans at San Jacinto and captured Santa Anna, who was released to secure Mexican recognition of the independence of Texas. The Mexicans rejected this and Houston was elected president of the independent Republic of Texas. There were resolutions from both houses of the Congress for recognition of Texas, which Jackson, uncharacteristically, was hesitant to do. He wished to honor treaty obligations with Mexico and claimed not to wish a war with that country, though he would normally find such a prospect appetizing. He was more concerned with causing a split in the Democratic Party between pro- and anti-slavery forces, but on his last full day as president, March 3, 1837, Jackson did send a chargé to Texas in an act of quasi-recognition. This was another time bomb that Jackson would leave for his successors.

The National Republicans of Henry Clay and John Quincy Adams, favoring protective tariffs and a strong federal government, including a national bank, and cool to the spread of slavery, merged with former Democrats opposed to Jackson's Bank policy, and with the more prosperous southern planters and northern industrialists, who found Jackson a dangerous rabble-rouser. They all joined, very implausibly, with southern opponents of Jackson's anti-nullification policy, to form what was called, at Clay's suggestion, the Whig Party. The remnants of the previous election's Anti-Masonic Party (which had carried Vermont in 1832) joined the Whigs, a catchment of all those fragments that had been scattered in all directions by the onslaught of the Jackson juggernaut. In Congress, they were a relatively coherent group led by Clay and Webster and Calhoun, who were well-settled into their long domination of the Congress. But in the country, they were an incongruous hodgepodge of elements awkwardly lined up in opposition to the galvanizing figure of the president, who carried the torch of national unity in the North and wore the mantle and laurels of the regional defender of slavery in the South, and was a war hero to all. Andrew Jackson remains one of the seven or eight most important presidents in the country's history—inventor of the spoils system, champion of the slaveholders, betrayer of the Indians, agent of financial disorder, but redeemer of an ill-considered war, leader of the populist Democrats, and conservator pro tempore of the American Union.

14. STRATEGIC REVIEW

It was 77 years from the start of the Seven Years' War to the reinauguration of Andrew Jackson, and in that time America had deftly moved through eight distinct strategic phases. Franklin had had the vision of the Great Power of the New World, and had fastened it admirably onto Pitt's vision of the British Empire to encourage the permanent expulsion of France from North America. This was the sine qua non to the possibility of American independence, which would have been impractical if France had remained in contention for control of the Great Lakes and the Mississippi and Ohio River valleys (1756–1763). For the fulfillment of Franklin's vision, France and Britain would both have to go from America, but France would have to go first.

When the king and the king's men refused to govern equitably as between the British of the home islands and of America, Washington's genius for guerrilla war (for it was genius and it was guerrilla war) was married to Franklin's diplomatic genius in enticing France self-destructively to the aid of republicanism, and to Jefferson's genius for presenting the quarrel in epochal, libertarian terms, and independence was won (1764–1783). Washington then displayed a political cunning and integrity and resistance to the temptations of force no triumphant general in an important country would show again until Charles de Gaulle patiently awaited the collapse of the French Fourth Republic 170 years later (1783–1787). Washington and Franklin sponsored the constitutional efforts of Madison, Hamilton, and Jay, and a stable and durable and adequately flexible system of government resulted (1787–1789).

Washington, Hamilton, and Adams launched the government of the new republic with surpassing insight and distinction, establishing strong economic policies and fiscal institutions, asserting federal authority and retaining sufficient military strength to be able to exchange non-aggression against Canada and the British West Indies for British liberality toward American commerce on the high seas, and used the status quo with Britain to lever a firm line against revolutionary and Napoleonic France (1789–1801).

The opposition came peacefully to power, often the litmus test of a new national regime. And Jefferson and Madison retained Hamilton's financial institutions and industrial policy, while expanding the country into the interior of the continent, broadening the franchise, and shrinking and decentralizing government. Their economic reprisals against Britain failed and Madison lost the opportunity to seize Canada, but at least registered again, in the otherwise pointless War of 1812, America's determined autonomy opposite Britain (1801–1817).

Monroe and John Quincy Adams continued the wiser policies of all their predecessors and seized the coat-tails and the elbow of their late British adversary, preponderant in the post-Napoleonic world, as tightly as Britain would embrace America when the correlation of forces between them tipped three-quarters of a century later. For the United States, it was solidarity in apparent equality with the only potentially threatening adversary, all in the interest of American hemispheric preeminence (1818–1829).

And Andrew Jackson would impose the acceptance of slavery where it existed and within its established latitude in implicit exchange for the inviolability of the Union, which the South, in its defensiveness about slavery, was already trying to redefine. Given demographic and economic trends, this would ensure the ability of the free states with skillful political leadership to prevail over the slave states, should the issue be forced, if the test of strength could be deferred by 20 or 30 years (1832–1860).

If these trends of growth and development could be retained and the slavery threat resolved, the United States, barely 80 years after Yorktown, would be one of the greatest powers in the world, as Franklin had foreseen. Of the founders of the country, Madison was the only one still alive in 1833, and he saw the danger and the promise. It would all be down to the next great leader of the American project, a raw-boned young Illinoisan, teaching himself law and wondering about slavery.

TWO

THE PREDESTINED
PEOPLE, 1836–1933

James K. Polk

CHAPTER FIVE

Slavery
The House Divided, 1836–1860

1. THE PRESIDENCY OF MARTIN VAN BUREN

Jackson respected the tradition of the founders and did not seek a third term (though like all of them, he could have won one), and he urged Martin Van Buren as his successor. Van Buren was nominated by the Democrats, with, for vice president, Colonel Richard M. Johnson, the supposed killer of Tecumseh and a successful militia leader and colorful figure who cohabited with a black woman, to whom he was not married, just a few blocks from the slave market in Washington. The disparate elements of the Whig movement could not agree on a candidate, so they adopted the tactic of nominating regional candidates in the hope of denying the Democrats a majority and pushing the election to the House of Representatives (where the likely Democratic majority would have elected Van Buren anyway). The dissident anti-Jackson Democrats nominated Hugh L. White of Tennessee; the New England Adamsites nominated Daniel Webster; and the Anti-Masonic elements reached back 25 years to try to tap the Jackson formula of the military hero above politics and chose Colonel Richard Johnson's old commander, General William Henry Harrison, victor of Tippecanoe and Moravian Town.

The election was essentially a referendum on Jackson, and Van Buren won, 762,000 to 550,000 for Harrison, 145,000 for White, and 41,000 for Webster. Van Buren had about 51.5 percent of the total vote but won more easily in the Electoral College, 170 votes to 73 for Harrison, 26 for White, and 14 for Webster. None of the four candidates for vice president was successful, so, for the only time in American history, the issue was decided by the Senate, where Richard Johnson was elected. Van Buren would be the only person in the history of the country, apart from Jefferson, who held the offices of president, vice president, and secretary of state. He had been state senator, U.S. senator, governor, and minister to Great Britain to boot, a political roué of great charm and cunning and no principles at all, and more of a maneuverer than a leader. After the four Virginia plantation owners and the two Boston academic lawyers, the country would alternately elect presidents who were generals or political wheelhorses, as it descended the slippery slope toward civil conflict.

No formula short of the three-fifths rule would have attracted the South into the Union; no alternate strategy to Jackson's, varied by Clay's compromises, was going to keep the country together until 1860. Only a war in the 1810s would elevate Andrew Jackson to the point of electability, no one else could have devised and implemented his formula for preserving the Union, and the United States could not have become the greatest power in the world without the South. American history has been like a bouncing (American) football, in unpredictable directions, dependent again and again on indispensable and often unlikely individuals, elevated improbably. Beyond its natural resources and its Constitution, few Americans could explain why the United States has been such a felicitous country, but almost all of them sense that it has been.

The U.S. economy, after Jackson's draconian tinkering, hit the wall in 1837. Federal land sales collapsed, declining by almost 90 percent, foreclosures occurred in large numbers with the invalidation of the former notes used as consideration for land sales, and then commodity prices declined precipitously, especially cotton (by about half). In New York and other cities, there were mass protests against unemployment and food and fuel prices. New York's main flour warehouse was ransacked. The relative absence of paper money created deflation, but the reliance on the banknotes of state banks made it very hard to monitor the money supply, and the lack of any supervision of financial institutions led to a great many bank failures, which was a condition facilitated and made more destructive by the disappearance of a large national bank. Van Buren advocated a paper currency, unsuccessfully.

The slavery debate, which would never subside for long, until, as Lincoln said, "every drop of blood drawn by the lash is repaid by a drop of blood drawn by the sword," flared up again with debate over petitions for the abolition of slavery and of the slave trade in the District of Columbia. The southern view was that endless discussion of the morality of slavery was abrasive to the well-being of the Union. Southern members of the Congress, led by Calhoun, considered these petitions insulting. When Senator James Buchanan of Pennsylvania, a distinguished ambassador and future secretary of state and president, had moved such a petition in January 1836, Calhoun had moved that such petitions be barred. Buchanan achieved a compromise by establishing their right to be presented and their automatic rejection, including of his own petition. (This was a little like Calhoun's fierce denunciation of the tariff he himself presented, in 1828.) In the House of Representatives, former President Adams defended the right of abolitionists to petition, and was anti-slavery, but believed the Congress had no power to abolish slavery, as it had been established and implicitly accepted by the Constitution. Resolutions were passed in 1836 and 1837 receiving but tabling without debate any resolutions about slavery, including ones declaring that the Congress had no right to deal with slavery at all and that it was inexpedient for the Congress to discuss the status of slavery in the District of Columbia. There was a good deal of discussion among southern members of the Congress regarding a resolution endorsing the legality and permanence of slavery, and declaring that if it were not passed, this would justify secession. Such a resolution was never proposed, but hypotheses ending in the right or desirability of secession were becoming more frequent. The murder of the abolitionist editor Elijah Lovejoy in Illinois in November 1837 caused a noteworthy inflammation of debate.

In December 1837, Senator Benjamin Swift of Vermont presented resolutions opposing the admission of Texas or any other new state as a slave state and upholding the right of Congress to deal with the slave trade in the District of Columbia. This brought forth John C. Calhoun, ever the supreme fire engine of southern legislators, with a series of resolutions at the very end of 1837 that reaffirmed the compact theory of the Union (which implied a right to secede or nullify legislation); asserted that the federal government had to resist all attempts by one part of the Union to use it against the domestic institutions of another part; and prohibited attacks on the institution of slavery and declared attacks on slavery in the District of Columbia to be a "direct and dangerous attack on the institutions of all the slave-holding states." The fact that Calhoun got all this adopted demonstrates the extent to which the South was blackmailing the North already with the specter of secession. Even Clay, who was a slaveholder but also a supporter of the move to encourage slaves to move to Liberia (a supposedly sovereign African country created for them by American altruists who wanted slavery to end by emigration back to Africa) and a moral critic of slavery, periodically condemned abolitionists as insouciant about provoking a civil war. In debate in 1839, when advised by Senator Preston of South Carolina that he could lose support in the North, Clay uttered his most famous words: "I trust the sentiments and opinions [I expressed] are correct; I had rather be right than be president." In 1844, John Quincy Adams, in one of the signal achievements of his very long and distinguished career, gained the repeal of the gag rule, which facilitated shutting down debate, and which he had consistently rejected as "a violation of the Constitution of the United States, of the rules of this House, and of the rights of my constituents."

Foreign affairs were relatively quiet in the Van Buren years, as Jackson's last secretary of state, John Forsyth, who had been an anti-Calhoun Jackson loyalist from Georgia, continued in that office under the new president. There were some frictions with Britain, over asylum given to the Canadian rebel William Lyon Mackenzie, and over a disputed lumbering area between Maine and New Brunswick (Aroostook). Popular sentiment flared up from time to time, but Van Buren enforced existing agreements and the well-traveled General Winfield Scott patrolled the border to prevent private-sector liberators of Canada from crossing. When they did sneak into Canada they were captured or put to flight promptly. Van Buren played it sensibly and the Aroostook question was referred to an arbiter and resolved by treaty in 1842.

2. THE LOG CABIN AND HARD CIDER ELECTION

The Whigs held their first nominating convention at Harrisburg, Pennsylvania, in December 1839. Though Clay was the logical choice, his support of a protective tariff alienated many natural supporters. Clay led initially, but the convention renominated General William Henry Harrison, the now 68-year-old hero of the Indian wars and the War of 1812. Harrison did not have a long record on policy and was acceptable to all the jostling factions under the Whig umbrella. John Tyler, a nullificationist who had broken with Jackson over the veto of the renewal of the charter of the Bank of the United States, and had resigned as senator from Virginia rather than follow the instructions of the Virginia legislature to vote for Benton's bill to expunge the censure of Jackson, was chosen for vice president. He was a slaveholder and his views on most issues diverged sharply from those of his running mate and most of the delegates at the convention, and he would soon illustrate the dangers of using the vice presidential nomination exclusively for ticket-balancing.

Van Buren was renominated by the Democrats on a straight Jacksonian platform—support of slavery and opposition to a national bank. There was much opposition to Richard Johnson, partly because of his flamboyant miscegenation and adultery, and no one was chosen for vice president; Van Buren left it to the states to put up whomever they wished, a unique confession of electoral weakness by an incumbent president seeking reelection. The election quickly turned into a sophisticated political public relations job by the Whigs, touting Harrison as a war hero and simple man of the people and the frontier, born in a log cabin, whose favorite beverage was cider. It was the Log Cabin and Hard Cider campaign, under the slogan "Tippecanoe and Tyler too." Policies were entirely avoided, apart from the Whigs unloading denigration on Van Buren as the author of the tenacious economic recession. Van Buren was falsely portrayed as a snobbish aristocrat living in "the palace" at the taxpayers' expense.

Beyond that, it was all parades, slogans, banners, placards, campaign buttons, and other innovations, and was the most substantively vapid presidential campaign in the country's history up to that time. Harrison won by 1.275 million votes to 1.129 million for Van Buren, about 53 percent to 47 and 234 electoral votes to 60. Van Buren had not been an important president. He was an interesting and capable machine politician in New York, and a wheeler-dealer on an international scale. Charming and astute, he was an unprincipled fox completely preoccupied with getting, rather than filling, an office, the exact opposite to John Quincy Adams. Van Buren did not vanish from the scene, and retained great popularity and influence among the Democrats, whose cause he had so long and ably advanced. The 1840 vote was the first presidential election since 1796 that had not been won by some sort of Democrat (two terms each for Jefferson, Madison, Monroe, and Jackson, and one for Adams, then a National Republican, i.e. non-Jackson Democrat).

Harrison had a fairly strong cabinet, with Daniel Webster at State (after Clay declined to take the post again), the capable John Bell in the War Department, and John J. Crittenden of Kentucky as attorney general. Most except Webster were Clay loyalists. Harrison has been rather misrepresented as a bumpkin. He was an able and intellectually curious man. Unfortunately, he put a wide range of ideas into his loquacious inaugural address, contracted a cold that escalated gradually into pneumonia, and died after only a month in office, on April 4, 1841. He was a considerable man and might have made a capable president. At 68, he was the oldest man elected to the office up to Ronald Reagan 140 years later. Unfortunately, the Whigs now paid the price for being such a broad church. The new president, John Tyler, the last Virginia slaveholder to hold the office, did a competent job rebutting suggestions that since he had not been elected president, he did not have the right to the full powers of the office. But he was an anti-Jackson Democrat, and so, especially as an accidental occupant of the White House, had virtually no support in the Congress or the country. It was only a month after inauguration day and no one had voted for him as president. Squeezed between Clay and the Jacksonites, he would try, without success, to attract a following.

In June, Clay introduced in the Senate a series of resolutions that amounted to the Whig program: a national bank, revenue-producing tariff protection, and the distribution of the proceeds of sales of public lands. In 1841 the Congress passed two bills setting up a new national bank, within the District of Columbia, but Tyler, who had broken with Jackson over the bank, vetoed both bills because they required states specifically to dissent, rather than specifically to adhere—absurdly narrow grounds to dispose of such hard-fought legislation. All of Tyler's cabinet resigned in protest at the president's vetoes, except Webster. He too retired in May 1843, to be replaced by Abel P. Upshur, the navy secretary.

3. THE TYLER PRESIDENCY

Never far from the surface, the ubiquitous slavery issue became prominent again in the *Amistad* case, in which slaves on a Spanish slave galley mutinied and were taken by an American warship to New London, Connecticut, where their status was litigated. John Quincy Adams successfully argued for their freedom at the Supreme Court of the United States. A further maritime controversy arose in March 1842, when an American brig, the *Creole*, sailed from Hampton Roads,

Virginia, and the slaves mutinied, killed a white sailor, and forced the crew to steer the ship to Nassau, Bahamas. The British freed all the slaves except those who were directly responsible for the murder, who were charged and detained. Secretary Webster demanded the return of the slaves as the property of U.S. citizens. The British ignored the demand, which was eventually settled for the payment of $110,000, 13 years later. It showed the strains on the country when a man who did not approve of slavery, Daniel Webster, felt it his official duty to write belligerent notes to Britain for the return of self-liberated slaves. Congressman Joshua Giddings of Ohio offered a series of astringent anti-slavery resolutions that caused the southerners and their allies in the Jackson settlement (whereby, like Webster, the North loyally supported the right of the South to retain slavery) to pass a vote of censure against Giddings. He resigned his Ohio district and was reelected with a heavy majority in a special election, demonstrating with startling clarity where northern opinion was, whatever arrangements their leaders were making to overlook the strains slavery caused within the country.

Following the defeat of the Whig program in the Congress, Henry Clay retired from the Senate and devoted himself altogether to organizing the Whigs, who now suffered the discomfort of having a president elected as a Whig who was seeking the Democratic nomination for reelection. Clay's retirement address on March 31, 1842, was one of the Senate's great emotional occasions. His successor as Whig leader in the Senate, John J. Crittenden, said it "was something like the soul's quitting the body."[1] Clay and Calhoun embraced in silence, and Clay left the Senate chamber, to which he had been first elected 36 years before. Jackson thought it was the end of Clay, politically: "The old coon is really and substantially dead, skinned and buried."[2] No, he was not, fortunately for the United States.

Webster's principal achievement in this term (the first of two) as secretary of state was to return to one of the principal objectives of such esteemed former architects of American diplomacy as John Jay and John Quincy Adams, and put relations with Great Britain on a thoroughly normal and current basis. This was facilitated by the departure from office of the Jackson entourage in Washington, and of Lord Melbourne and his brother-in-law, Lord Palmerston, in London and their replacement by the more amenable Sir Robert Peel. Lord Ashburton was sent as a special minister by Peel to the United States, which now had 18 million people, a population slightly larger than Great Britain's, and whatever its interne-

---

1. Robert V. Remini, *Henry Clay: Statesman for the Union*, New York, Norton, 1991, p. 609.
2. Ibid. p. 610. (The raccoon was the symbol of the Whig Party, as the elephant and the donkey are today of the Republicans and the Democrats.)

cine contradictions, now an important country that had to be taken seriously. The discussions were conducted in a very cordial and businesslike atmosphere, and of the 12,000 square miles in the disputed Aroostook area between Maine and New Brunswick, 7,000 were signed over to the U.S. This was a little less than it would have gained from the mediation of the king of the Netherlands in 1831, which the Senate had rejected by one vote in 1832. The entire border was clarified through to west of the Great Lakes, and various further agreements were made re extradition, navigation rights on shared rivers, and the joint suppression of the slave trade on the west coast of Africa (slavery had been abolished in the entire British Empire 10 years before), and the British made a very cautious quasi-apology for two incidents in the aftermath of the Mackenzie rebellion in Upper Canada (Ontario), in 1837. What became known as the Webster-Ashburton Treaty was ratified easily in the Senate, and Webster retired as secretary of state, and was followed by Upshur, the navy secretary. Upshur suffered the unique misfortune of being killed in February 1844, the only secretary of state to die violently, when on a cruise to demonstrate an immense naval gun on a steam-powered warship, the gun exploded. The cruise and test-firing were designed to impress and frighten the Mexicans, with whom relations had worsened. In the circumstances it did not succeed in that objective. Upshur was replaced by Calhoun, as Tyler was desperately cobbling a reconciliation with the southern Democrats, to reposition himself there and in the far-fetched hope of gaining the Democratic presidential nomination, since Clay clearly had a lock on the Whigs. (The Whig Party had expelled Tyler from membership anyway.) As Congress had repealed the Independent Treasury Act, this meant that throughout Tyler's term the handling of the government's money was at the exclusive discretion of the secretary of the Treasury.

The Oregon boundary would soon arise as a new hobgoblin in Anglo-American relations, as the area between the Rocky Mountains and the Pacific Ocean from the 42nd to the 54th parallels had been under joint management by the two countries since 1818, and after the U.S. had treatied out Spain (1819) and Russia (1824). From (J.Q.) Adams on, the Americans had offered to saw it off at the 49th parallel, but the British wanted the Columbia River basin and access to Puget Sound. This impasse festered and became a national political issue at the approach of the 1844 election.

And the Texas question would not remain quiet for long. The northern political leadership regarded the settlements and revolutions and scheming with Mexico of the Americans in Texas as a plot to extend slavery within the United States through petitions for admission to the Union as a state. Rebuffed under Houston's successor as president of Texas, one Mirabeau Lamar, Texas exchanged embassies with France, the Netherlands, and Belgium (a state invented by Palmerston to keep Antwerp out of the hands of France or a Germanic power), and with Great Britain, from 1838 to 1840. Houston returned to office in December 1841, and the Mexicans ineffectually invaded Texas in 1842, but the British and French intervened diplomatically to mediate an end to that conflict. Britain and France both wanted Texas as an independent country, to restrain the growth of the United States. Ironically, the North became alarmed at the idea of a European satellite on the country's southern border just as the South became alarmed at reports that the British were going to try to bribe the Texans into the abolition of slavery in the young republic. Sam Houston had pressed exactly the right buttons to shift opinion in Washington toward annexation of Texas, an astute management of U.S. political opinion.

The deathless Santa Anna, who had lost a leg fighting a French incursion at Veracruz in 1838, and had given his leg a full state military burial, informed the U.S. in August 1843 that any attempt at annexation would be regarded as a declaration of war on Mexico. This was not a frightening prospect, but Houston had to tread warily, as British awareness that he was again seeking annexation could cause the withdrawal of their patronage and leave him with no cards to play opposite Washington or Mexico, to gain entry to the Union. Upshur assured Houston that over two-thirds of the Senate would approve incorporation of Texas in the Union, in April 1844. Houston and Upshur's successor, Calhoun, signed a treaty of annexation under which the United States would assure the defense of Texas while the treaty was being ratified. Tyler recommended annexation to the Senate, and mentioned the abolitionist danger posed by British influence in Mexico, a concern amplified by Calhoun's rebuke to the British minister in Washington, defending slavery. This stoked up northern concerns that it was a slaveholders' plot after all, and the treaty that had been signed in April was rejected decisively (indicating the shifting balance of domestic opinion on the slavery issue, and the increasing strength of the North in Congress) in June. Tyler's effort to annex Texas by joint resolution of the houses of the Congress, simple majorities rather than the two-thirds majority required in a Senate treaty ratification, was not brought to a vote before the Congress adjourned, leaving the matter in flux heading into the 1844 election. The British, in their effort to keep Texas out of the U.S., did succeed in securing Mexican recognition of Texan independence in May 1845, but they had been bypassed by events. The approaching conflict was every bit as absurd as the run-up to the last war on American frontiers 33 years before. This was where the Texas and Oregon issues stood as they were brought to the front burner for the election of a new president (as no party would own up to Tyler).

4. THE 1844 ELECTION

Coming into the 1844 election campaign, it was generally assumed that Van Buren had a lock on the Democratic nomination, and Clay on that of the Whigs. Despite his long loyalty to Jackson, Van Buren was suspected in the South of being opposed to the annexation of Texas and hostile to slavery. Southern party leaders obtained a letter from Jackson, published in a Richmond newspaper, supporting the annexation of Texas.[3] It was generally believed that in a much-publicized visit of Van Buren to Clay at his home at Ashland, near Lexington, Kentucky, in May 1842, Van Buren had agreed with Clay that Texas would be kept out of the next election campaign. This would have proved impossible even without Jackson's intervention, but the extreme delicacy of the issue again illustrated the extent to which slavery inflamed American public life. Very little could be done in many policy areas without rattling the sensibilities of northerners nauseated by the ownership of people and the untrammeled ability to exploit, overwork, whip, violate, and kill them; and the southerners' revulsion at what they regarded as hypocrisy and hysteria in attacking a regime recognized in the Constitution, practiced ultimately by 12 of the country's presidents, and based on the decency of southern gentlemen not to abuse their live property, any more than they would domestic or farm animals, and on what was presumed to be a racial inferiority of Negroes.

Clay had less to lose, as the Whigs were unlikely to gain much support in the South, but Van Buren risked splitting his party along straight regional lines. This was the inherent risk in the Jackson strategy: if spirits overheated over slavery, issues could endlessly be presented that could make cooperation impossible. More and more finesse and ingenuity would be required to avoid such a trap. On April 27, 1844, Van Buren and Clay published letters in different newspapers opposing annexation. Van Buren wrote that admitting Texas as a state would incite an unjustifiable war with Mexico, an argument that was a matter of indifference in the North and that deeply offended the South as the spuriously explained desertion that it was. Specifically, it forfeited the support of Jackson, still the party kingmaker at 77, who stated that the nominee should be a pro-annexationist southwesterner. It is inexplicable how Van Buren could have erred so badly. He should have supported annexation and finessed the slavery issue, if necessary by some stratagem such as admitting Texas as two states, one slave and one free. Opposing admission

---

3. This was a step Jackson had feared to take when he had the chance in his two terms, and was somewhat emulated by Dwight D. Eisenhower 125 years later, when he dodged Indochina completely but became a war hawk as an ex-president.

to a large and rich adjacent area settled by Americans in an expansionist America shouting itself hoarse with variations on its exalted and exceptional destiny was a suicidal misjudgment. Van Buren had to wave the flag and exalt nationalism over concerns about slavery. The Red Fox of Kinderhook had uncharacteristically blundered into a deadly trap.

Clay was just as clumsy but had less at stake. He claimed that such a move without Mexican agreement would lead to war. (This was a prospect that did not concern a single visible or audible person in the country after all they had seen of the peg-legged "Napoleon of the West"; no American conceived of the military rout of Mexico as a serious challenge—they weren't like the British and the Canadians.) He said it would be "dangerous to the integrity of the Union," which was partly true, but it would not be as dangerous as rejecting the request for annexation. And he said the majority of Americans didn't approve such a step, which was not true, as long as the question was not posed as an extension of slavery. Three days after the letters were published, Clay was unanimously nominated for president by the Whigs at Baltimore (where most nominating conventions took place until the rise of Chicago 15 years later). Theodore Frelinghuysen of New Jersey was chosen for vice president. Clay then started to skate around the issue by publishing further letters saying that he was not opposed to the annexation of Texas but felt that the passions of the anti-abolitionists made it a danger, and then that he was in fact an annexationist, as long as that could be effected peacefully and honorably, etc., and finally that the issue of slavery should be kept out of the discussion, as if that were in the slightest possible. Clay managed the issue more suavely than Van Buren, who faced it more squarely but squandered whatever credit he might have achieved for doing so by recourse to the mealy mouthed humbug about avoiding war with Mexico.

The Democrats also met at Baltimore, starting on May 27, and Van Buren led on the first ballot, but the requirement for a two-thirds approval of the nominees (which continued in that party until 1936) soon ensured that he could not be chosen, such was the antagonism to him in the South. The eminent historian George Bancroft proposed the 48-year-old former Speaker of the House of Representatives and governor of Tennessee (though twice subsequently defeated seeking that office), James Knox Polk. His name was placed in nomination for the eighth ballot and he was selected on the ninth. Silas Wright, an anti-slavery Van Burenite from New York, was nominated for vice president (the flip-side of what the Whigs had done in 1839 by nominating the pro-slavery nullificationist Tyler to run with the stronger Unionist, Harrison). Wright was invited by telegraph and declined by the same new medium, and instead ran successfully for governor of New York.

George M. Dallas, a Pennsylvania "doughface" (malleable northern respecter of what was known as the southern slave power), was selected. Tyler assembled his loyalist Democrats on the same day at Baltimore and they nominated him for reelection, but when it became clear that he did not have appreciable support, he withdrew in August, becoming the first of a string of six consecutive presidents not to run for a second term, and the third of a string of 14 out of 16 between Jackson and McKinley not to achieve a second consecutive term (three died in their first terms).

It had become a very difficult office in a severely divided country. Polk represented the annexation of Texas as a patriotic expansion that was already basically committed, and hewed to the Jackson line: slavery would continue where it was part of the culture but not inconvenience those where it was not, and the nation's rightful growth must not be throttled or deterred because of unfounded fears. Clay continued to represent himself as pro-annexationist on conditions that were vaguely formulated but could not possibly be met.

Polk became the first dark-horse president in the country's history, and won by a hair's breadth, 1.34 million votes to 1.3 million for Clay and 62,000 for the anti-slavery Liberty candidate, James G. Birney, or 49.7 percent to 48.3 percent to 2 percent. Birney polled almost 16,000 votes in New York state, where Polk won over Clay by only 5,000. The abolitionists had put the Jacksonian pro-slavery candidate in the White House. For all the support Clay won in the South, he would have been better off to say he was pro-annexation but anti-slavery, or at least for deferring until a later date the issue of whether there would be slavery in Texas. The slavery debate was becoming more desperately serious so quickly that even the country's most agile politicians could not adjust to it. If Van Buren had shown a little imagination over Texas, he would have been nominated. Once Polk was nominated, if Clay had shown a little more agile footwork, he would have been elected. The electoral vote was 170 to 105. If Clay had had 6,000 more votes in New York, or just taken 3,000 from Polk, he would have won. In the extreme winter of his presidency, three days before Polk's inauguration on March 4, 1845, Tyler annexed Texas by resolution of both houses of Congress, already ratified by the legislature and the voters of Texas. Tyler had been a scheming and indifferent president, who made a difficult position worse by his many-sided duplicity. As an ex-president, he would dishonor himself by serving in the provisional congress, and being elected to the permanent congress, of the Confederate States in 1861, just before his death in 1862, aged 71.

James K. Polk, an unknown quantity and not a flamboyant or prepossessing man, would shortly prove a very astute operator at all levels. As noteworthy figures in his cabinet he had former minister to Russia and U.S. senator from Pennsylvania James Buchanan, the ultimate doughface, as secretary of state; former governor and senator from New York, a close Van Buren ally, inventor of the phrase "spoils system," and leader of the relatively slavery-tolerant "hunker" faction in New York, William L. Marcy, as secretary of war; and historian George Bancroft, who had first proposed Polk as president, as secretary of the navy. Mexico broke off diplomatic relations with the United States at the end of March 1845, and decreed a sizeable augmentation of the armed forces. Apart from Texas, other problems between the two countries included border disputes; $2 million owed under various conventions and commissions by Mexico, and unpaid; and the contentious matter of Mexico's attempted expulsion of American settlers from California, where the Mexicans accurately foresaw another Texas-like incursion.

5. PRESIDENT JAMES K. POLK AND THE MEXICAN WAR

General Zachary Taylor was named commander of the Army of Observation at the end of May and was told to be ready to enter Texas when informed of a Mexican invasion of Texas after Texan accession to U.S. annexation. Taylor's army had only 3,500 men, a quarter of the forces Washington had had at Yorktown, and half the entire strength of the U.S. Army (which less than 20 years later would be 100 times as large). In July, Taylor advanced to Corpus Christi, about 150 miles from the Rio Grande. In November, Polk sent John Slidell as a special minister plenipotentiary to Mexico, on hearing that Mexico was prepared to resume diplomatic relations, and with a mission to buy California and New Mexico for up to $40 million, concede outstanding money claims, and make the Rio Grande the border between the two countries, incorporating Texas into the U.S. When there was a coup in Mexico at the end of 1845 (a frequent occurrence in that country), Slidell was not received and he departed in March 1846. He advised Washington that the Mexicans had been emboldened by confidence that the United States would soon be going to war with Great Britain over the Oregon boundary dispute. Taylor had moved forward to the Rio Grande in January 1846. In April, General Pedro de Ampudia, commanding 5,700 men, confronted Taylor and told him to withdraw or war would commence.

On December 2, 1845, the U.S. president had enunciated the "Polk Doctrine"—an elaboration of the Monroe Doctrine, by which he reserved exclusively to "the people of this continent" the determination of their "destiny," and declared that "We can never consent that European powers shall interfere to prevent such a union [as Texas and the U.S.] because it might disturb the 'balance of power' which they may desire to maintain on this continent," and that there would be no further "European colony or dominion" set up anywhere in North America. This was a clever amplification of the Monroe-Adams formulation of 21 years before. It swaddled American imperialism in continental defense and shifted the focus from the United States simply snatching a large chunk of a neighboring country to a forceful defense of North American prerogatives. North America for the North Americans was the fig-leaf placed over the American rape of its southern neighbor. Polk was waving the flag and inciting enthusiasm for "manifest destiny," a phrase coined by nationalist editor John L. O'Sullivan, and taken up by the *New York Morning News* at the end of 1845. Before hostilities began in earnest, Polk was trying to put a star-spangled disguise over the slavery implications of the Texas annexation (which would now include New Mexico and parts of the present states of Arizona, California, Nevada, Colorado, and Utah).

Polk showed astute strategic and tactical skill in moving to dispose of the Oregon dispute before matters boiled over with Mexico. In his annual message to the Congress on December 2, 1845, Polk claimed the whole of Oregon, recommended the end of the joint convention for Anglo-American occupation, and called for military protection of the Oregon Trail. This got his followers shouting "54°40 or Fight!" and created a bellicose atmosphere for conducting discussions with the British. The British requested renewal by the U.S. of the offer to saw in half the disputed territory, now shared altogether, by extending the 49th parallel as the border to the Pacific, except for the tip of Vancouver Island. Polk denied this but let it be known that if the British requested the resumption of talks, the U.S. would agree. A draft treaty drawn by the British reached Washington on June 6, 1846, and at the same time the British advised the Mexicans that they would not become involved in Mexican-American relations. The British draft was acceptable, extending the 49th parallel, assuring the navigation rights of both countries in the Strait of San Juan de Fuca, and granting the British maritime access to the Columbia River. Polk took the unusually cautious step of submitting the draft to the Senate, where it was overwhelmingly approved. He thus got rid of any possibility of a two-front war, produced an eminently reasonable compromise, and made it impossible for him to be stabbed in the back when at grips with Mexico by allegations of having sold out Oregon. He also brought back the Independent Treasury Act in August 1846, which wasn't a national bank, but wasn't the secretary of the Treasury personally managing the currency either, and thus put central banking on a sound basis before war had begun in earnest with Mexico, unlike the monetary chaos in the midst of which Madison had gone into the War of 1812.

On April 25, 1846, 11 of General Taylor's cavalrymen were killed by the Mexicans and Taylor reported to Washington that hostilities had begun. Polk called for a declaration of war on May 9, and this was voted 174–14 in the House, and a motion denying approval of Polk's action in occupying disputed territory and provoking Mexico was voted down 97–27. The president thus barely protected himself against the not-unfounded charge of warmongering, and the Senate passed the declaration of war 40–2. The initial actions were along the Rio Grande, where Taylor, though substantially outnumbered, defeated the Mexicans at Palo Alto and Resaca de la Palma, inflicting about a 1,000 casualties and suffering just 48 dead and 120 American wounded. The Mexicans were adequately brave and motivated, but under-equipped and under-trained, and the quality of their officers was poor. Mexico started with an undisciplined army of 32,000, while the United States bulked up its army from 7,000 to 104,000, though only 31,000 were regulars, as opposed to reservists sauntering in with their own rifles and a rather casual approach to military discipline.

Zachary Taylor and the timeless Winfield Scott, who had distinguished himself in the War of 1812 more than 30 years before, were the leading American generals. The benefits of Jefferson's military academy (West Point) were already evident, and among the junior officers in this war who would within 20 years achieve world fame and in some cases immortality were Captain Robert E. Lee, Lieutenants Thomas Jonathan Jackson, James Longstreet, Braxton Bragg, Ulysses S. Grant, William Tecumseh Sherman, George G. Meade, George H. Thomas, and George B. McClellan, and Colonel Joseph E. Johnston. The advantages of a professional, non-political officer corps would soon become clear to the whole world. This is one of Thomas Jefferson's achievements for which he has received insufficient credit.

President Polk and War Secretary Marcy, though their backgrounds were, respectively, southern legislative log-rolling and New York boiler-room machine politics, soon proved very capable war leaders. They sat down with General Scott on May 14 and worked out the war plan. General Stephen W. Kearny, with a cavalry regiment from Fort Leavenworth, was declared to be commander of the Army of the West and dispatched to take Santa Fe, New Mexico, and drive on to San Diego and Los Angeles, assisted by naval forces conducting minor amphibious operations on the California coast, and by groups of armed settlers. There was a certain amount of backing and filling in California, with both American and Mexican settlers staging revolts, but this phase of operations went off more or less as planned. Taylor would wage a battle of the frontiers and shatter the Mexican forces in front of him and take Monterrey and Buena Vista, and Scott would be landed from the sea at the great Mexican fortress of Veracruz and would move inland and occupy the capital, Mexico City. It was an imaginative, practical plan that was successfully executed, and was a stark contrast to the fantasies entertained in Madison's time of over taking Canada (which Jefferson had once mistakenly described as "a mere matter of marching," but in 16 presidential years, he and Madison had not assembled the boots or men for the march). There were internecine problems, as Taylor and Scott were known to be Whigs and Polk suspected them both (with reason, as it turned out) of trying to parlay military success into residency in the White House, and they suspected Polk and Marcy of withholding what they would need to enjoy complete victory. (Both generals ran for president in the next six years.)

Kearny arrived in Santa Fe on August 29, 1846, after scattering Mexican forces almost without firing a shot. He pressed on to Los Angeles, where he arrived on January 10, 1847. Colonel (as he became in the course of the action) John C. Frémont and Commodore Robert F. Stockton had subdued most of California by August 17 and suppressed a Mexican revolt by the end of September. Frémont received the surrender of the Mexican forces on January 13, 1847. A jurisdictional dispute broke out between Kearny and Frémont, and eventually Frémont was court-martialed for disobedience and mutiny. Polk upheld most of the finding but reinstated Frémont in the army, from which he then resigned. Frémont was the son-in-law of Senator Thomas Hart Benton, and this episode created serious frictions within the senior ranks of the Democrats.

Taylor captured Monterrey on September 25, and agreed to an eight-week armistice to resupply his forces. This annoyed Polk, who wanted the swiftest prosecution of the war possible. Taylor and Polk each imputed political motives to the other and Taylor published a letter in a New York newspaper criticizing the administration. Polk lost faith in Taylor's ability to win the war quickly and approved Scott's taking 9,000 of Taylor's men (his army had been bulked up significantly) to add to his Veracruz landing force.

Taylor ignored orders and marched on to Buena Vista, where he encountered the inevitable and inimitable Santa Anna at the head of 15,000 men. Santa Anna had told an American emissary in February 1846 that for $30 million, he would return from exile in Cuba and arrange the Mexican cession of Texas and California to the U.S. Polk did not approve the bribe but did allow Santa Anna's return through the American blockade. Once back in Mexico, Santa Anna accused the incumbent president, Herrera, of treason for trying to negotiate dishonorably with the United States, staged a coup, and installed himself as president again. He took up his old military command and tried to stop Taylor at Buena Vista. Santa Anna gave Taylor a respectable fight but had to withdraw on February 23, 1847, after losing about 500 dead, twice as many as the Americans. Marcy reprimanded Taylor for criticizing the administration publicly. Taylor remained at Monterrey without orders or more than bare supplies and retired from the army on November 26, 1847. He returned a hero to the United States, just in time for the election season.

It was never going to be possible to keep the politics of slavery out of the conduct of the war. Congressman David Wilmot produced an amendment, known to history as the Wilmot Proviso, which prohibited slavery in any new territory that might accrue to the United States from the current war. Several months of acrimonious debate ensued in both houses of Congress. The Democrats hewed to their line that the Mexican War was an entirely justified response to Mexican mistreatment of Americans in Texas, and to Mexican aggression. And the Whigs attacked it as simple imperialism, conducted in furtherance of slavery and unconstitutionally initiated. The southern view, as usual in these times, was given by Calhoun in the Senate on February 19 and 20.

The South refused to be defensive about slavery, and sought its positive protection. The constitutional compact and states' rights theories received their usual airing, and Calhoun expressed concern about the South losing its influence in the balance of events. He said that if that balance was lost, the result would be "Political revolution, anarchy, civil war, and widespread disaster," and added that "if trampled upon, it will be idle to expect that we will not resist it."[4] The Whigs gained a narrow majority of the House of Representatives in the midterm elections of 1846.

General Winfield Scott's amphibious landing near Veracruz, designed to end the war, was launched on March 9, 1847, as 10,000 men were put ashore in special landing craft. Veracruz, defended by 5,000 Mexican soldiers, surrendered on March 27. Scott set out for Mexico City, soundly thrashing Santa Anna at Cerro Gordo and taking over 3,000 Mexican prisoners. As a third of his army vanished when their terms of enlistments were up and many were sick, Scott paused for several months and was joined in August by General Franklin Pierce, bringing his strength back to 13,000 men. At Churubusco on August 20, Santa Anna fought hard and bravely, and took 7,000 casualties, but inflicted only 1,000 casualties on the Americans. Scott pressed on to the capital, and after the Battle of Chapultapec, occupied the city of 200,000 with only 6,000 soldiers on September 13 and 14. Santa Anna resigned as president and conducted a few more military operations

---

4.   Richard B. Morris, *Encyclopedia of American History*, Sixth Edition, New York, Harper and Row, 1982, p. 241.

and then was sacked as commander of the army. The old scoundrel again went into exile. (He would return yet again as president in 1853, but was chased out once and for all in 1855 and lived for a time in Staten Island, where he imported chicle for tires. This was unsuccessful but his partner, Thomas Adams, invented the "Chiclet" at great profit.)

Polk had sent the senior clerk of the State Department, Nicholas Trist, to negotiate peace terms, and squabbling immediately erupted between him and Scott. Trist was eventually recalled in November, but ignored the fact and negotiated and signed the Treaty of Guadalupe Hidalgo on February 2, 1848. The United States paid a total of about $18,250,000 to Mexico, and Mexico renounced everything north of the Rio Grande, Gila, and Colorado Rivers. It was a gigantic acquest for the United States, 1,193,000 square miles, almost 150 percent of the size of the Louisiana Purchase. The United States had suffered 1,721 dead in action or of wounds, 11,155 who died of disease, 4,102 wounded. The cost to the Treasury was $97.5 million; it was a good deal more onerous proportionately than the War of 1812, but the United States bagged another great chunk of a continent at a knockdown economic cost and with a bearable loss of life.

Polk presented Trist's treaty to the Senate with an ambiguous endorsement, given that it was unauthorized. The Senate ratified, 38–14, on March 10, 1848, and the opposition was from doughface Democrats led by Buchanan (despite his presence as secretary of state in Polk's administration), who now wanted to annex the whole of Mexico. It had worked as a splendid, cheap patriotic war after all, though there were absurd aspects to it (Santa Anna's presence virtually assured that), and much of it, including the peace negotiations, was conducted contrary to orders. The Wilmot Proviso was again defeated, and the Gadsden Purchase of 1853 picked up another 45,000 square miles, for $10 million. It was brilliant strategy by Polk. The growth of slavery was concealed in the glorious martial growth of the nation, and, as a bonus, gold was fortuitously discovered on January 24, 1848, in large quantities at Sutter's Mill, California, and over 100,000 adventurers and fortune-seekers flooded into the state (as it soon became) from all over the world by the end of 1849. If Polk had bungled the war effort as badly as Madison had, it would have been a disaster (though there was no chance that the Mexicans would prove as militarily proficient as the British and the Canadians). By settling Oregon first and devising a realistic war plan, Polk had gambled successfully, made an immense accretion of territory, and punted the slavery issue forward again for a few years, though the atmosphere in which it was endlessly discussed was becoming steadily more ominous. The awful reckoning slavery always portended could not now be long postponed.

6. THE 1848 ELECTION

The United States did not much notice it, but 1848 was a year of revolution and tumult overseas, as the French and German and Italian worlds seethed. In what was called "the Springtime of Europe," Clemens von Metternich, the Austrian chancellor and foreign minister for 39 years, was sent packing by the mobs in Vienna; Pope Pius IX, just launched into a pontificate of 32 years, was temporarily chased out of Rome by Italian reunificationists; the Orleans monarchy in Paris was driven out and replaced by the Second Republic, led by Napoleon's nephew; and there were uprisings across Germany and in Poland, Hungary, Denmark, Switzerland, Belgium, and even Brazil. The departure of Metternich, "the Coachman of Europe" and convening genius of the Congress of Vienna, was particularly striking and presaged the rise of a united Germany as Austria's replacement as the leading German-speaking power, while the upheavals in Italy foretold the unification of that country as well as of Germany.

In America, the slavery issue flared again when Polk, in August 1848, sent the Congress a bill for the organization in Oregon of a territorial government free of slavery. The rising star of the congressional Democrats as the great triumvirs of Clay, Webster, and Calhoun moved through the autumn of their days, Stephen A. Douglas of Illinois, responded to southern complaints that the Congress had no power to restrict slavery in the states with a measure keeping Oregon laws in place unless and until its own legislature changed them. This led to a bill extending the Missouri Compromise line, 36°30, all the way to the Pacific, which would reestablish slavery in New Mexico and southern California, where Mexican law had abolished it. Inevitably, Calhoun was soon on his feet making his usual arguments with an acidulous tone made more mordant by the unimaginable idea that Mexican laws would govern in the United States. After seven months of debate, Oregon was set up as a non-slave territory, but all attempts to deal with other areas failed of adoption by one house or other of the Congress. In the last months of his term, Polk would be unable to secure the admission of California or New Mexico as slave-free territories.

By the time this controversy subsided, the presidential campaign was well along. Polk, on his record, could easily have been reelected, but he was not well and declined renomination. (He died three months after the inauguration of his successor.) At the Democratic convention in (inevitably) Baltimore, the New York delegation split between the Van Buren "Barnburners," who opposed the extension of slavery, and the "Hunkers" led by Marcy, who were doughface appeasers of the "slave power." The Hunkers pledged their support to the nominees, but Van Buren's Barnburners did not. Polk declined to exercise any influence, and Jackson was dead (in June 1845, aged 78). The Andrew Jackson of the North (to scale), General Lewis Cass, an expansionist and Anglophobe, was nominated on a platform that replicated that of 1844, denied the right of Congress to consider the status of slavery in the states, and criticized any attempt to bring the status of slavery before the Congress. General William O. Butler of Kentucky was chosen for vice president.

The Whigs met at Philadelphia in June and Clay, Taylor, and Scott were the contenders. The generals had the advantage of lack of any political policy track record, and Taylor was nominated. He shared in the glory of victory in the Mexican War, but was an enemy of Polk, and thus enjoyed the best of both worlds for a Whig. And Senator Millard Fillmore of New York was nominated for vice president, the only one of the four main-party candidates for national office who was not a general, in the aftermath of this fine little war. (The nomination of high-ranking military officers for national office, as has been mentioned, was commonplace, but with two generals from the same party the Democrats were unique overachievers.) There was fear that Clay was too controversial—that though he was the father of the party and the greatest figure in the public life of the country, he was in the overwrought atmosphere not electable, as he had tried three times before unsuccessfully. Anti-slavery motions were voted down and Taylor ran on a thoroughly ambiguous platform. It was well-known that the Whigs were anti-slavery, but they dissembled altogether at this convention. The platform ignored the issues and praised Taylor for his martial and patriotic virtues.

The Barnburners (named after a legendary Dutch New York farmer so stubborn he burned his own barn down to get rid of the rats in it) met at Utica and nominated Van Buren for president and Henry Dodge of Wisconsin for vice president. Anti-slavery militants from other states, especially New Englanders, held a convention at Buffalo later in June, of what was called the Free Soil Party, which effectively adopted the Wilmot Proviso of no extension of slavery. Charles Francis Adams, son of John Quincy Adams, was nominated for vice president. The new party attracted the support of anti-slavery lawyers Charles Sumner of Massachusetts and Salmon P. Chase of Ohio. The Barnburners of Van Buren united with Free Soil, and the combined nominees were Van Buren and Adams (a memorial to the fluidity of political attachments, given Van Buren's role in assisting Jackson against his running mate's father). The party demanded full liberty to attack slavery, supported the Wilmot Proviso, favored federal internal improvements and free homesteads for settlers (to expand the country with free states and people), and took the slogan "Free soil, free speech, free labor and free men." It was a complete affront to the Jackson settlement with the South, and was headed by Jackson's then chief disciple, who had replaced Calhoun after he was purged as vice president. Van Buren had not taken his disembarkation at the hands of Polk and Jackson like a good sport.

Taylor won the election with the tired Whig version of the Jackson formula, trying, within what were now very narrow parameters, to express some reservations about the expansion of slavery. Taylor received 1.36 million votes to 1.22 million for Cass to 291,000 for Van Buren; he won the popular vote by 47 percent to 43 percent, to 10 percent, with 163 electoral votes to 127 for Cass. Van Buren, whose motives were an indiscernible amalgam of sour grapes and, in the one seriously principled moment of his career, real reservations about slavery and the aggressivity of its advocates, flipped the election to Taylor by taking most of the Democratic vote in New York. He ran 121,000 to 114,000 ahead of Cass in that state and delivered it to Taylor. New York determined the election, as it had in 1844.

As if slavery had not strained the comity of the nation enough, on January 22, 1849, 69 southern members of Congress, with Calhoun as their spokesman, presented an "Address" enumerating the "acts of aggression" of the North—principally exclusion of slavery from territories and making the return of fugitive slaves more difficult.

Polk went into his brief retirement and came to his early death on June 15, 1849, aged only 53. He was far from charismatic and was never a great public figure. He was plucked almost from obscurity as a dark horse in a deadlocked convention, but was an extremely capable and successful president, an able leader of congressional opinion, and a fine war leader. He moved through difficult times and among looming shoals with great skill and agility. He was devious and duplicitous, was indistinct to the country, and was pushing the Jackson formula, the best solution but an inglorious one, so he was not a great president. But he was one of the country's 10 or 12 ablest and most accomplished presidents. As a political, diplomatic, and war strategist, settling with Britain before dealing with Mexico, obscuring the expansion of slavery in patriotic jingo, conducting one of the most efficiently executed wars in American history, and extending the rather tawdry Jackson settlement (the only method to hand to preserve the Union) into the vast new territory he acquired, and into another decade, he earned more, and more grateful, recognition than he has received from posterity. In straight strategic terms, James K. Polk was as capable as any of the presidents who preceded him except Washington. But this was the last of the brilliant series of American strategic triumphs from the Seven Years' War on, before the ghastly specter of slavery was finally confronted. There would now be a demeaning decade of mealy mouthed dissembling, shabby compromise, and gamecock provocation before the awful reckoning so long delayed and feared. America and the world that was watching it held their breath.

7. THE COMPROMISE OF 1850

It was obvious that the issue of the organization of territorial governments and the admission of new states would be a battleground between the abolitionists, the less fervent dissenters from slavery, the accomplices of the slaveholders, and the defenders of slavery. Each time the issue arose, which was now over a wide range of questions involving the extent of federal authority and the nature of the Constitution, including, ominously, the indissolubility or otherwise of the Union, there was a rending debate, always resolved by an extension of the Jackson formula of the security of slavery in the South and Southwest, and the unacceptability of nullification or any secessionist movement. But the process was one of attrition of nerves, patience, and goodwill. The North tired of the South's effort, usually through the recondite but lugubrious spokesmanship of Calhoun, to impose equality of influence between the regions despite the steadily swifter demographic and economic advance of the free states, and of the misplaced righteousness with which a clearly despicable and fallacious system was defended. The South was endlessly embarrassed and provoked by northern condescension toward a southern society that the southerners loved, was legitimized by the Constitution, and worked much better and more fairly, they believed, than the northerners, in their smug hypocrisy, acknowledged. And the large group that wasn't overly excited about the issue, but endorsed the Jackson formula, wearied of the endless and increasingly vituperative circumlocution as the same points were bellowed back and forth ad nauseam.

It would be a mistake to imagine that the majority of northerners were especially disconcerted by the moral implications of slavery. There were many abolitionists who found slavery repugnant, but the great majority of northern Americans had no notions of racial equality and did not consider it the business of the North to dictate to the South how their society was organized, as there were then very few African Americans in free states. Most northerners would have found slavery conceptually distasteful, but there is no evidence that a significant percentage of them wished to force the issue or risk the Union to be rid of slavery. A great mythos developed that the Union armies more than a decade later were trampling through the South prepared, as Julia Ward Howe wrote in the *Battle Hymn of the Republic*, "to die to make men free." This was just another creation of the mighty American public relations system. But the frustration of the North, that slavery existed in the South but was not offensive enough to do anything about it, aggravated the ambiance of moral back-biting at every opportunity to rail ineffectually about slavery, until the South routinely threatened to secede.

Henry Clay returned to the Senate in 1849 after an absence of seven years, and on January 29, 1850, he presented a series of resolutions designed to resolve the problem durably and replace the constant friction with a clean-cut and practical regime that would give all factions except the abolitionists and secessionists most of what they sought. His resolutions would admit California as a free state; organize the rest of the territory taken from Mexico without restriction on slavery; change the boundary between Texas and New Mexico; assume federally the debt accumulated by Texas, which would renounce any territorial claims on Mexico; abolish the slave trade in the District of Columbia while confirming the legitimacy of slavery itself there; tighten the pursuit and return of fugitive slaves; and proclaim the lack of congressional authority to intervene in the interstate slave trade. The ensuing debate continued for eight months and was the longest, most intense, and at times the most intellectually and oratorically distinguished in the history of the United States Congress, before or since. It marked the summit and the end of the reign of the Clay-Webster-Calhoun Triumvirate. Other great figures made their last great interventions, such as Thomas Hart Benton, and still others who would lead the nation into and through the coming turbulence, such as Stephen A. Douglas of Illinois, Salmon P. Chase of Ohio, William H. Seward of New York, and Jefferson Davis of Mississippi (named after a man all three triumvirs had known), shone brightly.

Clay spoke on February 5 and 6 and emphasized that secession was not a justified or effective remedy for southern concerns, and that the preservation of the Union was in the interests of and the duty of all, and to that end, mutual concessions were needed and appropriate. Calhoun, gravely ill and on the verge of death, sat while his address opposing Clay was read for him by Senator Mason of Virginia, and he said, one last time, that the South had to have entrenched equality in the newly taken territories, in a constitutional amendment restoring the South's equality and ability to protect herself, "before the equilibrium between the sections was destroyed by the actions of this [the federal] government."

Calhoun died a few weeks later, on March 31. By the last comment, as he explained posthumously in his *Disquisition on Government*, he meant that the Constitution had always intended a de facto dual ratification for any important initiative, and that this was being steadily eroded by what he declined to recognize as the forces of history. Webster followed on March 7 with another of his mighty addresses, supporting Clay's resolutions, beginning that he was not speaking for his state or region but "as an American . . . I speak today for the preservation of the

Union. 'Hear me for my cause.'" He said that matters of soil and climate excluded any recourse to the economics of slavery in the territories under discussion, and that the subject should not arise at all. Calhoun's constitutional divinations were completely unrigorous; Washington, southern slaveholder though he was, spoke at all times of an indissoluble Union; Jefferson and Madison, though states' rights advocates and rather quavering in their approach to slavery, recognized slavery's moral frailty, and none of them ever hinted at an imposed equality between sections. Webster was close to the mark in implying that as states were admitted, as they would be, across the continent to the Pacific, there would be no economic rationale for slavery in them at all, quite apart from the moral concerns slavery raised, and that Calhoun's notion of stopping history, even as the body of the nation was divided into a northern torso and southern tail, was nonsense at every level, the death-bed revisionism of a formidable but irrational apologist for a morally bankrupt, doomed regime.

William H. Seward, a rising star of the anti-slavery Whigs, who would be a presidential contender and distinguished secretary of state, spoke on March 11 and opposed Clay's resolutions because he wanted slavery contained as if by the Wilmot Proviso: no new slave states carved from the territories. He was one of the leaders of the emerging consensus in the North, that slavery could be tolerated where it was but there was no excuse for tolerating its expansion, and Seward declared legislative compromises in general to be "radically wrong and essentially vicious." He didn't dispute that the Constitution implicitly accepted the legitimacy of slavery, but spoke of a "higher law" that justified avoiding protection of it. He was morally very arguably correct, but this was a considerable liberty in the realm of constitutional law, as long-standing legal conditions cannot simply be dispensed with because a later generation finds moral problems with them. Jefferson Davis opposed Clay's resolutions for the same general reasons as Calhoun, as did, to a large extent, Thomas Hart Benton. Chase opposed for reasons similar to Seward's. Douglas, and the late presidential candidate General Lewis Cass of Michigan, supported the resolutions.

The resolutions were sent to a select committee of 13 senators, chaired by Clay, which came back with an omnibus bill and a special bill abolishing the slave trade in the District of Columbia, on May 8. President Taylor, who opposed reorganizing the new territories, apart from California, into Utah in the north and New Mexico in the south, as was now the proposal, died on July 9 after over-strenuous July 4th celebrations. Vice President Fillmore succeeded him and was a less-ardent New York critic of slavery than his colleague Seward, and supported Clay's resolutions. Though Taylor was a more substantial figure than Fillmore, Fillmore was better suited to achieve a compromise, and once again, Providence had assisted the United States. Taylor might not have been an insuperable obstacle as Tyler and Polk would have been, but he would not have been much help to Clay either. Clay and Douglas, now the Democratic leader in the Senate, though only 37, worked through the summer (though Clay had to retire from overstrained health, and did not play a leading role in the Senate again) to get those who put the Union ahead of opposition to, or militant and integral defense of, slavery together behind a reformulated compromise, which was enacted in five laws between September 9 and September 20. Most of the Unionists who favored a Wilmot restriction on the spread of slavery came over to Clay and Douglas, joining the softer disapprovers of slavery and the doughface northern appeasers of the South, and some southerners who were content with half a loaf. Only the outright abolitionists, the dogmatic Wilmotites like Seward, and the quasi-secessionist Calhounites were outside the compromise coalition when the new set of bills was voted.

The new legislation admitted California as a free state by a heavy majority; divided the acquired territory between Texas and California into two territories, Utah and New Mexico, where, in the kernel of the compromise, applications for statehood from component parts could be accepted whether slavery was included or not, "as their constitution may prescribe at the time of their admission"; tightened the discouragement of fugitive slaves; and abolished the slave trade in the District of Columbia. The Fugitive Slave Act passed the Senate 27 to 10 and the House 109 to 76, illustrating that the North was more concerned with the conceptual irritation of slavery as an institution than with helping individual slaves rebelling against their state of hopeless servitude.

This act set up special U.S. commissioners who could issue warrants for the arrest of alleged fugitive slaves after a summary hearing solely on the affidavit of a claimant. Commissioners received $10 for every such application granted and $5 for every one refused, a clear and egregious incitement to the avoidance of a fair finding. The commissioners could form posses, and those accused of being fugitive slaves but denying it had no right to a jury trial or to give evidence themselves. Those abetting the flight of slaves, deliberately or negligently, were subject to fines of $1,000, indemnity of the economic value of the fugitive slave(s), and imprisonment for up to six months. It was a disgraceful law that effectively entrenched the principle that African Americans were subhumans without civil rights, unless they were emancipated, at which point they miraculously metamorphosed into citizens.

It was inherently absurd that an act of emancipation by the ostensible owner would transform an animal without rights and subject to starvation, sexual violation, whipping, or even murder, without recourse, into a citizen with civil rights

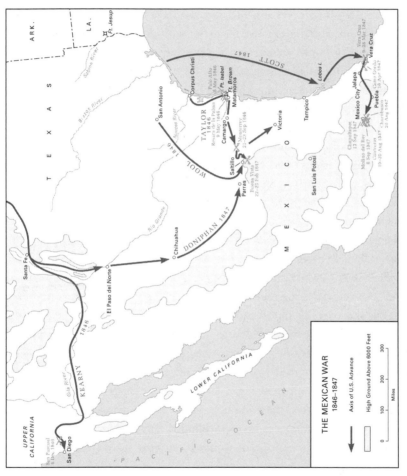

Mexican War. Courtesy of the U.S. Army Center of Military History

identical, theoretically, to those of the president of the United States. And the Fugitive Slave Act was a dramatic setback to human rights in America, considering that when Benjamin Franklin had been the president of Pennsylvania 65 years before, any slave who spent six consecutive months in that state was automatically free, and now all states were pledged to yield to these draconian enforcement procedures of the federal government. Northern abolitionists said from the start that they would not comply with the Fugitive Slave Act, and some states, such as Vermont, countered the Fugitive Slave Act with expanded guarantees of civil liberties. People trying to recover slaves were sometimes abused and hampered and the federal commissioners responsible for enforcement had a very difficult time in some northern states, and had problems getting local courts to enforce the act. There were riots, some entailing loss of life, in a number of northern cities, particularly New York, Boston, and Baltimore.

It was a high price for the Union but seemed to stabilize public policy and settle the political atmosphere. Secessionist candidates were defeated by Unionists throughout the South in elections in 1851, while the strenuous abolitionist Charles Sumner was elected U.S. senator from Massachusetts the following year. The Compromise of 1850, as it was called, contained a time bomb that could have been foreseen as mortally dangerous: the provision that each territory applying for statehood would determine itself whether it would be a free or slave state was an invitation to civil war in each state as the date of its application approached. Clay and Webster had done their best and they were great legislators and great patriots, but they were trying to palliate an intractable issue. Either slavery was morally acceptable or it was not. Endless expressions of distaste or disapproval among the free-state majority only provoked southern ambitions to secede; by not abdicating the right to denounce or restrict slavery, the North pushed the South toward the only apparent means available to it to secure slavery: the dissolution of the Union. And there was no method of ending northern discomfort with slavery except turning a permanent blind eye to it, which was impossible as long as it was expanding, or going to war to suppress it, or acquiescing in the break-up of the country.

Webster was right that it was nonsense to contemplate slavery in places where African American laborers were not more productive than Caucasian workers. There was no economic rationale for slavery in cooler climates than the cotton-producing South. Calhoun's demand for the imposition of a false equality of regions was preposterous, as people vote with their feet in such matters, and slave-holding was an odious system. And the demand for the establishment of slavery in places like New Mexico, where there was no possible economic use for it, was insolent. By not eliminating the recurrences of frictions, the Compromise of 1850 assured their escalation. This was clear enough with the publication in 1852 of Harriet Beecher Stowe's *Uncle Tom's Cabin*, a dramatization of the problems of the life of the slave that sold a completely unprecedented 1.2 million copies in a little over a year. The Compromise of 1850 bought time.

It would have been better to produce a continuation of the 1821 Missouri Compromise line to the California border, and to produce a magnanimous scheme whereby the federal government would incentivize emancipations generously, or even to impose a code of treatment that at least gave the slaves the rights accorded later by legislation against cruelty to animals. None of this would have been easy to pass, but it wasn't tried, and the Compromise was going to lead quickly to renewed and intense friction, though it earned Clay the title, with the usual American hyperbole, "the Great Pacificator" (as Calhoun, before he became a robotic and belligerent slavery apologist, was called "the Young Demosthenes," and as Webster was long known as "the Godlike Daniel"). As with all resolutions of tense impasses that are not comprehensive, such as the Versailles and Munich Conferences (Chapters 9 and 10), when the problems it had been hoped were settled rose up again, it was with increased venom and escalated hostility between the factions that had thought the problems composed.

As a solution and durable extension of the Jackson system, the compromise was a stopgap, but as strategy—and this may not have been in Clay's mind but it might have been in the thoughts of some others, possibly including Douglas—it was decisive to the survival of the country. In the ensuing decade, the U.S. population would increase by another 35 percent, from 23 to 31 million, 22.4 million in what would be the North (all but 448,000 free, and the slaves were in Kentucky, Missouri, and Maryland, and would be relatively easy to emancipate) to 8.7 million in the South, and of those, only 5.1 million whites. Even if Kentucky, Maryland, and Missouri, all contested states but with northern majorities, are divided between North and South, it only narrows the 22-to-5.1-million advantage of northern over southern Whites to about 21 to 6 million. In that decade, almost three million people arrived in the United States as immigrants, more than four-fifths to the North (plus all of the 800,000 immigrants who arrived in the first half of the 1860s). The northern states would mobilize more than three times as many men to their armed forces from 1861 to 1865 as the South and had a vastly larger industrial base to support an armed enforcement of the Union. Andrew Jackson and Henry Clay kept together for a further 30 years the Union that Washington,

Franklin, Jefferson, Madison, Hamilton, and Adams had founded and led for nearly 40 years, so that the greatest of all American leaders could make the Union "one and indivisible," and permanent, at last.

While the country was absorbed by the struggle for the Compromise, there were some foreign policy developments. Taylor's secretary of state, John M. Clayton, negotiated a treaty with the British minister in Washington, Sir Henry Lytton Bulwer (the Clayton-Bulwer Treaty), after both countries had been active in Nicaragua, preparing to build an isthmian canal between the Atlantic and the Pacific. The two agreed not to seek or assert exclusive control over, nor fortify, such a canal; guaranteed jointly the neutrality and security of any such canal; agreed to keep the canal open to the ships of both countries equally; and promised not to infringe on the sovereignty of any of the Central American states.

In December 1850, after the Austrian government's chargé in Washington, Johann Georg Hülsemann, registered a protest that the American diplomat A. Dudley Mann had encouraged Hungarian revolutionaries, Clayton's successor, Daniel Webster (back at State for a second time), wrote a bombastic letter in reply to Hülsemann, asserting America's right to support factions and movements in Europe that appeared, as did those of 1848, congruent with "those great ideas of responsible and popular government" that inspired the American Revolution. He went on grandly to inform Hülsemann that America had vastly rich and fertile lands compared with which "the possessions of the House of Habsburg are but as a patch on the earth's surface." This bumptious disparagement of what was still a substantial if polyglot empire, though it showed the unfamiliarity of even so worldly a man as Webster with accepted diplomatic style, also illustrated the disintegration of the residual Holy Roman Empire, just two years after the fall of Metternich. It was at about this time that this empire's condition was described as "hopeless but not desperate." These upheavals in Europe only reinforced the comparative eminence of august and unchallenged early Victorian Britain. The Hungarian revolutionary leader Louis Kossuth was accorded an immense reception when he arrived in New York in December.

There was a farcical expedition in 1851 against Spanish Cuba, led by General Narciso López, a Venezuelan-born Spanish general who had sided with the anti-Spanish faction in Cuba. López was apprehended and publicly garroted. Fifty Americans who accompanied López were executed and more than 70 others shipped back to Spain in unsatisfactory conditions and only released when the United States handed over $25,000 to cover reparations for the sacking by angry crowds of the Spanish consulate in New Orleans on August 21, 1851, following the execution of the 50 Americans. (The fiasco of the landing and the ransoming of the hostages presaged, at least to a slight degree, the debacle of American-backed guerrillas in the Bay of Pigs shambles in 1961, and the seizing of the American hostages in the U.S. embassy in Tehran in 1980–1981, Chapters 14 and 16.)

8. THE SLIDE TOWARD DISUNION

The Democrats met, again at Baltimore, in June 1852, and there was a fierce contest for the presidential nomination between the narrowly defeated (by Van Buren's spoiler anti-slavery candidacy) General Lewis Cass, senator from Michigan and former governor, minister to France, and secretary of war; Polk's able war secretary and former judge, senator, and three-term governor of New York, William L. Marcy; Illinois's capable and energetic Senator Stephen A. Douglas; and Polk's indecisive doughface secretary of state, James Buchanan of Pennsylvania. None of the four could get a majority of votes, much less the two-thirds majority required for nomination, so for the third straight Democratic convention a dark horse emerged, Franklin Pierce, former general and former U.S. senator from New Hampshire and now that state's governor. His views on slavery were not well-known, so he could be supported by all the factions, though all the leading candidates except Buchanan would have been better candidates and much better presidents. The vice presidential candidate was Alabama senator and former minister to France William R. King, who, although he and his family owned 500 slaves, was a Unionist and a moderate on the issue of slavery. King shared a house with James Buchanan for 15 years, and Jackson, in particular, had implied with his usual causticity that they were homosexuals, but that has never been substantiated.

The Whigs met in the same place as soon as the Democrats departed and also had a long struggle, between President Fillmore, who ran for reelection as champion of the Compromise of 1850; the anti-slavery general, Winfield Scott, who had fought in every American war (and significant skirmish) since 1812, and was the commanding general of the United States Army for 20 years; and the septuagenarian secretary of state, Daniel Webster. Finally, Scott prevailed on the 53rd ballot. This development eliminated any Whig support from pro-slavery elements and effectively divided the North between those who wanted to restrain or abolish slavery and those who were prepared to abide by the implicit but not unlimited expansion of it foreseen by the Compromise of 1850. The vice presidential candidate was Navy Secretary William Graham of North Carolina.

The platforms were virtually identical, but because Scott, though an upholder of the Compromise of 1850 and a Virginian, was known to be anti-slavery, and Pierce was a doughface appeaser of the South, though also a supporter of the Compromise, Pierce took the slave states en bloc and had the upper hand in the North, where the majority hoped the Great Compromise had solved the slavery controversy. Pierce was a distinguished general, who had served under Scott in Mexico, and as a governor and senator was a more apt campaigner (there was almost no physical campaign) than the stolid and rather guileless Scott, who was 71 and weighed about 300 pounds. Given his many advantages, it was not surprising that Pierce won with 1.6 million votes to 1.39 for Scott, 50 percent to 44 percent. (Almost all the rest went to the old Free Soil Party that Van Buren had led in 1848.)

The Compromise was holding, but its greatest authors were gone; Clay had died, aged 75, at the end of June, and Webster, who had contested the Whig nomination in June, died in October, aged 70. (Webster was succeeded as secretary of state by his most assiduous disciple, Edward Everett, former governor of Massachusetts and minister to Great Britain.) President Fillmore returned to be the most prominent citizen of Buffalo, New York, an undistinguished president, but one who had made a vital and positive contribution at a critical time by supporting the Compromise of 1850. He had also sent Commodore Matthew Perry to open the ports of Japan, an important mission completed by his successor. Douglas was now the leading figure in the Congress. The new vice president, William R. King, was suffering from tuberculosis, for which he went on a curative trip to Cuba. His condition worsened, and he was inaugurated by special act of Congress, at the consulate in Havana, and died after just 45 days in office at his home in Alabama, without ever having got back to Washington. The leading figures in the cabinet were the astute William L. Marcy as secretary of state and the strident Calhounite Jefferson Davis of Mississippi as secretary of war.

The Whigs had effectively become a party that could more or less tolerate the continuation of slavery if the Union depended on it but was opposed to its extension. They could no longer challenge successfully by selecting candidates who were fuzzy on the issue, as Harrison and Taylor, and in his way, Clay, had been. The Democrats were the sole continuators now of the Jackson settlement. There were many northern Democrats who were uncomfortable with the possibility of any expansion of slavery outside cotton, tobacco, and sugar-producing areas. The old Whigs had effectively disintegrated and gravitated toward a new party, alongside the anti-slavery Democrats and the Free Soilers.

On March 31, 1854, Commodore Matthew Perry, whom President Fillmore had sent to Japan, signed an agreement (Treaty of Kanagawa) opening two Japanese ports to the U.S. Perry brought gifts, including a miniature railway and telegraph, which did impress the locals. This was the beginning of the process that brought Japan out of its isolation and turned it very quickly into one of the world's Great Powers. In June of 1854, the Canadian Reciprocity Treaty resolved many and long-standing fishing disputes, essentially by opening up the waters of each country to the fishing of the other.

Between 1855 and 1860, there would be a series of private attempts led by the adventurer William Walker to take control of Nicaragua to promote an isthmian canal. Pierce professed not to approve the initiative, but Walker purported to be the president of Nicaragua from 1855 to 1857, during which time his emissary was received by Pierce, seeming to legitimize what was again looked upon in the North as another effort to extend the frontiers of slavery illicitly, out the back door of America in an unjustifiable act of aggression. This was reminiscent of the hostile Whig take on the Mexican War. Walker was chased out by Commodore Cornelius Vanderbilt, who owned the local railway. Walker returned a hero to the South, and reinvaded Nicaragua in 1857 unsuccessfully. The whole Ruritanian farce would come to an end with another invasion in 1860, in Honduras, where the local authorities defeated, captured, tried, and executed Walker with commendable efficiency. American public thinking on slavery had by then vastly transcended this type of farcical gasconade.

Pierce was a fine-looking, good-natured, charming, and well-intentioned man, and had been a competent general of division and was a popular governor of New Hampshire. Selected by the Democrats because of the ambiguity of his views and thus the possibility of selling him to a wide range of voters on the omnipresent slavery issue, he had poorly thought-out opinions and little grasp of the strong tides and currents that swept over the country, and no real principles from which to try to hold the country together. Jackson had been a strong and decisive leader, albeit with some primitive opinions; Van Buren was a cunning operator with flashes of principle; Tyler was muddled and inept and unscrupulous in method, though dogmatic in policy matters; and Fillmore was better but clumsy; but they were accidental presidents. Polk was as sly as Van Buren and more discerning, though less formidable than Jackson. Taylor equivocated well and didn't last long.

But Pierce was a weak leader at a dangerous time. To hold together the coalition that elected him, he would need a sophisticated knowledge of the background and political landscape of the country, and be settled in his views and effective in their implementation, as only Jackson and Polk were, among the presidents of the time; and as Clay, and up to a point, Webster, Douglas, Benton, and the one-term Illinois congressman Abraham Lincoln were among the legislators. Pierce missed on all counts, and he and his successor would reveal the vulnerability of the Jackson system. It always depends on leadership, whether the political center is a fulcrum of strength or a vortex of weakness. Jackson and Polk were border-state southerners who knew the South but had held federal offices (army commander and senator for Jackson, Speaker of the House for Polk), and they broadly understood the shoals around them and the possibilities available.

Of the 1852 Democratic contenders for president, Douglas and Cass, though worrisome, would have been better than Pierce and Buchanan, yet Pierce and Buchanan were the next presidential nominees. Scott and even Fillmore (and certainly Webster, had he lived) would have been better than Pierce and Buchanan, but in seeking obscurity of views and therefore comparative invulnerability from steadily angrier factions, the all-conquering Democratic Party fell into the hands of people whose views were indiscernible, not because they were calculatedly subtle and enigmatic but because they didn't really have any fixed point of conviction to work from and had no idea how to navigate the dangers that loomed at every hand. The baton of leadership had passed from the clever and ferocious Jackson to the cunning Van Buren and Polk, to the palsied hands of Pierce, and would go on to the equally incapable Buchanan.

Van Buren was all tactics and no strategy. Polk was a very astute tactician and a brilliant strategist. Pierce and Buchanan had no tactical or strategic skill. Jackson, Clay, Webster, and Polk were now dead, and Lincoln had not yet arisen. The descent to insurrection and civil war would now enter its last act. America was sleepwalking toward the edge of a cliff.

9. KANSAS AND NEBRASKA

The time bomb in the Compromise of 1850, in the impetuous grip of Douglas, began to sizzle ominously when Douglas presented the Kansas-Nebraska Act in January 1854. This measure adopted the principle of "squatter-sovereignty," or "popular sovereignty," leaving it to the territories themselves to determine, when they had the population necessary to be credible as states, whether they wished slavery within their own borders or not. This not only invited extreme friction as partisans of both sides jostled for the local majority, it explicitly repealed the Missouri Compromise line of 36°30 and agitated the North while whetting the appetite of the South by opening the specter (or to the slave states, the prospect) of slavery spreading all over the country, and the entire United States being dragged backward, contra-historically, into a dark age that would degrade and fragment all the proud claims of the founders of the republic based on the "inalienable rights" and "self-evident truths" that "all men are created equal." It had been enough of a stretch to keep this majestic canard going while over 10 percent of the whole population were slaves, but this was a mortal threat to the collective political self-esteem of the majority, who may not have been overly concerned with the fate of individual African Americans in bondage but were not prepared to be thought of, by themselves or anyone else, as believers in the backward malignancy of slave-holding. The Kansas-Nebraska Act was passed after three months of bitter debate, formally renouncing any congressional or federal oversight of slavery.

Stephen A. Douglas was a brilliant legislator and a passionate believer in democracy and was not personally an appeaser or sympathizer to slavery. He believed that the people were always right and that the people would do the right thing. It was one of the catastrophic errors in American history, and Pierce was not a sufficiently authoritative leader of the nation to see that this was just civil war on the installment plan and that with so overarching and preoccupying an issue, only the federal Congress and administration could balance the factions and regions and keep the Union functioning. Douglas believed that the economic and cultural absurdity of slaves in Kansas and Nebraska would kill slavery in those states, but without offending the South, to whom the door had not been closed other than by the impeccable operation of the free suffrage of the free inhabitants. He is also thought to have been fishing for southern support, with an inexplicable unawareness of how seriously he could alienate his northern supporters. And he was allegedly rushing the development of central and northern states to facilitate a trans-continental railway from Chicago, rather than the southern route that was being pressed by the war secretary, Jefferson Davis of Mississippi, with the usual torpid endorsement of the disconnected president.

The Kansas-Nebraska Act lit fuses in all directions; the New England Emigrant Aid Company was established, and promoted emigration of anti-slavery settlers to the territories approaching statehood, including 2,000 settlers in Kansas in the next couple of years. Secret societies promoting slavery arose in response, importing partisans of slavery. The "Appeal of the Independent Democrats" virtu-ally fragmented the Democratic Party at a stroke, as large numbers of anti-slavery Democrats deserted their party, having little more regard for Douglas than for the post-Calhoun leadership in the South. But the biggest shoe to fall came down in mid-July 1854, when a group of influential Whigs, anti-slavery Democrats, and the remnants of the Free Soil movement met at Jackson, Michigan, and formed what they called the Republican Party, and called for prohibition of slavery in the territories, repeal of the Kansas-Nebraska Act and the Fugitive Slave Act, and the abolition of slavery in the District of Columbia. It was obvious that if the Whigs could trade their token vote in the South for the more sizeable anti-slavery Democratic vote in the North, revitalized as Republicans, a much more sonorously American name than the Whigs (the British party of Walpole, Pelham,

Melbourne, and Palmerston), they could take the role of natural governing party from the Democrats, who had held it since Jefferson's time, and smash the Jackson settlement, leaving the Democrats either split between southern slaveholders and Douglas populists or confined to the South, and in either case clamoring for the spread of slavery around the country, while the Republicans became preeminent outside the South and demanded the irreversible retrenchment of slavery. That would not be a division that could be healed within the legislative process as Clay had so artfully done, or even by a clever balance of sticks and carrots, as Jackson and Polk had managed. America was in sight of the brink.

It could be assumed that most of the Whigs, such as Seward, who with Thurlow Weed had overthrown Van Buren and Secretary of State Marcy's Albany Regency and disapproved even the Compromise of 1850 as too accommodating of the South, and Salmon P. Chase of Ohio, Abraham Lincoln of Illinois, and all the abolitionists, such as Charles Sumner—dynamic and purposeful and very able men, not tired, deracinated trimmers like Pierce and Buchanan—would rally to the Republicans, as they did. Meetings like the one in Jackson, Michigan, took place across the North in 1854 and 1855.

Lincoln first achieved national attention with two speeches, in Springfield and Peoria, in October 1854, in which he spoke in conciliatory terms of the South, acknowledged its constitutional right to slavery, but opposed slavery in free territory and proposed its very gradual abolition by the creation of conditions that would make that natural. He favored a less draconian Fugitive Slave regime that would restore due process. From these early days, he was carving a constituency that would grow steadily larger, in peace, and war, and posterity, and eventually include almost 100 percent of the population, for the patient, inexorable imposition of what was morally right and politically practicable, without malice or demeaning compromise. He felt that slavery had to disappear, but that this objective could be indefinitely delayed to accommodate the acquired rights of the South and to spare the South humiliation and breach of established constitutional arrangements. His was a voice of reason, emanating from the bowels of semi-rural, semi-frontier America, but as all the world knows, it would grow clearer and less disputable, and more legitimate, and would finally be permanently revered, for its tactical astuteness and moral clarity, and for the always patient and never scolding or priggish nature of its message, and above all for its infallible eloquence and almost poetic, exquisite formulation. Though the proportions of the crisis threatening the nation were now obvious and mortal, only the most discerning could be confident that, as in previous American crises, a leader of the very great stature required to lead the nation through the gathering storm was already visible, and certainly audible.

While Lincoln was launching himself as a great and timely political orator to a national audience, the Pierce administration compounded the catastrophe of its support for squatter sovereignty and the scrapping of the Missouri Compromise. When an American merchant ship, the *Black Warrior*, was seized by Spanish officials in Havana because of innocuous errors in its manifest papers, war hawks in the Congress, both the slavery faction wanting a Mexican War sequel of easy additions to slave-holding territory, and those wishing to distract the factions of America by waving the flag about in another turkey-shoot mismatch of a hemispheric conflict, agitated for war. The American minister in Madrid, Pierre Soule, served the Spanish a strenuous ultimatum considerably in excess of what Secretary of State Marcy had authorized. (Soule, a French revolutionary fugitive and adventurer, had emigrated to the United States and become a senator from Louisiana before his appointment to Madrid.) Spain accepted Marcy's demand for an apology and reparations, but the secretary sent Soule to meet at Ostend (Belgium) with his ministers to France and Britain, John Mason and James Buchanan, in order to elaborate a policy for the acquisition of Cuba.

Soule was the chief author of the document that emerged, the so-called Ostend Manifesto, which called for the purchase of Cuba, as necessary to the security of the institution of slavery, and if the Spanish would not sell it, "we shall be justified in wresting it from Spain." Marcy rejected the manifesto and Soule resigned in December 1854, but its publication in March 1855 stirred outrage in the northern states over the apparent willingness of the administration to plunge into an unprovoked foreign war to defend and expand slavery. (The United States would not be averse to foreign derring-do to distract from domestic problems, and it would also develop a weakness for exporting some of its problems to neighbors, to avoid dealing with them: here slavery, a century later, drugs, where it would try to strangle supply rather than seriously punish demand.) Buchanan, the ne plus ultra and cul-de-sac of doughface moral enfeeblement and amoral appeasement of whatever quarter complained loudest, gained support in the South, enhancing his prospects as a presidential nominee, which had narrowly been denied him in 1852.

The general disintegration of the party system was illustrated and accelerated by the emergence of what called itself the American Party, generally known, from their password at clubhouses that sprang up like indigestible mushrooms throughout the country, "I don't know," as the Know-Nothings. It was an anti-immigrant party that particularly resented Roman Catholics, who because of emigration from Ireland during the Great Famine of the 1840s (nearly a million people fled to the United States), and in a steady stream from Italy and Bavaria and the German Rhineland, had become, by 1850, the largest single religious denomination in the country. It could reasonably be assumed that in terms made famous 110 years later by President Lyndon Johnson, the "frontlash" would be at least double the backlash; in exploiting anti-Catholic sentiment the Know Nothings would alienate not only the Roman Catholics but at least as many non-Catholics who would be offended by the bigotry of the movement.

All through 1855 and 1856, Kansas would be a bleeding sore for the whole country, envenoming even relatively staid opinion. Pro-slavery elements from neighboring Missouri were known as "Border Ruffians," and more than 5,000 of them secured the election of a pro-slavery legislature in March 1855. A pro-slavery legislature convened in July and enacted very pro-slavery legislation. The anti-slavery forces set up their own government at Topeka in October and enacted an entirely contrary, anti-slavery program. There were now two Kansas territorial governments legislating in exact contradiction to each other. There was frequent skirmishing between the parallel governments. Pierce made it a trifecta (after the squatter-sovereignty debacle and the Ostend Manifesto fiasco) by making it explicit in a special message to Congress in January 1856 that he favored the pro-slavery faction in Kansas. An outright civil war prevailed in Kansas from May to September 1856. The highlight of this discordant departure from the civic idyll recounted by de Tocqueville and others was the arrival of the anti-slavery militant John Brown, who, with the assistance of a raiding party consisting mainly of his own sons, hanged five pro-slavery leaders in the "Pottawatomie Massacre" in May 1856. There was now guerrilla war throughout Kansas, which took over 200 lives in November and December 1856, alone.

Congressional opinion divided sharply. The House supported admission of Kansas as a free state, but the Senate, where the slave states still held an equality of members, modified Douglas's bill and proposed a constitutional convention for Kansas. When Congress adjourned at the end of August 1856, there was still no recognized government of Kansas. In May, Charles Sumner, the abolitionist firebrand, had spoken vituperatively in the Senate on "The Crime Against Kansas" on May 19 and 20, 1856, disparaging several southern legislators, including South Carolina's Andrew Butler. On May 22, Butler's nephew, Congressman Preston Brooks, came upon Sumner in his Senate chair from behind, and assaulted him with a cane, causing a severe concussion and his absence from the Senate for three years, convalescing. Public anger in the North spiked again. With civil war in Kansas for months on end and grievous bodily harm being inflicted on the floor of the U.S. Senate, there is little wonder that Americans of all political persuasions thought that the whole process of government was disintegrating. Nothing that had occurred for some years bore the least resemblance to what Madison,

Hamilton, and others had had in mind for the brave new republic. Mere anarchy was abroad in the land, and in the Capitol itself.

10. BUCHANAN AND THE REPUBLICANS

The presidential campaign of 1856 was one of the most dismal in the country's history, as people completely inadequate to the immense crisis that threatened the Union contested for the nation's greatest offices. The American (Know-Nothing) Party met at Philadelphia in February and exhumed former President Millard Fillmore as their presidential candidate and Andrew Donelson of Tennessee as vice president. What was left of the rump of the Whigs supported the same candidates when they met at Baltimore in September. The American Party had not renounced its founding advocacy of the disqualification of Roman Catholics and the foreign-born from public office, nor the requirement of 21 years residence before the achievement of citizenship, but it didn't specifically reaffirm that platform either. It split over slavery and confined itself to platitudinous nativism. Fillmore dishonored his former great office, and even the vice presidency to which he was actually elected under General Taylor, by being the bowsprit of such a contemptible and schismatic movement.

The Democrats met at Cincinnati in June and chose Buchanan on the 17th ballot over Pierce and Douglas. Pierce had certainly earned rejection and did the honorable thing by allowing his party the opportunity publicly to repudiate him as incompetent, rather than skulking away. Douglas was much the ablest of the three and a sincere democrat and far from a fellow traveler of the slaveholders. But he had put the whole country into a desperate crisis. Buchanan was even less well-suited to deal with it than had been Pierce, who was at least an amiable man and a general. Buchanan was a decayed servitor, a shilly-shallying appeaser, whom Polk despised as his secretary of state for being unable to take a position and stick to it. (It didn't matter as Polk, like many successful presidents, reserved all important foreign policy matters to himself.) The 35-year-old two-term Kentucky congressman John C. Breckinridge was chosen for vice president. Breckinridge was talented but a militant supporter of slavery.

The Republicans met at Philadelphia later in June and unanimously made the eccentric selection of Colonel John C. Frémont, chiefly known as Senator Thomas Hart Benton's son-in-law, and for his swashbuckling in California a decade before, when he had been court-martialed but pardoned by Polk. Frémont was a 43-year-old topographical engineer who led numerous exploratory expeditions to the Far West and was widely known, respectfully, as The Pathfinder. He was an impetuous and erratic hothead, but was adventurous and brave, had earned military distinction, had evoked the expansion of the country, and was one of California's first U.S. senators, though he retired from that role after a year. He was an unambiguous opponent of slavery. New York's Senator William Henry Seward could have had the nomination, but his chief promoter, the strong-arm boss of New York state, Thurlow Weed, convinced him that a new party could not defeat the Democratic coalition and that it was better to aim for 1860. The vice presidential nominee was a former U.S. senator from New Jersey, William L. Dayton, who was supposedly popular with the Know-Nothings. (The runner-up was former congressman Abraham Lincoln of Illinois.)

The Republicans ran against "Bleeding Kansas," advocating the admission of Kansas as a free state, the restoration of federal authority over slavery, and the prohibition of slavery in the territories. The Know-Nothings were a drain on both parties, and in the Northeast many of them went for the Republicans, because they disapproved the aristocratic and slave-holding South. Elsewhere, it was more difficult to trace the voting pattern. The Republicans were a brand-new formation with an eccentric and controversial leader. Their motto was "Free Soil, Free Men, Frémont." The South would come in solidly for Buchanan, and it would have been astonishing if the winning party in 12 of the last 14 elections could not turn back a new party in a three-way race, and it did, 1.839 million to 1.335 million for Frémont to 875,000 for Fillmore, 45 percent to 33 percent to 22 percent; 174 electoral votes (all 14 slave states and 5 free states) to 114 for Frémont (11 free states) to 8 electoral votes, 1 slave state (Maryland) for Fillmore.

Pierce had been a disastrous president and would be a tragic ex-president. His marriage broke down, he sank into alcoholism, disgraced himself even more thoroughly than Tyler, a Virginian, by supporting the Confederacy in coming years, and died of cirrhosis in 1869, aged 64. Fillmore went back to Buffalo and lived uncontroversially, a patron of good causes such as the public library, and died in 1874, aged 74. Buchanan was popular in the South for recognizing Cuba at Ostend as essential to the security of slavery, and tolerated in the North as a stable conservator of the Union, albeit by appeasement of the secessionists. The majority of the free states had deserted the Democrats for the Republicans on their first try and with an odd candidate who was neither fish nor foul, neither military hero nor a public-policy proven quantity. A statesman was needed, which Buchanan was not.

Douglas had destroyed the Compromise he had helped Clay create, and while that was a grievous error, slavery had to be resolved; it was ultimately an intolerable evil and hypocrisy, and in precipitating the issue as he inadvertently did, Douglas forced its attempted resolution. He would play a unique role in also inadvertently elevating the indispensable savior of the Union and emancipator of the slaves. It was a terrible drama, and would have a sanguinary but noble end, and Douglas's role would be Shakespearean: tragic, honorable, and fortuitous. Buchanan was a final twist and trailer of a stale performance. (His cabinet was also undistinguished, except for, up to a point, Cass as secretary of state, but there would now be little of foreign affairs, and Cass did little and handed over for the last few months of the term to Attorney General Jeremiah S. Black.) All sensed that a mighty climax was now imminent. America was now an important country in the world and had called immense attention to itself for over 80 years, and had never ceased to absorb international curiosity and fire the imagination of observers everywhere. The suspense was constant; Armageddon was almost at hand.

11. DRED SCOTT AND LECOMPTON

There was no respite. Two days after the inauguration, on March 6, 1857, Taney's Supreme Court brought down another showstopper on the Fugitive Slave Act—the *Dred Scott* decision. Scott was a slave who had been taken to Illinois and Wisconsin, where slavery was illegal, and remained there between 1834 and 1838. He sued for his liberty in 1846 in Missouri, claiming to have been automatically emancipated by operation of the law in Illinois and Wisconsin. The first trial in Missouri favored Scott but he generally lost after that. There were three issues before the Supreme Court: whether Scott was a citizen of Missouri entitled to sue in the state's courts; whether he had gained his freedom and retained it on his return to Missouri; and whether the Missouri Compromise, which outlawed slavery in territories north of 36°30, was constitutional. The majority decided against Scott on all three counts, finding the Missouri Compromise unconstitutional 36 years ex post facto. The decision had been leaked to Buchanan, who had predicted in his inaugural address two days before that slavery matters would be "promptly settled." It was an appalling decision. Of course, once emancipated, slaves were citizens, and of course the emancipation did not apply only in some states and not others, and conferred the full rights of citizenship, including access to the courts. And the only possible contention that the Missouri Compromise was unconstitutional was based on the Kansas-Nebraska era, Calhounite claim that the federal government had no business being involved in slavery at all, a preposterous notion given that it was the issue upon which the future of the Union now depended.

Taney was a bigoted Jacksonite (though a Roman Catholic who might have been expected to be warier of the dangers of group discrimination), and the Court showed the problems that arise when one party, embarked on a controversial course on an overarching issue, has named virtually all the judges for 56 years. *Dred Scott* was an obvious travesty, a miscarriage of justice and a rape of equity, and was, along with popular sovereignty, another red rag to the northern bull, which would rather not have been disturbed, and another incitement of the South to demand the expansion of slavery throughout the territories.

The next bombshell to rock the nation came in the last months of 1857. The pro-slavery Kansas legislature wanted a pro-slavery constitution for the territory without recourse to a popular vote. The governor, Robert Walker of Mississippi, insisted on a legislative election, and that it be conducted fairly, though he was prepared to dispense with a popular referendum on the state constitution. The governor conscientiously threw out thousands of fraudulent ballots stuffed into boxes by the pro-slavery party. The free-state advocates emerged with a clear majority. The ensuing constitutional convention at Lecompton, Kansas, determined that the constitution would not be submitted to the people, but that only one clause would, which would determine whether slavery would be allowed in Kansas when it was incorporated as a state. If the vote on that issue was negative, then slavery would not "exist" in the state, but existing ownership of slaves, as *Dred Scott* had determined, would continue. This was another stacked deck for the slavery supporters, in the teeth of a clear majority in the territory.

Walker went to Washington to lobby Buchanan, who was determined to appease the South to hang on to his party. Stephen A. Douglas, conforming to overwhelming opinion across the North, came out in opposition to the Lecompton Constitution on December 9, 1857. Buchanan reneged on his previous guarantee to Walker and decided in favor of Lecompton, provoking Walker's immediate conscientious resignation. Free-state voters boycotted the December 21 vote on the constitutional slavery clause and the pro-slavers won, though about half their 6,000 votes were judged fraudulent. The free-state faction, evidently the majority, persuaded the acting governor to bring forward the opening of the legislative session, where it called for a clear vote on the Lecompton Constitution as a whole. This was held on January 4, 1858, and recorded an overwhelming majority against.

Buchanan, once embarked on his course, would not vary it, and proposed the admission of Kansas as a slave state, a shocking capitulation of the president to what was clearly a chronically minority view, in Kansas and in the country. Douglas repudiated the president and broke completely with him. Buchanan managed to put his bill through the Senate, but the House of Representatives, where the free majority in the country predominated, voted to resubmit the Lecompton Constitution for a free vote in Kansas. A new bill was proposed that provided for a new vote on Lecompton and, in the event of non-passage, continuation of Kansas as a territory until it had achieved a population of 90,000, which would qualify it for a seat in the House of Representatives. This bill passed and the vote was held on August 2, 1858, and yielded an 85 percent rejection of Lecompton. Kansas remained a territory until accepted as a free state in January 1861, just before the inauguration of Buchanan's successor. Except for the Republicans, who demanded an end to the appeasement of the slave states and the containment of slavery, this issue had been a disaster for almost everyone, including the southerners militant for an expansion of slavery in the territories or, in the alternative, secession. The ambivalent tyros, Pierce and Buchanan, had, with an assist from the reckless Douglas, destroyed the Jackson strategy that, with powerful help from Clay and Webster, had held the Union together for 30 years.

12. ABRAHAM LINCOLN

On June 16, 1858, Lincoln gave another historic address at Springfield, Illinois, where he applied the Biblical standard that "A house divided against itself cannot stand." He avoided disparagements of the South and stated his faith in the indissolubility of the Union, but said "it will become all one thing, or all the other." It was not a mystery which option he expected to prevail. Lincoln ran for the United States Senate from Illinois in the autumn of 1858 against Douglas and challenged him to a series of seven debates, between August 21 and October 15. They were formidable exchanges before large audiences in open-air meetings, and slavery was aired in all its aspects. At Freeport, Illinois, on August 27, Lincoln asked Douglas to explain "popular sovereignty" in the light of the *Dred Scott* decision. Douglas debunked *Dred Scott* by saying that the popular will would always prevail, as there could be no slavery without the application of police, who were subject to local control. This was entirely true, but outraged the South, which always assumed that authorities throughout the country would have to enforce slavery if the Supreme Court ordered it. Lincoln identified slavery as "a moral, a social, and a political wrong," although he denied that he thought African Americans were in fact the equal of whites (though he later changed this view).[5] Douglas dodged the moral issue, but virtually split the Democrats on the argument that local authorities

---

5.   In Lincoln's notes for speeches for September 1859, there appears: "Negro Equality! Fudge!! How long in the government of a God, great enough to make and maintain this Universe, shall there continue knaves to vend and fools to gulp, so low a piece of demagoguism as this?" *The Collected Works of Abraham Lincoln*, New Brunswick, New Jersey, Rutgers University Press, 1953, vol. 3, p. 399.

and voters in the territories could exclude slavery if they wished. The autumn elections produced heavy gains for the Republicans. Lincoln defeated Douglas in the popular vote, in that Republicans won a majority in the Illinois legislative elections; but since not all were up for reelection, the Democrats retained their majority in the legislature, which chose U.S. senators, and Douglas was reelected. Abraham Lincoln, having split the Democrats end to end like a rail, and more than held his own against the greatest Democratic leader since Polk, if not Jackson, became a national celebrity and a presidential contender. The Republicans took 29 of 33 congressmen from New York. The hard-pressed administration had lost control of the Congress.

On October 16, 1859, John Brown led a group of 18 men in a takeover of the federal arsenal at Harper's Ferry, Virginia, and planned to incite a slave revolt throughout the South. He held the arsenal for two days, but was then compelled to surrender by a force led by Colonel Robert E. Lee. No slaves rose and the effort was a complete failure. Brown was convicted and hanged on December 2. He had been supported by a number of northern abolitionist groups, and while few northerners approved of insurrection by slaves, Brown was widely admired as a man of conviction and principle, and the spectacle of such a desperate attempt, and such a severe end, given that he had not killed anyone, offended many, and kept the pot boiling.

In early 1860, Jefferson Davis presented a series of radical pro-slavery and quasi-secessionist resolutions to the Senate. Apart from the familiar Calhounite assertions, Davis pushed out a little further the gamecock southern view that Douglas had incited with popular sovereignty and the scrapping of the 36°30 demarcation from the Missouri Compromise. He said that neither Congress nor any territorial legislature had the license to impair slave-holding rights within the territories, that the federal government must protect the rights of slaveholders there, and that these matters could be determined only by state legislatures after admission to statehood. Thus, the whole vast middle of the continent should simply be thrown open to slavery as a matter of right and normal operation of the law, with no consultation with the inhabitants, and slavery must be aggressively protected by the government of the United States, a country the majority of the population of which clearly disapproved of slavery.

Most southern states claimed in one sort of public meeting or another the right to secede, and in South Carolina and Mississippi money was voted for the setting up of armed forces toward a military cover for exiting the Union. The South had taken up like fox hunters the call for expansion into the territories, and as the Republican Party was absolutely dedicated to confining slavery to, at the most generous, the Missouri Compromise line, it was generally agreed and often restated in the South that the election of a Republican president would be cause for secession, and if secession were resisted, war. On February 27, 1860, Abraham Lincoln made an impressive oratorical debut in New York City, at the Cooper Union. While the leading candidate for the presidential nomination was New York's Senator Seward, Lincoln, though relatively obscure and politically inexperienced, was intelligently clarifying the slavery issue and was emerging as a slightly exotic challenger, who had rendered the Republicans the mighty service of forcing Douglas, the Democrats' strongest leader, into irreconcilable differences with the South. As grave as the Union's prospects were, those of the Republicans were steadily more promising. At the Cooper Union, Lincoln demolished "popular sovereignty" and refuted the southern argument that the election of the Republicans would justify their secession. He condemned extremism on both sides, made a Clay-like appeal for reciprocal accommodation, recognized the gravity of southern threats to dissolve the Union, but made it clear that the extension of slavery, which the South now claimed virtually as a birthright, was completely unacceptable.

Lincoln had said before that he considered attempted secession a matter that had to be resisted by force if necessary, and that if it came to that, he was confident that the North would win. In a much-publicized address at Cincinnati on September 17, 1859, to a large audience that included many southerners who had come across the Ohio River from Kentucky to hear him, Lincoln said, addressing the southerners: "Will you make war upon us and kill us all? . . . I think you are as gallant and as brave men as live; that you can fight as bravely in a good cause, man for man, as any other people living . . . but man for man you are not better than we and there are not so many of you as there are of us. You will never make much of a hand at whipping us."[6] Lincoln was, after all, a frontiersman; he was very strong physically and had had no shortage of hand-to-hand combat. He was a man of peace, but not a pacifist.

The fact was that both sides were spoiling for a fight. The national government had been reduced to a dithering, hair-splitting, talking shop, impotently enduring endless threats bellowed at it from its constituents. The Jackson settlement was bound to turn into a shabby and unsustainable compromise when it was operated by weaklings who would never threaten to hang their vice presidents for treason and invade states of the Union as if they were foreign territory, as Jackson had

---

6. *The Collected Works of Abraham Lincoln, op. cit.*, p. 454.

done. The parties had put up steadily more ambiguous leaders to try to dissemble their way through the contradictions, and in the interest of attracting the South to him, Douglas, with the self-destructive abandon of a mindless opportunist, had seized on "popular sovereignty." Lincoln had forced him to keep his place as senator from Illinois by renouncing the main point of "popular sovereignty"—the right of slaveholders to their property in territories whatever the Congress or local governments thought of it. He had proffered the South more than the North was prepared to give, and then tried to take it back when Lincoln cut him off at the knees.

Unless the North was prepared to allow the South to withdraw, it would now come to war, and was like a classic series of aggregated grievances between two parties that can only be resolved by a fight, and a fight of unlimited length until one protagonist had beaten the other unconscious and stood over him in complete victory, or, in the case of the South, had so exhausted the North that it could not continue. Either the Union would break or the objecting party, the North, would have to beat the South into unconditional surrender.

Nothing less would clear the air, much less resolve the issue (as General U.S. Grant would explain, 20 years later, to German Imperial Chancellor Bismarck).[7] This could not be simply a successful dust-up. The South, in all its pride and courage, was chippy, swaggering, and disdainful. It could not be tamed like a disobedient child with a good birching, such as Germany, under Bismarck's leadership, would figuratively administer to the (almost unoffending but inadequately deferential) Danes, Austrians, and French. Nothing less would save the Union, which had so sonorously and loudly proclaimed itself the light unto the world and clarion of human freedom and dignity, the ark of deliverance of the rights of man, just one long lifetime before.

This was about to be the choice, acquiescence in the dissolution of the Union, northern suppression of the insurrection, or a successful southern war of independence. They were all bad choices for those who believed in the United States, but they were the only choices. The South didn't think the North had the will or ability to prevent the secession of the South, and many northerners thought so too. The task for the new president, if he wished to save the country—and the Republicans did, and were now almost certain to win, given the fragmentation they had engineered among their opponents—would be to persuade the North

7.   John Russell Grant, *Around the World with General Grant*, New York, Subscription Book Department, The American News Company, vol. 1, pp. 416–417.

to suppress the insurrection, and then do it, in the certain knowledge that the South would fight with the desperate courage and ingenuity of ferocious, brave people, proud of what they were defending, contemptuous of their opponents, a martial society much handier with horse and gun and rural travel than the more urban, polyglot North.

Abraham Lincoln

CHAPTER SIX

Civil War and Reconstruction
The Agony and Triumph of the American Union, 1860–1889

1. THE 1860 ELECTION

The Democrats met at Charleston, South Carolina, in April 1860. Jefferson Davis was now the principal heir to Calhoun, and the South demanded protection of slavery in the territories. It was not enough, as Calhoun himself had demanded, that the federal government have no role in these matters, or, as Douglas had proposed, that territories could vote for slavery if they chose. Now, the federal government had to sponsor and protect slavery in the territories, and slavery could only be repealed, if at all, when the territories became states. This mania cannot be entirely laid at the door of Douglas, but he opened the door for the monster of belligerent slavery to emerge. Douglas went as far as he could, advocating Calhoun's formula of congressional non-intervention in slavery, as well as adherence to Supreme Court rulings, including *Dred Scott*, and the takeover of Cuba (an outright act of belligerency against a foreign power). The southerners, who would have leapt for joy at the Douglas platform just a few years before, stalked out of the convention, which had failed to choose a nominee, and the official Democrats returned to Baltimore in June (after the Republican convention). Douglas was finally nominated there for president and he chose the relatively anti-secessionist former Georgia governor Herschel Vespasian Johnson as vice president. The southerners, representing 11 states, also reverted to Baltimore and chose Vice President John C. Breckinridge for president and transplanted North Carolinian Joseph Lane, senator from the new state of Oregon, for vice president.

The fragments of the continuing Whigs and the American Party (Know-Nothings) had met at Baltimore in May, constituted themselves as the Constitutional Union Party, dedicated to cooling slavery out by simply preserving the Union however the Supreme Court construed the Constitution as shaping it, and nominated former Tennessee senator and Harrison's war secretary, John Bell, for president, and Webster disciple and former secretary of state Edward Everett of Massachusetts for vice president. It was a wishful conjuration of an easy exit from the relentless and suffocating crisis.

Lincoln was instrumental in having Chicago chosen, for the first of scores of national conventions, as the place of the Republican convention in May. Lincoln largely packed the site, a new convention center nicknamed "the Wigwam," with supporters, and had the advantage of having been less militant in his comments than Seward and the other principal candidate, Salmon P. Chase of Ohio. It was clear that there would be two Democratic candidates running against the Republican nominee, whose victory should thus be assured. Given the disposition of electoral votes, all the Republicans had to do was win the northern states and they would win the election, albeit with a minority of votes, as Buchanan had had opposite Frémont and Fillmore in 1856, and Taylor against Cass and Van

Buren in 1848. To ensure that the party did well in the border states, and try to soften the antagonism of the southern secessionists, Lincoln was the best of the candidates. He also had the appeal of the self-made man, and of being his own man. Though born in a log cabin in Kentucky and an autodidact, Lincoln had built up one of the largest legal practices in the United States.

Seward had fought his anti-slavery corner well for a long time, and had been instrumental in uprooting the Van Buren–Marcy Albany Regency in New York. But Seward owed most of his career, and relied for most of the advice he followed on Thurlow Weed. Lincoln counseled himself. Seward had given some important addresses, including one famed for the identification, in 1858, of "an irrepressible conflict," but Lincoln had traveled tirelessly through the northern states, had met and established a rapport with most of the prominent Republicans, and by his series of brilliant, thoughtful, powerfully delivered speeches, had made himself conspicuously presidential.

Suddenly this new party, in the most dire circumstances the country had known since Valley Forge, was going to win, and what was needed was a thoughtful, strong, steady, profound leader. Chase had no campaign manager and had no idea of how to organize a campaign. Edward Bates, a prominent ex-Whig from Missouri, was the fourth candidate, but his campaign had largely been created by the publisher of the *New York Tribune*, Horace Greeley, in an act of vengeance against his former allies, Seward and Weed. These were substantial men, but they had never spoken of the immense crisis that loomed as Lincoln had, stirring audiences to their depths again and again with speeches like those in Illinois that had shaken the Democrats apart, and at Cooper Union.

The Republican Party had been organized mostly by its leaders in the principal northern states—Weed, Seward, and Greeley in New York, Chase in Ohio, Simon Cameron in Pennsylvania, and Lincoln in Illinois. Lincoln had been the soul of diplomacy and had no enemies, and had made himself friendlier with the other party barons than they were with each other; Seward and Weed had not even called upon Pennsylvania's Cameron, a kingmaker and favorite son from a very important state. And Lincoln had been the most articulate, frequently heard, and overpoweringly but unaffectedly eloquent evocator and voice of the ambitions and grievances of the opponents of the long and now rather sleazy Democratic confidence trick that tied slavery to Union. He was very well organized, including having altered rail schedules to bring tens of thousands of supporters from all over Illinois to Chicago in convention week.

Chicago had grown in less than 30 years from a fur and military post with barely 20 families, and wolves roaming the dirt streets at night, to a city of over

100,000 and the greatest grain, meat, and lumber market in the world; it was the breastplate of the mighty expansion across the continent of the United States. One of the principal trains bringing delegates and press from New York made the trip from Buffalo to Chicago in the astounding time of 16 hours,[1] frequently exceeding 60 miles an hour. The very progress of America and its explosive growth were mocked by the antiquarian primitiveness of the South.

On the first ballot, Seward led, 173½ to Lincoln's 102, 49 for Chase, and 48 for Bates; it was a Seward-Lincoln race. On the second ballot 188 for Seward to 183½ for Lincoln, and on the third ballot Lincoln came in at 231½, where only 233 was needed for a majority. A landslide of shifted votes put him across. In recognition of New England, Senator Hannibal Hamlin of Maine was chosen as vice presidential nominee. It had been, and still stands as, one of the most brilliant campaigns for a party nomination in American history. The party platform included all the old baubles of Clay's American System—the protective tariff for industry, liberal immigration, internal improvements, the Wilmot Proviso, an absolute prohibition of slavery in the territories, though new states were free to choose slavery—and it advocated a homestead law and a railway to the Pacific. America was to quell internal discordance and drive on to its promised greatness, inspiring and attracting the masses of oppressed Europe.

Republican victory was virtually a foregone conclusion; so was insurrection, and so, as Lincoln had warned, was war, and it would not be a slapstick war like much of what went on in previous wars with Indians, Mexicans, and even, at times, the French and the British. A terrible and total war impended, for the soul and integrity of America, to unbind it and attach it inexorably to an exalted and exceptional destiny, which it had long claimed for itself, or to cut it down to a humbled and truncated vision of itself, no longer master of the hemisphere, a heavily compromised success. The eyes of the world, which had never left America for long since Lexington and Concord, were riveted on her more fixedly than ever.

On November 6, 1860, Lincoln won 1.87 million votes (almost 40 percent), to 1.36 million (about 29 percent) for Douglas, 850,000 for Breckinridge (18 percent), and 590,000 for Bell (13 percent). Lincoln ran very strongly at nearly 40 percent in a four-way race, as was shown by his 180 electoral votes to 72 for Breckinridge, 39 for Bell, and just 12 for Douglas. Lincoln carried all 18 free states and no others. Breckinridge won in all 11 southern slave states except Virginia, which Bell won narrowly, and the border states between North and South broke:

---

1.   Doris Kearns Goodwin, *Team of Rivals: The Political Genius of Abraham Lincoln*, New York, Simon and Schuster, 2005, p. 237.

just Missouri for Douglas, Kentucky and Tennessee for Bell, and Maryland for Breckinridge. Breckinridge did not exceed 10 percent in any of the northern states, and Lincoln and Douglas (despite Douglas's mighty efforts to appease the South) had insignificant numbers of votes there. The country's regional divisions, away from the border between North and South, could scarcely have been more stark.

2. CIVIL WAR AT LAST

South Carolina's legislature voted to set up a state convention, which voted unanimously to secede from the Union on December 20, 1860, citing the election of a regional party, and of an anti-slavery president, and what it called the North's prolonged war on slavery. Mississippi, Florida, Alabama, Georgia, Louisiana, and Texas followed between January 9 and February 1. Virginia, Arkansas, North Carolina, and Tennessee voted that they would secede if any effort were made to coerce a seceding state to remain in the Union. There were 25 to 35 percent anti-secession minorities in Tennessee, Texas, and Virginia, even after the legislatures had voted to secede, but opinion firmed up quickly across the South.

The great American Union was crumbling as the handover from Buchanan to Lincoln neared. In his message to the Congress on December 3, Buchanan reiterated his notorious empathy with the slave states and declared the impotence of the federal government to prevent secession by force, on the advice of the attorney general, Jeremiah S. Black. (Black was rewarded for his pusillanimity by being named secretary of state when Cass left the sinking ship on December 14, 1860. Black said secession was illegal, but that coercion was also—a legally and practically absurd position that disgusted retired General Cass.) The legal argument about secession has always been fuzzy. Washington certainly charged the Continental Congress and the Constitutional Convention to produce an "indissoluble union," and it was hoped that this had been done. But the right of distinct units of a country to secede is frequently asserted and recognized, such as, in the nineteenth century, Belgium from the Netherlands and Texas from Mexico (not altogether spontaneously, as has been recounted), and in the twentieth century, Norway from Sweden, Ireland from the United Kingdom, Singapore from Malaysia, all the Soviet republics from Russia, and the Slovaks from Czechoslovakia; but none of these federations had anything like the voluntary origins or formal, consensual legitimacy of the United States. It is very difficult to find any legal rationale for the American states simply purporting to secede as if they had an untrammeled right at all times to promote themselves from subordinate jurisdictions in a federal state to sovereignty, merely by vote of a convention struck by act of the state legislature.

Since the legality of secession is not clear, Lincoln wisely chose to strengthen his legal position, both for posterity and opposite foreign powers, by arranging for the insurgents to begin the violence with an act of coercive aggression against the federal government. Between December 28, 1860, and February 18, 1861, state militiamen seized federal forts and arsenals in South Carolina, Georgia, Virginia, Alabama, Florida, Louisiana, Arkansas, and Texas, though without gunfire or casualties. When President Buchanan tried to send supplies to Fort Sumter in Charleston Harbor on January 5, in an unarmed ship, it was driven off by gunfire from Confederate shore batteries, again without casualties.

The Confederate States of America provisionally established themselves on February 4, 1861, at Montgomery, Alabama, with a states' rights affiliation of consenting states, and five days later, Jefferson Davis of Mississippi was elected president and Alexander Stephens of Georgia, who had opposed secession (along with Douglas's recent running mate, Herschel V. Johnson), vice president of the Confederacy. From February 11 to 23, Lincoln was on his famous train trip from Springfield, where he gave a memorable farewell, to Washington, with 14 stops along the way to greet well-wishers from the back of the train. In his inaugural address on March 4, he was conciliatory ("We must not be enemies"), but said that "No state, on its own mere action, can get out of the Union," making it clear that he did not accept the secessions that had been proclaimed. He also made it clear that violence need not occur, and that if it did, it would be the fault of the insurgents. Lincoln advised South Carolina that provisions only were on their way by ship to Fort Sumter at the mouth of Charleston Harbor, and South Carolina opened up withering fire on the fort from shore batteries on April 11. It surrendered on April 13. The South had opened fire on the North and galvanized opinion to suppress the revolt. There had been a good deal of waffling about, in Horace Greeley's words, not wanting "to live in a country where one part is pinned to the other by bayonets." This line of reasoning largely vanished after Fort Sumter was attacked (albeit no one was killed).

Lincoln announced the existence of an insurrection and called for 75,000 volunteers. This was seen as the signal of an imminent invasion, and Virginia, Arkansas, Tennessee, and North Carolina joined the Confederacy between April 17 and May 20, taking most of their serving U.S. Army officers with them, including Colonel Robert E. Lee, who opposed secession but felt his higher loyalty was to Virginia than to the U.S.A. (On that day, he declined General Winfield Scott's offer of command of the Union Army, and would assume command of the Army of Northern Virginia in June 1862, where he would become one of history's great commanders.) The 50 western counties of Virginia seceded from Virginia and were recognized two years later as the state of West Virginia (fulfilling Hamilton's old ambition to break up Virginia). The Union thus rejected the right of states to secede, but upheld the right of parts of states that opposed secession, when the majority in the state approved secession, to secede from the secessionist state and remain in the Union. Delaware, Maryland, Kentucky, and Missouri were slave states that remained in the Union, though there were close contests for the loyalty of the last three.

Lincoln had taken his opponents for the Republican presidential nomination into key government position—Seward as secretary of state, Chase at Treasury, Bates as attorney general—and he made the Pennsylvania Republican leader, Simon Cameron, secretary of war. (This last appointment was not a success, and Lincoln shortly replaced him with the forceful and abrasive, but effective, Edwin Stanton.) The 74-year-old Winfield Scott, a military hero for nearly 50 years, since America's first victories in the War of 1812, was still the commanding general of the U.S. Army. He cautioned against rushing into battle with raw recruits against southerners who would be more experienced with firearms, but congressional and press demands for a quick victory caused General Irwin McDowell to be sent forward at the head of 30,000 men to engage General Pierre G.T. Beauregard at Bull Run (Manassas), near Washington, on July 21, 1861. It started out well but ingenious improvisations by Confederate generals Joseph E. Johnston and Thomas J. Jackson, who earned the nickname "Stonewall" on that day, turned it into a victory for the South and a rout of the Union, with much of social Washington watching from a nearby height.

Lincoln traveled to West Point to get Scott's view. The ample septuagenarian said it would be a long and difficult war but was certainly winnable. Greater distances would eat up part of the Union's manpower advantage, and it would take some time to accustom Union draftees to the soldier's life that would come more easily to most Confederates. He produced—as he had for Polk 15 years before with his Mexican War strategy of Kearny's procession to California, Taylor's frontier action, and his own amphibious landing at Veracruz and march on Mexico City—a clever plan that was eventually executed. He advocated what was called an "Anaconda Plan" of strangling the South: a naval blockade along all its coast; constant pressure on its capital of Richmond from the main army defending Washington; attacks up and down the Mississippi from New Orleans and St. Louis to cut off Texas, Arkansas, and Louisiana; and then an offensive from Tennessee southeast through Georgia with the Armies of the Cumberland and the Tennessee, to cut the Confederacy in half again; and a northern pivot to roll up the Confederates between those armies and the Union Army of the Potomac between and around Washington and Richmond. Once again, he instantly identified the winning strategy, which succeeded as soon as Lincoln found the commanders who could carry it out. (Scott lived to see the Anaconda Plan completed, and died, full of honors, in 1866, aged almost 80, along with Washington and Nathanael Greene, one of America's three greatest general prior to those about to make their names.) Lincoln's first commanding general was George B. McClellan, a dashing officer who had won some early skirmishes in West Virginia.

As 1861 ended, the Union and the Confederacy were settling into what promised to be prolonged combat. Lincoln made it clear that he was conducting a war forced upon him, to preserve the Union, and that it was not a war to end slavery, though he would not tolerate the spread of slavery. Now he was armed with a plan of war; it remained to find the commanders and recruit and train the armies. The fact that many still regarded him as an ungainly bumpkin conferred the advantage of being underestimated.

Beyond the technical arguments about the indissolubility of the Union, and the general right to put down an insurrection, Lincoln invoked what amounted to a constitutional doctrine of eminent domain. Only the restoration of the Union would preserve the continuity of the great experiment of 1776, would continue to hold out the promise to the world of democratic government from the people upwards, and not devolved downward on men, whom he saw as essentially self-governing. If the South departed successfully, the United States would lose nearly 30 percent of its people and 40 percent of its territory, its momentum, mystique, national morale, and heritage of freedom; it would be hemmed about between British Canada and insolent rebels, as European countries are surrounded by rivals; and America's destiny to lead the world toward the attainment of the rights of man would be forfeit, as the dead and brutal hand of slavery crumpled the proclaimed principles of the Declaration of Independence. Until Lincoln had the armed might to crush the South, he would be vulnerable to the rationalizations and lapses of purpose of his people. If he could develop the first without being swamped by the second, he would save the nation that, in less time than now separated America from Yorktown, would save democracy in the world. Part of Lincoln's infallible eloquence was his unjingoistic conviction of America's predestined greatness and vocation to lead the world. His vision was accurate, as long as his self-confidence, which survived his frequent lapses into moroseness, was justified. A great and terrible drama was well underway.

3. ANTIETAM AND RELATIONS WITH THE BRITISH AND THE FRENCH

Abraham Lincoln issued his War Order No. 1, on January 27, 1862 (nine months after hostilities began), for a general Union offensive. In a pattern that was to become tediously familiar, McClellan ignored it. In what was to become a more agreeable tradition, his order was carried out beyond the call of duty in the west, where Generals George H. Thomas and Ulysses S. Grant advanced in January and February into Tennessee and captured Fort Donelson, where Grant shocked the South by taking 14,000 prisoners, and took Nashville on February 25. A sign of things to come was furnished when real blood was drawn at Shiloh, almost at the border of Tennessee, Mississippi, and Alabama, on April 6–7, where Grant took 13,000 casualties out of 63,000 Union soldiers engaged, and inflicted 11,0000 casualties on the Confederacy, including their commander, General A.S. Johnston, who was killed on the battlefield.

On April 26, 1862, a Union naval force under future admiral David Farragut landed General Benjamin Butler's forces, which took New Orleans. Only about 300 miles separated Grant from Butler, a narrowing window between the eastern and western Confederacy. The blockade of the Confederate coastline was already in force and being tightened, and the third of General Winfield Scott's Anaconda strategy components, the cutting off of the western Confederacy by driving down the Mississippi after taking New Orleans, was already underway. The second element, keeping the pressure constantly on Richmond, was off to a slow start.

In the east, Lincoln quickly tired of McClellan's excuses for inaction, and of McClellan personally. The general was a vain and insubordinate martinet, which Lincoln, who had a notoriously invulnerable ego, would happily have overlooked if the general had won something. Under Lincoln's orders to move on Richmond, McClellan chose to do so by an amphibious operation landed at the evocative locale of Yorktown on May 4. He moved slowly up the peninsula between the James and York Rivers, and a series of battles occurred between May and September. While this was happening, Stonewall Jackson moved brilliantly up the Shenandoah Valley between March and June, with about 20,000 men, outmaneuvering and defeating nearly 50,000 Union troops, until McDowell and local militia were forced to provide 30,000 troops for a possible defense of Washington.

McClellan got within five miles of Richmond but was stopped by General Joseph E. Johnston at the Battle of Seven Pines (Fair Oaks), May 31 and June 1, 1862. The Union had about 6,000 casualties, the Confederacy 8,000, including Johnston, who was seriously wounded, but recovered. The struggle for Richmond continued in the Seven Days' Battles around Mechanicsville from June 26 to July 2, where Lee made his debut as Confederate commander in Virginia. Both sides withdrew after this series of bloody engagements, in which the Union took 16,000 and the Confederacy over 20,000 casualties. If McClellan had had the determination of the war's last Union commander in the east, he would have held Lee's feet to the fire and might have broken the Confederacy's back. On July 11, Lincoln put the ponderous General Henry Halleck in as general-in-chief, with McClellan continuing as head of the Army of the Potomac. He consolidated the armies of Virginia and ordered a land approach to Richmond. Lee masterminded an ambush superbly executed by his able lieutenants, Generals Stonewall Jackson and James Longstreet, and defeated General John Pope at the Second Battle of Bull Run (Manassas) on August 29 and 30. Pope retreated to the defenses of Washington, was replaced by McClellan, and Lee invaded the North, entering northwestward into Maryland, apparently aiming to advance into Pennsylvania and isolate the Union capital. He took Harper's Ferry on September 15, capturing immense supplies of munitions and stores in the arsenal from which he had ejected John Brown on behalf of the Union just three years before, and taking 11,000 Union prisoners.

McClellan, in his brief but finest hour, overtook Lee near Sharpsburg, Maryland, on September 17, and on the bloodiest day of the war, at Antietam, the two armies divided nearly 25,000 casualties almost evenly. McClellan did not commit his reserves, as a bolder general would have done, given his numerical advantage, and Lee withdrew. McClellan did not try to press an advantage, but the day had important repercussions, at home and abroad.

At the beginning of the Civil War, the British establishment had largely favored the Confederacy, out of commercial connections to the textile industry, but underlying this leaning was a desire to see the Americans who had exited the British Empire so effectively and almost painlessly, having left the mother country the chit for evicting France from Canada, humbled and laid low.

Four outstanding past, present, and future prime ministers, of both major parties—Lord John Russell, Lord Palmerston, William Ewart Gladstone, and Robert Cecil, future Marquess of Salisbury, who between them had 11 terms as prime minister for a total of 42 years between 1846 and 1902—favored exchanging embassies with the Confederacy and, if need be, accepting war with America. It devolved upon cooler and relatively unestablished heads, including the Prince Consort, Albert (a German), and the leader of the Conservative Party in the House of Commons and overall leader for a total of 33 years, and twice prime minister, Benjamin Disraeli, to point out that the British government could not take a position in favor of slave-holding and secessionism, and that if it did, it would ultimately lose Canada and the West Indies whatever happened between the American North and South. Seward proved an energetic and sensible secretary of state, whose instincts were sound and who did not require much oversight from the president. Lincoln named as minister to London the very apt Charles Francis Adams, a scholarly diplomat and son and grandson of presidents, as close as America could come to an aristocrat, accredited to governments of British aristocrats. Adams admonished the foreign minister (and former and future prime minister), Lord Russell, not to engage in diplomatic intercourse with the Confederacy and secured a promise that he would not do so (having initially received Richmond's representatives). There had been a controversy in November and December 1861 when the Americans stopped a British merchantman and removed two emissaries from the Confederacy to Great Britain. Seward eventually rescinded the action on a technicality and the problem passed.

Following Antietam, the British and the French, who had been ramping up to recognize the Confederacy and propose mediation between the parties, realized that the war, which was racking up casualties on a scale that surpassed all but the Russian campaign in the Revolutionary and Napoleonic Wars, might not yield to such meddling. They desisted, resuming a state of watchful neutrality, though neutrality generally against the Union, tempered by the clear preference of the British working class for the Union, land of equality and absence of the decayed oppression of the class system. And Antietam emboldened Lincoln to issue his preliminary Emancipation Proclamation (on September 23), freeing all slaves in areas still in rebellion against the United States, as of January 1, 1863. On December 1, he asked for compensated emancipation, but that was declined by the Congress. To northerners uninterested in the plight of the slaves, he explained the measure as an incitement to revolt by the slaves, and a placebo to foreigners, i.e., the British and the French. He fended off complaints that emancipation would discourage the southern moderates with his attempt to compensate slaveholders. It was a deft tactical move, painlessly to stream together the two great purposes of the war, preservation of the Union and elimination of slavery, without offending those interested only in the former, by representing emancipation as an assist to the war effort.

There was jockeying in the western theater in the last half of 1862. General Beauregard's successor, General Braxton Bragg, like an angry hellcat, fought off all comers in central Tennessee, north and northwest of Chattanooga, until he narrowly lost the Battle of Murfreesboro to General Don Carlos Buell, with both sides splitting about evenly nearly 20,000 casualties. In the east, Lincoln finally became exasperated with McClellan's molasses pace and especially his failure to press the advantage after Antietam, and sacked McClellan, replacing him with General Ambrose E. Burnside. The new commander, rattled by Confederate cavalry general J.E.B. Stuart's daring October raids into Pennsylvania, led his army of 113,000 men against Lee's Army of Northern Virginia of 75,000 men, near Fredericksburg, midway between Washington and Richmond, on December 13, 1862. Lee beat Burnside off, inflicting over 11,000 Union casualties, against less than 6,000 himself. Lincoln sacked Burnside six weeks later, and replaced him with General Joseph Hooker.

Lincoln's Emancipation Proclamation, purporting to emancipate all slaves in areas in revolt as "then and forever free," came down on January 1, 1863. As it applied only to insurgent-occupied areas, it didn't have much practical impact but, again, sharply distinguished the combatants in the sight of the Europeans, where slavery was already an unappealing concept. The European desire to think of itself as compensatingly less raw and Darwinian than the United States, an amusing delusion in light of what would unfold in Europe in the coming century, was already a reflex. Lincoln knew that slavery was the cause of the war, though the abolition of it was not the real northern motive for pursuing the war. Emancipation, apparently almost meaningless, was successfully represented as a necessary tactical step to the president's supporters, without being a distraction to the real objective of suppressing a revolt, but it also united the practical objective and moral cause of the war. It was another of Lincoln's masterstrokes. The North was now bulletproof against both the charge of blasé non-concern about slavery and the domestic charge of spilling disturbing quantities of the Union's blood and treasure for a black population that most northerners did not consider to be entirely human, though most also considered the blacks to be victims of a system regarded as between distasteful and wicked. (It was both.) In thus aligning the two connected but not confluent Union war aims, Lincoln demonstrated again, as he had in his pursuit of the presidency, his unique mastery of the grand strategy of the war and of the causes that gave rise to it.

Lincoln's sure political instincts required him to deal with many ripplings of insurgency in his cabinet and Congress, but he never had much difficulty isolating plotters and disarming them with the inexorable logic of his position. Those instincts extended also to the British and the French. The British were never far from the temptation to assist in giving a comeuppance to the only country that had durably defeated and outsmarted them, and the French could never long resist the temptations of sheer opportunism, however elegantly they would dress it up as legitimate policy. In July 1862 the British had built for the Confederacy the CSS *Alabama*, a commerce raider. The United States lost hundreds of ships to the

Alabama and several other raiders, and more than 700 U.S. flag vessels changed to other countries of registration to avoid the risk; the country's merchant marine took more than 50 years to recover. This was the origin of the famous flags of convenience of Liberia and later, Panama. Events had moved sufficiently by April 1863, partly because of the Emancipation Proclamation, and partly because of northern military gains, that when another raider was completed in British yards, Adams delivered so strenuous a protest that the British government seized her (the *Alexandria*), but courts forced her delivery and release. The British had at all times to weigh the fact that if they pushed the Union too hard, they would be flung out of Canada and probably the West Indies. Whatever happened between the North and the South, Britain had no ability to defend Canada from the ever-growing Union Army, now nearly 500,000 men. The bemusement with which the British observed the start of the Civil War had given way to awe at the ferocity and courage of both sides, as even Palmerston acknowledged in Parliament several times. Britain had never in her history taken military casualties on the scale of those that were coming in every few weeks in the U.S. Civil War. However it ended, the implacable and uncompromising nature and astounding scale of the conflict commanded the attention and respect of all.

It was naturally a good deal more frivolous with the carnival government of Napoleon's nephew's Second Empire. Having ridden nostalgia about his uncle to the presidency when the Second Republic replaced the Orleans monarchy, when it was turfed out in the events of 1848, Louis Napoleon Bonaparte had, after four years, simply announced that he was emperor and had had it ratified in a trumped-up referendum. A charming scoundrel, Napoleon III disguised a weak chin with a well-trimmed goatee, and was an inveterate schemer, but without many other qualities that would remind anyone of his uncle, a demiurge and many-sided genius and one of the most immense personalities in all of human history. (In fame and mystique, Lincoln would become one of his very few rivals.)

Napoleon III proposed to mediate the U.S. Civil War, through his minister in Washington, in February 1863, but his good offices were roundly declined both by Seward and for good measure by the Congress, which with Lincoln's blessing dismissed even an offer of mediation as unacceptable "foreign intervention." France was still the country of Genêt and XYZ and had the greatest difficulty figuring out how to behave sensibly with the Americans. As he had less to lose in the Americas than Britain, Napoleon III had no compunction about building raiders for the Confederacy, and in 1864 he intervened in Mexico to place the Archduke Maximilian of Austria on the throne of that country. This was another example of the diplomatic stupidity of the French. By April 1864, the likelihood, though not a certainty until after Maximilian was installed, was that the North would win. And Seward and other American diplomats had left the French in no doubt that the United States would not tolerate a French puppet state in Mexico. If Napoleon had had a fraction of the skill at international affairs of Palmerston or Disraeli or Salisbury (three of Britain's craftiest and most diplomatically successful leaders), he would have promised the North any assistance in exchange for an expansion of French influence in Latin America, a share in the isthmian canal, and an expansion of French Guyana and the French West Indies perhaps. At the most difficult times, Lincoln might have been prepared to indulge such a thing. That would have lent the French gift of the Statue of Liberty 20 years later greater resonance. Maximilian's fraudulent empire ended tragically at the hands of Benito Juárez (the Lincoln of Mexico and namesake of Mussolini), and three years later Napoleon III's empire would end, appropriately, in farce, at the hands of Bismarck, continental Europe's greatest statesman since Richelieu. (Napoleon I being more of a conqueror than a statesman.)

4. THE TURNING POINT: VICKSBURG AND GETTYSBURG

The 1863 campaigns in the east began with the Union commander Lincoln named to replace Burnside after the Fredericksburg fiasco, General Joseph Hooker, attacking south against Lee's army and coming to grips with him at Chancellorsville, a few miles west of Fredericksburg, 50 miles southwest of Washington and north of Richmond. Hooker had 130,000 men, many of them now battle-trained (even if not many of the battles had been successful). Lee had only about 60,000, but he sent Jackson on a brilliant flanking move on Hooker's right and, with perfect timing, pushed the main Union Army back. Both sides took about 11,000 casualties, including Jackson, killed by the fire of his own sentries, on May 2. Hooker withdrew and followed McClellan and Burnside out of command and was replaced by Major General George G. Meade. While Union fortunes were discouraging, the Union was assembling a huge and well-trained and equipped army and Lincoln was changing generals after every defeat; he would come up with winners soon, because incoming Union commanders, as Scott had foreseen, now had a winning hand. One of the great turning points of world military history was almost at hand.

In the west, the South was holding the Confederacy together by blocking the North's southern drive down the Mississippi at Vicksburg, about 250 miles south of Memphis and 200 miles north-northwest of New Orleans. Vicksburg was a great fortress, defended with the usual tenacity of the Confederate Army. In a brilliant campaign from March to July 1863, Grant crossed the Mississippi into Louisiana, marched south of Vicksburg and brought his 20,000 men back north on Union ships on the river toward the back of Vicksburg, separating the two local Confederate armies, invested the city on May 22, and enforced a leak-proof siege of the fortress city. In the east, Lee, playing for European recognition, trying to demoralize the North, and concerned at the ever-increasing size and capability of the armies facing him, and of Grant's progress in the west, invaded the North, moving into Pennsylvania 50 miles north of Antietam and 100 miles northwest of Washington. Lincoln called for 100,000 volunteers, and considerably more men came forward into the Union recruiting offices.

Meade followed Lee, and the two armies met at Gettysburg, starting on July 1, 1863, as the siege of Vicksburg came to a climax. In a very complicated, desperately fought three-day battle replete with unit-sized acts of conspicuous courage on both sides again and again, the Confederacy made its supreme play at Gettysburg in Longstreet's assault on the Little Round Top on July 3. This would have turned the battle, if successful, but was repulsed after prolonged and intense fighting at close quarters, especially in the famous charge of Cemetery Ridge, where the Union prevailed with massed artillery and musketry at point-blank range. (This charge was one of Lee's few serious mistakes, and Longstreet made the effort only after expressing private misgivings.) Lee had no choice but to fall back on July 4, his retreat blocked by the swollen Potomac. Lincoln gave Meade a direct order to attack Lee with his back to the river, but Meade wavered. Lee escaped across the river in the succeeding days, but at the head of a defeated army.

Early on the morning of July 4, Vicksburg surrendered to Grant, who bagged 30,000 Confederate prisoners. Apart from the prisoners, both sides had taken about 10,000 casualties around Vicksburg. In three days at Gettysburg, the two armies had taken, together, over 50,000 casualties, nearly 60 percent of them Confederates, and counting the prisoners, over 100,000 casualties in the two actions. General Abner Doubleday said of Gettysburg: "Each house, church, hovel, and barn is filled with the wounded of both armies. The ground is covered with the dead."[2] The American aptitude for war would not be questioned again for a very long time. Spokesmen for government and opposition in the British Parliament paid homage to the ferocity and courage of the combatants. No one except Lincoln and the senior officers of both armies had imagined that the decisive climax of the American constitutional project could be such a noble and terrible combat.

---

2.   Goodwin, *op. cit.*, p. 533.

Three days were required to receive confirmation of the surrender of Vicksburg and the proportions of the Union victory at Gettysburg, and on the evening of July 7, thousands marched to the White House to congratulate the president, led by a regimental band. Lincoln appeared at the balcony, spoke of the glorious theme of the 4th of July, of the brave men who had died in the great victories of that and preceding days, and declared himself unable to improvise an address worthy of the historic occasion; he smiled, waved, and concluded jauntily, turning to the band: "I'll take the music."[3] On November 19, Lincoln would dedicate the cemetery at Gettysburg and deliver, in just 10 sentences, the speech he declined to try to improvise on July 4 from the White House balcony. It became perhaps the most famous speech in the history of the English language. He began on the uniqueness of America's foundation as a nation where "all men are created equal" and closed on the contribution of "these honored dead" that "government of the people, by the people, and for the people, will not perish from the earth." Both were slightly histrionic liberties, but close enough to the truth, and a gem of concise and overpowering simplicity and elegance on behalf, very artistically, of "those who here gave their lives that that nation might live." Lincoln always believed that the American idea would have died spiritually without the South. (His speech was also a contrast with the two-hour oration by Edward Everett that had preceded it, an admirable festive memorial of the traditional kind.)

On October 16, Lincoln, retaining Meade as commander of the Army of the Potomac, made him virtually a divisional commander by naming Grant over him, with the title of commander of the Grand Army of the Republic (evoking Napoleon's Grand Army, and it was now of equivalent size, with probably comparably competent middle officers). Grant was not Napoleon, but he was a very determined and capable general, as Lee knew. The western region was awarded by Lincoln and Grant to another general about to make world history, William Tecumseh Sherman.

The balance of the year yielded more good results for the North. Scott's Anaconda Plan of five points was now more than half complete: the naval blockade of the South was tight and effective; Grant was about to put maximum pressure on Lee; and the Union held all the Mississippi, and Texas, Louisiana, and Arkansas were cut off from the seven other Confederate states. (Tennessee had been largely occupied already.) At the Battle of Chickamauga (September 19–20), the Union

---

3. *Collected Works of Abraham Lincoln*, New Brunswick, New Jersey, Rutgers University Press, 1953, vol. 6, pp. 319–320.

commander, William Rosecrans, drew against General Braxton Bragg and the Union took 17,000 casualties and the Confederacy 18,000. George H. Thomas, appointed commander of the Army of the Cumberland, won at Chattanooga (Lookout Mountain-Missionary Ridge, November 23–25) against Bragg and Longstreet, with each side suffering about 6,000 casualties. The South was pushed almost completely out of Tennessee. Sherman prepared to march across Georgia from northwest to southeast, cutting four more states out of the Confederacy—Mississippi, Alabama, Georgia, and Florida—in the fourth phase of Scott's Anaconda Plan. Grant and Lee prepared for intense and bloody combat, total war, in the approaches to Richmond. As the Union's armies grew, its best generals came to the top, and the Confederacy was hacked down. Both sides fought with Lincoln's attempted reelection in November 1864 in mind. The defeat of the president was the Confederacy's last throw.

Following these victories, Adams told the British foreign secretary, Russell, that if the ironclad warships Britain was building for the Confederacy were delivered, it would be considered an act of war by the United States. The same message was conveyed to Napoleon III—about six naval vessels being built in French yards for the Confederacy. Britain and France (now that France had an interest in Mexico) were not prepared to bring down on their local interests the wrath of a nation that now deployed an immense, courageous, and brilliantly commanded army, and a considerable navy as well, and the contested ships were sold to neutral powers. The North had won the diplomatic wars; the South would receive no recognition from important foreign countries.

5. GRANT BEFORE RICHMOND, SHERMAN IN GEORGIA, AND THE 1864 ELECTION

Grant's drive toward Richmond, and Sherman's march through Georgia, both among the famous military campaigns of all history, began at the end of the first week of May 1864. Grant attacked toward Richmond while Butler approached it from the southeast. The Union armies had 140,000 men to 96,000 for Lee and Beauregard. In the Battle of the Wilderness, the agile Lee outmaneuvered Grant and inflicted 18,000 casualties to 10,000 of his own. Grant moved to go round Lee's flank at Spotsylvania, an action that cost another 12,000 Union casualties, about twice as many as Lee lost. Grant was not indifferent to casualties, but he did not believe Lee could stop him, and he thought he could force a battle at Richmond, where he could destroy or terminally enervate the Confederate Army. He pressed on south to Cold Harbor, only 20 miles east of Richmond, and attacked entrenched positions from June 1 to 3, losing 12,000 men on June 3 alone. After a month, he had lost 60,000 casualties, the size of Lee's entire army (not counting the 36,000 Beauregard deployed for the final defense of Richmond); but Lee had lost 30,000, half his army, and Grant could replace his losses and Lee could not.

Grant turned west, moving south of Richmond to cut it off from the rest of the Confederacy, and he laid siege to Petersburg, less than 20 miles south of Richmond, taking but inflicting heavy casualties and forcing Lee at all times to defend hard-pressed positions and preventing him from executing his skill at maneuver and imaginative and swift reconfigurations of formations. He planned to move past Richmond and take it from the rear, as he had Vicksburg. As the heavy slogging at Petersburg continued through the summer of 1864, Confederate cavalry general Jubal T. Early defeated Union forces in the Shenandoah Valley and came within five miles of Washington before troops sent back by Grant deflected Early, and the new commander of the Army of the Shenandoah, General Philip H. Sheridan, drove Early out of that valley and scorched it as he went. This group of army commanders, Grant with Sheridan under him on the Shenandoah, Sherman in the west with Thomas under him at the head of the Army of the Cumberland, were the senior command team to whom was entrusted the general offensive to end the war and the insurgency. They were a very strong group, as skilled as Lee, Johnston, Longstreet and Stonewall Jackson, had he lived. (Union armies were named after rivers, Confederate armies after states.)

Sherman's march through Georgia, with 100,000 men facing Johnston's 60,000, set out from Chattanooga. Johnston conducted a very capable, Fabian action of maneuver and harassment and managed even, lightly, to defeat Sherman at Kenesaw Mountain on June 27, about 100 miles south-southeast of Chattanooga. But Sherman's army was unstoppable and Sherman himself was too aggressive a commander to leave much for Johnston to attack, and on July 17 he arrived within 10 miles of Atlanta. Jefferson Davis foolishly replaced the cunning and unflappable Johnston with the impetuous John Bell Hood. Hood stood and fought before Atlanta on July 20 and 21, and was defeated and had to retire within Atlanta. Sherman invested the city, forced its evacuation on September 1, and occupied it the next day. On September 2, Sherman signaled Lincoln: "Atlanta is ours and fairly won." To the North, the enemy's greatest city had fallen. In southern lore, after victory was impossible and martyrdom was the objective, Atlanta was represented, in *Gone with the Wind* and elsewhere, as a Paris of the South wantonly desecrated and destroyed by northern war criminals. Sherman's rough-and-tumble notions of total war made such charges plausible. Sherman ordered Atlanta evacuated of civilians on September 7. Hood had ordered Confederate government buildings destroyed. Atlanta had only 14,000 people, but it was convenient to both sides to imply that it was a great metropolis. It was a rail and trans-shipment center and an important crossroads of the South, but the Lincoln reelection campaign represented its capture as breaking the back of the South.

The casualties of Grant's armies were not disguised from the public and were dismaying, and Lincoln, who was never overburdened by optimism, feared he might not be reelected. On July 4 he had pocket-vetoed (refused to sign) the Wade-Davis Bill, which proposed a radical and repressive reconstruction of the South and the treatment of its leaders as traitors. Lincoln had always planned as conciliatory an end as possible, as long as there was no ambiguity about the Union's victory and the South recommitted itself formally to the federal cause. Horace Greeley of the *New York Tribune*, an erratic man who at first had wanted to let the South go, published an attack upon Lincoln by the authors of Wade-Davis. Lincoln refused to allow uncertain electoral prospects to influence his conduct and ignored the obstreperous and insubordinate conduct of the radical members of his own party.

But it was clear that the Union was not far from victory. Sherman's seizure of Atlanta, signaling his intention to slice the South in two again, and Admiral Farragut's fine naval victory at Mobile Bay on August 5 ("Damn the torpedoes!" Farragut sank what was left of the Confederate Navy and landed soldiers who seized the last important Confederate Gulf port) again legitimized the Scott-Lincoln Anaconda strategy. Grant pinned down Lee while the naval constriction tightened and Sherman and Thomas tore the guts out of the Confederacy.

The Republican Party had met at Baltimore on June 7, and claimed to unite with the war Democrats and to call itself the National Union Party, as if it were a coalition. For this reason, Hamlin was not renominated for vice president, and was replaced by Andrew Johnson, the Tennessee Democratic senator who had remained loyal to the Union. Lincoln's slogan was "Don't change horses in the middle of the stream." The Democrats met at Chicago on August 29, and even though Sherman captured Atlanta while the convention was in progress, it adopted a "Copperhead" (defeatist and instant peace) platform seeking the immediate cessation of hostilities "on the basis of the Federal Union of the states," a preposterous flim-flam job. As their candidate to stand on this platform the Democrats chose General George B. McClellan, whom Lincoln had fired for not following up on his victory of Antietam. While McClellan claimed to disavow the feeble and cowardly platform, he certainly tried to exploit war weariness and pessimism. The tradition of a peace party had been carried with great integrity and rigor by De Witt Clinton for the Federalists against Madison in 1812, and by Henry Clay for the Whigs against Polk in 1844, but this was a dishonorable candidate standing on a dishonorable platform.

With that said, it must not be imagined that enthusiasm for the purposes of the war was universal. Attempts to conscript Union forces were not overly successful, and the armies were mainly filled by volunteers. There were four separate drafts, in July 1863, and March, July, and December 1864; but those allowed draftees to gain an exemption by paying $300 or recruiting a substitute. A total of 1,500,000 men were drafted, reduced by credits for having volunteered or having accepted alternate employment to 941,000, of which 776,000 were actually conscripted. Of these, 161,000, or 21 percent, failed to report, and 311,000 were exempted for physical or other reasons, another 38 percent; 87,000, or 11 percent, bought exemptions, and the number replaced by substitutes reduced the number of draftees who actually served to 43,000, or 6 percent. But 834,000 men volunteered, and the total number who served, as volunteers, substitutes, and draftees, was 997,000. At the first draft in July 1863, just 10 days after Gettysburg and Vicksburg, there were four days of draft riots in New York City, with widespread looting and the lynching of several African Americans, which required the infusion of several regiments of Meade's Army of the Potomac to restore order. The rioters were mainly Irish. While there were great working-class reservations about the war, and also by northerners with close southern connections, the response of volunteers was immense. The famous songwriter Stephen Foster composed a song about Lincoln's request for 300,000 men in 1863 with the refrain: "We're coming, our Union to restore; Coming Father Abraham, 300,000 more."

Lincoln's policy was hard-pressed at times, in the population, in the Congress, and in foreign capitals, but he always managed enough support to have the manpower to conduct the war, and enough success to prevent being shackled by radicals in his party and to deter direct foreign confrontations. His strategic management was masterly at every phase, as the secession crisis grew, as he split the Democrats in the debates with Douglas, took the Republican nomination from under the nose of Seward, arranged for the South to attack the Union, folded emancipation into the main war aim of preservation of the Union, and implemented Scott's strategy by identifying and promoting gifted commanders from well down in the ranks when the war began, all the while out-maneuvering domestic opposition and foreign scheming, and speaking and writing publicly of the country's war aims with unforgettable eloquence. So unassuming and free of egotism was he, that like a great circus performer, it was only obvious after he had left the stage how brilliant his strategic conceptions, command decisions, and tactical initiatives had been. That, coupled to the nobility of his cause, his infallible mastery of English, and his profoundly sympathetic personality, explains and justifies Lincoln's immense and universal prestige.

McLellan took Senator George H. Pendleton of Ohio for vice president, but by the time their convention adjourned, it appeared to be clear that Lincoln was winning the war and would win the election. And he was reelected, 2.218 million votes, including over 70 percent of members of the armed forces who voted, to 1.813 million. The overall margin was 55 percent to 45 percent. No one else had ever run for president of the U.S. in the middle of a war that had begun in his term, and it was a very respectable result. The only sequel would be Franklin D. Roosevelt in 1944, and he defeated Thomas E. Dewey by a slightly narrower percentage (though few members of the armed forces, 10 percent of the whole population, who would have voted strongly for Roosevelt, were able to vote (Chapter 11)).

6. THE END OF THE WAR AND THE DEATH OF LINCOLN

The election sounded the death-knell for the South. Sherman ordered that Atlanta be burned to the ground on November 7 (the day after the election), the city having been evacuated, but was persuaded by the city's leading Roman Catholic clergyman (Sherman was a semi-Roman Catholic and he had a son who became a Jesuit priest) to spare the city's churches and hospitals. It was still a dramatic, and for the South, traumatizing conflagration. It conformed to the grim and stern Lincoln-Grant-Sherman view that nothing less than a comprehensive and total defeat would eliminate in spirit as well as fact the vocation to independence of the South. Sherman departed the smoking ruins of Atlanta (about 70 percent of it was razed) on November 14 with 60,000 men stretched out on a front 60 miles wide, to march the 300 miles to the sea at Savannah. Sherman's orders were to "forage liberally on the land and destroy anything of military use to the enemy." Practically everything was destroyed—crops, buildings, roads, railways, bridges. Sherman occupied Savannah on December 22, having scorched to ashes and utterly destroyed most of Georgia. Savannah was not disturbed, and Sherman strictly reimposed discipline, having turned a blind eye to the most rapacious looting on the five-week march. The reality of what the war had become shocked even some northerners, startled the world, and profoundly shook what was left of southern morale.

Hood gave up fighting Sherman and moved to Sherman's west all the way back into Tennessee, thinking he might strangle Sherman's communications (not that it would have much mattered, as his armies took what they wanted on their route of march). It was a mad and desperate plan. Hood encountered Union general John Schofield in an engagement won by the Union, and then his errant, purposeless army came face-to-face with Thomas's seasoned Army of the Cumberland at Nashville, where Sherman had sent Thomas to rid him of Hood. Hood's army was completely destroyed and fragmented into disparate groups of stragglers and deserters and guerrillas. More than 20,000 Confederates were removed from the war in one way or another. Mississippi, Alabama, Florida, and Georgia were now separated from the Confederacy and Tennessee entirely occupied by the Union. The Confederacy was now reduced to Virginia and the Carolinas. Grant was south of Richmond and grinding Lee's army in the siege of Petersburg, and in the final phase of the Anaconda Plan, the dreaded Sherman turned north and drove into the Carolinas, wreaking even greater havoc than he had in Georgia. Lee reversed Davis's error and brought back the South's most talented general, next to Lee himself, Joseph Johnston, with the unenviable task of halting Sherman's juggernaut with much inferior forces. The Union navy employed amphibious forces to seize Fort Fisher and shut the port of Wilmington, North Carolina, in January and February 1865, and what was left of the Confederacy was racked by riots and demonstrations against shortages, speculation, skyrocketing prices, evaporation of income, and heavy casualties.

Sherman had eliminated South Carolina as a functioning state by the end of February and fought and won his last battle with Johnston at Bentonville, North Carolina, on March 19 and 20. But Johnston fought admirably and retired in good order despite Sherman's lack of reluctance, unlike Union generals earlier in the war, to give chase and set reserves on the retreating enemy. Grant's nine-month siege at Petersburg, as he had planned, had finally almost strangled Lee's army. Grant was deploying 115,000 battle-hardened veterans to Lee's 54,000, many of them new recruits. On April 1, Lee attacked at Five Forks, near Petersburg, but was repelled by Sheridan, and Lee had Davis called out of a church service and advised that he had ordered the immediate abandonment of Richmond and Petersburg. (At the Hampton Roads Conference on February 3, Lincoln himself met with Confederate vice president Stephens, an initial opponent of secession in 1861. Davis had instructed Stephens to insist on recognition of southern independence as a condition for peace, a mad delusion at this point, and the conference ended after a couple of hours.)

Davis fled his capital as Lee went to Lynchburg and prepared to try to embark his army, now reduced to 30,000 men, by rail to North Carolina to meet with Johnston for a final stand against the overwhelming encircling forces of Grant and Sherman. Grant moved like a cat on his trail and Sheridan blocked Lee's routes to the west and south. The Army of Northern Virginia was almost out of food and ammunition. Sheridan telegraphed Lincoln: "If the thing is pressed I think Lee will surrender." Lincoln instantly replied to Grant, quoting Sheridan's telegram and adding: "Let the thing be pressed"

Grant, his armies now sensing victory so keenly that, as he wrote, the infantry foreswore rest and rations and "marched about as rapidly as the cavalry,"[4] invited Lee to surrender. Lee asked for terms, and the two met at Appomattox Court House on April 9, 1865. As befits great generals and exemplary gentlemen, it was without histrionics or even negotiation, and was entirely courteous. They reminisced discursively about "the old army," and on request by Lee, Grant gave his terms and then wrote them, and Lee accepted straightforwardly. His army was now crumbling from famine and desertions, including the colonel, sole survivor of his regiment, and owner of the house where Grant was billeted, who dropped out near his home and surrendered personally to the Union commander. Grant permitted Confederate officers to retain their horses and sidearms and did not ask for prisoners. All weapons of war and ammunition were surrendered, the Army of Northern Virginia ceased operation, and all officers gave their word that no one would resume hostilities. The commander of the Union Armies ordered that 25,000 full rations be issued at once to their late and distinguished enemy. The Army of Northern Virginia self-demobilized and its survivors returned home, after visiting the Union quartermaster and commissary exactly as Union troops would. Grant ordered an end to what began as a 100-gun salute of victory, and ordered there be not the slightest gesture of exultation nor any act disrespectful of, as he put it, "a foe who had fought so long and valiantly, and had suffered so much for a cause, though that cause was, I believe, one of the worst for which a people ever fought, and one for which there was the least excuse."[5]

Johnston continued as best he could, but Sherman occupied Raleigh, North Carolina, on April 13. The Confederacy was almost entirely occupied and Johnston was effectively surrounded, and without ammunition or stores. He surrendered his army of 37,000 on April 17, despite the itinerant and deranged Davis's poor wail of appeal to continue. Sherman, as magnanimous in victory as he was remorseless in battle, gave his gallant and resourceful adversary even more generous terms than Grant had accorded Lee. (Sherman and Johnston became friends, and Johnston died 26 years later from pneumonia contracted from attending Sherman's funeral and burial, under-clothed for the raw northern weather. He was 84, 13 years older than Sherman, and he said Sherman would have done the same had the roles been reversed.)

The supreme figure of the great and terrible drama and providential redeemer of America, including the South, did not survive the war to win the peace. In what

---

4.   U.S. Grant, *Personal Memoirs of U.S. Grant*, New York, Charles L. Webster, 1885, p. 624.

5.   Ibid. p. 630.

many consider the greatest of all his oratorical triumphs, Abraham Lincoln said in his second inaugural address on March 4, 1865, that "The progress of our arms, upon which all else chiefly depends, is as well-known to the public as to myself and it is, I trust, reasonably satisfactory and encouraging to all. With high hope for the future, no prediction in regard to it is ventured. . . . Fondly do we hope, fervently do we pray, that this mighty scourge of war may speedily pass away" (a line of poetry). "Yet if God wills that all the wealth piled up by the bondsman's two hundred and fifty years of unrequited toil shall be sunk, and that every drop of blood drawn with the lash shall be paid by another drawn with the sword, as was said three thousand years ago, so still it must be said 'The judgments of the Lord are true and righteous altogether.' With malice toward none, with charity for all . . . let us strive on to finish the work we are in, to bind up the nation's wounds, to care for him who shall have borne the battle, and for his widow and his orphan, to do all which may achieve and cherish a just and a lasting peace among ourselves and with all nations."

This in the plainest and most powerful terms was Lincoln's strategy for America: the complete, unarguable, bone-crushing defeat of secessionism, and abolition of slavery, which he called "a peculiar and powerful interest," and the eventual determination that it is an evil that must be ended, for which purpose "He gives to both North and South this terrible war as the woe due to those by whom the offense came." Lincoln made no effort to restrain Sherman's depredations, but wished a generous peace of forgiveness and reconciliation. Lincoln was initially prepared to pay something to slaveholders for emancipation, to pick up some of the Confederate debt, and to readmit the southern states to the Union easily, as long as they pledged loyalty to the Union. He never regarded the insurgents as traitors. He knew that such a reconstituted Union would emerge immensely powerful, economically, militarily, and morally, that no power would ever dare to meddle in the Americas again, and that it would not be long before the Europeans, so complicatedly and finely balanced between themselves, would be soliciting America's assistance to one side or another there, rather than presuming to offer mediation and imagining the Americas were any rightful province of their interest.

The world was, indeed, appropriately awed by the ferocity of what was, if the various Revolutionary and Napoleonic Wars are divided up into a series of wars of shifting coalitions, the greatest war in the history of the world. The U.S. Civil War produced 360,000 Union and 300,000 Confederate combat deaths, about 90,000 civilian deaths, and approximately 475,000 wounded, military and civilian. The Union had almost four times the free population and twice as many combatants as the Confederacy, and roughly three-fifths of the 1.25 million total casualties, about 4 percent of the total free population, North and South, black and white, men, women, and children. No foreigners had foreseen the vehemence and fury of the struggle, or had imagined the emergent might of the victorious armies. Those who had thought America the light of the world, now knew it to be so. Those who had lamented the moral palsy of slavery behind the Jeffersonian message, rejoiced. And those who had doubted the strength, as opposed to the diplomatic agility, polemical talent, and geographic good fortune of the Americans and their leaders, saw the strength of the American people, of their devotion to their country and its ideals, and were struck almost dumb by the genius and humanity of their leader.

Lincoln visited Richmond on April 4, arriving by ship, first a flotilla, then the captain's launch, and finally, so heavy was the wreckage and mass of dead horses and undetonated torpedoes in the water, by rowboat. The conquering president was completely unruffled and found it reminiscent of the man who had come to ask him for a post of consul in a great foreign city and gradually scaled back his requests to humbler and humbler positions, and finally to the gift of a well-worn pair of trousers.[6] As he stepped ashore, many African Americans greeted him on their knees and Lincoln helped raise them up, and said "You must kneel to God only and thank him for the liberty you will hereafter enjoy." Demonstrating that he had never ceased to be the president of the United States, he walked two miles to Jefferson Davis's office, with security provided by a black regiment, and followed by a large and mainly black crowd of well-wishers, and was regarded from windows with neutral curiosity. He sat in Davis's desk chair without a hint of triumphalism, asked for a glass of water, and authorized the convening of the Virginia legislature, as long as it repealed the act of secession and removed Virginia's armies from the war (which were done). The butler said Mrs. Davis had told him, just two days before, to make the official residence ship-shape "for the Yankees."[7]

Apart from Lincoln's folkloric standing, his pure strategic achievements for the nation are rivaled among his predecessors only by Washington. The Union was impregnable, slavery's blight and shame had been erased as a bonus to suppressing the insurrection, and the United States was rivaled only by the British Empire and Bismarck's Prussia as the world's greatest power, and it had a hemisphere practically to itself. There was no balance of power in the Americas, only American power. Now the United States could receive floods of eager European immigrants, crank up its laissez-faire economy, and swiftly achieve an industrial scale of which the world had never dreamed. Lincoln (and Grant and Sherman) had severed the ball-and-chain

---

6.   Goodwin, *op. cit.*, p. 719.
7.   Ibid.

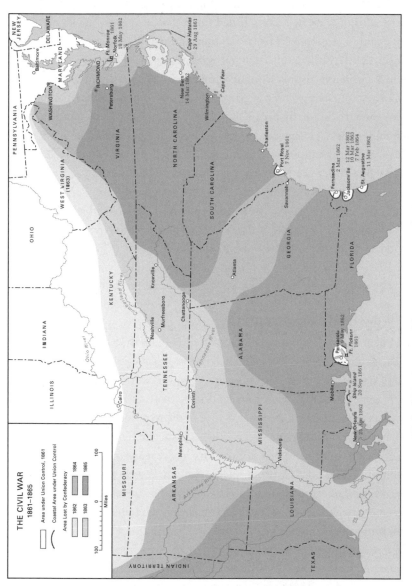

US Civil War. Courtesy of the U.S. Army Center of Military History

from the nation's ankle, and America could be America, and accelerate toward the summit of the world's nations.

As all the world knows, Abraham Lincoln was assassinated at Ford's Theatre in Washington on April 14, 1865, dying the following day. There is no need to emphasize further what he accomplished for America or expatiate much on his personal qualities, other than that he was then and remains the supreme and most deserving beneficiary of the American star system, surpassing even Washington. He was morose but never lost his sense of humor, proud but without vanity, utterly scrupulous without being a bit priggish or even above a political ruse, intellectual but down-to-earth, scholarly but an autodidact, the ultimate self-made man but without chippiness or aggression. He was always saddened and never angry at the betrayals and disappointments he endured, and was not worn down by a nagging wife or the premature death of two sons. He was, as the next great Republican president, Theodore Roosevelt, said, "Quiet, patient, mighty Lincoln," who lived and suffered, and died for the people and saved the Union by lending it his strength. Public grief throughout the North surpassed in universal intensity any such impulse in the history of the country.

A terrible ordeal was ending, a prolonged period of immense spontaneity and growth was about to begin. America was unbound, before a limitless horizon.

7. AMERICA AND THE WORLD

Vice President Andrew Johnson, who was discovered on the night of April 14 in a drink-taken condition (and had taken his oath as vice president in that condition the month before), assumed office. Seward, who was wounded in an attempt on his life that was part of the same plot by disgruntled southerners, recovered and continued as secretary of state for the balance of the term. As a Democrat who had only been 45 days the vice president, and as a self-taught Tennessean, Johnson was little-equipped to quell the designs of the forces of revenge in the North who had given Johnson's great predecessor problems enough. A great struggle loomed and soon began for the reconstruction of the country, but the almost vertical rise of America comparative with other states was practically a certainty. It had refurnished its reputation as the land of freedom and opportunity, and the policy of almost unlimited acceptance of immigration from Europe, which had assured the victory of the free over the slave states by swift population growth, and the steady westward movement of people and economic development guaranteed that the United States would soon assume an immense scale. Battles over reconstruction would retard the advance of the African American community and create constitutional frictions between the executive and legislative branches of the government, but nothing could now stop the inexorable and accelerating rise of America.

From 1865 to 1900, the population of the United States increased from 35 million to 76 million (while the British population increased from 24 million to 35 million, and the French from 38 million to just 39 million after losing two provinces to Germany), and America accepted over 13 million immigrants. Under the Homestead Act of 1862, 160-acre parcels of farmland were distributed virtually free to settlers, and the railway companies, which expanded geometrically across and all over the country, advertised in Europe for farmer-settlers and sponsored hundreds of thousands of them. The average per capita annual income of non-farm workers grew in this period by 75 percent, and the GDP grew in absolute terms by about 400 percent in those 35 years, net of inflation (which was minimal), and grew annually at an average rate of over 5 percent, gaining nearly 7 percent per year through the 1880s. These were unheard-of growth rates for a country that before it had even rebuilt the most war-damaged areas of the South was already the wealthiest in the world.

Corporate structures evolved creatively and capital markets grew wildly to accommodate this tremendous growth, fueled not just by immigration but by enhanced production techniques in adaptation of raw materials, such as steel refining, and by mass production to feed an ever growing and always more prosperous market. The United States was at the cutting edge of innovation in every field, and even as the frontier moved west and became more urban and orderly, it harnessed the spirit of boundless optimism and endless growth to those of predestined national greatness and the innate superiority of rampant American capitalism. It was well into the twentieth century before the United States started to entertain any notion of leveling the playing fields of commercial opportunity. From 1865 to 1900, railway mileage in the United States increased from about 32,000 miles to approximately 140,000 miles. Thanks in part to the Bessemer open-hearth process, American steel production increased in the same period from a few hundred thousand tons more than 30-fold to over 10 million tons, and more than doubled again to 24 million tons in 1910, by far the largest production of steel of any nation.

From 1789 to 1861, the United States was aspirant, vigorous, but fragile. From 1865 to 1900, it grew from one of the world's most important countries, with the British and newborn German empires, to a giant, with the same peers, but in no material sense subordinate to them. And it grew from the homogenization of the implacable problem of slavery and the new security of national unity, even with great human and physical carnage remaining to be removed and outgrown, to being a great power in the whole world—from a promising if insecure striver before the Civil War, and a stable but fatigued state after it, to a mighty incumbent growing with a force and speed and confidence that had neither parallel nor precedent, and promised to make the twentieth century a time of almost unimaginable expansion and achievement for America.

The period from 1865 to 1871 was also a time when most of the Great Powers of the coming hundred years reconfigured themselves. In this, too, America led by forcibly reenlisting dissentient parts and abolishing slavery, in 1865. In 1866, Bismarck's Germany humbled the Austrian Empire, established itself as the premier German state, and effectively forced the Habsburg Empire (which Webster had prematurely derided in the Hülsemann letter in 1851) to accept a dualist structure that made Austria and Hungary equal in the governance of the detritus of the Holy Roman Empire, which are today, apart from Austria and Hungary, the Czech Republic, Slovakia, and parts of Slovenia, Poland, Romania, Serbia, Croatia, Bosnia, and Italy.

In 1867, Canada, a string of British colonies and centrifugations from Britain, France, and America along the U.S. border, was formed into a self-governing affiliate state of Great Britain, pledged to cooperation between French- and English-speaking communities and to the construction of a trans-continental railroad that would be the basis for the settlement of a country as large, though it was unlikely to be as populous, as the United States. Canada would be a long time developing a strong and confident national personality, but in terms of resources it was as rich as the United States, with only a tenth of America's population. The foundation was laid for Canada to become, as it did in the last third of the twentieth century, one of the world's most important economies.

In 1868, Japan, shaken by Fillmore and Pierce's opening of its ports, peacefully underwent the Meiji Restoration, in which all governmental authority was reconstituted in the emperor, who had a universal mandate to take Japan into the world and ensure that its strength was adequate to repel the sort of Western imperialism and meddling that had so aggravated the Chinese. Japan swiftly rose to be one of the world's Great Powers and, next to the United States, the greatest in the Pacific.

In 1870, Italy, after 50 years of struggle and internecine conflict, ably led by Giuseppe Garibaldi and Camillo Benso, Conte di Cavour, got clear of the influence of the Austrians and the French (largely because of Bismarck's actions against both those powers), and confined the pope's influence to an entirely sectarian one, and became a united kingdom. Italy, too, joined the Great Powers, though not in the first rank. In 1870 and 1871, Prussia decisively defeated France, took Napoleon III prisoner at Sedan, and, after a heroic siege, occupied Paris and proclaimed the

Prussian Empire at the Palace of Versailles. The Bonapartes were finished, and France became a republic again, without Alsace and Lorraine, which Bismarck seized, but full of revanchist energy and cultural creativity. Beaten soundly twice in one lifetime, first by a British-led coalition and then by Prussia alone, with Bonaparte emperors chased out and Paris lengthily occupied both times, France had paid a heavy price for its political instability. The Battles of the Plains of Abraham and Waterloo, and actions in India had assured that there would be many times as many English- as French-speaking people in the world.

France remained a Great Power and magnetic culture, but was overshadowed by Prussia and would have an empire confined to Britain's leavings, unable to challenge Britain on the high seas and requiring allies to maintain its reduced territorial integrity opposite the great German army. Its primacy in the nearly two centuries from Richelieu to Napoleon I could not be retrieved. As long as Bismarck ruled in Berlin, France would be somewhat isolated, having squandered Richelieu's greatest bequest to France—the fragmentation of Germany, which both Napoleon and Metternich had conserved—but she would be a key ally in any counter-balancing coalition against Germany, of the kind the British could normally be relied upon to help to assemble.

Britain and Russia, the bookends of Europe, remained aloof from the fermentation in the midst of Europe and in North America. But in the realignment after 1871, the British and German Empires and the United States of America were the world's greatest powers, France and Russia were next, Japan, Austria-Hungary, and Italy after that. Spain and Turkey and China were in decline, and physically important and foreseeably of independent significance was Canada. For some time, leading Americans remained entirely aloof from this sort of consideration. The country grappled with the reconstruction of the South and did the necessary to facilitate breakneck economic and demographic growth. No power claimed a right of intervention in the Americas now, and the United States was not much interested, in any political way, with what it regarded as the tawdry and primitive squabblings of Europe, or the incomprehensible folkloric aberrations of the Orient. America had no rivals and no enemies, and had only to do what came naturally to it and what it did very effectively: admit the seekers of better lives from other lands, populate its interior, work hard, and grow with astounding speed into a Brobdingnagian giant among nations.

In less than a decade, the political maps of Europe and North America and the Far East were redrawn, but not, as in 1815, by agreement of the leading statesmen; rather by the competing policies and surging ambitions of statesmen. Where the European leaders after the Revolutionary and Napoleonic Wars joined to impose an agreed peace, 50 years into the Pax Britannica, Lincoln, Bismarck, Cavour, Palmerston, Thiers, and others (including the founder of Canada, the very capable John A. Macdonald) changed the world in consequence of less general wars and the riptides of international political trends and events. It was a process that could not be expected to maintain a general peace indefinitely, unless Britain and Germany could reach a comprehensive understanding to contain their natural rivalry. If they could not, the United States would ultimately hold the balance of power, whether it wished it or not.

8. RECONSTRUCTION

The problems of Reconstruction preoccupied the United States for about 15 years after the Civil War, without impeding its economic development or political integrity. Lincoln had contended that the Confederate states had never actually left the Union, as force of arms eventually confirmed, and stayed as free as he could of the "pernicious abstraction" of constitutional dogmas. Lincoln favored amnesty for all but a very few of the former rebels, as long as they took a firm oath of loyalty to the Union, and acceptance back into the full perquisites of statehood in all Confederate states where 10 percent of the residents who had voted in 1860 had sworn an oath of loyalty to the Union and the state had voted emancipation (which was, in any case, accomplished by constitutional amendment in December 1865). In the Wade-Davis Bill, which Lincoln had killed by non-signature in 1864, the Congress had sought to make readmission of states conditional on more than half the electorate taking such an oath. Arkansas and Louisiana had qualified for readmission under Lincoln's terms in 1864, but Congress refused to seat their representatives. The vindictive fervor of the Republican congressional leadership was inflated by fears of a revived Democratic Party that, it was assumed, would be more secure in the hearts of southern voters than ever after the Republicans had crushed the late effort to quit the Union. President Johnson, Tennessee Unionist Democrat, was now left like Tyler 25 years before without a party behind him (but he was a much more honorable and principled man than Tyler). He was in conflict from the start with the Radical Republicans who controlled the Congress. It was a difficult and unstable position from the beginning.

Starting on May 29, 1865, Johnson began to amnesty Confederates who took the loyalty oath, and well-to-do individuals and some other particular categories had to petition the president personally. He was generally quite obliging. He organized provisional governments for the remaining states that had seceded, and provisional governors were authorized to hold conventions of those who had been elected by those who had taken the oath. The conventions were expected to abolish slavery specifically and repudiate the states' war debt. By April of 1866, all states had complied and in his message to the Congress in December 1865, Johnson announced the restoration of the Union. The Republican congressional leaders, led by Thaddeus Stevens of Pennsylvania, had other ideas. They declined to endorse Johnson's actions and set up a committee of 15 (nine congressmen and six senators). Stevens considered the returning southern states to be "conquered provinces," and Senator Charles Sumner declared that they had "committed suicide." These men took the position that only the Congress could readmit states and determine the conditions required to do so.

On the other side, the old Confederate states set up stringent vagrancy and curfew laws to curtail the movement of African Americans and to negate as much as possible the consequences of their emancipation. Congress had set up the Freedmen's Bureau in March 1865 to assist emancipated slaves, and its activities were expanded to administer southern lands that had been abandoned in the wake of General Sherman's armies' devastating pass through Georgia and the Carolinas, and to provide military commissions to try those accused of restraining the rights of the emancipated in drumhead proceedings. Johnson vetoed these measures as ultra vires to the Congress in the absence of any state concurrence, and a violation of the Fifth Amendment requirement of due process for those whose military trial was proposed. The Congress overrode his veto in July 1866. In April 1866, Congress passed the Civil Rights Act, and confirmed it over Johnson's veto. The act affirmed the citizenship of former slaves, an apparently redundant procedure made necessary by the absurd and infamous *Dred Scott* decision. (Roger Taney had died in 1864, after 29 years as chief justice. And Lincoln had replaced him with Salmon P. Chase, who was closer in his views to Stevens than to Johnson.)

The Court eventually struck down the Civil Rights Act as unconstitutional, but the Fourteenth Amendment enabled the provisions of the act, and revoked the three-fifths clause of the Constitution, which had attributed more congressmen and electoral votes to the southern states. Congress made the ratification of the amendment a condition of readmission to the Union. Tennessee accepted these conditions and was readmitted, but the other southern states balked. The midterm elections in November 1866, partly in reverence for the late president, ironically, and partly on approval of the Stevens hard line against the South, gave the Republicans majorities exceeding two-thirds in both houses of Congress, from which almost the whole South remained absent. The first Reconstruction Act, passed over Johnson's veto in March 1867, divided the South into five military districts, which were deemed to be under martial law. To regain their status as states, the states of the South were to summon new conventions by universal suffrage of adult males, guaranteeing the freedom to vote of blacks and ratifying the Four-teenth Amendment. The subsequent Reconstruction Acts authorized the military to enroll the voters and to promulgate new state constitutions, regardless of the numbers of people participating. Johnson did as the new laws required, sending 20,000 soldiers and militiamen into the South, and 703,000 blacks and 627,000 whites were deemed to be voters. New conventions in the southern states met in 1868 and guaranteed black civil rights and disqualified ex-rebels from voting. By now only four southern states had not completed the readmission process. The Congress required them to ratify the Fifteenth Amendment to the Constitution, forbidding disqualification of voters for reason of race, color, or former servitude, and by 1870 they had done so.

In February 1868, the Congress, which had virtually taken over the authority of the executive branch by preventing the president from appointing Supreme Court justices and requiring that all military orders be subject to the approval of the commander of the army, and prohibiting the president from removal of officials confirmed by the Senate without approval of the Senate, impeached Johnson on 11 counts of defiance of the Congress and for bringing "disgrace and ridicule on the Congress." The effective cause was Johnson's dismissal of Secretary of War Edwin Stanton, a tiger whom even Lincoln sometimes had some difficulty restraining. (This was, in the abstract, preposterous, and Congress had managed to bring disgrace and ridicule upon itself.) Never was the tragic and untimely death of Lincoln more keenly felt. Johnson survived the spurious assault on May 16, 1868, on a vote of 35–19, one short of the two-thirds majority required for conviction. Johnson was inept at putting his case to the public, and suffered badly from being perceived as a southerner and a poor substitute for his illustrious predecessor, but he was, withal, the legitimate president who was trying to carry out Lincoln's policy and was, in every case, on the right side of the Constitution. The impeachment was a mockery and an outrage, saved from being a coup d'état only by the courage of a few senators and the fair conduct of the Senate trial by Chief Justice Chase.

In foreign affairs, Johnson had to deal with an invasion of Canada by a few hundred Fenian Irish Anglophobes at Niagara Falls in May 1866. This and a suc-cessive attack were easily repulsed by the Canadians, and the Fenian leaders were eventually arrested by U.S. border authorities. On February 12, 1866, which would have been Abraham Lincoln's 57th birthday, Seward delivered the French minister in Washington an ultimatum demanding the withdrawal of French forces from Mexico, after Johnson had dispatched General Sheridan at the head of 50,000 veterans of the Grand Army of the Republic to the Mexican border. Napoleon III

obediently abandoned the insane enterprise; his protégé Maximilian, the putative emperor of Mexico, bravely remained behind and was taken into custody
by the Mexican guerrillas led by Benito Juárez, and executed by firing squad on
June 19, 1867. This was a conspicuous humiliation for France, and illustrated
the distinction between Napoleon III, an uncalculating adventurer, and his uncle,
who led French arms from Portugal to Russia, and whose legend of conquest and
wise law-giving generated the nostalgic pride that enabled Napoleon III to win
election as president of the Second Republic, and recognition as France's second
emperor. In December 1866, Seward negotiated the acquisition of Alaska from
Russia for $7.2 million, a sum appropriated by the House of Representatives, with
the encouragement of generous bribes from the Russian minister in Washington,
whose government considered Alaska a costly liability of which they were well
quit. A U.S. Navy captain, William Reynolds, discovered Midway Island, 1,130
miles west of Hawaii, and claimed it for the United States. None could imagine
that its name would be immortalized 76 years later, as a decisive turning point in
the struggle for the Pacific in the greatest war in human history.

9. ULYSSES GRANT AS PRESIDENT

The Republicans met at Chicago in May 1868 and nominated General Ulysses
S. Grant for president almost unopposed, and House Speaker Schuyler Colfax of
Indiana for vice president, on a platform that repudiated Johnson and endorsed
the radical reconstruction of the South. The Democrats met in New York in July
and after 22 ballots chose former New York governor Horatio Seymour for president, and the former Union general Francis Blair of Missouri as vice president.
Seymour had opposed Lincoln as too belligerent in 1860, and had placated the
anti-draft rioters in New York in 1863. The Republicans "waved the bloody shirt"
and stood on Grant's prestige as supreme commander of the Union armies and
the just successor to Abraham Lincoln. Seymour, a benign but indecisive man, was
portrayed virtually as a traitor, and Blair did further damage to the Democrats with
a hysterical campaign against alleged Republican pandering to African Americans,
who were described as a "semi-barbarous race of fetishists and polygamists" who
would be unleashed, to subject white women to their "unbridled lust." Grant
won, by 3 million to 2.7 million, 53 percent to 47, and took 26 of 34 states, 214
to 80 electoral votes. In all of the circumstances, it was not an impressive victory
by Grant, and shows the innate moderation of a very large number of Americans,
toward both the Confederacy and the emancipated slaves. (As before the war,
Democrats had more sympathy for the southern whites than for blacks, and with
Republicans it was generally the other way round.)

Johnson departed Washington fairly unlamented, but had himself reelected U.S. senator from Tennessee—again, as in his impeachment trial, by only one vote in the state legislature; returned to Washington; and, after being left to languish for some time, finally got to give a stirring and plausible vindication of his public career and to warn about the state of Reconstruction in Louisiana. He was very warmly received in the Senate, including by some who had voted to impeach him as president, but he died soon afterward, in July 1875, aged 66. Andrew Johnson was an odd character, and far from an apt leader, but he stood for the Union in a secessionist state, and for reconciliation against a hurricane of mindless revanchism, and he was able to render some assistance to both fine causes. He was never tainted by the corruption that afflicted the post-Lincoln Republicans and always identified with the common people, of whom he was certainly an exemplar. William Henry Seward, Lincoln's closest collaborator and one of the founders of the Republican Party and a very able secretary of state in the difficult times of the war, who helped eject France from Mexico and bought the future state of Alaska, retired with distinction in 1869, ending an esteemed public career of 40 years.

Grant briefly appointed Lincoln friend and influential congressman Elihu Washburn as secretary of state, in which office he served only 12 days before retiring to become minister to France. He performed prodigies in this role, assisting in ending hostilities after the Siege of Paris at the end of the Franco-Prussian War. He was followed as secretary of state by Hamilton Fish, a distinguished lawyer, opening a new phase in American foreign policy management. Prior to the resolution of the Civil War, the United States, always sensitive to its position in the world as it made its way, alternated career foreign-service men (Jefferson, Monroe, J.Q. Adams, Buchanan) with powerful domestic politicians who could be relied upon to judge the compatibility of foreign policy objectives and domestic achievability (Randolph, John Marshall, Clay, Van Buren, Webster, Calhoun, Everett, Marcy, Cass, Seward). Now, unbound from the ambiguities of the slave interest and secure in the world's perception of the United States as a mighty and unified and rising nation, the powerful politicians were more often spelled by noteworthy lawyers, foreign policy being, it was imagined, reduced to mere negotiation of technical points in a demarcated world where the United States took what it wanted in its hemisphere and relations with other continents tended to be niceties of secondary importance. The Grant administration was little troubled with foreign affairs; Fish successfully negotiated the claims arising from British building and delivery of Confederate commerce raiders (the *Alabama*, etc.) for $15,500,000, far less than Sumner and the Radicals were seeking. The arbitration was something of an international-law pioneering act, as the tribunal included land-locked Switzerland, the new kingdom of Italy, and Brazil, an insignificant country in maritime terms. Grant's desire to annex the Dominican Republic was not ratified by even the cabinet, much less the Senate, and Fish had to make do with vague noises about the Monroe Doctrine. He did get compensation for the Spanish execution of some Americans on an arms-running ship to the Cuban rebels in 1873 and gained approval of a treaty with Hawaii assuring that no Hawaiian territory would be surrendered to a third power, in 1875.

The Grant administration funded the national debt; regularized specie payment and the circulation of paper money; frustrated a scheme to corner the gold market by Jay Gould and Jim Fisk, working with Grant's brother-in-law, a lobbyist whom the president repudiated; and prosecuted the graft-ridden regime of New York's Tammany Hall[8] boss, William M. Tweed. Grant set up the Civil Service Commission to reduce the excesses of patronage and sale of favors and services, but the first head of the commission resigned when his recommendations were ignored. Though the president's own probity was never at issue, he was unfamiliar with the antics of low-level political operatives, and scandal recurred in many places. When he ran for reelection in 1872, Grant replaced Vice President Colfax with Senator Henry Wilson as nominee, because Colfax was implicated in accepting stock from Credit Mobilier, a construction company formed to build the Union Pacific Railway, whose stock was used to encourage helpful politicians. Unfortunately, Wilson accepted stock as a gift from the same source as did, allegedly, rising Republican star congressman James A. Garfield of Ohio.

Grant was reelected in 1872 over the erratic publisher of the *New York Tribune*, Horace Greeley. Greeley began as a liberal Republican splinter nominee, complaining against corruption in the Grant administration, and about the continued Union Army occupation of the South, which was undoubtedly a very corrupt, and sometimes oppressive, regime. The Democrats also nominated him, but Greeley proved a naïve campaigner, prone to wild claims and easily embarrassed by some of the odd editorial positions he had taken over the years. His running mate, Missouri governor B. Gratz Brown, an old anti-slavery ally of Thomas Hart Benton and the previous Democratic vice presidential candidate, Francis Blair, further embarrassed the campaign with his conspicuous alcoholism, at one point in a campaign picnic trying to butter a watermelon. Grant stood as the victor of the war, a hero and a wise president untouched by the shortcomings of some of his

---

8. Tammany Hall was the headquarters of the New York City Democratic political machine into the second half of the twentieth century. Aaron Burr was one of the founders. It was traditionally an Irish American organization, but grew large Italian and Jewish branches also.

officials, and was massively supported by some of the lions of the private sector, including John Jacob Astor and Cornelius Vanderbilt. Grant won, 3.6 million to 2.8 million, 56 percent to 44 percent, 286 electoral votes to 86. (Greeley died after the election but before the Electoral College met, and his votes were scattered among Brown, future vice president Hendricks, and others.)

The secretary of the Treasury, W.A. Richardson, resigned in 1874 to avoid censure by Congress, and Grant intervened personally to prevent the conviction of his private secretary, General O.E. Babcock, for participating in an embezzlement scheme in the collection of tax on bottled liquor. The secretary of war, W.W. Belknap, resigned in 1876 to avoid impeachment for taking bribes in the sale of Indian trading posts. (The whole Bureau of Indian Affairs was honeycombed with corruption for many decades.) Apart from the repeated problems of lassitude over official conflicts of interest, it was a competent administration that allowed the country to get on with economic growth, pell-mell industrial expansion, and settlement of the West, despite the death of General George Armstrong Custer and 264 of his cavalrymen, killed at the Battle of the Little Big Horn on June 26, 1876, in the Black Hills of South Dakota, after 15,000 gold prospectors had invaded Indian territory. (This was effectively the last armed stand of the Indians.) The failure of the financial house of Jay Cooke in 1873 caused a financial panic that required about two years for a full recovery. But taxes and debt were both steadily reduced and Grant represented victory, peace, and prosperity. The Civil Rights Act of 1875 banned all racial discrimination, but in 1883 the Supreme Court ruled that the federal government had no ability to protect civil rights from the actions of individuals, as opposed to state governments, which did have such a right (but in the South were unlikely to use it). Federal efforts to protect the civil rights of African Americans now effectively stopped for almost 80 years.

10. THE 1876 ELECTION, HAYES, GARFIELD, ARTHUR, AND CLEVELAND'S FIRST TERM

In 1876, the leading Republican for the presidential election was the former Speaker of the House and senator from Maine, James G. Blaine, known to his followers after his nominating speech as "the plumed knight." He was a formidable figure, but was successfully smeared for alleged skullduggery with railway promoters, and the nomination went to General Rutherford B. Hayes, governor of Ohio. Congressman William A. Wheeler of New York was nominated for vice president. The Democrats chose Samuel J. Tilden, the distinguished reform governor of New York, and Senator Thomas A. Hendricks of Indiana. Even with large numbers of African Americans now voting in the South, the Democrats were assured of victory there because of the en bloc white adherence to the enemies of the Union Army and Radical Reconstruction. In the rest of the country, although there was a northern bias for the Republicans as the party of victory in war against the tawdry collection of Democratic doughfaces and defeatist Copperheads before and during the war, the large numbers of immigrants flooding into the great cities meant that the makings of Democratic victory were there for a strong candidate whose loyalty could not be impugned. General McClellan, the do-nothing army commander fired by Lincoln, had had the impudence to run against Lincoln on a defeatist platform in 1864; Horatio Seymour, who wanted a partial appeasement of the South in 1860, vocally criticized Lincoln's war policy, and placated the New York anti-draft rioters, was not a presentable candidate in 1868 against the commander of the Grand Army of the Republic (Grant). Greeley was a flake who first opposed the war and then urged all manner of will-o'-the-wisp ideas on Lincoln, and was not a serious candidate in 1872. But Tilden was a serious candidate. The Democrats won 14 of 16 presidential elections from 1800 to 1856 with variations of the Jackson formula of assuring but containing slavery and guaranteeing the Union. The Republicans won 14 of the next 18 elections as the party of the Union, victory, emancipation, and maximum economic growth. But many of those elections were not foregone conclusions, as most of the earlier Democratic victories were, as first the Federalists and then the Whigs collapsed and vanished. Once the Democrats got free of candidates tainted with ambiguity on the mighty cause of the Union, as McClellan, Seymour, and Greeley were, they won the South and could compete strongly in the rest of the country, and when they did not fall into the hands of factional leaders, ran closely with the Republicans, including in the five elections starting in 1876.

The election of 1876 would be seminal for the Union. Tilden won the popular vote, 4.28 million to 4.04 million. The Republicans contested the results in Florida, Louisiana, and South Carolina, and the Democrats contested Oregon. The three southern states were the only ones still under the control of the Radical Republicans, backed by the Union Army. In all the other states of the South, the Radicals had been jettisoned by the voters as the plundering and perversity of military-backed rule alienated the majority, even where substantial numbers of white voters were still unregistered. Debt levels had risen by several hundred percent in almost all of the southern states, though it must be said that large expenses were required, especially in Georgia and the Carolinas, to repair war damage. Almost all the southern states had set up school systems for African Americans and the regime of slavery had been replaced by one of segregation. Ironically, the elimination of the three-fifths rule from the Constitution, which had credited the southern states with three-fifths of the slave population for purposes of calculating the number of their congressmen and Electoral College members, was even more favorable to the South. Those states prevented the African Americans, though emancipated, from voting, and yet they were entirely counted for congressional districting and Electoral College purposes. As so often happens, those who seem to lose, win. The South could have negotiated as late as 1863, compensated emancipation and won the representation of the African Americans in the Congress and the Electoral College without allowing them to vote.

In 1876, Hayes would need all the contested electoral votes to be elected. The Constitution was ambiguous about counting the ballots: the vice president of the United States was to open the Electoral College ballots in the presence of both houses of Congress and the votes would then be counted. The Senate was Republican and the House Democratic, and each could be assumed to count in a partisan way. Congress navigated through the problem with an Electoral Commission, of five congressmen, five senators, and five Supreme Court justices, four designated in the bill, two appointees of each party. The fifth justice was to be chosen by the other four, and it was understood that it would be Justice David Davis, an independent, but he was chosen U.S. senator from Illinois and his place on the commission was taken by Republican appointee Joseph P. Bradley. Bradley had initially leaned to Tilden, who almost undoubtedly won the election, but finally, barely a week before Inauguration Day, came down for Hayes by refusing to "look behind the results," enabling Hayes to win the election 185 electoral votes to 184. The Oregon decision was undoubtedly correct, as the Democratic governor of Oregon illegally disqualified a Republican elector. But the southern results, based on Republican Reconstruction election boards rejecting large numbers of Tilden votes for extremely suspect reasons, despite the antics of Democratic "rifle clubs" to intimidate black voters, were probably unjust. (Such a counting problem would be addressed by legislation in 1887, giving the states the authority to determine where their electoral votes rightfully went.)

Tilden was a very distinguished and upright man and he agreed to abide by the decision, and carried his party with him, on condition that Hayes and his senior partisans agree to withdraw the armed forces from the South, name at least one southerner to the cabinet, and provide a generous allocation for internal improvements—physical reconstruction from war damage, in fact—in the southern states. Hayes also, a Union general and respected governor, was a man of integrity and honored his word to the letter. He appointed Joseph Key of Tennessee as postmaster general and withdrew all Union Army personnel from the South within two months of his inauguration. The era of "the carpetbaggers" and Union soldiers in the South, supporting African American officeholders, saw governments that varied in quality from place to place and that were sometimes pretty patchy and corrupt. It was a difficult aftermath to a terrible war, but the 1876 election result, though it contradicted democracy, was, due to the statesmanship of both candidates, but Governor Tilden in particular, an important step in the reunification of the national spirit. Henceforth, the South was solidly Democratic for the next 80 years, because the Democratic nominees always won, and when the Democrats controlled the Congress, approximately half of those years, the principal congressional committee chairmen, on the basis of seniority, were almost always southerners. For the losing side in such a bitter and protracted struggle, the South emerged, after a brief period of subjugation, with a very strong blocking position in the U.S. Capitol, and played it astutely, a new refinement to American federalism. Hayes appointed as secretary of state William Maxwell Everts, his counsel through the post-electoral struggle and one of the country's most eminent barristers, in the same tradition as the outgoing Hamilton Fish.

Grant is generally credited with promoting African American rights and almost wiping out the Ku Klux Klan, and restoring sound currency. He was ineffective in combating a severe recession in his second term and was too loyal to corrupt officials of his administration. His retirement was marred by a business failure in a company led by his son. Grant was wiped out financially, paying off the Vanderbilt family with personal mementos of his military career. Diagnosed with inoperable throat cancer, he completed his memoirs just before his death in July 1885, aged 63; they were published by his friend Mark Twain, had a huge critical and commercial success, and restored his family's fortunes. U.S. Grant is generally reckoned an outstanding general, an admirable man, and now, a moderately capable if uneven president.

The Hayes presidency was the most tranquil since that of John Quincy Adams. The Bland-Allison Act of 1878 required Treasury purchases of silver, but only at $2 million per month, which was not inflationary. Hayes alienated the Republican bosses of New York by suspending New York port customs collector Chester A. Arthur and his naval assistant, Alonzo B. Cornell, nominees of New York Republican boss Senator Roscoe Conkling. This and the president's scrupulous conduct of civil service hiring constituted a distinct advance in probity of government after the patronage free-for-all tolerated by the indulgent President Grant. Hayes also retained, by vetoing Democratic riders to appropriation bills, the right of the president to use the armed forces to assure fair congressional elections, frustrating southern Democratic designs to impose even more outrageous vitiations of electoral democracy in that region, not so much against the diminished Republican

Party of the South as against the few liberal Democrats who raised their heads in that unwelcoming post-bellum ambiance. The African Americans were already effectively excluded by a welter of poll taxes and literary tests.

In foreign policy, the only noteworthy developments were three 1880 treaties. Under the Samoan Treaty, the United States concerted with Samoan chieftains to keep Germany from construing Chancellor Bismarck's famous claim to "a place in the sun" as entitling it to take over Samoa. The U.S. assumed some non-exclusive rights and set up some facilities in the port of Pago Pago. In the Madrid Convention, the United States joined European powers in restricting extra-territorial rights of Moroccans; the French and Germans were already maneuvering competitively in and around Morocco. Hayes made the minimal response politically possible to complaints about Chinese immigration, replete with wails of alarm over the "Yellow Peril" and so forth, with the Chinese Treaty, which amended the existing arrangement and gave the U.S. the right to "regulate, limit, or suspend" but not terminate the right of Chinese laborers to emigrate to the United States. In light of the unusual nature of his election, President Hayes had foresworn reelection and as was his custom, adhered to his word. He was an unexciting but competent and respectable chief of state. For the purposes of this book, he followed the sensible strategy of the era, reduced internal tensions, modestly cleaned up government, and by benign passivity facilitated the meteoric rise of the population, prosperity, and industrial might of America; in his way and time, an almost ideal president. He and Tilden showed that America, despite the horrible war and heavy-handed occupation of a third of the country and the corruption that abounded, retained what George Orwell would call, in another time and country, a government of decent men.

The Republicans met at Chicago in June 1880, and the convention became a battle between the "stalwarts," by which was meant those who wanted to take office again waving "the bloody shirt" of war and Union, fading a bit after 15 years, as a cover for relatively self-interested and patronage-tainted government, and the reformers. Senator Roscoe Conkling led the stalwarts, though he knew he would not be a presentable candidate for president himself, and championed a return to the piping days of the indulgent hero, U.S. Grant. Their chief opponent, though he was a tarnished reformist candidate because of his alleged coziness with railroad promoters, was the former Speaker James G. Blaine. A third candidate, and a more authentic reformer by the probity of his conduct, was Treasury secretary John Sherman, who made a subliminal appeal to the perpetual warriors because of his iconic warrior brother, the scourge of the South, General William Tecumseh Sherman. The general summarized his career in the famous words "It is only those who have neither fired a shot nor heard the shrieks and groans of the wounded who cry aloud for blood. War is hell." When approached about succeeding Grant as Republican presidential candidate, Sherman replied with his usual lack of ambiguity: "If nominated I will not run, and if elected I will not serve." He would have been a more a capable executive than Grant, whom he always refused to upstage, having said: "Grant stood by me when I was crazy, and I stood by him when he was drunk, and now we stand by each other."

The convention see-sawed between the three candidates for 35 ballots, but Blaine and Sherman withdrew in favor of Major General James Abram Garfield of Ohio (who was Sherman's campaign manager) on the 36th ballot and he was nominated. Born in a log cabin in Ohio, a scholar and classics lecturer at Western Reserve Eclectic College, he was a widely respected general, with a distinguished combat record, especially at Shiloh, and had been Rosecrans's chief of staff. Garfield was a somewhat radical but very scrupulous and independent-minded nine-term congressman, and was elected by the Ohio legislature to be a U.S. senator in 1880, having succeeded Blaine as minority leader of the House of Representatives. He thus ran for president as congressman and senator-elect. As a sop to the stalwarts, Garfield chose Chester A. Arthur, whom Hayes had fired as New York customs collector, for vice president. The Republican platform was a pastiche: tariff protection for industry, civil service reform, veterans' benefits, and restrictions on Chinese immigration, all pretty superficial tangible or policy payoffs to different voting blocs.

The Democrats met at Cincinnati later in June and nominated General Winfield Scott Hancock for president and former congressman William H. English, a Democratic opponent of Buchanan and Douglas over "popular sovereignty" before the war, for vice president. The Democratic platform was practically identical to the Republican, though it sought a tariff for revenue only, as opposed to protection of American industry. Hancock was a military hero of the Mexican War and the Civil War, named after the man who was his Mexican War commander and for 15 years commanding general of the U.S. Army, and who lived to see his namesake a hero of Gettysburg and very admired corps commander of the Army of the Potomac. Hancock's General Order 40 in 1867, restraining military intervention in Louisiana home rule, made him popular in the South, while his steadfastness as a Union commander made him a hero throughout the North. Garfield ran the first front-porch campaign and it was clearly going to be a very close election, as had been 1876. The popular vote, with no significant disputed ballots anywhere, was the closest in U.S. history: 4.453 million for Garfield to 4.444 million for Hancock, and according to some counts, the margin was as low as 2,000. The

Greenback Labor Party polled 300,000 votes for James B. Weaver of Iowa, on a platform calling for protection of labor rights and issuance of increased volumes of paper money. The electoral vote was 214 for Garfield to 155 for Hancock. It could not have pushed the election to Hancock, as Weaver only made the difference in Indiana. Hancock graciously attended Garfield's inauguration and continued to serve in the army, from which he had only taken a leave of absence, and was still commander of the Atlantic District, headquartered on Governor's Island, New York, when he died, not yet 62, in 1886. He also served as president of the National Rifle Association. (This would be the last election won by a Republican without the adherence of California until George W. Bush in 2000.)

The main issue in Garfield's presidency was the continuing struggle with the stalwarts. Garfield appointed Blaine secretary of state, and then affronted Conkling by appointing a Conkling opponent, William Robertson, as port collector in New York. Conkling and his fellow stalwart New York senator, Thomas Platt, blocked the appointment until May and then resigned as senators, but were not reelected by the New York legislature. This was a considerable victory for Garfield, who had spoken supportively of civil service reform in his inaugural address. Garfield had begun well, but was shot by a disgruntled office seeker, Charles J. Guiteau, on July 2 at the Washington railway station, and died on September 19.

Chester A. Arthur became president amid national misgivings that he would be a stalwart front for renewed corruption, but he determined to govern differently to what had been forecast. Most of Garfield's cabinet retired, including Blaine, and former senator from New Jersey Frederick T. Frelinghuysen became secretary of state. Both Blaine and Frelinghuysen were in the tradition of party barons who brought some domestic political influence, rather than any demonstrated foreign policy expertise, to the office. Robert Lincoln, the late president's son, continued to serve, as he had Garfield, as secretary of war. Most of Arthur's other appointees were not identifiable stalwarts either. Arthur appointed a Tariff Commission and successfully championed its support of tariff reductions; pushed through Garfield's civil service reform, in the Pendleton Act of 1883, which required civil service examinations and apportionment of offices according to the populations of states; made a strenuous effort to separate civil service appointments from the flow of campaign funds; and supported the building of a modern, steel-hulled United States Navy, starting with three modern heavy cruisers.

It continued to be a quiet time in foreign affairs; Blaine had made various unsuccessful efforts to mediate disputes between Chile, Bolivia, and Peru, between Costa Rica and Colombia, and between Mexico and Guatemala, and his invitations to a peace conference were canceled by his successor. Arthur had a full exchange of embassies with Korea in 1882, and the United States signed the Geneva Convention on the treatment of the wounded. The U.S. agreed with the establishment of the Meridian at Greenwich in East London and with the abolition of the slave trade in the Congo in international conferences on those subjects in 1884. Pax Britannica quieted the whole world and America's corner of the world was preternaturally quiet.

Arthur was suffering from Bright's disease and was not well, but signified his desire to be renominated in 1884. He was passed over in favor of Blaine, but left office widely respected, even by such skeptics as Mark Twain, as an honest and capable leader. He died less than two years later, aged 56. Blaine took as his running mate a former Illinois senator, General John A. Logan (making this the 10th consecutive election and 15th of the last 16, and 21st of the 25 in the country's history, in which a senior military officer would receive electoral votes for national office).

The Democrats met in Chicago a month after the Republicans and nominated New York governor and former Buffalo mayor Stephen Grover Cleveland for president, and former governor and senator Thomas A. Hendricks of Indiana for vice president. The ensuing campaign was one of the most unsavory and irresponsible in American history. The Democrats claimed that correspondence they flourished about proved Blaine's corrupt arrangements with railway lobbyists while Speaker of the House. The Republicans accused Cleveland of having, while a bachelor, fathered an illegitimate child, which he acknowledged. Reform Republicans led by Edwin L. Godkin of the *New York Post*, Carl Schurz, leader of the German Americans of Missouri and a former U.S. senator, and Charles Francis Adams Jr. defected from Blaine to Cleveland. Tammany leader and New York boss John Kelly deserted Cleveland, but Samuel D. Burchard, a leading New York Protestant clergyman, called upon Blaine and denounced the Democrats as the party of "rum, Romanism, and rebellion." This stampeded New York's Irish and Italian communities back toward Cleveland, who carried his home state of New York by 1,149 votes out of 1,125,000 cast in the state, and won the election, 4.91 million votes to 4.85 million for Blaine, and 219 electoral votes to 182. New York swung the election, even more dramatically than Van Buren's spoiler vote against General Lewis Cass had done in 1848.[9]

---

9. Cleveland would prove a durable presidential figure, as would a succession of those who followed him. In the 31 presidential elections from 1884 to 2004, a candidate bearing the name Cleveland, Bryan, Roosevelt, Nixon, Dole, or Bush would win electoral votes to national office in 27 of them and be elected in 17 of them, on 12 occasions as president.

Vice President Hendricks died in November 1885, and two months later presidential succession was changed to go, in the event of the vacancy of the presidency and vice presidency, to cabinet members in the order of the creation of the departments, starting with the secretary of state. For that post Cleveland had selected longtime Delaware senator and former antiwar Democrat Thomas F. Bayard. He had had little foreign policy background, but again, there was little foreign policy to be formulated. Taxes levied to pay for the Civil War continued in place and generated large budget surpluses. Cleveland proposed tariff reductions but was rebuffed by Congress. Cleveland did accelerate the naval construction program and within 15 years the United States had the third navy in the world, after Britain and Germany. The Interstate Commerce Act of 1887 addressed problems of exploitation by railways of monopolies and regulated price schedules, with reasonable latitude to railway companies. Cleveland vetoed army pensions that were just pay-offs to the veterans' lobby, subsidized state agricultural scientific research, and repealed the Tenure of Office Act, which had been the basis of the impeachment of Andrew Johnson. Cleveland initially approved the return of captured Confederate battle flags to the Confederacy, but then rescinded approval, an issue the Republicans, ever ready to seize on any pretext for reviving the now tired glories of the Civil War, amplified in a completely irresponsible manner. By treaty with Hawaii, the U.S. gained the right to a fortified naval base at Pearl Harbor in 1887, and frictions with Britain and Germany over Samoa continued, with Britain aligning itself alternately with the other two, and all three retaining a naval presence there. Disputes with Canada over fishing in the Bering Sea and elsewhere led to some friction, and the Bayard-Chamberlain Treaty of 1888, though rejected by the Republican-led Senate, gave the Americans some rights in Canadian ports that had been ceded by the British, who retained control over most Canadian foreign relations.

In June 1888, Cleveland was renominated at St. Louis, and chose the 74-year-old former Ohio senator Allen Thurman as his running mate. Two weeks later, the Republicans, meeting in Chicago, chose former Indiana senator Benjamin Harrison, grandson of the ninth president, as their presidential candidate, and the wealthy former congressman and minister to France Levi P. Morton for vice president. (Morton had declined the vice presidency in 1880, thus passing on the succession to Garfield, but Garfield's assassin, Guiteau, was allegedly miffed that Morton had been named minister to France in preference to him.) The sole substantive issue in the election was the tariff, which Cleveland wished to reduce. The Republicans were massively financed and did their best with promises of increased veterans' (of the Union Army) pensions, and the nonsense about the Confederate flags. The British minister, Sir Lionel Sackville-West, unwisely answered a letter falsely claiming to be from a naturalized Englishman seeking advice on how to vote, with the insinuation that Cleveland would be better for British interests. The Republicans pulled this canard out of the hat on October 24 and the minister was expelled from the country the same day, but the Republicans made a good deal of hay out of it. For the third time in four elections, the Democrats won the popular vote, 5.54 million for Cleveland to 5.44 million for Harrison, and also for the third time in four elections the Republicans won anyway, 233 electoral votes to 168, as Harrison surprisingly won Cleveland's home state of New York by 14,373 votes out of 1.32 million cast, taking its 36 electoral votes. Once again, as in 1848, 1880, and 1884, New York state swung the election.

Cleveland had been another good president and he was not through yet. Nor was the Plumed Knight, James Gillespie Blaine, back again as secretary of state as the United States continued its serene ramble toward world power on the wings of rails and steel (assisted by naval construction), adding 7 percent annual economic growth and half a million new immigrants a year. Its population, at 62 million, had almost doubled in the 24 years since the end of the Civil War; in the lifetime of the narrowly defeated vice presidential candidate, Allen Thurman, it had multiplied eight-fold. It was all happening exactly as Franklin had foretold to his British friends a century before. The vertical rise of America was seen by all astute observers, including Europe's two greatest statesmen, Germany's Chancellor Bismarck and Britain's Prime Minister Salisbury, as the preeminent geopolitical phenomenon of the world. In London and Berlin and elsewhere, the comparative strength of the country moved appreciably according to the expertise of government policy. The ascent of America, like the system itself, was from the bottom up, like a volcano; the identity of the leaders, since the end of the great crisis of the Union, was almost incidental, and no one knew what mighty power remained unseen, constantly accumulating, below and within this amazing country.

Theodore Roosevelt

CHAPTER SEVEN

A New Great Power in the World, 1889–1914

1. BENJAMIN HARRISON

The presidency of Benjamin Harrison was one of the least eventful in the country's history. The administration attempted to deliver for its constituencies and against its opponents. It produced another Force Bill, which would enable federal invalidation of measures designed by white southern Democrats to prevent the emancipated slaves and other African Americans from voting. The bill cleared the House but the southern Democrats already had enough votes in the Senate to prevent its passage there.

What Abraham Lincoln called "the bondsman's 250 years of unrequited toil" was to be replaced by a century of segregation, an interim regime of separation and inequality, subordinacy but not slavery, in the South and much of the North. As the reassertion of white control in the South occurred (and not by antebellum patricians like Thomas Jefferson and Robert E. Lee, rather the gritty southern petty bourgeoisie and soon-to-be-infamous "white trash" of southern life, the elements most fearful of black emancipation and equality), large numbers of southern African Americans began to move to the great cities of the North and Midwest. They weren't well-received or instantly successful there either, but segregation was less severe and there was no hint of a deprived proprietary interest in the attitude of whites, but increasingly one of suspicion and disrespect. The route up from slavery, despite the bloodbaths already endured, would be slow and steep, long into the future.

The administration had greater success with its payoff of the "old soldier" vote. The Dependent Pension Act of June 1890 assured the pension to anyone who served 90 days in the Union armed forces who was disabled, mentally or physically, in combat or after, regardless of the reason, as well as to minor children, dependent parents, and working widows. In this presidential term, the annual cost of pensions rose over 60 percent, from $81 million to $135 million, and the number of pension recipients increased by 1895, contra-intuitively, given that the Civil War had then been over for 30 years, from 676,000 to 970,000. The veterans' associations of the Grand Army of the Republic were, in fact, a well-paid front organization for the Republican Party. It was the tangible response to Lincoln's call "to care for him who shall have borne the battle, and for his widow and his orphan," and it began the service pension, whose legitimacy in the United States would not be questioned again.

The Sherman Anti-Trust Act of July 1890 was a gesture to placate concerns about outright monopolies being created in various industries and charging what the traffic would bear to an exploited American public, while often applying wanton economic muscle to the management side of labor relations. The act declared to be illegal "Every combination . . . trust . . . or conspiracy in restraint of trade or commerce among the several states" or internationally. The federal government was authorized to move legally to dissolve trusts (monopolies), which now controlled the oil, whiskey, sugar, and lead industries, among others. This act mirrored similar initiatives in many of the states and responded to well-founded public concern about the dangers of exploitation of customers and employees. But there was no definition in the act of any of its key terms, and until the practice was established of pursuing authentic concerns, it bore the character more of tokenism than of reform. From 1890 to 1901 only 18 suits were launched under the act, and four of those were against labor unions. Showing their customary ingenuity, American industrialists and corporate lawyers quickened their pursuit of monopoly control of whole industries with holding companies, pooling agreements, informal price-fixing or geographic demarcations, or, as in the glass and aluminum industries, concentration of patent rights.

There was a severe decline in agricultural prices, due partially to protectionist activity by principal trading countries, including the McKinley Tariff of 1890 (guided through Congress by William McKinley of Ohio), which raised tariffs to 49.5 percent, and western agrarian and silver-mining interests only approved that tariff in exchange for concessions to the silver-mining industry. Under the Sherman Silver Purchase Act of July 1890, the federal treasury was obligated to buy 4.5 million ounces of silver per month at current prices, and pay for them with notes convertible into gold or silver at the Treasury's option. This was a form of inflation to combat recessive economic conditions and to spread money around an aggrieved (and normally Republican) area in the West and Southwest. These conditions gave rise to great discontent in the agrarian areas of the West and South, and a good deal of political fermentation, including efforts to unite militant farm and labor organizations in what became known, and persisted intermittently for more than 50 years, as the Populist, or Progressive, movement.

The foreign policy concerns of the Harrison administration were also less than earth-shaking. Cleveland had dispatched commissioners to a conference in Berlin about Samoa. Like most aspects of U.S. foreign policy in this time, it was a somewhat absurd episode. Cleveland told the Congress (January 15, 1889) that the matter was "delicate and critical," but two months later a feared naval confrontation between the U.S., Germany, and Great Britain was avoided when the combatant ships were overwhelmed by a hurricane in Apia harbor, destroying the German and American ships (three each) and sparing only the British vessel. (Had there been an exchange of fire in harbor, the collateral damage would have been considerable, but it is not clear at whom, if anyone, the British warship would have been firing.) In June 1889, it was agreed in Berlin that Samoa would be "independent and autonomous," but with a three-power protectorate and an agreed "adviser" to the king of Samoa.

Blaine's first International American Conference met in Washington starting in October, 1889. All the Latin American countries except the Dominican Republic were present. (Canada was not.) Blaine's proposals for a customs union and a dispute-resolution mechanism were not accepted, but the International Bureau of American Republics, which became the Pan-American Union, was established as a permanent office for exchange of information.

There were opera bouffe incidents with Italy and Chile. Following a trial of Mafia suspects in New Orleans in October 1890, which led to acquittals, a mob broke into the city jail in March and lynched 11 detainees, including three Italians. Blaine deplored the actions but rejected Italy's demand for indemnity and prosecution of the mob, as it was a State of Louisiana matter. Both sides withdrew their ambassadors and made unfriendly noises, but the incident was resolved by a payment of $25,000 in April 1892. The rebels in the Chilean civil war of 1891 sent a vessel to San Diego to collect arms and munitions. The ship was intercepted and escorted back to San Diego, but then released, as there was no violation of the Neutrality Act (which did not apply to civil wars). The rebels won the war and American sailors on shore leave were attacked by a mob at Valparaiso in October 1891, and two American sailors were killed. A public exchange of acerbities and demands ensued, and Blaine threatened a total breach of diplomatic relations and Harrison in his message to Congress in January 1892 virtually threatened war. The Chileans thought better of this and apologized, and paid an indemnity of $75,000 to close the incident.

Alone among the world's Great Powers, the United States had no serious business to conduct diplomatically. It stood noisily on its dignity when offended in the Americas or the Pacific, and could always extract an unembarrassing resolution of small matters, but rarely intersected in any significant way with another important country. In 1892, a dispute developed between the United States and Great Britain over seal hunting in the Bering Strait, separating Alaska from Russia. The problems had started when Americans accused Canada of poaching in 1886. After a sharp exchange of notes with Great Britain, a power that could not be as lightly treated as Chile or even Italy, the matter was referred to an international tribunal of French, Swedes, and Italians, who decided, establishing a long tradition of European resentment of American assertions of sovereignty, that the Canadians and British were right, and the United States eventually (in 1898) paid an indemnity of $473,000. These were terribly trivial matters compared with Bismarkian maneuverings, the revanchist agitations of France, Britain's tenacious hold on the delicate balance of power, and Japan's muscle-flexing in the Far East. James G. Blaine had retired as secretary of state for reasons of poor health in 1892, and was succeeded by John W. Foster, a respected career diplomat, whose son-in-law and grandson, Robert Lansing and John Foster Dulles, would also be secretaries of state.

The 1892 election season was riven by the Populist campaign, led by James B. Weaver, who had almost held the balance between Garfield and Hancock in 1880 and was nominated for president in St. Louis in February 1892. Farm prices were still depressed and there had been widespread labor disturbances in 1892, especially the Homestead Strike in July, in which seven people were killed at a Carnegie Steel plant in Pennsylvania, and Carnegie's manager, Henry Clay Frick, was attacked and wounded in a plot led by socialists Alexander Berkman and Emma Goldman. The platform was a recession-born mish-mash of Know-Nothingism and Progressivism. It included calls for expansion of the money supply by $50 per capita (which would have been spectacularly inflationary), unlimited issuance of silver coinage, sharp curtailment of the private banks, nationalization of the rail and telegraph and interstate shipping systems, a graduated income tax, direct election of U.S. senators (instead of by the state legislatures as the Constitution had provided), a referendary form of government, shorter working hours for all categories of labor, and restricted immigration. It was, as such movements often are, a mixed bag of enlightened and reactionary and quirky policies.

The Republicans met at Minneapolis in June, and renominated President Harrison and chose Whitelaw Reid of New York (editor of the *New York Tribune* and a friend and protégé of Horace Greeley) for vice president. (Harrison blamed Levi Morton's mismanagement of the Senate for failure to pass the Force Bill reenfranchising African Americans in the South and sought a change of vice presidents. Morton returned to private life and, apart from one term as governor of New York, soldiered on in ever-increasing prosperity to his death in 1920 on his 96th birthday.) The Democrats met at Chicago two weeks later and renominated Grover Cleveland, the party's candidate for the third consecutive time, with Adlai E. Stevenson of Illinois for vice president. (Stevenson, as Cleveland's first-term assistant postmaster general, had made himself a beloved figure to Democrats by firing 40,000 Republican postal workers and replacing them with southern Democrats. His name would be made more famous by his grandson, who ran two stylish (but unsuccessful) campaigns for president in the 1950s, partly singling out for attack the foreign policy of Secretary of State John W. Foster's grandson, John Foster Dulles.) The main issue was again the tariff, with Cleveland vaguely proposing reductions.

On election day, Cleveland won 5.54 million votes to 5.19 million for Harrison and 1.03 million for Weaver, 46 percent to 44 percent to 9 percent. (The Prohibitionists gained 271,000 votes, as alarm at alcoholism was becoming quite vocal.) McKinley's tariff and economic conditions generally in agrarian areas cost Harrison the election, as most of the Weaver voters were natural Republicans. Grover Cleveland was about to become the only person in American history to have non-consecutive terms as president. The outgoing secretary of state, John W. Foster, had had a foreign policy background and prior to that, the last secretary who could make this claim was Buchanan, who had been secretary of state under Polk. Since then, the holders of the office had been beneficiaries of political payoffs by the president to powerful faction heads (Clayton, Webster, Everett, Marcy, Cass, Seward, Washburn, Blaine, Frelinghuysen, Bayard), or had been prominent lawyers (Black, Fish, Everts). Cleveland followed now in both traditions, first with Walter Q. Gresham, who had been Arthur's postmaster general and secretary of the Treasury, before becoming an appellate judge and defecting to Cleveland and the Democrats. When Gresham died in 1895, Cleveland would select Richard Olney, a former attorney general, best known for taking injunctive action against the Pullman strikers in 1894. In these times, even the Democrats were closer to the capitalists than to the workers, and unions were looked upon as un-American radicalism. Benjamin Harrison had been a mediocre, but not a bad, president. He is one of the more forgettable figures to hold that office, but executed it with more distinction than Pierce or Buchanan, and than several of his eventual successors.

2. CLEVELAND'S SECOND PRESIDENCY

The U.S. economy was rocked by a new perturbation when the London merchant bank Barings failed and there was a disorderly unloading of American securities, causing a stock market crash with some panic selling, aggravated by a reduction in federal government revenues from reduced imports attributable to the McKinley Tariff and the increased expenses of the selective welfare system provided by the engrossed military pension scheme. U.S. gold reserves descended below $100 million on April 21, 1893, and declined further to $80 million in October. Nearly 500 banks and about 15,000 commercial institutions failed in 1892–1893. By 1897, one-third of railway mileage was in the hands of receivers. Amidst these tidal changes, Darwinian upheavals occurred in the economic well-being of millions, but nothing undermined the inexorable advance of the size of the American economy.

Cleveland determined to stop the diminution of gold reserves and summoned a special session of Congress for the summer of 1893, which repealed the Sherman Silver Purchase Act. This was a bitter battle that split his party (the Democrats) almost as grievously as Douglas had done with the Kansas-Nebraska Act and "popular sovereignty" in 1854. Gold reserves dipped to $41 million and attempts to float bond issues failed. Cleveland called on legendary financiers J. Pierpont Morgan and August Belmont, who underwrote a $62 million issue, on which they trousered a $7 million profit. The Populists and bimetallists became very agitated, and when that facility expired, reserves dipped again to under $80 million. The administration did float a public issue directly and confidence in the inviolability of the gold standard hovered through the 1896 election and then revived strongly.

The advocates of silver, bimetallists, took the agrarian and working classes out from under the more conservative Democrats, especially in the East and South, and after the period from 1876 to 1892 when the Democrats won the popular vote in four elections out of five, and only lost in 1880 by 7,000, the political landscape shifted again. Just as the ability of the Republicans to win by waving the "bloody shirt," quoting Lincoln, and paying off everyone related to a Union army or navy veteran was groaning to an end, they attached themselves like limpets to hard money, pure capitalism, individual enterprise, the ruggedness of the American spirit, and the alleged clear path to patriotism and godliness. There were great agitations by groups of unemployed, often calling themselves "armies." Coxey's Army, led by Jacob Coxey of Massillon, Ohio, called for a march of the unemployed on Washington in late 1893. In April, about 400 of them had arrived and they presented a petition calling for a job-creating public works program to dispense up to $500 million. Coxey and his chief collaborators were arrested for trespassing at the Capitol and the movement dispersed and disintegrated. American confidence in the inexorable rise of their country and the invincible strength of meritocracy was not going to be shaken easily. The mighty engine of growth soon resumed and swept up most of the malcontents in its train.

American economic and demographic growth was astounding throughout the period from the Civil War to 1929, but it moved in lurching fluctuations, and unevenly between industrial sectors. What grew consistently was the Gross National Product of the country and the per capita income derived from it, but within those exhilarating surges, there were sharp graphic changes in all directions. Consumer prices (1910–1914=100: Warren-Pearson Wholesale Price Index) moved from the end of each administration: 1865 (Lincoln) 132; 1869 (Johnson) 97.7; 1877 (Grant) 56; 1885 (Arthur) 56.6; 1897 (Cleveland) 46.6; 1901 (McKinley) 56.7; 1909 (Roosevelt) 70; 1913 (Taft) 70; 1921 (Wilson) 154; 1923 (Harding) 100.6; 1929 (Coolidge) 95.3. Throughout this time there were huge accretions of industrial capacity and output, and the price fluctuations did not necessarily imply increases or declines in prosperity, as there was little inflation, and declining prices generally meant increasing investment in supply. Stock prices (U.S. Bureau of the Census, taking 1926 as 100), moved: 1877 (Grant) 24.8; 1893 (Harrison) 43.9; 1897 (Cleveland) 35.2; 1913 (Taft) 63.8; 1921 (Wilson) 64.2; 1923 (Harding) 67.7; and the huge rise in the twenties, 1929 (Coolidge) 190.3.

In foreign affairs, the chief issues of the second Cleveland administration were further afield than the paltry concerns of fish and seals and the lynching of a few people that had inconveniently arisen in the nearly 30 years since Seward had expelled Napoleon III from Mexico. The United States had owned tropical fruit plantations and used the naval anchorage and replenishment station of Pearl Harbor, near Honolulu, for some years. The large, and mainly American, planters had generated a revolution in 1887 that produced a rather liberal and easily suggestible (to their interests) government. The damage done by the McKinley Tariff to Hawaiian sugar interests coincided with the defeat of the pro-American political faction and the accession of a patriotic leader, Queen Liliuokalani, who revoked the liberal constitution and assumed powers to rule by royal decree. The leading American plantation owner, Sanford B. Dole, whose name would soon become famous in the kitchens of America, staged a coup in 1893, and the American minister, John L. Stephens, by prearrangement, purported to legitimize this movement and ordered the landing of a small number of Marines from the visiting cruiser *Boston*, supposedly to defend American life and property. The Marines effortlessly occupied government buildings, raised the U.S. flag over them, proclaimed the Hawaiian Islands a U.S. protectorate, and recognized Dole as president of Hawaii. A treaty of annexation was composed, but filibustered by Democrats and not ratified by the Senate while Harrison was president. Cleveland withdrew the treaty in March 1893, and appointed a commissioner to investigate the whole status of Hawaii. The commissioner, ex-congressman James Blount, a liberal Democrat, withdrew recognition of the Dole regime, hauled down the American flag, and excoriated Stephens and the Dole-led planters, and said that the majority of Hawaiians were opposed to annexation.

Cleveland sent a new commissioner with orders to restore Liliuokalani, as long as she restored the 1887 constitution; amnestied the rebels (i.e., Dole and his friends); and honored the debts of the Dole administration. Dole magnificently improvised that as the United States (under Harrison) had recognized his government, the actions of Blount and Cleveland were an intrusion in the internal affairs of a foreign country. Cleveland declined recourse to force to remove Dole and restore the queen, deplored Dole's actions, but recognized his government in August 1894. It was an absurd cakewalk that left the world's other major powers gape-mouthed at American amateurism and naïveté.

Another somewhat silly and overblown controversy blew up over the border between British Guyana and Venezuela, which became important because of gold discoveries in the disputed area. Britain had taken over the largest part of Guyana from the Dutch in 1814, during the War of 1812, as the Netherlands was liberated from Napoleon's First Empire, and 10 years before the Monroe Doctrine was proclaimed. The British had surveyed the border in 1840 and produced a line that was not accepted by Venezuela. After the gold discoveries in 1887, Britain withdrew its 1840 proposal and claimed areas to the west of it; Venezuela rejected this claim, severed relations with Britain, and asked for U.S. mediation, which Britain declined. Cleveland's last secretary of state, Richard Olney, produced a very robust amplification of the Monroe Doctrine, claiming that any British attempt to pressure Venezuela constituted a violation of the Monroe Doctrine. Olney flexed America's muscles with scarcely more diplomatic subtlety than Daniel Webster had employed in his letter to the Austrian minister Johann Hülsemann in 1850. He advised the eminent British prime minister, Lord Salisbury, that "the United States is practically sovereign on this continent, and its fiat is law upon the subjects to which it confines its interposition. Why?" (as if he were conducting a tutorial with the British leader, who was in his third term as prime minister of the world's greatest empire, after having spent two highly successful years as foreign secretary). And then Olney graciously answered: "It is because, in addition to all other grounds, its infinite resources combined with its isolated position render it master of the situation and practically invulnerable as against any or all other powers."

Salisbury replied, with the suavity of his office and the confidence of the head of the Cecils, probably Britain's greatest and most influential family since Elizabethan times and through three dynasties and the Cromwell interregnum, that Great Britain did not recognize that the Monroe Doctrine had anything to do with it, since at issue was a border that antedated that doctrine. He declined the American offer of arbitration and all but invited Olney to be gone. Salisbury was technically correct, and Olney was bumptious, but Britain could not win this argument and was being challenged in naval strength and in several colonial areas by Germany, whose impetuous emperor, Wilhelm II, was encouraging Afrikaner resistance to Britain in the powder keg of South Africa. (Wilhelm had rashly dismissed Bismarck after 28 years as imperial chancellor and minister president of Prussia, in 1890.)

Cleveland presented the correspondence to the Congress and announced that he would appoint a commission to determine the just demarcation between Venezuela and Britain, and added that the United States would resist by force any British attempt to take more than what his commission recommended. Salisbury belatedly realized that it was time to throw this crisis into reverse, since the Americans were being so testy and bellicose about it, and he devolved it to the colonial secretary, Joseph Chamberlain, who declared that war between the two countries "would be an absurdity as well as a crime," adding that "The two nations are more closely allied in sentiment and interest than any other nations on the face of the earth." It had been British policy since the near-collision during the U.S. Civil War to maintain excellent relations with Washington; they were now natural allies and it was notoriously obvious that the United States was growing more powerful in absolute and relative terms every year.

It was astounding how this trivial episode stirred war fever in the United States. The 37-year-old president of the board of police commissioners of New York, Theodore Roosevelt, revealed his cowboy belligerence, writing: "Let the fight come if it must. I don't care whether our seacoast cities are bombarded or not. We would take Canada. If there is a muss, I shall try to have a hand in it myself! . . . It seems to me that if England were wise, she would fight now. We couldn't get at Canada until May, and meanwhile, she could play havoc with our coast cities and shipping. Personally, I rather hope that the fight will come soon. The clamor of the peace faction has convinced me that this country needs a war."[1] This was nonsense from every angle; the British could probably defend Canada quite well unless the United States reconstituted at least half of the strength of the old Grand Army of the Republic, and could reduce to rubble every American city on every ocean coast, from Seattle to San Diego, Galveston to Pensacola, and Jacksonville to Boston, for as long as pleased them. Further, from the British standpoint, it would be insane, as Chamberlain wrote, to get into war with the United States over such a trivial issue. Theodore Roosevelt would soon become one of the great executants of American strategic policy, and would be very successful. At this point, he was just a blustering, ill-tempered schoolyard pugilist.

Since the Civil War there had been almost no strategic thinking. But Captain Alfred Thayer Mahan became the father of the great American entry into the world with his epochal study *The Influence of Sea Power on History 1660–1783*, published in 1890. Within a few years, both Roosevelts, and a great many others, including the chief strategists of Britain and Germany (these three continuing to be the world's three greatest naval and maritime powers, and the three greatest powers generally), would be Mahan's disciples. Mahan provided a strategy for the United States just as its immense economic and population expansion caused it to burst out of its adolescent gamecock confinement to the Americas and the

---

1.   Daniel Ruddy, *Theodore Roosevelt's History of the United States*, New York, Harper Collins, 2010, p. 218.

eastern Pacific, as the Arthur-Cleveland-Harrison naval build-up (partly as an aid to the steel industry and to shipbuilding generally) made the U.S. an important naval power, and as expansionist opportunity presented itself. The United States had been growing exponentially by every measurement for 30 years. It was almost time for it to prorupt into the world.

The Venezuela Boundary Commission met in January 1896; Britain cooperated with it and the contending countries agreed in a treaty of January 1897 to submit their disagreement to a board of arbitration. In October 1899, the board reported out along the lines the British had claimed in 1840, but not agreeing the extension the British had claimed in 1887. Both sides accepted the award without rancor. Both Britain and the United States had by then been engaged in real combat in much more important matters. Olney did upgrade U.S. ministers to ambassadors, and legations to embassies, a symbolic act but in the diplomatic realm where symbols have some importance.

The Republicans met at Pittsburgh in May 1896 and chose Governor William McKinley of Ohio for president and Garret A. Hobart, Republican national committeeman from New Jersey, for vice president. McKinley's rise was engineered by his chief benefactor, financier and industrialist Marcus Alonzo Hanna, Republican Party chairman and campaign manager. The platform supported a high tariff, annexation of the Hawaiian Islands, and adherence to the gold standard, though it was suggested that the lot of the silver interests could be furthered through agreements with other countries. The pro-silver Republicans seceded and held their own convention, at which they endorsed the Democratic nominees. The Democrats met at Chicago in July and it was clear from the start that the bimetallists were in control of the convention. The party's platform proposed the free coinage of silver at the ratio of 16-to-one of gold over silver; demanded lower tariffs; condemned monopolies and injunctions against labor organization; and flirted with a tax on high incomes. It was a rather radical set of positions.

The principal Democratic bimetallist orator, William Jennings Bryan, 36-year-old former congressman from Nebraska, editor of the *Omaha World-Herald*, "boy wonder of the Platte" and soon to be "the Great Commoner," swept the convention with one of the great partisan harangues of American history, ending "You shall not press down upon the brow of labor this crown of thorns. You shall not crucify mankind upon a cross of gold." Bryan took as his running mate Arthur Sewall, Democratic national committeeman and wealthy banker and railroad director, of Maine. (The vice presidential fight, between Sewall and Hobart, was between national committeemen and was publicly seen as a battle between two luxuriantly mustachioed running mates of clean-shaven presidential nominees.)

Bryan was nominated also by the People's Party (Populists) and the pro-silver Republicans. The pro-gold Democrats quit, as the pro-silver Republicans had, and they, like the Prohibitionists, had their own nominees. Bryan set a new style of campaigning by barnstorming the country and giving more than 600 speeches. He was already a famous and popular bimetallist orator before the convention and built on his forensic reputation. McKinley replied with aphorisms to the press and passersby from the verandah of his home in Canton, Ohio, while Hanna financed the election and most of the major newspapers excoriated Bryan as a radical, a revolutionary, and an anarchist.

America was not ready for such a revolution; the Democrats had entered a cul-de-sac, and McKinley won 7.04 million votes and 271 electoral votes, to Bryan's 6.47 million votes and 176 electoral votes. The other candidates combined polled barely 300,000 votes. It was roughly 52 percent to 46 percent to 2 percent, and was the first substantial popular-vote victory the Republicans had enjoyed since Grant routed Greeley (who dropped dead a few weeks later) in 1872, while there was still a restricted electorate in the Union Army–occupied South. The Republican cycle of 14 election victories out of 18 between 1860 and 1928 would now enjoy its greatest phase, with 7 victories in 9 elections, none of them close, and the 2 defeats attributable to a rending split between the two leading Republican faction heads in 1912.

Stephen Grover Cleveland went into honored retirement, and died in 1908, aged 71. He was a courageous and principled president who stood for honesty in government and adherence to international law, but was somewhat out of step with the chauvinism and muscularity of America on the steep rise. Yet, even he strode to the bully pulpit and rattled his saber at the British over the silly issue of Venezuela's border (which was none of America's business anyway), having cranked himself to a state of near-belligerency over the fatuous issue of Samoa. As mayor of Buffalo, governor of New York, and president of the United States, Cleveland was unchanged: modest, guileless, good-humored, intelligent, unimaginative, and distinguished in conduct and motive; a good president for uncomplicated times, as had been Hayes, Arthur, and probably, had he lived, Garfield. The times were about to become more complicated as the mighty nascent power of America eased itself into the wider world, like a large man stepping gingerly into a bath.

3. WILLIAM MCKINLEY AND THE SPANISH-AMERICAN WAR

McKinley named the aging lion (73) of the Senate, and brother of the great general, John Sherman of the president-elect's home state of Ohio, as secretary of state (opening up a Senate seat for his champion, Mark Hanna, to which the

Ohio legislators elected him). McKinley appointed as deputy secretary of state his longtime Canton friend and intimate adviser William R. Day, a prominent local lawyer, who would succeed Sherman. McKinley thus followed the recent tradition of a party bigwig with no foreign policy background, followed by a lawyer with an equal absence of such background. McKinley's term was overshadowed by Cuban matters from the start. An insurrection against Spanish rule erupted in February 1895 and was followed with much interest in the United States. For a time in the 1850s, as was recorded in Chapter 6, the Democrats advocated the absorption of Cuba by the United States under no color of right except the desire to expand slavery as a sop to the South without riling the North by carving a slave state out of American territory. Americans had taken a dim view of Spanish colonial rule in the Americas since before the successful uprisings of Bolívar, San Martín (Argentina), and other Latin American revolutionaries in the first quarter of the century. This continued to be the case, and the moribund colonial administration of Spain was a dead hand in the Americas that offended the United States in a way that the presence of the British and French and Dutch, advanced and democratic countries and relatively enlightened colonial administrators, did not. The Cuban revolutionaries adopted the technique of burning down sugar fields and refineries, including some owned by Americans, in order to attract American intervention.

The Spanish replied with their then usual, heavy-handed and medieval inflexibility, by assigning suppression of the rebellion to General Valeriano "Butcher" Weyler (as the American media quickly labeled him, in collusion with the Cuban rebels, and not without some reason). Weyler produced a counter-scorched-earth policy and, without the slightest pretense to due process, committed large numbers of people, including women and children, to concentration camps, where malnutrition, disease, and rough treatment by custodial officers was commonplace and infamous. The U.S. Senate and House, in February and March 1896, conferred a status of legitimate belligerent on the Cuban revolutionaries and offered American good offices in establishing Cuban independence. The Spanish naturally considered that after nearly 400 years, they had some standing in Cuba and that if Cuba was ever to achieve its independence, Spain could confer that status on the island without any help from the Americans.

The American public attitude to Cuba was influenced by and tied up in one of the great circulation wars in the history of the daily press, between Joseph E. Pulitzer's *New York World* and William Randolph Hearst's *New York Journal*. Both newspapers achieved unheard-of circulations of around—and in Hearst's case—above a million a day, partly on the basis of flamboyantly written, artistically sketched, and sometimes luridly exaggerated or invented descriptions of Spanish outrages and atrocities. Hearst rescued a supposedly savagely raped convent girl who, once in the good life of New York, lost no time getting up to speed with the racy life of her liberator. Hearst had supported Bryan in 1896 and had no influence with McKinley, but he stirred opinion. And McKinley did have a war-hawk faction in his party, led by the young Theodore Roosevelt, now assistant secretary of the navy, and Henry Cabot Lodge, scion of a great Boston Brahmin family and senator from Massachusetts. In their energy and inventive stridency, they somewhat resembled the young Henry Clay, on England, 90 years before.

A relatively liberal government was installed in Madrid in October 1897, which recalled Weyler, granted partial autonomy to the Cubans, released imprisoned Americans, and cleaned up the concentration camps. As usual in such vortexes, the insurrectionists professed to be offended by tokenistic tricks, and the loyalists condemned the authorities for cowardly appeasement and rioted, demanding retention of Weyler. On February 9, 1898, Hearst published a letter that Cuban revolutionaries had stolen from the mails in Havana, addressed privately by the Spanish minister in Washington, Enrique Dupuy de Lôme, to a Cuban friend, in which he wrote that McKinley was "weak and a bidder for the admiration of the crowd, besides being a would-be politician who tries to leave a door open behind himself while keeping on good terms with the jingoes of his party." Dupuy de Lôme cabled his resignation to Madrid as soon as the letter was published. What he wrote was not altogether inaccurate, but he failed to note that walloping Spain was not only an easy option for the United States but that, somewhat incited by Spain's primitive conduct, it would be politically advantageous to McKinley and serve the interests of an America about to flex its great muscles in the world.

This was where things stood when, six days after the Dupuy de Lôme episode, the U.S. battleship *Maine*, sent to Havana supposedly to protect American lives and interests in Cuba, abruptly blew up in Havana harbor at 9:40 on the fine clear evening of February 15, 1898, killing 260 officers and men. Hearst and most of the rest of the media went into orbit, while the administration urged calm and the avoidance of leaping to conclusions, and appointed an admiralty board of inquiry, which five weeks later attributed the explosion on the *Maine* to an underwater mine of uncertain provenance. Hearst propagated the jingo cry "Remember the *Maine*!" and Congress voted a special defense appropriation of $50 million. McKinley showed admirable restraint and resisted public and congressional pressure to go to war at once. The American minister in Madrid assured the Spanish on March 27 that the United States had no designs on Cuba and sought a cease-fire within Cuba and the disassembly of the concentration camps. The Spanish agreed to these terms on April 5 and 9, but on April 11 McKinley asked for "forcible intervention" to establish peace in Cuba. This was a rather mealy mouthed back-step into war, presumably revealing an unconvinced president swayed by public opinion and by reflections on the easy partisan and geopolitical gains from hammering the flaccid and inert corpus of the Spanish Empire, which had been in gradual decline for 300 years since the defeat of the Spanish Armada in 1588.

On April 20, 1898, the Congress voted to recognize the independence of Cuba, demand the withdrawal of Spanish forces from Cuba, empower the president to use the army and the navy in pursuit of these aims, and to renounce any ambitions to govern Cuba, whose future would be determined by the population of Cuba. It was the ultimate political free lunch: the United States would help banish primitive imperialism and sought nothing for itself. It would take advantage of the weakness of Spain to masquerade as continental liberator, champion of freedom, and disinterested protector of human rights and national autonomy. The rest of what was more or less a charade, though any replacement of Spanish by American influence in the remaining fragments of the Spanish Empire would be a full step forward, unfolded quickly. McKinley signed the congressional war resolution on April 20, and gave the Spanish an ultimatum to withdraw at once from Cuba and grant its independence, or the U.S. would resort to force. Spain broke off relations with the U.S. the next day, and the United States imposed a naval blockade on Cuba the day after that.

On April 24, Spain completed its hot-headed, bull-headed blunder, as if in a time machine, into war with a country three full centuries ahead of it in all respects, 10 times as powerful, and 98 percent closer to the theater of activity, and declared war on the United States. The United States declared war the next day, retroactive four days to when it had commenced acts of war. Spain, the dimming, fading, superannuated fighting bull, had been prepared by the local Cuban picadors, goaded by the onlookers, fortified by dreams of bygone grandeur and requirements of honor, provoked by the cocky and histrionic matador, blinded and enraged by the red cape, and charged, delivering its head and neck and lungs to the mighty sword-thrust of its insouciant enemy. The Spanish-American War was such an uneven match, it went almost entirely according to (American) plan.

Commodore George Dewey commanded the U.S. Asiatic Squadron, consisting of four cruisers, which effectively rented facilities from the British at Hong Kong. When Dewey learned of the American declaration of war, he sailed his already fully stocked ships for Manila, and entered Manila Bay in the predawn of May 1, 1898. He opened fire on the 10 Spanish ships he took unawares there, at 5:40 a.m. ("You may fire when ready, Gridley."), and by early afternoon had sunk, destroyed, or captured all the Spanish ships and killed 381 Spanish sailors, suffering no significant damage and only eight wounded men himself. Dewey (promoted by the Congress to the sonorous title Admiral of the Navy) blockaded Manila and awaited the arrival of land forces to seize the Philippines, which, like Cuba, were already seething with insurrection. By the end of July, almost 11,000 American marines and soldiers had arrived and had contacted and arranged coordination with the rebels, led by Emilio Aguinaldo, whom Dewey returned to the Philippines from the exile where the Spanish had banished him. Manila was occupied by Americans and insurrectionists on August 13, and the Spanish surrendered the following day. If they had not so hot-headedly declared war on the United States, they would have lost Cuba but not the Philippines.

By this time, the main Spanish navy, having sailed from Spain to Cuba, was destroyed off Santiago by a superior American force led by five modern battleships, on July 1, 1898. The Spanish lost 474 sailors killed and 1,750 captured, to 1 killed and 1 wounded American. In the land action in Cuba, 17,000 men of the regular army and volunteers, most famously Theodore Roosevelt and Leonard Wood's Rough Riders, a cavalry regiment, were disembarked near Santiago on June 26, and succeeded in taking El Caney and San Juan Hill on July 1. These engagements did involve serious fighting and the United States suffered over 1,500 casualties. Roosevelt led his men on foot up San Juan Hill against heavy fire and took the heights above Santiago. Theodore Roosevelt became an instant and permanent American hero. (He was awarded the Congressional Medal of Honor nearly a century later, by President William J. Clinton, and about 50 years after his son, Theodore Junior, was awarded the same honor by their cousin, President Franklin D. Roosevelt, for his conspicuous courage in the 1944 Normandy landings. The only other family with father and son winners of the Congressional Medal of Honor, the MacArthurs, also gained them in the Philippines, General Arthur MacArthur evicting the Spanish in 1898 and General Douglas MacArthur in resisting the Japanese in 1941–1942.)

This effectively doomed the Spanish presence in Cuba, and on July 26 the Spanish inquired of the talented French ambassador in Washington, Jules Cambon (later ambassador to Berlin and, with his brother Paul, one of the architects of the Entente Cordiale between Britain and France), to find out American terms for peace. A protocol was signed on August 12 involving the relinquishment of Cuba by Spain and the cession of Puerto Rico (which the United States had occupied without opposition on July 25); the Philippines would be discussed later.

The Treaty of Paris of December 10 confirmed the cession of the Philippines to the United States, for $20 million, and Spanish assumption of Cuban debts of nearly $400 million. The secretary of state was now the talented and urbane John

Hay, once private secretary to Abraham Lincoln. William Day, a jurist at heart, had accepted appointment to the U.S. Supreme Court. Hay did have an extensive background in foreign policy, having been in the Paris, Madrid, and Vienna legations, as well as Rutherford Hayes's assistant secretary of state and McKinley's ambassador to Great Britain; he was very conscious of rising American strength in the world, and had many influential friends in the principal countries of Europe, as did the war secretary, Elihu Root. These men, along with Senator Lodge and, as he was elected in November 1898, New York governor Theodore Roosevelt, represented a new mentality nearing the summit of American affairs. They knew the trans-Atlantic world and would not be content with America simply ruling the Americas. It was as great a power as Britain and Germany and would act accordingly. They had all read Captain (later Admiral) Mahan's works, and Roosevelt had worked with Mahan in the Navy Department, and a new era of American assertiveness, of which the drubbing just administered to Spain was a harbinger, was about to open. The United States also took Guam, and for good measure had occupied Wake Island on July 4 and formally annexed Hawaii on July 7.

There was a considerable debate over the Treaty of Paris, with the Republicans waving the flag around and claiming that if the United States did not take over the Philippines, undesirable foreigners would. Most Democrats and the Populists were uneasy about the takeover of non-contiguous territory peopled by non-whites. William Jennings Bryan came to the aid of the administration, urging ratification and saying that the disposition of the Philippines could be determined in the following presidential election. With Bryan's help, the Senate ratified 57–27, just two votes more than the two-thirds needed. This, coupled with the ratification of the takeover of Hawaii, by a simple majority in a joint resolution, did indicate that the expansionists and colonialists were beginning to assert themselves over the isolationists and militant opponents of racial dabbling. The United States had mobilized 274,000 men to serve in the war, of whom relatively few got anywhere near belligerent activity. There were 379 battle deaths and 1,604 wounded, but 5,083 deaths from exotic diseases. The war cost $250 million, not much to pick up the Philippines, Cuba, and Puerto Rico, as well as Wake and Guam. But this was the last of America's carnival wars. Hereafter, it would have more serious opponents. (The Spanish fought bravely but their techniques and equipment were obsolete.)

Aguinaldo announced a new insurrection when he learned that the United States would not be quitting his country so quickly. The Filipino rebels had a disjointed and under-equipped force of about 70,000, and the United States deployed 70,000 trained or semi-trained soldiers to suppress the uprising. They saw off organized resistance by 1899, and reduced Aguinaldo to skulking about in the hills and jungles, darting out to stage minor ambushes, until he was captured in March 1901. A commission McKinley had set up urged eventual independence of the Philippines, but not until the U.S. had adequately prepared the country for full nationhood. At least it was acknowledged that the sun would be setting on this empire. A second commission, presided over by federal appellate judge William Howard Taft, in April 1900, gradually installed an entire government, largely headed by natives, in the Philippines, and provided a very enlightened administration. In June 1901, military government was ended in the Philippines, except in a few areas where insurrection continued. The U.S., in its relatively brief and confined try at it, proved a progressive colonial power.

Apart from Romania's 1915 declaration of war on Germany, which was at least induced by British bribes that were paid, and did leave Romania much expanded, after crushing defeat and occupation for three years of self-sought martyrdom on the side of the victorious powers, modern history records few examples of such mad plunges into mortal national combat in conditions of impossible disadvantage as Spain's against the United States. It would be another, though the last, of America's easy little hemispheric flexings of muscle at the beach. Strategy or, more accurately, spontaneous impulse to organic growth, had equipped America to be a great world power, just 109 years after George Washington was inaugurated as its first president. Actually playing that role successfully would require relearning the international strategic finesse of the country's greatest early diplomats, Franklin, Jay, Monroe, and John Quincy Adams.

The half-century from the Civil War to World War I were for America almost a reversion to the spontaneous strategy of national development and self-absorption that first awakened the founders of the nation. The energy of the Revolution and the early years, which had yielded to the long and ultimately terrible crisis of slavery, and then the raw-boned surging adolescence of this period, were soon to give way to the need for the consistent judgment and self-interested discipline of a great and mature nation. These stages succeeded each other with a rapidity and on a scale that was outside European experience, even where, as with Richelieu, Peter the Great, and Bismarck, Great Powers were swiftly made from quickly expanded but long-established cultures and nationalities. As it always has claimed, America was exceptional.

4. THE REELECTION AND ASSASSINATION OF PRESIDENT MCKINLEY

Japan had been flexing its muscles in the far Pacific, and had started, as was natural given the vulnerability of China at this time, with the Sino-Japanese War of 1894–1895. This threw wide open the gates of China and began a scramble of European powers building on their rapacious activities of some decades, to follow Japan in opening up spheres of influence in China. The United States initially declined to join in such indignities, but soon became concerned that the Europeans and Japanese would carve up all China and leave it out. Britain had offered the United States cooperation in Chinese matters in 1898 and 1899, but had been rebuffed. Hay had friends who had served in the British diplomatic service in China and he became somewhat well-informed about Chinese matters. In September 1899, he wrote the Russian, British, German, French, Italian, and Japanese governments asking for assurance that Chinese government tariffs and other arrangements would not be altered by whatever spheres of influence were being established, and that there would be no discrimination against any other foreigners in those spheres. This was a rather naïve questionnaire, to which he received rather evasive replies, but, in a time-honored gesture, Hay claimed to have achieved complete concurrence, and waving the official responses from the other six powers about, he declared the "final and definitive" acceptance of what was known as "the Open Door policy" in China.

Predictably enough, in the spring of 1900 xenophobic nationalism swept intellectual and clerical circles in China, and the Boxer Rebellion, dedicated to the expulsion of the "foreign devils" (not to mention the "long-nosed, fat-eyed barbarians"), erupted and quickly led to the seizure of the Chinese imperial capital at Peking. The foreign legations were besieged, and only relieved by an international force on August 14, 1900. The foreign powers exercised their usual heavy-handed will and extorted from China (September 1901) an indemnity of $333 million, of which the American share was to be $24.5 million. Hay issued another of his aerated circular letters to the powers enumerating everything that was supposed not to happen in China, and claiming to be upholding Chinese national dignity and the Open Door policy, which was not, in fact, compatible with any recognizable notion of Chinese sovereignty. Although there was a good deal of flimflam and wishful thinking in Hay's position, the United States excused China from most of its indemnity to the U.S. and China dedicated much of its unpaid balance to paying for the education of promising Chinese university students in the United States. The battle for Chinese control of its own affairs would continue, often with great loss of blood and physical destruction, through most of the first half of the twentieth century. But 100 years after the Boxer Rebellion, China was back as one of the world's greatest powers, in a remarkable and unique act of national regeneration.

From May to July 1899, a conference took place at The Hague under the auspices of the czar of Russia, Nicholas II, exploring arms limitations and seeking a regulation of methods of warfare. It proved impossible to restrict the use of poison gas and of balloons in war, and to impose weapons levels, but the Permanent Court of International Arbitration was established. The United States accepted a formula of dispute resolution through mediation and arbitration, but would not hear of compulsory arbitration or application of any such process to activities within the Americas, which it effectively reserved the right to sort out as it pleased. There were further small steps to absorb the new empire. Samoa was finally divided between Germany and the United States, with Britain being compensated elsewhere, and Pago Pago became an American naval base. And the Foraker Act in April 1900 established civil rule in Puerto Rico as an American territory like Alaska and Hawaii.

Foreign affairs had dominated McKinley's term, and almost the only legislative initiative of note was the Gold Standard Act of 1900, which reinforced the golden barricades against the bimetallists at the approach of the election. These had been years of high economic growth and broad and general prosperity. The Republicans met at Philadelphia in June and renominated President McKinley without opposition. Vice President Hobart had died in 1899, and to the consternation of the eastern machine politicians, especially from New York, Governor Theodore Roosevelt was nominated for vice president. The governing party's platform supported the gold standard, a protective tariff, and, suffused with the fruit of their "splendid little war" and its acquests, an isthmian canal in Central America, with the slightest concern only for the fact that it would have to be cut through the territory of another country.

The Democrats met at Kansas City in July and renominated William Jennings Bryan and former vice president Adlai E. Stevenson on a straight bimetallist platform. Silver had become a metaphor for western interests, the little man across the country, and resistance to Wall Street and the exploitive overlordship of eastern finance, although any practical connections between these causes and the bogeyman were tenuous. The Social Democrats, succeeding previous parties of the left, had met at Indianapolis in March and nominated, for the first of several star turns in the role, former railway worker and labor agitator Eugene V. Debs for president and Job Harriman of California for vice president. There were the usual Prohibition and other splinter-group candidates.

Bryan campaigned against imperialism and for the silver reform; McKinley was slightly more energetic than he had been four years before, and emphasized "the full dinner pail" as well as the easy part of imperialism: hammering a derelict colonial power and looking a good deal more liberal and full of a civilizing mission than the European colonial powers. Bryan was the exponent of the grumbles of the fringes of American society; McKinley was the candidate of American satisfaction: peace, effortless military victory, prosperity, accretions of territory, all manner of good fortune rolling in for America. McKinley led all the way and on election day the president became only the sixth man to win two consecutive, contested presidential terms, 7.22 million to Bryan's 6.36 million, 209,000 for the Prohibitionist, and 95,000 for the socialist Debs; 51.5 percent to 45.5 percent, to 3 percent to all the others, and 292 electoral votes to 155 for Bryan. The Democrats were still in the cul-de-sac of frightening too many satisfied people to vote against them without attracting enough unsatisfied people into voting for them.

In March 1901, the Platt Amendment was adopted, which supplemented what Cuban legislators had adopted as a regime for an independent Cuba in a constitutional convention that the United States had requested. The amendment, which was adopted as part of Cuba's constitution, and as a matter of treaty, provided that Cuba would never impair its independence by treaty opposite any foreign power; that Cuba would not borrow beyond its apparent means to service debt; and that the U.S. was authorized to intervene to ensure the survival of Cuban independence and the rule of law. The Cubans dutifully agreed to cede naval installations to the United States. The Platt Amendment was added to the treaty to ensure the permanence of the residual American rights, although the amendment itself was abrogated in 1934.

On September 6, 1901, President McKinley was shot by an anarchist, Leon Czolgosz, at the Pan-American Exposition in Buffalo. For a time he appeared likely to recover, but primitive hygienic standards aggravated the problem and McKinley died on September 14, of complications from his treatment. The vice president, vacationing in the Northeast, was advised by a mounted park ranger that the president's condition was deteriorating, and entrained at once for Buffalo. Roosevelt was in transit when McKinley died, and he was inaugurated shortly after he arrived in Buffalo. At 42, he was the youngest person ever to hold the office of president of the United States, and remains so.

McKinley was a popular and sensible if somewhat unimaginative president. He was an unenthused imperialist, but did not balk at expansion as Cleveland had; was close to monied industrial interests but not a tool of them. He was another of the group of presidents between Grant and Roosevelt who wanted to let America be America as it grew exponentially, nudging it here and there to reduce patronage in the civil service, build more warships, and avoid economic nostrums like bimetallism, more concerned about union agitation than economic combinations, but not oblivious of the concerns raised by either. Theodore Roosevelt, after passivity in the presidential office through the 36 years since the death of Lincoln, was altogether different, and abruptly raised the curtain on a new age of America's consciousness of itself and of its presence in the world.

5. PRESIDENT THEODORE ROOSEVELT

Roosevelt's diplomacy, through the capable and like-minded Hay, turned first to Panama. The Clayton-Bulwer Treaty of 1850 had assured equality between Britain and the United States in any isthmian canal linking the Atlantic and the Pacific, and forbade the fortification of such a canal, and promised the abstention of both powers from violations of local sovereignty in Central America. McKinley's Hay-Pauncefote Treaty of February 1900 and Roosevelt's second Hay-Pauncefote Treaty of November 1901 revoked the Clayton-Bulwer Treaty, envisioned an American canal that would be open equally to all nations; a canal that would be neutral territory in all respects, though under U.S. auspices; and a canal that the United States would be conceded the right to fortify. The Hay-Herran Convention was negotiated in January 1903 with Colombia, of which Panama was then a province, and provided that for $10 million and an annual rental of $250,000 the U.S. would receive a renewable 99-year lease on a canal zone six miles wide across the narrowest part of the isthmus of Panama. The U.S. had also arranged to buy the assets of the Panama Canal Company.[2] It was on the basis of that company having lowered its price from $109 million that the Congress opted for the Panama rather than the Nicaragua route. But the Senate of Colombia, unlike the U.S. Senate, did not ratify the Hay-Herran Convention, because it reasoned that if it waited another 18 months, the charter of the Panama Canal Company would expire and Colombia, and not the company, would receive the $40 million the United States was prepared to pay for the company's right of way and charter.

Unfortunately, Theodore Roosevelt chose to regard this not as an astute business decision but rather as a personal and national affront, and ordered a naval squadron to the Panamanian coast to assure the "free and uninterrupted transit" between the oceans guaranteed by the Treaty of New Granada of 1846, while encouraging a coup d'état by locals whipped up by shareholders of the Panama Canal Company, led by the French adventurer Philippe Bunau-Varilla. In fact, the revolution consisted effectively of the small railway owned by the company refusing to conduct Colombian forces into Panama while wealthy locals proclaimed Panama's independence, on November 3. Roosevelt, with his fleet intimidating

---

2.   This was the Interoceanic Canal Company (later the New Panama Canal Company) founded by the French in 1876, after the success with the Suez Canal, completed in 1869. It excavated about a quarter of the canal length, and had very valuable maps and surveys, but had not been a financial success.

Colombian central authorities from advancing on foot in the absence of rail transport, recognized the new country. Then the resourceful Bunau-Varilla, a founding shareholder of the company who had sold McKinley and Hanna on the virtues of the Panama route, presented his letters of credence to Roosevelt as minister of the Republic of Panama to the United States on November 13, and granted the Canal Zone in perpetuity to the United States through the Hay-Bunau-Varilla Treaty also of November 13 (a busy, well-planned day for him).

It was a crisply executed opera bouffe banana-republic farce. Work on a canal was begun almost at once, though interrupted in 1905 to effect improvements in resistance to malaria and yellow fever, which had killed many canal workers. A lock canal of 40.3 miles was built between 1906 and 1914 at a cost of $365 million, under the supervision of Colonel George Washington Goethals of the Army Corps of Engineers. The political facilitation was shabby, but it was a great engineering achievement and a triumph of Roosevelt's in reinforcing the overwhelming pre-eminence of the United States as the hemispheric power and becoming, with Great Britain, one of only two great naval powers in both the Atlantic and the Pacific.

In July 1902, Congress passed Roosevelt's Philippine Government Act, which put the government of the Philippines in the hands of the Taft Commission, headed by U.S. Court of Appeals judge William Howard Taft of Cincinnati. After 1907, when the Philippine legislature was elected, Taft and his commission served as the upper house of the legislature. Taft was an enlightened governor and the regime was undoubtedly an unrecognizable improvement on the Spanish colonial government, in modernizing efficiency and in respect for the individual and national rights of the population.

And in 1904, after the British and the Germans had suffered default on a loan to Venezuela and asked Roosevelt if he objected to their bombardment of Venezuelan coastal cities as an encouragement to the Venezuelans to pay their debts, with no ulterior motives or colonial ambitions, Roosevelt agreed, and also agreed to transmit a proposal for arbitration to The Hague Tribunal, which was accepted. Similar problems arose with the Dominican Republic, and what became known as the Roosevelt Corollary resulted, in which it was accepted that "Chronic wrongdoing or impotence may . . . require intervention by some civilized nation, and in the Western Hemisphere . . . may force the United States, however reluctantly, in flagrant cases of such wrongdoing or impotence, to the exercise of an international police power." The United States, despite the lack of support by the Senate, administered Dominican customs collection and debt repayments from 1904 to 1907. By this time and by these methods, Roosevelt pushed American dominance of the Americas (except for Canada) about as far as even the most imperious interpretation of the Monroe Doctrine would allow.

Considerable interest had arisen over the precise line of the boundary between the Alaska Panhandle and the Canadian province of British Columbia after the Klondike gold rush of 1896. Canada invoked the Anglo-Russian Treaty of 1825, which set the border at the outer edges of the peaks of the Rockies, while the United States invoked a line between the heads of bays and inlets along the coast. That would assure U.S. retention of the harbors. In January 1903, the U.S. and Great Britain signed an agreement confiding the determination to a joint commission consisting of three Americans, two Canadians, and the Lord Chief Justice of England and Wales, Lord Alverstone. Alverstone cast his vote with the Americans, and the matter, which had never been more than an irritant, was settled in America's favor, to the annoyance of the Canadians, who felt they had been put over the side by the mother country, but accepted that the higher interests of empire could not accommodate trivial disputes with the United States.

By this time, the United States had become such an immense power in the world, and was led by such a dynamic and aggressive president, and Britain was in such an intense contest of naval construction with Germany, that the British national and imperial interest required almost open-ended deference to the United States. France and Russia were in alliance against Germany and Austria-Hungary (Hungary having acquired parity with Austria, largely through the cunning political infighting, accompanied by extraordinary skills in the Habsburg salons and boudoirs, of the dashing and formidable Hungarian premier and foreign minister, Count Andrássy, with the help of Bismarck). Italy was loosely attached to the Berlin-Vienna alliance, and the Entente Cordiale between France and Britain was growing steadily more intimate, ancient foes now reconciled in the shadow of German military and naval might, with Alsace-Lorraine part of the German Empire and the German navy laying keels of ever larger battleships almost as swiftly as the British. The impetuous young Emperor Wilhelm II, after dismissing Bismarck as chancellor, had allowed the alliance with Russia and the isolation of France to lapse, as he became embroiled in the Habsburg-Romanov contest for the South Slavs and gratuitously challenged Britain's supremacy on the seas, the one concern that could always be relied upon to drive Britain into the camp of a rival's enemies.

Roosevelt himself was the first American president since John Quincy Adams (though Buchanan almost qualified) who had traveled extensively in Europe and had a sense of America's relations to Europe. In his early twenties he had written the definitive history of the naval campaigns of the War of 1812, and he and Admiral Mahan were among the six authors of the official history of the Royal Navy, because of their undoubted scholarship in the field. Mahan had been an indifferent sea commander, but when tapped for the Naval War College at Newport in 1866, intensified his studies and began his exposition of the strategic importance of sea power by illustrating the Roman advantage over the Carthaginians in the Punic Wars: Rome could transport its forces by sea while Carthage had to cross North Africa to the west from what is Tunisia and then cross to Spain and approach Italy through Spain and France. His *Influence of Sea Power on History, 1660–1783* (*see* pp. 273–274), published in 1890, strategically explained the rise of Britain.

These men provided a serious and academically learned basis for American strategic policy and supported an international presence for America far exceeding the confines of the New World. Mahan presciently pointed out that the Philippines could not be defended against a militarist Japan, and an informal understanding was made between Roosevelt and the Japanese that the American occupation of the Philippines and the aggressive Japanese occupation of Korea and Formosa would be reciprocally tolerated (the Taft-Katsura Agreement of 1905). Roosevelt strenuously accelerated U.S. naval construction, which only enhanced the United States's position as holder of the key to the world balance of power, a position Britain had largely vacated by entering into alliance with France and Russia against Germany and its allies. Less than a century after Britain had successfully assisted, exhorted, and bankrolled the Prussians, Russians, Austrians, Spanish, and Swedes against Napoleonic France, ending French hegemony in Europe, Britain's weight, committed entirely to the assistance of France and Russia, might not be sufficient to counter and deter the great power of Germanic Europe, Bismarck having undone the work of Richelieu, Germany's great fragmentor, and reconstructed a Teutonic power in Central Europe of immense strength and uncertain benignity.

The rise of Germany to parity with Britain and the comparative decline of France, punctuated by decisive defeats by Pitt in Canada, Wellington on the French frontier, and Bismarck at the gates of Paris, left the nascent and mighty industrial and demographic and still almost revolutionary republican force of America as the arbiter of the fates of nations and alliances in the Old World, on the opposite sides of both major oceans. To proclaim America's new vocation, Theodore Roosevelt sent the main American battle fleet, painted white and popularly known as The Great White Fleet, on a goodwill mission around the world in the last year of his presidency. It was admirably within the U.S. tradition of astute public relations, being much noticed in the world, and it fired the imagination of many Americans who had not been in the habit of thinking much beyond their own sea-girt borders.

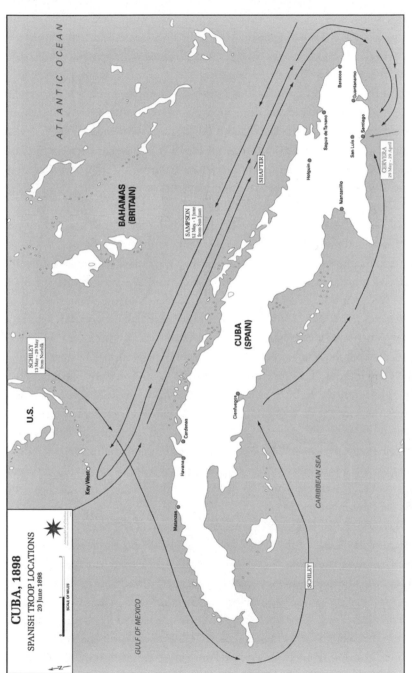

Cuba in the Spanish-American War. Courtesy of the Department of History, United States Military Academy

Roosevelt, unlike his predecessors since Lincoln (with the partial exception of Grant, whose strategic perceptions were famously acute and well-known but hadn't been much applied outside the United States), saw, relished, and exploited these changes. He had been a puny youth who had overcompensated by making himself, from sheer willpower, a barrel-chested rancher, frontiersman, and roustabout in the badlands, as well as a big-game hunter, and was an academic whose treatment of historic and strategic subjects achieved renown well beyond the British acceptance of the fairness and perception of his account of the naval operations in the War of 1812. His compulsive bellicosity has been mentioned in the Venezuelan–British Guyana border dispute. As New York City police commissioner, he was given to arbitrary round-ups of people out for a stroll late at night, on the grounds of aggressive suspicion. He was always quick to anger and more prone even than Jackson to escalate personal quarrels to feuds and fights to the death, and national disagreements to war.

He was a flamboyant campaign orator, referring to Bryan as a "human trombone." And he had almost superhuman energy, with mixed results. On one occasion, while he was giving a speech, he was the subject of an assassination attempt, but the bullet was largely absorbed by a book in his breast pocket and did penetrate his chest. There was a commotion as the gunman was subdued, and Roosevelt finished the speech. And once he became so enthused chopping trees that he chopped down those to which the telegraph lines to his house were attached, rendering him incommunicado as he awaited an important message. He had, in the French expression, the fault of his qualities. But with his bullying and simplistic aggressivity, there coexisted a high and well-informed intellect and a very strong sense of the national destiny, benign global mission, and the unsulliable honor of America. He was a brave and intelligent man, and also a very belligerent and impulsive one. The office, as well as the times and the voters, appeared to have sought the statesman.

In domestic affairs, Roosevelt's principal initiative in his first years as president was to assert the power of the federal government over the monopolies that had arisen in many of the country's industries. Failing to gain Senate approval of a policy to curb the trusts, as they were known, he ordered the attorney general, Philander C. Knox, to prosecute and seek the dissolution of Northern Securities, a railway holding company assembled by the epochal financier J. Pierpont Morgan. In August and September 1902, Roosevelt conducted a whistle-stop railway tour of New England and the Midwest whipping up public support of his policy, which he clearly defined as friendly to private enterprise, but not to monopolistic threats to the public interest. He benefited from the intractable position of the coal mine owners during the anthracite coal strike of 1902, and in 1904 the Supreme Court of the United States approved the administration's prosecution of Northern Securities. Roosevelt strengthened this policy with enabling legislation, including the Expedition and Elkins Acts, and artfully presented his policy as "a Square Deal" for the country.

The Republicans met in Chicago in June 1904, and President Roosevelt was nominated by acclamation, with Indiana Senator Charles W. Fairbanks, an orthodox McKinley conservative, for vice president. The Democrats met in St. Louis in July, and were in a demoralized state in the face of Roosevelt's immense popularity. They could not face a third straight nomination of Bryan, and Cleveland, the nominee for the previous three elections, had retired. Cleveland and other gold-standard Democrats from New York successfully put forward the candidacy of the chief justice of the New York Court of Appeals, Alton B. Parker, who chose the 80-year-old Henry Gassaway Davis, the oldest major party nominee to national office in American history, a former senator and millionaire coal mine owner from Virginia, for vice president. It was a gold-standard platform, which alienated the Bryanites and echoed Roosevelt's views on the trusts, but was almost silent about Roosevelt's assertive foreign policy. It was a tired and nondescript pair of nominees to challenge such a forceful and refreshing and successful incumbent. The Socialists ran Eugene Debs again, and the Prohibitionists, with unintended irony, a Silas C. Swallow.

There was never the slightest doubt of the outcome, and on election day Roosevelt won, 7.63 million to 5.1 million for Parker, 412,000 for Debs, 259,000 for Swallow; 56 percent to 38 percent to 6 percent for the lesser parties. The electoral vote was 336 to 140, as Roosevelt took every state outside the old Confederacy. On election night, Roosevelt gave the ill-considered and fateful promise not to seek renomination. He was the fifth president to inherit the office in midterm through the death of the incumbent, but the first to be reelected in his own right (unlike Tyler, Fillmore, Andrew Johnson, and Arthur, of whom all but Johnson sought renomination unsuccessfully), a pattern that would now be followed in the next three such cases (Coolidge, Truman, and Lyndon Johnson). It was the most one-sided U.S. presidential election victory since James Monroe ran for reelection without organized opposition in 1820.

6. ROOSEVELT'S SECOND TERM

John Milton Hay, one of America's most capable secretaries of state, died on July 1, 1905. He was an urbane and witty man, and got on well with Roosevelt. The distinguished jurist, and McKinley's and Roosevelt's war secretary, Elihu Root, succeeded him, and maintained the high standard set by Hay, though he was a reversion to the secretary with a legal rather than diplomatic background. Root had been succeeded as war secretary by William Howard Taft, who returned from a highly successful and imaginative term as governor of the Philippines.

War had broken out between Japan and Russia over spheres of influence in China, and especially Manchuria, and the Japanese had mauled the Russian fleet badly. Roosevelt opposed a lop-sided victory by either side, in order to assure the continuance of American preeminence in the far Pacific, and he expressed concern for the preservation of the Open Door policy in China. The Japanese requested and the Russians accepted his mediation in May and June 1905, and Roosevelt convened the peace conference at Portsmouth, New Hampshire, in August. A treaty emerged after only a few weeks, securing Japan's position in Korea and confirming its succession to most of Russia's commercial and railway rights in Manchuria, giving Japan the southern half of Sakhalin Island, but denying Japan an indemnity from Russia. Roosevelt's mediation role was executed knowledgeably and fairly, and he was awarded the Nobel Peace Prize in 1906. Roosevelt maintained good relations with both powers and reached a "gentlemen's agreement" with Japan in 1907, in which Japan promised to withhold passports from migratory laborers bound for the U.S. This was Roosevelt's response to a good deal of concern in the western states about "the Yellow Peril" represented by Oriental immigration. It was a genteel and civilized response to ugly racist agitation. The Root-Takahira Agreement of 1908 would formally confirm "the status quo" in the Pacific and uphold the Open Door policy in China but also that country's independence and integrity. (Given the extent of foreign meddling in China, this was just a placebo.)

The next evidence of risen American influence and the aptitudes of its current president came in the Moroccan crisis of 1906. France had coveted Morocco for some time, to add to its colonial occupation of Algeria and Tunisia, and had negotiated British and Italian approval of its assumption of a protectorate status over Morocco. (Britain and France formally signed the Anglo-French Entente in 1904, one of history's most important and successful alliances, in the furtherance of which even the king and emperor, Edward VII, had played a role, with a very successful state visit to Paris in 1903.) Germany was the chief opponent, and the German emperor, Wilhelm II, as was his wont, set himself up as the champion of Moroccan independence, as he had of Dutch Afrikaner independence in South Africa, a conflict that required Britain three years to win.

Wilhelm made a speech at Tangier in March 1905 advocating Moroccan independence, and in the ensuing controversy asked for a conference on Morocco and invited Roosevelt to secure French participation. Roosevelt, though reluctant, was concerned that a full imbroglio on this subject could provoke a general war in Europe, given the interlocking alliances that could easily trip off reciprocal declarations of war among the Great Powers. He arranged a conference at Algeciras, Spain, and secured acceptance of a protocol in April 1906. Under this arrangement, the independence and borders and economic stability and commercial accessibility of Morocco were secured, but France and Spain were put in charge of Moroccan domestic security, and the command and training of police. This was an acceptable arrangement and preserved everybody's dignity, though it effectively delivered control of Morocco to France, and Roosevelt took the unnecessary step of having the Algeciras convention ratified by the Senate, which did so on condition that it not be misunderstood as departure from traditional American non-involvement in the affairs of Europe.

Roosevelt had suggested a general peace conference in 1904, but that had been postponed by the Russo-Japanese war. Czar Nicholas II took up this cause himself and the result was the Hague Peace Conference from June to October 1907. Roosevelt's hopes for a world court were not successful, but there was a formal agreement that powers outside the Americas would not try to employ force against countries in the Americas for the collection of debts. This confirmed Roosevelt's redefinition of the Monroe Doctrine in the Venezuelan and Dominican debt crises, which effectively conferred on the United States the sole authority to apply force to anyone in the hemisphere, except Canada, which was understood to be a stable, unoffending and close ally of Great Britain. Europe was on a hair trigger for war and no European power cared a farthing or a fig for what went on in Latin America, but all were anxious not to antagonize the United States of America. In November and December 1907, Root succeeded in holding a conference in Washington that ended war involving several of the Central American republics. (Costa Rica, Guatemala, Honduras, Nicaragua, and El Salvador, as well as Mexico and the U.S., attended.)

In domestic matters, Roosevelt continued his reform agenda into his second term. In 1906, he approved and had adopted the Hepburn Act, which strengthened the Interstate Commerce Commission and authorized it to prevent monopolistic exploitation by railways; the Pure Food and Drug Act, which outlawed and penalized false packaging and labeling and the sale of seriously defective food and pharmaceuticals; and the Meat Inspection Act, which required sanitary conditions in meat-packing establishments and forbade the sale of contaminated meat. This was not an ambitious reform program by the standards of other advanced countries. Bismarck, in order to shut down labor radicalism and militant unionization, had provided unemployment insurance and pensions for the working class, and Britain under Disraeli and Gladstone had legislatively improved working conditions and housing standards, and legislation was promised by the incoming Liberal government of Sir Henry Campbell-Bannerman in 1905 for unemployment insurance and pensions. This and more would be presented, with a moderate income tax to pay for it, by the chancellor of the Exchequer, David Lloyd George, in 1909 and 1910. There would be nothing like this in the United States for another 30 years. But Roosevelt was concerned to be, and be seen as, a reformer and innovator.

Another of the president's passions was conservation. He was a hunter, ornithologist, and lover of nature, and a believer in the strenuous outdoors life. In the course of his administration, 148 million acres were set aside as national forest lands, 80 million acres of mineral lands were withdrawn from public sale, the Inland Waterways Commission and National Conservation Commission were established, and public awareness of the value of natural resources and the dangers of spoliation were greatly increased by a White House Conservation Conference in May 1908.

The one significant blemish on this very successful administration was the financial panic of 1907, which reduced the Dow-Jones Industrial Average (which at time of this writing stands at over 14,000, though that reflects a great deal of inflation) to 8, a brief reduction of over 70 percent, and led to urgent requests to J.P. Morgan to assist in stabilizing financial markets, which he did. An acquisition of a distressed competitor by United States Steel Corporation was permitted, with an assurance of no anti-trust consequences, and the Aldrich-Vreeland Act was passed in 1908, authorizing semi-currency to be issued by regional banks backed by government securities, and establishing a National Monetary Commission, which eventually (1912) recommended the establishment of the central bank, the Federal Reserve. (Nelson W. Aldrich, the co-sponsor of the act, was John D. Rockefeller's son-in-law, and his nephew and namesake, Nelson A. Rockefeller, would be a four-term governor of New York and the 41st vice president of the U.S.) The crisis passed quickly, but President Roosevelt was revealed as having not the remotest idea how the financial markets, or monetary policy generally, functioned.

Elihu Root retired as secretary of state to run successfully for the position of U.S. senator from New York in 1908, and was replaced by the under secretary, Robert Bacon, in 1909. Bacon was a Harvard friend of Roosevelt's and had long been a close junior associate of J.P. Morgan's. Roosevelt had been a highly popular and successful president, and he adhered to his pledge not to seek reelection. He sponsored as a Republican candidate, Secretary of War Taft, who was nominated, along with New York congressman James Schoolcraft Sherman (no relation to the secretary of state or the general) for vice president. The Republican platform promised tariff reform, conservation, and vigilance against trusts. Foreign policy did not figure too prominently in the campaign. The Democrats, reeling from the debacle of the previous election, went back to William Jennings Bryan for the third time, and a twice-defeated candidate for governor of Indiana, John F. Kern, for vice president. Bryan's platform avoided a direct promise of bimetallism, and pledged war on the trusts and a reduction of tariffs. The Socialists renominated Debs.

The Republicans were very popular and Roosevelt left no one in any doubt of his support for Taft, a distinguished Ohio appellate judge, very capable governor of the Philippines, and competent (if not overly busy) war secretary. The Republicans won their fourth consecutive term, 7.68 million votes for Taft to 6.4 million for Bryan, 421,000 for Debs, 253,000 for the Prohibitionists. (The Populist thunder was always stolen by the mighty Nebraska orator and crusader, Bryan.) Taft won 52 percent to 43 percent for Bryan and 5 percent for the others, 321 electoral votes to 162 for Bryan, the Democrats again bottled up in the unforgiving, seg-regationist South. The Republicans retained control of both houses of Congress; they were providing the country imaginative, sensible government, economic growth, and rising prestige in the world. The legal tradition in the State Depart-ment was reinforced by Taft's selection of Roosevelt's attorney general, Philander C. Knox, as secretary of state. Knox had been counsel for Andrew Carnegie, Andrew Mellon, and Henry C. Frick, and his presence, along with Bacon's in Roosevelt's administration, indicated the limitations of Roosevelt's trust-busting militancy.

7. PRESIDENT WILLIAM HOWARD TAFT

The leisurely and commercially oriented style of the elephantine Taft (the only U.S. president who weighed over 300 pounds) was quite a contrast with Roosevelt. His principal initiative in foreign policy was the transmutation of the Open Door into what became known as "Dollar Diplomacy," in which the administration intervened directly with the Chinese to have American banking groups inserted in consortia for the construction of railways with European and other interests in China and Manchuria. The Russians and the Japanese demarcated spheres of influence between themselves in Manchuria, in contravention of the Open Door, in order not to be trespassed upon by the Americans, and they did so with the agreement of the British and the French, who had effectively divided the whole mass of China, with Manchuria divided between Russia and Japan and the rest split up between the Western powers. American bankers declined to enter into arrangements that would attract the disapproval of foreign powers, and generally lost interest in China as a business venue. Taft and Knox had been incited to their actions by the bankers' agent, Willard Straight, a financial adventurer, who, in the tradition of such deal facilitators, had limited support from the various parties he was trying to bring together. The whole exercise was a rather crude intrusion in the affairs of China and of the principal foreign powers engaged there not closely attached to the defined interests of the American private sector in China. It forfeited some of the prestige Roosevelt had earned, with Hay and Root, for crisp execution of sensible and even imaginative policy in the area (despite Hay's fantasies about the benignity or even existence of the Open Door).

More successful was the resolution of the timeless Newfoundland fisheries issue, which was referred to the Hague Tribunal in 1910 and became subject to a reasonable compromise that was accepted in good heart by both sides. If Taft and Knox managed to settle one long-standing dispute with the British and the Canadians on America's northern border, they exacerbated another, with the Central Americans. The prominence of financial considerations in the determination of foreign policy achieved indecent depths in Nicaragua. That country was still considered a possible site for an inter-oceanic canal, if there were a desire to construct one in competition to the U.S. canal in Panama. In June 1911, following a routine coup d'état, the Knox-Castrillo Convention was concluded, surrendering the control of Nicaraguan customs and an open-ended right of intervention to the United States, which also undertook the administration of Nicaragua's national debt. Before the Senate could act on this, Nicaragua defaulted on a loan from a British banking group, and Knox handed over control of that country's finances to an American banking group who then advanced $1.5 million to the hard-pressed regime, and took over the national bank of Nicaragua and the state railway system (rudimentary as they were). But the Senate, which, with the House, changed hands to the Democrats in 1910, rejected the Knox-Castrillo agreement and a similar arrangement with Honduras. (As the Democrats had the entire congressional delegation of the Old South, they often had majorities in both houses.)

Dissatisfied Nicaraguans eventually revolted against the collapse of their little country into helpless tutelage by the United States. Taft landed a force of Marines to protect American interests. Knox attempted a treaty that would pay Nicaragua enough ($3 million) to clear its financial problems and would unwind the more draconian measures, in exchange for exclusive and permanent rights for a canal (though the Panama Canal was nearing completion), but the Senate balked. The U.S. Marines settled in for a long stay to assure their country's interests and supervise financial arrangements (a less storied and rhapsodized use of the Marine Corps than Jefferson's suppression of the Barbary pirates or Polk's seizure of the capital of Mexico) for more than 20 years, to 1933. As a parting gift to the Nicaraguans, the United States helped install the Somoza family in charge of Nicaragua, and they remained, rather oppressively, and almost uninterruptedly, from 1936 to 1979, until they were replaced by the quasi-communist Sandinistas. A future president (the next Roosevelt) would famously describe the original Somoza as "a son-of-a-bitch, but our son-of-a-bitch," and it fell to a later president, Ronald Reagan, to assist in sending "the little colonel in the green fatigues," the Sandinista leader, Daniel Ortega, packing. American policy in Nicaragua throughout this period cannot be judged a triumph of progressive liberality.

The administration's commendable attempt at virtual free trade with Canada, in the teeth of general tariff increases and the attraction to Canada of preferential trade arrangements with the British Empire, came unstuck with the defeat of the Canadian Liberal government of Sir Wilfrid Laurier and its replacement by a less pro-American Conservative government led by Sir Robert L. Borden. (Both Canadian prime ministers were capable leaders, but contrary to the conservative view, reciprocity, as it was called, was an imaginative policy by Taft and Knox. It was ultimately more than replicated by free-trade arrangements entered into between the two countries in 1989 at the behest of the Conservative leader in Canada then, Brian Mulroney.) Knox also tried to maintain Root's network of 25 arbitration treaties, but these were gradually whittled down by exceptions made for various categories of national interest.

The United States was already trying to counter rising Japanese influence in the Far East, which led to complications with Britain. The British, in conformity with their customary policy of organizing and operating a balance of power, had been something of a sponsor of Japan, for which country it had (very profitably) built a substantial navy, until the Japanese felt able to design and build their own ships. The British had been in the habit of looking on Russia as a potential intruder on their vast Indian empire, and were commercial rivals of the United States in the Far East, so the arrival of Japan as a major indigenous power with which Britain had no natural rivalry was a welcome development. The Anglo-Japanese Alliance resulted, and was a demonstration of the astuteness of the British Foreign Office, as Britain was the first of the Great Powers to recognize the geostrategic potential of Japan.

The rise of Germany, and its abrupt and relentless pursuit of a naval construction competition that constituted the greatest and most sustained threat to British naval supremacy since the Spanish Armada three centuries before, changed that, and all other British strategic considerations. Russia had allied itself with France, in response to Austria-Hungary's effort to bar Russian advances in the southern Slavic nations that tentatively emerged after the forcible retirement of the Turks, and Britain had allied itself to France to contain the Germans. Since the Triple Entente (Britain, France and Russia) and the Triple Alliance (Germany,

Austria-Hungary, and loosely, Italy) were so closely balanced, and as has been evident in other matters, the British opened a long campaign of appeasement of the United States, presciently based on the possibility that the great and soaring weight of America could be necessary to repulse Germany in the end; British strategic thinking and practice were reconfigured to meet the direst threat. The patronage of Japan would have to yield to truckling to the Americans and the new intimacy with Russia, warming to its highest point since both powers were in the death grips of war with Napoleon a century before.

When the Anglo-Japanese Alliance came up for renewal in July 1911, the British inserted the clause that neither party would be bound to engage in war with a third party with which it had a general arbitration agreement. With commendable alacrity, Knox negotiated, in less than a month, general arbitration agreements with Britain and France, who welcomed any enhanced cordiality with America and were not going to be drawn into war with it in any conceivable circumstances. The correlation of forces had changed unrecognizably since the agonies of Jefferson and Madison a century before over impressments of American sailors and seizure of American ships and the imposition of blockades on the United States by both Britain and France (Chapters 2, 3, and 4). These agreements were ratified by the Senate in March 1912, after Republican senator Henry Cabot Lodge, a close friend of Theodore Roosevelt's, agitated for exclusion of certain Oriental sensibilities and a reservation to allow for the now immensely broad official interpretation of the Monroe Doctrine that effectively gave the United States suzerainty over the entire hemisphere except Canada. Lodge added to this, in a resolution of August 1912, what became known as the Lodge Corollary, viewing with "grave concern" acquisition or occupation of strategically important areas, as defined by the U.S. Senate, anywhere in the Americas, by any entity the Senate judged to be inconveniently close to any government from outside the Americas. This was directed at the proposed Japanese acquisition of a large area with sea access in the Mexican province of Lower California, and the proposed acquisition was abandoned as a result. Trans-Pacific Japanese-American tensions had already begun, and would escalate sharply over the next three decades.

In domestic affairs, Taft had a respectable reform record; he prosecuted twice as many anti-trust cases as Roosevelt had (90 to 44), and had a more aggressive attorney general in George Wickersham than the oligarchic fellow-traveler Philander Knox had been. Taft attacked Rockefeller's Standard Oil Company and James Buchanan Duke's American Tobacco Company, and took another swing at Carnegie's old United States Steel Corporation, alleging, in effect, that in the Panic of 1907 Roosevelt had been swindled by Morgan into allowing the acquisition of a distressed competitor by U.S. Steel. This was an insane political initiative by Taft, who did not enjoy a fraction of the public support of Roosevelt, though he did enjoy more support from the barons of the Republican Party, who had always been more comfortable with the Hayes-Garfield-Harrison-McKinley conservatives than with the populist, uncontrollable, and often brilliant Roosevelt. Early in his term, Taft supported the tariff increase in the Payne-Aldrich Tariff, and in a speech at Winona, Minnesota, on September 17, 1909, called it "the best bill that the Republican Party ever passed." This was another ham-handed slap at Roosevelt, to whom Taft owed his elevation to the cabinet, and nomination and election to the presidency. Wisconsin's reform Republican senator Robert M. La Follette became an anti-Taft, pro-Roosevelt insurgent and led the adoption of tariff reductions from 1911 to 1913, which Taft vetoed.

Taft set up a Commission on Efficiency and Economy (in the federal government) and reduced federal spending by over $40 million in his first year in office. He proposed a disciplined budget procedure that was decades ahead of its time. Taft reverted to almost Cleveland-like resistance to some categories of patronage, and offended the Rooseveltians as a result. He also reviewed federal government expenses personally and meticulously, which saved money but also offended many claimants on his support. In the last year of his term, he submitted a detailed budget that was unprecedentedly comprehensive, but that the Senate, controlled by Democrats and inhabited by Republicans who were led by Rooseveltians like Lodge, ignored. His recommended methods were widely emulated in the more intelligently governed states, and led to the Budget Act of 1921, and subsequent reforms.

Taft also allocated telephone, telegraph, cable, and wireless operations to the Interstate Commerce Commission (Mann Elkins Act); set up a postal savings bank (deemed to encourage savings in a risk-free place by making mail collection and bank deposits a one-stop shop); made the transportation across state lines of underage women for immoral purposes a federal felony via the Mann Act; and required the publication of campaign contributions to congressional candidates. These all gave a patina of reform to his regime, but he had blundered into needless quarrels with the mighty ego of Roosevelt, who returned from one of his adventurous overseas trips in June 1910 and announced in an address at Osawatomie, Kansas, on August 31, 1910, a "New Nationalism," which included the view that private property was subject to the requirements of the public interest.

The next bone of contention was that Interior Secretary Richard Ballinger disputed the legality of Roosevelt's closing of the sale of some hydroelectric generation sites. Roosevelt's director of the U.S. Forest Service, Gifford Pinchot, publicly accused Ballinger of harming the conservation program in favor of private financial interest, and Taft fired him in January 1911. The Democrat-controlled Senate inquiry absolved Ballinger of wrongdoing but gave him a very rough ride, and he resigned in March 1911. The 1910 elections produced some noteworthy results, including the election of one of America's foremost educators and political scientists, the first non-clerical president of Princeton University (1902–1910), Thomas Woodrow Wilson, as governor of New Jersey.

8. THE TAFT-ROOSEVELT SCHISM AND THE 1912 ELECTION

The Taft-Roosevelt split was now irreconcilable and revealed the weaknesses of both men, but not their strengths. Roosevelt was an irrational egotist who sought opportunities for fault-finding and offended sensibilities. Taft had never run for elective office before, had no political skills, was guilty of ingratitude to his benefactor, and had no idea how to avoid abrasions with him. In January 1911, the Progressive Republicans met in Washington and virtually withdrew from the Republican Party, demanding direct election of U.S. senators; choice of presidential candidates by primary and not boss-dominated conventions; a comprehensive system of referendum and midterm recall by plebiscite; and tighter laws against corrupt practices. The goal was acknowledged to be the nomination of La Follette in place of Taft. This was not going to work, but it illustrated Taft's incompetence at keeping a political coalition together. In December 1911, Roosevelt let it be known that he would seek the Republican nomination against Taft, and in February he confirmed that he was a candidate. He won primaries in six states, and won the conventions in four others. The governing party was severely divided between Taft and Roosevelt supporters, with La Follette's followers and the Wisconsin senator himself having declared for Roosevelt. But the majority of delegates were controlled by party bosses and were chosen arbitrarily.

The Republicans met at Chicago in mid-June and seated Taft delegates over Roosevelt ones in many states where Roosevelt's partisans were in the majority. Taft and Sherman were renominated on a complacent platform that lauded the administration's record and promised continuity. Roosevelt said the nomination was fraudulent and declared: "We are at Armageddon and I fight for the Lord." Six weeks later, the insurgents met again in Chicago and nominated Roosevelt for president and Governor Hiram W. Johnson of California for vice president, on a platform that replicated that of La Follette of the previous year, and added tighter anti-trust regulation, the vote for women, improved working conditions by legislation, popular referendary reversal of judicial decisions, and a reduced tariff.

In the interregnum between the two Republican conventions, the Democrats had met in late June in Baltimore aware that they were almost certainly choosing the next president, given the disarray among their opponents. William Jennings Bryan stood again for the fourth time, against Woodrow Wilson and the Speaker of the House, Beauchamp "Champ" Clark of Missouri. When it became clear that Bryan could not do it again, he threw his support to Wilson as the more reform-minded candidate, and in one of the great ironies of American politics, the thrice-defeated nominee effectively named the next president. (If he had sat out 1908, when he had little chance, he would have been elected in 1912 and the world would be different, though probably not better.) The Democratic platform was distinct from Roosevelt's only in Wilson's advocacy of a more drastic tariff reduction and his condemnation of all monopolistic trusts, which he held could not be cured of their damaging effects by regulation alone, as they were inherently harmful. Foreign policy was scarcely mentioned. Wilson was selected on the 46th ballot, and Indiana governor Thomas R. Marshall, a witty and engaging but otherwise unexceptional politician, was nominated for vice president. The Socialists again nominated Eugene V. Debs and the Prohibitionists again chose Eugene W. Chafin. It was a lively campaign. Vice President Sherman became the seventh holder of his position to die in office, on October 30, 1912.

Wilson won, 6.29 million to 4.13 million for Roosevelt to 3.48 million for Taft. Debs's vote ballooned to 897,000 and Chafin's was 206,000. It was 42 percent for Wilson to 27 percent for Roosevelt to 23 percent for Taft to 8 percent for the others, and three-quarters of that for Debs; the electoral vote was 435 for Wilson, 88 for Roosevelt (Johnson was vital in winning for them the key state of California by a hair's breadth), and only 8 for Taft. Though he would be a minority president, given that he was running against two previously elected presidents and a very strong fourth-party candidate, Wilson did well, and ran several points ahead of Lincoln's vote in a four-candidate race against less serious opponents in 1860. If Roosevelt's and Taft's votes, and also Wilson's and Debs's, had been combined in a straight two-party race, the Republicans would have won their narrowest victory since Harrison in 1888. Roosevelt was the strongest third-party candidate in history, but he was also the only previously elected and undefeated ex-president to head a third party.

Taft, a little like John Quincy Adams and U.S. Grant, had suffered from comparative lack of partisan political experience, and was tactically inept. But he was a tolerably capable president, though in foreign policy he and Knox had been caricatures of money-seeking allies of American business, rather than astute internationalists like Roosevelt, Hay, and Root, or at least a competent opportunist like McKinley, or tenacious idealist like Cleveland. He had had no national strategy at all, despite his service abroad as a proconsul and in the War Department, and unlike the two presidents who bracketed him.

If Roosevelt had just left Taft alone, he could have easily succeeded him in 1916; he was as impatient and egocentric as Taft was insouciant and clumsy. As Taft's presidency ebbed away, the Constitution received its Sixteenth Amendment, authorizing a federal income tax, and shortly after the installation of the new administration (in May 1913), the Seventeeth Amendment was adopted, providing for the election of U.S. senators by direct popular vote in the states, taking that power from the state legislatures. Roosevelt would be a formidable leader of the opposition and Taft would return with distinction to the judiciary and become the only person in American history to be both president and chief justice of the United States, and the founder of a political dynasty.

Wilson prepared to govern, and in return for his having served the party as nominee (and helped Wilson invaluably to the nomination), Wilson named William Jennings Bryan, who was otherwise completely unqualified, secretary of state. More important, as time would reveal, and presaging the greatest American political dynasty of all, Wilson named as assistant secretary of the navy, a position the nominee's cousin had held, the 31-year-old New York state assemblyman Franklin Delano Roosevelt. The young Roosevelt would absorb all there was to learn from his cousin (and uncle-in-law), Theodore, and from his own president, and add volumes to that, in the next third of the century, when the whole world would hang in the balance on his decisions and their execution.

9. WOODROW WILSON'S FIRST TERM—DOMESTIC REFORMS, AND MEXICO

Woodrow Wilson was the son, as well as, on his mother's side, the grandson, of Presbyterian ministers; a graduate of Princeton and Johns Hopkins; and a formidable academic and educator, acclaimed professor, political and governmental historian, reform president of Princeton University, and reform governor of New Jersey. He was not as great a polymath as Jefferson, nor a linguist like John Quincy Adams, but he was a prodigious intellect, a powerful writer, and, unlike the other two, a formidable orator. And despite Theodore Roosevelt's endless lampooning of him as a feeble and waffling theoretician, he was a forceful and imaginative executive. Though his presidency would end in tragedy and infirmity, he remains a great historic figure, denied his honor and largely unheeded, but impossible to minimize or ignore, who looms hauntingly in the modern history of America and of the whole world.

His inaugural address called for the reinforcement of free competition, better treatment of the disadvantaged, conservation, and more efficient and businesslike administration of government, a combination and extension of the better policies of Roosevelt and Taft. On April 8, 1913, he became the first president since John Adams in 1800 to appear in person at the Congress, and advocated tariff revision. Wilson was an authority on comparative government and was not an unambiguous admirer of every aspect of the separation of powers in the U.S. Constitution. In coming, as head of the executive government, to address the legislators, he was in some measure emulating an aspect of the parliamentary system that he admired, that the executive sat in the legislature. (Wilson has paid a price in the opinion of subsequent historians, for insufficient cheerleading for the Constitution.)

In December 1913, after six months of debate, and fierce opposition from the commercial banking system, the Congress approved the Federal Reserve Act, the first comprehensive reform of American banking since the Civil War, and reestablishment of a central bank after Jackson's abolition of the charter of the Bank of the United States in 1836. Twelve district banks were set up in regional centers around the country as depositories for nationally chartered banks that were required to join the system, and for whichever state banks chose to join. The Federal Reserve Board set the discount rate (the rate at which money was loaned to the banking system), which controlled credit in the country. The district banks rediscounted the paper of local banks, which subscribed to the capital of the district banks and participated with the Federal Reserve in choosing directors of the district banks. The district reserve banks issued commercial paper that was counted as part of the money supply, against deposits by adhering banks and backed by a 40 percent reserve of gold. It was a comprehensive and very successful organization of the banking system, which put the United States, with Great Britain and the Bank of England, at the forefront of sensible monetary policymaking and credit administration. Most of the balance of Wilson's reform program was contained in the Federal Trade Commission Act and Clayton Anti-Trust Act of September and October 1914. The Federal Trade Commission was a bipartisan body empowered to enforce and monitor anti-trust rules, and the Clayton statute substantially expanded, clarified, and made more enforceable the Sherman Anti-Trust Act of 1890.

In foreign relations, Bryan opened his tenure in the State Department, in keeping with his unworldly, evangelical idealism, with the pursuit of treaties with the nations of the world assuring that all disputes would be referred for settlement to a permanent investigative commission, which would report within a year, during which there would be an obligatory (but completely unenforceable) "cooling off" period. Twenty-one such treaties were ratified, almost all of them with Latin American and Caribbean satellite states of the U.S.

Much more complicated, and instructively more intractable, were the problems of Mexico, which erupted into the lap of the United States following the overthrow of the 34-year dictatorship of President Porfirio Díaz in 1911, and Díaz's departure from Mexico. Díaz was another amiable scoundrel, only marginally more pure of motive, if significantly less absurd a mountebank, than General Antonio L. de Santa Anna, subduer of the Alamo and unsuccessful opponent of Sam Houston and of Winfield Scott. Díaz achieved great material progress for Mexico and coined the famous lamentation that Mexico was "so far from God and so close to the United States,"[3] but he ignored social reform and was inappropriately close to the big landowners and foreign investors. Santa Anna, Benito Juárez, the authentic and relatively disinterested patriot who overthrew the French in Mexico and executed the "Emperor" Maximilian, and Díaz were the three leading figures of Mexican public life from independence to 1911, principal political figures in the country from, respectively, 1833 to 1855, 1858 to 1872, and 1877 to 1911. Díaz was a successful leader in many ways, but after 34 years his regime was ripe to fall.

The opposition to Díaz was led by Francisco Madero, a moderate reformer and classic Kerensky type (Kerensky was the initial leader of the Russian revolution in 1917), who unleashed forces he could not control. Madero was overthrown and executed by the reactionary front for foreign and large domestic investors, led by Victoriano Huerta, in 1913. Wilson refused to recognize Huerta, whom he rightly saw as very unrepresentative of Mexican popular opinion, and preferred the less tainted Venustiano Carranza.

There was the usual sort of absurd incident that long bedeviled American relations with its "sister republics," as successive American presidents hopefully referred to them, when an American shore party at Tampico, on April 9, 1914, seeking only some supplies, strayed into an excluded area and was arrested. They were promptly released, but the U.S. squadron commander, Admiral Henry T. Mayo, in the sort of conduct that has irritated relations with Latin America for nearly two centuries, demanded a formal apology, punishment of the officer responsible, and a 21-gun salute to the American flag flying above Tampico. Huerta refused; Wilson allowed himself to be persuaded that he had to support Mayo in order not to advantage Huerta, and the apology was provided, but not the salute. Wilson secured the authority of Congress on April 22, 1914, to use force to redress grievances, and Bryan had just advised that a German ship carrying munitions was approaching Vera Cruz, in contravention of the blockade Wilson had taken it upon himself to impose. American ships and Marines bombarded and occupied Vera Cruz, and

---

3. The prime minister of Israel in the late seventies, Menachem Begin, at a high-level Israeli-Mexican meeting in the 1980s, joked that Israel had the opposite problem: "So close to God and so far from the United States."

Huerta broke off relations, Wilson having managed to unify Mexican opinion against the United States. Wilson did accept the mediation offer of Argentina, Brazil, and Chile, and at a meeting in Niagara Falls, Ontario (Canada), in May and June, the mediating countries proposed the retirement of Huerta, his replacement by a reform government, and no indemnity to the U.S. Huerta refused and had himself elected president; neither the mediating powers nor the U.S. accepted this, and Huerta resigned a few days later.

A month later, General Álvaro Obregón led a Constitutionalist army (the Carranza party) into Mexico City, and Carranza was recognized as president by the United States and other countries. Carranza's supposedly loyal lieutenant in the north, Francisco "Pancho" Villa, revolted, as did the leading warlord in the south, Emiliano Zapata. Carranza and Villa traded control of Mexico City as chaos prevailed in much of Mexico from 1915 to 1917. In his freebooting activities, Villa ignored the Mexican-U.S. border, other than as a refuge when Carranza and Obregón's loyalists succeeded in chasing him right out of the country. On January 10, 1916, Villa murdered 18 American mining engineers whom Carranza had invited to help reopen mines, and Villa's forces killed 17 Americans in a raid against Columbus, New Mexico, in March.

Wilson had tried to fob off the whole Mexican imbroglio, including these unhappy episodes, with a policy of "watchful waiting," but these outrages blew the lid off that humbug and, as happens from time to time in American affairs, the Congress got well ahead of the president in aroused belligerency. Wilson mobilized 150,000 militia to guard the Mexican border, and authorized, with Carranza's arm-twisted approval, a punitive raid into Mexico by General John J. Pershing at the head of 15,000 men. It was essentially a fiasco, aroused immense hostility in Mexico, and made a hero out of Villa, and Carranza rejected Wilson's unctuous attempts at agreed withdrawal and joint guarantees of the border. Finally, in early 1917, as European war threatened to involve the United States, Wilson quietly withdrew American forces, and Pershing prepared to head a hundred times as large a force against a thousand times as formidable an enemy.

Former president Huerta died of cirrhosis of the liver in 1916, as he approached the U.S.-Mexican border from the American side, with a view to launching another coup. (His nickname was "the jackal.") Carranza was elected president, and recognized, in 1917, and successfully arranged to have Zapata murdered in 1919. But Obregón turned against him and President Carranza was assassinated in 1920. Villa made peace with Obregón and retired to luxury, but was also assassinated in 1923. Obregón had a legitimate and very successful term as president from 1920 to 1924, and was succeeded by the talented and devious General Plutarco Calles in

1924. Consecutive terms were not permitted, but President Obregón was elected to succeed Calles in 1928, but was, in conformity with the now well-established tradition, assassinated before being reinaugurated the third of four presidents of Mexico to die violently, a record rarely challenged in any semi-serious jurisdiction since Roman times.

Calles remained the power in the country, and was known as *Maximato* until the election of General Lázaro Cárdenas in 1934. Calles founded the Partido Revolucionario Institucional, which ruled until 2000 in a virtual one-party state (and was democratically restored in 2012). He also conducted an anti-clerical campaign, known as the Cristero War, in which nearly 100,000 people were killed, including nearly 5,000 priests. Calles on the (anti-clerical) right and Zapata on the left, and Villa in the lore of outlawry, continue to be revered figures. These matters are recounted here because Mexican-American relations became an inter-mittently recurring matter of concern in Washington—little wonder, given the tumultuous devolution of events in Mexico and the illegal entry of perhaps 20 million Mexicans into the United States in the last half of the twentieth century.

10. WORLD WAR I

The Panama Canal opened officially on August 15, 1914. The Congress had passed a statute excluding U.S. flag ships from tolls, and the British objected that this was a violation of the Hay-Pauncefote Treaty, which promised equal treatment for all countries. Wilson agreed with the British and had the Panama Tolls Act repealed. It was presumably not entirely coincidental that the British thereafter approved everything the United States did in Mexico. By this time, the Great War had begun. Crown Prince Franz Ferdinand of Austria was assassinated by an anarchist, Gavrilo Princip, in Sarajevo, Bosnia, on June 28, 1914. Princip was acting for the Black Hand, a Serbian Pan-Slavic group, and the Serbian government was somewhat aware of the conspiracy, though it took no direct part in it. The German emperor gave Austria what he called "a blank check" to deal with Serbia as it wished. The Austrians investigated thoroughly but failed to find evidence of Serbian government complicity. The world was outraged and sympathetic to the Habsburgs. President Raymond Poincaré and Premier René Viviani of France visited St. Petersburg, July 20 to 23, and the French urged a strong hand to restrain Vienna. As soon as the French leaders had left the Russian capital, Austria served its ultimatum on Serbia, demanding suppression of hostile (to Vienna) organizations and publications, and dismissal of hostile officials, prosecution of accessories to the plot, sanitization of school curricula, and abject apologies. Serbia's reply was apparently conciliatory but evasive, and declined the requirement of prosecutions.

Serbia was the leader of Pan-Slav opposition to Austro-Hungarian incursions into the South Slavic lands grudgingly and forcibly vacated by Turkey, and Russia aspired to be the champion of the Slavs against Vienna, as it had been against the Turks. The British foreign secretary, Sir Edward Grey, proposed a conference on Austro-Serb problems, which France and Russia accepted but Austria-Hungary declined as unsuitable to matters of the honor of their empire, and they were supported by Germany. Both Vienna and Berlin believed the czar was bluffing, and Austria-Hungary declared war on Serbia on July 28. There was perfervid maneuvering, as France urged a strong response on Russia, and Berlin promised not to enter France or Belgium if Britain remained neutral. The British government declined. Between July 29 and August 3 all the five main powers were raising the ante while offering conditional reductions of tension but inching toward general mobilization, including a Russian order of full mobilization, which was then reduced to mobilization against Austria-Hungary only. This still attracted a German ultimatum to cease preparations for war on the German frontier, which caused a Russian reescalation, and Germany declared war on Russia on the evening of August 1. Belgium declined to give Germany free passage on its territory and was invaded by Germany, and Germany declared war on France on August 3. Britain declared war on Germany on August 4 and Austria-Hungary declared war on Russia on August 6. Italy declined to join the war, though some weeks later Turkey joined the war on the side of the Central Powers.

Almost all the leaders of the five initial Great Power belligerents were erratic and reckless about what they were getting into, like children playing with dynamite, without a thought of the human and material damage they might be about to cause. The expectation was for a brief war. The United States had talented ambassadors in the major capitals, who reported events accurately, but the United States was not consulted and claimed no right to intervene diplomatically. Wilson declared U.S. neutrality and on August 19 asked his countrymen to be "impartial in thought as well as in action." The British were more responsible and wary, but knew that they could not tolerate a German victory over France, Russia, and Belgium, and entered what their leaders feared would be an unprecedented hecatomb, with the capable foreign secretary, Grey, famously remarking: "The lights are going out all over Europe; we shall not see them lit again in our lifetime."

Woodrow Wilson

CHAPTER EIGHT

The Crisis of Democracy
*World War, Isolationism, and
Depression, 1914–1933*

1. THE WESTERN FRONT

The German war plan, devised by Field Marshal Alfred von Schlieffen, the former chief of the German General Staff, was to advance in overwhelming strength along the Channel coast of Belgium and France ("Let the last man on the right brush the Channel with his sleeve!") and encircle Paris from the north and west, severing Britain from France, and France from its capital. Schlieffen, like America's Admiral Mahan, was a student of the Punic Wars and wrote a learned treatise on Hannibal's masterpiece of encirclement, the Battle of Cannae, which was emulated in his plan for France and was partially revived in the great German blitzkrieg in France a generation later. The French plan, Plan XVII, devised by their commander, (subsequent) marshal Joseph Joffre, was to advance into the lost provinces of Alsace and Lorraine, and then into Germany. The Germans aimed at a quick knockout of France, while holding the eastern front against the Russians with relatively light forces.

Although Schlieffen's last words allegedly were "Keep the right wing strong!," his successor, Field Marshal Helmuth von Moltke, nephew of the victor of the Franco-Prussian War, weakened the right wing and revised the German plan to pass before Paris. After about two weeks of war, it became clear that the Germans were advancing well beyond the French in the north, and the French attack in Alsace and Lorraine was repulsed. Recognizing late, but not quite too late, the great danger in which France suddenly was, Joffre, with imperturbable coolness, abandoned his long-prepared Plan XVII and devised a new one, which consisted of a hasty but orderly retreat, keeping his armies intact, and surprising the Germans with a defense of Paris that would, if necessary, be fought to the last cartridge and the last man.

Moltke considered a French recovery impossible as his armies rolled inexorably toward Paris, and began to detach a few divisions and send them by rail to Russia. When the German armies arrived on and just north of the Marne, just 15 miles from Paris, they were attacked from the north and west and south with unsuspected force. Units totaling 1.485 million German soldiers and about 1.1 million Allied soldiers, 90 percent of them French, were engaged, and in five days of intensive fighting, the French, dramatically reinforced at the height of the battle with the Paris militia dispatched to the front in 600 requisitioned Paris taxis, defeated the Germans, who fell back 40 miles. The armies then extended their fronts to the English Channel and the Swiss border, and settled into more than four years of horribly bloody trench warfare, where the advantage was with the defense, and attacks were in the face of massed machine gun and artillery fire on both sides. There would be decisive fighting on the Russian and Turkish fronts, but in the greatest theater, in France, blood-letting would be without precedent and beyond imagination, and without decisive result. In the five days of the first Battle of the Marne, each side would endure 250,000 casualties, a ghastly prefiguring of the horrors and prodigies of courage and sacrifice to come.

It was quickly a stalemate. The French and the Germans, in their supreme struggle, a declining France and surging a Germany, met where the addition of the British Commonwealth forces and the unshakeable determination of France enabled that country to hold its own against what was now a larger and stronger German Empire. As the war continued on in sanguinary indecision, Europe's great nationalities bleeding themselves white (including Italy, which was unwisely seduced by offers of Allied favors and territorial gains in the Alps and on the Adriatic, to enter the war in 1915, though the horrible nature of the war was by then clear), it was inevitable that thoughts should focus on the United States, the mighty unengaged power, which had excluded itself from European affairs or interests in the Monroe Doctrine of 90 years before but possessed the power to determine the victor.

The British, although the Germans had built a formidable navy, announced an absolute blockade of Germany, which they shortly extended to include neutral countries that could pass on imports to or receive exports from Germany overland or in coastal waters—Netherlands, Denmark, Norway, and Sweden. The agreed but unratified Declaration of London of 1909 detailed items that could be embargoed in war, but these did not include foodstuffs and other goods not normally regarded as the sinews of war. We were now in an era of total war, and Great Britain was not about to relax its blockade policy, which had been rigorously exercised since the Seven Years' War, now more than 150 years before. On August 6, 1914, in the first few days of the war, Secretary Bryan asked that the belligerents accept the Declaration of London as written.

The Central Powers agreed, unsurprisingly, and the Russians and French said they would conform to the British position, which was also unsurprising, since without the British, the German navy would have prevailed over them without much difficulty. (France had the world's fourth navy, after Britain, Germany, and the U.S., but it was a distant fourth and concentrated in the Mediterranean.) The British, on August 20, 1914, accepted the Declaration, but with a radical expansion of what it considered contraband. This scandalized Bryan, who thought it smacked of the British attitude during the Napoleonic Wars, which led to the War of 1812. His sharp rejoinder was intercepted by Wilson's confidant in international affairs, (honorary) colonel Edward Mandell House, and toned down to a warning to the British of the severe effects on American public and political opinion of too restrictive a blockade. The British quietly ignored the warning and in November 1914 declared the North Sea a war zone and mined it entirely. This again outraged Bryan, who considered the British antics to be in no way less hostile and belligerent than the German recourse to submarine warfare against merchant shipping, which began in earnest when Germany declared the waters around the British Isles a war zone in retaliation, in February 1915.

The Bryan position had some merit, but in practical terms American trade with the Central Powers had been about $170 million in 1913, while trade with France and Britain in the same year had been about $800 million—a figure that ratcheted almost vertiginously upwards from there, to about $3 billion in 1919, while trade with Germany and Austria-Hungary declined in the same period by over 99 percent, to under $2 million. The U.S. banking industry was also something less than even-handed. It was obvious that whatever happened, Great Britain was not going to be conquered and her loans could always be collected, if needs must, from prosperous bits of her empire that could come within the maw of America, such as the hardy perennial in the American appetite, Canada, which had been salivated over intermittently by American leaders since Washington and Franklin and Jefferson. Canada was now independent, but there were extensive British assets in it. By April 1917, the American financial community had made loans to or bought bonds from Britain, France, Italy, and, to a slight degree, Russia, totaling $2.3 billion. This was a much more profitable version of the high-handedness of the British on the high seas than Jefferson and Madison had had to contend with.

The British position was made a good deal more tolerable by the typically abrasive methods of the Germans. The British were imposing an embargo, running ships into port, inspecting them, but not threatening American lives or property. The Germans warned on February 4, 1915, that neutral ships would enter the war zone around the British Isles at their own risk. Six days later, the United States, showing favoritism certainly based on kinship, the democratic bona fides of the British and French, their status as the defenders rather than aggressors in the war, and, not to be altogether put out of mind, their status as huge and profit-generating importers and borrowers, responded to Germany that attacks on American ships and the endangering or taking of American lives on the high seas would be considered "an indefensible violation of neutral rights." Germany would be held "strictly accountable." This was uneven treatment of the warring powers, but the Germans were threatening to sink ships and the British were only claiming a right to embargo certain cargoes.

The issue came quickly to a head with the German sinking, by submarine-launched torpedoes, off the coast of Ireland on May 7, 1915, of the great British liner *Lusitania*, former holder of the Blue Riband as the fastest trans-Atlantic ship, and one of the world's six or seven greatest ships, with the loss of 1,198 lives, including 124 Americans. American opinion was outraged. And so was the president. He drafted a diplomatic note that Bryan signed with reluctance, on May 13, demanding that Germany cease unrestricted submarine warfare, express regret at the sinking of the *Lusitania*, and offer reparations for the loss of American lives.

The German reply, on May 28, justified the incident on the grounds that the ship was armed and that it was carrying contraband. (It was unarmed, but carried a shipment of rifles and munitions, though not in significant quantities for a ship of 35,000 tons.) Wilson was dissatisfied with this and drafted a supplementary note, which rejected the German rationalization and demanded specific pledges against repetitions. Bryan resigned rather than sign the note, as he feared that it could involve America in the war. His resignation was tendered and accepted on June 7, 1915, and he was replaced at once by the counselor of the State Department, Robert Lansing (son-in-law of Benjamin Harrison's second secretary of state, John W. Foster). Wilson and Lansing followed with a third note on July 21 telling the German government that any future sinking of passenger vessels would be regarded as "deliberately unfriendly," an outright threat of war.

U.S.-German relations were further shaken by American discovery of a list of check stubs for payments to 126 identified German agents (who were then rounded up) in the United States, in the luggage of German attaché and future chancellor Franz von Papen, who was accused of fomenting sabotage, and eventually of trying to blow up the Welland Canal (in Canada). Germany was deemed responsible for several acts of sabotage in the United States while the U.S. was a neutral country, an utterly insane activity. Papen and others were deported from the United States in December 1915. Chastened by Wilson's sacking of Bryan and threatening war on Germany if it did not curtail its submarine activities, Germany ordered its submarine forces to leave all liners alone and focus on enemy warships, freighters, and tankers. Germany apologized to the United States in October 1915 for the sinking of the British liner *Arabic*, in which two Americans died.

2. DIPLOMATIC INITIATIVES

In Latin America apart from Mexico, there were the usual financial collapses and outbreaks of chaos to address. Haiti's president was assassinated in July 1915, and the country was mired in debt. Wilson dispatched the Marines, under the command of the racist war-lover General Smedley Butler, who treated all Haitians as virtual chimpanzees. Haiti became a protectorate of the United States, unable to adjust its tariffs or subscribe loans without American approval, while the United States collected and assessed tariffs and excise duties. An agreement with Nicaragua was finally agreed, in February 1916, granting the U.S. exclusive rights over an isthmian canal, though the canal in Panama was functioning well. When financial mismanagement and civil disorder again gripped the Dominican Republic in 1916, Wilson occupied the country and it was administered by U.S. naval officers until 1924. On January 17, 1917, the United States would buy the Danish Virgin Islands for $25 million.

Wilson had sent Colonel House to London, Paris, and Berlin in February 1915, and he held inconclusive talks with the leaders of those countries; he returned to see them a year later, to explore the possibilities of peace again. If neither side scored a decisive breakthrough, they would either stalemate and keep fighting until they had no more soldiers to kill, or the balance would have to be tipped by a current non-combatant, and only the United States had the power to do that. (Japan was a powerful enough country to make a difference, but it had no way of influencing events in Europe.) Wilson showed considerable foresight and imagination in suggesting peace terms, as his formidable mind focused on the challenge of ending this terrible war without the United States being drawn into it. In consequence of House's 1916 visit, a peace plan emerged consisting of enhanced German colonial rights and reduction of naval construction, restoration of occupied areas, including Alsace-Lorraine, and the complete expulsion of Turkey from Europe, including the handing over of Constantinople to Russia. Wilson communicated to Britain's Foreign Secretary Grey that if Britain, France, and Russia accepted such terms and the Central Powers declined them, the "United States would probably enter the war against Germany." Neither the Allies nor the Central Powers bit at this prospect, though it would have been much better for all of them if they had. Both sides still thought they could win the war, and the carnage continued. The 10-month Battle of Verdun, the greatest in the history of the world up to that time, was already well underway; it would inflict over a million casualties, about 700,000 dead, more French than German, but the French army held the city and forts of Verdun and forced the Germans back.

By now, a considerable agitation for war had arisen in the United States. A Preparedness Movement arose, in various almost paramilitary organizations, operating boot camps for volunteers, especially at Plattsburgh, New York. Theodore Roosevelt, Henry Cabot Lodge, and previous and future cabinet secretary Colonel Henry L. Stimson were among the leaders of the movement. They ranged from advocates of vigilance and readiness to deal with war should it be unloosed on the country to outright interventionists invoking the solidarity of the English-speaking peoples and of the great American and French republics. Senior British and French officials, including former prime minister Arthur James Balfour (now foreign secretary) and former French army commander Marshal Joseph Joffre, received very enthusiastic welcomes when they visited the United States. In February 1916, Secretary of War Lindley Garrison and Deputy Secretary Henry Breckinridge abruptly resigned from the administration in protest against Wilson's refusal to institute peacetime conscription, the exact opposite to Bryan's concern of a rush toward war when he resigned a year before, which indicated that Wilson was holding the solid center of public opinion. The new secretary of war would be the mayor of Cleveland, Newton D. Baker.

On the other side, there were hyperactive peace groups, including, starting another tradition of prominent American businessmen who fancied themselves endowed with talents for international mediation, Henry Ford, who sent a "peace ship" to Europe, which accomplished nothing worthwhile. He proved the forerunner of such self-nominated corporate ambassadors as Cyrus Eaton in the fifties and Armand Hammer in the eighties. In Congress, there were moves to prevent Americans from traveling on armed vessels, as the Germans announced they had the right to sink merchant vessels that were armed.

Wilson faced these measures down, and defended the prerogatives of his office, and after the *Lusitania* showdown, he urged preparedness. He told an audience in Philadelphia just three days after the *Lusitania* was sunk that "There is such a thing as a man being too proud to fight; there is such a thing as a nation being so right that it does not need to convince others by force that it is right." Roosevelt in particular raved and fumed in stentorian tones that this was pusillanimous claptrap, and it was a pious sentiment that didn't have unlimited appeal. Americans generally wanted to avoid war if they were not provoked intolerably. It was a terrible war and the United States was economically flourishing as a neutral supplier to the Allies. But these were questions of practicality and self-interest, not pride and virtue. Wilson did conclude after the *Lusitania* incident that the country had to be ready for anything, and presented the Congress a comprehensive plan of enhanced war-making power, on December 7, 1915.

In March 1916, the German Navy torpedoed a French ferry boat in the English Channel, the *Sussex*, injuring several Americans. Wilson and Lansing considered this a violation of the pledge given after the sinking of the *Arabic*, and Lansing recommended breaking off diplomatic relations with Germany. Wilson declined to do that, but had Lansing inform the talented German ambassador in Washington, Count Bernstorff, that relations would be severed if Germany did not avoid such provocations. The German reply promised change if its opponents respected international law.

The National Defense Act of June 1916 raised the regular army from 175,000 to 223,000, called for a fully trained militia of 450,000, and raised defense production orders and capability. Britain purported to blacklist American companies that traded with its enemies, in July 1916, and Wilson replied with legislation authorizing refusal of entry to, or exit from, any U.S. ports of any ship that discriminated against any American company. He also sent the Congress, which approved it, the highest naval construction and maintenance budget in the country's history. (In a moment of exasperation, on September 24, 1916, Wilson said to House: "Let us build a navy bigger than Britain's and do what we please.")[1] Britain rapidly desisted from any such provocation as had been threatened. It was an infinitely stronger America than Jefferson and Madison had led a century before, but Wilson also dealt with all aspects of the international crisis a great deal more capably than they had. This was where the country stood opposite the warring powers as it entered another presidential election campaign.

3. THE 1916 ELECTION AND UNRESTRICTED SUBMARINE WARFARE

The Republicans met at Chicago in June and nominated Supreme Court justice and former New York governor Charles Evans Hughes for president and former vice president (under Theodore Roosevelt) Charles W. Fairbanks of Indiana for vice president. Hughes had been on the high court for the last six years and had been a moderate and reform governor of New York, and so was acceptable to followers of both former Republican presidents, Taft and Roosevelt. The party platform played everything down the center and called for readiness but avoidance of adventurism. The Democrats met at St. Louis a week later, and renominated President Wilson and Vice President Marshall without opposition, lauding the president's reform program, his defense of American honor, and his avoidance of the slaughter in Europe. The slogan "He kept us out of war" was the rallying cry and was endlessly bandied about. It resonated well with most people, though Irish and German Americans resented a policy perceived as too friendly to Britain. The Progressives nominated Roosevelt, but he declined and supported Hughes, as then did most of the Progressives. The Socialists nominated Allan Benson by postal ballot, as Eugene Debs sat this election out. The Democrats accused Hughes of excessive reliance on "hyphenated-Americans," implying people of compromised loyalty to the country, especially German and Irish Americans,

---

1.   Conrad Black, *Franklin Delano Roosevelt: Champion of Freedom,* New York, PublicAffairs, 2003, p. 80.

but it was a relatively civilized campaign between two very urbane men. Some western states had accorded women the vote, and Wilson's implicit promise to stay out of the war was especially popular with them.

On election day, Wilson won 9.13 million votes to 8.54 million for Hughes, 585,000 for Benson, and 221,000 for the Prohibitionists, and won 277 electoral votes to 254 for Hughes. It was 49 percent for Wilson to 46 percent for Hughes and 3 percent for Benson. Wilson's popular-vote margin appeared sufficient, but the result came in very late, as it was decided by California. Hughes had failed to appear for an appointment with the governor of the state, former Progressive vice presidential candidate Hiram W, Johnson, who had been instrumental in carrying the state for Roosevelt in 1912. For this reason, Johnson withheld his endorsement from Hughes and Wilson took California and its 13 electoral votes by 3,773 popular votes, and was reelected—only the seventh man, of 27 who had served as president, to win two consecutive contested terms, and the first Democrat to do so since Jackson, 84 years before. Because of his reservations about aspects of the U.S. constitutional system, Wilson had planned, if Hughes had won, to appoint him secretary of state and resign with Marshall, to make Hughes president at once and not wait about, fussing impatiently, until March for his inauguration.

In September, Ambassador Count Bernstorff had asked whether Wilson would use his good offices to try to reconcile the parties if Germany undertook to restore Belgium. Wilson deferred consideration of that until after the election (instead of using the opportunity for electoral purposes, as many subsequent presidents might not have been able to resist the temptation to do). Wilson prepared a peace plan in November, but before presenting it, his soundings found the Allies implacably hostile to any peace overtures. Germany publicly declared on December 12 the willingness of the Central Powers to enter into comprehensive peace talks. The Allies refused because of German refusal to state peace terms in advance, but in fact they thought they were winning and were not interested. On December 18, Wilson asked the belligerent powers to state their war aims. Germany refused to do so, but the Allies, in a joint statement, demanded German withdrawal from all occupied territories, with indemnities and reparations; the liberation of all Italians, Czechs, Slovaks, Slavs, and Romanians from government by Austro-Hungarians; the expulsion of Turkey from Europe; and a new security regime for Europe guaranteeing the borders of all countries. The statement was vague about a reconstruction of Poland, and required the restoration of Alsace-Lorraine to France. On January 22, 1917, Wilson told the Congress that there would need to be an international organization to assure the peace, and called for "peace without victory." It was a perceptive concept that only a peace that did not harvest the seeds of revenge would be durable, and that such a peace would enable the world to use the terrible destruction of the current war as an effective deterrent to a return to general war.

On February 1, 1917, Emperor Wilhelm II made one of the most catastrophic errors of modern times, and the German government announced a return to unrestricted submarine warfare, with no regard to the nature or nationality of ships. The General Staff was persuaded, and persuaded the emperor (but not the civilian government) that Britain would break under the pressure before the United States could make its presence in the war in Europe felt. Wilson severed relations with Germany two days later, recalled his ambassador from Berlin, and expelled Bernstorff. The Congress passed a resolution of support on February 7. Germany allowed one American ship a week to go to Britain under conditions to be outlined, but this was obviously completely unacceptable. The first American merchantman sunk under this regime was the USS *Housatonic*, on February 3.

On March 1, a message was sent by the German foreign minister, Alfred Zimmermann, to the German minister in Mexico instructing him that if the U.S. looked likely to enter the war he should suggest to the Mexican government an alliance with Germany, for which Mexico would be rewarded with the restoration of territory lost in the Mexican War. The message was intercepted and decoded by British naval intelligence, and given to the U.S. ambassador in London, Walter Hines Page, who sent it to Lansing, who on Wilson's order promptly released it to the press. American ships were being sunk regularly by German submarines on the high seas, and relations had clearly passed the point of no return. Having just been reelected on the slogan of keeping the country out of war, Wilson was waiting for his own reinauguration and a few more provocations to stir American opinion to prodigies of outrage, before leading America into the greatest war in history.

All through the period since the sinking of the *Lusitania*, the assistant secretary of the navy, Franklin D. Roosevelt, had been playing a duplicitous double game with his cousin, Theodore Roosevelt, Senator Lodge, and Lodge's son-in-law, Congressman Augustus Gardner, chairman of the House Foreign Affairs Committee, while professing complete loyalty to Wilson and to his direct chief, Navy Secretary Josephus Daniels, an outright pacifist. The younger Roosevelt was guilty of a campaign of leaks to the press through his Machiavellian and gnomish assistant, Louis McHenry Howe, that carried policy disagreements to the edge of outright treachery. He had no more use than his famous cousin did for Wilson's pious humbug about being "too proud to fight." Though he would not have agreed with TR's description of Wilson as a "sophist . . . a logothete . . . a real doctrinaire," and "not a real man," he agreed that there was no doubt where America's interest lay and that a German victory, which could occur if there were not American intervention, would be a disaster for civilization. (The younger Roosevelt knew Germany well, and spoke German fluently.)

On March 11, 1917, Franklin Roosevelt met in the afternoon with Wilson's intimate adviser, Colonel House, who favored participation in the war, and in the evening with Republican participationists TR, General Leonard Wood (former proconsul in Cuba), Elihu Root, J.P. Morgan Jr., and the mayor of New York, John P. Mitchell. This was a tour de force in double-dealing. His experiences would be invaluable 25 years later, in even more desperate conditions for the world.[2]

In February and March 1917, Wilson armed American merchant vessels, following a 403–13 approval in the House of Representatives of Wilson's request. And after a filibuster in the Senate by, as Wilson called them, "a little group of willful men," led by Robert La Follette, Wilson and Lansing determined that he had the authority to do it without Senate approval. In Russia, a general revolt in the political classes and much of the officer corps led to the abdication of the Czar and the Romanov Dynasty, at first in favor of Prince Georgy Lvov's provisional government, and then a moderate, democratic, republican government led by Alexander Kerensky, with the Bolsheviks led by V.I. Lenin in sinister opposition, fomenting the next phase of their pursuit of a totalitarian, Marxist revolution. Russia continued, unsteadily, in the war, and the Kerensky interlude, as it soon proved to be, at least spared the Western Allies the embarrassment of an undemocratic Russia as an ally. As German sinkings of American vessels continued, Wilson consulted his cabinet (in another gesture to British methods of governance) on March 20, and it was unanimously agreed that there was no choice but war. At last, America was moving to the center of the world stage.

The fiasco in Mexico and routine interventions in the Caribbean gave no indication that Wilson had any strategic thoughts. But he had captured the essence of enduring peace; a war so terrible to be a deterrent against future wars must not incite insupportable ambitions for vengeance and redress, and the peace must be preserved by an international organization. It was a brilliant vision—the most imaginative insight into world affairs any leader of a great nation had ever had, almost a jingo of righteousness.

Theodore Roosevelt's naval construction, isthmian canal, and international activism, and Woodrow Wilson's transformation of a response to maritime aggression into a crusade against belligerency and revanchism and in favor of international law, organization, and civility, were the first two forays of America into a foreign

---

2. Black, *op. cit.*, pp. 77–80.

policy aimed at world influence: the big stick and bully pulpit, and the evangeliza-tion of militant democracy and constructive internationalism.

Neither would prove immediately consequential. But Theodore Roosevelt's most important relative, who would also prove to be the most talented member of the Wilson administration, would learn the necessity of possessing military strength from his quasi-uncle and cousin, and of selling a moral mission in foreign policy initiatives from his president. He would blend the two successfully and impose this dual character on American foreign policy thereafter. Franklin Delano Roosevelt would prove the true heir and continuator of both TR and Wilson, enemies of each other though they were, would be more successful in the world than either, and would win more elections as president than the two combined.

4. THE UNITED STATES ENTERS THE WAR

President Wilson delivered his war message to the Congress on the evening of April 2, 1917. Gaunt and dressed in black, ignoring the thunderous applause elicited by his eloquence, Wilson galvanized the nation, even a temporarily respectful Theo-dore Roosevelt, with his intellect, erudition, and articulation. "The world must be made safe for democracy. . . . the right is more precious than peace . . . . To such a task we can dedicate our lives and our fortunes, everything that we are and everything that we have, with the pride of those who know that the day has come when America is privileged to spend her blood and her might for the principles which gave her birth and happiness and the peace which she has treasured. God helping her, she can do no other." The declaration of war was voted and signed on April 6. To a world exhausted by a horrible war, America promised peace through the victory of the Western powers, buoyed by the mighty trans-Atlantic democracy, a victory of liberal reform, republican rule, and constitutional monarchy, over the dead hand of the authoritarian monarchies of Central and Eastern Europe. It would become a war to end war, and to, as the president stirringly said, "make the world safe for democracy." Life and meaning and purpose were imparted, at this very late date, to the unspeakable carnage in which tens of thousands died every few days on all sides, for years, to move an army commander's headquarters a few miles closer to Berlin or Paris or St. Petersburg, Vienna, Rome, or Constantinople.

The American entry into the war came as Allied fortunes were being severely stretched. The Germans sank 881,000 tons of Allied shipping in March 1917. And the failed offensives of the French in Champagne in April and of the British and Canadians in Flanders from June to November 1917, of Brusilov's Russian offensive against the Germans in July, and the rout of the Italians at Caporetto north of Venice in the late autumn, while the Bolsheviks seized power in St. Petersburg, organized a communist dictatorship, and left the war in March 1918, all presaged a mighty effort by Germany to win the war in the west, having transferred her entire eastern army to France, before American reinforcements could turn the tide.

In 19 months, Wilson raised the size of the United States Army from 200,000 to 4,000,000, with a navy of over 500,000; 2.8 million men were drafted and nearly 2 million volunteered. There were 500,000 American soldiers in France in May 1918, and they arrived throughout most of the last year of the war at the rate of over 200,000 a month, over 300,000 in July 1918 alone. The American Expeditionary Force under General John J. Pershing grew to 2.1 million men, of whom nearly 1.4 million were engaged combat forces. It became a race between the concentration of all German forces and arriving American forces on the Western Front, as well as a struggle against submarines in the Atlantic.

As the Great War escalated to its sanguinary and desperate climax, the British replaced H.H. Asquith as prime minister with the more energetic David Lloyd George at the head of a coalition government in December 1916. The French handed almost unlimited power to the 76-year-old veteran of the Paris Commune and the long battle over the Dreyfus affair, Georges Clemenceau, in November 1917. As Russia left the war and the Germans began their supreme play for victory in the west in March 1918, the Allies agreed on the appointment of Ferdinand Foch as generalissimo and supreme commander of the Allied armies, and in August, as he launched his great offensive, he was named Marshal of France. Pershing retained command of the American army, which was kept integral and contiguous, as were other Allied armies, but Foch assumed command of the entire theater, the greatest host in human history (up to that time), over 6,000,000 soldiers by November 1918.

The United States was not an Allied, but rather an "associated," power, as Wilson wished to retain the independent moral authority to propose a compromise peace. As the terrible year of 1917 unfolded, others followed Wilson's lead in trying to lift up the hearts of their embattled and much-widowed and orphaned populations with war aims that would inspirit a final and decisive sacrificial effort. Alexander Kerensky took office in Russia in May and called for a peace based on the self-determination of all the nationalities of Europe (the fragmentation of the Austro-Hungarian Empire in particular but not including the ethnic minorities of Russia). In August, Pope Benedict XV commended to the leaders of the warring powers a peace without indemnities, the renunciation of war and its replacement by disarmament and arbitration, the complete freedom of the seas, and the evacuation of Belgium and other occupied territories. When the Bolsheviks seized power in St. Petersburg and in Moscow in November 1917, they published secret treaties with the British and French that had the semblance of imperialist designs, and they redoubled their call for universal revolt and the worldwide solidarity of the laboring classes.

Woodrow Wilson returned to Congress on January 8, 1918, to enunciate his Fourteen Points. It was a world-shaking charter: open and openly negotiated covenants of peace; absolute freedom of the seas; tariff reduction and equality of trade; reduction of national armaments to the lowest point adequate for domestic security; impartial adjustment of all colonial claims, with equal weight to the native peoples and colonizing powers; evacuation of Russia and her self-determination; evacuation of Belgium; restoration of Alsace-Lorraine to France; the redrafting of Italy's borders to include all ethnic Italians except the Swiss; autonomous development for the peoples of Austria-Hungary; evacuation of Romania, Serbia, and Montenegro, and access to the sea for Serbia; opening of the Dardanelles, with self-determination of peoples governed by Turkey, but a secure and sovereign Ottoman Turkey; an independent Poland with access to the sea; and a general association of nations on the basis of equality of rights of all nations, regardless of size and strength.

It was an electrifying and prophetic program, which had the initial intended effect of inspiring the world but also contained the ingredients of disillusionment and havoc. The Germans would accept only if it was clear they were losing the war; so at the point, if it could be achieved, where the Americans turned the tide in favor of the Allies, the Germans would have to sue for peace on the basis of their diminished prospects, and the United States might have to threaten a separate peace to get Anglo-French agreement to any such terms as these. Neither power would accept the colonial or disarmament provisions; the British would not unreservedly accept unconditional freedom of the seas, since they controlled most of them, and the French, if victorious, would never trust the Germans to stay disarmed, nor make Germany's military renascence easier by disarming themselves. Sundering the Austro-Hungarian and Ottoman Empires had its appeal as an idea, but would create far more difficult and often lawless states than those being atomized had been. And any such total immersion in internationalism as this, especially any adherence to the multilateral assembly of nations that was envisioned in the last point, would be such a change of pace for America that it would require intensive lobbying of the opposition—not a tactic that commended itself to Wilson's authoritarian and didactic temperament, nor one that would be easy with such obdurate and fierce personalities as Roosevelt and Lodge.

Wilson's ability to rely on the Republicans, bearing in mind that anything like this would have to be a treaty requiring two-thirds of the senators for ratification, was not helped by his dismissal of Roosevelt's request to be allowed to lead a division of volunteers into the war, as he had the Rough Riders, with Leonard Wood and others, almost 20 years before in Cuba. TR was now 58, half-blind, and overweight and unfit after his 1913 trip up the Amazon, where he contracted some tenacious local ailments. Wilson thought that his predecessor was inspired by a *Boy's Own Annual* fable of what war was like and remarked that it was no longer "the charge of the Light Brigade." It was, in some respects, a nonsensical idea, but it held interesting political possibilities.

Wilson could, in effect, have bargained this favor for Roosevelt's support of his peace plan, if he had been prepared to preview some of it at this point, and could even have struck some sort of arrangement with Roosevelt, as Franklin D. Roosevelt would have done, and later did expediently and usually ephemerally, with any number of Republicans and dissident Democrats. But Wilson had no sense of political tactics, and was, rather, concerned with devising and imposing intellectual formulations that were profound but very complicated to implement. He was also a very inflexible personality, and a Virginia Presbyterian, afflicted with the racial attitudes of the South (unlike Theodore Roosevelt, an urbane world traveler and enlightened Lincoln Republican, who famously invited the eminent African American educator Booker T. Washington to dinner in the White House).

The addition of American shipbuilding capacity and of the U.S. Navy to the supply of men and materiel to the war zone tightened the blockade of Germany and defeated the German submarines, on behalf of which the German General Staff and emperor (over the protests of the civilian government) had provoked American entry into the war. Having driven Britain into the arms of the French with his colossal naval construction program, Wilhelm II used his fleet only for three days in the entire war in the spring of 1916, drawing an immense and inconclusive battle with the British Grand Fleet (Jutland), following which, the German High Seas Fleet returned to port and remained there for the duration of the war. Wilhelm, though not an unintelligent man, had notoriously impulsive and self-indulgent judgment and was one of the most catastrophically error-prone leaders in modern history, at a cost of countless millions of lives and his own throne and dynasty.

With American forces, relatively untrained but physically strong and in high spirits, pouring into the French Atlantic ports at 50,000 men a week, the Germans launched their supreme offensive on March 21, 1918. They attacked in great strength toward the rail and supply center of Amiens, with the plan of splitting the French and British armies and wheeling northward to the Channel and forcing the British into the sea. It was at this point that Foch was given the supreme command of all Western Front Allied armies. The Germans launched a new attack on April 9, west of Lille, with the same general objective as at Amiens, but progressed only about 17 miles against continuing fierce resistance and at heavy cost. The next German thrust was on May 27 to the south of Amiens, and it captured Soissons and got to within 50 miles of Paris, but did not break through French ranks. From June 9 to 15, the Germans attacked in salients east and north of Paris, but as always in this war, they encountered fanatical French resistance as they got close to the French capital.

By this time, Americans were playing a significant part in the defense and fought with much-remarked bravery and success at Cantigny, 50 miles north of Paris, where nearly 30,000 Americans were engaged. After these exertions, the German army had returned to the Marne, after an absence of four years. As a long war was presaged by the remarkable French recovery on the Marne in 1914, largely because of the immovability of Foch's army in that battle, the generalissimo earned his marshal's baton and opened the final offensive of the war by repulsing the Germans at the Marne again, with the assistance of 270,000 Americans. The salient between Soissons and Reims that threatened Paris was eliminated by August 6. Two days later, the British moved all their forces forward, with the Canadians and Belgians and over 50,000 Americans, pushing the Germans back from near Amiens.

A series of offensives involving all the Allied armies now erupted steadily along the whole front from the Channel to the Swiss border, and by early November the Allies were at a ragged line that ran from Brussels to Namur, Luxembourg, Metz, and Strasbourg, and the Germans had been cleared from Alsace and about half of Lorraine. On the southern front, the Italians, reinforced by French units, decisively defeated the Austro-Hungarians at Vittorio Veneto in late October. The Central Powers swiftly disintegrated. Bulgaria surrendered on September 30; a new German government, through the Swiss, asked Wilson on October 2, as did Austria on October 7, for an armistice followed by a peace conference based on the Fourteen Points. (The timeless Habsburg emperor Franz Joseph had died in November 1916, at age 86, after a reign of 68 years. He had begun in the revolt that swept out Metternich and lived almost but, mercifully, not quite, to the end of the 703-year rule of the Habsburgs.)

5. THE ARMISTICE

It was at this late point, when the war was effectively won, that Wilson could act, but the French and British responded that they had not been consulted about the Fourteen Points and did not agree with all of them. Wilson also delayed responding to the Germans, because he would not deal with a German government that he was unconvinced really represented the German population. The German fleet, which had had the comparative good fortune to be inactive for virtually all of the war, mutinied at Kiel on November 3; Austria surrendered on November 4; after a revolution broke out in Bavaria on November 7, the emperor abdicated and fled to the Netherlands on November 9, and a republic was declared on November 11. Wilson did threaten a separate peace (and had House tell Lloyd George and Clemenceau he would send the British and French war aims to the Congress); finally on November 5, the British and French accepted the Fourteen Points as a basis of negotiation, but with the provisions that they would determine what freedom of the seas actually consisted of and that Germany would have to pay reparations for war damage in territories from which they withdrew. Wilson agreed to this and transmitted, via the Swiss, the conditions to the Germans, whose government was now in a state of chaos, and authority for negotiating an armistice was delegated to Marshal Foch. German military delegates met with him on his campaign railway car in the Compiègne Forest on November 8, and the armistice was signed early on November 11, and took effect on the 11th hour of the 11th day of the 11th month of 1918.

Under its terms, Germany would evacuate all occupied territories, the left bank of the Rhine, and the bridgeheads of Mainz, Cologne, and Coblenz; the Allies retained a full right to claim damages; all submarines would be surrendered and the entire German fleet would be interned in British ports; the treaties of Brest-Litovsk and Bucharest (when the Germans conquered Romania, which had been induced by the British into declaring war on Germany in 1915) were abrogated; all German aircraft, tanks, and heavy artillery were to be destroyed; prisoners of war and deportees were to be returned; and Germany was to hand over 150,000 railway cars, 5,000 locomotives, and 5,000 trucks. So ended the greatest war in history. Sixteen million people had died and 21 million had been wounded. Of the main combatants, the dead and wounded totals, including civilians, were, in millions of people: Russia, 3.3 and 4.95; Turkey, 2.92 and 0.4 (indicating poor medical facilities); Germany, 2.47 and 4.25; France, 1.7 and 4.27; Austria-Hungary, 1.57 and 3.6; Italy, 1.24 and 0.95; the United Kingdom, 1.0 and 1.66; the United States, 117,000 dead and 206,000 wounded, and more than half the American dead were from the terrible pandemic of influenza that swept the camps at the end of the war.

Wilson began at once to make serious tactical errors; he called for a Democratic Congress in the midterm elections and was sharply rebuked by the voters, who delivered both houses to the Republicans, irritated by what was seen as a violation of his pledge to avoid politics. Roosevelt jubilated that "Mr. Wilson has no authority to speak for the American people" and denounced "his Fourteen Points and his four supplementary points and his five complementary points." He issued his statement from Roosevelt Hospital, where he was convalescing, but he died 10 weeks later, aged just 60, leaving Wilson unchallenged in American public esteem, but on a slippery slope of overheated expectations.

If Roosevelt had not weakened his health with his Amazon trip in 1913, he would almost certainly have lived longer, and, healthy, would have been the Republican presidential nominee in 1920, and would have been elected. His quarrel with Taft, splitting of his party, denigration of Irish and German Americans as insufficiently American, and extreme vitriol in reference to a distinguished incumbent (who replied with equally damaging, if less bombastic, strictures) all indicated that Roosevelt could not live easily with his mistaken pledge in 1904 not to seek reelection. If he finally had been reelected, he would presumably have been more temperate in his conduct. He was widely mourned as a gifted and popular leader. Wilson announced on November 18 that he would attend the peace conference in Paris in person, and that he would take no one from the Senate, nor any representative Republicans, with him. The conference opened on January 18, 1919.

6. THE PARIS PEACE CONFERENCE

It was clear from the outset that Clemenceau, Lloyd George, and the Italian premier, Vittorio Orlando, were not going to cooperate with Wilson's relatively altruistic view of the late enemy. Wilson's tactic was to gamble on acceptance of the League of Nations, as the new world body was to be called, before everything else, and the other terms could follow. The Allies accepted this sequence only on condition of various concessions, and the tug of war began between Wilson's attachment to the League and the desire of the other Allies to pick the carcass of the Central Powers. Wilson gave a draft of the Covenant of the League to the conference plenary session and returned to the United States on February 24. He had a dinner meeting with leading members of the Congress, which was a rather stormy session. Thirty-nine senators, more than enough to block passage, expressed their desire on March 2 to kill the League in its existing form. Their legal draftsman was Philander Knox, Taft's secretary of state and Roosevelt's attorney general, though Taft himself was pro-League. Two days later, Wilson declared in New York that any such effort would kill the entire peace agreement, and he returned to France on March 13.

The next day, in Paris, he was presented by Marshal Foch, who enjoyed great prestige as commander of the victorious armies, with a demand for heavy but unspecified reparations by Germany and Allied occupation of Germany to the Rhine, or at least the creation of a neutral Rhineland buffer state. Wilson refused and called for the liner *George Washington* to return to take him and his party back to America. He also had preliminary symptoms of acute stress. Foch and Clemenceau reduced their demand to a temporary occupation of parts of Germany, and Wilson promised a defensive treaty in which Britain and the U.S. would promise to come to France's assistance in the event of an unprovoked attack on her by Germany. This was really the key to the future: an American guarantee of France and Britain would probably have deterred even the lunatic government that eventually did rule in Germany. The Senate leaders expressed grievous reservations about the arrangement from the start and Wilson concentrated entirely on the Allies and not at all on the equally treacherous and even more intractable problems under the dome of the United States Capitol.

The Italians demanded specific performance on the Treaty of London, which had brought them into the war in 1915, under which they were to move their border up to the Brenner Pass, which would bring 200,000 German-speaking Austrians into Italy. Wilson agreed to this before the demographers on his staff could warn him that this was contrary to his national-ethnic self-determination policy. The further Italian demand of the Adriatic port of Fiume, promised in 1915, was unacceptable to Wilson, and the Italian leaders, Premier Orlando and Foreign Minister Sidney Sonnino, walked out. Wilson then appealed directly to the people of Italy for a fair peace. Orlando and Sonnino did come back in May, and Italy did succeed in taking Fiume by negotiation with the new kingdom of Yugoslavia, but for Wilson to squander this much credibility and capital on a trivial matter with the Italians left little room for optimism that he could deal with the much more formidable leaders of much stronger countries, Britain and France, or the faction heads of a U.S. Congress that was now almost in open revolt. Italy was only asking for what it had been promised, before there were any Fourteen Points, and Italy had taken 10 times as many war dead as the United States had. If it had been as confident of its martial ability as the other conferees were, it would just have taken what it wanted, but in these conditions, that would have been hazardous, though the poet and aviator Gabriele d'Annunzio took Fiume and was only dislodged by the Italian Navy, after governing for a year in proto-fascist manner, in 1920.

More of a problem were the Japanese, who had taken advantage of the war to enter it on the Allied side in August 1914 and confine their war-making activities to trying to take over permanently all German interests in China, especially the province of Shantung. The European powers were not minded, during the war, to argue the point, though the United States did, and the ambiguous Lansing-Ishii Agreement of November 1917 gave what Lansing considered temporary, and the

Japanese emissary, Viscount Kikujito Ishii, considered permanent, "paramount" interests in China, based on the enunciation that "territorial propinquity creates special relations." Of course, this was diplomatic humbug, and at the Paris Peace Conference Japan demanded, and did not receive, a declaration of racial equality, and then faced an attempt by the other powers to divide German interests in China between all of them, although Japan had taken those interests over and browbeaten China into a quasi-acquiescence in that.

Wilson finally acceded to Japan's demands, since, as a practical matter, there wasn't much to be done about them, on the condition that Japan acknowledged that Shantung would revert to China apart from economic rights. The Open Door and China's territorial integrity were sanctimoniously reiterated, but were, in fact, being steadily whittled away. The United States was the only country that made even the slightest pretense of concern for the Chinese interest in these matters. (If Japan had rallied to the Allies for any other than completely self-serving purposes, such as by sending two divisions to fight in France, or even against Turkey, she could have established a claim to all of Germany's Pacific islands and a much-enhanced status in the councils of the world. Portugal, though hardly a heavyweight country militarily, bravely volunteered modest forces for the Western Front, though her own interests were not in play and the Portuguese were only responding under their centuries-old treaty with Britain.)

The Allies had deployed 195,000 soldiers to Russia from 1918 to 1920, led by 70,000 Japanese, ostensibly to protect their interests, but really to seize an eastern chunk of Russia. The second largest contribution was from the Czech Republic—Austro-Hungarian prisoners of war whom the Bolshevik leaders released to return to the Western Front via Vladivostok, to join the Western Allies against the Central Powers. Most of them did not embark and instead engaged in the Russian Civil War against the Bolsheviks. The British landed 40,000 men at Archangel and Murmansk to secure vast supplies that had been deposited there and to assist the White Russians in their struggle with the Bolsheviks. The United States sent 24,000 men, and there were French and Canadians as well as, in the Caucasus Greek contingents, but it was a shambles and was never coordinated nor united by any mission statement. The Western powers left in 1920, and the combination of Soviet military success and American diplomatic pressure forced Japan back to its prewar frontiers in 1924.

Wilson tried to conciliate the reasonable Republicans such as Taft, by agreeing that the U.S. would refrain from participation in the mandate system, which was to provide for administration over seized German colonies; would oppose League interference in tariffs and immigration; would assure that there would be no interference with "regional understandings," such as the Monroe Doctrine; and would assure that any country could withdraw from the League on two years' notice.

7. THE TREATY OF VERSAILLES

The Treaty of Versailles was presented to the Germans on May 7 as a fait accompli; there would be none of the negotiating for which its emissaries had prepared. The treaty fixed responsibility for the Great War on Germany; took away from Germany Alsace-Lorraine, the western provinces of what became Poland, all colonies, and, until its future should be determined by plebiscite in 1935, the Saar; assessed reparations that later aggregated $56 billion; and imposed unilateral disarmament on Germany. The Covenant of the League of Nations was attached to the treaty. This established the secretariat at Geneva; set up an assembly and a council, on which the permanent members would be the U.S., Britain, France, Italy, and Japan; and pledged member states to avoid war, disarm, submit disagreements to the League, impose sanctions on aggressor states, and set up a Permanent Court of International Justice. Germany, under great protest, signed it on June 28, a week after its navy had scuttled itself at Scapa Flow, where it had been concentrated after the armistice. Over 70 ships, including 16 battleships and battle cruisers, were sunk, a pitiful end to a great fleet that antagonized Britain and was never, except for two inconclusive days, put to any practical use. It was the capstone of Wilhelmine strategy. Wilson departed France as soon as the treaty was signed, and returned to the United States on July 8, and submitted the Treaty of Versailles to the Senate on July 10, 1919.

This had been the first attempt at so comprehensive a reorganization of the world since the Congress of Vienna in 1815, and was the first attempt the United States had ever made to participate in deliberations that affected the whole world, or any part of it outside the Americas. Wilson had bet on the epochal peace-making and imposing possibilities of a world organization, and in order to achieve European and Japanese adherence to it, had sacrificed any pretense of a peace without victory or without vindictiveness. In the great struggle between France and Germany, France had made an astonishing comeback from the debacle of the Franco-Prussian War, but a united Germany, the bequest of Bismarck, was a larger population and France could be secure only if the alliance with the British and Americans was solid. Wilson assumed that Germany could be suitably rehabilitated as a democracy. Although the principal Allies were milling about with expeditionary forces in Russia, where a civil war was in progress, Wilson considered recapturing Russia for the family of civilized nations to be a project for the future, after the disposition of more urgent business.

Woodrow Wilson was a pioneer in international organization, and if the League could be set up and the United States drawn into the world to support the maintenance of peace in the principal regions of the world, democracy might be safe after all, as he had promised. The battle now turned to the United States Senate, where Wilson was just starting to realize that there could be a substantial problem. The Democrats were pretty solidly with the president, and the moderate Republicans, led by Lodge, would participate in the League, under conditions, though it has always been difficult to determine if Lodge was sincere or just masquerading as seeking to support the president on the fulfillment of unacceptable conditions. Unfortunately, Wilson's inflexibility made Lodge's opposition relatively easy to dress in comparative moderation. And the western isolationists, the "Irreconcilables," were led by Hiram Johnson, William E. Borah, and Robert M. La Follette. Wilson agreed to interpretative reservations that would not require the consent of other signatory countries, but these were insufficient for the hard-line isolationists, who held up consideration of the treaty until September 10.

Wilson set out on a speaking tour in the interior and west of the country to promote the treaty, on September 4, and Borah and other Irreconcilables conducted their own tour, paid for by wealthy Republican stalwarts Andrew Mellon and Henry Clay Frick. Wilson, a formidable, if overly erudite, public speaker, was well-received wherever he went, but on September 25, at Pueblo, Colorado, his health broke down, and he returned to Washington, where he suffered a massive stroke on October 2. He was no longer physically capable to act as president, and his judgment had been damaged also. On November 6, 1919, Lodge reported out a bill that included 14 reservations, but at least the United States would have joined the League and turned its back on isolationism. On November 18, in a letter to supporters, Wilson dismissed Lodge's bill as the "nullification" rather than ratification of the treaty. It was voted down the next day, as was unconditional acceptance (53–38). If Wilson had endorsed Lodge's version, it would have passed easily. The British and French, desperate for any American involvement as guarantors of Western European democracy, would have leapt like gazelles at almost any American ratification, no matter how hemmed about with escape hatches. But Wilson, barely compos mentis, resisted flexibility even when his wife suggested it. He even vetoed a declaration that the war with Germany was concluded.

A functioning and non-delusional Wilson might have made his deal with Lodge, as there were only 13 Irreconcilables. Mrs. Wilson largely controlled the government now, and allowed her husband only a few minutes a day of normal exposure to business, so fragile was his condition. By not publicly admitting the extent of Wilson's incapacitation, she denied him the public sympathy he would have received, and also denied the government the adequately effective leadership able-bodied and clear-headed cabinet members could have given. None of them remotely approached Wilson's stature or intellect, but they were passably competent and decent men who would have done the necessary. If Vice President Marshall had declared Wilson incapacitated, he could have taken over the management of the government and he and Lansing, bandying about the name of the stricken president, could probably have got Lodge to help adopt most of what Wilson was seeking. Lodge objected especially to Article X of the League Covenant, which committed the League to resist aggression and was construed by Lodge as meaning that American forces could be committed to combat without a vote of the U.S. Congress. This was nonsense in fact and was largely just illustrative of the personal antipathy between Lodge and Wilson, and of Lodge's desire to find an issue for the Republicans to win with in the 1920 elections.

In February 1920, the Senate, given the importance of the issue, agreed to reconsider the treaty, but positions had not changed, and Wilson, who was almost eager to die fighting for his treaty, would brook no compromise. He had just enough authority left to prevent all of the Senate Democrats from deserting to the Lodge compromise, and for good measure fired Lansing, for having convened the cabinet without notice to Wilson, though no business was transacted in the president's name. Bainbridge Colby, who had served Wilson as a legal adviser at the Paris negotiations, was appointed to replace Lansing as secretary of state.

8. THE 1920 ELECTION

Wilson asked the Democrats to make the 1920 election "a solemn referendum" on the League of Nations, and when they convened at San Francisco in late June they did endorse the League and the treaty, but professed a willingness to consider "reservations making clearer or more specific the obligations of the United States." The Republicans had met earlier in June in Chicago, and as they were split between the western Progressive isolationists and Irreconcilables, and the Taft, Root, Hughes wing of enlightened juridically minded easterners, the Republicans waffled and opposed the League but not "an agreement among the nations to preserve the peace of the world." The Republican convention was deadlocked for some ballots and then the party bosses, meeting in the original "smoke-filled room" in the Blackstone Hotel, settled upon the innocuous, genial, and probably suggestible or even malleable Senator Warren Gamaliel Harding of Ohio for president, and the taciturn governor of Massachusetts, Calvin Coolidge, who had gained popularity in the midst of the Red and anarchist scare by breaking a police strike in Boston, for vice president.

The Democrats, after 44 ballots, chose the governor of Ohio, James M. Cox, and the dynamic and evocatively named Assistant Secretary of the Navy Franklin Delano Roosevelt for vice president. The Socialists nominated Debs again, despite the fact that he was serving a 10-year prison term for sedition because of his lack of enthusiasm for the war effort. The Prohibitionists nominated a candidate again, although, in one of the most insane policy initiatives in its history, the United States in 1919 had already ratified the Eighteenth Amendment to the Constitution prohibiting the sale of alcoholic beverages, thus reducing most of the entire adult population to the status of lawbreakers and handing over one of America's greatest industries to organized crime, some of whose leading figures now became more prominent folkloric figures than its politicians.

The country was already settling into an era of unbridled absurdity and this election was not a solemn referendum on anything. The mood was one of frivolity, punctuated by reflexive fear. Because of Bolshevik propaganda and a modest spike in labor militancy, Attorney General A. Mitchell Palmer organized a full-scale Red Scare and on January 2, 1920, had 2,700 suspected communist agitators arrested in dragnets around the country. The Republicans promised "a return to normalcy." The country didn't want to hear any more of Woodrow Wilson's Old Testament call to greatness nor any talk of a Covenant with anything, except a speakeasy and the stock market. Harding ran a front-porch campaign and just rode the trend. Wilson, so recently the conquering hero, was thought a quavering, peevish, churlish old man, hiding in the White House. There was a recession in the country, and considerable doubt about what the purpose of entering the war had been.

Harding won, 16.15 million to 9.15 million for Cox and 920,000 for Debs. (The Prohibitionists won 189,000 votes, even though Prohibition was already in effect.) The electoral vote was 404 to 127. The Republicans had almost 62 percent of the vote to 34 percent for Cox to just over 4 percent for the others. Given the Democratic hold on the South, it was a remarkable victory for a mindless, no-name Republican good-time-Charlie campaign, and a heavy rejection of Wilson. The great expansion of the franchise was due to the granting of the right to vote to women. Harding chose Charles Evans Hughes as secretary of state, and he and Andrew Mellon at Treasury and the international engineer and aid administrator Herbert C. Hoover at the Commerce Department would be the stars of the administration. Once in office, the Republicans showed no disposition at all to internationalism, and Harding lost little time in burying League participation once and for all.

This astonishing cameo appearance by America on the world stage had suddenly arisen in the brilliant mind of Woodrow Wilson, as the predestined role of America to lead the nations of the world to durable peace. And it had swiftly vanished in the fickleness of the American public and the academic unsuitability of Wilson to the vagaries of the checks-and-balances political system. He has been much disparaged for excessive idealism and for tactical mismanagement of his ambitions, and he has also been criticized for insufficient reverence for the Constitution of the United States. But he grasped that the United States could never embark on foreign enterprises without some idealistic as well as practical basis to them, and that the world could not be safe for democracy without the United States in the front lines of those defending it. As for the Constitution, he can't be claimed to have foreseen the problems of gridlock in Washington or the prevalence of interests throughout the Congress, but he certainly had premonitions of these problems.

His presidency ended pitifully, with him shrunken and delusional. But he remains a haunting and compelling figure, courageous, eloquent, without opportunism, and stricken with misfortune, as well as flawed by impolitic hubris. He was a prophet; he was the first person to inspire the masses of the world with the vision of enduring peace, and though several of his most distinguished predecessors had vaguely referred to America's vocation to lead and the world's eventual dependence on it, it fell to him to try to effect that immense change in America and the world. He was a very able war leader and a decisive influence in preventing German victory. That he did not win the peace does not deny him the great homage he deserves for seeing so clearly the need for American intervention and for a new structure of international relations. America was briefly struck by infelicity. Without the breakdown of his health, Wilson might have got America into the world; and a healthy Theodore Roosevelt would have led America into the twenties to a very different and more observant drummer than Warren Harding.

For the world, this sudden appearance and withdrawal of America opened a long era of blaming the United States for every conceivable ill in the world. America was perceived and represented as a great cuckoo bird that might fly out of its hemisphere at any time making loud and portentous noises and then abruptly return, slamming the door behind it. It conformed to European desires to imagine that, despite its undoubted power, it was a silly, vulgar, and irresponsible place. The Wilson interlude on the world stage had been brief and had ended badly, but without it, the Allies would not have won the war, and the United States would not so surely and capably have come to the rescue of the Old World when it blundered, by its own errors, into war again, after, as Foch predicted, "a twenty-year armistice." Wilson failed, but he was the co-victor of World War I and, in a way, of World War II, and no one else, except possibly Winston Churchill, can make such a claim.

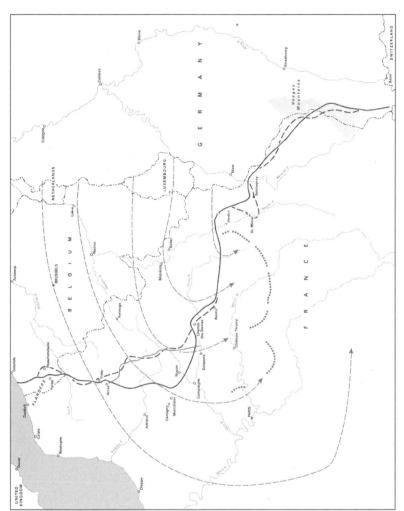

Western Front in WWI. Courtesy of the U.S. Army Center of Military History

Wilson permanently altered American foreign policy from the bantam rooster, Yankee Doodle rodomontade it had been under Jackson and in Daniel Webster's letter to Hülsemann in 1850 (Chapter 7), and the hemispheric prowling and growling that had gone on from the expulsion of the French from Mexico in 1867 to Wilson's own ludicrous punitive mission in Mexico nearly 50 years later. Its appearance among the Great Powers, though fleeting, showed the more astute observers, such as British foreign secretary Sir Edward Grey, that America was "a gigantic boiler. Once the fire is lighted under it, there is no limit to the power it can generate." The Republicans through the twenties pretended that they could substitute the sonorous espousal of peace and disarmament in place of contributing usefully to the correlation of democratic, stabilizing forces. Nothing would happen in the twenties while Germany and Russia were pulling themselves together, but if democracy failed in Germany and a nationalist government resulted, Communist Russia would hold the balance in Europe, an event that could cause almost all Europeans to become rather nostalgic for the Americans.

9. WARREN G. HARDING AND CALVIN COOLIDGE

The Harding administration made its first symbolic enactment of its anti-League substitute for pursuit of the peace process by responding to Irreconcilable senator Borah's resolution requesting a conference to discuss naval disarmament. It invited all the major powers except the German and Russian pariahs to Washington for that purpose, and also to discuss Pacific and Far Eastern questions. The American delegation was headed by Hughes, Root, and Lodge. Hughes was elected conference chairman and proposed not only a limitation of naval construction but the scrapping of large numbers of warships. Since the German fleet had already destroyed itself and the Russians were not invited, it was an orgy of self-enfeeblement by the victorious Allied powers. The U.S. agreed to scrap 645,000 tons, Britain 583,000 tons, Japan 480,000 tons, and so forth, and ratios of capital ships (over 10,000 tons and guns of more than 10-inch diameters) were to be 5 U.K, 5 U.S., 3 Japan, and 1.67 each for France and Italy. There was to be a 10-year moratorium on new capital-ship construction. There were separate treaties governing use of submarines, banning asphyxiating gases at sea, recognizing reciprocally rights in the Pacific, abrogating the Anglo-Japanese Treaty, and pledging all against the aggression of any power; there was the usual claptrap about guaranteeing Chinese independence and territorial integrity and the Open Door, which was itself a mockery of Chinese sovereignty; restoration to China of some control over her customs and of Shantung and Kiachow from Japan; and there were some agreements governing trans-Pacific cables. U.S. Senate ratification was heavily conditionalized. (The Chinese attended and had a ragtag of assets in what they called their "water force." They successfully rebutted the sarcasm of the upstart Japanese at the conference.)

The Pacific and Chinese provisions were ignored, as was Japan's pledge to naval moderation. The net effect was simply to deprive the major Western powers of 1.3 million tons of warships, including more than 20 capital ships that could have been useful in future conflicts, such as in convoy protection and support for amphibious landings. Nor should the British have been in such a hurry to allow the United States parity with it in naval forces. The initial American reaction was prideful euphoria that it was contributing importantly to world peace without surrendering sovereignty to the League. Of course, this was a mirage.

The next great issue was war debts. The United States was owed $10,950,000,000 from the various European powers, and the British and the French early proposed that they cancel their debts in exchange for their cancellation of debts from others, including German reparations. Wilson and his successors refused. The American attitude was summed up in Coolidge's rhetorical question: "They hired the money, didn't they?" However, financial realities imposed themselves very inconveniently. The World War Foreign Debt Commission was set up in February 1922, and a 62-year payback with an interest rate of 2.135 percent was agreed. In 1924, Italy arranged the elimination of 80 percent of its debt and an interest rate reduction to 0.4 percent. In 1926, the French achieved a 60.3 percent reduction, and a rate of 1.6 percent.

A parallel process governed German reparations. The Treaty of Versailles had set up the Allied Reparations Commission, which in 1921 fixed German reparations at 132 billion gold marks. The Germans severely devalued their currency, and the commission granted moratoria in 1923, but Germany was twice declared in default. On January 11, 1923, the French and Belgian armies occupied the Ruhr, and by late 1923, the German currency was worthless and the French franc had declined by 25 percent. At the end of the year, General Charles Gates Dawes of Chicago was named as head of a German Reparations Commission, and the following year he produced the Dawes Plan, which Germany accepted. It provided for reorganization of the Reichsbank under Allied supervision, and staged payments, from 1 billion gold marks in the first year to 2.5 billion in the fifth year, and an 800-million-mark international loan was arranged for Germany. The Allies were lending Germany much of the money to be repaid to them. It was agreed that the United States would receive a quarter of German reparations (a grossly exaggerated sum, compared with the claims of other powers, especially France). It was part of the naïve spirit of the time that Dawes achieved great popularity and prestige for this plan, which was not really enacted, though it at least punctured the balloon of immense reparations that would repay the Allies every cent they had expended.

In domestic affairs, Mellon cut taxes and the country snapped out of its recession; there were some reforms in the meat-packing industry, and Mellon followed the Taft administration's lead in setting up a serious budgetary process. The Fordney-McCumber Tariff of 1922 drastically raised tariffs on manufactures and agricultural products, and brought instant retaliation. Harding pardoned the Socialist leader, Debs.

Warren Harding, an amiable man, completely unqualified for his office, died of a pulmonary embolism in San Francisco on August 9, 1923, on his way back from a trip to Alaska. He was 57, and was widely lamented as a pleasant and good-natured personality. Vice President Calvin Coolidge succeeded him. About six months after Harding died, it came to light that his administration had been immersed in some widespread scandals, especially the secret leasing of the Teapot Dome and Elk's Hill oil fields to private interests, when they were supposedly reserved to the navy. There were other problems, and the secretary of the interior, Albert B. Fall, and the attorney general, Harry M. Daugherty, were indicted, and Fall was convicted, of taking a bribe. The amounts were not substantial, and there was certainly no suggestion of wrongdoing by Harding himself. Like U.S. Grant, he didn't have good judgment about how to manage politicians in charge of large flows of cash and the distribution of great financial preferments.

Woodrow Wilson died on February 5, 1924, having never recovered any ability to concentrate or remain active for more than a few minutes. Though not immensely popular personally, he was widely admired and his death was observed with respect. Of the main protagonists in the great contest of 1912, the only survivor was Taft, who, robust despite his immense girth, would remain a well-respected chief justice until he died in 1930, aged 72, and was succeeded by Charles Evans Hughes.

There was peace and prosperity and the Republicans were popular. Coolidge was quiet but emphatic in his terse remarks, and notoriously uncommunicative. The Republicans met in Cleveland in June 1924, and nominated President Coolidge and, for vice president, Charles G. Dawes, recognizing the prestige he had supposedly earned for his short-lived reparations deal with Germany. The platform supported continued reduced taxes and spending, high tariffs, and vague platitudes about international action for the avoidance of war.

The Democrats met in New York later in June and the party split between the governor of New York, Alfred E. Smith, a self-made, self-educated reform governor and the first Roman Catholic to make a serious challenge for the presidency, and William Gibbs McAdoo of Tennessee, Wilson's son-in-law and a former secretary of the Treasury. The racist Ku Klux Klan endorsed McAdoo, who did not renounce its support, and it made for a stormy convention in Madison Square Garden, where the forces of Governor Smith had packed most of the hall. Smith frankly renounced Prohibition as nonsense, and McAdoo stood as the Prohibitionist candidate. The most electrifying moment of the convention was the nomination of Smith by Franklin D. Roosevelt, as "the happy warrior of the political battlefield." Roosevelt had been stricken by polio in 1921, and lost the use of his legs. He approached the microphone on crutches, his legs in stiff braces, in a hushed stadium, and received a huge ovation, as did his ringing address putting Smith in nomination.

The convention went 103 ballots before settling on the rather conservative John W. Davis of West Virginia, former solicitor general and ambassador to Great Britain. The platform denounced the Ku Klux Klan and the corruption of the Republicans, and supported the League of Nations and a lower tariff, but was otherwise non-committal. It dissembled on the Prohibition question. In a final gesture to the bimetallists, William Jennings Bryan's brother Charles was chosen as vice presidential candidate.

Disgusted with the conservatism of both parties, and especially the Democrats, as well as by the Democrats' internationalism, the Conference for Progressive Political Action, a grouping of agrarian and labor interests, met at Cleveland in July and nominated Robert M. La Follette of Wisconsin for president and Senator Burton K. Wheeler of Montana for vice president. Their platform called for nationalization of railroads and electric power, an unrestricted right to strike, collective bargaining by farmers and workers, tighter securities regulation, and improved working conditions, and condemned Republican corruption and Mellon's pandering to the wealthy. It was a peppy left-wing program, but if the Democrats had not been so fragmented, they should have corralled most of these votes.

It was clearly going to be another big Republican year, and Coolidge won 15.7 million and 382 electoral votes to 8.4 million and 136 electoral votes for Davis and 4.8 million votes and 13 electoral votes for La Follette—54 percent to 29 percent to 16 percent. The country was booming, but it was uneven, and increasing amounts of family stock market and consumer spending was borrowed. For the time being, the country was happy with the Roaring Twenties as they unfolded, a national commitment to the good life, and abroad, gestures of pacific intent in a world still exhausted by the Great War and without animosity to America, which under the influence of the motion picture was becoming the constant spectacle of the whole world.

Very little happened in the Coolidge administration. Immigration was abruptly curtailed. This would have tragic consequences a decade and more later, when persecution of minorities, especially Jews, would force millions to try to flee Europe. The United States had admitted over a million immigrants in six separate years before World War I, and had admitted between 300,000 and 800,000 in each of the first five years of the twenties. Until huge numbers of undocumented Latin Americans began flooding into the country decades later, immigration after 1930 would not exceed 200,000 again for 20 years. One of the great engines of American growth was being shut down. There were further tax cuts in 1926 and 1928.

William Jennings Bryan, the old war-horse of bimetallism, pacifism, and resistance to Darwinian teaching (in the famous Scopes trial in Tennessee about the teaching of evolution, in early 1925), died on July 26, 1925, aged 65. His time had certainly passed (although his brother Charles had been the Democrats' vice presidential candidate the year before), but he was seen as a great populist and folkloric figure who, except for Theodore Roosevelt and Woodrow Wilson, had stirred American public life more than anyone since Lincoln.

Frank B. Kellogg, former senator and ambassador to Great Britain, became secretary of state in 1925. Here again, almost nothing happened. It was, in all things, an era of misplaced overconfidence. All through the twenties, the United States continued to vacillate and dither on the issue of the world court. Harding, Coolidge, and their successors favored it, and Root even produced an admission formula that virtually made American adherence conditional on not having an adverse judgment, but still it was blocked by Borah and others in the Senate. The great accomplishment of the Kellogg regime in the State Department was the Kellogg-Briand Pact, of 1927, in which France and the United States agreed to "outlaw war as an instrument of national policy"; this agreement was subscribed to by virtually every government in the world (62 nations), and there was the usual drenching shower of euphoria. (Aristide Briand, one of the Third Republic's champion politicians, had 11 terms as prime minister between 1909 and 1929, and served seven consecutive years, ending with his death in 1932, as foreign minister.) The sole sanction for the outlawry of war was the power of moral opinion in the world against violators. Of course, it was nonsense.

It continued to be the conventional wisdom among Republicans that prosperity was permanent, peace was inviolable, and America's existence was serendipitous. Herbert Hoover even revived Clay's phrase "the American System" to describe America's almost unique prosperity, the exclusion of African Americans and 20 percent of the white population being overlooked. It was still a generalization of prosperity that only a few countries with much smaller populations, such as Canada, approached. In strategic terms, there was no strategy; America had the key to prosperity and was far from potential conflict. It had no enemies and had a strong navy to keep undesirables at a distance. Everything would just continue to improve; it was the American way, the American system.

The 1928 election campaign took place in this halcyon atmosphere. Coolidge declined to run again and at the Republican convention in Kansas City in June, Commerce Secretary Herbert Hoover, of Iowa and California, widely identified with the great boom of the twenties, was nominated for president, with Senator Charles Curtis of Kansas for vice president. The platform envisioned federal assistance to farm prices and retention of high tariffs, and promised greater prosperity than ever, "a chicken in every pot, a car in every garage." Prohibition and abstention from the League were strongly supported.

The Democrats met in Houston later in June, and Franklin D. Roosevelt again nominated the now four-term governor of New York, Alfred E. Smith. He was chosen on the first ballot, and Senator Joseph T. Robinson of Arkansas was selected as vice presidential candidate.[3] The Democratic platform made noises similar to the Republicans about farm prices, supported increased powers of collective bargaining for labor, and pledged to enforce Prohibition while seeking its repeal, an artless straddle that offended everyone. It also sought increased federal control of hydroelectric power and the immediate granting of independence to the Philippines. The real issues were that Smith was a Roman Catholic and the Democrats opposed Prohibition. Smith had a flamboyant New York manner of dress, with rather loud suits and a derby hat. He had a large red nose, indicating perhaps his liking for prohibited drink, prominent gold fillings in his teeth, and a broad, Lower East Side New York accent. He had been a brilliant governor and had a rapport with urban dwellers, but he was a localized candidate in a time when there was great suspicion in Protestant America of the Roman Catholic Church as sinister, stuffed with hyphenated Americans, and directed by obscurantist Italians.

The country continued to be prosperous and at peace and it was hard to find too many discontented people. Hoover spoke like TR of "rugged individualism" as well as the "American System," of ever greater prosperity and prestige for the nation. It wasn't an original theme, but it wasn't a very vulnerable one, either, in these golden days. At the election, Smith more than topped the combined vote four years before for Davis and La Follette, but Hoover won, 21.4 million and 444 electoral votes to 15 million and 87 electoral votes for Smith. Even the Democratic control of the South was shaken by the anti-papist bias. It was 58

---

3.   This was the beginning of the Democratic practice of nominating a northern liberal for president and a southerner (usually somewhat conservative and segregationist) for vice president, which made for some incoherence in ticket-balancing, and continued for more than 30 years.

percent to 41 percent (a closer contest than Cox or Davis had managed in the previous elections). It turned out that the most important result of the evening was Franklin D. Roosevelt's narrow victory in succeeding Smith as governor of New York, even as Hoover carried the state against Smith. Smith had beseeched Roosevelt to run, against his own wishes, as he was still convalescing, but at the end of the night, Roosevelt had replaced Smith as the country's leading Democrat. That position might not have been worth much during these three consecutive Republican landslides, the latest that party's 14th victory in 18 elections starting with Lincoln in 1860. It looked permanent, and unshakeable, but it wasn't, and Roosevelt would rise quickly, and have undreamed-of staying power.

10. HERBERT HOOVER

Very few people have been inducted into the presidency of the United States with such a high reputation and enjoying such personal prestige as was Herbert Hoover. A Quaker mining engineer born in Iowa whose youth was spent in Oregon and California, Hoover, then 54, had worked very successfully as a gold and zinc engineer in Australia and China, learned Mandarin, invented a new process for extracting zinc from gold tailings, and written seminal texts on mining that are still authoritative today. He became very famous in his profession, and as he was in Europe when World War I broke out, became a natural candidate to assist in the distribution of food aid to invaded Belgium. He raised large contributions of foodstuffs and money for the civilian population of Belgium, and undoubtedly contributed vitally to the saving of many thousands of lives. He replicated this feat on a larger scale in Central Europe at the end of the war, and was responsible for saving the lives of millions of people, including a large number of Russians.

Hoover was extremely famous and had been sought by Wilson as his successor. Hoover allowed that he could not become a member of a party whose only member in the town where Hoover was brought up (West Branch, Iowa) had been the town drunk. He had reservations about Warren Harding, but endorsed him and was rewarded with the Commerce Department, a new cabinet position that Hoover turned into a great symbol of the ever-rising prosperity of America. He intervened in other departments and with the private sector and became a champion of business efficiency and of government-industry cooperation. He eventually constructed a splendid group of buildings for the Commerce Department, which remain a monument to him. He and Taft were the only presidents elevated directly from the cabinet in the twentith century, and the only presidents who had never previously held either elected public office or high military rank.

As his secretary of state, Hoover selected Colonel Henry L. Stimson, the governor of the Philippines, secretary of war under Taft, and Coolidge's special representative to the perennial shambles in Nicaragua. He continued the tradition of lawyers running the State Department, but was an enlightened internationalist with a good deal of experience abroad, including as an artillery colonel in the Great War.

11. THE 1929 CRASH

The new administration was quickly overwhelmed by the burst of the immense speculative bubble in the stock market, in October 1929, which wiped out 90 percent of stock market values over the following three years and precipitated the worldwide Great Depression, which laid low the economies of all advanced countries. Commodity prices, and the cost of living generally, had stopped rising in 1927, and residential construction, automobile production, sales and production of consumers' durable goods, and most categories of industrial investment had leveled or declined slightly. But stock market prices had continued to rise steeply, largely on an immense spike of retail buying on margin (i.e., with unpaid balances of sale, the loan secured by the underlying stock market value).

The commodity price index moved from 100.6 in 1923 to 95.3 in 1929, while the corresponding stock price index rose from 67.7 in 1922 to 190.3 in 1929. These numbers continued downward to 65 and 48, respectively, at the end of 1932. The Dow Jones Industrial Average, which had briefly been at 8 during the Panic of 1907, which President Roosevelt had asked J.P. Morgan to help resolve, had risen to 321 in October 1929, and descended gradually to 34 at the beginning of March 1933.

There was no commercial justification for such a vertiginous rise in the twenties, which was based on the optimism of the times and the propagation of the doctrine that everything was going up and getting better and that borrowing to invest in the growth implicit in the future was almost a sure thing. Statistical economic reporting was sporadic, unrigorous, and under-publicized, and the inherent vulnerabilities of the economy were grasped only by the most astute or intuitively sensible investors. They were rewarded for their restraint and foresight, but the millions of impetuous and unwary, and tens of millions of mere bystanders to the markets, paid a terrible price.

Hoover's approach to relief was based on principles of rugged individualism, an inability to grasp the gravity of the crisis, and an unwarranted conviction that prosperity would return automatically as part of a cycle. It didn't. Hoover literally convinced himself that the people who were reduced to selling apples prospered.

Hoover was in favor of decentralized relief, and throughout his administration, there was no direct federal assistance to the unemployed. In October 1930, a year after the initial crash, and the beginning of the steep economic downturn, Hoover sponsored a program of voluntary and local assistance, to "preserve the principles of individual and local responsibility." In December, he requested $150 million for job creation through public works. There were other half-measures, but the crisis generally deepened, with occasional misleading rallies that led to unjustified optimism that the worst was over.

The people were looking for leadership and hope, and Hoover, despite his great talent and warm humanity, was cruelly unfitted for the task so unkindly thrust upon him. He was unable to think in terms beyond voluntarism, local relief, and exhortations of an apparently soulless character to pull up socks, buckle down, and so forth. And Hoover had no political skill at all, as might have been foreseen from his lack of political experience. When a commission he had struck, headed by Taft's attorney general, George Wickersham, favored substantial changes to Prohibition, Hoover declared himself opposed to repeal. This was an astounding position, given the utter failure of the attempt to enforce temperance.

Veterans agitated for prepayment of bonuses voted to them, and when the measure was approved by the Congress, Hoover vetoed it as extravagant and likely to reward many who were not in need. This led eventually to the catastrophic fiasco of the "Bonus March" of 17,000 veterans on Washington in the spring of 1932. The government offered to pay their way home and most accepted the offer, but 2,000 refused to leave their squatters' camp on Anacostia Flats, and when the District of Columbia police tried to remove them, four deaths resulted. Hoover called on the army to move them out, and the chief of staff of the army, General Douglas MacArthur, assisted by his aides Lieutenant Dwight D. Eisenhower, who counseled moderation, and Lieutenant George S. Patton, who urged severity, cleared them out without loss of life, using cavalry, tanks, and infantry with fixed bayonets. This was not a good political image-builder.

The Republicans lost control of the Senate in 1930, after controlling it for 12 years, and lost 52 congressmen, and then several more after the election, through death and special elections, and Texas Democrat John Nance Garner replaced Theodore Roosevelt's son-in-law, Nicholas Longworth, as Speaker. Roosevelt was reelected governor of New York by the unheard-of margin of 725,000 votes. Hoover moved late to try more substantial relief measures. In February 1932, he set up the Reconstruction Finance Corporation, which was capitalized at $500 million, with authority to borrow up to $2 billion. The RFC was authorized to invest in financial institutions, including farm mortgage associations, as well as railways and building-and-loan societies. It could issue tax-free bonds and was designed chiefly to fight deflation rather than absorb the unemployed directly.

The RFC was strengthened by the Relief and Construction Act in July 1932, authorizing further borrowings of $1 billion, and was tasked with financing local public works schemes, which would engage the unemployed. The Federal Home Loan Bank Act, also enacted in July 1932, was designed to assist families with delinquent mortgages and encourage a revival of residential building, but with only $125 million it was, like the rest of Hoover's program, too little and too late. By the end of 1932, industrial production had declined by almost half from 1929, and by March of 1933 the banking and stock and commodity exchange systems had collapsed and were shut down almost entirely. There were between 15 and 17 million unemployed, about one-third of the entire work force, and farm and residential mortgage foreclosures threatened more than 40 percent of the whole population.

Herbert Hoover had famously said, shortly after the first stock market reversals in 1929, "The economy is fundamentally sound," and by late 1932 was promising that "Prosperity is just around the corner." By this time, Hoover had convinced himself that the economic crisis was an international phenomenon that had descended more or less like a malignant act of God, that he was blameless, and that what was needed was concerted international action to maintain strong currencies and avoid inflation and, as far as possible, deficits. In the light of subsequent history, it is clear that his policy prescriptions were the worst that could have been devised: income tax increases in 1930 to reduce the deficit, the shrinking of the money supply by the Federal Reserve Bank of New York, and the Smoot-Hawley Tariff of 1931, which raised duties to stratospheric levels, assuring retaliation. But economics, inexact and notoriously dismal science though it is, was quite rudimentary at the time and Hoover must not be judged by contemporary standards of knowledge of the role of the money supply and other factors in the level of economic activity, though he could certainly have been more imaginative and less dogmatic.

Manufacturing industry was confined to the domestic market, and agricultural exports were bought by the government at unsustainable prices and dumped in the world market, where the produce was bought with loans granted by the United States, on which the borrowers generally defaulted. It was an utterly futile policy, impoverishing American farmers and foreign consumers, and famishing disadvantaged Americans. Other advanced countries were also hard hit by the Depression. The United States was the most relatively contracted economy, because the speculative bubble had been larger there, and Hoover's Republican notions of self-help resisted public assistance on the scale that electorates in Canada and

Western Europe more promptly demanded. There were also, at the end of Hoover's term, the first stirrings of rising militarism in the world, in Japan and in Germany, which led to increases in the armed forces and the defense-production industries in those countries, soaking up the unemployed, and soon provoked similar measures in other countries in response to them.

12. INTERNATIONAL ECONOMICS AND ARMS CONTROL

In this unpromising ambiance, Stimson did manage to maintain a consistent foreign policy, and a somewhat more substantive one than Hughes's policy of unilateral disarmament by the democracies, and Kellogg's claim to have banned war. The first priority was the collapse, yet again, of the reparations scheme, the Dawes Plan (Chapter 10). Dawes, an eccentric figure who as vice president had quarreled with Coolidge, and who was comptroller of the currency under McKinley and a general of engineers in World War I, was now directing the RFC, which invested $50 million in Dawes's City National Bank of Chicago. This did not prevent it from going under a year later, and Dawes concluded his public career as a well-regarded ambassador to Great Britain. The Young Plan, named after industrialist Owen D. Young, reduced German reparations to $8 billion, payable over 58 years. This was a hopeful effort to catch the moving target of increasing economic distress, but in June 1932, the Lausanne Conference scrapped 90 percent of the remaining reparations (and Germany declined to repay more than a fraction of that the following year).

Parallel to this was the collapse of war debt repayments to the United States. The booming economy through most of the twenties, after the crisis of German hyper-inflation, enabled Germany to pay some reparations to France and Britain, which sent them on as war debt mitigations to the United States. The onset of the decline of business activity in the United States, the shrinking of the American money supply, and the reescalation of tariff wars assured that the contagion of economic deflation afflicted every country where the government did not intervene to raise spending, assure liquidity, and stimulate consumer demand.

The Italian Fascist government of Benito Mussolini, who had seized power in 1922, somewhat enhanced the military and engaged in showy public works projects as well, to absorb the unemployed and assure the absence of misery. Italy remained a private, if not exactly a free, enterprise economy, and avoided the worst of the Depression, though it was only a somewhat prosperous country in the northern industrial heartland between Genoa, Turin, and Milan.

The Japanese combated the Depression with a straitjacket of economic controls and the mobilization of all unallocated manpower by the armed forces and for defense production. In the Soviet Union, where Lenin had died in 1924 and was succeeded by Joseph Stalin, whole categories of the population were starved to death or otherwise liquidated in the drive to collectivization and the implementation of the command economy. Some formidable feats of engineering in public works were achieved, and much heavy industry was added and modernized. Apart from recalcitrant constituent groups or those deemed ethnic or class enemies of the regime (and their numbers were considerable and their fate terminal, as Stalin, in the course of his 29-year dictatorship, murdered at least 20 million of his countrymen), basic food, medical care, education, and shelter were available to the continuing population. But the collectivist drive consecrated most effort to building the infrastructure, industrial base, and military strength of the Communist regime. Stalin did achieve prodigies of productivity by eliminating millions of people and arbitrarily overvaluing production. None of the Soviet government's statistics could be believed, and it was impossible to make valid comparisons with other countries.

Banking and currency crises began in earnest in 1931, with the failure of a large Austrian bank, an attempted bail-out of Austria by the Bank of England, heavy withdrawals of deposits in German banks, and Britain's abandonment of the gold standard on September 21, 1931. Hoover proposed a one-year moratorium on reparation and war debt payments in June 1931. Most countries that were affected agreed promptly, but France, always suspicious of anything that might advantage Germany, dithered for a month, in which time the German banking system effectively collapsed. All banks in Germany were closed by the middle of July. The banking system was adequately reinforced by the German Central Bank to resume functioning more or less normally after a couple of weeks, but Europe's largest economy was in steep decline and social unrest was already severe, as the Communists and Adolf Hitler's National Socialist German Workers' Party (Nazis) crowded the Catholic and Protestant center parties. French premier Pierre Laval visited Hoover in October, and it was agreed that the moratorium was likely to continue for the balance of the Depression.

From January to April 1930, a resumed naval disarmament conference sat at London, attended by the five main naval powers and victorious principal allies of the Great War. Stimson headed the U.S. delegation, accompanied by, among others, Navy Secretary Charles Francis Adams, descendant of two presidents and grandson of Lincoln's minister to London. France refused to agree to parity for Italy, but the U.S., U.K., and Japan agreed on a continuation of a 10–6 ratio on capital ships and 10–7 on other vessels, except submarines, where parity was agreed. As a result that was shortly to prove to have been unwise, the British scrapped five capital ships, the Americans three, and the Japanese one. A decade later, there would be ample reason to regret this false measure of peace promotion. The League of Nations convened a follow-on disarmament conference in Geneva in February 1932, where the U.S., demonstrating the continued prevalence of the delusional Republican faith in the uncomplicated attainability of world peace, proposed the abolition of all offensive weapons. Naturally, this proposal sank without trace (Japan had already begun its aggressive war in China), and Hoover countered with a proposal for a 30 percent reduction in all armaments.

In October 1933, Germany, under Hitler's new government, had announced its withdrawal from the conference and from the League of Nations. The conference finally broke up in the spring of 1934, having failed to accomplish anything. There would be another attempt in 1936, where Britain, France, and the U.S., which should long since have been rearming themselves, agreed on a few limitations that were easily evaded because of the aggressive build-up of Japanese, Italian, and German naval forces. There would be little talk of arms control after that for nearly 40 years.

Even these early efforts at limiting the size of battleships were not successful. The powers, except Japan, who renounced its adherence at the end of 1934, were pledged not to exceed 35,000 tons in the displacement of new battleships. The British *King George V* class, American *North Carolina* class, French *Richelieu* class, German *Bismarck* class, and Italian *Littorio* class ships all exceeded that limit, by from 10 percent (Americans and British) to nearly 20 percent (the Germans). The Japanese, having had the decency to renounce this hypocrisy entirely, constructed the two largest battleships in history, the *Musashi* and the *Yamato*, each 73,000 tons. It proved impossible even to verify the size of these huge ships of the treaty countries, which required years to build. Verifying arms-control agreements in respect of aircraft and missile-launchers, relatively small, mobile, and concealable weapons, would be a desperately complicated matter in the next generation, when some reciprocal effort was made at control of these much more compact and destructive armaments.

13. JAPAN AND THE BEGINNING OF WAR

In September 1931, Japan occupied the principal cities of Manchuria, and systematically extended its control over southern Manchuria by January of 1932 and of the whole province by September, when Tokyo purported to recognize the puppet state of Manchukuo. This was a bare-faced violation of the Washington treaties, the Kellogg-Briand Pact, and the League of Nations Covenant. This was the first serious test of the League's ability to deter or roll back aggression. In January 1932, Stimson sent identical notes to China and Japan, stating that the United

States would not recognize any arrangement or act that might "impair . . . the sovereignty, independence, or territorial and administrative integrity of . . . China" or, inevitably, flogging the same spavined horse as all his predecessors since Hay, "the Open Door." Of course there had been no open door to China for years; it was just another figment of the roseate imagination of America's diplomats. This became known, rather portentously, as the Stimson Doctrine of non-recognition of any territories or agreements obtained by aggression.

The British government, four days after Stimson's pronunciamento, announced that it had full faith in Japan's assurances that the Open Door was intact; what would soon enough become the infamous British policy of appeasement of the dictators had begun. At the end of January, Japan bombarded and seized Shanghai, China's largest city. Stimson proposed to Sir John Simon, the British foreign secretary, a joint protest based on the Washington treaty, but Simon opted for action through the League. Stimson stated that the United States would stand on its treaty rights in the Far East, the beginning of what would prove a very durable practice of the United States taking a harder line against anti-Western and anti-democratic governments than the British or the French. (In what subsequent events and Stimson's role in them would prove to be an irony, he publicly wrote the ambassador in London, Dawes, that the United States "does not intend to go to war with Japan.") In October, in something of a victory for Stimson, the League adopted his doctrine, and in May, in a League victory achieved by the non-League U.S.A., Japan withdrew from Shanghai. This invites renewed consideration of whether the League of Nations could have been substantially more effective if the United States had adhered to it, instead of just to the Hughes-Kellogg aerated waffling about scrapping battleships and outlawing war.

In October 1932, the League's Lytton Commission produced the report of its inquiry into the dispute in Manchuria. It condemned Japan's aggression, but recognized Japan's rights in Manchuria and indulged in the sophistry of recognizing Manchuria as an "autonomous" state under Chinese "sovereignty" but Japanese "control." Words had lost their meaning in the placation of Japan, but despite this accommodation, Japan withdrew from the League in March 1933, a few weeks after the Lytton Report was adopted by the League of Nations' general assembly. The disintegration of the world had begun again.

14. THE POLITICS OF DEPRESSION

As the election season began, it was clear that in the desperate economic circumstances, the administration was going to have a very difficult time. The Republicans met at Chicago in June 1932 and renominated President Hoover and Vice President Curtis without significant dissent, on a platform that called for sharp reductions in government expenses, the sanctity of the gold standard and a balanced budget, vague alterations to Prohibition, enhanced tariffs, and continued restraint of immigration. Hoover had given a lot of attention to a world economic conference that would open in London in the spring of 1933, and set great store by this. Preliminary indications were that it would be another effort by the governments of the world to agree that they were all blameless in the face of an economic whirlwind that was virtually an Old Testament plague. There was already a good deal of discussion about pegging the principal currencies together, which was both impractical and almost irrelevant to the main problems of the Depression. The administration's leaders, including Andrew Mellon, who left the Treasury and replaced Dawes as ambassador in London, did not grasp that only expansion of the money supply, and liberalization of spending and trade, would alleviate the Depression, though it would also induce inflation. There was a grim choice between depression and inflation, but under no scenario could the United States go much longer without massive aid to the indigent and be confident of avoiding widespread disorder.

The Democrats met in Chicago a week after the Republicans had left the city, and struggled for the last time with their rule that required a two-thirds majority to nominate a candidate. The 1928 nominee, Alfred E. Smith, though he had not held a political office since being succeeded by Franklin D. Roosevelt as governor of New York, still had the support of the eastern urban party bosses. Roosevelt clearly had the lead, but there was a third candidate, Speaker John Nance Garner of Texas, whose candidacy was invented by media owner William Randolph Hearst, because he was an ancient foe of Smith's when Hearst had been active in New York politics himself, and believed Roosevelt was apt, as a Wilsonian, to be too much of an internationalist. Hearst was somewhat Anglophobic, and his newspaper chain published a regular column by Hitler (though Hearst was philo-Semitic and in his annual visits to Berlin through the thirties remonstrated with Hitler about the evils of anti-Semitism).

In the event of deadlock, there was much talk of a compromise candidate, such as former war secretary Newton D. Baker. Wilson's son-in-law and Smith's rival at the 1924 convention, William G. McAdoo, was the favorite-son candidate from California but was also under Hearst's influence, as he was running for the Senate there and Hearst was the state's largest newspaper publisher. Roosevelt led the first ballot, and his political operatives, Louis McHenry Howe and James A. Farley, had held back enough support to assure modest rises on the subsequent two ballots. At this point, financier and Roosevelt backer (and father of a future Democratic president) Joseph P. Kennedy succeeded in telephoning Hearst at his magnificent palace near San Luis Obispo, California, and warned him that if he did not wind down Garner and McAdoo, Baker or Smith might get the nomination. Roosevelt had already cravenly, his wife and some other intimates thought, made a rather isolationist speech clarifying his position in order to settle Hearst down. Hearst accepted Kennedy's advice, and Garner withdrew and, with the help of veteran congressman Sam Rayburn, delivered the Texas delegation to Roosevelt.

When the balloting recommenced, the alphabet quickly brought on McAdoo, who delivered California's entire delegation to Roosevelt, who was nominated at the end of the fourth ballot. In accord with the deal with Hearst, Garner was chosen for vice president, although he would have preferred to remain as Speaker. (And as he lived to be 98, he might have held the office for a very long time; he later dismissed the vice presidency as "not worth a pail of warm piss." When asked by Roosevelt if he had any advice on how to win the election, he responded: "Stay alive until November.") The party platform was a mélange of conservative and reform measures, including reductions in government expenditures and a balanced budget, unemployment and old-age insurance under state laws (without a hint of how to pay for them), participation in the international monetary conference that Hoover was touting, higher farm prices, flexibility on tariffs, the repeal of Prohibition, and the regulation of complex corporate structures and utilities and of securities and commodity exchanges.

The Socialists nominated Norman Thomas for president, and the Communists nominated William Z. Foster, neither for the first time nor the last.

Roosevelt had referred in a speech, while he was seeking the nomination, to "the forgotten man at the bottom of the economic pyramid," and he broke a long tradition by coming in person, by airplane, to the convention to accept the nomination. He told the convention and the country: "I pledge you, I pledge myself, to a New Deal for the American people." It was an electrifying message. Roosevelt was a very talented orator and he ran an energetic and aggressive campaign that edged close to suggestions of profound changes to assure a more equitable distribution of wealth, but was careful to refer to such measures only as last resorts. In different addresses he called for both increases and reductions of tariffs, and finessed it with explanations that these were bilateral matters that varied with each country, product, and commodity.

Hoover campaigned doggedly, writing his own thoughtful speeches, excoriating Roosevelt as a charlatan and a radical and referring to his slipperiness on many policies as "the nightmare of the chameleon on Scotch plaid." But Hoover was promising grim continuity, no change, and no believable hope. He was still claiming that the long forecasted and desperately awaited rally had started, and warned that the election of Roosevelt and the promulgation of his New Deal would mean that "the grass will grow in the streets of a hundred cities, a thousand towns; weeds will overrun millions of farms." Roosevelt described the shantytowns of the itinerant indigent on the edge of every city in America as "Hoovervilles" and accused the administration, unanswerably in the circumstances, of having failed, of having "worshipped the golden calf," of having been manipulated by "the money-changers in the temple," and of having lost all hope, imagination, and capacity to lead.

On election day, Roosevelt won 22.8 million votes, 57 percent of the total, and 472 electoral votes, to 15.8 million, 40 percent, and 59 electoral votes for Hoover. Thomas received 885,000 votes and Foster 103,000. These were very modest proportions of the vote for left-wing parties, compared with most other democracies, where radical parties were a serious threat.

Between Roosevelt's election and inauguration, the German president, Field Marshal Paul von Hindenburg, was induced to name Adolf Hitler chancellor. The centrist parties and wealthy businessmen assumed that Hitler could be controlled and would be a useful bulwark against the Communists. The second assumption was correct, but Hitler effortlessly and swiftly outmaneuvered all other faction heads and established a totalitarian dictatorship, uniting Hindenburg's position with his own as fuehrer in 1934, when the 86-year-old marshal-president died and the old Germany was laid in the grave with him. A process of remilitarizing Germany and putting what was left of the Treaty of Versailles to the shredder began at once.

The rise of Hitler had a very negative effect on Mussolini, who, having been fairly responsible, began to put on the airs of a conqueror. France elected a democratic socialist government in 1934, while former premier Laval sidled up to fascistic elements and the French Communist Party drew almost 20 percent of the vote. The Third Republic was less stable than ever. In 1936, Spain would erupt in a terrible, three-year civil war that would take a million lives, between fascists led by General Francisco Franco and a Communist-led coalition. In Britain, after the collapse of the Labour government, King George V had urged the rather plodding Labour Party prime minister, Ramsay MacDonald, to form a coalition government, which was mainly composed of Conservatives. Hitler and Stalin soon dominated or intimidated almost all of continental Europe except France, and they had no shortage of supporters in that country. Since the collapse of Wilson's efforts to bring the United States into the League of Nations, the world had been on a strategic holiday. The failure to make a serious peace with Germany, to come to terms with Soviet Russia, to set up an international organization with any muscle, to get a grip on tariffs, or even manage the economies of the major countries responsibly soon laid low the economy of the whole world and brought forward threats to Western democracy far more worrisome than the overgrown child, Wilhelm II.

In the United States, the expansion of the stock-speculating population vastly beyond what it had been before World War I made the crash infinitely worse. And the chaos of war and depression had made aggressive dictatorships fashionable. Britain and France were about to be outgunned by the dictators. And more even than in 1917, when Russia, Italy, and Japan had all been allies, albeit tired or remote allies, they were all now hostile to the democracies, and the beseeching eyes of the British and the French, and the attention of all, would soon be fixed on America, beleaguered though it now was.

Roosevelt would be taking his place in a world suffering acute economic distress and where the democracies, for the security of which millions had died in a hecatomb of war that had ended less than 15 years before, were in full retreat. His promise of change, his uplifting oratory, and even the courage he had shown in overcoming polio to seem much more mobile and robust than he really was inspirited the world in this worst of times, when other democratic governments seemed so tired and ineffectual, especially compared with the dynamism of the dictators. As his inauguration approached, American economic conditions lurched to new depths. The index of industrial production fell to an all-time low of 56, barely half where it had been in 1928. In less than three years, more than 5,500 banks had closed, taking down with them deposits of over $3 billion. Banks began closing, by state order, starting with Louisiana in early February 1933, and by inauguration day on March 4 almost every bank in the country and all its economic exchanges were closed, or banks were reduced to minimal individual withdrawals. Hoover insistently asked Roosevelt to pledge publicly to abandon the embryonic New Deal program and pledge to uphold Hoover's fetishistic attachment to the gold standard and the avoidance of major relief commitments. The president-elect declined. For his inauguration, there were army-manned machine-gun nests at the corners of all the great federal buildings in Washington for the first time since the Civil War. America and the world were in desperate straits.

THREE

THE INDISPENSABLE
COUNTRY, 1933–1957

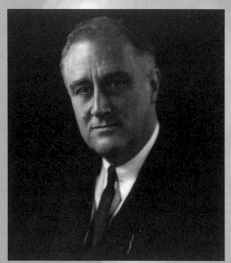

Franklin D. Roosevelt

CHAPTER NINE

Toward America's Rendezvous
with Destiny, 1933–1941

1. THE STRATEGIC HERITAGE AND PROSPECTS OF AMERICA IN 1933

The world was gasping and the great power of the New World was in danger of the complete collapse of its economic, and possibly even its political, system. Of Roosevelt's 30 predecessors as president, only Abraham Lincoln had taken office in such daunting circumstances. This narrative has proceeded fairly densely through 175 years since the start of the Seven Years' War, in which Benjamin Franklin had felt the need to urge Britain to ensure that the metropolitan French did not return to Canada. As the entire American project teetered, and the country brought in a new leader to try to resuscitate what had been 65 years of vertiginous expansion in every field and by any measurement since the Civil War, it is an opportune moment for a brief pause to assess the strategies of the rise and stall and prospects of America.

In the mid-eighteenth century, America was a haven for seekers of a freer and more prosperous life than was commonly available in Europe. As it had almost 30 percent of Britain's population toward the end of that period, and a higher standard of living, it was an important geopolitical entity, but Britain got little from it, and protecting it was onerous. A few Americans of international stature, most conspicuously Benjamin Franklin and George Washington, had an idea of what a powerhouse America could, relatively quickly, become. William Pitt, Earl of Chatham, had the geopolitical vision to add to the British manipulation of the balance of power on the continent, traditional since the time of Cardinal Wolsey and Henry VIII, 225 years before, the concentration on the navy and amphibious operations necessary to gain control of the world's oceans and most desirable places of empire. He led Britain to victory in Canada and India, the Caribbean, West Africa, and everywhere on the high seas.

Chatham's successors completely bungled the comprehensible need to get America to pay a representative share of the cost of clearing France out of North America. And Franklin, Washington, and other talented men, especially Jefferson, Hamilton, Madison, Adams, John Jay, John Marshall, James Monroe, and even the revolutionary drummer boy Andrew Jackson, determined that America would do better without being a British dependency. In an astonishing sequence of individual accomplishments, Washington held an improvised, scarcely paid army together for seven years, identified some talented subalterns, and moved with genius at the beginning and end of the conflict and with agility and tenacity as required in between, while Franklin, incredibly, persuaded the absolute French monarchy to join a war for republican democracy and imperial secession.

Jefferson packaged up a tax and jurisdictional dispute as the dawn of human liberty and individual rights, and Madison and Hamilton and Jay wrote the new nation a brilliant and novel Constitution whose adoption was secured by the persuasive eminence of Washington and Franklin. Washington, by his character and sagacity, created a distinguished presidency, in which most of the above-mentioned followed him; Jay and Marshall built a strong federal state from the bench; and Hamilton foresaw and designed the economic destiny of a country that in barely a century would operate on an economic scale that the world had not imagined possible The strategy was to achieve and glorify independence and secure it with functional political institutions, and it was an entirely successful strategy, brilliantly executed.

The new republic was splendidly launched; Jefferson and Polk each added as much territory as the Thirteen Colonies had had at the nation's outset, at minimal cost. The nation's Achilles' heel, even as it grew to be one of the world's major powers, alongside centuries-old kingdoms, was slavery, symbol of the civilization of the southern half of the country. Jackson decreed the compromise of slavery's legitimacy and the indissolubility of the Union, and his great rival, Henry Clay, helped produce compromises in 1820, before Jackson entered public life, and in 1850, after Jackson had died, that enabled the Union to survive until the slave-holding part of the country was reduced by natural growth to a quarter of the free population. The strategy was to preserve the Union, to exalt growth over internecine differences until the strength of the Union was insuperable within the country. It was a clever strategy, executed well up to the death of Clay, and was ultimately successful, though only by a hand's breadth.

When the Union was strong enough to suppress an insurgency, a new leader, at the head of a new party, was elected on the promise that the rights of slaveholders would be protected but that slavery could not expand into areas where it was uneconomic and foreign, and when this was confirmed as unacceptable to the South, proceeded with judicious cunning until the South initiated hostilities. In a prolonged masterpiece of sage and benign execution, Lincoln kept foreigners at bay, built a mighty army, promoted outstanding generals, emancipated the slaves (prospectively, as 95 percent of them were in rebel states), so that the abolitionists and those who cared only for the Union were both satisfied, as the proclaimed emancipation incited slave resistance in the South. Lincoln won, slavery was abolished, the Union was saved and automatically became one of the most powerful nations in the world, just 82 years after its independence was achieved. A providential leader appeared with an unassailable intellectual and moral position and applied adequate pressure for long enough to crush the forces of disunion and start to "bind up the nation's wounds." The tactics of founding the new party, taking it over, and leading it to victory, and the strategy of formulating the issue and the execution of the conduct of the war, were all masterpieces of surpassing brilliance and nobility.

There followed a third of a century in which the national leadership was almost irrelevant; there was no need for a providential Washington, Jackson, or Lincoln. Immigration was open, the economy was unfettered, and millions of people poured from the bowels of European famine and oppression and pogroms into this astoundingly fecund country. They pledged allegiance to Madison and Hamilton's Constitution, and they or their children made their way in the English language, and the organic growth of America, in its sustained swiftness and scale, surpassed anything in human history. The strategy was to let America be itself, and it was a brilliant strategy, the more so because it required almost no execution at all.

Just 50 years after the United States had crushed Mexico, it even more easily routed Mexico's former colonial master, Spain, albeit only in overseas outposts. Theodore Roosevelt seized Panama and built the inter-ocean canal, arbitrated between the Russians and Japanese, pacified the Philippines, built up the United States Navy to be the third in the world after only the British and German Empires, and painted that navy white and sent it round the world.

And Woodrow Wilson, the desiccated but erudite and eloquent intellectual, intervened to assure the victory of the democracies in history's bloodiest war, and created a vision of international cooperation, collective security, and the evangelization of democracy and national self-determination that briefly inspirited the war-ravaged world. More durably, he inserted a requirement in U.S. foreign policy of reasonable virtue as well as clear national interest. Without both those ingredients, ambitious foreign undertakings by American administrations are not really possible. Both Roosevelt and Wilson emphasized that the United States would now be an influence in the whole world, by its power and its moral authority. Roosevelt carried a big stick; Wilson at least had a big stick to hand, and both, in different ways, fired the imagination of the world. The strategy was the tentative assertion of American influence in the whole world, notice that the American era was imminent. Neither strategy had been thought out and Wilson's execution was faulty, but they were both on to something, and the unnatural abstention of America from the world had to end.

Wilson lost his health and his judgment and was repudiated, and there followed a false era of hedonism and foreign policy posturing, and economic insouciance. By 1933, the economy had crashed, and the American idea was more violently afflicted than ever in its history. The Civil War had threatened the nation's integrality, but not the future of its constitutional democracy in 70 percent of the country.

Now, the whole laissez-faire economic system that had fueled the meteoric rise of the nation and the individualistic philosophy that had idealized it were at risk.

There came now Franklin Delano Roosevelt to revive American optimism, reassert the nation's exceptionalism, reform the system sufficiently to renew it and revive its inexorable rise, to restore America's exalted destiny, and to lead it to its rightful place, as Benjamin Franklin had foreseen 175 years before, at the head of all the nations and peoples of the world. Up to now, there had been incremental strategies to create and conserve the nation, to preserve it against insurrection and the evils of slavery, and to bring it to the attention of the world and show the world some of the power of American industry and idealism. Now there was a grave challenge, and meeting the challenge would take America to the summit of the world, as a Manichaean struggle was approaching between the conservators and evocators of Western democracy and Judeo-Christian values, and the totalitarian apostles of racism, paganism, and Marxist materialism. American strategic thinking up to this point had been designed to build and promote America. Now, all that had been achieved had to be redeemed from the depths of economic and psychological depression and swiftly deployed to hold the battlements of the West in a world approaching a mortal crisis. America's rendezvous with what no longer seemed a manifest destiny was almost at hand.

2. THE NEW DEAL

At his inauguration on March 4, 1933, Roosevelt said that his primary task was "to put people to work." He promised bold experimentation, celebrated "the warm glow of national unity," and observed that "There is plenty, but a generous use of it languishes at the very source of the supply." And he rejoiced that "Our problems, thank God, concern only material things," having asserted that "This great nation will endure as it has endured, will revive and will prosper. . . . The only thing we have to fear is fear itself, needless, unreasoning, unjustified terror." He declared a general bank holiday, arranged for special banknotes to be available to cover excessive withdrawals, and began the reopening of the banks in stages by the district Federal Reserve banks, as they reached a point of designated invulnerability. Within three days of the end of the four-day bank holiday, three-quarters of the country's banks had reopened. The Federal Reserve merged some banks and the RFC eventually became a preferred shareholder in many of them, withdrawing as conditions allowed. In the first of a great many such occasions, Roosevelt addressed the nation by radio in what were called "fireside chats," in which he explained government policy in simple, familiar, and even intimate terms, and carried the country with him. The banking measures were an unqualified success and were shortly reinforced by a federal government guarantee of bank deposits.

Roosevelt called a special session of Congress that sat until June, in what became known as "the hundred days." Roosevelt slashed government salaries and pensions to correspond to deflation, repealed Prohibition, and attacked joblessness with programs that directly, and through grants to states and municipalities, absorbed more than seven million of the 17 million unemployed in conservation and public works (what would today be called infrastructure) projects. Farm prices were supported by a program of voting among groups of farmers (according to what they farmed) a roll-back of production in exchange for payments that assured an adequate food supply at survivable prices. A competitive government alternative to private hydroelectric power was provided by the Tennessee Valley Authority, which was the forerunner of massive rural electrification, and included a general plan of flood and drought control, irrigation, canals, and industrialization across seven southern states. More than a million urban home mortgages and several hundred thousand farm mortgages were refinanced. There was a complicated system of agreeing on codes for pay scales by industry, cartels in pricing and collective bargaining to raise both prices and wages were tolerated, and basic wages and working conditions and hours were improved. The country departed the gold standard, though gold was retained to complete intergovernmental transactions. The stock market reacted very appreciatively to all this, and it was clear throughout that Roosevelt was carrying public opinion for his program, which initially enjoyed almost universal support.

There had been very little inflation in Western Europe or America from the late eighteenth century to the World War I, but there had been intermittent severe economic retractions. Roosevelt was moving decisively to alleviate a terrible economic depression, but he was using public spending and the devaluation of the dollar to fight deflation. It was a justifiable decision; public morale firmed up and the country endowed itself with immense accretions of assets: parks, highways, airports, public buildings, bridges and tunnels, and ultimately warships and munitions, while unemployment was massively alleviated, all at bargain cost. Roosevelt was a traditional hard-currency advocate, but he started the United States, following the major European powers, down the slippery slope away from stable currency value and into the temptations of inflation.

In 1934, Roosevelt set up the Securities and Exchange Commission to regulate stock exchanges and the sale of securities issues, and various corporate practices. It responded to general disgruntlement with the excesses of Wall Street in the twenties, but was not intended to be too restrictive. Roosevelt installed as its first chairman the flamboyant (and ethically doubtful) financier Joseph P. Kennedy, answering the question of an incredulous journalist about his nominee: "Set a thief to catch a thief." In 1935, the administration established the Social Security Board to preside over a comprehensive, joint-contributory system of unemployment and old-age and survivor insurance and pensions, and relief for the destitute, and assistance to a range of social services for the most needful. This brought the United States fairly level with social programs in other advanced countries and completed a program of providing a safety net for all the victims of the Great Depression.

By late 1936, unemployment had declined from about 17 million, 33 percent of the work force, to about 10 million, 18 percent of an expanded work force, and the vast New Deal workfare programs absorbed more than seven million more in public works and conservation projects, another 14 percent of the work force, and the remaining 4 percent were supported by unemployment insurance. Comparative statistics with other countries are misleading, as, from 1935 on, Britain, France, Germany, Italy, and Japan were drawing steadily larger numbers of people into their armed forces and defense industries, who were counted as employed, while American participants in workfare programs, doing more productive work for the state than military drilling and munitions making, were not. Yet each category of state employee was, in strict economic terms, artificial, and a form of public sector pump priming. Workfare benefits were distributed equally to whites and African Americans, though the work units were segregated, and this was something of an upward revolution for the black communities.

In 1935 and 1936, Roosevelt put through modest tax increases on large personal and corporate incomes to fend off redistributionist movements that sprang up outside the traditional political parties. He engaged in a certain amount of rhetorical fireworks about completely imaginary groups of wrongdoers—"economic royalists, malefactors of great wealth, munitions makers, war profiteers," and so forth. There were no such groups, but by channeling the anger and frustration of the time into a cul de sac of fictitious categories of unnamed people, Roosevelt preserved the moral integrality of the nation, so he could concentrate its hostility on the true enemies of America, Nazi Germany and Imperial Japan. Had he named wealthy people, as some of his opponents did, as public enemies, civil strife would have ensued. By the end of 1935, the immediate crisis of food and shelter for millions of families was under control, and industrial production and consumer prices had increased more than 40 percent and stock prices had more than doubled since inauguration day.

There was no question of the strength of the U.S. currency or its financial system generally. The president was set at the head of a broad political coalition and enjoyed the support of a larger percentage of Americans than leaders in other important democratic countries commanded.

3. FRANKLIN D. ROOSEVELT AND THE WORLD

By the mid-thirties, foreign affairs were resuming an importance they had not had since the dying days of the Wilson administration. The new secretary of state was 11-term Tennessee congressman and then senator Cordell Hull. He had no particular qualifications for the position, but Roosevelt thought his popularity in Congress would be helpful. The president had a low opinion of the State Department from his service in World War I, and intended to conduct his own foreign policy. Roosevelt was fluent in French and German and knew Britain and the other principal Western European countries well. He had many friends and connections in the British Isles, France, and Germany.

In his inaugural address, Roosevelt exercised in many places his knack for the catchy phrase, including by promising the hemisphere that America would be a "good neighbor." This was not altogether the conception of the country that Latin Americans had held. In December 1933, Hull supported a pact at the Montevideo hemispheric conference that abjured armed intervention, which Roosevelt publicly endorsed as henceforth the policy of the United States, a revocation of his cousin's attitude and a considerable relief to many of the Latin American countries accustomed to the arrival of the U.S. Marines on the feeblest pretext. Roosevelt and Hull's emphasis was on pan-American solidarity against any outside interference. Roosevelt was always concerned about German and Italian penetration of the large ethnic communities of those nationalities in Argentina and Brazil.

Roosevelt sent his school friend, and one of the few American diplomats he respected, Sumner Welles, as ambassador to Cuba in 1933, and Welles negotiated a truce between feuding factions and virtually installed what would prove a nearly 30-year preeminence of Fulgencio Batista as the Cuban leader. Roosevelt arranged a reduction in the tariff on Cuban sugar and approved the repeal of the Platt Amendment of 1901, which had constrained Cuban finances and authorized the United States to intervene in that country under almost any pretext. Roosevelt withdrew all American forces from Haiti in 1934, and in 1936 agreed to the renunciation of many of the inequities of the Hay-Bunau-Varilla Treaty of 1903 with Panama. Roosevelt effectively acknowledged the full sovereignty of the Latin American states on condition that they resisted any influences from outside the hemisphere.

The London Economic Conference opened in June 1933. The gold bloc, led by France, Italy, and the Netherlands, but joined by Britain, although it had abandoned the gold standard, sought a fixed rate of exchange with the dollar, which Roosevelt profoundly suspected as an effort to overprice the American currency, and which he considered impractical between gold-backed and free-floating currencies. He thought the other leaders, like Hoover, were focusing on secondary issues and that each nation had to put its own unemployed back to work by stimulating its own economy and reviving the velocity of transactional activity. He instructed Hull to avoid any agreement except bilateral tariff reductions, as he was, at heart, more a free trader than a protectionist, favoring lower prices for lower income earners over special protection for manufacturers, as long as the dollar was fairly valued opposite other currencies. Roosevelt effectively blew up the conference with messages sent via the cruiser *Indianapolis* from his summer home at Campobello, New Brunswick, Canada, to which he had returned, by self-navigated sailboat (through dense fog in a remarkable feat of memory of the waters and sail navigation), for the first time since he had been evacuated from it with polio 12 years before. The *Indianapolis* fired a 21-gun salute as Roosevelt's sailboat emerged from the fog, and thousands of well-wishers lined the shore and welcomed him back.

In November 1933, after Stalin, on Roosevelt's invitation, had sent foreign affairs commissar Maxim Litvinov to Washington, the United States and the Soviet Union exchanged embassies, under a treaty in which the USSR. promised not to disseminate propaganda or otherwise interfere in domestic American affairs. There were also promises of fair treatment of American citizens in Russia and a supposed prospect of agreement on Russian indebtedness to the United States. In a pattern that was to become familiar, Stalin reneged on all aspects of the agreement, and the anticipated spike in trade between the two countries did not materialize. Stalin discouraged imports, apart from sophisticated military hardware, which Roosevelt was not prepared to sell him (until conditions had changed radically almost a decade later), and Russian goods were not of sufficient quality to be marketable in the United States. Neither country lacked raw materials or natural resources.

Roosevelt received a steady stream of prominent Europeans, and followed European affairs closely. He believed from the beginning that Hitler would prove impossible to contain, and urged a robust resistance to Nazi advances on Britain, France, and even Italy, until Mussolini delivered himself over to Hitler like a trussed-up partridge. British prime minister Ramsay MacDonald visited in 1933, essentially on economic matters, but he was already very worn down and had no real support in the coalition the king had created for him. The talks were cordial, but came to nothing. The visit of French premier Edouard Herriot was no more productive, as French premiers came and went with great frequency. German finance minister Hjalmar Horace Greeley Schacht (his father had lived in the United States during the Civil War) also visited early in Roosevelt's term, and advised that

Germany would not be paying any debts or reparations. Roosevelt conversed with him in German, and concluded that although he was not a militant Nazi, and was economically literate, he was an authentic German nationalist of the kind that Roosevelt had known since his mother had taken him to the Wagner Ring Cycle in Bayreuth in 1896 (when he was 14 and concluded that the Germans were falsely romantic racist warmongers), and Schacht confirmed Roosevelt's conviction that Germany was bent on a terrible revenge on her former foes.

Roosevelt listened to Hitler's principal speeches in his office, with his entourage. The Fuehrer was interrupted frequently with massed shouts of "Sieg heil!" (Victory), and the Germans only provided the translation at the end of his remarks, sometimes in a sanitized form. While the Nazi crowds were screaming their support, Roosevelt would give his colleagues his own translation. He well knew how to stir an audience, but was appalled by what he described as Hitler's "shrieks, and the huge crowd responding like animals."[1]

Italy invaded Ethiopia in May 1935, and the League of Nations again failed to take any action. The Ethiopian emperor, Haile Selassie, was jeered disgracefully by Italian delegates when he addressed the League of Nations. Roosevelt urged Britain and France to intervene, but those powers, instead, placated Mussolini in the hope of wooing him away from the embrace of Hitler. The Hoare-Laval Pact, partitioning Ethiopia and deferring to Mussolini, was so distasteful in both countries when it was leaked by a French newspaper that both foreign ministers lost their jobs, but the policy of appeasement continued.

The U.S. Congress was heavily influenced by western isolationists, who were fierce supporters of the New Deal but parted company with Roosevelt's Atlanticist inclinations. As tensions increased in Europe and the Far East, Roosevelt deftly moved to conciliate the southern conservatives in his party who had been unenthused by the New Deal but favored a strong military and were, for reasons going back to the Civil War, well-disposed to the British and the French.

Congress passed a Neutrality Act in 1935 and again in 1936, which urged the president to embargo arms shipments and loans to belligerents. Roosevelt signed the measures, but warned that they were more likely "to drag us into war than to keep us out." There was a new Neutrality Act in 1937 that extended the law to the Spanish Civil War, as the previous acts were confined to wars between nations. Roosevelt was under heavy pressure from the liberal community, which was his principal constituency, to support the Republican Loyalists in Spain, the leftist

1.   Franklin D. Roosevelt, letter to Margaret Suckley, September 26, 1938, author's collection.

parliamentary majority that resisted the fascist rebels led by Franco and were generally known as the Nationalists.

About two-thirds of Americans supported Franco's Republicans, who were very anti-clerical, but four-fifths of American Roman Catholics supported Roosevelt and almost 90 percent of them supported the Nationalists. Ever mindful of the need to preserve the strength of his governing coalition of American voting blocs, Roosevelt was privately happy enough to acquiesce in the naïve meddling of congressional isolationists; he did not judge Spain a sufficiently important issue, nor so clear a choice of preferred outcomes, to strain the unity of his party. Roosevelt went to great lengths to keep the Roman Catholic community, almost a quarter of Americans, and especially their episcopal leadership, on board. When Chicago's George Cardinal Mundelein arrived by ship in Naples for an ad limina visit to the pope, Roosevelt had the U.S. ambassador's train convey him to Rome, and on one occasion a visiting U.S. naval squadron at Naples fired a 17-gun salute in his honor, on orders from the president, via the navy secretary.

The battle lines were already being drawn between Roosevelt's view that the best guarantee of peace was to arm America and support the democracies, and the isolationist view that no belligerent should be supported and that any defense beyond an adequate navy was excessive and somehow an incitement to war. The absurdity of the isolationist position and the president's unfailing skill at rallying opinion were bound to tell, but Roosevelt trod warily, but artfully, through the late thirties.

In 1936, in contravention of the Treaty of Versailles, Hitler occupied the Rhineland militarily, and the French and Belgians did nothing. Roosevelt wrote a close cousin that if France did not occupy Germany up to the Rhine, "in two years, Germany will be stronger than France and it will be too late."[2] The British and the French rightly pointed out that all Roosevelt could supply was exhortations to a strong and hazardous policy by them, not tangible assistance. But Roosevelt responded, to the ambassadors of both countries, that he could not possibly rouse American opinion against Nazi and fascist aggression if the British and the French supinely accepted it. As always, geography, which put America far from any possible rival, was as friendly to it as it was unfriendly to the comparatively gentle countries that were proximate to Germany and Russia.

4. ROOSEVELT'S SECOND TERM

The Republicans met at Cleveland in June 1936, and nominated Governor Alfred M. Landon of Kansas for president and former Cuba Rough Rider and publisher

---

2.   Franklin D. Roosevelt, letter to Margaret Suckley, March 8, 1936, author's collection.

of the *Chicago Daily News*, Colonel Frank Knox, for vice president. Their plat-form attacked the New Deal and accused Roosevelt of running roughshod over the rights of the Congress, of profligate spending, of unconstitutional legislation, and of usurpation of the role of private enterprise. No repeal of key legislation was proposed, though some tax reductions were promised, with unspecified expense reductions. The Democrats met at Philadelphia later in June and renominated Roosevelt and Garner, abolished the requirement of two-thirds approval of nominees (which had bedeviled so many conventions), and supported the administration with intense enthusiasm. In a fighting acceptance speech to more than 60,000 party loyalists in Franklin Field, Roosevelt said that "This generation of Americans has a rendezvous with destiny."

A third party of malcontents of left and right, calling itself the Union Party nominated Republican congressman William Lemke on a platform of conserva-tive populism. The chief inspirations for this grouping had been the colorful and astute boss of Louisiana, governor and senator Huey P. Long, and the Michigan priest with a vast radio audience, Father Charles E. Coughlin. Long had been assassinated in September 1935, but Coughlin became so vituperative in his hos-tility to Roosevelt that representations were made to Rome. The second-highest figure in the Church (and next pope), Secretary of State Eugenio Cardinal Pacelli, spent the entire 1936 election campaign in America, enforcing the Vatican's gag on partisan commentary by Coughlin.

Former Democratic presidential nominees John W. Davis and Alfred E. Smith, and Wilson's last secretary of state, Bainbridge Colby, supported Landon, but they were completely passé, and had had little national support anyway. In a New York campaign wind-up at Madison Square Garden, Roosevelt excoriated the familiar bogeymen of war profiteers, economic royalists, and so forth, claimed to "welcome their hatred," and promised that he had "only just begun to fight." The issue was never really in doubt, and Landon was reduced to claiming that the government would default on Social Security payments. Roosevelt parried his assailants by claiming to be a "true conservative" saving the free enterprise system by repairing its inequities. Roosevelt knew that America had to have generally contented working and agrarian classes or there would be civil disorder and chronic social injustice and wastage of human resources. On election day, he was returned to office in one of the greatest victories in the country's history, 27.8 million votes (61 percent) and 523 electoral votes to 16.7 million votes (37 percent) and 8 electoral votes (Maine and Vermont) for Landon and 892,000 (2 percent) for Lemke. Roosevelt, who had gained strength in both houses of the Congress in the 1934 midterm elections, did so again in 1936, for the fourth consecutive time. He was deemed to have defeated the Depression and had an immense mandate to enact the rest of his program.

In America, at least, democratic leadership was vigorous and purposeful, a strong rival in world opinion to the endless claims of success and predestination of Hitler, Mussolini, and Stalin. These were the most arresting leaders of the Great Powers. To reinforce his insistence on repulse of totalitarian influences in the Americas, Roosevelt attended the Buenos Aires Inter-American Conference in December, and went on to Montevideo and Rio de Janeiro, and was received by huge and wildly enthusiastic crowds in all three capitals. In his speeches there he celebrated inter-American solidarity in the rejection of any aggressive extra-hemispheric intrusions. When Brazilian president Getúlio Vargas told Roosevelt as they motored through heavy crowds in Rio that some of his compatriots accused him of being a dictator, Roosevelt replied: "So do some of mine." He assigned Welles to negotiate agreements with Vargas to displace any German influence in Brazil, and the United States declined to criticize Vargas's assumption of nearly dictatorial powers in 1937, and pledged substantial economic assistance, effectively conditional upon the expulsion of any pro-German predilections, conditions that were accepted in treaties concluded in 1939. (Roosevelt's suspicions of the ambitions of Germany were confirmed when he encountered an old German battleship in the Caribbean as he returned on his ship from Rio; his disquietude was only slightly alleviated when the German bridge noted the presidential standard flown by Roosevelt's heavy cruiser, and sent all hands on deck in formation, and came about, and respectfully fired a 21-gun salute as Roosevelt's squadron passed.)[3]

The principal issue in the first year of the new term was Roosevelt's assault on the Supreme Court, which had overturned key measures of the New Deal. Roosevelt was happy enough to see the last of the National Industrial Recovery Act, with its industrial codes and unenforceable regulations, but he was concerned that the justices might attack Social Security and the Tennessee Valley Authority, two of the greatest legislative accomplishments of his government. He produced the Judiciary Reorganization Bill, which called for the expansion of the Supreme Court from nine to up to 15 justices if the incumbents declined to retire at age 70; the addition of up to 50 judges of other federal courts; the direct evocation to the Supreme Court of all constitutional challenges to federal legislation; automatic rights of government attorneys to be heard in such cases; and the assignment of additional district judges to clear overcrowded dockets.

---

3.   Franklin D. Roosevelt, letter to Margaret Suckley, November 24, 1936, author's collection.

This started out as a measure to alleviate overworked judges, but as it ran into difficulties in the Congress, Roosevelt took over direct championship of it and aggressively attacked the Supreme Court as a band of superannuated reactionaries who had no idea of the powers necessary for the Congress and the administration to defend the country against the ravages of the economic crisis, or to enact social policy for which there was a wide national consensus. One of the most conservative justices, Willis Van Devanter, retired, and the Supreme Court upheld the constitutionality of Social Security and a number of other New Deal measures. Roosevelt could have added a couple of justices, but he did not move until after the Senate majority leader, Joseph T. Robinson of Arkansas (vice presidential candidate with Smith in 1928), died on July 14, 1937. Roosevelt agreed to some procedural reforms but abandoned the expansion of the courts. This fracas opened up deep fissures within the governing coalition, and slowed the momentum of Roosevelt's legislative program. But he had the pleasure of appointing seven of the nine justices in the next four years, and the Supreme Court caused him no more problems.

On October 5, 1937, on his way back by train from a trip to Hawaii, Roosevelt addressed a giant crowd of 750,000 people in Chicago and called for a "quarantine" of aggressive states. He espoused collective security by the democracies, and in a tactic that he was to pursue successfully for several years, he went out well ahead of public opinion, denied that anything had changed, and waited for opinion to close in behind him. The atmosphere was further inflamed on December 12, 1937, when the Japanese, as was clear from film shot by Americans, deliberately attacked the American gunboat *Panay* in a Chinese river, killing two Americans and wounding 30. Hull demanded a formal apology, reparations, and believable assurances that there would be no further provocations, on December 14, and the Japanese complied entirely the same day. The talented U.S. ambassador to Tokyo, Joseph Grew, another school chum of Roosevelt's, had already protested against Japanese violations of the wilted heirloom of the dying months of the previous century, the Open Door. The Japanese had the candor to reply on November 18 that the Open Door was an "inapplicable" dead letter, and Hull responded on the last day of the year that the United States did not recognize what Tokyo and Berlin (who were allied, along with Italy, as of November 1936) called "the new order." (Roosevelt, who was the real leader of resistance to the Rome-Berlin-Tokyo "Axis," said: "It is not new, and it is not order.")

The new domestic political configuration was revealed in the controversy over the Ludlow Resolution in January 1938, which called for a constitutional amendment requiring a national referendum before war could be declared, other than after an invasion of the territory of the United States or its territories. Polls indicated that over

70 percent of Americans favored the measure, but Roosevelt violently attacked it as likely to facilitate the violation of "American rights with impunity," and it was rejected.

Roosevelt had always been reticent about deficit spending and only engaged in it to the extent he thought necessary for alleviating the Depression. Following the 1936 election victory, he endorsed the budget-balancing faction in his party, led by Treasury Secretary Henry Morgenthau and many of the southern Democrats in the Congress whom he now needed to support his foreign and defense policy. The workfare programs were scaled back in the hope that the private sector could now pick up the slack, but a relapse occurred and continued into 1938, in which the unemployment rolls again grew by several million. In April 1938, having given this policy option what he considered a fair try, Roosevelt relaunched the New Deal and immediately increased the public works and conservation employment programs by 1.5 million people, devoted up to $6 billion to new spending programs, and made the first of many major increases in defense outlays, including $1 billion for new battleships, aircraft carriers, and cruisers, totaling about 1.25 million tons of new heavy warships. There were also tax reductions on business, sponsored by Roosevelt's adversaries but unopposed by him, in May 1938. All this activity quickly induced a resumption of economic growth and employment, and the ground lost was all regained and more by late 1939.

5. RISING TENSIONS IN EUROPE

In March 1938, Roosevelt's Good Neighbor policy passed an important test when Mexican president Lázaro Cárdenas nationalized the American and British oil companies in Mexico. Hull, on Roosevelt's instruction, made it clear that he had no objection as long as reasonable compensation was paid. This was in marked contrast to the histrionics of the British, who threatened reprisals, although American sensibilities and international realities prevented them from going too far with such threats. Cárdenas expressed great relief and repeatedly praised Roosevelt in public, the first such occurrence in the 115-year history of relations between the two countries. Roosevelt was mindful of the complaint of his warmongering old friend Smedley Butler, ex-commandant of the Marine Corps, that he had been deployed around Latin America by American fruit and mining companies. He would end this system. Roosevelt had also approved a timetable for the independence of the Philippines in 1935, and Manuel Quezon was elected the country's first president. It was intended that full independence would be achieved on July 4, 1946.

Also in March 1938, Hitler annexed Austria. It was clear from the almost delirious reception given him when he returned to the country of his birth that very many Austrians, and likely a sizeable majority, agreed to absorption of the truncated state into the German Reich. There had been a contentious meeting between Hitler and the Austrian chancellor, Kurt von Schuschnigg, who made massive concessions to Hitler's bullying but announced a referendum when he returned to Vienna. Hitler professed to find this intolerable, and when Mussolini, who had blocked a German takeover of the country in 1934, approved Hitler's action, Germany invaded and met no resistance. Hitler gave a fiery speech to a wildly enthusiastic crowd packed into the square in front of the Imperial Hotel, where he had worked as a sweeper of floors and steps for the coming and going grandees of the capital of the Habsburg Empire 25 years before. Again, the British and French failed even to protest. Roosevelt, on his own authority, gave asylum to 17,000 Austrians, many of them Jews, whose passports were canceled by Germany. (It was 88 years since Daniel Webster had dismissed the Habsburg Empire as trivial and decrepit in the Hülsemann letter. Chapter 5).

Seizing Austria had merely whetted Hitler's appetite, and there was not the briefest respite before he began demanding the integration into the Reich of the Sudeten Germans of Czechoslovakia. His technique was to single out an offending neighboring country, especially if it had an irredentist German population that he would claim was being mistreated, as he did with the Sudetenland, like a lion selecting a wildebeest, then to terrorize it with belligerent speeches and threats and military maneuvers, and then to demand concessions (that usually meant the effective demise of the target country). In the spring of 1938, it was the turn of the Czechs, and Hitler started ramping up his complaints and demands.

Czechoslovakia was an artificial state sliced out of the Austro-Hungarian Empire at the Paris Conference; Bohemia and Moravia (Czechs) and Slovakia were patched together in an elongated country that stretched from Bavaria to the Soviet border. It included approximately two million Sudeten Germans in the western tip of the country, adjacent to Germany, and in territory where the Czechs had built extensive fortifications, foreseeing from whence a challenge to the new country might come. There was no doubt that most of the Sudetenlanders preferred to be in Germany, but there was no significant discrimination against them where they were. Czechoslovakia and Austria were the only countries sliced out of the Habsburg Empire that were serious functioning democracies.

As Hitler proceeded to tear off and digest chunks of that empire, it not only demonstrated the proportions of the mistake in carving up that amorphous (or as future British prime minister Winston Churchill later described it, "bovine") empire in 1919, but even exposed Bismarck's error in conducting the anti-Catholic Kulturkampf. If Imperial Germany had divided the Habsburg Empire unevenly (in its favor) with Russia, and made a durable arrangement with that country, it would never have faced a two-front war. It was always going to be difficult to reconcile the Habsburg and Romanov interests in Central Europe, but Germany and Russia could have partitioned it on generally ethnic lines, with Russia taking most of the Slavs and Germany taking Romania, the Czechs, Hungary, and part of Yugoslavia.

Hitler torqued up the pressure through the spring and summer, and provoked a couple of incidents. Czechoslovakia had been guaranteed by France, Britain, and the Soviet Union, which should have been sufficient to deter Hitler, but, as was his custom, he quickly detected the weakness underlying the Western democratic governments, and the unfathomable cynicism of Stalin. Hitler's threats reached a crescendo at the annual Nuremberg rally in late summer, where he explicitly threatened, to great enthusiasm from his partisans, to take the Sudetenland by force. In the midst of this choreographed terror campaign, British prime minister Neville Chamberlain asked Hitler to receive him, which the German leader did, at Berchtesgaden, near Nuremberg, where he had a mountain-top chalet, on September 15. Hitler made various demands, and Chamberlain returned to London and managed over the next few days to secure agreement on most of them. On September 22–23, he returned to see Hitler at Bad Godesberg on the Rhine, where Hitler raised his demands; Chamberlain returned to London amidst a general gloom that Europe might be on the brink of war.

Roosevelt was in frequent touch with his principal ambassadors in Europe, and told the British ambassador in Washington, Sir Ronald Lindsay, that Britain had to shed its "We who are about to die" attitude if it expected any encouragement from the United States. He told Lindsay that if Britain and France concerted with the Soviet Union and the Balkan countries and threatened imposition of a blockade on Germany, he would announce that the United States would observe the blockade and would supply the British and French war materiel at advantageous prices. He told his ambassador in Madrid, the historian Claude Bowers, who was dispiritedly watching the approach of Franco's army as the Civil War neared its dreadful end, that he opposed concessions of principle, and disagreed with the appeasement of Hitler; he thought that if Chamberlain really managed to buy peace, he would be a hero, but doubted that would be the outcome.

The threat of war apparently rattled even Hitler, and after final appeals from the pope, Roosevelt, and others, Mussolini suggested to Hitler that he could get what he wanted without war and he might wish to do so. Hitler deferred his announced general mobilization on September 28, and invited Mussolini, Chamberlain, and the French premier, Edouard Daladier, to join him in Munich for a conference the next day. This was communicated, in a dramatic moment, to Chamberlain as he was addressing Parliament about the crisis. He interrupted his address to read the cable that had just arrived from Hitler inviting him to Munich, and advised the House of Commons of its contents and that he would accept. There was immense relief. The Munich Agreement of September 29, 1938, required the Czechs to hand over the Sudetenland at once, and the Great Powers guaranteed the succeeding, emasculated Czechoslovak state.

This was a fantasy, of course, as Poland and Hungary then each tore a chunk out of the stricken country. Stalin was ignored throughout, and Chamberlain considered, from start to finish, that he was better off trying to work with Hitler and Mussolini than paying any attention at all to Roosevelt, whose overtures, including an invitation to confer, he coldly rebuffed. (One such episode contributed to the resignation of the promising young foreign secretary, Anthony Eden, 41, in early 1938.)

Chamberlain has been reviled by posterity, and not without reason, but he could not possibly have taken Britain to war to prevent the right of Sudetenlanders to be Germans. Neither the British nor the French public would have countenanced war, nor should have, for such a cause. But he should have achieved as much solidarity as possible with Stalin and Roosevelt (as his successor did, and they were the only non-fascist Nazi leaders of Great Powers who had some idea of what they were doing), and held the line for a staged handover of the Sudetenland and a real guarantee of the continuing Czechoslovak state. Instead, Chamberlain revived Disraeli's entirely justified phrases from the Congress of Berlin in 1878, when he had stood up to Bismarck and emerged with more than he had originally sought (including the island of Cyprus, which he had not particularly coveted): "Peace with Honour" and "Peace in our time."

He should have spoken cautiously and warned of the need for vigilance, and he did in fact increase aircraft production, which proved critically important two years later. But he seized the euphoria of the occasion and elected to be an international hero, a small evanescent Woodrow Wilson, without the ascetic intellectualism and moral and military authority, but uplifting the world with a vision of peace, whose realization was left entirely in the hands of the most psychotically belligerent statesman in history. (Wilson was never interested in appeasing anyone.)

Winston Churchill, veteran parliamentarian and a prominent member of four former governments, led a small parliamentary opposition to the Munich Agreement, which he called an "unmitigated defeat," and said that Britain faced "the bleak choice between war and shame" and predicted "We shall choose shame and then war." He warned that this was the first of many offerings from a bitter cup of humiliation unless Britain regained "the martial vigour . . . of olden time."[4]

---

4.   Martin Gilbert, editor, *Winston S. Churchill: Companion Volume V*, Part 3, *The Coming of War 1936–1939*, London, Heinemann, 1982, pp. 1117, 1155.

Roosevelt told his ambassador in Britain, the singularly inappropriate Joseph Kennedy (an indiscreet semi–fascist sympathizer whom Roosevelt had appointed as an Irish joke and to get him out of the United States), that he could express no congratulations to the British government on Munich, other than for himself and not his government, and then only verbally. As Chamberlain emplaned for Munich, Roosevelt sent him the ambiguous message, "Good man." He still hoped for something less than the complete sell-out that occurred.

The world was still relaxing from the settling down of the war scare when a Polish Jew assassinated an official of the German embassy in Paris. Germany erupted in officially orchestrated riots and pogroms, called "Kristallnacht," the night of broken glass (November 5, 1938), because of thousands of shattered Jewish storefronts. Dozens were killed and dozens of synagogues were burned down, as Nazi anti-Semitism achieved new depths of violence and repression. The Jewish community was made to pay the whole cost of cleaning up after the disturbances, and suffered the imposition of new confiscatory taxes and restrictions.

It has never been clear, other than rank opportunism, what the source of Hitler's animosity to the Jews was, but it was not as repugnant a policy at the time as it became, because it was not clear in what murderous atrocities it would end, and anti-Semitism, in milder forms, was widespread. The Jews were widely regarded as the descendants of Christ-killers in the more perfervid Christian circles, and as commercial and professional sharpers by less righteous philistines. There were frequent Western complaints about Hitler's mistreatment of the Jews, and he replied by offering to send the German Jews "in luxury liners" to any liberal democracy that would welcome them. There were no takers. The Latin American dictators, the Turks, and Franco, once in power in Spain, were more generous refuges than most of the Western democracies, and, as usual, Hitler closed in quickly and effectively on the weakness and hypocrisy of Western inter-war democratic leadership.

Roosevelt had a defensible record in reception of fugitives from Nazi Europe, ultimately accepting over 100,000 Jews, about 15 percent of the Jewish population of Germany. But with the Jews as with the Spanish Civil War, he would not be maneuvered into fragmenting the broad political mosaic he had assembled that provided him a permanent majority, in public opinion, the Congress, and in presidential elections, throughout his long reign (for reign it was). Most Americans disapproved of any physical or civic discrimination against Jews, but most also opposed the admission of large numbers of outsiders, perhaps especially Jews, to the United States. Similar attitudes prevailed in Britain, Canada, France, and other democratic countries.

Following Kristallnacht, Roosevelt pulled his ambassador (Hugh Wilson) from Berlin, and Hitler withdrew his from Washington, the able Hans Dieckhoff, just before Roosevelt expelled him. Dieckhoff (who was infinitely more capable than his brother-in-law, Hitler's insufferable and very limited foreign minister, Joachim von Ribbentrop) had warned Hitler that Roosevelt was mortally hostile to Nazism and was capable of being the first president to seek a third term, and of using his position as commander-in-chief to provoke war through naval incidents, if Germany were at war with Britain. A few weeks after Kristallnacht, Roosevelt told a public forum on the radio and in widely distributed newsfilm that "There can be no peace as long as there are millions of innocent wayfarers hounded from country to country with no place to lay their heads."

In one of his few political miscues, Roosevelt set out to purge his party, in the midterm elections of 1938 of some of its legislators who had failed to give his programs what he considered adequate support, including Georgia senator Walter George, Maryland senator Millard Tydings, and New York congressman John O'Connor. He knocked off O'Connor, but his personal intervention against the two senators did not appreciably reduce their popularity and both were renominated and reelected. The Republicans gained 81 congressmen and seven senators, but that still left the Democrats in firm control of both houses. Roosevelt would be more dependent on southern Democrats, whose views on treatment of African Americans, including on anti-lynching laws, he deplored, but the southerners would be amenable to his plan to shift the focus of his workfare and unemployment-reduction programs from public works to defense production of munitions, aircraft, and warships.

6. THE DESCENT TO WAR

Chamberlain's honeymoon was short and Munich was revealed as a false dawn in March 1939, when Hitler summoned the Czech president, Emil Hacha, to Berlin, and his deputy, the elephantine air force Reich Marshal Hermann Goering, chased him physically around a writing table until Hacha collapsed, and on revival signed a request for German intervention in Bohemia. It was an even more undignified and outrageous interview than had been Hitler's with Schuschnigg a year before. Hitler invaded and occupied Bohemia and Moravia, without resistance, but certainly unwelcomed by the Czechs, despite the solemn guarantee of the remains of that country by the signatories of the Munich Agreement, five months before. Slovakia and Carpatho-Ukraine, the other constituent parts of Czechoslovakia, declared their independence, and Czechoslovakia ceased to exist. Later in March, Hitler sliced the ethnically German province of Memel out of Lithuania, arriving in a sea-sick condition on a German armored cruiser to take possession personally of this new acquisition. His statement after Munich that he had "no more ter- ritorial demands to make in Europe" was thus laid bare as completely fraudulent, and he was no longer confining himself to assimilations of ethnic Germans. He immediately identified Poland as his next target and began public threats and demands for Danzig and the Polish Corridor, that country's access to the Baltic Sea. Compounding their previous errors, Chamberlain and the French, at the end of March, guaranteed Poland if that country were attacked. Chamberlain apparently believed that Poland would be a greater military power than the Soviet Union, the country with which the British and the French, whatever they thought of Bolshevism, should have been concerting policy.

Finally, very late, Chamberlain sent a diplomatic mission to Moscow to explore arrangements with the Soviet government. Unknown to Chamberlain, Stalin had lost all regard for the British and the French, having witnessed in astonishment their endless retreats before Hitler, for whom he had conceived considerable admiration, which was reciprocated. (They were, with Mao Tse-tung, the most formidable totalitarian dictators in history.) On April 7, Mussolini, desperate to keep up with Hitler, invaded and occupied Albania, and on April 15, Roosevelt sent identical letters to Hitler and Mussolini (via the king of Italy for protocol reasons as the king was chief of state and technically the analogue of Roosevelt and Hitler). He asked them if they could assure the world that they had no designs on 31 countries and areas in Europe and the Middle East.

Hitler took the unusual step of addressing the Reichstag, with Goering, in his capacity as its president, sitting behind him lolling in laughter in his chair while Hitler recited all 31 places of interest in a mocking tone and then gave an acidulous response that "You, Mr. Roosevelt, may think that your interventions will succeed everywhere"; he continued with a self-conscious description of the contrast between mighty America and cramped Germany and of his own success compared with what he implied was the lethargy of the Roosevelt administration, which had come to office just a month after Hitler. The German government had extorted assurances from most of the countries Roosevelt referred to that they had not felt threatened, and he essentially told Roosevelt to stay out of European affairs. As Roosevelt suspected might happen, while Hitler enjoyed himself and amused his countrymen, Americans were offended at seeing their president held up to ridicule for posing what most Americans considered a reasonable question.

The slide toward war accelerated now. Britain's King George VI and Queen Elizabeth visited Canada and the United States in May and June 1939, and made a very good impression. They had been coming to Canada, and Roosevelt invited them to visit the U.S. also as a goodwill and relationship-building gesture, as he had given up on Chamberlain. The American public found the royal couple attractive and unpretentious, and Roosevelt, who had known this king's father and brother (George V and Edward VIII), found them intelligent, conscientious, and unaffected. Like most people, they were impressed by Roosevelt's overpowering personality and his evident mastery of American public affairs and opinion, as well as his familiarity with the complicated European arena. The trip was a huge success. Roosevelt drove them to the royal train at the little Hyde Park railway station near his Hudson River home. Large crowds on both sides of the river sang "Auld Lang Syne," and Roosevelt called out "All the luck in the world." Ten weeks later, Britain was at war.

The Anglo-Russian negotiations proceeded desultorily, while Hitler sent the Wilhelmstrasse's crack diplomatic negotiators secretly to Moscow. Roosevelt was cruising in northern waters on the USS *Philadelphia*, in late August 1939. He was in the habit, when he wished to take a holiday, of requisitioning a heavy cruiser and purporting to visit defense installations while in fact fishing and playing cards with his cronies (and waiving, for his party and himself, the rule he had brought in when assistant secretary of the navy in World War I against alcohol on the ships). He received an alert that the German foreign minister, Ribbentrop, was about to go to Moscow, and Hull requested his immediate return to Washington. Roosevelt sent a message to Stalin at once, warning him that if he made an arrangement with Hitler, Hitler might overwhelm France and would then turn on Russia. The Russo-German pact, which included public clauses of reciprocal non-aggression and neutrality in the event of attacks by third parties, and a private agreement on the partition of Poland between them, should Germany attack that country, was signed on August 23. The effect was electrifying, considering the long and acrimonious hostility between the two regimes and Hitler's pose as a bulwark against both Bolshevism and the Asiatic hordes of central and eastern Russia. (An amiable Stalin told von Ribbentrop: "Your Fuehrer and I have poured pails of dung over each other's heads but I want you to know I think he's a hell of a fellow.")

Roosevelt sent the customary message to the parties proposing conciliation, under no illusions about the effect of it. Germany invaded Poland in overwhelming strength on September 1. Britain and France declared war on Germany on September 3, the Soviet Union invaded Poland on September 17, Warsaw fell to the Germans on September 27, the country was partitioned between the invading powers on September 28, and the last organized Polish resistance was crushed on October 5. It was a swift and horrifying demonstration of German military efficiency, with heavy use of armored (tank) divisions and heavy tactical aerial bombing, including the indiscriminate bombing of residential areas. Roosevelt declared American neutrality but did not ask Americans to be "neutral in thought," as Wilson had in 1914. He spoke to the Congress and called for avoidance of any reference to "a peace-party—we are all part of it," but he called for repeal of the Neutrality Acts in order to permit military sales to the Allies, and this was accomplished on November 4.

On October 11, Professor Albert Einstein (with whom Roosevelt always spoke in German) informed him of the possible development of an atomic bomb and Roosevelt began to take the project directly into the War Department. On October 14, the Soviet Union attacked Finland, but suffered a bloody nose for several months before overwhelming Russian forces finally forced the cession of a Finnish province. The British and the French considered sending forces to assist the Finns, and were preparing to do so when the Finns were forced to negotiate. Entering into combat with the Soviet Union would have been an unimaginable catastrophe for the Allies. Winston Churchill and Anthony Eden had been recalled to government by Chamberlain, Churchill in charge of the navy, the position he had held at the start of the World War I. And Roosevelt, relieved to have a warrior in a position of influence in the British government, initiated direct correspondence with Churchill, as he found Chamberlain hopeless and antagonistic. Hitler made a peace offering, proposing that the combatants end the war with exactly what they now possessed, no concessions by Germany, Britain, or France. Even Chamberlain was no longer interested, having been so bitterly disillusioned by Hitler's bad faith and barbarity.

Roosevelt sent Under Secretary of State Sumner Welles, for whose talents (unlike Hull's) he had considerable regard, on a mission to Rome, Berlin, Paris, and London in February and March 1940, to see if there were any prospects for peace. He found Mussolini full of bluster, Hitler disingenuously professing preparedness to make peace or war, the French sullen and demoralized, and the British grimly determined, but with no idea of how to win a war, and no prospects of an early peace. Roosevelt had long been convinced that Hitler was a compulsive warmonger who was determined to provoke war, and he doubted that Britain and France, without Russia, could contain Germany as they had, by the narrowest margin, until Russia collapsed, in World War I. In these circumstances, there is little likelihood and no evidence that Roosevelt had any intention of retiring after two terms, as his distinguished predecessors had done. He had written that France could not tolerate remilitarization of the Rhineland in 1936, and that Germany would soon be stronger than France. He had warned Stalin about facilitating Germany's initiation of war, and he had no confidence in the ability of Chamberlain or any French leader in sight to wage war successfully against such a satanic war leader as Hitler at the head of such a military machine as he had built. He doubted the ability of any discernible coalition to defeat Germany without the eventual participation of the United States.

7. THE GERMAN BLITZKRIEG, WINSTON CHURCHILL, AND THE FALL OF FRANCE

Roosevelt was considering these facts and how, if he were to seek a third term, he would engineer it without scandalizing American concerns about too long an incumbency, when Hitler seized Denmark and invaded Norway, in April 1940. An Anglo-French expeditionary force landed in Norway in mid-April but was forced to evacuate after 10 days. The British would return to Narvik at the end of May, but would again be forced to withdraw 10 days later. It was another snappy, professional German military operation, and it precipitated a confidence debate in the British House of Commons that revealed too many defections from Chamberlain's Conservative Party for him to continue. Though the foreign secretary, Lord Halifax, was considered for the succession, he was tainted by appeasement and did not feel he could govern from the unelected House of Lords. Winston Churchill was the obvious choice, and on May 10, 1940, King George VI invested him with practically unlimited power as head of an all-party national unity government, in what, with the invasion of the Netherlands, Luxembourg, Belgium, and France that morning, was now an unlimited emergency.

The German campaign plan, called "Sickle-sweep," devised chiefly by Field Marshal Erich von Manstein, but with Hitler's personal collaboration, was brilliantly conceived and executed. The Germans struck through what had been thought to be the impassable Ardennes Forest with swift-moving mechanized units, and wheeled right, opposite to the World War I Schlieffen Plan, and drove to the sea, completely separating the British, Belgians, and northern French armies from the main French army around Paris and along the Rhine, in the heavily fortified and underground Maginot Line. The Belgians capitulated on May 28, and 338,000 British and French soldiers were evacuated by hundreds of craft of all kinds between May 28 and June 4, from Dunkirk across the English Channel, as the retreating armies tenaciously defended the perimeter and the Royal Navy and Air Force retained air and sea superiority in the Channel. They left their equipment behind, and Roosevelt immediately (and without consultation in the midst of the intense run-up to presidential elections) sent Britain a full shipment of rifles and machine guns and munitions to rearm the evacuated forces and enable them to defend the home islands if necessary.[5]

The German army outnumbered and outgunned the remaining French by more than two to one and on June 5 launched a general offensive southward to sweep France out of the war. Italy declared war on France and Britain on June 10, an event that Roosevelt described as striking "a dagger into the back of its neighbor." Churchill and the French premier, Paul Reynaud, made increasingly urgent appeals to Roosevelt to announce that the U.S. would enter the war (which Churchill knew, certainly, to be completely out of the question), as Reynaud was now wrestling with a defeatist faction that wished peace at any price. His government evacuated to Bordeaux, and Paris, declared an open city, was occupied by the German army on June 14. The 84-year-old Marshal Henri-Philippe Pétain, the hero of Verdun, succeeded Reynaud as premier on June 17 and asked for German peace terms.

France surrendered in Marshal Foch's railway car where the 1918 Armistice was signed, at Compiègne, on June 22. The long battle between the French and the Germans was apparently over, in Germany's favor, as it crushed and humiliated and disarmed France and occupied more than half the country, including Paris. The Third Republic, which had presided over the greatest cultural flowering in French history and had seen the country victoriously through the agony of the World War I, ignominiously voted itself out of existence at the Vichy casino on July 10, 1940. The fascist sympathizer Pierre Laval would govern in the German interest in the unoccupied zone, in the name of the senescent marshal. Virtually all France, initially, knelt in submission before the Teutonic conquerors, as they marched in perfect precision down the main boulevards of all occupied cities, resplendent in their shiny boots, full breeches, shortish, tight-waisted tunics, and coal-scuttle helmets. Not since Napoleon crushed Prussia in 1806 had one Great European Power so swiftly and overwhelmingly defeated another. And in this case, the occupier intended to stay, and most of France was annexed to Germany, including Paris. Appearances were deceiving, however.

A pioneering advocate of mechanized and air warfare and junior minister in the Reynaud government, General Charles de Gaulle, with practically no support, and representing only the vestiges of France's national spirit and interests,

---

5.   As was referred to in Chapter 2, the theory has arisen that Hitler deliberately withheld pressure on the Dunkirk perimeter to make it less humbling for Britain to accept subsequent peace terms. There is no evidence to support this, and if all available German armor had been committed to the assault, it is not clear that it would have much hastened the fall of the beachhead against the total effort of the Royal Navy and Air Force, which would certainly have been more than a match for German mechanized forces, especially if heavy units of the Royal Navy had been deployed for close-up shore bombardment.

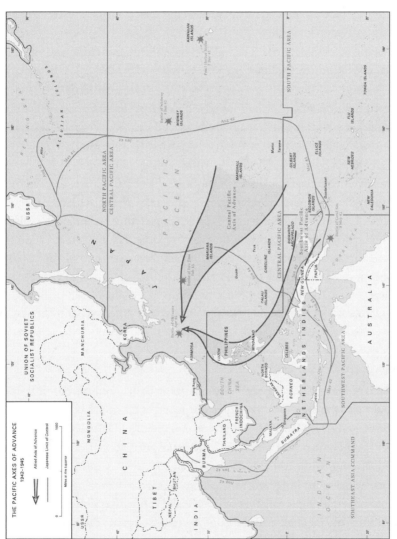

WWII Pacific. Courtesy of the U.S. Army Center of Military History

flew to England on June 18, and declared by radio to his countrymen: "France has lost a battle; France has not lost the war." He announced the formation of the Free French movement, which would continue the war. As Churchill said, he carried "with him, in his little aircraft, the honour of France." The major players of the greatest drama in modern history were all in place: Stalin, Hitler, Roosevelt, Churchill, and now de Gaulle.

As the tide of war swept over Europe, Roosevelt kept requesting and receiving increased allocations for military preparedness. As the war began, he installed General George C. Marshall, over many senior officers, to be chief of staff of the United States Army. Marshall urged Roosevelt to mobilize opinion for an increased defense budget and he assured the general that Hitler would take care of that. This was what happened, as Roosevelt ordered eight battleships, 24 aircraft carriers (there were only 24 afloat in the world, almost all in the British, Japanese, and U.S. navies), and an annual aircraft production of 50,000 (five times German production). The remaining workfare programs were entirely given over to defense production. It was the strategic coup of completing victory in one arena (elimination of unemployment) by focusing on the next target (arming America until it was an incomparable military superpower). Unemployment declined by 500,000 per month for the balance of the year and into 1941; that battle was over and won at last. Among the workfare projects were the two soon-to-be historic aircraft carriers, *Enterprise* and *Yorktown*. Unemployment had vanished completely, even in the relief programs, by the autumn of 1941.

8. THE THIRD TERM

Roosevelt had kept his countrymen entirely in the dark about his political intentions, and there was teeming curiosity about whether he would break a tradition as old as the Republic and seek a third term. As the Soviet Union occupied Latvia, Lithuania, and Estonia, bringing to 14 the number of countries that had been occupied, starting with Ethiopia, Roosevelt staged another of his political masterstrokes, by firing his isolationist war secretary, Harry Woodring, and bringing into his administration preparedness advocate and former Republican secretary of war and state Colonel Henry Stimson and, as navy secretary, the previous Republican candidate for vice president and comrade in arms of Theodore Roosevelt, Colonel Frank Knox. The enlistment of these two prominent Republicans gave the administration the character of a coalition. Eight days later, the Republicans met at Philadelphia and nominated dark-horse utilities executive, Wall Street lawyer, and public intellectual Wendell L. Willkie, originally from Indiana, for president, and Senator Charles L. McNary of Oregon for vice president. The Republicans attacked the New Deal without proposing to disband any of it and pledged to stay out of war, but supported aid to the democracies and resistance to any European intrusions in the Western Hemisphere.

Still Roosevelt kept his own counsel, though it is now obvious that he was planning to seek reelection. The Democrats met on July 15 at Chicago, and Roosevelt gave the convention keynote speaker, Senate majority leader Alben W. Barkley of Kentucky, a message to read in his address. It contained the usual references to Roosevelt's fervent ambition to return to his "home on the Hudson" (which is bunk, because if that is what he had wished to do, he would have done it), and said that he had no desire for a third term and that the delegates should feel free to vote for anyone they wished. Anyone obviously included him, and by prearrangement, a barrel-chested official of the Chicago Democratic municipal machine, which had packed the convention, bellowed into a microphone in the basement that was connected to every loudspeaker in the convention hall: "We want Roosevelt!" The convention erupted in Roosevelt demonstrations, singing "Happy Days Are Here Again," "Franklin D. Roosevelt Jones," and other Roosevelt songs, while the voice from the basement recounted every state and large city in the country as a place that did "want Roosevelt."

As a spontaneous move against the wishes and without the knowledge of the incumbent, it was a fraud, of course, and was largely perceived to be so, but it did reflect the party's wishes and was a reasonable facsimile of a draft. Roosevelt addressed the convention by special hook-up from the White House, after he inflicted on the convention the mad choice of the mystical leftist Henry A. Wallace, agriculture secretary, as his vice presidential candidate. Roosevelt said that the war emergency would prevent him from campaigning, but that he reserved the right to intervene in the electioneering to correct "campaign falsehoods," with little doubt that he would purport to find some. With that he embarked on a country-wide tour of defense installations that was publicized as much as campaign appearances and had most of the characteristics of them.

The Battle of Britain for the air superiority that would be necessary for any German invasion of England, given the overwhelming strength of the Royal Navy and the certainty that it would fight with desperate courage to defend the home islands, began on August 8 and continued to late October. Roosevelt would replace British aircraft losses, but the U.S. did not have a fighter plane that was competitive with Britain's superb Spitfire and Hurricane or Germany's Messerschmitt 109. In the course of the battle, Goering shifted targets from aircraft factories and airfields to night bombing of cities, especially London, in order to reduce the number of German planes being downed. This tactic brought German losses beneath the level of their aircraft production but assured the replacement of British losses also, and while bombing civil populations shook British morale, it did not crack and the attacks outraged world, and especially American opinion.

In the three months ending October 31, the British lost 915 aircraft but recovered most of the air crews, and the Germans lost 1,733 aircraft and lost all the aircrews over Britain. With their aircraft production holding and unlimited resupply from the U.S., it was clear that Britain had won the great air battle and would not be invaded. Churchill, a mighty orator, repeatedly roused his countrymen and stirred the whole world with Demosthenean tours de force on world broadcasts, including his immortal exhortation as France quit the war: "Let us so bear ourselves that if the British Commonwealth and Empire should last for a thousand years, men will still say, 'This was their finest hour.'" They did and it was. He concluded a broadcast in October: "We are still awaiting the long-promised invasion. So are the fishes." This was not an idle challenge; the capital ships of the Home Fleet were deployed to southern ports, and without air superiority a German invasion force would have gone to a watery grave and any shore parties that landed would have met a reception unlike any that the German army had had since 1918.

Roosevelt sent the British 50 aged destroyers in mid-campaign, and began extending American territorial waters from three miles to 1,800 miles, and ordered the navy to reveal the presence of any German ship to the British and the Canadians. He also secured the first peacetime conscription in the country's history, of a million men, which he called, taking a word from the Revolutionary War, "a muster." Willkie campaigned with great energy and focused on his claim that Roosevelt would lead the country into war. The young men of America, he said, "are already, almost at the boats." In fact, in retrospect, it appears that Roosevelt's idea was to do whatever was necessary to keep Britain in the war, arm America to the teeth, and intervene when the Germans had been enervated by attrition, somewhat as had happened in 1917. Toward the end of the campaign, Roosevelt emerged and gave some memorable campaign speeches. On October 28 in New York's Madison Square Garden, he added the names of Republican congressmen "Martin, Barton and Fish" to a recitation of reactionary opponents and the crowd, after the first instance, shouted out their names as he got to them. "I have said again and again and again that your sons will not be sent into any foreign wars" (Boston, October 30). His defeatist ambassador in London, Kennedy, returned late in the campaign, to, it was widely thought, endorse Willkie, but Roosevelt had him intercepted when his Clipper flying boat landed at New York and brought directly to the White House with his wife, where Roosevelt persuaded him, allegedly by promising to further the political careers of Kennedy's sons, to endorse him, which Kennedy did in a national radio broadcast a few days later (which Kennedy insisted on paying for himself).

Roosevelt solemnly promised to stay out of war, advocated peace through strength, was supported by Willkie in calling for assistance to Britain and Canada, and smeared the isolationists as, in effect, Nazi sympathizers. His courtship of the Roman Catholics (and particularly his refusal to buckle to the prevailing enthusiasm to support the Republicans in the Spanish Civil War) produced a handsome reward as New York's Archbishop Francis J. Spellman, who replaced the deceased Cardinal Mundelein of Chicago as America's most powerful clergyman, issued a statement that was read in every Roman Catholic church in America, asserting that "It is better to have strength and not need it than to need it and not have it. We seek peace, but not a peace that consists in a choice between slavery and death." It was a clear endorsement of Roosevelt's policy, without naming him. At the decisive moment, the leadership of that Church delivered all it had for the president.

On election day, Roosevelt won, 27.2 million (54.5 percent) and 449 electoral votes, to 22.3 million (44.5 percent) and 89 electoral votes for Willkie. The Democrats made modest gains in the congressional elections. On December 29, 1940, in one of the most famous of all his fireside chats, Roosevelt addressed more than 70 percent of the country, and said that "No dictator, no combination of dictators" would deter America from being "the great arsenal of democracy." Messages to the White House ran 100 to one in support of the president and he moved into his unprecedented third term with an approval rating of over 70 percent.

His sure-footed strategic agility had been an astounding tour de force through a complete political cycle. He had recruited the western isolationists to assist him in adopting programs to put the people back to work, renovate the nation's infrastructure, stabilize agriculture, assure the foundations of contented agrarian and working classes, and inspirit the nation. There were, from the Quarantine speech in October 1937 through his reelection, a series of almost faultless sequential steps toward the fulfillment of his grand strategy for America, the world, and, incidentally, himself. The war emergency ended the Depression as he ditched the Progressive isolationists upon whom the New Deal had depended and replaced them with the southern advocates of massive defense and aid to the British and the French, attracted prominent Republicans to the administration, and brought in the greatest armament program in world history.

The fall of France made the United States central, even more than in 1917, in the triumph of democratic government and the free enterprise economy, in the world. Roosevelt would assure Britain's survival and await in hopefulness a German immersion in Russia (which he had predicted to Stalin) and a deepening Japanese immersion in China, until the time was right for a mightily armed America to assert itself. In the supreme crisis of modern times, as in the supreme crisis of the Union 80 years before, and at the contentious birth of the republic 85 years before that, the head of the American people and state was a leader of surpassing political and strategic genius. The best was yet to come.

9. THE FOUR FREEDOMS AND LEND-LEASE

Now installed for an indefinite duration at the head of the nation, Roosevelt, in his State of the Union message on January 6, 1941, staked out much of the country's future international strategy. He outlined Four Freedoms as America's goals, implicitly for the whole world: freedom of speech and expression, freedom of worship, freedom from want, and freedom from fear. And in describing the world crisis, he uttered the defining words: "We must always be wary of those who with sounding brass and tinkling cymbal would preach the 'ism' of appeasement"; the United States must never be (and has not been) an appeasement power, and must escalate its promotion of democratic values.

The massive defense build-up continued apace, and secret staff talks began in Washington with the British, in the eventuality of both countries being at war with Germany and Japan. The principal conclusion in the early phase was that Germany was the more powerful and dangerous adversary and that whatever the circumstances of the issue being joined, primary concentration would have to be on the defeat of Germany. With the territory and populations Germany had now occupied, the Greater Reich had an ostensible population as great as that of the United States, 130 million, and an industrial capacity not greatly inferior. Only 60 percent of these people spoke German, but if Germany were allowed undisturbed possession of most of France and Poland and its other neighbors for two generations, its position would be irreversibly solidified. Such an expanded Germany, under totalitarian Nazi direction, was a menace to all civilization. Japan was a formidable nuisance but had little capacity seriously to discommode the West beyond the Central Pacific and the borders of India, apart from whatever it might attempt in Asiatic Russia.

In the year ending March 31, 1941, Allied merchant shipping losses to German submarine warfare had totaled about 2.3 million tons, which exceeded British shipbuilding capacity and strained food and some war supplies. Roosevelt transferred some naval units from the Pacific to the Atlantic and publicly designated almost two-thirds of the North Atlantic as America's "sea frontier" and a "Neutrality

Zone," by which he meant that the U.S. Navy would attack any German or Italian warship on detection, and advise the Royal and Canadian navies of their position.

Roosevelt's closest collaborator, Harry Hopkins, former director of his work-fare programs and now the secretary of commerce, and his friendly opponent in 1940, Wendell Willkie, both visited Britain in February 1941, and both made an excellent impression in Britain and took an excellent impression back with them. Hopkins told Churchill that Roosevelt was determined "at all costs and by all means, to carry you through" the war,[6] and described the American voters as 10 to 15 percent Nazi or Soviet sympathizers, who sheltered behind Lindbergh and professed neutrality but wanted a German victory; 10 to 15 percent, represented by Kennedy, who wanted to help Britain but were pessimistic and didn't want any risk of America entering the war; 10 to 15 percent, including Knox and Stimson, who thought war with Germany inevitable and wanted to get on with it; and 60 percent who favored all aid short of war, even if it risked war. He said Roosevelt had all the last two groups and some of the Kennedy faction, about 75 percent of the people, and was essentially in the war faction himself but knew the value of a united public opinion in wartime. Just before he left Britain, Hopkins, implicitly speaking for his leader, told Churchill, in the presence of a number of dinner companions: "Whither thou goest, I shall go; where thou lodgest, I will lodge; your people are my people and your God my God, even to the end."

And Willkie delivered to Churchill a hand-written message from Roosevelt that included a verse from Longfellow that, he wrote, "applies to you people as it does to us." Churchill read it on a world broadcast: "Sail on O ship of state; Sail on O Union strong and great; Humanity, with all its fears, with all its hopes for future years, Is hanging breathless on thy fate." Churchill responded with Clough's poem, beginning "Say not the struggle naught availeth," and ending "Westward look, the land is bright." The Western world was fortunate to be led at this decisive hour by two men who well represented, by their culture and beliefs and personalities, the civilization they were defending. And both countries were fortunate to have leaders so unusually conversant with the history and geography of the world's principal powers, and to have a background in directing a large navy in wartime.

The president's notions of neutrality were given a new and even more elastic definition with the Lend-Lease Act, presented in February as a result of Churchill's urgent advice to Roosevelt that Britain would not be able to pay cash for military

---

6.   Conrad Black, *Franklin Delano Roosevelt: Champion of Freedom*, New York, PublicAffairs, 2003, p. 616.

purchases much longer. Roosevelt took one of his restorative sea cruises, on the USS *Tuscaloosa* (he had been an avid sailor all his life), and conceived the idea of "lending" Britain and Canada whatever they needed, in exchange for the United States taking out leases on various locations in Newfoundland and Bermuda and the Caribbean to establish bases. Obviously, the concept of "lending" ammunition and warplanes and such in the midst of a world war, with any hope of having them returned, as borrowers are expected to do, was far-fetched, but Roosevelt defended it with his customary panache. He explained to the press that it was like lending "your neighbor your garden hose if his house is on fire." This was nonsense, of course, but when questioned further, Roosevelt asked the reporter if he knew the difference between a horse and a cow, and claimed that the distinction between a loan and a gift was just as obvious.

With heavy-duty arm-twisting from the White House, the measure passed both houses (skillfully floor-managed in the Senate by Foreign Relations Committee chairman Walter George, whom Roosevelt had tried to purge in 1938) on March 11. Most Republicans voted against, which makes it clear that if Willkie had won the 1940 election, though he would have favored aid to Britain, it is unlikely he would have devised such an imaginative scheme, and unlikely that he would have succeeded in passing it. The one occasion when someone sought a third presidential term in the United States was one when it was uniquely essential to Western civilization that he succeed. As often happens in its most dire moments, fortune smiled, consistent with the American traditional belief that when it matters most, God does bless America.

Lend-Lease assistance over the next four years would total over $50 billion. It was a brilliant scheme, and was proclaimed to be so even by Stalin, and the British Parliament voted a resolution of unreserved gratitude to the United States for what Churchill described as "the most unsordid act in the history of any nation." It made it clear that what Hitler had already described (accurately) as the "moral aggression" of American assistance to Britain, on the Atlantic and in its supply role, meant that Germany and the United States were already, in all respects except a general exchange of fire, at war. Hitler had to face that he had no chance of suppressing Britain by invasion, any more than Philip II in 1588, Choiseul in 1760, or Napoleon in 1804 (Introduction and Chapters 1 and 3). The Royal Navy was insuperable without air superiority, which was unattainable with the strength of the Royal Air Force backed by a blank check from America's immense aircraft production industry. British determination and courage, and American industrial might, would keep Britain durably in the war.

10. THE RUSSO-GERMAN WAR

If he was going to face the British and the Americans, Hitler began to shift from an offensive to a tenacious mode, and considered the thought that his best move would be to knock Russia out of the war now, to ensure that Germany controlled all of the European mainland. He would then be sure of not having to fight a two-front war, and the British and the Americans, to launch a successful attack on a Europe entirely dominated by Hitler, would probably need as many as 50,000 warplanes, 500 divisions, and the amphibious forces to land them, and would then have to slog from their starting point to Berlin to win. To Hitler's mind, which did not permit any moral considerations at all, a completely unprovoked and unannounced attack on Russia had its merits. It would be an immense gamble, but Hitler had taken those all his career, and had always succeeded.

If Hitler had followed up his peace overtures of October 1939 and July 1940 with placatory actions and the unilateral suspension of acts of war, he might have made it impossible for Roosevelt to rouse the American public from its isolationist torpor, and might even have lulled the British back into acquiescence. Had he had any of the moderate judgment of a Richelieu or Bismarck, he would have done that, but it would have deprived him of the fanaticism, the rigid totalitarianism, and the preparedness to risk all that were his strength and appeal, as well as, ultimately, his undoing. It was not in Hitler's character. An invasion of the USSR, by his standards of strategic calculation, made some sense, but not at that time and not the way he did it. It would have made much more sense to pour forces into North Africa, instead of the paltry four divisions he gave the brilliant Afrika Korps commander, Field Marshal Erwin Rommel (to add to seven less serviceable Italian divisions), in order to take the Suez Canal and occupy the oil-producing areas of the Middle East. He could thus have supplied Japan with oil, which would have eliminated the coercive aspect of the oil and scrap metal embargo Roosevelt imposed on Japan. It would have enabled Japan to ignore America and join a German attack on Russia. Roosevelt could not have secured, and would not have wished, a declaration of war to defend Stalin.

And since he had an alliance with Japan, Hitler could have coordinated actions against Russia with Japan. Japanese foreign minister Yosuke Matsuoka visited Berlin and Moscow in March and April 1941, proposing a four-power pact, including Italy. Hitler, for his own reasons, not only ignored that but failed to give him any indication of his thinking about the USSR, and lost the opportunity to concert a Japanese attack on the Russian Far East. By this time, the key strategic ingredient for Japan was Roosevelt's embargo of aircraft and aircraft parts and aviation fuel, and his reduction of oil sales to Japan, as Japan imported 85 percent of its oil—80 percent from the United States. Roosevelt was not prepared to reopen supplies unless Japan showed some disposition to withdraw from China and Indochina (which it began occupying after the fall of France, and formally absorbed in July 1941). With the United States shutting down as a supplier of oil, Japan had to be supplied from either the Dutch East Indies (later Indonesia), which were also closed to it by Roosevelt's intervention, or the Middle East, where supplies were controlled by Britain, or the Caucasus fields of the USSR. Neither Churchill nor Stalin was prepared to lubricate Japanese expansionism, any more than Roosevelt was.

If Hitler was not prepared to make a serious effort to seize the Middle Eastern oil fields and close the Suez Canal to Britain, he should at least have promised the Japanese that if they joined him in an attack on the USSR, and avoided war with the United States, which would have occurred if Japan had seized the Dutch East Indies, he would open up the Caucasus oil fields to them. Matsuoka would personally have been well-disposed to any of this. He was quite outraged at American obduracy, even though he had been raised in Portland, Oregon, and Oakland, California, and was a Christian (and ostentatiously disagreed with Hitler's anti-Semitic policies). Thus unalerted, Matsuoka went on to Moscow and signed a non-aggression pact with the USSR, though neither party could be trusted to adhere for one day to any pact it made.

Instead, Hitler kept his allies completely in the dark and prepared for the supreme gamble in the east, with some uncertainty, given the scale of the undertaking. He compared Russia to Wagner's *Flying Dutchman*—it was impossible to know exactly what would happen. As Hitler prepared for the onslaught against Russia, British and American intelligence reported great activity indicating such a move, which was duly handed on to the Soviet government by the British and American embassies in Moscow. Stalin ignored all of it.

Hitler had prepared by reducing all the Balkans to client states, but his plans were interrupted in March by Mussolini's ill-considered invasion of Greece, a mad enterprise for no good object, which enabled the fierce Greeks to give the ill-assured Fascist invaders a bloody nose reminiscent of the Finnish response to Stalin. Then, under the influence of British and American intelligence, a coup in Belgrade overthrew the pro-German government and abrogated the rather subservient treaty that had just been signed with the Reich. Hitler invaded Yugoslavia and then Greece, as Churchill had withdrawn 60,000 soldiers from North Africa to assist the Greeks against the Italians. The Germans overwhelmed the Yugoslavs and the Greeks and pushed the British into the boats, first in Greece and then by paratroop attack in Crete, as they had the year before at Dunkirk. Rommel had been enabled to launch an offensive that drove the British back into Egypt, but Hitler's timetable for an invasion of Russia was delayed by almost two months, as it took to the end of April to secure Greece. This would prove crucial. (It must be said that no outsider had had such success in quelling the endless conflicts of the Balkans as Hitler did. Bismarck had warned that "The Great Powers must not become involved in the quarrels of these sheep-stealers." Yet in the ensuing four years, Yugoslavia suffered 1.6 million war dead, 600,000 fighting the Germans and the Italians, and the other million fighting each other.)

Roosevelt occupied Greenland, with the approval of the junior-level Danish government in exile (a former consul was the most authoritative free Dane that could be found), as the U.S. would occupy Iceland, with the approval of that country, in July, and on May 27 Roosevelt declared a state of unlimited national emergency and closed all German and Italian consulates in the United States. He was behaving exactly as Hitler's last ambassador to Washington, Hans Dieckhoff, had predicted, and as Hitler had come to expect. It all confirmed him in his view that in order to be secure in his gains, he had to remove Russia from Europe and obliterate it as a threat to his rear, before Roosevelt came all the way into the war and he and Churchill concerted a three-way attack on the Reich with Stalin. It had a certain logic, but as is notorious, it was a catastrophic error. But if Hitler's calculations went awry, Roosevelt's did not. A Russo-German war, if it could be kept going, and an early German victory prevented, could open a German artery in the east and cause a war of attrition that would facilitate a decisive British-American stroke in the west.

The former chief of staff of the U.S. Army, now the commander of the armed forces of the Philippines (which Roosevelt nationalized into U.S. forces in July 1941), General Douglas MacArthur, had visited the Soviet general staff in 1932, and told Stimson (then Hoover's secretary of state and now Roosevelt's secretary of war) that Stalin had got rid of most of his best officers in his purges and replaced them with "Jewish commissars without the brains or requirement for command."[7] The Russians had done well against the Japanese in "border incidents" that involved up to 10 divisions, but had fared poorly against the Finns. But it was a vast and populous country and the Russian masses had never been easy to defeat when defending the motherland. Now, as Western intelligence, including the Vatican, was abuzz with reports of an imminent German assault, everyone except Stalin, who clung to his alliance with Hitler to the end, and the Japanese, who were

---

7.   Black, *op. cit.*, p. 321.

kept in the dark by everyone, knew that everything hung in the balance as Hitler unleashed Operation Barbarossa on June 22, and invaded the USSR with 180 divisions, with the Finns and Romanians, along a 2,000-mile front.

As always, the Germans enjoyed complete surprise and made rapid advances, encircling Russian armies in the Ukraine and Belarus in the first six weeks of the war and bagging about 1.3 million prisoners. Stalin was immobilized for the first few days, and his armies fell back everywhere, badly battered. In the Ukraine there was considerable initial enthusiasm for the Germans. But the Red Army did not crack entirely and showed no disposition to stop fighting. Its retreat continued into Russia, but slowed and remained orderly. Stalin had no difficulty replacing dead, wounded, and captured soldiers from the vast pool of the USSR's manpower. He took to the radio—a much rarer occasion for him than for Hitler, Churchill, and Roosevelt, who were, unlike Stalin, great natural orators—and invoked the traditions of Holy Mother Russia, having, to encourage traditional patriotic incitements, exhumed the Russian Orthodox Church that he had been trying to obliterate for the past 15 years. He spoke for the Russian masses (although a Georgian himself) when he avowed in his radio address: "The Germans are inundating our motherland like a plague of grey-green slugs. We will kill them, kill them all, and plough them under the sod." Roosevelt promised assistance to the Soviet Union on June 24, and on July 12 Britain and the USSR signed a mutual-defense agreement that included arms supplies to the Russians and a joint promise of no separate peace with Germany. (Britain had learned from France that such a pledge did not necessarily mean much.)

As Roosevelt edged toward war, the state of relations with Japan began to have a bearing on relations with Russia. When Japan completed its takeover of Indochina in July 1941, Roosevelt imposed a complete embargo on sales of scrap iron (the basis of much Japanese steel production, as it had access to little iron ore) and oil, including from the Dutch East Indies (which he effectively controlled because the Dutch government in exile, including the Queen, Wilhelmina, knew that they would never see the Netherlands again without the involvement of the United States). The oil embargo would only be lifted on the basis of specific export permits, tanker by tanker. This was going to force Japan either to scale back its continuing invasion of China and vacate Indochina, or attack to the south to obtain sure oil supplies from the Dutch East Indies, which the United States had already warned would be an act of war. (Roosevelt would not have had a united country declaring such a war, but giving Japan that ultimatum increased the likelihood that if it attacked the Dutch East Indies, it would attack the United States, too, which would unite American opinion.) The relevance of this to Russia was that if there were no sign of an American entry into the war, and the Germans overran Moscow and Leningrad, the temptation of Stalin to make a separate peace as Lenin and Trotsky had done in 1917, and to retire to Asia and await a favorable moment to return to Europe, would be great. He was not prepared to go on taking up to 10,000 casualties a day just to please Churchill and Roosevelt, not that he was much concerned about casualties for humanitarian reasons, but if he was going to quit the war, he wanted to salvage as much of the sinews of war, including his army, as he could. All aspects, and almost all major protagonists in the world struggle, were treacherous, except Churchill and Roosevelt, and they were not Eagle Scouts either (fortunately).

The Germans had all the Ukraine underfoot by mid-August, and had arrived at the gates of Leningrad by late September, as they drove into the Crimea. Hitler moved his central army group to the south and then back to the central front against Moscow, whose outskirts the German army approached as the winter took hold in mid-November. This was an impressive advance, but the German General Staff had anticipated even faster progress and assumed the disintegration of the Red Army, as the French, who had fought so valiantly in World War I, crumbled under the mechanized and aerial assaults of the German war machine in 1940. Instead, Russian resistance stiffened. It was a barbarous war, as German violations of the Geneva Convention, in the east, were ignored, and millions of prisoners of war, including one of Stalin's sons, were murdered on both sides.

The Germans committed horrible atrocities on the civil population, as Hitler acknowledged the campaign as a genocidal assault on the Slavic lumpenproletariat and peasant masses, and announced publicly that the entire population of Leningrad would be liquidated when the city, Peter the Great's majestic capital on the Baltic, was captured. Apart from the moral depravity of such assertions, they had a predictably reinforcing impact on resistant Soviet morale. The barbarity of the Nazi Gestapo rule in the Ukraine swiftly turned the welcome of the Germans into enervating guerrilla war. Unspeakable brutality occurred constantly, on a general scale, on both sides. The two mighty and evil totalitarian dictators were locked in a death struggle. That did not, however, preclude a separate peace, even if it meant Stalin's retreat across the Urals into Asia, if he could not see any prospect of a second front in the west.

11. THE ATLANTIC CHARTER

Churchill and Roosevelt, who had met only twice before, at the end of the previous world war, occasions from which Roosevelt retained an unpleasant memory of Churchill as a bibulous snob, and which Churchill did not remember at all, had a seaboard meeting on Placentia Bay, Newfoundland, August 9 to 12. Both leaders were accompanied by their senior military service chiefs, and the discussions took place on the USS *Augusta* and HMS *Prince of Wales*. Churchill, as he later said, courted the American president more assiduously than any woman had ever been wooed. Roosevelt had both a Yankee skepticism about British Tory imperialism and a fundamental Anglophilia, bolstered by his admiration for the eloquence and implacability of the British prime minister over the 14 months of his tenure through gravely critical times.

Churchill, though a veteran of 40 years in Parliament and nine different cabinet posts, had not always been popular and had never led a party in a general election. As a politician, Churchill had admired Roosevelt's mastery of the American political scene and the originality of his domestic program. And as first minister in a coalition, who had to spend much of his time keeping the king and Parliament informed and consulting with his cabinet and with the leaders of the main Commonwealth countries, especially Canada, Australia, and South Africa, Churchill envied and admired Roosevelt's status as the thrice-chosen chief of state, head of government, and commander-in-chief of the world's most powerful country, who seemed to have a permanent majority of the people behind him, and never seemed to consult with anyone about anything. They were the two greatest political personalities and statesmen of, certainly, the democratic world of the twentieth century and had many private interests in common, as well as a complete identity of immediate strategic interests. They got on very well, and Roosevelt wrote his cousin that Churchill reminded him in temperament of the ebullient mayor of New York, Fiorello H. La Guardia.[8]

Hopkins was now the head of the Lend-Lease program and had traveled back with Churchill to the conference on his battleship, having visited, and been impressed by, Stalin. It was agreed that Averell Harriman, who was helping coordinate the Lend-Lease program, and Churchill's former minister of aircraft production during the Battle of Britain, the Canadian newspaper publisher Lord Beaverbrook, would conduct a joint mission to Russia and assess Russia's war needs. Churchill outlined his view of the future development of the war, which emphasized maritime blockade, amphibious attacks around the perimeter of the kind Britain had conducted since Chatham's time (rarely with success), aerial bombardment, and aid to resistance groups conducting guerrilla war. He expressed doubt that there would be any need for the deployment of large armies in Western Europe. Roosevelt and Marshall did not believe a word of it and, presumably,

---

8.   August 9, 1941, author's collection.

Churchill didn't either, and was just trying to make participation in the war seem less onerous to the Americans.

Marshall replied for the Americans, very deferentially, as the British "were at this business every day, all day," but said that he believed that if America entered the war, there would be no alternative to invading France and driving on into Germany. This would be the source of considerable strategic differences between the two governments as the war unfolded. The British leadership, including Churchill himself, had all been active on the Western Front in World War I and dreaded a return to the terrible bloodbaths of France and Flanders. The Americans, not having gone all the way through that war, motivated by the advance of mechanized and air warfare creating greater mobility and giving the advantage to the offense, as Germany had often demonstrated in the last two years, and with the stupefying tank and aircraft production capacity of their country in mind, and the natural directness of the American temperament, favored a strike at the heart of Germany by the shortest route, and the assembly and concentration of the force necessary to achieve it. Churchill somewhat enjoyed being a war leader, and was imbued with the British tradition of continuing in wars for a long time, secure from invasion, and now generally in control of their own airspace. British elections could be postponed indefinitely, and there had not been one since 1935. If the Americans entered the war, they would be on a different military and political timetable.

There was considerable discussion about Japan, as Churchill was desperate to get the United States into the war by any aperture, even the Pacific. Roosevelt was still not in any hurry to enter the war, as long as it looked like Russia could hold out. Churchill urged Roosevelt to stop all oil shipments to Japan, but Roosevelt preferred to keep some, a trickle, on a shipload-by-shipload basis, so as not to put the Japanese right to the wall. The two leaders agreed to the Atlantic Charter, which pledged them to seek a postwar world where there would be a renunciation of national aggrandizement, and of territorial changes without the consent of the populations involved. The charter advocated the right of peoples to choose their own form of government; freer trade and emphasis on the general improvement of standards of living throughout the world; freedom from want and fear and of the seas; and the disarmament of aggressive countries. It was a pretty lofty and aerated program, and it raised the question of how Churchill proposed to apply the choice-of-government provision to the constituent parts of Britain's vast colonial empire. But it was an expression of solidarity between a country up to its eyes in war and another officially at peace, and was a sonorous program in contrast to the brute force of the Germans and Japanese (not to mention Mussolini's brutish antics and Stalin's subversions and aggressions, prior to being assaulted by his esteemed Nazi ally).

12. THE UNITED STATES AND JAPAN

While Roosevelt was meeting with Churchill, the House of Representatives, despite the prodigies of the very able Speaker Sam Rayburn, renewed peacetime conscription only by 203 votes to 202. Roosevelt's absence from the capital even for a couple of weeks caused slacknesses in the leadership. When he returned to Washington, Roosevelt discovered that, having made a great deal to Churchill of the need to retain some supply of oil to the Japanese, his under secretary of state for economic affairs, Dean Acheson, a hawk, had taken it upon himself to reject every request for an oil export permit the Japanese had made. There was, as he confidently put it, in the absence of a policy ordered by the president, a practice determined by him, Acheson (who would be one of the country's most competent secretaries of state under Roosevelt's successor). He had been under secretary of the Treasury, but had been fired by Roosevelt in 1934, supposedly for indiscretions, which he had not committed, but really for debating with Roosevelt about the price of gold; he had been brought back to government in 1940 after publicly asserting that the president had the right to sell Britain destroyers on his own authority without reference to the Congress. Roosevelt determined to raise Acheson's "practice" to a thoroughgoing policy. The question of whether Japan would go to war against the United States and Britain would come to a head simultaneously with the determination of whether Stalin could hold the Germans at Moscow and Leningrad.

In the autumn of 1941, tensions rose steadily in the Atlantic and the Pacific at the same time that the battle for Russia's greatest cities intensified. A German submarine attacked a U.S. destroyer on September 4; a week later Roosevelt announced publicly his previously issued "shoot on sight" order against Axis ships in what he had now defined as American waters (extending two-thirds of the way across the Atlantic). In October, after two American destroyers were attacked by German submarines and one was sunk, with the loss of more than a hundred American lives, Roosevelt asked Congress, which agreed, for authority to arm merchant vessels and gave a Navy Day speech on his cousin Theodore's birthday (October 27), in which he said that Americans "had taken their battle stations," that Hitler had fired the first shot, but that what "matters is who fires the last shot." What he did not say was that the American destroyers had been depth-charging the submarines that torpedoed them and had initiated hostilities.

By this time American decrypters had broken the Japanese diplomatic code and Roosevelt and Hull routinely saw messages to the Japanese embassy in Washington when the ambassador did or even before. A special representative arrived on November 20 and demanded that the U.S. withdraw its championship of China, reopen normal commercial and credit relations with Japan, assure Japan access to Dutch East Indies oil, and reduce American naval presence in the western Pacific. Hull made the standard American demands for respect of the sovereignty and equality of all countries, and for the status quo in the Pacific and Japanese withdrawal from China and Indochina. It was obvious and confirmed by diplomatic cables from the embassy to Tokyo that the two sides were not going to agree, and the U.S. ambassador in Japan, Joseph Grew, had warned on November 17 that the United States should be prepared for a sudden Japanese attack anywhere in the Pacific.

Roosevelt met the Japanese ambassador and special envoy on November 17, and outlined what he called a modus vivendi, which would in six-month renewable installments revive the sale of American oil and rice to Japan. The Japanese would send no more forces to Indochina or Manchuria, would leave the Thais, British, and Dutch alone, and would not join in any war between the United States and Germany. The Japanese ambasador took this seriously and asked for an outline in writing, and requested Tokyo to defer any further drift to war. The Japanese government acceded to its envoy's request, but Britain and China both objected when advised of the state of discussions, as both sought American entry into the war at once and by any means. American intelligence showed the movement of Japanese forces away from the Soviet border, and the Soviet government was advised of this. Stalin then withdrew almost all of his 400,000 troops in the Far East for the final battles of the year for Leningrad and Moscow. (The Trans-Siberian Railway was in nearly constant use, moving nearly 20 divisions westward.)

The Soviet government evacuated Moscow to the east but Stalin remained in the Kremlin and made sure this was known to the population. Roosevelt had to consider whether to force the issue with Japan or de-escalate and increase the risk of Stalin making peace with Hitler, whether he saved his main cities or not. Even conceding Ukraine and Belarus would afford Germany a thick *cordon sanitaire* and leave Hitler almost impregnable in Western and Central Europe. Roosevelt did not commit the modus vivendi to writing, and cable intercepts indicated that the countdown to war in Tokyo began again.

On November 27, the United States warned the British government that an attack by Japan in the Pacific was imminent and repeated warnings to all U.S. Army and Navy units in the Pacific that war was probably at hand and ordered maximum vigilance and preparedness. Roosevelt had moved the Pacific battle fleet from California to Pearl Harbor in the Hawaiian Islands in May 1940, and, via the chief of naval operations, Admiral Harold Stark, had sent the commander of the Pacific Fleet, Admiral J.O. Richardson, a description he had received from Churchill of the successful British aerial attack on the Italian battle fleet at anchor in Taranto in November 1940. It described the technique for firing aerial torpedoes successfully in the shallow waters of anchorages. Richardson had criticized Roosevelt for moving the battle fleet to a more exposed harbor, and had ignored Stark's recommendation to put torpedo nets out to protect the battle fleet when in Pearl Harbor. Roosevelt replaced him with Admiral Husband E. Kimmel as commander of the Pacific Fleet in January 1941. It was assumed in Washington that the Hawaiian Islands were in a state of full readiness—that there were torpedo nets around anchored ships and full air patrols throughout daylight hours 250 miles out from Pearl Harbor in all directions.

The U.S. requested an explanation for Japanese military activities, and four days later Roosevelt wrote Emperor Hirohito urging peace. That evening, December 6, he received a decryption of a message from the Japanese government to its envoys in Washington, who had requested a meeting with Hull for the following afternoon. The last paragraph was omitted until the following morning, but when Roosevelt read the cable, he gave it to Hopkins, who was with him in his study, and said: "This means war."[9]

Roosevelt's economic recovery program deserves a 67 percent grade as economics, an 80 percent for showmanship and morale-boosting, and 95 percent for castastrophe-avoidance. His war-preparation strategy was almost flawless genius. He subtly transferred one leg of his political support from western and midwestern liberal isolationists to southern, conservative, military preparedness advocates and quasi-Atlanticists. At the same time, he steadily strengthened hemispheric solidarity by reassuring the Canadians and outbidding Germany for the adherence of the Latin American dictators. He held the support of the one-quarter of Americans who were Roman Catholics in part by declining to support the anti-clerical Republicans in the Spanish Civil War and by other deferences, and the Roman Catholic episcopate delivered all it had for him at the end of the 1940 election campaign. Roosevelt's draft for a third term had been based on the promise of peace through strength and all aid short of war for the democracies, as the surest way to stay out of war, while telling the British and Canadian leaders that he would make war without declaring it. With Lend-Lease, the designation of two-thirds of the North Atlantic as a "Neutrality Zone" where the U.S. Navy

---

9. Black, *op. cit.*, p. 679.

attacked German ships on detection, and the arming of American merchantmen, he was effectively conducting undeclared war.

Roosevelt completed the elimination of the Depression with the greatest arms build-up in world history, assisted Russia to resist Germany when it was attacked by that country, promised to do whatever was needed to keep Britain in the war, pushed the Japanese imperialists to the wall with his oil and scrap metal embargoes, and when it seemed that Russia might buckle without a sign of armed relief from the West, invited a treacherous attack by Japan.

Every element of an intricate plan for worldwide victory over Nazism and Japanese imperialism, and the emergence of the United States as the preeminent power in the world after comparatively affordable investment and sacrifice in war, had been hatched and implemented by Roosevelt without real consultation with anyone, and with consummate skill. He had already established with the British that in the event of war, priority must go to the defeat of Germany by the invasion of Europe in France. All was now in readiness for a brilliantly executed war.

In 190 years of American history, only Benjamin Franklin's manipulation of the British and then the French while Washington conducted a successful guerrilla war and Jefferson won an epochal propaganda victory, and Lincoln's masterly mobilization of northern opinion and arms to preserve the Union, to which he appended the emancipation of the African Americans (and in a sense the whole country) from the bondage of slavery, bore comparison with Roosevelt's strategic triumph from 1937 to 1945.

This triumph was about to be consummated by his conduct of the war. And no other power in the world in the same period had remotely approached the accomplishment of such immense strategic victories as America's in the Seven Years' and Revolutionary Wars, the Civil War, and what was about to occur in the World War II, each vastly enhancing the standing of the country in the world.

Franklin D. Roosevelt
George C. Marshall
Winston Churchill

CHAPTER TEN

The Victory of Democracy in the West, 1941–1945

1. DAY OF INFAMY

The Japanese attacked Pearl Harbor the next morning just after dawn, with 353 aircraft from six aircraft carriers, in two flights. They achieved complete surprise and sank three battleships that settled upright by counter-flooding, capsized one, and grounded one. Three others were only lightly damaged and would be back in service in a couple of months. One would be back in about 15 months, two in about 18 months, and two were total losses. The American aircraft carriers were at sea and were undamaged. About 120 American planes were destroyed and approximately 2,300 Americans were killed. The United States retained nine operational battleships (plus the three that would be back in a couple of months), and had four nearing completion and four more under construction, compared with 12 Japanese, none damaged, but none on the slipways.

On December 10, the Japanese sank a British battleship (the *Prince of Wales*, which had brought Churchill to the Atlantic Conference in August) and a battle cruiser (*Repulse*), and the same week the Italians, in a bold attack by human-operated torpedoes in Alexandria, sank two other British battleships upright, in revenge for the debacle at Taranto 13 months before.

But the British retained 11 capital ships in working order, compared with nine for Germany and Italy combined, and eight aircraft carriers to none for its European enemies. The British had two battleships under construction, and the two damaged at Alexandria would return to service in a few months. The United States and Japan were approximately even in carrier forces. As the Japanese launched an ambitious offensive east and south in the Pacific, the United States would be able to move large numbers of land-based aircraft to the larger nearby islands. The naval balance was strained but not dire, though the submarine war in the Atlantic was very dangerous.

The Japanese emissaries arrived in Hull's office at 2:05 on Sunday, December 7, about 25 minutes after the attack had begun, and Roosevelt had told Hull to give no indication of prior knowledge of the attack, in order to give no clue of the cracking of Japanese codes. Hull excoriated his visitors for the content of their message and dismissed them. Japan attacked Malaya, Hong Kong, the Philippines, Guam, and various other islands in the next few days. It had begun badly, and MacArthur inexplicably allowed a substantial B-17 bomber force to be destroyed on the runway at Clark Air Base in the Philippines. (He blamed it, not altogether plausibly, on his air force commander, General Lewis H. Brereton, whom he described, with some justice, as a "blundering nincompoop," yet did not sack him.)

Roosevelt addressed a joint session of Congress the following day, beginning "Yesterday, December 7, 1941—a date which will live in infamy . . ." Later in his brief address, he completed his strategic formula begun in his State of the Union message from the same place 11 months before, "we will make very certain that this form of treachery shall never endanger us again." The United States would not be an appeasement power, would promote democratic values, and would thereafter maintain an effective deterrent power. It did so, and it was not until 60 years later that America's enemies devised the technique of attacking it with a terrorist mission that could not be directly linked to any country. It has successfully deterred attack by any other nation since the "Day of Infamy."

The dispute with Admiral Richardson over repositioning the Pacific battle fleet from San Francisco to Pearl Harbor created a potential vulnerability for Roosevelt, though Richardson's insouciance about a torpedo attack and Admiral Kimmel's feeble response to repeated warnings were serious derogations from orders. Kimmel and the local army commander were replaced and Admiral Chester W. Nimitz was appointed commander of the Pacific Fleet. The theory has persisted that Roosevelt knew of the attack and did nothing to warn his local commanders. He didn't know exactly where the attack would come and repeatedly warned all American commands throughout the Pacific. He had every reason to believe Pearl Harbor would be on high alert; he loved the navy, and was horrified as he heard the extent of the damage. He would never have been complicit in the death of American servicemen and could have stirred equal outrage against Japan even if the attack had been repulsed with minor damage, as it should have been. (Richardson, Kimmel, and Stark, who also came in for some blame, soldiered on in militant self-defense to the ages of 95, 86, and 91.)

2. EARLY MONTHS OF TOTAL WAR

Hitler, followed, as always, by Mussolini, declared war on the United States on December 11, in a rambling, hate-filled, and somewhat deranged fulmination. He was not obliged to under his alliance with Japan, but presumably concluded that Roosevelt was certain to find some pretext now to go to war against Germany and preferred to take the initiative. Hitler seemed to believe that the United States was a Jewish-directed country, and that Roosevelt was manipulated by Jewish doctors through "negro" orderlies. The whole theory was completely mad and, though it is irrelevant, Roosevelt's doctors were not Jewish. (More problematical was the outright quackery of Hitler's own medical advice.) Hitler knew nothing of America apart from what he learned reading the cowboy novels of Karl May, who had never set foot in the United States, and what May wrote was composed in prison. When war came with the United States, Hitler took this as his cue to liquidate the European Jews, as he had often threatened to do, as if this were somehow a quid pro quo for a war that he had, himself, declared on the U.S., albeit after some provocation from Roosevelt. The Wannsee Conference a month later formulated the plan to exterminate the Jews.

The Red Army beat back the Germans from Moscow and Leningrad and started a general counter-offensive. Roosevelt had entered the war at the head of an absolutely united people. He had come into the war before he had wished, and had lost some old battleships, but he had achieved the greatest consensus ever assembled for a war in the United States; the lost ships were not material to the outcome of the world struggle, and unless Germany could knock the Soviet Union out of the war in 1942, Germany and Japan were certain to be overwhelmed by the combination of the forces of the United States, the USSR, and the British Commonwealth and Empire. The vast military capability that would be required was already well-advanced in preparation, and in General Marshall, General MacArthur, and Admiral Nimitz, Roosevelt had already put in place three of his four key commanders, and on Marshall's urging, he soon identified the last, about-to-be-promoted General Dwight D. Eisenhower. Roosevelt had taken a giant step to an American-led, largely democratic world. The Axis was doomed as long as the British and the Americans incentivized Stalin adequately to stay in the war, and the key now was to occupy Germany, as well as France, Italy, and Japan, before the Soviets could, or, in the case of France and Italy, before the local Communist parties could seize control of them. Despite the losses at Pearl Harbor, Roosevelt, having determined that the victory of democracy depended on the continuation of Russia in the war to take most of the casualties against Germany, made a perfect entry into the conflict.

Winston Churchill came at once to America and received a generous reception when he addressed the Congress on December 26, even from former isolationists. He said, of the Japanese, to thunderous applause: "Do they not realize that we shall never cease to persevere against them until they have been taught a lesson that they and the world will never forget?" The Atlantic Charter, agreed in Newfoundland in August, was called the Declaration of the United Nations and was signed by 26 nations, including the principal allies, in Washington on January 1. The government of Free France was not invited to sign, because Roosevelt was continuing his embassy in Vichy, a regime he despised, but that he imagined might yet furnish him some advantages. His ambassador, his old navy friend Admiral William Leahy, was relatively friendly with Pétain, and he and Roosevelt had conceived the idea that Charles de Gaulle was an anti-democratic mountebank. Subsequent events would prove otherwise.

On Christmas Day, 1941, a Free French squadron of a couple of small warships had occupied the small islands of St. Pierre and Miquelon, off the Newfoundland coast, which Chatham had left with the French to service their fishing fleet at the end of the Seven Years' War (Chapter 1). Churchill and the long-serving Canadian prime minister, W.L. Mackenzie King, who were both in Washington, were completely unruffled by this, but Cordell Hull was inexplicably overwrought and demanded of them and of Roosevelt that they all chastise de Gaulle for unauthorized belligerency in the American hemisphere. Even Roosevelt, who was unreasonably skeptical about de Gaulle's motives and aptitudes (he distrusted political generals, starting with MacArthur), couldn't stir himself to much outrage about that. The main communication cables from the U.S. and Canada to Europe went through St. Pierre and Miquelon, and there was some suspicion that Vichy was monitoring the traffic and passing on messages to Germany. The secretary of state ricocheted around Washington in a righteous lather for the last week of 1941, but was rebuffed by all three leaders. King and Churchill were bemused by Hull's tantrum, and de Gaulle took no notice of it at all. Roosevelt paid little attention to Hull at the best of times.

American industry and manpower were rapidly transformed to complete mobilization. Gigantic annual production schedules were decreed, including 60,000 aircraft in 1942 and a staggering 125,000 in 1943; 45,000 tanks in 1942 and 75,000 in 1943; and six million tons of merchant shipping in 1942 and 10 million in 1943. When this was revealed to the Congress by Roosevelt on January 6, 1942, to perhaps the greatest applause he had ever received in Congress, Hitler expressed total incredulity. (All targets were exceeded.) It was soon clear that the United States would wage war on a scale the world had never imagined to be possible. The armed forces swiftly grew to 12.47 million, including an army of nearly 250 divisions, an air force of 125,000 planes, and a navy of 30 fleet carriers, 70 escort carriers, and 25 capital ships (battleships and battle cruisers).

An extended conference between Churchill and Roosevelt was very cordial and deferred the resolution of the differing views on the timing of an invasion of Western Europe. The British thought the American leaders oversimplified the creation of large and capable fighting forces and the Americans thought the British too cautious and unaware of the power of American mass production, of both the sinews of war and of combat-ready troops. They also considered the British overly traumatized by the bloodbath on the Western Front in World War I. The Americans expected France to be cleared almost as quickly as it was occupied, and in an overwhelming counter-application of air power and mechanized forces.

The Japanese advanced quickly in Malaya and the Dutch East Indies and 70,000 British surrendered to Japanese forces of inferior numbers on February 15. The Japanese had occupied all of the island of Java, including the capital of the

Dutch East Indies, Batavia, by March 9, the day they also occupied the capital of Burma, Rangoon. They moved on from Java into New Guinea. In the Philippines, the Japanese occupied Manila on January 2, but MacArthur conducted a skillful retreat in the Bataan Peninsula, from his headquarters on the rocky island fortress of Corregidor in Manila Bay. MacArthur defeated the Japanese invading force in late January and the invasion stalled for a month while reinforcements were brought in. MacArthur left Corregidor and arrived in Australia on March 17, after following a direct order from Roosevelt to withdraw personally, having ignored his first order to do so. He insisted on going by torpedo boat, rather than a submarine, to demonstrate that the Japanese naval blockade could be broken.

The renewed Japanese offensive cleared Bataan on April 9 and forced the surrender of Corregidor and its garrison of 11,500 by MacArthur's successor, General Jonathan Wainwright, on May 6. The American defense had lasted five months, a respectable performance in the circumstances, especially compared with the British fiasco in Malaya and Singapore and the earlier debacles in Western Europe against the Germans. Roosevelt awarded MacArthur the Congressional Medal of Honor, America's highest combat decoration. Marshall, an old rival of the recipient, sponsored the award, and MacArthur had been tenacious and agile after losing his air force on the runway, but it is hard to reject the suspicion that Roosevelt was partly motivated from concern for MacArthur's ability to cause political problems by blaming Roosevelt for the fall of the Philippines, even though American strategists from Mahan on had considered the islands indefensible from a Japanese attack. (It remains a mystery why the Corregidor forces weren't substantially or entirely evacuated, at least to Mindanao, where they could have joined Filipino guerrillas whom the Japanese never succeeded in eliminating.)

On April 18, in a strike personally commissioned by Roosevelt, General James A. Doolittle flew B-25 bombers off an aircraft carrier, briefly bombed a completely astonished and unprepared Tokyo, and continued on to land in unoccupied China. On arrival in Australia, MacArthur took command of the Southwest Pacific theater and scrapped the Australian plan to defend Australia in the interior of that country. He said Australia must be defended in the Solomon Islands and that the Japanese must not be allowed to set foot in Australia. This proved to be the correct strategy. The Japanese were forced to delay their offensive in New Guinea by the Battle of Coral Sea, May 7–8, conducted entirely by carrier forces, with the ships out of sight of each other. It was a narrow American victory, although the United States lost the large aircraft carrier *Lexington*. The Japanese lost one carrier and two others were damaged, and it lost almost a hundred aircraft, to 69 for the United States. This forced Japan to defer its attack on Port Moresby, New Guinea, from where it was proposed to invade Australia. On June 3–6, 1942, the United States, having now cracked the Japanese naval codes, anticipated the attack on Midway Island, caught the Japanese force changing from bomb-loaded to torpedo-loaded planes below decks when the Japanese had belatedly discovered that there were American carriers in the area, and sank four Japanese aircraft carriers, losing only one of their own. It was one of history's decisive naval battles and forced Japan back in the Central Pacific, and assured the safety of Hawaii. The Australians stopped the Japanese advance on Port Moresby in September, and the Americans launched their main offensive to push them back from Australia with their attack on Guadalcanal in the Solomon Islands in August. This struggle continued to February 1943, and included several naval battles that ultimately led to a decisive American victory on land and sea. (Several of the new American battleships, rushed to completion, performed very capably in these actions and won gunnery duels with Japanese capital ships, and sank two of them.)

The Russians pushed the Germans back to the Ukraine and western Russia from January to the end of April. There were extensive Anglo-American summit and staff conferences in April and May, as the two groups of leaders differed about the timetable of a return to Western Europe. Churchill, visiting Washington, was assuring Roosevelt and Marshall of the tenability of the British position at Tobruk, Libya, in May, when a message was brought in for Roosevelt, which he handed on to Churchill without comment, advising that the British and Australian garrison there had surrendered, to a smaller investing force of Rommel's. Roosevelt's only comment was "What can we do to help?" and he and Marshall dispatched 600 Sherman tanks to Egypt on fast freighters around the Cape of Good Hope. They proved very valuable, but not until Rommel, a very agile commander, pushed the British and Commonwealth forces back to El Alamein, about 100 miles west of Cairo. The British held here, on a fairly narrow front between the Mediterranean and the Qattara Depression, which was practically impassable. In the air war, Britain, which had been fighting for its life in the skies of England two years before, now began 1,000 bomber raids over German cities, starting with Cologne on May 30, 1942, Essen in the Ruhr industrial heartland the next day, and the port of Bremen on June 25. The British staged another of their fruitless coastal raids, at Dieppe on August 19, with 6,000 mainly Canadian troops, almost 60 percent of whom were killed, injured, or taken prisoner.

Marshall proposed an attack of 40,000 in northern France, and Churchill argued that they would be repulsed and crushed by the Germans and he was not prepared to make such a sacrifice just to please Stalin, who was agitating for a western front. Churchill proposed attacks in the Mediterranean, starting with

North Africa, and Roosevelt eventually agreed to this, and imposed the decision on Marshall, who feared, with some reason, that the British were trying to suck the Americans into Africa, Italy, and the Balkans, and avoid a cross-Channel attack into France and on to Germany. That intelligent fear did not excuse him from the terrible idea that anything useful could be accomplished by landing 40,000 men in France, where the German Wehrmacht would have eliminated them in quick time, a rare conceptual blunder by the American chief of staff (also the chairman of the Combined Allied Military Chiefs, putting him ultimately at the head of the combined U.S.–British Commonwealth forces of 25 million men).

Marshall and Hopkins were sent to London, and Roosevelt, who generally deferred to Marshall, ordered him to be more cooperative with the country's principal ally. He recognized that until the United States had the preponderance of Allied forces in the theater, it was going to be difficult to take control of theater policy away from the British. The argument in favor of North Africa was to attack Rommel's rear, take away Pétain's empire there and probably set the Germans on the Vichy regime in unoccupied France, increase pressure on Mussolini, send a cautionary message to Franco and Salazar in Spain and Portugal not to consider any derogation from neutrality, and increase the flow of supplies to Russia through the Dardanelles and the Middle East. Roosevelt hoped to launch the attacks, called Torch, in Morocco and Algeria in late October, before the midterm elections, but declined to accelerate the timetable when Marshall advised that a full rehearsal would be necessary, which would push the landings into November.

The Germans defeated the Russians before Kharkov in May and launched their summer offensive, emphasizing a drive to the Caucasus oil fields in the south, on June 28. They moved steadily east, crossed the Don River, and reached Stalingrad on the Volga on August 22, 1942. Ten days later, having captured Sevastopol, in the Crimea, after an eight-month siege, they attacked amphibiously into the South Caucasus. American and even British supplies were flowing into the Soviet Union in vast quantities, and Churchill embarked on a "raw task" in August, making the hazardous trip to Russia, via Gibraltar and south and then east across the Sahara to Cairo, where he appointed Generals Harold Alexander and Bernard L. Montgomery as commanders in Egypt. As agitation for independence in the vast Indian Empire had flared up again, Churchill also boldly ordered the imprisonment of the Indian leaders Mahatma Gandhi and Jawaharlal Nehru. He was tackling all the raw tasks at once. Churchill then went on to Moscow via Tehran. Churchill's chief of the Imperial General Staff, Field Marshal Sir Alan Brooke, stared out of the aircraft window and detected only one Soviet slit trench barring the way to the German armies approaching the Caucasus.

This was the first meeting between Churchill and Stalin. Churchill bluntly told Stalin there would be no landings in Western Europe in 1942, but attempted to interest Stalin in the North African landings. Stalin picked up the purpose of such landings instantly but excoriated Churchill for, in effect, cowardice, along with Roosevelt, for being afraid to face the Germans in serious combat. He said the Red Army was taking 10,000 casualties a day and asked why the British were "so afraid of the Germans." Churchill improvised a response that Eden (who had been recalled to government by Chamberlain and was now Churchill's lieutenant), Brooke, and the American ambassador to the USSR, Averell Harriman, considered the greatest speech of his entire long and brilliant career as a forensic orator and debater. He reminded Stalin that he (Stalin) and Hitler had started the war, that Britain and its Commonwealth were left completely alone for a year to cope with the Germans, and that he and Roosevelt were rendering every assistance they could to the Russians, having warned Stalin of the impending German attack and been ignored by him, and that he had not come this distance to be insulted, but rather to create a working relationship, as the Allies were sure to win if they did not fall out between themselves.

Churchill's interpreter was unable to translate the torrent of words (and Churchill fired him that evening), but Stalin's interpreter, Vladimir Pavlov, persevered and finally Stalin stood up, raised his arm, and said that he didn't really believe Churchill but deferred to his unconquerable spirit. The visit closed with an amicable drinking bout until 3:30 in the morning, and Churchill took off at dawn for the long return via Tehran. Stalin said he had prepared a nasty surprise for the German drive to the south, but Brooke believed the Germans would overwhelm the Russians, as Marshall believed the Germans would win the battle for Egypt and take the Suez Canal. The civilian leaders, Churchill and Roosevelt, thought differently, on both fronts, and were correct.

3. THE TURNING OF THE TIDE

All of the chief theaters came to a head in November 1942. On November 4, Montgomery launched a preparatory artillery offensive and then a general attack at El Alamein that forced Rommel back out of Egypt by November 12. On November 8, MacArthur's former chief aide, and Marshall's former chief of war planning, General Dwight D. Eisenhower, commanded the Torch landings, at Casablanca, Morocco, and Oran and Algiers, Algeria. The Anglo-American forces were largely embarked directly from the United States, and made a relatively uncontested descent on French North Africa, as the Vichy forces put up token resistance before concluding that the tides of war indicated that too strenuous a resistance would be inappropriate. The slippery, political French admiral, Jean François Darlan, was in North Africa visiting his son, who had been stricken with polio. In order to shut Vichy down, as Pétain, despite Roosevelt's efforts to placate him by invoking what Churchill called "the rather tired pieties of World War I," ordered resistance, Roosevelt had Darlan appointed as nominal governor in North Africa (and had his son treated at his Warm Springs Polio Foundation in Georgia). A French military-political farce ensued: de Gaulle was the only French leader apart from Pétain who had any support, but the Americans were trying to support General Henri Giraud, a limited but patriotic escapee from Nazi imprisonment, while handing titular authority to Darlan, a former Vichy premier. Churchill's chief of the defense staff, Brooke, accurately summarized the three: "Giraud has integrity but is not intelligent; Darlan is intelligent but has no integrity; and de Gaulle has high intelligence and high integrity, but an impossible and dictatorial personality."

The Germans invaded Vichy France, and the French fleet at Toulon scuttled itself rather than join the Allies or be captured by the Germans, or even sail to a neutral port. It was, as de Gaulle wrote, "the most sterile suicide imaginable." The British and American forces entered Tunisia on November 15 to try to cut off Rommel's retreat. They were too late for that and the battle of Africa was reduced to a fierce and prolonged rearguard action by the Germans in Tunisia. The political confusion was rationalized somewhat by the assassination, by a French monarchist, of Darlan on Christmas Eve, 1942. (The monarchists were an eccentric faction in French affairs 112 years after the final overthrow of the Bourbons.) Roosevelt had some friends to the White House on New Year's Eve, and privately screened the about-to-be-released film *Casablanca*, starring two of his most fervent Hollywood supporters, Humphrey Bogart and Claude Raines. He was about to depart for a conference with Churchill, de Gaulle, and Giraud at Casablanca, and expressed the humorous concern that he might encounter as cynical and confused a group of Frenchmen as the epic film depicted.

The naval battle of Guadalcanal, November 12–15, was a decisive American victory, which ensured that the Japanese would not be able to contest the island much longer, and had been definitively prevented from invading Australia. Henceforth, MacArthur would advance northwestward toward the Philippines, and Nimitz, the Central Pacific commander, would advance due west through the Marshall Islands and to Saipan, Guam, and toward the home islands of Japan. Roosevelt's immense naval construction programs and the Midway and Solomon Islands naval victories would now confer constantly lengthening naval superiority on the United States in the Pacific.

What became the greatest land battle in the history of the world, surpassing even Verdun, raged all through the late summer and autumn at Stalingrad. At the height of the battle in November, there were about 2,000,000 men engaged, perhaps 60 percent Russians, and including 200,000 Romanians and 100,000 Italians supporting the Germans. There were about 25,000 artillery pieces and 2,000 airplanes, evenly divided, and 1,500 tanks, 900 of them Russian. Ultimately, there were 1.1 million Russian and 840,000 Axis casualties, including approximately a million dead. It came to savage hand-to-hand fighting in the rubble of the city, and in the piercing cold of the Russian winter. The Russians attacked the German flanks, largely protected by the Romanians, on November 19, in overwhelming force. The Romanians put up a fairly spirited fight, but the Russians closed behind the German Sixth Army and surrounded it. Hitler would not hear of a break-out retreat.

The United States had gone to accelerated development of an atomic bomb in August 1942, having agreed on a full sharing of information with Britain (which did not, in fact occur, as Roosevelt determined that since the United States was spending most of the money, it would retain the science). The Manhattan Project created a separation plant at Oak Ridge, Tennessee, relying on the hydroelectric power of the TVA (Chapter 10), a bomb development laboratory at Los Alamos, New Mexico, and a plutonium production facility at Hanford, Washington. As progress was made, the possibilities of a military use of such a bomb loomed steadily larger in the minds of Roosevelt, Stimson, and Marshall.

In the 1942 congressional elections, the Democrats lost 46 congressmen and nine senators but retained their majorities in both houses, and legislation was much less disputatious in wartime. Roosevelt's acquiescence in Marshall's Torch timetable probably cost him 20 congressmen.

As 1942 ended, the Germans were trapped at Stalingrad and in inexorable retreat in North Africa, and the Japanese were being forced off Guadalcanal and pushed westward across the Pacific. The mighty American war engine was producing all categories of military equipment, munitions, and necessities in astonishing quantities, and the three main Allies (counting the British Commonwealth and Empire as one) had nearly 40 million men under arms.

The almost unspoken British-American strategy of leaving most of the heavy lifting against the Germans to the Russians, while contributing importantly in other theaters and as suppliers, is illustrated by the comparative scale of these decisive battles. Where Stalingrad engaged millions and produced nearly two million casualties, and a million dead, most of them Russians, El Alamein involved 310,000 troops, almost two-thirds of them British, and caused 45,000 casualties, two-thirds of them German and Italian. And Guadalcanal engaged fewer than 100,000 men, over 60 percent of them American, though the ferocity of the fighting is indicated by the fact that the Japanese suffered 31,000 dead and only 1,000 captured, and the United States 7,100 dead and only four captured. Defeating the Axis in Africa and at the gates of Australia were extremely important events, but they involved barely 2 percent of the Allied casualties that the Russians sustained at Stalingrad alone, and accounted for just 1 percent of the number of Axis casualties the Russians inflicted at Stalingrad. From this point on, the Germans and the Japanese and, while they lasted in the Axis, the Italians, were in almost unbroken retreat.

4. DIVERGENT WAR AIMS

With the momentum residing now with the Allies, 1943 would be a year of almost constant conferences, as the noose tightened around the necks of the Germans and the Japanese, and the Big Three—Roosevelt, Churchill, and Stalin—maneuvered toward the postwar world each sought. It would shortly be confirmed that the British were reluctant to shift the focus of operations from the Mediterranean to northern France, as the Americans insisted was the only way to defeat Germany. Beyond the question of military strategy to achieve victory, the three leaders all sought different outcomes. Churchill, who had been active in European politics and diplomacy for nearly 40 years, from when he became an under secretary for colonies in Sir Henry Campbell-Bannerman's government in 1905, wished to restore a balance of power in Europe, whose scales could, as throughout the last 400 years, be tipped by Britain. This would require the reconstruction of France, and de Gaulle, uncommonly difficult though he was (and violent though his disagreements with Churchill often were), was essential. And it would require a politically cleansed and reconstituted Germany and Italy, and a durable arrangement with the United States, preferably with the retention of some U.S. forces in Western Europe, a closer relationship than had been envisioned at the end of the previous war and that had been rejected in the byzantine complexities of the American congressional ratification process.

Stalin saw the door open to Western Europe, and oscillated between morbidly suspecting that Churchill and Roosevelt were just trying to promote attrition between him and Hitler, to leave a mountain of German and Russian war dead in Eastern Europe and the protagonists exhausted, and, if the Anglo-American Allies would, as they promised, seriously attack Germany in the West, seeing the opportunity for an unprecedented Russian thrust into Central and even Western Europe. Roosevelt did believe that Russia would be relatively exhausted after the war, and that the British Empire and other colonial empires would disintegrate, especially because of the defection of relatively sophisticated units like India, and he was determined to keep the United States permanently involved in Europe and the Far East in order to prevent overseas aggressors from gaining control of those theaters and threatening the national security of the United States.

Roosevelt saw that if the United States were not engaged in the world, the strength of the democracies would be critically divided, and there would be the danger, as there had been in both World Wars, that without American assistance the other democracies could be overrun and the United States would, as Roosevelt had said in his "Great Arsenal of Democracy" address on December 29, 1940 (Chapter 10), be "living at the point of a gun." He also expected the United States to emerge from the war as overwhelmingly the most powerful country in the world. To disguise its preeminence and cloak it in collective action, as well as to convince his previously isolationist countrymen that the world was not as dangerous a place as it had been, and to fulfill the Wilsonian requirement of a measure of idealism in a coldly realistic design, he sought a more effectual successor to the League of Nations: an international forum where the victorious powers would have the status of world policemen, armed with the right and the strength to intervene against aggressor states before they gained any traction.

In this spirit, he sought trusteeships for colonial territories, which would emancipate them to independence when they were ready, and foresaw that China, despite its present primitive and war-torn condition, would become one of the world's Great Powers, and should be recognized in advance in that role (although it was in the midst of a civil war between the Nationalist forces of Chiang Kai-shek and the Communists of Mao Tse-tung and Chou En-lai, which was pursued by both parties with more determination than the war against the Japanese invader).

Also complicated was the status of France. Churchill considered the revival of France essential to keeping Russia out of Western Europe, and de Gaulle the only French leader who could achieve that. Roosevelt was something of a Francophile, and spoke the language tolerably well, but he had been so shocked by the parliamentary bedlam and irresolution of the latter Third Republic, and by the astonishing collapse of the French state and army in 1940, that he was disinclined to believe that any French revival was in the cards, or that the obdurate de Gaulle, who had emerged from complete obscurity, as he put it himself, to "assume France,"[1] had any credentials to lead such a renascence. De Gaulle desperately wanted to be treated as the representative of the French national interest traditionally was—as the leader of a great and durable nation—and he sought to entice Churchill to a

---

1.   Charles de Gaulle, *War Memoirs*, New York, Simon and Schuster, 1955, p. 88.

more European and less Americocentric perspective, but he could not compete with Roosevelt for Churchill's attention. And he sought to be treated by Roosevelt as America treated Britain, but he was more keenly aware than anyone that France's recent history and current circumstances did not justify such treatment, so his only method of achieving attention and adding a cubit to France's status was to impress his allies with his powers of obstructionism and intractability. All agreed that in this activity, de Gaulle possessed preternatural genius (which he would continue to display for many years).

For the first four months of 1943, the German Afrika Korps was bottled up in Tunisia, reinforced by Hitler with constant airlifts of troops, as he believed he was deferring an invasion of Italy. Eisenhower and the Allied high command were happy enough to have him pouring first-class German troops into a theater where he couldn't win (and where if he had done the same a year earlier he would have taken the Suez Canal and the oil of the Middle East). The Allies might have been able to shut down the airlift, but didn't seriously try to do this. For Hitler to sacrifice forces in a lost cause in Africa while prohibiting a break-out effort by his surrounded army at Stalingrad was insane. He should have pulled out of both places and used the African forces to reinforce the Russian front.

The Soviets drove the Germans westward through the winter and the early spring in Russia, while the Americans, under MacArthur in the Southwest and Nimitz in the Central Pacific, pushed the Japanese steadily west. The joint chiefs had devised and both Pacific theater commanders very skillfully executed an island-hopping strategy, by which many Japanese garrisons were bypassed and stranded, as the United States' naval advantage grew steadily longer. A Japanese garrison of nearly 250,000 was stranded in Rabaul as MacArthur swept past it toward the Philippines. (Roosevelt, in the most important direct leader's intervention in naval construction of the war, ordered a class of 10 heavy cruisers to be altered in the shipyards and completed as the *Independence* class of aircraft carriers. They entered service in 1943 and accelerated the attainment of U.S. naval superiority.)

Eisenhower, as the Allied commander in North Africa, quickly achieved prodigies of seamless integration of a binational command structure, proving himself an outstanding soldier-diplomat, and made some sense out of the steaming political bouillabaisse of French North African politics. He and other senior Allied officials gave Darlan a mighty funeral in the Algiers cathedral and saluted Darlan's coffin as it preceded the cardinal-primate of Africa down the cathedral steps, but he recognized at once that de Gaulle was the only serious French political leader, and opened a good relationship with him that would take both men through 25 years, to the highest distinctions and offices within the gift of their countrymen.

5. THE CASABLANCA AND TRIDENT CONFERENCES

The first of the major conferences of 1943 was the meeting at Casablanca from January 14 to 24. General George S. Patton had commanded the landings there and was responsible for the security of the Anglo-American military and civilian leadership, meeting within range of German air strikes from Tunisia. There was a stark difference between American ambitions to invade northern France as soon as possible across the English Channel and British desires to probe what Churchill had been describing since his visit to Stalin in August 1942 as "the soft underbelly of Europe" in Italy and the Balkans (although a glance at a topographical map showed that it was nothing of the kind, especially if the mountain ranges were being defended by experienced German troops as they soon would be). The debate was sharpish at times, especially between Marshall, a taciturn but very intelligent and direct and efficient man, preeminently an organizer, and Brooke, a fast-talking and somewhat peremptory Ulsterman who indulged himself in the usual British conception that the Americans were novices at serious war, and had wildly naïve notions of their ability quickly to transform millions of farm boys and office and factory workers into capable fighting forces.

Eisenhower's achievement, from now to the end of the war, in getting senior British and American officers to work together quite smoothly, was a remarkable one. He was almost the only senior American officer who had any affection for the British, as Patton and the commander of the United States Fleet, Admiral Ernest J. King, detested the British, and even Marshall regarded most British generals as weak and afraid to fight. And none of the senior British apart from some of their liaison officers and perhaps Alexander, some of the RAF commanders, and Admiral Andrew Cunningham, Britain's greatest sea leader and Mediterranean commander, could abide the American senior officers. Montgomery and Brooke professed to regard Marshall and Eisenhower as completely incompetent, apart from clerical tasks. Fortunately, the officers on each side were somewhat in awe of the government leader on the other side, and Churchill and Roosevelt let their service chiefs fight it out between themselves, holding over them the Damoclean sword that if they were unable to reach agreement, the whole matter would be settled by the political leaders, a prospect that was so frightening it galvanized the generals and admirals of both countries into cooperative action.

The fact was that the Americans were correct. Roosevelt was concerned that if there were not serious progress in Western Europe, Hitler and Stalin could still make a separate peace, and that he would be sent packing in the 1944 election. He understood the British abhorrence of a bloodbath in northern France and in

Flanders, because of the horrors of the trenches of World War I, but he believed that mechanized and air war made trench warfare completely impractical and that American war production and manpower would provide the Allies overwhelming superiority. In all of this he was correct, and the Germans and Russians did have preliminary settlement talks in Stockholm in the summer of 1943, as Stalin was at pains to tell his allies when they finally met at the end of 1943.

It was agreed at Casablanca, after much acrimony between Brooke and Marshall, that with Eisenhower in command, the Allies would invade Sicily and the boot of Italy as soon as Tunisia was cleared, but supposedly without prejudice to an early cross-Channel invasion. This was, in fact, a victory for the British war plan, because it would be impossible now to launch an invasion of northwest Europe in 1943. Roosevelt and Marshall reasoned that it would have to be deferred to the spring of 1944, by which time the United States would have the preponderance of ground and air forces in the theater. Roosevelt determined that he and Churchill would have to meet with Stalin and convince him that they were serious about invading France, that the invasion of Italy would have to do in the meantime, and as an added earnest he declared to the press on behalf of both leaders that they would require the unconditional surrender of Germany and Japan. There has been much criticism of this decision, but the treatment soon accorded to Italy made it clear that something less onerous could be obtained if the incumbent government were disposed of, and it did offer slight reassurance to Stalin and remove some of the sour taste of the rather sleazy arrangements with Darlan.

De Gaulle and Giraud joined the conference, de Gaulle only after, on Roosevelt's suggestion, Churchill threatened to cut off all assistance to him. They agreed to a joint government of liberated North Africa, and it did not take de Gaulle, as both Churchill and Roosevelt, once he got a look at both men, agreed would happen, to outmaneuver the politically unskilled Giraud and reinforce his position as the leader of the combatant French, which now included a substantial Resistance in metropolitan France, and most of the French Empire except for Indochina. There was a joint meeting of Churchill and Roosevelt and de Gaulle and Giraud, who dutifully shook hands for the cameras. Churchill wrote: "The pictures of this event cannot be viewed, even in the setting of these tragic times, without a laugh."

Churchill sent Foreign Secretary Anthony Eden to meet with Roosevelt on March 13 and 15, 1943, and they had an extensive discussion. Roosevelt was very aware of the possibility that Stalin intended to seize large chunks of Europe. He had no difficulty awarding Russia part of Poland and compensating Poland with part of Germany, or with Russia taking back part of Finland and the small Baltic states (Latvia, Lithuania, Estonia) that it had held for 200 years prior to 1917, though he hoped for a referendum there, "even a rigged one."[2] He didn't see any point in trying to deny Stalin possession of what Russia had formerly held when he was certain to occupy it militarily anyway. Roosevelt was skeptical of any early French recovery, and made a number of "feckless" suggestions for creating new states in the Rhineland and elsewhere. He correctly doubted that the components of Yugoslavia would long cohere. Eden noted that "Roosevelt was familiar with the history and geography of Europe" and "He seemed to see himself disposing of the fate of many lands, allied no less than enemy. He did all this with so much grace that it was not easy to dissent. Yet it was too like a conjuror, skillfully juggling with balls of dynamite." Eden insightfully thought him like a stamp-collector (which he was), musing about separating and attaching states, but was impressed by his knowledge and reassured that he had no illusions about Stalin. (Roosevelt had assured British economist and emissary Lord Keynes that he was far from being "an automatic supporter of the Soviet Union" and had acknowledged to Archbishop Spellman that Eastern Europe was likely to be dominated, at least for a time, by the Soviet Union.)[3]

The German Sixth Army of 300,000, terribly afflicted by combat, hunger, and the elements, surrendered on February 2, 1943. The Russian advance to the west continued into the spring, and the British and the Americans finally secured the surrender of 250,000 Axis troops in Tunisia and the end of the war in Africa, on May 13. This was another heavy blow to the Axis, shortly following the debacle at Stalingrad. In the two actions, the Germans and their allies lost 750,000 men, and they could not replace such losses as the Russians and even, had the need arisen, the Americans could. MacArthur cleared New Guinea between January and September 1943, and Japan's senior admiral and architect of the Pearl Harbor attack, Isoroku Yamamoto, commander of the Combined Fleet, was killed when his plane was shot down on a tour of the Dutch East Indies, on April 18. He had attended Harvard University and been the naval attaché in Washington, and had warned against attacking the United States because of its industrial might. Nimitz, receiving code intercepts, asked Roosevelt's authority to shoot Yamamoto's plane down, which Roosevelt was happy to give. The Japanese had occupied a couple of the westernmost Aleutian Islands, midway between Japan and Alaska, but they were cleared out by American and Canadian troops between March and August.

The most extensive Anglo-American conference of the entire war took place at Washington, with weekend side trips to restored historic Williamsburg and the

---

2.   Conrad Black, *Franklin Delano Roosevelt: Champion of Freedom*, New York, PublicAffairs, 2003, p. 826.
3.   Ibid. p. 855.

Catoctin Mountains, from May 12 to 25, 1943. There was another ding-dong battle over the comparative merits of the Channel and Mediterranean operations. Churchill was for the Channel crossing "as soon as there are reasonable prospects of success," but agreed with Brooke that that could not happen until 1945 or 1946, because, as Brooke said, there were not 80 French divisions to join in against Germany. This was nonsense, as the United States would provide the difference, but Brooke didn't have confidence in instantly created American forces. The Americans thought air superiority would reduce the numbers of soldiers needed on the ground. The Americans made it clear that Italy could become "a vacuum" that would suck in Allied forces all through 1944, and that this was "not acceptable to the United States." The standard American gambit was that they were not prepared to stuff their forces into Britain while the British pursued imperial objectives in the Mediterranean, and that if the cross-Channel operation were not launched on a timely basis, they would decamp to the Pacific (where there would be no argument with anyone about how their forces were deployed).

Marshall and Brooke and their comrades made a sustained effort to be sociable and informal in leisure moments and the effect was very positive. All were reassured to see a human side of senior officers whom they had formerly found rather flinty and unremitting. Roosevelt and Churchill separated themselves from the service chiefs during the breaks and, as always, their relations, on which all else chiefly depended, were entirely cordial, despite strategic and philosophical differences. After a very convivial weekend at Williamsburg, it was ostensibly agreed that the Western Allies would invade northern France on May 1, 1944, and that an invasion of Italy would assist, rather than replace or defer, the French operations. This did not prevent a good deal of British waffling and evasive maneuvering through the balance of the year and even into 1944. Seven divisions would be ready for transfer from Italy to the French operation from November 1 on, at Marshall's call. Marshall had raised his planned deployment to almost 600,000 men from the Sledgehammer sacrificial offering of the previous year, of 40,000, a sizeable improvement but still not adequate to clear the Germans out of France. It was already clear that the war would be won by whichever of the Soviet Union or the West bagged Germany, France, and Italy, and the Americans were concerned that there not be what Roosevelt called "a lengthy pecking away at the fringes of Europe"[4] that would enable Russia to come farther into Europe than was desirable or preventable.

---

4.   Black, *op. cit.*, p. 831.

There was a very discursive discussion about China. Everyone agreed with the American commander in China, the acidulous General Joseph Stilwell, that Chiang Kai-shek was "a vacillating, tricky, undependable old scoundrel who never keeps his word." Churchill didn't want to do anything "silly" just to please Chiang, but Roosevelt was convinced, again quite presciently, that China would soon enter one of its cyclical upturns and be one of the world's Great Powers again. Brooke dismissed Stilwell as "a hopeless crank," living off Marshall's patronage. Marshall defended Stilwell as "a fighter," which even Brooke admitted, but Marshall went on to contrast him with British "commanders who had no fighting instinct and were soft and useless."[5] The Chinese ambassador to the U.S., and Chiang's in-law, T.V. Soong, told the conference that China would make a separate peace with Japan if it did not receive adequate assistance. Roosevelt and Churchill did not take that threat seriously, but agreed to increased assistance to that country anyway.

6. KURSK, THE FALL OF MUSSOLINI, AND THE FIRST QUEBEC CONFERENCE

In another of history's greatest battles, and the greatest tank battle and one of the greatest one-day air battles in history, the Germans failed in their effort to launch a third consecutive summer offensive at the Battle of Kursk from July 4 to August 23, 1943. Soviet intelligence had warning of the German effort to close off the salient and built defenses in depth back 250 kilometers, 10 times the width of the Maginot Line, at the anticipated points of attack, in nine different fortified and entrenched lines of defense. Unlike his usual practice, Hitler followed the obvious course, as the salient was conspicuous on the front, and delayed for six weeks bringing in new tanks. Germany had nearly 800,000 men, 3,000 tanks, 10,000 artillery pieces and mortars, and 2,000 aircraft engaged, against 1.9 million Russians with 5,000 tanks (initially), 25,000 artillery pieces and mortars, and almost 3,000 aircraft at any time, as losses were replaced. In the course of the battle, though it was a heavy defeat, the Germans demonstrated their remarkable war-making ability by inflicting 1,041,000 Russian casualties while taking 257,000 themselves, and knocking out 8,000 tanks and 3,600 aircraft, while losing 1,040 tanks and 840 aircraft themselves. Unlimited Russian manpower and supplies from the United States, as well as their own large aircraft and tank production, told. It was the last German offensive in the east, and demonstrated again the immense scale of the war in Russia, compared with those in the Mediterranean and the Pacific.

---

5.   Black, *op. cit.*, p. 833.

The British, Americans, and Canadians invaded Sicily on July 10, 1943, in the greatest amphibious operation in history up to that time. Field Marshal Alexander was the operational commander, under Eisenhower's ultimate command, and Montgomery and Patton were the battlefield army commanders. The Allies landed 160,000 men and 600 tanks to meet 40,000 Germans and 230,000 Italians with 260 tanks. The fall of Messina on August 17 to Patton signaled the end of resistance on the island; the Allies had taken 22,000 casualties to 10,000 Germans and 132,000 Italians, approximately 80 percent of them prisoners captured uninjured as Italy's commitment to Mussolini's ill-considered plunge into war crumbled.

In the midst of the action, on July 25, Italy's King Victor Emmanuel III dismissed Benito Mussolini as premier after 21 years of his dictatorship and, having smarted under his condescensions throughout that time, had him arrested, and named Marshal Pietro Badoglio, a slippery political roué as unreliable as but more likeable than Darlan, as prime minister. (Badoglio had been one of those responsible for the catastrophic Italian defeat at Caporetto in 1917, which he went to great lengths to hide in subsequent official records, and was ambassador to Brazil and Duke of Addis Ababa for his contribution to the Abyssinian campaign in 1936. He was a thorough-going scoundrel, precisely what the times required.) Badoglio ordered the dissolution of the Fascist party on July 28 (having long been one of its grandees).

The first Quebec Conference, between Churchill and Roosevelt and their service chiefs, attended in slight part also by Canada's Prime Minister King, took place between August 11 and 24, 1943. It was largely concerned with campaigns in Burma and China, confirmed the decisive turn in the Allies' favor of the Battle of the Atlantic against German submarines, and again envisioned landings in France the following spring and summer on both the Channel and Mediterranean coasts. But there was again great American unease, as Churchill kept grasping for alternatives, including an invasion of Norway that his own staff regarded as mad. Both sides recited their now familiar scripts, but matters started to turn just before the arrival of the leaders, when Brooke led what amounted to a consciousness-raising session. He acknowledged that the Americans thought the British were not really committed to the cross-Channel operation (Overlord it was and henceforth here will be called), and that the British thought the Americans were so preoccupied with it that they would charge into Europe regardless of the strategic facts. The Trident formula was amplified and it was agreed that Overlord would proceed on schedule, that the invasion of Italy would follow the clearance of Sicily, and that a standard of professional evaluation of the need and efficacy of reinforcements as between the respective operations would thereafter be applied. Marshall emphasized that Roosevelt "understood the importance of capturing Berlin."

The eccentric British guerrilla leader in Burma, General Orde Wingate, was introduced by Churchill and quickly became the Americans' favorite British general by his swashbuckling style and combative instincts. The presentational highlight was royal relative and Churchill protégé Admiral Louis Mountbatten, who had just been appointed commander in Burma, showing the possibilities of specially treated blocks of ice to serve as stationary aircraft carriers. He demonstrated this by firing a revolver at the blocks. The untreated block of ice was reduced to bits and pieces, but the treated block was resistant, causing a bullet to ricochet around the room, narrowly missing several of the senior officers present. Aides outside the meeting room were briefly concerned that Anglo-American relations had deteriorated to the point that their military chiefs were exchanging fire with their own side arms. (Churchill and Roosevelt were not present.)

The Allies invaded the mainland of Italy with the British thrust across the Strait of Messina on September 3, followed on September 9 by American landings under General Mark Clark at Salerno, 30 miles south of Naples. What ensued was almost as farcical as the pell-mell events in North Africa among the French political factions after the Allied landings at the end of 1942. The Italians, under the king and Badoglio, had surrendered to the Allies on September 8. The Italian navy, including 4 battleships, 5 cruisers, 12 destroyers, and 33 submarines, surrendered to the British, mainly at Malta, between September 8 and 10, despite German air attacks that sank the battleship *Roma*, on which the fleet commander, Admiral Carlo Bergamini, and 1,350 sailors, perished. Churchill, always as magnanimous in victory as he was implacable in combat, and a lover of Italy, directed that the Italian ships be received with the utmost respect and courtesy, and that the whole process be filmed for projection in Italy to contrast British with German treatment of Italians. The Germans seized Rome on September 10, and Victor Emmanuel and Badoglio fled to Brindisi. German paratroopers sprang Mussolini on September 12, and on September 15 he proclaimed a Fascist republic in the areas of the hasty German occupation of Italy. On October 13, the king and Badoglio declared war on Germany, making Italy a co-belligerent, the only one of the scores of countries engaged in World War II that had been on both sides of the war.

The first senior three-power meeting took place at the foreign ministers' conference in Moscow from October 19 to 30. This was the only time that Roosevelt allowed Hull to deal with senior British and Soviet officials. Eden and the Soviet foreign commissar, Vyecheslav M. Molotov, were present, and Stalin met with the foreign ministers several times. The invasion of Italy, capture of Naples, toppling of

Mussolini, and surrender of Italy and its switching to the Allied side all somewhat placated Stalin, who, after the victories of Stalingrad and Kursk and the continuing Red Army drive westward, was, in any case, less concerned about the activities of the Western Allies. He had constantly to decide whether he sought the weakening of Germany from Western attacks in France and Italy, or their continued abstention from a major offensive in the west to facilitate a greater Russian seizure of Central and even Western European territory, depending on the progress of the Russo-German War. The conference reaffirmed Anglo-American determination to invade France in 1944, failed to make much progress on the issue of who was to govern Poland after its anticipated liberation by the Red Army, set up a tripartite European Advisory Commission in London to determine the future of Germany, and envisioned an international organization of "peace-loving nations . . . for the maintenance of international peace and security."

The continuous British concurrences in plans to invade France in May 1944 were misleading, and the Americans, including Secretary of War Stimson, who visited London in August 1943, told Roosevelt that the "shadows of Passchendaele and Dunkerque hang too heavily over" the British, who were giving the cross-Channel landing only "lip service." He said they still felt that Germany could be "beaten by attritions," but that sort of "pin-prick warfare" would not "fool Stalin."[6] It is hard to exaggerate the extent to which the British leaders were scarred by their experience of the Western Front in World War I and also their fear of the German army. As the casualty figures from Stalingrad and Kursk demonstrated, the Germans did have an astonishing aptitude for war, and it is little wonder that Churchill and Roosevelt were grateful to be able to leave most of the ground war against Germany to the inexhaustible reserves of manpower of the Soviet Union, where the most brutal conscription and military discipline were imposed, and Stalin's totalitarian regime was not overly concerned with casualties, as long as the Soviet Union could translate battle deaths into expanded territory.

The British still thought the Americans blasé about the implications of conducting war with Germany, though by now they acknowledged the overwhelming strength of the Americans in armor and in the air, as well as a numerical manpower advantage on the ground. Roosevelt thought that once the Western Allies were established in France and rolling east, the Germans would fight to the last cartridge in the east but surrender relatively easily in the west, to benefit from the comparative civility of the Western Allies, who observed the Geneva Convention,

---

6.   Henry L. Stimson and McGeorge Bundy, *On Active Service in Peace and War*, New York, Harper, 1947, pp. 431–438.

as Germany did with them, in contrast to the unspeakable reciprocal savagery on the Eastern Front, where nearly five million prisoners of war were murdered, the majority by the Germans. The American encounters with the Japanese were somewhat similar to the Eastern Front, as the Japanese did not observe the niceties with prisoners, and preferred to die than to be captured. As at Guadalcanal, at Tarawa on November 20 to 23, 1943, Nimitz's 35,000 marines took about 10 percent casualties, while the Japanese suffered almost 100 percent casualties, with nearly 4,000 dead and only 17 men taken prisoner. This pattern would become steadily more pronounced and the numbers of defenders larger as the Americans closed in on the home islands of Japan.

7. THE CAIRO AND TEHRAN CONFERENCES

This year of conferences reached its climax at the Cairo and Tehran conferences, between November 22 and December 1, 1943. Both Western leaders approached the conferences on large warships, Roosevelt on the new and very powerful battleship *Iowa*, and Churchill on the sleek and venerable battle cruiser *Renown*. Churchill was fluish and Brooke recorded that he was in foul humor, threatening dire consequences if the Americans did not support his Mediterranean ambitions. (At one point, Churchill, in night attire, shouted out the window of the governor's residence in Malta to startled passersby to be quiet and to stop disturbing his rest.)[7] Roosevelt opposed any efforts by the recently established European Advisory Commission to demarcate occupation zones in Germany because of his theory, which he explained to his staff in a shipboard meeting en route, that, once across the Rhine, the Allies might be able to conduct "a railroad invasion of Germany with little or no fighting,"[8] as the Germans gave way while fighting fanatically in the east. He tore out a map from a copy of *National Geographic* magazine in the admiral's wardroom and marked out with a pen the zones of occupation that would be acceptable if there had to be any. He had the Western and Russian zones meeting at Berlin.

Roosevelt disembarked at Oran and flew to Cairo via Tunis, where he conferred with Eisenhower, and Churchill docked at Alexandria. The Cairo Conference began November 22 with an absurd meeting with the Chinese, led by Chiang and his scheming, feline wife. The Burmese theater commander, Mountbatten, gave a confident presentation (without use of side arms, unlike at Quebec), and when Brooke invited the Chinese to comment, there was what he called "a ghastly

---

7.   Keith Eubank, *Summit at Tehran*, New York, Morrow, 1985, p. 144.
8.   Black, *op. cit.*, p. 854.

silence." The Chinese had had advance copies of Mountbatten's presentation, but had no idea how to respond to it. Brooke suggested they withdraw and consider if they had any questions and comments. It was a complete shambles, but Roosevelt, though he recognized Chiang's limitations, wanted to make the conference a success for him, to strengthen his hand opposite the Japanese and the Communists. A communiqué was eventually issued promising increased assistance to Chiang.

The Americans wanted to give Chiang the plum of taking the Andaman Islands, but the British dismissed this as nonsense, and Churchill championed his latest hobby horse, the taking of the Mediterranean island of Rhodes, which, he claimed, would help bring Turkey into the war. At one point, Churchill grasped Marshall by the lapels and exclaimed, "Muskets must flame." Marshall replied, at a distance of six inches, that "Not one American is going to die on that Goddamned beach," Rhodes. There were pleasant dinners on American Thanksgiving Day and Churchill was impressed that the United States provided a turkey dinner for all 12 million of its servicemen, wherever they were in the world. Roosevelt sang the Marine Corps anthem, accompanied by a military band. Brooke, a churchgoer, dutifully attended an American Thanksgiving service at the Cairo Anglican cathedral, which he described as "a sad fiasco" (unlike the service he had attended at Williamsburg, where he found the liturgy and homily acceptable and the women well turned-out). But these outings did improve and stabilize the ambiance.[9] After fierce arguments, neither Rhodes nor the Andaman operation was pursued.

The British and Americans left the Chinese behind and flew to Tehran to meet Stalin. After one night at his legation outside the city, and a Soviet claim that they had uncovered a plot to kill all three leaders, Roosevelt accepted Stalin's rather than Churchill's invitation to stay in his embassy, as his own security detail had recommended he move into the city center. Ostensibly he chose the Soviet embassy because it was roomier, but in fact because Roosevelt was relying on Stalin to resolve the Overlord/Italy debate once and for all. He feared that Stalin might, after his Stalingrad and Kursk victories, support Churchill's plans for activities in the Balkans, in order to have a clearer path through Germany and into France. He arrived at the Soviet embassy on November 28, and Stalin immediately requested to visit him in his rooms. Roosevelt correctly assumed that his suite was bugged, that all conversation would be recorded, and that the personnel assigned to serve him (who were obviously carrying firearms) were secret police. In fact, Stalin had entrusted the task of recording conversations to the son of his much-feared police minister, Lavrenti Beria. Even Stalin described the bugging to young Sergio Beria as

---

9.   Black, *op. cit.*, pp. 832, 859.

"delicate and morally reprehensible."[10] Roosevelt spoke with his suspected auditor's sensibilities in mind. The Grand Alliance was off to an uneasy start. Sergio Beria later wrote that Stalin assumed that Roosevelt thought he was being overheard. Stalin questioned Beria very closely about Roosevelt's tone of voice and exact words. Beria claimed that he recorded Churchill beseeching Roosevelt not to commit to a date for Overlord, and Roosevelt telling Leahy that he was not going to "pull the chestnuts out of the fire for the British Empire." Roosevelt liked and admired Churchill but thought him a romantic, and not a man in close touch politically with his countrymen, trying to maintain an empire that could not long survive. With Stalin, an extremely cunning and ruthless cynic, it was, from the start and to say the least, scarcely a relationship of mutual trust.

At this first meeting, Roosevelt and Stalin were accompanied only by their interpreters, the redoubtable Pavlov and the deputy chief of the Russian desk and future eminent American diplomat Charles E. Bohlen. The contrast between the leonine patrician Roosevelt in an elegant blue suit in his wheelchair, and the five-foot, five-inch Stalin, with bushy hair, sallow, pockmarked complexion, a partially deformed left arm, unruly mustache, and stained and broken teeth, could hardly have been greater. After a discursive review of de Gaulle, whom Stalin sagely described as "an authentic representative of the soul of France," though "unrealistic" (Stalin had never met him at this point), and India, about which Stalin did not take the bait and said that the castes and cultures of the subcontinent made it very complicated (Roosevelt had for a time bombarded Churchill with gratuitous comments about the need for Indian independence, a meddlesome distraction he should not have inflicted on the British leader in the middle of the war), there came the most important moment of the conference. Roosevelt casually presented the northern France (Overlord) option and the Balkan option favored by Churchill, and Stalin emphatically confirmed his preference for Overlord. Though buoyed by the turn of fortunes on the Eastern Front, as Roosevelt had hoped, Stalin still felt he needed a main Allied effort in the west to be sure of victory in Europe, from which he would gain more than from a negotiated separate peace, toward which, as Stalin was about to confirm, there had been overtures from the Germans. Of course, any peace between Germany and Russia could always be torn up without notice again, as had been the last one.

After a few minutes, they adjourned their meeting for the first plenary session. As the only chief of state present, Roosevelt was the chairman of all meetings (Stalin's innocuous rubber-stamp president Mikhail Kalinin and King George VI

---

10. Black, *op. cit.*, p. 864.

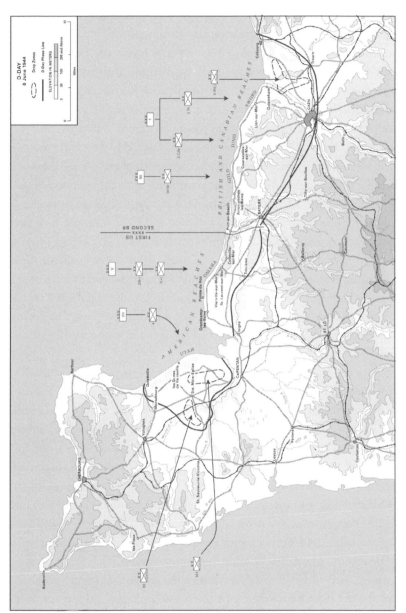

WWII Atlantic. Courtesy of the U.S. Army Center of Military History

were the analogues). All three leaders made opening statements referring to their great opportunity and duty, and Roosevelt gave a summary of the military situation in all theaters from the American standpoint, concluding with "the most important theater, Europe." He spoke of Overlord as a strong American commitment, and said that it was delayed to May 1 only because the English Channel is "such a disagreeable body of water." He blamed prior delays on difficulties with collecting enough landing craft. He said that for reasons of manpower, the British and Americans had to choose to some extent between committing forces to Overlord or to the Mediterranean and would be governed by what Stalin and his chief of staff, Marshal Klimenti Voroshilov, said would be of greater use to the Soviet Union. (Voroshilov was an old Bolshevik loyalist of Stalin's completely out of his depth trying to match strategic military insights with Brooke and Marshall.)

Stalin supported the American view, as he had told Roosevelt he would. He said that the Russian general Alexander Suvorov in 1799 had established that it was impossible to invade Germany from Italy. He said the Italian campaign was of secondary importance to Russia and there could be no decisive outcome there, that he doubted Turkey would enter the war, and that the Balkans were of more interest but a long way from the heart of Germany, and rugged country. "We Russians believe that the best result would be a blow at the enemy in northern France. Germany's weakest spot is France. The Germans will fight like devils to prevent such an attack."[11]

Churchill's ambivalence could not now continue. He expressed his support for Overlord, but said Britain could contribute only 16 divisions, not an impressive figure to the Russians or even the Americans, and an inexplicable conference gambit. Churchill expected Rome to fall in two months (it would take over six months) and saw a domino theory involving Turkey and the Balkan countries, and asked Stalin's detailed views. Stalin questioned him closely but courteously and after some minutes back and forth said that after the capture of Rome, the Italian effort should be continued in southern France and the invasion there should join forces with the Overlord armies and proceed into Germany. "Overlord should be the basic operation for 1944." (He here volunteered that he had had peace overtures from Germany and preliminary discussions in Stockholm.)

Brooke claimed in his diary that Stalin only supported Overlord because he assumed the Germans would throw the Western Allies into the sea, as they had done a number of times to the British, and that this would be the best of all worlds for him: Germany heavily distracted in the west, but the British and

---

11 Black, *op. cit.*, p. 866.

Americansdefeated, enabling Stalin to continue indefinitely into Europe.[12] It was assumed that Stalin was also angling for Communist Party takeovers in France and Italy. (Roosevelt peremptorily rejected Stalin's request for a place on the Italian Control Commission, though he did allow the Italian Communist leader, Palmiro Togliatti, into the provisional government as a minister without portfolio, with philosopher Benedetto Croce.) Brooke wrote in his diary for November 28 that "The conference is over when it has only just begun. Stalin has got the President in his pocket." This was the beginning of the myth, largely propagated by the British, though not by Churchill himself, that Stalin had duped Roosevelt. Brooke may have been correct that Stalin expected Overlord to fail, but it was Roosevelt who had triumphed, in causing Stalin to advocate precisely the course that assured the West the bulk of the geopolitical assets of Europe, and denied them to Russia. Churchill's Adriatic option would have facilitated Stalin's designs. Stalin and Churchill had inadvertently championed courses of action that were detrimental to the interests of both. Roosevelt had performed a remarkable diplomatic feat.

Correctly judging Overlord's likely success and recruiting his country's postwar rival to secure the reluctant adherence of his great but, on this issue, mistaken ally was an astoundingly successful maneuver. The next day, Roosevelt again met privately with Stalin and outlined the international organization he had in mind. Stalin wasn't much interested, but he was clearly prepared to go along with such a fig leaf for the Great Powers (among whom he did not number China or France), but was very concerned about the permanent demilitarization of Germany. That appeared to be the subject of Stalin's only fear and desire, apart from seizing as much of Europe as he could. Stalin's next line of attack in the plenary sessions was to impugn the credibility of Overlord if no commander had been designated. Churchill and Roosevelt promised that the commander would be named within two weeks. Stalin questioned Churchill's commitment to Overlord and Churchill growled back that he was committed to it as long as certain conditions were met. The British leader had boxed himself into a corner by playing games with the Americans until Roosevelt had to dragoon Stalin into settling the issue.

On the evening of November 29, there was a disagreeable incident over Stalin's suggestion that 50,000 German officers be shot out of hand. Churchill strenuously objected and stormed out of the dinner, but Stalin, in conciliatory mode, fetched him amiably back. The two leaders embraced. In private conversation, Roosevelt, in complete friendliness, advised Churchill to remember that he was now (for

---

12. Black, *op. cit.*, p. 870; Sir Alexander Cadogan, *Diaries*, New York, Putnam, 1972, p. 582; Lord Alan-brooke, *War Diaries: 1939–1945*, London, Weidenfeld and Nicholson, 2001, pp. 483–485.

the first time) a party leader and would have to fight an election as soon as the war was over, which they believed would be within two years. He told Churchill that if he didn't produce a social and political vision for his war-weary people, he could lose. Churchill would have done well to listen to Roosevelt, the all-time heavyweight champion of democratic politics.

On November 30, Winston Churchill's 69th birthday, it was agreed by the British and American chiefs that Overlord would take place by June 1, provided the Russians launched a major offensive in the east to coincide with it and prevent Hitler from transferring units from east to west. Churchill had a private meeting with Stalin and tried to recoup lost ground by pledging to Overlord 500,000 of Britain's best troops, 4,000 aircraft, and the Royal Navy's entire Home Fleet, the most powerful naval force in the Atlantic. The United States, the Battle of the Atlantic having been won, would be sending 150,000 soldiers a month to Britain. Churchill's birthday dinner at the British embassy that evening was a very jolly affair that continued through endless flattering toasts, including Stalin's deep admiration for American aircraft production of 10,000 a month. It ended at 2 a.m.

It is alleged by Frances Perkins, Roosevelt's labor secretary, that Roosevelt claimed to have disparaged Churchill the next day to ingratiate himself with Stalin, having apologized in advance to Churchill for doing so. No one else who was present—and almost all the British and Americans who wrote memoirs of the conference—recalled any such episode, so it probably didn't happen. But what possessed Roosevelt to tell Miss Perkins such a story (she was a generally reliable source) is disconcerting.

The generals and admirals departed to sightsee in Jerusalem, leaving the leaders to discuss political matters. Roosevelt largely absented himself from a discussion of Poland, though he said that he approved moving Poland's eastern and western borders 250 miles to the west and giving East Prussia (Konigsberg) to the Russians. He was unwise to tell Stalin he wanted no reference to these arrangements until after the next U.S. election, 11 months away, because of Polish American voters. But it didn't matter, as Stalin did not believe a word of Roosevelt's and Churchill's comments on what they could do in their domestic political environments. He assumed that such formidable leaders could do what they wanted and regarded these democratic niceties as nonsense, like the schoolboy claiming the cat ate his homework.

A communiqué was agreed that pledged to enlist the world to the elimination of "tyranny, slavery, oppression, and intolerance," and claimed that the three leaders departed Tehran "friends in fact, in spirit, and in purpose," a serious liberty, which conformed to Churchill's assertion, in the most famous line of the conference and in another context, that "The truth deserves a bodyguard of lies." Stalin later told the Yugoslavian communist politician Milovan Djilas that "Churchill would pick my pocket for a kopek; Roosevelt only dips in his hand for larger coins."[13]

Roosevelt and Churchill went to Cairo and met with Turkish president Ismet Inonu. He was extremely resistant to the idea of entering the war. Churchill and Eden accompanied him to the airport and Inonu embraced and kissed Churchill. Eden remarked that that was all they got from him. Roosevelt departed for Tunis. He had asked Marshall what he would prefer, between continuing where he was or commanding Overlord. Marshall, with his usual selflessness, declined to express a preference, because he did not think his wishes should be thought relevant. Roosevelt said he would be uneasy without Marshall at his side, and in Tunis appointed Eisenhower the Overlord commander, Churchill having agreed that it was Roosevelt's decision and that either Marshall or Eisenhower would be entirely acceptable to the British.

If Stalin had sided with Churchill on a Balkan campaign, he would have ended up with most of Germany and would have had a crack at a communist France. Tehran was one of the greatest triumphs in the history of Western diplomacy; Roosevelt's was on a par with Franklin's in Paris in 1778 (Chapter 3). Having a man of Stalin's cunning and cynicism advocate something detrimental to his territorial ambitions in Central and Western Europe because he underestimated Western military capabilities was a colossal achievement. Roosevelt flew to Palermo to review troops and encourage General George S. Patton (whom he considered "a joy"), as Patton had had to apologize to his army for slapping a demoralized but otherwise uninjured soldier in a field hospital. He flew on to Dakar, where the *Iowa* awaited him, and returned from there to the United States, arriving back at the White House on December 17. The war would now be a countdown to the invasion of Western Europe, followed, if that were successful, by a race to Berlin.

8. THE RETURN OF THE ALLIES: D-DAY

As 1944 opened, the forces of Stalin, MacArthur, Nimitz, and Alexander were all in inexorable progress toward their objectives, Berlin, Manila, Tokyo, and Rome. The Germans retreated from Leningrad at the end of January, ending a siege of 29 months, in which the Russians lost a million soldiers and a million civilians, and suffered nearly 2.5 million wounded and critically ill from famine or exposure. The Russians recaptured Odessa on April 10 and Sevastopol on May 9. MacArthur's forces seized most of the Admiralty Islands in March and invaded Dutch New Guinea in

---

13. Black, *op. cit.*, p. 865.

April. Nimitz's marines took Kwajalein in February, and landed at Saipan, nearly 2,000 miles west of Honolulu on June 15 (where the Japanese would lose 30,000 dead out of 31,000 defenders, many incinerated or asphyxiated by flame-throwers in caves where the U.S. Marines had chased them, or suicide victims as they leapt from cliffs rather than suffer the indignity of being captured). The Allies made an amphibious landing at Anzio, 30 miles south of Rome, on January 22, but instead of exploiting their advantage, dug in, and were almost dislodged by the Germans. From March to May, the Allies breached the German Gustav Line, especially at Monte Cassino, and approached Rome, which fell to the Americans on June 4, without significant fighting within the city.

The European Advisory Commission (set up at the Moscow foreign ministers' meeting in October 1943 to deal with German matters), which Roosevelt tried to discourage from doing anything until the Western Allied armies were well established in France and at least approaching Germany, was galvanized to action by the Russians and British in early 1944. It met in London and was chaired by the third-ranking member of the British Foreign Office (after Eden and Permanent Under Secretary for Foreign Affairs Cadogan), Sir William Strang, who had assisted Chamberlain at Munich and led the ill-fated mission to try to negotiate arrangements with Russia in 1939. The other members were the U.S. and Soviet ambassadors in London, John G. Winant and Feodor Gousev. Winant was assisted by George F. Kennan, a Russian expert and career diplomat, who would go on to great distinction as the original architect of the West's postwar strategy to counter the USSR.

Winant was slightly aware of the Tehran agreements that would move the western borders of the Soviet Union and Poland each more than 200 miles to the west, but no one else in the State Department was, including Hull. And Strang and Gousev knew nothing about those agreements, and Winant was under orders from Roosevelt not to breathe a word about them. While the Western nightmare was that Stalin would make a separate peace with Hitler (the Russo-German Stockholm discussions after Stalingrad and Kursk were not revived, but that was mainly because Hitler was not interested), the Soviet nightmare was that Hitler would be disposed of by the Germans, who would make a separate peace with the British and the Americans as the post-Mussolini Italians did. The particular British concern was that, as Churchill had explained at Tehran, the British contribution of manpower on the ground in Germany would be only a quarter of the American total (if the Canadians were lumped in with the British, which Roosevelt knew was not how the Canadians perceived themselves), and about 10 percent of the Russians, and the British would end up with a postage stamp of an occupation zone.

The commission met on January 14, and Strang presented a plan that gave the three powers almost equal zones and left Berlin 110 miles inside the Russian zone. Winant countered with Roosevelt's hastily executed design on the *National Geographic* map on the USS *Iowa*, which was the only instruction he had, from the Joint Chiefs (to whom Roosevelt had given it on the ship), confining Russia to the east of Berlin, with the eastern and western Allied zones meeting there. The U.S. had 46 percent of prewar Germany, Britain 34 percent, and the Soviet Union only 20 percent. Gousev rejected Winant's plan as completely unacceptable, and presumptuous, considering that in Europe, the West only had forces in Italy, where they were not overly numerous by Russian standards, nor advancing very quickly.

Winant and Kennan requested more information from Washington so they could support the president's plan, but never received anything useful, as the other powers became impatient. Finally Kennan returned to Washington, naturally received no enlightenment from the State Department, and requested an audience with the president, which was accorded in mid-March. Roosevelt said he would clarify matters. The British and the Russians agreed on a version of their own, similar to Strang's and giving almost equal zones to the three powers, leaving Berlin inside the Russian zones, but with British and American zones of Berlin and three assured access routes to Berlin from the western zones of Germany. Roosevelt was "irritated"[14] but on May 1 sent Winant an instruction to accept the Anglo-Russian fait accompli.

As events unfolded, about 10 million Germans fled before the advancing Red Army, carrying Germany on their feet and ox carts into the Western world, and thus securing most of Germany and more than 75 percent of Germans for the West. This fulfilled a primary objective of the Western leaders, and incidentally was something of a coup for Britain in attaining such a large German occupation zone, given the relatively small size of British forces engaged in Germany. (In fairness, the British did provide a much larger share of air forces in the war against Germany, the bulk of the forces in Italy, and the great majority of the naval forces in the European theater.) But if Strang had been less proactive, Roosevelt's ambition to enable the Western armies to take advantage of tougher German resistance in the east than the west, which Stalin also anticipated, would have been achieved. In his memoirs, Strang lamely claimed concern that the Russians would stop on the Polish-German border and leave it to the West to finish off Germany, that the Western commanders were concerned about having too large a part of Germany to occupy, and that the division was "fair." The first two assertions are a

---

14. George F. Kennan, *Memoirs 1925–1950*, Boston, Little Brown, 1967, pp. 170–171.

complete fabrication, and the British thereafter, especially Montgomery, blamed the Americans for not taking a larger part of Germany, and fairness was the last criterion anyone was concerned about and was not for a secondary official like Strang to judge.

General Dwight D. Eisenhower arrived in London to set up the Supreme Headquarters of the Allied Expeditionary Force on January 16. The intensive bombing of Germany and of military targets in France in preparation for Overlord had begun on January 11 and ramped up steadily. On March 6, 800 American bombers dropped incendiary bombs on Berlin. As Eisenhower elaborated his plans and organized his command structure, Churchill wrote Roosevelt three times that he was "hardening" for Overlord. Eisenhower took Marshal of the Royal Air Force Sir Arthur Tedder as his deputy commander, and three other British officers as service commanders: General Montgomery, Admiral Sir Bertram Ramsay (who had commanded the Dunkirk evacuation), and Air Chief Marshal Sir Trafford Leigh-Mallory. The plan eventually evolved to land in Normandy, well to the west of the narrowest part of the English Channel, and promote the ruse that it was a diversionary landing. Nearly 7,000 ships, including nearly 5,000 landing craft, and 12,000 aircraft would be involved, as three American, three British, and one Canadian division would come ashore, and three airborne divisions, two American and one British, and a Canadian brigade, would descend behind the beaches, 10 divisions on the first day, D-Day. Artificial harbors would be created by sinking cement barges, and over one million men would be disembarked in the first four weeks. It was the greatest single military operation in the history of the world and was masterly in concept, as it would be in execution. The target date was deferred, and problems of weather caused further delays. Finally, before his entire staff, after predictions of slightly improved weather, and a final moment of consideration, at 4 a.m. on June 5, 1944, Eisenhower uttered the deceptively simple words "OK, let's go."

On the evening of June 5, 1944, as Roosevelt spoke to the world about the liberation of Rome, and welcomed Italy back into the civilized world, Churchill and de Gaulle were having the most severe of all their many disputes. Churchill had advised de Gaulle two days before that in any dispute between France and America, Britain would always side with America. This was not a surprise, but was a rather insensitive comment. De Gaulle considered that Eisenhower's statement, to be given a few hours later announcing the Allied landings in France, effectively referred to France as if it were enemy territory, and that the Allies proposed to flood France with "counterfeit money," dispensed by the Allied soldiers. Eisenhower had made the point to Churchill and Roosevelt on June 3 that he was about to set forth to liberate France without the active support of the only Frenchman who could be of any military assistance to the Allies. De Gaulle, in the circumstances, had withheld the French officers who were to accompany the Allied airborne divisions and assist them with the local populations, and was declining to address the French people on the invasion unless France were treated like an ally and he were treated as the spokesman for France that Britain had officially recognized him to be for nearly four years.

De Gaulle's ambassador to the British, Pierre Vienot, was trying to smooth matters over and fetched up in Churchill's bedroom with Eden at one in the morning on D-Day, June 6. There was a frightful scene as Churchill, on one of the most momentous nights of his life, had consumed more alcohol than usual and had retired earlier than usual. Vienot said that there was a misunderstanding and that de Gaulle would certainly speak to the French people through the BBC. Churchill harangued Vienot for nearly two hours, accusing de Gaulle of "treachery in battle" and of not appreciating the sacrifice of the young British, Americans, and Canadians who were already embarked to go forth and liberate France. Vienot finally declared that he would not be spoken to in this way and left at 3 a.m., returning to de Gaulle, who was staying in the Connaught Hotel. Churchill then awakened an aide and shouted down the telephone to him that de Gaulle would not be allowed into France and would be returned to Algiers, if need be, he added in a magnificent flourish, "in chains."[15]

The aide ignored this and went uneasily back to sleep as if after a nightmare, but de Gaulle, advised by Vienot of Churchill's tirade, was satisfied at having inflicted on his host such an uncontrollable and sleep-depriving rage, and told Vienot to assure the British that of course he would speak to the French and send whatever support people he could. (Most of the initial airborne divisions were already over France, approximately 13,000 men.) When Eisenhower's statement was broadcast at 3:32 a.m. Eastern Time in the United States, as the British were making their way to work, de Gaulle issued a statement entirely supporting the invasion and announcing his presence in "this old and dear England; where else could I be?" The BBC announced all day on its French service that de Gaulle would speak in the evening, although de Gaulle refused to show his remarks in advance to the British.

---

15. Black, *op. cit.*, p. 941.

9. THE BATTLE OF FRANCE

The landings went better than had been feared, other than with unforeseen problems for Americans scaling cliffs at Omaha Beach. The Allies took about 6,000 casualties on the day, but landed successfully at all five beaches (two British, two American, and one Canadian), and penetrated inland beyond their initial targets. Casualties were not heavy among the airborne troops, for whom a casualty rate of up to 80 percent had been feared. The remarkable total of over 132,000 Allied soldiers landed on D-Day. Roosevelt had been awakened by his wife, to whom Marshall's telephone call at 3:30 a.m. was directed by the White House switchboard, as she was unable to sleep. Roosevelt had White House employees called in to work at 4 a.m. Throughout the United States, church bells and school bells pealed constantly, large crowds gathered in almost all public squares, and houses of worship of all denominations held almost continuous services in favor of the cross-Channel operation on D-Day and succeeding days.

De Gaulle spoke to the French, with Churchill listening in his office, prepared at any moment to pull the plug on his obstreperous colleague by telephone hookup with the BBC. It was soon clear that there would be no need for such a draconian and almost unthinkable intervention. De Gaulle summoned "the sons of France" to do their "simple and sacred duty to fight the enemy by every means in their power." He was generous in his references to the Allies, spoke as the civil and military authority of France, and said to his countrymen: "From behind the cloud so heavy with our blood and our tears, the sun of our greatness is reappearing." Churchill, well over his violent rage against de Gaulle 18 hours before, with tears streaming down his face, demanded of an incredulous aide: "Have you no sentiment?" Roosevelt gave one of his greatest addresses a few hours later, beginning "Our sons, pride of our nation, this day have set upon a mighty endeavor" and ending with the prayerful hope that America's sons and allies would produce "a peace invulnerable to the scheming of unworthy men."[16]

The landings achieved complete surprise and the ruse that Normandy was only a diversion was assisted by conspicuous air and sea activity in the nearer Channel ports, and by large numbers of dummy tanks and trucks and tent camps. And the conspicuous presence of General Patton, the Western general the Germans feared most, around Dover was successful and played a role in Hitler's withholding two armored divisions from the real invasion area. In Normandy, overwhelming Allied

---

16. *The Public Papers and Addresses of Franklin D. Roosevelt*, 1944–1945 Volume, *Victory and the Threshold of Peace*, New York, Harper, 1950, p. 153.

air and sea superiority made it difficult for German counter-attacks to take hold or the torrential influx of men and vehicles and stores to be interdicted or contested at all. There was fierce fighting in the *bocage* hedge country of the Norman interior, but it became clearer each day, and certain within 10 days, that the Allies could not be evicted. The German theater and Atlantic defense commanders, Field Marshals von Rundstedt and Rommel, told Hitler on June 17 that it would be impossible to contain the Allies in their beachhead. Within three weeks, more than a million men, 172,000 vehicles, and over 600,000 tons of supplies had been landed. By September 5, the Allies had landed 2.1 million men and 3.47 million tons of supplies, and the Americans continued to send two divisions a week to the front, and could do so almost indefinitely.

Stalin launched the offensive he had promised to synchronize with Overlord on June 23, moving a million men forward on a 450 mile front in Belarus, taking Minsk and entering Poland, and promptly installing his puppet Communist Polish government in Lublin. Stalin may, as the British suspected, have pushed for Overlord at Tehran because he thought it would fail, but at the end of June, completely unprompted, he issued a statement praising it and the strategic bombing campaign that had preceded it. He referred to the "brilliant successes" of Eisenhower's forces and added, "The history of war does not know of another undertaking comparable to it for breadth of conception, grandeur of scale, and mastery of execution." This was nothing less than the truth, from a source not much given to hyperbole in praise of others. This was an immense vindication of the strategic judgment of the American leadership, and of Eisenhower's command decisions. The combined power and prestige and perception of benignity of America and its president were now approaching a scale never before attained in the Western world. It was an astounding surge in the fortunes and standing of the economically and psychologically depressed country whose headship Franklin D. Roosevelt had taken 11 years before.

One of the few spirited disagreements Roosevelt and Churchill had took place in mid-June through early July over the proposed landing in southern France, which Churchill objected to because it would take six divisions from his beloved but somewhat sluggish Italian campaign. He was prepared to sacrifice the divisions to an amphibious landing up the Adriatic to Trieste and what he called the Ljubljana Gap into Austria, but Eisenhower countered him at Roosevelt's request. He did not believe there really was a Ljubljana Gap or that the Germans could not prevent a breakthrough there as they had in Italy. And he believed the southern French landings would lead to a quick progress up the Rhône Valley and a linkup with his armies in northern France, cutting off a good many Germans in France and ideally moving quickly to the Rhine.

Churchill dismissed the southern French action—Anvil, as it was called, and later Dragoon—as "bleak and sterile" and likely to lead to a costly defeat or at least stalemate. He even suggested that moving French divisions to France would unduly assist de Gaulle's ambitions, a rather disingenuous argument. Roosevelt replied to Churchill on June 29 that "The Rhone corridor has its limitations, but it is better than Ljubljana and is certainly far better than the terrain over which we have been fighting in Italy. . . . My dear friend, I beg you, let us go ahead with our plan." Churchill was so upset, he initially considered resigning, but thought better of it, and dejectedly wrote back, "We are deeply grieved by your telegram" and quoted Montgomery's skepticism about the operation. (Montgomery was motivated entirely by anti-Americanism.) Churchill, as he had recently written Mrs. Churchill, was already discountenanced by the inexorable rise of America: "It has always been my wish to keep equal, but how can you do that against so mighty a nation?"[17]

Roosevelt replied instantly and in very conciliatory manner to Churchill; the landings went off as scheduled on August 15, with Churchill gallantly watching from a destroyer offshore; and once again Roosevelt and Marshall and Eisenhower were entirely vindicated. The 10 divisions eventually involved moved swiftly up the Rhône Valley, joined with the northern armies near Dijon on September 11, cut off nearly 100,000 German soldiers in southwestern France, and reached the Rhine at Belfort on September 14. They facilitated Eisenhower's double-envelopment of the Ruhr in early 1945.

On June 23, the Soviets launched their main summer offensive, involving over two million men on a front stretching 800 miles south from Leningrad. It moved inexorably toward Poland. The Germans began launching V-1 semi-guided missiles at southern England on June 14, succeeded by the more powerful V-2 on September 7. The Allies broke out of their beachhead area on June 18, and seized the damaged port of Cherbourg on June 27. The British would take Caen on July 9 and the Americans St. Lo on July 25, and Patton, who took over the Third Army after his service as a decoy had run its course, cut off significant German forces in Brittany by August 10.

The long-awaited and tortuously prepared visit of Charles de Gaulle to the United States finally began on July 6, 1944. Even de Gaulle was impressed by the overwhelming confidence and power of America, and by Roosevelt's "glittering personality," but added, "As was only human, Roosevelt's will to power cloaked itself in idealism." It was almost incomprehensible to de Gaulle that Roosevelt

---

17. Black, *op. cit.*, p. 954.

really was an idealist, given how cynical and ruthless he was in his methods, and also how overwhelming was now his and his country's power. This was a complicated relationship, as de Gaulle sought a restoration of the unquestioned status as a coequal Great Power with Britain and America that Clemenceau had enjoyed with Lloyd George and Wilson. Churchill was prepared for this, but never to the point of considering France a rival to America for Britain's affections. Roosevelt liked and knew France, which accentuated his disappointment in the French collapse in 1940, and the shameful performance of many Frenchmen, including most that Roosevelt knew personally.

De Gaulle understood the debacle of 1940 better than anyone, having loudly warned of the dangers of the military and political policies that led to it. But he wanted an instant resurrection of France based on its historic standing and not the contemporary correlation of forces. Time was to some degree on his side, as France was in the process of being liberated, chiefly by the exertions of the Americans. He oscillated between aggravating the British when, as he put it, "Mr. Churchill felt some of the spirit of Pitt in his own soul," and trying to entice Churchill back into an Entente Cordiale that would be entirely independent of the Americans. It was, for a time, an impossible position, as France had infinitely less stature in the world than Britain and Roosevelt didn't owe him anything. And it was the beginning of what de Gaulle later aggregated into a comprehensive foreign policy: that the Anglo-Saxons didn't really care about Europe but France did and would take care of Europe, as it could make bilateral arrangements with both Germany and Russia, in the interests of Europe and at the expense of the British and the Americans, while professing absolute solidarity with Britain and America in times of crisis.

It was also the relaunch, after five years of frantically importuning the United States for assistance, of the post-Versailles practice of blaming the United States for everything. Thus, de Gaulle implied in his memoirs, it was American isolationism that caused the fall of France, and nearly 30 years later it would supposedly be American policy in Vietnam that caused the general strike that paralyzed France in 1968. Roosevelt supposedly conceded too much to Stalin, another part of the confidence trick that France and not the Anglo-Saxons was the guarantor of Western Europe. De Gaulle claimed that these conversations convinced him, as if he had been unaware of it before, that "in foreign affairs, logic and sentiment do not weigh heavily in comparison with the realities of power; that what matters is what one takes and what one can hold on to; that to regain her place, France must count only on herself." Roosevelt replied: "We shall do what we can, but it is true that to serve France, no one can replace the French people."

It was a successful visit, as Roosevelt tendered de Gaulle a state luncheon and proposed two generous toasts, and thereafter declared that he and de Gaulle had mended fences. In his public remarks, he denounced "troublemakers" who had stirred up problems between his guest and himself. Roosevelt realized that he had underestimated de Gaulle and confirmed full recognition of him as the leader of France, pending democratic confirmation of that fact, and warmed to the idea of assisting France, as Churchill had long proposed, in reassuming an important role as a more reliable ally, whatever its failings, than the Germans, Russians, or Italians. Roosevelt had moved just in time, because six weeks after de Gaulle left the United States (for "the beloved and courageous" Canada, as de Gaulle described it, with some irony, given his subsequent mischief in that country), he was welcomed with immense fervor by millions of Parisians in a manner that made it clear that he spoke unquestionably for France. The private and public references of Roosevelt and de Gaulle to each other, and the correspondence between them, would hereafter be quite cordial. The consequences of the ups and downs of the Roosevelt-Churchill problems with de Gaulle would echo in the relations of the three countries for the rest of the twentieth century. Had those men stayed in office for a few more consecutive years, they would doubtless have worked it out, but in less than two years, all were gone, Roosevelt permanently.

The Germans vacated Paris and it was occupied by the Allies on August 24, and Charles de Gaulle made his historic walk down the Champs-Elysées the following day at the head of all the notables of France, however they had spent the last four years ("Two steps behind, please, gentlemen," he said as he started down the great boulevard). In his remarks, to millions of jubilant Parisians, he amplified the double myth that France had never left the war and had contributed very largely to its own liberation. This was a fraud, though a useful one in rallying all the non-communist forces in the country, especially the numerous Pétainists, to ensure that there was no possibility of a coup by the communist underground armies, which may have been almost as numerous as the Gaullist Resistance.

10. CLOSING IN ON GERMANY AND JAPAN

By this time, there had been a number of other developments on other fronts. On June 22, Roosevelt's benefit bill for veterans, known to history as the G.I. Bill of Rights, one of the most successful measures of his entire presidency, was passed. It gave every serviceman a free year of post-secondary education for every year in the armed forces, and provided virtually interest-free loans for ex-servicemen to set up a small business or to buy a farm. For years after the war, a very large proportion of American university students were veterans, and the unemployed youth that

Roosevelt had cycled through his workfare programs and then conscripted, and who had been led to victory by outstanding theater commanders in a just and necessary war, now became a highly motivated and patriotic middle class. This was the sort of program that Roosevelt had recommended to Churchill at Tehran as good in itself but likely necessary to assure reelection.

Roosevelt journeyed to Hawaii later in July to meet with his Pacific theater commanders, Admiral Nimitz and General MacArthur, to concert the end-game strategy against Japan. MacArthur, who had famously promised to return to the Philippines, wished to do that, while Nimitz made himself, with no great enthusiasm, the proponent of the ambition of his irascible colleague Admiral Ernest J. King to bypass the Philippines and invade Formosa. (Roosevelt said he had promoted King, an argumentative Anglophobe, to be fleet commander because he understood King "cut his toenails with a torpedo-net cutter and shaved with a blowtorch."[18] He was a very crusty character and now held the scepter of the seas; when Nimitz's mighty Pacific Fleet set sail in the last months of the war with over 20 battleships, 30 fleet carriers, and 70 escort carriers, it carried 400,000 sailors and over 4,000 aircraft.) It was a cordial meeting, as Nimitz and MacArthur got on well and Roosevelt was a respected patron of both, despite his suspicions of MacArthur's political maneuvering. When he returned to Washington, Roosevelt decided in favor of MacArthur's plan, as the United States owed something to the Philippines, and Formosa was a long way through open seas, with a still significant Japanese navy prowling about, and the bombing of Japan could be accomplished from other islands in the western Pacific that Nimitz's forces were already approaching.

While he was on his way to embarkation for Hawaii from San Diego, the Democrats, at Chicago, renominated Roosevelt by acclamation for a fourth term. As Henry Wallace, an obscurantist leftist mystic, was clearly a hazardous occupant of the vice presidency, he was dumped, with a minimum of ceremony but with elaborate Rooseveltian cynicism and dissembling, for Missouri's Senator Harry S. Truman. Roosevelt made his choice known when his train stopped briefly in Chicago on his way west, though he did not leave the train. The Republicans had met three weeks before in the same city and had nominated New York's 42-year-old governor, Thomas E. Dewey, for president and Ohio senator John W. Bricker for vice president.

Both parties supported some notion of postwar international organization. It was impossible to attack the Roosevelt administration, as the president had led the

18. Black, *op. cit.*, p. 703.

country out of the Depression that most Americans blamed on the Republicans, had been vindicated in his assistance to the democracies from 1939 to 1941, was considered to be blameless in the U.S. involvement in the war, and had managed all aspects of the war with conspicuous success. And the invasion of the Philippines was planned for before the election. The only issue the Republicans could find was Roosevelt's health, which had visibly deteriorated, though he was only 62. His doctor, Ross McIntyre, whom he had promoted from navy lieutenant and White House duty medical officer, because of his successful treatment of Roosevelt's sinus condition, to vice admiral and surgeon general of the United States Navy, assured the country that FDR was good for another term. Roosevelt resented the attacks on his health, and to spike the rumors had a two-hour motor trip through the four main boroughs of New York City in an open car on a raw and rainy day, October 21, 1944. More than three million New Yorkers stood for an extended period in the rain, up to 30 deep, just to catch a glimpse of the president as he passed at 20 miles an hour in his open car.

The interesting and controversial aspect of the election was that the southern senators and congressmen, virtually all Democrats, who had supported every aspect of Roosevelt's national security and war policy, were concerned to prevent the more than 500,000 southern African American servicemen from voting, and so joined with the congressional Republicans to restrict voting in the armed forces, which contained over 10 million eligible voters, to only about 25 percent of them, by spurious requirements. It was assumed that the great majority would vote for the commander-in-chief. Roosevelt did not wish to split his party, and he was going to carry the southern states anyway, without the young black servicemen. But he accused the Republicans of denying the right to vote to the armed forces and generally served notice that the mistreatment of African Americans had to stop. There had been several nasty racial riots during the war, and the issue, whose moral unacceptability Roosevelt well recognized, was festering. The G.I. Bill of Rights, like the prewar workfare and agricultural price support programs, though segregated, applied equally to all eligible candidates regardless of pigmentation, and constituted a tremendous breakthrough for African Americans.

Roosevelt and Churchill met again at Quebec from September 11 to 16. Churchill, called upon by Roosevelt to kick off the conference, generously allowed that Anvil (Dragoon, the landings in southern France) had been a great success, and that the Italian campaign had not, as he had feared, been "ruined," and was proceeding quite well. There were no strategic disagreements between the two sides at this conference, and there was an unspoken recognition throughout that it was not really a meeting of equals, but Roosevelt and Marshall managed it with exquisite tact, and even Brooke, in his generally rather acidulous diary, was quite upbeat. The conference met as the Warsaw Uprising was being crushed by the Germans while the Red Army stood, inert, on the other side of the Vistula, declining to render assistance. The Poles had only staged the uprising when the Russians were across the river, to facilitate the liberation of Warsaw. Stalin would not even allow the Western Allied air forces to drop assistance to the Poles in Warsaw and land in Russia. It was a grim foretaste of Stalin's notions of the political future of Eastern Europe. Most of Warsaw was reduced to rubble, and 200,000 Varsovians, one-fifth of the population of the city, died in the heroic uprising.

Roosevelt allowed his Treasury secretary, Henry Morgenthau, to propose a plan for the "pastoralization" of Germany, its reduction to a deindustrialized state. The British were at first quite skeptical but became more interested when what was in contemplation was shown to be the elimination of a great deal of competition for British industries. Roosevelt had told his cabinet committee on Germany that Germans should be deprived of indoor plumbing and prevented from wearing uniforms, in a considerable feat of deadpan advocacy. He didn't take the issue seriously, other than its potential as a bargaining chip with Stalin, who had made it clear at Tehran how much he feared a revival of German militarism. Although the European Advisory Commission agreement on German occupation zones was confirmed at this meeting, it was clear that most of Germany and most Germans would be in Western hands at the war's end, and that the Western Allies had the power to deliver or withhold a full demilitarization of Germany. The conference continued for a few days at Roosevelt's home at Hyde Park, before Churchill and his party returned home from New York on the great liner *Queen Mary*.

The Western Front as it moved into eastern France was organized into the Northern, Central, and Southern Army Groups, commanded by, respectively, Montgomery, General Omar N. Bradley, and American general Jacob Devers. Montgomery had the Sixth British and First Canadian Armies (18 divisions); Bradley had the U.S. Ninth, Third, and First Armies (46 divisions), and Devers had the U.S. Thirteenth and French First Armies (24 divisions). There were also five airborne divisions and a number of other divisions available to Eisenhower's headquarters and involved in mopping up pockets of Germans in the French interior and assuring logistics. Eisenhower's armies continued to grow as they approached and entered Germany, and Patton's Third Army, in particular, badly mauled the Germans in the center of the front. Unfortunately, Montgomery's agitation for a larger role and Churchill's concern to take down the German V-2 launchers that were raining a good deal of devastation on England led to a diversion of supplies from Patton's fast-advancing forces to the north, as Montgomery attempted an outflanking maneuver into Holland, led by 34,000 airborne troops. The Western Allies entered Germany at Eupen on September 12. The Americans took Nijmegan, but the British were defeated at Arnem (the "bridge too far"), and the operation was not a success. The Germans opened the dikes and flooded much of Holland, threatening the entire civil population with starvation, and the Canadians cleared the Scheldt estuary and opened the vital port of Antwerp in October. The Americans took Aachen, the first substantial German city to be occupied, on October 2, and Patton had occupied Metz and Strasbourg, French Rhine fortress cities, on September 22 and 23.

In the east, the Russians occupied Talinn, Estonia, on September 22, and Königsberg and Belgrade, Yugoslavia, a month later (with, in Belgrade, collaboration from communist and anti-communist Yugoslav partisans). In the Pacific, the American return to the Philippines was initiated by the naval victory of the Philippine Sea on June 19 and 20, in which three Japanese aircraft carriers were sunk and many other vessels damaged. On October 20, MacArthur's forces invaded the central Philippines at Leyte, smoking out the Japanese Combined Fleet in a desperate gamble that led to the greatest naval battle of the war in several separate actions in and near Leyte Gulf, October 23–25. The Americans destroyed the Japanese navy as a coherent fighting force, sinking three battleships, four aircraft carriers, and nine cruisers and nine destroyers, with light losses themselves. It was a welcome present for Roosevelt, one week before the election. The battle for the Philippines continued to February 23 and caused severe damage to Manila, but was never in doubt.

Winston Churchill was in Moscow visiting Stalin from October 9 to 18. Roosevelt asked that Harriman be included, and advised Churchill and Stalin that he considered this meeting preliminary to the scheduled meeting between the three leaders in the Crimea in February, and said he would not be bound by any agreements from these meetings in Moscow. Stalin, who assumed that Churchill would be bringing whatever he and Roosevelt had concerted at Quebec, replied that Roosevelt's position "does not seem to correspond with reality."[19] As his armies were already in Central Europe, he presumably meant the reality of what the Red Army was about to impose on "liberated" territory, and of the geographic misfortune of those countries that found themselves between Germany and Russia. (Churchill did not reply at all to Roosevelt, a rarity in their voluminous correspondence.)

Churchill and Eden met with Stalin on the night of their arrival, and Churchill opened with "Let us settle our affairs in the Balkans. Don't let us get at cross-purposes in small ways." He suggested that the Soviet Union have 90 percent of the

19. Black, *op. cit.*, p. 1004.

influence in Romania and 75 percent in Bulgaria, that it be 50–50 in Yugoslavia and Hungary, and that Britain have 90 percent of the Great Power influence in Greece. While this was being translated for Stalin, Churchill wrote it out on a piece of paper and handed it to his host. Stalin "took his blue pencil and made a large tick upon it, and passed it back to us. It was all settled in no more time than it takes to set down." Churchill said: "Might it not be thought rather cynical if it seemed we had disposed of these issues, so fateful to millions of people, in such an offhand manner?" He suggested burning what he later called the "naughty" piece of paper, but Stalin told him to keep it. In his memoirs, Churchill claimed that these were only temporary arrangements, but that is completely implausible. Churchill well knew the nature of his host, and if it had been temporary, the demarcation would not have been "fateful to millions," nor even "naughty."

In fact he hadn't struck a bad bargain, as Stalin was going to take what Churchill conceded anyway. But Molotov bullied Eden into raising the Soviet position in Hungary to 75 percent, and even then, Stalin raised his status in Romania, Bulgaria, and Hungary to 100 percent and stoked up a civil war under the noses of the British and the Americans in Greece. Churchill didn't tell Roosevelt exactly what had happened but told him there was a need to resolve Balkan issues to avoid civil war there (though civil war resulted in Yugoslavia as well as in Greece).

In the light of subsequent revisionist history, including most ingenious revisions by Churchill himself in his voluminous memoirs, it is worth noting that if Churchill hadn't dragged Britain's heels on Overlord and distracted the Americans with all the bunk about the "soft underbelly" and "Ljubljana Gap," and hadn't thrown in with Russia at the European Advisory Commission's demarcation of occupation zones in Germany, the Western Powers would have ended up with almost all of Germany, at least the Czech part of Czechoslovakia, and Hungary.

The atmosphere at the conference was very cordial; Stalin arranged for a great ovation for Churchill when they attended the Bolshoi Ballet and Opera, and saw him off at the airport, an unprecedented courtesy. "He made several expressions of personal regard which I feel sure were sincere." Doubtless they were, and Mr. Churchill deserved no less, but Stalin's cordiality is hardly surprising: Churchill had legitimized the rape Stalin was about to commit, though refusal to do so would not have prevented it.

11. THE 1944 ELECTION AND THE BATTLE OF THE ARDENNES

Roosevelt campaigned as he had in the 1940 election, in the last three weeks, and spoke to very enthusiastic and large crowds in the great cities of the East, Northeast, and Midwest, including a dramatic appearance, under a spotlight in an otherwise darkened Soldier Field in Chicago, before 120,000 people (where Mrs. Sullivan, the mother of five sons who had perished in a cruiser, was introduced to great applause). His tour of New York City and vigorous stump appearances silenced the only issue the Republicans had: Roosevelt's health. Dewey was a comparative upstart and Roosevelt ran as the conqueror of the Republican Depression, of Republican isolationism, and of the Germans and the Japanese. There were only 2.691 million military votes out of more than 12 million eligible, but Roosevelt won, for the fourth time, 25.6 million votes (54 percent) to 22 million for Dewey (46 percent), and 432 electoral votes from 36 states to 99 from 12 states for Dewey. It was a very respectable performance by Dewey against so invincible an opponent, but if the armed forces had been able vote in representative numbers, Roosevelt would undoubtedly have won by at least as great a margin as he had over Willkie in 1940. (Willkie and McNary had both died, so if Willkie had won in 1940, the president on election day would have been the Republican secretary of state, possibly Herbert Hoover.)

On December 16, Hitler launched a major offensive in the west, out of the Ardennes Forest in poor winter weather that neutralized the Allies' air advantage. The German attack involved about 500,000 men, nearly half of the 55 German divisions that had retreated to the Rhine before Eisenhower's 96 divisions. The German plan was to overrun Allied supplies, especially tank fuel to resupply themselves, and proceed all the way to Antwerp, which had recently been cleared by the Canadians, in an attack that resembled the drive to Dunkirk in 1940. As in 1940, they were attacking out of the Ardennes against a relatively under-defended section of the Allied line, and one held by newly arrived American troops. Allied intelligence, especially from Patton's Third Army, had warned that a German attack was possible, and Eisenhower had pulled Allied stores and supplies back from the front.

The Germans achieved almost complete tactical surprise, and advanced about 50 miles in the first week, when the weather kept the Allied air forces out of the fight. Patton wheeled his Third Army north and the 101st Airborne Division fiercely defended the surrounded Belgian fortress city of Bastogne. American resistance stiffened steadily, and Patton crashed into the German southern flank on Christmas Day and relieved Bastogne the next day. Eisenhower committed all his reserves to Bradley's Central Army Group, and gave command of the American Ninth Army, partly separated from Patton by the German advance, to Montgomery, who, after his usual methodical preparation, attacked the northern side of the German salient on January 2. The Allied line regained its original position on January 21. Germany had taken about 120,000 casualties to about 90,000 for the Allies, 77,000 of them Americans, including 21,000 prisoners. Germany lost about a third of its air force, 1,500 planes, after the weather lifted following Christmas. It had been the usual highly professional operation by the Germans, but the correlation of forces was now too lopsided and the quality of the Western armies too well-developed for any prospect of successfully resisting in the west. The senior Allied commanders, Eisenhower, Bradley, Montgomery, Patton, and McAuliffe (in Bastogne), all performed admirably.

As 1944 ended, it was clear that Hitler would not be able to continue in the war for more than about six months. In both Europe and the Pacific, World War II had reached its final phase. The Allies were unstoppable; victory was at hand on every front. The Western Allies were on the Rhine and almost to the Alps and they had almost entirely occupied France and Italy. The Americans were approaching Japan from the east and southeast. The Russians were still not in Warsaw. Stalin would not be denied some spoils, but an immense strategic victory for Western democracy seemed imminent.

Harry S. Truman

1. YALTA

The Russians launched a general offensive on January 12, occupied Warsaw on January 17, and reached the Oder River, south of the border of Poland and Germany but only about 200 miles from Berlin, on January 23, 1945. Alexander and Clark had pushed the Germans into the extreme north of Italy. MacArthur's forces entered Manila on February 5. This was where the Allied armies were when Churchill, Roosevelt, and Stalin met at Yalta, in the Crimea, starting on February 4. Roosevelt was accompanied, apart from the service chiefs, by his new secretary of state, the former chairman of United States Steel Corporation, Edward Stettinius, who had been Hull's under secretary when Hull retired in November 1944 (the longest-serving secretary of state in U.S. history); by James Byrnes, the head of the Offices of Economic Stabilization and War Mobilization; and by Roosevelt's daughter, Anna. After introductory remarks from the leaders, and summaries of the Eastern and Western Fronts in Europe, Italy, the Pacific, and Burma, the conference dealt with great application with a succession of complicated points. It was agreed that France would receive an occupation zone of Germany carved out of the British zone and would join the European Advisory Commission and the Allied Control Commission in Germany; that Nazi war criminals would be punished, Germany disarmed, and the German general staff dissolved; and that reparations were to be determined by the Allies and paid by Germany. The United Nations Organization would be set up by the five founding powers (China and France as well as those present) at San Francisco, starting on April 25. (Roosevelt would have it set up and running before the war ended, and have equal numbers of Republicans and Democrats on the American founding delegation, to avoid the shambles that befell Wilson.)

The Yalta Declarations on Liberated Europe and on Poland promised democratic government with free elections, with, in Poland, "universal suffrage and secret ballot." In Yugoslavia, the Communists under Josip Broz Tito and the regent for the Karageorgevich monarchy would be encouraged to cooperate, as Churchill had proposed (with no practical likelihood of success).

It was agreed that the foreign ministers of the Big Three would meet every three or four months for an indefinite period, and that unity between them was "a sacred obligation." There was a slew of protocols and secret clauses, including relaxation of the Montreux Convention, assuring easier movement of Soviet vessels sailing to and from Soviet ports through the Bosporus, and the return of all prisoners and displaced civilians. As about one million Soviet citizens were serving with the German armed forces, Stalin wanted these people back to imprison or execute them. In practice, the Americans accepted their assurances that they were German, or whatever nationality they claimed, but the British, in the spirit of

Colonel Nicholson in the film *The Bridge on the River Kwai*, dutifully shipped back a large number of Soviet defectors to Stalin's gruesome mercies.

The Soviet Union undertook to enter the war against Japan within two or three months of the end of the European war, and the USSR would receive back all that Russia had ceded to Japan at the end of the Russo-Japanese war of 1904–1905 in the Treaty of Portsmouth, brokered by Roosevelt's cousin Theodore (southern Sakhalin, the Kuril Islands, which had in fact been ceded in 1875, but not the Russian suzerainty of the Manchurian railways and the harbor of Port Arthur). Roosevelt was adamant that all Stalin could have was a lease, because China was another of the five designated permanent members of the United Nations, and he would not be a party to inflicting on China a return to colonialism. The entry of Russia into the war against Japan (which would require abrogation by Stalin of the Russo-Japanese non-aggression pact of 1941, not a great conscientious problem for any of them), was a high priority to the U.S. Joint Chiefs. It was clear from their battles with Japan on the islands approaching Japan itself that no Japanese, even most civilians, would be taken alive, and it was feared that if atomic weapons, which were scheduled to be tested in about five months, did not work, Allied casualties in an attack on Japan itself could be as great as one million. The Soviet Union was to receive three votes at the United Nations, for Russia, the Ukraine, and Belarus. The British Dominions were all entitled to votes, and it was agreed in secret side letters to Roosevelt by Stalin and Churchill ("My Dear Franklin") that the United States, if there were any domestic political embarrassment, could also have three votes. (In what would become a controversial matter, the alleged former Soviet spy Alger Hiss, who was in the American delegation at Yalta, made only one recommendation, to oppose granting the USSR three votes in the UN.)

The conference ended very cordially on February 11, and everyone, even the usually acidulous diarists Brooke and Cadogan, was quite satisfied with it. Roosevelt made it clear to intimates that he knew how easily its agreements could be violated, but he had what he needed most: the international organization with which he was going to defeat the isolationists and exercise through a façade of multilateralism America's preponderant influence in the world; the solemn Declarations on Poland and on Liberated Europe, which if violated by Stalin, would justify strenuous U.S., U.K., French, and (if adequately bribed by the Americans) Chinese counter-measures; and the assurance that, if necessary, Russia would take a sizeable share of the casualties incurred in subduing Japan.

Immense controversy has arisen about this conference, but the West got everything it wanted. As the Roosevelt biographer Ted Morgan has pointed out, "If

Yalta was a sell-out, why did [Stalin] go to such lengths to violate the agreement?"[1] Roosevelt was not well at Yalta, but his mental powers were unaffected, as all who worked with him, especially Bohlen and Stettinius, attest. His plan was to await the development of atomic weapons and then hold Stalin's feet to the fire: the West would guarantee the permanent defanging of Germany (if not Morgenthau's mad "pastoralization" plan), a large economic aid package for Russia, and entire respectability for Stalin and his regime as one of the world's very greatest leaders of a co-equal superpower with the United States. And if that were not adequate incentive, Germany would be rearmed under Western tutelage, there would not be a cent of assistance, Stalin and his murderous regime could continue as the civilized world's pariah, and, as Roosevelt had discussed with Stimson in August 1944, the United States would consider the potential for its status as holder of a nuclear monopoly, to accomplish "the necessity of bringing Russia . . . into the fold of Christian civilization."[2] Roosevelt and Stalin parted on the cheerful agreement that they would "meet again soon, in Berlin." They were not to meet again.

2. THE FINAL OFFENSIVES

Eisenhower's armies launched their offensive to end the war in the west starting on February 8, with the British and Canadian invasion of Germany from Holland, followed by Patton's attack across the Saar River on February 22. The American Central Army Group prorupted into the Ruhr Valley on February 23, and took Cologne and Dusseldorf on the Rhine, and the bridge across the Rhine at Remagen, all on March 7. A full Allied offensive across the Rhine, by boat and by air, was successfully carried out starting March 23, and Eisenhower's grand double envelopment of the Ruhr, the industrial heartland of Germany, was executed from March 24 to April 18, culminating in the surrender of 325,000 German soldiers.

The only Central European country that had not been mentioned, at Tehran, at Yalta, in Churchill's meeting with Stalin in October 1944, or otherwise, was Czechoslovakia. The Russians were soon in control of most of Slovakia, but Bohemia and Moravia, including Prague, which was undamaged by the war, were unclaimed, and it has never been explained, including in the memoirs of the principal figures in the drama, why the Western Allies did not occupy Prague.

In the Pacific, Nimitz invaded Iwo Jima, a volcanic island about 700 miles from Japan, which, when captured, would make Japan much more accessible to air attack from American B-29s. There were 18,000 Japanese defenders, in

---

1. Ted Morgan, *FDR: A Biography*, New York, Simon and Schuster, 1985, p. 735.
2. James MacGregor Burns, *Roosevelt: Soldier of Freedom*, New York, Harcourt, 1970, p. 459.

a heavily fortified and camouflaged network of bunkers and artillery and heavy machine gun emplacements, connected by 18 kilometers of tunnels. The Americans arrived in an armada of 450 ships, attacked the entire periphery of the island for three days with the full continuous broadsides of 20 battleships at point-blank range, supplemented by heavy aerial bombing throughout that time, starting on February 19. A total of 70,000 marines were landed. Given the correlation of forces, the Japanese had no chance of repulsing the attack, but they held out until March 17. The Americans took about 4,500 dead and 15,300 wounded. The 18,000 Japanese defenders, who had, as at Saipan, to be incinerated or suffocated in their caves and bunkers with sustained assault from flame-throwers, all died, except for 216 taken prisoner, most of them while unconscious from wounds. It could be reasonably inferred that the defense of Japan itself would be a matter of suicidal tenacity to the last woman and ambulatory child, if atomic weapons did not obviate a conventional assault and occupation.

This apprehension was reinforced with the battle for Okinawa, just 360 miles from Japan, which began on April 1. The United States had 23 battleships, counting the British Pacific Fleet, which had been beefed up, as the German navy was now almost extinct. The Allies had scores of fleet and escort carriers and again opened with a carpet bombardment of several days. The Japanese attacked the Allied fleet with 1,500 kamikaze (suicide) planes, and damaged several aircraft carriers and sank several destroyer escorts. An effort to attack with surface ships, led by the world's largest battleship, the 73,000-ton *Yamato*, was foiled by American carrier forces, which attacked the *Yamato* with over 300 planes and sank it with 15 torpedo hits, all on the same side to prevent counter-flooding, and 21 heavy bomb hits. They sank almost all the escorting vessels too, and the Japanese lost 3,700 sailors, to only 12 American airmen, on April 7.

Okinawa was defended by 120,000 Japanese, and the invaders landed 183,000 experienced and heavily armed shock troops. The battle continued to June 21, though it was generally a mopping-up operation for the last month. The Allies (95 percent Americans) suffered over 12,000 dead and 38,000 wounded. Japan achieved a 100 percent casualty rate, 113,000 dead and 7,000 wounded. No able-bodied Japanese were captured. There were more than 100,000 civilians killed, as the Japanese forces dispersed among the native (mainly Japanese) population. This bloody campaign confirmed that only atomic weapons, which would be tested in New Mexico a month after the end of the Okinawa campaign, could prevent a horrible bloodbath in the main islands of Japan.

In Germany, the U.S. Ninth Army, part of Bradley's Central Army Group, reached the Elbe on April 12. The Russians launched a drive on Berlin on April

13, and arrived in the eastern outskirts of the shattered German capital on April 24. The end of the Third Reich was at hand.

3. THE DEATH OF PRESIDENT ROOSEVELT; PRESIDENT TRUMAN AND THE POTSDAM CONFERENCE

Franklin Delano Roosevelt died of a cerebral hemorrhage at his winter home at Warm Springs, Georgia, on April 12. He was only 63. Vice President Harry S. Truman was sworn in as president several hours later. Winston Churchill spoke nothing but the truth when he said in his parliamentary eulogy on April 17: "In the days of peace, he had broadened the foundation of American life and union. In war he had raised the strength, might, and glory of the Great Republic to a height never attained by any nation in history. . . . All this was no more than worldly power and grandeur had it not been that the causes of human freedom and social justice, to which so much of his life had been given, added a luster [to him and his achievements] which will long be discernible among men. . . . In Franklin Roosevelt there has died the greatest American friend we have ever known, and the greatest champion of freedom who has ever brought help and comfort from the New World to the Old."

Roosevelt had infused an economically and psychologically depressed nation with his own vitality, had led it with consummate talent and astuteness, step by step, to overwhelming economic, military, moral, and popular cultural preeminence in the world, and to the brink of victory over every foreign and domestic enemy. He was exhausted in his fourth term, and was thinking of retiring just before he died, but President Roosevelt had made it America's world to lead, a world largely safe for democracy, at last, as long as the United States was involved in it. He would have been proud that he headed the official list of America's war dead on April 13, as commander-in-chief of the mighty and everywhere victorious armed forces of the United States.

For some days, Churchill had been bombarding Roosevelt with messages urging him to send the U.S. Ninth Army on to Berlin, blissfully oblivious of the European Advisory Commission agreement on occupation zones in Germany, which his government had proposed. He continued this campaign with Truman, who had never been informed by Roosevelt about anything, and had to make decisions of historic and global importance in haste. Fortunately, the new president was a man of courage, sound judgment, and a decisive temperament. He referred Churchill's importuning to Marshall, who consulted Eisenhower, although it was a strategic decision of national foreign and security policy, not a properly military matter. Eisenhower said that he would of course carry out any orders he received, but that he understood the United States was bound by the EAC zones, and did not personally see why he should sacrifice the lives of American, British, Canadian, and French soldiers to take territory that would then be handed back to the Russians.

It is possible that had Eisenhower known that Stalin was already violating the Yalta agreements and his spheres-of-influence agreement with Churchill, and snuffing out any independence in the territories occupied by the Red Army, and had he known of the imminent testing of atomic weapons, he might have given a different opinion. But the opinion he did give was the view of the Joint Chiefs (Marshall, King, Arnold of the Army Air Force, and Leahy), as they didn't want to alienate the Russians unless they knew the atomic bomb would work and that they would not need the Russians to take up to half of the million casualties anticipated in subduing Japan. Taking Berlin and holding it would have been an act of brinkmanship, and Stalin had three times as big an army as Eisenhower. American and British domestic opinion would not have accepted a show-down confrontation with Stalin, whom they had been conditioned by the successes of the Red Army and the apparently satisfactory meetings at Tehran and Yalta to regard positively, if warily. Roosevelt needed the United Nations established and the United States firmly installed in it, while Allied unity was intact, so that he could complete the rout of the isolationists and sell his argument to his countrymen that the world was no longer as sinister a place as it had been, and that American involvement in the world was necessary to keep it so.

Roosevelt had already put on hold the $6.5 billion economic aid package he had dangled before Stalin, pending Soviet compliance with the Yalta Declarations on Poland and on Liberated Europe. And the permanent demilitarization of Germany, which even without Berlin would be 75 percent in the hands of the West, thus could be easily reversed and Germany put back on its feet and tied in with de Gaulle's France, Churchill's Britain, a post-Fascist, non-communist Italy, even Franco's Spain, and the always Russophobic Turks as, with American assistance, a counterweight to Russia—an American-led and infinitely more powerful revival of the German and Japanese Anti-Comintern Pact.

As the Reich was overrun, death camps were liberated and the proportions of Nazi infamies—12 million people murdered in the camps, half of them Jews—horrified the world. Eisenhower ordered that all the camps liberated in the West be filmed, that the world not be inherited by Holocaust-deniers. He wrote that the most moving experience of his life was when he visited the Buchenwald death camp and human skeletons, seeing his five-star insignia as supreme commander of the Allied armies, bravely saluted him. (He came to attention and crisply returned the salute.)

Trying to escape Italy in a German army truck, wearing a German army uniform, Mussolini, whom the Roman crowds had cheered with adulation for nearly 20 year, was apprehended by partisans and shot with his companion, Clara Petacci on April 28. Their corpses were hoisted, upside down, in a Milan square, and mutilated and desecrated by a mob. Hitler, taking note of the Duce's inelegant end, remained in his bunker in Berlin until the Russians were almost overhead, and having ordered that his corpse and that of his just-married wife, Eva Braun, be burned, committed suicide with a handgun on April 30. Most of the rest of the Nazi leadership committed suicide, except for Ribbentrop, who was executed for war crimes, along with a number of others after the Nuremberg trials, which had been envisioned at the Potsdam Conference. Grand Admiral Karl Doenitz was designated by Hitler in his will as his heir, and set up a government in Flensburg, near the Danish border. They held cabinet meetings for a few days, in which the ministers for policy areas that were now completely esoteric, such as agriculture, spoke as if there were still anything left to govern. Doenitz's only interest was to permit as many as possible of his fellow German servicemen to surrender to the Western Allies, and he ordered all units to surrender on May 8. The European war was over.

If it was going to be necessary to turn American opinion against Russia, it would take a little while for comprehensive demonization of the Kremlin and its chief occupant, and a grievance more worrisome to Americans than the treatment of former pro-fascist dictatorships like Romania and Hungary, or the formerly corrupt and anti-Semitic dictatorship of Poland. Most of the criticism of the Yalta agreements is a chorus of otherwise discordant anti-American elements, echoed by anti-Roosevelt Americans. This frequently grotesque canard suited disgruntled British imperialists, anti-Anglo-Saxon Gaullists, liberal Western appeasers of Russia of the Brandt-Trudeau variety, Eastern Europeans claiming an American obligation to risk war for them, as the British and French had for Poland, and in the United States the oft-defeated Republicans and those who made a career in the fifties of peddling one version or another of the Red Scare.

It is generally reckoned, by Bohlen and others, that Roosevelt, because of his immense prestige in the world, and his unfaltering leadership of American opinion, would have succeeded more quickly than Truman did in stirring American opinion to resist and contain Russia. But Truman and his successors—initially the strategic team recruited by Roosevelt, including Marshall, Eisenhower, MacArthur, Acheson, Kennan, Bohlen, and others—did adopt and execute the containment strategy, which secured the ultimate completion of the World War II: victory in the Cold War and the defeat of international communism and the disintegration of the Soviet Union.

It must be recorded that Stalin's decision to initiate the Cold War by violating almost every clause of the Yalta agreements was, next to Japan's attack on Pearl Harbor (Chapter 11) and Wilhelm II's recourse to unrestricted submarine warfare in 1917 (Chapter 9), the most catastrophic strategic error of the twentieth century. If he had finessed the occupation of Eastern Europe, at least until American forces had departed Europe and he had the American aid package, and the Soviet Union, too, had atomic weapons; and if his successors had had the intelligence of the Chinese Communists, to abandon economic communism but retain authoritarianism, Russia could have been a durable rival to the United States, though certainly an underdog.

Considering where the poor world was gasping in the summer of 1940, with Germany, Japan, Italy, and France all in undemocratic hands and hostile to the British and the Americans, it was an astounding feat to bring all those countries into, or back into, the West as flourishing democratic allies, while Stalin, who took over 90 percent of the casualties for disposing of Hitler, gained only a fleeting domination of a poor and hostile patch of Eastern Europe. At the end of World War II, Roosevelt and Churchill played their cards well; the appalling errors were made by Stalin. The Soviet Union barely survived the Nazi-Soviet Pact; it would not survive the Cold War, which Stalin soon insouciantly began.

President Truman journeyed by ship to Europe to meet with Churchill and Stalin at Potsdam, near Berlin, in July 1945. In flying from Antwerp to Berlin, Truman was struck by the terrible devastation of Germany, with almost all roads, bridges, and towns smashed and most fields razed and scarred. Truman had allowed Stettinius to attend the organizing conference of the United Nations in San Francisco in late April and May, but eased him out as secretary of state in June and made him first U.S. ambassador to the United Nations. He was replaced as head of the State Department by James F. Byrnes, former civilian director of war mobilization and industry and, prior to that, United States senator from South Carolina and associate justice of the Supreme Court of the United States.

Truman and Churchill met for the first time on the morning of July 16, for two hours, and got on very well. Truman wrote that he was suspicious of Churchill's "soft soap" about how much he had liked Roosevelt and admired America, but considered the British leader "a most charming and very clever person."[3] Truman toured the shattered wreckage of Berlin, but declined to visit Hitler's bunker, as he

---

3. David McCullough, *Truman*, New York, Simon and Schuster, 1991, p. 412.

did not wish the Germans to think he was gloating in victory. Truman was some-what depressed by the horrible devastation of what had been, after Tokyo, London, and New York, the fourth-largest city in the world, though, as he said to Byrnes and Leahy, who accompanied him, the Germans "had brought it on themselves." While Truman was touring Berlin, as he learned that night, the atomic bomb had been successfully tested at Alamogordo, New Mexico, producing "a light not of this world." The 77-year-old war secretary, World War I artillery colonel Henry Stimson, personally delivered the coded top-secret message to Truman, as soon as it arrived. The implications of it were instantly clear to both doughty veterans of the Western Front of 1917 and 1918.

The next morning, Truman was sitting at his desk in the house allotted to him when he looked up to see Joseph Stalin at the doorway, with Molotov and the interpreter, Pavlov. Truman got up and approached, shook hands heartily, and later declared himself surprised that Stalin, at five feet, five inches, was "a little bit of a squirt." Truman was joined by Byrnes and Bohlen. After a taciturn start, the two leaders got on well. Stalin said he was sure Hitler had escaped to Spain or Argentina, and promised again to enter the war against Japan (which had asked Stalin through its ambassador in Moscow to broker a peace with the Allies) by August 15. Truman spontaneously invited Stalin and his party to stay for lunch, and it became quite convivial, Stalin warmly praising the California wine. Like Roosevelt, Churchill, and de Gaulle, Truman found Stalin courteous, equable, direct, "honest—but smart as hell." He concluded, "I can deal with Stalin."[4]

The first plenary session began later that day, with Truman accompanied, in addition to Byrnes, Leahy, and Bohlen, by the Stalin sycophant and former ambassador to Moscow Joseph Davies, a seriously unfortunate choice. (George Kennan judged Davies and Joseph Kennedy in London the two most disastrous appointments in the history of the U.S. diplomatic service.) As with Roosevelt, Truman was the only head of state present, and was elected chairman of the conference. Truman was well-prepared and started into a detailed agenda, quickly arriving at the point that the "obligations" under the Yalta Declarations on Poland and on Liberated Europe "have not been carried out." He called for the immediate inclusion of Italy in the United Nations. Churchill objected, invoked Roosevelt's reference to Mussolini's "stab in the back," and pointed out that his country had been fighting the Italians for two years before the Americans arrived in Africa.

Truman responded to Churchill's complaints of moving too quickly with a self-effacing statement of reverence for Roosevelt and determination to maintain the good

---

4.   McCullough, *op. cit.*, p. 419.

relationship with America's allies, and this theme was taken up by Churchill and Stalin. The first session showed the American and Soviet leaders to be businesslike and incisive, where Churchill, who had been rather discursive, loved conferences as only a parliamentarian could and as Truman and Stalin, who were executives and not legislators (though Truman had been a senator for 10 years, he had not been a particularly active debater), could not. Churchill and Stalin objected to China having anything to do with the peace of Europe, and Stalin ominously said he wanted assurance of adequate reparations from Germany, and wanted to discuss the future of Poland, as well as three subjects that had not been raised in previous conferences: taking half of what was left of the German navy, Russia's share of colonial trusteeships, and the status of Franco's Spain. (The last two were completely out of the question, and came as bolts from the blue. Giving Stalin a couple of African colonial trusteeships might have made it more difficult for the postwar communists to romance what became the Third World.)

On July 18, Truman had a very cordial meeting with Churchill, after which Churchill wrote that the new president "seems a man of exceptional character." Truman went on to a second lunch with Stalin, replete with Russian toasts, and Stalin told Truman of the Japanese peace overture (of which the Americans were, by intercepts and decryptions, already aware, but Truman was impressed by Stalin's openness). But at the session later that day, Stalin bluntly said, "We cannot get away from the results of the war." He was referring to the advance of the Red Army. Churchill made both Truman and Stalin impatient by his loquacity on the subjects of Poland and Germany. Truman was not prepared to discuss dividing up what little was left of the German navy until Japan had been defeated, and he was not prepared to talk about Spain, saying that he had no affinity for Franco but that he didn't want to take part in another war in Spain. "There have been enough wars in Europe."[5] It had not been a good session, but Truman held a very jaunty party that evening for the other leaders.

Truman met with Eisenhower and Bradley. Eisenhower was opposed to continuing to try to entice the Russians into the war against Japan, although he realized they would enter it as soon as they could, whatever the U.S. wanted, to gain territory. Eisenhower also opposed using the atomic bomb, for moral reasons, as he thought Japan already defeated. Bradley made no recommendation. Truman abruptly offered to help elect Eisenhower president. The general declined interest. Full reports now arrived of the power of the atomic bomb. Truman sent Stimson

---

5.   McCullough, *op. cit.*, p. 427.

to tell Churchill, who called it "the Second Coming in Wrath."[6] At the July 21 session, Stalin asked diplomatic recognition for Romania, Bulgaria, and Finland, and Truman replied that "We will not recognize these governments until they are set up on a satisfactory basis." Truman demanded that the severance of a chunk of Germany to Poland, as had been agreed at Tehran, but that was part of the Russian occupation zone under the EAC agreement, did not justify Soviet violation of the Yalta Declaration on Poland, and should be taken into account in any thought of reparations. His strong stance, prompted in part by the atomic news, greatly pleased and impressed Churchill.

Truman met with Churchill and the senior military figures of both countries on July 24, and it was agreed that the atomic bomb would be dropped within two weeks, and that the likeliest target was Hiroshima, the southern headquarters for Japan's home defense forces. The plenary session that day was difficult and robust. Churchill and Truman demanded recognition of Italy but declined to recognize Romania, Hungary, or Bulgaria until, as Truman put it, "the satellite governments are reorganized along democratic lines as agreed at Yalta." Stalin replied, crystallizing the problem, "If a government is not fascist, it is democratic." Churchill was having none of it and contrasted Italy, a free society with a free press, with Romania, where the British embassy was like a prison. "All fairy tales," said Stalin. Churchill demurred. Truman strongly supported Churchill, who expressed his gratitude to his inner circle.[7]

At the end of the plenary session on July 24, Truman walked around the conference table and said to Stalin and Pavlov that the U.S. "had a new weapon of unusual destructive force." Stalin said he hoped it would be used with good effect on the Japanese. Churchill, Bohlen, and other senior Western delegates watched closely and, like Truman, were surprised that Stalin was indifferent and not at all curious, and did not raise the matter again in the conference. Already, in fact, Stalin knew what was afoot from his espionage network, especially from the scientist Klaus Fuchs, who was in New Mexico and feeding vital information to the Soviet Union's nuclear program. That evening, Stalin ordered acceleration of the Soviet Union's own nuclear program.[8]

Churchill left the conference on July 25, to receive the results of the British general election, taking Eden and Labour Party leader Clement Attlee (who made no impression on Stalin or Truman and went through the fierce July heat in a

6. McCullough, *op. cit.*, p. 432.
7. Ibid. p. 445.
8. Ibid. p. 443.

three-piece wool suit). Contrary to expectations, but not to Roosevelt's warning at Tehran nor Churchill's own forebodings at the end, Churchill was defeated. Stalin said, "Democracy must be a wretched system to replace a great man like Churchill with someone like Attlee." Charles de Gaulle wrote of Churchill that he had "lost neither his glory not his popularity thereby; merely the adherence he had won as guide and symbol of the nation in peril. His nature, identified with a magnificent enterprise, his countenance, etched by the fires and frosts of great events, were no longer adequate to the era of mediocrity."

The conference resumed, but nothing was accomplished. Truman had pushed a proposal for the opening of all seas, oceans, rivers, canals, and other waterways, but Stalin was opposed. Truman hoped that the next meeting would be in Washington. Stalin replied, in Russian, "God willing," a rare invocation of the deity by the unsuccessful former seminary student. It was all very cordial, but Truman, though he had liked Stalin, thought him "that little son of a bitch," and Stalin thought Truman "worthless."[9] They were not to meet again either. Truman had a very pleasant meeting in Plymouth harbor on his way home with King George VI, a sensible, unpretentious, and very popular monarch. Neither man sought or expected the great offices they held, but both acquitted them valiantly. The Cold War was about to break out, as soon as the existing war ended.

4. THE BEGINNINGS OF THE COLD WAR

There was a race between the United States dropping the atomic bomb on Japan and the Soviet declaration of war on Japan, as the American military and civilian leaders, though certain Stalin would seize what had been conceded to him in the Far East at Yalta, no longer wished any Soviet presence in Japan. The atomic bomb was dropped on Hiroshima on August 6, one week after Japan rejected the Potsdam Conference's demand for Japan's surrender. The Soviet Union declared war on Japan on August 8, and invaded Manchuria with almost a million men that Stalin had hastily moved back to the Far East after the surrender of Germany. Approximately 100,000 people were killed and 60,000 injured at Hiroshima, yet the Japanese were still not prepared to throw in the towel, so the United States dropped a second atomic bomb on the naval port of Nagasaki, killing about 70,000 and injuring slightly fewer people than three days before, but leveling the city.

The next day, at the conclusion of what must rank as the most catastrophic week in the military history of any country, following Emperor Hirohito's address to the nation stating that "Events have not gone altogether as we would have wished"

---

9.   McCullough, *op. cit.*, p. 452.

and asking his subjects to "think the unthinkable and endure the unendurable," Japan accepted to surrender unconditionally as long as the emperor retained the Chrysanthemum Throne. The United States accepted the Japanese surrender on August 14, and did so formally on Nimitz's flagship, the battleship USS *Missouri*, in Tokyo Bay on September 2. General Douglas MacArthur had been appointed military governor of Japan, and accepted the Japanese surrender on behalf of the United Nations. He subsequently informed the Russian representative that he would arrest and imprison any Soviet personnel whose presence in Japan he had not authorized, thus securing, with Germany, France, and Italy, the last great strategic national prize of the war for the West.

World War II was over. The United States had suffered 322,000 dead and 700,000 wounded, in armed forces of about 13 million. Approximately 70 million people had died as a result of the war, about 24 million military dead, including over five million prisoners of war, and 46 million civilians. Among the principal combatants, the Soviet Union suffered 9.5 million military deaths and 14 million civilian; China 3.5 million military and 12 million civilian; Germany 5.5 million military and two million civilian; Japan 2.1 million military and 750,000 civilian; Poland 5.5 million civilian; and there were more or less 500,000 combined military and civilian deaths each in the United Kingdom, France, and Italy. The total number of wounded or victims of war-related illnesses must have been well over 100 million people. The United States emerged from the war as the possessor of half the entire economic product of the world and of a nuclear monopoly, as the founder of the United Nations, and as by far the most powerful and esteemed nationality in the world by almost any measurement. Its strategic management, combining conventional force, diplomatic ingenuity, and Wilsonian moral high-mindedness, had been almost faultless, from Roosevelt's Quarantine speech in 1937 through Potsdam.

Truman ended Lend-Lease on August 21; $50.6 billion of assistance had been dispensed, and $7.8 billion returned. A further 50-year loan of $3.7 billion at 2 percent was granted to Great Britain, but the Soviet account, $11.1 billion advanced and $2.2 billion back in reciprocal payments, was never settled. Given the scale of Soviet combat deaths, military and civilian, and the damage the Soviet armed forces did to Germany, the United States could never be accused of making a bad bargain.[10] Not only did the Russians take over 23 million dead, it is unlikely

---

10.   In the course of the war, the U.S. provided the USSR with 385,833 trucks, 51,503 jeeps, 7,056 tanks, 5,071 tractors, 1,981 locomotives, 11,158 freight cars, 14,834 airplanes, 2,670,000 tons of petroleum products, and each Soviet soldier more than "one-half pound of fairly concentrated food per day." Vincent

that any Western democracy could have endured losses on anything like such a scale and continued in the war. Nearly 15 percent of the entire population was killed, an even larger percentage wounded, and more than three-quarters of the populated area of the country was destroyed. The continental United States, of course, was untouched, except for the ineffectual shelling of a couple of Pacific coast lighthouses.

The year ebbed away with the heavy Stalinist tyranny bearing down ever more stiflingly on Eastern Europe. The first of the promised meetings of the Council of Ministers was held at London from September 11 to October 2, and failed to generate peace treaties with Italy, Bulgaria, Hungary, and Romania, largely because Molotov disputed the right of the Chinese and the French to be present. The second meeting of the Council was in Moscow from December 16 to 26. There was a wide-ranging discussion, but all decisions were deferred to a peace conference of the 21 Allied nations.

General Marshall retired from the army in December, and after only six days to enjoy his retirement, Truman telephoned him at home and asked him to become special ambassador to China to try to resolve the Chinese Civil War between Chiang Kai-shek's Nationalists and Mao Tse-tung's Communists. Marshall replaced Hoover's war secretary, Patrick Hurley, who was one of the many Republicans Roosevelt had recruited into his government. Hurley was a blustering and belligerent old bull moose, who announced his retirement as ambassador in a speech to the National Press Club, an hour after he had told Truman that everything was fine and that he would be returning soon to China in his official capacity.

The Paris Peace Conference was held in three stages, from July to October 1946. The principal Allies agreed on the peace treaties, but the whole process broke down over the Russian objection to anything much more than an observer role for the smaller Allied countries. Finally, in New York in November and December 1946, Secretary of State Byrnes reached agreement with Molotov on the peace treaties that had long been under discussion. All the former Axis countries (Italy, Romania, Hungary, Bulgaria, and Finland) paid reparations to the Soviet Union and some other countries, and Hungary, Romania, and Finland conceded some territory to Russia. Italy yielded the Dodecanese Islands to Greece, and Fiume and the Adriatic coast east of Trieste to Yugoslavia; Italy even paid reparations to Ethiopia and Albania, as well as to Russia, Greece, and Yugoslavia. Libya's independence was recognized.

J. Esposito, editor, *West Point Atlas of American Wars*, New York, Praeger, 1959, vol. 2, text accompanying map 41.

On February 9, 1946, Stalin, who gave a real public speech only once every two or three years, declared publicly that communism and capitalism were incompatible and that another world war was certain. He ordered a tripling of national defense production, and predicted another capitalist depression in the fifties and a resumption of armed conflict then. It was an astonishingly inept and ill-considered address. Even had his predictions of the travails of capitalism been correct, it is not clear what would have motivated Stalin to volunteer his militant hostility in this way. Subtle and clever though he was, he seemed not to realize how much stronger he would have been if he had succeeded in anesthetizing the United States, which wanted nothing more than to withdraw from Europe, disarm, and get back to civilian and semi-isolated existence. Byrnes said on February 28 that the United States "could not stand alone if force or the threat of force is used contrary to the purposes and principles" of the charter of the United Nations. The United States was moving deftly to line up independent world opinion behind a defensive stance opposite Soviet threats and aggression. The Soviet Union had not withdrawn from Manchuria or from northern Iran, which at this point seemed in the same category of wrongfully occupied territories as the Eastern European states whose independence, sovereignty, and free democratic elections Stalin had co-guaranteed at Yalta.

On March 6, 1946, Churchill, having been invited by Truman himself, and accompanied by him in Roosevelt's old armored railway car, the *Ferdinand Magellan*, and introduced by the president, spoke at Westminster College in Fulton, Missouri. He wrote his speech carefully and shared it in advance with Truman and his entourage. The president approved it entirely. Churchill said that he admired the Russians and personally liked Stalin, but that "From Stettin in the Baltic to Trieste in the Adriatic, an iron curtain has descended on Europe. Warsaw, Berlin, Prague, Vienna, Budapest, Belgrade, Bucharest, and Sofia, all these famous cities and the populations around them lie in what I must call the Soviet sphere, and all are subject in one form or another, not only to Soviet influence but in a very high and, in many cases, increasing measure, to control from Moscow." He explained that the Soviets did not want war, but victory without war. There was nothing they respected so much as strength and nothing they so despised as weakness, and what was needed was a union of the Western democracies, especially the United States and the United Kingdom. Truman, sitting beside him, smiled appreciatively and frequently applauded.

The immediate reaction in the country was negative, the noted pundit Walter Lippmann calling it "an almost catastrophic blunder." Truman then, uncharacteristically, waffled and told Henry Wallace, now the secretary of commerce (a post for which he had no qualifications and from which Truman shortly fired him, for his pro-Soviet views, as he had fired long-serving interior secretary and one of the leading figures of the New Deal Harold Ickes for impugning his integrity and Treasury secretary Morgenthau for debating his decisions), that Churchill had "put me on the spot." He told the press he had "no comment" on the speech and wrote Stalin offering to send the battleship *Missouri* to pick him up and bring him to America and accompany him to the same campus to speak his mind. Stalin declined. This was not the Truman known to history and the persona he cultivated as fearless, pugnacious, and courageous, generally a fair description. Churchill, as in warning the world about Hitler 10 years before, was unerringly accurate. The phrase "iron curtain" entered into the language and into history. He was strongly supported from the start by Harriman, Leahy, Acheson, and Secretary of the Navy James V. Forrestal. These people all regarded Byrnes as too accommodating of the Russians.

In February, George F. Kennan wrote what became known as "the long telegram" from the embassy in Moscow, 8,000 words on the irreconcilability of the U.S. and the USSR, stating that the Russians were neurotically suffused with feelings of inferiority, and were, under the Communists, "committed fanatically" to the impossibility of "peaceful coexistence," and to a desire to disrupt the domestic tranquility and destroy the international standing and credibility of the United States. He believed that the Communists were just the latest of a long line of Russian regimes that would force the country to pay for an immense military power beyond the means of Russia to support, to provide security for their "internally weak regimes."

In May 1946, Truman had to deal with a revolt by the labor leadership that had long been a pillar of the Democratic Party, when strikes in the railway and coal industries broke out. Truman tried hard to broker agreements, but eventually moved to draft the rail workers into the army, whereupon the two-day-old strike collapsed, and two days later the coal miners and management settled. The Republicans gained control of the Congress for the first time since 1928, in November 1946, as the country was having trouble adjusting to the change from the magnificently confident and mellifluous Roosevelt to the unpretentious and direct but slightly underwhelming Truman. (Among the congressmen elected for the first time in 1946 were future presidents John F. Kennedy, Richard M. Nixon, and Gerald R. Ford.)

Byrnes, feeling out of step with the increasing hard line of the administration, resigned, and was replaced on January 21, 1947, by General George C. Marshall, a man of such prestige that his appointment restored some of the diminished standing of the administration. Marshall asked Acheson to remain as his under secretary of state, which Acheson did, and the two made one of the greatest combinations in the history of American foreign policy.

Marshall's mission to China had not been a success. The Communists were steadily gaining strength, the Nationalist government was inept and incompetent, and Marshall's brokering of a cease-fire and a brief coalition government was unwittingly modestly helpful to the Communists. It was difficult to warm to the Communists, who were full of anti-American venom, yet it was impossible to have any faith in Chiang Kai-shek, who was, as Stilwell had described him at Quebec and Cairo in 1943, a treacherous, cowardly, double-dealing scoundrel, trying to play the Japanese, Americans, and Communists off against each other.

On February 21, 1947, Prime Minister Attlee sent Washington a message that Britain could no longer afford to maintain the defense of Greece, and that the following month it would withdraw the 40,000 troops that had been deployed to prevent a communist victory in the civil war that Stalin had pledged, in the meeting with Churchill in October 1944, to avoid by conceding Britain 90 percent of the influence in that country. On March 12, Truman addressed an emergency session of Congress and asked for $400 million in aid to Greece and Turkey, and warned that failure to act decisively and at once would imperil Europe, the Middle East, and all of Asia. He enunciated what became known as the Truman Doctrine, of containing Soviet expansion by assisting countries that were resisting its aggression, whether overt or by subversion.

On April 9, with the assistance of prominent Republican senator Arthur Vandenberg, David E. Lilienthal was confirmed as head of the Atomic Energy Commission, despite claims from Republican leaders, including Robert A. Taft and John Bricker, that Lilienthal was a communist, an unfounded allegation. And on April 22 and May 9 the Senate and the House of Representatives passed overwhelmingly the bills for assistance to Greece and Turkey. Truman had persuaded America to begin the preemptive rescue of Europe from the menace of Soviet Communism.

In response to the temper of the times and the Red Scare that was being whipped up by the Republicans, egged on by J. Edgar Hoover, now completing his first quarter-century as director of the FBI, Truman approved (reluctantly) a screening of federal employees. The Civil Service Commission examined the files, over the next four years, of three million government employees, and the FBI investigated 14,000. A total of 212 were dismissed as being of questionable loyalty. No espionage was uncovered and no one was indicted. It was, as Truman famously said, a "red herring," but it was an integral part of rousing America from its customary political torpor and focusing public opinion on the Soviet threat, which was a fiction within America except for some scientific espionage, but very real almost everywhere else. (One of the reasons Truman had moved Stettinius out as secretary of state so quickly was that he had returned unexamined a Soviet code book that detailed that country's espionage activities in the U.S.)

5. SAVING WESTERN EUROPE

At the Moscow foreign ministers' conference in March and April 1947, Marshall and Bevin failed to make any progress with Molotov over Germany, as the Soviets wanted a centralized, jointly managed Germany from which the Soviet Union would extract $10 billion in reparations. Beyond that, Marshall concluded, they wanted as much chaos and misery as possible in Western Europe, in the hope of the victory of local Communist parties. Molotov, i.e., Stalin, particularly wished to encourage a prolonged state of poverty and dislocation in Germany. Marshall decided in the light of his visit with Stalin and his weeks of fruitless discussion with Molotov, whom he knew to be acting under Stalin's strict orders, that he had been mistaken in his view, developed at Tehran and Yalta and Potsdam, that Stalin could be negotiated with successfully. Marshall had received as he left Washington a State Department memo warning that economic conditions in Europe were much worse than he had feared. Stops at Berlin and Paris on the way home shocked him, both visually and from descriptions he received from resident American experts. He spoke to the nation on April 28, and said, "The patient is sinking while the doctors deliberate." He told Kennan to assemble a meeting of State Department specialists at once, and prepare a report.

Truman had been considering economic assistance for some time and on June 5, Marshall, having cleared it with Truman first, delivered a convocation address at Harvard University, which had largely been written by Bohlen, based on Kennan's report. Marshall was careful to avoid any polemics, and said, "Our policy is not directed against any country or doctrine, but against hunger, poverty, desperation, and chaos. Its purpose should be the revival of a working economy in the world so as to permit the emergence of political and social conditions in which free institutions can exist." He declined any ambition "to draw up unilaterally a program designed to place Europe on its feet economically. That is the business of the Europeans." Marshall was calling on the Europeans to work out their own needs with U.S. assistance, and he was implicitly leaving it open for the Soviets to accept such aid, on their own behalf and for their satellites. Marshall said that "the whole world's future hangs on proper judgment, hangs on the realization by the American people of what can best be done, or what must be done."

Immense controversy arose in the United States and corresponding hopefulness in Europe; Truman started a challenging selling job in the Congress, and a conference was swiftly organized in Paris with the prospective recipients. Stalin had told Molotov to object to any pooling of capital that implied Russian resources being spent in Western Europe, and also to object to the American requirement for a detailed accounting of how American taxpayers' money was being spent. On this unhopeful note, Molotov stormed out of the conference, denouncing what was officially called the European Recovery Program as a "vicious American scheme for using dollars to buy" influence in Europe. Under pressure from Moscow, all the satellite countries would decline to participate, including Czechoslovakia, which, having not been covered by any of the wartime or postwar conferences, had fallen under a communist-dominated coalition. It remains a mystery that normally loquacious memoirists among the Western leaders, including Churchill, Eisenhower, and Truman, skirted around without touching how the Czechs, at least, fell between the cracks. (Slovakia was certain to be occupied by the Red Army.)

This was another disastrous blunder by Stalin; in pulling out and attacking the U.S. plan, he assured its passage by the Republican-led Congress and painted Soviet Communism as a retrograde, dictatorial empire of brute force and economic stagnation, against the American-led forces of democracy and economic growth. When the international political game evolved from hurling millions of soldiers westward while pursuing chicanery in international conferences and subversion, to the rights and welfare of the war-weary masses of the world, Stalin's heavy-handed treachery and authoritarianism were exposed and uncompetitive, especially against the collective efforts of the brilliant strategic team that Roosevelt had assembled and that flowered under an equally courageous but less suave and domineering president. The Marshall Plan (Truman typically refused to take the credit for it), as it was soon known, was as brilliant and imaginative a policy as Lend-Lease had been.

It was indicative of the times that the Congress overrode Truman's veto of the Taft-Hartley Act, which banned the closed shop and political contributions from unions, required audits of unions and anti-communist loyalty oaths from union leaders, and made unions liable for breaches of contract. On July 25, 1947, the Congress did pass Truman's comprehensive National Security Act, setting up the Air Force as an independent service, uniting the War and Navy Departments into the Department of Defense, setting up the National Security Council, and enhancing the status of the Central Intelligence Agency. (Navy secretary James V. Forrestal was the first secretary of defense.)

On September 18, 1947, Andrei Vishinsky, Soviet deputy foreign minister, denounced the U.S. government as "warmongers" in the United Nations General Assembly, and on October 5, Moscow announced the creation of the Cominform, successor to the Comintern (Communist International) that Stalin had theoretically discontinued in 1943 as a sop to Roosevelt and Churchill. On November 29, the United States and the Soviet Union pushed through the United Nations a resolution approving the partition of the Palestine Mandate into predominantly Jewish and Arab areas. Britain announced it would withdraw its 50,000 soldiers from Palestine within six months, and pressures immediately arose within and on the United States in particular for and against the creation of a Jewish state. Marshall and Forrestal were strongly opposed, because of the animosity it would cause in the Arab world, and Forrestal emphasized that the United States did not have the military personnel to replace the British in the area, which the Pentagon estimated would require 100,000 men, more than three times what was available.

On February 25, 1948, a coup d'état in Prague installed the Communists and on March 10, Jan Masaryk, the Czech foreign minister, who had been through the Munich betrayal 10 years before, apparently committed suicide, though rumors have abounded ever since that he was murdered by the Communists, and successive subsequent investigations have come to different conclusions. The coup and Masaryk's death, however it happened, dramatized the steadily rising tension in Europe. On March 17, Truman addressed a joint session of Congress, cited the Soviet Union as a menace to peace which sought the conquest of all Europe, and asked for immediate passage of the Marshall Plan and restoration of the military draft.

The Italian election of April 18 was an unprecedented slanging match between the Christian Democrats led by Alcide De Gasperi and the Communist-dominated Popular Front led by Palmiro Togliatti. There was considerable violence in northern Italy and the Christian Democrats accused the Communists of seeking to seize the nation's children and turn them into witnesses against their parents in criminal proceedings. The two leading parties were heavily funded by the CIA and the Soviet Union, and Pope Pius XII intervened decisively, implying that a vote for the Popular Front was an act of self-excommunication. ("When you cast your ballot, God sees you; Stalin doesn't" was the popular formulation.) It was a clear victory for the Christian Democrats, 48.5 percent to 31 percent, and the Socialist Party soon flaked off the coalition with the Communists.

On May 14, the United States recognized the new state of Israel as soon as it was proclaimed, after a rending struggle within the government in which General Marshall said he would vote against Truman in the next election if he went ahead with it. Marshall never again spoke to Clark Clifford, a champion of Israel, Truman's chief assistant and a future secretary of defense, and one of Washington's greatest power brokers for 50 years.

On June 11, 1948, Republican senator Arthur Vandenberg of Michigan presented and had adopted a resolution authorizing military alliances with regional collective-security groups, in furtherance of the United Nations Charter. On June 23, the Western Allied Powers in Berlin enacted currency reforms in West Berlin, contrary to the Soviet ambition to circulate Russian currency throughout the city. The next day Stalin abruptly closed the land access from West Germany to West Berlin. The United States, with full British and French cooperation, began the air supply of the 2.1 million residents of West Berlin. It was well understood that East bloc interception of Western aircraft would be considered an act of war. On June 28, Truman ostentatiously sent two squadrons of B-29s to Germany, which were assumed to be there to execute an atomic attack on Russia if provoked. (This was a ruse, as the aircraft were not equipped to carry atomic bombs, but the Russians never discovered that.)

This was another disastrous error by Stalin, seeming to break his undertakings, threaten war, and strangle the prostrate city of Berlin, in which there were no military targets. And he failed; he was clearly afraid of the power of the United States, and after 321 days, he abandoned the effort and reopened land access to West Berlin from West Germany. The United States had ceased its industrial dismantling of Germany in May 1946, as that policy had never been anything but a sop to Stalin anyway, and henceforth the objective in Germany was to resurrect it as a powerful, democratic ally in the constellation of states determined, under American leadership, to keep the Russians out of Western Europe. The British and American occupation zones were merged administratively on December 2, 1946. And the coordinated policy was the swiftest possible resuscitation of Germany as a democratic, stable, industrial power.

6. THE PEOPLE'S TRIUMPH

As the Democratic convention neared, there was great disillusionment with Truman. He had spoken in favor of civil rights for African Americans, which seriously rattled the South, and his hard-line Cold War stance had driven off Henry Wallace and the left; Wallace had publicly criticized Truman and was promptly fired. There was a stampede to draft Eisenhower, who had retired as army chief of staff and was now president of Columbia University. Eisenhower was not interested, but Roosevelt's ne'er-do-well sons and liberals Claude Pepper of Florida, Chester Bowles of Connecticut, and Hubert Humphrey, mayor of Minneapolis; Auto Workers' leader Walter Reuther; southerners Senator John Sparkman and South Carolina governor Strom Thurmond; and bosses Jake Arvey of Chicago, Mayor William O'Dwyer of New York, and Frank Hague of New Jersey all started screaming for Eisenhower (whom none of them knew, and who had never been a Democrat). Truman was nominated anyway, with Senate Majority Leader Alben W. Barkley of Kentucky for vice president, after midnight at Philadelphia on July 15. The event was celebrated by the release of a large number of long-cooped, agitated, and incontinent pigeons, portrayed as doves of peace, including the two that landed on former (and future) Speaker Sam Rayburn's glabrous head.[11] It was generally assumed that the Republican nominees, Governor Thomas E. Dewey of New York and Governor Earl Warren of California, would win easily. Humphrey had moved to pass a pro–civil rights resolution, and when Truman finally addressed the convention, he was direct, tough, and feisty, and portrayed the campaign as the underdog, the working people, the small farmer, against the slickers, the privileged in their country clubs, and the ancient enemies of everything he and Roosevelt had done to save the country, in the last 15 years, from the Republicans' Depression and isolationism. It was an instant reinvigoration, and he ran a very spirited campaign.

Two days later, the "Dixiecrats," as they called themselves, southern segregationists, nominated Thurmond for president and Governor Fielding Wright of Mississippi for vice president, and two weeks later, in the same hall in Philadelphia where the Republicans and the Democrats had met, the Progressive Citizens of America, in the biggest convention of all, nominated Henry Wallace for president, and the "Singing Cowboy" of Idaho, Senator Glen H. Taylor ("Oh Give Me a Home By the Capital Dome"), for vice president. Wallace refused to repudiate his communist support, and his platform opposed the Marshall Plan, the Truman Doctrine, and the draft, and advocated unilateral nuclear disarmament. Acidulous commentators H.L. Mencken and Dorothy Parker, and even perennial Socialist candidate Norman Thomas, denounced Wallace as a communist dupe. His candidacy effectively sank at the outset.

Truman embarked on his historic, 22,000-mile "whistle-stop tour" of the country in Roosevelt's well-traveled railway car, the *Ferdinand Magellan*, on September 17. The polls were unfavorable, but the reception, everywhere in the country, was very positive. Everywhere he sounded the theme of the dauntless underdog, and the Dewey campaign responded with torpid overconfidence. The president generally began: "I'm Harry Truman, I work for the government, and I'm trying to keep my job." The crowds grew and called out "Give 'em hell, Harry," and he did. He was greeted by over a million people in New York on October 29. Closing polls showed Truman had narrowed Dewey's lead to five

---

11. McCullough, *op. cit.*, p. 642.

points, and the commentariat—Alistair Cooke, Walter Lippmann, Drew Pearson, Marquis Childs, the Alsops, and H.V. Kaltenborn—were, as usual, all chanting the conventional wisdom: that Truman would lose badly.

The 1948 election is generally reckoned the greatest electoral upset in American history: Truman took 24.2 million votes, 49.6 percent of the total, and 303 electoral votes, to Dewey's 21.99 million votes, 45.1 percent of the total, and 189 electoral votes, to Thurmond's 1.18 million votes, 2.4 percent of the vote, and 39 electoral votes, and Wallace's 1.16 million votes, 2.4 percent, and no electoral votes. Truman won Ohio, Illinois, and California by a total of just 57,000 votes, and if any two of those states had gone to Dewey, Thurmond could have forced the vote to the House of Representatives (where the Democrats were again in control and Rayburn assumedly could have saved the election for Truman). General Marshall, who with uncharacteristic pique had threatened not to vote for Truman over his support of Israel, wrote him: "You have put over the greatest one-man fight in American history." This was almost certainly true and the world had now to take note of a determined, sage, and very considerable reelected president. Harry Truman was assured of a challenging second term, but probably would not have wished it any other way.

7. THE FALL OF CHINA

The new term opened very smoothly. General George C. Marshall, facing a kidney operation, retired, and was replaced as secretary of state by the very experienced and capable Dean G. Acheson. It was clear that Truman had outwitted Stalin with the Berlin airlift, which, when the blockade was lifted on May 12, 1949, had been broken by nearly 278,000 flights bearing 2.33 million tons of supplies. On April 4, what became the most successful alliance in world history, the North Atlantic Treaty Organization (NATO), was launched. The United States, Canada, Britain, France, Italy, Belgium, the Netherlands, Luxembourg, Denmark, Iceland, Portugal, and Norway initially joined in a pact that an attack upon one was an attack upon all. The subsequent clause left some liberty about what steps would be taken by each member in response to such attack, but it was effectively, a United States military guarantee for the other countries. In 1952, Greece and Turkey would join, and in 1955, the fate that Stalin had feared, West Germany would join. Many other countries followed.

As time passed, the United States would station 300,000 men of their armed forces in Western Europe, and the revival of Western European prosperity and purposefulness would steadily build a formidable defense against any assault from the Red Army, backed by the entire worldwide arsenal of the United States, nuclear and conventional. Roosevelt's policy of American engagement in Europe and the Far East, and the containment policy originally envisioned as the response to Soviet bad faith by George Kennan, took shape and gained strength, and the domestic Communist parties in Western Europe failed to dislodge the democratic parties.

On the same day the Berlin blockade was lifted, May 12, the Allied powers recognized the sovereign state of the Federal Republic of Germany (West Germany), with its capital on the Rhine, at Bonn, largely because it was the home of Germany's leading statesman, Christian Democrat Konrad Adenauer, who had been mayor of Cologne before the Nazi era, and had been persecuted during the Third Reich. Adenauer became the Federal Republic's first chancellor. One of the greatest acts of statesmanship of the postwar world in the twentieth century would be Adenauer's rejection of Stalin's offer of reunification of Germany in exchange for Germany's neutrality between the Soviet and Western blocs. Adenauer said that Germany would remain with its allies and would eventually be reunified anyway, as did occur, and he carried German opinion with him.

When Truman first started exploring, with Acheson, the possibilities for such an alliance, the Dutch had been chiefly concerned with retention of Indonesia, which was impossible; the French with subjugation of Germany, which was impractical; and the British with spiking the mystique of communism by making a success of democratic socialism in Britain, which, as Truman gently pointed out, was not going to deter Stalin's armed forces, even if it were a success domestically (and it wasn't). The Americans led the new alliance with great distinction, and Eisenhower retired from Columbia University to become the first military commander of NATO, and did his now very predictably inspired job of putting together a multinational, smoothly operating command structure for NATO in Paris.

In the Far East, MacArthur was proving an extremely deft and imaginative governor of Japan, instituting women's rights, a democratic political system, and a free market economy, while preserving the emperor, with whom he developed a good relationship, and adapting Western reforms to Japanese folkways. He was deeply respected in Japan, and very attentive to the sensibilities of the Japanese. There was no Soviet presence in the country at all, except for a very modest military liaison office. MacArthur and other American experts in the area regularly warned Truman and his senior colleagues of the deteriorating situation in China. Mao Tse-tung's Communists, better organized and galvanized by an ideological faith, steadily gained against Chiang Kai-shek's corrupt and very compromised Nationalists. It was clear from Stalin's comments at Tehran and Yalta and Potsdam that he had no great affinity for Mao or the Chinese Communists generally, but in the

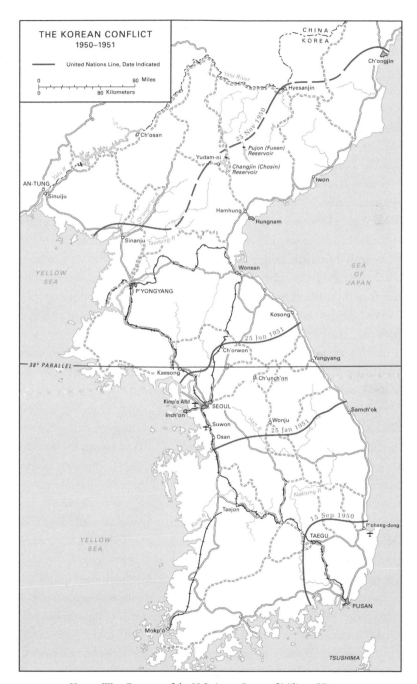

THE KOREAN CONFLICT
1950–1951

⎯⎯⎯ United Nations Line, Date Indicated

0 _____ 80 Miles
0 _____ 80 Kilometers

CHINA
KOREA

Ch'ongjin

Yalu River

Hyesanjin

25 Nov 1950

Ch'osan

Pujon (Fusen)
Reservoir

Yudam-ni

Changjin (Chosin)
Reservoir

Iwon

AN-TUNG
Yalu R.

Sinuiju

Hamhung

Hungnam

Sinanju
Taedong R.

Wonsan

SEA
OF
JAPAN

P'YONGYANG

Kosong

25 Jun 1951

YELLOW
SEA

Ch'orwon

Yangyang

⎯ 38° PARALLEL ⎯

Kaesong

Ch'unch'on

Kimp'o Afld

SEOUL

Samch'ok

Inch'on

Suwon

Wonju

Osan

25 Jan 1951

Han R.

Naktong R.

Taejon

Kum R.

15 Sep 1950

P'ohang-dong

TAEGU

YELLOW
SEA

PUSAN

Mokp'o

TSUSHIMA

Korean War. Courtesy of the U.S. Army Center of Military History

acutely defensive atmosphere that was developing, fed by reports of Communist espionage, the specter of a Communist takeover in China was a very disturbing one.

The Red Scare was fueled by espionage controversies, which began with the defection of the Soviet cipher and coding clerk in the embassy in Ottawa, Canada, Igor Gouzenko, in September 1945. The information he dumped into the lap of the Canadian authorities, the FBI (as the CIA was just being assembled from the war-time Office of Strategic Services), and British MI5 led to the apprehension of Klaus Fuchs, the Americans Julius and Ethel Rosenberg (arrested in 1950 and executed on June 19, 1953), and ultimately the British spy ring of Guy Burgess, Donald MacLean, Kim Philby, Anthony Blunt, and John Cairncross. There were television programs in the United States dramatizing the Red Menace and constant warnings that anyone's friends, neighbors, or even relatives could be communist spies. J. Edgar Hoover was making provocative speeches around the country about the Red Menace and New York's Francis J. Cardinal Spellman claimed the country was in imminent danger of a communist takeover. This was preposterous; there were very few American communists, even fewer Soviet agents, and none of them in any positions of influence, but it rattled public confidence, though it helped produce the political support for a water-tight containment policy against the Soviet Union.

Former State Department official Alger Hiss was accused by *Time* magazine assistant editor Whittaker Chambers of having spied for the USSR in the thirties, and after he denied it, he was, by the efforts of California congressman Richard M. Nixon, indicted for perjury on December 15, 1948. The tense atmosphere was escalated and the capital shocked by the suicide of just-retired Secretary of Defense James V. Forrestal, who jumped from a 16th floor window at Bethesda Naval Hospital on May 22, 1949. He had had a depressive breakdown, but rumors abounded for a time that he had been murdered in a communist conspiracy (like Jan Masaryk in Prague the year before). Forrestal was succeeded by Louis A. Johnson, who moved quickly to cut costs but antagonized virtually everyone, and General Omar N. Bradley wrote that "unwittingly, Mr. Truman had replaced one mental case with another."[12]

By mid-1949, it was clear that Chiang Kai-shek was finished and was being routed by Mao Tse-tung. *Time* and *Life* publisher Henry R. Luce, who had been born to Christian missionaries in China, and believed in Chiang and his Wellesley-educated Christian wife, led the charge in support of the Chiangs, backed by an army of church and Republican groups, and by General Douglas MacArthur, who

---

12. McCullough, *op. cit.*, p. 742.

wrote for Luce's mass-circulation publications at times. On August 4, 1949, the State Department published a document of over 1,000 pages on the history of U.S.-China relations, with particular emphasis on 1944 to 1949. In a foreword, Dean Acheson wrote that more than $2 billion had been given to Chiang, who was dismissed as corrupt and incompetent. Acheson concluded that the impending fall of China was the result of "internal Chinese forces . . . which this country tried to influence but could not." Truman told Senator Vandenberg: "We picked a bad horse."[13] Republican demagogues, including California senator William Knowland and Wisconsin senator Joseph R. McCarthy (who had defeated Robert La Follette Jr., in a 180-degree ideological turn for Wisconsin), were not going to let Truman and the Democrats off that lightly.

As the Chinese Nationalists circled the drain, Stalin detonated an atomic bomb, on August 29, 1949. This led to an anguished, semi-public debate about whether the United States should proceed to a "super bomb," the hydrogen bomb. This controversy was only resolved in favor of doing so on January 31, 1950, when Truman was satisfied that the Soviet Union would proceed to the same destination. The hydrogen bomb was tested by the United States on January 11, 1952, and it possessed the potential to be as much as 1,000 times more powerful than the atomic bombs dropped on Hiroshima and Nagasaki.

In the meantime, Mao Tse-tung proclaimed the People's Republic of China on October 10, 1949 (the 24th anniversary of the revolution of Chiang Kai-shek's brother in-law, Sun Yat-sen, although the relationship was posthumous to Sun), and almost all fighting had ceased on the Chinese mainland by December. Chiang had removed to Taiwan, and declared Taipei the temporary capital of the Republic of China. The United States Seventh Fleet, sailing from Japan, effectively assured Taiwan's security from invasion, permanently thereafter, at least to the time of this writing.

8. THE COMMUNIST ATTACK IN KOREA

On January 12, 1950, in an address to the National Press Club, Acheson described the American defense perimeter. But by not mentioning South Korea he implied that it was outside the perimeter. Korea had been arbitrarily divided at the 38th parallel for the purposes of deciding whether the Japanese occupying forces should surrender to the United States or the Soviet Union. The demarcation had been decreed by two junior officers in the Pentagon one night in the summer of 1945, one of them, then Colonel Dean Rusk, a future secretary of state. The South had

---

13. McCullough, *op. cit.*, p. 744.

two-thirds of Korea's population and a rather larger area, and was a little larger than the state of Indiana.

The junior senator from Wisconsin, Joseph R. McCarthy, announced in a speech to Republican women in Wheeling, West Virginia, on February 6, 1950, that he had in his hand a list of 205 "known communists" in the State Department. He made similar speeches a few days later, in Salt Lake City and Reno, claiming that there were 57 "card-carrying communists" in the State Department, and this allegation received a good deal of publicity. Not long after, he gave a five-hour harangue in the Senate, and his allegation levitated to 81 communists in the State Department. He never produced a shred of evidence, had no evidence, and was treated with considerable skepticism in most of the media. But he struck a chord with a large echelon of opinion in a fearful America. McCarthy multiplied his fantastic allegations, denigrating Truman, Acheson, and ultimately Marshall. Some Republican senators, smarting from their decades out of office, lent support to McCarthy, even though they must have known what slanders his charges were. It is illustrative of the poor level to which public debate had sunk that anyone could take seriously allegations of treason against Acheson and Marshall, and of senescence against Truman himself, reducing him to manipulation by traitors.

On April 7, 1950, National Security Council Report No. 68, largely written by long-serving foreign and defense policy official Paul Nitze, under Acheson's supervision, was handed to Truman, and warned that "This Republic and its citizens, in the ascendancy of their strength, stand in their deepest peril" because of wholly inadequate military strength to enforce its containment policy, given that, at that point, the Soviet Union was expected to achieve atomic parity within a few years. Truman was still considering how to respond to this strenuous rearmament recommendation from his national security team, including the senior military officers, when North Korea abruptly invaded South Korea on June 24. It was assumed that this was a Soviet-prompted aggression, in part motivated by its exclusion from Japan, and Truman was determined that it had to be responded to firmly and at once. He remembered Manchuria and Ethiopia and the disastrous consequences of the democracies not helping the victims of aggression by dictators. The United Nations was an American invention and "In this first big test, we just can't let them down," Truman said.[14]

On June 27, with almost unanimous support from Congress by voice vote, and the complete solidarity of his national security group, military and civilian, and as North Korean tanks entered the South Korean capital of Seoul and North Korean

14. McCullough, *op. cit.*, p. 779.

leader Kim Il Sung promised to "crush" the South, Truman ordered full air and naval support of the South. MacArthur was already calling for ground intervention, and was causing concern about his independent-mindedness, even in the mind of Louis Johnson, who was generally considered a loose cannon himself.[15] Johnson, having just returned with Bradley from Tokyo, advised Truman to be very precise in any orders he sent MacArthur.

At 10:45 on the evening of the 27th, the United Nations supported a resolution backing the United States action. Stalin and Molotov had made another serious error: their ambassador at the UN had been pulled in protest against the continued occupation of the Chinese Security Council chair and General Assembly membership by the Nationalists. For the first time, an international organization had approved military action. Acheson's January 12 speech was resurrected by some and blamed for inciting the belief that the United States would not defend South Korea. The secretary's omission of Korea was injudicious, but it is unlikely that Stalin, Mao, and Kim Il Sung relied on it overly in unleashing such an onslaught.

American opinion of every hue and source was practically unanimous; Walter Lippmann, James Reston, Joseph and Stewart Alsop, Thomas E. Dewey, Cordell Hull, all the influential newspapers and magazines, and an avalanche of uncontradicted messages from the public, spontaneously backed the president. Eisenhower said, "We'll have a dozen Koreas soon if we don't take a firm stand."[16] At 3:30 a.m. on June 30, MacArthur reported to the Pentagon from Korea, where he was inspecting the situation for Truman and Bradley, that the South Koreans could not hold with air and sea support alone, and that two American divisions were needed at once. Truman responded immediately and authorized the movement of the forces MacArthur requested, from his occupation divisions in Japan. The Americans, as they arrived, and the South Koreans, were outnumbered three-to-one by the North, which was heavily armed and was spearheaded by a large number of the formidable Russian T-34 tanks. It was monsoon season in Korea and the temperature was steadily above 100 degrees.

MacArthur was now the United Nations theater commander (in Tokyo) and was conducting an orderly withdrawal, stretching North Korean supply lines and preparing a relatively solid defensive perimeter in the south of the peninsula. He had asked for 30,000 men at the beginning of July, and on July 9 for another four divisions. The UN forces were conducting a distinguished rearguard action and they yielded barely 100 miles throughout July. On July 29, the tactical battlefield

---

15. McCullough, *op. cit.*, p. 779.
16. Ibid. p. 781.

commander, General Walton Walker, ordered his forces, around Pusan at the southern extremity of Korea, to "stand or die." There would be no retreat—as he put it, "No Dunkirk, no Bataan."[17]

On July 19, Truman effectively doubled the defense budgetary request for the year in progress. The congressional appropriation for defense for 1950 had been $13 billion; Truman's supplementary request increased it to $25 billion, and it would be $48 billion for 1951 and $60 billion for 1952. Truman had lost confidence in Johnson by this time, not only for his abrasiveness and hostility to Acheson, but particularly because of the complacency with which he had been slashing the defense budget. (Harriman, who had replaced Winant as ambassador to Britain and then Henry Wallace as secretary of commerce, and was now Marshall Plan administrator, told Truman that Johnson was hoping to force Acheson out and replace him with Harriman himself.) And Truman had long objected to MacArthur as "a play actor and bunco man,"[18] though he did not question his military talents. There was clearly a substantial problem in the president's senior defense team.

By early August, the Pusan perimeter of 130 miles had been extensively fortified and heavy reinforcements of men and materiel had been shipped and airlifted into it. Harriman and Deputy Army Chief of Staff Matthew Ridgway and Air Force Deputy Chief of Staff General Lauris Norstad were sent by Truman to see MacArthur in August 1950. (It remains a mystery what Harriman, a railway heir and Roosevelt supporter of uneven performance in his long and varied public career, was doing in all these roles.) MacArthur had made a much-publicized trip to Chiang Kai-shek at the end of July, and Harriman was sent to tell MacArthur that he would get everything he needed but had to avoid any inflammation of the Chinese situation, and especially any encouragement to Chiang to invade China or otherwise reactivate the Chinese Civil War.

MacArthur took advantage of the visit of Ridgway and the others to propose a brilliantly imaginative plan for smashing the North Koreans in a stroke. MacArthur completely converted the three men (who were not gullible and were not acolytes of his) to his plan to make an amphibious landing at Inchon, near Seoul and 200 miles north of Pusan, and cut the peninsula in two, decapitating almost the entire North Korean army engaged around Pusan, which would then be enveloped on both sides and pounded mercilessly from the air. It was an especially risky operation because Inchon had 30-foot tides, and the landings would have to be conducted at high tide right at the sea wall; there were no beaches to land

---

17. McCullough, *op. cit.*, pp. 788–789.
18. Ibid. p. 793.

on. MacArthur thought the risk would ensure surprise, and was aware that this was how the Japanese had conquered Korea in 1895. Harriman, unshaven and hungry, went directly from his returning plane to the White House to brief the president, who listened carefully and then sent him to see Bradley.

The tides would be ideal on September 15. There were now 100,000 defenders in Pusan and the battle there was turning, though by mid-September the U.S. had taken 15,000 casualties. Truman was outraged by a statement MacArthur made to the Veterans of Foreign Wars supporting, in his usual florid superlatives, the defense of Formosa. The actual statement was unexceptionable, but Truman and Acheson were afraid that any encouragement of Chiang could lead to an ill-considered attempt to return to the mainland. Despite his reservations about MacArthur, and the opposition of Bradley, whom Truman respected, the president approved MacArthur's Inchon plan on August 28. Truman, perhaps more clearly than ever, demonstrated his clarity of judgment and gift for command decisions. He saw the genius of the plan and felt the prospects outweighed the risks, although his personal relationships would have inclined him to Bradley. Ridgway, whom Truman liked and respected, might have been an influence, as he recommended the action. On September 12, Truman fired Louis Johnson as secretary of defense and replaced him at once, and one more time, with General George C. Marshall, despite Marshall's characteristically thoughtful warning that he was still being blamed for the fall of China. MacArthur's attack at Inchon proceeded three days later.

The operation was a bone-crushing success, the supreme pinnacle of Douglas MacArthur's career as one of the great military commanders of modern times. He landed nearly 70,000 men from 262 ships in a little over an hour; Inchon was taken in less than a day, Seoul recaptured in 10 days; and Walker broke out of the Pusan perimeter and in less than two weeks most of the North Korean army was killed, wounded, captured, or surrounded and doomed. On October 1, 16 days after the landing, the United Nations had moved from the desperate perimeter of Pusan to the 38th parallel and had annihilated the North Koreans. Rarely in the history of war had there been such a quick turn in so large a combat. Truman cabled his senior serving general (equal rank to Marshall and Eisenhower and, as of September 22, Bradley, though he had opposed the operation): "Well and nobly done."

There was general agreement in Washington among the highest circles around Truman, including Marshall, Acheson, and the newly elevated and converted Bradley, that MacArthur should be authorized to cross the 38th parallel. His mission was changed to destruction of the North Korean armed forces, and the invasion of the North was approved by the United Nations, still operating without the

Russians, in the first week of October. There were diplomatic reports that Mao's premier and foreign minister, Chou En-lai, was warning of Chinese intervention in the event of such a push, but this was dismissed as bluff in the heady aftermath of MacArthur's smashing victory. United Nations forces crossed the 38th parallel going north in great strength on October 9.

Truman and MacArthur had a storied meeting to discuss strategy in light of recent events, on Wake Island on October 15. Contrary to their expectations, they got on well, and met for less than three hours. Truman took off his jacket and invited others to do the same, and when MacArthur asked if the president minded if he smoked his pipe, Truman responded that he did not and had probably had "more smoke blown in my face than any man alive."

MacArthur, as usually happened when he addressed military matters for which he was responsible, was overwhelmingly prepared and completely persuasive. He held the group spellbound with his summary of the theater, and predicted that Pyongyang would be occupied within a week and his army evacuated back to Japan by Christmas, and that the United Nations would be able to hold country-wide elections before the end of the year. He rated the chances of Chinese intervention as "very little." He said the Chinese had only 125,000 men along the Yalu and no air force. The Russians, he volunteered, had 1,000 warplanes in Siberia but no significant land forces, and he doubted that Soviet air power and Chinese troops could be successfully coordinated. MacArthur said the 60,000 North Korean prisoners of war were "the happiest Koreans in all Korea," as they were well fed and clean. He expressed incomprehension at the French problems in Indochina and thought that they only lacked an aggressive general. MacArthur was warm in his praise for Truman and the support he had received from all parts of the administration, and Truman more than fully reciprocated in his praise of MacArthur's generalship. Truman referred to MacArthur in his communiqué as "one of America's great soldier-statesmen" and expressed the same views in a world broadcast from San Francisco on his way home. MacArthur, on hearing the president's address, cabled his respectful gratitude. It was a reciprocal love-in from which no one present dissented.

9. THE CHINESE INVASION OF KOREA

On November 1, Truman learned that there were strong intelligence reports that there were Chinese Communist troops across the Yalu, as many as 20,000 of them. In fact, there were more than five times as many; they marched by night, and rested, heavily camouflaged, during the day. Any Chinese soldier who moved when an Allied reconnaissance plane flew over was executed. (That day was unseasonably hot and Truman took a nap after lunch, during which two Puerto Rican nationalists attempted to invade Blair House, where the Trumans were staying while the White House was being renovated, and assassinate the president. They did not gain entry and were both killed, but not before they killed a member of Truman's security unit.)

On November 24, MacArthur was in Korea, unruffled by intelligence reports that there were now over 30,000 Chinese troops in North Korea. He had divided his forces into two separated armies advancing up each coast of the Korean peninsula, with the plan of encircling whatever enemy forces there were in between them, another bold but risky plan. On November 28, the Chinese invaded with 260,000 men, despite MacArthur, with Truman's approval, having bombed the Korean ends of the bridges across the Yalu. MacArthur quickly called for massive reinforcements and authority to bomb Manchuria, bring in Nationalist Chinese troops, and blockade the Chinese mainland. This was the beginning of a fundamental parting of the ways, as the National Security Council met on November 28 and it was agreed that the objective was to avoid a war with China as well as with Russia and to get out of Korea with honor. Marshall said that going to full-scale war with China would "fall into a Russian trap." Truman opposed anything that would embarrass MacArthur in the face of the enemy, but he and his theater commander now differed on the purpose of the war in Korea. MacArthur wanted to smash the Chinese army in Korea, bomb its industrial base, such as it was, to rubble, and generally punish the new People's Republic with a severe military defeat. Truman, Marshall, Acheson, and Bradley wanted to revert to the original purpose of the UN "police action" and hold the 38th parallel for the South and conduct a limited war only until that end was attained. It was a legitimate strategic disagreement that would ramify gravely through the next 25 years and the next five American presidencies.

At his press conference on November 30, Truman strongly defended MacArthur and in answer to questions about the atomic bomb, said, "There has always been active consideration of its use." This was a serious error, unless Truman were really prepared to threaten use of atomic weapons, which he was not, and which flew in the face of his decision to wind down the war to holding the 38th parallel until a cease-fire could be restored, after whatever conventional attrition. His contention, and that of his senior national security advisers, down to the talented second level of Kennan, Bohlen, and Nitze, and Ridgway on the military side, was that Korea was not worth an all-out conventional war with China, that atomic weapons were in fact out of the question, that there was a danger of Soviet responses in East Asia and in Europe, and that the objective was avoidance of defeat and not victory.

The contrary view espoused with growing insubordination by MacArthur, but also favored by most Republicans, including that party's senior foreign policy expert, John Foster Dulles, and upcoming Senate star, Richard M. Nixon, was that the expansion of the war by China had to be replied to by a counter-expansion and not by retreat and a grasping for an "honorable" accommodation on the Korean peninsula. (Nixon had just defeated the glamorous actress and mistress of Democratic senator Lyndon B. Johnson of Texas, Mrs. Helen Gahagan Douglas, by 700,000 votes, calling her "pink down to her underwear"—a simultaneous netting of the Red-baiters and the male locker room, to which she replied by coining the phrase "Tricky Dick.")

It has been fashionable to endorse the Truman view these 60 years since. But MacArthur made a serious point that a draftee army could not be asked to risk the lives of its soldiers for less than victory. It is now clear, as Chou En-lai confirmed 20 years later to Richard Nixon, that Stalin would not have lifted a finger to help China, and the United States possessed overwhelming atomic deterrence. The United Nations forces could have destroyed a Chinese army of 300,000, or any conceivable larger number, and inflicted a grievous wound on the People's Republic as it was still puling in its cradle. And it could have eliminated the hideous and venomous asp of the Kim regime in Pyongyang at the outset of what proved a binge of more than 60 years in disturbing and threatening the peace of the whole world (as this is written, with threats of nuclear self-empowerment).

It cannot be easily resolved whether Truman or MacArthur was correct, but there are good arguments for both. Even the judicious but emotionally pro-Truman David McCullough, author of a well-regarded Truman biography (much cited in this chapter), laments that Truman didn't fire MacArthur as soon as the Chinese attacked. But the point could just as well be made that instead he should have adopted MacArthur's policy while sternly warning the general never to speak out of turn again. And if he had had to part with Acheson or Bradley or even Marshall, he could have replaced them, won in Korea, and, had he wished, been reelected and served longer as president than anyone except his predecessor. (More than two terms had now been legislated as unconstitutional by the Republicans, out of office almost a whole generation after the defeats they had suffered at the hands of Roosevelt and Truman.)

Marshall was not particularly needed at the Pentagon, and Robert Lovett, who succeeded him, would have been perfectly adequate had he assumed the office a year earlier. Acheson was a very able secretary of state, but he had contributed at least as much to the Korean imbroglio post–November 1950 by his January 12 speech to the National Press Club as MacArthur had by carrying out his orders from Truman and the UN, from which neither Marshall nor Acheson dissented. And Bradley, a popular soldiers' general, but out of his depth in the same exalted five-star company as Marshall, Eisenhower, and MacArthur, to which he was elevated for mistakenly opposing the epochally brilliant Inchon operation, was completely dispensable and easily replaceable, unlike MacArthur, whose dismissal the limited-war and orderly-retreat advocates now persistently demanded, in a buzz that was constantly in the president's ears.

Truman was a man of good sense, high courage, absolute integrity, keen intelligence, and impeccable sense of duty, but he uncharacteristically erred in trying to support MacArthur while endorsing a policy that MacArthur cogently opposed. MacArthur had either to be backed in his recommended policy or told that he would have to mend his ambitions to conform to the administration's views or retire back to the military government of Japan, where all conceded his effectiveness. By allowing the chasm between himself and the theater commander to widen, Truman gave hostages to the Chinese, and created a fissure that would require measures to resolve that were so draconian that they terminated, prematurely and acrimoniously, the careers of both men, a great general and a distinguished president.

British prime minister Clement Attlee, at the first mention (by Truman) of atomic weapons, rushed across the Atlantic with his coat-tails trailing behind him, to offer to broker America's evacuation of Korea. British military units were loyally and capably serving (in modest numbers) in the United Nations forces in Korea, but the British were chiefly concerned not to provoke the Chinese to attack Hong Kong or to increase the pressure already being asserted in the so-called civil war in Malaya (which the Chinese stoked up but the British were resourcefully fighting). Truman declined and said that there would be no use of nuclear weapons, but that he would rather be ejected in honorable defeat than enter the cowardly negotiations that Attlee was offering, though he stressed his confidence that no such fiasco was in prospect. The allies were panicking as dissension sapped Truman's own inner circle.

10. TRUMAN AND MACARTHUR

Field commander Walton Walker died in an automobile crash on December 23, 1950, and MacArthur requested, and Truman immediately agreed on, General Matthew Ridgway as his replacement. Ridgway arrived on Christmas Day and was given absolute authority over his command by MacArthur and began a very swift shaping up of what had become a rather shaggy and demoralized army. The

New Year, 1951, opened on this relatively upbeat note as Ridgway started to reenergize his command, but MacArthur and the Joint Chiefs were all asking for the use of atomic weapons in Manchuria, a step Truman would not countenance. In strictly military terms, the senior officers were correct; atomic weapons would have ended the Chinese intrusion in Korea and Stalin would not have attempted a reprisal. But there were larger, humanitarian and policy considerations, and the ultimate potential of productive relations with China (which Truman lived to see) to be considered. And the service chiefs had to be weaned away from the facile reflex of demanding use of the ultimate weapon whenever something disagreeable happened. No retaliation would have occurred then, but Truman sagely saw that the United States could not revert to atomic weapons whenever the conventional going got rough, and be confident that it would never be the recipient of the use of such arms. The United Nations was not going to be pushed back to Pusan, but there was no visible way to end the war except by a variant of what MacArthur was proposing, including use of Nationalist Chinese forces and conventional bombing of Manchuria. MacArthur was in fairly open disagreement with the administration, with a good deal of encouragement from the service chiefs and the Republicans and southern Democrats, in a way that Truman's ambivalence had somewhat encouraged. It had become a policy schism that was becoming increasingly necessary, and difficult, to heal.

Truman wrote MacArthur on January 13—expressing what Acheson, who had been fired for insubordination by Roosevelt and was at least as pig-headed as MacArthur, considered "infinite" (i.e., excessive) "patience," that "great prudence" must be shown not to involve "Japan or Western Europe in large-scale hostilities," even envisioning the possibility that "if we must withdraw from Korea, it be clear to the world that that course was forced on us by military necessity and that we shall not accept the result politically or militarily until the aggression has been rectified." This was the crux of the command problem: Truman was correct not to consider the use of nuclear weapons, but he should not have contemplated—and there was no military reason to consider, and MacArthur assured him there was no reason to fear—being evicted from the peninsula. Truman should have called for an expanded conventional war. There was no reason not to respond to the direct aggression by China. In those respects, though not in declining to dissent from the Joint Chiefs' proposed nuclear hip-shooting, MacArthur was correct. But Truman was the commander-in-chief; presidents have the constitutional duty to exercise their best judgment and the right to make mistakes, and insubordination from any commander is intolerable. MacArthur was getting perilously close to it, egged on by hawks of both parties in Congress, and not subject to serious efforts at dissuasion by the Joint Chiefs or even Defense Secretary Marshall, who both had the authority to contradict the theater commander in the name of the president.

Truman declared a national emergency, imposed wage and price controls, and completed the quadrupling of the defense budget in the course of the year to over $50 billion. On January 17, Marshall read Truman a report over the telephone from Korea that Ridgway was confident that he could repel any attack, and that no evacuation of Korea was in prospect. The theory has arisen that MacArthur had forecast being pushed out of Korea and that Ridgway was responsible for a miraculous resurrection of the Eighth Army.[19] This is not sustained by an analysis of the cables. The CIA had made that claim, but MacArthur had said that "Under the extraordinary limitations and conditions imposed upon the command in Korea . . . its military position is untenable, but it can hold if overriding political considerations so dictate, for any length of time up to its complete destruction" (which would only occur if suicide attacks from the Chinese continued indefinitely and his own losses were not replaced). MacArthur disagreed with a defined objective short of victory, and disputed the morality of asking draftees to risk and give their lives for an objective short of victory, but he never suggested that he could be thrown out of Korea, unless he were abandoned virtually as he had been at Corregidor nine years before.

Ridgway commanded his army very well and aggressively, and retook Seoul on March 15, and regained the 38th parallel at the end of that month. He had 365,000 men (counting the South Koreans and other allies) to 480,000 for the enemy, which, given United Nations air superiority, made any eviction from Korea inconceivable. But MacArthur wanted a united Korea, and was accused by Acheson in particular of "fighting the Pentagon" while "Ridgway was fighting the enemy." This was an unfair allegation. MacArthur was the theater commander and cannot be excluded from credit for retrieving the situation yet again; he enjoyed the substantial agreement of a waffling Pentagon (including two other five-star generals, Marshall and Bradley), and was far from morose at the gains of his own forces, contrary to the claims of his opponents.[20]

Truman submitted a draft cease-fire proposal to the 17 other UN allies in the UN on March 21, and MacArthur was sent the highlights of it the day before. The MacArthur faction concluded that Truman had lost his nerve, and the Truman faction shortly concluded that MacArthur had taken leave of his senses, as he issued a statement on March 24 threatening to expand the war by blockading

---

19. McCullough, *op. cit.*, p. 834.
20. Ibid. p. 835.

China and conventionally bombing the Chinese interior, which he predicted would produce the collapse of the People's Republic. (He was not, contrary to some of the cacophonous name-calling that ensued, threatening or advocating the use of atomic weapons.)

The die was cast and Truman, whatever the strategic rights and wrongs, had to assert the authority of his office, within the U.S. command structure, and vis-à-vis his allies, who undoubtedly preferred the Truman to the MacArthur view (except for the South Koreans and Nationalist Chinese, who were the most important allies in the war), and also to be clear to the Chinese and the Russians. Acheson, Marshall's under secretary, Lovett, and Bradley, along with juniors such as Rusk, wanted MacArthur fired, and Truman was enraged, but on March 14, the Gallup organization put the president's popularity at 26 percent. MacArthur had immense prestige and he was offering victory in a war that had now inflicted 169,000 casualties on the South Koreans and 57,000 on the United States (and barely 3,000 on all the other allies together).

Truman was commissioning research on Lincoln's dismissal of General McClellan in 1862 (Chapter 6), as if there were the slightest comparison between the generals or the circumstances, but the issue blew up on April 5 when Republican House leader Joe Martin (the durable subject of FDR's "Martin, Barton, and Fish" speech in 1940, and once and future Speaker of the House) read in the House an exchange of correspondence he had had with MacArthur in the previous month. MacArthur had not described as confidential his reply to Martin's request for his "views" on a speech censorious of the administration that Martin had given, and in his reply MacArthur agreed that the Nationalist Chinese should be used and stated that "There is no substitute for victory."

Despite the obviously impossible impasse, Truman kept his own counsel, Marshall and Chief Justice Fred M. Vinson (Vinson's role in this is even more incongruous than Harriman's or Rusk's) urged caution, the Joint Chiefs were divided (as usual throughout these matters), and even Acheson was hesitant, while Speaker Sam Rayburn was non-committal. They were all afraid to bell the cat. Truman's entourage was full of hot-headed advice about disposing of MacArthur, which was certainly understandable. But Truman could easily have retrieved matters even at this late date by warning MacArthur in dire terms and inciting the inference in the camps of friends and foes that he and MacArthur were coordinating a stick-and-carrot approach to the Communists; Mao and Stalin were so morbidly suspicious, they probably assumed that that was what was happening anyway.

On April 8, the Joint Chiefs finally concluded that MacArthur had to go, because he had divided his forces (though he had sought and received the authority to do so), because he had launched his November offensive without adequate intelligence (though he was relying on the CIA, which he did not command and which had a wholly inadequate capacity to assess guerrilla activities and forces), because the Chiefs had concluded that MacArthur had lost confidence in himself (a gratuitous and utterly fatuous observation entirely beyond their capabilities and authority to make), and because of MacArthur's insubordination toward the president, but not to them, since he had contravened no instructions from the Joint Chiefs. The last was the only legitimate ground they invoked, and the erratic and sometimes Iago-like activities of Bradley are suspect here, as he had opposed Inchon and undercut MacArthur. There were also a lot of irritating junior-level busybodies, led by Harriman and Rusk. They were constantly demanding MacArthur's dismissal, although the only standing they had was Truman's practice to consult rather widely, unlike most other successful U.S. presidents. (Roosevelt almost never consulted anybody about anything, and when he did, he rarely paid any attention to the advice he received.) At the last minute, Truman, who had been convinced that MacArthur wished to be fired, suddenly became almost neurotic that he was going to resign and so held a press conference at 1:00 a.m. on April 11 to dismiss MacArthur, having sent Secretary of the Army Frank Pace to Tokyo to hand the general personal notice of his dismissal and spare him the embarrassment of having such a message come through lower-level communication channels.

The outcry exceeded even what had been anticipated. Thousands of longshoremen walked off their jobs, four state legislatures condemned the president, and a unanimous Republican congressional leadership called for an impeachment inquiry and invited MacArthur to address a special session of Congress. The Los Angeles city council adjourned for a day of "sorrowful contemplation of the political assassination of General MacArthur," and flags throughout the country were lowered or flown upside down. A few senators, Walter Lippmann, the *New York Times*, the *Washington Post*, and other liberal media, as well as the British and the French, who had token forces in Korea, supported Truman. MacArthur received overwhelming popular welcomes in San Francisco when he arrived on April 17 and in other cities, and addressed the Congress on April 19.

It was one of the most eloquently formulated and delivered speeches in American history. Though best remembered for the ending, invoking a barrack ballad about how "Old soldiers never die," the core of the address was his statement "I know war as few other men now living have known it, and nothing to me is more revolting. But once the aggressions of an enemy have forced war upon us, there is no alternative but to apply every available means to bring that war to the swiftest possible victorious conclusion at the minimum possible cost in American and allied lives. . . . In war, there is no substitute for victory."

He buttressed this with what he called "my understanding that the above views are shared by practically every military commander familiar with the Korean theater including our own Joint Chiefs of Staff." By this time everyone in the administration was fighting for his life against the tide of MacArthur support, and Truman, Marshall, and Bradley had to, and did, get the Chiefs into a goal-line defense of the president. On April 20, MacArthur received the greatest personal welcome in American history, a stupefying turnout of an estimated 7,500,000 cheering supporters in New York City.

Hearings on Korea and the dismissal of MacArthur opened before the Senate Armed Services Committee, chaired by Democratic senator Richard B. Russell of Georgia, on May 3. MacArthur was eloquent but unphilosophical, completely self-absorbed, and incapable of admitting a possibility of his own error, and he parried all questions about strategic problems that could be triggered by events in the Far East or in other theaters, such as Europe. Marshall and the Joint Chiefs testified under intense but very courteous questioning for 19 days. To all but the lunatic McCarthyite right, Marshall's prestige was as great as MacArthur's, and Marshall spoke of MacArthur, whom he had sponsored for the Congressional Medal of Honor nine years before, as a great soldier and commander for whom he had "tremendous respect." Marshall emphasized that the administration had not renounced a possibility of easy victory (which is not what MacArthur had suggested), and compared it to the "notable victory" in Berlin (the airlift), which had taken five months longer to achieve than the current duration of the Korean War. (They were hardly comparable, as Marshall was perfectly aware, since a shot had not been fired nor a casualty sustained in the Berlin airlift.)

Marshall implied, but did not say, that the choice was between saving South Korea and tolerating the continued existence of North Korea, and a much wider and possibly world and atomic war. This was just speculation, and in the light of subsequent events is known to be mistaken, and should have seemed so then. Stalin was in no position to exchange atomic fire with the U.S., and no one was going to help Mao Tse-tung, whose staying power after 30 years of civil and foreign war in a primitive country was not unlimited. Even if his reserves of manpower might have appeared so, his numbers of adequately trained forces were very limited. The United States could have turned the entire Soviet Union into a radioactive rubble heap in a few days at minimal risk to itself, though the reluctance of Truman to consider such a denouement was to his credit. But he should have remembered who he was dealing with in Stalin, who would certainly take such a threat seriously, as the Chinese did when Truman's successor made it two years later.

Bradley followed, and uttered the most famous line of the hearings—that following MacArthur's recommendations would "involve us in the wrong war, at the wrong place, at the wrong time, and with the wrong enemy." Strategically, MacArthur was correct, and Bradley's quip was bunk. It would not have been so difficult to expel China from Korea, and the failure to do so has inflicted the terribly tedious and vexing burden of North Korea on the world for all posterity to date. MacArthur was not adequately advised of the change in mission statement from the reunification of Korea that he was ordered to effect after salvaging the campaign at Inchon, to the limited war to hold the 38th parallel after the Chinese intervention. Truman had every right to conclude that getting rid of North Korea was not worth the cost, as his successor also concluded, but he and his entourage should have been more careful about endlessly professing to think it was a choice between the 38th parallel and a world—atomic, or otherwise prohibitively terrible—war.

Truman and his admirers have translated the firing of MacArthur into a triumph of selfless courage, but it was both unnecessary and a disaster. The ultimate issue was insubordination, but it should not have been allowed to develop as it did, and the absolute, belatedly recognized, and negligently aggravated necessities of a great office should not be mistaken for courage, as Truman's partisans have claimed, with general success. The fact that Harry S. Truman certainly was a courageous man and president makes his dithering and ultimately overreaction in this case the more disappointing. Truman should have moved earlier to curtail MacArthur's undoubted egomania, as the inexhaustibly confident patrician, Roosevelt, did a number of times (resolving one disagreement with the point that he, not MacArthur, had been elected president, though allegedly allowing that it could have been a case of mistaken identity). Truman should have warned MacArthur to accept administration policy as it evolved or retire gracefully back to Tokyo. Sacking him from all positions in the middle of the night was a shabby, fearful, and spiteful act. All the nonsense about the two men cracking up was terribly undignified, considering their stature—MacArthur compared himself to the music critic who had panned Margaret Truman's talents and received a threatening letter from her father; Bradley had compared MacArthur to Forrestal, ultimately an acutely paranoid suicide case.

Truman allowed the problem to fester, and insisted on collegially involving the sorcery of a lot of tinkering aides, to the point that when he finally cut the painter, these two great men destroyed each other's public lives ignominiously and prematurely, and took Marshall and Bradley and Acheson into permanent retirement with them. Of that whole brilliant echelon of Roosevelt's top strategic team, only Eisenhower, in Paris setting up NATO, survived intact politically, and he inherited the full distinguished legacy of the Roosevelt-Truman decades (although he would to some degree technically run in opposition to it).

Truman eventually claimed to have written a letter to himself on April 9, 1950, upholding the tradition of two presidential terms, which only Franklin D. Roosevelt had departed from, and which was now enforced by constitutional amendment, though Truman was specifically exempted. He may have written the letter, and his word should not be lightly challenged, but whether he had intended to retire or not, he certainly did not intend to retire as a result of acute, if unjust, unpopularity. That was what he now faced, and MacArthur toured the country for months attacking Truman in very destructive terms. The creation of such a political debacle cannot be seen as anything but a regrettable swan song for a great general and a distinguished president. As for MacArthur, General Charles de Gaulle, a military admirer but not an acquaintance of MacArthur's, and a cordial postwar colleague of Truman's, correctly described MacArthur in a speech of April 15, 1951, as "a general whose boldness was feared after full advantage had been taken of it."[21]

The Korean War settled down very close to the 38th parallel from July 1951 until six months after the inauguration of Truman's successor, during which time there were fairly continuous negotiations and fierce fire-fighting along the line. Many of the Chinese and North Koreans did not wish to be repatriated, which snarled discussions beyond even the unimaginable intractability of the Chinese and North Korean Communists. The MacArthur fervor subsided, but he continued to be more popular than Truman or Marshall. As the war in Korea dragged on, the Truman-Acheson-Marshall-Bradley policy appeared less successful. It did prevail over MacArthur's "no substitute for victory" policy, and it left an Achilles' heel for future open-ended involvement in Asiatic military quagmires by unwary American civilian and military leaders.

At the rise of the national state in the sixteenth century, there had been four Great Powers in the West—England, France, the Holy Roman Empire, and Turkey. A hundred years after that, the Empire had broken in two, Spain and Austria, and Russia had joined the group. In the eighteenth century, Spain and Turkey fell away, but Prussia emerged. And in the nineteenth century, Prussia became Germany, and Italy, Japan, and the United States joined the ranks of the Great Powers. World War I eliminated Austria, and World War II elevated the U.S.A. and the USSR, and the British, French, Japanese, and Italians, and later the Germans,

21. Conrad Black, *Richard M. Nixon: A Life in Full*, New York, PublicAffairs, 2007, p. 171.

were effectively client states of the United States, though not without influence in that role, especially Britain and France.

Two long lifetimes after Yorktown (162 years), and one after Appomattox (80 years), America dominated most of the world, challenged only by a large, strange country perversely and militantly advocating the antithesis of America's message. The dialectical confrontation of Hegel and Marx was at hand: against America's exceptionalism, individualism, free enterprise, and invocation of a benign Providence was the totalitarianism, atheism, and command economy of Russia and its puppet states. The Americans blinked almost in disbelief that they could be affronted so forcefully by such heresies, but they rose quickly to the challenge of delivering the world from a new dark age. They would contain the threat, until the threat relented, gave way, and collapsed.

Mobilizing a worldwide containment effort on the recently isolationist Americans would require infusing the country with anxious determination, creating atomic bomb shelters, maintaining conscription, and deploying forces all over the world. The Communist takeover of China and penetration of many intellectual circles, and America's nuclear saber-rattling and official encouragement of some level of domestic paranoia, all made it seem a closer contest that it really was. The ideologically confused, bloodstained regime in the Kremlin was now all that stood in the path of America's unchallenged, rather gently asserted supremacy in the whole world. America was entering the last lap of the quarter-millennium progression from threatened colony to junior partner in the British Empire, to fragile new republic, regional power, Great Power, Greatest Power, co–Superpower, Supreme Power. To the founders and greatest renovators of the American project, not much of this brilliant, almost vertical, trajectory would have been a surprise.

Dwight D. Eisenhower

CHAPTER TWELVE

The Red Scare and the Free World, 1951–1957

1. THE REPUBLICAN RENAISSANCE AT LAST

The balance of Truman's presidency was an anti-climax, and the principal feature of it was the worst of the Red Scare and the McCarthy era, though Truman deserves no discredit for either. The senator from Wisconsin, on June 14, 1951, in an eight-hour address in the Senate, the last couple of hours to an almost empty chamber, directed the most outrageous allegations that had probably ever been heard there, against General Marshall in particular, accusing him of causing, by his treachery and incompetence, every Communist success since the Bolshevik Revolution. His universally respected conduct as army chief of staff and chairman of the Combined Allied Military Chiefs in World War II (setting him officially at the head of the 25 million soldiers, sailors, and airmen of the United States and British Commonwealth) was reviled as a series of failures culminating in the gift of Eastern Europe to Stalin. His service as Truman's emissary in China was held responsible for the Communist victory there, and his time as secretary of state and of defense was deemed responsible for other failures, including Communist victories in Czechoslovakia and North Korea. It was, said McCarthy, "a conspiracy on a scale so immense as to dwarf any previous such venture in the history of man . . . so black that, when it is finally exposed, its principals shall be forever deserving of the maledictions of all honest men."[1] It was fantastic that a sophisticated democracy could indulge such heinous calumnies in its legislature without the accuser being subjected to compulsory mental examination. And it was only made possible because of the terrible schism between the followers of Truman and those of MacArthur. The McCarran Act in September 1951, passed over Truman's veto, required registration of communists and communist-front organizations, the internment of communists during national emergencies, the prohibition of their employment in any national defense industries, and the ineligibility for entry into the United States of anyone who had ever been a member of a totalitarian organization. (Of course, the problems of definition made the whole statute absurd.)

After these rending events and with a state of emergency and a foreign war dragging on, it was unlikely that the Democrats could win a sixth straight election, something that had happened only once before in the U.S. in an era of competing political parties (Lincoln, Grant, Hayes and Garfield, riding victory in the Civil War, and the last two elections were effectively draws, Chapters 7 and 8). When Thomas E. Dewey, the Republican nominee against Roosevelt and Truman, was elected to a third four-year term as governor of New York in November 1950, he

---

1.   Speech by Senator Joseph McCarthy, June 14, 1951, in *The Congressional Record: Proceedings and Debates of the 82nd Congress, First Session,* vol. 97, part 5.

forswore any further interest in seeking the presidency and declared his support for General Dwight D. Eisenhower, who had retired as army chief of staff succeeding Marshall and became president of Columbia University in May 1948.

One month after Dewey's announcement of his support, Truman asked Eisenhower to take over the military command of the just-founded North Atlantic Treaty Organization. Eisenhower went to extraordinary lengths to pretend complete lack of interest in the presidency and to masquerade as a draftee to the office. It should be the Republicans' turn, Dewey was out of the race, and the favored candidate for that party's nomination was Republican Senate leader and son of the former president and chief justice, Robert A. Taft of Ohio, an intelligent but rather colorless man, admired by colleagues but not overly accessible to public enthusiasm, and generally rather isolationist.

Eisenhower, to those who examined his career closely, was a political operator and soldier-diplomat of rare virtuosity. Having served as MacArthur's understudy as chief of staff and in the Philippines, he returned to the United States on the outbreak of World War II and quickly attracted the just-promoted Marshall's attention and became his chief of war plans; then commander of the invasions of North Africa, Sicily, and Italy; commander of Overlord and of the Allied Expeditionary Forces in Western Europe; army chief of staff; president of Columbia; supreme commander of NATO—an astonishing career path, from Abilene, Kansas, to SACEUR in Paris, with the White House beckoning. There had been almost no setbacks and there were almost no audible enemies or serious critics. Ike, as he was always known, was well-liked by Roosevelt, Truman, Churchill, de Gaulle, even Stalin (and Churchill, aged 76, had just led the British Conservatives back to office, and de Gaulle was awaiting his opportunity, which would come). Dwight Eisenhower brilliantly combined the amiable, smiling, golfing, avuncular model politician with the five-star generalissimo and victorious military commander.

His plan for the supreme office consisted in eschewing any interest in it if Taft would promise whole-hearted support for NATO. This was a brilliant plan, because he didn't tell Taft about it, and while Taft wished him well, he professed to be uncertain if he favored dispatching four or six American divisions to Europe. Had Eisenhower told him that with Taft's full support, i.e., for six divisions, he, Eisenhower, would permanently withdraw from politics, Taft, though even more guileless and less opportunistic than Truman, would almost certainly have provided that support to assure himself the Republican nomination that he had twice before sought unsuccessfully. In any case, the senator's preliminary support for the dispatch of four divisions or six to Europe was a completely implausible reason for making such a career decision, and was only revealed after Taft was dead and Eisenhower had won the prize in question. The whole story is piffle.

Eisenhower, as in his career as a whole, was midway between his mentors, MacArthur and Marshall; he wanted political office almost as ardently as did MacArthur, but unlike his old chief, knew how to seem disinterested, and looked almost as disinterested as Marshall really was, but was as politically ambitious as MacArthur, if much more subtle. He was an amiable and fine-looking man, but lacked MacArthur's great oratorical talents (although he was a better writer).[2] In fairness, if Dewey had won in 1948, as he should have, given his advantages, and had won a second term, it is doubtful that Eisenhower would have leapt into political life at the age of 66 in 1956. He wanted the presidency, but on his own timetable.

As the Republican nomination in 1952 approached, it became clear that it would be a close race for delegates between Taft as the candidate of the party regulars, and Eisenhower as the public favorite and choice of the lean and hungry Republicans most tired of Democratic incumbency. In the southern states, which always voted Democratic, the Republicans didn't hold primaries and party locals chose the delegates, who naturally had the same votes at a convention as the delegates from other states that the Republicans had a real chance to win in a general election. The party elders in southern states favored Taft, but there were competing slates of Eisenhower supporters, and it would all come down to which group of delegates the convention would seat. The three-term governor of California and 1948 vice presidential candidate, Earl Warren, hoped for an even split between Taft and Eisenhower and his own victory as a compromise candidate. To this end, he stood as a favorite son and required that all California delegates be pledged to him.

Eisenhower, despite all his coy protestations, was in intense discussion with the Dewey forces that backed him. The only player who played a more adept game of political maneuver than Eisenhower was the 39-year-old junior senator from California, Richard M. Nixon. He pledged personal, private, verbal loyalty to his leader in the Senate, Taft; signed a loyalty pledge to Warren to assure his membership in the California delegation (which would not be his ex-officio as a U.S. senator from California); but privately arranged with Dewey that if he could deliver California's votes to seat the Eisenhower delegates at the convention from the contested southern states, Dewey would press his nomination for vice president on Eisenhower. Nixon was already a well-known and active campaigner around the country, having been the nominee of both the Republicans and the Democrats in his congressional district in 1948 and after the conviction of Alger Hiss in the

---

2.   Conrad Black, *Richard M. Nixon: A Life in Full*, New York, PublicAffairs, 2007, p. 183.

perjury proceedings that Nixon's questions had generated and his much publicized victory over Helen Gahagan Douglas in 1950 for the Senate.

Truman wrote Eisenhower in December 1951 asking his political intentions and the general wrote back from Paris on New Year's Day, 1952, in longhand, that "You know, far better than I, that the possibility that I will ever be drawn into political activity is so remote as to be negligible."[3] Five days later, Senator Henry Cabot Lodge publicly established the Eisenhower-for-President campaign, and the day after that, Eisenhower said he would accept the nomination if chosen. He won the New Hampshire primary a few weeks later, and shortly after that his supporters held a rally of 30,000 people for him in Madison Square Garden. Dewey smoked him out in early April with a message that if he didn't get off the fence and stop pretending he was George Washington waiting for a draft (not that Dewey used that phrase), MacArthur would be nominated—a complete fiction, but a nightmare for Eisenhower (because of the cordial but intense rivalry that had developed between them) that propelled him back from Paris.

Nixon boarded Warren's convention train bound from Sacramento to Chicago at Denver on July 3, and went through the train urging every delegate to move to Eisenhower on the second ballot. Taft, with five contested state delegations supporting him, was about 100 delegates ahead with a little over 100 pledged to Warren, but those were really honeycombed by Nixon. There were about 150 undecided. At the California caucus meeting on July 6, Nixon seized the microphone unannounced after the other California senator, William Knowland, had called for a divided California vote on the seating of Taft and Eisenhower delegates, to try to promote a stand-off between them. Nixon said this would be sleazy and self-defeating, and that despite his great respect for Taft, he believed the Republicans had to do the right thing: obey the people's will. He added, incidentally, that only Eisenhower could win and that he was not interested in going down as a Republican for the sixth straight time.[4]

This essentially stampeded Warren's delegates from under him, and led to Eisenhower winning the contested delegates and the convention, even though Taft, in a final throw, let it be known that if nominated, he would select MacArthur for vice president. Had Nixon not been so effective an infiltrator, Taft would have won the nomination, MacArthur might well have put him across in the election, and, as Taft died in August 1953, MacArthur could have been president after all, at the ripe age of 73. (He lived until 1964, in excellent health until about 1961.)

---

3.   Black, *op. cit.*, p. 184.
4.   Ibid. p. 202.

MacArthur was the convention keynote speaker, but gave an uncharacteristically flaccid speech.

The young Cassius, Nixon, was playing a subtle high-stakes game among men who were already world-historic figures. Eisenhower was nominated, Dewey championed Nixon, who was invited aboard by Eisenhower, and they ran on a platform that condemned Truman's handling of Korea and China without exactly endorsing MacArthur, advocated reduced spending, debt, and taxes, promised retention of the Taft-Hartley right-to-work and open shop law, and implied some sympathy for the McCarthyite fiction about a Democratic sell-out to Stalin, though neither candidate touched that hot iron and both stayed well clear of McCarthy himself. (Eisenhower knew what bunk the Yalta Myth was, as he showed when he reminded the Russians of their failure to honor their Yalta obligations throughout his dealings with them as president.)

While Eisenhower was not really drafted, Adlai E. Stevenson, the governor of Illinois and Roosevelt's assistant secretary of the navy, who had not, in fact, sought the nomination, was drafted by the Democrats. An eloquent, liberal intellectual and grandson of Cleveland's second vice president, he conducted a stylish and articulate campaign. The Democrats integrally supported the Roosevelt-Truman record, opposed Taft-Hartley, and retained the championship of civil rights for African Americans from Truman and Humphrey four years before, but reverted to the previous practice of nominating a segregationist southerner, Senator John J. Sparkman of Alabama, for vice president. Nixon had to endure a tense controversy over a so-called slush fund that was not, in fact, improper, and was less controversial than the personal financial arrangements of both Eisenhower and Stevenson. Eisenhower was not overly supportive, but Nixon saved his nomination with a dramatic, if rather mawkish, speech in which he referred to the gift of a dog, Checkers, to his young daughters.

Eisenhower disappointed many by speaking in Wisconsin and excising from his text, after it had been distributed to the press, a planned defense of General Marshall in the home state of his chief accuser, McCarthy. Stevenson spoke shortly after at the University of Wisconsin and said: "Disturbing things have taken place in our land. The pillorying of the innocent has caused the wise to stammer and the timid to retreat. . . . The voice of the accuser stills every other voice in the land. . . . If General Eisenhower would publicly embrace those who slandered General Marshall, there is certainly no reason to believe that he would restrain those who would slander me."[5] It was an uncharacteristic act of outright cowardice by Eisenhower.

On October 24, Eisenhower portentously announced: "I shall go to Korea" (with no hint of what he would do when he got there). On election day, Eisenhower and Nixon won 33.9 million votes to 27.3 million votes for Stevenson and Sparkman, 442 electoral votes to 82, 55.5 percent to 44 percent. The Republicans narrowly won control of both houses of the Congress, although Senator Wayne Morse of Oregon quit the Republicans over Eisenhower's deference to McCarthy and desertion of Marshall. Eminent Republican international lawyer John Foster Dulles, legal counsel of the American delegation at the Paris Peace Conference in 1919, briefly Hitler's lawyer in the U.S. in 1933, partial author of the Japan Peace Treaty, grandson of Benjamin Harrison's second secretary of state, John W. Foster, and nephew of Wilson's, Robert Lansing, would be the new secretary of state. (It was a remarkable family. Dulles's brother, Allen, was head of the Central Intelligence Agency, 1953–1961, and his son, Avery, a religious convert, was an eminent theologian and ultimately a cardinal.)

Harry S. Truman left office with a minority of Americans approving his performance, but was soon and is now durably regarded as a capable president and a man of unpretentious courage and integrity and wisdom. His command decisions on the atomic bomb, Berlin, NATO, the Marshall Plan, and Korea were all correct, important, and successful. In his homespun forthrightness and simplicity, he was in all respects the flip side of his elegant and devious predecessor. Truman was the average man, who in his capabilities was far from average, thrust up from the people; Roosevelt was the invincible aristocrat, ruling indefinitely and at his own pleasure by a combination of divine right, popular will, and natural aptitude, calling everyone by their first names, as Acheson pointed out, with the suave assurance of a Bourbon king, making no distinction between "the secretary of state and a stable boy."[6] It had been impossible, as Ernest Hemingway remarked, to reply to Roosevelt because of his overwhelming personality and almost absolute power. They had both been fine presidents and it had been a time of immense accomplishment, as America advanced from the depths of the Great Depression to overwhelming power, influence, and responsibility.

---

5. Black, *op. cit.*, pp. 265–266.
6. Conrad Black, *Franklin Delano Roosevelt: Champion of Freedom*, New York, PublicAffairs, 2003, pp. 312, 1129.

2. PRESIDENT DWIGHT D. EISENHOWER

The president-elect made a very short visit to South Korea, and soon made it known to Chinese Premier Chou En-lai, through the Indian government, that if the long-snarled cease-fire talks did not move, the use of atomic weapons would commend itself to him. On July 27, 1953, a Korean armistice was signed at Pan Mun Jon, and general warfare along the 38th parallel has been avoided since, though there have been many relatively local violations. This raises the question of why Truman did not try the same tactic. The Korean War cost 53,000 dead, missing, or captured American servicemen, and 93,000 were wounded, 170,000 South Korean military personnel were killed and 450,000 were wounded, while 750,000 South Korean civilians were killed and 230,000 were injured. About 300,000 North Korean military personnel were killed and 300,000 wounded, and 1.55 million civilians were killed or injured; the Chinese suffered approximately 400,000 military deaths and 500,000 injuries. After the French Revolutionary and Napoleonic Wars and the World Wars, it produced the greatest number of deaths of any conflict since the Thirty Years' War in the seventeenth century.

The subsequent spectacular growth of the South Korean economy to a sophisticated trillion-dollar model of modern industry in a well-functioning democracy, and more than 15 times the level of prosperity of the North, which wallows yet in desperate poverty, famine, and tyranny, reinforced the success of the Truman administration's initial objective to preserve the South from aggression. Eisenhower, despite the inflamed rhetoric of much of the Republican Party, effectively continued Truman's policy and had much more in common with his policy and personality than with MacArthur's, and took a number of occasions to emphasize his extremely high regard for George C. Marshall (to whom he owed his astounding rise from obscurity to world-historic command positions). Eisenhower would suavely anneal the national schism, and apply his diplomatic skills to conserve almost all the achievements of the Roosevelt-Truman years while leading the Republicans back to the mainstream of American political life after decades of almost flat-earth marginalization where Roosevelt's political cunning and chicanery and policy genius had confined them.

Joseph Stalin died on March 5, 1953, after a harsh and violent dictatorship of 29 years, and a divided regime succeeded him, leading to a rending but almost bloodless factional struggle for power. (Stalin's chief assistant Poskrebyshev and the police minister, Lavrenti Beria, were executed, but other members of losing factions were retired; Molotov eventually became director of a hydroelectric power dam in Siberia, after 30 years near the summit of Soviet life.) After a couple of years,

Nikita S. Khrushchev emerged as the party secretary general, the most important position in the USSR, and was a less sinister figure than Lenin or Stalin, his only predecessors.

Eisenhower had been authorized at the Yalta Conference to enter into direct contact with the Soviet high command, which in practice meant Stalin, in order to avoid accidental conflict as the two gigantic Allied army groups approached each other in Germany and Central Europe. And Stalin was so impressed with the conception and execution of the cross-channel invasion of France that he invited Eisenhower to Moscow in May 1945, and they got on quite well. While Eisenhower considered communism to be unutterable nonsense, he believed that it would be possible to deal with the Russians. And he was disgusted with the fear-mongering of McCarthyism that effectively presented communism as a virus or poison that could be secretly inserted in the drinking supply or the breakfast cereal of the children of America. He was in fact very critical, privately, of all his old chiefs except Roosevelt—Marshall for forcing coalition government and a false cease-fire on Chiang, Truman for being too squeamish about threatening draconian reprisals on China, and MacArthur for being too publicly and verbally trigger-happy about atomic weapons and for his rank insubordinacy.

Ike, as he was known to friends and to the American public, combined fiscal restraint with military purposefulness by proposing and enacting two policies that were popularly known as "more bang for the buck" and "brinkmanship." He wished to build on America's lead in nuclear weapons and their delivery capacity, and to roll back the vast personnel costs of large standing forces, especially the army. Though he had reached the highest possible rank in the U.S. Army, Eisenhower considered the navy and the air force better investments because they projected American power; he thought the retention of large standing armies was not altogether necessary and that it would be much cheaper, and more effective, and more conducive to economic growth and broadening prosperity, to restrain defense costs and focus them on massive retaliatory power of the most devastating kind, which would also stimulate advanced scientific research and sophisticated manufacturing.

Eisenhower also enhanced the role of the CIA and had no hesitation in using it to turf out unfriendly governments in several countries, starting with Iran. The eccentric leader of that country, Mohammed Mossadegh, who frequently appeared at public occasions in his pajamas, and burst into tears in the middle of speeches from his balcony, and accepted the support of local communists, had nationalized the Anglo-Persian Oil Company. The British responded by shutting down the largest oil refinery in the world, at Abadan, declared any acquisitions of Iranian oil to be the purchase of stolen property, and promised to sue any such buyers in British or foreign courts. Mossadegh was astoundingly inept to be impeded in this way, and had only to take a leaf from the book of Lázaro Cárdenas in Mexico in the late thirties and pay a somewhat reasonable compensation, even in notes, and line up sales in advance to countries who wouldn't care what Western courts thought of anything. Instead, he endured a crippling loss of revenue and beseeched Eisenhower to help him against the British. Now that Churchill was back in office in London, the chances of Eisenhower siding with Mossadegh in such a dispute were less than zero, especially with the young pro-Western Shah in opposition and conspicuously available to take back absolute power.

As Eisenhower considered nuclear war out of the question, conventional war horribly expensive in lives and money and possibly unwinnable against the Russians and Chinese, and stalemate unacceptable, he warmed up to the CIA, headed by Dulles's brother Allen, as a low-budget, high-effectiveness alternative. Eisenhower authorized a coup against Mossadegh, which consisted of the CIA operative for Iran, Theodore Roosevelt's grandson, Kermit, dispensing over a million dollars among military and tribal leaders to organize protests and stage a coup when the time came. Mossadegh passed a good deal of progressive legislation, for land reform and broadened education, but also rigged a 99.99 percent win in a referendum on whether to grant him absolute power for a year. The Shah showed no great staying power, forcing Mossadegh's resignation and then rejecting it, resisting cooperation in a coup and then giving way, and at the height of tension, removing to Rome for the summer of 1953. The British didn't have the resources to arrange a coup for themselves, and Churchill bombarded Eisenhower with messages to get rid of Mossadegh, lest the Russians succeed in Iran (as he had bombarded Truman in 1945 to scrap the German demarcation zones and the spheres of influence in Eastern Europe he had approved over American objections).

Iran was a Ruritanian farce in an important country, a rich oil state on the borders of the Soviet Union. Kermit Roosevelt prepared the ground well, under the nose of the naïve Iranian leader, who was thrown out by his own military on August 19, 1953. It was the smart move, but has been much criticized, and is yet. It was a crisp professional operation, and the Shah proved an effective and modernizing ruler. Of course there is room for legitimate debate about whether the United States would and should have done better by working with Mossadegh and not promoting and sustaining regime change. But once having done so, it had to back its protégé. The problem was not dispensing with Mossadegh, it was giving insufficient support to the Shah 25 years and five presidents of the United States later. Eisenhower and Dulles assured, through Kermit Roosevelt, that the

British monopoly on Iranian oil would be knocked down to 40 percent, a share equal to that of the United States. (The Anglo-Persian, later Anglo-Iranian, Oil Company, and then British Petroleum (BP), would carry some long-term baggage as President Barack Obama, elected in 2008, would publicly disapprove Eisenhower's overthrow of Mossadegh and BP's role, and BP would not escape controversy, as Obama would become extremely censorious about the company's conduct in the 2009–2010 Gulf of Mexico oil spill.)

On December 8, 1953, Eisenhower, after conferring with Churchill and the French premier, Joseph Laniel, in Bermuda, addressed the United Nations General Assembly, and proposed a division of available nuclear fissionable material between the U.S.A., the USSR, and the U.K., which would be handed over to the International Atomic Energy Agency, whose establishment he urged under UN auspices, for sharing for peaceful purposes with all the countries of the world. It was a rather visionary idea, and was exceedingly well received when he presented it. Even the Russians applauded, but they then shilly-shallied, and the International Atomic Energy Agency was only set up in 1957. This was the "Atoms for Peace" plan, but the Russians, again with the heavy-handed clumsiness that had distinguished all their activities since they became one of the world's two superpowers, ultimately refused, as they had refused participation in the Marshall Plan.

Eisenhower deftly managed to reduce U.S. defense expenditures by relying more on atomic development, and got peace in Korea by threatening nuclear war, yet he took over and championed the cause of international civilian use of atomic energy, and de-escalation of the Cold War. It was a clever policy, spanning brinkmanship and peaceful sharing of atomic power for peaceful purposes, as Eisenhower was himself simultaneously a golfing, barbecuing grandfather, and the five-star general who crossed the Rhine, enveloped the Ruhr, liberated many of the death camps, and, as much as Stalin, drove Hitler to suicide.

Eisenhower also dispatched Nixon (whose trip with other congressmen to Europe in 1947 had greatly strengthened support for the Marshall Plan) on a 70-day, 20-country tour of the Far East and South Asia, starting October 5. Nixon was always massively briefed, and was so on this occasion, and had, as passing decades would show, great aptitude for foreign relations. Eisenhower entrusted Nixon with the mission of telling South Korean president Syngman Rhee that he absolutely must not provoke a renewal of the conflict with the North. Nixon also closely studied the successful British techniques in dealing with the Chinese Communist–inspired civil war in Malaya. Nixon stayed with the British commander and governor, Field Marshal Sir Gerald Templer, and they developed a warm mutual appreciation that would resonate importantly more than 15 years later. Nixon went on to Vietnam and was as unimpressed with the French plan to deal with their insurrection as he had been struck by the intelligent planning and execution of the British.

He delivered Eisenhower's message to Rhee, and in a wide-ranging interview with Japan's great survivor, Emperor Hirohito, urged Japan to begin rearming at once (only nine years after he had earned two battle starts fighting Hirohito's armies at Guadalcanal, Bougainville, and Green Island). In a seven-hour meeting with Chiang Kai-shek, Nixon disabused him of any idea of going back to the mainland. In Burma, he originated his technique, which would become familiar on every continent except Antarctica, of going into the midst of crowds of demonstrators and disarming them with knowledgeable conversation. He was very impressed with Philippine president Ramon Magsaysay, and considered Indonesian president Sukarno a corrupt and degenerate cynic and buffoon. Both were accurate insights. He intensely disliked Indian prime minister Jawaharlal Nehru, and his daughter, Indira Gandhi, as pompous and ineffectual hypocrites claiming transcendent cultural and humanitarian virtue for their ramshackle, poverty-stricken country. He finished his tour with excellent visits with the Pakistani leader, Field Marshal Mohammed Ayub Khan, and with the recently reinstalled Shah of Iran, thereafter a life-long friend.

Nixon and his wife demonstrated a strong grasp of all they saw and made excellent impressions personally on all their hosts (and on the traveling American press contingent), other than Nehru, who, after Nixon promised aid to Pakistan, called him "an unprincipled cad." Many of these encounters would have important consequences. Nixon addressed the nation at Eisenhower's request on December 23, 1953, and spoke of the danger of communist infiltration and insurrection in Malaya, Indochina, Indonesia, the Philippines, and Burma, as well as the divisions of China and Korea, presaging Eisenhower's soon-to-be-coined domino theory—that if one of these countries went down, it would take others. Nixon strenuously recommended to Eisenhower and Dulles a South East Asia Treaty Organization, modeled on NATO, and work began on this at once.

Nixon and Dulles were essentially in favor of using Chiang's forces in Korea, drawing the Red Chinese army into the peninsula as MacArthur had proposed, cutting them off, and crushing them from all sides and the air, while conventionally bombing China's fragile industrial capacity, and administering a stinging military defeat on China. They also wanted comprehensive aid to anti-communist forces in the area, to be conducted and directed as the British were in Malaya: not colonial holding operations like the French were attempting in Indochina, which were hopeless, but as Western support for indigenous, democratic, and anti-communist forces, as was being successfully carried out in Europe. Eisenhower agreed that more attention had to be paid to Asia (he had, after all, spent four years with MacArthur in the Philippines, albeit, as he later rather snidely said, "studying theatrics" from his chief). But Eisenhower did not want to use American ground forces in Asia again, and while he invented the domino theory, he was a cautious judge of how much effort was warranted in the case of each unit in the sequence. Indochina was clearly coming next, and fast.

Eisenhower was effectively fine-tuning the containment strategy, with the astute eye of a proven military analyst and commander, and very successful soldier-diplomat at the highest levels in war and peace but also as a very successful politician. He was admirably qualified to consolidate the gains of Roosevelt and Truman, having served both those presidents with great distinction.

3. INDOCHINA

By early 1954, the condition of the French in Indochina was becoming very dis-quieting. France could generally hold its own against the Viet Minh (Vietnamese Communists led by Ho Chi Minh) but such a war was very costly for the French, who were constantly seeking U.S. assistance, and threatening an indefinite delay in the approval of the European Defense Community if they did not receive it. The Defense Community was the integration of NATO military forces (including a rearmed West Germany) that Eisenhower had been pushing since he was the first NATO Supreme Allied Commander, Europe (SACEUR). This issue and Indo-china became ensnared in France's ancient preoccupation with Germany, which France was having some difficulty considering as a friend. In his first months as president, Eisenhower had told the French that American assistance in Indochina was conditional on France finding a "forceful and inspired" military leader in Vietnam, and on France promising independence and getting out from under the opprobrium of seeming to fight a colonial war. France had had a first-class commander, General (posthumously Marshal) Jean de Lattre de Tassigny, who had commanded the French First Army of 10 divisions in Eisenhower's sweep through France and into Germany almost a decade before. De Lattre had won several victories against the Viet Minh, and had military matters fairly stabilized when he had to retire because of cancer (shortly after his only son had died in action under his command), and he succumbed quickly to the illness, dying in January 1952. (Eisenhower, de Gaulle, though he was not present, and Montgomery were among the honorary pallbearers at the mighty state funeral from the Invalides to the Arc de Triomphe to Notre Dame.)

On the second point, the French knew that their real enemies were the independentists within Indochina, though they were being supported by the Russians and the Chinese. Unlike the British, who knew such a war to be unwinnable, the French were determined to hang on to what they could, even if they dragged down European defense and the security of France itself in doing so. Eisenhower was not prepared to commit America to defend French colonialism, and with the administration's "New Look" of fewer men and greater firepower and air and sea forces, there was not the manpower to fight in Asia while maintaining an integrated conventional and nuclear deterrent in Europe, which remained the principal theater, as had been agreed since the beginning of the Anglo-American staff talks in 1939.

Apart from some desperate appeals by the French (a little like Reynaud's to Roosevelt in 1940), there was no thought of nuclear weapons in Indochina. Eisenhower rejected Walter Bedell Smith's recommendation of insertion of Nationalist Chinese forces (which Smith had made to Acheson in 1950 over Korea). Eisenhower considered that this would just draw the Chinese into Indochina and create another open artery such as Korea had been. (He was certainly correct then, but Bedell Smith, MacArthur, and others had been correct in Korea, where the Communist Chinese were already invading in large numbers. There would also, eventually, be an argument for using Taiwanese in Vietnam, after more than 300,000 Communist Chinese were dispatched to North Vietnam in non-combat roles; Chapter 14.) Eisenhower wanted Britain to join him in providing air assistance and materiel for the French, as long as they could make a plausible claim that self-government for Vietnam, Laos, and Cambodia lay at the end of it. This conformed with current views of collective security and America's refusal to promote colonialism, and should see the communists off. But Churchill, who, at 79, was erratic and rather intractable, claimed that only the English-speaking people mattered and that he didn't care what happened in Asia.

The French asked for 25 B-26 bombers and 400 technicians to assist in operating and servicing them. They claimed they were going back on the offensive under de Lattre's successor, Raoul Salan, and that the fortress at Dien Bien Phu was impregnable. Salan was a drug-addicted scoundrel, and no great military genius, a very inadequate replacement for de Lattre. As one of Eisenhower's biographers, Stephen Ambrose, put it: "Eisenhower found it difficult to see how the French putting their most famous units into a fortress surrounded by high ground that was held by the enemy constituted taking the offensive." He gave them 10 B-26s, which were certainly not going to provide a balance of victory.[7] By March, French

7.   Stephen E. Ambrose, *Eisenhower: The President*, New York, Simon and Schuster, 1984, p. 175.

optimism had evaporated and their chief of staff, General Paul Ely, came urgently to Washington seeking help. Eisenhower agreed to the sale of some C-119 planes that could deluge the area around Dien Bien Phu with napalm and make the ant-like movements of the guerrilla enemy more detectable.

Eisenhower made it clear to Ely, as his capable ambassador in Paris, Douglas Dillon, did to the government of Laniel, that there would be no consideration of direct American intervention unless France subscribed entirely to the EDC and did the necessary to make it universally understood that this was not a war for preservation of the colonial status quo. He also said to intimates and wrote in his memoirs that jungle warfare was very difficult, no American units were now familiar with it, that casualties would be heavy, and that an influx of Western soldiers would "probably have aggravated rather than assuaged Asiatic resentments."[8] The president showed both his military expertise and his spectacular talents at tactical political maneuver, by seeking a national debate on the issue of intervention in Indochina in the context of joint action with the British, the French, the Australians, the components of Indochina itself, and also forces from Thailand, the Philippines, and New Zealand. It was on these terms that Eisenhower couched any possible direct American involvement. He was confident that the national debate would oppose intervention, that the Congress would balk, and that no one not already in the war (i.e., France and the Vietnamese, Laotians, and Cambodians) would contribute one soldier, and meanwhile the French were not meeting his initial conditions. Salan, a devious French army careerist, was not up to commanding such a difficult theater, and the French were becoming defeatist and were dragging their heels on EDC.

All this activity of Eisenhower's was an elaborate, incomprehensible ceremony, as his press conferences often were, designed to confuse everyone but hold the president invulnerable, in this case, to screams about "losing Indochina." He did not now think a partitioning could be avoided, and hoped that at that point, an independent South Vietnam could be assisted to defend itself against the communist North. It was *déjà vu* from Korea, but with the knowledge gained from that struggle.

Eisenhower and Dulles suspected the French had decided to try to use the upcoming Geneva Conference, supposedly about Korea, to negotiate themselves out of Indochina, where Eisenhower wanted to preorganize a Western stance. On April 5, 1954, Ambassador Dillon reported that Ely claimed the U.S. had agreed

---

8.   William B. Ewald Jr., *Eisenhower the President: Crucial Days: 1951–1960*, Englewood Cliffs, New Jersey, Prentice Hall, 1981, p. 119.

to drop two or three atomic weapons on the Viet Minh. This was nonsense. As the conditions at Dien Bien Phu worsened, Eisenhower took the position that the U.S. would not intervene without allies in a collective-security operation. Eisenhower sent the Joint Chiefs chairman, Admiral Arthur Radford, to have another try with Churchill, but the old warrior said that if Britain hadn't fought for India, it wouldn't fight for French Indochina either. This was pretextual waffling from an aging man, but there weren't going to be any allies apart from those desperately calling for their own rescue.

At his April 7 press conference, Eisenhower laid out the domino theory very graphically, but on the basis that they would only start falling on the abandonment of all of Southeast Asia. His plan was to avoid being drawn into a lost battle in North Vietnam, lay the defeat on the stupidity of the French and the balkiness of other allies, do a preemptive hosing down on excessive alarm about the imminent debacle at Dien Bien Phu, but warm up opinion for the activation of the SEATO Nixon had proposed setting up, and the organization of collective security in the Far East, with the Indochinese domino being whatever could be salvaged from the communists in the current struggle the French were about to lose.

The Geneva Conference opened on April 26, and Dien Bien Phu fell on May 7 (with a loss of 13,000 men—3,000 French and 10,000 pro-French Vietnamese). The French lost fewer of their own people than the Americans under General Horatio Gates did at Camden in 1779 (Chapter 2), and the whole garrison was barely half the number of American prisoners taken at the start of the Battle of the Ardennes (Chapter 10), but the international left played it up the way the North implied in 1864 that Atlanta was a city of 500,000 (instead of 14,000, Chapter 6).

Eisenhower found it incredible that "a nation which had only the help of a tiny British army when it turned back the German flood in 1914 and withstood the gigantic 1916 attacks at Verdun could now be reduced to the point that she cannot produce a few hundred technicians to keep planes flying properly in Indochina. . . . The only hope is to produce a new and inspirational leader—and I do not mean one that is 6 feet 5 and who considers himself to be, by some miraculous biological and transmigrative process, the offspring of Clemenceau and Jeanne d'Arc."[9] Of course de Gaulle was the only alternative to the communists as the Fourth Republic floundered from crisis to crisis. And Roosevelt's canard about Le Tigre and St. Joan, coined in a letter to his cousin from the Casablanca Conference 11 years before,[10] was becoming desperately tired by this time. Only de Gaulle

9. Ambrose, *op. cit.*, p. 183.
10. January 14, 1943, author's personal collection.

had the prestige, cunning, and ruthless determination to restore French greatness, and Eisenhower at least avoided the Rooseveltian parlor game of trying to unveil and buff up implausible rivals to him such as the scoundrel Admiral Darlan and the ludicrous General Giraud. On his own authority, which he technically did not possess (and which caused French writer François Mauriac to wonder if de Gaulle were mad), de Gaulle called for a national demonstration at the Arc de Triomphe following Dien Bien Phu, in remembrance of the sacrifices of the French Army, but observed as he emerged from his car that "The people have not really turned out." They would turn out in the next crisis, Algeria, already looming.

Eisenhower's handling of the crisis was his usual astute mélange of caution, self-immunization from reproach, and both tactical and strategic insight. Vice President Nixon spoke to the American Society of Newspaper Editors on April 16. In response to the question of whether he would favor insertion of American forces to protect against a communist takeover of Indochina if the French pulled out, he said that he would, and added, "I believe the executive branch of the government has to take the politically unpopular decision of facing up to it and doing it, and I personally would support such a decision."[11] This caused, as it was intended to, quite a stir, as Nixon was trying to propel his chief forward by the small of the back and the scruff of the neck into a more forceful posture in Southeast Asia.

Eisenhower had his press secretary, James Hagerty, hose down the controversy without embarrassing Nixon. Despite ingenious and persistent efforts, Nixon could not persuade Eisenhower to budge. If the United States had carpet-bombed the area around Dien Bien Phu while airlifting out its 13,000 defenders, it would have spared France great humiliation and demoralization, and would have redounded to the immeasurable benefit of the old France-America alliance, which would soon assume greater importance than it had since the times of Wilson and Clemenceau. And if America were ever to be involved in Indochina, it should have been when France was an ally and before Ho Chi Minh had turned the majority of Vietnamese into fierce warrior-robots. Eisenhower implicitly conceded the partition of Vietnam, but drew the line there and set up SEATO to strengthen all the post-partition dominos. The ominous strategic mystery was whether half of Vietnam was practically salvageable at an acceptable cost.

Joseph Laniel's government was defeated in the French National Assembly on June 12, and he was replaced by the highly intelligent but leftish Pierre Mendès-France, who promised to secure peace in Indochina by July 20. This convinced

---

11. Claude Mauriac, *The Other de Gaulle*, London, Angus and Robertson, 1973, p. 356.

Eisenhower that a complete sell-out was in the offing, and he pulled Walter Bedell Smith, the under secretary of state, his representative at the Geneva Conference and wartime chief of staff, and the U.S. had only an observer status at Geneva thereafter.

Laniel had favored the European Defense Community, which was the only framework yet devised for rearming Germany, the fear of which was almost the only reprisal that had caught Stalin's attention and had caused Roosevelt to indulge Morgenthau's nonsense about the pastoralization of Germany. Mendès-France was ambiguous and even Churchill and Eden, who arrived in Washington in late June, were waffling about it; the British were not much more enthused about a rearmed Germany than the French and the Russians were. Although Eisenhower now found Churchill sluggish, largely deaf, and with limited powers of concentration, he had enormous admiration and affection for him (which was largely reciprocated), and offered the British leaders a deal: if Britain would support the EDC, the United States would supply Britain with more atomic bombs to ensure that their bomber force could be fully utilized in the event of such a conflict. And they should agree on Geneva terms: independence for Laos and Cambodia and withdrawal of all Viet Minh forces from those countries, and a division of Vietnam at the 17th parallel. The tired British leaders were ambivalent.

The Geneva Conference ended on July 21. The U.S. did not sign, but did not imply that it would obstruct the conclusions of the conference. Dulles, who was in Geneva but did not attend the conference, famously refused to shake hands with Chou En-lai, and when interrupted in his bath with the news that China was prepared to release all Korean War prisoners and normalize relations, without hesitation and on his own authority, Dulles declined. The agreement was a climb-down for the Chinese and the Americans (the French were now almost incidental). The Viet Minh could take all of Vietnam if new forces beyond France's capabilities were not inserted, and the Republican and southern Democratic hawks, including the Joint Chiefs, endorsed the perfect compromise of staying out of Indochina but launching an atomic attack on China, which would supposedly avoid the partition of Vietnam—an insane proposal. Meanwhile, to put the feet of the British and the French to the fire, Eisenhower had Lyndon Johnson, William Knowland, and Nixon put through the Senate, which they did by unanimous vote, a measure authorizing the president to take any steps necessary to "restore sovereignty to Germany and to enable her to contribute to the maintenance of peace and security." It was almost back to Woodrow Wilson's threat of a separate peace with Germany in 1918; if the British and French did not get on board, the Americans would rearm Germany, outside a pan-European military command, but as a full partner in NATO, and even America's chief ally in Europe just nine years after the surrender of the Third Reich.

While Churchill and Eden were in Washington, Chou En-lai and Mendès-France were meeting in Geneva. They settled on the compromise the British and the Americans were agreeing, but with the provision that there would be Vietnam-wide elections within two years on the issue of unification. This was a fig leaf of face-saving for France, as Ho Chi Minh was certain to win such elections with a unanimous vote from the North, in the familiar communist manner. Chou said he would deliver the Viet Minh if Mendès-France could deliver the Americans.

But that was not what Eisenhower agreed to; Dulles now bustled about recruiting adherents to SEATO, and rounded up Britain, France, Australia, New Zealand, Thailand, the Philippines, and Pakistan. The CIA reported that Ngo Dinh Diem was the only possible non-communist South Vietnamese leader who had any support, and the Americans recognized him and Eisenhower sent him a letter in September, with an aid mission designed to prop up a durable non-communist, independent South Vietnam. This made a Swiss cheese of Geneva from the start, as South Vietnam was recognized as a permanent state by the United States and its entourage, and South Vietnam joined SEATO, and the Geneva Accord had stipulated that neither Vietnam would be in an alliance. (Of course, this was also a fraud, given Ho's relations with China and Russia.)

It is easy to forget, given how successful it ultimately was, how fragile NATO was even five years after its founding. It was convenient for the French to blame their decisive defeat in Vietnam on the U.S., and on August 30, the National Assembly in Paris rejected the European Defense Community. Eisenhower suspected that there were substantial elements of French opinion that would entertain defecting to an alliance with the Soviet Union. But, as always, he was ready with his contingency plan and ordered the immediate convening of a NATO meeting where the United States rammed through the election of Germany to the alliance as a fully sovereign (and effectively forgiven) state. The French, having been soundly trounced by the communist elements of their former Vietnamese colonial subjects, blamed the defeat on the Americans, who had given plenty of advice on how to avoid it and generous tangible support. They kicked the United States mindlessly on the shins by threatening to blackball Germany in NATO (denuding the defense of France itself, if the United States did not salvage their lost colonial escapade in Indochina). France was rewarded by being put over America's knee and given a further international public thrashing as Germany, the Nazi pariah and rubble heap of just nine years before, was parachuted into NATO and seated higher up the table than France. This was all effected under the observant eyes of the British.

If Churchill lamented his loss of what he fancied to be equality of influence with Roosevelt (Chapter 11), he could scarcely fail to notice where the correlation of forces within the Western Alliance stood now. France had learned little of how to manage its relations with the United States since the fiasco of the Citizen Genêt and XYZ affairs (Chapter 3), and Napoleon III's intrusion in Mexico (Chapter 6).

Even at this remove and after the end of the Cold War, it is not clear whether the MacArthur-Nixon-Dulles faction or Eisenhower and Truman were correct about Korea and Vietnam. If the Americans had imported 200,000 Nationalist Chinese into Korea, conventionally bombed Manchuria, and interdicted Chinese reinforcements across the Yalu by air, whether before or shortly after Stalin's death and with the Kremlin in disarray, Communist China would have been severely chastened in its infancy, and would not have enjoyed the moral victory it claimed in fighting the United States and United Nations to a standstill. It is not clear that peace would have taken appreciably longer or cost significantly more American lives than was actually the case. And, again, the world would have been spared the pestilential nuisance of the belligerently deranged Kim dynasty in Pyongyang.

And if Eisenhower had acted like a real ally at Dien Bien Phu and helped avoid a French debacle, he could presumably have reached an arrangement that Indochina would become the independent democracies of Cambodia, Laos, and South Vietnam as well as North Vietnam, and that the United States would assist the French in helping the South Vietnamese government resist the communists, as the British were doing in Malaya. SEATO would be set up, the other countries would provide some forces, as most of them eventually did, and France would wholeheartedly support the EDC. Dulles should have shaken hands with Chou En-lai; he was a good deal more civilized than many people Dulles fraternized with, and they should have moved to normalize relations with China as soon as favorable terms were available; nothing was gained by waiting for almost 20 years.

It was a powerful argument for Eisenhower to say that he ended the Korean War and kept the U.S. out of Vietnam. But 10 years later, as an ex-president, he was a Vietnam hawk, urging a strong stand in Vietnam after his successor had allowed Laos to be transformed into a conduit for North Vietnamese infiltration of the South, and after the French had become friendlier with the Asian communists than they were with their ancient American ally. Like most Oriental politics, it is very complicated.

4. THE CIA IN CENTRAL AMERICA

As the Geneva Conference droned on, there occurred in Central America another farce of the kind that had been recurring at short intervals for over a century. In

Guatemala, the democratically elected reformist government of Jacobo Arbenz was proposing relatively moderate land reform, but accepted support from the local Communist party. Arbenz nationalized some of the acreage of the United Fruit Company (of which Allen Dulles had been a director, and of which even Eisenhower's secretary, Ann Whitman, was a shareholder, though it is unlikely, despite leftist insinuations, that these facts altered official policy). A CIA operation was cooked up by Eisenhower, the Dulles brothers, and a couple of senior CIA operatives, in which a designated colonel, Carlos Castillo Armas, was suddenly proclaimed by a friendly radio station in Honduras as a challenger for the presidency. A "front" was alleged to exist, headed by Castillo Armas, which in fact consisted of 150 hired hands of the usual ragged CIA insurgent variety. To call them soldiers of fortune would exaggerate both their levels of energy and discipline and the clarity of their motives. The Swedish ship *Alfhem* docked in Guatemala on May 15, 1954, with a cargo of Czech artillery, rifles, and side arms, which Dulles and Eisenhower immediately denounced in the most stentorian terms, with the inevitable bandying about of the Monroe Doctrine. In fact, this equipment wasn't for the army, which Arbenz realized was being bribed by the Americans and was unreliable; it was for a people's militia he was setting up.

Castillo Armas's "front" was claimed by the Honduran radio station the CIA operated to have "invaded" Guatemala, and a completely fanciful account was then disseminated, over the air and in the world generally, to the effect that a war of liberation was raging in Guatemala, and moving ever closer to the capital, Guatemala City. In fact, Castillo Armas moved six miles inside the Guatemalan border and went into permanent bivouac in the jungle, in the Church of the Black Christ. There was no front, no war, and certainly no uprising. Eisenhower himself calculated that the way to frighten Arbenz was air power, and he approved giving two P-51s to Nicaraguan dictator Anastasio Somoza, who would then give Castillo Armas the two P-51s he already had. (This was the same Somoza whom Roosevelt had described as "a son of a bitch but our son of a bitch.") Eisenhower authorized CIA pilots to fly from Managua Airport and do some precise bombing in Guatemala. He had also authorized a blockade of Guatemala and asserted the right of search and seizure on the high seas. This inflamed the ire of the British and the French.

Arbenz requested the United Nations to take up the matter, and the British, scandalized at the threat to seize ships on the oceans, and the French, none too pleased at the failure of the Americans to help them in Indochina, let it be known that they would support Arbenz at the UN, including in the dispatch of observers to Guatemala. These would quickly unearth the proportions of the U.S. presence in these shenanigans, and Eisenhower told his UN ambassador, Henry Cabot Lodge, to tell the British and the French that the U.S. would veto (for the first time the U.S. would use a UN veto) any such initiatives, and that if the British and French threw in with Arbenz, the United States would reevaluate its views about Egypt, the Suez Canal, and North Africa (Algeria, Tunisia, and Morocco were all in varying stages of revolt against the French). The British and French thought better of it, abstained, and there was no need for a U.S. veto; Arbenz fled at the prospect of Eisenhower turning up the pressure as far as he had to, resigning on June 27, 1954. Churchill and Eden arrived in Washington June 25, and Eisenhower had a blunt talk with them about their meddling in the Americas.

Eisenhower had been decisive in Guatemala, and may have spared the U.S. political inconvenience, but there was the appearance of being too wedded to the United Fruit Company, which had been effectively deploying U.S. forces in Latin America for decades, and was not the hemisphere's most enlightened employer. The United States might have begun sooner to try to recruit moderate reformers in Latin America, and it is not clear if Arbenz really had any communist sympathies or not, though there is reason to believe that he was a slightly Kerensky-like figure, with an academic interest in Marx. Castillo Armas was assassinated, for unknown reasons, in 1957. Eisenhower was correct to expel the British and French from Latin America (yet again), and it is hard to get too excited about his ejection of a somewhat suspect government, but he was straying a long way from Roosevelt's public relations success of the Good Neighbor, or even Harry Truman's much-admired visit to the graves of Mexican soldiers who died in the Mexican War with the U.S. in 1848. If the objective was to keep the communists out of the hemisphere, and not just stop the pretentious blunderings of Whitehall and the Quai d'Orsay, America was going to have to do better than this, and Eisenhower did send Nixon to visit South America comprehensively, later in his presidency. As usual, Nixon, who soon emerged as the administration's star foreign policy thinker (not excluding Dulles or Eisenhower himself), came back with some serious proposals, but there was already a lot of water over the dam by then. (Eisenhower himself eventually toured South America and was very respectfully received, but the whole political nature of the continent had shifted by then.)

5. EISENHOWER'S ASTUTE POLITICAL INSTINCTS

A front where Eisenhower was unambiguously successful was in the expunging of the influence of Senator Joseph R. McCarthy, who had become more and more erratic. Once he attacked Eisenhower, and expanded the "twenty years of treason"[12]

12. Black, *op. cit.*, pp. 298, 302.

he professed to find in Roosevelt and Truman, to include the incumbent, matters proceeded swiftly. McCarthy announced public hearings to investigate charges of subversive infiltration of the U.S. Army. Eisenhower made it clear that no subpoenas from McCarthy to the army would be responded to, and that anyone who responded to any such subpoena could consider doing so in a letter of resignation as a government employee. Eisenhower had had enough and imposed an absolute privilege as commander-in-chief and retired holder of the army's highest rank and commands, and dismissed the complaints even of his own Republican congressional leaders. Nixon as president of the Senate, and the Democratic Senate leader, Lyndon B. Johnson, organized a censure vote, which passed against McCarthy 67–22 on December 2, 1954, after McCarthy had denounced his opponents as "handmaidens of Communism."[13] McCarthy disintegrated into alcoholism and inconsequentiality, and died, aged 48, on May 2, 1957. It had been a very strange era, an aberration of overreaction and demagogy, which enjoyed the durability it did only because American official policy required that the people be severely frightened by the Red Menace; a certain amount of frothy excess, with the American love of the spectacle and relative procedural flexibility, was almost inevitable.

An aspect of the unsettled climate even of American military opinion was the frequency of requests from the Joint Chiefs of Staff for atomic attacks on China. America and the world were fortunate that in Dwight D. Eisenhower there was a leader who knew exactly how to deal both with trigger-happy generals and admirals, and with bellicose congressional leaders (he said of his Senate majority leader, William Knowland, that he "has no foreign policy except to develop high blood pressure whenever he mentions the words 'Red China'").[14] Eisenhower patiently repeated to the JCS, headed by Admiral Radford, that an atomic attack on China would swiftly lead to nuclear war with the Soviet Union, which would leave the Eurasian land mass from the Elbe to Vladivostok and from the Arctic shores of Siberia to the northern border of Vietnam, except, it could be hoped, Hong Kong, a smoldering ruin of lethal radioactivity, famine, devastation, and scores or even hundreds of millions of corpses, and what did his bemedalled friends (though less bemedalled than he, had he chosen to receive the Joint Chiefs in his full kit) suggest as the civilized world's next step after that? Answer came there none.

Eisenhower, beneath his deliberately contorted syntax and generally amiable exterior, was a very complicated and sophisticated tactician and strategist. He knew from his dealings with Stalin and Zhukov in 1945 that the Russians would

---

13. Black, *op. cit.*, p. 308.
14. Ambrose, *op. cit.*, p. 202.

take brinkmanship, the threat of massive retaliation, seriously, and that he could embrace that policy and cut defense spending, run a sensible federal budget, and even cut some taxes. But when the military high command started grabbing for the nuclear toys he slapped them down and told them such a war was out of the question unless the Soviets or the Chinese initiated hostilities against a vital American interest, such as a NATO country or Japan. Thus, his answer to Korea was to threaten nuclear weapons to get the status quo ante that Truman had been unable to close on without believable atomic threats. His answer to Vietnam was not to touch France's egomaniacal pursuit of a colonial beau geste, not to go in without allies, but to announce that the dominos started at the demarcation line between Communist North Vietnam and a newly independent South Vietnam.

Apart from trying to spare the French the Dien Bien Phu debacle, Eisenhower should have accepted at least discussions with Chou at Geneva, though they would have had to be conducted by a subtler mind than Dulles's—Nixon, or even some bipartisan combination of MacArthur, Acheson, Bohlen, and Kennan. China might have traded normalization and reasonable assurances such as were made by Nixon 17 years later, over Taiwan, a Korean peace treaty, and the People's Republic's assumption of the Chinese seat at the UN, in exchange for a 20-year separation of the two Vietnams. But this is conjecture; Eisenhower tried to reason with the French, got Germany into NATO, and salvaged the possibility of half a loaf in Vietnam. He took a risk in violating the Geneva Accord, by which the U.S. was not bound, and SEATO was not ultimately successful. But by the time Vietnam was unified more than 20 years later, the communists had been massacred in Indonesia and defeated in Malaya; South Korea, Taiwan, and Singapore were all tremendous economic success stories; and the United States had constructive relations with the People's Republic. The resolution of the West German question, though not by Eisenhower's preferred formula of an integrated European army, was by far the most important strategic outcome of the match, though it had nothing to do with China. As usual, Eisenhower, while seeming cautious and not especially dynamic, had deftly played an indifferent hand; he had taken a swipe at his principal foe, Stalin's fractious successors, by elevating Germany; had matched wits evenly with the very cunning Chou En-lai; had brushed off the French, who were at this point impossible; and had sent a polite, firm message to the British, while quietly routing the domestic extremists. The Cold War had just begun, but was already very complicated. America had a deceptively subtle leader, and the times demanded no less.

6. THE FORMOSA STRAIT AND VIETNAM

On September 3, 1954, the latest Chinese initiative to aggravate the United States and roil the waters in the Far East, devised with almost fiendish imagination, began. China started shelling the tiny offshore islands of Quemoy and Matsu, which instantly became household words throughout the world. The nearest of the islands is closer to the Chinese mainland than Staten Island is to Manhattan. They are rock piles, historically attached to China, that Chiang had stuffed with soldiers and used as jumping-off points for the harassment of Chinese coastal shipping, and for raids on the mainland. Chiang claimed that the fall of Quemoy and Matsu would severely compromise the security of Taiwan itself, and the Joint Chiefs disagreed with that assessment, but averred that they could not be defended without American assistance. This was complicated by the fact that the waters among and between the islands and China, at their narrowest points, were not accessible to the principal ships of the U.S. Seventh Fleet, because of the deep drafts of its heavy units, in particular the giant aircraft carrier *Midway*.

Admiral Radford and his colleagues on the Joint Chiefs visited the president in Denver on his summer holiday on September 12 and for the third time in less than six months recommended the use of atomic weapons on China, and also the deployment of American forces on the islands. Eisenhower wouldn't hear of it; he said that if war broke out, Russia, not China, would be the main counter target, and he lectured them forcefully on the requirements of constitutional govern- ment and the need to obtain congressional approval for the use of such weapons, especially in so abstruse a cause. The implications of the fact that the Chiefs, the successors of MacArthur, Marshall, Eisenhower, Nimitz, and Bradley, would be so relaxed about precipitating millions of people into eternity for such nonsensical strategic assets are disquieting. Roosevelt would have had the self-confidence, and Truman the gritty independent-mindedness and Missouri skepticism, to refuse them; but even better was Eisenhower's dismissal of Radford's requests as military, moral, strategic, and constitutional foolishness. Senior military officials can always impute the non-cooperation of civilian chiefs to their strategic philistinism and civilian squeamishness; this is much more challenging with a president who reached the highest possible rank in the combat U.S. Army, successfully commanded the greatest military operation in world history, and received the unconditional sur- render of the nation's enemies in Western Europe.

The usual suspects fell for Chiang's response to Mao and Chou's tweak. Senator Knowland demanded a naval blockade of the whole Chinese coast. To the shouts of Knowland and McCarthy and their claque about the "honor of America,"

Vietnam War. Courtesy of the U.S. Army Center of Military History

Eisenhower replied that he was well familiar with that honor and did not construe it as being "insensible to the safety of [American] soldiers."[15] In December, he signed a mutual-defense treaty with the Nationalist Chinese that made an attack on either an attack on both, but confined the definition of Nationalist China to Taiwan and the Pescadores. Chiang agreed formally not to initiate hostilities with the People's Republic unilaterally, conforming with the message Nixon had been sent to deliver to Chiang and Syngman Rhee the year before. The Chinese bombardment of Quemoy and Matsu continued for the rest of 1954, steadily intensifying, and there were repeated requests from Chiang, the Republican right, and the JCS to take drastic action. Eisenhower privately recommended against Chiang putting "more and more men on those small and exposed islands."[16] At a news conference in late November, Eisenhower answered a question about using military intervention in response to Chinese mistreatment of American POWs in Korea by saying that he had written "letters of condolence . . . by the thousands, to bereaved mothers and wives. That is a very sobering experience. . . . Don't go to war in response to emotions of anger and resentment; do it prayerfully."[17]

Five times in the course of 1954 he had been asked by military and State Department advisers and congressional supporters to go to war in Asia, usually with a sprinkling of atomic bombs upon China: in April and again in May as the Dien Bien Phu surrender approached, in late June when the French claimed the Chinese air force was about to attack them, in September at the beginning of the shelling of Quemoy and Matsu, and again in November when China revealed the conditions in which it detained captured American airmen.

The ink (none of it American) was scarcely dry on the Geneva Accord when problems began to bubble up from the nascent but unproclaimed state of South Vietnam. Allen Dulles had sent the astute intelligence colonel Edward Lansdale (model for the good official in the novel *The Ugly American*) to harass the Viet Minh and assess Diem in the autumn of 1954. Lansdale reported that the Viet Minh were going to take absolute control of the North very quickly, and that Diem's efforts to install himself were proceeding with difficulty, and in November Eisenhower appointed the distinguished combat general J. Lawton Collins as ambassador to what the president called "Free Vietnam." Collins was given command over the entire American mission in the new country and the mission statement to assist in building and preserving its sovereignty. Lansdale had warned that when it became

---

15. Ambrose, *op. cit.*, p. 214.
16. Ambrose, *op. cit.*, p. 230.
17. Ibid. p. 230.

clear that the elections Chou and Mendès-France had set up at Geneva, to be held after the two-year decent interval to save a little decorum for France did not occur, Diem would have an insurrection, and to the extent that North and South Vietnam were separate countries, a war, on his hands.

For Eisenhower to approve the cancellation of the elections, and send a four-star general to Saigon with a clear mandate to reinforce the permanent independence of South Vietnam and help it build an army and fight the war that Collins warned was about to begin again, was a very serious step into what would prove a tragic adventure. Eisenhower met with Collins on November 3, just before his departure for Saigon, and told him that he wished to emulate the examples of Greece and South Korea and assist the South Vietnamese to be able to defend themselves. Eisenhower had complained that the French, after his old comrade de Lattre de Tassigny died in 1951, wanted American aid but would not listen to American advice. He transferred a $400 million package of military assistance to France to South Vietnam, and told Collins to disperse it according to his best judgment (and Collins was as distinguished a general as de Lattre, and infinitely more so than Salan). Many questions remain over these decisions, especially if, despite all the business about dominoes, Eisenhower would not have been better off to keep his hands off South Vietnam and announce that the French had fumbled away all Indochina and that the dominoes started at Malaya, Thailand, and other sturdier and more coherent states; and if he was going to take a stand, if he could not have taken it while France was still a factor in Indochina, trading evacuation from Dien Bien Phu and even the insertion of some forces, in exchange for a durable French military commitment to the newly independent non-communist Indochinese countries.

Eisenhower sent Dulles to Europe in September 1954 to arrange Germany's election to NATO. He agreed with West German chancellor Konrad Adenauer that the German army would not exceed 12 divisions, that West Germany would not seek nuclear weapons, and that control would reside with the NATO commander (SACEUR, the post Eisenhower had set up). Dulles carried out his mission skillfully, and the threat remained, if France did not come on side, that the United States would finally make a bipartite arrangement with West Germany. The French National Assembly and the U.S. Senate ratified the arrangements, and the integration of the Federal Republic of Germany into the Western Alliance in April 1955 was one of the greatest of Dwight D. Eisenhower's many historic achievements, as military commander and as president.

The French, in one year, had managed their greatest military defeat—apart from 1940 and Bismarck's capture of Napoleon III at Sedan in 1870—since

Waterloo, if not Napoleon's defeat in Russia in 1812, and had fumbled their way into secondary position as a continental European ally behind Germany, the mortal and genocidal enemy of less than a decade before. Eisenhower bore in mind at all times that Europe was the key theater and Cold War battleground, and that too aggressive or impetuous a policy in the Far East would spook America's allies in Western Europe, where communism was militating within a hundred miles of the Rhine in East Germany, and seething and fermenting in more than 20 percent of the population in France and in Italy. America and the Western world were well-served by his world view, as they were by the U.S. president's disposition to discount the alarms and bellicosity of his Joint Chiefs.

In the off-year election in November 1954, the Republicans lost control of both houses of the Congress fairly narrowly, and Sam Rayburn and Lyndon Johnson began the exercise of an iron control over the House and Senate that would continue to the end of the decade. They were two of the legendarily capable leaders in the history of the Congress, on a par with Clay and Webster (as managers not orators). Eisenhower gained general bipartisan support, apart from the more extreme members of the reactionary Republican right, for his strategic policy of containment in Europe through American-led alliance, the arming of infiltrated countries (building on the Truman Doctrine), a reduction of American military manpower, and a steady build-up of air, naval, and atomic superiority, while prompting counter-subversion through the CIA wherever a country was threatened and seemed susceptible. This was the "New Look," which many senior officers and some Republican hawks criticized, but which preserved the peace and avoided large deficits and tax increases.

New Year's Day, 1955, was an occasion for mutual threats of war from Chou En-lai and Chiang Kai-shek. The Communists seized a couple of the small islands in the Formosa Strait. Eisenhower broke new constitutional ground in asking Congress for authority to use any level of force, including atomic weapons, that he judged necessary, for the defense of Formosa and the Pescadores, and "closely related localities," the identification of which would be left to the president. Eisenhower produced the "Formosa Doctrine," which like many of his forays into the prosaic, especially at press conferences, was designed to be incomprehensible: Chou called it a war message and Chiang complained that it did not cover Quemoy and Matsu. Eisenhower made it clear to the Joint Chiefs and the congressional leaders that he would only use the degree of force he thought necessary to defend Formosa and the Pescadores, and that on no account would he allow an attack upon mainland China or be dragged into the Chinese Civil War by Chiang. The timeless leaders of the House, Speaker Sam Rayburn and minority leader and former Speaker

Joe Martin, jammed it through without debate, 403–3. There was a resolution in the Senate curtailing Eisenhower's authority, but this was brushed aside and Johnson and Knowland put the president's measure through after three days, 83–3. Eisenhower, in a remarkable vote of confidence, was given a blank check, even to blast China with atomic weapons if he thought the national interest justified it.

In almost identical letters to the NATO commander, General Alfred Gruenther, and to Winston Churchill (who was finally about to retire as prime minister, after nine years and over 30 years in government and 54 years in Parliament), Eisenhower wrote that Europeans consider America "reckless, impulsive, and immature," but reminded them that he had to deal with "the truculent and the timid, the jingoists and the pacifists." Where Roosevelt flattered whom he had to, dissembled when he felt it necessary, and sailed through like a monarch, and Truman took the best decision as each came up, crisply and clearly, Eisenhower was always mindful of the political landscape and maneuvered in a grey zone of complicated syntax and personal discretion, aware of the poles between which he had to operate.

Churchill was skeptical about anything to do with East Asia, and really cared only about Hong Kong and Malaya. He didn't believe the version of the domino theory that Eisenhower tried to sell through a visit by Dulles—a rather pious, overserious, and uncongenial man to send as an emissary to Churchill, unlike Acheson, who liked a drink and was very witty and much more articulate than Dulles. Churchill and Eden didn't buy any of it, and thought the U.S. should try to negotiate the handover of Quemoy and Matsu for a guarantee not to bother Formosa, which, as Eisenhower said, was "more wishful than realistic." In post-colonial terms, the British had no idea at all of how to deal with East Asia, and had no resources to be a factor there anymore.

Dulles went from London to the Far East and said when he returned to Washington that he doubted the Nationalist Chinese army would remain loyal to Chiang if the Communists invaded, and that if it was the president's decision to defend Quemoy and Matsu, atomic weapons would have to be used. There was a great deal of concern, even among conservative Democrats like Johnson, about betting too much on strategic rubbish like Quemoy and Matsu. Truman's favorite general, Matthew B. Ridgway, now the chief of staff of the army, told congressional hearings that he opposed Eisenhower's "New Look" of fewer troops and more firepower, atomic and otherwise. Eisenhower was sorely tempted to sack him, as Truman had fired MacArthur, but didn't, partly on the advice of Dulles.

Hard as it is in retrospect to believe that these trivial islands could have created such a war agitation, it was a period of intense strain. Finally, on April 23, Chou gave in Bandung (Indonesia) a very conciliatory speech, Eisenhower responded somewhat in the same spirit, and the shelling of the islands was reduced, and stopped altogether in May 1955. The whole episode is generally reckoned a great Eisenhower victory, as the bombardment stopped and Chiang retained Quemoy and Matsu. It was not a triumph in preventing an invasion of Formosa, as there was no chance China could have achieved that successfully with the U.S. Seventh Fleet in the Formosa Strait (which Eisenhower had beefed up with three additional aircraft carriers). But it was a triumph in picking a showdown where he could not lose, providing himself the flexibility to avoid a Dien Bien Phu at Quemoy and Matsu, which is probably why Mao and Chou did not attack the islands in human waves—because the U.S. had no prestige invested in them. He had faced the Chinese down at no cost in American lives, and had maintained the confidence of all strata of American opinion except the extreme pacifists and screaming war hawks, who could not, between them, have exceeded 10 percent of opinion.

7. OPEN SKIES

There had not been a high-level meeting between the U.S. and the USSR for almost 10 years, since Potsdam. The United States declined to meet with the Soviets until they showed some sign of being in earnest. Following the resolution of the Formosa Strait impasse, Eisenhower said that he would accept agreement on a peace treaty with Austria as a sufficient sign of Russian seriousness. All four powers did agree to evacuate Austria, which would be a neutral state that would organize its own defense. A four-power summit meeting was then convened for Geneva, starting July 18, 1955.

The summer of 1955 was the first time the world had generally breathed easily since that of 1929. In 1955, Detroit built and sold almost eight million cars, but only New York, Chicago, and Los Angeles had highways around them, and apart from the Pennsylvania Turnpike there were scarcely any four-lane inter-city highways in the country. Eisenhower was from the interior of the country (Abilene, Kansas), and had admired the advanced highways in Germany when he had been military governor there. In July 1954, Eisenhower had Nixon unveil the greatest public works project in the country's history, a 10-year, $50 billion interstate highway program. This would revive the internal-improvements controversies of 125 years before and recall aspects of Roosevelt's New Deal, workfare projects. And it would soak up what unemployed there still were, as the country shook off the last vestiges of depression and war and enjoyed almost full employment, only 1 percent inflation, a balanced budget, and the Cold War seeming, two years after the death of the gruesome Stalin, to settle down. Peace and prosperity had returned after whole or partial absences of over 25 years, and unlike in the twenties, the United States was now engaged everywhere in the world.

There had been some proposals by both the Soviet and the American side for military inspection teams on the ground in both countries, at highway crossings and such, but Eisenhower was skeptical that they would accomplish much, after he had seen how surreptitiously the Chinese had moved around in Korea. He had been very aware of the advances in aerial reconnaissance since he was the theater commander in Europe, and had been for some months working up some proposals for reciprocally opening up each country for air inspection by the other. The U-2 high-altitude, Mach 2 aerial reconnaissance plane was almost ready, and rocket-launched satellites that could perform the same function would be ready within a few years. Eisenhower thought it an idea whose time was coming anyway. Eisenhower addressed the nation on the eve of departure for Geneva and claimed a desire only to change the atmosphere for the better between the superpowers. Though not a religious man, he concluded by urging the entire nation to pray for peace. (He had also called for a prayer at his inauguration, a time-honored gambit for American leaders—even, or perhaps particularly, the less religiously observant of them.)

The Soviet delegation was headed by Nikita Khrushchev as Communist Party chairman; the new premier, Nikolai Bulganin; the ancient foreign minister, V.M. Molotov; and Eisenhower's war-time colleague, the defense minister, Marshal Georgi Zhukov. Eisenhower soon discovered that Zhukov was exhausted and diminished and nothing like the powerful figure he had been. Despite having been elected on a platform that heaped denigration on the Yalta Conference for having given Europe away to Stalin, and having told his Republican congressional leadership that there would not be another Yalta, Eisenhower opened the conference with a stern demand for specific performance of the Soviet Union's promises from Yalta, specifically in the Declarations on Poland and Liberated Europe.

The opening sessions were fairly acrimonious, but the social occasions were quite convivial. Eisenhower, because of his position and great military prestige, was certainly the leading figure there, and, like Roosevelt and Truman before him, was the only chief of state, and so presided. Churchill, who loved summit conferences, had finally retired, and Eden led the British. The French were led by Mendès-France's successor, the very capable Edgar Faure. But France had suffered too many defeats in the previous 15 years to carry much weight.

Several days into the conference, after trying to revive the "Atoms for Peace" proposal, Eisenhower, Eden, and Faure rejected Khrushchev's proposal for an Austria-like solution to Germany: reunification and neutrality. This indicated the degree to which the West really had won the war: Stalin took most of the casualties against Germany, but the West had the overwhelming majority of the Germans, and West Germany vastly outperformed the Communist East. The powers agreed on more cultural exchanges, and then Eisenhower made his pitch for what was called his "Open Skies" proposal. The British and the French were very positive. Though the Russians were at first non-committal in Bulganin's reaction, he was followed by Khrushchev, who dismissed the idea as just an espionage attempt. It was here that it became obvious, as would soon be confirmed, that Khrushchev was emerging as Stalin's successor as dictator of the country. As Eisenhower had hoped, there was a lightening of atmosphere, and Khrushchev and Bulganin had made it clear that they wished to visit the U.S.A.

Eisenhower gave the conference a rather platitudinous wind-up, claiming to have come to Geneva because of "my lasting faith in the decent instincts and good sense of the people who populate this world of ours." He spoke to the country on television on his return, pledged that there had been no secret deals, acknowledged that there had been no progress on the divided nations of Germany, Korea, China, and Vietnam, but said that the atmosphere was relatively upbeat and that it could be built upon from there. Eisenhower was proving to be a fortunate, as well as a capable, if cautious, often devious, and idiosyncratic, president. He suffered a modest heart attack on September 24 while on holiday in Colorado, and was in hospital for six weeks, and convalesced at home into the New Year, 1956.

8. THE SUEZ CRISIS

Eisenhower carefully considered whether to seek reelection at age 66, in light of his recent indisposition, and he did the modern U.S. presidential candidate's obligatory semi-public consultation of family and advisers, receiving the inevitable harvest of sycophancies, cresting with his brother Milton's concern that the country might be so concerned about his health that it would defeat him at the polls in order to increase the likelihood of greater longevity. His advisers felt that no one else could defeat the Democrats, which was nonsense, considering that Nixon would effectively draw the election in 1960 against a stronger candidate than Stevenson. Eisenhower said he would "hate to turn this country back into the hands of people like Stevenson, Harriman, and Kefauver." (Harriman had been elected governor of New York, by 11,000 votes out of over 5.1 million cast, against Irving Ives; Estes Kefauver was a prominent Democratic senator from Tennessee, and they were all quite respectable politicians.)[18] A few years before, Eisenhower had described the Democrats as "Extremes of the left, extremes of the right, with corruption and political chicanery shot through the whole business."[19] (He was speaking of Roosevelt, Truman, Rayburn, and Johnson; what he might have thought of Jesse Jackson, George Wallace, and George McGovern intimidates the imagination.)

Eisenhower, as is customary with incumbent American presidents, thought himself indispensable, and when assured by his medical team that he was up to it, he determined to run again, and then inflicted an agony on Nixon about reselecting him as vice president—pretty shabby treatment of a loyal and capable vice president who had been instrumental in securing Eisenhower's nomination over Taft in 1952. Eisenhower was not indispensable and after his heart attack he slowed down considerably. He certainly had a good record to run for a second term, but four years later he would be the oldest president in history up to that time, and would seem pretty tired.

In January 1956, the new British prime minister, Anthony Eden, came to Washington for substantive talks with Eisenhower. Eden had known Eisenhower well since the North African campaigns of 1943; had served three separated terms as foreign secretary since 1935, totaling 12 years, plus six years as shadow foreign secretary; had worked closely with Churchill for 16 years; and had dealt in detailed negotiations with Hitler, Stalin, Roosevelt, Mussolini, Truman, Chou En-lai, de Gaulle, and almost everyone else who had been prominent in the world in the last 20 years. The British wanted to abandon the pretense that anyone except Mao Tse-tung's Communists governed China, but agreed to support Diem's refusal to hold Vietnam-wide elections, for the official reason that the North had violated the Geneva Accord (which it had, but the real reason was that Ho Chi Minh would have won 100 percent of the vote in the North from nationalist enthusiasm and by application of the usual communist electoral methods, and perhaps 20 to 30 percent in the South).

Eden was mainly concerned about Egypt and its leader, Colonel Gamal Abdel Nasser, who had seized power in 1954, two years after he and other officers had ousted the absurd and dissolute British puppet, King Farouk. Eden had lost confidence in Nasser, whom Eisenhower had thought something of a reformer. Dulles intervened that he feared Nasser was a tool of the communists, but Dulles suspected that of a wide swath of leaders, from Nehru to Mossadegh to the unfor-

---

18. Ambrose, *op. cit.*, p. 282.
19. Blanche Wiesen Cook, *The Declassified Eisenhower*, Garden City, New York, Doubleday, 1981, p. 77.

tunate Guatemalan Arbenz. This was an implausible complaint, because Dulles himself had approved a demand of cash payments for $27 million of arms Nasser had made the year before, driving him into the arms of the Czechs, who sold him the arms on credit. Eden reminded Eisenhower and Dulles that selling any arms to Egypt violated the Tripartite Pact between their countries and France to do nothing to aggravate hostilities between Israel and the Arabs.

Of course, this too was nonsense, as it just made the Arabs dependent on the Soviet bloc as arms suppliers. It was a figment of the neo-colonial imagination of the British and the French that they could long maintain the Middle East in a relatively disarmed state. Eden now proposed that Britain take the lead in the Middle East, and that the U.S. join the British-sponsored Baghdad Pact, which linked Pakistan, Iran, Iraq, and Turkey, to block Russia's way to the south, and make it a military alliance. The Israelis and Egyptians both thought the Baghdad Pact directed against them, and Eisenhower and Dulles thought they would irritate the Israelis and the Arabs by joining it. This was a bit rich, considering the mess Britain had made of the admittedly complicated problem of Palestine, where they had effectively promised the same territory to the Jews and the Arabs in 1917, and mismanaged the balance between them for 30 years afterward. Further, the administration had quietly undercut the British position in the Middle East from its start, and rather as Roosevelt had imagined that the Russians and the Vichy French preferred the Americans to the British, Eisenhower and Dulles had an evangelical notion of the boundless goodwill the United States deployed in the Middle East compared with the British and the French. Of course the Arab nationalists had no use for any of them, and to boot, the Israelis hated the British, whom they considered responsible for the deaths of hundreds of thousands of Jews who would otherwise have successfully fled prewar Europe for Palestine (with, unfortunately, some reason).

Eisenhower now sent the man he (inexplicably) favored to succeed him, Deputy Defense Secretary Robert Anderson, to start the lengthy process of shuttle diplomacy between Nasser and the first prime minister of Israel, David Ben Gurion. Eisenhower authorized Anderson to offer both countries large amounts of money to compose their differences. The U.S. was prepared to guarantee Israel's UN-approved borders of 1948, but Ben Gurion was not prepared to retire to them. Anderson offered resettlement of the Palestinian refugees throughout the Arab world, but Nasser declined to agree to such a "destruction of a people."[20]

---

20. Ambrose, *op. cit.*, p. 317.

Eisenhower wished, after the failure of Anderson's mission, to continue being neutral between Israel and the Arabs, but he was now suspicious of Nasser's pitch to pan-Arab feeling, which, with encouragement from Dulles, he suspected to be vulnerable to communist subornation. He wrote in his diary on March 8[21] that he would work to separate Saudi Arabia from Egypt, which he thought was wandering off the reservation toward Moscow, in order to reduce the ability of a USSR-Arab alliance to blackmail Western Europe, which was heavily dependent on Arab oil, into enfeeblement of the Western Alliance. Eisenhower badly misjudged the requirements of alliance in the Middle East, though Eden, especially, was in a delusional zone if he thought Britain capable of leading anyone anywhere in that region. The French, at war with the North African Arabs in Algeria especially, and friendly to Israel, were more sensible. While the constellation of people and events promised to put great stress on the Western Alliance, it would have been hard to imagine the proportions of the fiasco that was coming.

With that said, Eisenhower again demonstrated his acute strategic judgment, as he saw at the outset the real issue from the standpoint of American interests was to keep oil flowing to Europe, restrain the Europeans from neo-colonial nostrums, be more alluring to the main Arab powers than the Soviet Union was, promote Arab divisions, and try anything that might damp down the Arab-Jewish blood feud. Tactically, while he was right not to embark in any idea of Eden's for trying to organize the Middle East, he gave up a bit prematurely, as time would show, the possibility of keeping Egypt out of the hands of the Russians. In his diary he expressed confidence that if Egypt could be rather isolated in the Arab world and its only important ally were the Soviet Union, "she would very quickly get sick of that prospect."[22]

At a meeting with very senior foreign and military policy officials, including Dulles, Admiral Radford, and Defense Secretary Charles Wilson (none of whom knew anything about the Middle East), Eisenhower took a long step into darkness by approving Dulles's advice to warn Nasser he could not walk arm-in-arm with the Russians and retain most-favored-nation status with the U.S. He proposed fumbling and punting forward negotiations about the great project of the Aswan High Dam, which was supposed vastly to increase Egyptian agricultural production; suspending the distribution of CARE aid to Egypt; increasing support to the Baghdad Pact without joining it; and accelerating discussions with the Saudis by offering extensive military assistance. It was a jumbled, self-contradictory mélange

---

21. Ibid. p. 321.
22. Ambrose, *op. cit.*, p. 317.

of proposals, putting forth a number of incomplete initiatives with that love of confusion that was so evident in Eisenhower's responses to the press. Wooing the Saudis was a good idea, to undercut Nasser, secure Europe's oil supply, and generally fragment the Arabs (at which they do not usually require much encouragement). But beyond that, it was a pastiche, inadequately thought through in comparison with Western European and even Far Eastern policy.

Eisenhower and Dulles should have realized the danger of Moscow stepping up to finance the Aswan project, which was a straight humanitarian development project of no military relevance. Stopping the shipment of CARE packages transposed to Eisenhower, his administration, and the country, the appearance of a Scroogian Presbyterian humbug and hypocrite, which was, unfortunately, not entirely a caricature of Dulles. This and the decision to back Diem's lunge for an independent South Vietnam were steps that would greatly, and not very benignly, influence freighted decades to come in both regions. Eisenhower was a good foreign policy strategist, as he had been a fine military strategist, but where he had also been a very competent military tactician, he was, in foreign affairs, unlike in politics and congressional relations, very uneven, and Dulles, though an estimable man in many ways, was not a good choice to fill in where the president himself had an unsure grasp.

Nasser quickly discovered, if he had not known them already, the political virtues of anti-Americanism. He withdrew recognition of Chiang and transferred it to Mao Tse-tung's regime at the end of May. On June 20, 1956, Eisenhower sent the head of the World Bank, Eugene Black, to Cairo to try to close the Aswan deal with Nasser, who layered in new conditions that the president considered unacceptable. The proposed deal included a grant of $70 million and a loan on favorable terms of $200 million. Eisenhower welcomed the opportunity to pull out, and when Nasser sent a message on July 19 accepting the American proposal of the previous month, Eisenhower had Dulles inform the Egyptian ambassador that day that the deal was off.

Nasser responded by nationalizing the Suez Canal on July 29 and taking over its operations. Eden, who had been making threatening noises for some time, was apoplectic and called for drastic measures. Eisenhower was not overly concerned and sent veteran diplomat Robert Murphy to London and Paris to cool out the British, warn both countries not to connect this to the Arab-Israeli confrontation (i.e., recruit the military assistance of Israel), and propose a conference of maritime nations. Eisenhower and his entourage thought Eden, who advised the president on July 31 that Britain intended to take military action to "break Nasser," was overreacting, and suspected him of reaching too quickly for a military option in pursuit of what were to some degree quasi-colonial objectives. He also feared that Nasser was a plausible spokesman for Arab resentment of the West and for some legitimate Arab aspirations, and that he was "within his rights"[23] to take the canal. He didn't believe that Egypt would have much problem operating the Suez Canal, but feared that the seizure of it would incite similar ambitions by the Panamanians. And he also thought that such a military measure as Eden was planning would shut off Arab oil to Europe and require the redirection of some oil from the Americas to Europe, causing the imposition of rationing of gasoline in the United States.

At this point, Nasser was the only actor in this drama that was making any sense. The Arabs weren't going to stop oil shipments to countries like Germany and Italy, which played no role in this; Iran certainly, and probably the Saudis and the Gulf states and emirates, would not touch a boycott; and none of the oil-producing countries had much affection for the Egyptians, and resented Nasser stirring up their populations underneath them. The idea of rationing in the U.S. to send oil and gasoline to Britain and France was absurd. And Eisenhower could not have imagined that Panama had any insane notions of its ability to evict the United States from the Panama Canal. Britain had withdrawn 80,000 troops from the Suez Canal area by agreement with Nasser, leaving it a sitting duck, and Egypt was no great military power, but was a large country. Panama (Chapter 8) was a tiny jungle state with no armed forces and completely dependent on the U.S., which had more than adequate defense forces in the legitimately constituted Canal Zone. (In the past 10 years, Britain had withdrawn over 300,000 of its armed forces from Greece, India, Palestine, and Suez, indicating how unwieldy the key units of its Empire had become, and in some cases, had long been.)

Eden had taken leave of his senses; Britain and France couldn't occupy Egypt, a country of nearly 30 million people, or reestablish themselves by force in durable control of the Suez Canal, and had no evident ability to dispose of Nasser, which, if it could be done, would inflame the Arab world dangerously. But a conference, which Eisenhower sent Dulles to London to set up, was just Eisenhoweresque shilly-shallying and muddying the waters while tempers supposedly cooled. It was a completely inadequate response. Dulles was a little better, saying that Nasser must be made "to disgorge his theft," but that the British had gone into both World Wars on the assumption that the U.S. would come in after to save them, and were about to gamble that the same thing would happen again. (In fact, they entered the World War I with no thought of the

---

23. Ambrose, *op. cit.*, p. 332.

U.S., and it would be inaccurately flattering to Chamberlain to think he had any such thoughts in 1939.)

The British and the French certainly had the military ability to take back the canal, but had no ability to leave 200,000 troops there indefinitely to hold it. On August 12, the president and Dulles met the congressional leadership. Senate leader Lyndon Johnson said that the U.S. must support its allies and assist them in non-military ways. Eisenhower disagreed, but assured the senators and congressmen that he would not "stand impotent and let this one man get away with it." Dulles likened Nasser to Hitler and then left for his conference in London. Eisenhower had a dilemma but wasn't doing anything serious to deal with it. Dulles got an 18–4 vote at his conference in favor of requiring that the Suez Canal be operated by an international board, and a committee chaired by Australia's veteran prime minister Robert Menzies was delegated to try to sell the concept to Nasser.

To keep his place as vice president, Nixon, who had occupied the post with distinction, had to have recourse to surreptitious campaigns for write-in support as vice president in the uncontested Republican primaries, and faced other indignities, to resolve Eisenhower's sadistic ambivalence about his suitability to continue. At one point, Eisenhower tried the bizarre gambit of suggesting that Nixon should wish to stay on as vice president only if he thought that he, Eisenhower, would not survive the term. Nixon overcame Eisenhower's ambivalence, perhaps augmented by the president's reluctance to acknowledge how much he owed Nixon for having been nominated in 1952. They were renominated by acclamation at San Francisco, to face Stevenson again, and Senator Estes Kefauver, and the president took a brief summer holiday. Overseas events proceeded apace.

Menzies arrived in Cairo on September 2. Nasser offered freedom of passage of the canal and equitable tolls, but refused to consider handing back control to anyone, as Eisenhower had foreseen. In correspondence with Eden over the next week, Eisenhower wrote that there could be no thought of force until the matter was referred to the United Nations, that Eden should end British mobilization and the withdrawal of British citizens from Egypt, that American opinion would not support force, that British huffing and puffing was strengthening Arab support for Nasser, and that Britain could not economically sustain prolonged military operations and the loss of Middle Eastern oil. He wrote that Eden would solidify Arab, African, and much Asian support for Nasser and would open the door of the Middle East to Russia, and that there were opportunities to divide the Arabs and undermine Nasser over time.

He was correct in much of this, but Britain and France could have made short work of Egypt militarily (they were still, next to the superpowers, the world's two strongest nations militarily), there was no likelihood of a serious or leak-proof oil embargo (most of the exporters had no other source of income), and Eisenhower was in no position to get too exalted about how to handle Egypt, as he precipitated the problem by ducking out of the Aswan Dam project. It was a futile exchange, as Eden replied with warnings about a new Munich. He understood the dangers, but "we have many times led Europe in the fight for freedom. It would be an ignoble end to our long history if we tamely accepted to perish by degrees." This was all moonshine, as Eden was hardly "fighting for freedom" and the end of British history was hardly at hand. Eisenhower replied more sensibly, mentioning super tankers that would make Suez less of a lifeline, and proposed unspecified economic pressures and the subsidization of increasing fissures in the Arab world.[24] But Eden had reached a compulsive and hyperactive condition and Eisenhower was just dispensing bromides and palliatives. He could more profitably have dealt with the French, who were really just playing along to kick the Arabs in the shins and in solidarity with their great arms purchaser (largely with American money), Israel. French cynicism was a point of practical strength compared with Eden's ravings and Eisenhower's havering.

The next move was Dulles's Suez Canal Users' Association, a classic Dulles improvisation, which proposed to pilot ships through the canal in both directions and withhold payment of transit tolls. His proposal was, as he knew, absurd, but he formulated it so complicatedly (using similar techniques of dissembling and obfuscation as his chief) that he forced prolonged negotiations on the parties. These had scarcely begun when the British pilots abandoned their posts on September 14 and Nasser replaced them at once with Egyptian pilots, who kept the canal going at a slightly heightened rate of activity. Eisenhower let Eden know that any thought of force now was "ridiculous" and that he should accept Nasser's offer of compensation.

The British and the French rather publicly mobilized their forces on Cyprus all through September. On October 8, Eisenhower told Under Secretary of State Herbert Hoover Jr. (who had replaced General Walter Bedell Smith) that he would not countenance a plan that from the correspondence appeared to be a coup d'état or even assassination attempt on Nasser, told him to issue an official statement in the most unambiguous terms that the United States would not agree with any act or threat of war in the Middle East, and told him to announce that the U.S. would immediately begin construction of 60,000-ton tankers that would reduce British

24. Ambrose, *op. cit.*, p. 339.

and French dependence on the Suez Canal for oil and reduce the revenues of the canal. He directed the State Department to devise a plan, "any plan,"[25] that might have some interest for Nasser, and to try to involve Nehru and the Organization of African Unity in the issue. It was illustrative of Eisenhower's natural talents at enmeshing the most improbable entities, for which he normally had little use (he couldn't abide Nehru but Nehru seemed to have a good relationship with Nasser, and the OAU was essentially a Black African organization that would have no leverage on Nasser), in controversies to confuse them, weigh them down, slow them up, and prevent bad and hot-headed things from happening. (Nasser and Nehru and Yugoslavia's Tito would be the leaders of the world's neutralist movement, and Nasser was briefly the head of the OAU a decade later.)

In mid-October, on a joint approach from Britain and France (whether sincere or just a diversionary fig leaf for what was coming has never been determined), UN Secretary-General Dag Hammarskjöld worked out six principles, including some concept of internationalization of the Suez Canal. But before Hammarskjöld could organize a visit to Nasser, another crisis blew up in Eastern Europe.

9. REVOLT IN BUDAPEST AND WAR IN THE MIDDLE EAST

Following the release of Khrushchev's Twentieth Party Congress address denouncing Stalin, riots erupted in Poland in June, and the puppet satellite regime was thrown out and replaced by Wladyslaw Gomulka, whom the Soviets had forced out as a Titoist in 1948 and imprisoned in 1951, and who was only spared execution by the death of Stalin in 1953. (Tito had established Yugoslav independence from the USSR, though the country remained a communist dictatorship.) On October 22, the disturbances spread to Hungary, and the following day, the premier the Soviets had forced out as a loyalty risk (to them), Imre Nagy, was restored to office. Nagy promised democratization and a rising standard of living, and the Soviets dispatched forces from their occupation units in Hungary to Budapest to "maintain order."

Events now moved quickly, with spontaneous uprisings around Hungary and freedom fighters blowing treads off Soviet tanks with Molotov cocktails. (Molotov himself accompanied Khrushchev and other Soviet leaders to Warsaw, where Gomulka promised adherence to the Soviet foreign policy line, as long as he could experiment somewhat in internal policies, and this was agreed.) In Budapest, Nagy announced Hungary's withdrawal from the Warsaw Pact and its neutrality in the Cold War. The Soviet ambassador in Budapest, Yuri Andropov (subsequent

---

25. Ibid. p. 351.

chairman of the Soviet Communist Party), purported to discuss the withdrawal from Hungary of the five Soviet occupation divisions.

These proved not to be good-faith discussions, but while they continued, Eisenhower and Dulles exchanged rather smug comments about how the collapse of the Soviet subjugation of Eastern Europe was coming rather more quickly than had been expected, and implicitly, that all their bunk about "liberation and rollback" from Republican postwar lore was unfolding as they had promised and demanded on Radio Free Europe and the Voice of America. Like most communists who have any notion of comparative democracy, particularly those in the Soviet bloc between the defection of Tito, who had a powerful and battle-hardened army and close connections to the neighboring West in 1949, and the rise of Gorbachev in 1983, Nagy was completely naïve about Soviet responses to national independence movements. But in this case, the president of the United States and his secretary of state, for all their experience and worldliness, were not much wiser.

While all was hopefulness and self-congratulation—and U.S. intelligence reported Israeli mobilization and assumed Israel was about to attack Jordan, which had just formed an alliance with Egypt and Syria, which the British and French might use as some sort of pretext for seizing the canal—the British and French governments embarked on what must rank as one of their most insane military adventures in their very crowded national histories. Despite U-2 overflights and strenuous efforts to crack the codes in the heavy traffic between London, Paris, and Tel Aviv (three of America's closest allies, and the U-2s had to fly from Germany because Eden would not allow overflights of Russia from the U.K., such was the state of what 10 years before had been the Grand Alliance), the CIA had been completely foxed by their allies, the chief Anglo-French triumph of the campaign.

On October 28, Israel attacked not Jordan but Egypt, in the Sinai. Radford thought it would take them three days to seize the Sinai, and that that would be the end of it. Dulles said that Egypt would close the canal and shut down the pipelines, and then the British and the French would intervene to protect their oil supplies.[26] Eisenhower had warned Ben Gurion not to try anything, but his powers of moral dissuasion with the Israeli leader were no greater than with Eden and the French. The American leadership was stuck on the notion that their chief allies were convinced the U.S. would always "pull their chestnuts out of the fire." It is generally assumed that the British didn't believe their great ally and honorary citizen, General Eisenhower, would desert them; the French believed that NATO's greatest champion would not desert his two main NATO partners, and

---

26. Ambrose, *op. cit.*, p. 357.

Ben Gurion assumed that the United States would not undercut Israel at election time (they were nine days from the U.S. election). But all they really wanted was for Eisenhower to stay on the sidelines while they beat the stuffing out of Nasser.

Eisenhower determined that the U.S. must put principle above traditional attachments and that he must ignore any political considerations arising from the election, though he doubted the American people would throw him out over such an issue anyway. He issued a statement on October 29 upholding the section of the Tripartite Agreement of 1950 (Britain, France, and the United States) that they would side with the victim of aggression in the Middle East, leaving no doubt that this was Egypt. He ordered that the British be advised that although they had a legitimate grievance against Egypt, it did not justify the drastic step they had taken, and that the U.S. would present the UN with a cease-fire resolution in the morning. The British chargé, J.E. Coulson, was summoned (the ambassador had returned to London), and Eisenhower asked that the British government be informed at once of his views.

Only on October 30 did the U.S. administration understand the proportions of the Anglo-French-Israeli action. Ben Gurion sent a message in the morning saying that Israel's existence was at stake and there was no thought of stopping, much less retreating. Eden and the (ostensibly Socialist, though in France political labels are deceiving) French premier, Guy Mollet,[27] exchanged messages with Eisenhower, and explained that the Tripartite Declaration was invalid because of changed circumstances. Eisenhower suspected Churchill's "mid-Victorian hand" in this (completely unjustly), and speculated that the French thought that this action might somehow assist them in Algeria, where there was a widespread and bloody Arab insurrection.[28]

At midday on the East Coast, the British and the French gave Egypt a very severe 12-hour ultimatum. Finally, it was clear: unless the Egyptians and the Israelis each withdrew 10 miles from the banks of the Suez Canal, Britain and France would occupy the canal and keep it open. Israel, of course, accepted at once, and intended to retain the Sinai, and to be allowed transit of the canal.

Eisenhower may be said, finally, to have captured the essence of it when he said on that afternoon, though Eden was now at least trying to explain his and his allies' actions to the U.S. president after a two-week silence: "I've just never seen Great Powers make such a mess and botch of things. Of course, in a war,

---

27. Mollet had replaced Faure a few months before; such was the revolving door of the Fourth Republic—four premiers in less than three years.
28. Ambrose, *op. cit.*, p. 359.

there's just nobody I would rather have fighting alongside of me than the British. But—this thing! My God!"[29] He considered it, from the start, "the biggest error of our time, outside of losing China" (which he largely, and unfairly, blamed on his revered old chief, Marshall).

The next morning, Eden won a confidence motion in the British House of Commons, 270–218, which would not normally be considered adequate to continue with such a risky operation by a recently reelected government. But Russia announced that it would withdraw its forces from Hungary and respect the sovereignty of the East European states as it had promised to do at Yalta, and apologized for its past behavior. Eisenhower, while his closest colleagues rejoiced, again showed his worldliness by finally expressing doubt about Soviet sincerity.

It was not too late for Eden and Mollet to pull back, and they could certainly extract some concessions from Nasser now, but Eden ordered the attack to begin; British planes bombed Egyptian cities and military targets. Nasser did manage to sink a number of ships in the Suez Canal, effectively blocking it. Eisenhower spoke to the nation and the world at 7 p.m. on Halloween. He said the U.S. would economically assist Eastern European countries if they asked for it, but assured the Russians that he would not try to recruit them as allies; said the U.S. sought peace with Arabs and Jews; and spoke warmly of Britain and France and Israel, but said the United States had not in the slightest been consulted about this action, and that while the powers that undertook it had the right not to consult America, America had, and would exercise, its right to dissent from their initiative. The United States sought peace and the rule of law. It was an effective and statesman-like address that showed Eisenhower's grasp of longer-term strategic goals to keep the Western Alliance together through the outbreak of insanity in London. (Paris and Tel Aviv weren't risking anything; France and Israel were both more or less at war with the Arabs, and could make it up with the Americans anytime.)

The American leadership was correct to be annoyed with its allies, but if Eisenhower hadn't pulled out on the Aswan Dam, Nasser would never have seized the canal as he did. If the U.S. had lifted a finger to help France avoid a terrible humiliation in Vietnam two years before, the French would have consulted. And if Dulles had been more congenial with the British (both Churchill and Eden found him grating, humorless, unimaginative, and full of sanctimony, and didn't notice his good points, especially his fierce anti-communism), and had earned their confidence as Acheson and Marshall and most subsequent secretaries of state did, Britain would not have put such strain on the alliance with such a hare-brained plan.

---

29. Ibid. p. 360.

(Dulles underwent an emergency cancer operation on November 4, and Hoover was acting secretary for the balance of these crises.) At least Eisenhower made sure that Lodge, the ambassador to the United Nations, got the U.S. resolution in first, to avoid a much harsher condemnation of the three renegade warrior nations by a Russian motion. The French and the British, and then the Russians, vetoed resolutions, including American ones, at the UN that they found disagreeable.

After 10 days of some disorder in Budapest and elsewhere, and ostensible negotiations, the Hungarian negotiators were seized; 17 more Soviet divisions were inserted into Hungary, as 80 percent of the Hungarian army had deserted rather than suppress the population, and the Red Army occupied Budapest in the predawn hours of November 4. Eisenhower had been correct to smell a Soviet rat, and only now, with Soviet tanks a few hundred yards away, did Nagy ask for military assistance from the international community—no one in particular, claiming it had been promised by Radio Free Europe. (It had been, implicitly, but not in these circumstances, and a radio propaganda station couldn't officially bind the nation to war, even with all Dulles's belligerent fantasies about liberation and rollback. And Nagy was seeking help from an international group, not just the U.S.)

The fact is, the U.S. could have airlifted some assistance to the freedom fighters, but didn't even do that, so risk-averse was Eisenhower (as he had been when he let the Soviets take Prague and recommended against taking Berlin, in 1945, because he feared accidental conflict with them). It would have been worth a try for Eisenhower to propose a reciprocal scale-back of the alliances—Poland and Hungary, and possibly Greece and Denmark, joining Finland, Austria, and Yugoslavia as neutral states with no foreign forces on them, with guaranteed Soviet access to its occupation zone in Germany, and perhaps some cap on West German force levels. If the divided Kremlin had refused, it might at least have squeezed more political juice out of the lemon and seemed less of a betrayal of the forces of freedom behind the Iron Curtain. If Nagy had acted like Gomulka and not just announced Hungary's withdrawal from the Warsaw Pact, he might have accomplished something durable, but he had no idea of world affairs and no idea what forces he was dealing with, especially with a war underway in the Middle East.

The British and the French finally landed in Egypt on November 5, paratroopers preceding amphibious landings around the northern end of the Suez Canal. The Soviet premier, Nikolai Bulganin, wrote to Eisenhower, threatening force, by implication including atomic attack, on Britain and France, if their alleged aggression did not cease, and proposing to Eisenhower that the USSR and the U.S. take joint military action in Egypt, a mad idea that could not have been meant seriously. Bulganin naturally avoided all mention of his country's brutal reoccupation of

Budapest the day before, and Eisenhower responded almost at once, with a statement that any Soviet military intervention in the Middle East would be resisted with military counter-force from the United States, and made it implicitly clear through channels, to all parties, that any attack on Britain and/or France would be treated as a direct act of unlimited aggression against the United States itself and would be responded to with instant and maximum force. That stopped the Kremlin's references to the possible imminence of World War III. Eisenhower wrote in his diary of moving to "help the refugees fleeing from the criminal action of the Soviets," and claimed that landlocked Hungary was "as inaccessible to us as Tibet,"[30] which, as a glance at the map shows, is self-justificative eyewash. And he scarcely lifted a finger to help the 200,000 refugees, despite Nixon's going to the border and on his return pleading with Eisenhower and Rayburn to help them. The U.S. filled an upgraded quota of 21,000, and eventually nearly 60,000 more, and the refugees were generously received in Canada, Australia, and elsewhere.

As America went to the polls, international grand strategy had been reduced to tragicomic farce on a scale rarely plumbed in modern history, though not chiefly by American actions.

10. REELECTION AND DE-ESCALATION

America voted on November 6, as the Syrians blew up oil pipelines from Iraq to the Mediterranean (it might have been too technologically challenging just to shut them and collect the through-flow for themselves). Eisenhower had scarcely campaigned and left that, as he left most distasteful tasks, to his vice president. International crises had made it a lively campaign. Stevenson had started out with an inane set of military proposals for abolition of the draft, a nuclear test ban, and an enhanced program of missile development. Eisenhower replied that the end of the draft would leave the United States in default of its military commitments, that a nuclear test ban would cause a great deal of missile development activity to be wasted, and that every rocket scientist in the country was already working overtime on developing the military potential of missiles of all sizes.

Stevenson had been under secretary of the navy in World War II, but had no executive authority or specialized knowledge of military matters and was demolished in one well-publicized press conference by the incumbent, who did not have to remind Americans that his combined credentials as a war planner and theater and alliance commander were probably greater than that of any person since Napoleon. Stevenson was reduced to informing the public, most directly on election eve, that

---

30. Ambrose, *op. cit.*, p. 30.

Eisenhower's health was so parlous that a vote for Ike was a vote for Nixon, an uncharacteristically tasteless and politically futile sally (and Eisenhower eventually outlived Stevenson, who was 10 years younger, by four years).

As always in international crises, the nation rallied to the president. There had never been any doubt about the election, and Eisenhower and Nixon won by 35.6 million and 57.4 percent of the vote, with 457 electoral votes and 43 states, to Stevenson and Kefauver's 25.7 million, 42 percent, and 73 electoral votes from five states. The Republicans even took most of the South (despite the ruling of the Supreme Court declaring racial segregation of schools unconstitutional, which Eisenhower made it clear he would carry out, albeit without enthusiasm). As an endorsement of the incumbent, it was, next to Roosevelt's in 1936, the greatest since Monroe ran unopposed in 1820, as Eisenhower polled slightly ahead of Jackson in 1832, Grant in 1872, and TR in 1904. But the Rayburn-Johnson control of the Democratic Congress was undisturbed, and Eisenhower was the first president to win an election and face a hostile Congress in both houses since General Zachary Taylor in 1848. The country detected the president's (justified) disdain for his party's congressional leadership—Knowland and the other reactionaries.

On Election Day, Eisenhower ordered the first stage of mobilization—recall of all military personnel from leave—and was delighted to get a call from Eden saying a cease-fire was acceptable to Britain, as he claimed that the British and the French already controlled the canal. Eisenhower expressed great pleasure and said that the UN peacekeepers would be led by Canadians, as he didn't want any of the permanent Security Council members involved, because that would put Russian soldiers on the Suez Canal. (It was a White House plan that Lodge gave to Canadian external affairs minister Lester Pearson in the corridors of the UN, as Canada was a reliable ally that would be more acceptable to the neutral nations. Pearson happily ran with it, won the Nobel Peace Prize and the leadership of his party in 1958, and was elected prime minister of Canada in 1963.) Eden asked how the election looked, and the president responded that he had been focused on the Middle East and Hungary and that "I don't give a damn how the election goes. I guess it will be all right."[31]

The Suez crisis ended on the shabby note of Eisenhower destabilizing the British currency and enforcing an oil embargo on Britain and France until their forces were out of Egypt, and telling his ambassador in London, Winthrop Aldrich (John D. Rockefeller's son-in-law and a financial backer of Eisenhower), to scheme with Harold Macmillan and Rab Butler, the two candidates to succeed

---

31. Ambrose, *op. cit.*, p. 369.

Eden, who was deemed to be finished, and enabling Macmillan to tell Eden that the British pound would collapse if American demands for withdrawal were not met. This was something of an exaggeration but providential for Macmillan's ambition to ditch Eden and take his place, which he did. Almost all Ike's great British wartime comrades, from Mr. Churchill down through the upper military ranks at the time of D-Day (Britain's last amphibious operation, which had enjoyed masterly planning and execution), wrote to Eisenhower asking for a gentler treatment of Britain, and Eisenhower responded to all in sorrowful but amiable inflexibility. (Thus, Macmillan largely owed his ultimate success to Eisenhower, and Pearson his to Lodge, and Eisenhower, despite his demiurgic back-digging efforts to disguise it, largely owed his original nomination to Nixon; the beneficiaries of this vital career assistance, as happens in politics, were uniform in their ingratitude.)

Eisenhower was stirred by the Middle East crisis to advocate what became known as the Eisenhower Doctrine, which enabled the president to extend military and economic assistance on his own authority to countries menaced by communist subversion. The Congress only approved the military part of it, and the only significant difference with Truman's Doctrine was that Eisenhower's extended throughout the Third World, though it was aimed primarily at the Arab world as a rival to Nasser's rising influence. He invited a procession of Third World leaders to Washington, starting with Nehru and peaking at King Saud, whom he had been promoting as a rival in the Arab world to Nasser. Saud proved a shy man of medieval views, unsuitable to rival Nasser at stirring the Arab masses, but important as a source of oil for Europe. (Eisenhower was not brilliant at judging political horseflesh; his preferred candidates to succeed himself were Treasury Secretary Anderson and his capable but completely non-political brother Milton Eisenhower, president of Johns Hopkins University.) He again had recourse to coercion when he supported a congressional measure to stop private assistance to Israel if it did not withdraw from Gaza. These positions were broadly correct, and when Israel did occupy Gaza, from 1967 to 1993, it was terribly tumultuous and burdensome. The Israelis announced their withdrawal on March 1, 1957.

The crises had almost completely passed by the beginning of 1957. America's allies had been trounced by American intervention, and the hob-nailed Soviet jackboot had crushed freedom's windpipe in Hungary, but the Western Alliance had been preserved. As usual, Eisenhower had been perceptive and sound in his strategic judgment and analyses of the events as they unfolded, but contrary to his performance as a military commander, he had been ponderous and unimaginative in decision-making. He could have caused much greater inconvenience to the Russians over the Hungarian uprising, should not have driven Nasser into the arms of the Kremlin with the Aswan Dam decision, and could easily have preserved more dignity for his allies, mad though their Suez caper was. His attack on the British currency and his oil embargo after the cease-fire to hasten the Anglo-French departure were gratuitous and unfriendly acts, and neither the bonhomous "I Like Ike" gaiety of his reception of Eden's surrender, nor the diaphanous whitewash he and his principal biographer, Stephen Ambrose, slap onto these events, disguise these facts.

This would be the last time an enfeebled France would have to endure such demeaning treatment. Charles de Gaulle's long-awaited (particularly by him) hour was about to strike, and Eisenhower would live to see the Franco-American relationship shift unpleasantly. Ike was a safe pair of hands, and he consolidated and gained Republican acceptance of the achievements of Roosevelt and Truman. If given long enough, he could come up with interesting ideas, like Open Skies and the interstate highway system, but he was getting a bit smug and slightly old in his attitudes. No president except possibly Monroe had had a better second than a first term. Eisenhower had rendered immense service to America and the world, but was entering an Indian summer that would be relatively undisturbed and rather unexciting. But he retained to the end the essential strategic sense to preserve America's commanding preeminence in the world, and to avoid impetuosities that would bedevil some of his successors. Most of the world resumed its long march back to normalcy. The Eisenhower years were the best the United States and most of the West had known, at least since the twenties and possibly ever. These six presidential terms of Roosevelt, Truman, and Eisenhower had produced steadily rising prosperity, and under American leadership, the slow advance of democracy in the world. The United States had led the West to victory in the World War II, while Russia took most of the casualties; imposed a containment policy on Soviet Communism; and, with Open Skies, begun the de-escalation of the Cold War. No other country could have done any of it.

FOUR

THE SUPREME NATION, 1957–2013

John F. Kennedy

CHAPTER THIRTEEN
Peace and Prosperity, 1957–1965

1. A PROFUSION OF TROUBLE SPOTS

On September 25, 1957, Eisenhower sent the 101st Airborne Division, the fabled "Screaming Eagles," to Little Rock, Arkansas, to integrate Central High School, emphasizing that he was enforcing the law, not militarily assaulting the social institutions of the South. Eisenhower saw less clearly than had Roosevelt and Truman the moral palsy of segregation and its harmful effects, though Nixon warned of the damage segregation was doing to America's standing in the world and ability to compete with international communism, especially in African countries. Powerful senator Richard Russell of Georgia accused Eisenhower of using "Hitler-like storm trooper tactics,"[1] illustrating how deep the problems supposedly settled by the Civil War remained. All that had really been settled was that no state could secede. (The *Brown v. Board of Education* case that caused the Supreme Court of the United States to outlaw segregation had been argued by John W. Davis, Democratic presidential candidate of 1924, for the segregationists, and by future and first African American Supreme Court justice Thurgood Marshall for the complainants.)

On October 4, 1957, Eisenhower was completely blindsided by the successful Soviet launch into orbit of the world's first man-made satellite, the *Sputnik*. Eisenhower was again completely out of touch with the depth of concern that immediately arose in the United States that it was being scientifically and ultimately militarily outdistanced by the Soviet Union. The whole American education system, industrial base, and military strategy were instantly placed under intense scrutiny, with Eisenhower implausibly assuring everyone that all was under control. On November 25, after intense discussions with backbiting military chiefs and budget hawks and defense hawks wanting to bust the budget to counter the perceived Soviet missile charge, Eisenhower had a stroke in his office. (He quickly recovered.)

And in December, the long-awaited and much prepublicized launch of an American satellite led to a liftoff of the Vanguard rocket just two seconds before it fell back onto its launcher and blew up with a tremendous report, before the news cameras of the world. There was suddenly a revenance almost of the acute paranoia of the McCarthy era, with Khrushchev bouncing around the world claiming that the entire American defense commitment to manned bombers was obsolete and that communism would sweep the world on the wings of triumphant Marxist physical and social science. There was rising criticism of Dulles's intractable foreign policy, and in retrospect, he was largely blamed for the Western fiascoes in Hungary and Suez. Eisenhower was aware that he, the president, was

---

1.   James C. Duram, *A Moderate Among Extremists: Dwight D. Eisenhower and the School Desegregation Crisis*, Chicago, Nelson-Hall, 1981, pp. 159–160.

the author of those policies, even if Dulles, who was relatively inaccessible to the generous feelings of others because of his incessant, boring obsession with communism, was a convenient lightning rod. Eisenhower was too astute a politician not to notice that the administration needed some new policies, an infusion of energy, and a bit of panache. But he ignored a series of suggestions by Richard Nixon, including stimulative tax cuts.

Though Eisenhower came back quickly from his stroke, he was clearly not an energetic leader. He responded to Bulganin's request for a summit meeting in the United States, which Dulles typically considered a plot to plant spies in the country, with a suggestion of a prior foreign ministers' meeting. There was much talk of arms control and test bans, and Eisenhower tried to get a consensus in his administration to declare a moratorium on nuclear testing, but was disturbed by the utter inflexibility of the head of the Atomic Energy Commission, Admiral Lewis Strauss (who had just managed to have the security clearance of one of the fathers of the atomic bomb, J. Robert Oppenheimer, lifted), and the new defense secretary, Neil McElroy. Even Dulles argued strenuously that something had to be done or the Soviets would win a clear propaganda victory, as the CIA had advised that a unilateral test suspension by Russia was believed to be imminent.

On March 27, 1958, Khrushchev pushed out Bulganin and consolidated the offices of premier and Communist Party chairman, as his predecessors, Lenin and Stalin, had done. On March 31, 1958, with the U.S. administration still dithering, Khrushchev announced a unilateral test ban. The Russians had just concluded a series of tests and would need some time to set up for new ones, and Khrushchev reserved the right to resume tests if the Americans and the British continued to test. It was a brilliant coup that, along with the *Sputnik*-Vanguard episode, gave Russia a stinging double defeat of the United States that continued to rattle the serenity of Eisenhower's era of peace and prosperity and made the Russians seem dynamic and the emergent world force, just five months after the brutal subjugation of a briefly free Budapest. (Imre Nagy had been betrayed, seized, and hanged by the Soviet secret police, to complete the wickedness of the affair.)

Dulles persuaded Eisenhower to propose technical talks toward a lasting test-ban treaty with the Soviets, and Khrushchev accepted. It was a positive turn and Dulles, who was instrumental in achieving it, was generally derided for delaying it. Dulles even successfully argued for restraint in defense spending, a policy that Eisenhower approved, especially after the CIA acknowledged that it had unwittingly multiplied by three the number of intercontinental bombers the Soviet Union possessed and had brought forward by some years the date of commissioning of their intercontinental ballistic missile capability.

But American embarrassments continued. On January 31, 1958, the United States finally put up its first satellite, *Explorer 1*, but it weighed only 31 pounds. In March, the navy got a Vanguard missile to work, but its satellite only weighed three pounds; in May, the Russians successfully launched *Sputnik III*, which weighed 3,000 pounds. Eisenhower's policies of having the three main armed services all competing in the missile field had been a costly failure. In April, and against his own wishes, because he wasn't much interested in space but was very concerned with national defense, Eisenhower recommended the creation of the National Aeronautics and Space Administration. Eisenhower was so preoccupied with balancing the budget (the deficits were very small) that he refused to increase funding for education, although the public had been whipped into a frenzy that the Russians were educating themselves toward world domination through science. One point where he did hold the line was bomb shelters, which he dismissed as a complete waste of money, as he considered massive retaliation to be the only sensible defense policy.

The correlation of forces within the Western Alliance began to shift with the return to power in France of General Charles de Gaulle, after 12 years waiting for the Fourth Republic to stumble to an end. France would quickly cease to be the unstable and irresolute country it had been, ricocheting from one colonial imbroglio to the next. It was only a few months before de Gaulle produced a new constitution that gave France a strong executive, effectively by the brilliant stroke of creating a very strong presidency with a renewable seven-year term, which was in effect a monarchy, thus reconciling in his Fifth Republic the struggle between, on one hand, four monarchies and three quasi and restored monarchies, and, on the other, four republics and three quasi republics, which had tumbled pell-mell on and after each other since the fall of the Bastille 169 years before. He won overwhelming approval for his constitution and for his election as president, relaunched the currency, began a nuclear program, and implied that France would accept status as a Great Power or would effectively withdraw from any integrated notion of NATO. Eisenhower cautioned Dulles as he was about to emplane for Paris that "de Gaulle is capable of the most extraordinary actions."

Khrushchev started agitating about Berlin, demanding recognition of East Germany, and proposing that all Berlin be declared an open city under UN auspices. Faithful to their recent practice of insane suggestions, the JCS proposed that if problems arose on the highway accesses to West Berlin, the U.S. be ready with a force of one division to fight its way into Berlin. Eisenhower was incredulous that his armed services chiefs could propose such a foolish plan, as the Red Army in Germany could dispose of a single American division in a day.

As Eisenhower impatiently waited for anything to happen with his Doctrine, Egypt and Syria purported to merge into one country—the United Arab Republic—and in July the entire Iraqi royal family and the eight-term prime minister, Nuri as-Said, were murdered in the most barbarous fashion. (Said attempted to flee, disguised as a woman but wearing men's shoes, and was apprehended, executed, and buried. His corpse was disinterred by angry mobs, dragged through the streets, hung upside down and mutilated like Mussolini's, then burned.) There was a long dispute between the two leaders of the Maronite Christians in Lebanon, Camille Chamoun, the president, and Fouad Chehab, head of the diminutive army (9,000 men of uncertain loyalty). The Christians traditionally held the presidency and the Muslims the position of prime minister, and the president did not take a second term, and Chamoun wished to change that. He repeatedly asked for American military intervention in Lebanon, claiming Egyptian and Syrian infiltration. Jordan's youthful King Hussein made the same claim—"the two little chaps," British prime minister Macmillan called them. UN Secretary-General Hammarskjöld, who was a good deal more effective than most of his successors in that role, arrived in Beirut on June 18 and was unable to find much evidence of infiltration. The concerns in Jordan, according to Macmillan, were better founded, and Hussein sought British and American assistance.[2]

Eisenhower and Macmillan, who had had a good deal to do with each other during the war, put their relations back together quickly. Macmillan was a cagey, slightly seedy Edwardian manipulator, unlike the overearnest and emotional Eden and the overpowering romantic genius Churchill. The Iraqi coup, on July 14, clearly sounded the deathknell of the Western policy to keep the Arab countries poor and dependent on the West. By now, the Middle East was becoming an armed camp, with the nationalist Arabs being supplied by the Russians, the pro-Western Arabs by the British and the Americans, and the Israelis by the French (who were paid by Israel largely with money provided by both the tax collector and the private sector of the United States).

The U.S. Sixth Fleet began landing an American division in Lebanon on July 15, 1958. The action demonstrated Eisenhower's peculiar brilliance again. There was no real reason for the invasion, and it had nothing to do with the Eisenhower Doctrine, which referred to foreign aggression or infiltration. He wasn't intervening against anyone and took absolutely no casualties. He was just trying to impress Nasser, as well as his supporters and those in the region, such as Saud, to whom America was a suitor, as well as to shut down Democrats accusing him of being

---

2. Stephen E. Ambrose, *Eisenhower: The President*, New York, Simon & Schuster, 1984, p. 471.

indulgent to "Reds and fellow travelers" and so committed to massive retaliation that the United States had no capacity for flexible response. Eisenhower always resented allegations that he, of all people, had shortchanged or mismanaged the military. Chamoun lost the election to Chehab and the Americans were all gone from Lebanon in October, and Eisenhower wrote in his diary that the operation effected "a definite change" in Nasser's attitude to the U.S. On July 17, the British landed 2,200 paratroopers in Jordan, as reinforcement to the king in any way he wished to use them. Both the Jordanian and Lebanese crises ended quickly.

Like Quemoy and Matsu, it was a brilliant Eisenhower initiative, an over-whelming response to an imagined threat, no enemy, no casualties—a virtual confrontation, as if in a pantomime. And Quemoy and Matsu conveniently flared up again; Chiang had stuffed one-third of his army into the ridiculous islands, over 100,000 troops. The Chinese began heavy artillery bombardments and naval interdiction of supplies to the islands on August 25. Chiang wanted to escalate, as did Dulles and the new JCS chairman, General Nathan Twining, who both recommended the use of tactical nuclear weapons on Chinese airfields. Eisenhower refused and Twining tried the back door, proposing that the commander of the Seventh Fleet be given authority to use any degree of force he judged appropriate. Eisenhower bluntly refused to delegate such war-making authority. Lunacy was breaking out in the national security establishment again. Eisenhower spoke to the nation on September 11, 1958, and said that there would be no appeasement, but that he did not believe there would be war either.

None of America's allies was prepared to support the United States in strong measures over such worthless islands, and 50 percent of Americans did not approve such a strenuous defense of them. Dulles, apprised of this, wondered if NATO and SEATO were "falling apart." The president sent Dulles to Formosa to suggest that Chiang take most of his forces off the islands, and to promise to supply him with landing craft to make it appear that he was ready to invade the mainland if conditions there indicated the disintegration of the People's Republic. Chiang declined but did issue a statement renouncing force as a method of regaining the mainland. Discussions were carried on between the American and Communist Chinese ambassadors in Warsaw, and following Chiang's declaration, the Chinese announced they would only bombard the islands on odd days of the month, prompting Eisenhower to wonder if "we were in a Gilbert and Sullivan war."[3] Once again, at no risk and no loss, Eisenhower looked strong and his quavering allies looked like ninnies.

---

3. Ambrose, *op. cit.*, p. 485.

Although all polls showed the president remained very popular in the country, there was now a recession, and Eisenhower ignored Nixon's warning that if he didn't cut taxes it would worsen and cost the Republicans dearly in the congressional elections. In November, the Democrats gained 12 Senate seats and 49 congressmen. The only bright spot for the administration was the victory of Eisenhower's assistant and former Roosevelt under secretary of state Nelson A. Rockefeller over Averell Harriman as governor of New York by 660,000 votes. Rockefeller was a formidable personality, though Eisenhower thought him too inclined to buy expertise rather than acquire it himself. Rockefeller appeared to be the only possible rival to Nixon for the nomination in 1960, while on the Democratic side the reelection of Massachusetts senator John F. Kennedy by a formidable 864,000 votes presaged the first serious challenge for the presidency by a Roman Catholic since Alfred E. Smith in 1928. Eisenhower was an old-fashioned budget-balancer, although he managed to balance it only once, and told the JCS that if the fiscal integrity of the country wasn't protected, "procurement of defense systems will avail nothing."[4] He asked whether, with the Strategic Air Command, with IRBMs being installed in Europe and Polaris ICBM submarines and other, land-launched ICBMs being built, along with dozens of fleet aircraft carriers, the JCS were not going overboard for superfluous massive retaliation.

As 1959 dawned, Cuban rebel leader Fidel Castro approached Havana, and the dictator who had dominated the country for more than 25 years, Fulgencio Batista, departed (his pockets heavy laden with the spoils of office). Eisenhower was disappointed to find a sharp discrepancy between the State Department and the CIA over whether the incoming forces led by Castro were communist-dominated; State thought not, Central Intelligence thought they were. It soon emerged that Castro was a communist himself and proposed to impose a communist government. The usual response to irritants in Latin America, the intervention of the Marines, was recommended, but Eisenhower, in the light of Castro's popularity in Cuba and throughout Latin America, once again was a voice of reason over the trigger-happy hot heads who abounded in the administration and Congress, not to mention the armed forces. Eisenhower, in mid-January, approved exploration of covert actions to diminish Castro's popularity in Latin America and to destabilize his regime in Cuba. In July, the CIA would still consider an acceptable relationship with Castro possible but problematical, and the State Department was still of the view that Castro was "interesting," in Under Secretary Christian Herter's word, and a formidable leader, but naïve and erratic. Though Eisenhower would not

---

4. Ambrose, *op. cit.*, p. 496.

countenance military intervention, he was skeptical that a workable relationship could be found with Castro.

2. THE END OF THE DULLES ERA, THE STATE OF THE WESTERN ALLIANCE, AND EISENHOWER'S PEACE OFFENSIVE

John Foster Dulles was diagnosed with incurable cancer in February and soldiered bravely on for a while, but resigned on April 13, recommending Herter as his replacement. Eisenhower accepted the resignation with profound sadness, and appointed Herter. Dulles died a brave death on May 25, 1959, and most of the world's principal foreign ministers, including Russia's Andrei Gromyko (who would be foreign minister of the Soviet Union for nearly 30 years), attended his funeral. Dulles is difficult to evaluate historically; he was very hardworking and well-informed and knew a great deal about almost every country in the world. He was a resolute anticommunist but not a warmonger, and deserves credit for maintaining America's alliances well. His advice was generally judicious, and he retained the president's confidence throughout.

He was not over-endowed with imagination, flexibility, conviviality, or a sense of public relations, all valuable attributes in a foreign minister, but he was generally successful, and the administration's failures, especially the shabby treatment of misguided allies in Vietnam and Suez, the breach with Nasser, and the failure to do anything about the Hungarian uprising, were Eisenhower's errors and not his. He was guilty of paying no attention to Latin America (where Nixon was almost stoned to death by mobs in Caracas in 1958) and of the unnecessary prolongation of frigid relations with China, but in the principal areas he had to deal with, he was solid and always avoided the trigger-happy and fiscally profligate tendencies of the Joint Chiefs and the defense establishment. He was a formidable secretary and must be reckoned rather successful at conducting his considerable part of the Cold War, but probably should have retired at the end of the first term. He does rank somewhere among Monroe, John Quincy Adams, Seward, Hay, Root, Stimson, George Marshall, Acheson, Henry Kissinger, George Shultz, and James Baker, as one of the important holders of that office. (Many others, of course, were important public figures but not especially in that office, including Jefferson, John Marshall, Madison, Clay, Webster, Calhoun, Cass, Blaine, Sherman, Bryan, Hughes, Colin Powell, and Hillary Clinton.)

Christian Herter, who was born in France, attended the Paris Peace Conference as Dulles had; served under Herbert Hoover in relief work and then in the Commerce Department; had six terms in the Massachusetts legislature and five terms in the House of Representatives, where he led the Herter Commission (including freshman Richard Nixon) to Europe to support the Marshall Plan; served two terms as governor of Massachusetts; and became Dulles's under secretary and then succeeded him. He was a competent journeyman but was less informed than Dulles and had no comparable relationship or background with the president.

As Eisenhower got into the home stretch, after the slap on the wrists of the midterm elections, and sailing his own ship alone in foreign affairs without Dulles, he decided to try to build on his Open Skies plan and de-escalate the Cold War. Khrushchev and Macmillan were agitating for a summit meeting (Macmillan entirely for domestic political reasons, as he would be returning to the voters in 1959 and wanted the country to have forgotten all about Suez). Khrushchev kept extending his deadlines for Western withdrawal from Berlin (which the Soviets would also vacate but would make Berlin a UN-guaranteed international city and sign a separate peace with East Germany). Eisenhower kept dangling a partial test-ban treaty before the Russians, starting with a ban on atmospheric tests, never rejected a summit meeting (though he did not think it would accomplish anything), and teased further delays out of Khrushchev over Berlin and East Germany.

Eisenhower explained to congressional leaders and the JCS, who wanted more vigorous action, that he considered it his duty, derived from the Declaration of Independence, to facilitate the "pursuit of happiness" and not to upset the public unduly.[5] In the Berlin Crisis of 1958–1959, he again showed his astonishing ability to seem to fumble his way smilingly through problems while in fact steering a carefully planned course between jagged facts and personalities, defending vital interests, conceding nothing, but giving no offense and good-naturedly rolling things forward. His ability to defuse crises, whether by negotiating from strength with recourse to discrete threats (Korea), dodging them altogether as a bad option (Vietnam), seizing on dramatic action in cases where he could not lose because they were either absurd (Quemoy and Matsu) or imagined (Lebanon) and looking strong doing it, or just dissembling and cautiously offering incentives while running out the clock, as in Berlin, was among Eisenhower's greatest strengths as president.

Eisenhower adopted, in mid-1959, the rather bold position that if intercontinental ballistic missiles were successfully deployed, intermediate missiles in Western Europe might not be necessary, especially when close to the Soviet borders, such as in Greece, a site he judged "very questionable" for missile deployment.[6] He rejected the argument that would later be adopted in the United States and the principal Western European states, that any war between the USSR and NATO

---

5.   Ambrose, *op. cit.*, p. 511.
6.   Ibid. p. 533.

should not be conducted directly between the United States and the Soviet Union over the heads of the European allies. And he also adopted the position, which would soon be taken up by his successor, that missiles close to the Soviet Union itself, such as in Greece, could be withdrawn in exchange for nondeployment of Soviet missiles in comparably close places to the United States (such as Cuba).

In July 1959, Eisenhower invited Khrushchev to the United States, intending a brief stay after the Soviet leader addressed the United Nations in New York in September. He entrusted veteran diplomat Robert Murphy with the personal issuance of the invitation, conditional on some progress in the Geneva arms-control and test-ban talks. Murphy didn't express the condition and Khrushchev accepted for a 10-day visit. To allay concerns in the capitals of America's principal allies, Eisenhower undertook a brief flying visit on the new presidential jet aircraft to Bonn, London, and Paris.

He found Adenauer very preoccupied with the French imbroglio in Algeria, where several hundred thousand French soldiers were now engaged in trying to suppress an Arab insurrection. About 10 percent of the Algerian population was European and loyal to France, and another 20 percent or more were Arabs who cooperated with the French and had placed their bets on the permanence of French rule. Algeria was officially a province rather than a colony of France. Adenauer was convinced the communists were behind the revolt and that if Algeria fell to them, all North Africa would. Eisenhower, who had considerable experience of the area in 1942 and 1943, thought Adenauer's alarms excessive. Macmillan was affable and relaxed but urged a comprehensive test-ban treaty, regardless of deficiencies of inspection, presumably for political reasons, as his election was now imminent. Given verification difficulties with underground tests, Eisenhower wanted to start with a ban on atmospheric tests only, as these generated most of the radiation.

Eisenhower found Charles de Gaulle as difficult as he had foreseen, though he sympathized with many of de Gaulle's views. De Gaulle had already proposed a tripartite agreement with Britain and the U.S. that would effectively assure a common worldwide strategy and foreign policy and would give the French a veto on any use of NATO nuclear weapons based in France. The first idea was impractical for several reasons, as it conferred on France and to a degree Britain an influence greater than anything to which they had a rightful claim. It also would have made operating the Western Alliance extremely difficult as the suspicions of the Germans and Italians, in particular, would be severely agitated. And it would mandate a level of external influence on American policy that would never be acceptable in the United States, as de Gaulle had not provided a resolution mechanism where the powers were at odds. The American military and civilian leadership both rejected the notion of a French veto on use of NATO nuclear weapons based in France, so de Gaulle ordered their removal, which was occurring during Eisenhower's visit. But privately, Eisenhower could see de Gaulle's point, and the principle he was pursuing was soon generally agreed in NATO. Of course, the host countries had to have the authority to determine if they could be the source of nuclear attacks on others, as was recognized after a few years.

Eisenhower had considerable sympathy for the French position in Algeria, but was militant that the United States must not throw in its lot with colonialism and the suppression of indigenous national forces. De Gaulle had not given up his hope that he might eventually, with the help of the Germans, entice the British to think more as Europeans than as Atlanticist Anglo-Americans, and he still had the wartime delusions of the revenant grandeur of France, though it was just starting to recover political stability under his leadership and constitution and was deeply mired in the Algerian War. Yet there might have been the possibility of some sort of placation of him that would have made France a closer ally—by conceding the joint approval of nuclear missions from NATO countries (what became known decades later as the two-key system) and by establishing some sort of NATO executive direction that would have included two other rotating countries and involved various bilateral guarantees for Germany and several other allies. Instead, Eisenhower only lamented the demise of the European Defense Community and asked de Gaulle to consider reviving it. This was the integrated European armed forces under American command and was at least as impractical an idea as anything the French leader was proposing. De Gaulle declined, but American leaders continued almost mindlessly to favor Euro-integration (civil and military) long after the end of any need to encourage it in order to make the Europeans better Cold Warriors.

Eisenhower did assure his hosts that they had nothing to fear in his meetings with Khrushchev, and the trip was a great personal success. He pulled immense crowds, about a million wildly cheering and spontaneously attending people lined the roads from the airports into London and Paris and hundreds of thousands in Bonn, a remarkable feat in London only three years after Suez. He and Macmillan appeared together on television in London and spoke ex tempore in conversation. It was a very successful occasion. He returned to Washington on September 7, just a week before Khrushchev's arrival.

Khrushchev told the United Nations that the Soviet Union favored a complete abolition of all weapons, nuclear and conventional, in just four years, but had no suggestions for an inspection system and presented a fall-back proposal for a serious effort to close the test-ban agreement. He had a cross-country tour of the

United States and two days of talks with Eisenhower at Camp David. His general position was that neither side wanted war, but there was no progress at all on the substantive issues of the test ban and Great Power relations in Germany, the Middle East, and Far East, other than Khrushchev's relaxation of any deadline for progress on Berlin. At one point when Khrushchev proclaimed his ability to rout the conventional forces of NATO in Berlin and West Germany, Eisenhower instantly replied: "If you attack us in Germany, there will be nothing conventional about" our response.[7] The visit generated what was called "the Spirit of Camp David" and was a modest improvement in atmospherics.

Eisenhower spent almost three weeks in December on a trip to Rome, Ankara, Karachi, Kabul, New Delhi (with side trips, including to the Taj Mahal), Tehran, Athens, Tunis, Paris, Madrid, and Casablanca. He again pulled tremendous crowds in almost all the countries, including India. He met again with de Gaulle and went over de Gaulle's concern, expressed in a November letter, that the United States and the Soviet Union could level Europe without hitting each other, in the event of war between them, and could even reach a grand accommodation that would be to the detriment of Western Europe. He was really pitching this to a European constituency, to push again France's claim to being the true defender of Europe and the unreliability of the Anglo-American allies without a stronger European (i.e., French) influence on the Alliance. There was a grain of plausibility in this, but for the most part French policy was an infelicitous aggregation of misplaced grandiosity, paranoia, and confidence tricks. Eisenhower remonstrated with him and did well assuaging his concerns, but he could not eliminate the temptations and advantages to de Gaulle of continuing to posture as an authentic European redoubt against both the Soviet Communists and the Anglo-Saxons, who would, however, as need arose, be a splendid ally of Washington and London in a crisis, if not for even slightly disinterested motives. It was essentially a fraud, but de Gaulle was a statesman of great stature, who was thus a more consummately adept charlatan.

By early 1960, the problem with Cuba was becoming quite aggravated. Castro was almost certainly a communist and was whipping up great hostility to the United States in his interminable addresses to huge crowds in Havana. He executed hundreds of alleged Batista supporters in procedures that made no pretense to due process, and had seized some American property. The traditional American recourse in such matters, after the dispatch of the Marines more or less at the behest of the United Fruit Company and similarly avaricious corporate ambassadors of the

---

7.   David Eisenhower and Julie Nixon Eisenhower, *Going Home to Glory: A Memoir of Life with Dwight D. Eisenhower, 1961–1969*, New York, Simon & Schuster, 2010, p. 86.

U.S., was to declare a violation of the Organization of American States prohibition of communist infiltration in the Americas. But Castro was too cunning to be overtly in violation of that, and too popular in Latin America, where he invoked ancient prejudices against the gringos and did not just hurl Marxist shibboleths, to enable imposition of such an accusation on the OAS. Eisenhower was warned that he could not move against Castro without doing the same against right-wing Dominican dictator Rafael Leonidas Trujillo.

The CIA produced some very trivial suggestions for destabilizing the Castro regime—demolishing sugar refineries and so forth—and then some exotic but absurd and unsuccessful methods of assassinating Castro, including poisoned cigars and exploding seashells. There were growing numbers of angry Cuban refugees in Florida, and Eisenhower authorized a program to find a suitable exile leader and alternate government, to support destabilization efforts in Cuba, to establish a clandestine organization there, to launch a major propaganda offensive against Castro, and to create a paramilitary force for guerrilla action. In February 1960, Eisenhower made a moderately successful trip to Argentina, Brazil, Chile, and Uruguay, as well as Puerto Rico. As always, he pulled large and friendly crowds, but they weren't as full of gratitude and solidarity as those of Paris and London. This was going to be a very durable and complicated problem. The United States would pay a price for ignoring, for the 20 years since Roosevelt's Good Neighbor policy was subsumed into World War II, the festering sores and antagonisms of Latin America.

Eisenhower was now preparing what he hoped would be the crowning achievement of his presidency, in arms control and Cold War de-escalation. He told a meeting of the National Security Council on March 24, 1960, that he would effectively accept a Soviet counterproposal of acceptance of a supervised and verified ban of all atmospheric, underwater, and large underground nuclear tests and a voluntary, unverified end to small underground tests. The JCS, Defense Department, and the Atomic Energy Commission were horrified, but the president pointed out to them that the U.S. was already using the peaceful program, Plowshare, which also revealed military applications, and that it would be inappropriate to be too self-righteous.[8] He was prepared to accept an unverified moratorium on small underground tests for up to two years but emphasized that a treaty was necessary to stop the endless construction and deployment of utterly absurd numbers and throw weights of nuclear warheads, to the detriment of more productive uses of resources in both countries. Once again, General Dwight Eisenhower applied his

---

8.   Ambrose, *op. cit.*, p. 565.

immense knowledge of military affairs, and insight into the military and defense personality, to shape national policy in a sensible and placatory direction.

3. THE U-2, THE PARIS SUMMIT, AND THE END OF THE EISENHOWER PRESIDENCY

All was in readiness for the summit meeting in Paris when a U-2 aerial reconnaissance overflight of Russia was authorized by Eisenhower and did not return. The American leadership assumed that the plane crashed, and eventually referred to a routine, high-altitude meteorological flight, on the assumption that the pilot was dead. Khrushchev did nothing to undermine this claim and let the Americans reinforce the fraud about weather flights. On May 8, Khrushchev revealed that he had the plane and the pilot, and still the Americans persisted in their pathetic attempt at deception. Instead of saying that such flights occasionally occurred, were always authorized by him personally, were not a patch on Soviet espionage in the West, confirmed American missile superiority, and would not have been necessary at all if the Russians had accepted Eisenhower's Open Skies proposal, the Americans waffled and, at Herter's instigation, denied that the aircraft had had any authority to overfly the Soviet Union. The leading figures of the administration were scrambling and fussing and running for cover, and Eisenhower, on May 9, approved the acknowledgement of a broad authority for such overflights.

Played to perfection by Khrushchev, it was a humiliating, shaming, public relations disaster for America, and caused the partial disintegration of Eisenhower's reputation as a cool, upright, highly capable Cold War commander. Khrushchev raised the temperature further by threatening to destroy the bases in neighboring countries from which the flights were launched. Khrushchev publicly professed to believe that Eisenhower did not know about these flights, in order to portray him as a fuddy-duddy unable to control American militarism and tempt him further into deception. Eisenhower said that Soviet conduct required such overflights and that Khrushchev's histrionics revealed "a fetish about secrecy." With Khrushchev demanding a public apology from Eisenhower, which the American president made clear would not be forthcoming, the two men and Macmillan departed for the Paris summit conference on May 14. Eisenhower met first with de Gaulle and Macmillan. Though the proportions of the fiasco were hardly comparable, it could not have been a more different atmosphere than that which followed Suez. Eisenhower said: "I hope no one is under the illusion that I am going to crawl on my knees to Khrushchev." De Gaulle smiled and said: "No one is under that illusion," and referred to Khrushchev's threat of attack on America's allies. Eisenhower replied: "Rockets can travel in two directions." Macmillan expressed agreement and de Gaulle added: "With us it is easy; we are bound together by history." Eisenhower was suitably moved and grateful for the solidarity of his allies, and said so, but the summit conference, in which he had placed such hopes, was over before it began.

It did convene, and Eisenhower had intended to reply to a six-page demand Khrushchev had served on de Gaulle, calling for American apologies and so forth. Khrushchev stood up and started shouting accusations against Eisenhower and the United States. De Gaulle interrupted him and said the acoustics in the room were excellent and that there was no need for Khrushchev to raise his voice, and had his own interpreter say it to spare Khrushchev's translator the embarrassment. Khrushchev started up again and quickly regained his former volume and complained of being overflown. De Gaulle again interrupted him and said that France had been overflown 18 times in the previous day by the satellite "you launched just before you left Moscow to impress us." Khrushchev concluded his diatribe by withdrawing his invitation to the American leader to come to Russia. Eisenhower replied that he need not have gone to such lengths to withdraw his invitation, and that he hoped that they could now discuss serious matters. Khrushchev and his colleagues stood up abruptly and left. Eisenhower moved to follow them out and de Gaulle grasped his elbow and said: "I don't know what Khrushchev is going to do nor what is going to happen, but whatever he does and whatever happens, I want you to know that I am with you to the end." As always in stressful times, de Gaulle (and Macmillan too, though less dramatically) was elegant in his solidarity, and his last words to Khrushchev were "Don't let me detain your departure." De Gaulle was the leading figure of the aborted conference, but he had spoken nothing but the truth when, a few months earlier, he had "told Dwight Eisenhower that whatever the outcome of the conference, he [Eisenhower] would take with him into retirement the esteem of the whole world."[9]

The effort to de-escalate the Cold War and produce a test-ban treaty fizzled, and there was only snarling, rather than any useful dialogue, between Moscow and Washington for the rest of Eisenhower's term. He had planned to visit Russia and then Japan after the Paris summit; when the Russia visit was canceled, he decided to go to the Philippines, Korea, Formosa, and then Japan. But Japanese communists staged such demonstrations against the mutual-defense treaty that was about to be ratified that the feeble Japanese government asked that Eisenhower's visit be postponed, instead of putting down the riots and asking the people for the reception their distinguished visitor deserved. The combination of the *Sputnik*

---

9.   Charles de Gaulle, *Memoirs of Hope, 1958–1962*, London, Weidenfeld and Nicholson, 1972, p. 244.

debacle, the U-2 shambles, and the fizzle of the Tokyo trip made the latter Eisenhower presidency seem tired and bumbling, though the president retained his great popularity, in America and the world.

But his time was passing, and his chief associates, Herter and CIA director Allen Dulles, were also old and irresolute. The balance of his presidency was an anticlimax. Eisenhower was insensitive to requests from Nixon, who was trying to succeed him as president, and from others, for increased attention to space exploration, which the president considered a waste of money. And he effectively tolerated the continuation of the nonsense about a missile gap, based on *Sputnik* and Khrushchev's bravura; it was a complete fraud, and Eisenhower, given his great military prestige, could have debunked it easily, but he was somewhat enervated by the abrupt end of his détente-seeking summitry.

There were alarms about Castro, agitation for drastic action from Nixon and others, which Eisenhower sensibly resisted, and about the Congo, which Belgium granted its independence but which immediately fragmented, with a pro-Belgian faction continuing to control the mining-rich Katanga region. Eisenhower had the intelligence to avoid support of colonialism, and while the U.S. had a hand in a coup against the new government led by Patrice Lumumba, it had nothing to do with his assassination.

John F. Kennedy and Lyndon B. Johnson were the Democratic nominees in 1960, and Richard Nixon was easily chosen, despite his chief's shilly-shallying, and he took Henry Cabot Lodge for the vice presidential slot. Kennedy was assured of the votes of the country's Roman Catholics, about a quarter of the population, and deftly managed to campaign against religious prejudice, although the Republicans never tried to fan any, and Kennedy convinced just enough Protestants that they had to vote for him to prove to themselves that they were not bigots. It was a stylish political maneuver. The official result was a Kennedy victory of 34.22 million votes to 34.11 million for Nixon and 303 electoral votes to 219, and 15 for Virginia's Senator Harry F. Byrd. If the votes are distributed exactly in Alabama, rather than giving Byrd's nearly 300,000 unpledged Democratic votes to Kennedy as a fellow Democrat, Nixon almost certainly won the popular vote. Nixon was also almost certainly cheated of Illinois, where Kennedy won by 9,000 votes out of 4.8 million votes cast and some ballot boxes in Chicago were never found. The Democrats won nine states and the Republicans four by 1 percent or less. The election was effectively a draw and no one will ever know who really won, but Kennedy was the ostensible victor and Nixon rejected even Eisenhower's urging to have a judicial recount. Nixon has not received the credit he deserved for sparing the country such an ordeal of uncertainty.

Kennedy and his young family and entourage were immensely convivial and full of what they called "vigor"; and it was certainly time for a new generation. At 43, Kennedy was the youngest man ever elected president of the United States (he was 27 years younger than Eisenhower, 19 years younger than Eisenhower at his first election, though a year older than Theodore Roosevelt when he succeeded McKinley), and his administration was full of strenuous young people. The sober and well-tried Dean Rusk, wartime colonel, holder of a variety of secondary foreign policy positions under Truman, and president of the Rockefeller Foundation, became secretary of state.

The end of the Eisenhower administration was a sad, dwindling twilight, but it should not have been. In the 100 years and 20 presidencies between Rutherford Hayes and Ronald Reagan (counting Cleveland twice, as is the custom, because his terms were not consecutive), Eisenhower, Theodore Roosevelt, and Calvin Coolidge were the only presidents who retired in good health and good standing with the voters, and of those, Eisenhower was the only one who became president by being elected to the office. His were years of peace and prosperity. He got out of and stayed out of wars, made the first start toward de-escalation of the Cold War with Open Skies, and made immense contributions to knitting the country together and renovating infrastructure with the interstate highway program and the St. Lawrence Seaway.

He was studiously ambiguous, as a deliberate tactic to feel his way through foreign and domestic problems, did nothing to dismantle the New Deal, but cavorted with the Republican country club reactionaries as if he were one of them. He did little to reduce wartime tax rates, reform the welfare system, or grasp the soaring possibilities in embracing the space program. He failed to silence a lot of impudent mythmaking about a missile gap when he had in fact been a wise steward of the nation's defenses, keeping them strong, avoiding the reckless bellicosity of the service chiefs, resisting the temptation to overspend, and finally, in his farewell message, cautioning against the relations between the senior officers and the defense production industries. (This was later misrepresented by the left as cautioning against a virtual coup by the service chiefs and munitions and armaments makers, when he was really concerned about undue extravagance in the acquisition of unneeded and hideously expensive weapons systems.)

He had an inadequate notion of civil rights but enforced the law decisively and led the Western Alliance with consideration and diplomatic skill, despite his botch of Suez, an insane enterprise by the British and the French, yet one that should not have led to those countries being durably sandbagged as Great Powers. Until the U-2 fiasco, he dealt better with the Soviets than any president except

Nixon and Reagan, and despite his cool reception to most of his ideas, worked better with de Gaulle than any of the other five U.S. presidents who dealt with him, except Nixon.

It was a personal failing that he was much less helpful in making Nixon president than Nixon had been in making him president, and he was not particularly loyal to his supporters, unlike most of the presidents who came shortly before or soon after him. But he maintained his popularity better than any modern president except Roosevelt and perhaps Reagan. Despite his lack of imagination and his ambivalence, he was a sage and capable and in all respects reliable holder of his great office in very tense times, where a less steady and experienced leader could have got the country into real problems, as some of his successors shortly did. The whole world benefitted from his refusal to be stampeded or hoodwinked by the armed services chiefs.

Beneath his amiable and avuncular exterior, Eisenhower was always a cunning operator, as different in method from Roosevelt's sphinx-like, aristocratic charm masking immense ambitions and devious acts as from Truman's blunt and courageous decisiveness, which could quickly become pugnacity. All were effective and between them provided seven consecutive terms of very successful high-level strategic direction. The condition of the world and of the place of the United States within it from 1933 to 1961, due essentially to the capability of these three presidents, would have been unbelievable at the start of the period. Probably the closest parallel to it in duration of good government and influence on the whole (known) world is provided by the five consecutive benign Roman emperors, Nerva, Trajan, Hadrian, Antoninus Pius, and Marcus Aurelius (96–180 A.D.; Roman emperors didn't have term limits). The next 20 years would be very tumultuous.

4. PRESIDENT JOHN F. KENNEDY AND THE NEW FRONTIER

The Kennedy era came in with panache and a refreshing emphasis on renewal, reexamination of previously accepted truths, and an apparent infusion of energy into the top ranks of government. The president's eight-year-younger brother, Robert, a former aide to Senator McCarthy, would be attorney general. He was not qualified for the position on the basis of his legal career, as Eisenhower's Brownell and Rogers or Roosevelt's Cummings, Murphy, Jackson, and Biddle had been. But he was unprecedentedly close to the president and very committed to several important policy goals, including civil rights and a crackdown on organized crime.

There had been extensive concerns about the phenomenon of the Kennedys. The new president's father had been a harum-scarum financier, flamboyantly putting motion picture companies together and capitalizing on the speculative susceptibilities of the stock market in the era before strict rules about the accuracy of prospectuses or the retention of escrowed stock. He was an effective chairman of the Securities and Exchange Commission and an adequate chairman of the Maritime Commission. He was a poor choice as ambassador to Great Britain, as he supported the appeasement movement ostentatiously and became a semi-public defeatist about the ability of the British to survive the war. He had been effectively blackballed by Roosevelt and Truman and Eisenhower. John F. Kennedy was parachuted easily into the congressional district held by the famous Boston politician and four-time mayor James Michael Curley in 1946. In 1952, Ambassador Kennedy laid out a large campaign fund to take advantage of incumbent Henry Cabot Lodge's preoccupation with the Eisenhower campaign effort and paid Senator McCarthy, a family friend, not to intervene in the state. Kennedy won and was overwhelmingly reelected in 1958.

Kennedy had a distinguished war record as a torpedo boat captain and won a Pulitzer Prize for a book he wrote about American senators who had risked their careers to make courageous decisions of principle. But it was suspected and later came to light that the book had been largely ghostwritten for him. Kennedy and his glamorous wife did not suffer from public reservations about their Roman Catholicism, a concern that had generally eroded, and they were responded to by much of the population like movie stars, or even rock stars, and were publicly friendly with a number of prominent entertainers, including Angie Dickinson and Marilyn Monroe (with both of whom the president and the attorney general had sexual relationships) and Frank Sinatra.

There were vague suggestions, through the senior Kennedy, Sinatra, and shared romantic relations, of links to the underworld. There have also come to light a number of questions about the new president's health. He had been a sickly youth and due to war wounds had a chronically painful back. He took a heavy cocktail of prescribed medicine, including hormones, steroids, animal organ cells, vitamins, enzymes, and amphetamines, which sometimes cause hyperactivity, nervous tension, impaired judgment, sudden mood swings, and sexual cravings verging on satyriasis. Little of this, apart from the friendliness with actors and actresses, was publicly known at the time, and it was, on balance, a refreshing change from the patrician Roosevelt, the down-to-earth Truman, and the avuncular General Eisenhower. The Kennedy era, from its ambiance and style and energy, was different from the start and has been unforgettable since.

Kennedy's inaugural address on January 20, 1961, is surpassed only by Lincoln's two addresses and Franklin D. Roosevelt's first inaugural ("Nothing to fear but fear itself"), as the most famous in the country's history. He urged Americans:

"Ask not what your country can do for you; ask what you can do for your country" and promised to "pay any price, bear any burden . . . oppose any foe" in the cause of freedom. This promised a sharp change from Eisenhower's policy of trying to limit and stay clear of actual exchanges of continuing fire while threatening to use atomic weapons on a range of categories of aggression. Where Eisenhower talked a saber-rattling line, and did so successfully in gaining peace in Korea, he stayed clear of attempts to involve the U.S. in war in Vietnam and in the Formosa Strait. From the start, Kennedy appeared to be expressing a preparedness to use conventional military activity more actively and, in Eisenhower's expression, less "prayerfully" than the former administration, but to be prepared to forgo incitement of nuclear envy by the Kremlin by not demanding continually larger throw weights and more numerous launch platforms for nuclear weapons. It has not been entirely clear how fully these views were embraced or what level of sophisticated analysis went into the development of them.

The new defense secretary, Robert McNamara, the former head of Ford Motor Company, was an ambitious architect of change from the start, seeking to standardize warplane types and advocating a new notion of allowing the USSR to achieve nuclear parity with the United States, creating a defense formula of "Mutual Assured Destruction." The rationale for this was that it would make nuclear war practically impossible, as neither side could be under the slightest illusion that the result of conflict would not be the destruction of everyone. Critics of this view would claim that it would only incite the Soviets to an accelerated buildup to try to gain absolute nuclear superiority. And critics of McNamara's quest for a standardized warplane claimed, with some justice as it turned out, that aircraft flown from aircraft carriers have to be lighter and that those flown from the land should have larger bomb or missile-launch capacities. These problems emerged gradually and in very awkward circumstances.

The conventional national security team was fairly orthodox, and welcome after the sclerosis of Herter and Allen Dulles (who unfortunately was kept on at the CIA). Dean Rusk as secretary of state was not a radical departure from the past and was an articulate, expressionless spokesman for whatever was afoot. Adlai Stevenson, who would have been secretary of state had he not responded to the incitements of Eleanor Roosevelt and sought the nomination himself for the third time, was a very pacifistic and urbane figure at the United Nations, where he replaced Henry Cabot Lodge, the late vice presidential candidate, who would soon become the envoy to the coming, and altogether predictable, hot spot of South Vietnam. The national security advisor was Colonel Henry L. Stimson's old aide, McGeorge Bundy, a Harvard eminence, and his deputy was Walt Whitman Rostow, a tough anti-communist of a largely economic background. Kennedy transformed the White House decision-making apparatus from a layered command structure that Eisenhower had had, to one where almost all initiatives came back to the president from their originators, even if they were well down in the organization. Many relatively untried and rather academic people were directing a new government in a novel way. When Vice President Lyndon Johnson told Speaker Sam Rayburn (who had served in Congress since Wilson's time) how impressed he was with many of these bright young people, Rayburn responded: "I'd feel a whole lot better about them if just one of them had run for sheriff once."[10]

In emphasizing a less confrontational and more upbeat approach to the exigencies of the Cold War, Kennedy early in his administration set up the Peace Corps, which was intended to be an adjunct to foreign aid, to be helpful to those in need of it, and to stress the desire of the United States to live peacefully with all countries. He installed his brother-in-law, R. Sargent Shriver (husband of his sister Eunice), as the head of the Peace Corps, in which eventually 200,000 Americans served in 139 countries. It is not easily quantifiable, but it assumedly had a positive effect on America's relations with the world. It amplified the upbeat nature of the Kennedys, though to cynics it also appeared to be the substitution of the politics of the Eagle Scout for the generally harsh and unsentimental realities that control international relations.

Trying to retrieve Roosevelt's cordial atmosphere of the Good Neighbor in Latin America, he also set up the Alliance for Progress in Latin America, and put Puerto Rico's capable governor Luis Muñoz Marín at the head of it. It was a public relations success, and received over $20 billion from the U.S. through the decade of the sixties. Its goals were to foster economic growth and investment, literacy, better health care, and democratic government in Latin America, and it set the goal of 2.5 percent annual GDP growth rates. That objective was achieved, and there were large advances in literacy, but the Alliance was not a political success under future U.S. presidents. The funds commitment was not adequate to be vital to a whole hemisphere, and critics remarked that American business extracted far more in dividends from Latin America than the U.S. government was reinvesting in it.

On May 25, 1961, a month after the Soviet Union put aloft successfully the first man in space, President Kennedy enunciated the goal of putting a man on the moon and returning him safely to earth before the end of the decade. As he put it a few months later: "We choose to go to the moon." It did fairly quickly eliminate concerns about who was leading the space race, put a stop to the drivel about

---

10. David Halberstam, *The Best and the Brightest*, New York, Random House, 1972, p. 53.

the missile gap, and certainly uplifted the imaginations of a great many people. And it would prove a very thoroughly developed and administered program that continued under three presidents and achieved all its objectives.

5. THE BAY OF PIGS, THE VIENNA SUMMIT, AND THE BERLIN WALL

The Kennedy foreign policy quickly became embroiled in relations with the Soviet Union, especially in regard to Cuba and Berlin. Cuba had been a lively subject of conversation in the latter days of the Eisenhower administration. As Nixon and Kennedy debated in the two months before the 1960 election, Kennedy accused Eisenhower and Nixon of tolerating a festering communist sore right under America's nose, "eight minutes by jet" from Florida. Nixon was privately imploring Eisenhower to do something to appear more protective of American interests and get him out from under Kennedy's charges of a feeble and appeasing policy. Eisenhower replied that some covert activities could be engaged in, but that Castro was not violating the OAS Charter and was popular in Latin America, and that if the United States just moved on him militarily, it would be illegal, would cause tremendous problems in Latin America, and could lead to the assertion of extreme pressures by Khrushchev on the West, especially in Berlin. Nixon, in a policy straitjacket, managed a superb series of replies to Kennedy, accusing the Democratic nominee of being a trigger-happy amateur. Nixon called Castro a "pipsqueak demagogue" but said that a direct military attack was unjustified and would be a disaster. Nixon didn't believe a word of what he was saying to Kennedy, but delivered it very effectively. Eisenhower had asked for the recruitment of a charismatic leader-in-exile from the émigré community around Miami, but they were mainly aggrieved professionals and well-to-do people who were full of rage but not very representative.

On April 16, 1961, following through on Kennedy's promises of decisive action against Cuba, Kennedy and Allen Dulles authorized the landing of 1,500 armed and trained Cuban refugees at the Bay of Pigs on the south coast of Cuba. They achieved surprise but lost some of their force on uncharted coral reefs. There was some air support, mainly from B-26s, which were no match for the faster aircraft Castro had. Castro also had an army of 25,000, the core of it his loyalists who had driven Batista out. The Cuban government counter-attacked forcefully on April 17 and a somewhat disorganized retreat began. It was over on April 19; 118 of the 1,500 invaders were dead and about 1,200 captured. The Cubans had suffered several thousand dead, but it was a stinging humiliation for the United States. Kennedy took responsibility publicly, and privately felt he had been completely misled by the CIA with predictions of a popular rising such as one would achieve just putting a match to a tinderbox. Allen Dulles replied that he assumed that the administration would prevent a defeat by the insertion of forces if necessary, as Eisenhower had done with Arbenz in Guatemala. They both were out of their minds to imagine anything could be achieved with such a trivial force. *Sputnik*, the U-2, and the cancellation of the Japan trip had been embarrassments for Eisenhower, but this was an absolute debacle that set Khrushchev crowing from the rooftops of the world, of righteousness, invincibility, and triumphant predestination. Kennedy returned to the drawing board.

He traveled to Paris in May and had a very satisfactory meeting with Charles de Gaulle, who found him open-minded, well-informed, very courteous, and accompanied by an excessively gracious, attractive wife quite proficient in French. Kennedy was on his way to meet with Khrushchev at Vienna, on June 4, and de Gaulle warned him that Khrushchev would be extremely bombastic and abrasive and that he should simply ignore that and be firm. The Vienna meeting was not a success. The stylish American president was slightly nonplussed by the obese, demonstrative, boisterous Russian. Khrushchev was pushing his plan for a separate peace with East Germany and the withdrawal of all the occupying powers from Berlin, and preferably Germany, under conditions of German disarmament. The problem came down to what it had been for over 15 years: the Russians, having made the Nazi-Soviet Pact with Hitler that started the World War II, found the Nazis at their throats less than two years later, had to endure most of the human and physical cost in subduing Hitler, but at the end of it found themselves facing a rearming Germany, fully backed by the British and the Americans, and by a swiftly rising France in the hands of a leader who had completely outmaneuvered the French Communist Party that Stalin had used to immobilize the country for decades, including during the German blitzkrieg of 1940. And about 3.5 million East Germans had reached the West through Berlin, and Khrushchev saw what the Soviets had managed to seize of Germany slipping away. He said: "Berlin is a bone in my throat."

Kennedy did not agree to anything imprudent at Vienna, and warned Khrushchev that any effort to strangle Berlin would lead to war. He and his entourage did feel that he had not replied at all adequately to Khrushchev's belligerent provocations, and that Khrushchev would take away from the meeting a sense that Kennedy was weak and inexperienced. This he did, and his threats against West Berlin, where large numbers of people were defecting to the West every week, would now increase. Eisenhower had been the first American statesman to draw a possible connection between Cuba and Berlin, when he warned that Khrushchev might imagine he had the right to deploy missiles to Cuba, as the U.S. had to Greece and Turkey. Both areas, Berlin and Cuba, increasingly became strategic sore points through 1961.

Kennedy came back strongly and in a speech in July announced a $3.25 billion increase in the defense budget, including the retention of 200,000 more draftees. He was explicit, as he had been with Khrushchev in Vienna, that an attack on West Berlin would be considered an attack on the United States and would be an act of war. The speech was well-crafted and well-delivered, and all polls showed that it was endorsed by 85 percent of Americans. The following month, the Soviets began cordoning off East Berlin with barbed wire, as people in unprecedented numbers fled westward. To reassure West Berliners of America's commitment to that city, Kennedy sent Vice President Johnson and others by land through the checkpoints to East Berlin. On August 13, 1961, Khrushchev began the construction of the Berlin Wall, as he stopped the subway traffic between the two halves of the city. There were no legal grounds for tearing the wall down, and while all the Western Allies supported the preservation of West Berlin, they were not prepared to go to what would almost surely be a nuclear war to assure the ability of Germans to move freely between the sections of their country that were demarcated by the victorious Allies at the end of a terrible war unleashed by the Germans. A complete impasse was avoided, as the West did not try to demolish the wall and Khrushchev did not interdict traffic between West Germany and West Berlin.

6. VIETNAM AND THE CUBA–MISSILE CRISIS

In the transitional briefings for the new administration, Eisenhower had warned Kennedy that Indochina was a serious and growing problem, and he described Laos as "the cork in the bottle,"[11] by which he meant that the key was to stop the flow of communist forces and supplies down what was already known as the Ho Chi Minh Trail from North Vietnam into Laos and on to South Vietnam. It became a very intricate set of many trails, some of them virtual full-scale highways, that delivered and supported the huge North Vietnamese commitment to the war in the South. Kennedy made a defining decision when in March 1961 he changed the American objective from a "free" to a "neutral" Laos. As the quasileader of the opposition, Richard Nixon, pointed out, this was just "communism on the installment plan."[12] And as the country's two senior retired generals (Dwight D. Eisenhower and Douglas MacArthur) separately warned, it would be impossible

---

11. Ambrose, *op. cit.*, p. 614.
12. Conrad Black, *Richard M. Nixon: A Life in Full*, New York, PublicAffairs, 2007, p. 570.

to win in the South if the flow of northern reinforcements and supplies through Laos could not be stopped.

Kennedy did redefine the relationship with South Vietnam from "support" to a "partnership" and sent Vice President Johnson to Saigon in May 1961 to explain the level of American commitment to President Ngo Dinh Diem. There was a good deal of political and social assistance, and through much of 1961 and 1962 a lot of unutterable nonsense about fighting communism by building bridges and schools and clinics. All that mattered was who could occupy the land and control the population. The president steadily increased the number of "advisers," which included some special forces and a fair amount of military hardware, in a total mission of about 13,000 by late 1963. He authorized increased military assistance by a national-security memorandum of early 1962, and there were a number of initiatives, including defoliation of large areas, to try to make the guerrillas a less elusive target. Vietnam continued to suppurate unsatisfactorily through 1961 and 1962; it would not go away and could not be stabilized by half measures, as Ho Chi Minh felt he had been effectively guaranteed the country at Geneva in 1954, and that the two-year layover was just a face-saver for the French. Though it is difficult to be precise about what Kennedy really thought, or how his views evolved, he appears at the least to have wished to keep Saigon afloat until after the 1964 elections and then make the decision of whether the country was worth an all-out effort, which would require the insertion of sizeable forces, incurring serious casualties.

East Berlin continued to be walled off and there were painful and awful incidents of individuals trying to escape and being shot down by East German guards, provoking huge and emotional demonstrations on the western side of the wall, which was officially called the "Anti-Fascist, Protection Rampart." And there were no serious efforts to restrict air and land access from the West to West Berlin. But suddenly, Cuba erupted as the most direct and highest-stakes confrontation of the entire Cold War. It was reported to Kennedy on October 16, 1962, that U-2 photographs revealed Soviet missile launchers in Cuba, and that they were more likely for offensive than defensive missiles. Kennedy was faced with the stern choice of removing the missiles by force, which would involve the exchange of fire, and possibly heavy, or even atomic, fire with the USSR; asserting some level of prohibition but signaling that an exchange could be negotiated; or simply acquiescing in the deployment of Soviet missiles in the Americas. The last was out of the question by any measurement.

A third of those at the National Security Council meetings urged an immediate aerial attack on the sites. The negatives to that were that there was a chance that

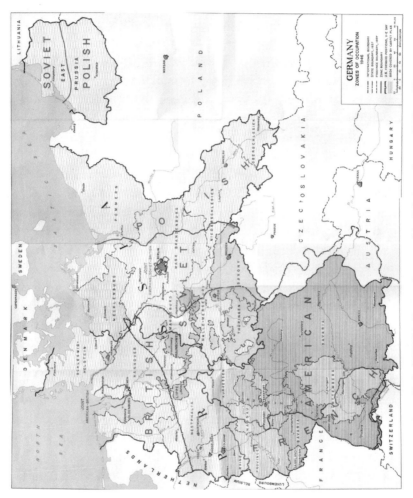

Demarcation at End of WWII in Europe. Courtesy of the U.S. Army Center of Military History

the air raids would not detect and destroy all the sites, and that the remaining ones could launch a nuclear attack on the U.S. And however it went in Cuba, Khrushchev would have to reply in a place where he had the edge—most obviously, Berlin. He could also attack American missile sites close to the USSR, such as those in Turkey. There were some people present who were concerned about unannounced bombing (as at Pearl Harbor, though the circumstances were hardly comparable), and some foreign leaders were, as America's allies often are, irresolute and full of caution. (Kennedy sent Dean Acheson to brief General de Gaulle, who assured Acheson that he did not need to look at the aerial photographs, that he would take the word of the president of the United States as he had that of his three predecessors, and promised his complete support of whatever course Kennedy followed. De Gaulle summoned the Soviet ambassador, who replied, "This will probably be war." De Gaulle said, "I doubt it, but if it is, we will perish together. Good day, Ambassador," and dismissed the Russian envoy.)[13]

This development was particularly galling, because Gromyko had promised on behalf of his government that there would be no missile deployment in Cuba. It was decided to impose a naval quarantine on all sea traffic to Cuba, which the United States Navy certainly had the ships to enforce, and did so on October 24, two days after Kennedy sent a private message to that effect to Khrushchev and advised the nation in a clear and effective television address of the circumstances and of his action. There were four days of unsuccessful messages between Kennedy and Khrushchev, and a request from U Thant[14] that both sides undo the steps they had taken in Cuba. Khrushchev accepted to do that but Kennedy declined. After four days, on October 28, and after the U.S. had stopped and searched a Soviet vessel without incident, Khrushchev undertook to remove the missiles and have that verified by United Nations inspectors, and the United States undertook not to invade Cuba and privately agreed to withdraw the intermediate missiles from Greece and Turkey, and later claimed that, although both those countries requested that the missiles remain, the sites were obsolete and were being replaced by missiles launched from the Mediterranean by Polaris submarines.

A considerable dual myth has arisen about this celebrated and hair-raising episode. The first is that it was a great strategic victory for the United States. It certainly appeared so, as it appeared that the Russians meekly withdrew when Kennedy imposed his quarantine. But it had been a fear in the Soviet bloc that

---

13. Black, *op. cit.*, p. 438.
14. U Thant was elected to succeed Hammarskjöld, who died in an air crash in the Congo in 1961, while secretary-general of the United Nations.

the United States, as had long been its custom in Latin America, might invade Cuba, and that option was given up. And as Khrushchev pointed out, before the crisis arose there had been American missiles in Greece and Turkey but no Soviet missiles in Cuba; and at the end of the crisis, there were no American missiles in Greece or Turkey, and continued to be no Soviet missiles in Cuba and there was an American guarantee not to invade Cuba. The explanation of the Polaris submarines is bunk; the submarines were being commissioned anyway and carried longer-range missiles, and the land-based missiles in Greece and Turkey were an added threat and were withdrawn over protests of the host countries, which weakened NATO in both countries. It was an apparent defeat for the Soviet Union but at best was, in all respects except public relations a draw for the United States. De Gaulle professed, as was his wont, to find it indicative of American untrustworthiness as defenders of Europe if the United States itself were under threat.

The second myth, and a more consequential one, was that this was a masterpiece of sophisticated and novel crisis management, based on the Critical Path method devised at Harvard University (where the president, Bundy, and much of the rest of his entourage were alumni). This held that virtually scientific calculation determined that with the application of a given amount of pressure the result was predictable. Apart from the self-serving hauteur of this fable, it was propagated on the back of another American intelligence failure: completely unknown to the CIA, the Pentagon, and the White House, there were two full Russian divisions in Cuba, and the warheads needed for the missiles were in-country, so the quarantine was, so to speak, locking the barn door after the horses had come in. While the quarantine was on, the local Soviet commander could have fired away to his heart's content and demolished Florida, Georgia, and Alabama, at least, and the land invasion, which some of the military but very few or none of the civilians advocated, would have succeeded eventually, but crushing two divisions of the Red Army would not be like taking over the customs house of the Dominican Republic in the 1920s. Unfortunately, the theory that the Kennedy administration was on to a new level of sophisticated decision-making took hold among the putative possessors of it and led them far astray in years to come, as they wandered down the paths opened up by the president's inaugural promise to "bear any burden . . . oppose any foe," etc. The hour of hubris was coming, soon.

What was reassuring and a great presidential accomplishment was that Kennedy, doubtless informed by the Bay of Pigs disaster, had learned a little of the skepticism about the promises of senior officers that had come so naturally to Eisenhower. Kennedy reasoned that a land invasion could be very complicated and dangerous; an air-to-ground attack on the identified sites could work but would almost certainly produce a military reaction elsewhere, probably wouldn't take down all the launchers, and he at least wasn't certain that the Russians had not got any missiles to Cuba. It is an academic question, as war was avoided and the Cold War ended happily for the United States and its allies eventually, but if Kennedy had attacked the missile sites by air and left it that any attack on West Berlin continued to be a casus belli as far as the West was concerned, and that missiles would, in due course, be updated and not withdrawn from Greece and Turkey, and that any further deployment of offensive weapons to Cuba would be prevented by whatever means were necessary and in the meantime the quarantine continued, he would probably have won a greater victory. But this is the perfect vision of hindsight (though some, such as Nixon, advocated it at the time), just as various more benign scenarios of Vietnam are hindsight, and even some of Korea, though they were also quite audible in 1950 to 1953. More practical and less humbling to Khrushchev would have been promising no invasion of Cuba for withdrawal and permanent nondeployment of missiles in Cuba, leaving Greece and Turkey out of it.

Kennedy did manage the crisis well, gained great stature in the country and the world, and scored some gains in the midterm elections a few days later, including the defeat of Richard Nixon in his quest for governor of California, where he very likely would have won without the tension and happy ending of the Cuban Missile Crisis.

In December 1962, Kennedy allegedly told Johnson's successor as senate leader, Mike Mansfield, that Vietnam might be a lost cause, but that after what had been committed there already, if he now abandoned it, there would be a McCarthy-like Red Scare and he would not be reelected, but that he could pull out after he was reelected.[15] It is not certain that he believed this. If he had explained what he thought the war would cost and said that the smart move was to dodge that one and start Eisenhower's dominoes off one country further on, such as Thailand or Malaysia, or both, the country would have bought it, especially as he could still blame the whole shambles on France, with a slight donkey-kick to Eisenhower. On the other hand, the communists were now a huge threat in Sukarno's oil-rich but ramshackle Indonesia, the world's seventh most populous country, which really was a big domino. The strategic decisions that awaited in Vietnam, and could not be long postponed, were very difficult.

In August 1963, the Diem government in Saigon, as Henry Cabot Lodge arrived as the new ambassador, began a crackdown on Buddhist monks protesting

---

15. Richard Reeves, *President Kennedy: Profile of Power*, New York, Simon & Schuster, 1993, p. 444.

what they claimed was Diem's despotism. This resonated very strongly in the United States and there was widespread unease about what America was doing to assist an ally whose conduct caused pacifist Buddhist clergymen to incinerate themselves. Lodge was asked to persuade Diem and his brother to retire, and failing that, to let it be known to Diem's generals that a coup would be in order. (A subsequent president, Nguyen Van Thieu, told the author, on October 1, 1970, that it was very difficult even to get fuel for his tanks in October 1963, so tightly had the United States clamped down on the regime.) There were contacts between faction heads and the U.S. embassy and repeated exploratory missions from Washington to Saigon to try to sort out the discrepant reports from the Defense Department, which claimed that substantial progress was being made, and the State Department, which reported that the country was being lost to the communists.

On November 1, one of Saigon's more egregiously political generals, in intimate contact with everyone from Ho Chi Minh to the Pentagon and the State Department, effected a coup, removing Diem and his brother and murdering them both. The U.S. administration approved a coup, but not the murder, though it might reasonably have surmised that such a fate was eminently possible. Diem had been put in place by Eisenhower, Nixon had represented the United States at his inauguration, and he had been a reasonably competent president in horribly difficult times. The initial reaction in Washington was almost euphoric, and it was assumed that this would clear the way for the triumph of democracy in South Vietnam. The implications of the United States acquiescing in the overthrow and murder of the ally it had encouraged to tear up the Geneva provision for pan-Vietnam elections, and with which it professed to set up an anti-communist "partnership" within SEATO just two years before, were not confidence-building for America's Asian allies.

It will never be known what Kennedy would have done had he been reelected to a second term; he had ordered the withdrawal of 1,000 men (out of about 16,000) from the mission in Vietnam by the end of 1963. This writer's suspicion is that he would have found the whole proposition so uncertain, the military advice so questionable, and the political difficulties of reversing Laos neutrality and cutting the Ho Chi Minh Trail so daunting, in the world and in the country, when feeding untold tens of thousands of draftees into such a dodgy mission, that he would have made the most elegant exit he could have, and simply said that taking a stand there would have been the stupid option. This was no Quemoy and Matsu, and even there, Eisenhower had no troops on the ground. But this is conjecture. This was where things stood at the end of the Kennedy presidency.

On June 26, 1963, Kennedy spoke in West Berlin to a wildly applauding audience of over two million and uttered the famous words "Ich bin ein Berliner" (I am a citizen of Berlin), which he held, in contemplating Khrushchev's hideous wall, to be the proudest claim a free man could make. "Freedom has many difficulties and democracy is not perfect, but we have never had to put a wall up to keep our people in." It was a memorable speech and Kennedy's suavity, courage, and eloquence made him very popular in the world. (As he left Berlin, he told an aide, "We will never have another day like this one, as long as we live."[16] He didn't.)

Kennedy had taken up the torch of a nuclear-test-ban treaty, originally Stevenson's idea, in 1956, which Eisenhower had ridiculed successfully and then exhumed in the last year of his presidency, only to have it torpedoed by Khrushchev in his histrionic reaction to the U-2 incident. They had agreed at Vienna that they should restart this process, and in July 1963 Kennedy sent the ageless Averell Harriman back to Moscow, where he had been the ambassador 20 years before, to negotiate such an agreement. By this time, newly launched American satellites had confirmed that the missile gap was nonsense and that the American position was superior. This unfortunately did not bury McNamara's enthusiasm for allowing a complete Soviet catch-up, to make agreement easier, rather than to tempt the Russians with the prospect of outright nuclear superiority. An agreement was reached, which the U.K. but not France immediately endorsed, banning nuclear tests on the ground, in the air, or underwater, but not underground. It was a substantial achievement in restricting radioactive contamination and counts as a solid accomplishment of the administration.

7. THE DEATH AND LEGACY OF JOHN F. KENNEDY

In domestic policy, President Kennedy ambitiously called his program the New Frontier, to continue the New Deal, and sought tax simplification and reductions, unequivocal civil rights for African Americans, greater funding for education, and universal medical care for the elderly. Despite the presence of the legendarily able manipulator of the Congress, Vice President Lyndon Johnson, as president of the Senate, nothing significant had been enacted when John F. Kennedy was assassinated with a telescopic rifle while riding in an open car beside his wife, past very friendly crowds in Dallas at midday on November 22, 1963.

This grisly scene was almost exactly captured on film and was, in its impact on the country, the most horrible single episode in American history, rivaled, if at all, only 38 years later with the suicide aircraft attacks on the World Trade Center

---

16. Reeves, *op. cit.*, p. 537.

towers in New York. There was a splendid and poignant funeral, distinguishedly attended in bright, crisp, autumn weather, with the late president's young family unforgettable in their poise and dignity, a piercingly sad and crystalline moment in the lives of all the hundreds of millions of people who watched it on television. Charles de Gaulle, Ethiopia's Emperor Haile Selassie, and Ireland's 83-year-old president Eamon De Valera were the senior foreign mourners. Elder statesmen Eisenhower and Truman were reconciled when they met before the obsequies, after more than a decade of a frosty lack of rapport. But there was no contact between them after that.

John F. Kennedy's presidency is hard to categorize definitively. Certainly, he was an intelligent, apt, stylish, dynamic, and popular leader, probably more admired in the world than any modern American president except Franklin D. Roosevelt. He was a very charming public and private personality, and despite the Bay of Pigs fiasco, was never much embarrassed, even to the extent Eisenhower had been by the *Sputnik* and U-2 episodes. The Bay of Pigs was such a shambles, no one could really credit that it was the United States putting out a serious effort, and it had been erased by the Cuban Missile Crisis, even if this was not the decisive victory pretended by Kennedy's posthumous mythmakers (and they were numerous and perfervidly active, not least with Jackie's bunk about his administration having been some sort of "Camelot" idyll).

President Kennedy renewed American government and carried forward the highest traditions of the three distinguished presidents who preceded him. Unlike them, he saw the benefit of higher growth through lower taxes, and moved the Democratic Party to the imaginative center in economic terms. He put the federal government squarely on the right side of civil rights and made an important contribution to addressing this policy with the extreme determination it required, after what can only be called preliminary, though vital, steps under Roosevelt, Truman, and Eisenhower. He and his wife brought immense elegance and glamour to the office, which raised public and international interest in it, even if this did invite some of the frippery and evanescence of the American star system to attach itself to the headship of the nation and the Western Alliance.

In strategic terms, he held the line well in Europe, but had no real idea of how to deal with de Gaulle, and though he impressed and got on well with the French leader, he could not get beyond the American bugbear about trying to make all Western military forces effectively subaltern resources of an American-led alliance, even promoting a completely fanciful notion of an Atlantic Nuclear Force, which would put British and French forces practically into locally manned squadrons of the U.S. Navy. He didn't grasp Europe's desire to be allied, and even subordinate, but not strategically subsumed, and had no idea of de Gaulle's potential for intellectually and oratorically plausible mischief, which Roosevelt and Truman and Eisenhower had discovered when Kennedy was a lieutenant commander in the Pacific. There was nothing to suggest that he would be more than a competent continuator of the Western Alliance, though doubtless a suave and personable one.

He never really focused on the Middle East, and where his record lurches off into unknowable or disquieting hypotheses is in the Far East and in nuclear strategy. He should never have run any risk of seeming to be partly responsible for the murder of Diem. It is unlikely that he would have plunged into Vietnam with ground forces, and certainly unlikely that he would have done so without a clear mandate. But the nonsense about fighting Ho Chi Minh with social work, like the breeziness about assisting in the ejection of the long-standing American protégé, Diem, when the Buddhists at one pagoda held a few full-press immolations, was both objectively bad and amateurish strategic management. He had largely given away Vietnam when he gave a green light to turn Laos into a superhighway for infiltration, and though his management would probably have been better than that of his immediate successor, he is not completely free of blame for the failures of the ensuing administration, stuffed as it was with his choices for high office, starting with Johnson, Rusk, McNamara, Bundy, and Rostow.

In nuclear strategy there was also room for concern. He opened the gates to "bear any burden" and effectively abandoned Eisenhower's policy of keeping defense expenditures under control while maintaining and extending nuclear superiority, ducking land wars, building and helping indigenous forces, and threatening to turn Russia and China into charnel houses if they crossed the double white line of American national interest, while offering Atoms for Peace, Open Skies, and other confidence-building measures. To the extent Kennedy endorsed—as he appeared to do in his inaugural address and in subsequent Defense Department and National Security Council position papers—letting the USSR build up to American nuclear attack capabilities, and also the possibility of U.S. involvement in more than one local war at a time, he was disposing of his greatest deterrent on the false supposition that this would encourage Soviet reasonableness, while handing the client, robot states of Moscow and Beijing the ability to draw American draftees into war and send them home in large numbers in body bags.

The fact that these infelicitous and strategically disastrous events befell his successors, whom he had named and installed and tended to listen to, does not convict him of their failings. And he does appear to have been a man able, especially after the Bay of Pigs, to override advice, but he can't be entirely exonerated from those errors or cleared of suspicion that he might have partially committed them, either. He also deserves some credit for the great advances in tax reform and reduction, and in civil rights, and medical care for the elderly, which he ineffectually proposed and his successor enacted. On balance, and as far as he went, John F. Kennedy was a good and beloved president, who remains yet in the hearts and imaginations of the nation and the world, nearly 50 years after his tragic death.

9. PRESIDENT LYNDON BAINES JOHNSON

Lyndon Johnson was a Washington legend 15 years before he moved into the White House. The variety of personalities and backgrounds in the succession of the Atlanticist, multilingual patrician Roosevelt; the hardscrabble, night law school Man from Missouri, Truman; the plain man of Kansas become conqueror of continents and leader of transoceanic alliances, Eisenhower; the rich, smart, brave, and charming son of plutocracy and of Irish Catholic exclusion, Kennedy; and the poor but irresistible Texas legislative and commercial wheeler-dealer, Johnson, showed as nothing else could the immense variety but rigorous coherence of the unimaginably diverse and powerful nation the United States had become in the 180 years of its independence.

Johnson was a large, overpowering, tactile, and crude man, with a tremendously effective way of bringing those whom he could influence into line. He knew the vulnerability of everyone—their ambitions, foibles, and weaknesses—and was one of the all-time, supreme masters of the logrolling, back-scratching American political system. His technique and personality were well-known before he became president and he applied them with maximum force to the waverers, along with the bandying about of the name of the late president, to get through the civil rights act that Kennedy had presented but that was being filibustered in the Congress. Johnson crushed the filibuster and the historic act passed.

In the spring of 1964, at Ann Arbor, Michigan, in accepting an honorary degree from the University of Michigan, Johnson enunciated his "Great Society" program, which essentially consisted of massively increased assistance to the needy of all descriptions, as well as particular assistance to disadvantaged blacks, while cutting everyone's taxes. It did not foresee the corruption of the teachers' unions, and was naïve about what unmarried African American men would do with the captive money paid to the mothers of their children.

With much of what was left over of the New Frontier passed, the Republicans nominated the conservative senator Barry M. Goldwater of Arizona for president, and the Republican party chairman, Congressman William Miller, a pool hall owner from Lockport, New York, as vice president. Johnson was renominated for president at Atlantic City, New Jersey, on his 56th birthday, August 27, 1964.

The long-serving liberal senator from Minnesota, Hubert H. Humphrey, was the nominee for veep. It was an epochal night for the Democratic Party. Adlai Stevenson eulogized Mrs. Eleanor Roosevelt; Roosevelt's long time party chairman, James A. Farley, eulogized Speaker Sam Rayburn (both had died in 1962; Rayburn had been Speaker a total of 17 years, and one of the leaders of the House of Representatives for a decade before that). And Robert Kennedy eulogized his brother, drawing heavily from apposite quotes from Shakespeare. All spoke well, and none, nor Johnson either, would be seen at a Democratic national convention again, they who between them had been key figures at Democratic conventions for more than 30 years. The party barons and notables appeared on the balcony overlooking the sea, and on the beach a mighty fireworks converted night into day. Lyndon Johnson, with all the powers of incumbency, the martyrdom of his predecessor, and his call for civil rights, playing well, and facing a not overly distinguished opponent on the far right, seemed to have all the power in the land, as he waved at the tens of thousands of people beneath him. He did, but in the way of politics, he soon yielded much, to hubris and to nemesis.

After a lackluster campaign, in which the Democrats tried to frighten the country with the possibility of Goldwater repealing Social Security and governing for the exclusive benefit of the Republicans' wealthiest supporters, as well as blowing up the world by reckless mismanagement of atomic weapons, the people spoke, appropriately and in a mighty voice: 43.1 million votes for Johnson to 27.2 million for Goldwater, 61.1 percent to 38.5, and 486 electoral votes to 52. It was one of the greatest landslides in American history. Apart from Johnson and Humphrey, the big winner of the night was former attorney general Robert F. Kennedy, elected U.S. senator from New York (where he had not lived and could not vote). He was a challenger in the wings against Johnson from the start. Despite the debacle, the Goldwater movement has remained a turning point and force in American history, as the right recaptured the Republican Party for the first time since Coolidge and pledged it to smaller government. The country knew it was, for now, going cock-a-hoop for the Great Society, but millions wondered what would happen in South Vietnam. The answer would not be a comforting one.

On balance, and by most measurements, the United States had risen steadily in the world under four consecutive talented presidents through 30 years. Lyndon Johnson had been in Washington throughout that time, having arrived as an aide to a congressman in 1932. (He was elected congressman in 1937, senator in 1948, and majority leader of the senate in 1954.) The United States was now an unrecognizably rich and confident country. Its rivals of 30 years before were now junior allies. Its only persistent rival was not really its peer. (In the midst of the

1964 election campaign, the Soviet leadership sacked the bumptious and erratic Khrushchev and replaced him with the more stable and apparently less bellicose Leonid Brezhnev as general secretary and Alexei Kosygin as premier. Unlike Lenin and Stalin, Khrushchev did not die in office, and there were no liquidations following the transition.)

The immense power of America ensured that its errors could ramify widely, but its potential to lead the world further toward wider democracy and greater prosperity was unlimited. Russia and China were antagonists, and the world was full of treacherous problems. But America was approaching the high-water mark of America's century.

Richard Nixon

CHAPTER FOURTEEN

Vietnam and Détente
The Beginning of the End of the Cold War, 1965–1973

1. THE GREAT SOCIETY

President Johnson formulated his legislative plans with great breadth of vision, and after passing Kennedy's civil rights and tax reduction bills, and winning his overwhelming reelection, he presented and jammed through the Congress a flurry of social measures, including the Voting Rights Act (putting teeth into the federal guarantee of the right of African Americans, in particular, to vote) and a raft of measures connected to what was officially described as the War on Poverty. These included the Higher Education Act of 1965, which poured federal money into the promotion of education.

Johnson had briefly been a school teacher in the early 1930s in Depression-era southwest Texas, and had great faith in the propositions that education was the key to eliminating poverty and that money was the key to better education. He broke the barrier against the funding of private schools, a taboo that Kennedy, as a Roman Catholic, had been afraid to touch, and his initiatives improved the physical plant and educational materials available to the nation's schools. Unfortunately, time would determine that the persistence of poverty had much more to do with family stability and social conditions than with access to education. And educational standards in fact declined over time.

There was a raft of welfare programs and alterations that assisted poor areas of the country but inadvertently undermined the family, especially in the African American community. Medicare was enacted to assist the elderly and Medicaid for the economically disadvantaged, and these programs were popular and durable. The tax reductions proved more helpful in encouraging and generalizing prosperity, by stimulating economic activity and private-sector job creation. Johnson also radically altered the pattern of immigration. As a product of the Texas Hill Country and the areas that had received a good deal of poor Mexican migrants, he changed the ratios and was the chief generator of a sharp evolution in American immigration. In 1970, 60 percent of foreign-born immigrants were from Europe, but in 2000, this had declined to 15 percent. The numbers of first-generation immigrants quadrupled from 1970 to 2007, from 9.6 million to 38 million. (These trends were greatly accentuated by the deliberately tolerated entry into the country from Mexico of 15 million or more illegal or underdocumented Latin Americans in the last third of the twentieth century.)

There was a pervasive spirit of support for the end of racial discrimination in all forms and for adherence to the equality of rights and opportunity that infused the founding texts and sustaining national self-image, not to say mythology, of America. This heady atmosphere was topped up by steady major achievements in space exploration, as Johnson financed and promoted first the Gemini and then the Apollo program and the United States edged ever closer to a manned landing on the moon, which Kennedy had promised before the end of the decade. A military intervention in the Dominican Republic in 1965, though it aroused some protest in liberal circles, was quickly followed by a fair election and democratic stability and was seen everywhere as a success. By mid-1966, however, all was overshadowed by Vietnam.

2. VIETNAM, THE GROWING CRISIS

As Johnson entered office, there were 16,000 American "advisers" in South Vietnam. The South Vietnamese army had received a good deal of equipment and training from the Americans and had some respectable fighting units, but the victorious Viet Minh army that had won at Dien Bien Phu had been pouring through Laos and into South Vietnam in heavy numbers and were fully supplied by the Russians and the Chinese, since Eisenhower recognized the permanence of South Vietnam in 1956, and particularly since Kennedy accepted the "neutrality" of Laos in 1962. South Vietnam could not, on its own, resist the North Vietnamese and Viet Cong (essentially the Viet Minh from the South) without either massive American military assistance or a vast program of conscripting, training, and equipping an autonomous anti-communist army.

Eisenhower drew the line for the start of the dominoes at the 38th parallel, but did not do the necessary to equip Diem as quickly as possible. Kennedy poured in more advisers, but saw that the war was being lost. Under the mistaken advice of Lodge, Kennedy had imagined that getting rid of Diem would enable a more democratic and popular leader to conduct resistance to the communists. It only made the Americans appear treacherous and brought on an era of acute instability in Saigon, as the communist forces vacuumed up large areas of the interior. If this country was going to be defended, something would have to be done soon, and it would have to go far beyond pep talks, arms shipments, building schools, and social work.

The dominoes weren't obviously going to fall in all directions from Saigon. Thailand seemed to be stable; the Switzerland of the East, it had been bullied by Japan into declaring war on the U.S. after Pearl Harbor, but accompanied its war message with the assurance that it would commit no warlike acts, and did not. The British and their local allies had largely won the civil war in Malaya. Taiwan, with the U.S. Seventh Fleet in the Formosa Strait, was secure and prospering, as were Japan and South Korea. The Philippines was adequately stable, though no model of civic management, and of course, Australia and New Zealand were flourishing Commonwealth democracies. Burma was almost incomprehensible, a hermit country of gentle people but uncertain governance.

The wild card was the potentially biggest domino of all, Indonesia. Oil rich and with thousands of islands and 100 million people, Indonesia had been governed since Dutch rule by the dissolute international posturer Kusno Sukarno, whom Nixon so disapproved when he visited him in 1953. Sukarno's system of "Guided Democracy" was a tenuous balance of the Indonesian Communist Party, led by D.N. Aidit; the military, led by Defense Minister General Abdul Haris Nasution; Suharto, his chief of staff; and politically active elements of the Islamic hierarchy. While Lyndon Johnson considered what to do in South Vietnam, having been elected in his own right, promising to prevent South Vietnam from falling to the communists, but also to avoid having "American boys doing what Asian boys should be doing," the political fabric of Sukarno's corrupt and economically backward 20-year rule was tearing apart, as the three factions began scrapping and assaulting each other. Most of the senior staff of the armed forces were kidnapped and murdered, and General Nasution only narrowly escaped a communist hit team (by jumping over the back wall of his house, breaking his leg). This was the point of no return; General Suharto raised his standard against the Communists, and the military joined forces with political Islam.

A gentle and cheerful people, the Indonesians, famously, run amok occasionally and become wantonly and brutally violent. This was what happened for about a year after May 1965. Sukarno remained as a figurehead as the Communist Party was declared a national enemy and became a subject of a very determined extermination effort. Approximately 600,000 people were murdered, most of them allegedly Communists, including Aidit, seized and summarily executed while trying to escape on a motorcycle. The Communists were massacred and disbanded, and more than 1.5 million people were arrested. Sukarno was stripped of power, deposed in 1967, and put under house arrest, and he died in 1970. Suharto became president in 1966 and joined with the Sultan of Jogjakarta as Islamic leader, and set the country on a new course of pro-Western foreign policy and an economic program of growth and spreading prosperity, largely devised by capitalist American economists from the University of California. Indonesia was politically reliable by mid-1966, but the American buildup in Vietnam, which may well have emboldened military resistance against Sukarno and the Communists for whom he was then fronting, was still in its early stages.

President Johnson had revoked President Kennedy's order to reduce the number of American advisers in Vietnam by 1,000, just four days after taking office. He had always been something of a conventional hawk, having floor-managed the Formosa Resolution giving the president a military blank check; urged upon Eisenhower support of the British and the French against Nasser in 1956; and urged strong action against Cuba in 1960; and he now soon expressed concern that if "we don't stop the Commies in Vietnam, tomorrow they'll be in Honolulu, and next week in San Francisco."[1] This was the Red Scare combined with the Yellow Peril.

The Gulf of Tonkin Resolution of August 1964 gave Johnson the authority to deploy such force as he considered necessary "to repel armed attack," a slightly more explicit formulation than the Formosa Resolution. The origins of the Gulf of Tonkin Resolution remain controversial. On August 2, 1964, the U.S. destroyer *Maddox* was attacked by three North Vietnamese torpedo boats, and three torpedoes and some machine-gun fire were ineffectually aimed at the *Maddox*. An American fighter plane from the carrier *Ticonderoga* sank one of the torpedo boats and Johnson issued a severe warning. On August 3, in heavy weather, the *Maddox* and the destroyer *C. Turner Joy* (named after the chief Pan Mun Jon, Korean War peace negotiator) were patrolling in about the same place as the previous day's incident. They believed they had been attacked, though they were not certain, and reported the incident, and Johnson was doubtless in good faith when he solicited the very broad resolution from the Congress. He bombed North Vietnamese coastal and air facilities. Whether the American ships had been attacked or not, it was a very slender legal basis for the eventual American war effort in Vietnam.

Vietnam was the strangest and most unsatisfactory war in American history. By 1965, when Johnson had finally to decide what to do about it, Indochina had attracted the attention of five consecutive presidents. Roosevelt, Truman, and Eisenhower were determined not to assist France back into colonial rule; Roosevelt had proposed a United Nations trusteeship until it and other colonial territories were ready for self-government, though he told Stalin that in the case of Indochina, that could take decades. (Stalin thought his timetable would need acceleration.[2] Truman largely ignored it, though American diplomats and agents, and the French, warned him of communist advances there. Eisenhower found the French so pigheaded in their suicidal battle for retention of their doomed empire, he couldn't do much until they had been defeated and expelled from the country. But then he drew the line in the jungle and proclaimed the inviolability of the state whose legitimacy he championed, in contradiction of the Geneva Accord, where the United States was not bound, but which had been approved by its principal allies.

Kennedy just did the necessary to prevent a collapse without making any effort to turn the tide, whose direction was clear to all. The Laos Neutrality Accord, as

---

1.   A much-quoted comment; Mrs. Lyndon Johnson confirmed to the author that her husband occasionally expressed such sentiments.

2.   Conrad Black, *Franklin Delano Roosevelt: Champion of Freedom*, New York, PublicAffairs, 2003, p. 1060.

has been mentioned, facilitated the communist invasion of the South. The best guess is that Kennedy was not prepared to intervene with heavy force to keep Vietnam divided, but he and his successor agreed to address the issue after the 1964 election. Johnson's reaction to the developing Indochinese crisis bore from the start the stigmata of catastrophe.

As someone who had watched with much admiration how Roosevelt had gone deeper and deeper into war while professing only to maintain peace, he seemed to have taken away the message that as president he could pursue his domestic agenda, expensive though it was, while conducting an ever-growing war. The conditions were incomparable: Roosevelt was maneuvering into war on his own schedule, after arming his country to the teeth after the principal adversary and most doubtful ally (Germany and Russia) had enervated each other, and after the British and their Canadian affiliates had fought heroically for over two years; the entry to be triggered by a monstrous provocation that would unite the nation and enlist it until an absolute victory had been won.

With Johnson and Vietnam, there was never a declaration even of the existence of a state of war, only an escalation of force levels; never a stated determination to achieve victory, just a lot of ever more ungalvanizing official waffle about "a limited war by limited means, for a limited objective." Washington was achieving independence; Lincoln was suppressing insurrection and later emancipating the slaves; Wilson and Roosevelt were making the world safe for democracy, and, in an international framework and a regional context, Truman was also. And all were responding to overwhelming provocation and all were determined to persevere until their military objectives were achieved, and all did so, though Truman's Korean objectives fluctuated upwards for a few weeks, before settling back down to the status quo ante in response to the direct Chinese intervention.

Polk was expanding slavery with the Mexican War while skillfully avoiding a rending crisis between slave and free states by wrapping it in the manifest destiny of the Stars and Stripes. And McKinley had a private sector–confected accidental provocation and a humanitarian mission to administer an effortless thrashing to the hapless Spanish.

With Johnson and Vietnam, America was sleepwalking into its fourth deadliest war without a casus belli, with only a gradual increase in belligerency, and no clarity of objective. From 15 to 25 percent of the country was doubtful of the moral justification, or at least the human costs of the war, and more than half, once war was afoot, wanted to pursue it single-mindedly to a defined victory. Lyndon Johnson never really made it clear that he wanted to win enough to do what would be necessary to win. Lyndon Johnson, so immensely accomplished in the congressional arts, fell victim to the overconfidence of the strategic advisers he inherited from Kennedy, and their cocksure conviction that they had the key to precise, calibrated problem-solving. And he and his entourage and the nation fell victim to the glib promise of the confident morn of John F. Kennedy's inauguration, that any price, any burden, would be borne and any foe opposed, in freedom's name.

3. AMERICA AT WAR IN ASIA

Johnson raised the number of American military personnel in Vietnam from 16,000 to 184,000, from the beginning to the end of 1965, and to 385,000 in 1966, 486,000 in 1967, and 536,000 in 1968. He privately called it "a bitch of a war" and was haunted by the casualties, which got to 400 dead a week, spiking at the worst of the combat to twice that. It was the first war in history that was on television in the living rooms of the world every day. A vigorous debate arose in the United States over choosing between "guns and butter." The administration solemnly asserted its ability to do both. Casualties rose with force levels and the theater commander, General William Westmoreland, compounded other problems by sending increasing numbers of men, as they arrived, on search-and-destroy missions, assuming that the more of the enemy could be lured into the South and killed, the more quickly the war would end. This was probably the greatest blunder of U.S. military history. Generals MacArthur (who died in 1984) and Eisenhower warned against ground war in Indochina, but both stressed that if such a war must be fought, the flow of men and supplies from the North had to be stopped by closing the Demilitarized Zone (DMZ) on the 17th parallel and extending that through Laos, whatever the terms of the 1962 Neutrality Agreement (completely ignored by the North, which was hardly a surprise to Kennedy and Rusk, the American authors of the agreement.)

Unlike the practice in previous wars, draft calls were for a defined period, and combat duty tours were 6 months for the officers and 12 months for the lower ranks, not a great morale booster, and when a tour was over, the beneficiary of the elapsed time gratefully departed, even if he was exchanging fire with the enemy. Because of the immense lengths to which the American government went to make the lives of the Expeditionary Force in Vietnam as comfortable as possible, there was an unusually high percentage of support forces to combat forces, or "trigger-pullers." Johnson himself exploded about "Ban Deodorant and Coca-Cola squads," as there were not 200,000 combat troops and airmen even when there were over 500,000 Americans in country.

None of these command errors must take away from the great effort and many battlefield successes of the United States and its allies (the South Vietnamese became steadily stronger, the 50,000 South Koreans were very tough troops, and the Thais, Filipinos, and Australians provided modest numbers of competent forces). The full level of North Vietnamese and Viet Cong casualties will probably never be known, but must certainly have exceeded a million dead. But Ho Chi Minh and his chief collaborators were not interested in casualties. Contrary to Westmoreland's calculations, there were no such pressures on North Vietnamese society from these horrifying casualties as would have afflicted any Western society. Similarly, though the United States bombed the North, Johnson had the mistaken idea that he was always on the verge of applying more pressure than the enemy could endure. U.S. intelligence had no concept of how fanatically trained and determined North Vietnam was after more than 15 years of Ho Chi Minh's people's paradise.

In the aerial bombing of an enemy it is quite in order to rule out certain targets for humanitarian reasons, but the air defenses and resupply routes and sources have to be destroyed and the infrastructure of the enemy reduced to rubble and maintained in that state. The Soviet Union provided the North with sophisticated antiaircraft defenses and the United States kept applying and reducing bombing pressure, which had the sole effect of emboldening the enemy, facilitating the resupply and redeployment of antiaircraft missiles, and unnecessarily deflating the morale of American airmen, who were superbly professional and about whose safety the president cared deeply (to the point of frequent insomnia). In addition, there were 300,000 Chinese support personnel in North Vietnam, liberating an equal number of North Vietnamese to serve as cannon fodder in the war in the South. Especially after the uproar over MacArthur's suggestion of using Nationalist Chinese in Korea, there was not a thought to utilizing them here, even for the equivalent purpose of freeing up more South Vietnamese to fight the enemy.

As the war continued, draft calls increased, and Johnson moved to cancel university deferments, so it was not just the working classes and black ghettoes that were furnishing the involuntary soldiers but the middle class and upper-income groups as well; discontent with the war began to ripple very audibly. As the body bags returning the dead came back in increasing numbers and optimistic reports from the Pentagon and the high command in Saigon continued to pour forth, what became known as a "credibility gap" developed and seriously compromised the moral authority of the administration and the president. President Johnson had had less experience of direct military involvement than any holder of his office since Coolidge. Even Hoover (who died in 1964, aged 90 and a respected elder statesman, the Depression long forgotten), though a civilian, had seen a great deal of World War I in Europe. Lyndon Johnson was a congressman at the outbreak of World War II and served briefly in the armed forces, and was in combat, in that he was in a noncombat position on an aircraft that did come under Japanese fire. President Roosevelt ordered all members of the Congress to depart the armed forces (unless they cared to resign as legislators, which was also not particularly encouraged, and FDR had a high opinion of the young LBJ), and the theater commander, General MacArthur, did not miss the opportunity to award a silver star for combat bravery to the returning congressman. (It is not for contemporaries to asperse Johnson's war service or MacArthur's motives; the congressman volunteered, served, was in harm's way, and was demobilized by the commander-in-chief, but some thought it a slightly slender pretext for the third-highest combat decoration.)

Whatever the reasons, Lyndon Johnson, a vehement and strenuous man, highly intelligent and anything but complacent, and in some respects an outstandingly capable president, was a poor war leader. He was always wobbling between more and less war and lost the support of both the hawks and the doves, of all but those prepared to give their president a blank check. In October 1966, when his polls had slipped badly and the midterm elections threatened to sweep out a great many of the crop of Democrats carried in on the landslide of two years before, Johnson met in Manila with the new president of South Vietnam, the capable General Nguyen Van Thieu. They agreed on the formula of the withdrawal from the South of all nonindigenous forces. This was the confession, instantly noted by all close observers, including those in Hanoi, Beijing, and Moscow (and Saigon and Washington), that Johnson was throwing in the towel. If all Ho Chi Minh had wanted was to win the war, he would have taken the deal, withdrawn, waited for six months after the American withdrawal, and then launched all his forces in a direct invasion of the South, with no possibility that the United States would again set a toe in that scalding cauldron of Oriental blood and tears.

Ho Chi Minh, born in 1890, an early communist, who had lived in New York, Boston, London (where he supposedly worked for the renowned chef Escoffier), and Paris, and for prolonged stages in Moscow and various parts of China and Thailand, had been one of the eminent figures of international communism at least since he took the leadership of the nascent Vietnamese communists in about 1943. He had led a life of frequent hardship, danger, and illness, and was a fervent believer in communism as the vehicle and carrier of the forces of history. He had petitioned Wilson for Indochinese independence at Paris in 1919 but did not receive a hearing, and he concluded that it had fallen to him to turn world history decisively. He would not accept merely the reunification of Vietnam. He would press on and decisively defeat the United States of America, the world's leading capitalist power, and establish the inevitability of the communist triumph over all mankind. There is no other conceivable explanation for his rejection of Johnson's offer of victory with a face-saving exit for the United States (in time for LBJ to be reelected, get back to the Great Society, and become the longest-serving president of the U.S. except FDR, a modestly more dignified exit than Mendès-France had arranged at Geneva in 1954 as the U.S. had certainly not been defeated as France had). Johnson had set forth to prevent the communist takeover of South Vietnam, and was now facing catastrophe on such a scale that he had neither the mind nor the stomach to win, had been let down by his inherited Kennedy-appointed advisers, had been misled by his generals, and had an opponent who wanted to throw the Americans into the South China Sea and didn't care if he had to sacrifice illimitable quantities (for the North Vietnamese soldiers were a commodity) of men to do it.

In the off-year elections, the Republicans picked up 47 congressmen, three senators, and eight governorships, including Ronald Reagan in California, where he defeated the incumbent, Edmund G. Brown (who had ridden the Cuban Missile Crisis to victory over Nixon four years before), by over a million votes. Nelson Rockefeller became only the second person (after Thomas E. Dewey) to win three consecutive four-year terms as governor of New York. By 1967, the national atmosphere was of endless violence, demonstrations, mobs screaming obscenities at the police, the ingratitude of students and finally favored African Americans, and, overhanging everything, a war that the country seemed not to be winning and that the enemy seemed to have no interest in ending, even on favorable terms. All over the world, there were anti-American demonstrations in front of U.S. embassies and burnings of American flags. It was hard to reconcile with the long-standing American self-image of God's own country, the envy and pride of all the world. Not knowing what to do next, Lyndon Johnson kept raising the draft calls for Vietnam.

Johnson had, with great courage and legislative skill, taken a giant step in the emancipation of the former slaves, but in doing so, he had forfeited the support of the white majorities in the South, which had voted for the Democrats since that party was founded by Jefferson and Madison 175 years before. And the white liberal majority that had been mobilized by the nonviolent protests of Martin Luther King, crystallized in the parliamentary genius of Lyndon Johnson, were wary of racial violence and rising crime rates. Johnson had been fiscally responsible and there was not a debt problem and, as always, war stimulated economic activity.

4. STRATEGIC REASSESSMENT

Robert McNamara had persuaded the president of the wisdom of his idea of simply allowing the Soviet Union to reach parity with the United States in nuclear throw weights and launch vehicles, even as America streaked ahead of Russia to the moon. The defense secretary believed that this would encourage substantive arms-control negotiations, and when he referred to the nuclear balance he proudly called America's declining level of superiority in numbers and deliverable destructive capacity of nuclear weapons a beneficial development, even an achievement. Eisenhower's policy of shrinking the personnel and devoting most of the military budget to the achievement of ever more sophisticated technology in delivery systems and invulnerability of retaliatory power, while capping defense spending at quite affordable levels, had been turned upside down. As if the bitter fruit of the Kennedy inaugural promises of burden-bearing and indiscriminate defense of the barricades of freedom were to send huge draftee armies into quagmires at the ends of the earth while America's city cores burned, it all seemed to have been a terrible wrong-turning. And MacArthur's view that draftee armies cannot be asked to give their lives for anything less than victory, in anything less than a high and direct national interest rose up like a cobra's head over the whole harsh national public policy debate.

Despite McNamara's generous gift of nuclear parity to the Soviet Union, there was no dividend in enhanced arms-control discussions. The Kremlin planned to blink momentarily in incredulity as it sped past the U.S. and became the world's greatest power. Robert McNamara, like most of the Kennedy group, as the evidence poured in of their miscalculations, bailed out, leaving their president to face the discordant music in ever greater solitude. McGeorge Bundy, like McNamara himself, and the lesser claque of bright and best young men who had so dazzled the virtual frontiersman and alumnus of Southwest Texas State Teachers' College, Lyndon Johnson, scurried out the back door of the White House into the long grass and, in many cases, into the burgeoning antiwar movement.

In June 1967, as it became clear that Egypt and Syria were about to attack Israel, Israel staged a preemptive strike. It smashed the Egyptian air force, occupied all of Sinai up to the Suez Canal, as it had in the Anglo-French scam of 1956 (Chapter 12), and pushed the Syrians back beyond the Golan Heights. As King Hussein of Jordan was persuaded by Egypt's Nasser to fly to the aid of what was represented as Egypt's victory (like Mussolini coming to assist in Hitler's great victory in the west of 1940), Israel seized all the West Bank of the Jordan River and ended the division of Jerusalem, taking the Temple Mount and the Western Wall. It was a great victory, but Israel became an Alsatian goose, too full of Arabs. It occupied Sinai, Gaza, the West Bank, and the Golan Heights, giving Israel in its new borders a population that was only about 60 percent Jewish. Since Israel could not expel the Arabs it governed, there were obvious demographic problems. Further, since the only Palestinians the King of Jordan could now claim to represent were the majority of his own countrymen, he soon handed over (though officially only in 1971) being the spokesman of the Palestinians to the head of the Palestine Liberation Organization, the disheveled, bewhiskered, incomparably devious, and almost imperishably ubiquitous Yasser Arafat. For all seekers of a reasonable peace, it would prove a very poor trade, from a plucky king to an unmitigated terrorist.

It also opened up a fissure in the ranks of the West. Charles de Gaulle had exited the Algerian War in 1962 and 1963, having to make war also on the fiercest partisans of a French Algeria, led by General Raoul Salan, who went underground but was eventually captured. De Gaulle now appeased the radical Arabs and became something of a hero to Nasser and others, and stirred up resentment against the British and the Americans. He vetoed British entry into the Common Market, made France the first leading Western power to exchange embassies with Communist China, and for good measure visited Canada as an invited state visitor in July 1967, as that country celebrated the centenary of its status as an independent confederation, and urged the French Canadians to secede and set up their own country. Having failed to bring Eisenhower or Kennedy to the virtues of French equality with the Anglo-Saxons in the leadership of the West and, to be fair to him, having failed even to generate a serious, good-faith discussion about reforms to the Western Alliance, he again set out, as he had a quarter-century before, to show what chaos he could provoke. He had lost none of his talent in this regard.

In July 1967, Soviet premier Alexei Kosygin came to the United States and Canada and met with President Johnson at Glassboro, New Jersey. They had far-ranging discussions and seemed to get on well, and there was no doubt that in this first Soviet-American summit meeting since Kennedy underwhelmed Khrushchev at Vienna in 1962, Johnson was well prepared and forceful, but nothing except a brief improvement in ambiance and atmospherics resulted from the talks. Cuba was assisting in pouring drugs into the United States, Ho was prepared to sacrifice his country's brainwashed manhood to push America out of Vietnam, America was torn by rioting and violence, and one of the leading Republicans in the Senate (George Aiken of Vermont) told Johnson to "declare victory and leave." The domestic left said of the ambassador in Saigon, Ellsworth Bunker, that they would "blow Ellsworth out of his bunker," and when LBJ was reported as saying he did not know how to get out of Vietnam, they helpfully replied: "By plane and by boat."

5. THE EMBATTLED ADMINISTRATION

By the autumn of 1967, the Johnson administration, which had bestrode the world with such unchallenged authority two years before, appeared helpless.

Incapable of prosecuting the war to win it or just cutting the painter and going, with no plan to alleviate draft calls and American casualties without "being the first American president to lose a war" (Madison's War of 1812 was something less than an uncontested triumph), the Johnson administration just floundered. Johnson poured in another 100,000 draftees, as if, with America erupting in antiwar demos in every town and city every week, that would intimidate Ho to throw in the winning hand he believed (correctly if Johnson didn't play his hand better) that he held.

McNamara, who had been an eager proponent of the war for several years, recognized that the existing policy was not working and in November 1967 recommended to Johnson freezing troop levels, ceasing the of bombing of the North, and handing over the war in as rapid stages as possible to the South Vietnamese. This was a bridge too far for Johnson, who had offered a slightly less obvious victory to Ho Chi Minh a year before and been rebuffed. But McNamara was finished and had lost all faith in what he was and had been doing, and announced his retirement on November 29, 1967. The leader of the opposition within the Democrats, Senator Robert Kennedy, had followed the trajectory of most of the Kennedys: from hawk to dove as the policies they had advocated failed and could be blamed on the hapless inheritor Johnson, who had been conducted into the quagmire by the Kennedy entourage and was now left there to be reviled as an usurper and a Texan oaf. Not since Woodrow Wilson had a president descended the mountain so swiftly and uncomfortably in foreign policy matters (though on the economy, the Depression gave Hoover an even more precipitate sleigh ride).

Johnson brought in to replace McNamara the legendary Washington insider and fixer Clark Clifford. Clifford had been an aide to President Truman, and played a role in encouraging the founding of the State of Israel, probably a role much exaggerated in his memoirs (though he did attract the monumental wrath of the secretary of state, General Marshall). Clifford had well measured the temper of political opinion and was already headed for the exit when he arrived at the Pentagon. Kennedy greeted the announcement of Clifford's appointment with a comparison of him to "Attila the Hun." Bobby need not have been so alarmed; Clifford, McNamara, and Kennedy had all been on the same Vietnam treadmill leading from bellicosity to the virtues of placation.

Johnson sent Clifford and General Maxwell Taylor (originator of the now not so sonorous "limited war by limited means for a limited objective") on a fact-finding mission to Vietnam. They came back still satisfied the U.S. was winning but, according to Clifford, much less convinced that there were any dominoes around to worry about. Johnson had wasted the 15 months since the failure of his Manila peace offer and just produced more of the same that put him deeper down the well. There would have been plenty of time and public support to intensify bombing of the North, dedicate the U.S. effort to closing down the Ho Chi Minh Trail and cleaning out the sanctuaries and supply depots in Cambodia, and training the South Vietnamese how to win the war and equipping them to do so. Westmoreland had effectively shouldered them (ARVN, as the South Vietnamese army was called) aside and underemphasized the Truman and Eisenhower Doctrines' championship of local self-help.

It would also have been possible to bring in some Nationalist Chinese in non-combat roles to release some South Vietnamese to active duty and some Americans for withdrawal. And it would probably have been possible to move 50,000 more South Koreans to Vietnam and replace them at home with 50,000 Americans, whom the South Korean leadership, the tough General Park Chung Hee, would have been happy to have as insurance along the 38th parallel. With these steps, the United States would have put the North under intolerable pressure from the air, would have strangled the insurrection in the South, and would have been able to withdraw 150,000 Americans fairly quickly, reduce draft calls and casualties, and convince the majority of Americans that the war could end tolerably well and soon. But unlike Lincoln, who read a great deal about war once he was in one, and wrote dozens of insightful orders, Johnson knew nothing about it and was not a wise judge of senior officers. When he did consult General Omar Bradley, Bradley was, as he had been when second-guessing MacArthur in Korea, a pessimist and told Johnson to "lower your sights."

It had become a strategic impasse that could not continue. As MacArthur had told the Congress 16 years before, "War by its very nature has as its object victory and not prolonged indecision; in war there is no substitute for victory." Johnson had to produce a believable plan for affordable victory, or let it be known to Hanoi that the U.S. would leave in a cease-fire as long as its prisoners were returned, failing which it would bomb North Vietnam, as was often said in mockery of official braggadocio, "into the Stone Age." Fight to win or leave at once; anything in between was an illusion, a desecration, and defeat made more unendurable by needless and humiliating prolongation.

In the closing months of 1967, Westmoreland made a number of much-publicized statements of great satisfaction and confidence, and American public opinion did firm up appreciably. It is now known that the battering the North had taken had created deep divisions in its high command, and that the Soviet Union was urging a return to less costly guerrilla war and a policy of agreeing to negotiations and then assuring that they didn't accomplish anything. On the communist side, all powers, including the North Vietnamese, were happy to go on feeding the slaughter, but in fact it could not be sustained indefinitely. The Americans were closer to victory than they realized. Westmoreland discounted that the NVA-VC could launch a countrywide offensive, and had been suckered to some degree by a decoy action at the northwest outpost of Khe Sanh, where he concentrated heavy forces as the international left, on cue from Hanoi, kept likening it to Dien Bien Phu.

Hanoi proclaimed a cease-fire for the Vietnamese holiday period, which Thieu observed for only 36 hours, but the Americans gave more leave than usual. West-moreland and his southern corps commander, General Frederick Weyand, did post extra elite forces in and around Saigon on high alert, a most valuable decision. The fabled Tet Offensive began just after midnight in the first hours of January 31, 1968, on all the corps-area military command points and later in the day, after nightfall, on Saigon and many smaller places. The communists targeted especially the Presidential Palace, the U.S. embassy, the ARVN headquarters and other senior command points, and the main radio station. The only one they even managed to enter was the radio station, and they held part of it for six hours, but the lines to the transmission tower on the outskirts were immediately cut, and transmission, under massive security, was resumed at the tower after a brief lapse. The NVA had a recording of Ho proclaiming the liberation of Saigon and calling for the whole population to rise, and they had assumed that large elements of the population would rise. The Vietnamese people had seen and felt the heavy tread of this terrible war ebbing and flowing over them for nearly 30 years, going back to the arrival of the Japanese, and they were not much interested in rising up for or against anyone.

At the national palace and the various military command centers, security quickly overwhelmed the attackers and killed all of them. In the U.S. embassy, the attackers blew a hole in the wall of the compound and 19 sappers entered but could not get into the chancery or outbuildings, and all were killed by sunrise. The initial brunt of most of the fighting outside Saigon was taken by ARVN, who fought quite respectably and were almost nowhere put to rout. The elite Allied units of all nationalities were deployed decisively to the trouble spots in order of need. The fighting continued for several weeks in the first phase, and there were guerrilla activities into the early spring. The greatest individual combat zones were at Hue, the ancient imperial capital, and at Khe Sanh. At Hue, the communists attacked with nearly 10,000 troops and took much of the old walled city, but the South Vietnamese and the Americans hung on in their command headquarters and eventually, after both sides poured in heavy reinforcements, the communists were expelled completely and the South Vietnamese flag raised over the Palace of

Perfect Peace in the Citadel. The communists lost about 5,000 combat dead and the Allies about 700, over 500 of them ARVN. Mass graves of about 2,000 people who had been executed in groups were discovered and the precise composition of these grim residues of war have never been determined. There seem to have been some South Vietnamese shooting parties abroad, but most of the deaths were certainly at the hands of the communists, including some of their own agents whom, in the highest Stalinist tradition, they chose to liquidate rather than have their identity unearthed as active, talkative agents.

In the Khe Sanh area, the communists did attack a few days before the Tet Offensive but never got past the perimeter and lost 8,000 dead to about 900 Allies, more ARVN than U.S. In the entire offensive, the North and the VC lost over 45,000 dead and 60,000 wounded (few of whom could return to combat), compared with 9,000 Allied dead and 20,000 wounded, about a third of them American. It was a great Allied victory and a deadly defeat for Hanoi, but the Americans, who had been flying blind through this whole conflict, forfeited the ability to enlist their own public and sell a coherent narrative of what they were doing and how it was going to end. Robert McNamara was checking out, patting himself on the back for sitting on his hands until the USSR had got upsides in the nuclear competition, and effectively counseling, semi-privately, throwing in the towel on Vietnam. Clifford was coming in having already come to a similar opinion. There was no one in the inner councils of the administration—and Westmoreland was too shaken by the assault, tarnished by his strategic blunders—who could see it for what it could be. Someone who understood war better and knew how to execute a ruse de guerre would have said that overconfident statements by Westmoreland and others had been tactically designed to draw the communists into a trap, that they had taken the bait and been decisively defeated, and that there would now begin a permanent and irreversible drawdown, toward the provision by South Vietnam of the manpower for its own self-defense, like other countries in the region, and toward the all-volunteer armed forces of the United States. Just before Tet, the North Koreans seized an American intelligence ship in international waters, the *Pueblo*, and the United States was thoroughly embarrassed by one communist puppet state as it was in mortal combat with, it was assumed to be, another.

Tet was Lyndon Johnson's passport to another term as president, but instead, he crumbled. He could not persuade the country that Tet had not been a disaster but actually a great victory. The country lost hope, the media eroded, and the world's greatest power, mighty and courageous, wallowed in the ignominy of strategic error, compounded by a puritanical incompetence at improvisation afflicting its senior leadership. CBS chief news reader and former war correspondent Walter

Cronkite, with his bedside manner like a country doctor and a luxuriant mustache that comforted the nation as Marshal Pétain's had the French, walked through the dining room of the Majestic Hotel in Saigon in army helmet and fatigues, and announced to the country that he had lost hope in the war.

In the New Hampshire primary, where Johnson had allowed a stand-in, Senator Thomas McIntyre, to be in his place on the ballot, in what was another considerable victory, Johnson won 49 to 41 for the antiwar challenger, Senator Eugene McCarthy of Minnesota, an eccentric but intelligent and witty campaigner who had been barnstorming the state for months. Four days later, Robert Kennedy, who had been hanging back, aware of the practical impossibility of defeating an incumbent president for the nomination, felt shamed by McCarthy's performance into jumping off the shelf. From Portland, Oregon, where he was campaigning, Richard Nixon watched Robert Kennedy's candidacy announcement and, prophetically, said to an aide: "Very terrible forces have been unleashed. Something bad is going to come of this. God knows where this is going to lead."[3] Kennedy claimed to be entering the fray lest "America lose the moral leadership of this planet." America's claim to holding this leadership had become quite threadbare already, and would continue to shrink.

Westmoreland took the occasion to ask for 206,000 more soldiers, and he could not have been unaware that any such further infusion was completely out of the question. Westmoreland was kicked upstairs to army chief of staff and replaced by a very talented tank general and protégé of General George S. Patton, General Creighton W. Abrams. On March 31, 1968, President Johnson addressed the nation, announced a bombing pause over the North, invited the enemy to peace talks, and concluded: "There is division in the American house now. . . . I will not seek, and I shall not accept, the nomination of my party for another term as your president." The president of the United States had been chased from office by a ragged little Vietnamese communist, a goateed former salad-mixer for Escoffier.

6. THE 1968 ELECTION

It was a terrible year for America, and it would get much worse. But it must be remembered that at one time or another, Lyndon Johnson, Robert Kennedy. Hubert Humphrey, Nelson Rockefeller, Ronald Reagan, and Richard Nixon were all running for president, as well as secondary people such as McCarthy, George Romney, and Alabama governor George Wallace. There probably has never been such a profusion of distinguished candidates; beleaguered and divided though the

---

3.   Conrad Black, *Richard M. Nixon: A Life in Full*, New York, PublicAffairs, 2007, p. 518.

country was, its moral leadership open to much question, the United States still commanded the almost unlimited attention of a world addicted to its spectacles, even more than in Jefferson's time, and no less for their often very violent quality. The civil rights leader Martin Luther King was assassinated on April 4 in Memphis; he was 39. King had had the genius to forgo violence and appeal exclusively to the innate and decent knowledge of most American whites that it was immoral to treat African Americans as an inferior species, and that it made a complete mockery of the constitutional ideals that continued to be bandied about as the light unto the world in matters of civil rights and human dignity. White America obviously possessed the ability to crush the African Americans but not the moral disposition to do so when they were only fellow citizens nonviolently seeking what had been promised to them more than a century before after a terrible and cathartic war.

Just two months later, the same fate befell Robert Kennedy, in Los Angeles, at the end of his victorious primary campaign in California (a primary in which the incumbent governor, Ronald Reagan, ran ahead of all other candidates combined in both parties, although Nixon and Rockefeller were only write-in candidates). King remains one of the great black leaders of all times and places; Robert Kennedy is an enigma. To his enemies, he was too much like his authoritarian and unscrupulous father, and was too comfortable with Joe McCarthy, and too quick to tap Martin Luther King's telephone and audit Richard Nixon's mother's taxes. His choirboy and family-man pieties did not sit well with his endless womanizing, and it was never clear to what extent the grace of his conversion on Vietnam was a conscientious change of mind or just rank opportunism. Yet, he was a courageous, patriotic, and idealistic man, and in this terrible year 1968, millions of Americans identified with him and will always look back on his brief and tragic campaign as one of the defining moments of their lives.

While this violent election campaign unfolded in the United States, in France the Gaullist regime, celebrating its 10th anniversary, was suddenly overwhelmed by student demonstrations and a general strike. De Gaulle was on one of his state visits (to Romania), urging the locals to revolt from the yoke they were under and take their lead from the disinterested font of civilization led by himself (it was essentially the same message, from Bucharest to Phnom Penh to Rio de Janeiro to Montreal). The original issue was overcrowding of campuses, and then in the unique foible of the French that requires them every so often to interrupt their splendidly comfortable and stylish lives to tear up paving stones and hurl them at the police, the country indulged more and more radical provocateurs until black and white flags were everywhere and people were screaming insanities and were being cheered to the rafters, "even unto Notre Dame" (as Napoleon, who well knew, and exploited the trait, said). There was great suspense, as de Gaulle had made France perhaps the world's third most influential country, with a delicate world power balance between the Soviet Union and an America so distracted and mired in Vietnam, and undergoing the pains of long-repressed racial frictions. The Communists held about 20 percent of the French votes and were very active in the anti-Gaullist activities, and tiresome though de Gaulle was to those he targeted, especially the English-speaking countries, he was generally reliable in the severest crises and his resurrection of France as a powerful state was a great benefit to the West. Its disintegration now would be a far more serious setback than anything that might happen in Indochina.

In one of the last great triumphs of his tumultuous career, which spanned three French republics as well as interim regimes, he waited until he judged that the ancient French spirit of avarice would cause the bourgeoisie to grasp that these riotous shenanigans might actually cost them something, and then he ostentatiously flew to visit the commander of the main French army, on the Rhine, the loyal Gaullist paratroop general and victorious veteran of the Battle of Algiers, Jacques Massu, assured himself of the loyalty of the notoriously heavyhanded (when it intervened in civil affairs) French army, and returned to Paris to make a five-minute speech, on May 30, 1968. It was audio-only on the strike-bound national ORTF network, with just a still picture of the president of the Republic on the television screens of the nation. He began: "As the sole legitimate repository of national and republican power, I have, in the last 24 hours, considered every means—I repeat, every means—for the conservation of that power." He dissolved the National Assembly for new elections, which would be held on the normal timetable unless what he called the forces of "totalitarian communism" proposed to "prevent the people from expressing themselves, as they have prevented the students from studying, the teachers from teaching, and the workers from working." He explicitly threatened, in that eventuality, rule by personal decree, which the Constitution (which he effectively wrote) authorized, and imposition of martial law by the army, well accustomed to imposing it in less genteel places, such as North Africa. The opposition collapsed. There was no possible resistance to de Gaulle's promise of free elections fairly facilitated by overwhelming force, all in conformity with a constitution almost 90 percent of the public approved less than a decade before. Where 500,000 people marched down the Champs-Elysées demanding that de Gaulle go, on the morning of May 30, 750,000 marched back up the boulevard in the early evening, demanding that he remain (doubtless scores of thousands were in both marches). This was a decisive defeat for the international left.

The Republicans met in Miami in early August and nominated Richard Nixon for president over Rockefeller and Reagan, and the somewhat reactionary governor of Maryland, Spiro Agnew, for vice president, as Alabama governor George C. Wallace was running as an arch-segregationist independent candidate, and Nixon had to hold some of the South and border states to win. The Democrats met in Chicago in August in a riot-torn convention, where the New Left exploited the reactionary stupidity of the mighty Richard Daley political machine, which ruled the city with an iron fist, with provoking and outrageous demonstrations without permits and endless goading and taunting of the police. Vice President Hubert Humphrey was nominated safely enough over McCarthy (in the absence of the two leading candidates, Lyndon Johnson and Robert Kennedy). Senator Edmund Muskie of Maine (a Roman Catholic) was chosen for vice president.

As the Chicago drama was unfolding before the astonished eyes of a world that had no idea what surprises, grim or diverting, would emerge from the boiling cauldron of America from one week to the next, the Soviet Union and some of its compliant satellites abruptly invaded the Czech region of Czechoslovakia (Bohemia), all along its borders with Iron Curtain countries, and by a long succession of giant transport planes, disgorging thousands of Soviet troops at Prague Airport on August 21. It was done much more professionally and less violently than the precedents in Warsaw, East Berlin, and Budapest, and the reform leader, Alexander Dubček, was removed from office but not physically abused. There wasn't much other powers could do about it, but it was, in strictly opportunistic terms, a welcome leitmotif for the United States after all the horrors of Vietnam, racial disturbances, and assassinations and political violence that had beset that country.

Nixon had a heavy lead at the start of the election campaign, but Humphrey ran a plucky race and gradually the antiwar left rallied to him, while the Johnson Democrats, led by the president himself, stuck with Humphrey out of loyalty. As the race narrowed in the polls, the third-party vote for Wallace began to diminish, as third-party votes in the U.S. usually do. With the election very close coming into the last week, Johnson and Nixon, two of the toughest and least scrupulous political leaders in the country's history, resorted to new levels of electoral skullduggery. Nixon throughout the campaign had largely dodged the Vietnam issue by saying, "I have a plan," often patting his suit breast pocket as if it held the plan, and purporting to observe a moratorium on political discussion of Vietnam because the North Vietnamese and the Viet Cong had followed the advice of the Russians and were "negotiating" in Paris with the Americans. In fact, they were just arguing about the shape of a table, as the South Vietnamese refused to negotiate with the Viet Cong.

Nixon assumed all through the campaign that Johnson would try to pull it out for Humphrey by fabricating some peace breakthrough at the end. And some officials of the Nixon campaign, especially Anna Chennault, the widow of Chiang

Kai-shek's friend and commander of the Flying Tigers air support group in China during the war, were friendly with the South Vietnamese ambassador in Washington and with President Thieu himself.[4] Johnson was tapping the telephones of the embassy of his South Vietnamese ally, as well as of Nixon and his senior campaign officials, and even of his own vice president and his party's candidate, Humphrey. He was trying to get evidence of someone illegally conducting foreign policy (the Logan Act), but the Republicans steered clear of that.

Finally, on October 30, just six days before the election, time ran out and Johnson went on television to announce the long-awaited, providentially timed, and completely spurious breakthrough. Thieu had consistently refused to attend any such talks and didn't need Nixon to tell him that his government had a better chance with the Republicans than the Democrats. So Johnson said that the North Vietnamese had agreed to respect the DMZ (not a huge concession, since almost all their supplies came down the Ho Chi Minh Trail through Laos or through the port of Sihanoukville and the jungles of Cambodia anyway), and that they would not attack South Vietnamese cities. Johnson delicately said that the Viet Cong and South Vietnamese were "free" to attend.

Thieu cracked this farce wide open on November 2 by stating that he would not be a party to such an attempted sellout. Nixon announced yet another "personal moratorium" on Vietnam campaigning but had his campaign co-manager, the lieutenant governor of California, Robert Finch, issue a statement that he was "surprised" that Thieu was not in place—i.e., that it was just an election stunt. Nixon interrupted his personal moratorium on November 3 to say that he personally didn't question Johnson's good faith, but that Finch had every right to consider the president's action a political trumpery if he wished. Johnson took to referring to Finch as "Fink," as if he didn't know what his name was, and on election eve, as Nixon and Humphrey were on competing nationwide telethons, Nixon referred to the latest intelligence showing increased North Vietnamese infiltration (a complete falsehood). There were no serious voting irregularities, unlike 1960, when Kennedy probably stole the election, or 1876, when Hayes certainly did when a deadlock was broken by a congressional commission. But in electoral mores, Johnson, on behalf of the unoffending Humphrey, and Nixon, had scraped the barrel. In a tragic time, with 400 conscripted servicemen dying every week and violence all over the country, the sacred privilege of the ballot was exercised at the end of a spectacularly reprehensible effort to manipulate the

---

4.   Anna Chennault was romantically involved at the time with Thomas Corcoran, former chief of staff of Franklin D. Roosevelt and law partner of Humphrey's campaign co–manager, James Rowe.

election. Johnson had been more egregious than Nixon, and Nixon's desire not to be robbed again is understandable, but it was an outrageous burlesque of popular consultation. Nixon won, 31.77 million votes to 31.27 million for Humphrey and 9.9 million for Wallace, or 43.4 percent to 42.7 percent to 13.5 percent, and 391 electoral votes to 191 for Humphrey and 46 for Wallace.

7. PRESIDENT RICHARD NIXON

The transition was cordial and Johnson returned to his ranch under, as he called them, "the tattered skies of Texas." He had been vital to the 1960 election, directed the space program well, and rendered great and irreplaceable service to the amelioration of racial justice and relations. Some of his social programs were beneficial, and the scale of them was noble in intention. He had little idea of the subtleties of foreign policy and no concept of what he was getting into in Indochina, nor of how to build necessary domestic and foreign support for a war and sustain it, nor of how to conduct it. When he virtually won at Tet, he despaired, lost all faith in the military command, and gave up his war and his office: a gigantic, tragic, important, and, at his best, outstanding president. He had been one of Washington's greatest figures for 30 years.

Richard Nixon was the first president to be elected to office without his party in control of either house of Congress since Zachary Taylor in 1848. He inherited a nation in turmoil in a world of immense complexity. He chose the former (Eisenhower administration) attorney general, William P. Rogers, as secretary of state, but he detested the foreign service and considered Rogers a friendly placeman who would keep things quiet while he reoriented foreign policy. By far the most important of his appointments was of Harvard professor and German refugee from the pogroms of the Third Reich, Henry A. Kissinger, as national security advisor, succeeding McGeorge Bundy and Walt W. Rostow. Nixon and Kissinger's association would be one of the most remarkable and fruitful in the history of American government.

There were antiwar protesters throwing garbage at the new president's car as he went to the inaugural parade reviewing stand, to which Nixon and his wife responded by opening the roof of the car and standing to acknowledge the crowds, a widely appreciated gesture. While he was still reviewing the parade, Kissinger arrived with some executive orders for Rogers to sign, drafted by him and Nixon, effectively assuring that the national security advisor would see all policy matters and could require material from the State and Defense departments.

Though no one except Nixon and Kissinger knew it, this was a massive reshaping of the conduct of foreign policy. The times were so contentious, and Nixon himself such a controversial figure, because he had ridden the relatively sober aspects of the Red Scare to high office and manipulated himself from there into national office, and had been left by Eisenhower to do the dirty work for the administration politically, Nixon could not count on much slack from the Democrats. And that party, having led America into Vietnam, was now dominated by those who wished to be rid of it at any price. Nixon would have only the shortest interval before traditional post-electoral amnesia would take over and leave it as his war.

Despite all his rather amusing posturing about having a "plan" for Vietnam, neither he nor Kissinger, both of whom had visited there a number of times, had much idea of what to do, and they began by making a perfectly reasonable offer to Ho Chi Minh, not yet realizing that Ho not only wanted the whole country, he wanted the distinction of administering a bone-crushing military defeat on the United States as well, and thought he was halfway there with the tremendous antiwar protests in the U.S. Nixon proposed joint withdrawals, free elections, and so forth, and later received what he called a "quite frivolous" reply from Ho (who died on September 2, 1969, a few months short of his 80th birthday). Nixon had let it be known through channels that if he did not receive a substantive proposal from the North within a year of his election, he would take unspecified radical measures. The months went by with no sign of any movement, but the scale of the war was reduced, as the enemy was replenishing his losses from the Tet bloodbath.

Richard Nixon had been fascinated by and heavily involved in foreign policy for more than 20 years before he became president, and had been instrumental in leading the Republicans away from their post–Theodore Roosevelt isolationist roots. As vice president he had made many foreign visits all over the world and had become quite convivial with leading foreign statesmen, including de Gaulle and Adenauer. Despite the State Department, the Foreign Relations Committee of the Senate, and most columnists advising against it, Nixon went to Europe from February 23 to March 3 and had an extremely successful visit. The Europeans had seen little of Johnson and didn't much like what they did see. They liked Kennedy but those were relatively halcyon days. There was sentimental respect for Ike, dislike for Dulles, and admiration, from a distance, for Truman. Nixon was overwhelmingly prepared and had long had the habit of memorizing speeches and delivering them entirely from memory, and the Europeans were impressed by his fluency and foreign policy knowledge. (Nixon had a remarkable memory; he had played the piano since his childhood, but never read music, and memorized hundreds of compositions, including whole concertos.)

He was formidably informed and diplomatic with the NATO Council in Brussels, in meetings with British government leaders and prominent people, and with Queen Elizabeth. So it went in Germany and Italy, and then in extensive private discussions with de Gaulle. The French leader confirmed what the British prime minister, Harold Wilson, had said (having recently met with Soviet premier Kosygin), that relations between Russia and China had deteriorated very badly, although Kosygin and Brezhnev, when they deposed and replaced Khrushchev, had tried to improve those relations.

Since he had first met Nixon as vice president, de Gaulle had appreciated how knowledgeable Nixon was about foreign affairs, and was grateful for his deferences to him. Some of the meetings between them on this visit were at the Palace of Versailles, from which place de Gaulle claimed, in a wild exaggeration on the facts, "Louis XIV ruled Europe." De Gaulle was correct in insisting on European nuclear deterrent forces, lest any Soviet-American dispute simply devastate Europe without directly endangering the homelands of the protagonists. (The unspoken European preference, if it came to it, was that the Americans and the Russians should slug it out between themselves and over Europe's head.) Nixon sensibly argued for conventional deterrence in Europe and battlefield nuclear weapons, which would do great damage where forces clashed but avoid the devastation of the whole continent. The two views could be reconciled, and it went much better than with the tedious repeated and unrealistic demands of Eisenhower and Kennedy that Europe simply fold its forces into conventional subordinacy to the Americans.

De Gaulle proposed gradual American negotiation out of Vietnam, which Nixon took as indicating de Gaulle's desire to use America's distraction in Vietnam to facilitate the complicated East-West and intra-Alliance balance of power that de Gaulle had been gaming so effectively. (Nixon well remembered when France's entrapment in Algeria had hobbled it in the world.) He diplomatically returned to Italy for separate meetings with Pope Paul VI, which went very cordially, and after receiving an initially skeptical but soon almost rapturous press in Europe, reflected in the media at home, Nixon and his large party returned, and the president's handling of a lengthy press conference on his return was widely praised.

Nixon next attacked the strategic-arms mess that Kennedy, Johnson, McNamara, and Clifford had left. With great dexterity, Nixon announced his wish to revive arms-control discussions with the Soviets, which Johnson had deferred after the Czech invasion; reduced the defense budget by $2.5 billion, the first such reduction in 10 years; and called for development of a partial anti-missile defense system, which should placate the hawks and the doves and not overly fluster the Russians. To journalists' questions, Nixon sagely pointed out that Russian leaders had always been preoccupied with defense and would perfectly understand. In fact, they were always concerned about American technological advantages and this was the beginning of what would be a major turn in the Cold War by emphasis on anti-missile defenses, three presidencies later.

On March 19, 1969, Nixon had a fine reconciliation with the greatest living former secretary of state and his former enemy, Dean Acheson, and they agreed that Johnson had made a mistake committing large numbers of ground forces to Vietnam starting in 1965. Nixon had a further flurry of meetings with world leaders following the funeral of Dwight D. Eisenhower (where he was the eulogist), on March 30. As usual, de Gaulle was the principal focus of Nixon's attention, and this would be the last meeting they would have. De Gaulle was now more clearly advocating that the U.S. announce it was leaving Vietnam and get on with taking its lumps as a defeated power, which, though he did not put it this way, he thought would be good for it and for everyone else. Nixon had other ideas. De Gaulle also urged early meetings with the Soviet leaders. Nixon was in no hurry for those either, until he had strengthened the U.S. hand in the world. Charles de Gaulle would retire the following month, and died in November 1970, just short of his 80th birthday, and was succeeded by his former premier, Georges Pompidou.

On May 15, the North Koreans shot down a U.S. intelligence-gathering aircraft well offshore, and Nixon responded by sending a large naval squadron, including the nuclear aircraft carrier *Enterprise*, into North Korean territorial waters and stating that, "It will be the practice of this administration to give only one warning, and North Korea has been warned." There were no problems with the North Koreans after that. On June 8, Nixon met with Thieu at Midway Island and announced an immediate withdrawal of 25,000 men from South Vietnam. He promised Thieu massive assistance to help the South fight the war, but a reduction in the American effort to fight it for them. It wasn't much of a start, but it was a start, as student demonstrations began to ripple and bubble around the country just before the end of the university year. At a press conference on June 10, Nixon was asked about Clark Clifford's statement that the administration should aim at withdrawing 100,000 men by the end of 1970. Nixon said that Clifford had been secretary when force levels and American casualties had reached their highest point; he "had his chance and didn't move on it. I would hope we could beat Mr. Clifford's timetable." (He did.)

Nixon used veteran French diplomat Jean Sainteney as a go-between with Ho Chi Minh, and Kissinger began a long sequence of secret meetings with the North Vietnamese in Paris. Nixon and Kissinger both traded on Nixon's reputation as a fierce Cold Warrior and potential "madman" in threatening drastic measures if there were not real progress by November 1. He went to the mid-Pacific in July to watch the splashdown of the spacecraft returning the astronauts from the long-promised moon landing, and at Guam enunciated what became the "Nixon Doctrine," almost indistinguishable from Truman's and Eisenhower's doctrines, pledging assistance to countries defending themselves against aggression. He continued on to Manila, Jakarta, Bangkok, and Saigon, where he met with a throng of soldiers. He continued to New Delhi and Lahore, Pakistan (where he liked the Pakistani president, General Yahya Khan), and returned via Romania, where he emulated de Gaulle in encouraging the Romanian leader, Nikolai Ceausescu, to take his distance from the Russians. (Nixon received an immense popular welcome; these visits always aggravated the Russians.)

8. THE SILENT MAJORITY

The problem with Nixon's plan of a reasonable approach to North Vietnam and granting to November 1, 1969, to respond reasonably was not only that it was impossible to reason with Hanoi but that this gave the Democrats in Congress time to disown their war and hang it in the public's mind on Nixon. Student demonstrations started up again and something calling itself the Vietnam Moratorium began holding mass demonstrations, though nonviolent ones, on the ides of each month. There were 20,000 demonstrators in Washington and 50,000 in New York on October 15, 1969. Any political consensus in Washington was melting away, and even the Republicans' new Senate leader, Hugh Scott of Pennsylvania (Everett Dirksen, who had followed Knowland in 1958, had recently died), proposed a unilateral cease-fire.

Richard Nixon had run out of time; his bluff had been called by post-Ho Hanoi; they didn't believe he could force a satisfactory end; the Democrats were pretending it was his war and most were for just getting out. He was one of the few people who thought a non-communist Vietnam could still be salvaged, and Henry Kissinger, at least until recently and probably still, was a "decent interval" advocate, who thought that if the U.S. could depart and Saigon could stay afloat for a couple of years, the credibility of the U.S. would not be too much shaken. The concept of spending lives for such a cynical objective was contrary to the American ethos, as MacArthur had demonstrated (and Truman was, after all, saving half of Korea), and if whatever was done to provide the interval wasn't at least plausibly represented as having a chance of maintaining a non-communist South Vietnam, public and congressional opinion would not hold. There had been no bombing over the North for 20 months, since Johnson announced his retirement, and no concessions from the North had resulted. There was no argument for continuing to appease the North if any argument could be advanced for continuing to pursue the war.

The long-considered response to North Vietnamese intransigence was Operation Duck Hook, which was a resumption of heavy bombing of military sites in the North; attacks on the Ho Chi Minh Trail, including, potentially, on land; the mining and closing of Haiphong harbor; and the seizure and elimination of communist depots and sanctuaries in Cambodia. As Nixon did not confide in anyone, neither Kissinger nor the rest of his entourage had any idea of Nixon's plan to mobilize Middle America behind his plan, whatever it was. And much of the administration had been shaken by the strength and stated intentions of the Vietnam Moratorium. Nixon thought he could rally support for a sensible policy, unlike almost all his advisers (excepting a few military staff), and Kissinger advised in a memo on October 17, that "no quick and decisive military action [seemed] attainable, and that there [was] not enough unanimity in our administration to pursue so daring and risky a course" (as Duck Hook). This wasn't really the question, which was whether Nixon could build and hold opinion for a policy that he could represent as a winning strategy at an acceptable cost. The American public were, for the most part, not overly concerned with North or even South Vietnamese military and civilian casualties; they did not want to continue indefinitely in a war that was costing American lives and treasure and didn't seem to be getting closer to an acceptable outcome, and in which their credulity had been abused by their military and civilian leadership. And the party that had plunged the country into the war now wanted to wrench it out.

Nixon had decided against escalation, and in his memoirs cited the death of Ho Chi Minh, which he thought might produce more moderate leadership; much-reduced recent American casualties; and the advice he had received from Sir Robert Thompson, one of the chief architects of the British victory over the communists in Malaya, whom Nixon had known since he visited him in 1953. Thompson said that escalation would cause immense international controversy without addressing the issue of whether the South could, with American material assistance, defend itself. Britain had never had 10 percent of the force levels in Malaya that the U.S. now had in Vietnam, and while his advice in counter-guerrilla activity was worth listening to, staking the whole policy on the advice of a retired British military officer from a scarcely analogous theater 15 years before is no excuse. (Thompson had also given President Johnson a great deal of advice about Vietnam that had proved to be mistaken.)

None of this resonates very believably; if Nixon were going to rally Middle America, the stronger and more purposeful the military effort, consistent with improving prospects and reducing American casualties, the better his argument for doing so. At the least, maintaining Johnson's bombing concession 20 months after it had failed to produce any quid pro quo from the enemy made no sense (as Nixon acknowledged in his memoirs, and both he and Kissinger later regretted that they had not hit Hanoi hard from the outset). Yet, despite all the errors of successive administrations, a chance remained.

Nixon received a final request from Gromyko, via his ambassador in Washington, Anatoly Dobrynin, to pull out of Vietnam, on October 20. Nixon reminded Dobrynin that Johnson only granted the bombing halt because his former ambassadors to Moscow, Harriman, Bohlen, and Llewellyn Thompson, all told him that Moscow could not assist in finding a peace settlement while the United States was bombing a socialist country. President Nixon finally addressed the country and laid out his Vietnam strategy on November 3, 1969. It was a memorable speech. "I have chosen a plan for peace and I take responsibility for it." If it succeeded, "what the critics say now won't matter. If it does not succeed, anything I say then won't matter." He described all he had done to try to reach an agreement, revealed for the first time (even to Kissinger) the correspondence with Ho Chi Minh, and said that Hanoi had not, and would not, show "the least willingness [to make peace] while it is convinced that all it has to do is wait for our next concession, and the next concession after that one, until it gets everything it wants." He outlined his Vietnamization plan, to hand over the war to the Vietnamese in accord with the Nixon Doctrine, while retaining air support. He told the young: "I respect your idealism." (He did not in fact, and considered them shirkers and cowards masquerading as having moral qualms about the war, but was doubtless truthful in saying: "I want peace as much as you do.")

Then he addressed "the great silent majority of my fellow Americans—I ask for your support. . . . The more divided we are at home, the less likely the enemy is to negotiate at Paris. Let us be united for peace . . . and against defeat. . . . Let us understand: North Vietnam cannot defeat or humiliate the United States. Only Americans can do that." It was an electrifying address: over 80,000 messages of support arrived almost instantly, 300 congressmen and 58 senators coauthored resolutions of support, 77 percent of the people supported his Vietnamization policy, and the president's approval rating jumped from 52 to 68 percent.[5] A few weeks later Nixon announced the withdrawal of 60,000 Americans from Vietnam. If he had announced 100,000 in his speech over a slightly longer timetable and announced Duck Hook as well, he would not have had appreciably less support. Withal, though it was very late, this was leadership and clarity at least, and the great majority of Americans would rather hand the war to the South than the

---

5. Black, *op. cit.*, pp. 635–638.

South to the North if their president said it had a chance of success. He did, and it did, if events in the next presidential term had gone differently.

Nixon moved to shore up and strengthen his silent majority in other ways, promoting locally negotiated school desegregation in every state, not just singling out the South, and sparing the country the unimaginable disaster of enforcing court orders to transport school children all around the great cities of America into racially different areas to promote racial balance. He also founded the Environmental Protection Agency and (largely motivated by his poor youth, when his family had to take their holidays in public parks) vastly increased the number and quality of national parks.

In a 40,000-word foreign policy summary in February 1970, entirely composed by Nixon and Kissinger, a "just settlement" was stated as the goal in Vietnam, and an "architecture of peace" was sought which would be more than "the absence of war" and would include a "normal and constructive relationship" with China. The report referred to "nuclear sufficiency," an inspired concept that consisted of seeking emphasis on defensive systems, while retaining equality of throw weights but exploiting American technological advantages, especially in putting Multiple, Independently Targeted Reentry Vehicles (MIRV) in individual warheads, thus effectively reopening a favorable missile gap. It would not arouse the doves, would placate the hawks, and would incite the Soviets to negotiate while the U.S. steadily gained strength. It was all very sophisticated strategic planning.

When the new French president, Georges Pompidou, arrived for a state visit in February 1970 and was jeered by Jewish opponents of France's pro-Arab policies in several cities, Nixon went out of his way to be seen in public with the French leader. Kissinger continued his secret meetings in Paris with North Vietnamese negotiator Le Duc Tho ("Ducky," Kissinger called him) all through 1970, but the North was immoveable. They didn't believe for a minute that the South could defend itself: "If you couldn't win with 500,000 of your own men, how do you expect the puppet troops to do the fighting? Ducky asked."[6] Cambodia's carnival prince Sihanouk was sent packing in March 1970, after 16 years, and Soviet premier Kosygin, who disliked him, had the pleasure of telling him this at Moscow Airport, as he saw him onto his plane. Sihanouk's prime minister, Lon Nol, a pro-American general, sacked the North Vietnamese and Viet Cong embassies in Phnom Penh, closed the port of Sihanoukville to war supplies, and demanded the departure of the 60,000 North Vietnamese and Viet Cong soldiers in the country. He had nopower to enforce this and Hanoi ignored it, though the closing of Sihanoukville was a notable inconvenience to them.

---

6.   Black, *op. cit.*, p. 660.

9. THE CAMBODIAN INCURSION

On April 30, 1970, Nixon again addressed the nation and told the world of his decision to intervene directly in Cambodia, with the South Vietnamese, to eliminate the enemy military sanctuaries. (He had explained privately, to Rockefeller, that a leader took as much flak for unpopular half-measures as for doing them completely, so he might as well do it right.) He assured the country that it was a measure to secure the integrity of Cambodia, not violate it, and that the forces making the incursion would be withdrawn promptly. He added: "It is not our power, but our will and character that is being tested. . . . We live in an age of anarchy. . . . We see mindless attacks on all the great institutions which have been created by free civilization in the last 500 years. Even here in the United States, great universities are being systematically destroyed. . . . If, when the chips are down, the world's most powerful nation, the United States of America, behaves like a pitiful, helpless giant, the forces of totalitarianism and anarchy will threaten free nations and free institutions throughout the world. . . . I would rather be a one-term president and do what I believe is right than to be a two-term president at the cost of seeing America become a second-rate power and to see this nation accept the first defeat in its proud, 190-year history."[7]

He again carried the country, comfortably enough, though opposition to his action was close to 30 percent, and in a regrettable incident at Kent State University, Ohio, on May 2, four demonstrating students were killed by gunfire from panicky National Guardsmen. Nixon telephoned the bereaved families and deplored the incident, but the televised spectacle shocked the nation, and the subsequent grand jury investigation was a whitewash of the National Guard. The country was also troubled at this time by revelations of a massacre of 567 civilians at My Lai, Vietnam. Nixon handled the issue well with his comment at the last press conference of 1970 (December 8) that the generous spirit of almost all the 1,200,000 Americans who had served in Vietnam must not be sullied by such incidents and that anyone convicted of such incidents would be punished.

There were widespread demonstrations but, for the first time, there were large demonstrations in favor of the administration, including over 100,000 people in New York on May 20, after hard-hatted construction workers had several times beaten up students and other demonstrators carrying Viet Cong and North Vietnamese flags and desecrating American symbols, including urinating on the famous statue of George Washington in the New York financial district. Nixon, a

---

7.   Black, *op. cit.*, pp. 670–671.

skilled and hardball political operator for 25 years, well knew how to polarize the country along an uneven division in his favor. The great majority, whatever they thought of the war, had no patience for adulation of the communist enemy and wanton desecration of the emblems and heroes of American patriotism.

On June 30, 1970, the White House revealed that in the Cambodian action, which ended on schedule, the U.S. had lost 344 dead and the ARVN 818, not the thousands that even his own secretaries of state and defense (Melvin R. Laird) had predicted. It was claimed that over 13,500 enemy soldiers had been killed or captured, as well as over 22,000 guns, 15 million rounds of ammunition, and a formidable 14 million tons of rice, and that 12,000 enemy buildings and bunkers had been destroyed, including, Kissinger deadpanned, what was presumed to be the enemy headquarters, a large, wooden, five-sided structure. Only a third of enemy forces in Cambodia had been eliminated, but this was the sharpest and most effective military initiative the Allies had ever taken in Vietnam, and, as Nixon told the press, at least six months of comparative tranquility had been bought.

In the autumn of 1970, there was a series of unconnected events that Nixon and Kissinger met with agility. They stood ready to support Israeli intervention to help King Hussein of Jordan against a Syrian intervention, but Hussein eliminated the entire Syrian tank force from the air and chased the Syrians out. Israel would not be welcome. It was then that Hussein signed over leadership of the Palestinians to the completely unfeasible terrorist Yasser Arafat and his PLO. In Chile, the voters gave Marxist candidate Salvador Allende 36.3 percent of the vote and 80 of 200 members of the Congress, which would secure his election in a three-way race, and Nixon began considering methods of undermining the tenuous result, as he had, with good reason, no faith in the adherence of a communist to the constitutional niceties, once in office.

Nixon made a peace proposal in Vietnam on October 7, with the midterm elections in mind, a stand-still cease-fire and the withdrawal of all nonindigenous military forces from the South followed by internationally supervised free elections. It was like LBJ's Manila proposal of 1966, but again Hanoi rejected it, presumably because it still thought it could defeat the U.S. itself. In a brief trip to a few European capitals, Nixon had a much more agreeable visit with the old fascist Francisco Franco in Madrid than with the almost equally old communist Tito in Belgrade, and better than either with the pope and the new British prime minister, Edward Heath, but the trip was overshadowed by the death at age 52 of the Egyptian president, Gamel Abdel Nasser. Nasser had been a failure at everything except manipulating the Great Powers and inflaming the Arab masses. The new president, Anwar Sadat, would prove much more amenable to serious progress in stabilizing the Middle East.

In the midterm elections, the Republicans, after Nixon made a whirlwind tour of 30 states (in the last year of his presidency, Johnson could not go anywhere except military bases without demonstrations), gained two senators and lost nine congressmen, a very respectable showing. Adlai Stevenson Jr. was elected governor of Illinois, Congressman George H.W. Bush was defeated for U.S. senator from Texas by Lloyd Bentsen, Eugene McCarthy retired, Hubert Humphrey came back to the Senate for a fourth term, and Conservative James Buckley was elected as senator from New York. By the end of 1970, Nixon had reduced force levels in Vietnam to 335,000, down 215,000 from when he entered office, and far ahead of Clark Clifford's rather gratuitous recommendation to aim for a reduction of 100,000 by then.

10. THE OPENING WITH CHINA

During the United Nations General Assembly in September, Nixon made conciliatory overtures to the Chinese Communists, via Pakistani president Yahya Khan, as he always did in his talks with Ceausescu. On December 9, the Pakistani ambassador in Washington handed over to Kissinger a letter from Yahya summarizing a conversation with Premier Chou En-lai, in which Chou said it would be sensible for a senior American official to visit China. Nixon had cast this bread upon the waters even before he was president, in a conciliatory passage on China he wrote in *Foreign Affairs*, the publication of the Council on Foreign Relations. Nixon had long recognized that China could not be excluded from the world, and he knew that to force Hanoi to stop imagining it could defeat the Unites States, as opposed to just the South Vietnamese, at least one of the communist giants had to be weaned away from bankrolling and arming that effort. He was also confident that opening up relations with China would assert irresistible pressures on Russia to be more cooperative in other areas, though as with Hitler and Stalin in 1942–1944, if too much advantage were taken of the dispute between the dictators, they would be capable of composing their differences. Nixon, as the chief conceptualizer and architect of this arrangement, knew it had to be managed with extreme caution. Now, he and Kissinger immediately composed a letter to Chou proposing comprehensive talks at the highest level.

On February 8, 1971, as congressional action had barred U.S. ground forces in Laos, Nixon browbeat Thieu into sending 30,000 men to cut the Ho Chi Minh Trail. Of course the force was of wholly inadequate strength (like Marshall's

Sledgehammer in France in 1942, Chapter 10), and though ARVN started out all right, they soon met with superior forces, before reaching their objective of Lam Son. Nixon devised the ruse de guerre of helicoptering onto the target, claiming victory, and then packing up the operation just in time to avoid an ARVN massacre. It was clever but it didn't fool either Hanoi or the American media, who saw the ragged condition in which the ARVN units returned. On April 9, having already announced a further 50,000 reduction in manpower, Nixon told the country that U.S. force levels in South Vietnam would be down to 184,000 at the end of 1971, an almost two-thirds reduction since he entered office, and ARVN appeared to be doing a tolerable job of holding its position.

Three days before, in what was a considerable breakthrough, and, as it turned out, by direct order of Mao Tse-tung himself, the U.S. Ping-Pong team, at the end of an international tournament in Japan, was invited to tour the People's Republic. It was such an obscure gesture, few outside the White House and the Kremlin took any notice of it. The Chinese released long-held prisoners; there were further secret contacts in different capitals; and Mao gave a relatively conciliatory interview to American longtime fellow traveler Edgar Snow. Two giants were almost indiscernibly winking and twitching at each other across a crowded and unobservant world. On May 18, as Soviet-American relations warmed, with the U.S. no longer asking Moscow to apply any pressure on Hanoi, and Moscow uneasily detecting some movement in U.S.-China relations, an outline was announced of a comprehensive arms-control agreement between the two superpowers.

On June 2, again via the Pakistani channel, Chou reported that Mao would be delighted to welcome Nixon to China, and that for a preparatory and organizing visit Chou would welcome a designated senior official, who was soon confirmed to be Kissinger. Eight days later, unannounced, Nixon ended a 21-year trade embargo on China. He was conducting an extremely delicate and intricate minuet on a high-wire, with consummate skill. The country was heavily distracted by the publication of the Pentagon Papers, purloined from the Defense Department by a disaffected Vietnam expert, Daniel Ellsberg, and published in successive newspapers. The government tried to enjoin publication, but the papers were disparaging of the Kennedy and Johnson administrations, not of Nixon's.

Henry Kissinger departed on July 1 on his Asian trip to Saigon, Bangkok, New Delhi, and Pakistan, where he feigned illness and was conveyed to the airport in disguise in an old car driven personally by the Pakistani foreign minister, in the dead of night, and then flew to Beijing. Kissinger and Chou agreed that American forces could leave Taiwan if China promised not to invade the island, a sober and fair communiqué was worked out, largely by Mao, and Chou promised not to grant entries to any more American politicians who were seeking them until after Nixon's visit.

Kissinger left Beijing after a completely successful visit on July 11, recovered from his pretended stomach flu in Northern Pakistan, flew on to Tehran, and, by prearrangement, sent on the maximum security line from the U.S. embassy there the preagreed one-word message to Nixon, delivered to him by General Alexander Haig, "Eureka." At 7:31 p.m., July 15, 1971, Richard Nixon electrified the world with an unscheduled announcement on all radio and television outlets in the United States, as an identical announcement was made in Beijing. It was stated that Kissinger had been invited to China by Chou En-lai, had visited and expressed Nixon's interest in visiting China, and that Chairman Mao Tse-tung had cordially invited the president, who was happy to accept and would go to China before his scheduled visit to the Soviet Union in May 1972. Every government in the world except Pakistan was thunderstruck. The timing of the trip was to ensure that Nixon had maximum leverage on Mocow when he went there. He had all the world powers in a row; it was a remarkable feat for a country that just 30 months before was riot-torn, was diplomatically inactive, and saw no exit from Vietnam.

On August 13, 1971, Nixon rounded up his economic officials and advisers and brought them to Camp David for a serious discussion of how to avoid inflation and rev up the economy in the year before the election. He said that conditions had changed and that no one should be bound by past positions. He announced the next evening a package of investment credits, excise tax reductions, a 5 percent reduction in the number of federal employees, a 10 percent cut in foreign aid, a 90-day wage and price freeze, a 10 percent tax on all imports, and a suspension of the gold convertibility of the dollar. It was a bold program that responded to the renewed international interest in effectively buying gold from the United States at discounted prices. It could be assumed to stop inflation temporarily (until after the election), stop the foreign pickpockets, stimulate the economy, but introduce an age of relatively little discipline between currencies, when they would have no value at all, except opposite each other. He concluded that "Whether the nation stays Number One depends on your competitive spirit, your sense of personal destiny, your pride in your country and yourself."[8] It was a popular program that again confounded the Democrats, who thought Nixon incapable of price controls and were gearing up to accuse him of being soft on inflation. Europe and Japan were accustomed to exploiting a high dollar with cheap exports, while undermining the dollar by exploiting its convertibility. Nixon

---

8.   Black, *op. cit.*, p. 743.

ended this. In removing the dollar from any standard of comparative measurement other than its value opposite other free-floating currencies, he was opening the floodgates to more easily disguised inflation, a temptation future administrations could reasonably be assumed to have trouble resisting. He should, after the dust had settled, have reintroduced some disciplinary yardstick for intergovernmental transactions, even a blend of gold, oil, and consumer necessities.

In the autumn of 1971, East Pakistan (originally Bengal and later Bangladesh), separated by a thousand miles across India from West Pakistan, was agitating for independence from the West and had voted accordingly in December 1970 (97 percent for Mujibur Rahman's Awami League). Nixon's ally Yahya Khan had persuaded himself that both China and the U.S. would come to his aid against India, and Nixon suspected the Russians of inciting the Indians and the Bengalis. He cut aid to India, but general disorder broke out when Mujib declared East Pakistani independence. Yahya unleashed the 70,000 soldiers he had deployed in the East, and hundreds of thousands of East Pakistanis were killed and millions fled to India. The United States and China wanted to be helpful to Yahya, but there were limits to what they could reasonably do against such a strong sentiment of national expression, and in the face of Yahya's brutal and unimaginative response to it.

Indian prime minister Indira Gandhi visited Washington in November 1971 and had a very unsatisfactory exchange with Nixon. She pledged to leave West Pakistan alone but required that the violence cease in East Pakistan and that the refugees who had poured into her country in millions be permitted to return. It was not an unreasonable position, but Nixon suspected her of fomenting the violence in the East and of having designs on the West. At the end of November, guerrillas armed and trained by the Indians entered East Pakistan and the Indian army came a few miles across the East Pakistan border, ostensibly to maintain order at the request of the local authorities (a complete fabrication). Gandhi was duplicitous and Yahya was delusional, an unpromising state of affairs for the subcontinent, and on December 3, Yahya insanely launched an ineffectual attack on the Indian air force. It did little damage but gave the Indian leader all she needed to launch an all-out invasion of East Pakistan. The Indians decimated the Pakistani air force, enjoying superior numbers.

Nixon blamed India for escalating the crisis, Pakistan for starting the war, and the Russians for inciting the Indians. He warned the Soviet Union and India against any attack on West Pakistan, and moved a nuclear aircraft carrier task force to the Bay of Bengal. Nixon used the visiting Soviet agriculture minister and then the direct hotline to Brezhnev to send his warning. This was the best he could do for

Yahya. On December 10, Kissinger gave the Chinese ambassador to the UN a full sheaf of aerial photographic reconnaissance of Soviet force dispositions all along its Asian borders from Turkey to the Far East. On December 16, the Pakistani army in East Pakistan surrendered to overwhelming Indian forces, having put up a respectable fight in a dubious cause. It all settled down quickly but lengthily embittered relations between India and the U.S.

Nixon met with the principal West European leaders at different temperate places in December, assured them of America's solidarity with Europe, and agreed to a revaluing of currencies that enabled him to cancel the 10 percent import surcharge in his August economic message. Nixon told all three leaders—France's Pompidou, Britain's Heath, and West Germany's Willy Brandt—that the five geostrategic points with the industrial and military strength to influence the world were the United States, Western Europe, Japan, Russia, and China. As head of one, he was concerned to strengthen his alliance with Europe and Japan, detach China completely from Russia, and then, from a position of strength, negotiate de-escalation of tensions and a reasonable working relationship with Russia. All the European leaders purported to understand, and concurred. It was perfectly correct and skillfully executed pure strategy. The great challenges to the United States since it had become the world's greatest power had come from Nazi-dominated Western Europe (1938–1944) and the Russia of Stalin, Khrushchev, and Brezhnev since then; an economic challenge from a friendly Japan was already developing, and a Chinese rivalry was predictable eventually. The United States dealt effectively with each as it arose.

As the election year of 1972 opened, Nixon announced a withdrawal of another 70,000 Americans from Vietnam by May, which would leave only 69,000, a reduction of 88 percent from when he entered office. He awaited the Democrats' claim that this was insufficient and that total withdrawal should be offered, and it was not long in coming. Senator George McGovern, one of the leading candidates for the presidential nomination and almost an outright pacifist, demanded that Nixon offer total withdrawal in exchange for release of American prisoners of war. Nixon then, on January 25, 1972, revealed Kissinger's secret negotiations in Paris and hammered the Democratic peace candidates with the fact that Hanoi had not only been offered what McGovern and the others accused Nixon of not offering, but had rejected it. He said that "the only reply to our plan has been an increase in troop infiltrations and communist military offensives in Laos and Cambodia. We are being asked publicly to set a terminal date for our withdrawals when we already have offered one in private. . . . If the enemy wants peace, it will have to recognize the important difference between settlement and surrender."[9] As usual, Nixon outsmarted his critics.

President Nixon and his party of over 300 landed at Beijing Airport on February 21, 1972, and Nixon descended the gangplank and offered his hand to Premier Chou En-lai, concluding the handshake offered by Chou and rebuffed by Secretary of State John Foster Dulles at Geneva in 1954 (Chapter 12). Shortly after his arrival, Nixon and Kissinger (but not Rogers) met with Mao Tse-tung and Chou En-lai at Mao's home. The photographs of their warm handshake astonished the world more than any such burial of the hatchet since Stalin smiled benignly on the handshake between Molotov and Ribbentrop at the Kremlin in August 1939.

For the next week, as they traveled about China, Nixon and Chou En-lai conducted an itinerant summit meeting that ranged widely and was entirely cordial. Nixon was so overwhelmingly informed and conscious of the historic character of the occasion, he was the undoubted star of the session, the public parts of which were telecast live to the United States. The principal formal agreement was that there was only one China and that Taiwan was part of it, but that there would be no reunification of China by force. Nixon made the point that the Chinese would prefer American forces in Japan to a remilitarized Japan, and that if China could prepare its self-defense better, the United States would be able to reduce its defense expenditures. He was explicit in his offer to assist China in the event of Soviet attack, and Chou was implicit in his indication of determination to discourage North Vietnam from imagining it could defeat the United States itself. Nixon said: "We are not going to walk out of [Vietnam] without an agreement. . . . [Otherwise] the U.S. would be a nation that would . . . deserve nothing but contempt before the peoples and nations of the world, whatever their philosophies." The visit was accurately described by Nixon in the closing banquet as "a week that changed the world";[10] it was an overwhelming triumph, and incited the mutually hoped-for unease in the Kremlin.

11. RELATIONS WITH THE USSR

On March 30, North Vietnam launched an all-out assault on the South, hoping to move before there were any consequences to the Nixon visit to China or his upcoming visit to Moscow and while the weather still was unfriendly to air operations. They invaded directly across the DMZ and from Laos and Cambodia, with 150,000 North Vietnamese regulars and 200 of the latest Soviet tanks. It was an

---

9. Black, *op. cit.*, pp. 767–771.
10. Ibid. pp. 787, 791–792.

even greater offensive than that at Tet in January 1968, when there were 500,000 American servicemen in country. Nixon ordered massive air attacks on the North, accused the Joint Chiefs of cowardice, defeatism, and their own flake-out in Vietnam, said the "air force is not worth a shit,"[11] an uncalled-for overstatement from the commander-in-chief, and threatened to fire the high command if they didn't carry out his orders for a comprehensive aerial pummeling of the enemy.

He added 85 B-52s, an aircraft carrier, and nearly 500 fighter-bombers to the air-strike capability in and around North Vietnam. Finally, on April 16, Nixon dispensed with Johnson's failed bombing halt of four years before and darkened the skies of North Vietnam with American warplanes. They smashed the air defenses and the harbor facilities at Haiphong (damaging four Russian ships), and bombed selectively in Hanoi. The bombing attacks were raised steadily and maintained at 1,000 air strikes a day in the North, an unsustainable assault on such a small and relatively primitive country trying to conduct a war on its neighbor, and provided almost instant and massive close-air support to ARVN, taking the full brunt of the communist offensive on the ground. Nixon made it clear to everyone, including the public, that he would punish the North Vietnamese and was not concerned with whether the Soviets canceled his invitation to them for May (as Khrushchev canceled Eisenhower's over the trivial U-2 affair 13 years before).

Richard Nixon, now heavily backed by public opinion, was defending the credibility of the United States, and said that his office would not be worth holding if he was chased out of Vietnam by the communists, who had treated his every conciliatory gesture with contempt for three years. Now they had gone too far. The inexhaustible and brilliant diplomatic troubleshooter Henry Kissinger, dispatched to Moscow on April 20 after Nixon had delayed his departure for two weeks, to set up the state visit to the Soviet Union, reported that Brezhnev claimed no foreknowledge of the North Vietnamese attack and didn't care how severely the Americans blasted North Vietnam. In discussions with Gromyko, he moved the parallel discussions between arms-control specialists a long way forward from where they had arrived at Helsinki.

Kissinger returned on April 25 and he and Nixon worked out the retuning of their strategy: the greatest arms-control agreement in history (though Nixon always thought arms control a fraud because the Russians always cheated and the U.S. could always win an arms race, so there was no reason to curtail it, a point proved by subsequent president Ronald Reagan); a slight caution to the Chinese with an upbeat visit to Moscow; and the decision finally to unload on the Vietnamese

11. Black, *op. cit.*, p. 796.

communists from the air as the president had been advocating since he was Citizen Nixon seven years before.

As the outcome in South Vietnam hung in the balance, Nixon ordered the closing by aerial mines of Haiphong harbor and the direct destruction of all military targets in North Vietnam, including every trace of the country's rudimentary rail and highway network. Still unflustered by what was widely assumed to be the imminent cancellation of his visit to the Soviet Union and the arms-control agreement, he spoke to the nation on May 8. He summarized the Kennedy-Johnson escalations, his staged withdrawals, and his frequent and completely unrequited efforts at peace agreements in public and private negotiations. And he summarized the escalation of the air war, which he promised would destroy the entire war-making potential of the North and would continue until there was a peace agreement, including a return of prisoners of war. This was a tacit admission, as Johnson had made in 1966, that the NVA could remain in South Vietnam. With China having deserted Hanoi's higher ambition to drive the U.S. out and Moscow apparently more concerned with the triangular relationship with Washington and Beijing than with encouraging Hanoi's war ambitions, the diplomatic objective now conformed to military and diplomatic realities at last.

The liberal press and the peace Democrats attacked Nixon's escalation, but the Silent Majority held firm, as Nixon had withdrawn American forces and was clearly being assaulted by a totalitarian regime in violation of international law, and the South Vietnamese were now defending themselves quite courageously. Moscow reaffirmed its invitation to him, and he departed Washington for Moscow on May 20 after ordering an increase in air strikes on North Vietnam from 1,000 to 1,200 every day he was in the USSR He and his very large entourage landed at Moscow on May 22, and on the first state visit of a president of the United States to the Soviet Union, Nixon was greeted with maximum ceremony and respect and conducted in a vast motorcade to the Kremlin Grand Palace, over which the U.S. flag now flew beside that of the Soviet Union.

The key issue of the summit talks was Strategic Arms Limitations (SALT), and Nixon supported Kissinger and the professional arms negotiators led by Gerard Smith, to agree on equal launchers and throw weight, but exempt multiple-warhead regulation (MIRVs) and intercontinental bombers, thus appeasing the doves while retaining the ability to overstrain Soviet financial resources and quiet the hawks. (It was all even more symbolic than the space race, since both countries had a vastly excessive nuclear capability for any conceivable purposes.) Agreement was reached and signed on May 26, including anti-missile defense systems, and leaving out American MIRVs and long-range bombers. It was a brilliant agreement for the United States.

Nixon went on to Leningrad, eloquently addressed the Soviet people and the world in a conciliatory televised address, had a very cordial windup with Brezhnev, went to Kiev, called upon the Shah of Iran, and returned to Washington on June 1 and went directly to address the Congress, which greeted him with abundant and cordial respect. By this time, the South Vietnamese, with no American help on the ground, had defeated and repulsed the communist offensive. The Nixon (or Truman or Eisenhower) Doctrine was working. There had never in American history been such a sequence of strategic policy successes, apart from the unfolding of World War II after May 1942. Nixon had won the war of the United States against North Vietnam and was within sight of retrieving a non-communist South Vietnam, as ARVN had demonstrated it could hold with heavy U.S. air support. This was astounding progress since Johnson had thrown in the towel with his Manila proposals six years before. Nixon was now hoping for more than a decent interval after the end of direct American involvement in the Vietnam conflict.

12. THE 1972 ELECTION AND THE CLIMAX IN VIETNAM

What now took place was unprecedented in America—a bipartisan dual suicide. Pacifist George McGovern defeated Hubert Humphrey in the California primary and was assured of the Democratic nomination, which he did win on July 13. The Democratic convention in Miami was a shambles that saw votes cast for fictitious characters and Mao Tse-tung for vice president, and where McGovern only got to speak at 3 a.m. The vice presidential candidate, Thomas Eagleton, had to withdraw because of earlier mental health problems, and was replaced by Kennedy in-law and former War on Poverty director and ambassador to France, Sargent Shriver. The Democratic platform called for immediate purification of the environment whatever the cost in unemployment, higher income taxes for everyone above the average national income, drastic defense cuts and immediate, unconditional withdrawal from Vietnam, unlimited busing of school children to achieve racial balance in each school regardless of geography or the wishes of parents, a guaranteed annual income for every American, and immediate amnesty for all draft dodgers and deserters. Running against the most successful single presidential term at least since Roosevelt's third term 30 years before, the Democrats chose a very mediocre candidate to run on an insane platform that not a third of the population could possibly have endorsed.

For the first time in decades, running in his own right, Nixon was going to enjoy a landslide. More than that, the Democrats had committed themselves to a nomination process that fragmented their party, expelled the bosses (and even refused to seat the mayor of Chicago, Richard J. Daley, who had won the 1960 election for Kennedy), and distributed power to unrepresentative blocs of affirmative-action-selected delegates. Following 40 years of distinguished candidates (Smith, Roosevelt, Truman, Stevenson, Kennedy, Johnson, Humphrey), the Democrats would not produce an impressive, or for the most part even serious, candidate for president or vice president for 20 years (except for Senator Lloyd Bentsen, the vice presidential candidate in 1988). George Meany, the head of the AFL-CIO, the principal labor confederation, which had declared its neutrality in the election for the first time in history, allowed that he would not vote for either candidate but that his wife and daughters were voting for Nixon.

Meanwhile, a group of overeager Republicans, responding to what they and the Nixon forces generally thought was an unscrupulous, unpatriotic Democratic Party favored by liberal media, broke into the Democratic National Committee headquarters in the Watergate building in Washington and were apprehended by police on June 14. Nixon had not known anything of this mad enterprise, nor, specifically, had anyone close to him, and it was so ludicrous that for a long time even the Democrats and the national media didn't think such an astute operator as Nixon could possibly be dragged into it. Unfortunately, instead of delegating the matter to someone to keep it away from the presidential office and shut it down as best he legally could, Nixon became directly involved in strategies for dealing with it and repeatedly misled the public and the press about his involvement, which came to light when a tape recording system in his office and on some of his other telephones was revealed and its recorded contents were subpoenaed. It is still not clear that Nixon did anything illegal, but once the media and his partisan opponents got a glimpse of Nixon's vulnerability, they pursued him relentlessly, he continued to mishandle the problem, and executive authority evaporated day by day.

Nixon made the further error of spending all the vast resources of his party in this election year on his own campaign, and for the first time since 1946 did not lift a finger to help Republican congressional candidates and scarcely campaigned personally at all. Had he elaborated the program he had championed for decades, including welfare and health care reform, tax reductions and simplification, and a strong but sane environment policy; added a referendum on the Vietnam peace terms he insisted on; and spread the party's money around the congressional races and campaigned hard for his party's candidates, he would probably have withstood even the tactical errors he made handling Watergate, inexplicable as they were.

Kissinger continued the formerly secret but now revealed talks in Paris, and the North Vietnamese finally recognized that they could not defeat the United States: that Nixon was about to smash his pacifist opponents, had induced Beijing and Moscow to defect from Hanoi, had adequately supported ARVN to beat the communists on the ground, and was now battering the North with over a thousand air strikes a day that could not be endured indefinitely and that were arousing no protests at all in America. (The American public, within reason, didn't care what Nixon did to the North; it was only concerned about American casualties, and these had almost stopped). By the time Nixon was renominated (1,327 to 1) at his convention in Miami on August 22, Le Duc Tho had accepted the last published American peace terms and had agreed with Kissinger, who had undoubtedly managed very difficult negotiations with impossible interlocutors with great skill, on an October 15 date of peace. There would be an elaborate formula for subsequent elections in South Vietnam, which all sides would ignore.

By October 10, Kissinger had pushed Le Duc Tho a little further back than what Nixon had offered in January, while McGovern went on national television to say that he would end all aid of every kind and withdraw completely from South Vietnam on inauguration day. Even the *New York Times* remarked that McGovern was advocating harsher terms for the U.S. and Saigon than Hanoi was now proposing. Kissinger returned to Washington on October 12, and as peace appeared imminent, Nixon finally cut the bombing of the North to 200 sorties a day. Nixon and Kissinger were trying to bring Thieu into line, but he was demanding the complete withdrawal of northern forces from the South. Nixon had let pass the ability to turn any part of the election into a referendum on a peace settlement. However great his own victory, the Democrats would hold the Congress.

Ironically for a president about to win the greatest plurality in American history (unsurpassed even 40 years later), time had run out for Richard Nixon. He couldn't browbeat Hanoi into more concessions, would have to force the issue with Thieu, and would soon be facing votes to cut off the war in Congress now that he had made the Democrats' war terminable on his own previously stated terms. On November 7, 1972, Richard Nixon won over McGovern, 47.2 million to 29.2 million, 60 percent to 37.5 percent of the vote, and lost only Massachusetts and the District of Columbia. The electoral vote was 520 to 17. The Republicans won 12 congressional seats but lost two senators. It was a presidential landslide comparable only to Roosevelt's in 1936 and Johnson's in 1964, in the whole history of contested American elections starting in 1824.

Nixon had only to inauguration day, 14 weeks, to get a peace signed in Vietnam. He managed the recalcitrance of Thieu by raising the ante one more time, as the deadline of the now completely post-Johnson congressional Democrats to withdraw American support closed in on them. The U.S. was threatening the North with massive escalation if they did not accept revised American terms and the South with abandonment of the war if they did not accept the terms. It was a delicate game. Kissinger took Thieu's exceptions to the draft agreement to Paris on December 4, and they were rejected. Kissinger and Nixon both went into overdrive, Kissinger carrying on arduous negotiations with the Chinese in Paris in the evenings and with Le Duc Tho during the day, while Nixon pulled out all the military and diplomatic stops, raising the intensity of bombing beyond any previous levels. He remined Haiphong harbor and resumed heavy bombing in Hanoi on December 14, and the bombing was moved to 1,500 strikes per day on December 18. The Soviet ambassador in Hanoi told North Vietnamese, premier Pham Van Dong on December 23, with American bombs falling near the prime minister's office, shaking the building and requiring raised voices, that Hanoi had to accept American terms. Mao Tse-tung himself told the Viet Cong foreign minister the same thing on December 29, calling those who held out "so-called communists, and bad guys."[12]

The next day, Hanoi announced that it would resume the Paris talks on January 8, and signaled privately that they would accept the revised American terms. These chiefly consisted of wording changes demanded by Thieu, as Kissinger (for security reasons) had been using North Vietnamese interpreters, and the Vietnamese version contained many insulting references to Saigon and Washington as, respectively, "vassals" and "pirates." After a final mighty flourish of B-52 deluges, Nixon suspended the bombing of the North on January 18, and was reinaugurated on January 20. President Lyndon Baines Johnson, just 64, died on January 22 (and was accorded a state funeral and widely praised as a master of the Congress and the greatest champion of civil rights since Lincoln). On January 23, Nixon announced to the nation and the world that the Vietnam War was ending with a cease-fire on January 27, with the withdrawal of the 24,700 remaining U.S. personnel (down 96 percent from where it had been four years before), and with the return of prisoners. He referred generously to Johnson.

Almost two million Americans had served in Vietnam and 58,000 had died there, and about two million Vietnamese also died on both sides combined, military and civilian, a blurred distinction in such a war. Probably Eisenhower should either have helped the French and led the resistance in 1954, though it would have been difficult just a year after Korea, or not guaranteed an independent South

---

12. Black, *op. cit.*, p. 853.

Vietnam in 1955. Kennedy was still trying to figure out what to do when he was assassinated. Johnson's intervention can be justified and probably helped defeat the communists in Indonesia, but the inadequate congressional authorization and the inept strategic plan of the general staff of the army, not seriously interdicting the flow of men and supplies from the North, cannot be justified. Lyndon Johnson, in his reluctance, could never decide if he was really at war.

Nixon was much the most effective of all of the American presidents in Vietnam, but he should have moved to cut the Ho Chi Minh Trail and resumed heavy bombing of the North and imported Nationalist Chinese in noncombat roles to compensate for the Chinese Red Army personnel in the North, as he announced Vietnamization in 1969. He submitted the peace agreement to the Senate, which ratified it without significant opposition. The president hoped that this would commit the country to respond to the next North Vietnamese offensive, as it had at Tet in 1968 and in April of 1972, with massive air power. He abolished conscription a few months later.

Richard Nixon had averted the disaster that loomed in 1968, and withdrew from Vietnam with honor. Tragically and unimaginably, Watergate replaced Vietnam as the national crisis, and snatched defeat back, after Nixon had come close to retrieving victory. The Republican Nixon had resurrected the Democrat Johnson after they had fought one of the shabbiest electoral contests in history; and the Democrats betrayed Johnson, destroyed Nixon, and emasculated themselves. Not even Greek dramatists, tragic or comic, had imagined this plot.

Ronald Reagan

1. THE WATERGATE DELUGE

Despite its great achievements and the high prestige of the reelected president, the Nixon administration disintegrated very quickly as the Watergate story unfolded amidst a host of minor campaign and administration officials turning court and partisan-dominated congressional committee hearings into confessionals, launching endless accusations of "campaign dirty tricks," financing liberties, cynical motivations, steadily further up the chain, in the manner of the American plea-bargain system. Immunities for prosecution or sweetheart sentences are traded for incriminating evidence, no matter how uncorroborated and unrigorous, against higher-ups. It was not long before the process backed into the side doors of the White House and Nixon's own chief aides appeared to have had some involvement, if not in illegal initial activity, in trying to conceal the extent of it.

The Congress doesn't have to respond to the procedural rules of a Justice Department prosecution (which do not impose much of a restraint at the best of times), so it was not long before the president's former White House counsel, John Dean, who had been involved in some illegal activity he did not tell the president about, was chirping like a canary flying backward at three o'clock in the morning to the Senate Select Watergate Committee and on national television and radio in the most destructive manner possible. He testified with oleaginous sanctimony, despite the ancient seal of lawyer-client privilege.

Practically the only Nixon underling on the domestic political side who did not crack eventually was G. Gordon Liddy, a heroically motivated lawyer and political soldier who had periodically suggested blowing up the Brookings Institution and other lively initiatives. Even when sentenced to 35 years in prison, he did not alter his testimony, gave a military salute as he left the court, and early in his stay in prison beat up a fellow inmate for the unauthorized borrowing of his toothbrush. (His sentence was radically reduced and he went on to great success as a radio talk-show host and after-dinner speaker, for more than 35 years.) The endless flow of Watergate revelations pushed the soap operas off the air, and the business of government soon became extremely difficult.

The people actually arrested in the Watergate complex, after entering the Democratic National Committee office illegally, testified that their legal fees and family expenses were being paid by someone but they were not sure who. This could not possibly stand. Judge John J. Sirica didn't believe it and sentenced very severely to encourage reconsideration, and he encouraged the Congress to get to the bottom of the question. The Republican strategists had to know that the source of these funds would be revealed and that refusal to reveal them was just going to lead to aggravated charges of perjury. There is no evidence that Nixon knew anything about any of this at this point, but as if morbidly attracted to the subject because he (correctly) doubted that the managers in place had any idea of how to deal with it, he did ask enough to be somewhat informed, all recorded on devices he had placed in his office and telephones, and publicly denied that he knew what he was finding out. There is nothing unconstitutional about presidents not telling the truth, and all presidents are guilty of that at times, but it is a certain method of squandering political capital when it happens on a large scale and comes quickly to light. By not cleaning out the lawbreakers himself, he was leaving it to the courts and to the Democrats in the Congress to do it. He had to either get rid of anyone whose conduct was legally suspect or destroy the tapes, get rid of the most vulnerable of the apparent offenders, and be prepared to stonewall at a defensible point. The first would have been better, as well as more creditable, but by doing neither, Nixon himself sank into the quagmire. On April 17, 1973, Henry Kissinger, who had had nothing to do with any of it, said in a taped conversation: "You have saved this country, Mr. President. The history books will show that when no one will know what Watergate means."[1]

The Congress passed the War Powers Resolution, severely restraining the president's ability to conduct war, and a 180-degree turn from the passivity of the Congress as Roosevelt committed acts of war against Germany in 1941 and from the blank check it gave Eisenhower in the Formosa Resolution in 1955, largely replicated for Johnson in the Tonkin Gulf Resolution of 1964. This was a matter of questionable constitutionality but, at time of writing, has not been tested, and was more a rebuke of Johnson than of Nixon, but it altered the president's traditional latitude as commander-in-chief, by requiring congressional authorization for combat deployment within 90 days. Nixon's veto was overridden, but some subsequent presidents (including Clinton in Kosovo and Obama in Libya) have ignored the resolution.

On April 30, 1973, Nixon's two closest collaborators, John Ehrlichman and Bob Haldeman, resigned; the attorney general, Richard Kleindienst, retired; and White House counsel John Dean (who was trying to blackmail Nixon while trading incrimination of him to the prosecutors and congressional committees for personal immunity) was fired. A special prosecutor was appointed, the rabidly partisan Democrat and Kennedy family friend Archibald Cox.

The rampaging Watergate congressional hearings were suspended during the official visit to the United States by Soviet leader Brezhnev and the long-serving foreign minister Gromyko, starting June 16. It proved impossible to make any real progress on a further arms limitation agreement (SALTII). The summit moved to

---

1. Conrad Black, *Richard M. Nixon: A Life in Full*, New York, PublicAffairs, 2007, p. 887.

California on June 23, and Brezhnev, after retiring, and then telling Nixon's valet that he wanted to resume discussions, told Nixon that the Middle East was about to blow up. Sadat had already evicted the Russians from his country but was loudly proclaiming that war was imminent. Nixon immediately saw the potential for negotiating a comprehensive agreement with Brezhnev and the two superpowers and America's principal allies imposing it. Nixon feared that Arafat, the Syrians, and other comparative newcomers could prove a great deal harder to deal with even than the Russians had been, especially now that the Kremlin could see its influence fading in the area since the death of Nasser. Nothing immediately came of it, and though the atmospherics of the meeting were good, the summit was only a modest success. (In California, the Soviet leaders stayed in Nixon's house, Brezhnev and Gromyko sleeping in the Nixon daughters' bedrooms.)

At the end of July, a case against Vice President Spiro Agnew arose, of his having taken at least 40 separate bribes and kickbacks in his previous position as governor of Maryland. After a good deal of negotiation, he resigned in exchange for non-prosecution, pleading nolo contendere, which is not an admission of guilt, and paid a $10,000 fine. There is sometimes difficulty determining when political contributions have been made in exchange for official favors. Agnew was not widely respected, and Nixon replaced him, not with either of the two leading stars of his party, Nelson Rockefeller or Ronald Reagan, but with the widely liked and respected but unexciting Gerald R. Ford, a 13-term Michigan congressman and Republican House leader. While this was unfolding, William Rogers retired as secretary of state in August and Henry Kissinger was confirmed as his replacement without difficulty the following month.

The existence of Nixon's taping device had been revealed by one of the White House witnesses on July 16, and subpoenaed. Nixon apparently did not understand that the courts might order their complete surrender, and having lost the opportunity innocuously to destroy them, declined various methods of somewhat reasonable compromise, including a private hearing by Senate Watergate Committee chairman Sam Ervin, ranking Republican Howard Baker, and Cox, who agreed not to reveal anything irrelevant to their investigation. Many of the tapes were favorable to Nixon, but some were legally worrisome, and many contained more coarse language and ethnic slurs than Nixon would want in the public domain. The hostile press, led by the *Washington Post*, the *New York Times*, and the main television networks, were already deluging the public with spurious charges against Nixon of underpaying taxes, zealously tapping telephones (including that of his own brother) and almost what Franz Kafka famously called "nameless crimes." In April 1974, the Internal Revenue Service, after a campaign of leaks, disallowed

Nixon's agreed tax-deduction for the contribution to the National Archives of his vice presidential papers, but the National Archives kept the papers. This was outright theft, and Nixon had only been following in the steps of his predecessors, from Eisenhower to Johnson and (now Senator) Humphrey. In the circumstances, he gamely paid the assessment (though litigation by him and his literary executors for return of the papers was ultimately successful).

2. REVOLUTION IN CHILE AND WAR IN THE MIDDLE EAST

In Chile, communist fellow-traveler Salvador Allende, having pledged not to alter or violate the Constitution, had been inaugurated as president in 1970, and as copper, the staple of Chile's economy, was at the bottom of its normal price cycle, there was 15 percent unemployment and 30 percent inflation. Allende responded with the usual Marxist policy prescription: he nationalized the largest farms and estates and the copper and banking industries, with minimal compensation; decreed a 40 percent wage increase for workers in all industries; and ordered a freeze in prices. The completely inevitable chaos ensued. Opposition members of the National Congress were excluded and a virtual Marxist dictatorship, replete with intimidation of the media and opposition legislators, was being set up. There was considerable violence, and both the Congress and the Supreme Court of Chile declared Allende's conduct unconstitutional and generally illegal.

On September 11, 1973, the chiefs of staff of the armed forces revolted, seizing the National Congress, government buildings, radio and television stations, and railway and bus terminals, and attacking the presidential palace with tanks and artillery, storming it with elite troops, and killing or capturing everyone within. Allende allegedly committed suicide with a machine gun given to him and inscribed and engraved by Fidel Castro, but this is contested and he may simply have been murdered or killed in an exchange of fire. Weeks of mopping up and skirmishing followed, several thousand people were murdered, 30,000 were detained, and a large number were barbarously tortured. Allende and his followers were not abstainers in this and the attempt to whitewash them as pacifistic social reformers is a nauseating fraud, but the armed forces, led by General Augusto Pinochet, committed most of the excesses.

There have been many allegations against Nixon and Kissinger of being impli-cated in this violence, but nothing has ever been proved or even believably argued to support this, including under subsequent Chilean governments led by demo-cratic socialists. The United States certainly made it clear to the Chilean military that it would not oppose a coup, and there is no doubt that Nixon, who knew Latin America fairly well after a number of highly publicized visits there, considered that the entrenchment of a communist regime in a major Latin American country would be a strategic disaster. It must also be said that Pinochet then ran, for 15 years, the most successful government in Latin America. He brought in a group of Chilean alumni of George Shultz and Milton Friedman's University of Chicago administration and economics faculties, denationalized, deregulated, cut taxes, reduced union prerogatives, welcomed foreign investment, and generated consistently high economic growth rates that sharply increased living standards and lifted up most people who had been in poverty. In 1988, Pinochet, having restored a free parliament, held a referendum on his own continuation as president, against all parties combined, and lost, 55 to 43 percent. He retired, handed over to an elected Christian Democrat, and continued for five years as commander of the armed forces. In geopolitical terms, the Nixon-Kissinger Chilean policy, though it was probably not determining on the ground, was (other than in human rights terms) a complete and important success, and did, ultimately, restore the democracy that Allende had overthrown.

Egypt and Syria attacked Israel during the Jewish Yom Kippur holiday on October 6, and achieved complete surprise. The Syrians pushed the Israelis off the Golan Heights in south Syria, and the Egyptians crossed the Suez Canal and pierced the Bar-Lev Line, which Israel had represented as almost impenetrable, and came a short distance into the Sinai. Both Brezhnev's warnings and Sadat's threats had proved well-founded. The Israelis had always assumed that they would not have to face more than a brief war with the Arabs, and went through aircraft, tanks, and ordnance with disconcerting speed. Nixon resupplied the Israeli air force with combat planes and Kissinger made it clear that any Arab attempt to intercept them as they were flown to Israel would be regarded as an act of war. Nixon presciently foresaw that Arab success could produce a reentry of the Soviet Union, as the Arabs' armourer, into the region, but he sought to help ensure a good showing by Israel without the humiliation of the Egyptians or the Russians, as had occurred in 1967, but with a sufficiently respectable Arab showing to encourage all parties onto the path of a durable peace. He said to Kissinger that Israel could not "get away with just having this thing hang over for another four years and have us at odds with the Arab world. We're not going to do it anymore."[2]

There followed a contest of airlifts with the Soviet Union, which the United States easily won with its superior air transport capacity, and Nixon told his entourage that he would take complete responsibility for the anticipated Arab oil embargo. By October 20, the Israelis had cleared the Syrians back off the Golan

2.   Black, *op. cit.*, p. 924.

Heights, had recrossed the Suez Canal in two places, and had surrounded the Egyptian army in Sinai. This was enough for Brezhnev, seeing his hopes of reentry to the Middle East on the wings of Arab military victory disappear, to propose a cease-fire in place and invite Kissinger to Moscow to work out a durable regional agreement. There was a lack of agreement between Nixon and Kissinger as the secretary of state left for Moscow on October 20. Kissinger didn't believe a broad settlement could be reached, and thought it better to complete the expulsion of the Russians from the region, and feared that Nixon underestimated the difficulties of reaching and imposing such a settlement. The Arab states, led by Saudi Arabia, had reduced oil production starting on October 17.

Kissinger went to Israel for one day and told the Israelis they had to agree to a cease-fire and could not force the surrender of the Egyptian army in Sinai. On October 22, a joint U.S.-Soviet resolution in the UN Security Council passed, mandating a cease-fire in place. Israel continued to squeeze, and on the 24th, Sadat became so desperate he asked for joint Russo-American military intervention. (All parties agreed that UN peacekeepers were a nuisance and an irrelevancy and should be avoided.) Nixon would have nothing to do with such a request and on October 24, Brezhnev sent a message to Nixon that if the U.S. didn't agree to joint action, the USSR would inject forces unilaterally to impose the cease-fire. Nixon and Kissinger and the National Security Council responded with a heightened state of military alert, the dispatch of two aircraft carrier combat groups (*Franklin D. Roosevelt* and *John F. Kennedy*) to or toward the Eastern Mediterranean, preparation for the dispatch of an airborne division to the region, and the return to the U.S. for integration into the Strategic Air Command (i.e., for possible attack on the USSR) of 60 B-52s from Guam.

This level of saber-rattling was effective. Brezhnev said no more of his threat to intervene unilaterally, a third UN resolution, cosponsored by the Soviet Union and the U.S., was adopted, and Kissinger muscled Israel into acceptance without closing the ring completely on the Egyptian army in Sinai. It was another strategic success for the United States, the more remarkable for occurring in the midst of an explosion in the Watergate crisis. Nixon had come up with a compromise whereby Senator John Stennis of Mississippi would check the tapes against the White House transcripts. Nixon claimed that his attorney general, Elliott Richardson, and Senators Ervin and Baker had agreed to this (but, unfortunately, for once a White House conversation was not taped), and Richardson and Ervin reneged. Richardson resigned after he refused to fire the special prosecutor, Cox, although Nixon asked him to remain while there was an international crisis; the deputy attorney general, William Ruckelshaus, resigned, but in the manner of early film comedies, Nixon declined his resignation and fired him instead. The acting attorney general, Robert Bork, fired Cox, without taking a position on the matter but because he accepted that the president had the constitutional right to fire anyone in the executive branch of the federal government. There were a great many calls in the Congress for impeachment and hearings on that subject began, in the usual spirit of incandescent partisanship, in the House. If Nixon had just lamented the impasse, he might have got something close to a reasonable compromise, but by pulling the trigger on Cox and the senior officials of the Justice Department, he ignited the issue far beyond his ability to manage. All this unfolded while the Yom Kippur War was in progress and the cease-fire was being negotiated in a time of great international tension.

Nixon was the second (after Eisenhower) of many U.S. presidents to call for a restoration of energy independence, but nothing came of it, then or under the next seven presidents, as the strategic vulnerability of the United States steadily increased. The price of oil rose 400 percent in a few months, taking gasoline prices and the rate of inflation up with it. The Democrats wanted gas rationing, but Nixon, who had worked in the wartime Office of Price Administration before joining the navy in World War II, resisted this as a catastrophic idea.

On January 17, 1974, in a prodigious feat of personal diplomacy, Henry Kissinger negotiated a mutual withdrawal of the Israeli and Egyptian armies and won the confidence of both sides. He was emerging as a very widely admired and dazzlingly talented foreign minister and not just an extremely capable executant of a brilliant foreign policy president.

On March 18, the oil embargo ended, but the oil-exporting countries were already addicted to high-priced oil. Egypt and the United States reopened diplomatic relations after a lapse of seven years and more than a decade of frosty relations before that, after the Eisenhower-Dulles pullout on financing the Aswan Dam project and Nasser's flight into the arms of Khrushchev. And on May 29, Kissinger completed the brokering of the Israeli-Syrian forces disengagement, which has stood, unviolated, at time of writing, for 38 years.

On April 5, 1974, French president Georges Pompidou died in office. Nixon attended his funeral and, as he had been at the memorial service for de Gaulle in the same place (Notre Dame Cathedral) five years before, was by far the most prominent figure among the very large number of heads of state and government present. He remained three days in Paris and met with many foreign leaders in the opulent U.S. embassy, on the Faubourg St. Honore between the British embassy that had been "bought" by the Duke of Wellington after Waterloo, and the Elysée Palace, residence of the president of the Republic. De Gaulle's former finance minister Valéry Giscard d'Estaing was elected the third president of the Fifth Republic a few months later.

Nixon started a Middle East tour in Cairo on June 12, and he and Sadat stood in an open car (despite Nixon's phlebitis, heat of over 100 degrees, and the avoidance of open cars by U.S. presidents since the assassination of Kennedy in 1963) and were cheered by dense crowds numbering well over a million on the way from the airport to the presidential palace. It was quite a turn in U.S.-Egyptian relations. There was a series of accords on secondary matters with Egypt, and Nixon went on to meet with King Faisal of Saudi Arabia. Nixon was unsuccessful in urging Saudi support for the reestablishment of King Hussein as representative of the Palestinians rather than Arafat, but he parried the king's championship of the 1967 borders. Faisal promised a quick reduction in the price of oil. Nixon continued on to a very cordial meeting with the Syrian president, Hafez al-Assad, and restored diplomatic relations with that country, then proceeded to Israel, where he told Premier Yitzhak Rabin that the United States would no longer give Israel an open-ended guarantee. There was an emotional exchange at the state dinner with the recently retired Golda Meir, whom Nixon praised and who replied in an impromptu toast that "Richard Nixon is a very great American president." The tour concluded with a very satisfactory visit with Jordan's King Hussein and Nixon returned to the United States on June 19.

3. WATERGATE, THE LAST ACT

Former junior and middle-level White House officials were now being routinely given prison sentences, usually for perjury in denying their knowledge of the Watergate break-in before it occurred, or in muddying the waters about it when it had first been exposed. It was all coming down to the tapes. Nixon, having failed to destroy them, underestimated their explosive content, and botched many opportunities to compromise regarding their use, was almost certainly going to be ordered by the Supreme Court to surrender them.

In accord with his 1972 agreement with Brezhnev, Nixon made the annual visit to the Soviet leaders starting on June 27. The president was received with immense ceremony and cheered by large crowds all along the route in from the airport to the Kremlin. Two days later they removed to Yalta, only a few miles from where Roosevelt, Churchill, and Stalin had met 29 years before. Brezhnev wanted a Russo-American nonaggression pact, but Nixon was wary, because he thought it was really an effort to isolate the Chinese. It was a very convivial occasion, but again, little tangible progress was achieved. Nixon's now almost rabid domestic enemies, deranged with blood lust whatever the facts and consequences to world affairs and the domestic constitutional balance and the institution of the presidency, having vocally feared that Nixon would give the national security store away in the Kremlin for domestic political advantage, now professed to be disappointed that he returned almost empty-handed on July 3.

On July 24, the Supreme Court voted 8–0 (future chief justice William Rehnquist abstaining as a former employee of the Justice Department) that Nixon had to surrender all the tapes. The key was the June 23, 1972, tape that his enemies were about to represent as "a smoking gun." In fact, he had authorized Haldeman, Ehrlichman, and Dean to suggest to the director and deputy director of the CIA, Richard Helms and General Vernon Walters, that they ask the FBI to desist from investigating the Watergate affair because it might, through the Cubans who made the break-in, back into the CIA operations against Cuba. Helms and Walters said that they would obey a direct order from the president but would not act otherwise. Nixon declined to take it further (and it was a fatuous idea of Haldeman's, a former advertising executive, anyway, since the local prosecutors were investigating, not the FBI). This was nothing to impeach a president for, but the crisis had to end, and the fact that it was not (and is not) clear that Nixon violated the law, or that he committed an impeachable offense, was now beside the point. He had been crucified by his opponents and the tension in Washington was intolerable. The distinguished British author Muriel Spark wrote a novel, *The Abbess of Crewe*, that was a parody of Watergate, about the theft of a thimble in a convent. She was correct; it was nonsense, but it was inexorable.

At 9 p.m. Eastern Time, on August 8, 1974, Richard Nixon delivered, despite unimaginable pressure, from memory and with complete composure, an entirely dignified and eloquent address, admitting no crimes but acknowledging serious errors and the impossibility of continuing in these circumstances, and said that he would resign as president the following day at noon. It was a formula that would be durable and successful: errors but not crimes, and his status in historical regard would rise steadily, after the initial explosion of recriminations. He could have fought through a Senate trial; there was no longer anything negative to emerge, and the House Judiciary charges against him were partisan bunk, except possibly for the authorization of money paid to defendants in exchange for altered testimony. But he might have been removed by the required two-thirds majority of the Senate, and if he had squeaked through, would have had no moral authority to fill the next two years and five months of his term. All conceded that Nixon had spoken with dignity; he departed after an emotional and affecting address to the White House staff the next day, and a brief serenity settled on the capital and the country.

Thus passed from the scene, though not for long from public life, one of the most talented and unusual figures in American history. Richard Nixon seemed a rather ordinary man, and attracted and retained a following of tens of millions of ordinary people to whom, as to him, little came easily, and who never ceased to persevere, often against more glamorous, facile, advantaged, and wealthier people (the Kennedys, Rockefellers, Stevensons, etc.). This bond with ordinary people, many of whom would be routinely described as strivers or even losers, was the constituency he never lost. He built this invisible bloc of the struggling middle and working class into an immense following that never deserted him, to and after his death, and was one of his three great accomplishments. The second was that he was one of America's most effective presidents, who calmed a terribly divided and riot-torn country at war when he took the headship of it in 1969. He was rivaled only by Franklin D. Roosevelt, Harry S. Truman, Ronald Reagan, and, in a sense, Woodrow Wilson, as the most strategically astute and imaginative president in the country's history. And third, in being the subject of the arousal of the puritanical conscience of America by his opponents, which destroyed his career, and by maintaining that he had committed errors but broken no laws, Nixon took back the control of that puritanical conscience and turned it against his oppressors. He remains one of the presidents Americans are most interested in, and though dead more than 15 years, he gnaws now at that conscience that so assaulted him. In the last and greatest of his many comebacks, he had largely regained public esteem by the time of his death in April 1994, aged 81. All his successors as president attended his funeral, by the Nixon Library and birthplace in Yorba Linda (suburban Los Angeles), and Henry Kissinger, the last and most intimate of the eulogists, unforgettably captured the deceased as one who had come from an improbable place. "He achieved greatly, and he suffered deeply. But he never gave up. . . . he advanced the vision of peace of his Quaker youth. . . . He was devoted to his family. He loved his country. And he considered service his honor." Richard Nixon did not always seem to be of this world; both very ordinary and even awkward, sometimes banal, and yet an imperishable demiurge. He will linger in the American consciousness for a very long time.

4. PRESIDENT GERALD FORD

On August 9, incoming president Gerald Ford spoke with great sensitivity, graciousness, and insight, said that "our long national nightmare is over," and asked for prayers that the man "who had brought peace to the world" would enjoy it himself. He chose for vice president Nelson Rockefeller, who was confirmed after unnecessarily belligerent hearings, and Henry Kissinger continued as secretary of state. These men, with Donald Rumsfeld in defense and William Simon at the Treasury, provided capable and distinguished leadership as the country settled down from the unprecedented hysteria and national neurosis of Watergate. Ford granted Nixon a full pardon on September 8, 1974, as the ex-president fought for his life against blood clots, and the vindictive mood of the country punished Ford in the midterm elections for his decency. The year ebbed uneventfully away.

Inflation soon became the chief preoccupation of the administration, and there was agitation for both spending reductions and tax cuts. The economy was rather uncertain into 1975, and so were many foreign areas. A Portuguese military faction had overturned the semi-fascist dictatorship that had ruled for 42 years, in April 1974, and an internecine struggle between pro- and anti-communist forces seesawed back and forth in senior military circles for almost two years, before the pro-Western faction, with heavy input from the CIA and the Holy See, prevailed.

Turkey had landed forces in Cyprus in the summer of 1974, to protect the Turkish minority, and the always prickly Greek-Turkish relationship put great strains on NATO. At the end of November 1974, Ford and Brezhnev met at the Far Eastern Soviet city of Vladivostok. There was a tentative agreement to try to balance the different throw weights and launch vehicles of strategic nuclear weapons, as so-called nuclear units were devised for negotiating purposes. But the Russians had to face the fact that though they had gross parity, the Americans had superior technology and quality of weapons. The pace of discussions was not assisted by the fact that Brezhnev suffered at least one minor stroke in the course of them. The points of concurrence took many years to aggregate into a serious agreement.

The follow-up discussions with Israel and Egypt after the disengagement were so sluggish, even under the relatively reasonable new premier, Yitzhak Rabin, that Ford informed Rabin in March that he was "reassessing" U.S. policy in the region, and all U.S. aid to Israel stopped from March until there was finally some movement at the end of the summer, and an interim Sinai agreement was arranged under Kissinger's constant and ingenious efforts, in September.

In the meantime, the North Vietnamese staged their long-awaited third major invasion of South Vietnam. Unlike the first such lunge, at Tet in 1968, there were no U.S. ground forces to repulse them; and unlike the second offensive in April 1972 to disrupt the triangular arrangements Nixon was making with Beijing and Moscow, there was no U.S. air power to assist. And the Democrats, whose war it had been, voted down any military assistance to the South. It was the unalloyed capitulation of America, renunciation of its long war effort, and the abandonment of an ally that had endured over 500,000 war dead fighting a former common enemy. Lack of Democratic enthusiasm for any participation in that war is understandable, but the Senate had ratified the peace agreements when there were explicit promises to assist the South in the event of an enemy breech of the agreement, which was universally anticipated. Nothing short of another massive air campaign was going to save Saigon this time, but this brutal abandonment of the anti-communist cause in South Vietnam 20 years after Eisenhower had sent Nixon there to pledge support for the "first domino" was irresponsible by the standards of great powers.

If Eisenhower had dictated sensible cooperative terms to France in 1954 in exchange for assistance and then arranged just part of the country for Ho Chi Minh and legitimized the rest; or if he or Kennedy had introduced SEATO forces along the DMZ and in Laos to prevent the communist subversion of the South, and Kennedy had not handed Laos to the communists for conversion into the greatest land arms route in history with the agreement of 1962; or if Johnson had entered on a direct congressional authorization, pushed Vietnamization from the start, had soldiers stay for longer tours and, again, followed MacArthur's and Eisenhower's advice and stopped the infiltration along the Ho Chi Minh Trail; or if Nixon had done the same as soon as he was inaugurated and after Johnson's phony peace breakthrough failed to achieve anything; or even, just possibly, if the Senate had not scuttled Indochina in 1973–1975, it would probably, or at least might, have ended satisfactorily.

As it was, tragedy metastasized: hundreds of thousands were massacred in the South, almost a million mainly Chinese Vietnamese fled the South in boats, and hundreds of thousands drowned, and perhaps two million people perished in the Killing Fields of Cambodia. Because of the failures of the U.S. political class and military high command, and the ability of the generally weak American left to misrepresent the motives and moral relativism of the powers at war, all Indochina was doomed to a horrible, heartbreaking fate. Nixon, by great dexterity and at times courage, had avoided the defeat of the United States itself. But it suffered a distinct strategic setback, captured graphically by terrible pictures of American helicopters departing the rooftops of Saigon with their erstwhile allies desperately clinging to the runners. It was the hour of America's greatest ignominy. The United States would ultimately accept about 200,000 Vietnamese refugees (including Nguyen Van Thieu).

Civil war broke out in Angola in earnest at about this time, as the Portuguese empire collapsed and the home country was itself a closely contested battleground between competing communist and pro-Western factions. The Soviet Union and Cuba (which sent tens of thousands of troops, some of them with a refueling stop in Canada) aided one faction, the U.S. another, and the South Africans supported both the U.S. protégés and another faction. This war went on for 15 years, and by the time the originally Russian-sponsored contender won, the Cold War was over, oil had been discovered in Angola, and the standard of living rose swiftly.

The Italian Communist Party made substantial gains and there was a good deal of disturbing speculation about bringing it into government. The Soviets were emboldened in their always teeming efforts to incite communist takeovers of vulnerable countries in Latin America and Africa.

President Ford did put on something of a show of strength when an American merchant ship, the *Mayaguez*, was seized by Cambodian communists in May 1975. He dispatched helicopter forces to retake the ship and liberate the crew, which they did. It was a bit of a Pyrrhic victory, as two of the helicopters crashed, having made some errors in the approach and approximately as many servicemen were killed as sailors were rescued, but it was a successful show of force. A greater success came in August of the following year when North Korean soldiers killed two American soldiers who were routinely pruning a tree in the zone between the two Koreas. Kim Jong Il, the dictator's son, managed to have this accepted by a conference of the unaligned as an attempted invasion of the North. Ford sent heavy military units into no-man's-land to continue routine gardening, and B-52s repeatedly overflew the parallel at low altitude. It had the desired effect.

The United States and Canada and almost all European countries participated in the Helsinki Accords in July and August 1975. The effect of the Accords was generally thought to be morally to respectabilize the Soviet Union, and they didn't really accomplish much except involve the Kremlin in a discussion of the subject. The so-called Decalogue, which was the agreed document from the conference, guaranteed freedom of thought (which is in any case difficult to interdict) and of conscience and religion (slight progress for the communists), but did not refer to freedom of expression or of political leadership selection. It guaranteed nonintervention in the affairs of each country, which was, of course, as much an assurance of untroubled despotism as anything else, but might, in theory, make outrages like Budapest in 1956 and Prague in 1968 more difficult. Helsinki did give rise to Human Rights Watch, an avowedly leftist organization that would surpass even Amnesty International in its whitewash of the international left.

Ford had a cordial but not especially productive visit to China in December 1975. He and Kissinger did their best to hold the line and keep the alliance in good order, but it was a difficult time. The negotiation of the possible handover of the Panama Canal to Panama arose after lengthy agitation by de facto Panamanian leader Omar Torrijos. Panama was (Chapter 7) an artificial country sliced out of Colombia by Teddy Roosevelt because the Colombians were being shirty about what to charge for the right to build an isthmian canal. The whole policy of détente with the USSR, including what was held to be a charade of a human rights conference, the spectacular fall of Vietnam, the alleged over-placation of

China, and now the plan to give away the Panama Canal to the original banana republic, revived the fissures in the Republican Party between the old Goldwater and Rockefeller factions. Gerald Ford, a good and brave and conscientious man, was not a sufficiently galvanizing or ingeniously cunning leader, as Eisenhower and Nixon had been, to keep those factions together.

5. THE 1976 ELECTION

The leader of the liberals, Nelson Rockefeller, was now the vice president and was tarred with the perceived shortcomings of the administration, and Ford, though personally appreciated for his human qualities, was seen by the Nixon-haters as beholden to the former president and too quick to give him a pardon. The Democrats, having buried Johnson and canonized the Kennedys, were now in the hands of pacifistic naifs. Though they would allow Mayor Richard Daley back at their convention and pay him homage as a party elder, unworldly righteousness now reigned. So shaken was the country by the debacle of Vietnam and the shambles of Watergate, so convinced was most of it that both were the result of intolerably sleazy politics and politicians, the Democrats had become an aggregation of innocents and the Republicans a house sharply divided at the bifurcation between left-center and medium-right.

For president, the Democrats nominated the former governor of Georgia, James E. (Jimmy) Carter, who ran effectively as a Washington outsider, never having held a position there. The last president who could claim outsider status was Woodrow Wilson. Humphrey, Johnson, and Kennedy, and even McGovern had been Washington veterans for many years before becoming contenders for the presidency. Carter took Humphrey's successor as senator from Minnesota, Walter F. Mondale, for vice president, heavily emphasized the alleged corruption and undoubted cynicism of the Watergate Republicans, and opened up a large lead in the polls before the Republicans' convention, in Kansas City in late August.

The leader of the conservative Republicans was no longer the stolid Goldwater from the relatively small state of Arizona. It was now the twice-chosen governor of California, Ronald Reagan, mocked by his opponents as an ex-actor, but a hypnotic public speaker and public relations genius who sold conservatism as no one else could. He entered the race against Ford and won a number of the primaries. He ran the incumbent president the closest race to the convention of anyone who had attempted the same step since Theodore Roosevelt, a former president after all, running against President Taft in 1912 (Chapter 7). Ford won the convention, but felt obligated to disembark Rockefeller as vice president and chose the sharp-tongued senator from Kansas (where there weren't many voters and which always voted Republican), Robert Dole. Ford won the nomination, though fairly closely, but Reagan made the convention wait about 15 minutes before he emerged to give one of his rousing political orations, while scarcely referring to the nominee. If Ford didn't win the election, Reagan would be waiting and ready four years later.

Ford trailed by 33 points as the campaign started but campaigned pluckily and made telling arguments against Carter's rather simplistic view of the world. It was a mediocre election, fought between uninspiring candidates, who played out the exhausted morality play of bombed-out, post-Vietnam, post-Watergate American public life. The country was just starting to recover from deep self-inflicted wounds, aggravated by misplaced sanctimony. (In 2001, the John F. Kennedy Library Foundation awarded the John F. Kennedy Profiles in Courage Medal to President Ford for pardoning Nixon, who had always got on well with all the Kennedys except Bobby, including the father. In making the award, Senator Edward M. Kennedy said that while he had opposed the Nixon pardon at the time, he now recognized that it was the just and correct decision. Teddy Kennedy, having drowned one of his assistants in a drunken car accident in 1969 and fled the scene of the accident, was not a natural source for Solomonic moral judgments, but in this case he was surely right, and it was a gracious tribute to the 87-year-old Ford.)

The Democrats were accusing the Republicans of being unprecedentedly corrupt (which they weren't; Kennedy and Johnson, not to mention some old-timers, gave them plenty of precedent), and proposed a cure of puritanical altruism that was going to cause the leaders in the Kremlin and the Forbidden City to split their sides in laughter; the country was see-sawing between the excessively stigmatized and the unpromisingly righteous, while the national media patted itself endlessly on the head and back for exposing (i.e., exacerbating) two of the greatest disasters in American strategic and political history, Vietnam and Watergate.

Jerry Ford made it a close election, as Hubert Humphrey had in 1968, and Harry Truman had in 1948, all gallant fighters. Apart from Watergate and the Nixon pardon, there were only two other issues: Ford was offering Vietnam draft evaders a conditional transfer to an honorable discharge, and Carter offered an unconditional pardon to dodgers and deserters. America, still trying to detoxify itself from the 20-year Indochinese nightmare, leaned to Carter's proposal. There was a return, for the first time since 1960, to televised debates, and although Ford generally did well, he at one point said that the "Poles don't consider themselves dominated by the Soviet Union." Carter and his partisans represented this as unawareness on the part of the president of the presence of the Soviet army in Poland, and of the location of the headquarters of the Warsaw Pact. Ford wasn't verbally agile (and neither was Carter), and he should have expressed himself more unambiguously, but this was only an infelicitous choice of words. Although Ford was a distinguished athlete and an alumnus of the Yale Law School, he could be caricatured as a bit of an oaf and not overly intelligent. LBJ, the master of the destructive barb, said of Ford on separate occasions that "Jerry played football too often without his helmet," that he "couldn't fart and chew gum at the same time," and that he "couldn't pour piss out of a boot if the instructions were written on the heel." Carter wasn't as amusing as Johnson, but almost as nasty, and perceptions are crucial in politics. Ford paid for his presentational problems.

On election day, Carter won, 40.8 million (50.1 percent) to 39.2 million (48 percent); 297 electoral votes to 240, though Ford won 27 states to 23 plus the District of Columbia for Carter. It was a completely clean election, and if 11,000 votes had changed sides, or Ford had polled 22,000 more in Ohio and Wisconsin, Ford would have won. It was almost as close as the 1960 and 1968 elections, though unlike those, with an ethically unexceptionable campaign. Gerald Ford had never sought nor expected to be president, entered the office in very difficult circumstances, and was, in his unpretentious plainness, a distinguished president. He had had no thought except what was good for the country, and had a long and happy retirement, ultimately living longer than any other president of the United States; he died in 2004, aged 93 years and five months, universally honored for his character, personality, and service. Unfortunately, this was also effectively the end of Henry Kissinger's public career, though he sometimes was consulted by future presidents of both parties. He was too great a talent to have been left underutilized, and was only 53. He continued as a world-renowned and historic figure, but, for different personal reasons, future Republican presidents did not invite him back to the State Department.

6. PRESIDENT JIMMY CARTER

The world was not sure what to expect from a president calling himself Jimmy, a successful peanut farmer and Naval Academy graduate who was an understudy of the father of the U.S. atomic submarine program, Admiral Hyman Rickover, and an authority on naval nuclear propulsion and submarine design, now the cornerstone of America's nuclear deterrent. He had served on surface vessels as well and had been a well-regarded junior officer (as had Kennedy, Nixon, and Ford, though they were all in combat). President Carter was the first person from the Old South to hold that office since John Tyler. (Zachary Taylor and Woodrow Wilson were from Virginia but left in their mid-twenties, and Lyndon Johnson's Texas wasn't the Old South.) Carter was a very pro–civil rights governor in a state that had been fairly retarded in treatment of African Americans for an unconscionable length of time, though he was not otherwise a particularly distinguished governor.

He quickly paid for his unfamiliarity with the operations of the Congress, in particular contrast to his four predecessors, who between them had served 80 years at the Capitol before becoming president (including the last three as vice president). Almost none of his ambitious domestic program gained any traction at all, including his endlessly repeated promises of tax reform.

In foreign and defense policy, however, where the president does have much more latitude, his imprint was visible, and uneven. His secretary of state was veteran lawyer and public official Cyrus R. Vance, an able but very conciliatory foreign policy expert, balanced by the more hawkish national security advisor, the learned and forceful Polish-Canadian Harvard academic, Dr. Zbigniew Brzezinski. (It says something distinctive and flattering about America that two of its greatest modern foreign policy experts were men of such distant and unlikely provenance as Kissinger and Brzezinski.)

Carter started with his unconditional pardon of draft evaders and deserters on inauguration day, and immediately began withdrawing forces from South Korea. This was quickly opposed by the armed forces committees in the Congress and he was widely advised that anything that might encourage North Korean adventurism was a bad idea. In the end, he only withdrew a few thousand of the American troops in South Korea. In his first budget, Carter slashed defense spending by six billion dollars and, in a major address a few months into his administration, said that the country must get over its "irrational fear of communism." Most Americans, unlike in the McCarthy era, were not afraid of communism, but were a good deal more skeptical than their president about the motives of the Soviet Union. (The people were right.)

From the start, he emphasized human rights in foreign countries, including allies. This is always a controversial matter, disputed between those who emphasize morally neutral strategic interest and those who emphasize the moral high ground. It has been an almost constant irritant to Sino-American relations. At a certain point, some regimes become too odious for almost anyone, as Pol Pot's Khmer Rouge Cambodians, who murdered over a quarter of the entire population, did even for the Chinese and Russians. But short of such an evil government, there is room for legitimate debate about the point of crossover between national interest and maintenance of political and moral standards. It is likely that Carter's emphasis on human rights may have caused many countries to be less casual about oppression of their citizens, but it is also undeniable that the policy brought serious geopolitical inconvenience on the U.S., without accomplishing any significant improvement in the political quality of the lives of the populations Carter was sincerely trying to help.

He sided openly with the Sandinistas in Nicaragua, essentially a communist front with no more regard for civil rights than communists normally have, against America's longtime docile and corrupt protégé, the Somoza family (FDR's famous "He may be a son-of-a-bitch, but he's our son-of-a-bitch," Chapter 9). The United States certainly could not go on being identified with the Somozas, as Eisenhower realized about the Dominican Republic's Rafael Leónidas Trujillo in the late fifties (Chapter 13). But assisting worshipful puppets of Castro provoked severe communist infiltration in Central America and required Carter's successors to expend a great deal more effort and political capital in that region than it would normally justify.

Even more destructive to American interests was Carter's appeasement of the fundamentalist Islamic opponents of the Shah of Iran, and his pressure on the Shah to yield ground to the Islamist leader, the Ayatollah Ruhollah Khomeini. What possessed the U.S. president that an Islamic believer in a fundamentalist Muhammadan theocracy was any sort of legitimate democratic opposition escaped the comprehension of most observers and of all of posterity. Khomeini was militantly anti-Western, anti-Semitic, anti-Christian, and an absolutist of the most primitive kind. It became clear fairly early on that the Shah could only deal with the problem by a combination of force and generosity, which he had the military and paramilitary force and the oil income to do. Carter discouraged him from that and in the end, as Brzezinski put it, "threw him out like a dead mouse," in 1978. He did not even permit the Shah to enter the United States after he had abdicated, though he had been a fiercely loyal American ally since he had met with Roosevelt at the Tehran Conference in 1943 (Chapter 10) and particularly since Eisenhower had restored him to his throne in 1953 (Chapter 12). He had ignored the oil embargo five years before. (Carter did relent a year later, when the Shah sought entry for medical reasons.) Human rights in Iran deteriorated and the country regressed in every respect, becoming an even greater nuisance to the civilized world than the North Koreans. In this instance, Carter's policy was self-destructively foolish and the fate of America's relatively respectable allies, from Diem and Thieu to the Shah and others to come, was noted.

Carter did complete the giveaway of the Panama Canal in 1977, and the Senate ratified it. The canal would have to be widened and deepened, and was no longer useful for large tankers, aircraft carriers, and even cruise liners, but it is not clear why Carter didn't settle on some system of co-ownership. The U.S. had a clear title, unlike the British and French at Suez (Chapter 12), though it must be remembered that it was Ford and Kissinger who started down this path.

The U.S. had occasion to invade Panama and seize a successor president and try him as a common criminal 12 years later (the trial and imprisonment a dubious enterprise legally, but that is addressed later in this chapter).

President Carter's greatest achievement, and a great personal triumph, was the Camp David agreement of 1978 between Egypt and Israel and their formidable leaders, President Anwar Sadat and Prime Minister Menachem Begin. This secured the Israeli withdrawal from Sinai, the reopening of the Suez Canal after 11 years, the exchange of full recognition and embassies between the two countries, and a promise by Begin to produce a formula for Palestinian self-rule. As Egypt was the most populous and historically significant of the Arab powers, this was an immense step forward for normalization of relations between the Jewish state and the Arab world. As part of the arrangement, the United States pledged extensive annual assistance, military and otherwise, to both countries, cementing the abject Soviet expulsion from Egypt.

Sadat had been an agitator for Egyptian independence in British times, and was Nasser's vice president when the president suddenly and prematurely died in 1970. He had succeeded in inflicting a momentary defeat on Israel in crossing the Suez Canal in 1973 at the outset of the Yom Kippur War, which—through Nixon and Kissinger's intervention with Golda Meir to prevent the destruction of the overexposed Egyptian army that had accomplished this (considerable) feat— enabled Sadat to be the liberator of the Sinai, who took back the Canal, and took the leadership of the Arab world back from the proponents of endless war with Israel (a policy easier for those who didn't actually have to do battle with Israel).

Menachem Begin, a fugitive from the pogroms of Eastern Europe, the head of the violent independentist organization Irgun, and 29 years the leader of the opposition in Israel against all the preceding prime ministers in the country's history, had also moved a long way. He had been an advocate of a greater, Biblical Israel, with an ancient and expansive notion of its rightful extent. Regrettably, he gave no substance to the Palestinian autonomy plan, which, when it finally emerged, was, as one knowledgeable commentator on the Middle East put it, "the right of the Palestinians to take out their own garbage."

Sadat would be assassinated in 1981 by the Muslim Brotherhood, chiefly motivated by the Camp David agreement. And Egypt lost stature, as its economy stagnated and its population grew, and the oil states, especially Saudi Arabia, became steadily more influential. But that takes nothing from President Carter's achievement in brokering the greatest advance there has been in Arab-Israeli relations since Israel was created (in 1948, before many of the Arab states were fully independent).

President Carter went to Vienna in June 1979, to meet with Leonid Brezhnev, and signed there a SALT II agreement along the lines that Ford and Kissinger had negotiated with Brezhnev and Gromyko at Vladivostok. There was criticism at once that the United States was conceding too much nuclear equality to the Soviet Union. As if by delayed reaction, there was a backlash against McNamara's reverence for Mutual Assured Destruction (MAD), and the aggressive return of the Russians to public ruminations on the inevitable triumph of Soviet Communism as the wave of the future and force of history. Carter's placation of the communist powers was creating unease across the American political and national security establishment.

The SALT II agreement was assured of a rugged passage, as by some measurement it did give the Soviet Union superiority (in numbers), though it didn't entirely dilute Nixon's inspired notion of "nuclear sufficiency"—technological superiority and multiple warheads. But that could not be publicly argued, and Carter was immediately on his back foot, contending with the bipartisan Committee on the Present Danger, supported by most of the intellectually serious national security experts from the Kennedy and Johnson administrations, most of the southern Democrats, big defense Democrats led by Senator Henry Jackson of Washington, and virtually all the Republicans, except a few New York liberals. (Nelson Rockefeller had died in January 1979, aged 70, confirming Ronald Reagan as the almost certain leader of the Republicans in the next election.)

SALT II was in trouble with congressional and public opinion when the whole Carter policy of almost militant altruism hit land mines under each foot in the last days of 1979. In November, Khomeini's regime stormed the U.S. embassy in Tehran, an outrageous violation of international law, and seized 52 hostages with diplomatic passports within. Carter made his natural appeals to international opinion, courts, and organizations, and was generally supported everywhere. But a popular late-night network news program began, entitled *America Held Hostage*, and continued to telecast every weeknight for the life of the crisis. Carter made occasional purposeful statements such as "The honor of America is more important than the lives of any individuals." But he appeared impotent, to a degree completely unprecedented in the history of his country and his office. At least Lyndon Johnson was making war on North Vietnam, however ill-advisedly in tactical terms, and poor James Madison finally went to war with Britain, as did Wilson with Germany. Carter made pious statements and earnest entreaties, but Khomeini ignored him as if the president of the United States had no more deterrent or moral authority than the president of Albania or Paraguay. Carter continued the Democratic policy followed to some extent by all their presidents since Jefferson, except Roosevelt and Truman, of not seeming to wield an adequately large or versatile stick to defend the entire national interest.

And on December 26, 1979, the Soviet Union invaded Afghanistan. Leonid Brezhnev had enunciated the Brezhnev Doctrine (even Soviet leaders were resistless against the temptation to have a doctrine named after them, however portentous the phrase might be in the circumstances). This held that any country that became "socialist," i.e., communist, would be retained in that condition, if necessary by the application of Soviet military force. This outrageous concept was invoked in the aftermath of the oppression of Czech liberalism in August 1968. Now Brezhnev was pushing it further, in implicit disregard for the deterrent strength of the United States, by invading a neighboring country that it claimed had adopted socialism and was being threatened by internal and external reactionary forces.

This was by a wide margin a more unwise, not to say morally reprehensible, action than the American commitment of large-scale forces to the defense of South Vietnam. It was not only the first naked aggression the Soviet Union had committed against a neighbor since Stalin seized a chunk of Poland and the Baltic states of Latvia, Lithuania, and Estonia under the Nazi-Soviet Pact, and then for good measure invaded Finland a few months later, in 1939 and 1940. It was also, in Talleyrand's famous formulation, immoral, and also an error. It is almost inconceivable that the Soviet leadership could have undertaken such a mad enterprise. The secret of Afghan independence was that it was so lacking in geopolitical interest as a landlocked country with almost no natural resources, was so rugged and mountainous, and its population was so resistant to outsiders, it was never worth the huge commitment of forces that would be necessary to suppress it. The British had come to this conclusion 75 years before.

Now the Soviets not only antagonized the Muslim world and provoked the Western Alliance, and blundered into a geopolitically useless and indigestible place ("a porcupine," as Hitler said of Switzerland), it did so with completely inadequate forces. The Kremlin replicated, on a smaller scale but even more egregiously, Johnson's error of entering ambiguously into foreign war. There was no rationale, no serious measurement of the risk-reward ratio, an inadequate commitment of forces, no exit strategy, and no possible justification even if the Afghans had not risen in revolt, as they instantly and almost universally did.

An unlikely informal coalition, including the United States, Britain, China, Saudi Arabia, Pakistan, Iran, and Israel began assisting the Afghan rebels, mainly Islamists even more primitive in their social outlook than Khomeini. The Soviet occupation force of 100,000 was pinned down to the major centers and could soon move between them only in armored columns. The United States distributed so many over-the-shoulder ground-to-air missiles that the Soviet helicopter forces took terrible losses. It was, almost from the earliest days, a disaster for the Russians, but it again made Jimmy Carter look weak to his countrymen as an election year dawned.

Carter had two other problems—indecisiveness and a faltering economy. There was a pattern that made the country and its allies uneasy, of Carter taking an initiative and then reversing it. For some time the administration publicly alleged that the Soviet Union was developing a nuclear submarine base at Cienfuegos, Cuba, something Nixon and Kissinger had looked at closely but finally decided wasn't really happening and should not become the cause of a superpower dispute. Carter eventually came to the same conclusion. For several days he was publicly dispatching a carrier group to the Indian Ocean, led by the USS *America*, but then ordered it, also publicly, without explanation, to make a 180-degree turn.

Much more worrisome and disruptive of the Western Alliance was that Carter pressed hard for the attachment of neutron warheads to NATO's short-range missiles in Europe; warheads that killed people by radiation but did comparatively minimal damage to inanimate structures such as buildings. The Soviet propaganda apparatus and its docile believers in the West took up the hue and cry that this was inhuman. Western leaders such as West German chancellor Helmut Schmidt went to great lengths and political inconvenience to hold the line, and then Carter abruptly decided that it should not be done, essentially for the reasons the Russians and their allies and dupes had been alleging.

The Tehran hostage crisis took a further nasty turn in April 1980, when Carter ordered a helicopter rescue effort and it was a complete fiasco due to poor intelligence, though without loss of life. Secretary of State Vance resigned, revealing this only after the mission, because he believed that if the hostages were freed, Khomeini would just seize 50 other Americans in Iran, randomly. He was succeeded by the 1968 vice presidential candidate, Senator Edmund Muskie of Maine, a man of no particular foreign policy credentials. This mishandling of a severe affront to the United States was not an acceptable quality of strategic leadership, for the United States or the Western Alliance. The American public, even if they could rarely be precise about it, sensed this.

The sharp renewed increase in oil prices provoked galloping inflation while economic activity slowed and the U.S. economy was afflicted by stagflation, almost double-digit inflation and unemployment, and the Federal Reserve chairman, Paul Volcker, determined on a policy of high interest rates to reduce economic activity, collapse inflationary pressures, and essentially ignore the short-term impact on unemployment.

7. THE RISE OF RONALD REAGAN

Ronald Reagan swept almost all the primaries in 1980 and was easily nominated for president by the Republicans in Detroit. Former Texas congressman, CIA director, representative to China, ambassador to the United Nations, and Republican Party chairman George H.W. Bush ran a respectable but distant second. There was a movement to ask President Ford to stand for vice president, but Reagan refused to shed any of the constitutional authority of the office he sought, and Ford was not lusting after a lower office than he had already held, and Reagan chose Bush for vice president. Carter faced a strenuous but strangely disorganized and poorly explained challenge from Senator Edward Kennedy and lost a few of the big primaries, but won renomination, with Mondale, without serious difficulty.

Conventional liberal national opinion was that Reagan was a shallow if attractive and eloquent superannuated film actor; it disdained his landslide victories as governor of California and assumed that Carter, as a substantial chief executive and incumbent president, would be elected, as all incumbents had been since Hoover. Congressman John Anderson of Illinois, a liberal Republican of the Rockefeller stripe, but not a well-known figure, ran as a third-party independent. Reagan conducted an extremely professional campaign. The themes were that Carter was an ineffectual, gullible weakling, so out of his depth that he was endangering world peace by creating irresistible temptations for the Russians. The hostage crisis and the Afghan invasion were endlessly cited as evidence of his unsuitability to be president. The economic problems were dumped entirely at his door because of his inability to influence oil prices, his betrayal of America's ally the Shah, who always pierced any anti-Western oil cartel, his enfeeblement of the armed forces, and his supposed appeasement of the Soviets. The Democrats portrayed Reagan as a simplistic, right-wing extremist who would make an ass of himself and endanger world peace. Carter was referred to informally as a peanut farmer by one side, and Reagan, with equal disdain by the other, as an actor. (One of his more vocal and articulate critics, the writer Gore Vidal, said that it was "an injustice to call Reagan a 'Grade B actor.' He is one of the greatest actors in world history, who played in a lot of Grade B movies." Vidal particularly harped on Reagan's performance in *Bedtime for Bonzo*.)

The Democrats ridiculed Reagan's campaign promises of higher defense spending and reduced income taxes, which he said would accelerate economic growth rates sufficiently to avoid an unacceptable deficit (more or less what happened). Unable to catch Reagan in the polls, Carter gambled everything on a debate, late in the campaign, believing that his detailed knowledge of issues and Reagan's perceived breeziness and imprecision would reveal the challenger as light for the office both were seeking. Reagan proved to be well-versed in the issues, and had some debating techniques that were damaging to Carter ("There you go again"). Reagan concluded by asking that the voters consider, as they exercised the "sacred privilege of the ballot," if they and their families and the country were "better off than you were four years ago." Reagan added a little to his lead and closed the campaign with some overpoweringly eloquent addresses and a saturation advertising blitz hammering the theme "The time is now for strong leadership. If not us, who? If not now, when?"

On election day, Reagan won decisively, 43.9 million votes (51 percent), to 35.5 million votes (41 percent) for Carter and 5.7 million votes (6.6 percent) for Anderson. Reagan won 489 electoral votes and 44 states to 49 electoral votes, six states, and the District of Columbia for the president. The Republicans gained control of the Senate for the first time in 28 years, since Eisenhower, in his first campaign, drew the Senate, leaving (vice president) Nixon with the deciding vote. Reagan chose as secretary of state Kissinger's former deputy at the National Security Council, and Nixon's chief of staff, vice chief of staff of the army, and Ford's Supreme Allied Commander (NATO) in Europe, General Alexander M. Haig. He was a tough Vietnam combat veteran and an apparently splendidly qualified choice; he had performed well in all his previous positions.

Carter and Muskie did manage to negotiate the release of the Tehran hostages, although they were only freed a few minutes after Reagan was inaugurated, on January 20, 1981, and Reagan graciously invited Carter to welcome the hostages back to the West in Germany on behalf of the nation. The country had cured itself of the nostrum of an almost overly trusting foreign policy.

Ronald Reagan was one of the most astonishing characters ever to occupy the presidency of the United States. The son of an unsuccessful shoe salesman in downstate Illinois, he graduated from an obscure local college, Eureka, and held only six jobs in his career: lifeguard in Tampico, Illinois; baseball announcer in Des Moines, Iowa (California-bound in the Great Depression); film actor (including six terms as head of the Screen Actors' Guild); vice president for public and personnel relations of General Electric Corporation; governor of California; and president of the United States. He was less than a month short of his seventieth birthday on his inauguration, the oldest of any newly inaugurated president in the history of the country. He had been an ardent Democrat, who was driven into the Republican Party by the antics of the left in Hollywood after World War II, as the Cold War broke out, and further propelled along that path by the experience of 90 percent marginal income tax rates (most people in that bracket could find methods of reduction or exoneration). Reagan became one of the spokesmen for the new conservatives, was more flexible and much more articulate than Goldwater, and had been backed by a group of wealthy California Republicans for governor in 1966. He was an effective and popular governor. When radical students occupied the main campus square at Berkeley, he had the National Guard clear it with fixed bayonets, and there were no injuries. When he went to places where there were large demonstrations being restrained by state policemen with locked arms, he made a point of shaking hands with each one of the policemen and ignoring the demonstrators just two feet away.

Reagan was a very affable man and was universally charming, but he was, in the words of media proprietor Rupert Murdoch to the author, "a cunning old peasant." In a benign reenactment of a familiar plot, his financial backers probably expected to retain more influence on him than they did. He smiled amiably, but would steer his own course, and had the confidence and the intuition to follow his own instincts. Ronald Reagan did not change his views to lure voters; the nation, between 1965 and 1980, came steadily, almost imperceptibly, to him. In a sense, the office had sought the man, and he assumed the office with a clear and comprehensive program to (once again) let America be America. "The only welfare system we ever had that worked was a job," he declared, and when asked his plan for the Cold War, he replied, "We win and they lose." He soon made it clear that there was a new mood in the White House, the Pentagon, and the State Department. There would be no return to détente, and the United States immediately began a massive arms buildup of all forces, and a plan to assist anti-communist guerrillas and shatter the Brezhnev Doctrine of the permanence of communist rule once established with the (inevitable) Reagan Doctrine, almost indistinguishable from those of Truman, Eisenhower, and Nixon; and he began with increased arms shipments to the Afghan guerrillas and to the Nicaraguan Contras, who opposed the leftist Sandinistas, who had replaced the Somoza government in Nicaragua and aided leftist guerrillas in El Salvador.

Reagan thought that the Kennedy and Johnson Democrats and Nixon and Kissinger, and certainly Carter, had been too deferential to the Russians, and that the Soviet Union was not really a plausible rival to the U.S.—that its economic system was, as he put it, "Mickey Mouse," the political system was oppressive, and the whole country was a cauldron of barely suppressed ethnic and economic conflicts and too stagnant to keep pace if the U.S. would shake Vietnam and Watergate out of its psychology and act boldly but not impetuously. Where Nixon and Kissinger were chess grandmasters, Reagan was a poker player, but also of surpassing skill.

8. PRESIDENT RONALD REAGAN

Reagan began his term with the advancement of two simple concepts, a sharp acceleration of America's military capacity and a sizeable reduction of income taxes, on the theory that this course was vindicated by the Kennedy-Johnson tax cuts and that revenue would actually grow from increased economic activity and produce less fervent efforts at tax avoidance and evasion. The defense buildup included building 100 new warships and recommissioning the *Iowa* class battleships as both naval artillery and cruise missile launching platforms; building the B-1 bomber as a successor to the B-52 (a program Carter had canceled); and completing the M-X missile, which Reagan christened the Peacekeeper, a maximum-range intercontinental missile with 10 independently targeted warheads (i.e., the equivalent of 10 missiles and the cornerstone of Nixon's wonderful euphemism of "nuclear sufficiency"—sufficient, that is, to frighten the Soviets).

The Reagan administration continued to negotiate with the European NATO allies the deployment of intermediate-range missiles in those countries to reply to the Soviet SS-20s, whose launch sites were already being set up in significant numbers in Eastern Europe. Personal income taxes were broadly cut by 25 percent. He sent a powerful message when 13,000 air traffic controllers (whose union, PATCO, had supported Reagan in the 1980 election) struck illegally; he gave them, as government employees, 48 hours to return to work, and then fired the 90 percent of them that did not obey the order, on August 5, 1981. Flights were reduced in number and military air controllers were substituted, and there were no mishaps. This dramatic step indicated with great clarity that a new hand was on the government, replacing the uncertain grip of his predecessor.

The progress of Reagan's program was assisted by his great aplomb in coping with an assassination attempt on March 30, 1981, in Washington. As he left a hotel after a midday speech, he was wounded in the chest by a bullet from an assailant who also shot the president's press secretary, a member of his security unit, and a municipal policeman. The president, though he had a collapsed lung and a bullet only about an inch from his heart, walked into the hospital, where he was driven at speed, though he had to be assisted into the operating room. He removed his oxygen mask to say to the gathered group of doctors and emergency nurses: "I hope you're all Republicans." The presiding doctor (a Democrat) responded with equal gallantry that at that moment, all Americans were Republicans. The president recovered quickly and addressed the Congress four weeks later to prolonged and thunderous applause, and in the face of his enhanced popularity, his congressional opponents were resistless against his taxing and spending cuts and increases in defense outlays.

Reagan developed a comprehensive strategy for squeezing the Soviet Union and forcing the end of the Cold War. He opened close relations with the Vatican, concerting policy with the Holy See's secretary of state, Agostino Cardinal Casaroli, and through his ambassador to the Vatican, William Wilson. Wilson was a member of a subcommittee of the National Security Council that specialized in coordinating anti-communist activities with the Roman Catholic Church. When Casaroli came to lunch in the White House early in Reagan's term, he told the president and secretary of state and other select luncheoners that there were approximately 100 million Roman Catholics behind the Iron Curtain who took their religion seriously, almost all of whom detested communism, and that the (Polish) pope (since 1978), John Paul II, intended, without urging impetuosity on the faithful, to tighten the screws on the Soviets. Like most Poles, the pope was unimpressed with communism and especially the Russian-imposed version of it in Poland, and the Polish and Ukrainian and Russian Uniate Catholic communities were particularly strong and aggrieved at communist religious and national oppression. This was a break from relatively placatory recent popes, other than Pius XII in 1948 and Paul VI in 1976, when, on each occasion, the Italian Communist Party made a determined charge to join the government or even lead it in that country, and they responded strongly (Chapter 11, and earlier in this chapter).

Later in 1981, the United States imposed sanctions on communist Poland in response to the imposition of martial law in that country to combat militancy from the Catholic industrial unions. The United States and the Holy See also cooperated in Central America and elsewhere in Latin America. Reagan regularly disparaged the Soviet Union, ending what had effectively been a condition of unilateral verbal disarmament, describing it as "an evil empire" in a widely telecast speech on June 8, 1982, and on March 3, 1983, as a "sad, bizarre chapter in human history whose last pages are even now being written."

Reagan extended increased assistance to the anti-Russian resisters in Afghanistan, and to the pro-Western factions in the civil wars in Angola and Mozambique, as well as, eventually quite controversially, in Central America. Reagan was annoyed by Soviet industrial espionage in the U.S., and he authorized CIA director William Casey to develop a complicated plan, ostensibly devised by the private sector, for the collection and pipeline-transmission of natural gas from a large gas-producing area, designed to generate such pressures that it would blow up the whole field. This was represented as a superior and very advanced design, which was deliberately allowed to get into the hands of Soviet agents. Reagan and Casey were vastly amused about a year later when one of the largest non-nuclear explosions in history was recorded in the principal gas-producing region of Siberia. This humiliating fiasco drastically reduced the Soviet appetite for industrial espionage.[3]

There were personality differences between the president and the secretary of state, and General Haig retired from that office in July 1982 and was replaced by George P. Shultz, a former marine combat captain and dean of business administration at the University of Chicago; Nixon's labor secretary, budget director, and secretary of the Treasury; and president of the engineering giant Bechtel Corporation. He was as well-qualified as Haig and temperamentally more emollient.

The president played what proved to be a decisive card on March 23, 1983, when he outlined his Strategic Defense Initiative, a plan for building a defensive anti-missile shield that was a combination of ground-launched and space-based missile-interception systems. It was ridiculed widely by the left and even the center in the United States as "Star Wars" (after the series of successful science fiction movies of that name that had recently been produced) and criticized by most of America's allies as "destabilizing" of the equilibrium that Democratic presidents had promoted with the USSR As Reagan suspected, most of America's allies were happy with an apparent equal correlation of forces between the two super-powers, because it enabled them to exercise maximum influence of the delicate balance between them, with minimum effort. The chief exception to this was the formidable Conservative British prime minister Margaret Thatcher, with whom Reagan developed a warm and close rapport, starting with American support of the British in the brief war that country had with Argentina over the strategically unimportant Falkland Islands in 1981. (This did not prevent Thatcher's foreign secretary, Geoffrey Howe, from referring, ill-advisedly, to SDI as "a Maginot Line," an unfounded comparison.)

Despite the shrieks of impracticality and provocation of the domestic and international left, Reagan, as was his custom, carried U.S. public opinion with his plain and eloquent arguments that it was a completely defensive, conventional (no nuclear aspect) system and innocently asked what possible objection anyone could have to it. He said it was chiefly designed to deal with accidental missile firings, or the missiles of rogue states of the future. Groups of concerned scientists, the spiritual heirs of those scientists who had righteously opposed the development of the atomic bomb, claimed that space launch platforms of up to 45,000 tons would have to be sent into orbit. This was preposterous, but it was beside the point, because Reagan's target was the psychology of the Kremlin and the Soviet

---

3.   Reagan's entire range of carefully designed harassments of the Soviet Union is well described by Martin and Annelise Anderson in *Reagan's Secret War,* New York, Crown, 2009.

economy. He correctly judged that the Soviet Union must be spending a back-breaking share of its wheezing command economy on its military capability and that Russian fear of American military-scientific prowess would incite Kremlin paranoia, already inflamed by the mighty Peacekeeper missile.

The Soviet leadership saw the possible compromise of their nuclear deterrent capability. This was precisely what Reagan had intended. It was nonsense, because the science to shoot down missiles was bound to stay behind the science of propelling offensive missiles to their targets for a long time, and no sane person would conceivably embark on nuclear war on the assumption that he had a leak-proof nuclear missile defense. Again Reagan, though not a chess player, was a brilliant poker player, and as it became clear that American opinion supported the president and bought into his peaceful intentions, and he achieved initial funding for his program, the Soviet leadership became steadily more obsessed with, as they considered it, the mortal threat of SDI to their world status by negating the strength of their nuclear capability. In his more playful moments, Reagan even suggested he would share the technology with the USSR, an utterly absurd prospect, yet one that he carried off with great, apparently earnest, and brilliant histrionic virtuosity, (as one might expect from a retired professional actor).

And he lost no opportunity to embarrass the Russians and make the most of their heavy-footed errors, as when they shot down a South Korean airliner, KAL 007, killing hundreds of passengers, when it accidentally entered Soviet airspace in the Far East, on September 1, 1983. Reagan called it a "massacre," and it was outrageous, but was clearly not an intentional downing of a civilian airliner, just a trigger-happy response by a pilot to a nighttime intrusion. (The American cruiser *Vincennes*, on July 3, 1988, would have even less excuse for shooting down an Iranian civil airliner on a familiar flight path on a scheduled flight to Dubai, in Iranian airspace, in broad daylight, with antiaircraft missiles, killing 290 civilians.) Reagan in his first four years showed no interest at all in meeting with the Soviet leaders, as all his predecessors since Roosevelt had done. Leonid Brezhnev had died in office on November 30, 1982, after 18 years as general secretary of the Communist Party of the Soviet Union, and was succeeded by former KGB (secret police) director Yuri Andropov (who had masterminded the crushing of the Hungarians in 1956). But his health was fragile from the outset, and he died on February 9, 1984, and was succeeded by Konstantin Chernenko, who was 75 and evidently far from robust.

The Reagan administration's Middle East policy was not overly successful, and doubtless suffered from the assassination, by Islamist fanatics, of Egyptian president Sadat on October 6, 1981. Because of recurrent rocket attacks and sabotage missions across Lebanon's southern border into Israel, that country invaded Lebanon and drove the Palestinian guerrillas into Beirut in June 1982, where the Israelis shelled them quite destructively. A UN resolution secured a cease-fire and a multinational force including 800 U.S. Marines was inserted to ensure that Palestinian terrorists did not reoccupy the south of the country. The French arrived on June 22 and the Americans on June 25. They were withdrawn after a short cooling-off period. After the Lebanese Phalange (Christian far right) massacred hundreds of Muslims in the Sabra and Shatila camps, a larger multinational force including 1,800 Marines was reintroduced. A relatively novel form of warfare for the international powers was encountered when suicide bombers crashed an explosives-filled car at the U.S. embassy on April 18, 1983, killing 17 Americans. Despite heavy precautions, a much deadlier strike came on October 23, when 241 Marines were killed in a suicide bombing of their barracks near Beirut Airport.

Support for the mission collapsed and Reagan saw that there was no alternative to pouring forces into an absorbent and terminally inflamed area of the world or pulling out as gracefully as possible. He chose the second and all American forces were out of Lebanon on February 26, 1984. But in the meantime, he scored an Eisenhower-like free goal, largely distracting his countrymen by invading the Caribbean island nation of Grenada two days after the bombing in Beirut, so he was able to address the nation simultaneously on both subjects. Grenada was a Commonwealth country of 100,000, where Queen Elizabeth II was the monarch. The prime minister, Maurice Bishop, had been murdered and the whole population was under house arrest, and there was a developing Cuban presence in the country. The neighboring island countries, led by Dominica, urged intervention, and the United States occupied the island with the Marine contingent on the aircraft carrier *Independence*, supplemented by other air- and sea-borne forces from several states, totaling 7,600 invaders, on October 25.

The incoming Americans were fired upon by a Cuban warship bearing the somewhat irritating name *Vietnam Heroica*, and it conferred great pleasure on many Americans to reduce that vessel to submerged fragments with an instant hail-fire of air-to-surface missiles. Though criticized by Britain and some other countries, it was a useful diversion and was generally popular in Grenada itself and in the U.S., and American forces were withdrawn completely after a few months. The United States suffered 19 dead and 116 wounded. Margaret Thatcher complained of the action as an unwarranted intrusion that annoyed her country at a time when she was campaigning against fierce opposition to deployment of NATO (i.e., U.S.) intermediate-range missiles in Britain. It was one of the very rare disagreements between Reagan and Thatcher, and it is not clear why Reagan did not try to involve a British component in the operation to make it a joint venture, other than his haste to put an easy victory on top of the tragedy in Beirut. Reagan took a number of opportunities for risk-free demonstrations of American military power, sinking in increments a significant part of the Iranian navy when that country challenged the U.S. fleet in the Persian Gulf, and shooting down Libyan fighters when they entered the declared airspace of a U.S. Sixth Fleet aircraft carrier battle group in the Mediterranean.

By the end of 1983, inflation had virtually stopped, net job creation was running at about 250,000 per month, and unemployment was in steady decline. The public enjoyed lower taxes, and though budget deficits had been larger than at any time since World War II, they were now in decline and sharp decline as a share of GDP. The country had been heartened by Reagan's jaunty eloquence, and apparent reestablishment of the credibility of the United States and its alliance system after the tumult and irresolution of the previous 20 years. He and George Bush, who had filled his position with distinction, were renominated without opposition, and the Republicans presented the 1984 election as an occasion to celebrate "Morning in America." It was the first authentic peace-and-prosperity reelection campaign since Eisenhower's in 1956 (and if that were exempted because of the Suez War and the Hungarian uprising just before the election, the comparison would go back to Hoover in 1928).

The Democrats nominated former vice president Walter F. Mondale, after a close battle with Senator Gary Hart, which was highlighted by Hart challenging the press to find him with a woman not his wife, which they managed to do several times. It was nonsense, of course, but the Democratic nomination was unlikely to be worth much more than it had been in 1904 (against TR), 1924 and 1928 (against Coolidge and Hoover), 1956 (Eisenhower), and in 1972 against Nixon. Mondale tried to spice up his prospects by choosing for vice president the first female and fourth overt Roman Catholic (after Kennedy, Muskie, and Shriver) to be nominated for national office, New York congresswoman Geraldine Ferraro. She was a lively and scrappy candidate, but some of the questionable business connections of her husband were exploited for partisan purposes. Reagan and Bush were massively financed and organized and were unassailable on their record, and Mondale made his life more difficult by promising tax increases and suggesting a rather cap-in-hand approach to the Kremlin on arms control. The highlight of a bland campaign was when, in answer to a question, Reagan said in a debate that he would "not hold my opponent's comparative youth and inexperience against him" (Reagan was 17 years older, and the oldest major party candidate ever to seek the office, 73).

On election day, Reagan and Bush won another historic landslide, 54.5 million votes (58.8 percent) and 525 electoral votes (the highest total in history) to 37.6 million votes (40.6 percent) and 13 electoral votes. Mondale won his home state of Minnesota by only 3,764 votes. The Republicans gained 16 congressmen and lost one senator, but the control of neither house changed hands. It was a completely clean, courteous, good-natured election, with none of the acrimony and skullduggery that had been a feature of most elections since Eisenhower's time.

9. SECOND TERM AND ASSESSMENT OF RONALD REAGAN

Konstantin Chernenko died on March 10, 1985, and was succeeded by Mikhail S. Gorbachev. The Soviet Union finally had a leader appreciably below the age of 60 for the first time since the young (and in his macabre way, dynamic) Stalin of the twenties and thirties. Gorbachev had had responsibility for agriculture and had traveled to a number of non-communist countries as a rising Kremlin figure, including a tour of large western farms and ranches with Canada's Pierre Trudeau, and had conversations with Margaret Thatcher that she found quite promising. On April 8, 1985, he stopped the deployment of SS-20 intermediate missiles in Eastern Europe, to confuse the imminent NATO deployment of U.S. Pershing and ground-launched cruise missiles. He also dusted off the old saw invoked by half the Western leaders and all the post-Stalin Russian leaders about banning all nuclear weapons, as if this were remotely feasible and would actually make war less rather than more probable. Reagan was on a much more sensible line with the creation of nuclear defenses, but it would shortly be clear how sensitive a point this was with the new leaders of the Kremlin. The venerable Andrei Gromyko was finally removed as foreign minister after 28 years and elected president, replaced by the foreign policy untested Edward Shevardnadze of Georgia.

Gorbachev announced a policy of openness ("Glasnost") and of restructuring ("Perestroika"), which included a determined crackdown on the grave national problem of alcoholism, the denunciation and scattered prosecution of corruption, which was pandemic in Soviet government, the introduction of contested elections for some party offices, and the acceptance of private ownership of some small businesses. These steps were widely applauded in the West, and doubtless welcomed domestically, but there is no evidence that Gorbachev had any idea how vulnerable the Soviet system was to such shock therapy. It was a tremendous patchwork of ethnic and tribal groups and more than half the population of the USSR were not Russians. Ethnic and sectarian attachments die with difficulty when they are violently attacked, as by Stalin, rather than subsumed into a new world of egalitarian prosperity, as the North and South American and Australian immigrants from Europe were (and they retained their religions and as much connection to their native culture as they wished).

Reforms on this scale are always hazardous, and for a time, no matter how well-managed, the transitory regime has many of the worst aspects, and few of the best, of both the old era and the one to which the state aspires. This brought down the Shah, as the most tenacious and generally oppressive of the old coexist very awkwardly with the vulgarity and *arrivisme* of the new. Instead of following Deng Xiao-ping's model in China of massive economic reforms forced through by a state and party apparatus of scarcely loosened authority, Gorbachev tried comparative democratization without substantive economic changes. The move against alcoholism was almost as much a disaster as Prohibition had been in the United States in the twenties. The black market took over, and while alcoholism declined somewhat, government revenues plummeted.

Reagan assisted this process with one of his most successful Middle East initiatives: he sold Saudi Arabia sophisticated military hardware formerly not available to Arab powers, including a fleet of AWACS radar detection planes, in exchange for a private promise from the Saudi king of a reduction in oil prices. Saudi Arabia, because of its preeminence in OPEC, was able to deliver on this, and the oil price, which was $30 per barrel in November 1985, had fallen to $12 by March 1986. Oil was the chief Soviet export, as its manufactures were of inadequate quality for export and its other natural resources were uncompetitively expensively extracted and generally surplus to the world's requirements (apart from small quantities of gold and diamonds).

This initiative was coincident with the first Reagan-Gorbachev meeting, at Geneva, in the house of the Aga Khan, the Ishmaelite leader, in November 1985. It was very cordial and a public relations success for both leaders. It was the first summit meeting in six years; Reagan promised full reciprocity in any genuine reduction of tensions and move to cooperation, but made it clear that the United States would never accept an inferior military status to any other country, and there seemed to be a similarity of view on arms reductions and Afghanistan between the two leaders. There was a divided view for a time in the senior councils of the West (Gorbachev had met the West German and French leaders too) whether the new Soviet leader was trying to gull the West into relaxed vigilance, or was really about to dismantle the authoritarian capabilities of the Soviet state, unaware of what a shambles of economic and jurisdictional meltdown was likely to occur.

In January of 1986, Gorbachev proposed the removal and nondeployment of all intermediate missiles from Western and Central Europe, and conjured yet again the benign fable that cannot fail to cross the lips of the world's leaders for long, of the complete abolition of nuclear weapons by 2000. Ronald Reagan was happy to join him in these endeavors, though with oft-expressed wariness about the believability of any Soviet leader. In July 1986, Gorbachev pledged to withdraw from Afghanistan. On October 11, 1986, Gorbachev and Reagan met at Reykjavik, Iceland, and Gorbachev, with no prior hint of such an ambitious plan, proposed the complete abolition of all nuclear weapons except tactical battlefield nuclear systems, along with anti-missile defenses, for which, he claimed, there would then be no need.

Reagan, who was an idiosyncratic idealist and sentimentalist, as well as a sly old man now 75, professed to take the first option seriously, though he pointed out that he could not speak for his British and French allies, which were also nuclear powers. (There were also the Chinese, Indians, and Israelis and soon Pakistan and South Africa to think about, as well as all the nuclear-capable powers, dozens of them.) Reagan rejected scrapping his anti-missile defense program, but warmed up the almost equivalent fable of sharing it with the Soviet Union. This surrealistic exchange continued for two days, and then Reagan broke off the talks and the two leaders parted amicably enough, but in an atmosphere of disappointment. American allies were horrified, including the redoubtable Margaret Thatcher, who, when asked if she was for a "nuclear-free Europe," instantly replied that she was for a "war-free Europe."

But Gorbachev had fatally shown his hand, his acute fear of SDI; Reagan had called him, in poker parlance, and it was clear that the United States was finally in a commanding position in the Cold War. Its economy was booming while Russia's was floundering, and in defense terms, mighty America, led by a tough but humane and sometimes slightly dreamy leader, who yet possessed great moral integrity, a consciousness of his strength, and a genius at holding national opinion behind him, was about to spend the Soviet Union to the mat and develop absolute military superiority while professing only the elimination of the horrible specter of nuclear weapons. It ranked with the greatest foreign policy initiatives of Roosevelt, Truman, and Nixon, as a brilliant stroke of pure grand strategy.

Unfortunately, Reagan, as his tide appeared to crest, was suddenly threatened by a bizarre episode that would be known as the Iran-Contra scandal. A number of American civilians had been seized by the militant Islamist organization Hezbollah, supplied and to some extent directed by the Iranian and Syrian governments, in Lebanon, and Reagan, who was susceptible to emotional human appeals, had overlooked or more likely condoned the sale of arms to Israel, which sold them on to Iran, supposedly in exchange, apart from the cash payment, for the release, one by one, of the hostages in Beirut. Even more unfortunately, it didn't stop there, and after a time, Colonel Oliver North, an aide to the national security advisor, Robert (Bud) McFarlane, had rerouted the profit on the arms sales—which Israel (to the destruction of which state the Iranian government never ceased to aspire) faithfully remitted from Iran—to the assistance of the anti-Sandinista Contras in Nicaragua. Support of the guerrillas had sometimes been approved by the Congress and sometimes forbidden, and there is not a clear basis to the constitutional ability of the Congress to determine such things.

One of the many unpleasant consequences of the Watergate affair was that the impeachment of the president became much easier to contemplate (and threaten) than it had been, and policy differences were routinely criminalized, especially when the White House and the Capitol were in different partisan hands, as was the case between 1969 and 2003 in 21 years with the Senate and 26 for the House of Representatives. An aircraft delivering arms to the Contras was shot down and the crew interviewed by officials of the Sandinista government. The story surfaced in an Arabic newspaper in Beirut in the first days of November 1986, and was endorsed by the Iranian government, which represented it as an act of cowardly and hypocritical boot-licking by the United States, especially when it emerged that McFarlane had turned up in Tehran in a disguise with a Bible for the Ayatollah Khomeini inscribed by Reagan.

It was a pitiful and farcical story, and the president's almost indestructible domestic popularity descended almost 20 points, very abruptly. There was much hip-shooting talk of "constitutional crimes" and so forth. In the midterm elections in 1986, the Democrats gained five House seats and eight Senate seats, taking control of that chamber for the first time in six years. Reagan at first told the country, in November 1986, that he had not traded arms for hostages. He set up the Tower Commission (Republican senator John Tower of Texas, General Brent Scowcroft, and former senator and secretary of state Edmund Muskie) to look into the whole affair. North and his comely assistant, Ms. Fawn Hall, had destroyed some of the relevant documents, and the commission was unable to determine exactly how much Reagan knew about it all.

Reagan admitted in March that what he had approved, arms sales to Israel, had "deteriorated" into trading arms for hostages. He professed to have known nothing about the shipments of arms to the Contras. The CIA director, William Casey, suffered a stroke just before he was to testify before a congressional committee, and died without recovering. Watergate investigative reporter Bob Woodward of the *Washington Post* claimed to have entered Casey's hospital room and interviewed him briefly and secured an acknowledgement of guilt, but Casey was unconscious and his room heavily secured at the time; this appeared to be an extension of the author's talents for mythmaking, which were well enough demonstrated in the Watergate affair.

On June 12, 1987, Reagan visited West Berlin for the 750th anniversary of Berlin, and made almost as well-remembered a comment in a speech at the Berlin Wall as John F. Kennedy had made there almost exactly 24 years before: "Mr. Gorbachev, tear down this wall!" and repeated it several times as he labored the iniquity of it. Reagan had earned the esteem of the Germans, not least because when he visited the Federal Republic two years before and it was revealed that there were some Waffen SS draftees' graves in a cemetery he was scheduled to visit, Reagan resisted the urgings of the Congress, his staff, and even his wife, kept to the visit (though he added a stop at the Bergen-Belsen concentration camp first), and said that those conscripted into service for the Third Reich who gave their lives in combat at a young age were also victims. Reagan's moral, as well as his physical, courage were evident and were the source of much of his great popularity.

After this, there were some indictments, and some misdemeanor convictions, in the Iran-Contra imbroglio that led to fines and eventual pardons, and the whole matter dried up and the president's popularity revived, but it was a discordantly harebrained and absurd interlude. It did not alter the correlation of forces between the United States and the Soviet Union, however. And on November 24, 1987, at Geneva, an INF (Intermediate Nuclear Forces) agreement was signed, reversing and avoiding the deployment of all such weapons in Western and Central Europe. This was a remarkable strategic victory for Reagan, Thatcher, and West Germany's Chancellor Helmut Kohl, who had held fast to their deployment schedules. They traded the nondeployment of missiles for the removal of a larger number of Soviet missiles that had already been deployed. And the American Pershing mobile missiles were not, in fact, as yet fully developed, and the ground-launched cruise missiles the U.S. would now not be deploying could just as easily be launched from American warships based in European ports and American aircraft flying from European bases.

There was another very cordial summit meeting in Washington, in December 1987, and in February 1988 Gorbachev promised the complete Soviet evacuation of Afghanistan within a year. The Soviets did leave within a year, having taken 28,000 combat dead for no remotely justifiable reason, and devastated much of the country. The puppet government they left behind was quickly overrun by the mujahedeen and Taliban the Americans in particular had armed, and the pro-Soviet regime crumbled in the next several years and its leaders either fled or were summarily executed.

Soon after the Afghan departure announcement, Gorbachev withdrew the Brezhnev Doctrine and declared that all the former satellite states were free to do as they wished as autonomous states. Soviet foreign ministry spokesman Gennadi Gerasimov, playing off the popular Frank Sinatra song "My Way," called this the "Sinatra Doctrine," an amusing send-up of the penchant of Soviet and American leaders to lay claim to having established a doctrine. The collapse of the Soviet bloc and of the Warsaw Pact were widely predicted and were clearly presaged. President Reagan visited Moscow for another of his rapid-fire summits with Gorbachev in May 1988, and gave a well-received address at Moscow University praising the virtues of free enterprise. Many Western Sovietologists were now predicting the imminent collapse of the USSR itself, as leaders of the constituent republics and other more local jurisdictions were reorganizing in random and unprecedented ways. The USSR was like a jalopy going at excessive speed and starting to fall apart. Gorbachev never lost his faith in socialism and claimed all his reforms were designed to strengthen it. Though he had seen the astounding productivity of western Canada's large farms, he never fully decollectivized Soviet agriculture. He did not grasp, then or subsequently, that the notion of "communism's human face" was completely impractical; if it wasn't totalitarian, or at least very authoritarian, it could not be imposed at all, and however it was imposed, it didn't work very well. And this fact Ronald Reagan grasped with perhaps more conviction than any other American president.

The Democrats nominated three-term Massachusetts governor Michael S. Dukakis for president and distinguished Texas senator Lloyd Bentsen for vice president. Dukakis was an intelligent and articulate man but appeared somewhat desiccated during the fall campaign. Bentsen was witty and knowledgeable and impressed the voters. Vice president George H.W. Bush won a fairly spirited nomination race with the Republican leader of the Senate and 1976 vice presidential candidate, Robert Dole, and chose as his vice presidential nominee Senator J. Danforth (Dan) Quayle of Indiana. Quayle had a good policy record and was quite amiable but seemed to lack gravitas and had some difficulty explaining why he spent the Vietnam War in the National Guard. He survived the grilling of the White House press corps and the national media, but never entirely got over the impression that he was a lightweight. The campaign was not very elevated, and the Republicans, under their chief strategist, Lee Atwater, lampooned Dukakis for his opposition to the death penalty, belief in paroling convicts, and opposition to obligatory recitations of the Pledge of Allegiance (which Bush and Quayle then mechanically and solemnly uttered at the start of all their campaign appearances no matter how mundane).

Like Eisenhower in 1960, had the Constitution and age (Reagan was now a sprightly 77) allowed it, the president would certainly have been able to win a third term, and Bush ran, essentially, as his stand-in and heir to his achievements and popularity. On election day, Bush and Quayle won safely enough, 48.9 million votes (53.4 percent) and 426 electoral votes from 40 states to 41.8 million votes for Dukakis and Bentsen (45.7 percent) and 111 electoral votes from 10 states and the District of Columbia. The Congress was almost unchanged, with Democratic gains of one Senate and two House seats. It was the fifth Republican victory in six presidential elections starting in 1968.

Mikhail Gorbachev had made his last meeting with Ronald Reagan while they were both in office when he came to New York to address the United Nations in December. He announced a 500,000-man unilateral reduction in the Red Army. It was a fine capstone to a very productive, if rather unequal, relationship, and Gorbachev got off to a very good start with the president-elect (whom he had already met a number of times). By this time, large parts of the USSR itself were in disintegration mode. Popular Front, non-communist coalitions had gained control of the Baltic states and there was irredentist and separatist violence in the three Caucasus republics, Georgia, Azerbaijan, and Armenia. In October and November 1988, Latvia, Lithuania, and Estonia all declared themselves to be legislatively sovereign, and declared their native languages and their traditional flags to be official. Gorbachev flew directly back from Washington to Armenia, which had been devastated by an earthquake, and was understandably incensed to be besieged by protesters complaining of mistreatment of Armenians in Azerbaijan, especially in the district of Nagorno-Karabakh, which sought to secede from Azerbaijan and unite with Armenia. There was immense agitation in both republics and daily demonstrations of up to 500,000 people in Baku, the Aziri capital. Gorbachev imposed a curfew on Baku (a city of two million) on December 5, and would have to try to impose order in Nagorno-Karabakh in February with paratroopers and a tank regiment, after it purported to secede from Azerbaijan.

It is always a matter of skill whether the political center is a position of strength or weakness, and Gorbachev, advocating socialism and union of the country, was caught between conservative communists who feared liberalization would kill communism and reformers who did not believe communism could be reformed. This was Gorbachev's insoluble dilemma, because both groups were correct.

Ronald Reagan left office with a high approval rating. Though the only important domestic accomplishment in his second term was a bipartisan tax reform bill, he avoided the usual lame-duck problem with the great progress that he steadily made with the Soviet leader throughout his second term. Reagan had sharply lowered the personal tax rates of all taxpayers, and had produced very high rates of productivity increase (almost 4 percent per year for most of his time as president) and over 18 million net new jobs. Reagan's reinvigoration of America's economy and national morale, coupled to his massive strengthening of the American military and then his masterstroke of proposing development of an air-tight missile defense, had severely rattled the three infirm septuagenarians who preceded Mikhail Gorbachev as Soviet leader. His calm firmness, gift for self-deprecation, constant good humor, sure political instinct, remarkable human qualities, absence of any officiousness or pomposity, and his unblustering espousal of good intentions impressed the nation and eventually the world. His almost hypnotic eloquence as an orator (he was in fact a benign demagogue, though his opponents tried to minimize his talents as those of a "good communicator"), as well as his exploitation of the addiction of his opponents to underestimate him, made him one of the most formidable politicians and outstanding presidents in the nation's history. (Former defense secretary and longtime Democratic insider and Washington fixer Clark Clifford called him "an amiable dunce," but Clifford didn't think much of Eisenhower, either.)

Reagan stuck to prosperity through the economic growth of free enterprise and lower taxes, and peace through strength. He delivered both and his standing as a president became clearer after he had retired and the scale of his achievement towered over the simplicity of his methods. Ronald Reagan was fortunate in having Margaret Thatcher, Pope John Paul II, Helmut Kohl, and Trudeau's successor in Canada, Brian Mulroney, as allies, and Mikhail Gorbachev as the eventual Soviet leader opposite him. But that takes nothing from his status as probably, next to (in chronological order only) Washington, Lincoln, and FDR, the greatest American president. He was revered as an ex-president and mourned by the whole nation when he died, aged 93, in 2004, after a long bout with Alzheimer's disease. For the first time, foreign leaders (Margaret Thatcher and Brian Mulroney) were among the eulogists at the state funeral of an American president.

10. PRESIDENT GEORGE H.W. BUSH

George Bush was formidably qualified to be president: after being a well-decorated combat navy aviator while only 20, in World War II, a Yale alumnus, and a successful businessman, he served two terms in the House of Representatives and ran two unsuccessful but very respectable campaigns for the U.S. Senate in Texas; served as ambassador to the UN, Republican Party chairman, representative to China, and director of the CIA; and became only the sixth person to serve two full terms as vice president. He would be, as Richard Nixon wrote, "a good man with good intentions . . . [but] no discernible pattern of political principle . . . no political rhythm, no conservative cadence, and not enough charismatic style to compensate."[4] He did, however, have a considerable aptitude for foreign policy and was well-respected personally by other national leaders. His secretary of state would be former White House chief of staff and Treasury secretary under Reagan, the very capable Houston lawyer and Bush's political manager, James A. Baker. They had inherited a winning hand from their retired leader and didn't have to wait long for America's only remaining rival in the world to fold.

The erosion of the Soviet Union and the Soviet bloc accelerated dramatically. In March and April of 1989, there were the first free party elections in Russia since 1917 (and there hadn't been any for positions of real authority before that). Gorbachev claimed that 84 percent of those elected were Soviet Communist Party candidates, but their party loyalty was soft in many cases. Two leading new legislators were Russian patriotic leader and reformer Boris Yeltsin and scientist and dissident Andrei Sakharov. Gorbachev was desperately struggling to maintain ultimate central authority even as he yielded jurisdiction to the constituent Soviet republics. He did address the European Parliament at Strasbourg on July 6, 1989, and raised a subject that clearly indicated where he would like to take Soviet foreign policy if he could keep his country together, when he spoke of "our common European home." He was well-received, but this was the old ploy, much used by de Gaulle and his followers, of playing the continental solidarity card against the U.S. connection (except, of course, when American intervention was necessary to protect or liberate Europeans from each other, as it had been for the last 40 years). It could have been a real distraction to the West if Gorbachev's own position had been stronger.

Whatever he thought of the satellite countries, he was too preoccupied to pay much attention to them now. On August 19, 1989, the democratic Catholic journalist and intellectual Tadeusz Mazowiecki was installed as prime minister of Poland, after the Solidarity labor movement backed by the pope had forced compromises on the government. Institutional democratic reforms followed quickly. In October, Hungary legislated itself to be a democratic republic; the Soviet Union pledged by treaty to withdraw; Imre Nagy and his followers, whom the Russians and their Hungarian followers had executed in 1956, were reinterred with state honors; and the borders were opened to the West. On November 9, the government of East Germany (the German Democratic Republic) announced that the barriers between East Germany and the West would be opened, and the Berlin Wall (the "Antifascist Protection Rampart") was swarmed over by huge crowds on both sides, chipped at, and soon attacked and pierced by heavy equipment. The East

---

4.   Black, *op. cit.*, p. 1049.

German state, which in 1953 had "lost confidence in the people," dissolved. The Czechoslovak communist state progressively disintegrated through the autumn and formerly imprisoned dissident and intellectual Václav Havel was elected president on December 29. The reform leader deposed by the Soviet intervention in 1968, Alexander Dubček, returned as parliamentary speaker.

The 24-year dictatorship of Nicolae Ceausescu and the entire Communist Party government in Romania ended most dramatically of all. Ceausescu addressed a large crowd in the chief square of Bucharest on December 21, 1989, condemning dissent in a provincial town. The crowd booed and jeered and he fell silent, tried to regain attention, promised everyone a raise, and retreated inside, barricaded in the party headquarters by the crowd overnight. As reports came in of the state falling apart throughout the country, his elite forces suppressed and injured many demonstrators, the defense minister committed suicide, and the armed forces deserted. Ceausescu emerged again on December 22 to try to speak, and the crowd threw stones and bottles at him. The protesters smashed down the doors of the building and only missed lynching their ostensible leader and his wife by a few seconds, as they fled from the roof by helicopter. The army closed the airspace and the helicopter had to land. The Ceausescus were arrested by local police and held until a military unit arrived. The first couple was held for three days, then given a perfunctory drumhead "trial," found guilty of a vast range of offenses from embezzlement to genocide, taken to a wall while Ceausescu sang the "Internationale," and executed by firing squad. At least, unlike many other deposed leaders who were executed in this narrative, from Mussolini to Nuri as Said (Iraq) to Najibullah (Afghanistan), their corpses were not displayed and desecrated.

Apparently indifferent to the collapse in shame and shambles of the rule Stalin imposed and his successors maintained on Eastern Europe, contrary to Stalin's commitments at Yalta in 1945, Gorbachev had another very jovial summit meeting with Bush, at Malta in early December. Also in December, the United States, supposedly motivated by the shooting of an American serviceman and the suppression of the results of free elections, seized Panama City with 24,000 troops who had been airlifted to the Canal Zone (which had not yet been vacated under Carter's treaty with Panama). The authoritarian president, Manuel Noriega, a former CIA operative, was chased into the residence of the apostolic nuncio, and eventually surrendered to U.S. forces (who did not violate the Vatican's diplomatic privilege). The democratically elected president, Guillermo Endara, was installed and the removal of Noriega appeared to be popular with the Panamanians and is justifiable.

Bush's transportation of him to Florida, where he was then tried in U.S. criminal court as a racketeer and drug dealer, was a more questionable enterprise. At time of writing, 23 years later, Noriega, who was handed over to France after 20 years in prison in Florida, and imprisoned by the French for a sequential set of grievances, is back in Panama under house arrest. There have been worse injustices inflicted on more sympathetic national leaders, but the legality of trying the president of a foreign country as a common criminal after seizing him by military force is questionable, though no one has much seemed to care about it, so distasteful a character was he. By this time, Cuba had been such a conspicuous economic failure and notoriously oppressive state, Castro's incumbency was useful to the United States as illustrative of the failings of communism in Latin America. Gorbachev had tired of this open artery also, and stopped paying all Castro's bills.

Lithuania and Moldova professed to secede from the Soviet Union in February 1990, and Estonia and Latvia in March. There were jurisdictional disputes between the central government and most of the republics throughout the year, and Georgia announced its secession in October. East Germany proved to be completely ungovernable without being walled and fenced off from the West and overseen by the Red Army, and Baker and Bush, with the cooperation of host Brian Mulroney, turned an Open Skies conference in Ottawa in October 1990 into a meeting between both Germanies and the four postwar occupying powers, and agreed to the reunification of Germany. This was very skillfully strategized by Chancellor Kohl, but the diplomatic skills of Bush and Baker were essential, as Prime Minister Thatcher and the fourth president of the Fifth French Republic (since 1981), François Mitterrand, true to the entrenched attitude of the foreign policy establishments of both countries, opposed German reunification.

Gorbachev himself was unenthused about it, but there was not a great deal he could now do to prevent it. All three powers had had good reason to fear a united Germany over the last 120 years. But of the Western Great Powers, the United States did not fear a united Germany and was pledged to achieve reunification, and Bush and Baker managed the negotiations with exquisite tact and persuasiveness. The reunification of Germany and the continuing recession and internal weakness of Russia changed the political equation in Europe. Helmut Kohl, probably the greatest federal German leader after Bismarck and Adenauer (obviously Hitler is in a special category of brilliance and evil), was sincere in his promotion of "a European Germany and not a German Europe."

Although the integration of the mismanaged East into the Federal Republic has been abrasive and complicated, it was necessary, had been promised, and was achieved gracefully by all the other countries involved. The event demonstrates again the statesmanship of President Truman and the other authors of the containment strategy, and of European statesmen starting with Churchill and de

Gaulle, in putting West Germany back on its feet and treating it as a respected and trusted ally. The Franco-German Friendship Treaty negotiated by de Gaulle and Adenauer and concluded in 1963 was a landmark that Schmidt and Giscard d'Estaing and Mitterrand and Kohl elaborated. (It included a preamble promising continued cooperation with NATO and pursuit of German reunification, though de Gaulle was lukewarm about both.) Eisenhower's almost unilateral election of Germany to NATO and the Franco-German Friendship Treaty were made possible by Adenauer's successful rejection of Stalin's offer of reunification in exchange for Cold War neutrality. In the positive evolution of Germany's international status, all of these statesmen conducted themselves with distinction.

11. THE FIRST IRAQ WAR

On August 1, 1990, Iraq, under its dictator, Saddam Hussein, invaded and occupied the oil-rich sheikhdom of Kuwait. Margaret Thatcher, vacationing in the United States, concerted with President Bush a vigorous response. It has been a matter of some contention exactly what the U.S. ambassador to Iraq, April Glaspie, said to Saddam when they met on July 25. She did say that the United States had no position on Arab-Arab disputes, nor on Iraq's border claims, although she referred to Iraqi troop concentrations on the Kuwaiti border. In the circumstances, she could have made more cautionary noises, but it would not have been reasonable for Saddam to conclude there would be no intervention if he invaded. Saddam was not reasonable.

He rejected demands for his withdrawal, was warned repeatedly, and was condemned in the United Nations, the Arab league, and elsewhere. Bush and Baker organized an immense coalition including all of NATO, most Middle Eastern countries except Jordan and Israel, and many other nations, ultimately amassing well over 500,000 soldiers and massive air and sea power, most, though certainly not all of it, American. Bush observed the War Powers Act, and after vigorous and often eloquent debate, both houses of the Congress authorized the use of force to liberate Kuwait. Every few days, television viewers throughout the world would see film of families waving goodbye to loved ones among the 6,000-person crews of giant American aircraft carriers and the 2,550-man crews of huge reconditioned battleships as they departed their home ports for the Persian Gulf. Saudi Arabia was officially the co-head of the coalition with the United States, and contributed a co-commander, though in fact the entire effort was commanded by American general Norman Schwarzkopf.

On January 17, 1991, carpet bombing with unprecedentedly precise weapons began on military targets throughout Iraq and in Kuwait. All Iraqi air defenses were quickly silenced and the Iraqi air force fled to Iran (a country on which Saddam had unleashed an unsuccessful aggressive war in which approximately a million people were killed, from 1980 to 1988, and Iran did not return the Iraqi airplanes). There were over 100,000 sorties, and the allies lost a total of 75 airplanes (most flight crews survived). Throughout this time, the Iraqis were lobbing Scud missiles at Israel, hoping to provoke an attack that might shake loose America's Arab coalition partners. The U.S. and the Netherlands deployed Patriot anti-missile weapons that brought down most of the Scuds, which were not very effective anyway. Israeli prime minister Yitzhak Shamir made it clear that if Iraq launched chemical or bacteriological weapons against Israel, he would reply with nuclear weapons, and added, "Israel asks no one to fight its battles." There was no such escalation.

This was the first recourse to ground combat on a large scale that the United States had undertaken since the terrible tragedy of Vietnam, and there was great concern that Iraq's ostensibly large and well-armed army could put up fierce resistance and inflict heavy casualties. This did not happen. With Saddam still spitting defiance though his army had been pummeled and almost immobilized from the air, on February 24 allied forces invaded in overwhelming strength in Kuwait and Iraq, with close and heavy air support from several directions, spearheaded by elite forces of a number of countries, including U.S. Marines and air cavalry, the British SAS, and the French Foreign Legion.

The Iraqis were quickly expelled from Kuwait and in full retreat when Bush and his commanders accepted a cease-fire after just 100 hours. Saddam renounced ambitions on Kuwait, but was allowed to remain in power in Baghdad, though a no-fly zone was enforced against the Iraqis over their northern, Kurdish, territory. The allies suffered 392 dead and 776 wounded, against Iraq's approximately 30,000 dead, 75,000 wounded, and hundreds of thousands of prisoners. (The allies apparently surpassed the previous record for imbalance of casualties between land combatants, generally accepted to be held by Alexander the Great, who allegedly killed 50,000 Persians and captured over 100,000 others, at a loss of fewer than a thousand men himself, on one day, at nearby Gaugamela, on October 1, 331 B.C.) The conception and execution of the operation, diplomatically and militarily, by President Bush; secretaries Baker and Dick Cheney (Defense); and the chief of staff, General Colin L. Powell, and General Schwarzkopf, were all at the very highest standards of professionalism, and were universally recognized to be so. As the Soviet Union collapsed, the United States led the most "splendid little war" (in allied casualties, not scale of operations) in its history. Bush's approval rating rose to about 90 percent. The contrast between the superpowers could not have been greater, as their long rivalry neared its end.

More controversial were allowing Saddam to remain at all and not doing more to assure the end of the repression of the Kurds. Bush and his chief collaborators claimed that if they had taken Baghdad, they would have had to govern the whole country. This is a bit flimsy, since they wouldn't have needed to occupy Baghdad, but just to overrun most of the country, liberate the Kurds, and demand Saddam's departure. (And they did end up running the whole country anyway, starting in 2003.) Margaret Thatcher had lost the support of an appreciable number of her own Conservative members of Parliament, and retired earlier in the year, but was replaced by her chosen successor, John Major. Major was a good ally and sensible prime minister, but did not have the influence in the coalition and with Bush personally that Thatcher had had. It was not long before Saddam was portraying himself to the Arab masses as a David to the American Goliath, a great survivor, and even a plucky chap, all of which was preposterous, but not unsalable to such an impressionable and hero-starved audience. The fate of the dissentient Kurdish population was a gruesome one, despite the allied no-fly zone.

12. THE END OF THE COLD WAR

In January 1991, Gorbachev had recourse to traditional Soviet repressive methods in Georgia and Latvia, but his heart wasn't in it, and he wasn't prepared to kill people as Stalin and Khrushchev and even occasionally Brezhnev had done. On March 17, 1991, 76.4 percent of Soviet voters ostensibly voted to remain in a reformed Soviet Union, although the Baltic republics and Georgia and Armenia voted to secede and Moldova abstained. But on June 12, Boris Yeltsin, who had defected from the Communist Party and sought full democracy, denationalization and decontrol of all industry and agriculture, and the Russian secession from the Soviet Union, was elected head of the Russian Republic with 57 percent in a free vote. He was now a very serious rival, in terms of legitimacy to speak for the Russians, to Gorbachev.

There were some final traditional exertions. President Bush came to Moscow for a summit meeting in July 1991, and he and Gorbachev signed a Strategic Arms Reduction Agreement (START), which had been under negotiation for almost a decade, and pledged a reduction in nuclear weapons of the two powers by about 30 percent. On August 1, President Bush stopped in Kiev, the capital of Ukraine, the second most populous of the Soviet republics, and spoke to the legislature there, suggesting the virtues of renewed federalism. He emphasized that it was not

America's place to intervene in the relations between the different governments in the USSR and that he was not doing so. But he did praise Gorbachev while urging full freedom for Ukraine, and implied that something short of the complete disassembly of the USSR would be desirable. (Former Nixon speechwriter and lexicographer William Safire called this, a bit harshly, "the Chicken Kiev speech.")

And on August 19, while Gorbachev was on holiday in the Crimea, there was an attempted coup d'état led by his vice president (Gennadi Yenayev), prime minister (Valentin Pavlov), defense minister (Dmitri Yazov), and secret police (KGB) chief (Vladimir Kryuchkov). They purported to put Gorbachev under house arrest, and suspended elections, most of the media, and all political activity. It was astonishing that Gorbachev could be betrayed by his senior collaborators (just the sort of event that Stalin liquidated almost all of his closest comrades to prevent almost 60 years before). The launch of the New Union Treaty, which would grant the republics autonomy with a common president, common foreign and defense policy, and common market, was planned for August 20, but had to be deferred. Boris Yeltsin led the resistance to the coup and bravely appeared in public in front of the Russian Republic government building before large and supportive (to him) crowds.

The coup collapsed on August 21 and Gorbachev returned, but he now had no moral or jurisdictional authority. He was the father of democracy throughout the USSR and was much admired in the world, but had completely lost control of events and owed to Yeltsin whatever position he retained. Events were almost running free, though not, fortunately, in the control of the formidable Soviet nuclear arsenal. Except for Georgia (the homeland of Stalin and Shevardnadze), which had already declared itself independent in 1990, all the republics declared their independence between August and December 1991, ending with Russia on December 21. On Christmas Day, without histrionics or serious recriminations, Gorbachev resigned as president of the Soviet Union and declared that the office had ceased to exist. On December 26, the Council of the Soviet Union voted recognition of the dissolution and the end of the Union of Soviet Socialist Republics, and then voted to dissolve itself. Over the Kremlin, the hammer and sickle was lowered and the prerevolutionary flag of Russia was raised.

Unimaginably, and with breathtaking swiftness, the Cold War, the Soviet Union, and international communism passed into history. All of the 10 U.S. presidents from the second Roosevelt to the first Bush, five of each party, deserved credit, though not equally, for what was the greatest and most bloodless strategic victory in the history of the nation-state. Without so much as a pistol shot ever being exchanged between them, the Soviet Union simply expired, unable to continue in the impossible competition to which Stalin committed it, against the United States. His violation of his Yalta pledge (1945) to the freedom and independence of Eastern Europe, and resumed agitation and subversion against the West throughout the world was, next to the Japanese attack on Pearl Harbor and other targets in 1941, and to Kaiser Wilhelm II's recourse to submarine attacks on American ships in 1917, the greatest world-significant strategic blunder since the Napoleonic Wars. It was the more surprising coming from such a cunning leader as Stalin.

All three terrible mistakes were underestimations of the United States, which grew steadily in strength and importance, other than during the early years of the Great Depression, throughout the twentieth century.

It was only 208 years since the British conceded three million Americans (including 500,000 slaves) their national independence—less than the time between George I and George V, or between the accessions of Louis XIV and Napoleon III. With most of an immense and stupefyingly rich continent open to it, armed with the English language, the Common Law, a democratic tradition, a revolutionary launch, Jefferson's heroic mythos, and Madison and Hamilton's Constitution, and brilliantly led when necessary, the United States had completed a rise without the slightest parallel or precedent in the history of the world.

It had operated since the World War I on a scale the world had never seen or imagined before, and its economic, military, and scientific might and political and popular cultural influence inundated the whole world, without any recourse to traditional conquest and imperial subjugation. And at the hour of its supreme victory, there was not a hint of triumphalism or condescension, officially or among the public, only relief that the Cold War was over and that the threat that had created such paroxysms just 40 years before had gone. Gorbachev and Yeltsin, and Russia generally, continued to be respected in the United States, and this mighty apotheosis, by a normally somewhat demonstrative, not to say boastful, people, was assimilated with gracious modesty, making it even more monumental because no monuments were erected to it, though they would have been justified. America was at the summit of the world, unchallenged in its mastery, in its time, and in all of preceding history.

Barack Obama

CHAPTER SIXTEEN

Waiting for the Future, 1992–2013

1. NEW RIVALRIES

With the collapse of the Soviet Union, there was a sharply reduced need for strategic innovation or even vigilance in the U.S. government. Richard Nixon, when he startled the world with his overture to China in 1972, had told his principal European allies (Chapter 14) that there were five areas capable of influencing the world, militarily and economically—the United States, Western Europe, Russia, Japan, and China. He said that Western Europe and Japan were solid allies of the United States and that he wished to reinforce the detachment of China from Russia and then deal with Russia from strength. In 1992, Russia retained less than half of the population, though most of the physical expanse, of the former USSR, and all pretense at cooperation with the former Soviet republics quickly melted, except, to a degree, with Belarus and a couple of the Asian republics.

Russia itself was in a shell-shocked condition. Boris Yeltsin privatized almost everything, but on the basis of rank favoritism, and instantly created a notorious infestation of "oligarchs" who soon became familiar and generally rather coarse figures in the high-spending cities and resorts of the West. The transfer of nuclear weapons proceeded fairly well, and at least without disaster. Russia was reduced to renting its old Black Sea naval base of Sevastopol from Ukraine. The missile and air forces and the large navy that Khrushchev and Brezhnev had built after the Cuban Missile Crisis in 1962 deteriorated and shrank, and the Russians no longer had the means or physical plant to conduct an arms race, in quantity or quality, with the United States. Yeltsin was a brave and sincere man but, like many of his countrymen, a chronic alcoholic. Yeltsin abruptly resigned in 1999 and was succeeded by Vladimir Putin, the premier, who had a KGB background, and has continued as the principal Russian political figure, either president or prime minister, since.

The much-feared famines and utter devastation of Russia did not occur in the early Yeltsin years, and Putin is generally conceded to have restored order, rebuilt income levels, largely completed the transition to a private enterprise economy, and produced high economic growth rates. He restored a nationalist foreign policy that has steered Russia to a nettlesome inconstancy, endlessly seeking more deference than it can now, on the basis of its geopolitical strength, legitimately claim. Russia again showed its imperishability and stoic genius of survival, a nation much punished in the severity of its climate and inborn grimness of its people (though not without bursts of exuberance). And it pays the price of having had, by Western standards, almost no experience of good government. Most its few successful rulers were barbarously harsh, particularly Peter the Great and Stalin, and as has been described, Stalin doomed Russia's great charge to world power by opening an unwinnable contest with America. Like all of Europe but to a relative extreme, Russia has a declining birthrate. High oil and other commodity prices have helped, though at time of writing they seem unlikely to continue. But Russia still has no reliable political institutions, and Putin is a fairly shameless despot, though not heavy-handed by the standards of most of his predecessors. Russia is in its way immutable, and one of the world's greatest cultures, but it does not now possess the stability, critical mass, or demographic trajectory to be believable as a coming source of great influence, or more than a self-important and rather abrasive regional power, albeit across most of the immense region of Eurasia.

To the extent that it was followed at all, the Russian threat to America's primacy was succeeded by that of Japan, which, with apparently insuperable Oriental cunning, did a complete back-flip from the militarism and absolutism that led it to disaster at and after Pearl Harbor. It entrusted its entire defense to the United States, and built an industrial powerhouse based on quality of manufacturing, especially automobiles and other engineered products, and an ingrained, rigorously imposed national discipline. For a few years in the nineties, there was a good deal of talk of an irresistible triumph of Japanese industry and finance, a notion the Japanese collective leadership and opinion leaders helped to incite. When President Bush led the great alliance he and James Baker had constructed into the Gulf War in 1991, there was very audible speculation in prominent Japanese circles that if it were not successful, Japan would surpass the United States in economic might and international prestige, continuing, almost perversely, to leave the great burden of military defense almost entirely to the account of the Americans.

The nadir on the American side of this competition came on January 8, 1992, when President Bush vomited and fainted at a state dinner tendered to him by Japanese premier Kiichi Miyazawa. The premier had welcomed Bush to Japan in condescending words about the economic difficulties the United States was enduring, and the banquet incident, which followed an unsuccessful game of doubles tennis against the Japanese emperor and crown prince, were given considerable symbolic significance, for a time. Japan appeared set to become the manufacturing and even financial giant of the world, and redeployed its vast export revenues and the fruit of the high savings rate of the Japanese (about 25 percent, against almost none in the U.S. and between 5 and 10 percent in other advanced Western countries) in steadily more prominent foreign investments, such as Rockefeller Center in New York.

Japanese real estate values skyrocketed and Japanese banks and industrial groups (*zaibatsu*, vast conglomerates, four of which, working intimately with the government, controlled almost the entire private sector) were the largest in the world. But their financial reporting was inadequate, the state was too much implicated in the operation of the private sector, leadership in all sectors of Japanese life was too collegial to respond quickly to crises, and the country had bought into the notion of Japan as a superstate and didn't recognize a mighty inflationary bubble. It all came down in shambles in the late nineties; the manufacturing exports continued, but real estate and other values crumbled and the Tokyo Stock Exchange evaporated by over 75 percent. Japan resumed its former status as an important country, but gradually indebted itself as its birthrate declined and it was unable to reignite an economic boom. (Rockefeller Center was repossessed by its former owners.) And Japan was steadily undercut by its fiercely competitive local rivals, especially South Korea and Taiwan, and in financial terms, Singapore and, while it remained outside China (until 1997), Hong Kong.

The next putative candidacy for rivalry to the U.S. for world leadership, though it was, in spirit, even less inherently hostile than that of Japan, was Western Europe's. And like Japan's, Western Europe's defense had been largely in American hands throughout the Cold War. Although the implosion of the Soviet Union led to sharp American force reductions in Europe, it was also followed by a much greater withering of most of the defense capability of Western Europe, except for the modest number of submarine-launched nuclear missiles of the British and the French. Thus, opposite both the Japanese and the Europeans, American military primacy became even more pronounced in the 20 years after the Soviet breakup. Europe steadily integrated, through the handover of more powers to the European Commission in Brussels and to the European Parliament in Strasbourg.

To the Eurocrats, as they were called, from the smaller countries such as Belgium and the Netherlands, it was the opportunity to rule a large jurisdiction. There was a brief, euphoric, pan-European sense of fraternity and the jubilant end to many centuries of horrifying internecine European strife. And to the Euro-integrationists in France and Great Britain, such as Edward Heath, British prime minister 1970–1974, and Jacques Delors, Mitterrand's finance minister and head of the European Commission, though they and few others would publicly say so, it was the dream of the revival of a Eurocentric world. After the horrors of World War I, and the failure of the chief Western European powers to reach a durable accord at Munich, the one occasion where they met (Chapter 9), and the hideous reprise of World War II, Western Europe had had to endure the soft hegemony of America, its chief liberator from Hitler, to prevent the domination of Stalin and his successors, which would probably have been as harsh as Hitler's, to judge from the unhappy fate of Eastern Europe. But with the collapse of the Soviet Union, it was furtively reasoned, America could now be dismissed with thanks, and the Western Europeans could stand on each other's shoulders and reestablish the Eurocentricity of the world after a painful lapse of a century.

Of course, it was utter nonsense; after a good deal of lively debate, Britain refused to chuck the political institutions it had developed and that had served it well for nearly a thousand years, for the earnest, untried *dirigisme* of Brussels and the talking shop of Strasbourg, with vague powers and 11 languages, before eight more languages came in with the addition of the former Soviet satellites and Baltic republics. And it didn't want its often intimate and vital relationship with the United States, especially under Churchill and Roosevelt and Thatcher and Reagan, subsumed into the much less amicable relations of America with France and Germany.

The French were anti-integration under de Gaulle, who believed he could dominate Western Europe as long as Britain was excluded (he vetoed its entry in 1962), and Germany was divided and still self-conscious about the unspeakable atrocities of the Third Reich. Though he was doubtless sincere, as a World War I prisoner of war (taken when wounded and unconscious amid the slaughter of Verdun), de Gaulle flattered the Germans, and when he visited Germany spoke in heavily accented but comprehensible German (like Churchill's French), which he had learned as a POW. Under Pompidou, the French were more expansive and admitted Britain to the Common Market, but were for autonomous member-states under subsequent presidents France was more driven by the pan-European bug but believed that it could be closer to Germany than were the British, and to the British than were the Germans, and somehow could manipulate the whole continent. (The French have rarely in their national history lacked an overconfident sense of their ability to prevail intellectually, as long as they weren't too bedeviled by the Anglo-Saxons.)

In the same measure that the United States, unlike the British and the French and the Russians, did not fear a united Germany, Germany feared a Europe without the close alliance of the United States, the only power that was friendly, democratic, and so strong that it could discourage the rivalries within Europe. And the federal chancellor who accomplished German reunification, with indispensable help from George Bush and James Baker, had lost his father, uncle, and brother in France in the World Wars, and feared what a solitary Germany could do. Helmut Kohl restored the capital of Germany to Berlin, and was haunted by the close proximity to each other of the architectural remnants of successive failed regimes—Frederick the Great's Brandenburg Gate, the Hohenzollerns' Cathedral, Bismarck's Reichstag, Hitler's bunker, and Stalin's immense embassy in East Berlin, all within a few hundred yards. He was sincere in calling for "a European Germany and not a German Europe."

The high-water mark of the European idea was the launch of the euro in 1999, the common currency in which ultimately 17 of the 27 European countries (at its fullest expanse, at time of writing) participated. But the endless regulations of the minutiae of everyday life, in the name of community, grated on many. The natural rivalries between the major European powers, though all in the context of friendly peoples, eroded any sense of unity. The social democratic emphasis on the public sector and a safety net for all created a continental lethargy and sluggish job creation, and curtailed economic growth. When the Eastern European states were admitted, they all sought the U.S. military guarantee implicit in NATO membership more fervently than any participation in what was now called the European Union. The southern Eurozone states, Greece, Italy, Spain, and Portugal, all signed false prospectuses to secure their admission at higher values to their soft national currencies than proved to be justified, causing immense financial strain near the end of the first decade of the new millennium. And Europe, suffering an insufficient birthrate, to avoid declining population, replaced the unborn with largely Muslim immigration, importing a serious problem that led to a great deal of urban violence in the early years after 2000. A Europe of convivial neighboring states won the adherence and commendation of all, but as a coherent power in the world, it gained no traction.

The cycle had evolved, in descending order of scale of threat to the United States. The first European challenge, Nazi Germany, was mortally dangerous, as Roosevelt saw as early as 1936, when he warned against French toleration of the remilitarization of the Rhineland. Hitler's Greater Germany had as great a population (though 40 percent of it did not speak German) as the United States and an inferior but not uncompetitive industrial capacity. And Italy, unoccupied France, Hungary, Romania, Yugoslavia, Slovakia, Spain, and Portugal were fascist satellites. The mortal conflict with Hitler, the physical brunt of which was borne by Stalin's Russia, was followed by the serious but uneven rivalry of Soviet Communism, until it collapsed from the unbearable weight of the self-imposed competition with the United States. Japan seemed to have a formula for remaining a military protégé of America and taking advantage of its low military obligations while striking a mortal threat at the industrial and financial core of American strength, but apart from the quality of its engineered products, the threat was made of straw and was quickly blown away. And the idea of the rivalry of a united Europe was a wild surmise unsupported by any practical foundation.

This left only China, of the potential centers of rival economic and military strength Nixon had identified in 1972. China was large and historic, and was starting from very far back. Chou En-lai died in January 1976, followed seven months later by Mao Tse-tung. The customary rending struggle for power followed, in which there emerged the twice-purged veteran of the Long March, Deng

Xiao-ping, who gained effective control of the government in 1977 and held it for 15 years, and remained the most influential figure in the country to his death in 1997, aged 92. He invented what was called socialist capitalism, and other hybrid names that essentially promoted an economy that was about half free and half command and state-planned, in a political structure that was less authoritarian than Mao's but a party dictatorship. There were not the wild lurches into mad and destructive derailments like the Great Leap Forward of the fifties, when Mao had everyone trying to produce steel in their backyards, or the Great Cultural Revolution of the seventies, when millions of people were displaced, humiliated, beaten, and killed. (Deng was under house arrest and his son was defenestrated, becoming a paraplegic.) The then second figure in the Party, standing briefly between Mao and Chou, Lin Piao, was such a helpless cocaine addict he had to breathe motorcycle fumes to clear his head. He supposedly attempted a coup in 1971, was inadvertently betrayed by his daughter, fled by plane, and died when the airplane crashed in Mongolia, whether by running out of fuel (the unlikely official version), by pilot error (the unlikely Mongolian version), or from attack by pursuing Chinese warplanes.

It was from this teeming firmament that Deng emerged to reinvent communism and lead China toward its potential status as a world power, which it had enjoyed at several stages in its incomparable history, though in a smaller, in the sense of less-explored, world. By encouraging entrepreneurship, plowing the resources of the state into economic investment, welcoming foreign investment, and radically modernizing key industries, Deng had the pleasure of seeing China achieve astonishing economic and social progress. The brutal suppression of the freedom demonstrators in Tiananmen Square in 1989, though it is not clear that Deng ordered it, temporarily compromised his authority, but as throughout his career, he persevered. He had inaugurated, as Khrushchev did in Russia, the removal of senior officials without inflicting physical harm on them, and the maneuvering that continued in the highest Chinese circles to the end of Deng's life did not lead to bloodshed (with the likely exception of Mao's widow, who died in prison and may have been informally executed) or vast public campaigns of denunciation.

China passed Japan as the second largest economy in the world in 2010, and had about 40 percent of U.S. GDP, and in terms of purchasing power parity within the country, almost 70 percent, though only about 15 percent per capita. The Chinese navy was starting to build aircraft carriers, as the Soviet Union had (and as Hitler started to do but did not complete any). The pattern of geopolitical challengers setting out for naval rivalry with the incumbent holder of the scepter of the seas is a familiar one, from the Persians and the Turks to the Spanish, the

Dutch, Napoleon, Wilhelm II, and Khrushchev. As a policy, it has been no more successful, and much more costly, than Britain's historic addiction, from Pitt to Churchill, to undermanned amphibious landings around the perimeter of Europe.

China cannot be underestimated, and has the historic mentality and experience of a Great Power that has not faded in that immense and ancient people, as it has in Spain, where world power depended on distant colonial possessions. But, as with previous challengers to the U.S., there has been a tremendous gush of unthinking and premature acclaim; China has a completely corrupt political system with no worthwhile institutions, and a governing philosophy and national goals and political ethos that are made up ad hoc and very difficult to enforce over such a vast, sullen, skeptical population. Not one published financial or economic figure can be believed, it is still mainly a command economy, and although China has performed admirably as a developing country pulling hundreds of millions of people out of a primitive and desperately poor life into a burgeoning contemporary economy, there are still many hundreds of millions of people living as they did 3,000 years ago. The radical and often stylish evolution of Shanghai and Beijing in particular have impressed the world, as did China's emergence from nowhere to win the 2010 Olympic Games (in Beijing and in monumental stadia designed by the world's most illustrious architects).

But there are almost no general social services, and terrible internal stresses. The reduction of its problem of overpopulation can only be accomplished by such restrictive birth control that there will be a prolonged problem of aging. China will face the same problem as Europe, Russia, and Japan—an aging, declining, more welfare-dependent population—though at least it is by choice and a smaller population is objectively desirable. Opposite a determined America, China will have a very long and difficult time achieving real geopolitical parity.

As Europe wrestles with its financial woes, Germany is emerging as a semi-giant, at the head of a core of strong-currency nations, including Austria, the Czech Republic, the Netherlands, Poland, the small Baltic countries, and Scandinavia, about 190 million people and about half of American GDP. Such a bloc, astutely led, could establish some level of preeminence over most of Europe, including France (which has become very erratic) and Russia.

2. GEORGE BUSH AND BILL CLINTON

President Bush's post–Gulf War popularity quickly eroded, as much of it was relief that there had not been heavy casualties or prolonged combat in the Gulf War; Iraq had everything that Vietnam had not—an unquestionable cause, a precise and achievable goal, overwhelming force, a complete constitutional and international mandate, a huge coalition, volunteer armed forces, and a simple exit strategy. But a moderate recession settled in and Republicans remembered Bush's preelection pledge of "no new taxes" after he acquiesced in tax increases to reduce the deficit. He had called Reagan's economic proposals "voodoo economics" in the 1980 primaries, and Republicans were now Reaganite. The president's support in his own party was soft, and Ross Perot, an opinionated Texan billionaire, ran a largely self-financed populist campaign against Bush's free-trade policies, including the Free Trade Agreement with Canada in 1989 and the much more controversial North American Free Trade Agreement, NAFTA, including Mexico, which was only adopted just after the 1992 election. Bush recalled his able secretary of state, James A. Baker, to take charge of his reelection campaign and replaced him for the last few months of the term with career foreign policy specialist and former Kissinger protégé Lawrence Eagleburger.

Bush's answer to a worsening economy was a rather vacuous plea to a joint session of Congress and to the country to spend more. He paid a price for not ever having been an electoral politician. He had had a fairly tough race for his congressional district when he first ran, but after that, despite the important positions he held appointively and by clutching Reagan's coattails, he never really clicked with the public.

Perot was a populist who flowered suddenly after the main party nominations had been locked up by the president against populist dissident Pat Buchanan, and by five-time Arkansas governor Bill Clinton for the Democrats over a diverse field including a rather offbeat campaign by former California governor Jerry Brown. Perot's campaign was launched with a tremendous television blitz as soon as the primaries were over, and he was fishing especially after the popularly disaffected of both parties with an eclectic platform of a balanced budget, free choice of abortion, tightened gun control, a stricter war on drugs, protectionism, greater emphasis of environmental protection, and electronic referenda to promote direct democracy. He had led some important task forces on education and drugs in Texas; had, unlike Clinton, opposed the Gulf War; and ran a campaign pitched to a disconnected group of constituencies of right and left.

The country was uninspired by its president and unconvinced by his chief challenger, and Perot made greater inroads than any third-party candidate since the scarcely comparable Theodore Roosevelt in 1912. Perot was running for a time ahead of both parties' likely candidates but abruptly withdrew in July after Bill Clinton was nominated by the Democrats at their convention in New York. Clinton selected Senator Al Gore of Tennessee as his vice presidential candidate, and enjoyed a tremendous bounce from his convention, where he presented himself as a "New Democrat," who had supported the Gulf War and criticized the budget deficit. He claimed that too many people had been disadvantaged by Reagan-Bush policies favorable to the prosperous but indifferent to those less well-off. Perot claimed that he did not wish to push the race into the House of Representatives. However, he was back two months later, claiming he had been forced out by Republicans who had threatened to disrupt his daughter's wedding.

The Republicans met in Houston and got only a modest lift from their convention. It was not clear when Perot reentered the race which of his opponents was the principal victim of his depredations. It was illustrative of the clumsiness of the Republican campaign (after the death in 1991, aged only 40, of hardball Bush strategist Lee Atwater) that it accepted a three-way debate, failed to take measures to arrest the economic slide, and largely focused on Clinton's peccadilloes and draft avoidance. Bush (somewhat understandably) never knew what to make of Perot, whom Clinton sideswiped with his pitch to the people of modest incomes and insecure employment, "I feel your pain." It was an appalling blunder for Bush to get so detached from the Reaganite foundations of the modern Republicans that he lost chunks of it not only to Clinton but even to an unstable political charlatan like Perot, who never provided a word of specificity for all the facile promises he made. On election day, Clinton won, 44.9 million votes (43.1 percent) and 370 electoral votes from 32 states and the District of Columbia to 39.1 million votes (37.5 percent) and 168 electoral votes from 18 states, and 19.7 million votes (18.9 percent) and no states for Perot.

George Bush had been a competent and, in foreign policy terms, a good president, but a generally unexciting one. Though he did not know the people well, he was a respected and well-liked ex-president, who was soon seen clearly as a gentleman and patriot who had served the nation valorously in war and intermittently and with distinction through many important positions all the way to its highest office, for nearly 50 years.

Bill Clinton was a very astute politician, and one of the new group of presidential politicians who had never had any real career except politics, nor any real ambition except to be president. Such men as Taft, Wilson, Hoover, Eisenhower, and Reagan were very famous because of completely separate careers they had had before seeking any public office. Truman, Carter, and Bush had had other careers, and Franklin Roosevelt had been sidelined for seven years mitigating a terrible affliction (polio). Harding, Coolidge, Johnson, and Ford went early into politics (after war service, in Ford's case), but none of them was aiming for the White House; and Kennedy and Nixon, who were, at least won some battle stars, got round the world a bit, came from prominent centers (Boston and Los Angeles), and had been a long time in Washington. Bill Clinton ran unsuccessfully for congressman at age 28, was elected attorney general of Arkansas at 30, and governor at 32.

As president, he raised taxes and balanced the budget, lost a battle for comprehensive medical insurance waged by his wife, lost control of both houses of Congress in 1994, and didn't have much legislative impact after that, though he did eventually sign a welfare reform measure that undid some of the excesses of Johnson's Great Society programs, though it was chiefly sponsored by Republicans. The country's numbers on economic growth, job creation, reduction of welfare rolls (largely because of the Republican-led reforms), unemployment and inflation (under 5 and 3 percent), and poverty (under 12 percent) were all good, but there is some dispute about how much of these gains came from a peace dividend on the end of the Cold War and a reduced defense requirement, and how much from the long buildup of Reagan's tax reductions and productivity increases. Clinton did start the country down the road to chronic balance-of-payments deficits and to officially mandated and legislated noncommercial residential housing mortgages, which, with low interest rates, led to a terrible surplus of housing with no owners' equity in it and an enormous quantity of worthless mortgages a decade later.

He had no difficulty being reelected in 1996 over the Republican candidate, Senate leader and 1976 vice presidential candidate Robert Dole and his running mate, Jack Kemp, a former New York congressman and a leading advocate of tax cuts (also a former very talented professional football quarterback). Dole was witty but inconsistent, and an erratic campaigner, who wasn't an agile debater and didn't have much to shoot at, given the general prosperity and lack of foreign problems at the time of the election. His stock answer to many questions in the debates began with a reference to having "a modest foundation," a fact that rarely turned out to be relevant to the subject he was supposedly addressing. Implausibly, Ross Perot ran again, for no explicable reason and against a more popular and politically connected president than George Bush had been. Clinton and Gore won with 47.4 million votes (49.2 percent) and 379 electoral votes from 31 states and the District of Columbia to 39.2 million votes (40.7 percent) and 159 electoral votes from 19 states for Dole and Kemp to 8.1 million votes (8.4 percent) and no electoral votes for Perot (who mercifully took the hint and retired from politics). Clinton chose Warren Christopher, a Los Angeles lawyer and Carter's deputy secretary of state, for the State Department in his first term, and in his second term elevated the ambassador to the United Nations, Madeleine K. Albright, the first woman to hold that office. She was a colorful personality and less conventional than Christopher, but there was less serious policy management for these holders of that office than any since Coolidge's colleague, Frank Kellogg, who purported, with the French statesman Aristide Briand, to ban war as an instrument of national policy (Chapter 8).

Clinton dabbled in the little that came by in foreign affairs, rather fecklessly. The new administration was handed, in effect, a grenade with the pin pulled by Bush in Somalia. Bush had responded to acute famine and food shortages in that country by landing Marines to distribute food. This depressed local agricultural prices and led to some sniping at the Americans at about the time of the Clinton inauguration. The new administration, without giving it adequate thought, plunged into nation-building in one of the most unpromising, dysfunctional, and violent countries in the world. A few crossfires with the faction heads and a downed heli-copter, replete with the traditional public entertainment in the area of dragging the bodies of enemies through the street (American servicemen in this case), and Clinton reconsidered the plan and redeployed the nation-builders out of the nation.

He was happy to take some credit for the Oslo Accords in 1993, which brought the Israeli government and the Palestine Liberation Organization together for the first time. Arafat shook hands on the White House lawn with Yitzhak Rabin and Shimon Peres (then the Israeli foreign minister, but at different times prime minister, opposition leader, president, defense minister, and holder of many other posts throughout Israel's history). But Arafat ignored the agreement and it was only the occasion for some unilateral concessions from Israel. Clinton tried again in 2000, when Ehud Barak was Israeli premier, but Arafat blew the talks up and demanded the right of millions of claimed Palestinians to pour into Israel and inundate the Jewish state. He left Camp David to unleash the Second Intifada, which Barak's successor, General Ariel Sharon, put down very effectively.

There was rather ineffectual and unfortunate meddling in Haiti in 1994, and the promotion of a government that proved to be corrupt even by Haitian standards, and that conferred questionable preferments in its international telephone revenues on friends of the Clinton administration. There was complete inactivity from the U.S. and all outside major powers, except to some degree France, in Rwanda in 1994, where the French-backed Hutus massacred 800,000 Tutsis, about a fifth of the population, a tragedy on the scale of the Cambodian atrocities 20 years before.

The artificial federation of Yugoslavia, created at the Paris Peace Conference after World War I, and held together by the Serbian Karagorgevich Dynasty between the wars and by the agile nationalist communist Josip Broz (Marshal) Tito for 35 years after the World War II, gradually unraveled in the late eighties as the Serbians resumed a rather aggressive treatment of Croatian and Muslim minorities, especially in Bosnia. The head of the European Commission, Jacques Poos of Luxembourg, triumphantly announced in 1991, after violence erupted in

Slovenia, that "the hour of Europe has dawned," and that there was no place for the Americans, a view in which the Bush administration happily concurred. But it was only a few months before the Europeans were beseeching American assistance.

Ignoring Bismarck's famous admonitions that "The Great Powers must not become involved in the quarrels of these sheep-stealers," and that the Balkans "were not worth the bones of one Pomeranian grenadier," the Americans, particularly former secretary of state Cyrus Vance, did assist the Europeans with sanctions and negotiators and eventually with forces. A fragile agreement for Bosnia was negotiated under American auspices at (of all unlikely places) Dayton, Ohio, in 1995. This did not constrain Serbia from attempting to suppress Montenegro and seize Kosovo from an Albanian majority, which led to a NATO air war against the Serbs that eventually drove out of power in Belgrade the authoritarian regime of Slobodan Milosevic. But it was a strange conflict, NATO's first against Europeans, in which, to stay above antiaircraft missiles and try to avoid any casualties, NATO aircraft did not descend below 15,000 feet. Air-to-ground rocketry developed by the Americans was astonishingly accurate and was successful after a great deal of damage had been inflicted, but the concept of a war worth killing for but not dying for had worrisome implications, in what militarily sophisticated countries might do to more primitive countries. Russia and China condemned the operation and the United Nations never endorsed it, but it did achieve its objective.

Clinton had terrible difficulty getting approval from the Republican Congress to pay American dues to the United Nations, because of the general leftist, anti-American, anti-Israel, and pro-abortion stance of the organization, which was always too much for the Republican leadership. He finally had to agree to avoid any funding of abortion facilitation to get $800 million of the accumulated arrears paid and to save America's vote in the General Assembly. (The world organization had evolved unpredictably from the device Roosevelt had intended to lure America out of isolation and front America's preeminent influence in the world, mainly composed of the reliable votes of docile Latin American republics and cooperative British dominions. It had become a playpen for corrupt despotisms of the underdeveloped world to gambol about flaunting their often outrageous mockeries of human rights and puerile interstate behavior, thumbing their noses at the Great Powers.)

Clinton's most successful foreign policy initiative was essentially a flim-flam job called the "Partnership for Peace" that gave observer status at NATO to the former satellites and republics of the Soviet Union and had some of the superficial trappings of an extension of the alliance to all of them, including the Asian republics, but in fact provided full cover for an eastward expansion of NATO.

Poland, the Czech Republic, and Hungary joined in 1999, followed in 2004 by Slovakia (which had seceded from the now defunct Paris Peace Conference state of Czechoslovakia), Romania, Bulgaria, Lithuania, Latvia, Estonia, and Slovenia, all seeking an American military guarantee for their oft-violated and lengthily repressed independence. (In 2009, Albania and Croatia joined.)

The chief strategic significance of this was that Poland, whose independence had also been restored at Paris in 1919, for which the British, French, Canadians, and Australians had gone to war in 1939, and whose independence Stalin had promised at Yalta, was now relatively secure and solidly in the West. More important, the long tussle over whether Germany, the most powerful nation in Europe when united, and the heart of the continent, was an eastern- or western-facing nation, was completely resolved in favor of the West. Stalin said in 1945 that the long battle between the Germans and the Slavs had been won by the Slavs, but the division was, because of the overwhelming and benign intervention of the United States, along different lines: the democracies and the communists. Ten million Germans had fled westward ahead of the Red Army in the terrible last months of World War II (Chapters 10 and 11). An honored member of the Western Alliance, West Germany extended the West with reunification in 1990, but now the eastern border of Germany was no longer the outer eastern edge of the Western world. Poland and Hungary, brutalized in 1956, and the Czechs, betrayed in 1938 at Munich and overlooked by everyone except Stalin in 1945, and suppressed again in 1968, were rightly the first wave of post–Cold War members. Germany was entirely enfolded in the comfortable and cordial embrace of the West. In no other respect was the strategic triumph of the United States more benignly manifested, and Bill Clinton, like the 10 preceding holders of his office, played a valuable role in it.

Clinton also claimed a role in Irish affairs, which were still disturbed by agitation for secession from the United Kingdom in Northern Ireland, and allegations of mistreatment of the Roman Catholic minority there by the Protestants. The Irish Republican Army and various Protestant groups frequently resorted to violence. About 40 percent of Ulster (Northern Ireland) was strongly attached to the British Union, but prepared to entertain some compromises; 20 percent were unionists opposed to any compromise; 20 percent were somewhat secessionist, but ostensibly opposed to violence; and 20 percent were secessionist with no great aversion, or even an active disposition, to violence. Religion was really a pretext, though the secessionists were almost entirely Roman Catholic. It was a strange political culture that defined itself, as the militant Protestants did, by the right to stage provocative marches through Roman Catholic areas celebrating the anniversary of the most violent episodes of Protestant oppression of Roman Catholics in British, and especially Irish, history.

Clinton was certainly a partisan of peace, but oversimplified the problems, welcomed IRA leaders to the White House on St. Patrick's Day to sing "When Irish Eyes Are Smiling" and other Irish American ditties, and allowed his ambassador to Dublin, Jean Smith (President Kennedy's sister), to pretend she had some standing in Northern Ireland, though it was a province of the United Kingdom, America's foremost ally. Clinton may have made some contribution to the de-escalating but not definitive Good Friday Agreement of 1998 between the factions, and conditions did improve markedly, especially after the immense international revulsion against terrorism that came in the next few years. But President Clinton did go to the outer limits of what was appropriate in the affairs of two friendly sovereign countries (the U.K. and the Republic of Ireland).

This rising phenomenon of terrorism was, in the absence of rival states, the emerging challenge to the United States. Franklin D. Roosevelt had outlined the basis of future U.S. strategic policy in two sentences in addresses to the Congress at the beginning and end of 1941. In the State of the Union message of January 6, he said, "We must always be wary of those who with sounding brass and tinkling cymbal would preach the 'ism' of appeasement." And in his war message on December 8, he said, "We will make very certain that this form of treachery never again endangers us." The United States would not be an appeasement power and would thereafter maintain sufficient deterrent strength to dissuade any foreign power from direct attack (Chapters 9 and 10). These policies were followed by his successors; the United States has not, in the 1930s sense of the word, appeased offensive and antagonistic states, and no nation has dared to attack it directly since Pearl Harbor. With terrorism, enemies of the West and America in particular, but of governments generally, thought they had a way round this: the terrorist act launched by forces apparently unrelated to any particular country.

This got underway in earnest in Clinton's time, and especially as it proved possible to recruit people happy to kill themselves in the act. The opening gun in the United States was the truck-bombing in the basement garage of the World Trade Center in New York on February 26, 1993. It was apparently masterminded by an extremist Islamist sheikh living in New Jersey, who, with others, was successfully prosecuted. Seven people were killed and 1,042 were injured, but the plan, to weaken the foundations of the North Tower sufficiently to topple it into the other tower, bringing them both down, did not succeed.

The Clinton administration mobilized a coordinated antiterrorism effort, and doubtless prevented some tragedies, but its retaliatory actions were ineffectual.

An international military barracks, the Khobar Towers, in Dhahran, Saudi Arabia, was attacked with an explosive-laden tanker truck parked nearby, killing 20 (19 Americans), and injuring 372, on June 25, 1996. The U.S. embassies in Nairobi, Kenya, and Dar es Salaam, Tanzania, were almost simultaneously attacked by suicide truck-bombers in August 1998, on the model of the attack at the U.S. Marine barracks in Beirut, in 1983. In Nairobi, 212 people were killed and about 4,000 injured, and in Dar es Salaam, 11 people were killed and 85 injured. The great majority of the victims were local people, as only 12 Americans were killed, though the embassies were very heavily damaged. And on October 26, 1998, the U.S. Navy destroyer *Cole* was rammed by a small craft laden with high explosives in the harbor of Aden (Yemen), a suicide attack that killed 17 people and seriously damaged the ship. None of these attacks inflicted anything like the casualties that had been hoped, but when Clinton left office, it was an escalating pattern and a very sinister threat, though not directed exclusively at the United States, and of a lesser gravity than the armed hostility of a serious country. Clinton's response could have been much more effective.

The 2000 presidential election pitted the former president's son, Texas governor George W. Bush, who had won a spirited contest over Senator John McCain for the nomination, against incumbent vice president Al Gore, who had won the nomination over a strong challenge from New Jersey senator and former basketball star William Bradley. Bush took as his vice presidential candidate Dick Cheney, former prominent Republican congressman from Wyoming, White House chief of staff, and Father Bush's defense secretary, and Gore selected Connecticut senator Joseph I. Lieberman, the first major party Jewish nominee for national office (which did not appear to affect the vote at all). Bush appeared to lead narrowly through the campaign, but the poll result was 50.46 million for Bush and only 113 votes short of 51 million votes for Gore; 47.9 percent to 48.4 percent.

Florida was apparently won by Bush by 537 votes, about one 1/100th of 1 percent of the roughly five million votes cast in the state. The absentee military vote eventually raised Bush's margin to 900. Gore demanded a hand recount in four counties, and a ludicrous farce began of individual returning officers sharply disputing the acceptability of whether entire portions of ballots that were detachable, called "chads," had been fully removed. Family friend James A. Baker, former secretary of state and of the Treasury, who had managed George H.W. Bush into the vice presidential nomination, and then both of Ronald Reagan's campaigns and both of the elder Bush's, came to the rescue with a legal campaign.

The Florida Supreme Court ordered a hand recount of the entire state, which was impossible, not only for practical reasons but because scores or even hundreds of thousands of individual ballots could be contested judicially. This was ruled unconstitutional by the U.S. Supreme Court, 7–2. More controversially, in a 5–4 vote, the high court declared a "safe harbor date" of December 12 to accommodate constitutional requirements for the assembly of the Electoral College results for a January 20 inauguration, which effectively gave George W. Bush the election.

It was a questionable result, as the dates could be adjusted for technological realities, but any recount of ballots cast in the relatively primitive manner of some Florida counties would be a Gordian knot that would have to be sliced at some point. Because of the impossibility of judging the validity of so many individual ballots, it will never be known who won the 2000 election, which is probably even more problematic than the Kennedy-Nixon (and Johnson) election of 1960. This was the fourth time (after John Quincy Adams and Jackson in 1824, Rutherford Hayes and Samuel Tilden in 1876, and Benjamin Harrison and Grover Cleveland in 1888, Chapters 4 and 7) that a presidential candidate won with fewer votes than his chief opponent (though the same almost certainly occurred in 1960 as well, because of the misallocation of Alabama votes for a Democratic third-party candidate to Kennedy as official Democrat).

It would be unfair to impute the votes of the Supreme Court justices to the party of the presidents who chose them, but all five of the majority were Republican selections, though so also were two of the dissenters. It may not be unreasonable to suspect that if seven of the nine justices had been put forward by Democratic rather than Republican presidents, the key 5–4 vote could have been different. (If the justices put forward by the Republican candidate's father had recused, the vote would still have been 4–3.) Somebody has to win, and Bush was as likely to have won Florida as Gore. But to be absolutely sure, the whole state would have had to be repolled rather than recounted, which was impossible in the deadlines and would have been an unfair elevation of the prerogatives of the voters of Florida compared with other states. The system is imperfect, but it worked, and Gore, a somewhat wooden personality, responded graciously. (He went on to win a Nobel Peace Prize and make a substantial fortune as an alarmist environmental advocate.)

Clinton had been impeached in 1998, but condemned by comfortably fewer than the two-thirds of the Senate required for removal from office, over his sworn statements about a sexual relationship he had had with a young female White House intern. He had been sued civilly by other claimants of sexual harassment or misconduct, but these concerns, though tawdry and embarrassing to him and his great office, were not the sort of behavior the authors of the Constitution (some of whom were not paragons of connubial fidelity either) had had in mind for justifying the removal from office of federal officials. What should have occurred but didn't was a rejection of the practice of criminalizing partisan and policy differences between the president and the Congress, and a retroactive acknowledgement that neither the impeachment of Andrew Johnson nor the House Judiciary Committee vote to impeach Richard Nixon should have happened.

William Jefferson Clinton left office a popular and certainly not an unsuccessful president, but not an especially consequential president either. He probably accomplished less than any preceding president who served two full terms, except possibly Grant, and that is not certain, and of course Grant's status as a great figure of American history is based on his military career, which was at least as brilliant and about as important as those of Washington and Eisenhower. Clinton was highly intelligent, assiduous in policy terms, moderate, and popular in America and the world. He was well-served by the strategic triumphs of his predecessors and the economic head of steam stoked up by Ronald Reagan. If George H.W. Bush had been more politically agile and astute, he would have avoided the farce of Ross Perot's intrusion and would have reaped the full benefit of his strong leadership in the Gulf War and of Reagan's great accomplishments. But Clinton took the economic bonus and cannot be blamed for the good fortune of serving in less difficult times. He was, other than in his personal conduct, which is irrelevant for these purposes, a prudent leader who made few short-term mistakes. But he faced few strategic decisions and had little aptitude to think in those terms, did not reply adequately to the incipient terrorist threat, and began the economic erosion caused by the imbalance of payments and the overbuilding of housing whose financing was even flimsier than its construction standards. These chickens would feast on steroids and come home to roost with a terrible vengeance after Clinton had gone but before his wife could reclaim the White House as a Clinton family home.

3. GEORGE W. BUSH AND THE WAR ON TERROR

George W. Bush entered office with the usual goodwill of an incoming president and his party's narrow control of both houses of the Congress. His secretary of state was the very widely respected General Colin L. Powell, the first African American (in fact, Caribbean American) to hold that or any comparably high federal office. He was a former national security advisor and chairman of the Joint Chiefs of Staff and, like Eisenhower and Marshall, could have had the nomination of either party and almost certainly the presidency, had he wished them.

The Bush presidency got underway quietly enough, but the world was changed utterly by the terrorist attacks on the United States on September 11, 2001. Four groups of suicide terrorists seized control of airliners departing eastern airports for the West Coast, to ensure they were heavily laden with jet fuel, and then took the controls and directed them into their targets, killing themselves, everyone on board, and nearly 3,000 others, none of any significance to the militant Islamist cause they were promoting; hundreds were not even Americans. No one who watched television then or in the succeeding days can ever forget the news film of the two airliners, about 20 minutes apart, slamming into the tops of the two towers of the previously targeted World Trade Center. Even those assaults, though the airplanes throttled out and generated tremendous explosions, did not bring down the towers. But the structural spines of the buildings, though of great tensile strength, had not been designed to endure this intensity of heat indefinitely, over so many floors, and the world watched, horrified, on live television, as first one tower and, on the time lapse between the initial attacks, the other melted from the top 15 floors, the descending weight of the molten structure causing a concertina effect as each building began, almost majestically and with gathering speed, to descend to the ground.

The New York firemen performed prodigies of courage, and most occupants of the buildings were able to descend the staircases and escape, but very few who were in offices above the places of impact of the aircraft could be saved. Apart from pictures of the detonation of the atomic bomb and of the Nazi death camps, the filmed and pictorial history of human combat yields few spectacles so horrifying as those of the demise of the World Trade Center towers. In all of American history, only the film of the assassination of President Kennedy rivals these in impact. The third aircraft flew into the Pentagon, but not where the defense secretary's and Joint Chiefs' offices are, and the building was repaired quite quickly. A fourth aircraft was hijacked and was thought to be aimed at the U.S. Capitol or the White House, but passengers using their cell phones learned of the other suicide attacks and a group of male passengers tried to overpower the hijackers. In the ensuing struggle, the aircraft crashed in rural Pennsylvania, but at least no one was killed on the ground.

Palestinians cheered, though Arafat warned against it and purported to give blood in aid of the injured. Iranian and Iraqi official reaction was favorable and admiring. But almost all the world that was not inflamed in militant Islamic lunacy was appalled at this dark new chapter in human conflict—the mass, world spectacle of the suicidal massacre of the innocents. For the first time in its history of 52 years, Clause 5 of the North Atlantic Treaty was invoked and the NATO membership unanimously declared that all member countries had been attacked as a result of the September 11 (9/11) onslaught on America. The often tartly anti-American French highbrow daily, *Le Monde*, famously headlined: "Today, We Are All Americans."

President Bush, who had been in an elementary school in Florida promoting his education reforms when advised of what was at first assumed to be an accident, quickly flew to an air base in Louisiana, and then to the emergency command headquarters in Nebraska, where there were, in early hindsight, somewhat unseemly pictures of portly aides running with nuclear code boxes to the accesses to the underground nuclear-attack-proof control center. After a few hours underground, it was clear this was not a coordinated international threat, and Bush returned to Washington on his official aircraft, escorted by advanced U.S. Air Force fighters for the first time ever in domestic airspace. Bush spoke briefly to the nation late in the evening, and while it was not a particularly memorable address, he enunciated the principles that the United States would divide foreign countries between those who were its allies and those who were not, and that countries that assisted terrorism would be treated no differently than terrorists themselves. The world was not accustomed to seeing the United States as a victim country, and its president made it clear that it would not be a passive victim for long.

There was an almost unanimous U.S. consensus for severe countermeasures and, as always, the removal of the threat. Bush spoke well at a national memorial service for the victims at the National Cathedral and also in addressing the Congress and the nation. He warned strenuously against any reaction against Muslims in general, and ensured that a Muslim cleric was among the eminent clergy who spoke at the memorial service. Bush and his chief collaborators, including Vice President Cheney and Defense Secretary Rumsfeld, while grateful for NATO's solidarity, suspected some of the membership of rushing to America's side with a view to moderating its response by collegializing it. There was perhaps some truth to this, but such an open and strong endorsement from such a powerful group of countries should have been valued more highly as the great strategic asset and sincere act of solidarity that it was.

The organization responsible for most of the previous recent terrorist attacks, in Saudi Arabia, East Africa, and on the USS *Cole*, al-Qaeda, was soon happily taking responsibility for these attacks. The headquarters of the organization was known to be near the eastern frontier of Afghanistan, now a failed state still in civil war, after the shambles of the Soviet occupation and the arming of the fundamentalist Islamic groups (chiefly by the United States). The leader of al-Qaeda, Osama bin Laden, was in the habit of issuing belligerent videos, in which he complained of the Western presence in Saudi Arabia, and raged against the existence of the State of Israel. In the frustration of the Muslim Arabs, alleviated almost exclusively in some of the fortuitously oil-rich countries, militant Islam, a savage and deranged interpretation of that religion, had gathered some strength.

The wealthiest of the Muslim states, Saudi Arabia, was effectively a joint venture between the House of Saud and the Wahhabi sect of extreme Islam; and the informal arrangement was that if the Saudi royal family would finance the Wahhabis' massive proselytization across the Muslim world with traditional schools and cultural institutions, the House of Saud would be undisturbed in its incumbency. This was a precarious arrangement, and even if it didn't collapse in disagreement between the parties, as blackmail arrangements almost always do, it was going to lead to trouble with the West quite soon. It had.

The United States, accompanied by the British and soon other NATO forces, landed special forces in Afghanistan in early October, and the Taliban regime, which was already in difficulties with various aggrieved domestic groups, quickly collapsed and fled into the wild Northwest Frontier region of Pakistan, which the government of that country did not control. Clinton had attempted to impose sanctions on both India and Pakistan when those countries became nuclear powers, which did not deter them from achieving and building on that status, but did completely poison their relations with the United States. It left the United States with no serious ally in South Asia, as it had no major ally in the Persian Gulf (Iran and Iraq were almost equally antagonistic).

In the new circumstances, Bush courted the Pakistani president, General Pervez Musharraf, another in the long line of military rulers who periodically disembark inept and corrupt civilian leadership in that very difficult nation. It was well known that, in its obsessive hatred of India, Pakistan cultivated various Muslim extremist groups to assist it in the disputed territory of Kashmir, and to ensure limitations on Indian influence in Afghanistan. In fact, about one-third of the Taliban, the Haqqani faction, was largely financed by the Pakistani intelligence service, ISI. Bush wandered into the tenebrous thickets of Muslim politics without much of a road map. The Saudis responded somewhat seriously to the incentives given them to sever links with al-Qaeda. The Pakistanis gamed the circumstances and delivered much less than they were paid and had promised to do.

As is the custom in U.S. public policy, Bush declared a "War on Terror," as Johnson had his War on Poverty, and Nixon and Reagan the War on Drugs; both the last two wars have been lost, though inconclusively. Throughout 2002, the United States did discomfit al-Qaeda's operations in many places. Almost no government really appreciated domestic terrorists and America helped strengthen counterterrorist measures throughout the world. There were incidents here and there, some of them quite serious, especially at a bar in Bali on October 12, 2002, which killed 202 people (including 88 Australians) and injured 240; in the Madrid commuter train system on November 3, 2004, that killed 191 and injured 1,800 people; and a series of bombs on London Underground trains and a bus on July 7, 2005, that killed 52 and injured 700. But the United States relentlessly bore down on al-Qaeda and destroyed most of its organization and leadership, including bin Laden, who was killed in his own bedroom in Abbottabad, Pakistan, near the Pakistan army's headquarters on May 2, 2011.

It was clear by mid-2002 that the Bush administration had focused on Saddam Hussein in Iraq, and was threatening him in the most dire terms. It was believed that Saddam had developed, or was close to having, nuclear and chemical weapons, Weapons of Mass Destruction—WMD, as they were known. Certainly, Saddam did nothing to reduce the apparent probability that he did, as he darkly hinted in the Arab world that he was preparing a nuclear revenge for having been evicted from Kuwait, and he had completely refused to cooperate with United Nations inspectors, or even admit them until under intense and explicit military pressure from the United States.

Bush had a clear international law case for invading Iraq, as Saddam had been in violation of the cease-fire that ended the Gulf War on several important counts, and had ignored 17 consecutive UN Security Council resolutions demanding compliance with various agreed obligations. (In response to a rather porous regime of sanctions, he had worked out a corrupt system of exporting oil in exchange for assistance to children and the medically needful; huge amounts of graft flowed both ways and to unseemly places in the United Nations organization, on this scheme.)

Though Colin Powell made an extremely eloquent presentation at the United Nations, much of the world, though not much admiring Saddam, was skeptical about another Iraq War. Bush himself spoke to the General Assembly and made excellent points about assuring that the United Nations did not become an impotent talking shop as the League of Nations had been. But the UN WMD inspectors were now claiming to be receiving adequate cooperation in Iraq and finding nothing, and there was no casus belli remotely comparable to the invasion of Kuwait. Germany, France, and Russia were all holding hands in opposition to the American threats to Iraq. Britain and some other traditional allies such as Australia and Egypt were on side, but even Canada declined to join on this occasion. It is not clear why George W. Bush was in such a desperate hurry to attack Saddam, nor why Saddam did not do the necessary to make it clear that he had no WMD and end noncompliance with the Gulf War cease-fire. Subsequent examination of Iraqi official papers indicated that Saddam was mad, which was not altogether surprising. But the impetuosity of the American government remains a mystery.

The United States and Great Britain attacked Iraq overland and with amphibious and paratroop strikes on March 20, 2003, and moved quickly on Baghdad. The

Iraqi resistance was triflingly more determined than 12 years before, but was over-powered at every stage where it attempted to take a stance. The allies again only suffered a few hundred casualties while shattering the Iraqi army and occupying the entire country except the friendly Kurdish north, which was already in revolt against Saddam. The Kurds mounted an offensive in the north, with heavy air assistance from the allies, and the main unit part of the war ended after about 10 days as the Iraqi state disintegrated, while Saddam went underground. (He was captured, hiding in a foxhole near a rural farmhouse, on December 13, 2003, handed over to the new Iraqi government, and tried and executed, by hanging, which he faced with dignity, filmed on a mobile phone, on December 30, 2006.)

It was on seizing Baghdad that the United States committed one of the greatest military blunders of its history, almost on a scale with the failure to cut the Ho Chi Minh Trail (Chapter 14) and the failure of military intelligence to detect the infiltration of 140,000 or more Chinese guerrillas into Korea in 1950 (Chapter 11). The entire armed forces and police forces of Iraq, 400,000 men, were discharged, declared to be unemployed and without income, but not discouraged from taking their weapons and ordnance with them. It should have been obvious to the U.S. commander, General Tommy Franks; to the defense secretary, Donald Rumsfeld; to the head of the new occupation authority, Paul Bremer; and to the president himself that this would turn Iraq into a civil war zone for years to come. Most of the disemployed soldiers and policemen, however limited their capacity to do battle with the premier units of the U.S. Army and Marines and their allies, were capable of lending themselves out quite capably to the factions that now emerged throughout the country apart from Kurdistan, and escalating and maintaining a state of extreme violence for years. This is exactly what happened.

Bush and his administration now proclaimed the desirability of democracy everywhere, as democracies did not make war aggressively. It was almost as simple-minded a concept as Jimmy Carter's indiscriminate championship of human rights, no matter how much more repressive and hostile to the United States might be the successor regime to the one whose rights record had been found wanting. The Bush administration called for democratic elections in the Palestinian territories, and the more extreme Hamas defeated the admittedly distasteful Fatah (though it necessarily became less insufferable in November 2004 when Yasser Arafat, aged 75, died of natural causes after being effectively confined to his compound in Ramallah by the Israeli army for two years). The administration's promotion of democracy in Lebanon helped deliver that country to the extremists of Hezbollah, and their demands for democracy in Egypt contributed, at least marginally, to the fall of the Mubarak government, albeit in 2011.

The lionization of democracy as a system is unexceptionable and appropriate for the United States, but it was very late for an American administration to be claiming democracy as both a panacea and an original thought. Embarking on the reconstruction of Iraq as a democracy was the most ambitious and daunting task of nation-building the United States had ever undertaken. Instead of officially decapitating the Saddam regime and elevating some nontoxic middle-level military and civilian personnel of some apparent talent, and maintaining the military and police under new orders and commanders, as the occupation forces of Eisenhower in Germany and MacArthur in Japan had done, Bremer set about remaking the entire state.

Tribal, sectarian, ideological, and nationalist crosscurrents, each tendency armed to the teeth with the remnants of Saddam's security forces, tore the country to pieces and there was little progress in restoration of order, services, water supply, electricity or oil production, or other indices for several years, and the United States eventually sustained over 5,000 dead and 32,000 wounded in Iraq. It had also largely decamped from Afghanistan to Iraq, leaving its loyal NATO and United Nations allies to deal with what was essentially an American war there, though it was in a humanitarian cause, with insufficient forces. The allies and inadequate American forces conducted a holding action in Afghanistan for over five years, while pretending that the government of the country was reliable and somewhat democratic. (Led by a scoundrel, Hamid Karzai, it was a sinkhole of corruption that was so licentious that the hated Taliban made a serious comeback.)

What the United States should have done in Iraq, apart from allowing junior ministers and officers, under supervision, to bring their country forward in civic and governance terms, was offer to rebuild it in exchange for preagreed quantities of oil at a prefixed, mutually defensible price per barrel. They were castigated in the world for seeking oil, and did not gain a drop of it. In strategic terms, though there was perfectly adequate justification for disposing of Saddam, it was a disaster. It cost over $1 trillion, perhaps 40,000 American casualties, mired almost the entire U.S. conventional ground forces military capability in a morass for seven years, strained the Western Alliance, achieved little in the War on Terror, and inflated the price of oil without increasing supply.

Fortunately for Bush, the American public were still enjoying the aftermath of the crisp execution of the military operation when reelection time came around in 2004. Bush and Cheney were renominated without opposition, and the Democrats, after another lackluster campaign for the nomination, lapsing back into the general mediocrity of post-1968, pre-Clinton Democratic internecine politics, chose Senator John Kerry of Massachusetts for president and Governor John Edwards of North Carolina for vice president. They both had a lot of overgroomed hair on their topknots, but had little allure as candidates; Kerry was sanctimonious and humorless, Edwards glib and specious. Bush was not very charismatic, but he was comparatively solid, and Cheney, though afflicted by grimness, was clearly a very capable and experienced man, with impressive legislative, administrative, and private sector credentials. (He had been the head of the large international engineering firm Halliburton, which profited handsomely from the reconstruction of Iraq.)

Kerry ran into difficulty early when he tried to span the schism in his party over the Iraq War by explaining that he had supported the invasion but had then voted to withhold funds for the mission. It had come to this. Bush was no spellbinder and had spent most of the credit he had earned for responding quite well to the 9/11 attacks, pursuing the War on Terror vigorously, and adopting a serious program of tax cuts to ward off a postattack recession. Only his awkwardness and growing concerns about an Iraq exit strategy prevented him from running away with it, but at least he won the first clear majority since his father in 1992, and became the first president since Madison to be a second consecutive two-term elected president. He won by 62 million votes (50.7 percent) and 286 electoral votes from 31 states to 59 million votes (48.3 percent) and a strong 251 electoral votes from 19 states and the District of Columbia for Kerry. The Republicans retained control of both houses of the Congress comfortably enough, and George W. Bush became the first president since Franklin D. Roosevelt to win two consecutive terms and bring his party in with him both times in control of both the Senate and the House. Colin Powell retired, not a spectacular secretary of state but a very respected man and public official. He was replaced by the national security advisor, Condoleezza Rice, a talented, articulate, and ingenuous former provost of Stanford, and concert pianist. She was an African American Russia specialist, now an out-outmoded discipline, and had served as national security advisor in the first George W. Bush term.

The second Bush term was overshadowed by the Iraq involvement, as the project floundered with no visible progress through 2005 and 2006, and the country became impatient and handed both houses of the Congress back to the Democrats in November of 2006. A committee called the Iraq Study Group had been set up by the U.S. Institute for Peace, the Center for Strategic and International Studies, and the James A. Baker III Institute for Public Policy, essentially to give the president the most unembarrassing possible exit from what was assumed to be the hopeless imbroglio in Iraq. The membership was a formidable array of prominent people from each party, almost none of whom, except for Baker and to a point the co-chairman, former House Foreign Affairs Committee chairman Lee

Hamilton, knew anything about the Middle East. It was a political Murderers' Row, with Clinton insider and fixer Vernon Jordan, former New York mayor Rudolph Giuliani, and former Supreme Court justice Sandra Day O'Connor, but it was largely a try by the president's father's friends to save some face for the current president, while reminding him of how unwise he was implicitly to go beyond the ambitions of Papa Bush in the Gulf War in 1991. The recommendations were a pusillanimous wish list about negotiations with Iran and Syria, pushing a Palestinian-Israel settlement, and starting an immediate pullout from Iraq, as if any useful negotiations with those antagonists could be conducted while the United States cut and ran from the area.

The report was just a thinly whitewashed confession that the whole enterprise was a failure, dressed up by Baker as a bipartisan effort, which it was in the sense that the Democrats wanted a defeat and the Republicans, being apologists for Bush Sr., were consolable that the current president had not shown them up. Given that neither Bush would have been president without the applied talents of James Baker, he was entitled to this foray and clearly relished it. Condoleezza Rice was basically a defeatist also, and Rumsfeld was discredited by the time the ISG's report was known privately to the president.

Outwardly undismayed by the failure of his nation-building effort, George W. Bush vastly exceeded the humdrum confines of his normal limited grasp of grand strategy and its domestic political execution with the most brilliant foreign policy stroke of any president since Ronald Reagan came up with SDI as a means of fragmenting the self-confidence of the Soviet leadership. He sacked Rumsfeld right after the congressional midterm defeat and brought in one of the ISG members, former CIA chief Robert Gates, a chum of the president's father, to carry out a policy that was a 180-degree reversal of the inter-leg-tail retreat the ISG was proposing. The ISG report was revealed on December 12, 2006, and on January 12, 2007, the president announced a "surge," the reinforcement of the U.S. forces in Iraq with an additional 30,000 soldiers—as well as, though it was not publicly announced, a change in campaign tactics, based on greater cooperation with and reward for the tribal and regional chieftains of Iraq. By rejecting his father's friends' confession of failure and plucking one of its advocates to conduct a diametrically opposite policy, George W. Bush showed not only a Machiavellian sense of irony but the highest political courage and, since the policy actually worked, a blinding and unsuspected gift of statesmanship.

The surge was a success and control of the country increased quickly and the level of violence subsided equally quickly, and Bush was able to withdraw the additional forces by the time he left office in January 2009. The Democrats, who had overcommitted themselves to failure in Iraq, had to retrace their steps. George W. Bush was so inarticulate and had so strained public credulity and indulgence by this time that he gained little immediate credit for successfully reversing policy and changing the executants of it, but his action salvaged a respectable outcome of the mission from the stomach of ignominy, though it did not redeem all the bumptious hyperbole about the apotheosis of democracy. The question remained of whether Iraq would be a durable, secular, even slightly democratic confederation, or would fragment or degenerate into a corrupt despotism, even one subject to unsuitable Iranian influence.

4. THE GREAT RECESSION AND BARACK OBAMA

By this time, other grave problems had descended. The U.S. current-account deficit over the previous five years had ballooned to a cumulative total of over $3 trillion and was running at about $800 billion per year. Much more immediately sinister was that the Clinton embrace of the building trades and real estate speculators in the name of greater family home ownership, by ordering continued minimal interest rates and mandating residential mortgages unsecured by any equity and linked to irrationally inflated housing values, abruptly exploded with a report heard and felt round the world.

In the autumn of 2008, almost the entire private-sector-lending banking system of the Western world, except for prudent Canada, was instantly insolvent; the depositors were guaranteed, but the shareholders were at the wall, waiting for the fusillade. One of the recently retired leaders of the world's largest financial group, Citicorp, explained that "when the music's playing, everyone has to dance." Insurance giant AIG, already bedeviled by the New York attorney general, just elected governor, had to be rescued for issuing immense dollar quantities of insurance against default by these worthless "subprime mortgages." The requirement for monthly asset revaluations by most financial companies assured the triumph of short-sellers, as companies that were stretched to the 30–1 ratio of debt-to-asset values were steadily issuing equity at crashing prices to maintain their ratios.

The president's tocsin was "The sucker could go down," referring not to the electorate that had twice (or at least the second time) placed him in the world's greatest office of state, but to the $14-trillion U.S. economy. Though an inelegant formulation, hardly worthy of the proportions of the crisis, it was an accurate summation. Successive U.S. administrations had kept interest rates at negligible levels and encouraged consumption as well as residential home-buying (which in practice often meant individuals buying batches of homes with no equity commitment and low-interest mortgages, selling them when they went up in market value, and abandoning them and surrendering the keys when they went down). It was a political free lunch for Clinton (and even Bush), as they could speak of increasing home ownership at no apparent cost to the taxpayer. The American consumers had carried the luxury-goods industries of France and Italy and the engineered-products industries of Germany and Japan on their backs for decades, while American manufacturing and nearly 60 million jobs were outsourced to cheap-labor countries even as up to 20 million undocumented and poor migrants were tacitly allowed to enter the country to perform menial tasks.

The Clinton-Bush lack of rigor and discipline in the country's international accounts and regulatory standards, lassitude in immigration, and encouragement of consumer and municipal and state debt accumulation rolled over the world like a tidal wave, and the whole financial structure of America and Europe was instantly revealed in its ghastly infirmity. Most of the American automobile industry, which had conceded $30,000 of union pension and health-plan benefits for every car manufactured while producing clunkers instead of cars worthy of great trademarks like Cadillac, Lincoln, and Chrysler that had been respected everywhere in the world, was living off continued tariff protection for trucks and now went into bankruptcy at the speed of the contestants in the Indianapolis 500. Arizona had sold the state Capitol on a lease-back; states were releasing prisoners (in itself a good thing in what had become a carceral nation, but not for the right reasons). Suddenly, America had its pockets turned inside out and everything was crumbling.

And there were unusually worrisome aspects to the crisis. No one—bankers of all kinds, from the Federal Reserve to the lending and merchant banks; industrialists and academic economists (with a couple of exceptions); financial journalists, politicians, and Treasury officials—had foreseen what was coming. Not only was the country bust, and its private sector largely bust, and much of the population personally very stretched, but the mystique of American capitalism had been vaporized. The whole architecture of the American economy—based on consumer appetites and an addiction to the service industries (over $1 trillion a year in legal billings), on essentially superfluous spending that was a partially self-imposed taxation on the whole private sector, and on the unsustainable snobbery of preferring to work in skyscraper offices rather than in light, much less heavy, industry—wobbled. And even in the extreme winter of the problem, during the election campaign of 2008, almost no one said anything sensible about the proportions, causes, and possible remedies.

It was in this fraught atmosphere that the second Bush era came to an end. The Democrats had a gripping campaign between Senator Hillary Rodham Clinton (now of New York), wife of the former president, and Senator Barack Obama of

Chicago, the first (half) African American (and son of one Muslim parent) to make a serious run for the presidency. The Clintons were presumed to own the Democratic Party, as the last unambiguously and durably successful leaders of it since Roosevelt (though the Kennedys might have got there if JFK and RFK had not been assassinated). Senator Clinton won more votes and states in the primaries, but Senator Obama seduced his party and then the nation with a subtle formula that was never explicit, but was clear to the electorate: The great, white, decent, centrist majority of America, conscientiously guilty over the treatment of the African Americans after what Lincoln called "the bondsman's 250 years of unrequited toil" followed by 100 years of segregation and a slow upward incline since, could be rid of its guilt and, as a bonus, never have to listen to the charlatan leaders of the African American political community who had unworthily succeeded Martin Luther King, if it only elevated Barack Obama to the headship of the nation.

The large number of ex-officio superdelegates to the Democratic convention in Denver were seduced by this tacit bargain, and Obama was the ideal candidate to offer it. Though his pigmentation was African, neither his physiognomy nor his inflection and cadences were ethnically distinct. He was eloquent and a fine, athletic-looking man. It was certainly long past time the United States ended any reticence about selecting a non-Caucasian as its leader. And many Democrats clearly resented the proprietary attitudes of the Clintons, and probably the indignities Bill Clinton had brought on the presidency with his indiscretions and his intimate flirtations with perjury, though it was, on its face, bizarre to punish his wife electorally for his infidelities. Obama was nominated, and oddly chose as his running mate the malapropistic senatorial wheelhorse Joseph Biden of Delaware. The Republicans met in St. Paul, Minnesota, 10 days later, and nominated Senator John McCain, who had run George W. Bush a good race in 2000. McCain had been a valiant POW in North Vietnam and was a cantankerous and often maverick senator, and generally a fairly orthodox conservative on most issues. For vice president, he took the comely (in the way of a sexy librarian) Alaska governor, Sarah Palin, a capable debater and campaigner, though exposed in interviews to be thin on some foreign policy areas especially. But she was an imaginative choice and brought a lot of attention to the Republican ticket and she more than held her own with Biden in their debate.

As the economy imploded, Obama did not have to do much, as the times, the *Zeitgeist*, and the contrast between his own youth (44) and fluency and the shopworn quality of his opponent were all strong advantages for the challenger. When the economic crisis cracked open, McCain at first declared, in (Herbert) Hooverese, that the economy was sound (which it wasn't), on Monday; then excoriated corporate greed (as did almost everyone in both parties) on Tuesday; demanded the dismissal of the head of the SEC on Wednesday; suspended his campaign on Thursday to return to Washington for a White House emergency meeting about it on Friday; and said nothing at the meeting. He was a blunderbuss candidate whose time had passed, and all the stars were aligned for Obama. On election day he won, 69.5 million (52.9 percent) and 365 electoral votes from 28 states and D.C., and one from Nebraska (where three counties vote separately and directly choose a member of the Electoral College) to McCain's 59.9 million (45.7 percent) and 173 electoral votes from 22 states. The Democrats retained control of both houses of Congress.

George W. Bush left office quite unpopular and rather disdained for his bungled syntax, Texas mannerisms (as LBJ had been), and acoustically jarring diction ("the war in Eye-rack"). He had avoided a recession and led the nation effectively after the 9/11 attacks. He undoubtedly did terrible damage to the terrorist organizations, especially al-Qaeda, and the terrorist recurrences were much less serious and frequent than bin Laden and others had promised and many had feared. His next most important strategic initiative, and a very good one, was the July 2005 nuclear agreement with India, which broke the ice in that relationship and was topped up by a very successful presidential visit to India in March 2006. He was much disparaged in Europe, though so are most American presidents if there is any opportunity to do so (all the presidents since Roosevelt except Kennedy and, for a time, Nixon were frequently mocked in Europe). He had no idea of economic matters and completely abdicated when they suddenly boiled over. He did act generously to combat AIDS in Africa, but was often a somewhat dysfunctional president. He was far from great, but there have been many with fewer qualities and successes. And if Iraq finally emerges with any sort of reasonable power-sharing, his strategic influence, with democracy finally advanced by a major Arab country, could be quite positive and significant (though at time of writing, such an outcome did not appear the most likely).

Barack Obama chose his chief rival, Hillary Clinton, as secretary of state, and entered office with a broad mandate, though, as he did not have to say anything very precise in the campaign, an unspecific one. He continued, with apparent success, the withdrawal of forces from Iraq, but built up force levels in Afghanistan and revitalized the discouraged NATO effort there. And he approved the raid into Pakistan in 2011 that killed bin Laden, a long-sought and eminently justifiable objective of Americans. He was the most popular American president in Europe since Kennedy, but his appeasement of Iran, even as it hastened toward a nuclear military capability; his simplistically equivocal views on Israel; his apologies for some of his most esteemed predecessors (including, in different respects, Roosevelt, Truman, and Eisenhower); his promises of emulating European socialism; and his failure to produce any coherent Alliance policy all disappointed his countrymen. And four years of $1.5 trillion federal budget deficits took the national debt from the $10 trillion he inherited after 232 years of American history to $16 trillion in four years, although employment declined by five million jobs and there was no real economic recovery.

Unease grew that Obama did not really appreciate the highest qualities of America and was to some extent a factional and not national leader, as the office requires. His response to the economic crisis was a mighty Christmas cake of a "stimulus" package ($800 billion) for the delectation of the Democratic congressional committee chairmen, which did not prevent them from being dumped as the majority party in the House of Representatives in 2010 as the Republicans gained 66 congressmen. Obama's great transformative measure was a terribly expensive and controversial health care bill that broadened coverage but increased medical care costs for many, that was misrepresented as cost-neutral, and that generated a bitter legislative battle that produced little benefit for the governing party. American medical care was excellent for the 70 percent of people who had full-service coverage paid for by their employers but very patchy for the 100 million others, and the cost of American health care was $4,000 per capita more than in other advanced countries (Australia, Canada, France, Germany, Japan, and the U.K., whose overall health care standards were not inferior to those of the U.S.). The federal budgetary deficit was anticipated to continue unabated for a decade, and had all the characteristics, if not the official description, of an annual money-supply increase of 100 percent over the money supply when Obama was inaugurated. A demeaning chicken game between the administration and the Republican House of Representatives unfolded over several years about the competing merits of raising taxes and reducing expenditures.

Since gold had been entirely demonetized (by Nixon in 1971, Chapter 15), the major currencies had no value except against each other, and all the more-circulated currencies, led downward by the U.S. dollar, the euro, and the Japanese yen, were crumbling together. Imports of foreign-sourced oil grew from the 20 percent Richard Nixon viewed with alarm in 1973 (not to mention the 10 percent that worried Eisenhower in 1956) to 60 percent of a much larger level of consumption at five times the price less than 40 years later, but did decline to about 45 percent under Obama because of advanced drilling techniques, tighter fuel efficiency standards, and some conservative measures. Predictions for petroleum imports were optimistic, which indicated declining income for the world's most mischievous countries. But world markets soon showed a lack of confidence in the ability of the Obama administration to cope with these problems even as the financial stability of the Eurozone wobbled badly, and France stepped backward by electing a nondescript Socialist (François Hollande), on a platform of raising taxes and lowering the retirement age.

Obama seemed to think that by signaling that the United States was no longer under white Christian senior management, all countries that were not white and/or Christian could set aside their differences with it, as if international affairs were ever resolved on any basis except national interests. After the "shellacking," as he called the 2010 elections, voters were now turning the rascals out every two or four years.

5. SEEING AMERICA PLAIN

Barring a miraculous renascence of Obama's administration, which was fairly narrowly reelected in 2012 over another diffident republican challenger, W. Mitt Romney,[1] the United States seems to have lost its vocation for greatness in the absence of any rivals to it. After 1991, there wasn't much American strategic policy, because there wasn't much need for one. From 1756 to the end of the War of 1812, American leaders were establishing their country as a stable fixture in the world. Then, until the end of the Civil War, they were deferring or winning internal conflicts, preserving the Union. For the next 60 years, with the brief diversion of Woodrow Wilson's foray to turn the German emperor's provocations into the attempted evangelization of the world for democracy and world government, America was just growing, rapidly and by all measurements—the natural, thrusting, irrepressible growth of what the whole world now knew to be a predestined nation. And from the depths of the Great Depression to the end of the Cold War was what its greatest modern leader called America's rendezvous with that evidently approaching (though not exactly manifest) destiny. One adversary after another was laid low: economic and psychological depression, the threats of Nazism and Japanese imperialism, and then international communism. The country had run out of adversaries, except within, and a ragtag of terrorists abroad.

Almost two years before Richard Nixon enumerated his geopolitical reasoning for the outreach to China, he told Americans (in his Silent Majority speech of November 3, 1969) that North Vietnam "cannot defeat or humiliate the United States. Only Americans can do that." This was the real challenge to American

---

1. Obama and Biden received 65.47 million votes (51 percent and 332 electoral votes) to 60.78 million votes for Romney and his running mate, Congressman Paul Ryan of Wisconsin (47.3 percent and 206 electoral votes). Given the scope of the country's problems, there was little discussion of serious issues.

supremacy, the ability of the United States to sustain a will to greatness when it had nothing left to prove, no foreign power to surpass, and no serious direct or even remote threat from any other nation or coalition of nations. And this has proved a doughty challenge in the 20 years since the end of the Soviet Union.

The United States in 2012 was in full decline by all normal measurements. Its economy was sluggish, misoriented to discarded criteria of mindless consumption, low investment, and no savings; its justice system was corrupt and oppressive and produced 6 to 12 times the per capita number of incarcerated people as other prosperous democracies, on behalf of a war on drugs that is an exercise in hypocrisy and futility in which America has been more decisively defeated than in any war it actually waged. A rogue prosecutocracy terrorizes the country; it wins 99.5 per cent of its cases, 97 percent without a trial, so stacked is the judicial deck and withered the guarantees of individual liberties in the Bill of Rights. Forty-eight million Americans have a criminal record and there is minimal general recognition of the evils of the system.[2] It is less, but still significantly, dependent on oil-exporting countries that do not wish it well and use their price-gouging to promote worldwide anti-Western and particularly anti-American activity. Public education standards have eroded drastically, and most recent immigration has been illegal and of unskilled labor, as the springs of American ascent in the world, the more easily assimilable and comparably cultured Central and Eastern Europeans, have dried up, and in any case had the gate slammed in their face tragically, starting in 1925. American democracy is corroded, is based on the agitation of self-serving interests, and is in permanent election campaign, and presidential campaigns now require $1 billion or more for each side. The quality of national candidates and congressional leaders has declined precipitously.

In sum, American exceptionalism, which was always to a degree a fraud (because of the mistreatment of African Americans and the comparable democratic rights of the British, Dutch, Swiss, and Scandinavians), is now only a matter of the country's immense scale, and of the continuing credulity and dedication of the American masses. Dissident conservatives still celebrate the Tea Party, unaware of the questionable purposes of the original; most Americans still work hard and

---

2. Disclosure: I was charged with 17 counts of financial and related crimes in 2005, of which four were abandoned, nine rejected by jurors, four unanimously vacated by the Supreme Court of the U.S., and two spuriously and self-servingly retrieved by a lower-court judge whom the high court had excoriated but to whom it remanded the four counts for assessment of the gravity of his own errors. I was sent to prison for three years and two weeks, where I was a tutor and teacher, able to help over a hundred fellow inmates to matriculate. The chances that I would ever have committed a crime have always been less than zero, and I was able to assess the terrible imbalances and excess of contemporary U.S. justice.

believe in the revolutionary purity of their origins and the unique democratic values of their country. They are generally aware that America made democracy the dominant world political system, but not that the United States is not now a very well-functioning democracy itself.

But the United States has taken a good time for a setback. It has no rivals, and China will hit the wall of false financial reporting and unsustainable official corruption long before the difficulties of the United States induce any irretrievable decline in that country's status. America missed the opportunity to be more tightly connected to the rest of the Americas and thus have a more comparable demographic bloc for its economic progress than China or India. It could have had effective federal union with large parts of the hemisphere had it wished it, at different times and in different ways, including Canada and Mexico, by which acts it would have added 50 percent to its population and 150 percent to its treasure house of natural resources. But most of Latin America and certainly Canada are steadily gathering strength and are fairly well-disposed, or at least unthreatening, neighbors, but have no interest in being too intimately associated with the United States.

The United States is a country that takes less account of corruption and hypocrisy and is more susceptible, in Napoleon's phrase, to "lies agreed upon," than many other prominent nations (the Europeans and Japanese, after their appalling barbarism in the twentieth century, seem to have faced and accepted their guilt and shame). The United States remains incomparably the greatest and most successful country there has ever been. And though it is vulgar, banal, slovenly, and complacent, and most of its leadership cadres have failed it, it is neither lazy nor driven by a death wish. Historically, when the United States has needed strong leadership, it has found it. It does need leadership now, and it is not easily visible in the present sea of mediocre strivers. But America is threatened only by itself, and Americans, collectively, like themselves, and the country will come round. Someone will lead it on with a new purpose more galvanizing than just borrowing for the bovine satiety of fickle appetites, in politics as in consumer goods.

Richard Nixon was correct that only Americans can defeat and humiliate the United States, and eventually, when they see it plain and have some serious leadership again, they will recognize the impulse to self-destruction as un-American, and turn it into one of national renovation. God, Providence, fate, or the Muse have not withdrawn His or its blessing, and the Americans will return to the manifest destiny of being a sensibly motivated and even exemplary country again, long before they have forfeited to any other long-surpassed nation the preeminence in the world for which America long strove, which it richly earned, and which it has more or less majestically retained.

ACKNOWLEDGMENTS

I am grateful to Barbara for putting up with this distraction in our lives; to Robert Jennings for his early encouragement, and to Doug Pepper of Random House Canada, Roger Kimball of Encounter Books and *The New Criterion*, and Morton Janklow, for their encouragement at various stages, to Henry Kissinger for his generous Introductory Note and his sage advice as the work was in progress, to Stan Freedman, Ron Genini, George Jonas, John Lukacs, Andrew Roberts, Brian Stewart, the incomparable Bill Whitworth and Ezra Zilkha for their comments on the manuscript, to Joan Maida for greatly helping to organize the material, and to Heather Ohle, Lesley Rock, Lauren Miklos, and Jenny Bradshaw for their invaluable work in getting it ready for publication. They all deserve credit (if any is to be had), and no blame, for the resulting book, and I profusely thank them all.

—Conrad Black
Toronto, March 2013

INDEX